Messias Puer: Christian Knorr von Rosenroth's Lost Exegesis of Kabbalistic Christianity

Aries Book Series

TEXTS AND STUDIES IN WESTERN ESOTERICISM

Editor-in-Chief

Marco Pasi

Editorial Board

Jean-Pierre Brach
Wouter J. Hanegraaff
Andreas Kilcher

Advisory Board

Allison Coudert – Antoine Faivre – Olav Hammer
Monika Neugebauer-Wölk – Mark Sedgwick – Jan Snoek
György Szőnyi – Garry Trompf

VOLUME 28

The titles published in this series are listed at *brill.com/arbs*

Messias Puer
Christian Knorr von Rosenroth's Lost Exegesis of Kabbalistic Christianity

Editio princeps plena
with Translation and Introduction

By

Anna M. Vileno
Robert J. Wilkinson

BRILL

LEIDEN | BOSTON

Cover illustration: *Icon of Saint Zachariah*, Françoise Michel (2019), in honour of Zacharie de Sauvage, born on September 15, 2019.

Library of Congress Cataloging-in-Publication Data

Names: Knorr von Rosenroth, Christian, Freiherr, 1636-1689 author. | Knorr von Rosenroth, Christian, Freiherr, 1636-1689. Messias Puer. | Knorr von Rosenroth, Christian, Freiherr, 1636-1689. Messias Puer. English. | Vileno, Anna Maria, editor. | Wilkinson, Robert J. (Robert John), 1955- editor.
Title: Messias Puer : Christian Knorr von Rosenroth's lost exegesis of kabbalistic Christianity / editio princeps plena, with translation and introduction by Anna M. Vileno, Robert J. Wilkinson.
Description: Leiden ; Boston : Brill, [2021] | Series: Aries book series : texts and studies in Western esotericism, 1871-1405 ; volume 28 | Includes bibliographical references and indexes. | Text in Latin and English translated from Latin of Knorr von Rosenroth's commentary on the New Testament known in contemporary sources as Messias Puer, preserved in manuscript form at the Herzog August Bibliothek in Wolfenbüttel, identified as "hab. cod. Guelf. 126 Extrav."
Identifiers: LCCN 2020046129 (print) | LCCN 2020046130 (ebook) | ISBN 9789004426481 (hardback) | ISBN 9789004443426 (e-book)
Subjects: LCSH: Bible. Gospels–Commentaries–Early works to 1800. | Cabala–Early works to 1800. | Manuscripts. | Knorr von Rosenroth, Christian, Freiherr, 1636-1689. Messias Puer. | Herzog August Bibliothek. Manuscript. Cod. Guelf. 126 extrav.
Classification: LCC BS2555.A2 K6613 2021 (print) | LCC BS2555.A2 (ebook) | DDC 226/.07–dc23
LC record available at https://lccn.loc.gov/2020046129
LC ebook record available at https://lccn.loc.gov/2020046130

Typeface for the Latin, Greek, and Cyrillic scripts: "Brill". See and download: brill.com/brill-typeface.

ISSN 1871-1405
ISBN 978-90-04-42648-1 (hardback)
ISBN 978-90-04-44342-6 (e-book)

Copyright 2021 by Koninklijke Brill NV, Leiden, The Netherlands.
Koninklijke Brill NV incorporates the imprints Brill, Brill Hes & De Graaf, Brill Nijhoff, Brill Rodopi, Brill Sense, Hotei Publishing, mentis Verlag, Verlag Ferdinand Schöningh and Wilhelm Fink Verlag.
All rights reserved. No part of this publication may be reproduced, translated, stored in a retrieval system, or transmitted in any form or by any means, electronic, mechanical, photocopying, recording or otherwise, without prior written permission from the publisher. Requests for re-use and/or translations must be addressed to Koninklijke Brill NV via brill.com or copyright.com.

This book is printed on acid-free paper and produced in a sustainable manner.

To two young boys,
Hippolyte Mercure and Hector Zoroastre

Contents

Preface IX

1 **Introduction** 1
   1 *Messias Puer* 1
   2 The *Parallelismi Soharitici* 7
   3 The Evidence for the *Excerpta* found in *Messias Puer* 10
   4 Two Witnesses to the Text of *Messias Puer* 16

2 **The Manuscript** 18
   1 A Description of the Manuscript 18
   2 Hebrew Pagination 19
   3 The Absence of a Title Page in the Manuscript 19
   4 Knorr's Hand 21
   5 The Syriac Paper Slips 24
   6 From Manuscript to Print 24
   7 The Red Crayon Markings 27

3 **Changes to the Manuscript of *Messias Puer*** 31
   1 The Exceptional Tolerance of Sulzbach 31
   2 Self-Correction and Self-Censorship 33
   3 Changes of Speaker 37
   4 Charges of Judaising 40

4 **Biblical Texts in *Messias Puer*** 44
   1 The New Testament Text of *Messias Puer*: The Peshitta Text 44
   2 Orientalism and Biblical Studies 51

5 **The Intra-textuality of *Messias Puer*: Knorr Citing Knorr** 56
   1 The *Apocalypse Commentary* and the *Harmonia Evangeliorum* 57
   2 *Kabbala Denudata* 65
   3 *Adumbratio Kabbalæ Christianæ* 65
   4 The Question of Authorship 68

6 **Theological and Exegetical Innovation in *Messias Puer*** 71
   1 The Revolution of Souls 74
   2 The Lurianic Narrative of the Shards, the Sparks and Jeshuah as Saviour 80

     3   Messiah 93
     4   A Jewish Messianic Kingdom 96
     5   Mary and the Virgin Birth 99
     6   Finding the Sefirot in the Text of the New Testament 108

7 **The Edition** 114
     1   The Principles of the Edition 114
     2   Using the Apparatus 115

Text and Translation

Sectio I. Evangelium Sanctum Prædicationis Lucæ Evangelistæ, quod locutus est et prædicavit Græcè in Alexandria magna. Cap. I. 118

Sectio II. Evangelium Sanctum Præconium Jochanan Præconis, Quod protulit & prædicavit Græcè in Epheso. Cap. I. 134

Sectio III. Luc. I. 150

Sectio IV. Luc. I, v. 26–38 220

Sectio V. Luc. I, v. 39 266

Sectio VI. Matthæi Cap. I. v. 1–25. Evangelium Sanctum Prædicationis Matthæi Apostoli. 288

Sectio VII. De Nativitate & Circumsione Johannis, & Restituto Zacharia, ê Luca 1, v. 57–80. 394

Sectio VIII. De Nativitate, Circumcisione & Oblatione Christi. ê Luc. II, 1–39. 428

Sectio IX. De Adventu Magorum & Fuga Christi: ex Matth. 2. p. t. 496

Sectio X. De Sapientia Jesu Duodecennis in Templo Demonstrata è Luc. 2, v. 40–52. 538

Bibliography 559
Index of Terms and Nouns 583
Index of Biblical References 593

Preface

Christian Knorr von Rosenroth was born in 1636 in the vicinity of Głogów, a Silesian city in present day Poland. The son of a protestant pastor, Knorr enjoyed a classical education, embracing theology, philosophy and the study of ancient classical and oriental languages. His student dissertation, presented in Leipzig, was devoted to the "Theology of the Gentiles" as it may be gleaned from the medals and coins conserved from Greek and Roman Antiquity.[1] This rather curious work appears to contain the seeds of many of the interests later entertained by Knorr and to reflect an early stage of his interest in the ancient traditions sometimes called *philosophia perennis*. If von Rosenroth is best-known today for his *Kabbala Denudata*, a Latin anthology of kabbalistic texts partly taken from the Lurianic tradition, he did not confine his research to Kabbalah. A real "Renaissance man", he was productive as an author, translator, editor and commentator and took interest in fields as variegated as antique numismatics, medicine, biblical exegesis and landscape architecture.[2]

As was the custom at the time, Knorr travelled throughout Europe in order to complete his education.[3] Among the various countries that he visited—France, England and the Netherlands—his stay in Amsterdam seems to have been of particular importance for the future development of his thought.[4] During the Seventeenth Century the welcoming city of Amsterdam hosted a large and motley Jewish community, of many different tendencies. Amongst these, the Marranos, the Jews who had converted to Catholicism while living in Spain or Portugal and who were now in some cases returning to Judaism, played an important role in the numerous cultural transfers that took place at the time between Jews and Christians.[5] Through his meeting with a large number of

---

1 A manuscript version of his *Disputatio philologica de Theologia de Gentilis* is preserved in the Herzog August Bibliothek in Wolfenbüttel. Part of it was printed in 1660 in Leipzig, under the title *Dissertatio De Antiquis Romanor. Numismatib. Consecrationem Illustrantibus*.
2 For a convenient list of his works, see C. Knorr von Rosenroth, *Aufgang der Artzney-Kunst. Mit Beiträgen von Walter Pagel und Friedhelm Kemp* (Reproduction of Edition of 1683; Munich, 1971): pp. xxxii–xxxvii; and *Christian Knorr von Rosenroth. Dichter und Gelehrter am Sulzbacher Musenhof. Festschrift zur 300 Wiederkehr des Todestages*, ed. by I.M. Battafarano (Sulzbach-Rosenberg: 1989).
3 A record of this *peregrinatio academica* is still extant in the Herzog August Bibliothek, Cod. Guelf. Extrav. 253.1.
4 G. Van Gemert, "Christian Knorr von Rosenroth in Amsterdam. Die *Kabbala Denudata* und der niederländische Kontext", *Morgen-Glantz*, 16 (2006): pp. 111–133.
5 At the end of the Seventeenth Century an important network of knowledge transfer was woven around, among others, questions relating to the pre-existence of the soul and its rein-

scholars, Jews and Christians alike, who cultivated a deep interest in Kabbalistic studies, Knorr's interest in mystical Jewish literature was stimulated.[6] The city of Safed, in upper Galilee, was an important centre where different audacious and innovative kabbalistic systems were elaborated by leading Jewish scholars such as Moshe Cordovero, Salomon Alkabetz and Isaac Luria, the most prominent figure of Safedian Kabbalah. Kabbalistic texts began to spread to the common Jewish folk. The study of esoteric lore became popular in Europe even beyond the strictly religious sphere where it had been confined until then. Although we lack precise information about the textual sources of his work, it is probably that, while wandering through Europe, and especially in the Netherlands, Knorr gathered texts from the Lurianic tradition that would soon lie at the core of his kabbalistic anthology, *Kabbala Denudata*.

Furthermore, in the years 1662–1663 in Amsterdam, Knorr had the opportunity to encounter followers of the Sabbatean movement, which spread all over Europe in the wake of the messianic activities of Sabbatai Tsevi (1625–1676) the Jewish Messiah of Early Modern times.[7] Born in Smyrna, in present day Turkey, Tsevi was the leading figure of an extensive messianic movement that spread across Europe and North Africa. Despite his conversion to Islam in 1666, Sabbatianism remained a strong and influential trend in Jewish life throughout

---

carnation, to the eternity of Hell and to the idea of universal redemption (see: *Morgen-Glantz. Die Präexistenz der Seelen. Eine interreligiöse Debatte im 17. Jahrhundert*, ed. by G. Necker and R. Zeller, 24 (2014)). These debates erupted remarkably at the same time in both Christian and Jewish circles (see: D.P. Walker, *The Decline of Hell: Seventeenth-century Discussions of Eternal Torment* (University of Chicago Press, 1964) and A. Altmann, "Eternality of Punishment: A Theological Controversy within the Amsterdam Rabbinate in the Thirties of the Seventeenth Century", *Proceedings of the American Academy for Jewish Research*, 40 (1972): pp. 1–88).

6 Christian interest in Jewish esoteric and mystical traditions was not new. There is general historical agreement in tracing the origins of "Christian Kabbalah" to the Fifteenth Century. It is impossible to retrace that history here, but the reader should consult initially the works of F. Secret: *Le Zohar chez les kabbalistes chrétiens de la Renaissance* (Paris: Mouton, 1964) and *Les kabbalistes chrétiens de la Renaissance*, (Paris: Dunod, 1964). See also *Kabbalistes chrétiens*, ed. by A. Faivre et F. Tristan, (Paris: Albin Michel, 1979) and W. Schmidt-Biggemann, *Geschichte Der Christlichen Kabbala. Band I: 15. Und 16. Jahrhundert*. (Stuttgart-Bad Cannstatt: Frommann-Holzboog, 2012); *Band II: 1600–1660* (2013); *Band III: 1660–1850* (2013); *Band IV: Bibliographie* (2014).

7 On Sabbatai Tsevi and Sabbatianism, see the classical study of G. Scholem, *Sabbatai Sevi. The Mystical Messiah 1626–1676. With a New Introduction by Yaacob Dweck* (Princeton: University Press, 2016 [1973¹]). See also *Ha-halom ve-shivro. Ha-tenu'ah ha-Shabbta'it u-sheluhoteha: meshihiyut, Shabbeta'ut u-Frankizm*, ed. by R. Elior (Jerusalem, 2001), 2 vols.; M. Goldish, *The Sabbatean Prophets* (Cambridge, Mass., 2004); P. Maciejko, *Sabbatian Heresy: Writings on Mysticism, Messianism, and the Origins of Jewish Modernity* (Waltham, Massachusetts: University of New Hampshire Press, 2017).

the Seventeenth and the Eighteenth Centuries and inevitably provoked vigorous opposition from the rabbinic authorities. The extent of the consequential social unrest led inevitably to the involvement of the Christian authorities, who were solicited by other Jews to condemn Sabbatean adherents. This explosion of messianic fervour attracted the attention of several Christian scholars at the time, for example, the French biblical critic Richard Simon. According to some modern scholars, arguing from the concurrence of Sabbatianism and von Rosenroth's work, his publication of the *Kabbala Denudata* at the Palatine Court of Sulzbach where he was Privy Counselor needs to be considered in the light of the Sabbatean influence.[8] This period, the second half of the Seventeenth Century in Europe, was characterized by strong messianic expectations, in both Jewish and Christian communities, and many Christian millenarians took a serious interest in the Sabbatean movement. Without doubt, this messianic tension needs to be born in mind when we account for the genesis of the last work of Christian Knorr von Rosenroth, the *Messias Puer*.

Christian Knorr von Rosenroth was deeply rooted in the intellectual life of his time. He carried on epistolary exchanges with such personalities as the Cambridge Platonic philosopher Henry More, which were published in the first volume of the *Kabbala Denudata* in 1677. More had expressed his views on Kabbalah in 1653, in his *Conjectura Cabbalistica*, and when he became acquainted with Lurianic Kabbalah recently made available in Knorr's Latin translations, he reacted vigorously against its use in a Christian context.[9] Through Henry More, Knorr became acquainted with the thought of the French philosopher René Descartes, about whose work Knorr addressed many questions to his English correspondent.

Among Knorr's many connections we find G.W. Leibniz, whose friendship with Knorr has been illuminated particularly in the works of Allison Coudert. Until thirty years ago, Leibniz was considered as being quite indifferent to what were conceived as the "occultist" interests of Kabbalah. Though often presented as the incarnation of rationalism, the herald of modern science and mathematics, Leibniz was in fact attracted by the esoteric tradition of Judaism,

---

[8] This is for example the orientation suggested by Boaz Huss in his "The Text and Context of the 1684 Sulzbach Edition of the Zohar", *Tradition, Heterodoxy and Religious Culture: Judaism and Christianity in the Early Modern Period*, edited by C.R. Goodblatt and H. Kreisel (Beer-Sheva: Ben-Gurion University of the Negev Press, 2006): pp. 117–138. As we shall see below, this topic needs further exploration, due to the lack of really decisive evidence.

[9] The terms of the polemics are presented in A.M. Vileno, *À l'ombre de la kabbale. Philologie et ésotérisme au XVIIe siècle dans l'œuvre de Knorr de Rosenroth* (Paris: Honoré Champion, 2016): pp. 89–129.

and, in a world where philosophy, science and religion were hardly distinguishable, admired von Rosenroth's work. As the librarian of Duke Anthony Ulrich of Brunswick, Prince of Wolfenbüttel, Leibniz was well informed about the various publication projects of the *République des lettres*, and his correspondence preserves one of the very few early attestations we have of *Messias Puer* and its content. Leibniz was introduced to Knorr in 1671 when he was preparing his kabbalistic anthology by Knorr's friend and colleague Francis Mercury van Helmont. It appears that during one of his trips, in 1688, Leibniz spend a period with Knorr in Sulzbach and Leibniz's letters written during and after this stay attest his keen interest in Knorr's enterprise.[10]

A central role in Knorr's life was played by his friendship with the Belgian physician and alchemist Francis Mercury van Helmont. Knorr wrote the preface to the latter's *Alphabeti vere naturalis hebraici brevissima delineatio*, about the Hebrew alphabet and its usefulness in the education of people affected by deafness[11]. The collaboration of Knorr and van Helmont contributed to the publication of several works important for the intellectual history of seventeenth-century German culture: a German translation of Boethius' *Consolation of Philosophy*[12] and a translation of the medical *summa* of Jean-Baptiste van Helmont, Francis Mercury's father, the *Ortus medicinæ* among them[13].

The exact role that each of the two companions played in the Hebrew printing and translation programme of the circle of the Palatine Court of Sulzbach is still under discussion among scholars[14]. Was Knorr merely a compiler, (as he himself describes his function[15]) and just the translator of versions that

---

10 For a detailed account of the question, see A.P. Coudert, "Leibniz et Christian Knorr von Rosenroth: une amitié méconnue", *Revue de l'histoire des religions*, 213/4 (1996): pp. 467–484.

11 The full title reads "*Alphabeti vere naturalis hebraici brevissima delineatio. Quae simul methodum suppeditat, juxta quam qui surdi nati sunt sic informari possunt, ut non alios saltem loquentes intelligant, sed & ipsi ad sermonis usum perveniant.*" The text was published in a bilingual edition by A.P. Coudert, and T. Corse, *The Alphabet of Nature by F.M. van Helmont* (Leiden and Boston: Brill, 2007).

12 *Christlich-Vernunfft-gemesser Trost und Unterricht, in Widerwertigkeit und Bestürtzung über dem vermeinten Wohl-oder Überlstand der Bösen und Frommen* (Sulzbach: Lichtenthaler, 1667).

13 *Aufgang der Artzney-Kunst* (Sulzbach: 1683).

14 See volume 27, 2017, of *Morgen-Glantz*, dedicated to "Vater und Sohn Helmont", esp. G. Necker and R. Zeller, "Einleitung": pp. 9–22.

15 See "Excerpta ex Epistola quadam Compilatoris de utilitate Versionis Libri Cabbalistici Sohar" in *Kabbala Denudata I, Pars secunda* (Sulzbach, 1677): pp. 3–5 and A. Kilcher, "Einleitung—Die *Kabbala Denudata* in Text und Kontext", *Morgen-Glantz*, 16 (2006): pp. 9–14, p. 10.

were requested from him by van Helmont, who in that case would be the real initiator of the project? Or did Knorr take a fully active part in the projects? As we suggest in this book, Knorr may have been only a major participant to the anthological project as a translator, but his close acquaintance with the texts allowed him to assimilate kabbalistic doctrines to such an extent that he became able to produce personal and original works such as the major part of *Adumbratio* and, of course, his most prominent and original achievement, *Messias Puer*.

As we have seen, Christian Knorr von Rosenroth was a German Christian Kabbalist who distinguished himself by the translation into Latin of Hebrew mystical texts belonging mainly to the Lurianic tradition and collected in an anthology called *Kabbala Denudata* published between 1677 and 1684.[16] According to Gershom Scholem, the great twentieth-century scholar of Kabbalah, the kabbalistic system of Isaac Luria (1534–1572), the last stage in the historical development of Kabbalah, was characterised by strong innovative hermeneutics and was to become, through its reception in Hassidism, the most influential upon Jewish religious life until the present day—to such an extent that Lurianic Kabbalah can be considered today as the "official theology of Judaism"[17]. The quality of Knorr's translation work did not escape Scholem's notice any more than the reliability of his Hebrew sources.[18] Whenever it is possible, a comparison of the Hebrew text and Knorr's translation reveals the latter accurately to convey the meaning of the Hebrew. Furthermore, Knorr showed a desire fully to grasp the multiple meanings of Kabbalistic texts, as one may see in his *Loci communes kabbalistici*, a dictionary of the most commonly encountered Kabbalistic notions, each entry of which exposes several different possible interpretations. In this way, the text is never reduced to just a single possible reading.

---

16 The extent of the Lurianic character of *Kabbala Denudata* is the subject of much discussion. We would estimate that about half of the anthology belongs to the Lurianic tradition. The anthology was published in two volumes: *Kabbala Denudata I* (Sulzbach, 1677); *Kabbala Denudata II* (Frankfurt, 1684).

17 "The influence of the Lurianic Kabbalah, which from about 1630 onwards became something like the true theologia mystica of Judaism, can hardly be exaggerated." (G. Scholem, *Major Trends in Jewish Mysticism* (New York and Jerusalem: Schocken Books, 1954 [1941¹]): p. 284).

18 Scholem was particularly interested in a rather mysterious work, a mixture of Alchemy and Kabbalah, entitled *Esh Metsaref*, of which Knorr provided a translation broken up under separate heads throughout his *Loci communes kabbalistici* and which constitutes the sole surviving witness of the text. Scholem concluded that Knorr had used a Hebrew original (G. Scholem, *De la création du monde à Varsovie* (Paris: Cerf, 1990 [1984¹]): pp. 132 sq). About this tractate, see *infra*, p. 9 sq.

In addition to his translations and epistolary exchanges with notable contemporaries[19], Knorr also worked energetically on Christian Kabbalah. Some works, like *Adumbratio kabbalæ christianæ*,[20] probably produced in collaboration with his regular companion, Francis Mercury van Helmont and published in 1684 in the second volume of *Kabbala Denudata*, reflect his engagement in an intellectual programme aimed at re-interpreting Christian doctrines in the light of Kabbalistic teachings.[21] But, in addition to the singular and original production of *Adumbratio*, Knorr was also responsible for an edition of the Syriac New Testament printed in unvocalised square Hebrew letters in Sulzbach in 1684. This year of 1684 was thus important in Knorr's intellectual development for with this *Peshitta*, our author took an important step in the general development of his own research into Christian Kabbalah.[22] The significance of the Syriac Peshitta New Testament for Knorr was that he considered it was written essentially in the same Aramaic as the Zohar and thus allowed the New Testament to be understood in the light of Zoharic categories and doctrines.

This same year of 1684 saw the fruition of the next aspect of this important co-ordinated project of Knorr, namely the publication of an edition of the Zohar itself in Aramaic. In a certain fashion all of Knorr's publications since the first volume of *Kabbala Denudata* anticipated this publication which for a long time afterwards remained a work of reference for Hebraists[23]. In the Latin introduction to the Sulzbach Zohar, Knorr, in pedagogic mood, proposes a progressive approach to the reader: to become familiar with the un-pointed Aramaic which appears in Hebrew letters in the Zohar Knorr recommends

---

19 The correspondence between Knorr and Henry More was published in *Kabbala Denudata I*, "Pars secunda". It is probable that Knorr and More exchanged other letters that have not come down to us. See R. Zeller, "Naturmagie, Kabbala, Millennium. Das Sulzbacher Projekt um Christian Knorr von Rosenroth und der Cambridger Platoniker Henry More", *Morgen-Glantz* 11 (2001): pp. 13–76.

20 See: S.A. Spector, *Francis Mercury van Helmont's Sketch of Christian Kabbalism* (Leiden: Brill, 2012). The work enjoys a new modern translation by J. Rousse-Lacordaire, *Esquisse de la kabbale chrétienne* (Paris: Les Belles Lettres, 2018).

21 Vileno discusses at length the appropriate way to conceive the relationship between Kabbalah and Christianity in Knorr's thought (Vileno, *À l'ombre de la kabbale*, op. cit., pp. 253–257 *et passim*).

22 We have given a description of this edition of the Peshitta and its importance (A.M. Vileno and R.J. Wilkinson, "Die Peshitta von 1684 im Kontext des Werkes von Christian Knorr von Rosenroth als Beitrag zu einem 'kabbalistischen Christentum'", *Morgen-Glantz*, 28 (2018): pp. 201–230).

23 Huss, "The Text and Context of the 1684 Sulzbach Edition of the Zohar", *art. cit.*; Id., "Translations of the Zohar: Historical Contexts and Ideological Frameworks", *Correspondances*, 4 (2016): pp. 81–128.

PREFACE   XV

practice in reading the extracts of the Zohar published in the second volume of the anthology which give a vocalised text in the same Hebrew characters opposite a Latin translation and accompanied by commentaries. The exercise of reading the Syriac New Testament in square Hebrew type together with the Kabbalistic lexicon which is the *Loci*, should enable the reader to approach the text of the Zohar without difficulty.[24] A Zoharic reading of the New Testament thus becomes attainable.

The second volume of the *Kabbala Denudata* begins with a long preface in which Knorr, basing himself on authentic identifiable textual sources, sets out the history of the collection of the Zohar, as it is reported in Jewish tradition. Undoubtedly having himself an interest in the question, Knorr defended the antiquity of the Zohar.[25] Indeed to trace the Zohar back to Simon bar Yochai as tradition demands, entails placing it close to the time of Jesus.[26] It is then far easier to claim that the Zohar contains Christian truths. The principal

---

24 "*Si quem absterreat difficultas sive styli, sive materiæ hoc in opere propositæ, is sciat, in Tomo secundo Kabbalæ Denudatæ certos exhiberi in usum hujus Exercitii gradus. Textus enim Librorum qui vocantur Siphra de Zeniutha: Idra rabba, & Idra suta, quæ sunt Compendia totius Kabbalæ, ibidem proponuntur punctati, & in Sectiones atque paragraphos dissecti, unà cum Versione & Commentariis. Tres autem Tractatus initiales libri Sohar Editionis Mantuanæ ibidem pariter proponuntur, sed cum versione tantùm & Commentario. In quibus si paululum quis fuerit exercitatus; (præsertim si Novum Testamentum Syriacum literis Hebraicis impressum frequenter insimul perlegatur;) Opus hoc ipsum non punctatum sine versione, facilè intelliget; cum potissimum nec Commentario destituatur: & in Tomo primo Kabbalæ Denudatæ Lexicon etiam aliquale ad manus habeat, cum adminiculis necessariis aliis.*" ("Anyone who is repelled by the difficulty of the style or of the material contained in this work should know that in the second volume of Kabbala Denudata there are texts provided to be used as progressive exercises. The text of the books entitled Siphra de Zeniutha, Idra Rabba and Idra Suta—which constitute a summary of the whole Kabbalah—is given with vocalisation, divided into paragraphs and accompanied by a translation and commentary. The first three tractates of the Zohar in the Mantuan edition are similarly provided with a translation and commentary. If one practices a little with these texts (and especially if one at the same time regularly reads the New Testament printed in Hebrew Letters), one will very easily come to terms with this work which is neither vocalised nor furnished with a translation—though is still provided with a commentary. Finally the reader should have to hand the Lexicon found in the first volume of Kabbala Denudata, which offers other necessary assistance.") (C. Knorr von Rosenroth, "Lectori benevolo salutem!" in *Liber Sohar* (Sulzbach: 1684), without pagination).

25 This traditional date, adopted by Knorr, is in conflict with both the historical facts and current philology. These place the redaction of the Zohar at the end of the Thirteenth Century in Spain, whilst the traditional view attributes it to Simon bar Yochai, a second-century scholar, who lived in Palestine.

26 The title page of the second volume of *Kabbala Denudata* of 1684 describes the Aramaic of the Zohar as written "*in specie Idiomatis Terræ Israëliticæ tempore Christi & Apostolorum usitati*" (C. Knorr von Rosenroth, *Kabbala Denudata II*, (Frankfurt, 1684)).

object remains however to render the Zohar accessible to Latin readers, though Knorr's apologetic concerns are particularly clear in this year of 1684. However in addition to *Adumbratio kabbalæ christianæ* already mentioned, Christian Knorr von Rosenroth was also the author of a work entitled *Messias Puer*, which now with this edition can be seen to represent the final outcome of his Kabbalistic studies from a Christian perspective.

The work of Christian Knorr von Rosenroth enjoyed a wide and long-lasting reception. His kabbalistic anthology remained, until the end of the Nineteenth Century the principal if not the only one source through which readers could access kabbalistic studies without mastering the Hebrew language. Major scholars and intellectual personalities such as Adolphe Franck, Heinrich Graetz or Paul Vulliaud quoted Knorr extensively until the very beginning of the Twentieth Century.[27] Most strikingly, standing both in the tradition established by earlier Christian Kabbalah and also representing its last most significant monument, Knorr's work was responsible for taking Kabbalah out of the field of the Jewish Studies and introducing it into the larger field of Modern Esotericism and Occultism.[28] The kabbalistic library offered by Knorr, even though it often remained, so to speak, an unknown quantity under a well-known title, enjoyed such a wide fame that it progressively assumed a kind of mythical status itself. Beyond its historical and philological contribution in spreading kabbalistic texts through a wide European readership, the *Kabbala Denudata* also began to function as a kind of "warranty certificate" under the validation of which all kind of magical and esoteric texts circulated.[29]

---

27   Cf. A. Franck, *La kabbale ou la philosophie religieuse des Hébreux* (Geneva and Paris: Slatkine, 1981 [1843¹]): pp. 137, 256; H. Graetz, *Geschichte der Juden von den ältesten Zeiten bis auf die Gegenwart. Aus den Quellen neu Bearb* (Leipzig: O. Leiner, 1897): vol. 10, p. 267; P. Vulliaud, *Traduction intégrale du Siphra di-tzeniutha* (Paris: E. Nourry, 1930), with a Preface of Jean de Pauly. On Vulliaud, see further: J.-P. Brach, "Paul Vuilliaud (1875–1950) and Jewish Kabbalah" *Kabbalah and Modernity* edited by B. Huss, M. Pasi and K. Von Stuckrad (Leiden, Brill 2010): pp. 129–149.

28   To such an extent that, according to Andreas B. Kilcher, the "history of the foundation of Modern Occultism is in fact the history of the *Kabbala Denudata*'s reception into Esoteric Freemasonry during the last third of the Nineteenth Century and the first third of the Twentieth Century" ("Verhüllung und Enthüllung des Geheimnisses. Die *Kabbala Denudata* im Okkultismus der Moderne", *Morgen-Glantz* 16 (2006): pp. 343–383, pp. 361–362). The brief summary of this reception as reported here is partially based on Kilcher's study. See also B. Roling, "Erlösung Im Angelischen Makrokosmos. Emanuel Swedenborg, Die *Kabbala Denudata* Und Die Schwedische Orientalistik", *Morgen-Glantz*, 16 (2006): pp. 385–457.

29   Ibid, pp. 343–348. See also E. Asprem, "*Kabbalah Recreata*: Reception and Adaptation of Kabbalah in Modern Occultism" *The Pomegranate* 9/2 (2007): pp. 132–153.

Amongst the texts presented in Knorr's anthology, two attracted particular attention: a lost alchemical treatise known as *Esh Metsaref*, and a selection of excerpts of the Zohar. Indeed, the *Kabbala Denudata* remains famous in Hermetic *milieux* because it preserves the only available fragments of a "Compendium Libri Cabbalistico-chymici", the title of which Knorr spells *Æsch Mezareph*, literally the "Burning Fire", which deals with the Philosophers' Stone.[30] Quite quickly, these fragments were reassembled and published by an anonymous freemason in an English translation of 1714.[31] The history of the *Esh Metsaref* is surrounded by a halo of mystery. If most of the sources that Knorr used in his anthology are identifiable, the case of this alchemical tractate is more complicated. Despite its title, no Hebrew work is known under this name. This has given rise to a lot of speculation and animated research.[32] Basing himself on a close analysis of Knorr's translation, Scholem estimated that "the *tournures* as well as the content demonstrate in a very clear way that Knorr had at his elbow a real Hebrew manuscript and not some Latin version of the work"[33]. The *Burning Fire* builds on systematic parallels between the kabbalistic and the alchemical traditions. The rediscovery of the text by one of the most influential British Freemasons of his time, William Wynn Westcott, founder with Samuel Liddell MacGregor Mathers of the *Golden Dawn*[34], introduces us to the story of the latter reception of the *Kabbala Denudata* in the new context of nineteenth-century Hermeticism and its renewal through the perspective offered by Carl Gustav Jung.

To grasp this second important contribution of Knorr's *Kabbala* requires us to consider a major link in the chain of transmission of the *Kabbala* in its English version, Samuel Liddell MacGregor Mathers (1854–1918), one of the founders of the renewed *Golden Dawn* society, at the end of the Nineteenth

---

30 For a detailed account of the reception of the *Esh Metsaref*, see A. Kilcher, "*Cabbala chymica*. Knorrs spekulative Verbindung von Kabbala und Alchemie", *Morgen-Glantz*, 13 (2003): pp. 97–119.
31 *A Short Enquiry concerning the Hermetic Art by a Lover of Philalethes. To which is annexed a Collection from* Kabbala Denudata, *and translation of the Chymical-cabbalistical treatise intituled* Æsch Mezareph, *or,* Purifying Fire (London: 1714).
32 Scholem tells us of the disappointment of Hermann Kopp, a specialist of Alchemy, that he could not trace the work announced by Knorr on the title page of the first volume of the *Kabbala Denudata* (Scholem, "Alchimie et kabbale", in *De la création du monde jusqu'à Varsovie*, op. cit., pp. 99–168, p. 138). Indeed, *Esh Metsaref* does not appear as one clearly defined work, but instead is scattered in many fragments throughout Knorr's kabbalistic lexicon "Loci communes kabbalistici", in *KD I*, pp. 1–740.
33 Scholem, "Alchimie et kabbale", *art. cit.*, p. 139.
34 *A Short Enquiry concerning the Hermetic Art by a Lover of Philalethes*, op. cit. (quoted by A. Kilcher, "Verhüllung und Enthüllung des Geheimnisses", *art. cit.*, p. 351).

Century. In 1887 Mathers provided a translation of the three Zoharic tractates brought to light by Knorr, namely the *Sifra De-Tseniuta* (the "Book of the Concealed things"), the *Idra Rabba* (the "Great Assembly") and the *Idra Zuta* (the "Lower Assembly"). Mathers published his work under the barely innocent title of *Kabbalah Unveiled*.[35] Most probably, the success of the *Isis Unveiled* published some ten years earlier by Helena Blavatsky played a significant part in Mather's choice. His translation was itself translated into many European languages and hence reached a very large readership. The crucial point here is that these tractates reflected a particular trend in the history of Kabbalah, that of Lurianic Kabbalah. As noted above, Lurianic Kabbalah brought a wholly fresh contribution to the history of Jewish mysticism and paid a particular attention to the three Zoharic tractates chosen and translated by Knorr. They were subject to numerous commentaries by the members of the Lurianic School (a great part of which Knorr integrated in the second volume of his anthology) and were widely considered the most dense and sophisticated of kabbalistic texts. Knorr's chosen emphasis on Lurianic Kabbalah in his translations was handed down, through the latter French and English versions, to the larger readership of the Nineteenth Century. This particular transmission history of kabbalistic texts lead gradually to a greater focus on the Zohar, and more specifically, upon these three tractates, considered as a kind of "essential Zohar". Through the work of the French Occultist Éliphas Lévi, an even sharper focus fell upon the short tractate *Sifra De-Tseniuta*, the "Book of the Concealed Things".

Éliphas Lévi whose real name was Alphonse Louis Constant (1810–1875) played a crucial role (along with the activities of Mathers and his friends) in framing a new conception of Kabbalah.[36] Levi not only established a new occultist science articulated around the teachings of Kabbalah, he placed it

---

35   The classical Latin term *denudata*, comes from *denudare* and means "to expose", "to bare", or "to unclothe". In later Latin, the word assumed progressively the meaning of "explain". Though the two terms, *explain* and *bare* are close, the choice of *unveil* reflects the favour the latter enjoyed in the Occultist milieu of the Belle Époque.

36   For a first approach to Éliphas Lévi, see the classical study of C. McIntosh, *Éliphas Lévi and the French Occult Revival* (London: Rider, 1972) and the recent and very well informed J. Strube, *Sozialismus, Katholizismus Und Okkultismus Im Frankreich Des 19. Jahrhunderts: Die Genealogie Der Schriften von Eliphas Lévi* (Berlin: de Gruyter, 2016). On his link with Kabbalah, see F. Secret, "Du 'De occulta philosophia' à l'occultisme du XIXe siècle", *Revue de l'histoire des religions* 186/1 (1974): pp. 55–81; and *Idem*, "Éliphas Lévi et la kabbale", *Charis. Archives de l'Unicorne* 1 (1988): pp. 81–89; R.L. Uzzel, *Éliphas Lévi and the Kabbalah. The Masonic and French Connection of the American Mystery Tradition* (Lancaster U.S.: Cornerstone Book Publishers, 2006). See also; W.J. Hanegraaff, "The Beginnings of Occultist Kabbalah: Adolphe Frank and Éliphas Lévi" in *Kabbalah and Modernity* edited by B. Huss, M. Pasi and K. Von Stuckrad (Leiden: Brill 2010): pp. 107–128.

at the very core of his new system. The Zohar and in particular the *Sifra De-Tseniuta* became under his pen an "encompassing key"[37] that allows one to explain everything that occurs and the operating mode of all traditions. Kabbalah became here the source of all esoteric and religious movements and the most intimate explanation of everything. Many of Éliphas Lévi's works are orientated towards this explanatory goal, among others his (quite personal) French translation of the Zohar[38]. Here we encounter Knorr von Rosenroth again, since Éliphas Lévi based his translation on the Latin version of the Zohar published in the *Kabbala Denudata* and not, as he claimed, on the original text. Obviously, Levi did not have sufficient mastery of Hebrew and Aramaic to produce a translation by himself.[39] Éliphas Lévi none the less insisted repeatedly on the necessity of going back to source texts and not relying only on secondary literature that had been produced by previous Christian Kabbalists. In that perspective, he recommended his disciples to read Knorr's Zohar and we learn from his German editor and biographer that *Kabbala Denudata* became, from 1850 onward, Éliphas Lévi's bedside book.[40] In his *Dogme et rituel de la haute-magie* published between 1854 and 1856, Éliphas Lévi set up a systematic parallel between the kabbalistic tradition and the Tarot through his 22 chapters. There Lévi stated that the Zohar was "absolute secret knowledge"[41]. In 1896, the work reached the English readership thanks to the translation of Arthur Edward Waite, *Transcendental Magic, its Doctrine and Ritual*[42].

The close link established during the Nineteenth Century between Esotericism and Esoteric Freemasonry on one hand, and literature on the other hand, transmitted the influence of Knorr's work, though it became increasingly remote. Thus we find (as far as France is concerned) reminiscences of it deep

---

37 "allumfassenden Schlüssel" (Ibid, p. 353).
38 É. Lévi, *Le livre des splendeurs: contenant le soleil judaïque, la gloire chrétienne et l'étoile flamboyante: études sur les origines de la Kabbale avec des recherches sur les mystères de la franc-maçonnerie suivies de la profession de foi et des éléments de la Kabbale* (Paris: Chamuel, 1894). The work dates back to 1870 but was published posthumously in 1894.
39 By the way, it must be noticed that the same claim was made by Paul Vulliaud about his 1930 translation of the Zohar, where he in all probability relied, as did Lévi, on Knorr's work.
40 F. Werle, "Éliphas Lévi. Versuch einer Biographie", in É. Lévi, *Das Buch der Weisen* (Vienna: München-Planegg, 1928): p. 196 (quoted by Kilcher, "Verhüllung und Enthüllung des Geheimnisses", *art. cit.*, p. 355).
41 See, for example: É. Lévi, *Dogme et rituel de la haute-magie* (Paris: Niclaus, 1967), pp. 37, 49, 112.
42 A.E. Waite, *Transcendental Magic. Its Doctrine and Ritual by Éliphas Lévi. A Complete Translation of "Dogme et Rituel de la Haute Magie" with a Biographical Preface* (London: G. Redway, 1896).

in Joris-Karl Huysmans' literature of decadence and in the surrealism of André Breton and in Britain, in the work of Max Theon and Arthur Edward Waite. In the works of American freemasons like Albert Pike and Kenneth Mackenzie, the *Kabbala Denudata* became the foundation of the deepest *arcana* of the esoteric High Grades, whereas the revolutionary contribution of Helena Blavatsky offered for Knorr an unexpected posterity, now dechristianized and parallel to the recently discovered Oriental Tradition.[43]

In contrast with the many translations, compilations and editions he produced, Knorr left us very few original productions, the most significant until now having been his *Adumbratio kabbalæ christianæ*.[44] This makes it quite difficult for the scholar to enter the most intimate convictions and motivations of this discrete man who, as we have shown, nevertheless exerted a strong and long-lasting influence on the later developments of Western Esotericism. However, as will become evident in the following pages, Knorr's recovered *Messias Puer* introduces us into the final and most comprehensive formulation of his system of thought, through the systematic application of all his kabbalistic studies to the Syriac text of the New Testament. Indeed, as our apparatus to the Latin text makes clear, his *Kabbala Denudata* is omnipresent throughout his commentary, building a consistent world of references without which the complexities of this last work would remain impossible for the reader fully to grasp.

With the recovery of *Messias Puer*, there will now be scope for a detailed investigation of the manner in which Knorr presented several doctrinal matters and also opportunity to observe the development of his audacious and radical hermeneutic based on a complex but systematic and coherent re-reading of the Gospels. Both areas of innovation touch critically on the question of the relationship between Judaism and Christianity and offer an insight into Knorr's closely-argued exegetical deployment of the Lurianic doctrines in his engagement with New Testament texts as he sought to find a road to reconciliation between Judaism and Christianity.

Knorr had already demonstrated his mastery of traditional Jewish texts. But the *Messias Puer* is equally characterised by a linguistic component displaying a proficiency in comparative philology which is the basis for many of the text's developments. In practice, the Greek and Syriac versions are forensically compared to extract the interpretation at once most rich and also closest to

---

43 Kilcher, "Verhüllung und Enthüllung des Geheimnisses", *art. cit.*, pp. 374–383.
44 The question of the authorship of *Adumbratio* raises many delicate questions, which are discussed *infra*, esp. notes 209–210.

the letter of the text, a principal focus of Knorr. In this context the Syriac version is generally preferred. Knorr is however aware of the Arabic version, feels confident to prefer an Arabic etymology from a Lexicon, and to refer to other Arabic material at second-hand. He was also familiar with contemporary work on Ethiopia and Ethiopic texts. A fuller consideration of Knorr's new work will now enable him to be placed in the context of a wider Oriental philology.

Also, considerable attention is devoted in the *Messias Puer* to the circumstances of the production of the New Testament texts as well to the historical context of the events related therein. The Jewish tradition is here seen as the key to unlock the New Testament passages which had always resisted convincing interpretation. In this respect Knorr is evidently heir to the work of John Lightfoot in Cambridge (whose work he had beside him)[45] and his approach has similarities to Richard Simon's *Comparaison des cérémonies des Juifs et de la discipline de l'Eglise*[46] which in the same period turned to Hebrew texts to elucidate the traditional Christian Scriptures. The topics thematically developed by the *Messias Puer*, the sources exploited, as well as the deployment of its exegetical technique, thus place this work at the centre of research into Orientalism in the context of developing Biblical Criticism. Yet what is missing from Lightfoot is a positive appreciation of the religious value of the Mishnaic and Talmudic material he exploited in his reconstruction of the *realia* of New Testament times, and what is not found in Simon is the deep conviction that the Jewish mystical tradition is the bearer of the True Gospel. Both these convictions inform the newly recovered *Messias Puer*.

---

45   J. Lightfoot, *The harmony, chronicle and order of the New Testament, the text of the four evangelists methodized, story of the acts of the apostles analyzed, order of the epistles manifested, times of the revelation observed: all illustrated, with variety of observations upon the chiefest difficulties textuall & talmudicall, for clearing of their sense and language: with an additional discourse concerning the fall of Jerusalem and the condition of the Jews in that land afterward* (London, printed by A.M. for Simon Miller, 1655) and later in J.R. Pitman, ed., *John Lightfoot Erubin; or Miscellanies and the Harmony of the Gospels Parts I & II* (London: J.F. Dove, 1822). Knorr refers to Lightfoot's works in a letter (to Van Helmont?), where he asks that *The Harmony* be sent him. (Cf. Cod. Guelf. 30.4 Extrav, folio 47^r, Herzog August Bibliothek, Wolfenbüttel). We thank Rosmarie Zeller who drew our attention to this letter. Cf. also *infra*, chapter 4, notes 35 and 36.

46   Published in the second edition of *Cérémonies et coutumes qui s'observent aujourd'huy parmi les Juifs* (Paris: Louis Billaine, 1681).

CHAPTER 1

Introduction

1   *Messias Puer*

Towards the end of October 1687 the famous philosopher and polymath, G.W. Leibniz, left Hannover for Southern Germany and Vienna on a trip of several months. He arrived in Sulzbach, one of the old Imperial Towns of the Holy Roman Empire in the Oberpfalz, on the 30 December, but soon left to visit his friend J.D. Crafft in Bohemia. He returned to Sulzbach at the beginning of February 1688 for a stay of just two weeks during which he enjoyed discussions with Knorr and others[1]. He recalled these subsequently in his correspondence.

In a letter dated February 7/17 1688 to Leibniz from Christoph Daniel Findekeller (1634–1694) there is mention of *Messias Puer*. Findekeller was replying to a letter of Leibniz of 16/26 January 1688 now apparently lost:

> Pour ce qui est de Mr Knorr de Rosenroth, Directeur de la Chancelerie à Sulzbacq, il y a long temps, que j'ay de l'honneur de le connoistre par la voye de mon beaufrere, Glimper, qui lui avoit procuré l'amitié de feu Mr le Baron de Frisen; ce que vous me marquez de lui et de son manuscrit du Messias puer, sera quelque chose de curieux, quand il le mettra aujour, mais possible que ce Mss[t] ne restera dans la Bibliotheque de son Prince.[2]

---

[1] This chronology is proposed by M. Finke, *Sulzbach im 17. Jahrhundert Zur Kulturgeschichte einer süddeutschen Residenz* (Regensberg: Friedrich Pustet, 1998), p. 222, note 618. It is based on Leibniz's *Reise-Journal 1687–1688* (Hildesheim: Facsimile G. Olms, 1966) and K. Müller and G. Krönert, *Leben und Werke von Gottfried Wilhelm Leibnitz. Eine Chronick* (Frankfurt am Main: Vittorio Klostermann, 1969), p. 85. A different account is found in A.P. Coudert, *Leibniz and the Kabbalah* (Dortrecht: Springer, 1995): pp. xiii, 41, 46–48. She believes Leibniz spent longer there, but appears to accept that he may have returned in late February, following E.J. Aiton, *Leibniz. A Biography* (Bristol: Adam Hilger, 1985): p. 144.

[2] "As for M. Knorr de Rosenroth, the Director of the Chancellery at Sulzbach, a long time ago I had the honour of knowing him by way of my brother-in-law, Glimper, who had procured for him the friendship of the late Baron de Frisen; what you tell me about him and his manuscript of *Messias puer*, will be most interesting, when he brings it out into the light of day, but it is possible that this manuscript will not remain in the Library of his Prince." G.W. Leibniz, *Sämtliche Schriften und Briefe*, edited by Deutsche Akademie der Wissenschaften (Darmstadt and Berlin: Akademie-Verlag, 1923) 1.5: p. 55. The footnote is interesting: *"Knorr Messias puer ist nie erschienen. Nach Knorrs Tod besaß die Handschr. Fr. Merkur van Helmont, der das Werk in Amsterdam drucken lassen wollte."* ("Knorr's *Messias puer* never appeared. After Knorr's

To the German Lutheran theologian, Gerhard W. Molanus (1633–1722), Leibniz wrote from Munich on 24 (?) April 1688:

> *Absolvit Knorrius elegans opus cui titulum fecit,* Messias Puer, *in quo Christi Historia inde a conceptu usque ad disputationem in templo collatis Cabbalistarum locis pulcherrime ornatur.*[3]

In a letter of 30 August/9 September 1688 sent this time to the philologist Hiob Ludolph (1624–1704), the author of a history of Ethiopia, to whom Leibniz warmly commended Knorr's works, he once again described the *Messias Puer*:

> *Ostendit mihi jam prope confectum opus, cui titulus est:* Messias Puer, *ubi Historia Christi ab annunciatione ad baptismum usque, quae ab Evangelistis traditur cum aliunde, tum ex locis veterum cabbalistarum mirifice illustratur.*[4]

A few weeks after Knorr's death, mention of the work was also made in the *Monatlichen Unterredungen*:

> So will ich denn von einem andern Scripto etwas vorbringen/ setze Herr *Fulgentius* hinzu/ das mich und andere in grosse Verwanderung gebracht hat. Der hochberühmte Herr Cantzler zu Sultzbach/ dessen Nahmen die gantze gelehrte Welt kennet/ hat in den Rabbinischen/ sonderlich dem Geheimniß-vollen *Caballistis*chen Sachen/ eine unvergleichliche Wissenschafft. Seine *Kabbala denudata* und Liber Zohar weisen es klärlich aus. Allein das Werck/ so er ietzo unter den Händen und fast verfertiget hat/ wird es noch viel mehr bezeugen. Denn wie er in den *Cabbalisti*schen Büchern viel Zeugniße vor die Christlische Religion gefunden hat/ also

---

death Fr. Mercury van Helmont had the manuscript which he wanted to publish in Amsterdam.".) (K. Salecker *Chr. Knorr von Rosenroth* 1931 pp. VIII and 12 f.) The passage is also a valuable indication that the manuscript of *Messias Puer* and no doubt that also of its companion volume the *Excerpta* (see below) would have been housed in the Pfalzgraf's own library.

3 "Knorr has finished a remarkable work called *Messias Puer* in which the history of Christ from his conception up until the Disputation in the Temple is most pleasingly illustrated by a large number of passages taken from the Kabbalists." (Letter of 24 (?) April 1688 in *Sämtliche Schriften und Briefe*, op.cit., I.5, p. 109).

4 "He showed me an almost completed work, the title of which is *Messias Puer*, in which the history of Christ from the annunciation to his baptism, which is handed down by the Evangelists and others, is then wonderfully illustrated by passages from the ancient Kabbalists." (Ibid., p. 235).

hat er sie zum Theil in da obbelobte Werck gebracht/ welches die Überschrift haben soll: *MESSIAS PUER*. Darinnen wird die Historie Christi von der Verkündigung Mariä an biß auf seine Tauffe/ wie sie von denen Evangelisten beschrieben wird so wohl aus andern/ als zuförderst aus denen *Cabbalisti*schen *Scribenten*/ überausschön ud herrlich erkläret.[5]

A letter from Knorr's friend and collaborator Francis Mercury van Helmont to Leibniz who was working as librarian to Duke Anthony Ulrich of Brunswick, Prince of Wolfenbüttel (October 1696) has raised the possibility in some minds that the *Messias Puer* was amongst some of the works van Helmont was at the time trying to get printed in Amsterdam, but there is no specific mention of the *Messias Puer*:

Les escript de Mr. Knor de Rosenrot, qui SA. Ser^{me}. Monseig^r. Le Ducq Antoine Ulrich de Bronsvic demande pur Le faire imprimer. Je iuge a propos comme en peu de jours ispere daller a Amsterdam de Les prendre avecq moy pour voir si La ie les peu mieux faire imprimer quoy faisant Vous aures part de mesme ie doennerey a SA. Le Ser^{me} Je demeure Comme Vous saves, Monsieur.[6]

However writing his *Vitae Knorrianae curriculum* in 1718, 29 years after Knorr's death, Christian Theophil Unger considered the manuscript *in tenebris delitescit*, but not necessarily destroyed:

---

[5] "I would like to mention something from another writing" adds Herr Fulgentius, "that has brought great amazement to me and others. The renowned Chancellor of Sulzbach, whose name is known to the whole scholarly world, has an incomparable knowledge of rabbinic and particularly mystical kabbalistic matters. His *Kabbala denudata* and *Zohar* prove this clearly. The work he has now in hand and has nearly finished will alone provide much more evidence of this. For having discovered many testimonies to the Christian Religion in Kabbalistic books, he has put some of them into a praiseworthy work which is to have the title: *Messias Puer*. In it the story of Christ from the Annunciation to Mary up until his Baptism as described by the Evangelists is beautifully and masterfully expounded with the aid of other works, especially those of the kabbalistic writers." (*Monatliche Unterredungen Einiger Guten Freunde Von Allerhand Büchern und andern annemlichen Geschichten* (Leipzig, 1690), p. 482). Van Helmont also showed a copy to Eric Benzelius who refers to "Historia Evangelica" in his correspondence. Cf. J. Kunert, *Der Juden Könige zwei* (Unpublished Doctoral Thesis, Universität Erfurt, 2019), p. 363, note 1420.

[6] "The writings of M. Knorr von Rosenroth, which His Most Serene Highness Monseigneur Duke Anthony Ulrich of Brunswick asks to have printed: I shall decide about it when in a few days I hope to go to Amsterdam and take them with me to see if they can be better printed there. When I have done that you will be informed equally with His Most Serene Highness. I remain, as you know, Sir." (Niedersächsische Landesbibliothek, Hanover, MSS Helmont 389, f. 49, Ter Borg, October, 1696), quoted by Coudert, *Leibniz and the Kabbalah*, op. cit., p. 181.

Idiomate Rabbinico concinnavit de veritate Christianæ Religionis librum, Messias Puer dictum, quo mysteria fidei nostræ testimoniis ex ipsis Cabbalisticis monumentis erutis probare tentavit. Hucusque tamen in tenebris delitescit eximius ingenii fœtus & lucem publicam vix unquam videbit.[7]

Unger's notice guided later reports[8]. Van Gemert has demonstrated the direct and indirect dependence upon him on the part of the two earliest Dutch Universal Lexicons, A.G. Luïscius *Algemeen historisch geographisch en genealogisch woordenboek* (1724–1739) and the *Groot algemeen historisch, geographisch, genealogisch en oordeelkundig woordenboek* (7th ed. 1733) of David van Hoogstraten and Jan Lodewijk Schuer, both of which carry articles on Knorr. It is of cautionary value to observe how the description of *Messias Puer* grows in successive presentations of Unger's material into a vernacular title "*On the Truth of the Christian Religion*". Van Hoogstraten and Schuer have:

Zyne eigene schriften zyn: *Messias puer* of van de waarheid des Christelyken Godsdiensts, welken hy door de getuigenissen der Kabbalisten zoekt te bewyzen, en daarom ook het gehele werk, nog ongedrukt zynde, in Rabbynsche tale heeft vervaardigt.[9]

Louis Moréri's *Grand Dictionnaire Historique* (Basle 1740) is similarly dependent upon Unger, but also creates an alternative title:

Voici la liste de ses ouvrages: Messias puer, ou de la Vérité de la Religion Chrétienne, qu'il prétend prouver par les témoinages de la Science Cab-

---

7 "He compiled in the rabbinic dialect a book On the Truth of the Christian Religion called *Messias Puer* by which he attempted to prove the mysteries of our Faith from the witness taken from the kabbalistic monuments themselves. However, up until now, this exceptional product of his mind has remained hidden in the dark and has scarcly ever seen the public light of day." (C.T. Unger, "Vitae Knorrianae curriculum, ne pereat cum Historiae Litterariae Cultoribus communicat C.T.V [Christian Theophil Unger]", in *Nova Litteraria anni* MDCCXVII *in supplementum actorum eruditorum divulgata* [...] *auctore Io. Gottleib Kravsio*, ed. by J.G. Kraus, (Leipzig: 1718), pp. 191–200) The *Vitae ... curriculum* is mentioned in G. van Gemert, "Frühe niederländische Stimmen zu Christian Knorr von Rosenroth und ihr Kontext. Knorr-Artikel in Lexiken aus der ersten Hälfte des 18. Jahrhunderts", *Morgen-Glantz* 1 (1991): pp. 79–90, p. 84. In the same volume is a German annotated translation of the text: M. Finke and E. Handschur, "Christian Knorrs von Rosenroth Lebenslauf aus dem Jahre 1718", Ibid.: pp. 33–48.
8 Van Gemert, "Frühe niederländische stimmen", *art. cit.*, p. 84.
9 "His own writings are: *Messias puer* or Concerning the Truth of the Christian Religion, which he seeks to prove by the testimonies of the Kabbalists and so for this reason the whole work, which is still unprinted, is written in rabbinic dialect." (Quoted by van Gemert, Ibid., p. 83).

INTRODUCTION

balistique. (Tout l'ouvrage est écrit en langage rabbinique & se trouve encore en manuscrit.)[10]

The article on Knorr in the fifteenth volume of Zedler's *Universal Lexicon* of 1737 is similarly dependent and persists with Unger's unhelpful remark about the work being in *Idiomate Rabbinico*, which one assumes was simply a misunderstanding of the presence of the Syriac, but now (as with Moréri) the entire work is written *en langage rabbinique* rather than Latin. But of interest is how Zedler contrives to create yet another form of the title from a description of the text, this time in Latin, to supplement the vernacular expansion. This title may have come from the description in *Monatlichen Unterredungen* noted above, which in turn is similar to Leibniz's description:

> Seine eigene Schriften sind: Messias puer, ab adnunciatione Mariae usque ad Baptismus, oder von der Wahrheit der Christlichen Religion, die er sich durch die Zeugnisse derer cabbalisten zu erweisen bemühet und deßwegen auch das ganze Werck in Rabbinischer Sprache verfertiget, so aber noch nicht gedruckt ist.[11]

Evidently these notices have no independent value whatsoever.

At this point it may be helpful to consider the attestation of *Historiae Evangelicae initium, secundum quatuor Evangelistas* which we consider to be no more than a phantom work. The evidence for this work is primarily the printed fragment found in the Bayerischen Staatsbibliothek in Munich. It is without title-page, printer or place and has evidently been named in the catalogue in the absence of a title page in the conventional way by its first words, the heading on the first page[12]. On the first page appears a handwritten note giving the shelfmark: "Exeg. 567m Knorr" and a stamp underneath indicating the

---

10   "Here is the list of his works: *Messias puer*, or The Truth of the Christian Religion, which he claims to prove by the testimonies of Kabbbalistic knowledge. (The whole book is written in rabbinic language and is still in manuscript.)" (L. Moréri, *Grand Dictionnaire Historique*, vol. 5 (Basle, 1740): p. 833).

11   "His own writings are: *Messias Puer, From the Annunciation to Mary upto his Baptism, or Concerning the Truth of the Christian Religion*, which he endeavors to prove by the testimonies of their Kabbalists and for that reason also the whole work is written in the rabbinic language. But this is still not printed." (Quoted by van Gemert, "Frühe niederländische Stimmen zu Christian Knorr von Rosenroth und ihr Kontext", art. cit., p. 86).

12   On the first printed page, an initial autograph annotation "Vitringa ss Observat 138" refers to the *Sacrarum Observationum Libri Sex I* (Franeker, 1712) of Campegius Vitringa (1659–1722), page 128 (not page 138 as stated in the annotation) where in his "*Dissertatio Secunda de Sephiroth Kabbalistarum*" (pp. 125–174, p. 128) favourable mention is made of the *Kab-*

provenience of the book: "Ex donat Molliana". The exemplar comes from the collection of Karl Maria Ehrenbert Freiherr von Moll[13]. We know of no other remaining copies, but J. Fabricius in 1724 reported one:

> *Christiani* CNORRII *a Rosenroth Historia evangelica. Sine capite et calce: libellus enim caret rubro, & fine, quoniam auctor ei est immortuus. Introducitur autem Cabbalista catechumenus, qui quæstiones ex* IV. *evangeliis proponit, & Christianus ad eas respondet. Multa hic cabbalistica infarciri, nemo dubitabit, qui auctorem noverit.*[14]

A complete manuscript in the Herzog August Bibliothek in Wolfenbüttel upon which our edition here is based[15], which is undoubtedly the same work[16], is similarly without title page and is named from its opening words which were added by Knorr's hand, the heading on the first page. But otherwise the title *Historiæ evangelicæ initium* seems significantly unattested.

---

bala Denudata and of Knorr. Evidently the annotation was added by one who believed the book to be by Knorr.

13 *Historische Kataloge der Bayerischen Staatsbibliothek München. Münchner Hofbibliothek und andere Provenienzen*, ed. by S. Kellner and A. Spethmann (Wiesbaden: Harrassowitz Verlag, 1996): pp. 539–541.

14 "Christian Knorr von Rosenroth, *Historia Evangelica*. Without front or back material. Without a title, or an ending for the author died. A Kabbalist Catechumen is introduced who asks questions upon the Four Gospels and a Christian replies to them. The book is stuffed with a lot of kabbalistic material—at which no one who knows the author will be surprised." J. Fabricius, *Historia bibliothecae Fabricianae qua singuli eius libri eorumque contenta*, VI (Wolfenbüttel & Helmstadt, 1724), p. 526. The use here of almost the exact words *auctor est immortuus* ("The writer died") which appear in the anonymous handwritten note at the end of the BSB fragment [*auctor operi immortus est*] ("The writer of the work died"), makes one wonder whether this is not in fact the same volume. This is probably the case since Fabricius' *Historia* is a kind of bibliography of his own library and it seems quite possible that therefore the sole exemplar had passed through his hands. Fabricius was Professor in Altdorf, the regional University of Nuremberg, and may have known Knorr well. Knorr also enjoyed close relationships with Wagenknecht, another Professor in Altdorf. Later on, Fabricius was present in Wolfenbüttel, which is an additional link with the Court of Sulzbach. Our gratitude goes here to Rosmarie Zeller for this valuable information about the scholarly network surrounding Knorr.

15 Cod. Guelf. 126 Extrav.

16 Possibly the preserved printed version of the Bayerische Staatsbibliothek is the printer's proof copy made from the HAB manuscript. (This would perhaps account for the uncorrected errors in the Hebrew letters.) If we imagine the printing took place in Sulzbach, the most likely place, then we may conjecture that the proofs were first kept in the library of Sulzbach and subsequently bound together. Once again we are grateful to Rosmarie Zeller for this observation.

2 The *Parallelismi Soharitici*

In the preface to the second volume of *Kabbala Denudata* (1684), Knorr announced the imminent appearance, *Deo favente*, of a new work:

> Adjunxi autem, in gratiam illorum quibus allegare dicta Soharis voluptas erit, sive in Concionibus sive in scriptis aliis, parallelismum aliqualem dictorum quorundam Novi Testamenti, cujus usum alio tempore, Deo favente, exhibebo uberiorem.[17]

The same year, at the end of the short introduction which he placed at the beginning of his edition of the Zohar, he further announced:

> & si Dominus permiserit Parallelismos Soharisticos in N.T quàm proximè expectet.[18]

It is perhaps significant that we encounter no mention of the *Parallelismi* of Knorr in later works of the Seventeenth and Eighteenth Centuries, but evidently these two passages give Knorr's intention at the time to gather such an anthology of passages, even though they do not strictly entail that he actually did so.

Three years later (in 1687) Pierre Bayle (1647–1706), the French philosopher most famous for his *Dictionnaire historique et critique*, reported Knorr's work in progress in a notice which appears to combine both *Messias Puer* and the planned *Parallelismi* together as one work:

> Messias Puer, Ex Antiquitatibus Hebræorum, & in specie è Libro SOHAR ad Textum N.T. Syriacum illustrans cum Sesqui-Centuria Locorum, Textibus N.T. variè parallelorum, excerptum è Libro SOHAR cum Textu originario, & Versione Latina Opusculum, In gratiam convertendorum Judæorum kat' anthrōpon [*Greek for "ad hominem"*] conscriptum.[19]

---

[17] "I have added for those who may wish to cite Zoharic extracts, either in their public discourses or in other writings, parallels rather similar to some New Testament expressions, the use of which I shall explain more fully (God willing) at another time." ("Lectori philebræo salutem!" in *KD II*, pp. 1–38, p. 17).

[18] "If the Lord permits, he hopes to deliver *Zoharic Parallels to the New Testament* in as short a time as possible." ("Lectori benevolo salutem!" in *Liber Sohar*, op. cit.).

[19] "*Messias Puer*: A little work of extracts from ancient Hebrew texts and particularly from the Book Zohar compared with the Syriac text of the New Testament with 150 quotations, variously parallel to New Testament texts, taken from the Book Zohar, with the original

This full and detailed title is evidently not a reflection of the doxographic tradition we have just examined in the case of the Dictionaries. Nor is it merely a repetition of Knorr's stated intentions in 1684. Genuinely new information is presented in the specification of the use of the Syriac New Testament, the provision of both original text and Latin versions and in the statement of conversionary intent. The flourish of *Sesqui-Centuria Locorum* (One Hundred and Fifty Quotations) is likely that of the author, and accurately describes the *Centuria* as we have reconstructed them below. This is also our earliest report of *Messias Puer* and precedes Leibniz's notices.

Unsurprisingly, *Messias Puer* first mentioned by Bayle and the *Parallelismi* anticipated by Knorr have generally been understood to constitute one single sole work.[20] Indeed it would seem plausible that this was the intention when the title reported by Bayle in 1687 was created. However in the light of the full text of what is called *Historiæ evangelicæ initium*, there may be reasons to believe that Knorr's intention to write a single work of Zoharic parallels to the Syriac NT called *Messias Puer* was revised.

The manuscript of *Historiæ evangelicæ initium* allows us remarkably to observe its growth, correction and refinement up unto 1689, at least for the part covered by the BSB fragment. When the process was begun we cannot know precisely, but perhaps we may imagine work beginning after the statements of Knorr's intentions in 1684, the pivotal year which saw the publication of the second volume of *Kabbala Denudata* including *Adumbratio*, the Hebrew *Zohar* and the Syriac *Peshitta*.[21] In the uncorrected text of the manuscript there occurs an explicit mention of the *Parallelismi*:

---

text and a Latin translation. Written *ad hominem* to convert the Jews." (P. Bayle, *Nouvelles de la République des Lettres. Mois Janvier 1687* (Amsterdam, 1687), p. 332).

20 For example: "This was also the purpose of Knorr's lost work, *Messias Puer*, which contained comparisons between passages from the Syriac New Testament and messianic passages from the *Zohar* and the midrashim: *Messias Puer. E Antiquitatibus Hebraeorum et in specie e libro Sohar ad Textum Novi Testamenti Syriacum illustrans.* (…) Knorr announces this work at the end of his salutation to the reader in the *Zohar* edition: '& si Dominus permiserit parallelismos Soharisticos in N.T quam proxime expectet'" (Huss, "The Text and Context of the 1684 Sulzbach Edition of the Zohar", *art. cit.*, p. 129, note 29). Similarly: S. Campanini, review of *Francis Mercury van Helmont's Sketch of Christian Kabbalism*, edited by Sheila A. Spector, *Aries* 17/2 (2017): pp. 246–249, p. 246.

21 *Novum domini nostri Jesu Christi Testamentum syriace. Ditika khadasha* (Sulzbach: 1684). We have discussed the importance of this year for Knorr in Vileno and Wilkinson, "Die Peshitta von 1684 in Kontext des Werkes von Christian Knorr von Rosenroth als Beitrag zu einem 'kabbalistischen Christentums'", *art. cit.*

> *Loca autem nonnulla ê Libro Sohar, ubi de utroque Messia agitur, evolvi possunt in Parallelismis atque Excerptis Sohariticis ad Nov. Testamentum. Cent. 1. Loc. 62. usque ad 91.*[22]

This notice seems to preserve the title of the work announced by Knorr at the beginning of his 1684 *Zohar* mentioned above. It is also congruent with Bayle's title of 1687. However, a correcting hand, which we have identified as that of Knorr himself, subsequently deleted the title *Parallelismis atque Excerptis Sohariticis ad Nov. Testamentum* and replaced it in the margin by the single word *Excerptis*.[23]

A few lines later on folio 25ᵛ, the original title of the work (on the only other occasion it is mentioned) is again subject to correction:

> (*vide autem de his latius in Parallelismis & Excerptis Sohariticis Cent. 1. Loc. 54. n. 40.41.*)[24]

This is replaced by:

> (*Vide in Excerptis Cent. 1. Loc. 54. n. 40.41.*)[25]

References to *Excerpta* appear extensively throughout the whole of the manuscript. It is evidently a separate work to *Historiæ evangelicæ initium*, yet reference to it is both systematic and omnipresent. It is sadly evident that our reading of *Historiæ evangelicæ initium* today is hampered by lack of access to this book which was evidently intended as a sort of documentary archive to the *Historiæ evangelicæ initium*. Matters are often raised, but not further pursued because the interlocutors (and the reader) are simply referred to the relevant passage in the *Excerpta*. There is no hint in the *Historiæ evangelicæ initium* that the *Excerpta* contained any (of what we would call) Syriac.[26]

---

22 "Several passages from the Zohar which treat of both Messiahs may be found in *Zoharic Parallels to the New Testament with Excerpts*, Century 1, Quotations 62 to 91." (*Historiæ evangelicæ initium secundum quatuor evangelistas*, op. cit., folio 25ʳ).
23 Ibid.
24 "Also see more widely on these issues, *Zoharic Parallels and Excerpts*, Century 1, Quotation 54, notes 40 & 41."
25 "See in *Excerpts* Century 1, Quotation 54, notes 40 & 41."
26 Bayle says that Zoharic texts in the prospective *Messias Puer* were cited in the original and in Latin. This may possibly suggest that the manuscript of *Excerpta* also contained "Syriac" (i.e. Zoharic texts in Hebrew type) which may have been pasted in from pages of Knorr's 1684 Hebrew Zohar (much as pages from the 1684 Peshitta edition were pasted

It is our suggestion that at some point, probably after 1687, Knorr discovered that he could not practically deliver a work which contained both the full text of his accumulated Zoharic parallels and a close exposition of the Syriac Peshitta text of the New Testament. He therefore decided to split his material into two volumes. The Zoharic material he placed in a work called *Excerpta* and the exposition of the Peshitta he reserved for a work called *Messias Puer* which since almost its first appearance has confusingly been known by the replacement title *Historiæ evangelicæ initium*.

3 The Evidence for the *Excerpta* Found in *Messias Puer*

We have suggested above that after Bayle had given his accurate description of the work in progress in 1687, Knorr decided to divide his work entitled *Parallelisimi atque Excerpti Zoharitici ad Nov. Testamentum* into two. One part was to be a commentary on the Syriac Text of the New Testament passages on the early years of Messiah, *Messias Puer*, and the other a collection of essentially Zoharic extracts[27], henceforth known as the *Excerpta*. This proposition we believe may be strengthened by an analysis of the references made to the *Excerpta* in the *Historiæ evangelicæ initium*, which we consider to be, in fact, *Messias Puer* as it emerged after Bayle's notice but before Leibniz's mention.

References to the explicitly named *Excerpta* are found throughout *Messias Puer*. They are grouped (generally sequentially) into two groups: *Cent[uria] I*, which comprises 100 *loci* or extracts and *Cent[uria] II* which comprises just 50.[28] The collection thus satisfies Bayles' description "... *cum Sesqui-Centorum Locorum, Textibus N.T. varie parallelorum è libro* SOHAR ...". Great importance lies in the generally sequential nature of the references. *Messias Puer* begins with a reference to *locus* 1 and finishes with a reference to *locus* 150. Between the two, references are generally in sequence but with some disturbances. Where a group of *loci* are initially cited together (e.g. Cent. I Loc. 26–41 are described generally in folio 7^v as referring to angels, Cent. I Loc. 62–91 are described generally in folio 25^r as referring to both Messiahs), but subsequently specific ref-

---

into *Messias Puer*) or they have may been written out by hand. But it is also possible that the *Excerpta* had only a Latin text.

27   We know that the *Excerpta* did contain Talmudic material as well, from a remark in folio 40^r: "The passage from the Jerusalem Talmud is more extensively quoted in Excerpts 2. loc. 16".

28   For the first one hundred *loci* reference is usually made just to "Cent." Thereafter "Cent. I" and "Cent. II" are systematically distinguished.

INTRODUCTION 11

erence is made back to a particular locus within the larger group (as the topic later under discussion demands) then the sequence is interrupted, but only to return thereafter to the anticipated sequence. Also one or two references out of sequence probably arise because of the chance occurrence of some useful and citable material in an earlier or later passage. None the less, it remains quite incontrovertible that the order of topics treated in the 150 *loci* of the two Centuriae is the order of topics which emerges from the commentary in *Messias Puer* and is indeed determined by it. That is to say: the *Excerpta* are in the order *Messias Puer* requires. We would urge this as clear evidence that the two works were conceived together, but are now split, that is; that the combined work Bayle reported as being underway, was subsequently divided into *Messias Puer* and the *Excerpta*.

The following table shows how the numbered sequence of *Excerpta* generally follows that of the commentary in *Messias Puer*. The first number is that of the sequence of 150 *Excerpta* as reported in *Messias Puer*, the second column offers a list of the subject matter of the *Excerpta* in so far as this can be established from explicit mentions in the citations found in *Messias Puer*, and the third column indicates the numbers of the folios of the manuscript of the Herzog August Bibliothek of Wolfenbüttel (Cod. Guelf. 126 Extrav) on which each *Excerptum* is cited. Our argument depends upon the similarity of the sequences.

Centuria I		folio 2^r
Locus 1	Parable in Zohar to show mystical sense of oral Law	
Locus 2	Metathesis of "tannaim" into "mighty"	folios 2^r–2^v
Locus 3	br'šyt; "Abraham" means loved by God	folios 3^v–4^r
Locus 4	br'šyt	folios 3^v–4^r
Locus 5	br'šyt	folios 3^v–4^r
Locus 6	br'šyt	folios 3^v–4^r
Locus 7	br'šyt	folios 3^v–4^r
Locus 8	br'šyt	folios 3^v–4^r
Locus 9	br'šyt	folios 3^v–4^r
Locus 10	br'šyt; Kingdom called "Fear"	folios 3^v–4^r
Locus 11	br'šyt	folios 3^v–4^r
Locus 12	Illumination	folio 4^v
Locus 13	[29]	

---

29   An empty line after a locus number indicates that it is never cited.

(cont.)

Locus 14	Hepar, Esavus and the Heart of Jacob	folio 6^r
Locus 15	Foetuses enjoy intelligence	folio 52^r
Locus 16	Virgin Mother Lech Leha Crem 235	folio 32^r
Locus 17		
Locus 18	Birth-pangs of Messiah	folio 47^v
Locus 19	Hepar, Esavus and the Heart of Jacob	folio 6^r
Locus 20	Sterility	folio 7^r
Locus 21	Sterility; Daroma	folios 7^r; 5^v
Locus 22	Incense	folios 7^v; 11^v
Locus 23	Incense	folio 7^v
Locus 24	Quotation from Tamid on Daily Sacrifice	folio 7^v
Locus 25		
Locus 26	Angels	folio 7^v
Locus 27	Angels; Gabriel; Elijah became an angel	folios 7^v; 11^v
Locus 28	Angels	folios 7^v; 9^v
Locus 29	Angels; Gabriel	folios 7^v; 11^v
Locus 30	Angels	folio 7^v
Locus 31	Angels; Gabriel et seq	folios 7^v; 11^v
Locus 32	Angels	folio 7^v
Locus 33	Angels	folio 7^v
Locus 34	Angels	folio 7^v
Locus 35	Angels; Prayer; Elijah was Phineas	folios 7^v; 9^r–10^r
Locus 36	Angels	folio 7^v
Locus 37	Angels	folio 7^v
Locus 38	Angels	folio 7^v
Locus 39	Angels	folio 7^v
Locus 40	Angels	folio 7^v
Locus 41	Angels	folio 7^v
Locus 42		
Locus 43	Signs of Conception; strong liquor	folios 10^v; 12^v
Locus 44	Filled with the Holy Spirit	folio 10^v
Locus 45	Filled with the Holy Spirit	folio 10^v
Locus 46	Filled with the Holy Spirit	folio 10^v
Locus 47	The more secret missions of angels	folio 11^v
Locus 48		
Locus 49	High Priest forbidden to tarry in Temple	folio 12^v
Locus 50	Joy of commandment of purification	folio 12^v
Locus 51	Shekinah in tents of Sarah & Rebecca	folio 17^r

INTRODUCTION

(cont.)

Locus 52	Shekinah in tents of Sarah & Rebecca	folios 17^r; 48^r
Locus 53	Shekinah in tents of Sarah & Rebecca	folios 17^r; 48^r
Locus 54	Revolution of Souls; Bathsheba	folios 24^r; 25^r–26^r; 41^v
Locus 55	Revolution of Souls	folio 24^r
Locus 56	Revolution of Souls	folio 24^r
Locus 57	Revolution of Souls	folio 24^r
Locus 58	Revolution of Souls	folio 24^r
Locus 59	Revolution of Souls	folios 24^r; 6^r
Locus 60	Revolution of Souls	folio 24^r
Locus 61	Revolution of Souls	folio 24^r
Locus 62	Messiah; in Paradise	folios 25^r; 46^v; 52^r
Locus 63	Messiah	folio 25^r
Locus 64	Messiah	folio 25^r
Locus 65	Messiah	folio 25^r
Locus 66	Messiah; Virgin Mother; Lech Leha	folios 25^r; 14^r; 32^r
Locus 67	Messiah	folio 25^r
Locus 68	Messiah	folios 25^r; 34^v
Locus 69	Messiah; Galilee	folios 25^r; 34^v; 47^v
Locus 70	Messiah; Star	folios 25^r; 34^v; 46^v
Locus 71	Messiah	folio 25^r
Locus 72	Messiah	folio 25^r
Locus 73	Messiah	folios 25^r; 48^r
Locus 74	Messiah; Return under Messiah	folios 25^r; 35^r; 46^v; 47^v; 48^r
Locus 75	Messiah	folio 25^r
Locus 76	Messiah	folio 25^r
Locus 77	Messiah	folio 25^r
Locus 78	Messiah	folio 25^r
Locus 79	Messiah	folio 25^r
Locus 80	Messiah	folio 25^r
Locus 81	Messiah	folio 25^r
Locus 82	Messiah	folio 25^r
Locus 83	Messiah	folio 25^r
Locus 84	Messiah	folio 25^r
Locus 85	Messiah; Birth pangs	folios 25^r; 47^v
Locus 86	Messiah; Daroma	folios 25^r; 5^v
Locus 87	Messiah	folio 25^r

(cont.)

Locus 88	Messiah	folio 25^r
Locus 89	Messiah	folios 25^r; 2^r
Locus 90	Messiah; Gabriel; Merchabha	folios 25^r; 8^r
Locus 91	Messiah	folio 25^r
Locus 92	Mystical meanings of "Abraham" etc	folios 25^r; 17^v; 51^v
Locus 93		
Locus 94	Sterility of Good Works	folio 6^v
Locus 95	Sterility of Good Works	folio 6^v
Locus 96		
Locus 97		
Locus 98	Bathsheba and David	folio 26^r
Locus 99		
Locus 100		
Centuria II		folio 33^v
Locus 101	Circumcision	
Locus 102	Circumcision	folios 33^v; 34^v
Locus 103	Circumcision	folio 33^v
Locus 104	Circumcision	folio 33^v
Locus 105	Giving of names attributed to God	folio 34^r
Locus 106	Giving of names attributed to God	folio 34^r
Locus 107	Giving of names attributed to God	folio 34^r
Locus 108	Bridegroom's friend Gen Crem c43.1	folio 34^v
Locus 109	Bridegroom's friend Gen Crem c43.1	folio 34^v
Locus 110		
Locus 111		
Locus 112		
Locus 113	Being strong in the Spirit	folio 36^r
Locus 114		
Locus 115	Satan harming Israel after the census	folio 39^r
Locus 116	The Arab on the Messiah Berachoth 5a	folio 40^r
Locus 117	Job and Balaam born without foreskins	folio 43^r
Locus 118	Several called Messiah (JT) Berachoth 5a	folio 43^r
Locus 119	Day of Purification	folio 43^r
Locus 120	= Zohar Sect Vajickra c13	folio 36^r
Locus 121	Precept of the law of the firstborn	folio 43^r
Locus 122	Simeon saw Angel of Death before he died	folio 43^r
Locus 123	The righteous see Shekinah before death	folio 43^v

(cont.)

Locus 124	The righteous see Shekinah before death	folio 43^v
Locus 125	= Berachoth ch. 1 fol. 17a	folio 43^v
Locus 126	Balaam	folios 47^v; 44^v
Locus 127	Balaam	folios 47^v; 44^v
Locus 128	Balaam	folio 47^v
Locus 129	Balaam	folio 47^v
Locus 130	Balaam	folio 47^v
Locus 131	Balaam	folio 47^v
Locus 132	Balaam	folio 47^v
Locus 133	Balaam; Jer 35.16 speaks of Messiah	folios 47^v; 48^r
Locus 134	Jer 35.16 speaks of Messiah	folios 47^v; 48^r
Locus 135		
Locus 136	Boys conspicuous for their great wisdom	folio 51^r
Locus 137	Boys conspicuous for their great wisdom	folios 51^r–51^v
Locus 138	Boys conspicuous for their great wisdom	folios 51^r–51^v
Locus 139	Boys conspicuous for their great wisdom	folio 51^r
Locus 140	Boys conspicuous for their great wisdom	folio 51^r
Locus 141	Boys conspicuous for their great wisdom	folio 51^r
Locus 142	Concerning the name "Zohar"; Angels	folios 51^r; 1^r
Locus 143	Angels descending from the Creative World	folio 51^r
Locus 144	Assher's love of learning	folio 51^r
Locus 145	Mystical trads of the feasts from Tikkunim	folio 51^v
Locus 146	More allowed a man after 13th birthday	folio 51^v
Locus 147		
Locus 148	Another singular story of love of learning	folio 51^v
Locus 149	Reason for obeying parents in Zohar	folio 52^r
Locus 150	Father and Mother in the divine realm	folio 52^r

When Leibniz wrote to Molanus in April 1688, he made a natural distinction between two of Knorr's projects. References to them are separated by several lines. First he mentioned that Knorr had assembled a collection of Zoharic extracts:

> *Multa ex libro Zoar exerpta edi curavit, quibus Christiana etiam veritas comprobatur.*[30]

---

30 "He undertook to publish many excerpts from the book Zohar by which Christian Truth was indeed proved."

One takes *edi curavit* to refer to the production of the separate volume of the *Excerpta*, which no doubt, were kept in manuscript alongside the manuscript *Messias Puer* in the Ducal Library in Sulzbach when Leibniz visited in 1688.[31] Several lines later Leibniz refers to *Messias Puer* in the words cited above. They are now two different works. The *Excerpta* has been lost. But *Messias Puer* has survived.

4 Two Witnesses to the Text of *Messias Puer*

As we have seen the text of *Messias Puer* survives in two forms, the manuscript and a fragmentary printing. The manuscript of *Messias Puer* is preserved in the Herzog Augustus Bibliothek in Wolfenbüttel[32]. Findekeller's remark to Leibniz[33] indicates it was originally in the Duke's library in Sulzbach. Several books from the Sulzbach Library found their way to Wolfenbüttel, many through the hands of the Librarian Jakob Burckhard (1681–1752), who was himself born in Sulzbach.[34] But as far as the Cod. 126 Extrav. is concerned, we have no precise indication of how it reached Wolfenbüttel. The fact that the same binding and the same watermark on the end papers are to be found on other books of the same collection indicates that the text was probably still unbound when it arrived at the HAB.[35] The various items of the collection "Extravagantes" date

---

31 It is, of course, possible that this first reference to a collection of Zoharic fragments may refer to the early collections in *Kabbala Denudata*, but the use of the term *Excerpta* may more strongly suggest a reference to our collection.

32 Shelf Mark: Cod. Guelf. 126 Extrav. See: W.-D. Otte: *Die neueren Handschriften der Gruppe Extravagantes, 2. 90.1 Extrav.–220 Extrav.* (Frankfurt: Vittorio Klostermann, 1987): p. 80.

33 Cf. *supra*, chapter I, footnote 2.

34 These holdings are described in R. Zeller, "Der Nachlaß Christian Knorr von Rosenroth in der Herzog August-Bibliothek in Wolfenbüttel", *Morgen-Glantz* 16 (2006): pp. 55–71; for Burkhardt, see p. 56, note 4 and W. Arnold, "Jacob Burckhardt aus Sulzbach als Bibiothekar in Wolfenbüttel", *Morgen-Glantz* 19 (2009): pp. 53–70.

35 The manuscripts from the donation of Jacob Burckhardt (30.4; 149.13; 157.2 Extrav.) share the same style and technique of binding as 126 Extrav. (i.e. our manuscript). This style of binding occurs in the case of many more manuscripts which have no connection with Knorr and one should therefore conclude that this is the work of a local bookbinder. This conclusion is confirmed by a consideration of the watermarks. Cod. Guelf. 126 Extrav. has on end papers at the front and at the back the watermark CCG (a similar but not identical motif is: WZIS DE0945-Müller2858_3r ⟨Permalink⟩). The CCG occurs also on the end paper in the back of 30.4 Extrav.. In addition, manuscript 30.4 Extrav. has an unidentified watermark that does not occur in our 126 Extrav., but on the end papers of the other Knorr von Rosenroth manuscripts, 149.13 and 157.2 Extrav. All this suggests a relationship between

INTRODUCTION 17

back to the time of Duke Augustus, the founder of the library himself.[36] They were named "Extravagantes" because these were works which were omitted from an initial catalogue of the Guelf collection and consequently were called by established usage "Extravagantes".[37]

    these manuscripts, but says nothing about their history before their arrival in Wolfenbüttel. (Personal communication of Dr Sven Limbeck, 19.9.18.)

36   http://diglib.hab.de/?db=mss&lang=en&list=collection&id=extrav

37   The term was originally used in canon law for papal documents not included in the twelfth-century *Decretum Gratiani*, but none the less binding upon the Church.

CHAPTER 2

The Manuscript

1   A Description of the Manuscript

The manuscript (HAB. Cod. Guelf. 126 Extrav.) is in-octavo, bound in leather half-binding with leather corners, characteristic of both the Seventeenth Century and the HAB holdings of the same collection. There is a fly-leaf at the beginning and two pages at the end in a different paper which bears a watermark. Otherwise the codex comprises 52 folios recto / verso, that is 104 pages.[1] At the moment, the provenience of the watermark has yet to be identified. The codex is gathered in quaternions as can be seen from a close inspection of the spine and binding.

A striking feature of the pages of the manuscript is that each sheet is crossed by having been folded into four with a horizontal and a vertical crease.[2] The reason for this consistent feature is not obvious. Perhaps we should imagine that the creases arose from folding the sheets to facilitate their transmission backwards and forwards between Knorr and his secretaries. Or maybe the pages were folded to be sent to the printer, though it must be said that we do not in fact know where the BSB fragment was printed and it should be noted that all the pages are folded, not just those printed in the BSB fragment.[3] Although probably the BSB fragment was printed in Sulzbach where Knorr could supervize the printing process. Then, when Van Helmont tried to have the text printed in Amsterdam, maybe he folded the pages in order to carry them. A last possibility is that the pages were folded in order to be sent to Wolfenbüttel, where we assumed they were bound together.

---

1   The last two blank pages have also been numbered.
2   As has been noted by the author of the HAB Catalogue: "Alle Blätter des Manuskripts sind längs und quer gefaltet gewesen." (*Kataloge der Herzog August Bibliothek Wolfenbüttel*, op. cit., p. 80).
3   The sheets are written on both sides. Consequently folding them in four left no space for an address or for sealing wax, nor the possibility of folding them into themselves. One should therefore perhaps assume that they were sent, in whatever numbers, in an enclosing sheet folded around them and bearing an address. Examples of letters from Knorr's correspondence folded, addressed and sealed can be seen in HAB Cod. Guelf 30. 4. Extrav. See: http://diglib.hab.de/?db=mss&list=ms&id=30-4-extrav&lang=en

2   Hebrew Pagination

The manuscript carries pagination in Hebrew numerals (letters) on the bottom right-hand corner of given sheets. The sequence numbers the gathered quaternions and extends from an initial *bet* to a final *nun* on folio 52. There is no *alef*. (Thus *bet* appears on folio 4ʳ, *gimel* on folio 8ʳ and so on until *nun* appears on folio 52ʳ). The absence of an *alef* seems to indicate that the manuscript may have been deprived of its title page. This impression will be reinforced when we discuss below the fact that first quaternion does not have the right number of sheets. We shall notice a similar lack of title page in the case of the printed BSB fragment.

In addition the pages of the manuscript are marked in the top right hand corner of the recto with an Arabic numeral in red-crayon which has been overwritten in black ink. We shall argue below that this system of numeration appears to have been added in the context of the printing of the BSB fragment, and thus the Hebrew numeration should be considered the original pagination of the manuscript.

3   The Absence of a Title Page in the Manuscript

As we have seen the codex has no title page. The text begins with the title of the first section of the work *"Evangelium Sanctum Prædicationis Lucæ Evangelistæ, quod locutus est et prædicavit Græcè in Alexandria magna"*.[4] Above this, right at the top of the page has been added in a hand we identify as Knorr's *"Historiæ Evangelicæ initium secundùm quatuor Evangelistas. Sectio 1"* (Figure 1). If this addition followed the removal of the title page (which seems likely as it removed and replaced the previous marginal numeration "Sectio 1"), it would seem that Knorr himself chose this new title which subsequently entered the catalogues.

---

4   "The Holy Gospel of the Preaching of Luke which was spoken and preached in Alexandria the Great".

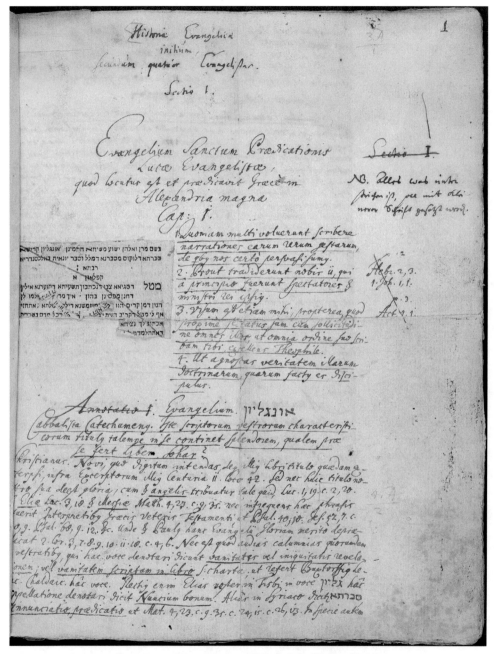

FIGURE 1   Codex Guelf. 126 Extrav. (Herzog August Bibliothek, Wolfenbüttel), folio 1ʳ.

4 Knorr's Hand[5]

The paper of the codex appears a little brown, but the text is perfectly legible. Several hands are apparent in the codex. The majority of the writing is in a humanist script which probably belonged to a secretary, a professional scribe such as Knorr would have at his disposal as an important functionary of the Court.[6] This first secretarial hand initially wrote a large part of the text. Knorr himself took over for half a page on folio 49^r (Figure 2) and a second secretarial hand continued from the second part of folio 49^r. A few lines in Knorr's hand are found on folio 50^r. He also wrote the four last pages himself (51^{r-v}, 52^{r-v}).[7] We are fortunate that Knorr's distinctive hand can be so confidently recognised, as it is found in several of his manuscripts. A list of these is available.[8] Conveniently Knorr's hand may be examined in Cod. Guelf 30.4 at folios 2^r–3^r (below); 3^v–3^r; 8^r–11^v; 34^r–35^v; 40^r–42^v; 47^r–48^v.[9]

The manuscript has a particular interest, however, not merely because Knorr wrote parts of it in his own hand. Rather it arises from his systematic and detailed correction of the work of the secretaries. We have preserved innumerable corrections, deletions and additions which permit us to follow Knorr's guidance of his text to its final form. This material provides a rare insight into the author's changes of mind and hesitations, to which we shall return shortly (Figure 3).

The text of the codex, within the generic constraints of a dialogue between a "Christianus" and a "Cabbalista Catechumenus",[10] constitutes a sequential verse-by-verse commentary on the Gospel accounts of the birth and early life of Christ. The comments address the Syriac Peshitta text of the Gospels, which was published by Knorr himself in 1684.[11]

---

5   We are indebted here to the meticulous analyses of Doktor Sven Limbeck of the Manuscript Department at the Herzog August Library, and for his invaluable technical guidance.
6   Knorr was Chancellor to the Court at Sulzbach and Privy Counsellor of Christian Augustus. He was appointed due to the good offices of his friend van Helmont (Finke, *Sulzbach im 17. Jahrhundert*, op. cit., p. 114).
7   The use of secretaries by Knorr need not be taken for granted. Cod. Guelf. 149.13 Extrav. contains works in Knorr's own hand in both German and Latin. They are a lot more difficult to read than the text prepared by secretaries in our manuscript, HAB. Cod. Guelf. 126 Extrav. It may be that Knorr chose to use secretaries because he intended to publish the work and so prepared a more legible text for the printer.
8   A convenient list of manuscripts in Knorr's own hand can be found in A. Fuchs, "Christian Knorr von Rosenroth. Ein Beitrag zu seinem Leben und seinen Werken", *Zeitschrift für Kirchengeschichte*, 35 (1914): pp. 548–583 at pp. 570–571.
9   See: http://diglib.hab.de/?db=mss&list=ms&id=30-4-extrav&lang=en
10 From his second appearance until the end of the text, he is referred to by the abbreviation "Cabb. Cat.".
11 Cf. *supra*, chapter 1, note 21.

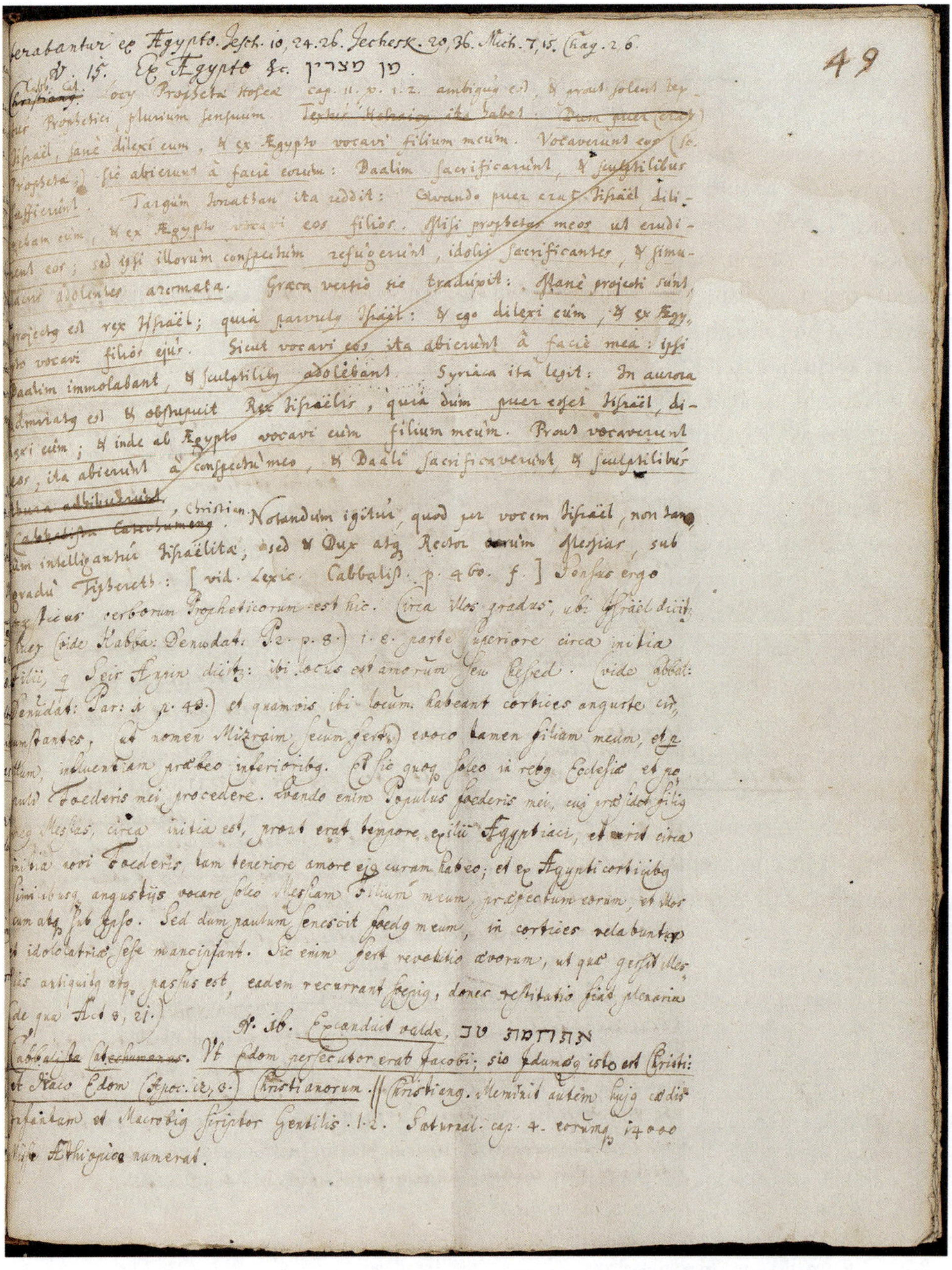

FIGURE 2   Codex Guelf. 126 Extrav., showing Knorr's hand in the first half-page of folio 49ʳ

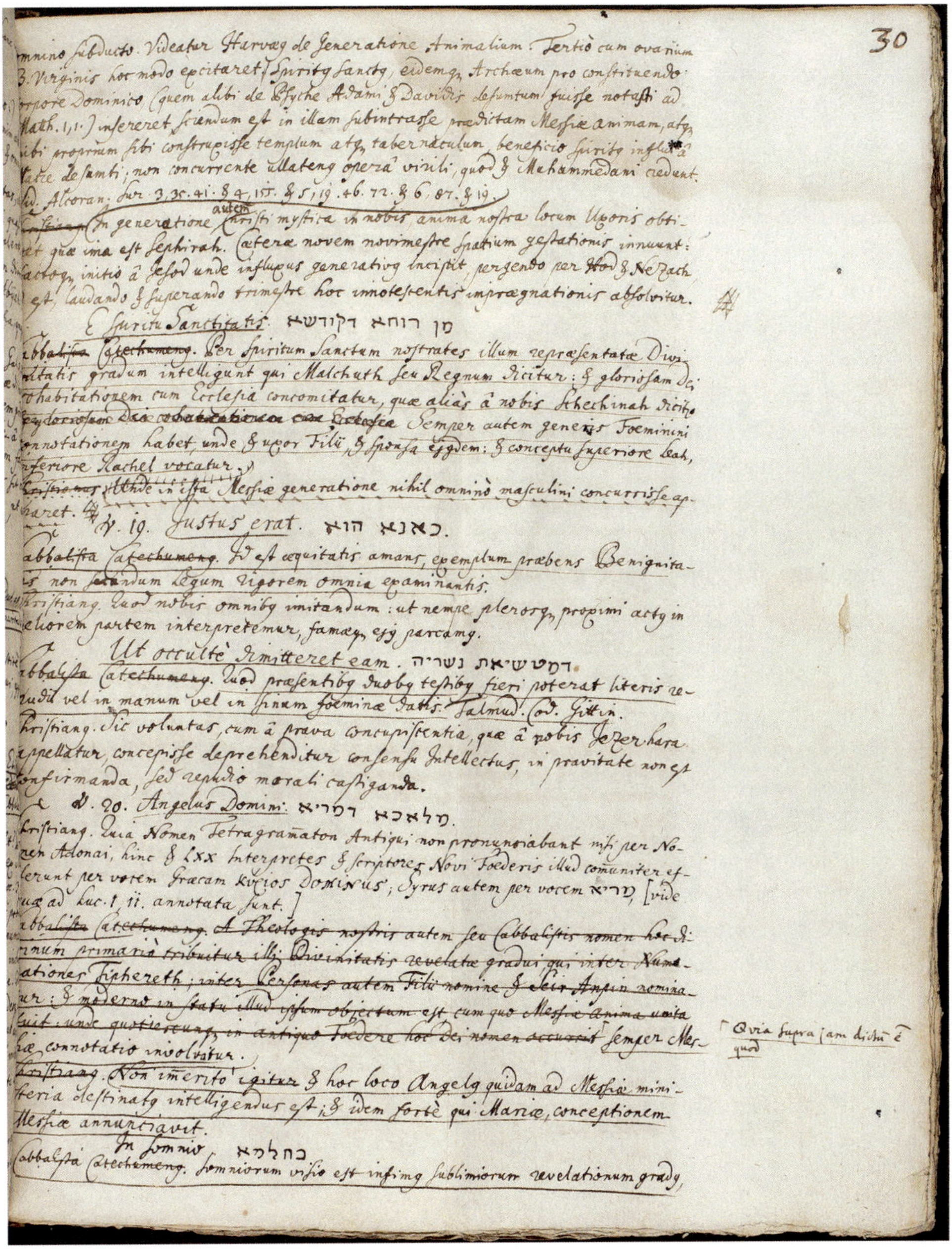

30

omnino subducto. Videatur Harvaeus de Generatione Animalium. Tertiò cum ovarium B. Virginis hoc modo excitaret Spiritus Sanctus, eidemque Archaeum pro constituendo corpore Dominico (quem alibi de Psyche Adami & Davidis desumtum fuisse notasti ad Math. 1,1.) insereret, sciendum est in illam subintrasse praedictam Messiae animam, atque ibi proprium sibi construxisse templum atque tabernaculum beneficio spiritus influxu à Patre desumti; non concurrente ullatenus opera virili; quod & Mahammedani credunt. Vid. Alcoran. Sur. 3.35.41. & 4,155. & 5,19.46.72. & 6,87. & 19.

Christianus In generatione autem Christi mystica in nobis anima nostra locum Uxoris obtinet quae ima est Sephirah. Caeterae novem novimestre spatium gestationis innuunt: factoque initio à Jesod unde influxus generativus incipit, pergendo per Hod & Nezach est, laudando & superando trimestre hoc innocentis impraegnationis absolvitur.

E Spiritu Sanctitatis מן רוחא דקודשא

Cabbalista Catechumenus. Per Spiritum Sanctum nostrates illum repraesentatae Divinitatis gradum intelligunt qui Malchuth seu Regnum dicitur: & gloriosam Dei cohabitationem cum Ecclesia concomitatur, quae alias à nobis Schechinah dicitur. Semper autem generis Foeminini connotationem habet, unde & uxor Filii, & sponsa ejusdem: & conceptu superiore Leah, inferiore Rachel vocatur.

Christianus Unde in ista Messiae generatione nihil omnino masculini concurrisse apparet. v. 19. Justus erat. כאנא הוא

Cabbalista Catechumenus. Id est aequitatis amans, exemplum praebens Benignitatis non secundum legum rigorem omnia examinantis.

Christianus. Quod nobis omnibus imitandum: ut nempe plerorumque proximi actus in meliorem partem interpretemur, famaeque ejus parcamus.

Ut occultè dimitteret eam. דמטשיאת נשריה

Cabbalista Catechumenus. Quod praesentibus duobus testibus fieri poterat literis repudii vel in manum vel in sinum foeminae datis. Talmud. Cod. Gittin.

Christianus. Sit voluntas, cum à prava concupiscentia, quae à nobis Jezer hara appellatur, concepisse deprehenditur consensu Intellectus, in pravitate non est confirmanda, sed repudio morali castiganda.

v. 20. Angelus Domini. מלאכא דמריא

Christianus. Quia Nomen Tetragrammaton Antiqui non pronunciabant nisi per Nomen Adonai, hinc & LXX Interpretes & Scriptores Novi Foederis illud communiter efferunt per vocem Graecam Κύριος Dominus; Syrus autem per vocem מריא [vide quae ad Luc. 1, ii. annotata sunt.]

Cabbalista Catechumenus. A Theologis nostris autem seu Cabbalistis nomen hoc divinum primariò tribuitur illi Divinitatis revelatae gradui qui inter Numerationes Tiphereth; inter Personas autem Filii nomine & Seir Anpin nominatur: & moderno in statu illud ipsum objectum est cum quo Messiae Anima unita fuit: unde quotiescunque in antiquo Foedere hoc dei nomen occurrit semper Messiae connotatio involvitur.

Quia supra jam dictum est quod

Christianus. Non immeritò igitur & hoc loco Angelus quidam ad Messiae ministeria destinatus intelligendus est; & idem fortè qui Mariae conceptionem Messiae annunciavit.

In somnis בחלמא

Cabbalista Catechumenus. Somniorum visio est infimus sublimiorum revelationum gradus,

FIGURE 3 Codex Guelf. 126 Extrav., folio 30r

5 The Syriac Paper Slips

Provision is made in the layout of the pages throughout the manuscript for the insertion of the text of the 1684 Sulzbach Peshitta to the several New Testament passages quoted at length for comment. There are seven cases where the text has been carefully cut from the pages of an exemplar and stuck into the manuscript. However in each of these cases the Peshitta text is scored through in the manuscript and it does not at any point appear in the printed fragment in BSB.

On the fourth occasion (folio 13^r) where the Peshitta text of Lk 1,26–38 is needed, the Syriac for the last two verses 37 and 38 is missing. However there is space for the two verses to be cut out and added to the space left. These two verses appear on the next page of Knorr's 1684 edition and so would have had to be cut from another sheet. On the sixth occasion (folio 20^v) where the Peshitta text of Mt 1.1–25 is needed, only the Syriac for verses 1–18 appears and there is no space left for the Peshitta of verses 19–25. These verses again fall on the next page of Knorr's edition. It would appear that the space required was significantly mis-calculated here. On the seventh occasion (folio 32^v) where Lk 1.57–80 is being cited, the Syriac is missing from the last part of verse 66 to verse 80, though it appears that space had been left sufficient for its insertion. Thereafter for the text of Lk 2.1–39 (folio 36^v), Mt 2.1–23 (folio 45^r) and Lk 2.40–52 (folio 50^v) spaces have been left for the insertion but there is no text inserted.

Several scenarios may be imagined to account for all this, but it would seem reasonably safe to conclude that plans entertained as the manuscript was drafted were dropped when it came to printing, perhaps because of the difficulties of printing, though these were hardly insuperable. We have suggested above that von Rosenroth was forced by practicalities to modify the project announced by Bayle of a commentary upon the Syriac text placed alongside his collection of extracts from the Zohar, and that this became finally *Messias Puer* and the ancillary collection (now lost, but to an extent reconstructable) of the *Excerpta*. It is possible that we should see a similar reduction of aspiration in the face of practicalities in the case of the once intended citations of the Peshitta.

6 From Manuscript to Print

The *Bayerische Staatsbibliothek* (BSB) exemplar is without title page, date or place. As we have seen above there seems to be no other copy of it and J. Fabricius' 1724 reference to the work may indeed be to the same volume.

THE MANUSCRIPT   25

The catalogue title of *Historiæ evangelicæ initium* is taken, as occurred with the manuscript, from the first words of the text which were added in Knorr's hand. It comprises about a hundred pages, but the printed text breaks off after the first part of folio 19ʳ and so represents only about a third of the text of the manuscript. It is a rather inaccurate printing of the final form of the manuscript.[12] It displays several orthographic variants, which are not of great significance (*ante hâc* rather than the manuscript's *antehac*; *eôdem* rather than *eodem*; *DEum* rather than *Deum*) and should not be a great surprise since printing houses often had their own orthographic peculiarities. Though the changes to the manuscript marked by Knorr are correctly made, the printed version has some graver faults. First, biblical references are often given incorrectly, although the correct form appears in the manuscript.[13] Then several words are incorrectly spelled, though they are correctly written in the manuscript.[14] Finally and more seriously, arising probably from ignorance rather than carelessness, numerous Hebrew words appear written quite incorrectly, though once again, the manuscript has the correct forms.[15]

We have mentioned an initial anonymous manuscript annotation indicating the work was recognised as Knorr's.[16] A final anonymous manuscript note comes at the end of the printed text which says that printing was broken off because of the death of the author: "*Plura non sunt impressa. Auctor operi est immortuus.*"[17] The catalogue of the *Bayerische Staatsbibliothek* gives no place of printing but dates the piece to 1690. It may however be that 1689 is more probable if the printing was indeed stopped by the death of Knorr in April of 1689.

---

12   The inaccuracy of the BSB exemplar can also be explained by the supposition that it is a first proof which had not undergone correction. That may partially explain, for example, why the words in Hebrew type are erroneously spelled.

13   BSB reads "Matth.1, 28" instead of "Matth.1, 18" on folio 10ʳ, "Dan. 10, 5–19" instead of "Dan. 10, 5–10" on folio 15ʳ, "Hebr. 13" instead of "Hebr. 1, 3" on folio 17ᵛ, "Act. 17, 18" instead of the correct "17, 28" on folio 17ʳ.

14   *naturam* instead of *naturarum* on folio 4ʳ; *generalite* instead of *generalitate* on folio 8ʳ; *Nercabhâ* instead of *Mercabhâ* on folio 8ʳ; *Talis* instead of the proper name *Talius* on folio 10ʳ; *eundem* instead of *eandem* on folio 11ʳ; *subjicenda* instead of *subjicienda* on folio 18ʳ.

15   אליחו instead of אליהו on folio 9ᵛ; וכ בית instead of בכ בית; מתים ("the dead") instead of מרים ("Mary") on folio 14ʳ! The printer's evident difficulty with the Hebrew here may be the reason why the Syriac text in Hebrew letters in the manuscript was ultimately omitted from the printed fragment. Clearly we must assume that for some reason the printing expertise which was available to Knorr in 1684 was not available to him in 1689.

16   Cf. *supra*.

17   "No more was printed, for the author of the work died".

At first glance, the state of the manuscript makes it hard to imagine it as the direct basis of the fragmentary printed edition. It is difficult to conceive that the printer, working normally rapidly and mechanically, could be able to include so many corrections and additions. However the most part of the corrections which appear in the first part of the manuscript are indeed well and truly represented in the printed edition in the *Bayerische Staatsbibliothek*. Two possibilities may be entertained: either there once existed an intermediate "clean" manuscript containing a "fair copy", but now lost, which the printer used; or the manuscript in the *Herzog August Bibliothek* could have been itself used, if one imagined that the author, Knorr von Rosenroth, actively participated in the printing process.[18] It is this latter possibility which should probably be preferred for several reasons: first of all this is what is suggested by the anonymous manuscript note which concludes the printed version in the *Bayerische Staatsbibliothek*—this clearly indicates the involvement of the author to the extent that the printing did not continue without him; also the collaboration of authors in the printing of their own works, particularly in the area of *Hebraica*, is well documented;[19] further all the corrections and additions which appear in the first part of the manuscript have been included in the printed edition; and then we may mention an instruction in German (presumably because addressed to the printer) in Knorr's own hand added to the first page of the manuscript indicating that all material underlined in the manuscript should be printed in smaller type.[20] This very much suggests that the manuscript did

---

18   The HAB Catalogue confidently describes the manuscript as *"Druck-vorlage"* ("A printer's copy") (*Kataloge der Herzog August Bibliothek Wolfenbüttel*, op. cit., p. 80).

19   S.G. Burnett, "Christian Hebrew Printing in the Sixteenth Century: Printers, Humanism and the Impact of the Reformation", *Helmantica: Revista de Filología Clásica y Hebrea*, 51/154 (2000): pp. 13–42, p. 28. In 1683 the Lutheran Johannes Holst (1648–1726), the assistant of the Reformed Christian printer, Abraham Lichtenthaler (who had first established a printing house in Sulzbach in 1664) set up his own press. Thereafter, Moshe ben Uri Shraga Bloch set up a Hebrew press which was to produce a long line of Hebrew books until it was closed in 1851. Both Christian Knorr von Rosenroth and Francis Mercury van Helmont were involved in its establishment. Bloch's first book was the Sulzbach Zohar *Typis Moysi Bloch & opera Johannis Holst Prostat Norinbergae apud Wolfgangum Mauritium Endterum*. Knorr also helped Bloch with the production of his *Sefer Chesed le-Abraham* by Abraham ben Mordecai Azulai (1570–1643) in 1685, as we shall see below. Thus Knorr's involvement in the printing process should therefore not necessarily be a cause for surprise. For Hebrew printing in Sulzbach, see M. Weinberg, "Die hebräischen Druckereien in Sulzbach", *Jahrbuch der Jüdisch-Literarischen Gesellschaft*, 1 (1903): pp. 25–32; Id., "Die hebräischen Druckereien in Sulzbach" *Verbesserungen und Ergänzungen* (Frankfurt: Sänger & Friedberg, 1923) and Huss, "Text and Context of the 1684 Sulzbach edition of the Zohar", art. cit., pp. 122–124.

20   *"NB. Alles was unterstrichen ist, soll mit kleinerer Schrift gesetzt werd[en]"*. ("N.B. Everything

in fact serve as the direct basis of the printing.[21] Finally, if one allows that the printer was well and truly confronted by the manuscript, this would explain the presence in the margin of the manuscript of a numeration of pages and gatherings in red crayon which generally corresponds to those of the printed edition. These marginal annotations of the printer cease to appear in the manuscript at the same point that the printed work also ceases—that is at folio 19^r.

However a more detailed comparison of the numeration of pages and gatherings in the manuscript with those of the printed version indicates less than total agreement and suggests that two pages may be missing from the beginning of the manuscript. The manuscript begins its notation with 3A/1, but the printed text with A/1. Possibly this may indicate the omission of a title page. A close examination of the manuscript, the binding and the sewing confirms the absence of the first page. The loss or suppression of such a title page seems to be the reason why the work was subsequently named in conventional fashion after the first words of its text, in this case *Historiæ evangelicæ initium*.

7 The Red Crayon Markings

The HAB manuscript has been marked with a red crayon. These marks almost (but not quite) entirely concern the relationship between the HAB manuscript and the BSB printed text. They gave the BSB signature and a BSB page number for the manuscript material which immediately *follows* the marking. They also indicate precisely the catchword which appears at the end of each printed page in anticipation of the beginning of the next.[22]

The signature relates to the gathering, in this case a quaternion. Four sheets are folded in half and placed inside one another. Together they comprise eight leaves and sixteen pages, but the order of the printed "pages" on the front and reverse of the unfolded sheets will not be that of the pages of assembled gathering (and some will be upside down). The annotation assists the printer, and also helps the binder get everything in order. The system used is simple: the

---

underlined should be set in smaller type"). The underlined passages in the manuscript are in italics in the printed edition.

21   We have suggested above that Knorr's use of secretaries in producing the manuscript may have been because he wished it to be legible for a printer.

22   Every page has a catchword except BSB p. 14. This seems to be because the next page begins with a half-line of Hebrew type, which would have been unnecessarily awkward to anticipate on the previous page (especially if, as we have suggested, the printer was not confident with Hebrew).

first quarternion is A and thus its first sheet is also A[23], the second sheet 2A, the third 3A, the fourth 4A: if these are in order, all the pages in the gathering will be. To these the page number of BSB is added.[24]

The manuscript begins with the annotation 3A/1; followed by 4A/2; [*deest*][25]; 6A/4; 7A/5; 8A/6; 9A/7 and on to 16A/14. One notices immediately that the *first* printed page of the BSB text was the *third* page of the gathering according to the annotation, but nothing precedes it in the printed text, nor are there any earlier sheets now extant in the manuscript.

The last printed page of the BSB text page 96 announced the beginning of gathering G, which would have begun on page 97. The manuscript has annotations 2G/98 and 3G/99 further marking the beginning of the new gathering, but the printed text stops at page 96.

The printing was demonstrably a success, at least to the extent that the pagination of the BSB is accurate and sequential and so is the order of the signatures. But it seems one or two slips occurred in the process. The paginator initially wrote 6.D/54 followed by 6.D/55 (which should have been 7.D/55) and then 7.D/56 and 8.D/57. Realising perhaps that he had two 6.Ds he corrected 8.D/57 to 9.D/57 to restore the sequence but left the two 6.Ds.

A more considerable muddle however appears at the beginning of gathering B. The annotations run Pr B / [15?[26]]; [*deest*][27]; Pr B/17; Pr B/18; [deletion: Pr?] B2/19; [*deest*][28]; 4B4/23[29] corrected to 4B/20; 6B/21; 7B/23[30]; 8B/24; 9B5[31]/25.

---

23 In fact in the manuscript annotations the first sheet of a gathering is called Pr B; Pr C; Pr D; Pr E; Pr F & Pr G. The Pr graph is written with an extended vertical line rising from the top of the /r/ indicating probably some form of *primus*.

24 The annotation 9B/25 anticipating printed page 95 is in fact written 9B5/25 indicating that the next printed page should carry the signature number B5 at the bottom, which it does. A similar instruction 4B4/23 indicating that page 23 should be marked with signature number B4 (which it is) was deleted when correcting other matters (Cf. *infra*).

25 The omission of this notation seems to be entirely a slip. There is only one other case where a new page in the printed text is not marked in the manuscript and that is at the end of BSB page 15.

26 The number is difficult to read, but the predictable 15 fits the traces.

27 There is no announcement of printed page 16 here in the manuscript where it is expected.

28 There is no announcement of printed page 19 here in the manuscript where it is expected

29 This annotation is correct in as much as page 23 should and does carry the signature B4. The problem is that it is out of sequence here.

30 Here the sequence is restored and continues correctly until the end with the exception of the two 6Ds mentioned above. But notice that the sequence is only restored by the omission on page 22 in the red annotations.

31 The 5 here on page 24 anticipates the beginning of B5 on page 25. The notation B5 is otherwise missing as explained above.

There are extant here 3 Pr Bs (excluding the possible deletion), where there should only be one; there are no manuscript notices anticipating printed pages 16 and 20 and the expected signature numbers B5 and B22 are missing. It may perhaps be suggested that it is the presence of simply too many Pr Bs that has necessitated the subsequent contrivances to restore the sequence. If this point is conceded, it may be asked why the master of the red-crayon felt forced to resort to three first pages to gathering B? May one perhaps suggest that this is a natural consequence of having begun the first gathering A with 3A/1 instead of Pr A/1? When the red crayon reached the end of the sequence for signature A, i.e. 16A, it was evident (from the pagination 16A/14) that there remained two pages of the gathering over. The multiplication of the Pr Bs was simply a way of filling those pages up—but an expediency which demanded the subsequent "fudge" to restore the order. We shall return below to the consequences of the first gathering beginning with 3A/1.

The question of when these annotations were made naturally arises. They have every appearance of being the marks of the printer. It may be suggested that they were made *after* the impression as a way of ensuring that all the material in the manuscript had been printed. In this case, however, it would seem that the details of the gatherings was quite unnecessary as all that was required was to mark the manuscript with the number of the printed page which bore its content. The precise noting of the catchwords may also seem rather overconscientious. Such an hypothesis, asserting that the marks are descriptive after the event, would also entail that at the end of the BSB text there were just three pages printed of gathering G and that these were then omitted from the printed edition. This is not impossible, of course, but perhaps under the circumstances of Knorr's possible indisposition we may imagine the printer reluctant to broach another gathering. It is perhaps more plausible to imagine the annotations prepared immediately before-hand by the printer for the guidance of the type-setter, or perhaps the type-setter making his own calculations of the amount of text he could get on a page and keeping his eye on the catchwords and signatures by a running tally. In the later case, one would consider the text marked up not long before the printing and the slight over-run in the markings at the end, merely an anticipation of a future gathering.

This view may take some support from the two red-crayon marks which are *not* to do with pagination. On folio 3ᵛ just above the annotation 14A/12 there appears a clear sign marking what is apparently to be the indentation of a sequence of numbers (beginning with the text "*1. Quia* ..."). In addition on the same page but a little lower down there occurs the very short Hebrew word *my* in Hebrew script, but surrounded by Latin. It could easily be mistaken, so the red crayon has marked *NB* in the margin as a warning. Evidently while this would be salutary during the printing, it would be totally otiose thereafter.

The manuscript is numbered with Arabic numerals in the top right-hand corner of the recto of every sheet. These are confidently drawn in black ink, but apparently over an earlier red crayon. It is possible that the underlying red numbers were placed upon the sheets of the manuscript by the printer at much the same time as the other red crayon markings. When the printer received the sheets, initially numbering the leaves sequentially would be an obvious precaution before marking up the signatures, the printed pages numbers and the catchwords. It would provide simple security and reassurance which could not be provided by the rather more abstruse numeration of the groupings of the manuscript by Hebrew letters mentioned above which is probably the work of Knorr himself. We may then imagine that after the manuscript's return from the only partially successful visit to printers, someone (perhaps the Duke's Librarian) considered it useful to reinforce the crayon numbers with black ink.

We have seen above evidence in the case of both the manuscript and the printed fragment that the title page has been omitted. Given the extreme discretion of Knorr, it seems possible that it was at some point thought a sensible precaution to suppress the title (though, mercifully, not to destroy the book). The absence of both title pages, however, does explain why the title was lost from both versions of the text itself which was then in both cases named conventionally for the opening words of its text which were apparently added by Knorr himself for this purpose. The title *Messias Puer* was preserved of course in the contemporary notices, but generally taken to have been lost. It is our hope that our edition will reunite the work with its original title and indicate something of the importance of that work in the appreciation of Knorr's corpus.

CHAPTER 3

Changes to the Manuscript of *Messias Puer*

1   The Exceptional Tolerance of Sulzbach

The fact that Knorr spent almost all his life, apart from his studies in Leipzig, Wittenberg and Leiden, in the Palatine Court of Sulzbach is significant. The specific historical context and the religious atmosphere of the Christian August's Palatine Court had a strong influence on Knorr's intellectual development. It was thanks to his friend van Helmont that Knorr first met the Count Christian Augustus.[1] Van Helmont had entered his service in 1650 as a private counselor on religious matters[2], in charge of moderating the interconfessional tensions that brought the protestant Count Christian August into opposition to his cousin Philip Wilhelm, Duke of Pfalz-Neuburg, a fervent Catholic (Count Christian August himself later formally converted to Catholicism). Van Helmont's implication in this controversy brought him before the Court of Inquisition, accused of Judaising. Van Helmont was convicted and imprisoned between 1661 and 1663. His liberation was due to the intervention in his favour of Count Christian August, who protested the religious orthodoxy of his counselor. Van Helmont's later life and publications, however, show very clearly just how very far van Helmont was from any kind of orthodoxy, philosophical or religious. The fact that Christian August was prepared to defend his counselor should also make us question his own rigour, though not necessarily his sincerity. It seems indeed that the Palatine Court of Sulzbach was a place of extraordinary tolerance, which was prepared to welcome all kinds of religious dissidents, whether Catholics or Protestants.[3] Different religious communities

---

1   For a characterisation of Christian Augustus' Court see V. Wappmann, *Durchbruch zur Toleranz: die Religionspolitik des Pfalzgrafen Christian August von Sulzbach 1622–1708*, (Neustadt a.d. Aisch: Degener, 1998); Id., "Juden, Quäker, Pietisten. Die Irenik des Sulzbacher Kreises 1651–1708" in *Union-Konversion-Toleranz. Dimensionen der Annäherung zwischen den christlichen Konfessionen im 17 und 18. Jahrhundert* edited by H. Duchhardt and G. May (Mainz: P. von Zabern, 2000): pp. 119–138; Finke, *Sulzbach im 17. Jahrhundert,* op. cit. and I.M. Battafarano, "'Ob die Juden von Natur stincken'. Thomas Browne und Christian Knorr von Rosenroth gegen die Gemeinplätze des Antisemitismus", *Morgen-Glantz* 2 (1992): pp. 51–63.
2   A.P. Coudert, *The Impact of the Kabbalah in the Seventeenth Century: The Life and Thought of Francis Mercury van Helmont (1614–1698)* (Leiden: Brill, 1998): p. 108.
3   "His support of spiritualist Lutherans like Fabricius, Brawe, and Florinus certainly suggested [...] that his allegiance to the Catholic Church was not what it should be. Christian August pur-

coexisted in the Palatine lands and the Count encouraged religious contacts between Catholics and Protestants by setting up a *simultaneum*, the sharing of the use of places of worship by both communities. The tolerance of Christian August also extended to the Jewish community as well, who were allowed permanent rights of settlement in 1666.[4] The consequences of this favorable climate are observable in cultural matters too: a printing press was established in Sulzbach which was to be of considerable importance in the printing and the diffusion of *Hebraica* and of Knorr von Rosenroth's own works. Fully to grasp the exceptional climate of tolerance, one has to keep in mind that the extraordinarily destructive Thirty Years War (1618–1648), which had ravaged particularly the Holy Roman Empire, was still vivid in everyone's memory and that anti-Semitism was widespread amongst both Catholics and Protestants. Knorr von Rosenroth was twelve years old at the end of the war and we know his family had had to leave their home because of the war. What is more, accusations of Judaizing were common at the time, as is demonstrated by van Helmont's trial. In this context, the atmosphere of the Palatine Court has been properly described as exceptional.[5]

Count Christian August's tolerance was inevitably confined to his own lands and, as is evident from the case of van Helmont, such local protection did not remove wider risks. In spite then of the favorable atmosphere in Sulzbach, we shall not be surprised to discover that Knorr did not write without considerable discretion and that the remarkable evidence of corrections to the manuscript of *Messias Puer* reveals a vigilant self-censorship.

---

sued a policy that had the express intention of turning Sulzbach into a haven for the unorthodox [...] many people with highly questionable beliefs settled there from 1658 onwards, drawn largely by van Helmont and because of the extraordinary degree of tolerance Christian August permitted." (Ibid., p. 55).

4   Allison Coudert quotes an honourable mention of Christian Augustus as a competent Hebraist with a special interest in Kabbalah and a defender of Jews against charges of murdering Christian children from the Lutheran Hebraist and correspondent of Knorr, Joseph Christoph Wagenseil: Coudert, *The Impact of the Kabbalah*, op. cit., p. 135. The correspondence between Knorr and Wagenseil is found in HAB Wolfenbüttel Cod. Guelf 30.4 Extrav. folios 1^{r-v}; 2^r; 3^{r-v}; 4^{v-r}; 6^r. Cf. P. Blastenbrei, *Johann Christoph Wagenseil und seine Stellung zum Judentum* (Erlangen: Harald Fischer, 2004): p. 28 and p. 111.

5   Allison P. Coudert described this in "The *Kabbala denudata*: Converting Jews or Seducing Christians" in *Jewish Christians and Christian Jews. From the Renaissance to the Enlightenment*, edited by R.H. Popkin and G.M. Weiner (Dortrecht: Springer, 1994), pp. 73–96. For a recent account inserting the Zohar project into the centre of Sulzbach reforms after the Thirty Years War: A.B. Kilcher, "The Theological Dialectics of Christian Hebraism and Kabbalah in Early Modernity" in *The Jew as Legitimation. Jewish-Gentile Relations Beyond Antisemitism and Philosemitism*, edited by D. J. Wertheim (Amsterdam: Palgrave Macmillan, 2017): pp. 47–62 at pp. 53–55.

2 Self-Correction and Self-Censorship

The manuscript of *Messias Puer* provides a remarkable document of Knorr's revision and correction of his developing work. Inevitably some corrections indicate the sort of editorial revision any author undertakes upon work in progress: avoiding repetition, clarification, minor expansion or abbreviation. Some corrections indicate perhaps an editorial revision of focus or emphasis, and yet others are more clearly motivated by a self-censorship which sought to make less controversial the impact of the final text. It is a specific aim of our edition that readers should be able to follow and assess for themselves all these corrections.

Evidently Knorr practiced a vigorous self-censorship of his own work. The numerous corrections revealed in the manuscript provide us with a privileged insight to his way of proceeding and his frequent hesitations.[6] The absence of a proper title-page is probably the first indication of Knorr's self-censorship.

We have ample evidence of Knorr's discretion and reluctance to put his name to his works, not least his use of pseudonyms, particularly Peganius and Rautner. Even in the remarks to the reader at the beginning of his 1684 edition of the Zohar, he hides behind the signature of "Collaborantes". This habit of publishing anonymously is mentioned also by Leibniz in his notes recording conversations with Knorr: "M. Rosenroth has published different things without his name".[7] The discretion of Knorr was loyally recalled by his son Johann Christian (1670–1716) in a letter to Daniel Georg Morhof (1639–1691), who at the time held the Chair of History in Kiel, after his father's death.[8]

---

6 The letters of Knorr in Cod. Guelf. 30.4 Extrav. (mentioned above) show a similarly detailed correction of the original text.

7 L.-A. Foucher de Careil, *Leibniz: La philosophie juive et la cabale* (Paris: Auguste, 1861): pp. 75–79, cited by Coudert, *Leibniz and the Kabbalah*, op. cit., p. 46.

8 *"Le souvenir, que vous conservez pour la memoire de feu Mr. mon Pere m'oblige en verité de vous en faire beaucoup de remerciments. Je ne manquerois pas aussi de vous envoyer quelques particularitez de sa vie et de ses veilles, si je ne craignois pas de troubler plûtot les cendres de mon Pere, au lie[u] d'éterniser son nom. Car comme de son vivant, par des raisons politiques, jointes a quelques autres mouvements de pieté, il n'a jamais voulu, que l'on sçache, quels ouvrages il ait mis au monde; ainsi vous jugerez bien, qu'apres sa mort j'ay trop de veneration pour la volonté, qu'il en eût, que de contributer à divulguer ce qu'il tachoit de cacher si soigneusement. D'ailleurs je ne sçaurois vous celer, qu'il y en avoit quelqu'uns de ses écrits, qui après sa mort eurent à essuyer des critiques ainsi rudes, que sanglantes, et quoique j'aurois pû confondre facilement ces mauvais Calomniateurs, il faut pourtant que je vous dise, que force considerations, aussi bien que de bons conseils de quelqu'uns de mes Amis, m'en dissuaderent. Ainsi j'aime mieux veritablement, que les choses restent, où elles sont. Si des livres, que feu Mr. mon Pere a fait imprimer,*

Because the title which appears in the catalogues was added by Knorr's own hand at the beginning of the manuscript text, we may conclude that it was Knorr himself who decided to remove the first pages of the manuscript, which in all probability carried the title as he had initially conceived it. The decision was not without its consequences, since it led to the loss of the text for more than 300 years. But the question of why Knorr ultimately rejected the title *"Messias Puer"* remains. To speak of self-censorship, one must be able to specify the dangerous charges to which a given title might give rise and provide evidence of the desire of Knorr to protect himself from such reproaches. But it is difficult for the modern reader to imagine that "The Child Messiah" could in anyway appear more subversive than "The Beginning of the Gospel Narrative". Perhaps Knorr found the latter title more conventional and more similar to the titles of other contemporary works?[9] It may also be that, if Jewish readers were in mind, the utter unfamiliarity of the phrase and the lack of any memorable consideration of Messiah as a child in Jewish tradition persuaded him that the title was

---

quelque'uns en été edifiées, ou qu'ils leur ont rendu bon usage, j'en suid bien aise et rends grace au Ciel: d'en faire connoitre l'Auteur au monde, ce me paroit pure vanité, dont je sçay, que feu Mr. mon Pere étoit fort éloigné." ("The recollection you preserve of the memory of my late father truely obliges me to thank you very much. I should not fail to send you some details of his life and his labours, if I did not fear thereby rather to disturb the ashes of my Father, than to immortalise his name. For as in his lifetime, for political reasons together with some other promptings of piety, he never wished that it should be known what works he gave to the world, so (you will well imagine) after his death I have too much respect for his wishes, than to assist in divulging that which he tried so carefully to hide. Moreover, I cannot conceal from you that there were some of his writings, which after his death had to endure criticisms so harsh and bloody that although I could have easily confuted these evil calumniators, I must tell you, however, weighty considerations, as well as the good advice of some of my friends, dissuaded me from doing so. So, I really prefer that things stay as they are. If by the books, which my father had printed, some have been edified, or have had good use of them, I am happy and thank Heaven. But to make the author known to the world seems to me to be pure vanity most uncharacteristic, I know, of my late father.") (Text cited in Zeller, "Der Nachlaß Christian Knorr von Rosenroths", *art. cit.*, pp. 56–57).

9   To cite but a few examples: D. de la Carrera, *Historia Evangelica metrice compacta ex ipsis Evangelistarum verbis* (Matriti, 1651); D. de Baeza, *Historia evangelica universa* (Friessem: 1684); R. Simon, *Histoire critique du Vieux Testament. Nouvelle édition qui est la première imprimée sur la copie de Paris, augmentée d'une apologie générale et de plusieurs remarques critiques* (Rotterdam: Reinier Leers, 1685); R. Simon, *Histoire critique des versions du Nouveau Testament: où l'on fait connoître quel a été l'usage de la lecture des livres sacrés dans les principales églises du monde* (Rotterdam: Reinier Leers, 1690); the several editions of A. Arnauld, *Histoire et concorde des IV Evangelistes, contenant selon l'ordre des temps, la vie & les instructions de N.S. Jesus-Christ* (Paris: Veuve Charles Savreux, 1669).

unsuitably unfamiliar.[10] On the other hand, Knorr's project of writing *Messias Puer* seems to have been well known to his contemporaries, as their notices cited above bear witness. Perhaps the author sought to cover his tracks and hide the most controversial aspect of the original title as we know it from the contemporary notices—namely that the work was a commentary upon the New Testament *on kabbalistic principles*—under the far more conventional title of *Historiæ evangelicæ initium*.[11] The strategy was evidently successful: no subsequent scholar seems to have taken any interest in the work at all.

The number of the corrections made to the manuscript indicates the extent of Knorr's self-correction. We have selected below examples of the most important and revealing changes, attempting where possible to indicate the various controversial issues which motivated his self-censorship.

One fundamental correction to the manuscript text, however, may not have been entirely of Knorr's choosing. That is the omission of the Syriac text which was stuck into the initial part of the manuscript. This did not appear in the BSB printed fragment. Where these passages do exist in the manuscript they are crossed through as are the accompanying marginal references designed to illustrate the text. We do not know why no attempt was made to print this material: whether it was the choice of Knorr, or the reluctance of the printer. Given however that we know of Knorr's aim to provide commentary specifically on the Peshitta text and of his own edition of the Syriac New Testament in 1684 and of the fact, as we have seen above, that the layout of the manuscript right to the end (though with some errors) seems designed to receive the extracts of the Syriac text, we may reasonably leave open the possibility that this impoverishment of his work was not deliberately chosen.[12]

---

10   We are grateful here to Carsten Wilke for a stimulating exchange about the figure of the Messiah in the Jewish tradition.

11   In this respect the title given by Bayle with its precise mention of the 150 Excerpts associated with *Messias Puer* seems to be the most reliable indication of what the original title may have been.

12   In the Introduction to his edition of the Zohar in 1684, Knorr told his readers that they needed to hand a copy of his Kabbalistic Lexicon (*"Loci communes kabbalistici"*) and also the other tractates gathered in *Kabbala Denudata*: *"In quibus si paululum quis fuerit exercitatus; (præsertim si Novum Testamentum Syriacum literis Hebraicis impressum frequenter insimul perlegatur;) Opus hoc ipsum non punctatum sine versione, facilè intelliget; cum potissimum nec Commentario destituatur: & in Tomo primo Kabbalæ Denudatæ Lexicon etiam aliquale ad manus habeat, cum adminiculis necessariis aliis."* ("If one practices a little with these texts (and especially if one at the same time regularly reads the New Testament printed in Hebrew Letters), one will very easily come to terms with this work which is neither vocalised nor furnished with a translation—though is still provided with a commentary. Finally the reader should have to hand the Lexicon found in the first volume of

On several occasions Knorr appears to excise from his work extended passages of technical material, which presumably he found upon reflection unnecessarily heavy and which (though quite proper matters of Biblical Introduction) did not much further his exegesis of the New Testament text in terms of Lurianic doctrine. Thus, Knorr deleted several pages of dense technical argument around the question of the original language of Matthew's Gospel at folio 21^r with the remark that he wished to avoid that debate: "*Controversiam tamen ipsam hic non tangebam*". The material deleted was a full and competent account of arguments from several points of view and came to a conclusion which was explicitly in agreement with that of Walton in the ancillary material to his London Polyglot. Evidently he subsequently felt that such a lengthy exposition of the *status quaestionis* was in the immediate context unnecessary.

Knorr also upon reflection shortened (on folio 47^r) some of his remarks upon the background of the Magi, perhaps also considering here that little was gained (and perhaps a certain prejudice produced) by dwelling upon the demonic worship of the Persians. Knorr's natural thoroughness (on folio 49^r) when dealing with all the versional variants in the text of Hos 11.1–2 ("Out of Israel have I called my Son") apparently subsequently struck him as excessive (and much the same could be found in Lightfoot)[13] and he abbreviated his remarks, though he left similar material in his nearby discussion of Jer 31.15 "A voice cries in Ramah" (on folio 49^v).

Two occasions perhaps remain where such judicious editorial pruning was *not* displayed. Both instances reveal Knorr's natural impulse to put down all that may be known about the details of New Testament *realia*, but without the compensating discipline of focused editing. Perhaps a little too long is spent in telling us of John the Baptist's desert (on folio 36^r), particularly as the material is confessedly merely taken from Lightfoot. But surely the most egregious incontinence in this respect is found in comment upon Lk 2.7 (on folio 40^r) when Knorr has an exaggeratedly extended discussion to persuade the reader that Jesus' manger was really a field-stall. Though even in that context, he does have the sense to delete a comment (on folio 42^v on Lk 2.20) which draws attention (after all of this long discussion) to the fact that the text does not actually say Christ was *born* in a field-stall, merely *laid* in one! No doubt he considered it better not to raise a difficulty which might not otherwise occur to the reader.

Kabbala denudata, which offers other necessary assistance"). ("Lectori benevolo salutem!" in *Liber Sohar*, op. cit.). Perhaps he might subsequently (had he lived) have advised them to have equally available a copy of his own 1684 Peshitta New Testament.

13 John Lightfoot (1602–1675), Rabbinic Scholar, Master of St. Catharine's College, Cambridge and Vice-Chancellor of the University.

Of a slightly different nature is the excision of a long exhortation (at folio 28ᵛ) to the several moral and spiritual virtues of Christian life worked up from the etymologies of the forty-nine names which appear in Matthew's genealogy of Christ. *Messias Puer* does remark elsewhere upon the importance of Christian living, but this section is rather long. It is certainly contrived and the fixity of its form makes it rather repetitive and predictable, but it is perhaps something of a *tour de force* and one has no reason to doubt that Knorr took the collective "meaning" of the roots of these names totally seriously and found them spiritually instructive. It was probably the length of the passage and its distance from the immediate concerns of exegesis which led to its excision.

3 Changes of Speaker

As we have seen, the *Messias Puer* consists of a dialogue between two characters, a "Christian" and a "Kabbalist Catchecumen". One editorial difficulty lies in the transcription and presentation of the changes which are made in the manuscript to the alternating exchanges between the two interlocutors. Many of the corrections made by Knorr are aimed at, in the most straightforward cases, changing the speaker. In other cases, they serve to "cut short" one speaker and give his words to the other.[14]

These changes of speaker indicate the progress of Knorr's careful structuring of his dialogue, but also fashion the presentation and role of the *persona* of the Kabbalist Catechumen. From the first folio, the Kabbalist Catechumen's contributions are corrected: *Legem Novam non admittimus* is replaced by *Legem novam non admittunt Hebræi*.[15] The change from the first to the third person plural emphasises the fact that the Kabbalist, who since *Adumbratio* has become a Catechumen, no longer identifies with the Jewish people.[16]

Within the stereotyped conventions of dialogues between a Jew and a Christian, the distribution of the speeches generally presents the Christian as the principal exponent, who teaches the Jew who is for his part invited to convert. But in *Messias Puer* the Kabbalist takes an active and constructive part in the development of the exposition and does not on the whole limit himself to asking questions which merely provide opportunities for long expositional responses from the Christian.[17] On several occasions it appears that the roles

---

14 The reader will find many examples of this in the Apparatus to the Edition.
15 "We do not accept the New Law" is replaced by "The Hebrews do not accept the New Law".
16 Other occurances of this are noted throughout the Edition.
17 For a recent survey of the conventions which characterise this stereotyped genre of a dia-

of pupil and teacher are themselves reversed, as in the case of folios 9ʳ/9ᵛ and 15ʳ/17ʳ, when the Christian after a brief question is treated to the Kabbalist's expositions. However towards the end of the text on folios 43ᵛ, 44ʳ, 45ʳ and 46ʳ the change of speakers is clearly intended to portray the Christian in the role of teacher of the Kabbalist whose role is progressively limited to asking questions. There can be little doubt that Knorr has upon reflection tactfully moved the burden of teaching away from the Kabbalist Catechumen and returned it to the Christian (as the conventions of the genre would normally demand). This promotes the appearance that it is the Christian who has truth to teach the Kabbalist, whereas before correction the text showed clearly that the Christian himself had a lot to learn.

But perhaps we should ask why, in contrast to the usual demands of the genre, the Kabbalist Catechumen was originally given such a prominent part in the dialogue? And why was this subsequently so consistently adjusted by Knorr in anticipation of publication? The original text conspicuously did not observe the conventions of the genre and the Kabbalist Catechumen provided most of the exposition. The answer to such a question must be merely speculative. One might hazard that because most of the material in the dialogue would be new to a Christian reader and is evidently Lurianic, Knorr naturally placed it in the mouth of the Kabbalist Catechumen. Subsequently, we may imagine, he came to feel this unwise and corrected his text to the expected convention.

More boldly one might imagine that behind the Kabbalist Catechumen there lies a real collaborator (and perhaps also a convert) whose substantial contribution to the collaboration lay, as one might expect, in the elaboration of kabbalistic interpretations of the New Testament text. It was this "reality" then (one would suppose) which Knorr effaced by his editorial rearrangement. But, sadly, we do not independently know of any such collaborator, or indeed even who Knorr's Hebrew teacher was.[18] One is also wary of assuming that Knorr could not have written *Messias Puer* on his own, a point we shall return to below.

---

logue between a Jew and a Christian, *Dialogue de Timothée et Aquila. Dispute entre un juif et un chrétien*, translated by S. Morlet (Paris: Les Belles Lettres, 2017): pp. xi–xvii. More extensively, see G. Dahan, *La Polémique chrétienne contre le judaïsme* (Paris: Albin Michel, 1991): pp. 57–95.

18 Boaz Huss remarked that we would understand Knorr better if we could identify his Hebrew teacher ("Text and Context of the 1684 Sulzbach edition of the Zohar", *art. cit.*, pp. 133–134). He conjectured that that teacher might be a Sabbatian, but, at least in *Messias Puer*, there is no positive support for that suggestion. The argument for Sabbatian influence is presented (though still without decisive proof) as an hypothesis in A.B. Kilcher, "The Theological Dialectics of Christian Hebraism and Kabbalah in Early Modernity", *art.*

Smaller adjustments apart from the exchange of speakers also appear eloquent. One deletion which must strike the modern reader as an extraordinary erasure of precisely the identity we do not hesitate to attribute to Knorr is found on folio 32ʳ in a comment on Mt 1.23. Here Knorr suppresses a mention of "Christian Kabbalists". It is naturally precisely in these terms that we understand Knorr's *œuvre*, but evidently he felt that his presentation of his convictions would not be helped by using such a clear and unambiguous notice of his intentions. It was more prudent, no doubt, not to draw attention to the possibility of such a clearly articulated programme.[19]

The original text commenting upon Lk 2.31 (on folio 44ʳ) has: "*illa revelatio illa Cabbalistarum qua ...*". On reflection Knorr evidently felt this betrayed too much of his own very positive evaluation of the Kabbalistic tradition (as *revelatio*). He therefore corrected the text to an anodine "*relatio*"![20] Here Knorr really does give expression to his own settled view of the Zoharic tradition, yet steps back from it with the characteristic self-censorship which we meet throughout the manuscript of *Messias Puer*. A clear statement of this conviction of the worth of the Zohar is found in *Epistola Compilatoris* (to Henry More):

> I considered that the great schism of the Christian Religion has no other cause than the difference of philological terms and metaphysical principles among the Christians [...]; therefore I concluded that I had to search after that ancient philosophy which flowered at the time of Christ among his disciples and which stems from the oldest sources of the Holy Oracle. When I was turning to search after this ancient doctrine of God and other spiritual and theological matters, I came across the oldest book of

---

cit., pp. 53–55. The issue here, of course, is specifically that of who taught him Kabbalah. Several scholars in Amsterdam have been proposed for the role (Thomas de Pinch (1614–1679); Isaac de Rocamora (1601–1684) or R. Meir Stern from Frankfurt) but there is no decisive evidence. As to Knorr's basic knowledge of the language, he probably acquired that during his time in Leipzig (1655–1660), where we know the language had been taught since 1519 and where Knorr founded a circle for the study of Hebrew and other oriental languages in 1660 (see *Infra*, chapter 4, footnote 39). The professors of Hebrew during his time there were Martin Geier (from 1639–1658) and Johann Adam Scherzer (from 1658–1667). Knorr also proposed a Hebrew language society in Sulzbach (perhaps rather like the Deutschgesinnte Genossenschaft of Philipp von Zesen (1619–1689) of which he was a member) in the Address to the Reader which he wrote at the beginning of Van Helmont's *Alphabeti vere Naturalis* of 1667 pp. 7–8.

19 The term "cabala Christiana" is not apparently employed much before *c.*1600. Heinrich Khunrath uses it in *Amphitheatrum sapientiae* (Hamburg: 1595) and in *Von Hylealischen, das ist Pri-materialischen Catholischen algemejnem Naturljchen Chaos* (Magdeburg: Gehne, 1597).

20 That is an "account" rather than a "revelation".

the Jews, the Book of Splendour [*i. e. the Zohar*]. Even though I questioned the age of this book in view of its division into chapters, I was aware that the chapters themselves and the teachings, which seem to be fragments rather, were very old and contained most ancient teachings and propositions.[21]

4 Charges of Judaising

The quest for a deeper understanding of the Hebrew language that is found throughout Knorr's work is yet more apparent in *Messias Puer*. The work displays a desire to place Hebrew in an expanded perspective which engages not only with several other Semitic languages (Syriac, Aramaic and Arabic) but also seeks to demonstrate the greater usefulness of Aramaic for its purposes in comparison with the usual Latin and Greek. The point of this linguistic exercise is to provide the Christian reader with direct access to a biblical text of both Old and New Testaments (unencumbered by intervening translation), which is expressed in terms significantly similar to those of the Zohar. Another consideration motivating this search is apparent in *Messias Puer*: the necessity of mastering the subtleties of the Hebrew text in the context of Christian polemics against Judaism. In practice, Jews frequently based their arguments resisting conversion upon their knowledge of the text of the Hebrew Bible. The traditional, often typological, exegesis whereby Christians found predictions of Jesus Christ in their "Old Testament" was countered by a divergent interpretation upon the part of Jews who considered the Christians incapable of understanding the nuances of the Hebrew text. Evidently it is to just such a challenge that *Messias Puer* seeks to respond.

However this interest in the study of Hebrew and the intense investment of effort it necessitates was far from enjoying universal approval and was

---

[21] "*Cæterum, cum tanta Religionum Christianarum divortia non aliunde orta esse suspicarer, quam à tanta Principiorum Philosophicorum, definitionumque Metaphysicarum inter Christianos diversitate* [...] *Illicò mentem subiit, illam ipsam indagare Philosophiæ antiquitatem, quæ ipsius etiam Christi & Apostolorum tempore viguit, & è cujus scaturigine quicquid ferè est Sacrorum oraculorum fluxisse videtur. Scrutatur igitur antiquas illas de Deo, cæterisque quæstionibus Pneumaticis atque Theologicis opiniones, in antuiquissimum illum Judæorum librum incidi quem Sohar, seu splendorem appellant; cujus antiquitatem, quamvis ob recentiorem capitulorum ejus compilationem oppugnari viderem, ipsa tamen capitula atque tradita, quæ fragmenta potiùs dicenda sunt, antiqua satis esse, & antiquissimas explicare opiniones atque hypotheses abunde reperi.*" ("Excerpta ex Epistola quadam Compilatoris de utilitate Versionis Libri Cabbalistici Sohar" in *KD I*, p. 3).

often thought suspect, Jewish language and Jewish religion being considered as inextricably linked.[22] Consequently anyone knowing Hebrew risked being suspected of practicing Judaism. In the context of the mutual hostility of Jews and Christians, the later did not consider that the language used by Jews might be of any use whatsoever. Finally the main reason for refusing the study of Hebrew was the fear of the establishment of any connection with Jewish religious conceptions which might threaten to damage Christian faith.

It is in this perspective that one should understand the accusation of Judaising so frequently levelled at Christian Hebraists. If the suspicion had long existed, it was particularly prevalent in Protestant Europe of the Seventeenth Century, where both Catholics and Protestants used charges of Judaising against each other, and Protestants against other Protestants. Knorr and his work were evidently not immune to the consequences of this situation and we find reflections of it throughout his writings. The tension evident in the works of Knorr between his attraction to Hebrew, his prudence in fear of these dangerous accusations, and the methods he uses to neutralise or deflect the risk are more easily understood if they are imagined as an "Art of Writing" as suggested by Leo Strauss[23]. In the context of his studies of Jewish and Islamic philosophy in the Middle Ages, Leo Strauss observed that the experience of living subject to forms of political and intellectual persecution led writers to avoid censure or condemnation by developing a "special language" which would enable them to develop their ideas, while at the same time concealing them. According to Strauss this "Art of Writing" is found most frequently amongst philosophers.[24] Strauss considered that that which the author allows to be understood "between the lines" constitutes, even if this evidently contradicts that which the author himself elsewhere affirms, the reality of his thought and the real depth of his conviction.[25] Knorr's work is characterised by a tension between confirmity to the ideological exigencies of his community—a Chris-

---

22 On this, see J. Friedman, *The Most Ancient Testimony: Sixteenth-Century Christian-Hebraica in the Age of Renaissance Nostalgia* (Athens: Ohio University Press, 1983): pp. 16 et sq.

23 L. Strauss, *Persecution and the Art of Writing*, 2nd ed. (Chicago and London: University of Chicago Press, 1988). For early discussion of the morality of dissimulation and a broad account of its history, see P. Zagorin, *Ways of Lying. Dissimulation, Persecution and Conformity in Early Modern Europe* (Cambridge, Mass.: Harvard University Press, 1990): especially pp. 255–288.

24 Strauss wrote after working on Maimonides. He further clarified his ideas and answered some of his critics in Id., "On a Forgotten Kind of Writing", *Chicago Review* 8/1 (1954): pp. 64–75.

25 It is the suggestive value of Strauss's remarks we allude to here: we are not concerned to promote his imaginative insight into a hermeneutic method.

tian community suspicious of anything having its origin in Judaism—and the necessity of sufficiently accomodating both his own intellectual coherence and his particular personal engagements. Recource to the "art of writing" permits simultaneously apparent conformity to community opinions and thus avoidance of the danger inevitably consequential upon a public expression on the part of Knorr of his admiration for Jewish tradition, but at the same time preserves for capable and understanding readers the philosophic burden of this literature.

Knorr's remarks upon the question of the utility of Hebrew Studies should be read bearing in mind this key to their understanding. Accusations of Judaising were rife at the time of the publication of Knorr's major works and his friend and collaborator Francis Mercury van Helmont had suffered their consequences a few years earlier. Paradoxically it was the current atmosphere of anti-Judaism which encouraged our author to present his work as an attempt to conform Judaism to Christian doctrine so as to avoid personal attacks. This same paradox was observed a long time ago by James Overfield when he offered a re-evaluation of the dispute which had opposed Reuchlin to the Dominican Pfefferkorn. Though this had previously long been considered a dispute between Scholastics and Humanists,[26] Overfield claimed it was anti-Judaism rather than anti-Humanism which was at the root of the proceedings targeting Reuchlin.[27] More recently Robert J. Wilkinson drew attention to similar struggles in the context of the 1553 burning of the Talmud and Andreas Masius' letter to Cardinal Pighino of the same year.[28]

In the same fashion, we observe with Knorr a tension between the need to conform to the demands of the society to which he belonged, and, on the other hand, the necessity of preserving both "the intellectual coherence of thought and individual integrity".[29] This tension is at the origin of numerous passages in

---

26   [129] So for example: C.G. Nauert, "The Clash of Humanists and Scholastics: An Approach to Pre-Reformation Controversies", *The Sixteenth Century Journal*, 4/1 (1973): pp. 1–18, p. 4; and the more detailed P.O. Kristeller, *Renaissance Thought: the Classic, Scholastic, and Humanist Strains* (New York: Harper and Row, 1961).

27   J.H. Overfield, "A New Look at the Reuchlin Affair", *Studies in Medieval and Renaissance History*, 8 (1971): pp. 165–207.

28   R.J. Wilkinson, *Orientalism, Aramaic and Kabbalah in the Catholic Reformation* (Leiden: Brill, 2007): pp. 91–94.

29   This type of dilemma, with which a writer might find himself confronted, was observed by C.G. Nauert in his work on Peter of Ravenna in the context of polemics between Scholastics and Humanists: "Peter of Ravenna and the 'Obscure Men' of Cologne: A Case of Pre-Reformation Controversy", *Renaissance. Studies in Honor of Hans Baron* (DeKalb, IL: Northern Illinois University Press, 1971): pp. 609–640.

the *Kabbala Denudata* where the writer argues in favour of the study of Jewish Literature and in which he wavers constantly between admitting the inherent difficulty of these texts—indeed the distaste they may provoke[30]—and the necessity of passing beyond this repugnance to a perception of their hidden wisdom. The number of oscillations in *Kabbala Denudata* between these two contrasted poles is astonishing and indicates the complexity of the question in hand. In view of the context of suspicion which we have described, this type of writing is evidently intended to disarm in advance the accusations of Judaising to which Knorr was liable. In this light, the negative criticisms of Kabbalah may be understood as part of the practice of an "Art of Writing". Under threat, Knorr developed a line of argument which superficially conformed to the common view that it was useless, indeed, dangerous, to devote oneself to the study of Hebrew texts. Just as Strauss suggested in other cases, this strategy had two goals: to escape from an ever-present threat which menaced any open expression of admiration for kabbalistic texts; but also to preserve the philosophic value of this literature for those capable of reading it.

This imaginative "key to reading" has a special interest in our case and appears to work on two levels; for the kabbalistic literature Knorr was studying was also founded on similar principles of discretion. Significantly, Leo Strauss when analysing this "Art of Writing" in Maimonides, called Maimonides (with a knowing paradox) *the first kabbalist*.[31]

30 Some statements about the difficulties faced by one who would take interest in the study of Kabbalah offer very emphatic and colourful formulations: "So without being intimidated by the extraordinary stylistic difficulty [of these kabbalistic texts], nor by the apparently inscrutable riddles, with which the [*Kabbala*] abounds, I undertook to follow this pathway, thereafter scattered with boulders, rough ground, chasms and precipices and so covered with mud that there is little surprise that most people abandon it, repelled by an unavoidable distaste. There is little surprise, then, that most turned away, driven off by this inevitable revulsion." (*"Non absterritus igitur incredibili styli ejus difficultate, nec abstrusissimis aenigmatum quibus scatet involucris, viam ingressus sum paucis tritam, à nemine, quod sciam, emensam, caeterum tot scrupis, salebris, voraginibus, praecipitiis, tantoque coeno refertam, ut mirum non sit quin plerique inevitabili territi fastidio, eam deseruerint."*) ("Excerpta ex Epistola quadam Compilatoris" in *KD I*, p. 3).
31 Strauss, *Persecution and the Art of Writing*, op. cit., p. 51.

CHAPTER 4

Biblical Texts in *Messias Puer*

1   The New Testament Text of *Messias Puer*: The Peshitta Text

The New Testament text upon which the commentary in *Messias Puer* is based is that of the Syriac Peshitta New Testament. This is the text found in Knorr's own Sulzbach edition of 1684: DYTYQ' ḤDT' *Novum Domini Nostri Jesu Christi Testamentum Syriace*, which he cited for the first time in his *Adumbratio* of the same year.[1] The book is a 12° volume of 192 leaves, printed in square unvocalised Hebrew letters and following the shorter New Testament canon[2] to which the printer has added an initial: *Ex Officina Johannis Holst*. MDCLXXXIV. *Prostat Norinbergae apud Wolfgangum Mauritium Endterum*[3]. The text from this edition has literally been cut from the pages of an exemplar and pasted into spaces left throughout the manuscript to receive them. Alongside the space dedicated to the Syriac papers slips—whether they were pasted in or not[4]—the text offers a Latin translation of the Syriac which is then used as the basis for Knorr's exegesis of the passage. This version is substantially different from the Vulgate and the differences are systematically noted in the edition[5].

The first printed edition of the Peshitta New Testament was produced in 1555 in Vienna by Johann Albrecht Widmanstetter (1506–1557), Orientalist and

---

[1] "The New Testament of our Lord Jesus Christ in Syriac". This edition is discussed more fully in Vileno and Wilkinson, "Die Peshitta von 1684", *art. cit.*

[2] For the question of the Syriac canons, see D.N. Phillips, "Les canons des nouveaux testaments en syriaque" in *Le Nouveau Testament en syriaque*, edited by J.-C. Haelewyck (Paris: Geuthner, 2017): pp. 7–26, esp. pp. 14–21 for the Peshitta.

[3] "From the print-shop of J. Holst 1684. Sold in Nürnberg at the shop of W.M. Endert." C. von Tischendorf, *Novum Testamentum Graece* (Leipzig: J.C. Hinrichs, 1894), vol. III, p. 820 mentions a second edition: *"Anno 1684 (cum novo titulo a. 1715) prodiit editio Sulzbachi typis impressa Norimbergae venum data, fortasse ex editione Antverpiensi anni 1575 repetita."* ("In the year 1684 (with a new title from 1715) he produced an edition printed in Sulzbach and put on sale in Nuremberg, perhaps taken from the 1575 Antwerp edition").

[4] Cf. *supra*.

[5] At points Knorr clearly had access to other editions. On Mt 2.23 (folio 50ʳ) the phrase "in the prophet(s)" is said to be vocalised contrary to the consonantal text, but Knorr's 1684 text is unvocalised. Also citations from the longer Peshitta canon clearly cannot come from his edition which presents only the shorter canon. The Peshitta Old Testament is cited in the commentary on Mt 2.15 (folio 49ʳ) for the text of Hos 11.1–2. This was available in Walton's London Polyglot.

Diplomat, using vocalised Syriac type.[6] Subsequently another edition appeared from Guy Le Fèvre de La Boderie, again in vocalised Syriac type, in Plantin's Antwerp Polyglot Bible. Guy Le Fèvre de La Boderie subsequently produced an unvocalised edition in square Hebrew letters in 1584 and this is the text used in Knorr's edition[7]. Syriac is a late, predominantly Christian, dialect of Aramaic. It arrived in Europe on the margins of the Fifth Lateran Council (1513–1515) where it was sponsored by Cardinal Egidio da Viterbo (1469–1532). The Cardinal was a noted Christian Kabbalist and imposed a kabbalistic interpretation upon the language from the very beginning though this was replaced in the later part of the Sixteenth Century with a more pragmatic emphasis upon the relationship of Syriac speaking Christians with Rome.[8]

Though not insensitive to historical periods or dialectal differences, early scholars of Syriac tended to stress linguistic continuities where we more habitually stress differences. An example of this is found in the work of the extraordinary French Orientalist, Guillaume Postel (1510–1581), who entertained a very promiscuous view of Aramaic, finding an unbroken continuity between the ancient language, the Aramaic of the Zohar and the later form of the language used by contemporary Eastern Christians[9]. This is perhaps most apparent in his idiosyncratic translation of the Zohar, which was printed while the Hebrew text itself was still in manuscript[10].

---

[6] For Widmanstetter in this context, see Wilkinson, *Orientalism, Aramaic and Kabbalah*, op. cit., pp. 137–169.

[7] For other printed editions of the Peshitta New Testament, see R.J. Wilkinson, "Les Éditions imprimées de la Peshitta syriaque du Nouveau Testament" in *Le Nouveau Testament en syriaque*, op. cit., pp. 269–289.

[8] For the Kabbalistic context of early Syriac studies, see Wilkinson, *Orientalism, Aramaic and Kabbalah,* op. cit. and Id., *The Kabbalistic Scholars of the Antwerp Polyglot Bible* (Leiden: Brill, 2007). For attitudes to Syriac at the end of the century, see Id., "Syriac Studies in Rome in the Second Half of the Sixteenth Century", *Journal for Late Antique Religion and Culture* 6 (2012): pp. 55–74.

[9] For a modern characterisation of Zoharic Aramaic: A. Rapoport-Albert and T. Kwasman, "Late Aramaic: The Literary and Linguistic Context of the Zohar", *Aramaic Studies* 4/1 (2006): pp. 5–19; Y. Liebes, "Hebrew and Aramaic as Languages of the Zohar", *ibid:* pp. 35–52; C. Mopsik, "Late Judeo-Aramaic: The Language of Theosophic Kabbalah", Ibid.: pp. 21–33.

[10] Judith Weiss's work on Postel's Zohar translation and his approach to Aramaic is fundamental: *Guillaume Postel's First Latin Translation and Commentary of the Zohar*, 2 volumes (PhD dissertation, Ben Gurion University of the Negev, 2013); Ead., "The Quality of Guillaume Postel's Zohar Latin Translation (1547–1553)", *Accademia: Revue de la Société Marsile Ficin* 15 (2013): pp. 63–82; Ead., *On the Conciliation of Nature and Grace. A Latin Translation and Commentary on the Zohar by Guillaume Postel (1510–1581)* (Jerusalem: The Hebrew University, Magnes Press, 2017).

Knorr did not insist upon a common view that the New Testament was originally written in Syriac,[11] though he did consider Syriac to be close to the vernacular of Christ[12]. He was quite familiar with the best contemporary philology had to offer him: the polyglot bibles and their various texts; contemporary chronological studies and rabbinic scholarship. He had Buxtorf's *Grammatica Chaldaica* at his elbow—but, because of his synthetic view of Aramaic, he read the Syriac New Testament as if it was the Zohar, *both linguistically and doctrinally*. Knorr thus contrived to establish, as it were, a common lexical domain across the Targums, the Zohar and the Peshitta. Usages across the dialects thus contribute equally to establishing the meanings and associations of chosen terms. Thus on Lk 2.11 (folio 41ᵛ) Knorr explains that "Jesus" means "saviour"

---

[11]   In the long deletion at the beginnings of his commentary on Mt 1 (folio 21ʳ), Knorr sets out his views on the original language of Matthew's Gospel (folio 32ᵛ on Mt 1.23) and also considers that of the Gospel used by the Nazaraeans and Ebionites. He also follows Walton in his *Apparatus to the Prolegomenon to the London Polyglot* (folios 22ᵛ–23ʳ) in deeming Christ's vernacular Syro-Chaldaean to be a Jerusalem dialect with similarities both to Biblical and Targumic Aramaic as well with continuities with the later Antiochene Syriac, though without many of the lexical items of the later (especially those taken from Greek). He accepts Guy Le Fèvre de La Boderie's suggestion that the distinctive Syriac script was adopted by Antiochene Christians to distinguish their Gospel from that used by the Nazaraeans and Ebionites. On occasion Knorr can find in Syriac a more precise rendering of the original (as in the spelling of Elisabeth (folio 6ʳ) or a more accurate meaning, as in the case of the Syriac preposition for "with" in Jn 1.1). J.C. Wagenseil wrote on this topic in *Exercitatio philologica de lingua authentica sive originali Novi Testamenti et praecipue Evangelii Matthaei* (Altdorf: Literis Schönnerstædtianis, 1691) and determined that Matthew wrote in neither Hebrew or Aramaic. Rudolf Martin Meelführer (1670–1729) similarly discussed the question in an Altdorf dissertation: *An Matthaeus Evangelium Graece scripserit?* (Altdorf: Literis Schönnerstædtianis, 1696). Johan Kemper produced his translation of a Hebrew Matthew in 1703 from a Syriac text printed in Hebrew characters, though it appears this was because he did not read Greek. There seems to be no reason to believe he thought Matthew wrote in Hebrew or Aramaic, see J. Eskhult, *Andreas Norrelius' Latin Translation of Johan Kemper's Hebrew Commentary on Matthew* (Uppsala: Acta Universitatis Upsaliensis, 2007), p. 422. For a broad survey of contemporary conceptions of Syriac, see R.J. Wilkinson, "Constructing Syriac in Latin: Establishing the Identity of Syriac in the West over a Century and a Half (c.1550–c.1700): An Account of Grammatical and Extra-Linguistic Determinants", *Babelao: Electronic Journal for Ancient and Oriental Studies* 5 (2016): pp. 169–283.

[12]   This question of Jesus' vernacular was extensively discussed in the later Seventeenth Century: for example, the two Jena theses, J. Reiskius, *Dissertatio philologica de lingua vernacula Jesus Christi* (Jena: Bauhofer, 1670) and J. Klaeden, *De Lingua Domini nostri Jesu Christi vernacula dissertatio* (Jena: Bauhofen, 1672) which are discussed in a larger context in M. Eskhult and J. Eskhult, "The Language of Jesus and Related Questions" in *KUSATU (Kleine Untersuchungen zur Sprache des Alten Testaments und seiner Umwelt)* 15 (2013): pp. 315–373, at p. 325.

and takes supporting citations from the Zohar, the Targums and the Hebrew Pentateuch. Simeon's enigmatic words in Lk 2.34 (folios 44^r–44^v) are explained from etymologies of Jesus name derived from both Aramaic and Syriac. In the case of the meaning of Herod's name in Mt 2.1 (folios 46^r–46^v) not only Aramaic and Syriac etymologies are evoked, but also one from Arabic, which is in fact preferred. The "transgressions" we have just noted here from Aramaic and Syriac to Biblical Hebrew and Arabic are not exceptional. Often the Syriac text is little more than a pretext for citing Biblical Hebrew material without further to do.

We have on a previous occasion described in detail the use made of the Peshitta by Knorr in both *Adumbratio* and the BSB printed fragment[13]. Those observations generally hold true for the rest of the manuscript, but we may supplement them with further examples. Considerable importance is attached (as we previously indicated) to the translation of the beginning of John's Gospel as the [First] Principle of Creation which introduces *Adam Kadmon*. Also the use of Syriac for Greek common nouns (like "kingdom", "glory", "wisdom" etc.) produces in effect proper nouns homonymous with the sefirot to great expositional advantage as we shall try to show below. Doctrinal issues are favoured by the Peshitta reading of Lk 1.42 (folio 19^r) "Blessed is the fruit which is in thy womb"—where the Vulgate has "the fruit of thy womb"—which avoids any suggestion that Mary may have contributed to the conception of Messiah. On Lk 2.41 (folio 51^r) the Syriac "his people" is judged preferable to the Greek "his parents" in removing any suspicion that Joseph may have been the father of Messiah.[14] On the other hand the Greek *en tois tou patros mou* "about my father's business" is preferred against the Syriac "my Father's house". The Syriac "people of his possession" is judged preferable at Lk 2.1 to the Greek "all the world" (*oikoumenēi*), although Knorr forgot to use that form in his previous long citation of Lk 2.1–18. In the chapter 3 of *Adumbratio*[15], Spector suggests[16] that the author has "emended" the Syriac of John 11.25 from "consolation" to "resurrection". The Peshitta text in fact has *nwḥm'* which is reproduced in the text of *Adumbratio* and which means "resurrection". However, the author may have seen in the word *nwḥ'* "repose" or "serenity", whence "consolation". Knorr appeals to this same connection between "resurrection" and "consolation" on Lk 2.25[17]. Less

---

13   Vileno and Wilkinson, "Die Peshitta von 1684", *art. cit.*
14   Similarly, see the remark on Lk 2.33 on folio 44^r.
15   III.43, p. 16 (Spector, *Francis Mercury van Helmont's Sketch of Christian Kabbalism*, op. cit., p. 53).
16   Ibid., p. 164.
17   *Historiæ evangelicæ initium*, folio 43^r.

momentously, Knorr on Lk 1.80[18] proposed a (not impossible) Syriac etymology for the word "Essene". The Syriac is called in support for Knorr's insistence on Lk 2.7[19] that the Bethlehem "manger" (Vulgate: *praesepium*) was in fact a field stall.

Following the authoritative statement of Bishop Brian Walton (1660–1661), the editor of the magnificent London Polyglot Bible (1654–1657) in his Apparatus to the *Prolegomenon* to the Bible, Knorr, as we have seen, held[20] the vernacular of Christ was a Jerusalem dialect comprising elements from Biblical and Targumic Aramaic (considered to be B.C.) and Syriac, though without many later lexical items (especially from Greek) found in later or Antiochene Syriac. This vernacular he refers to as "Syro-Chaldaean". This was the language Simeon spoke in Lk 2.30[21] and also the vernacular the Angel used in greeting Mary in Lk 2.10[22]. There he announced good tidings of great joy universally to all the world (*'lm'*) but the compiler of the Greek Gospel perhaps working from a fragmentary vernacular notice read this as "to the whole people (*'m'*)" thus propagating a far more restricted view of the scope of the benefits of the birth of Messiah.

Knorr takes some interest in the Syriac forms of proper names, though he is not always consistent in the forms he uses. He specifically denounces the Greek form of Elischeba's name as corrupt. In two cases points of substance are developed from Syriac names. Mary's name is expounded as it appears in the Peshitta [*mrym*] and understood as equivalent to *mryh* "The Lord is *yh*". Whilst *mryh* is an attested biblical Hebrew name, it is glossed here as comprising the Aramaic *mr* [= Lord] followed by the divine name. This plays upon the normal Syriac word for "the Lord" in the Peshitta New Testament, which is *mry'*. The evident fact that the last letter is an /m/ is explained by two arguments from contingency: either the /m/ was substituted for /h/ out of reverence for the divine name (as in the biblical case of Abijam for Abijah) or the final weak aspiration necessitated the adding of the /m/. This philological analysis is presented within the cadre of a reading of the meaning of all the names of Matthew's genealogy as a continuous text to which each name contributes an appropriate religious meaning or exhortation.[23] Mary's name (on the basis of the philological analysis just given) is construed as "and the will of the Soul sub-

---

18 Ibid., folio 36ʳ.
19 Ibid., folio 40ʳ.
20 Ibid., folios 22ᵛ–23ʳ.
21 Ibid., folio 43ᵛ.
22 Ibid., folio 41ʳ.
23 Ibid., folios 28ᵛ–29ʳ on Mt 1.17.

jects itself, passive and feminine, totally to God so that the Lord is God within it" (because of the statement "the Lord is *yh*" which is inside her name). The name of Martha (who was contrasted elsewhere with another Mary) is by similar reasoning given the opposite meaning, as if, rather than submissive, she were "the mistress", her name being taken as the Aramaic *mr* [lord] with a feminine noun ending. On Mt 1.23 the Kabbalist Catechumen subjects Mary's name to numerical scrutiny with some doctrinal point: "the name *mrym* [Mary] has a numerical value of twice that of [the Hebrew word] *'lmh* [virgin, as used in Isa 7.14], as if to say: she was a virgin before birth and afterwards too"[24]. The name of Jesus is also subject to numerical calculations at Mt 1.21[25] and at Lk 2.41[26].

From the very first edition of the New Testament Peshitta in 1555, it was common-place to remark upon the utility of the edition for the evangelisation of Jews. This was particularly so in those cases where Syriac type was not available and square Hebrew letters had (*faute de mieux*) to be used instead. Though the Privilege granted to the *editio princeps* forbade reproduction even in Hebrew type "*aut etiam Hebræarum usitatis formulis denuo exprimere*" for three years in the realms of Ferdinand I, Widmanstetter indicated in his introductory remarks to his appended Calendar of Festal Readings (κκ3) that at that time he had himself intended to produce such an edition: "*Hosce Novi Testamenti libros Hebraeorum literarum usitatis formis (dummodo vos consilii huius mei aeque ac laboris iam exantlati approbatores habeam) exscriptos, propediem edi atque pervulgari curabo*"[27]. The 1569 Peshitta edition of the Jewish convert and Biblical scholar, Immanuel Tremellius (1510–1580) had to be printed in (vocalised) Hebrew letters for lack of a Syriac font in Geneva, but the French orientalist, poet and pupil of Guillaume Postel, Guy Le Fèvre de La Boderie (1541–1598), in his 1584 Paris edition did not even vocalise his Hebrew letters. He sought to turn this to an advantage and remarks in his *Dedicatio* (p. xx) that the reason for not having vowel points on the Hebrew is to enable Jews to read it more as Hebrew or Jewish Aramaic and to make it as little different as possible from the language of their Talmud.[28]

---

24 At folio 32ʳ. On Mary, see further R.J. Wilkinson, "The Kabbalistic Treatment of the Virgin Mary in Christian Knorr von Rosenroth's *Historiae Evangelicae initium secundum quatuor Evangelistas*. A Provisional Description", *Accademia. Revue de la société Marsile Ficin* (forthcoming).
25 Folio 31ʳ.
26 Folio 51ᵛ.
27 "These New Testament books I shall soon have edited and distributed in the usual Hebrew letter font (provided only I have your agreement in this and approval of my hard work so far)". (J.A. Widmanstetter, *Liber sacrosancti Evangelii de Iesu Christo Domino et Deo nostro* (Vienna. Zimmerman, 1555), unpaginated at κκ3.)
28 Guy Le Fèvre de La Boderie, *Novum Iesu Christi D. N. Testamentum* (Paris: Benenatus, 1584): p. xx.

It is very much in this tradition that the Christian Philosopher in *Adumbratio* introduces his Peshitta citations: "In order that little by little we may be conformed to that dialect, we have on several occasions used quotations from it"[29]. The Syriac text is not only a similar dialect to Zoharic Aramaic; its use enables students (or perhaps their discourse) to "be conformed" to a form of expression more suitable for the proposed synthesis of Christian and kabbalistic doctrines. Thereafter in *Adumbratio* citations are taken from the Peshitta (in previous works Knorr had used the Vulgate)[30]. The importance given to this remarkable instrument for Jewish and Christian rapprochement underwent a noticeable development between 1684 and 1688/9. In *Adumbratio*, the use of the Peshitta New Testament permits no more than a "familiarity with this dialect" as we have seen, whereas in *Messias Puer* it is the very foundation of the interpretation developed by the two collaborating characters, since each verse, indeed each word is scrutinised in the Syriac version and evaluated against the Greek version, on occasion to the detriment of the latter. The advantage which is now systematically exploited is that Gospel Truth may be found in both the Zohar and in the Gospels in effectively the same language and the same idiom and that the idioms of the Peshitta may thus be considered to mirror, indeed to constitute tokens of, the very expressions of the Zohar—thereby providing a united linguistic field for exegesis and exposition. Thus, for example, ordinary New Testament common nouns like "kingdom", "glory" or "wisdom" may become the proper names of sefirot with enormous consequence for interpretation.

The Peshitta was published in the same year as *Adumbratio*. *Messias Puer* indicates the increased importance the work had assumed in the imagination of Knorr, an increased importance which alone explains its role in Knorr's last work, which is now known to us. In discussing the context of the Hebrew edition of the Zohar which von Rosenroth brought out in 1684, the same year in which he published both *Adumbratio* and the Peshitta New Testament, Boaz Huss wrote of the "Christian Messianic Mission" he considered to be the background to this year of publications.[31] One may perhaps be permitted further to observe that in the following year (1685), Christian Augustus granted a liberal

---

29 "[...] *juxta textum Syriacum qui scriptis vestris kabbalisticis maxime est conformis, unde ut paulatim in Dialecto conformemur aliquot citationes ex illo instituemus*" (II.§3). Our translation differs from that of S. Spector: "which conforms entirely to your Kabbalistic writers and from which we extract several citations to help us a little in this dialogue." (Spector, *Francis Mercury van Helmont's Sketch of Christian Kabbalism,* op. cit., p. 33).

30 For instance, in "Synopsis Liber Sohar" (in *KD II*), all New Testament quotations are drawn from the Vulgate, with very minor variations.

31 Huss, "Text and Context of the 1684 Sulzbach edition of the Zohar", *art. cit.*, discusses what he calls the "Christian Messianic Mission" on pp. 124–129. See also, W. Schmidt-Biggemann,

charter (which was subsequently renewed) awarding permanent residence to the growing Jewish community in Sulzbach.[32] Such a significant social development (at least for the small number of families involved) may no doubt have encouraged Knorr's enthusiasm for his programme of *rapprochement* in the years between 1684 and the completion of *Messias Puer*.

2 Orientalism and Biblical Studies

Messias Puer is (as it were) a laboratory in which Knorr may be seen developing his ideas. An attentive examination of the sources he used reveals a breadth unusual even for a Christian Hebraist. In addition to other Christian Hebraists (Johannes Buxtorf (1564–1629) and John Lightfoot (1602–1675)) or to the Jewish Grammarian, David Qimchi (1160–1235), Knorr had recourse to Hebrew literature of several genres. After references to Zohar (as collected in *Excerpta*) references to the Talmud are most numerous, then to the Targums (principally Targum Jonathan) and to the Midrashim. However, in addition to the classical Jewish exegetic works, one is struck by the presence of several works which stand out as being contemporary with Knorr. Knorr's interest in recent Jewish works was already evident in his study of Lurianic Kabbalah.[33]

"Knorr von Rosenroths missionarische Intentionen", *Morgen-Glantz* 20 (2010): pp. 189–204.

[32] See "[Jews in] Sulzbach", *Revue orientale*, edited by E. Carmoly, 3 (Brussels, 1843–1844): pp. 138–140, at p. 139; F. Skolnik, *Encyclopedia Judaica* (USA: Macmillan Reprints, 2006), s.v. "Sulzbach", 19 (Som-Tu): pp. 306–307; M. Weinberg, *Geschichte der Juden in der Oberpfalz* (1927): pp. 52–53; C. Weber, "Jüdisches Leben in Sulzbach und Floß im 17. und 18. Jahrhundert", *Morgen-Glantz* 22 (2012), pp. 115–143 at pages 119–120 discusses Knorr's involvement in this. See also R. Zeller, "Die Rolle von Franciscus Mercurius Van Helmont bei der Ansiedlung der Juden in Sulzbach", *Morgen-Glantz* 25 (2015): pp. 383–401.

[33] "*Scrutaturus igitur antiquas illas de Deo, caeterisque quaestionibus Pneumaticis atque Theologicis opiniones, in antiquissimum illum Judaeorum librum indici quem Sohar, seu splendorem appellant; cujus antiquitatem, quamvis ob recentiorem capitulorum ejus compilationem oppugnari viderem, ipsa tamen capitula atque tradita, quae fragmenta potius dicenda sunt, antiqua satis esse, & antiquissimas explicare opiniones atque hypotheses abunde reperi.*" ("I am about to show, then, that those ancient opinions about God and other spiritual questions and theological opinions, are expressed in that most ancient book of the Jews which was published as 'Zohar' (or 'Splendour'). Although I may seem to be contradicted over its age by the more recent collection of its chapters, nevertheless the chapters themselves and the material handed down (which are more properly called 'fragments') are sufficiently old and we notice that they explain the most ancient opinions and hypothesis.") ("Excerpta ex Epistola quadam Compilatoris de utilitate Versionis Libri Cabbalistici Sohar" in *KD I*, p. 3). Cf. also Vileno, *À l'ombre de la kabbale*, op. cit., pp. 83–85.

It is further exemplified here in *Messias Puer* by his knowledge of such works as the chronographical *Tsemach David,* the lexicon *Zer Zahav* and the kabbalistic commentaries *Emeq ha-melekh, Mayyan Chokhmah* and *Pardes Rimonim,* in addition to *Yalqut Reuveni* and *Chesed le-Abraham.*[34]

If Knorr's reputation as a Hebrew scholar needs no further emphasis, his engagement with Biblical studies also is equally well illustrated by the weight of scholarship brought to bear in *Messias Puer.* He appears to have had John Lightfoot's work at his elbow as he wrote[35] and the contrast between the two is instructive. The Master of Catharine Hall had pursued his Mishnaic and Talmudic studies without significant instruction from contemporary Jewish scholars. He was interested in establishing the chronology of Gospel texts and using the Jewish sources to illuminate the *realia* of first-century Palestine. He was not particularly sympathetic to contemporary Jews and certainly had no doctrinal interest in Jewish teaching other than seeing it traditionally as an inferior and obsolete anticipation of Christianity.[36] Von Rosenroth was quite different and was studying the far more advanced and difficult texts of the Zohar precisely for their doctrinal vision and in evident sympathy with local Jewish scholars. Nevertheless Knorr was well informed of several aspects of Lightfoot's work as he was of contemporary biblical linguistic, textual and chronographical scholarship as the annotations to the Translation seek to make clear. Hebrew chronographical texts are also mentioned in references to *Seder Olam* and citations from *Sefer Juchasin,* and we can see he had recourse both to J. Buxtorf's great *Lexicon chal-*

---

34 Several of these works appear in the catalogue of the Sulzbach library to which, consequently, we may have some confidence that Knorr had direct access. Which is not to say that substantial work does not remain to be done in establishing precisely which Hebrew sources he had at his disposal. The *Sefer Chesed le-Abraham* of Abraham ben Mordecai Azulai (1570–1643) was first printed in Sulzbach in 1685 by Moses ben Uri Schraga Bloch with the assistance of Knorr. The manuscript used is now Ms. Heb. 17 in the Universitätsbibliothek in Erlangen. The same year Imanuel Ataias printed another version for Meshullam Zalmon ben Abraham Berack of Gorice in Amsterdam. The text in this edition is both partial and faulty. Unfortunately it is this text which has been used by subsequent editors.

35 Similarities and differences between the two are illustrated throughout the annotations to the translation.

36 None the less Knorr was appreciative of Lightfoot and mentioned him with many other great Hebraists of history in *KD II*, p. 31 § 41: *"Et hâc ipsa lingua viri tot insignes utpote Origenes [et multi alii] Lightfootius atque alii non sibi modo ipsis famam comparavere immortalem; sed & Ecclesiae Christianae hanc accenderunt lucem, qua nobis adhuc, hac quidem in parte, frui concessum est."* ("And in this language so many distinguished men like Origen [and many others] Lightfoot not only acquired everlasting fame for themselves: but also the Christian Churches lit this light which even still today is given to us to enjoy in part.")

daicum and his work on Hebrew Abbreviations. In addition to Hebrew, Syriac was not an unreasonable expectation of a biblical scholar in the second half of the Sixteenth Century[37]. The Polyglot Bibles of Antwerp, Paris and London had made the biblical text available in several ancient oriental languages and sufficient grammars and lexica existed for those who wished to study them. The 1734 Catalogue of the library in Sulzbach (now in Munich) may give a partial picture of some of the "oriental" volumes once held there.[38] Knorr was also interested in the cognate ancient biblical languages.[39] Leibniz tells us of his interest in Hiob Ludolf's Ethiopic studies (and his remarks on a Samaritan letter and comparative alphabets[40]) and he cites the Ethiopian *Synaxarion* for the number of the Holy Innocents. Not all oriental learning was first hand however, and predictably we find erudition at second hand with the citation of Arabic sources taken from Samuel Borchardt (1599–1667), the French Protestant Biblical scholar and Orientalist, and an Arabic etymology for "Herod" taken from the *Lexicon Heptaglotton* of the Cambridge Orientalist Edmund Castell (1601–1686). His description of the language of Jesus is taken with acknowledgement (as we have seen) from Walton. These cases indicate that von Rosenroth was familiar with the best recent work in the field and able to use these resources properly and to advantage.

With respect to Knorr's Zoharic scholarship, *Messias Puer* again makes apparent the cumulative force of his researches over several years. Knorr gives extensive citations to previous Sulzbach compilations. First of all there is the *Excerpta* which we now are able in outline to describe, which was evidently a work designed to complement *Messias Puer*. But extensive reference is also made to the previous anthologies of texts in *Kabbala Denudata*, whence *Loci communes* in particular is a much exploited collection. The earlier works of collection and interpretation were applied to the exposition of the debate in *Adumbratio* (though again they are mentioned only by citation and not by

---

37 For Syriac Studies in the Seventeenth Century see Wilkinson, "Constructing Syriac in Latin", *art. cit.*

38 Cilian Joseph von Düring's 1734 *Novum Inventarium Bibliothecæ Sulzbaco-Palatinæ* (Bayerische Staatsbibliothek, Cbm Cat. 580, Respositorium A.) We have drawn attention in the annotations to the Translation to volumes used by Knorr which are found in this catalogue. We are indebted to Rosmarie Zeller for drawing our attention to this volume.

39 For Knorr's involvement with several friends in a "Collegium Glottologicum zum Studium der Judaistik und der orientalischen Sprachen" ["A Linguistic College for the Study of Judaism and Oriental Languages".] in Leipzig in 1660, see Zeller, "Die Rolle von Franciscus Mercurius Van Helmont", *art. cit.*, p. 391.

40 For a brief bibliography of early Samaritan studies, see Wilkinson, *Orientalism*, op. cit., p. 104, note 37.

quotation). On these grounds we feel emboldened to claim that *Messias Puer* may be regarded as the culmination of a programme of writing and publication which began at least by 1684, the year of the second volume of *Kabbala Denudata*, of *Adumbratio* and of the Sulzbach edition of the Peshitta New Testament.

The full force of Knorr's arguments and their textual support in the Zoharic texts is only really apparent to the reader who looks up the quotations. No doubt this was what the first (or at least, intended) readers would have been themselves obliged to do. *Messias Puer* cannot be read quickly: an experienced scholar of the New Testament may well be able to look at a long string of biblical references (such as Knorr provides) and recall most of the passages. It is far more difficult to imagine readers so familiar with the Sulzbach anthologies that they could so readily identify the passages in question. Not perhaps impossible; but the imaginable readers would probably be Jewish scholars who had themselves cooperated on the collection of the material in the first place. It was clearly to address the problem of mobilising and deploying this accumulated Zoharic erudition in the exegesis of the relevant New Testament texts that Knorr produced the *Excerpta*, as we have argued above. It is for these reasons that we have included in the Apparatus to the Edition extensive quotations from Knorr's previous kabbalistic works when they are cited by him. It is hoped that by explicitly displaying the intra-textual connections between these works that both the coherence and the goal of this body of work will become apparent and that more of the complexity of Knorr's thought may be appreciated by the reader.

Knorr was a very highly competent scholar of Hebrew and Aramaic and the Zohar collections. He also showed himself (like Lightfoot) interested in the chronological problems of Scripture (although in Knorr's case the interest was perhaps ultimately in the use of chronology in the interpretation of predicative biblical prophecies anticipating the events of the End)[41]; questions of history and original languages of canonical books and their production; the considerably different forms of the biblical text across the versions and the realities of life in New Testament times. One might be tempted here to draw a distinction between those matters which some would describe as von Rosenroth's "occultist" interests (contentious though such a retrojection may be) and his well-informed and technical biblical scholarship. This would be wrong. There

---

41   Lightfoot's Anglicanism showed little enthusiasm for eschatological anticipations. He was happy to deploy Jewish knowledge to illuminate New Testament *realia*, but without much sympathy for biblical or contemporary Jews. He was certainly not interested in a Jewish Messianic Kingdom.

is a case to be made for Knorr's importance in the development of a less traditional and confessional biblical studies and even in the emergence of less committed accounts of Religion. With that case, there also emerges the question of whether we should consider Esotericism had any role to play in these developments.

Guy G. Stroumsa's *A New Science: the Discovery of Religion in the Age of Reason* most informatively and stimulatingly traces the long history of this new discipline which he describes in his work, but it is clear that he dismisses "Esotericism" as a possible factor in this development: it was supposedly so boldly opposed to the newly-emerging Reason[42]. Stroumsa does not mention Knorr and his remarks on the contribution of symbolism are confined to the Renaissance (the symbolism of the later Athanasius Kircher being considered as anomalous and characteristic of the Renaissance rather than the Early Modern Period). It is not unreasonable (or uncommon), however, for Knorr to be considered an important representative of what we call, retrospectively for this period, "Esotericism". There are several indications, which, particularly when taken together, argue strongly for Knorr's inclusion in the broader picture of the development of biblical studies and in an account of the birth of this "New Science": his study of Religion, his deep philological consciousness and accuracy. Moreover, *Messias Puer* demonstrates that Knorr was highly interested in the concrete circumstances of production of the biblical texts and the project of their exposition in conformity with the relevant historical, sociological and material knowledge. All these preoccupations Knorr shared with his famous contemporary, Richard Simon (1638–1712), the French Oratorian Priest and Orientalist, almost universally recognized, at least in the French speaking world, as the "Father of Biblical Criticism". We may ask therefore: should we reconsider the limits of the Science of Religions (and maybe to extend them) in order to integrate the retrojected notion of "Esotericism" in some form into it, or should we expand our very provisional definition of "Esotericism" to cater for the extraordinary scholarship of Christian Knorr von Rosenroth?[43]

---

42   G.G. Stroumsa, *A New Science: the Discovery of Religion in the Age of Reason* (Cambridge Mass.: Harvard University Press, 2010): pp. 33–47.

43   Anna M. Vileno is grateful for discussion of these issues after her paper "Knorr's *Messias Puer*: between Western Esotericism and the Study of Religion" at the INASWE (Israeli Network for the Academic Study of Western Esotericism) Conference, held at the Hebrew University of Jerusalem on 30.5.2018.

CHAPTER 5

The Intra-textuality of *Messias Puer*: Knorr Citing Knorr

Messias Puer has remained in manuscript and in spite of its partial printing, does not seem to have much attracted the attention either of Knorr's near contemporaries (with the notable exception of Leibniz and a few others, we have discussed above) or later scholars. None the less, the work constitutes the final advanced state of completion of Knorr's considerable work as a Christian Kabbalist. *Messias Puer* constitutes probably one of the most rigorous applications of Kabbalah to the texts of the New Testament. Its recovery therefore may be expected to stimulate reflection upon his previous writings in the light of the final and coherent exegetical achievement of *Messias Puer*.

On consideration of the copious references made in *Messias Puer*, one is immediately struck by Knorr's constant recourse to the texts he had already anthologised in the two volumes of his *Kabbala Denudata* which appeared in 1677/1678 and 1684. We have argued above that *Messias Puer* was initially accompanied by a companion volume of *Excerpta*, which functioned as a source book of Zoharic material arranged after the order of topics in *Messias Puer*. In a similar way, Knorr made constant reference to material he had accumulated and printed over the previous decade or so. In this case it was not just a collection of extracts, but rather a body of substantial texts, some translations of Hebrew works, others written by himself (possibly with others) like *Adumbratio* or compiled to form a lexicon of key terms like *Loci communes*. *Messias Puer* is raised upon the foundations of these previous works and Knorr assumes the reader has them to hand to consolidate or develop points made in *Messias Puer*. One thus becomes aware of the cumulative force of Knorr's work and realises that *Messias Puer* is in fact the culmination of those previous labours which underpin the whole work.

From general considerations we may turn our attention to the relationships between *Messias Puer* and other earlier specific texts of Knorr. We shall start with two works which were not part of *Kabbala Denudata*, but preceded it, the *Apocalypse Commentary* of 1670 and the *Harmonia Evangeliorum* of 1672 which treats New Testament passages in essentially the same order as *Messias Puer* and offers a similar "world chronology" to that found in *Messias Puer*.

1 The *Apocalypse Commentary* (1670) and the *Harmonia Evangeliorum* (1672)

The Renaissance interest in Chronography was motivated by several related concerns. There was an initial compunction to bring universal history into accord with biblical narrative by reconciling it not only with the Europe's own Classical chronologies, but also with the chronological material provided from the "new worlds".[1] This latter data seemed to complicate matters by offering apparent corroboration of the pre-Adamic hypotheses of different human origins other than from the biblical Adam, which were becoming increasingly popular[2] and which were made notorious in 1655 by the *Prae-Adamitae* of the French diplomat and millenarian theologian Isaac de Lapeyrère (1596–1676) which was Englished the following year as *Men before Adam*. These accounts threatened the integrity of the biblical Adamic lineage[3]. Attempts to defend the scriptural chronology were made even more difficult by the striking differences in the chronologies of the Greek and Hebrew bibles.[4]

In response to this growing awareness of the need for universal histories, particularly in France, chronological studies flourished. Jean Bodin (1530–1596), the French jurist and political philosopher, wrote that "the most important part of the subject [of universal history] depends upon the chronological princi-

---

1 Mingjun-Lu, *The Chinese Impact upon English Renaissance Literature: A Globalization and Liberal Cosmopolitan Approach to Donne and Milton* (London: Routledge, 2015): pp. 89–92 used here. For his discussion of the Milton-Oldenburg exchanges on this topic, see pp. 116–118.
2 Paracelsus had claimed that "it cannot be believed that such newly found people in the islands are of Adam's blood", but rather must have come from "a different Adam". Giordano Bruno held "the black race / of the Ethiopians and the yellow offspring of America [...] cannot be traced to the same descent, nor are they sprung / from the generative force of a single progenitor". See *Readings in Early Anthropology*, edited by J.S. Slotkin (London: Routledge, 2012), p. 43.
3 On Lapeyrère, see D.N. Livingstone, *Adam's Ancestors Race: Religion and the Politics of Human Origins* (Baltimore: Johns Hopkins, 2008): pp. 26–51; R.H. Popkin, *Issac de La Peyrère (1596–1676). His Life, Works and Influence* (Leiden: Brill, 1987). Pages 26–41 deal with pre-Adamites. J.-P. Oddos, *Isaac de Lapeyrère (1596-1676)* (Paris, 2012); A. Pietsch, *Isaac La Peyrère* (Berlin, 2012)
4 The English Calvinist William Whitaker (1547–1595), exploiting these problems in confessional conflict and in support of the Hebrew, remarked in 1610: "there is the greatest difference between the Hebrew and Greek books in the account of dates and years" for "the Greek books reckon 2242 years from Adam in the beginning of the world to the flood, as we read in Augustine, Eusebius and Nicephorus' Chronology. But in the Hebrew books we see that there were no more than 1656. Thus the Greek calculation exceeds the Hebrew by 586 years." (*William Whitaker. A Disputation on Holy Scripture against the Papists*, edited by William Fitzgerald (Cambridge: University Press, 1849): p. 121.)

ple [...] a system of universal time is needed for this method of which we treat".[5] The French Jesuit Dionysius Petavius (1583–1652), whose work Knorr consulted, considered chronology "pure calculation of time" and thus quantitatively different from "history", for:

> History has as its own to possess fully the matter of deeds and to write down their order, usually with proofs, arguments, and witnesses, whence the order of individual years is established. Chronology indeed inquires after one thing, by what signs and marks each thing may be arranged in its years and times, and is nearly always content with that. It does not extend further than individual events.[6]

Chronology is for Petavius one of the four sciences—Physics, Astronomy, Music and Civil Divisions of Time—which have to do with Time.

The study of Time in this manner was decisively advanced by the great French scholar Joseph Scaliger (1540–1609) whose revolutionary *Opus novum de emendatione temporum* of 1583 quite transformed the subject. Treating both sacred and profane sources as of equal value, Scaliger created a single template which allowed him to integrate non-biblical data into the biblical schema and to extend that scheme into the future. He called this his "Julian Period".[7]

It would be inappropriate here to list the many authors of the period, both on the Continent and in England, who wrote on chronographical matters.[8] Suffice

---

5 *Jean Bodin, Method for the Easy Comprehension of History*, translated by B. Reynolds (New York: Norton, 1969), p. 303.
6 This is from the Preface of Petavius' *Rationarum temporum* (Paris, 1633), itself a version of his *Opus de doctrina temporum* (Paris, 1627). For Petavius' chronology, see D.J. Wilcox, *The Measure of Times Past. Pre-Newtonian Chronologies and the Rhetoric of Relative Time* (Chicago: University of Chicago Press, 1987): p. 205.
7 See *Opus novum de emendatione temporum* (Paris, 1583), p. 198. Fundamental to the study of Scaliger's chronology is A. Grafton, *Joseph Scaliger: A Study in the History of Classical Scholarship. Vol 2 Historical Chronology* (Oxford: Clarendon, 1993). There is an excellent summary in the same author's "Scaliger's Chronology: Philology, World History, Astronomy" in Id., *Defenders of the Text. The Tradition of Scholarship in an Age of Science (1450–1800)* (Cambridge Mass.: Harvard University Press, 1991): pp. 104–146 with notes at pp. 276–289. The Julian Period is explained at pp. 104–144. Also Wilcox, *The Measure of Times Past*, op. cit., pp. 198–199.
8 S. Mandelbrote, "'The Doors shall fly open': Chronology and Biblical Interpretation in England, 1630–1730", in *The Oxford Handbook of the Bible in Early Modern England, c.1530–1700*, edited by K. Killeen, H. Smith and R. Willie (Oxford: University Press, 2015): pp. 176–193; A. Grafton, "From 'de Die Natali' to 'de Emendatione Temporum': The Origins and Setting of Scaliger's Chronology", *Journal of the Warburg and Courtauld Institutes* 48 (1985): pp. 100–143; Id., "Tradition and Technique in Historical Chronology" in *Ancient History and the Antiquarian: Essays in Memory of Arnaldo Momigliano*, edited by M. Crawford and C.R. Ligota

it to note that Scaliger himself remarked to Seth Calvisius (whose chronological work Knorr also consulted) in a letter of 3 October 1605 that every year the Frankfurt Book Fair witnessed a new crop of chronographical books— *"Nullae Francofurtenses nundinae sine Chronologorum proventu"*.[9] Not that quantity brought unanimity: it has been noted that twenty-nine separate dates for the Creation of the World are found in the works of 108 early modern scholars broaching the topic.[10]

Chronographical studies had a particular interest for Knorr in their serviceability for the interpretation of biblical prophecy, particularly of the several periods specified in both the Book of Daniel and the Apocalypse.[11] He was also able to make use of Jewish chronographies like the *Seder Olam* and *Sefer Juchasin*. We can observe Knorr's exploitation of this material not only in *Messias Puer* but also in two works which anticipate Knorr's use of chronological data there for this purpose[12].

(London: Warburg Institute, 1995): pp. 15–31; Id., "Chronology and its Discontents in Renaissance Europe: The Vicissitudes of a Tradition" in *Time: Histories and Ethnologies*, edited by D.O. Hughes and T.R. Trautmann (Ann Arbor, 1995): pp. 139–167; Id., "Some Uses of Eclipses in Early Modern Chronology", *Journal of the History of Ideas* 64, 2 (2003): pp. 213–229; P. Nothaft, *Dating the Passion: The Life of Jesus and the Emergence of Scientific Chronology (200–1600)* (Leiden: Brill, 2012): esp. pp. 203–283. The publication of K. Macfarlane, *Hugh Broughton (1549–1612): Scholarship, Controversy and the English Bible* (Unpublished Doctoral Thesis, Oxford University, 2017) is also now anticipated.

9   "No Frankfurt fair goes by without its crop of chronologers". Quoted by Anthony Grafton, "Scaliger's Chronology", *art. cit.*, p. 105; 277.

10 C.A. Patrides, "Renaissance Estimates of the Year of Creation", *Huntington Library Quarterly* 26, 4 (1963): pp. 315–322 at pp. 316–317.

11 A. Seifert, *Der Rückzug der biblischen Prophetie von der neueren Geschichte: Studien zur Geschichte der Reichstheologie des frühneuzeitlichen deutschen Protestantismus* (Köln: Böhlau, 1990); I. Backus, *Reformation Readings of the Apocalypse* (Oxford: University Press, 2000); Ead., "The Beast: Interpretations of Daniel 7.2–9 and Apocalypse 13.1–4, 11–12 in Lutheran, Zwinglian and Calvinist Circles in the Late Sixteenth Century", *Reformation and Renaissance Review* 3 (2001): pp. 59–77; W.S. Reid, "The Four Monarchies of Daniel in Reformation Historiography", *Historical Reflections* 8 (1981): pp. 115–123.

12 One notes references to these works in HAB Cod. Guelf. 30.4, which contains twenty-two letters of Knorr's correspondence from the 1670s. See Zeller, "Nachlass", *art. cit.*, p. 59. There is also an extensive work, *Collegium über Universal Historie*, written in German in Knorr's hand which is found with two other works in HAB Cod. Guelf 149.13. Extrav., a volume from Knorr's library donated by Jacob Burkhardt. This may be the work to which Unger referred to in "Vitae Knorrianae curriculum" as "*de Intricatissimis dubiis chronologicis*" (p. 192) and which he considered to be lost. Knorr indicated his interest in these matters as early as his Dissertation, *Dissertatio de Antiquis Romanor. Numismatib. Consecrationem Illustrantibus*, op. cit. After the end of chapter 3 §15 he gives the *corollaria* of his work. The first is: "*An ex versione LXX. Interpretum, Codice Samaritico, Historiâ Josephi, Fabulis Rabbino-*

Knorr's commentary upon the Apocalypse, *Eigentliche Erklärung über die Gesichter der Offenbarung S Johannis* ... appeared in 1670 under the pseudonym of Peganius.[13] Knorr's systematic correlation of World History with the periods mentioned in the Apocalypse can be seen at a glance in the tabular presentation (*"Kurzer inhalt dieses Büchleins auf Chronologische Art vorgestellet"*). He finds three chronological sections in the Apocalypse. To the first period from the Destruction of Judaism to the Destruction of Paganism he allocates the absolute dates of 34 AC to 337 AC. The second period from the Destruction of Paganism to the demise of Spiritual Babylon runs from 379 AC to 1860 AC. The third period, from the Seventh Trumpet until the End, is not absolutely dated, but includes the 1000 year reign, the loosing of Satan and the war against Gog and Magog, after which comes "the Restoration of All Things".[14]

The *Harmonia Evangeliorum, Oder Zusammenfügung der vier H. Evangelisten* [...] *Dem ist beygefüget eine Chronologische Vorbereitung Uber das Neue*

---

rum et Antiquitatibus Chaldæorum, Ægyptiorum & Sinensium demonstrari possit, Natale mundi tempus vulgarem Aeram annis 1440 anticipare?" ["Whether it can be demonstrated from the Septuagint Translation, the Samaritan Codex, Josephus' History, Rabbinic tales and the Antiquities of the Chaldaeans, the Egyptians and the Chinese, that the period of the world's birth preceded the common era by 1440 years?"] To which the reponse was *"N*[*ego*]" ("I deny") (p. 32).

13 *Christian Knorr von Rosenroth Apokalypse-Kommentar*, ed. by Battafarano, (Bern: Peter Lang, 2004). For Knorr's understanding of World History as the History of Salvation, see pp. 197–205. Also, I.M. Battafarano, "Gott als hermetischer Dichter. Christian Knorrs von Rosenroth ingeniös-barocker Kommentar der 'Johannesapokalypse' (1670)", *Morgen-Glantz* 7 (1997): pp. 15–65; and Id. "'Denn wenn Gott brüllet / wer wollte nicht weissagen' Christian Knorrs von Rosenroth Deutung der Weltgeschichte als Heilsgeschichte im *Apokalypse-Kommentar* (1670)", *Morgen Glantz* 15 (2005): pp. 13–26; G. van Gemert, "Christian Knorr von Rosenroth und Petrus Serrarius Die Apokalypsekommentare in Deutungszusammenhang", *Morgen-Glantz* 11 (2001): pp. 205–227. Further: R. Zeller, "Knorrs Erklärung der Gesichter Johannis im Kontext der zeitgenössischen Apokalypse-Deutung", *Morgen-Glantz* 21 (2011): pp. 9–14; Ead., "Knorrs Apokalypse Deutung und England", *Morgen-Glantz* 21 (2011): pp. 107–133; G. van Gemert, "Knorrs Apokalypse-Kommentar und der niederländische Kontext. Breckling, Serrarius, Hiël und andere", Ibid., pp. 211–225; von Greyerz, K. "Das Nachdenken über die Apokalypse im England des späteren 17. Jahrhunderts", Ibid., pp. 15–38. There is also an English version: *A Genuine Explication of the Visions of the Book of Revelation: Full of New Christian Considerations wherein True and False Christendom is briefly and nakedly represented by A.B. Peganius* (London: W.G., n.d.) on which see W.G. Marigold, "Die englische Übersetzung von Knorrs Kommentar zur Johannesapokalypse und die Rezeption deutscher Erbauungsschriften in England in 17. Jahrhundert", *Morgen-Glantz* 8 (1998): pp. 171–196.

14 John Lightfoot's work was also important to Knorr in his study of the Apocalypse.

Testament[15] was published by Johann David Zunner in Frankfurt in 1672. The title-page suggests that the work had been made from an English *"Vorlage"* (*"Auß dem Englischen ins Teutsche übersetzt"*) and that this original was found in the papers of James Ussher, Bishop of Armagh (1581–1656) (*"Welche beyde Schrifften in Jacobi USSERI Ertzbischoffen zu Armach und Primaten in Irland / hinterlassener Bibliothec gefunden worden"*), though it must be conceded that it is not precisely clear just what is being claimed in this title page! There is nothing in Ussher's *Nachlaß* which might have served as such an original.

C.T. Unger's 1718 biography of Knorr none the less repeats this claim: *"Ejusdem est interpretatio Germanica Harmoniæ Evangelistarum ab anonymo Anglice conscriptæ & in musæo Vsseriano repertæ"*[16], but he also records contrary rumours: *"Dicitur ipse* Knorrius *auctor esse, & ista de Anglico confinxisse."*[17] The copy of the 1672 printed edition in HAB Wolfenbüttel (sign. Td 126) has more to say on this score in a handwritten note[18]:

> *"Autor hujus libri est Vir illustris* Knorr à Rosenroth, *Consiliarius, dum viveret, intimus Marchionis Sulzbacensis, Vir in literatura Orientali versatissimus. Dedit hoc opus* Helmontio, *Hebraicarum rerum ad superstitionem usque perito, cujus cura ac sumptibus ederetur. Obtulit Helmontius inspiciendum librum M[anu]sc[rip]tum Doctori* Fabritio, *Academiae Heidelbergensis Theologo. Qui editionem maturare suasit, addito gemino consilio, de titulo libri reformando, ac de opera castrando aliterque instruendo. Quod ad titulum attinet,* Autorem *verum dissimulandum, judicavit, ac pere-*

---

15   *"HARMONIA EVANGELIORUM, Oder Zusammenfügung der vier H. Evangelisten. Worinnen alle und jede deroselben Wort beydes nach Lutheri und der Englischen version in Ordnung gebracht / Doch mit sonderlichen Buchstaben unterschieden / und durch kurtze Vornemlich zu Erbauung deß Christlichen Lebens zielende Anmerckungen erkläret sind. Dem ist beygefüget eine Chronologische Vorbereitung Uber das Neue Testament / zu dessen richtigem Verstand nützlich zu gebrauchen. Welche beyde Schrifften in JACOBI USSERI, Ertzbischoffen zu Armach und Primaten in Irland / hinterlassener Bibliothec gefunden worden. Auß dem Englischen ins Teutsche übersetzt. Franckfurt / In Verlegung Johann David Zunners. Gedruckt bey Johann Andrea. ANNO M. DC. LXXII."*

16   "His too is the German translation of the Gospel Harmony made by an anonymous Englishman and found in Ussher's library". (Unger, "Vitae Knorrianae curriculum", op. cit., p. 193.)

17   "Knorr himself is said to be its author and to have put it together from the English." For this work, see M. Finke and E. Handschur, "Christian Knorrs von Rosenroth Lebenslauf aus dem Jahre 1718", *art. cit.*

18   We follow here G. van Gemert, "Zu Knorrs Evangelienharmonie von 1672 Vorlage, Verfasserfrage und Kontext", *Morgen-Glantz* 3 (1993): pp. 155–162, who has presented the evidence and shown the likely reliability of this testimony.

grinum eumque Anglum *subornandum. Atque ita* Usserii *umbra placuit, sub qua delitesceret Knorr à Rosenroth.* Textum *porro castravit Fabritius, eaque eliminavit, quae lectorem offendere posse videbantur, maxime, quae migrationem animarum concernerent. Versionem quoque* Lutheri *Germanicam inserere suasit, ne Lutherani nova versione absterrerentur.* Praefationem *addidit Doctor* Schuz, *i*[*uris*]*c*[*onsul*]*tus Francofurtensis, qui et sumptibus Helmontianis edidit.*
Sic
Autor, Knorr à Rosenroth.
Curator, Helmontius.
Castrator, Fabritius.
Editor, Schuzius."[19]

The printed copy in Yale substantially reports the same material but also purports to identify the source, Hermann van der Hardt (1660–1746) from 1690 Professor of Oriental Languages in Helmstadt:

Ex exemplo bibliothecae Guelpherbytanae cui Herm. von der Hardt manu sua sequentia adscripsit:[20]

Autor hujus libri est Knorr à Rosenroth, Consiliarius, dum viveret, intimus Marchionis Sultzbacensis, vir in literatura Orientali versatissimus. Dedit hoc opus Helmontio Hebraicarum rerum ad superstitionem usque perito,

---

19 "The author of the book is the illustrious gentleman Knorr von Rosenroth, intimate counselor, while he lived, of the Duke of Sulzbach, a man most versed in Oriental literature. He gave the work to van Helmont, skilled in Hebrew studies to the point of superstition, to have it printed at his own expense. Van Helmont offered the book in manuscript for inspection to Doctor Fabricius, a theologian at the University of Heidelberg. He advised rapid publication but added two recommendations: to change the book's title page; and to edit [emasculate] the work and arrange it differently. As far as the title page went, he thought to conceal the true author and attribute the work to a foreign Englishman. And so the ghost of Ussher was chosen, behind whom Von Rosenroth lay hidden. Fabricius then went on to edit [emasculate] the text and to eliminate those things it appeared could offend the reader, particularly those things about the migration of souls. He also persuaded him to insert a version of Luther's German [translation], so that the Lutherans would not be frightened away by the new text. The Frankfurt lawyer Doctor Schuz added a preface and published it at van Helmont's expense. So: Von Rosenroth wrote it; Van Helmont paid for it; Fabricius edited [emasculated] it and Schuz got it printed." (van Gemert, "Zu Knorrs Evangelienharmonie", *art. cit.*, p. 159).
20 "From a copy in the Wolfenbüttel library, to which Herm. von der Hardt added the following in his own hand".

cuius cura et sumtibus ederetur. Obtulit Helmontius inspiciendum librum M[anu]sc[rip]tum Doctori Fabricio, Academiae Heidelbergensis Theol. qui editionem maturare suasit, addito gemino consilio de titulo libri reformando, ac de opera castrando aliterque instruendo. Quod at [sic!] titulum attinet, autorem verum dissimulandum judicavit, ac peregrinum eumque Anglum subornandum. Atque ita Usserii umbras placuit, sub qua delitesceret Knorr à Rosenroth. Textum porro castravit Fabricius, eaque eliminavit quae lectorem offendere videbantur posse, maxime quae migrationem animarum concernerent. Versionem quoque Germanicam inserere suasit, ne Lutherani nova versione absterrerentur. Praefationem addidit Doctor Schütz Jureconsultus Francofurtanus, qui et sumtibus Helmontianis edidit.

Sic Autor Knorr à Rosenroht [sic!]
Curator Helmontius
Castrator Fabricius
Editor Schutzius.[21]

Evidently there are complex questions here which demand further attention, not least the bizarre notion of a scandalous German translation of an "English version".[22] Here, however, we shall confine ourselves to two pertinent features of this work as it relates to *Messias Puer*. First one should note the location of this earlier work of Knorr's within the field of Universal History and Chronology. The work begins with a time-line: *"Folget demnach eine Vorbereitung über das Neue Testament nemlich die Zeit-Rechnung / und ein kurtzer Begriff der ganzen Histori des Neuen Testaments"*[23]. The Chronology thereafter synchronises the Year of the World (W); the Year before the Birth of Christ (vC); the Year after Christ's Birth (C); the Regnal Years of mentioned Monarchs (K); the Weeks of Daniel's Prophecy (D) and the Year of the Gospel (E).

Obviously a well-established chronology is the basis for successful harmonisation.

---

21   Ibid, pp. 160–161.
22   The Lutheran version cited in the *Harmonia* is indeed precisely that, but the "English Version" which has been put into German appears to be the Vulgate rather carefully translated with words naturally omitted in the Latin being added in brackets in the German. The eighteen printed German language bibles which preceded Luther's translation (1522–1534) were all made from the Vulgate text.
23   "Here follows a [work] preliminary to the New Testament, namely a Chronological Calculation and a short Sketch of the whole of New Testament History" (*Harmonia Evangeliorum*, op. cit., p. 2).

We should also note that the *Gospel Harmony* itself in its first eight sections is the basis for the order of the New Testament passages treated in *Messias Puer*. Knorr suggests there that this order has the economic advantage of harmonisation; and then follows the sequence of his earlier work[24]. The order of the *Harmonia* is: Lk 1.1–4; Jn 1.1–14; Lk 1.5–56; Mt 1.1–25; Lk 1.57–80; Lk 2.1–38; Mt 2.1–23; Lk 2.39–52. The order of *Messias Puer* is: Lk 1.1–4; Jn 1.1–5 (slightly shorter than the *Harmonia* passage[25]); Lk 1.5–26; Lk 1.26–38; Lk 1.39–52 (the same text and order as the *Harmonia*, but broken into shorter sections); Mt 1.1–25; Lk 1.54–80; Lk 2.1–39; Mt 2.1–23; Lk 2.40–52. This pattern itself is found previously in Lightfoot in work repeatedly cited in Knorr's commentary.[26]

Within *Messias Puer* itself, Knorr's interest in the chronological aspects of World Chronology and eschatological dates are evident, for example, in passages treating of Zachariah's Ministry (folio 13^v); Matthew's Genealogy and several passages on Lk 2 (folios 37^v–39^v). The prophetess Anna's life history is related to these larger periods. However, one must not forget the complexities introduced into this discourse by the doctrine of reincarnation to which we shall return below. The interest in reincarnation which Knorr shared with several of his contemporaries was enriched by his innovative use of the theory of the revolution of souls as it had been developed in Lurianic Kabbalah. The originality and innovation of *Messias Puer* specifically here resides in the combination of the separate field of chronography with this esoteric doctrine achieved by recourse to Kabbalah.

We shall consider below the doctrine of a Jewish Earthly Messianic Kingdom, a striking feature of Knorr's eschatological expectations as it emerges from *Messias Puer*.

---

24 "Christianus. Prolegomena hæc præmitto, ut cætera Evangeliorum contenta juxta temporum seriem in unam coadunare possim harmoniam, unâque annotatione aliquando, si Deus concesserit, pluribus satisfaciam textibus." (*Historiæ Evangelicæ initium*, folio 1^r). ("Christian: I put this introduction first, so that I might be able to order the other things in the Gospels into one harmonious time sequence, and thus God willing, to treat several texts adequately with just a little added commentary".)

25 The passage is shortened in *Messias Puer* to avoid mention of the subsequent ministry of John the Baptist which falls outside the chronological limits of the work.

26 Conveniently in Lightfoot, *Erubin; or Miscellanies and the Harmony of the Gospels. Parts I & II*, op. cit.

2 Kabbala Denudata

The importance of citations from *Kabbala Denudata* in *Messias Puer* has been mentioned above. A rapid comparison of the works cited in *Messias Puer* with those collected in *Kabbala Denudata* indicates that the whole of the anthology was exploited by Knorr in *Messias Puer*. Three texts are most heavily cited: *Loci communes kabbalistici* published in the volume of 1677; *De revolutionibus animarum* and *Adumbratio kabbalæ christianæ*, both of which were published in the volume of 1684. *Adumbratio* is cited some thirty times throughout *Messias Puer*. There are more than a hundred references to *Loci* and these too are evenly distributed throughout the work. *De revolutionibus animarum*, a translation of the Lurianic treatise devoted to the doctrine of the revolution of souls, is cited most frequently (more than 130 times), but unlike the *Loci*, the *De revolutionibus animarum* is not cited regularly throughout the work but only in those passages concerned principally with this doctrine. As we have remarked all the other treatises in the anthology are cited with the notable exception of the exchanges with Henry More which appear in the first volume and More's other works which Knorr integrated into his anthology. It is thus very clear that Knorr made reference only to works which he had himself (partially?) edited (like *Adumbratio*), or translated (like *De revolutionibus*) or compiled (like *Loci*). The familiarity of the author with the cited texts is an important element for understanding the way in which *Messias Puer* was conceived and elaborated by Knorr. This is particularly relevant, as we shall see, in the case of *Adumbratio*.

3 Adumbratio kabbalæ christianæ

In many respects, *Messias Puer* appears as the counterpart of *Adumbratio kabbalæ christianæ* and both works will benefit from being considered together. *Adumbratio* was published anonymously in 1684 as a part of the second volume of *Kabbala Denudata*. *Messias Puer*, for its part, remained in manuscript form catalogued under a false title, as the original title page was not preserved. Both texts take the form of a dialogue between two characters who seem to have been carried over from the one work to other, yet undergo a subtle transformation between 1684 and 1688/9, as the *Cabbalista* and the *Philosophus Christianus* of *Adumbratio* become respectively a *Cabbalista Catechumenus* and a *Christianus*. The dialogue of 1684 opens with a statement of the Kabbalist according to which the two characters agree to draw up "a shared hypothesis" or at least an "hypothesis by which both [the Kabbalist] will be better able to understand [the Christian] doctrine and [the Christian Philosopher] will be able to grasp [the] enigmatic ways of speaking [of the Jews]" with the intention of achieving "the most pressing necessity" of the conversion of the Jews.[27]

Adumbratio comprises principally an exposition of Kabbalistic doctrines, particularly those of the Lurianic tradition.[28] Assuming a philosophic perspective, the two characters undertake to test the possibility of applying these particular doctrines to Christianity in search of equivalents which offer confirmation of the Lurianic system. The process is particularly striking in the case of *Adam Kadmon*, the "Primordial Man" where details are specifically and systematically compared with characteristics of Christ recognised in the Christian tradition. The exploitation of a hermeneutic of analogy allows *Adumbratio* to entertain a plurality of meaning which skilfully masks the subtle pressures applied to the text of the New Testament and thereby gives the impression of a convincing demonstration. The construction of the "shared hypothesis" is made possible by ignoring some specifically Christian themes and avoiding the usual stumbling blocks of the familiar genre of polemical dialogue. Specifically the Virgin Conception of Christ and the Passion are carefully avoided in *Adumbratio*.[29] Even when "the coming of Christ into the world"[30] is in question, the text confines itself strictly to the Father and his role in the introduction of the Son into the world.[31] This account is in no way innocent, since

---

27 *Adumbratio kabbalæ christianæ* (Frankfurt: Johannes David Zunner, 1684), p. 3. This enjoys an independent pagination and is usually printed with the second volume of the *Kabbala Denudata*. On this topic, W. Schmidt-Biggemann, "Knorr von Rosenroths missionarische Intentionen", *art. cit.*, pp. 189–204.

28 For an introduction to this school of Kabbalah, see G. Necker, *Einführung in die lurianische Kabbala* (Frankfurt am Main: Verl. Der Weltreligionen, 2008).

29 Two discrete mentions of the Virgin Mary appear in *Adumbratio* at pages 63 and 64. This last one is interesting: suddenly, the Christian Philosopher remembers that he promised to be brief: "*Quæ propterea saltem allegantur, ut [(juxta commune Regulam vestram; cum dicitis: Id quod accidit Patribus (i.e. supernis) accidit & liberis (i.e infernis)] appareat nihil esse absurdi, si Mater Messiæ dicatur Virgo, juxta Jesch. 7, vs. 14. De aliis autem Messianæ Nativitatis Circumstantis nihil hic addemus, ne nimiis digressionibus dilabamur à scopo propositæ brevitatis.*" ("It is more over claimed that [(according to your common rule when you say: 'That which happens to the fathers (i.e. above) happens also to the children (i.e. below)] there appears nothing unreasonable when the Mother of Messiah is called a virgin in Isa. 7.14. But about the other circumstances of Messiah's birth, we shall add no more, lest with too many digressions we slip from our target of agreed brevity.") We consider the treatment of the Virgin Birth in *Messias Puer* below.

30 The word *incarnatio* is never used of Messiah in *Adumbratio*.

31 Jn 16.28 is invoked here (*Adumbratio*, op. cit., p. 44). Allison Coudert considers the diminution of the role of Christ a characteristic of the intellectual ambience in which Knorr developed: "While in Paris Leibniz formulated a prayer which he thought the basis for a truly ecumenical religion, only to receive a shocked response from Arnauld, who rejected

it is conformed to the account of creation found in Lurianic Kabbalah which centres around the figure of *Adam Kadmon* (who also is "brought down into the world").[32] Moreover, the final chapters of *Adumbratio* which describe the final state of restitution use a language which pointedly avoids the habitual exegetical terms used of the redemptive role of Christ.[33] Matters present themselves in a very different guise just a few years later in *Messias Puer*. The Kabbalist, now become a Kabbalist Catechumen, cooperates actively and on equal terms with the Christian in the interpretation of the New Testament texts. He is no longer content merely to expound kabbalistic doctrine but actively seeks new interpretations of the Gospels which might be developed from the resources of Kabbalah. The Christian Philosopher also changes and becomes simply—that is completely—Christian as the writing moves from a consciously philosophical style to that of an essentially exegetical text. The manner of proceeding is quite different too: where *Adumbratio* frequently confined itself to the mere enumeration of parallel passages (sometimes of a purely formal relevance[34]), *Messias Puer* reveals itself to be far more innovative and creative, as we shall attempt to indicate below. This is because of the challenge introduced by the detailed examination of the biblical text and its previous interpreters which constrains the exegete (Knorr) to innovate if he is both to satisfy the requirements of the text and also to articulate a coherent theological reading from his own doctrinal principles. The philosophical questions were more easily dealt with in the freedom of *Adumbratio*'s imagined debate: now the debate involves the more intransigent words of the Gospel text and the demands they impose upon a persuasive exegesis.

---

it outright because it said nothing about Christ. Van Helmont's ecumenism went even farther than Leibniz's, to the point that he was pursued and imprisoned as a heretic. He believed that all men could be saved, whatever their religion, a sentiment that clearly undercut the unique role of Christ in salvation and embraced the Pelagian idea that an individual could be saved by his own efforts. As I will show, the same Pelagian implications appear in Leibniz's mature monadology and came from van Helmont and the Lurianic Kabbalah." (*Leibniz and the Kabbalah*, op. cit., p. 10).

32   The Hebrew verb is נשתלשל, "to drop through", "to lower".
33   The last chapters (10–12) are entitled: *"De statu postremæ Restitutionis, ejusque Gradu primo; De secundo Gradu Restitutionis Animarum; De duobus ultimis Restitutionis Messianæ Gradibus."* Chapter 11 specifically describes the fighting of Christ against the "Shells" in Lurianic terms. Also among the very rare mentions of the "suffering" or "sacrifice" of Christ, the crucifixion is never mentioned, except in the allegorical reading of "taking up one's cross" meaning "to follow Christ" (*Adumbratio*, op. cit., p. 64).
34   Vileno, *À l'ombre de la kabbale*, op. cit., p. 157.

4 The Question of Authorship

We have seen above that Knorr's own personal convictions are somewhat hidden in his anthologies of translations. We have also noted his discretionary preference for anonymity, though there is no substantial disagreement over his authorship of the *Apocalypse Commentary* which we have used. In the case of the *Harmonia*, we simply need a far better idea of what is going on in that obfuscated text before we use an assertion of Knorr's authorship to attempt to discover what he wished to say in it.

The question of authorship is far more contested in the case of *Adumbratio*, though it has generally been assumed it was rather the work of van Helmont.[35] Sarah Hutton argued for van Helmont's authorship[36] and Rosmarie Zeller has recently pointed out the tendency to attribute all works to Knorr and none to van Helmont.[37] In a recent monograph Anna M. Vileno while accepting the general difficulty of deciding the question argued that a good case could be made for asserting that chapter 3 of *Adumbratio* was principally the work of Knorr and that chapter 7 was principally written by van Helmont.[38] Most scholars would accept that there may have been some form of cooperation between the two friends.

In the case of *Messias Puer* the situation is far clearer. Whilst it remains possible that drafts of passages by van Helmont (or anyone else) may have been used to produce the secretaries' own drafts, that this was the case we shall

---

35 Sheila A. Spector called her English translation of *Adumbratio* without equivocation, "*Francis Mercury van Helmont's Sketch of Christian Kabbalah*".
36 S. Hutton, *Anne Conway: A Woman Philosopher* (Cambridge University Press, 2009): p. 204.
37 Zeller and Necker, "Einleitung", *art. cit.*
38 Vileno, *À l'ombre*, op. cit., pp. 132–135. Nor is this contention disproved by *Messias Puer*. One may notice that one chapter of *Adumbratio* which Knorr does *not* cite in *Messias Puer* is chapter 7, precisely that tentatively attributed to van Helmont. It is also the case (as we have just seen) that Knorr in *Messias Puer* does not once refer to Henry More's work which also appears in *Kabbala Denudata*. It is quite plausible to imagine that he did not cite these works because he had not written them himself and was thus not fully at home with their content. For a survey of problems of authorship surrounding Van Helmont's works, see Hutton, *Anne Conway*, op. cit., pp. 148–150. Concerning the *Adumbratio* in particular and the various elements of its composition, see *Ead.*, pp. 204–205, Vileno, *À l'ombre*, op. cit., pp. 132–135 and R. Zeller, "Die Lehre von der Präexistenz der Seelen bei Knorr und Helmont im Kontext der Diskussion in England", *Morgen-Glantz*, 24 (2014): pp. 133–154. The question of the precise relationship between Knorr and Van Helmont is extremely complex due to the habitual anonymity of both parties. Knorr was probably led to an interest in Kabbalah by Van Helmont. Sarah Hutton has shown Van Helmont to have been an indefatigable traveller maintaining numerous contacts well beyond Sulzbach who thereby enabled Knorr to keep abreast of the latest philosophical developments of his day.

never be able to know. We may however be quite sure that the correction of the secretaries' work was done by Knorr and that we are able to observe him refashioning his work in several ways as we have discussed above. There is no reasonable doubt that Knorr was in this sense the author of the manuscript, which contemporary testimony thought he had written, and that in all probability he attempted to see through the press.

It remains then to ask, does Knorr's undoubted authorship of *Messias Puer* create a presumption that he was also the author of *Adumbratio*?

It is clear that *Messias Puer* was intended as a companion piece to *Adumbratio*. Its very form as a dialogue (and the more developed relationship between the two characters) makes it explicitly clear that *Messias Puer* is a sequel to the earlier work. But this continuity of genre and of *dramatis personae* does not in any way entail identity of authorship. *Adumbratio* may (to an unknown extent) be a work of collaboration, but there is no reason to consider *Messias Puer* to be so. The evidence of the manuscript and of contemporary testimony is decisive. Furthermore the very nature of the scholarship displayed in *Messias Puer* is characteristic of Knorr rather than of van Helmont. There is no doubt of Knorr's abilities as a Hebraist (as we have seen above). There is less evidence of this for van Helmont. His work on the Hebrew Alphabet *Alphabeti vere naturalis hebraici brevissime delineatio* ... (1667) is most definitely *not* a work of Semitic philology or a study of Hebrew (as we would understand it), rather it is the assertion of a relationship between the shape of Hebrew letters and the anatomy of the human throat, which has indeed speculative implications for the "naturalness" of Hebrew as a language, but is not what we understand by philology.[39] Nor, even if we credit van Helmont with a substantial contribution to the more philosophical *Adumbratio*, would that show him equipped with the necessary knowledge of the Mishnaic and Talmudic material deployed in *Messias Puer* to present the *realia* of New Testament times or to have previously demonstrated kabbalistic expositional innovation. It is therefore not evident upon what basis we could claim that *Messias Puer* reflected his erudition or creative exegesis.

Finally we may perhaps return to the question raised above of whether Knorr was capable of being the sole author of *Messias Puer*. In considering the changes Knorr made to the distribution of material between the two conversationalists in the dialogue, we rashly speculated whether a real collaboration

---

[39] For Knorr's preface to this work, see Zeller, "Die Rolle von Franciscus Mercurius Van Helmont", *art. cit.*, pp. 390–391, and for a wider context, Ead., "Adamische Sprache, Natursprache und Kabbala. Überlegungen zur Sprachtheorie und Poesie in 17. Jahrhundert", *Morgen-Glantz* 6 (1996): pp. 133–154.

with a Jewish scholar might lie behind the *persona* of the Kabbalist Catechumen. We do not know, but we may consider whether such an hypothesis is necessary. On balance it would seem that the work Knorr had done before *Messias Puer* in anthologising for *Kabbala Denudata* and collecting the material in the enormous *Loci communes* (even if he were helped at some stage, which presumably would have been likely, if not indeed necessary) equipped him with the required fluency in the study of the Lurianic doctrines to practice their manipulation on his own. The question then remains whether he was individually capable of synthesising this material with the text of the New Testament. In this respect we may conclude that it would have been more likely for Knorr to be possessed of a thorough knowledge of the New Testament texts and the issues which arise from them in the history of their interpretation than a Jewish scholar. As much of the achievement of *Messias Puer* lies in the synthesis of the two systems and the achievement of a close reading of the New Testament in the light of the kabbalistic doctrines, it may be, in fact, easier to imagine that synthesis took place in the mind of one man, a man who had intimate knowledge of both Luria and the Christian New Testament. We would argue, therefore, that there is nothing in *Messias Puer* that can be shown Knorr could not have written, much that he might well have been the only person to be able to write, and no compelling reason to think he had an immediate collaborator. Contemporary testimony, as we have seen above, gives no hint that *Messias Puer* was a collaborative effort. We shall thus consider Knorr to be its sole author.

CHAPTER 6

Theological and Exegetical Innovation in *Messias Puer*

Messias Puer is a master-piece of exegetic creativity and ingenuity. In essence it is a harmonisation of two separate narratives which had not previously been brought into such a close relationship: the narrative of the Gospel passages chronologically ordered and the Lurianic narratives of Creation, the Soul of Messiah, Salvation, Reincarnation and his account of the divine Sefirot. The reader more familiar with the Gospel narrative will none the less observe that the apparently arbitrary responses of the dialogue—prompted by the contingencies of the Gospel text—do in fact cumulatively evoke the major doctrines of Luria to produce a coherent, integrated and utterly innovative interpretation of the text. For factual comment on the New Testament, History, Topography, Manners etc., Knorr was content to avail himself of the accumulated wisdom of contemporary Christian Hebraists and his sustained engagement with Lightfoot gives us a way to measure the rather prosaic banality of this material. But in textual exposition and doctrinal matters, the case is quite different. On many occasions the application of kabbalistic perspectives is totally new, simply because nobody previously had sought to read the New Testament in this perspective, nor had anyone else discovered the consequential difficulties and opportunities which the New Testament text read in this light provoked and to which Knorr proposed his own solutions. Perhaps an obvious point may be made here: believing and confessionally committed exegetes see their activities as essentially an extraction of meanings already existing within Scripture or the Tradition. To those without, all of this activity appears as a creation of meaning rather than the discovery of truths hidden from the foundation of the world. From outside, the teachings of the Jewish Kabbalists appear profoundly creative and Knorr's innovation in reading the New Testament in a Lurianic light is essentially a prolongation of that same creative exegesis. Nor was Knorr's reading confined merely to the passages from the Gospels, which are the ostensible subject of the commentary. Knorr's copious citations show us clearly in what sense he wished to read a large number of passages in Acts, the Epistles and the Apocalypse. Most central doctrinal issues are broached, though, as readers of *Adumbratio* have noticed, there hardly emerges much of a "*theologia crucis*". Yet Knorr does have an account of sin and evil in the world and an elaborated view of how Messiah brings salvation in the end to all.

And that salvation does involve Messiah's suffering at the hands of the "Shells". Messiah dies and is resurrected.

It is salutary to observe just how multi-dimensional and integrated Knorr's reading is. On occasion one of the interlocutors makes a comment and then his remarks are interpreted as a "mystery"[1] or as "Mystical Theology"[2] which provokes a psychological reading of the text—a prophetic mystery, however, is more likely to involve chronographic and prophetic time periods. On occasion, the conversation will progress to practical spiritual lessons worked up from the details of the text, as in the case of the large excision of the meanings of the forty-seven names in Matthew's genealogy of Jesus.[3] Similarly, at the end of comment upon Lk 1.38 at folio 18ʳ Knorr turns the people and events of the narrative just told into a "story of the conception of the Divine Life in the Soul". There is a coherent salvific structure behind these exhortations and, as one discovers elsewhere in *Messias Puer*, an elaborated psychology of the disturbances of the (tri-partite) soul as a basis for "Christian living".[4] Though Christian Kabbalah as a whole may be apparently more interested in theoretical rather than ethical questions, there can be no doubt of *Messias Puer*'s orientation towards becoming behaviour.

The dialogue also displays the integration of several key kabbalistic perspectives in the interest of a full account of the Gospel texts. The complexity of the exposition devoted in John the Baptist is remarkable: his parents' reincarnations are traced and the "mysterious" (*i. e.* sefirotic) associations of his father Zachariah's role and priestly family are made clear with respect to Chokhmah,

---

[1] See for example at folios 5ʳ/5ᵛ where Herod represents the Kingdom of Hepar, or the lower stomach, or Evil Desire. At folio 6ʳ Zachariah and Elischeba (after having being linked to *Foundation* and *Kingdom*) are made to teach a lesson about the acceptability to God of genuine prayer. Or see folio 18ʳ which similarly expands on the names and places in Lk 1.5–38.
[2] See for example at folio 15ʳ.
[3] Cf. folios 28ᵛ–29ʳ.
[4] Similarly, the first contribution of the Christian Philosopher in *Adumbratio* emphasises the importance of imitating the character of Messiah: *"Vereor autem, ne vel in limine te absterreat scopus meus, qui eo tendit, ut non tantum infinita Dei erga genus humanum propensio atque bonitas illustretur; sed etiam persona illa, quæ nobis Messias dicitur, ejusque vita, quoad ejus fieri queat, exaltetur; nec non sincera ejusdem imitatio cultusque Dei purus promoveatur; adeoque hypothesis ista omnia sublimiorum studiorum & actuum sectatoribus commendabilis fiat."* ("But I am afraid lest, even just upon the threshold, my goal may frighten you away, which aims not so much to illustrate the infinite inclination and goodness of God to the human race, but rather to exalt that personage who we call Messiah and his life (to the extent it could be his) and also to promote the sincere imitation of him and the pure worship of God, so that this hypothesis may be commended to the followers of all aspects of more lofty duties and actions".) (*Adumbratio kabbalæ christianæ*, p. 3).

Chesed and Hod. We learn of the descent of these Sefirot into "Foundation" (*Yesod*) and "Kingdom" (*Malkhut*) in the Coming of John. Prior to his coming the barrenness of Zachariah and Elisabeth had indicated the lack of holy illumination in "Kingdom" (*Malkhut*) (or Ecclesia). John, of course, was a *revolutio* of Elijah and also identified with Sandalphon. His birth involves a division of his soul which had not sunk in the fall of souls through sin. The division of his soul helps us understand how he was able in heaven to attend his own circumcision on earth, just as (we shall subsequently learn) Messiah was able to support "all things" during his humiliation on earth. John's birth proclaims liberty from the Shells, with enormous richness and complexity.

Yet Knorr is not totally without self-inhibition in his commentary as we shall hope to show. He appears reluctant to mention by name key terms in Lurianic Kabbalah, though we know from elsewhere that he was familiar not only with the terminology but also the doctrines. Certainly at no point does he offer a single fully integrated account of Luria and many aspects of that tradition go without specific mention. This observation should in part be mitigated by an appreciation of the significance of the citations made throughout the text and it is for this reason that these have been set out in full in the Apparatus. Interpretation of a given passage in *Messias Puer* requires *of necessity* that the cited passages be considered. None the less, some topics are not fully explicated. The question of the sense in which Messiah is divine is obviously of the very first importance and it is addressed in two passages we shall shortly consider. But briefly: one can see the way in which Knorr addresses the issue and what is his kabbalistic solution. But this is presented without a full and systematic presentation of the relevant kabbalistic notions and its significance is scarcely emphasised. No doubt the genre imposed its restraints and Knorr may have sought to spare his readers unnecessary difficulty, but though a daring and fundamentally innovative work, *Messias Puer* bears on its surface the evidence of Knorr's circumspection and prudence.

Short of a full expositional commentary, the footnotes to the translation are designed to provide the reader with such material as is necessary for the understanding of the text, though these will fall short of exposing all the doctrinal and exegetical innovation of *Messias Puer*. We have therefore selected several themes in the pages below to illustrate some of the distinctive feature of *Messias Puer* in this respect. Our intention here is purely descriptive, and our *editio princeps* does not also pretend to be a synthesised exposition or evaluation of Knorr's theology. Such a work will require more time and reflection and more scholars. We hope however to be able to at least indicate the exciting significance of *Messias Puer* in this respect.

1   The Revolution of Souls

The doctrine of the "Revolution of Souls" (reincarnation) is central to Lurianic Kabbalah and to Knorr von Rosenroth. We meet it in *Messias Puer* with respect to several individuals, but then on a larger chronographical and prophetic stage. From the very beginning of the book (folio 5ʳ) and frequently thereafter, one is referred back to the exposition of the topic in *De revolutionibus animarum* in *Kabbala Denudata*.

This treatise is entirely devoted to the exposition and exegetical application of the doctrine of the revolution of souls, central to Lurianic Kabbalah. The term comes from the Hebrew *gilgul* and *gilgul ha-nefesh* from the infinitive *legalgel* "to roll", "to revolve", whence the idea of "revolution". Scholem detected the first indication of the doctrine in the *Sefer ha-Bahir*, although the term does not itself appear there. *Bahir* introduces the concept in the context of reflection upon theodicy.[5] The doctrine also appears after a fashion in Zohar,[6] but is limited there to certain individuals in the context of sexual disorders and does not appear as a universal law applicable to everybody.

In the second half of the Sixteenth Century the doctrine of *gilgul* was emphasized by the Lurianic School and contextualised within a far wider perspective, namely that of the "Restoration of the World" which embraced a significant messianic dimension. According to the doctrine described by Hayyim Vital, all souls were once contained within Adam Kadmon, the "Primordial Man" (who is to be distinguished from Adam Rishon, the "First Man"). The "Primordial Man" is to be understood here as a cosmological figure. The successive revolutions of a soul do not depend exclusively upon a person's own deeds, but equally upon its "root", that is to say, the "root" of that specific soul within the cosmic body of Adam Kadmon, since originally, before being incarnated in a human body, the soul had existed within the body of Adam Kadmon. A soul enjoys solidarity with other souls which have their origin in the same part of *Adam Kadmon's* body and who thus share the same "root". The souls which had been distributed throughout the diverse organs and limbs of the Primordial Man (so that some were said to be from his head or his feet etc.) enjoyed greater or lesser status, dependent upon their place of origin.

---

5   Scholem, *Major Trends in Jewish Mysticism,* op. cit., pp. 280 *sq.* For a detailed discussion of the use of the Lurianic theory of the revolution of souls in the context of Knorr's messianic expectations, see A.M. Vileno, "Reincarnations of Messiah(s): Messianic Expectations in Christian Knorr von Rosenroth's Last Work", *Frankfurter Judaistische Beiträge* 43 (2019/20): pp. 73–96.

6   Zohar II, 99b.

In the account of Creation as imagined in the Lurianic tradition, the sin of the First Man ejected the souls (described as "sparks") into the material world, the world of the "shells". In this way particles of both Good and Evil became mixed together and it falls to mankind to make their sparks (i.e. their souls) ascend again back towards their Creator by keeping the commandments, so that they might separate Good and Evil and purge their souls from the Evil contracted by the sin of the First Man. This is the context of the "revolution of souls": these multiple incarnations are occasions for the restoration of the soul. In this perspective the *revolutio animarum* is not to be considered as a punishment, but rather as an opportunity for the reparation of sins previously committed. One can see clearly here how the question of theodicy was taken up and developed by Lurianic thinkers. The transmigration of the soul enables one to explain why certain of the righteous enjoy a state of felicity, whilst others suffer cruelly.

Furthermore, one should emphasise that the doctrine of the transmigration of souls constitutes a point of departure for a new way of interpreting the traditional texts (mainly but not exclusively) of the Bible, by emphasising the links which exist between characters of different epochs who, by reason of being incarnations of the same soul, share characteristics which can be explained in no other way.

This hermeneutic technique shares points of similarity with traditional Christian typology and it is precisely in this way that it is extensively exploited by Knorr.[7] The doctrine of the "revolution of the soul" reveals itself as most useful to our Christian Kabbalist—in the sense that it offers him the key to a coherent reading—and at the same time as valuable because it derives from Jewish tradition which enjoyed, in the eyes of a scholar like Knorr, an authority undeniably superior to the Greek tradition which also contained similar notions.

The doctrine of the revolution of souls is fundamental to numerous exegetical developments in *Messias Puer* and is deployed both with respect to individuals encountered in the New Testament text (amongst whom Messiah occupies a predominant position) and also with respect to groups of people (like the Magi or the Holy Innocents of Matthew chapter 2)—and is even used with

---

7 The doctrine of "the revolution of souls" as it appears in Jewish Hebrew Kabbalah seems to have been known to some Christian writers before the diffusion of Lurianic Kabbalah. There is an echo in the circle of Cardinal Egidio da Viterbo between 1530 and 1550. We know that Egidio translated (or had translated) the *Sefer ha-Bahir*. At roughly the same time in France, Guillaume Postel produced an annotated translation of *Sefer ha-Bahir* in which he took an interest in the doctrine of *gilgul*.

respect to events. The notion of the revolution of souls permits a reinforcement of the parallels proposed by more classical typology[8]. However this is not just an announcement of New Testament features detected in the Old Testament on the basis of symbolic parallels, but the assertion of a real ontological identity between people who lived at very different times from each other.

Thus the characteristics shared in common between Joseph the son of Jacob and Joseph the spouse of Mary[9] are to be explained by the fact that the latter is a reincarnation of the former. Similarly in the case of Mary who is assimilated to Eve by the intermediary of Miriam, the sister of Moses. At folio 15ʳ a marginal addition shows Knorr inserting Miriam the sister of Moses as a "link" between the first woman Eve and Mary, the mother of Jesus. Having established that Miriam was a reincarnation of Eve, the characteristics of Miriam and Mary are then compared. In addition to the fact that they have the same name, both of them received the Holy Spirit and sang a canticle. Moreover, each one was in her own way "a fountain of life"[10]. The figure of John the Baptist is the object of particular attention[11], doubtless on account of the parallel, amply exploited within the Christian tradition, between John's mission as forerunner and that of Elijah described in the Second Book of Kings. Mention of John the Baptist is the occasion for the Christian Kabbalist to distinguish between different types of reincarnation according to the part of the soul involved[12] and to emphasise the essential importance of this doctrine. In short: John the Baptist was not just someone who simply resembled Elijah, but was in fact Elijah himself.

---

8   As in the case of the relationship established between Eve and Mary.
9   *Messias Puer* recalls that both were described as chaste men and both of them received revelations by way of a dream. Furthermore both appear as a "nourisher", one of the Land of Israel and the other, according to Knorr, as the "nourisher" of Mary (Cf. folio 14ᵛ, on Lk 1.27).
10 "[...] it is said of Miriam, Moses' sister that by her mediation the miraculous spring followed the Israelite camp and that after her death this water dried up (Num 20.1–2, Numbers Rabbah *initio*). Much more [than this] can be said of the other Miriam, because by her mediation the Fountain of Salvation began to flow into Ecclesia (Jn 7.37; 1 Cor 10.4). The Reincarnation of Isaiah's prophetess was interposed [between the two Mariams] (Isa 7.14) and this is why (5) the [Hebrew] word *h'lmh* [virgin] is applied to each of the three of them Ex 2.8; Isa 7.14; Mt 1.23." (Cf. folio 15ʳ on Lk 1.27).
11 Cf. folio 9ᵛ.
12 "According to our teachers, one type is the Reincarnation of the Psyche which we call [in Hebrew] *Nefesh*, another, the Reincarnation of the Spirit or [in Hebrew] *Ruach* and [a third], that of the Mind or [in Hebrew] *Neshamah*. It appears (to attend also to your own text at the same time) that in John [the Baptist] there was a Reincarnation not of the soul but of the spirit of Elijah (according to the words of the Angel in Lk 1.17)." (Cf. folio 9ᵛ).

THEOLOGICAL AND EXEGETICAL INNOVATION IN MESSIAS PUER 77

Unsurprisingly, we find the same doctrine more consequentially asserted in the case of Messiah. Commenting on Mt 1.1 "Son of David", the Kabbalist Catechumen passes in review the biblical characters of Adam, Abraham and David. To demonstrate the single chain of these revolutions of the Soul of Messiah[13], Knorr appeals to several sources including Zohar and *Yalqut Reuveni*.[14] Elsewhere, Knorr's creative exegetical response to the New Testament texts is well exemplified in his treatment of the genealogy of Jesus which, though informed by contemporary discussions, innovates precisely in the introduction of the doctrine of the Revolutions of Souls into the set of possible solutions to the notorious exegetic problems there.[15] Thus Jesus, we discover at folio 24^r, may really be Son of Joseph by virtue of his descent from his maternal grandfather:

> **Christian** If I was dealing with one of the unbelievers amongst your people, I should be allowed to resort to first principles, namely that: (1) human souls exist before they are born; and (2) they can be born several times. That (3) the literal sense in Scripture should not be neglected; one may be able to pass over [from it] to mysteries.
>
> So what would be so absurd, if I had said that Joseph had truly been the father of Messiah; but specifically in the sense that his daughter, who had died a little before, was soon reborn from Heli (Lk 3.23) and was thus betrothed to Joseph? For if it could happen that those [souls], who had [once] been spouses, soon became son and mother—which is what the Zohar expressly teaches happened in the case of Levirate marriage—why should it not happen that those [souls] who were father and daughter should shortly thereafter emerge as spouses?—especially on the assumption of the perpetual virginity of Mary.
>
> And so, to speak first of all specifically about the third group [of the genealogy], there *are* fourteen generations, since [as has just been demonstrated] there was a generation between Joseph and Mary. (2) Specifically, also, this table achieves a demonstration that Jesus was a Son of David [by descent] from his grandfather i.e. Joseph.

---

13 On the concept of the "Soul of Messiah", see J.-P. Brach, "Das Theorem der 'messianischen Seele' in der christlichen Kabbala bis zur *Kabbala Denudata*", *Morgen-Glantz* 16 (2006): pp. 244–258.
14 Cf. folios 24^v/25^v.
15 The Kabbalist Catechumen on Mt 1.3 (folios 25^v/^{r}) has an explanation of the anomalous appearance of Zara in the genealogy offered in terms of expiatory reincarnation.

It goes without saying that the general intention of the work is a demonstration that the Christ recognised by Christians is the Messiah to whom all Jewish literature—biblical, talmudic or esoteric—alludes. Consequently the figure of Messiah appears continually throughout the book and we have emphasised here two cases where the doctrine of the revolution of souls was systematically applied to the question of Messiah, first with respect to the figure of Messiah himself and then in the rigorous analysis of his genealogy as it is presented in the Gospels.

Mention of the Ten Tribes and the massacred Holy Innocents develops a more general perspective upon the destiny of groups. This has quite unexpected consequences as in the case of the Magi. Comment on Mt 2.1 finds them to be reincarnations of Jannes and Jambres of the sons of Balaam and gives a plausible account of their souls' long progress, the prophetic powers of Balaam and also their own sensitivity to the challenge of the star. As there were (apparently) quite a number of them, it is suggested that some might be reincarnations of the lapsed kings of Israel and Judah.

The case of the Slaughtered Innocents in Mt 2.17 citing the prophecy of Jer 31.15 offers a quite innovative interpretative opportunity and Knorr's solution is surprising. Here one group of individuals is destined to be reborn to, in a certain way, "die better" after learning of the establishment of the New Covenant. Knorr is aware of the paradoxical nature of this type of reincarnation and refers the reader to *De revolutionibus animarum* for further details.[16]

Beyond the cycles of revolutions of souls, Knorr finds evidence of larger historical cycles which are not merely typologically similar, but involve the same souls in parallel struggles against the shards. He starts with the Soul of Messiah and Egypt. Commenting upon Mt 2.13, the Kabbalist Catechumen asserts:

> Just like the first exile of the Israelites (whose Leader was always the soul of Messiah) to Egypt, where according to Hebrew teaching the Shekhinah was exiled with them. Thus the first exile of Messiah himself is in Egypt so that his departure from Egypt might pre-figure the time now

---

16 "According to the teachings of your sages, this fulfillment cannot be better explained than by the re-incarnation of those who were once killed by the Babylonians in this very place and then had been reborn and were killed again. And since the souls are soon more fully to be restored and on account of Christ have now been taken from among the living, it is reasonable to believe that they were reborn as soon as possible and immediately after the establishment of the New Covenant and then after the pouring out of the Holy Spirit were illuminated by its gifts and through martyrdom obtained the final consummation. For such reincarnations, see Tract De Revol. Animarum, p. 423, §10." (Cf. folio 49ʳ).

present in which the people of Messiah can be lead out from spiritual straits (for this is the meaning of the word *mçrym* [Egypt]).

Towards the end of this extract Christian calls this "the Revolution of Ages", which doctrine asserts that "what Messiah did and suffered of old, those same things recur quite often until the Final Full Restitution".[17]

The doctrine of the "revolution of souls" thus transforms the conventional typology of the Gospels into an assertion of real continuity (of soul) between several different historical persons or groups, often with the same name. That the doctrine is applied to Herod will come now as no surprise, but it is then developed, after the fashion of the previous passage with respect to the Shell of Edom.[18] A succinct statement of the case is found on Mt 1.16 at folio 49^r: "As Edom persecuted Jacob, so this Idumaean [Herod] will persecute Christ and the Dragon Edom (Rev 12.3) [Rome] [will persecute] the Christians."

A longer and more developed passage on this theme to be found at folios 5^r/5^v displays the notion which is called this time the "Flow of Ages". It also nicely illustrates the rich complexity of Knorr's exegesis as he integrates various aspects of Lurianic teaching in his reading of the Gospel text and also his chronographical and prophetic interests. Knorr establishes that Herod was historically, as the son of Antipater, an Edomite. The progressive domination of Edomites over the Souls of the Jewish people (in correlation with the latter's place of origin within the body of Adam Kadmon) is described through their various historical experiences. Rome too is shown to have Edomite antecedents through Josippon's tale of Tzepho who disputed the right of primogeniture with Joseph and his brother at the tomb of Jacob. Tzepho in time founded an Edomite colony in Campania and became the first king of Rome.[19] Rome is identified as Edom in Isa 63.1 and as the Red Dragon in Rev 12.13. Returning to Herod himself, he is shown to be the reincarnation of Hadar the last king of Edom (Gen 36.39) as an example of the "Hypothesis of Revolutions" whereby there is nothing new under the Sun and "those who in a certain fated period were once famous and now believed to have appeared repeatedly in the theatre of this world." A "mystic" meaning may be perceived if we take a clue from the Zohar: Herod is linked (psychologically) to the Kingdom of Hepar or the Lower Stomach or Evil Desire. This explains his behaviour but also identifies him as a precursor of the man of sin in 2 Thess.

---

17 Cf. Ibid.
18 Reference is found to the shells of Moab and Egypt (On Mt 1.5 "by Ruth") at folio 25^v.
19 Turnus and the Rutuli in *Aeneid* Book 7 also attest to this Edomite origin.

Knorr comments here upon the name and role of Herod in Lk 1.5. The interest and originality of his development lies in the blending of individual and historical accounts by an application of the doctrine of the revolution of souls to groups. Such teaching seems to have analogies with other kabbalistic teachings about the *shemittot* to which Knorr refers as either the "Revolution of Ages" or the "Flow of Ages". It is noticeable however that Knorr does not use this specific term in *Messias Puer*, none the less an entry is dedicated to the concept in his *Loci communes kabbalistici*. The concept of *gilgul* spread significantly from the second half of the Sixteenth Century onwards, mainly due to the popularity of the Kabbalistic school of Isaac Luria. In this context, the transmigration of souls became much more widespread, flourishing in a general vision of the restoration of the world which, according to Scholem, included a strong messianic dimension.[20] The transmigration of the soul thus assumed both a collective and an individual dimension, since everyone became a participant in the process of general restoration.

2   The Lurianic Narrative of the Shards, the Sparks and Jeshuah as Saviour

When one studies a case of Cultural Transfer[21] such as Christian Kabbalah, an immediate question arises: should one give an account of the relevant texts as they appear within the Jewish tradition, or as they appear in the writings of the Christian authors who appropriated them? Or, to put it another way, should one emphasise the context of the reception or the context whence the transferred material was taken?[22]

---

20   Scholem, *Le messianisme juif* (Paris, 1974), pp. 97–102. For the identification of the doctrine of the *shemittot* and Knorr's "Flow of Ages", see Vileno, "Reincarnations of Messiah(s): Messianic Expectations in Christian Knorr von Rosenroth's Last Work", *art. cit.*

21   By "Cultural Transfer" one understands here: "un mouvement d'objets, personnes, populations, mots, idées, concepts ... entre deux espaces culturels (États, nations, groupes ethniques, espaces linguistiques, aires culturelles et religieuses). Objet nouveau de recherches, la théorie des 'transferts culturels' propose d'en analyser les supports et les logiques. Elle s'intéresse à tous les domaines possibles de l'interculturel, du métissage—zones frontières entre cultures, langues, systèmes religieux ou politiques". ("A movement of objects, people, populations, words, ideas, concepts ... between two cultural spaces (states, nations, ethnic groups, linguistic spaces, cultural and religious areas). A new object of research, the theory of 'cultural transfers' proposes to analyze cultural supports and logics. It is interested in all possible areas of interculturality, mixing—frontiers between cultures, languages, religious or political systems".) (B. Joyeux-Prunel, "'Les transferts culturels'. Un discours de la méthode", *Hypothèses* 1 (2002): pp. 149–162, p. 151).

22   Ibid, p. 153.

In the case of Knorr, should one then describe (say) the myth of creation as it was elaborated in the Lurianic schools, or rather choose the final finished product and present what our Christian Hebraist himself has to say about it in his work? One has no wish to impose an artificially abstract definition upon the varieties of Lurianic Kabbalah, but it may none the less be helpful to give below a brief account of the main points of Luria's doctrine. In fact we know that the various episodes which make up the Lurianic creation myth were well known to Knorr[23], although they do not always all appear explicitly in *Messias Puer*.

Any investigation of specifically Lurianic Kabbalah encounters a fundamental difficulty, which is that there is not a single unified account of the Lurianic narrative. Issac Luria—the kabbalist active in the town of Safed in Galilee between 1569–1572 who gave his name to the movement—wrote practically nothing. We learn of his thought necessarily therefore through the writings of his pupils, who each present a personal reading of the teachings of their master. The difficulty which the Lurianic corpus thus presents is emphasised by Lawrence Fine:

> While we tend to think of a creation myth in terms of a single, coherent narrative that can be told as one does a simple story, Luria's mythological teachings have not come down to us in this way. Instead, we discover a seemingly endless series of inordinately complex notions, presented in often fragmentary and conflicting versions by multiple authors and editors. [...] Not only do we encounter conflicts and contradictions between the versions presented by different authors [...] but we sometimes also find them occurring even among the different versions presented by a single individual.[24]

---

23 Several entries in the *Loci communes kabbalistici* are specifically dedicated to them: "Adam Kadmon" (pp. 28–31); "Tsimtsum" (pp. 665–666); "Kelipot" (pp. 675–676); "Reshimu" (pp. 693–694); "Shevirat ha-kelim" (pp. 478–480; 698–703); "Tikun" (pp. 732–736).

24 L. Fine, *Physician of the Soul, Healer of the Cosmos. Isaac Luria and his Kabbalistic Fellowship* (Stanford University Press, 2003), p. 124. Scholem similarly evokes this diversity amongst the manuscripts and the fact that three different versions of the Lurianic writings were put into circulation by the disciples of Hayyim Vital (Cf. Scholem, *Sabbatai Sevi. The Mystical Messiah 1626–1676*, op. cit., p. 182). Although it is scarcely possible to give an account of the extent of research addressing the many facets of Lurianic Kabbalah, the following are fundamental for an initial approach: Scholem, *Major Trends, op. cit.*, pp. 244–286; I. Tishby, *The Doctrine of Evil and of the Shard in the Kabbalah of Ari* (in Hebrew) (Jerusalem: Magnes, 1942); R. Meroz, *The Teachings of Redemption in Lurianic Kabbalah* (in Hebrew) (Hebrew University of Jerusalem, 1988); Ead., "Faithful Transmission Versus Innovation: Luria and His Disciples", in *Gershom Scholem's Major Trends in Jewish Mysti-*

The nature of the Hebrew sources which served as the basis of Knorr's work remains a fundamental problem.[25] We have the Sulzbach Library Catalogue, in as far as concerns the works subsequently transferred to the Bayerische Staatsbibliothek in Munich. But this latter is still in manuscript and has not yet been exhaustively investigated.[26]

As we have seen, Lurianic Kabbalah was transmitted in several versions, sometimes quite different from each other. Then question arises from which branch(s) of the tradition Knorr took his material. The *Loci communes kabbalistici* are in this respect an invaluable source of information. For in compiling them, Knorr, meticulous scholar that he was, indicated his source at the end of each entry in this encyclopaedia.[27] This permits us to see the sources which Knorr knew, in addition to those texts which he translated *in extenso* in his anthology, *Kabbala Denudata*.[28] In this way we can observe that his explanations of technical terms in Lurianic Kabbalah are taken from *Ets Hayyim*, "The Tree of Life". The presentation of the Lurianic descent from Adam Kadmon is said to be taken from "Ez Chajim Part. Ozaroth Chajim Tract. Adam Kad-

---

cism 50 Years After, ed. by P. Schäfer, J. Dan (Tübingen: Mohr Siebeck, 1993): pp. 257–273; M. Idel, "Concerning the Concept of *Tsimtsum* in Kabbalah and in Scholarship", *Mekhkarei Yerushalaym* 10 (1992): pp. 59–112; Id., "'One from a Town, Two from a Clan'. The Diffusion of Lurianic Kabbala and Sabbateanism: A Re-Examination", *Jewish History* 7, 2 (1993): pp. 79–104; S. Magid, "From Theosophy to Midrash: Lurianic Exegesis of the Garden of Eden", *AJS Review* 22, 1 (1997): pp. 37–75; Y. Liebes, "Myth vs. Symbol in the Zohar and in Lurianic Kabbalah", in *Essential Papers on Kabbalah*, ed. by L. Fine (New York: University Press, 2000), pp. 212–241; L. Fine, *Physician of the Soul* and his numerous articles on the ritual aspect of Lurianic Kabbalah (mentioned in the bibliography there: Ibid, pp. 454–455); G. Necker, *Einfürung, op. cit.*

25 Among the rare articles devoted to this topic, see K. Burmistrov, "Die hebräischen Quellen der *Kabbala Denudata*", *Morgen-Glantz* 12 (2002): pp. 341–376 and E. Morlok, "*De Revolutionibus Animarum* in der *Kabbala Denudata* und dessen lurianische Vorlage *Sefer haGilgulim* von Chajjim Vital (1543–1620)", *Morgen-Glantz* 24 (2014): pp. 1–18. On Herrera's texts in *Kabbala Denudata*, see G. Necker, *Humanistische Kabbala im Barock: Leben und Werk des Abraham Cohen de Herrera* (Berlin: De Gruyter, 2011): p. 11, notes 41–42.

26 We have indicated in footnotes the works cited by Knorr in *Messias Puer* which, thanks to the catalogue of 1734, we know were (then) found in the Sulzbach Library. Rosmarie Zeller with the assistance of Laura Balbiani has provided a list of the categories of classification into which the 4815 volumes were divided. Cf. R. Zeller, "Die Kataloge der Sulzbacher Hofbibliothek", *Morgen-Glantz* 19 (2009): pp. 311–392. This catalogue followed an initial catalogue of 1679 which is similarly available.

27 For an analysis of Knorr's lexicographic work in the *Loci*, see A.B. Kilcher, "Lexikographische Konstruktion der Kabbala. Die *Loci communes cabbalistici* [sic] der *Kabbala Denudata*", *Morgen-Glantz* 7 (1997): pp. 67–125.

28 It should be remarked that now, through the many works which are cited in it, *Messias Puer* offers us a new way of entry into the vast learning of Knorr.

mon"[29]. But this reference is not clear, to the extent that "Ozaroth Chajim" could perhaps designate a specific version of Hayyim Vital's writings, "which is to a large extent a concise version of the homilies in the original *Ez Hayyim*"[30]. But Knorr *also* makes reference here to *Ets Hayyim*. But the work we today recognise under that title is in fact the product of several reworkings of the text, either by Hayyim Vital himself or his pupils.[31] Another not insignificant difficulty arises, in addition to that of the identification of Knorr's sources. The transmission of Lurianic writings into Europe has been the subject of much debate since the pioneering work of Gershom Scholem. The Kabbalist Israel Sarug, claiming to have Luria's teaching, seems to have been responsible for the introduction of Lurianic Kabbalah into Italy in the last years of the Sixteenth Century.[32] But, problematically, pieces of works of Israel Sarug were attributed to Hayyim Vital.[33]

If Knorr never refers to Sarug's name, Hayyim Vital, the best known pupil of Issac Luria, is mentioned twice explicitly as the author of manuscripts which served as the basis for the commentaries of Zohar published in the second volume of *Kabbala Denudata*: "Partis secundae Tractatus quartus *qui est* in Siphra de Zeniutha *Seu* Librum mysterii commentarius è manuscripto à

---

29 "Loci communes kabbalistici", in KD I, p. 31. The entry devoted to "Tsimtsum" (Ibid., pp. 665–666) refers to the same treatise. Two other treatises are cited as references: "Etz Chajim Part. Ozaroth Chajim Tract. Olam Hannekudim" ("Kelipot", pp. 675–676); "Shevirat ha-kelim", pp. 698–703; "Tikun", pp. 732–736 and also "Etz Chajim Part. Ozaroth Chajim Tract. Olam Haakudim" ("Kelim", pp. 478–480; "Reshimu", pp. 693–694).

30 P. Giller, *Reading the Zohar: The Sacred Text of the Kabbalah* (Oxford: University Press, 2000): p. 23. This last version of Hayyim Vital's writings shows the traces of editorial work by Meir Poppers, one of Vital's pupils, and seems to have been the main source of the knowledge of Lurianic Kabbalah in seventeenth-century Germany. (Cf. Giller, *Reading the Zohar*, op. cit., p. 23 and Fine, *Physician of the Soul*, op. cit., pp. 16–17).

31 If the first version undertaken by Vital identified material attributable to Luria himself from other collections of commentaries, subsequent versions, due initally to his son Samuel Vital and to other disciples thereafter (Jacob Tzemakh, Meir Poppers) reorganised the different works by a thematic grouping: "They combined all of the *Zohar* commentaries, regardless of the stage of Luria's thought represented or whether their author was Luria, Vital, or someone else." (Giller, *Reading the Zohar*, op. cit., p. 24). On these complications, see Necker, *Einfürung in die lurianische Kabbala*, op. cit., pp. 47–52.

32 "On the whole, the spread of Lurianic Kabbalism was almost entirely due to the activity of another Kabbalist, Israel Sarug, who between 1592 and 1598 carried on a lively propaganda in the interests of the new school among the Kabbalists of Italy" (Scholem, *Major Trends*, op. cit., p. 257). Although, traces of Lurianic Kabbalah were already observable in Europe in the 1620s, before Sarug's presence in Italy: Cf., J. Avivi, "The Writings of Luria in Italy before 1620" (in Hebrew), *Alei Sefer* 11 (1984): pp. 91–134.

33 Giller, *Reading the Zohar*, op. cit., p. 204, note 99.

R. Chajim Vital juxta tradita R. Jezchak Lorja Germanie edito latinitate donatus: *In quo Magna ex parte etiam illustrantur ambo Tractatus, qui vocantur Idra, tam rabba sive major, quam suta sive minor*"[34] and "Partis Secundae Tractatus Quintus *qui continet* Tres tractatus initiales libri Sohar qui in Editione Mantuana referentur ad Praefationem; cum textu originario, pro majori exercitio Tyronum, non punctato, sed cum versione tamen, & commentariis, partim è Libro Sohare Chammah; partim è Manuscriptis à R. Chajim Vital juxta tradita R. Jizchak Lorja Germani editis."[35] It would appear here that Knorr was working on the basis of manuscripts which had come from Germany under the name of Hayyim Vital—but perhaps these were the works of Israel Sarug.

Other accounts of Lurianic Kabbalah are found in the *Kabbala Denudata*, such as the *Shaar ha-shamayyim* of Abraham Cohen de Herrera[36]. Then there is the *Emeq ha-melekh*, at the time "the most comprehensive compendium of Lurianic kabbalah"[37] and "the first printed work to bring a full-length exposition of the Lurianic kabbalah (that is, Sarug's version of it)".[38] The "Valley of the King" was printed in Amsterdam in 1648 and a Latin translation appears in the second volume *of Kabbala Denudata*[39]. Although this text is only rarely cited in *Messias Puer*, the author's insistence upon the messianic and eschatological dimension of Lurianic Kabbalah seems thoroughly to have penetrated Knorr's thought world—which was probably already well-disposed to receive it.[40]

---

34 "The Fourth Tractate of the Second Part which is a short commentary upon Siphra de Zeniutha or the Book of the Mystery from a manuscript after the tradition of R. Jezchak Lorja in Germany, printed in Latin by R. Chajim Vital: in which there is illustrated in great part the two tractates Idra Rabba (the Greater) and Idra Suta (the Less)".

35 "The Fifth Tractate of the Second Part which contains the three initial tractates of the Book Zohar which in the Mantuan edition make up the Preface, with the original text, for the greater exercise of beginners unpointed, however with a translation and commentaries, some from the Book Sohar Chammah and some from manuscripts printed by R. Chajim Vital after the tradition of R. Jizchak Lorja in Germany".

36 On Herrera, see G. Scholem, *Avraham Cohen de Herrera's* Shaar ha-shamayyim. *His life, his work and his Influence* (in Hebrew) (Jerusalem: Mossad Bialik, 1978); A. Altmann, "Lurianic Kabbala in a Platonic Key: Abraham Cohen Herrera's *Puerta del Cielo*", *Hebrew Union College Annual Cincinnati* 53 (1982): pp. 317–355; *"Le Portail des cieux"*, traduit et annoté par M. Attali, (Paris: Editions de l' Éclat, 2010); N. Yosha, *Myth and Metaphor. Avraham Cohen Herrera's Philosophic Interpretation of Lurianic Kabbalah* (in Hebrew) (Jerusalem: Magnes, 1994); Necker, *Humanistische Kabbala*, op. cit.

37 Scholem, *Sabbatai Sevi*, p. 528.

38 Ibid., p. 551.

39 *"Partis primæ Tractatus Secundus, Quae est Introductio Pro meliori intellectu Libri Sohar. E Scripto R. Naphathali Hirtz, F.R. Jaacob Elchanan; Quod vocat Vallem Regiam"*, pp. 151–346.

40 On Naphathali ben Jacob Bacharach, see Y. Liebes, "Toward a Study of the Author of *Emeq*

Contrary to what one observes in *Adumbratio*, the technical terms of Lurianic Kabbalah are absent from *Messias Puer*. On no occasion do the key notions of *tsimtsum*, *shevirat ha-kelim* or even *tikun* appear explicitly by name in the text. Moreover, although the different moments in the Lurianic drama are well and truly present in *Messias Puer*, they are never referred to by the usual kabbalistic vocabulary. On the other hand, we know that Knorr had fully mastered this technical repertoire, as is clear from the *Loci* which we have just been discussing, as well as from the numerous translations collected in *Kabbala Denudata*.

It is at this point that there arises the question of the readership envisaged by Knorr: the omission or concealment of technical terms could be seen as a literary strategy primarily intended to attract a Christian readers who one may well imagine might be put off by a strange terminology. One can also easily see that this would endanger the whole of Knorr's exegetical project by discrediting his (already extremely audacious) interpretation of the New Testament.

On the other hand, if one imagines that *Messias Puer* is aimed primarily at a Jewish readership, then the absence of the appropriate terms might well appear as an inappropriate omission: it would have the consequence of depriving the Jewish reader of potentially familiar, and therefore reassuring, references in the polemical context of the dialogue between the Kabbalist and the Christian. Yet, another consideration reinforces the impression that the text primarily seeks to address a Jewish readership: the observation that the Tetragrammaton and the other divine names are systematically written piously broken by an apostrophe in imitation of the usual Hebrew practice to prevent inadvertent articulation. One can understand that such a practice might be prudently adopted if the author was addressing a Jewish readership, but it makes very little real sense in a Christian context.

That having been said—and the two readerships are not necessarily mutually exclusive—one can also very easily imagine that Kabbalah (and perhaps particularly Lurianic Kabbalah) found little favour among the Jewish commu-

---

ha-Melech: His Personality, Writings and Kabbalah" (in Hebrew), *Mekhkarei Yerushalaym* 11 (1993): pp. 101–137. More specifically on the relationships between *Emek ha-melekh* and Knorr, see J.H. Chajes, "Durchlässige Grenzen: Die Visualisierung Gottes zwischen jüdischer und christlicher Kabbala bei Knorr von Rosenroth und van Helmont", *Morgen-Glantz* 27 (2017): pp. 99–147. See also P. Theisohn, "Zur Rezeption von Naphtali Herz Bacharachs *Sefer Emeq ha-Melech* in der *Kabbala Denudata*", *Morgen-Glantz* 16 (2006): pp. 221–241 and E. Baumgarten, "Comments on Rav Naftali Bachrach's Usage of Pre-Lurianic Sources", *Association for Jewish Studies Review*, 37/2 (2013): pp. 1–23.

nity, which may in itself have determined Knorr to adopt a prudent attitude and thus suppress excessive explicit mention of kabbalistic terms.[41]

The Lurianic system in spite of its enormous elaborated complexity may yet be considered, at heart, a metaphysical narrative or myth which in obvious and salient repects is different from the fundamental narrative of the Hebrew Bible. Lurianic scholars therefore were faced with an exegetical project of providing a midrashic reading of the Tanakh which would conform to the demands of their doctrines. Knorr faced a similar challenge in expounding the New Testament text in such a way that it might be seen to support the Lurianic narrative and be compatible with the Lurianic notions of the origin of souls, the fall of souls, the nature of evil, its defeat and the final "restoration". None of these narratives appear obviously on the surface of the New Testament and established Christianity had powerful and influential accounts of its own to offer in these areas which were manifestly not Lurianic. If however the kabbalistic tradition was indeed an ancient and authoritative *revelatio* (and not just a *relatio*)[42], then such a narrative might justifiably be presupposed and, if the New Testament was susceptible to interpretation in its light, the resulting "good news" would be salutary for both Jews and Christians—indeed offered the prospect of a shared common understanding of and participation in salvation.

The Lurianic account of Creation begins before the Creation described in Genesis and takes place in a sort of cosmological time with the initial act of Divinity which is called *tsimtsum*, "contraction" or "constriction". As in other traditions, the purpose of the Lurianic myth is to offer an explanation of how the One became Many, by a sequence of emanations similar to that of Neo-Platonism. The Divine retracted its essence from a point at its centre towards its extremities in a circular movement. The purpose of this was to clear a space where Divinity and the intensity of its light would be absent and in which the created world might find a place.[43] According to other versions of the same myth, the Divinity is described as being of a mixed nature, comprising at once within itself both positive and negative forces (*din*, "judgment" and *rachamim*, "mercy"). From this perspective, the purpose of creation was to purge the Divinity of the demonic forces which it contained.[44]

---

41 Scholem mentions several movements of opposition to Lurianic kabbalah, especially in the form taught by Israel Sarug. Cf. *Sabbatai Sevi,* op. cit., p. 87, note 134 and p. 210.
42 Cf. *supra*, p. 39.
43 The Lurianic account perpetuates a midrashic exposition according to which several worlds were created by the Divinity before our own and which were all destroyed because of the demands of Divine omnipresence (*Genesis Rabbah* 3.9).
44 Cf. Fine, *Physician of the Soul*, op. cit., p. 127.

After the contraction, a tiny quantity of divine light was none the less reintroduced into the space left void (called *tehiru*) because nothing can in fact exist within a total absence of the divine. The light was reintroduced in the form of a line and concentric circles from which *Adam Kadmon* the "Primordial Man" was formed who acts as an intermediary between the Divinity and the created world and who occupies a central place in the Lurianic system. From those residues of light which had remained present within the *tehiru*, there were formed the vases (*kelim*), destined to receive and hold the divine light. Here the Lurianic narrative takes a dramatic turn, for the vases, under the pressure of the intensity of the reintroduced light, smashed (an episode which is known as *shevirat ha-kelim*, the "shattering of the vases").

The shards of these vases fell towards the centre of the space from which initially Divinity had withdrawn, dragging with them sparks of light which remained attached to them. From a geometric perspective the retreat of Divinity had taken place from the centre towards the circumference and it was precisely the centre of this now empty space which became the place of creation. Thus the material world is a mixed world, the product of a combination of demonic material and sparks of divine light hidden and imprisoned within the gangue of material. Finally, the process of rehabilitation, the third panel of the Lurianic triptych, consists in the liberation of the sparks of light caught in the material shells (*kelipot*) which retain them until they can make their ascent back to the Creator. The passage from the One to the Many is here, then, conceived as something temporary, the objective being to recover the original unity in the One without differentiation.

With the creation of the material world related in the Bible, during the days that preceded the birth of the First Man (*Adam Rishon*), the divine components, that is, the sefirot and the *partsufim*, began their ascension and were close to reaching the level of unity with the divine realm that they had enjoyed before the breaking of the vessels, rising on high through the various worlds of Formation (*Yestirah*) and Creation (*Briah*), to reach the highest world of Emanation (*Atsilut*). Immediately after the Creation of the First Man, together with the occurence of the world's first Shabbat, this process of restauration could have been completed. However, the transgression of the First Man (*Adam Rishon*) provoked a dramatic fall within the material world. Since then, this universal restoration, the achievement of *tikun*, was constantly deferred. In consequence of the correspondence between the world above and the world below, each Sabbath is considered as an occasion propitious for the restoration of the world.[45] But the transgression of the First Man (*Adam Rishon*) had another fur-

---

45   Ibid., pp. 141–144.

ther consequence, important in the case of *Messias Puer*—it provoked the fall into the material world (*kelipot*) of the souls which were contained within the body of the Primordial Man (*Adam Kadmon*).

This vast mythological narrative and it successive embellishments are not presented in their entirety but are alluded to in part. Furthermore Knorr also wishes to harmonise this grand vision with very different New Testament passages on sin and salvation and the broader Christian understanding of these matters. The following passage indicates the difficulty Knorr faced in presenting such a narrative, for here the reader must be introduced to reincarnation, Adam Kadmon and Adam Belial and the opposing fallen and impure army under Samael. To some extent Knorr has to rely (as we have seen) on familiarity with his previous work. But the readers themselves must also accept the universal restoration wherein (similar to the heresy of Origen) even the worst of shards may be corrected and also understand the "forgiveness of sins" in the context of reincarnation as "freedom from the (appropriate) punishments". In this last respect the lemma of Mt 1.21 is significant. According to Knorr's translation of the Syriac, Jeshuah frees his people "from their punishments". The Vulgate, however, has "from their sins". The passage is from folio 31^v.

From their punishments

Christian Just as the Hebrew word '*wn*, sin or iniquity, is often used for punishment as in 1Sam 28.10; Gen 4.13; 19.15; Lev 15.1; 16.22 etc, so also is the Greek word *harmartia* as in Mt 9.2, 5, 6; Jn 1.29; 8.21, 24; 9.41; 15.22, 24; 16.8, 9. Likewise, the Syriac [word] *ḥṭh'* in all these places. So here we should understand the whole saving work of Messiah. Thus all types of ills, by which on account of their primaeval fall the souls of men are punished, are implied here. They are overwhelmed by the filthy Shards; they lack the primal light and influx; and are subject to the *Yetser ha-ra* or the Evil Impulse; and to death, to being born within various incarnations and envelopments; and to the torments of Gehennah etc. from all of which, but mainly from their proneness to sin, Messiah both wishes and is able to free them.

Kabbalist Catechumen If what our writers mean by the People of Messiah is to become clear we need here to explain more fully their theory of the Soul. The Man of Holiness, that is Adam the Protoplast, they consider as a single army of Souls; as if some Souls belonged to his head, evidently some to his eyes, some to his nose etc. and so on through his individual limbs. And to this [Adam] they oppose another—Adam Belial, the Man of Perversity, who himself is also like a body and [constitutes] a similar army under the leadership of Samael. This alternate and impure army, which had already previously fallen, prevailed in the Temptation in Paradise with the consequence that individual members [of this body], by specific sins, subjected to themselves the corresponding members in [the body of] Holiness. Our writers say that it soon happened that those Souls which had been in the Holy Man which fell under pollution, then descended into the World of Generation to become the People of the Covenant and the Israelites. But those who before then had already fallen under Samael, the Prince of unclean spirits and by the time of the Fall were mixed into the holy body of Adam, as they descended to [the world] of Generation wanted to escape into the Gentile peoples (Tract. *De Revol. Animarum*, 1§ 2, 14). This opinion is set forward a little more accurately in *Adumbratio*, chap. 10 § 6, 7, where it should be noted that according to this theory even the wickedness of the worse and the deviance of the shards can finally be corrected; so that in the Last Times of Messiah, that privation and inclination to evil which Scripture calls *Death* (truly the absence of the diviner nature) will be utterly borne away, so that there will be a Complete Restitution Isa 25.8; 1 Cor 15.26, 54, 55, 56.

First, therefore, by the People of Messiah we should understand the Souls of the Old Covenant reincarnated many times, until they are fully subject to Messiah. Second: all remaining Souls who sooner or later will be led to the New Covenant—until after reincarnated births and many punishments, God will be "all in all" 1 Cor 15.28.

A few years earlier *Adumbratio* had shown an interest in the question of original sin, its origin and transmission. The text developed the notion that sin, rather than being innate, was in fact acquired, as a result of upbringing at the hands of one's parents. Original sin was not, therefore, intrinsic to human nature. To clarify the issue, the Christian Philosopher of *Adumbratio* established there a distinction between the terms "sin" and "punishment". The term *peccatum*, from the Latin *peccare* means "to commit a fault, to fail, to do wrong" or even "to be faulty, to be defective". By contrast *poena* "punishment" has a primary sense of "a ransom intended to compensate for murder" and thence "compensation, reparation, vengence punishment, chastisement". The Greek word ποινή (*poinē*) has similarly a legal meaning of compensation arising from a delict committed. There is therefore a chronological relationship between the two terms since the punishment (*poena*) is the reparation demanded as a result of the sin (*peccatum*). What was the intention of the Christian Philosopher in establishing this distinction? Was it to declare that the "penalty" indicates reparation for a fault committed and not for a weakness inherent in human nature? Perhaps one may see here traces of Pelagianism. According to this doctrine man is capable of assuring his own salvation by his own means and his own sole merit, without the intervention of Grace. The existence of sin without personal responsibility was quite inconceiveable for Pelagians. In that respect one could say that they argued more as philosophers than as Christians.[46] This remark could just as well have been made of the author(s) of *Adumbratio* and *Messias Puer* especially as Francis Mercury van Helmont's attachment to Pelagianism has been amply demonstrated by the works of Alison Coudert.[47]

In short *Adumbratio* appears to deny the reality of *peccatum originale* which, according to the author(s) is merely a turn of phrase or a trope. Original sin in fact is only the penalty and not the fault. The distinction which is made here, together with the denial of the transmission of original sin by human generation, constitutes a major challenge to Augustinian doctrine.

More largely, *Messias Puer* in its account of the manner in which the process of salvation unfolds insists upon the perfectible nature of man which can be "taught" by Messiah. The following passage in commenting upon Zachariah's song concentrates specifically upon what is meant by salvation and gives a fairly full account of its various aspects:

> On "he might prepare his ways": see below on Mt 3.3. So we grasp the method of Messiah by which he intends first the restitution of the souls of Israelites and then the souls of proselytes too. And this Messianic method will be described in detail by the following verse 77. It requires that Messiah should give knowledge to or inform his people as the Supreme Rector of the Divine Assembly (see Tract. *De Revol. Animarum*, chap. 1, § 1, p. 244; *Adumbratio* chap. 1, § 5, 6; 2, § 13; 4, § 7 seq.; 5, § 2; 6, § 2; 8, § 2. And compare Jn 3.2; Mt 8.19; 12.38; 19.16; 22.16, 24, 36; 26.18 etc.). Also that: [the Greek] *sōtēria* [salvation] or [the Aramaic] *ḥy'* [life] i.e. the restoration of the saved soul or its *life* (does not consist in deeds as carefully as possible performed according to the norm of either Law since these are natural and not entirely free from primaeval sin, see *Adumbratio*, chap. 2, § 12 but) requires (1) the Remission of Sins which to be rightly understood requires us to note that:

---

46 A. Sage, "Le péché originel dans la pensée de saint Augustin, de 412 à 430", *Revue des Études Augustiniennes* 15, 1 (1969): pp. 75–112, p. 76.

47 Coudert, *Leibniz and the Kabbalah*, op. cit., pp. 8–10; 155; Ead., "Henry More, the Kabbalah, and the Quakers", in *Philosophy, Science, and Religion in England 1640–1700*, edited by P. Zagorin, R. Ashcraft and R. Kroll (Cambridge: University Press, 1992): pp. 31–67, p. 40; Ead., *The Impact of the Kabbalah in the Seventeenth Century*, op. cit., pp. 128 et *passim*.

(a) any given soul when first created was a shining globe (which could take on any form, including the human), but at the time of Adam's fall was taken captive by a certain dark Spirit of Impurity (See Tract. *De Revol. Animarum*, p. 248, §11, 12, 14) whose blackness obscured the light of the soul.

(b) that the soul being drawn down into generation, a large part of it was liberated from that darkness—drawn down, that is, into bright action which it previously lacked. However it retained many stains or remnants and parts of its perverter (it has parts which are a mixture of both souls and shards and *nitsutsot* or various sparks) which are ideas which come into existence with various affects i.e. the origins of the natural movements and organisation of the soul.

(c) that also various obfuscations enter the soul from outside. These are all connected with a spirit of the Shards and may cause us an influx of spirit either from food or drink or the incidence of a certain feeling from which notions are formed.

(d) that every action of the soul arises from an idea and if it is sinful it only matches the idea. For all the ideas in a soul, there are an equal number of spirits within it. And these are evil if the ideas are evil. (See Tract. *De Anima* by Rabbi Moses Cordovero, p. 146 *seq.*). These are the specific punishments for individual sins.

(e) that the remission of sins consists not so much in the forgetting of those acts, but also the removal of the punishments or the ideas of the shard spirits. This is what Mic 7.19 means when it says that sins "are thrown into the depths of the sea" *i. e.* those spirits which are the punishment of sins are shut into the depths of Great Abyss. So for these reasons the whole basis of the new Messianic way of proceeding is the remission of sins i.e. the removal of the punishments, which also removes those corrupting ideas which otherwise would produce many similar acts. This is the first requirement of life or the restoration of the soul.

But also required is (2) that saving restoration, the unique influx of the Grace of a merciful God, not merely for the remission of sins which we have just been discussing, but also to inform all the subsequent moral acts of the soul. So briefly the meaning of Zachariah's words is this: that Messiah will inform his people; the life of the soul consists in the remission of sins (as if he said "The Light of the Soul is restored by the removal of the darkness of the Shards") and in the mercy of the Grace of God (as if he said "This Light of the Soul cannot exist nor be increased unless born from the influx of the degree Tiferet [Glory]") to which is linked the [Aramaic] word *rḥm'* [mercy] and from the degree Chesed to which is linked the [Hebrew] word *ḥnnh* [Grace] and from the degree Binah to which is linked the[Aramaic] word *'lhn* [God]. (See Lex. Cabb., p. 680 & p. 109, n. 17; p. 110, n. 2,3,4; p. 111, n. 2.)

V78, 79 Now, finally, follows the last part of this prophecy which concerns the final completion of the Messianic kingdom. The meaning is that in a little while, by the gracious influx of the mercy of God, we shall be visited by that same Light of Messiah, not merely in its rising as now, but from on high, as at mid-day, to illuminate not only those whose soul has up to now been obscured by the stains of darkness, but also those who sit in complete darkness (i.e. who have not yet recognised the Light of Messiah that has arisen so far, or who are from the Jews of the modern dispersion; or are the descendants of the Ten Tribes) and in the shadow of death (i.e. who have up to now still to be converted from the Gentiles). But we who are already experiencing the beginnings of illumination he will lead to the way of complete prosperity. (See Lex. Cabb., pp. 717 *seq.* & Rev 21.23; 22.5; Isa 60.19, 20.)[48]

The detail of the manner in which Messiah will bring redemption and grant remission of sins focuses upon the origin of the shards from which the souls, which were created pure and without sin (as "shining globes"), must be freed. Sin is presented as coming from outside, as a stranger to the soul. This is the reason why sin which has come and attached itself to the soul, can simply be eliminated in the "removal of the punishments". Evidently we are here faced with a notion of Original Sin, which extends and refines, almost with a technical precision, the reflections initiated in *Adumbratio*. But the "removal of punishments" is only one stage in a process which is envisaged in stages by Knorr. For in fact there follows an educational stage wherein Messiah, not content merely to have removed punishments will teach people not to recommit sin and will "inform all the subsequent moral acts of the soul", developing here the figure of Christ as the merciful teacher *par excellence*.

---

48 At folios 35ʳ–36ʳ.

3　Messiah

Messiah is central to the New Testament texts under examination in the commentary and consequently to the focus of the exegetical investigation itself. As a distinguishing doctrine between Jews and Christians the topic of Messiah was crucial to the polemics between the two faiths. Knorr's presentation of the subject is not that of orthodox Christianity. Without denying the complexity of Christological and Theological disputes of the Reformation, nor the existence of dissident convictions, Christian accounts of the Messiah were for the most part Trinitarian and claimed allegiance to Nicaea. That is to say, Jesus Christ, the Messiah, was the third person of the Trinity incarnate in the Flesh. He was God from eternity and uncreated. The anathemas at the end of the Nicaean Creed specifically targeted the Arians who said "There was a time when he [the Son] was not"[49], which is precisely what Knorr insists upon. Like Arius, but in a very different idiom, he considered the Soul of Messiah was the beginning of Creation.

The doctrine of Messiah in *Messias Puer* is quite complex and comprises several parts. We shall not repeat here what has just been said about the Soul of Messiah or of *Adam Kadmon*, but both are essential to understanding Messiah as the "first-born of creation", his corporate nature, and the prospect of salvation, which as we shall see shortly involves a Jewish Millennial Kingdom. These themes will be incidentally expanded further in several passages we shall discuss below. Such is the inter-connected nature of Knorr's thought and exegesis.

In Mary there occurred the final reincarnation of the Nefesh (the lowest part of the soul) of David and the Nefesh of *Adam Kadmon* from which was formed the vital spirit of Messiah. Knorr seeks other categories to satisfy the apparent demands of the New Testament text that Jesus was in some sense "divine". In his discussion of the opening verses of John's Gospel, initially commenting on Jn 1.1 (*"The [First] Principle of Creation was the Word, and the Word Itself was with God and God was that Word"*) Knorr writes:

> **Kabbalist Catechumen** So it is not so much the divine nature of Messiah which this name asserts, as his created nature: and certainly, if I were to convert to your opinion, I would not say this began in [the womb of] Mary. Relevant here are *Adumbratio*, chap. 3 & chap. 7, para. 26.[50]

49　*Ēn pote hoti ouk ēn* [*ho huios*].
50　At folio 3ᵛ.

The important point here is that the life of Messiah did not begin in the womb of Mary. If the existence of Messiah had, in conformity with Kabbalah but contrary to Christian doctrine, a beginning in time, *Messias Puer*, on the other hand denies that that beginning was the conception of Jesus by Mary.

Similarly in comment on Jn 1.2, the question arises of the relation of Messiah to divinity. The Kabbalist Catechumen is equally insistent that Messiah's existence did not begin in Mary's womb, but goes on to speak of Messiah being united with Divinity from the beginning:

> Or does the word *bryšyt* here in Verse 2 really have another meaning: (…) that right from the beginning the Messiah had been united with Divinity; and that that Union did not begin with his state of lowliness?

Here the "state of his lowliness" is evidently his birth from Mary.

How that may be imagined is indicated in a passage we already examined above (On Mt 1.15 "Out of Egypt"):

> The mystical sense of the prophet's words is this: Around those degrees where Israel is called "Boy" (See Cabb. Denud., Part. 2, p. 8) *i. e.* the higher part around the beginnings of the Son which is called Zeir Anpin, is the place of Love or Chesed (See Cabb. Denud., Part. 1, p. 43) and, although the surrounding Shards have there a narrow place (as the name Egypt implies), nonetheless "I call out my Son and Boy" and through him provide an influx for lower creatures.[51]

Which may be compared with a passage (at folio 29ᵛ on Mt 1.15) we shall discuss more fully below:

> And although others fell, the Soul of Messiah itself in its wholeness remained always united with the divine degree called The Son and with which from the beginning the Soul of Messiah had joined itself (Heb 13.8). Thus, from the beginning of the Ecclesia, the whole economy of the Old Covenant was administered through the Soul of Messiah (1 Cor 10.4). Until at last, having put on human flesh, it was to appear and initiate the ministry of the New Convenant.

---

51   At folio 49ʳ.

The "divinity" of Jesus is accounted for by the steadfast unity of the Soul of Messiah with the "divine degree called the Son". The reader will find this corroborated by the various speculations on the significance of the name of Jesus in the context of the other divine names and particularly the Tetragrammaton in *Messias Puer*.[52]

The indication here of how Lurianic kabbalah deals with the central Christian issue of the "divinity" of the Son is quite crucial. The three passages we have just reviewed do not set out the full context in Lurianic thought, though there is an explanatory reference to *Kabbala Denudata*. What is in play here is the doctrine of *partsufim* ("faces"), fresh structures of the Godhead formed in the new spheres of Creation after the "breaking of the vessels" (*shevirat ha-kelim*). Two of the five *partsufim* are *Aba* and *Ima* (Father and Mother) to which Knorr refers elsewhere in *Messias Puer*. And also "the higher part around the beginnings of the Son which is called Zeir Anpin" (another of the *partsufim*). It is perhaps the work of another occasion to attempt a fully articulated account of Knorr's view of this key doctrine. Our point here is the comparative discretion of its presentation. There is little systematic preparation or presentation and the vital issue passes without anything like the emphasis one might expect. Knorr has done the work and has seen how a Lurianic Christology might be constructed, but the reader of *Messias Puer* (alas!) does not receive that full exposition.

Several passages which we shall meet below speculate on how Messiah might both "uphold the worlds" and yet (at the same time) be present here on earth. The Lurianic tradition had already solved that problem (we are told) in the case of Metatron. The problem occurs again when the Soul of Elijah attends his own circumcision when reincarnated as John the Baptist. The answer is that the two superior portions of the soul, *Chayah* and *Yechidah*, remain in heaven for the duration. The Yechidah of Messiah, however, had appeared in Samson, as we learn on Mt 2.19:

> For, amongst the Former Prophets is included the book of Judges, to which the evangelist seems to wish to point, and to draw a type of Samson from Judg 13.5. As if the Angel there had said: This acolyte of the Sun (which the name "Soham Schon" sounds like) will not only perform those feats, but in him, as Yechidah, at the same time will be a power of Messiah, the true liberator of his people, which was originally united with the degree Tiferet

---

52   A.M. Vileno, "Les noms divins dans l'œuvre de Knorr de Rosenroth: une présence voilée", *Accademia. Revue de la société Marsile Ficin* (forthcoming).

(which they call the Sun). And just like that hero, he will be a Nazirite and thus Messiah will be called by a similar name. Which is what happened.[53]

Knorr is well aware of the Jewish traditions of two Messiahs, indeed he anthologised the relevant passages in the lost *Excerpta*, as we saw above. He does not, however, see them as two different *personae*, but rather as aspects of the one Messiah.[54]

4   A Jewish Messianic Kingdom

It is evident from *Messias Puer* that for Knorr both prophecy and chronology provide the basis for his anticipation of a literal, material and political future Jewish messianic kingdom in Palestine. This involves an interpretation of several passages in a way not traditional and clear moments of disagreement with the more common reading of passages by Lightfoot, whose work Knorr seems to have kept an eye on as he wrote.

It is also evident that while *Adumbratio* addresses in several respects the "Final Restitution", it does not explicitly mention this physical and political restoration of the Kingdom of Israel. We are thus introduced in *Messias Puer* to an aspect of Knorr's eschatology perhaps only anticipated in the Apocalypse Commentary but one that intimately relates to the future destiny of Jews, as well as Christians. It is not perhaps entirely fanciful to imagine that this more positive and less supersessionist prospect for contemporary Jews was not entirely unrelated to the grant of rights of residence to the Jews of Sulzbach by the Duke in 1685, with which Knorr was much concerned and to which we have alluded above. The traditional Augustinian role for contemporary Jews was for them to be kept debased, desolate and dispersed as a punishment and also as an object lesson that God keeps his promises (or perhaps better, fulfils his threats). A recent account of Augustine has provided a more positive evaluation of his thought and has argued that it may even have had salutary effects.[55] Yet such a perspective in its consequences remains very different from the approach to contemporary Jews found in Christian Augustus' Sulzbach and to the rights

---

53   At folio 50ᵛ.
54   This is discussed more fully in the notes to the Translation and in Vileno, "Reincarnations of Messiah(s): Messianic Expectations in Christian Knorr von Rosenroth's Last Work", *art. cit.*
55   P. Fredriksen, *Augustine and the Jews. A Christian Defense of Jews and Judaism*, 2nd ed. (Yale University Press, 2010).

of settlement given to Jews there in 1666 followed by the liberal Charter of Privileges of 1685. Knorr was very much involved in the settlement.[56] He also expressed himself at length on what he considered to be proper toleration of contemporary Jews in the Forward *Lectori philebreo salutem* at the beginning of the second 1684 volume of *Kabbala Denudata*, in a section *De Toleratione Judaeorum inter Christianos* which contains 28 arguments for their tolerance.[57] There is a striking similarity between this text and similar arguments offered later by Knorr's correspondant Wagenseil.[58] The discovery of Knorr's conviction of an anticipated Jewish Messianic Kingdom in Palestine where Jews would be gathered and ultimately be converted, offers a forceful prophetic reason for this more liberal treatment of Jews: far from being perpetual wanderers, they were imagined as having an honourable future role to play in the eschatological drama.

In a first writing on Lk 1.55 at folio 19^v, Knorr allowed the Christian to express these hopes. On reflection, he adjusted the manuscript to have these controversial notions articulated by the Kabbalist Catechumen and permits the Christian himself no response, one way or the other, to these singular anticipations of a future Jewish kingdom. This is a very clear example of the self-censorship he exercised upon his work but also a further indication of his own expectations, as a Christian, of a future Messianic Age.

In the late Sixteenth Century, English theologians began to find both a typological fulfilment of the Exodus and a literal fulfilment of the Abrahamic covenant promises—and, indeed, the burden of the prophecies in Daniel and Revelation—in a restoration of contemporary Jews to Palestine.[59] There they

---

56   Weber, "Jüdisches Leben in Sulzbach und Floß in 17. und 18. Jahrhundert", *art. cit.*, at pages 119–120.
57   § 20-§ 48 pp. 20–38. These are discussed by Zeller, "Die Rolle von Franciscus Mercurius Van Helmont", *art. cit.*, pp. 393–396. The text of the forward transcribed by Erna Handschur may be found in *Morgen-Glantz* 16 (2006): pp. 17–54.
58   J.C. Wagenseil, *Hoffnung der Erlösung Israels* (Leipzig 1705: Nürnberg and Altdorf 1707).
59   For basic biography see N. Matar, "The Idea of the Restoration of the Jews in English Protestant Thought: From the Reformation until 1660", *Durham University Journal* 77 (1985): pp. 23–36; Id., "The Idea of the Restoration of the Jews in English Protestant Thought: From 1661–1701", *Harvard Theological Review* 78 (1985): pp. 115–148; Id., "The Controversy over the Restoration of the Jews in English Protestant Thought: 1701–1753", *Durham University Journal* 80 (1988): pp. 241–256; Id., "The Controversy over the Restoration of the Jews in English Protestant Thought: 1754–1809", *Durham University Journal* 87 (1990): pp. 29–44; S. Snobelen, "'The Mystery of this Restoration of all Things': Isaac Newton on the Return of the Jews" in *Millenarianism and Messianism in Early Modern European Culture Vol III*, ed. by J.E. Force and R.H. Popkin (Dordrecht: Springer, 2001): pp. 95–118, esp. pp. 111–112; R.W. Cogley, "The Fall of the Ottoman Empire and the Restoration of Israel in the 'Judeo-centric'

would convert to Christianity, establish a messianic kingdom and most usefully destroy the Turks. Andrew Willet (1562–1621) proposed such a restoration in his work *De Universali et Novissima Iudaeorum vocatione*.[60] He was imprisoned and his book burned. In 1608 Thomas Draxe published *The World's Restoration or Generall Calling of the Jews*, which again drew inspiration from the Apostle Paul's expression of hope in Romans chapters 9–11. Draxe anticipated the restoration of Jews to Palestine and their conversion. By pointed contrast, the King James Version of 1611 in its running chapter headings glossed the promises to Abraham not as a promise of territorial possession but of the first Advent: "Promise to Abram of Christ". Henry Finch's *The Calling of the Jewes A Present to Iudah and the Children of Israel*[61], written under the influence of Thomas Brightman, first connected this restoration with the destruction of the Turks or Muslims. Finch imagined the Euphrates would dry up (Rev 16.12) to let the returning Jews cross over, the Jews would be attacked by Gog and Magog ("the Turke") and suffer discomfort but then win victory in their own land. They would become a powerful kingdom ruling over other nations, though he too thought they would convert to Christianity. Sir Henry Finch was the uncle of Anne Conway of Ragley Hall with whom Francis Mercury van Helmont stayed (though it is uncertain whether she met Knorr during his scholarly wanderings in Britain). King James I took against this heresy, Finch was imprisoned and Archbishop Laud refuted his views as an old error of the Jews in a subsequent sermon before the King.[62] In 1639 Thomas Goodwin urged in *An Exposition of the Revelation*[63] that "the Turke" was to be overthrown to make way for the Jews, the Kings of the East, during the sixth vial, and finally to be destroyed during the seventh. George Foster, otherwise Jacob Israel, prepared himself to lead the restoration, prophesying the death of the Pope in 1654 and the defeat of the great Turk in 1656.[64]

On the Continent, Johann Piscator (1546–1625) argued for an entirely future millennium in his *In Apocalypsin Johannis Commentarius*[65]. Johann Heinrich

---

Strand of Puritan Millenarianism", *Church History: Studies in Christianity and Culture* 72, 2 (2003): pp. 304–332; A. Crome, *The Restoration of the Jews: Early Modern Hermeneutics, Eschatology and National Identity in the Works of Thomas Brightman* (Dordrecht: Springer, 2014): p. 150 for Henry Finch.

60 (Cambridge: John Legat, 1590).
61 (London: Edward Griffin, 1621).
62 See *The Works of the Most Reverand Father in God William Laud D. D.*, ed. by W. Scott (Oxford: J.H. Parker, 1867), (Vol. 1, Sermons), First Sermon 19.6.1621 pp. 1–31 at p. 17, with useful notes.
63 In *The Works of Thomas Goodwin* (Edinburgh: James Nichols, 1861), vol. 3, p. 62.
64 See his *The Pouring Forth of the Seventh and last Viall upon all Flesh and Fleshlines* ([London], 1650) pp. 56, 63, 65.
65 (Herborn, 1613).

Alsted (1588–1638) was particularly instrumental in introducing millenarianism into Reformation Europe, his early optimistic views becoming more pessimistic after the beginning of the Thirty Years War. His *Diatribe de mille annis apocalypticis* describes his view of the Millennium and the Conversion of the Jews.[66]

Passages in *Messias Puer* which evoke this doctrine include comments on Lk 1. 32 & 33 (at folio 17^r); Mary's Song at Lk 1.38 (at folio 20^r); Zachariah's Song at Lk 1.70 (at folio 35^r) and Anna's words at Lk 2.38 (at folio 43^v). There is also relevant material in the speculations about Christ's age of twelve when he disputed in the Temple in Lk 2.42 (at folio 52^r). It is perhaps a sign of Knorr's awareness of the controversial nature of this hope that an exposition of it arising from Lk 1.55 is taken by one of his many adjustments to the manuscript from the Christian and is given to the Kabbalist Catechumen (at folio 19^v).

5   Mary and the Virgin Birth

The Virgin Mary enjoys particular attention in *Messias Puer*.[67] This is not surprising in as much as the New Testament texts in question concentrate specifically on the birth of Messiah, the Annunciation and the preceding events, as well as the principal episodes of his childhood—events in which Mary naturally takes a significant part. A comparison of *Adumbratio* and *Messias Puer* enables us better to appreciate the specific characteristics of the latter. As far as Mary is concerned, if *Adumbratio* makes very little of her role in the coming of Messiah, *Messias Puer* confronts the reader with an interpretation both original and audacious. The importance of the Virgin Birth is emphasised, and the doctrine of Mary's *perpetual* virginity is also asserted, though that in itself is said not to be essential for Messiah's status. Commenting on Mt 1.24–25, we read:

---

66   *Sumptibus Conradi Elfridi*, Frankfurt am Main, 1627. For Alsted see: *Puritans, the Millenium and the Future of Israel: Puritan Eschatology 1600–1660*, ed. by P. Toon, 2nd ed. (Cambridge: James Clarke, 2002): pp. 42–56; The Third Appendix pp. 137–153 is still helpful for expectations of the Conversion of the Jews entertained in the seventeenth-century Netherlands; H. Hotson, *Johann Heinrich Alsted (1588–1638): Between Renaissance, Reformation and Universal Reform* (Oxford: University Press, 2000); Id., *Paradise Postponed: Johann Heinrich Alsted and the Birth of Calvinist Millenarianism* (Dordrecht: Springer, 2001).

67   For an initial account see Wilkinson, "The Kabbalistic Treatment of the Virgin Mary in Christian Knorr von Rosenroth's *Historiae evangelicae initium secundum quatuor evangelistas*. A Provisional Description", *art. cit.* The distinctive interpretation placed upon the theophoric name of Mary as a mixture of Aramaic and Hebrew has been considered above in discussion of the Peshitta text.

V24 And he took etc. *wdbrh*

Christian An example of the spiritual marriage of an illuminated Intellect with the Will of the Virgin for the heavenly generation of the divine life in us.

Kabbalist Catechumen This is rather [a matter of] company and assistance, involving no influx or cooperation, than real marriage.

V25 Until *'dm'*

Kabbalist Catechumen The Hebrew conjunction *'d* [until] and the Syriac *'dm'* [until] and the Greek *heōs* [until] do not always oppose a later time to an earlier one, as [can be seen in] in Gen 8.7; Gen 28.15; 1 Sam 15.35; 2 Sam 6.23; Job 27.5; Ps 12.3; Isa 22.14; Mt 12.20; 14.22; Mt 28 *at the end*.

Christian Joseph's continence does not lack a mystery for the human influx would cease forever at once, when there arose the excellence of a diviner nature.[68] But even if the testimony of Antiquity does not agree here, or if Mary did not remain a perpetual virgin, this causes no diminution in the authority of Jesus himself as Messiah.[69]

But although Knorr asserts the Virginity of Mary, he also denies her any part in the conception *whatsoever* and asserts her total "passivity". This is particularly clear in his translation of Lk 1.42. Here he provides his own translation of the Syriac Peshitta text which significantly differs from the Vulgate. Instead of the Vulgate "*et exclamavit voce magna, et dixit: benedicta tu inter mulieres, et benedictus fructus ventris tui*"[70] Knorr gives us, "*Et clamavit voce elatâ, dixitque Marjamæ: Benedicta tu inter mulieres: & benedictus est fructus, qui in ventre tuo*".[71] This is not merely a chance difference of translation, as becomes clear from the subsequent remarks of Christian:

So when he added *And Blessed is the fruit etc.*, he referred to the anointing of Messiah from which had flowed down Mary's blessing. And deliberately

---

[68] We understand here that the presence of a "diviner nature" in the womb of Mary terminally inhibited the "human influx" of Joseph.

[69] At folio 32ᵛ.

[70] "And he cried with a great voice and said: Blessed are you amongst women and blessed is the fruit of your womb".

[71] "He lifted up his voice and said to Mariam: Blessed are you amongst women and blessed is the fruit which is in your womb".

he said [*the fruit*] *which is in your womb* and not the fruit *of your womb* so that Mary would not consider herself the origin of so marvellous a conception, but rather as a receptacle and wet-nurse.[72]

A more technical account in folios 14^r–14^v again emphasises Mary's lack of any contribution to the birth:

> When souls are generated in the ordinary way, first of all from their parents, there is separated or transferred from the parents' vital spirit that bright particle, which is the immediate vehicle of the soul of the child or his vital spirit and which they call [in Greek] *archēgon* "progenitor" or "firstborn". The nature of this is semi-material so that it is held together by material food and drink and can be separated from the spirit of its parents. Since however in the same act [of coition] by which this [bright] particle is transferred from the parents into the Archegos ["progenitor" or "firstborn"], the spirit of the parents is in the affect of Desire which is the greatest movement of love, so by its own nature on account of its separation and the obfuscation of the mind born of this, it is flawed. Consequently the idea of this affect remains even in the transferred part and is the tinder of all ideas flaring up in the spirit from which [come] the other consequent affects which produce sins.
>
> When therefore such an unmediated vehicle or vital spirit had been prepared for the soul of Messiah, it clearly had to be absolutely void of any such notions. Consequently his Archegus was not separated by the coming together of the spirits of his parents which the *Yetser ha-ra* or "libidinous desire" always accompanies, nor from the soul of his mother alone, although she was a virgin, because her vital spirit did not lack the notions and the human motivations which are born from this [manner of generation][73]. It was for this reason that she was called away from the responsibility of teaching her son (Mt 12.47). Therefore in her case the Holy Spirit itself supplemented the innate spirit (in as far as it is the spirit of Messiah) and so mixed it with the Virgin's spirit that she was able to draw from it the highest spirit of the influxes, through the ever surpassingly powerful light of his more holy Archegus, so that no material ideas could arise in him with the influx.

---

72 At folio 19^r. On the same folio the passivity of Mary is once more evoked as a feminine characteristic, matched by a parallel reflection on the absence of an active virile intervention in the conception of Christ.
73 This appears to be incompatible with the Immaculate Conception of the Virgin.

So when there is call for comment on the phrase "Son of Mary and Son of God", we find on Mt 1.21, that Knorr is careful not to say that Messiah took of Mary's flesh:

> For she will bare a son etc. *t'ldy dyn br'*
>
> **Christian** Messiah is called the Son of Mary, as we have already noted elsewhere, on account of the fact that he took on flesh in her by the influx of the Holy Spirit. But he is called Son of God on account of being the first-born amongst the natures of the spirits and on account of his constant union with the divine degree which is called The Son (See *Adumbratio*, chap. 3, § 2; 8, § 6).[74]

For this reason Knorr needs to explain away the attendance of Mother and child at "their purification ceremony" in comment on Lk 2.22:

> The day of their purification *ywmt' dtdkythwn*
>
> **Christian** We have written out a passage about this in Excerpt Cent. II Loc. 19. By purification literally is understood a *declaration* of purity; from this it does not follow that Messiah was ever unclean nor his mother, but it needed to be done not for his sake but for the sake of the others, so that they would not be considered unclean.[75]

Knorr is happy to make use of the tradition that Mary had a pain-free delivery, but for the purpose of stressing the unique nature of this pregnancy in a way other than that in which the tradition had formerly served. In comment upon Lk 2.12 "And she brought forth her firstborn and wrapped him in swaddling clothes" he remarks on the miraculous nature of this: Mary was not exhausted like other mothers, but without the help of a midwife was able to proceed immediately after the birth to swaddle the child.[76]

The Christian's comments on Mt 1.18 at folios 29ᵛ–30ʳ give a long perspective on the soul of Messiah before it lodged in Mary's womb. He discusses its role as the First of Created Things before the world was made, the fall of the souls, at which time the Soul of Messiah was crucially linked "with the divine degree called 'the Son'":

---

74 At folio 31ʳ.
75 At folio 43ʳ.
76 Cf. folio 41ᵛ.

First it should be presupposed with all the Academy of your people that the soul of Messiah was not from Mary, nor did it have its beginning in her womb, but was the First of Created Things (Rev 3.14) and together with the whole race of spirits was created by God in a moment before the beginnings of the material world. That is why [the soul of Messiah] is specifically reckoned by your doctors amongst those things which were created before the foundation of the world. It is certain that [the Soul of Messiah] was the initial principle with which Moses began his account in Gen 1.1 and by which everything else was created, as John explains 1.1, 3 (see also Col 1.15, 16; 1 Cor 8.6; Eph 3.9; Heb 1.2). And although others fell, the Soul of Messiah itself in its wholeness remained always united with the divine degree called "the Son" and with which from the beginning the Soul of Messiah had joined itself (Heb 13.8). Thus, from the beginning of the Ecclesia, the whole economy of the Old Covenant was administered through the Soul of Messiah (1 Cor 10.4). Until at last, having put on human flesh, it was to appear and initiate the ministry of the New Convenant.

Secondly, let us assume from more accurate Science that all generation [comes] from an egg and that both in quadrupeds and in man it is their ovaries which are necessary for effecting generation, [together with] an excitement of the spirit which in the normal way comes from the seed and entirely overwhelms the mother's body. See Harvey *On the Generation of Animals*.

Thirdly, let us take it that when the Holy Spirit stimulated the ovaries of the Blessed Virgin in this way, in order to form the Lord's body, it inserted into her the Archaeus (which elsewhere you noted on Mt 1.1 had been drawn from the Psyche [Soul] of Adam and David). It is necessary to know that the aforementioned Soul of Messiah constructed for itself its own temple and tabernacle by the benefit of an influx of Spirit drawn from the Mother[77] and without the concurrence or work of any human male, which even the Moslems believe.

Alongside these passages which preclude any contribution of Mary to the conception of Messiah, the text introduces a far more elevated account of the birth of Messiah expressed in terms of a common interpretation of the sefirot and, in particular, the association of the ninth sefirah Yesod [Foundation] with

---

77   The Lurianic "Mother" (one of the "faces", see above) is meant here and not Mary.

the *membrum virile*. Thus the reply of the Kabbalist Catechumen to the Christian's question of which sefirah was connected to the phrase "full of grace" in Lk 1.28 strikes a distinctive note:

> **Christian:** To what grade of the Divine Numerations do you attribute this Grace?
> **Kabbalist Catechumen:** *tybwtʾ* [the Syriac word for "grace"] is derived from *twb* which means "good" and refers to various grades of divine influxes, particularly Kindness, Beauty, Foundation and Kingdom (See *Lex. Cabb.*, p. 368 *seq.*) with all of which Mary can now be considered to have been filled, but especially with Foundation from which comes conception.[78]

Mary enjoys the influx of several sefirot, but most particularly the sefirah Yesod is involved in the conception. This takes place not as human intercourse, but as a sefirotic influx.

This sefirotic gloss is reinforced by a connection established just a little earlier according to which Joseph, Mary's husband, is called the "nourisher" (*nutritor*) of Mary:

> [Cabb. Cat.] (...) it is noteworthy that the revelations given to each of the two [Josephs] were made through dreams (Mt 1.20; 2.13, 19) and, just as the Patriarch Joseph is called by our Kabbalists "Nourisher of the Land or of the Kingdom", so the other Joseph was the "Nourisher of Mary" who equally should be linked to the measure *of Kingdom*.[79]

The union of the ninth and tenth sefirot, that is, of Yesod and of Kingdom which represents equally the feminine aspect of divinity and the divine presence in the world, naturally evokes a sexual relationship. But this striking evocation of sefirotic congress is quite removed from any physical participation on the part of Joseph.

This passage may be illuminated by a comparison with a passage on the meaning of the name Zachariah found at folios 6ʳ/6ᵛ which links Yesod with Zachariah and Kingdom with the infertile Elischeba who is also related to Kingdom (or Ecclesia), but contrasts their case with the Birth of Messiah:

---

78 Folio 15ᵛ.
79 Folios 14ᵛ/15ʳ

> This name [Zachariah], which is derived from "Memory", I would relate to the degree *Yesod* [*Foundation*], according to the traditions of your Kabbalists (about which, see *Apparat. in Lib. Zohar*, Part. 1, pp. 308, 309). For in that state there was no illumination of your Church from this degree of *Foundation*, much less from the degrees of the higher lights. Even the degree *Kingdom* (which is said to have no light of its own, like the moon) was only able to illuminate [your Church] a little. If you wish to discover a secret [meaning] in this text, [notice] that Zachariah (who [is related] to *Foundation*) and Elischeba (who has to be related to *Kingdom* according to [*Loci communes kabbalistici*] 116 seq. *Apparat sup. cit.*) are said to lack offspring. But when (now prick up your ears!) Messiah came in the flesh, the illumination of *Foundation* had to be manifested, and that happened by the mediation of Zachariah.

A comment upon Lk 1.31 ("You will conceive in your womb") at folio 16^r further indicates that Joseph had no part in the birth:

> From this very phrase comes a striking confirmation of our oldest opinion about the pre-existence of souls, for a woman's conception with the assistance of a man can scarcely be understood here. Because what is conceived cannot be said to be due to motion, some substance is here necessarily implied. So clearly nothing is left that the Blessed Virgin could have conceived in her womb [other] than the soul of Messiah come down from a more sublime world to this the lowest of worlds (See on Mt 1.18).

A comment on Lk 1.34 "How will this be?" at folio 17^r indicates that Mary probably thought her conception would take place at the moment of the Annunciation. A comment at folio 15^v on Lk 1.28 "Our Lord is with you" indicates that was the case:

> Our Lord is with you *mrn 'mky*
>
> **Christian** What Lord is meant here and what is his presence like?
> **Kabbalist Catechumen** These words mean here: The Lord of Angels is with you. That is: Messiah himself is present having descended to you, just as he descended to Gideon (Judg 6.12) but with a far greater intimacy, so that now you can be called that city where the name JHVH is present (Ezek 48.35).

Knorr cannot have been unaware that many aspects of this account were vulnerable to charges of heterodoxy. Within the Roman Church the declaration of the Council of Ephesus (431) that Mary was to be venerated as *Theotokos* was generally observed, though the question of her immaculateness (whether she was preserved from the taint of original sin at her birth) continued to be debated—even after Sixtus IV had included it in the liturgical calendar and dedicated the Sistine Chapel to the Immaculate Conception in 1476—until immaculism was declared a dogma in 1854. Some of the early reformers seem to have maintained a fairly traditional piety towards Mary, and upheld the doctrine of the Virgin Birth but Calvin had doubts about the propriety of the use of *Theotokos* and many raised questions over intercession, the Assumption of the Virgin and devotional practices they considered idolatrous. Though Knorr argues hard for the Virginity of Mary and the absence of any contribution on the part of Joseph, he nevertheless allows Mary no part in the conception and christologically the divine presence in her womb is a created thing, the union of the Soul of Messiah and "the Son". This is perhaps "Arianism" and certainly not what was intended by the Council in calling Mary, *Theotokos*. Nor can Knorr be situated confortably in the debate over immaculism; because, as we have seen, he does not share the necessary doctrine of sin within which that debate was contextualised, though his comments on Lk 1.27 would seem to preclude immaculism. Mary does not appear to have an intercessory role in *Messias Puer* and her piety is an example of passive obedience, rather than of active intervention for the faithful. Perhaps in some of these later respects he shows the influence of his reformed background, but his doctrines are not orthodox Protestantism. Yet he is bold in his assertions and there is little chance of missing what he is saying.

Remarkably then he seems to have made only one adjustment in the manuscript which has to do with these matters. On page 89 of the printed fragment in the BSB one finds a explanation by the Christian of the Angels words to Mary at the Annunciation that the Holy Spirit would come and overshadow her.

> The Spirit of Messiah is considered either according to its created nature or according to its uncreated divinity. To the first you can easily attribute all those, as it were, local, actions and motions, although these too are [better seen] rather as manifestations of something previously already present, and not occurring quite as "coming", properly so called.

As we have seen the printed fragment in the BSB includes all the corrections made to the manuscript. In this case, Knorr's initial uncorrected comment was significantly different:

Hence Maria received the gift of prophecy; and all her spirit was made full of light (Mt 6.22) and [became] a pure receptacle to incarnate the soul of the Messiah. And the Holy Spirit established in her the Archegus or the vital spirit for [welcoming] Jesus. And there the vital spirit, implanted in her, formed small corpuscula for the benefit of the spirit to be infused from Maria.

The corrections of the manuscript offer us privileged access to the process of self-censorship to which Knorr submitted his work. Yet the reason for the excision is not obvious. This is not apparently the most contentious of his remarks, nor, is it the only technical discussion we have (e.g. the Archegus was mentioned previously in the passage at folio 14^v.). Perhaps, however, Knorr having sought to give an explanation of the Virgin Birth with the aid of small corpuscula formed in Mary considered he here presumed too much in offering such a detailed account of the operation of the Holy Spirit.

However it may be that Knorr is wrestling here with a problem not quite resolved in his account of the conception at folio 30^r on Mt 1.18. Crucially there he seems to advocate Harvey's ovism, whilst at the same time denying Mary any part in the process. He may have felt the physiology of the egg, which he seems entirely to accept, narrowed the problem of female contributions to conception either as menstrual blood or as female sperm which had been suggested by Aristotle and Galen respectively.[80] But where does the egg come from? In normal conception the ovaries are stimulated and in this case this was done by the Holy Spirit. But Mary cannot produce or contribute to the egg! In this case the Archegus (the Soul of Adam and David) or vital spirit was inserted into Mary for the purpose of [welcoming] Jesus. At this point Knorr observes that the Soul of Messiah, as he now calls it, "constructed for itself its own temple and tabernacle" by influence from the Mother (Ima, not Mary). If this "temple and tabernacle" is taken as *an egg* the problem may be solved. The small corpuscula implanted into Mary by the vital spirit, "for the benefit of the spirit to be infused from Maria" may be taken as providing a (non-human) source for the egg, temple and tabernacle of the Soul of Messiah. If this (admittedly conjectural) explanation has any validity, it would illustrate a remarkable congruence between contemporary medical explanation and occultist descriptions: Knorr offered his metaphysical account in full acceptance of Harvey. On this view we

---

80   For general accounts, P. Darmon, *Le mythe de la procréation à l'âge baroque* (Éditions du Seuil, Paris 1981) and M. van der Lugt, *Le ver, le démon et la Vierge. Les théories médiévales de la géneration extraordinaire* (Paris: L'Âne d'Or, 2004).

might explain the excision as either too technical, or even as raising a difficult solution to a problem which might be better left suppressed.

6 Finding the Sefirot in the Text of the New Testament

The use of the Syriac Peshitta as the base text for the commentary in *Messias Puer* (it was first cited in *Adumbratio*) is important for a whole dimension of Knorr's exegesis. The version commended itself to Knorr because he considered it shared its Aramaic vocabulary and idiom with the Zoharic texts. This enabled him to read several common New Testament nouns (e.g. kingdom, glory, wisdom etc.) as if they were the proper names of the sefirot (Malkuth, Tiferet, Chokhmah etc.) and so to deploy all the resources of the sefirotic relationships and connotations in comment upon the New Testament text.

But such explanations are not tied to specific vocabulary, although that often provides an opportunity to be exploited. Often a comment is followed by another detecting a mystery or some mystical theology in the verse in question and propting an account of things in the light of the sefirot. Thus at folio 2^r the connection of the oral Law with Kingdom and Wife is exploited in the case of the Gospels and "secret teachings" are brought out like a child from its mother's womb:

> If the oral Law is connected in Kabbalah to the Grade of *Kingdom* or of *Wife*, then just as a child previously concealed [within its mother's womb] is brought forth from a wife, in the same way the secrets of the Law are brought into the light from within [the oral Law]. [But now] by a far greater right are the Writings of the New Covenant connected to that same degree of *Kingdom* in which are manifested the secret teachings of the Kingdom of God, which had been hidden from the foundation of the world (Cf. Mt 13.11, 35; Rm 16.25; Col 1.26; Eph 3.9).
>
> So if someone asks: "Why did Jesus write nothing, when Moses did write?" a reasonable reply can be: the teaching of Christ is oral Law, which was spread by the gift of the Spirit rather than by that of the letter (2 Cor 3.3, 6, 7). And hence it can also be linked to the grade *Strength* or *Might*, just like the oral Law of Moses (conf. *Cabbal. Denud.*, Part. I, pp. 730 seq.).

But, naturally the sefirot are significantly evoked in matters of lofty theological importance. In discussion of the beginning of John's Gospel, it is asked why the *persona* of Messiah or *Adam Kadmon* as an expression of divinity is called "Word". Christian replies:

By calling him "Word" the whole of his Emanation is, as it were, brought to its completion. For just as in "word" there combine articulation, spirit, voice and speaker, so "diction" or "articulation" is linked by you to *Malkhut* (see in *Loc. Comm. dbwr, dbr, 'myrh* etc.); "spirit" to *Tiferet* (see *rwḥ*); "voice" to *Binah* and, in its own sense, to *Chokhmah* (see *qwl*); the "speaker" himself is concealed as *Keter* and the "breathing" in *Ein Sof*.[81]

In consideration of the statement that "the Word was God" we further learn (at folio 3ᵛ):

> **Kabbalistic Catechumen** The [Syriac] word *'lh'* [God] to which [the Hebrew] *'lhym* [*'elohim* (plural): God] is equivalent, (1) is indeed generally taken for all the Light, immanent in *Atsilut* from infinity, and communicated downwards from there; thus this name extends through the whole system, so that *Malkhut* and *Tiferet* (by contemplating *Gevurah* and *Hod*) and *Binah* [too] lay claim to it for themselves. Further, by reason of *my* (which is part of it) and also by reason of the 32 Paths of Wisdom, which are the 32 [occurrences of the name] *'elohim* in the account of Creation, *Chokhmah* too and *Keter* are brought back to it: but none the less (2) it is also used specially to suggest severity and judgment.

On Lk 1.32 at folio 16ᵛ Jesus is called "The Son of the Most High":

> **Kabbalist Catechumen** How do you explain this according to the doctrines of our teachers?
> **Christian** Here the name of the Highest or Greatest seems to me to indicate the Infinite God himself in so far as he is considered to be either outside the world of *Atsilut* or *Emanation* or is named within it by the notion of the Highest *Corona* (See *Lex. Cabb.*, pp. 223, 419, 683 and *Cabb. Denud.*, Part. 2, p. 7) so that there is not so much a relationship between Father and Son emerging between characters of the Kabbalists, as between *Ein Sof* or the Infinite and Adam Kadmon or Messiah. "He will be called" is the same as "he will be declared" (as in Mt 3.17; 17.5) and "he will be confirmed" (Rm 1.4; Jn 6.27; Heb 1. 3, 4, 5.)

It is a matter of wonder that the boy Jesus, though only a lad, still filled the Four Worlds (folio 51ʳ on Lk 2.40):

---

81   At folio 3ᵛ. Detailed comments are reserved to the notes to the Translation.

Kabbalist Catechumen Although the Supreme Lord of all Spirits was now [only] a boy, he still filled the Four Worlds.

Christian He was in heaven, though existing on earth (Jn 3.13). And that not just with respect to his divinity, but also with respect to the extension of the grades of his soul. And what prevents us from saying that here there is an allusion to these four degrees? The words "*The boy grew*" refer to the Creative World. The following "*and was strengthened by the spirit*" refer to the Formative or Angelic World as if the Holy Spirit (which doubtless is understood here, as in [the case of] John, since our Most Holy Lord was no less filled [with it] while still in the womb, in as much as he never lacked it) now shone with a light in him which befitted that Angelic World, or the souls living in those Palaces of Paradise. What follows: "and was filled with Wisdom" will be a reference to the Creative World. It is as if the sense was: "examples of such wisdom shone from him as are found only in the loftiest souls". Here it will be useful to examine some examples of boys conspicuous for their great wisdom (Cent. II Loc. 36, 37, 38, 39, 40, 41). And perhaps just as by the logic of the Formative World, the Angels descended upon him, so from the Creative World, from the greatest schools of all, there descended upon him more often certain souls, as such are quite often said to descend in the Zohar.

Jesus' very name (on Mt 1.21 at folio 31r) is described as a "Second Tetragrammaton" and is expounded in terms of its letters and their relation to the sefirot; and Messiah's kingdom will be established and an influx will descend from the most perfect union of the Grades *Tiferet* and *Malkhut* and there will be a restitution similar to the beginning in Gen 2.4. (folio 17r on Lk 1.32). That restoration may be described as "Peace on earth". At folio 42r on Lk 2.14 that is described in terms of a special influx between the Father and the Supernal Mother (the "faces") and between Malkhut and Yesod. Once again one may be allowed to point out that this analysis, prompted solely by the Gospel words, is Knorr's own innovation:

> I shall hardly err, if I say that these words ["Glory to God in the Highest"] present nothing other than an acclamation of praise to Messiah. They mean to say: "You, who have just been born, *are* 'Glory to God in the highest and over the earth peace and good will to men'": *i. e.* "You are the cause of these things" and thus they can properly be said to have praised. The same meaning occurs in the acclamation of Lk 19.38, "Blessed is the King who comes in the name of the Lord (*who is*) peace in the heavens and glory on high". Cf. Eph 2.14; 1.5. By this they imply that a double connection

is established to send forth a most abundant influx (see *Lex. Cabb.*, p. 305 and the passage from the Zohar adduced there), namely, that between the Father and the Mother (for *kbd* or Glory is the title of the supernal Mother when she receives an influx from Wisdom, or the Father (see *Lex. Cabb.*, p. 464) and also between Malkhut, which is called Earth (see *Lex. Cabb.*, p. 156) and Yesod in as much as it is called *šlwm* or Peace (See *Lex. Cabb.*, p. 465 & p. 717)). This, it says, results in the goodwill or positive opinion of the Father towards men. Here in the Hebrew no doubt the word *rzwn* (Benevolence) was used which gives rise here to a striking resonance with the [Hebrew] word *'rz* (Earth) (about which see *Lex. Cabb.*, p. 157 and especially p. 691 *seq.*) and introduces great illumination from the First Principle of Light.

Other characters in the Gospel narrative and the events involving them are seen in the light of the sefirot. The careful disection of Mary's Magnificat in Lk 1.46 at folio 19ᵛ indicates the complexities which Knorr can discover. The first part of the song is said to relate to Mary herself and comprise four parts. She builds it around the four letters of the Tetragrammaton and the four World Systems. These are correlated with the parts of her own soul, and then all is absorbed in a commentary on the appropriate sefirotic influences. John the Baptist as the "friend of the bridegroom" enjoys an illuminating influx from the "Hand of the Lord" (on Lk 1.66 at folio 34ᵛ):

> **Kabbalist Catechumen** We shall uncover a kabbalistic meaning at the same time. John as "the friend of the bridegroom" (as he is called in Jn 3.29) we place in the degree Yesod where Joseph is also located and the other righteous who led the bride to her husband. See the Zohar in Gen. Crem. c. 43.1 (towards the end) & col. 30 (towards the end), which passages are found in Excerpt Cent. II Loc. 8 & 9. So now the [five fingers of the] hand of the Lord which was with him will be the five degrees standing over him and illuminating him with their influx, namely: Gedulah, Gevurah, Tiferet, Netsach and Hod (See *Lex. Cabb.*, under *yd* [hand] p. 275).

Both the influxes of the sefirot and Knorr's chronographical and prophetic schema are combined to give an interpretation of the stages of Anna's life based on the words of Luke's text (at folio 44ᵛ on Lk 2.36):

> **Christian** Mystically here Anna denotes the Ecclesia of the Israelites, which around the time of its first beginning under Moses had an influx of Grace according to the meaning of the name, [Anna]. Anna was the

daughter of Phanuel (*i. e.* "of the faces of the name *'l* [El]") meaning she had illumination from all the degrees ranged under the degree of El (*i. e.* Chesed). She was of the tribe of Assher (*i. e.* Happiness) with Binah also, the supernal Mother, indeed Corona [Crown] herself, contributing her own light (see *Lex. Cabb.*, p. 166). "She then remained during the years of her virginity", until David transferred the Tabernacle of the Lord to Jerusalem when the Lower Jerusalem seems to have married her husband. If we count the years from then until the [first] Destruction of the Temple (and the removal of the Shekhinah which was the time her widowhood began) we get 467. (That is: 33 for David, 4 for Solomon before the Temple and 430 up to the Destruction of the Temple, according to the very accurate Lydiat). From this needs to be subtracted the 125 years of the wicked kings of Judah, leaving 342 years. Now 342 years constitutes the seven jubilee years [49 years] of her marriage. From the Destruction of the Temple to the Birth of Christ according to Lydiat's reckoning is 590 years, which equals as it were[82], the 12 jubilee years of her widowhood, or the absence of the Shekhinah. So Anna is said to have been a widow for 12 Years of Weeks [*i. e.* 12 × 7] or 84 years, but now the prophetess "went out" again *i. e.* she had access to the Shekhinah (Mal 3.1).

Finally we may consider the Magi to whom Knorr credits familiarity with lower degrees, commenting on Mt 2.11:

> **Kabbalist Catechumen.** I think so. But the matter is not without some mystery, for according to the Kabbalists gold usually refers to Binah [or Intelligence], Frankincense to Chokhmah [or Wisdom] and myrrh to Keter [or Crown] (see *Lex. Cabb.*, pp. 298, 493 and 517). What if the Magi knew something of the ancient traditions (although perhaps they had not risen above the degrees of impurity)? They seem to have grasped the seven lower degrees in Messiah, with which they wanted to unite the three highest degrees for an influx by far most favourable.[83]

It was a new and bold undertaking on Knorr's part to seek to find the Lurianic sefirot, not only in certain terms of the New Testament which in their Syriac forms evoked the Aramaic names of the sefirot, but also within the wider narratives of the Peshitta New Testament. This was an exercise almost

---

82   12 × 49 = 588.
83   At folio 48ᵛ.

entirely without precedent. It required a deep familiarity with the kabbalistic categories themselves and the self-confidence to undertake a flexible and creative manipulation of them in the face of the apparently quite alien text of the Gospels. It also required sufficient theological penetration to discover where such accounts might not only appear plausible to informed (Jewish or Christian) readers, but also might reasonably be considered *preferable* and to offer a more profound illumination of texts which had long been expounded in the light of more traditional Christian notions. The recovery of *Messias Puer* enables us to enlarge our appreciation of Knorr's Christian apprehension of Judaism in several formerly unappreciated ways, but it may be in his attempt to find the sefirot in the New Testament narrative that his work is at its most creatively original.

CHAPTER 7

The Edition

1 The Principles of the Edition

We present here the text of *Messias Puer* as it appears in the manuscript preserved in the HAB. The principal text has been transcribed with all the corrections found in its margins or within the body of the text noted in the apparatus. To the extent that the printed fragment (BSB) shows variants from the manuscript these are also noted in the apparatus. All the corrections to the manuscript are contained in the printed fragment, and consequently variants between the manuscript and the printed fragment are generally either orthographic or result from printers' errors. On occasion errors are made in biblical references in BSB and these are reported in the apparatus.

The main difference between the printed fragment and the manuscript (apart from the greater length of the manuscript) is that the extracts of the Syriac Peshitta text are not found in the printed fragment. One may wonder at the absence of the Syriac extracts from the printed fragment. It is quite possible that the fragment was printed in Sulzbach where previously the Peshitta New Testament had been printed *Ex Officina Johannis Holst.* MDCLXXXIV. Johann Holst (1648–1726) was the newly independent Christian printer also named in the foreword to the Sulzbach Hebrew *Zohar* of 1684.[1] One might have thought that the printers and expertise to print the Syriac in Hebrew letters were available in Sulzbach in 1689, but the question of why it was evidently not attempted to produce the more complicated format of the manuscript, must remain open.

For easier readability, the names of the persons in the dialogue have been printed in bold type, although this is a feature of neither the manuscript nor the printed fragment.[2] Text which is underlined in the manuscript appears in italics in our edition, as in the BSB fragment. Abbreviations are usually expanded. The punctuation is generally respected and the sometimes inconsistent use of capital letters is reproduced as it occurs. Letters which cannot be read in the manuscript, but which are obviously to be restored, appear in square brackets.

---

1 Before 1683 he had been Lichtenthaler's type setter. Cf. *supra*, chapter 2, footnote 19.
2 In the BSB printed fragment the name of Christian is printed in italics and his words in normal type. The reverse was adopted by the printer for the Kabbalist Katechumen; his name appears in ordinary type and his words in italics.

The folio numbers and the pagination of the printed fragment available for the early part of the text are given in the margin. Lines of the manuscript have been numbered and a vertical bar [|] appears in the text every five lines.

As we have said, our edition seeks to give as accurate a description of the manuscript as possible. In this respect an orthographic peculiarity deserves to be highlighted. The initial Hebrew letter *yod* in the case of the word "Israel" is rendered in Latin by a doubled "*ii*". Thus "Israel" both in the manuscript and the printed version of *Messias Puer* appears as "Iisrael". Rather being a simple error, this seems a spelling long adopted by Knorr. This peculiar spelling appears throughout the *Loci communes* and notably also in *Adumbratio*. One may reasonably conjecture that unusual orthography represents the pronunciation of the Hebrew with which he was in practice confronted. There are some rare attestations of this same orthographic peculiarity in writers from the end of the Seventeenth Century and the beginning of the Eighteenth.[3]

2 Using the Apparatus

The Apparatus is designedly full. It is intended to help the reader become acquainted with Knorr's manuscript and the transformations it underwent, but also to provide some indication of the significance of Knorr's sometimes rather succinct remarks and citations by displaying the relevant quotations in full. Knorr's *corpus* is nothing if not allusive, and cumulatively so. Thus much of the significance of *Messias Puer* will not be grasped if the reader does not appreciate the gathering force of the reference to, and then the application of, his previously assembled texts; or, indeed, to the prefatory arguments in previously works, most particularly *Adumbratio*, but also all the other Zoharic texts gathered, in anticipation, in *Kabbala Denudata*.[4]

The Apparatus seeks fully to furnish a description of the manuscript. In particular, it seeks to exhibit the changes made to the manuscript by Knorr's own editorial intervention. In addition, the apparatus seeks to show the evidence for the assertion that BSB is a printing of the corrected manuscript[5] and also to explain minor verbal or grammatical changes between the manuscript

---

3 For example in J. Marckius, *Scripturariae Exercitationes ad Quinque & Viginti Selecta Loca Veteris Testamenti* (Amsterdam: Borstius, 1709). Several examples may be found in the unpaginated preface *Benevolo Lectori Sal[utem]*.
4 Knorr himself draws attention to the importance of these internal references in his foreword to the 1684 Zohar where he encourages the reader to have at his elbow a copy of *Kabbala Denudata*. Cf. *supra*, Preface, note 24.
5 Two exceptions are to be noticed: on folio 5^r, *nempe* is lacking, as is an addition in margin (*ut antehac*), probably due to the printer's oversight.

and the printed version. The detail of the Apparatus also seeks to display the development of the manuscript in full and to account where possible for the major deletions, corrections and changes in the manuscript. In addition to being purely descriptive, the Apparatus also seeks to assist in the reading of the manuscript by providing intratextual depth by full quotation of citations from Knorr's previous Kabbalistic works. Rather than provide merely summary statements of Knorr's doctrines at appropriate points in the notes to the translation, we have attempted to display the internal coherence of his thought and the felicity of its exegetical application by setting out extensively in the apparatus throughout the edition the texts to which Knorr himself chose to guide his learned reader. The aim is to display the connected argument and the cumulative evidence which is brought to play in exposition. The reader of the translation, therefore, who may wish for further enlightenment from the Author on a topic, is encouraged to consult the relevant part of the apparatus to the edition where the passages Knorr cites are set out *in extenso*. Finally, the difference between the manuscript's biblical text and the Vulgate are reported in the footnotes. The Vulgate text used is the traditional Clementine edition, considered authoritative by the post-Trentine Catholic Church and in use in the German lands at the time.

Text and Translation

fol. 1ʳ

¹Evangelium Sanctum Prædicationis²
Lucæ Evangelistæ,
quod locutus est et prædicavit Græcè in
Alexandria magna.³
Cap. I.

1. ⁴*Quoniam multi voluerunt scribere narrationes earum rerum gestarum, de quibus nos certò persuasi sumus.*⁵

*2. Prout tradiderunt nobis ii, qui à principio fuerunt spectatores & | ministri rei ipsius.*⁶,⁷

*3. Visum est etiam mihi, propterea, quod proximè sectatus sum cum sollicitudine omnes illos, ut omnia ordine suo scribam tibi, excellens Theophile.*⁸,⁹

*4. Ut agnoscas veritatem illarum doctrinarum, quarum factus es discipulus.*¹⁰

---

1 Added at the top of the page, centred as if for a title: Historiæ Evangelicæ initium, secundum quatuor Evangelistas. Sectio I. A red pencil square bracket inserted into the text ([Historiæ) refers to an annotation in the right margin: 3.A/1. BSB has an initial annotation: *Vitringa ss Observat 138.* This is a reference to the *Sacrarum Observationum Libri Sex* (Franeker 1659–1708 and often afterwards) of Campegius Vitringa (1659–1722), the Dutch Protestant Professor of Oriental Languages at Franeker after 1680. The reference is apparently to Book 1 p. 128 (not 138) where in his *Dissertatio Secunda de Sephiroth Kabbalistarum*, favourable mention is made of the *Kabbala denudata* and Knorr: "[Kd] *Cuius Auctoris Opera, licet nomen suum quacunque tandem de causa presserit, aliunde satis intelleximus esse Illustrem Virum Christianum Knorrium B. L. a Rosenroth, cui itaque ob huius laborem gratias publice solvimus debitas.*"
2 In the right margin, an initial Sectio I. is deleted, probably after Knorr had indicated the general title, followed by the section number, at the top of the page (cf. previous note).
3 Handwritten note in the right margin, in German (presumably because addressed to the printer): NB. Alles was unterstrichen ist, soll mit kleinerer Schrift gesetzt werd(en). ("Everything that has been underlined must be printed in smaller characters").
4 On the left-hand side of the page is pasted in a printed fragment cut out from an exemplar of the Peshitta New Testament edited by Knorr in Sulzbach in 1684. The fragment is crossed out and does not appear in the printed version of the BSB. The attached fragment is not well preserved, the bottom part is lacking, presumably due to the crease of the page, which passed through the fragment approximately in the middle.
5 Vulgate: "*Quoniam quidem multi conati sunt ordinare narrationem, quæ in nobis completæ sunt, rerum.*" Vulgate texts cited for comparison are taken from the official Roman edition published under the authority of Pope Clement VIII in 1592. As a text of the Vulgate this may leave much to be desired, but it is more appropriate to compare Knorr with a common contemporary text, than (anachronistically) to cite a more critical modern one.

The Beginning of the Gospel History according to the Four Evangelists fol. 1ʳ

Section 1

The Holy Gospel of the Preaching of Luke the Evangelist which he spoke and preached in Greek in Alexandria the Great[11]

Chapter 1

1 Since many wanted[12] to write accounts of those things of which we are certainly persuaded[13],

2 in as much as those who were from the beginning witnesses | and ministers of this very matter handed [it[14]] down to us,

3 I too decided on that account, Excellent Theophilus, to write everything in its proper order for you, since I have followed them all most closely with care,

4 so that you might know the truth of those doctrines[15] of which you have been taught [Greek: katēchēthēs].[16]

---

6   Text in the right margin, deleted: v. 2 Hebr. 2, 3; 1Joh. 1, 1.

7   Vulgate: Sicut tradiderunt nobis, qui ab initio ipsi viderunt, et ministri fuerunt sermonis.

8   Text in the right margin, deleted: v. 3 Act. 1, 1.

9   Vulgate: Visum est et mihi, assecuto omnia a principio diligenter, ex ordine tibi scribere, optime Theophile.

10 Vulgate: Ut cognoscas eorum verborum, de quibus eruditus es, veritatem.

11 This is the traditional heading of Luke's Gospel in the Peshitta.

12 Vugate: "attempted".

13 Vulgate: "which were done among us".

14 Square brackets [...] indicate an addition of the translator. The Vulgate here has "the word".

15 It is probably not by chance that Knorr uses "doctrine" instead of the usual Vulgate "words" here. It possibly reflects his perception of Kabbalah as being a body of doctrines, more related to a philosophical system rather than to a specific religious teaching.

16 Knorr's Latin text differs considerably from the Vulgate. This is his own translation from the Syriac. He emphasises below the element of oral tradition (i.e the transmission of teaching from a teacher to pupils rather than individual study of material) to show that the Gospel is like Kabbalah. Knorr's "English translation" in his *Harmonia Evangeliorum, Oder Zusamenfügung der vier H. Evangelisten*, op. cit., p. 2 has explicitly "mundlich" here. The use of the word "catechumen" here is probably deliberately chosen to evoke the oral transmission of Kabbalah. Such a connection is later made by Jacob Rhenferd (1654–1712), Professor of Oriental Languages in Franeker, in his *Dissertatio de Stylo Apocalypseos Cabbalistica* in Id., *Opera Philologica* ... (Utrecht: Guiliemus van der Water, 1722), pp. 1–33, at p. 1: "*Cabbala* [...] *acceptionem notat, sive oralem aut viva voce traditam, auribusque perceptam doctrinam, seu illam institutionem quam Graeci* katēchēsis *appellant* ...".

[17]*Evangelium.* אוונגליון

Cabbalista Catechumenus. *Iste scriptorum vestrorum characteristicorum titulus talemne in se continet splendorem, qualem præ se fert Liber Sohar?*

Christianus. Novi, quô digitum intendas, deque illius libri titulo quædam excerpsi, infra Excerptorum illius Centuria II., loco 42. Sed nec huic titulo nostro sua deest gloria, cum & *angelis*[18] tribuatur tale quid, Luc. 1, 19 ‖ [19]c. 2, 20 & | *Eliæ* Luc. 3, 18 & *Messiæ* Matth. 4, 23; c. 9, 35. nec[20] infrequens hæc phrasis fuerit Interpretibus Græcis veteris Testamenti, ut Psal. 40, 10; Jes. 52, 7; c. 40, 9; Psal. 68, 9.12 &c. Unde & Paulus hanc Evangelii Gloriam meritò deprædicat 2 Cor. 3, 7.8.9.10.11.18; c. 4, 6. Nec est quod audias calumnias quorundam è vestratibus, qui hac voce denotari dicunt *vanitatis vel iniquitatis revelationem;* | vel *vanitatem scriptam in libro* sive charta; ut refert Buxtorffius Lexic. Chaldaic. hâc voce. Rectiùs enim Elias vester in Tisbi in voce גליון hâc

---

17 Deletion: Annotatio 1.
18 BSB: Angelis
19 A red pencil square bracket inserted into the text ([c. 2, 20) refers to an annotation in the right margin: 4.A/2.
20 BSB: Nec
21 The interlocutor in *Adumbratio kabbalæ christianæ* is a Kabbalist. In this work he has become a Kabbalist Catechumen and in this role shares collaboratively in the exposition of the New Testament with the Christian. His share of the contribution is much reduced by the subsequent allocation of many of his speeches to the Christian in the final form of the manuscript. "Christian" is probably not intended to recall the name of Christian Knorr de Rosenroth but rather to denote merely a generic "Christian" like the equally generic "Christian Philosopher" in *Adumbratio*. But perhaps Knorr enjoyed the possible double meaming.
22 Knorr's *Kabbala Denudata* is an anthology of Zoharic texts put into Latin. He published a Hebrew text of the Zohar in 1684 on which see Boaz Huss, "Text und Context der Sulzbacher Zohar", *Morgen-Glantz* 16 (2002): pp. 135–159, also appearing as "The Text and Context of the 1684 Sulzbach Edition of the Zohar" in *Tradition, Heterodoxy and Religious Culture: Judaism and Christianity in the Early Modern Period*, edited by C. Goodblat and H. Kreisel (Beer-Sheva: Ben-Gurion University Press, 2007), pp. 117–138. The classic treatment of previous Christian interest in the Zohar is François Secret, *Le Zohar chez les kabbalistes chrétiens de la Renaissance* (Paris: Durlacher, 1958; Paris: Mouton, 1964). For a brief narrative account of Postel's translation of the Zohar, which he considered written in *Chaldaica sive vulgaris Syriaca*, see Wilkinson, *Orientalism*, op. cit., p. 118, note 80. For a thorough investiagation of Postel's translation, see Weiss, *On the Conciliation of Nature and Grace. A Latin Translation and Commentary on the Zohar by Guillaume Postel*, op. cit.
23 Glory is apparently attributed to the gospel here because it is announced by Gabriel who stands in the presence of God (Lk 1.19) and because the shepherds "glorify God for the thing they had seen" (Lk 2.20).

Gospel ’wnglywn

Kabbalist Catechumen[21] Does this title of your characteristic [Gospel] writings | contain in it such splendour as the Book *Zohar* [which itself means "Splendour"] displays?[22]

Christian I know the book to which you refer and I have excerpted material concerning its title (see: Centuria II, Locus 42). But this title of ours is not without its own glory, for this is ‖ attributed to it by angels (Lk 1.19; 2.20)[23]; by | Elijah (Lk 3.18)[24]; and by Messiah (Mt 4.23; 9.35). Frequently the word [*euangelizomai*] was used by the translators of the Greek Old Testament: e.g. Ps 40.10[25]; Isa 52.7; 40.9; Ps 68.9, 12[26] etc.[27] Paul thus [rightly] proclaims the glory [*doxa*] of the Gospel (2 Cor 3.7, 8, 9, 10, 11, 18; 4.6). Nor should you dare [to repeat] the insults of certain of your own teachers who say that the word means *The Vain or Evil Revelation* | or *Vanity Written in a Book or on a Sheet* (as Buxtorff mentions in his *Lexicon Chaldaicum sub voce*[28]). More

p. 2

---

24   The verse refers only to the preaching of John the Baptist. He is considered typologically as Elijah in Mt 11.14, but for our author John is the reincarnation of the spirit of Elijah, as explained at length in folio 9ᵛ.

25   LXX 39.10.

26   LXX 67.9, 12.

27   Knorr follows the numbering of the Hebrew Psalter, though he is quoting from the LXX which is numbered differently.

28   *Johann Buxtorf P. Lexicon Chaldaicum Talmudicum et Rabbinicum I*, ed. by Bernard Fischer (London: Asher, 1875), p. 25 s.v. ’wnglywn is the source of all the information here, including the reference to Elias Levita's lexicon *Tishbi*. But the charge is much older: Amulo of Lyon (fl. 840), *Epistula seu Liber contra Judaeos ad Carolum Regem*, Patrologia Latina, vol. 116 (Paris: Migne, 1852), 170a §. 10 has: "*Evangelium, quod nos Graeco eloquio intelligimus bonum nuncium, ipsi propria lingua malitiosissime immutantes vocant* Havongalion, *quod interpretatur Latine iniquitatis revelatio, asserentes videlicet, quod non in eo mysterium salutis humanae, sed iniquitas, qua totus mundus in errorem mitteretur, fuerit relevata, nescientes (insani) quod etiam istud ab eis confictum vocabulum apertissimum iniquitatis eorum sit testimonium.*" The passage is cited as from Raban Maur in J.C. Wagenseil, *Tela ignea Satanae* (Altdorf: J.H. Schönnerstaedt, 1681), p. 52. Sebastian Münster, *Evangelium secundum Mattheum in Lingua Hebraica* (Basel: Henricus Petrus, 1537), p. 47 has: "*Est* euangelion *vox Graeca faustum significans nuncium et fausti nuncio praemium usurpaturque ab evangelistis pro ilia felici annuntione, qua Dei de Christo promissio praedicatur impleta, salus animarum mortalibus oblata, peccata hominum credentium in Christum illius sanguine et morte expiata etc. Hebraei pro hac voce usurpant* bswrh [*besorah*], *etiam si illa pro bonae et malae rei nuncio in Scriptura usurpetur.* [...] *Ceterum Iudaei nostrates, Christi et membrorum eius aperti hostes, hanc saluberrimam Evangelii vocem pervertentes vocant* ’wnglywn *idque per modum contemptus, perinde quasi iniquitates Christianorum sint revelatae in eo libro. Alii vocant* ’wnglywn—*id est revelationem vanitatis. Quod si hoc animo id facerent libenter ferre-*

appellatione denotari dicit *Nuncium bonum.* Aliàs in Syriaco dicitur סברתא,
annunciatio, prædicatio ut Mat. 4, 23; c. 9, 35; c. 24, 15[29]; c. 26, 13. In spe-
fol. 1ᵛ cie autem ||| denotat nuncium de adventu Messiæ in carnem, & pacto Novi
Fœderis pro sanctificatione credentium: sive id fiat prædicatione & orali
annunciatione, ut Rom. 1, 1.9; c. 10, 16. sive scripto & Historia, Mar. 1, 1. sive
quod nos tangit, professione & vita. 2 Tim. 1, 8. Conf. Mar. 10, 29 ubi habetur
סברתא. | Hoc loco idem est ac historia de Jesu Nazareno, qui est Messias. 5

[30]*Lucæ* דלוקוס

Cabb. Cat.[31] *Cur Lucam præmittis, ignotum hominem?*

Christianus. Prolegomena hæc præmitto, ut cætera Evangeliorum contenta juxta temporum seriem in unam coadunare possim harmoniam, unâ-
que annotatione | aliquando, si Deus[32] concesserit, pluribus satisfaciam tex- 10
tibus. Quam clarus autem, vel quam obscurus fuerit Lucas, nihil ad rem facit;
p. 3 sufficit quod in canonem sit receptus || à primis Ecclesiæ temporibus. Neque
enim & vos tam scrupulosi estis circa Doctores vestros; quorum verba in
Mischnah & Gemarâh allegata vobis omninò sunt authentica, quamvis de
personis illorum plurima disputentur | in libro Juchasin. Nihil tamen etiam 15
abjecti est in hoc nostro; Et Nomen quidem est latinæ originis, an â Patrono
assumtum, an aliunde, quis edisserat? Pro eo, Col. 4, 14; 2 Tim. 4, 11; Phil. 24
habetur לוקא & Act. 13, 1; Rom. 16, 21. לוקיוס: unum enim esse eundemque
quid obstat? Ipse autem[33] Pâtria fuit Cyrenæus, Act. 13, 1. professione medi-

---

    mus, nempe qui cupit recedere a malo, discat eum librum et is liber docebit eum vanitatem
    quam fugiat atque bonum quod faciat. Nunc autem hostili animo nostra sacra turpibus
    conspurcare nituntur nominibus."

29   The author probably meant verse 14 which has the appropriate vocabulary.
30   Deletion: Annotatio 2.
31   In the manuscript, the name of the character "Cabbalista Catechumenus" has been
    systematically abbreviated in "Cabb. Cat." from now on.
32   BSB: DEus
33   BSB: autem. In the printed version, the abbreviations are systematically developed.
34   Levita.
35   Knorr's *Harmonia Evangelorum* was printed anonymously by Johann Andreas in Frank-
    furt in 1672. The work is of relevance here because the order of the passages of Scripture
    found in *Messias Puer* follows the order of the *Harmonia*. The order of the *Harmonia*
    is itself based upon that of John Lightfoot, *The harmony, chronicle and order of the New*
    Testament the text of the four evangelists methodized, story of the acts of the apostles ana-
    lyzed, order of the epistles manifested, times of the revelation observed: all illustrated, with
    variety of observations upon the chiefest difficulties textuall & talmudicall, for clearing of
    their sense and language: with an additional discourse concerning the fall of Jerusalem
    and the condition of the Jews in that land afterward (London, printed by A.M. for Simon

SECTION I 123

correctly your Elias[34] in his [Lexicon] *Tishbi sub voce "glywn"* says this word denotes *Good News*. Elsewhere in the Syriac New Testament it is called *sbrt'*, "Announcement", "Proclamation" as in Mt 4.23; 9.35; 24.15; 26.13. But specifically ||| [the term] denotes the announcement of the Coming of Messiah in the flesh and the Covenant of the New Testament for the sanctification of believers; whether that was by preaching and oral proclamation (as in Rm 1.1, 9; 10.16) or by writing and narrative (Mk 1.1); or, which is relevant in our case, by "confession" and "way of life" (2 Tim 1.8. Cf. Mk 10.29 where *sbrt'* occurs). | Here also it means: the "Account of Jesus of Nazareth who is Messiah".

fol. 1v

Of Luke dlwqws

Kabbalist Catechumen Why do you start [our discussion] with Luke, someone unknown?

Christian I deal with this introduction [in Luke] first so that I can harmonise the other Gospel material in one temporal sequence and then with a single comment, | God willing, I can deal adequately with several texts at once.[35] But how famous—or how obscure—Luke was has no relevance. It is enough that [his Gospel] was received into the canon [of Scripture] ||| from the first days of the Church. Nor are you so fussy about your own teachers whose words in the Mishnah and Gemarah you claim are totally authentic, although there is a lot of dispute about just who they were in | the book *Juchasin*.[36] However there is nothing despicable about our [man]: his name is of Latin origin, whether he took it from his patron or from somewhere else, who can say? He is called *lwq'* [Luke] in Col 4.14; 2 Tim 4.11; Philem 24 and *lwqyws* [Lucius] in Acts 13.1; Rm 16.21. Why should both these names not refer to one and the same man? His home was Cyrene (Acts 13.1); his profes-

p. 3

Miller, 1655) and later in *John Lightfoot Erubin; or Miscellanies and the Harmony of the Gospels Parts I & II*, ed. by J.R. Pitman (London: J.F. Dove, 1822). John Lightfoot was Master of St Catharine's College (then Catharine Hall) Cambridge between 1650 and 1675. Daniel M. Welton produced a Leipzig dissertation on him in 1878, *John Lightfoot. The English Hebraist* (Leipzig: Ackermann and Glazer, 1878). He established his reputation on commentaries on the New Testament which drew upon his own considerable and almost entirely self-taught knowledge of the Mishnah and Talmud. Knorr had his work open in front of him as he wrote and his commentary engages in a running "conversation" with it, as we have tried to indicate below with selected quotations from Pitman's edition. For more on Knorr's *Harmonia*, see the Introduction.

36   *Sefer Juchasin* by R. Abraham ben Samuel Zacuto, the Portuguese Royal Astronomer and Mathematician (1452–1515?), was published in Tunisia in 1504, Cracow in 1581 and with a full Hebrew edition by Filipowski (London, 1857). It is a history from Creation to 1500 AD.

cus Col. 4, 14. natione Hebræus, quod Hebraismi | seu Targumismi testantur 20
plurimi, in scriptis ejus occurentes. Porrò quod è LXX Discipulis fuerit titulus
tradit hujus Evangelii[37] Arabici; nec apparet, quid opponi queat. Quod Antiochiæ scholam habuerit colligitur ex Act. 13, 1 quodque Pauli fuerit comes,
liber Actorum testatur & laus Pauli 2 Cor. 8, 18; c. 13. fin. quod autem[38] Alexandriæ isthæc scripserit, titulus Evangelii hujus Syriaci edocet; qui | an 25
postponendus sit opinioni Hieronymi, qui in Achaia[39] illum scripsisse Evangelium suum asserit, alii viderint. Nobis hic Autor ipso nominis sui etymo
amplissimum aperit campum ad Allegoriam *de Luce* latiùs pertractandam,
quod uno saltem verbo insinuasse sufficiat; & cum doctrinâ vestrâ minimè
est dissonum.

[40]*Voluerunt scribere* צבו דנכתבון 30

Cabb. Cat. *Ergone cætera Evangelia tunc temporis nondum absoluta erant?*
   Christianus. Omninò, juxta dictamen antiquissimæ hujus versionis Syriacæ, vel nondum abso- ||[41]-luta erant; vel ad manus Lucæ nondum pervenerant, ita ut | hoc Evangelium inter prima Novi Fœderis scripta referendum 35
sit.
   Cabb. Cat. *Jam de Autoritate scriptorum istorum agendum; cumque nec ad scripturæ hujus nec ad Ecclesiæ vestræ testimonia acquiescere, sed legem*

---

37 Correction: a sign is placed above the line which indicates that the terms should be inverted. BSB: Evangelii hujus
38 BSB: autem
39 BSB: Achaja
40 Deletion: Annotatio 3
41 A red pencil square bracket inserted into the text (abso[luta) refers to an annotation in the left margin: 6.A/4.
42 The Arabic text of the Gospels was first printed by the Medicean Press in Rome in 1590: Giovanni Battista Raimondi, *Evangelium sanctus Domini Nostri Iesu Christi conscriptum a quatuor Evangelis sanctis id est Mattheo, Marco, Luca et Iohanne*. Thomas Erpenius printed a complete Arabic New Testament (made from the Syriac) *Novum D. N.J. Christi Testamentum Arabice ex bibliotheca Leidensi, edente Thoma Erpenio* (Leiden: Typographia Linguorum Orientalium, 1616). The Arabic New Testament also appeared in both the Paris and the London Polyglot Bible. For the versions themselves: Hikmat Kashouh, *The Arabic Versions of the Gospels. The Manuscripts and Their Families* (Berlin: De Gruyter, 2011).
43 All possible New Testament verses relevant to Luke are being reviewed here. The verse in 2 Cor is generally taken as Paul praising Luke (though he does not mention his name). The reference "c13 *ad fin.*" is to the traditional subscription in Greek manuscripts of the standard Byzantine edition which has the epistle written by Titus

sion, a doctor (Col 4.14); and his people the Hebrews—evidence of which are the many Hebraisms | and locutions from the Targums found in his writings. Additionally, the title of the Arabic version of this Gospel hands down that he was one of the Seventy Disciples [Lk 10.1], and I cannot see what objection can be raised to this[42]. That he had a school at Antioch is gathered from Acts 13.1. That he was Paul's companion, the Book of Acts tells us along with the praise of Paul (2 Cor 8.18; 13 *ad fin.*)[43]. The title of this Gospel in Syriac teaches us that he wrote this present work in Alexandria. | Whether we should prefer the opinion of Jerome, who asserted that Luke wrote his Gospel in Achaea, let others decide[44]. For us, this [Gospel] writer by the very meaning of his [own] name opens the field right up for a broader treatment of the allegory of Light [*de Luce: as if from "lux"*] which this single word alone suffices to suggest and which scarcely differs from your own teaching[45].

They wanted to write çbw dnktbwn

Kabbalist Catechumen Does that mean the other Gospels did not yet exist?

Christian Well, according to the statement of this very ancient Syriac version, either ‖ they had not yet been written at all, or they had not yet come into the hands of Luke. | Consequently his gospel is considered among the earliest writings of the New Testament[46].

Kabbalist Catechumen Now we must deal with the authority of these Scriptures since our teachers acquiesce neither to Luke's testimony, nor to that of your Church, but rather admit the Law alone as the rule of salvation.

p. 4

---

and Lucas from Philippi. These subscriptions appear in the Geneva Bible (1560) and many editions of the KJV after 1611 but though influential are conjectural. Their assertion that 1 Cor was written from Phillipi is almost certainly wrong (1 Cor 16.8–9 was probably written from Ephesus) and there is no evidence in Galatians to support their assertion that it was written in Rome.

44 The reference is to Jerome's Prologue to the Gospel of Luke from the so-called Anti-Marcionite Prologues: "*Sancto instigatus Spiritu, in Achaiae partibus hoc descripsit evangelium*" ["Moved by the Holy Spirit, Luke wrote down this Gospel in parts of Achaia"]. For Jerome generally in this period, see Eugene F. Rice Jr, *Saint Jerome in the Renaissance* (Baltimore: Johns Hopkins University Press, 1985).

45 The importance of light becomes apparent from *Adumbratio*, chap. 2, § 8–11, p. 4 (Spector, *Francis Mercury van Helmont's Sketch of Christian Kabbalah*, op. cit., p. 33) and the extensive subsequent development of the matters there anticipated in summary.

46 The very content of Luke's prologue with its mention of previous texts discouraged early speculation on what we might call (in synoptic terms) Lucan Priority and that should not be read into the text here.

solam pro salutis normâ admittere queamus[47], *nunc quæro, quomodo hæc scripta ad legem referas? Legem enim antiquam | hîc proponi non dices, quia sexcenta & tria*[48] *præcepta Mosis sublata esse asseritis: Legem Novam non admittimus*[49]; *cum talem datum iri, ne quidem Propheta asserat, qui de novo fœdere vaticinatur. Jer. 31, 33?* 40

Christianus. Quid si dicerem, & hîc Legem proponi, sed oralem; & cui saltem minor esse nequeat autoritas, quam illis vestris Libris, quibus Lex Mosis oralis conscripta | dicitur, ut sunt scripta libri Sohar & Talmudica. Si enim (1.) Lex oralis Mosaica ||| primitùs scripto non fuit comprehensa, sed oretenus saltem tradita; donec urgente necessitate propter dispersionem Doctorum & Discipulorum scriptis consignaretur: Haud aliter sane Doctrina Novi Fœderis, primitùs nec à Christo, nec ab Apostolis scribendo, sed orali informatione tradita est, unde illud κατηχήτης | oretenus edoctus; sive אתתלמדת discipulus factus es, Luc. 1, 4. Conf. Act. 18, 25; 1 Cor. 14, 19; Gal. 6, 6. cum ||[50] Rom. 2, 18. Atque sic ipse quoque Christus mandabat discipulis suis Matth. 28, 19, μαθητεύσατε תלמדו discipulos facite, conf. Matth. 13, 52; c. 27, 57; Act. 14, 21. Donec propter διασπορὰν sive dispersionem, de qua Act. 8, 14; c. 11, 19 tandem scripta emanarent Evangelica; partim suâ sponte | scribentibus ipsis Apostolis & Discipulis; partim tradentibus illis, qui â[51] principio spectatores & ministri fuerant ipsius rei Luc. 1, 2 partim etiam jubente Domino Ap. 1, 19; c. 2, 1.8.12.18; c. 3, 1.7.14; c. 19, 9. Sicut in Idra Suta sub initium R. Schimeon F. Jochai disponit: R. Abba scribet: R. Eleazar Filius meus, profitebitur: reliqui autem socii mussitando meditabuntur in corde suo. Sohar in Deut. | Cremon. col. 557. Mant. fol. 287. (2.) Si Lex oralis proponit Legis Mosaicæ sensum internum occultum, mysticum, quod toties in Libro Sohar inculcatur, & in specie in festiva illa parabola, quam exhibui Centur. I[a] Loc. 1. Excerpt. certè similia Legis Mosaicæ mysteria, præsertim de Christo

---

47 Correction: queamus replaced by soleant nostrates.
48 Correction: tria replaced by tredecim.
49 Correction: admittimus replaced by admittunt Hebræi. The correction indicates that the Cabbalist, now being a Catechumen, is considered to be now set apart from the Jewish people. Cf. also *infra*, Sectio III, note 211 (perpenderetis replaced by perpenderent vestrates).
50 A red pencil square bracket inserted into the text ([Rom. 2, 18) refers to an annotation in the right margin: 7.A/5.
51 BSB: à
52 Traditionally Torah is considered to comprise 613 commandments.
53 Knorr published a Hebrew text of the Zohar in Sulzbach in 1684. However in *Messias Puer* whenever he cites the Zohar outside his collection of passages in Excerpta, he never refers to his own version, only to the Mantuan or Cremona editions. His own

So I now ask, how do you relate these writings to the Law? For you are not saying that the ancient [written] | Law is in question here, because you claim the 613 precepts of Moses have been done away with[52]; the Jews, [on the other hand], do not admit a new Law, since not even the Prophet [Jeremiah] who prophesied of a New Covenant asserted that [a new Law] was going to be given (Jer 31.33).

Christian What if I were to say that here the Law *is* in question—but *oral* Law, | the authority of which [here] cannot be less than those books of yours in which Moses' oral Law is said to be written, such as the writings of the Book *Zohar* and the Talmudic writings?

For (1) the oral Mosaic Law ||| was not originally reduced to writing, but rather handed down by word of mouth until under the pressure of necessity, or because of the dispersion of teachers and pupils, it was entrusted to writing. In quite the same way, the teaching of the New Covenant, was originally written down neither by Christ or by the Apostles, but was handed down orally. So [the Greek] *katēchēthēs* [in Lk 1.4] | [means] "taught orally" [and the Syriac] *'ttlmdt* "you became a disciple" (Lk 1.4. Cf. Acts 18.25; 1 Cor 14.19; Gal 6.6; with Rm 2.18). || Thus Christ himself also commanded his disciples in Mt 28.19 [in Greek] *mathēteusate* [and in Syriac] *tlmdw* to "make disciples". Cf. Mt 13.52; 27.57; Acts 14.21. Until (because of the [Greek] *diasporan* or Dispersion, concerning which see Acts 8.14; 11.19), finally the written Gospels emerged: some written by the Apostles themselves and the Disciples of their own accord |; others written down from the tradition of those who "from the beginning had been witnesses of the event itself" (Lk 1.2); some even at divine command (Rev 1.19; 2.1, 8, 12, 18; 3.1, 7, 14; 19.9). Just as [it says] at the beginning of *Idra Suta*: "R. Simeon ben Yochai *taught*; R. Abba *wrote down*; and R. Eleasar, my son, *proclaimed*: but the other companions meditated whispering to themselves in their hearts". (Zohar in Deut. | Cremona Col. 557; Mant. fol. 287)[53].

(2) If the oral Law teaches the inner hidden and mystical sense of the Law of Moses (which is what is taught so many times in the Book *Zohar* and specifically in that cheerful parable which I presented in Cent. I. Loc. 1 of the Excerpts[54]), then certainly secret teachings, similar [to those in the Law]

---

edition has both versions. The main one is the longer one of Cremona and references to the Mantuan version are marked by pagination inserted between the two columns of the text. It may possibly be that when Knorr does cite both editions, he is in fact referring to the cross references in his own edition. We are not aware of anywhere else at the time where the two editions were so conveniently set side by side.

54   Extensive reference is made throughout *Messias Puer* to this lost work, on which see the Introduction.

& satis Ecclesia ejus in scriptis Novi Fœderis occurrunt plurima, conf. Joh. 5, 39; Luc. 24, 27.44.45; Gal. 4, 24. sqq.; | Hebr. 4, 9.14; c. 7, 1; c. 8, 5; c. 9, 8; c. 9, 1. &c.&c. (3.) Si Lex oralis tradita fuit Mosi in monte[55] Sinai; profecto eidem etiam tradita fuerunt mysteria de Christo, unde & in monte apparens Domino nostro, cum ipso collocutus est de morte ejus Luc. 9, 31 (4.) Si Lex oralis sepem Legi statuit, ad elongandum hominem â[56]peccatis; idem certè Christus præstitit Matth. 5, 22.28.32.34.39.44. &c. (5.) Si Lex oralis in Cabbala | refertur ad gradum Regni, sive Uxoris, ita ut sicut ab ‖ [57]Uxore in lucem editur infans antehac[58] occultatus, eodem[59] modo ab illa in lucem emittantur Arcana Legis[60]: certè majori jure ad eundem Regni gradum pertinent Novi Fœderis scripta, in quibus manifestantur mysteria Regni Dei, quæ ab orbe condito fuerunt occultata, conf. Matth. 13, 11.35; Rom. 16, 25; Col. 1, 26; Eph. 3, 9. Unde si quis quærat: | *quare ipse Jesus nihil scripserit sicut Moses?* Haud immeritò responderi posset, doctrinam Christi esse Legem oralem, quæ spiritus beneficio propaganda potiùs fuerit quam literæ. 2. Cor. 3, 3.6.7. Unde non immeritò ad gradum Gebhuræ sive vehementiæ etiam referri potest, sicut Lex oralis Mosaica. Videatur Cabbal. denudat. Part. 1, p. 730. sq.

Cabb. Cat. *Cum autem tota sit Practica, & præter Prolegomena*[61] *ad salutem hominis moraliter instruendi necessaria, parum in se contineat Philosophiæ Theoreticæ; Unde petenda est pars residua Legis oralis Theoretica? Philosophia enim â Græcis gentilibus profecta obtrudi nobis non potest: Definitiones patrum*[62] *& decreta Conciliorum parem cum scriptura autoritatem*[63] *habere* | *inter vos nondum convenit?*

---

55 BSB: Monte
56 BSB: à
57 A red pencil square bracket inserted into the text ([Uxore) refers to an annotation in the right margin: 8.A/6.
58 BSB: ante hâc
59 BSB: eôdem
60 BSB: legis
61 BSB: Prelegomena. The correct transcription from Greek is indeed *pro-*.
62 BSB: Patrum
63 BSB: authoritatem
64 Pirke Avot 1.1. "Moses received the [oral] Law from Sinai and committed it to Joshua, and Joshua to the elders, and the elders to the Prophets, and the Prophets committed it to the men of the Great Synagogue".
65 Pirke Avot 1.1. "[The men of the Great Synagogue] said three things: Be deliberate in judgement, raise up many disciples, and make a fence around the Law". (*The Mishnah*

of Moses, also occur many times in the writings of the New Testament—particularly concerning Christ and often his Church (Cf. Jn 5.39; Lk 24.27, 44, 45; Gal 4.24 et *seq.* |; Heb 4.9, 14; 7.1; 8.5; 9.8; 9.1 etc.).

(3) If the oral Law was handed down to Moses on Mount Sinai[64], then, be sure, to him also was handed down the secret teachings about Christ—which is why [Moses] appeared to our Lord in the Mountain [of Transfiguration] and spoke with him about his death (Lk 9.31).

(4) If the oral Law established a Fence to the Law to guard a man from sin[65], so Christ did the same (Mt 5.22, 28, 32, 34, 39, 44 etc.).

(5) If the oral Law is connected in Kabbalah | to the Grade of *Kingdom* or of *Wife*, then just ‖ as a child previously concealed [within its mother's womb] is brought forth from a wife, in the same way the secrets of the Law are brought into the light from within [the oral Law]. [But now] by a far greater right are the Writings of the New Covenant connected to that same degree of *Kingdom* in which are manifested the secret teachings of the Kingdom of God, which had been hidden from the foundation of the world (Cf. Mt 13.11, 35; Rm 16.25; Col 1.26; Eph 3.9). p. 6

So if someone asks: "Why did Jesus write nothing, when Moses did write?" a reasonable reply can be: the teaching of Christ is oral Law, which was spread by the gift of the Spirit rather than by that of the letter (2 Cor 3.3, 6, 7). And hence it can also be linked to the grade *Strength* or *Might*, just like the oral Law of Moses (conf. *Cabb. Denud.* Part. 1, p. 730 *seq.*)[66].

Kabbalist Catechumen But since the whole [of Jesus' teaching] is practical and, with the exception of such introduction necessary for the moral instruction of a man for salvation, contains little Theoretical Philosophy, where should one look [within Christianity] for the theoretical material [which is found in] the oral Law?[67] You cannot impose the philosophy taught by the Greeks upon us: and you have not yet agreed amongst yourselves that the definitions of the Fathers and the decrees of the Councils have equal authority | with Scripture.[68]

Translated from the Hebrew with Introduction and Brief Explanatory Notes, translated by Herbert Danby (London: Oxford University Press, 1933), p. 446).

66 Note that the anthology *Kabbala Denudata* is referred to as "Cabbala Denudata" thoughout the *Messias Puer*.

67 The objection is that there is little in the New Testament accounts of Jesus' teaching which is not ethical and nothing which looks like extended kabbalistic speculation.

68 There is an echo here of contemporary confessional debates on the comparative authority of Scripture and Conciliar decisions.

Christianus. Ergò dum conversionem vestram intendimus, ad hominem vobiscum agemus & principia hæc theoretica assumemus ex antiquis Vestris
p. 7 Libris, de Lege orali temporibus Apo- ‖[69]-stolorum & Apostolicorum Virorum scriptis, quatenus illa cum phrasi Novi Fœderis consona sunt.

[70][*Certò persuasi sumus &c.*] מפסינן 45

fol. 2ᵛ **Cabb. Cat.** *Qualem nobis promittitis certitudinem?*

Christianus. Si quoad res gestas nihil vobis proponitur, quàm quod probabilitatis limites non excedit; & qualia in vestris quoque proponuntur scriptis: quoad doctrinam autem, nihil etiam quod non utrique Legi vestræ sit conforme; nonne rectè | facitis, si certè de his sitis persuasi? Atqui talia olim 5 proposita sunt â[71] scriptoribus Evangelicis. Unde hæc vox מפסינן, quæ accuratè exprimit vim phraseos Chaldaicæ, Pr. 6, 35; c. 1, 10. cujus sensus est *acquiescere, contentum esse*: item sensum vocis Græcæ hoc in textu πεπληροφορημένον conf. Rom. 4, 21; c. 14, 5; 2 Tim. 4, 17. & in specie Col. 2, 2; 1 Thess. 1, 5. ut sic ab initio statim insinuetur | prima Fidei pars, assensus scilicet, 10 indubitatus, cum fiducia indissolubiliter cohærens; quæ est character Christianismi primarius.

V. II. [72]*Tradiderunt* דאשלמו

Cabb. Cat. *Ergonè & vos traditiones admittitis, quas tamen rejicit Jesus*[73] *Matth. 15, 9?*

Christianus. Genuinas, originarias, nec intentioni Legislatoris oppositas 15 admittimus. Nec parva hîc nobis est cum vestratibus conformitas. Sicut enim
p. 8 traditiones apud vestrates vel erant ‖ [74]*Mischnicæ*, quæ in scholis Hierosolymitanis erant traditæ atque decisæ; vel *Barajethicæ* quæ extra illas. Sic distinctio similis erui potest circa tradita Christianæ fidei. Erat enim | Hie- 20

---

69 A red pencil square bracket inserted into the text (Apo[stolorum) refers to an annotation in the right margin: 9.A/7.
70 Deletion: Annotat. 4. Added: Certo persuasi sumus &c.
71 BSB: à
72 Deletion: Annotatio 1
73 BSB: JESUS
74 A red pencil square bracket inserted into the text ([Mischnicæ) refers to an annotation in the left margin: 10.A/8.
75 An important principle of the debate is established here. They will assume all kabbalistic teaching as long as the expression of the New Testament allows it.

SECTION I

Christian In that case, since it is your conversion we seek, we shall speak then *ad hominem* and assume the theoretical principles of your ancient books about the oral Law written down at the ‖ time of the Apostles and of their successors in as far as these agree with the expressions of the New Testament[75].

p. 7

45 *We are certainly persuaded mpsynn* ‖‖

fol. 2ᵛ

Kabbalist Catchecumen What sort of certainty can you promise us?

Christian If, as far as facts go, nothing is proposed to you other than what does not exceed the limits of probability; and is the same sort of thing as that which is also found in your own writings; and as far as doctrine goes, nothing [is proposed] which does not conform to each of your two Laws,
5 then surely you do right | if indeed you are persuaded in these matters. And in fact just such [circumstances] have been described by the Gospel Writers. Whence this [Syriac] word *mpsynn* which accurately expresses the force of the Aramaic phrase [found in the Targum to] Prov 6.35; 1.10 and which means "to acquiesce" or "to be content with". The Greek word *peplērophorēmenōn* has the same meaning (Cf. Rm 4.21; 14.5; 2 Tim 4.17 and particularly Col 2.2; 1 Thess 1.5.). So that, right from the start [of the Gospels] the principal part
10 of Faith is insinuated |—assented to, of course, undoubted and inseparably joined with trust—this is the fundamental characteristic of Christianity.

Verse 2
They handed over dꞌšlmw

Kabbalist Catechumen So do you admit traditions which Jesus rejected (Mt 15.9)?[76]
15 **Christian** We admit genuine original traditions which are not opposed to the intention of the Lawgiver. We are very much like your teachers in this. For your traditions are either ‖ those of the *Mishnah* which had been handed down and decided in the schools of Jerusalem or *Baraithas* which are additional to them.[77] A similar distinction can be found within the traditions of
20 the Christian Faith. The Apostolic School in Jerusalem | enjoyed the high-

p. 8

---

76 Jesus here rejects some Jewish teachings which he says (citing Isaiah in Mt 15.8 and making the point more sharply) they have made up and which "transgress the commandment".
77 Though the Mishnah was not written down until the Third Century AD, it reports the decisions of earlier scholars.

rosolymis Schola Apostolica summæ Autoritatis, Act. 11, 30; c. 15, 2.4.6.22.23; c. 16, 4. Sed & scholæ erant extraneæ, ut Act. 13, 1. ad quas spectabat vocatio gentium. Et si Doctores traditionum dicti תנאים per metathesin dicti fuêre איתנים fortes: quanto magis hi Nostrates. Vide Excerpt. Libri Sohar Cent. I. loc. 89. n. 1. & ibid. loc. 2.[78]

V. 111[79] קריב הוית יציפאית לכלהון

Proximè sectatus sum cum sollicitudine omnes illos.

Cabb. Cat. *Antiquus est mos iste sectandi eruditos; nihilne tibi occurrit simile in scriptis nostris?*

Christianus. De talibus, qui sectati esse dicuntur Viros studio Legis claros, | omninò historiæ etiam in Sohar occurrunt, vid. Excerpt. Cent. I. Loc. 54. n. 7.

[80]*Theophile* תאופילא

Cabb. Cat. *Quisnam fuit ille; & quænam*[81] *est significatio nominis hujus?*

Christianus. Lateat persona. Nominis duplex esse potest sensus, qui Deum | amat, & quem ‖ [82]Deus amat. In Sohar hoc in genere deprædicatur Abraham. Vid. Excerpt. Cent. I. Loc. 2. n. 5. conf. Jac. 2.23.

---

78 Added: Conf. Matth. 11, 12; Luc. 16, 16; Rom. 1, 16; c. 15, 19; 1 Cor. 1, 18.24; c. 2, 4.5; c. 4, 20; c. 12, 10.28.29; Gal. 3, 5; Eph. 3, 16.20; Col. 1, 11.29. &c.
79 Deletion: Annotatio 1
80 Deletion: Annotatio 2
81 BSB: quæ nam
82 A red pencil square bracket inserted into the text ([Deus) refers to an annotation in the left margin: 11.A/9.

SECTION I

est authority (Acts 11.30; 15.2, 4, 6, 22, 23; 16.4), but there were also schools elsewhere (so Acts 13.1) to which the called of the Gentiles looked. And if the teachers of [your] tradition called *tn'ym* [Tannaim[83]] were renamed by metathesis *'tnym* "the Mighty", how much more may these of ours be so designated! See Excerpt. Libri Sohar Cent. I Loc. 89 n. 1 & ibid. Loc. 2. Cf. Mt 11.12; Lk 16.16; Rm 1.16; 15.19; 1 Cor 1.18, 24; 2.4, 5; 4.20; 12.10, 28, 29; Gal 3.5; Eph 3.16, 20; Col 1.11, 29 etc.

Verse 3

25   *I have followed them all most closely with care qryb hwyt yçyp'yt lklhwn*

Kabbalist Catchecumen This duty of following scholars is ancient. Does anything like it in our writings occur to you?

Christian The stories about such [people], who are said to follow the men
30   distinguished in the study of the Law | all occur in the Zohar (Excerpts Cent. I Loc. 54 n. 7).

Theophilus t'wpyl'

Kabbalist Catechumen Who was he? And what is the meaning of his name?

Christian His identity is unknown. His name has two possible meanings:
35   "He who loves God" and ‖ "He whom God loves". |[84] In the Zohar, Abraham   p. 9
is described in this way (See Excerpt Cent. I Loc. 2 n. 5 Cf. Jam 2.23).[85]

---

83   The first generation of teachers whose oral decisions now appear written in the Mishnah.
84   Lightfoot, *Miscellanies and the Harmony of the Gospels*, op. cit., p. 115: "'Theophilus,' in Greek, is the same in signification with 'Jedidiah,' in Hebrew, the name of Solomon, 'the Lord's beloved'; or with the glorious title of Abraham, 'the friend of God'."
85   It is evident that the extracts in this work, the Excerpts, were arranged generally according to the order of topics discussed in *Messias Puer*. See Introduction.

[1]Evangelium Sanctum
Præconium Jochanan Præconis,
Quod protulit & prædicavit Græcè in Epheso.
Cap. I.

fol. 3[r]   [2]1. Principium Creationis erat verbum, & ipsum verbum erat apud Deum[3]; & Deus erat ipsum verbum.[4,5]

2. Hoc erat creationis principium[6] apud | Deum.

3. Omnia per manum ejus facta sunt, & sine eo ne unum quidem fuit, quicquid factum est.[7]

4. In ipso erat vita, & vita erat Lux filiorum | hominis.[8,9]

5. Et ipsa Lux in tenebris lucet, & tenebræ non comprehenderunt eam.[10,11]

V. I. [12]Principium Creationis בריישית

Cabb. Cat. Sicut Chaldæis vox בראשית non idem sonat | ac in Principio, sive per Principium, prout in Hebræo: quod docent exempla Jes. 41, 4[13]; c. 40, 21; c. 66, 9; c. 28, 29; 1 Sam 23, 5; Job. 41, 2.[14] ubi מבראשית est â[15] principio creationis; סדרי בראשית ordines principii creationis; בראשית[16] עובדי opera principii Creationis. Atque sic etiam in Sohar & alibi sæpiùs ימי בראשית | Dies principii p. 10 creationis; item מעשה בראשית opus prin- ‖-cipii [17]Creationis. Ita etiam Syrus

---

1   Added in the margin, on the left: Sectio II.
2   On the left-hand half of the page, a fragment cut from Knorr's edition of the Peshittta New Testament containing the Syriac version of the quoted passage in the Gospel of John is pasted in and crossed out.
3   BSB: DEum
4   Added in the right margin and subsequently crossed out: v. 1. 1. Joh. 1, 1.2; Apoc. 19, 13. Infr[a] 10, 33.36.
5   Vulgate: In principio erat Verbum, et Verbum erat apud Deum, et Deus erat Verbum.
6   Correction: creationis principium replaced by in principio. Knorr's correction aims at mitigating the boldness of the first formulation, which was very far from the Vulgate (Hoc erat in principio apud Deum). Knorr understands the *creationis principium* as Adam Kadmon or the pre-existent Christ.
7   Vulgate: Omnia per ipsum facta sunt; et sine ipso factum est nihil quod factum est.
8   Added in the right margin and subsequently crossed out: v. 3. Eph. 3, 9; Col 1, 17; Hebr. 1, 2. Infr[a] 5, 26 & 8, 12 & 9, 5 & 12, 46; 1Joh. 5, 11.
9   Vulgate: In ipso vita erat, et vita erat lux hominum.
10 Added in the right margin and subsequently crossed out: v. 5. Infr[a] 3, 19.
11 Vulgate: Et lux in tenebris lucet, et tenebræ eam non comprehenderunt.
12 Deletion: Annotatio 1
13 The Hebrew has here מראש, and the Vulgate *ab exordio*.

Section II
The Holy Gospel
The Proclamation of the Herald John
Which he advanced and preached in Greek in Ephesus[18]
Chapter 1 ‖

1 The [First] Principle of Creation was the Word[19], and the Word Itself was with God and God was that Word[20].
2 This [First] Principle of Creation was | with God.
3 Everything was made by his hand, and without him there was not one thing[21] which was made.
4 In him was Life and the Life was the Light of the sons | of man[22].
5 And the Light itself shines in darkness and the darkness does not overcome it[23].

Verse 1
The [First] Principle of Creation bryšyt

Kabbalist Catechumen As with Aramaic speakers, so in Hebrew, the word *br'šyt* does not mean | "in the Beginning" rather "The [First] Principle of Creation", as these examples indicate: Isa 41.4; 40.21; 66.9; 28.29; 1 Sam 23.5; Job 41.2, where [respectively] *mbr'šyt* means "from the [First] Principle of Creation", *sdry br'šyt* "the orders of the [First] Principle of Creation", *ʿwbdy br'šyt* "the works of the [First] Principle of Creation". And in the Zohar and elsewhere, quite frequently *ymy br'šyt* | [means] "the days of the [First] Principle

---

14 With the exception of the first two references, the others do not relate to the question of the origin of the principle or of the beginning.
15 BSB: à
16 Deletion of four words, now unreadable.
17 A red pencil square bracket inserted into the text ([Creationis) refers to an annotation in the right margin: 12.A/10.
18 This is the traditional heading to John's Gospel in the Peshitta New Testament.
19 Vulgate: "In the beginning was the Word". The translation of the Syriac given here is coherent with the exposition which follows.
20 So Vulgate "Et Deus erat Verbum". The Greek *kai theos ēn ho logos* which appears to use *theos* predicatively without the article may be more nuanced.
21 Vulgate adds "which was mad" here.
22 Vulgate: "light of men".
23 The text here follows the Vulgate "*et tenebrae eam non comprehenderunt*" in contrast to the lemma given below.

Interpres antiquissimus voce בְּרֵישִׁית *semper*[24] *utitur eodem modo, ut Matth. 19, 4.8; Marc. 10, 6; Joh. 8, 44; Hebr. 1, 10; 1 Joh. 1, 1; c. 2, 7.13.14. ubi* מִן בְּרֵישִׁית *est â principio Creationis. Quid hinc concludis?*

Christianus. Licebitne concludere; quod non tantùm antiquissimus iste interpres noster Evangelii Johannitici (sive Apostolus fuerit, sive è Discipulis Domini, prout quidam Marcum fuisse statuunt; sive alius quidam Vir Apostolicus, quod universalis omnium Ecclesiarum orientalium consensus approbat;) eodem sensu hanc vocem acceperit, quo tota tunc Ecclesia Judaica utebatur; sed & ipse Johannes | Apostolus ex linguæ potius patriæ sensu Evangelium suum sit exorsus, quam Græcanicæ, cujus sanè, ut è tota illius phrasi apparet non admodum fuit studiosus? Sanè accedit, quod ipse Christus Apoc. 3, 14. se appellet Principium creationis Dei.

Cabb. Cat. *Hoc præsupposito, confirmaretur nostra hypothesis*[25], | *quod hîc intelligatur istud principiatum primum unicum, â causâ primâ unicâ necessariò productum; quod deinde fuit principium omnium productorum reliquorum; videatur Philosophiæ Cabbalisticæ Dissertatio 2. per totum. Cabbalæ Denudatæ scilicet. Part. 3. p. 31. seqq.*[26] ||

[27]**Christianus.** Modò subintelligatur Messias, in illo philosophandi genere faciles | esse possemus.

Cabb. Cat. *Quid autem super voce* בְּרֵאשִׁית *annotant veteres in Libro Sohar?*

Christianus. Quamvis pleraque illorum parum faciant ad propositum nostrum; exercitii tamen philologici gratia, quædam collegimus in Excerpt. Cent. I. Loc. 3.4.5.6.7.8.9.10.11. |||

---

24   Correction: semper replaced by plerumque. The correction softens the claim.

25   The same expression, "our hypothesis", appears in *Kabbala denudata, II*, 1684 "Adumbratio kabbalæ christianæ", p. 26.

26   For this comment of the Cabbalist, cf. "Adumbratio kabbalæ christianæ", op. cit., p. 8. The "Dissertation of Kabbalistic Philosophy" he is referring to is the Latin translation of the *Puerta del Cielo* by Abraham Cohen de Herrera: "Liber Porta Cœlorum in quo dogmata Cabbalistica Philosophicè proponuntur & cum Philosophia platonica conferuntur", published in the *Kabbala denudata, I, Pars tertia*: "Probatur tredecim argumentis fortißimis (sic), quod à Principio primo immediatè emanaverit Principiatum Unum tantùm & perfectum." ("Dissertatio secunda", Cap. 1, p. 31).

27   A red pencil square bracket inserted into the text ([Christianus) refers to an annotation in the right margin: 13.A/11.

28   With this important exposition one should compare the material in "Adumbratio kabbalæ christianæ", chap. 3, §13, p. 9 (Spector, *Francis Mercury van Helmont's Sketch of Christian Kabbalah*, op. cit., p. 42) and the comments upon that passage in Anna

of Creation" and *mʿśh brʾšyt* "the work of the ‖ [First] Principle of Creation". So also the very ancient Syriac translator uses *bryšyt* frequently in the same way at Mt 19.4,8; Mk 10.6; Jn 8.44; Heb 1.10; 1Jn 1.1; 2.7, 13, 14 where *mn bryšyt* means "from the [First] Principle of Creation".[28] What do you conclude from this?

Christian May one not conclude: that not only this our very ancient [Syriac] translator of the Gospel of John (whether he was the Apostle [John] |, or one of the Disciples of the Lord (just as indeed Mark is thought to have been) or some other one of the Apostles—which the universal consensus of the Eastern Churches considers to be the case) understood this word [*brʾšyt* in Hebrew, *bršyt* in Syriac] in the same sense as the whole of the Jewish Ecclesia did at that time, and [secondly] that the Apostle John himself wrote his own Gospel in the idiom of his native language rather than in that of Greek, in which clearly, as is apparent from all his usage, he was not greatly learned. Clearly, too, [John] assents to that which Christ calls himself (Rev 3.14), "the Principium of the Creation of God".[29]

Kabbalist Catechumen This presupposition [of yours] | confirms our hypothesis that here is to be understood that Unique First One of the Principia, produced necessarily from the sole First Cause, which then was the Principium of everything else which was produced. See *Philosophiae Cabbalisticae Dissertatio 2 passim*; *Cabb. Denud.*, Part. 3, p. 31 et seq.[30] ‖

Christian We can easily see how Messiah is implied in that type of philosophising. |

Kabbalist Catechumen But what did the ancients have to say about the word *brʾšyt* in the Book *Zohar*?

Christian Although many of their remarks there have little to do with our proposition, as a philological exercise, we collected some of them in Excerpt. Cent. I Loc. 3, 4, 5, 6, 7, 8, 9, 10, 11. ‖‖

M. Vileno and Robert J. Wilkinson, "Die Peshitta von 1684", *art. cit.*, p. 219. There Genesis 1.1 is cited and both the Hebrew *brʾšyt* ("in the beginning") and the Syriac *bryšyt* are given, but translated *"per principium (i.e. Messiam) creavit Deus coelum & terram"*. The point here is that God created through the Principle (*Bereshit*) which is Messiah. Copious New Testament citations there indicate how several assertions of Christ's cosmic role in creation are now to be understood as congruent with, if not simply expressing, this understanding.

29 The Greek *archē tēs ktiseōs tou theou* and the Vulgate *"qui est principium creaturae"* can perhaps tolerate this sense. The Syriac (Harklean) text however has *wršyt' dbryth d'lh'* which seems undoubtedly temporal.

30 Reference is made back here to the more philosophic discussions of ultimate causality in "Adumbratio kabbalæ christianæ".

[31]*Erat verbum* איתוהי מלתא

Cabb. Cat. *Si Johannes per verbum intelligit Messiam seu personam illam, inter omnia producta primam, quæ â Nostratibus dicitur Adam Kadmon, cur Verbi appellatione utitur?*

Christianus. Ut ad vestrum potissimum me accomodem captum, rationes mihi inter alias occurrunt sequentes:

1. Quia sicut verbum est expressio rei ignotæ; ita Messias est expressio Dei infiniti, incomprehensibilis (Joh. 1, 18) & hoc sensu Cabbalistis vestris vox Breschith dicitur verbum, inter decem creationis verba numerandum: i.e. expressio quædam | objectorum sublimium incognitorum: ita in Epistola ad Hebræos c. 1, 3. Messias dicitur character. Et sicut Messias per appellationem Verbi dicitur expressio divinitatis; ita de eodem dicitur, quod omnia portet verbo, i.e. expressione virtutis suæ, Heb. 1, 3.

2. Verbi appellatione tota quasi exhauritur ipsius Emanatio: sicut enim in verbo concurrunt elocutio, spiritus, vox & loquens: ita dictio seu ǁ [32]elocutio à Vobis refertur | ad Malchuth; vide in Loc. Comm. [33]דבור, [34]דבר, [35]אמירה &c. Spiritus ad Thiphereth; vid. [36]רוח; vox ad Binah & suo sensu ad Chochmah, vid. [37]קול: ipse autem loquens occultus est Kether; Et inspirans, En soph.

3. In specie Messias communiter â Vestratibus olim referebatur ad Regni gradum qui communissimè vocatur Schechinah, & ordinariè verbum; vide in דבר loco citato | & Targum Gen. 28, 20.21; Ex. 19, 17; Jes. 1, 14.16; c. 45, 2; c. 48, 11; c. 49, 5.15; c. 51.5; Jer. 24, 6; c. 27, 5.18; c. 29, 14.23; Hos. 1, 7.9; Zach. 2, 5.

---

31   Deletion: Annotatio 2
32   A red pencil square bracket inserted into the text ([elocutio) refers to an annotation in the left margin: 14.A/12.
33   "דבור *Loquela*. Ita vocatur Schechinah Malchuth. Ratio est, quia Tiphereth vocatur Vox: ergò Malchuth *loquela* vel *elocutio*. Sicut enim locutio discriminat voces, & sonos syllabæ, ita Malchuth est manifestatio Tiphereth, & conspectus sonorum ejus. Ita autem vocatur ex parte Gebhurah: quia locutio semper duritiem refert, quamvis non excludantur cæteri gradus. [...]" (*Kabbala Denudata, I*, "Apparatus in Librum Sohar, Pars prima, nempe Loci communes kabbalistici secundum ordinem Alphabeticum concinnati, qui Lexici instar esse possunt", p. 243).
34   "דבר *Verbum*. Est Malchuth. Et huc pertinet illud Psal. 103, 20. *Fortes robore, facientes verbum ejus*. de quo vid. Sohar & Tikkunim. Sic quoque locus ille Psal. 110, 4. *Secundum verbum meum Malchizedek*; quæ est Schechinah; quæ vocatur *Verbum meum*, quia erat mensura Davidis. [...]" (Ibid., pp. 245–246).
35   "10. Sub eodem titulo אמירה in Pardes reperiuntur sequentia his verbis: Hoc in loco variant Interpretes. Quidam hanc vocem referunt ad *Malchuth*, adducto loco Psal. 68, 12. *Adonai dabit Sermonem*: Sicut phrasin דיבור *loquendi* referunt ad Gebhurah, ex hac ratione, quod Exod. 6, 2. dicatur: *Et locutus est Elohim ad Mosen*. Ubi phrasis *loquendi*

Was the Word ythwy mlt'

Kabbalist Catechumen If by "Word" John understood Messiah or his "persona", the first among all things produced, whom our sages call *Adam Kadmon*, why does he use the term "Word"?

Christian To better adapt myself to your capacity [I shall offer] the following reasons which amongst others occur to me:

(1) Because, just as a word is an expression of something unknown, so is Messiah an expression | of the Infinite and Incomprehensible God (Jn 1.18). In this sense your Kabbalists consider the word *Breschith* (called "Word") should be counted amongst the Ten Words of Creation *i. e.* as an expression of certain sublime [but] unknown objects[38]: so in Heb 1.3, Messiah is designated as a "character" [or "express image"]. Just as Messiah by the term "Word" is said to be an expression of divinity, so also it is said that "he upholds everything by the word i.e. by the expression of his power" (Heb 1.3).

(2) By calling him "Word" the whole of his Emanation is, as it were, brought to its completion. For just as in "word" there combine articulation, spirit, voice and speaker, so "diction" or ‖ "articulation" is linked by you | to *Malkhut* (see in *Loc Comm. dbwr, dbr, 'myrh etc.*); "spirit" to *Tiferet* (see *rwḥ*); "voice" to *Binah* and, in its own sense, to *Chokhmah* (see *qwl*); the "speaker" himself is concealed as *Keter* and the "breathing" in *Ein Sof*.

(3) Specifically, Messiah was commonly connected by your [teachers] to the Grade *Kingdom* [*Malkhut*] which is most commonly called *Shekhinah*, and ordinarily "Word". See on *dbr* loc. cit. | and the Targum on Gen 28.20, 21; Ex 19.17; Isa 1.14, 16; 45.2; 48.11; 49.5, 15; 51.5; Jer 24.6; 27.5, 18; 29.14, 23; Hos 1.7, 9; Zech 2. 5[39].

p. 12

---

combinatur cum Elohim, quod est in Prædicamento Gebhurah. [...] 11. Alii alio modo; Dibbur referunt ad Malchuth, & Amirah ad Tiphereth." (Ibid., p. 128).

36 "רוח *Spiritus*. Hæc vox nudè posita refertur ad Tiphereth, qui inter elementa nomen Aëris habet; cum medium teneat locum inter Gedulah & Gebhurah, Aquam & Ignem. [...]" (Ibid., p. 682).

37 "קול *Vox*; nullibi non ad Tiphereth pertinet. Sed datur *Vox interna*, quæ non auditur, nempe in Binah; & nihilominus tamen subintelligitur Daath in Istâ latens. קול ergò *Vox*, absolutè positu (sic), est Tiphereth: sed & omnes septem Sephiroth vocantur Voces, quæ sunt septem Voces illæ, quarum mentio sit Ps. 29, 3.4.5.7.8.9. Omnes tamen respectum involventes ad Tiphereth: sicut & in promulgatione Legis Eædem voces appellantur eodem respectu, ita ut Illæ sint sex Voces, & Ipse septima, qui omnes complectitur, sub mysterio ascensus ejus in Binah." (Ibid., p. 673).

38 The Ten Utterances ('*śrh m'mrwt*) by which the world was created are linked to the Ten Commandments ('*śrt hdbrwt*) of Ex 20 in Zohar, III, 11b.

39 The relevance of these quotations is not necessarily evident from the biblical text.

Et 4. hac ipsa[40] appellatione tota series historiæ creationis explicatur, ut sensus sit, quotiescunque in Genesi dicitur, *Et dixit*; toties involvi mentionem Schechinæ & Messiæ; ne exclusâ quidem voce בראשית. Et procul dubio huc respexit ipse Dominus | Joh. 5, 46 & Evangelista Luc. 24, 27. Conferantur initia Mosis (Hebr. 10, 7) & initia omnium Prophetarum.

Cabb. Cat. *Non igitur tantoperè divina Natura Messiæ hoc nomine innuitur, quam natura illius producta, quam profectò in Maria initium sumsisse minimè dicerem si ad vestras partes transirem*[41]. *Et huc pertinent loca Adumbration.* | *Cabbal. Christianæ c. 3. & c. 7.§. 26.*[42]

[43]*Erat apud Deum* איתוהי הוא לות אלהא

Cabb. Cat. *Fallor? An hîc innuitur intimà & quam vos dicitis personalis illa unio Animæ sive naturæ productæ Messianæ cum communicata sibi natura divina?* ‖[44] *particula enim* לות *Chaldæis & Syris denotat conjunctionem* | *& consociationem intimiorem.*

Christianus. *Sanè particula* πρός *respectum potiùs externum denotat; qualis in Christo neutiquam sufficit. Sed de Nomine* אלהא *quædam suggere.*

Cabb. Cat. *Vox* אלהא, *cui æquipollet* אלהים (*1.*) *generaliter quidem sumitur pro tota Luce, ab infinito in Aziluth immanante, & abhinc ulterius communicata;* | *unde hoc nomen extensionem quandam habet per totum illud systema,*

However the Targum's insertion of "word" gives them point e.g. Targum Isa 1.14. "Your new moons and your appointed feasts my Word hates"; Targum Isa 1.16 "Put away the evil of your doings from before the presence of my Word". The use of the Aramaic word *mmrʾ* [word] appears often to be just another way of saying "God" or "the Lord". There has none the less been much debate about whether it is a likely influence upon John's theology of the Word, though many scholars have considered this a blind alley. Its relevance has been argued for by Martin Mc Namara, *Targum and Testament Revised* (Grand Rapids: Eerdmanns, 2010), pp. 155–166; Id., "The Logos of the Fourth Gospel and the Memra of the Palestinian Targum (Ex 12.42)" now collected in his *Targum and Testament Collected Essays* (Tübingen: Mohr Siebeck, 2011), pp. 439–443. John Ronning, *The Jewish Targums and John's Logos Theology* (Peabody, Mass.: Hendrickson, 2010) offers support to this view.

40   BSB: hâc ipsâ
41   Deletion: si ad vestras partes transirem.
42   The third chapter of the "Adumbratio" is devoted to a systematic comparison of the characteristics attributed by the Lurianic tradition to Adam Kadmon and those attributed to Christ by Christian traditions. Chapter VII deals with the preexistence of souls, but a large part of it considers the nature of Christ, in order to demonstrate that it is both human and divine.

(4) By this term ["Word"] the whole sequence of the history of Creation is explained, as whenever in Genesis it is said "And He said" there is involved a mention of Shekhinah and Messiah—not to forget the word *brʾšyt*. And no doubt the Lord himself | looked back to this (Jn 5.46) and also the Evangelist (Lk 24.27). The "beginnings in Moses (Heb 10.7) and in all the Prophets" [mentioned in Lk 24.27] are here brought together.

Kabbalist Catechumen So it is not so much the divine nature of Messiah which this name asserts, as his created nature: and certainly, if I were to convert to your opinion, I would not say this began in [the womb of] Mary[45]. Relevant here are *Adumbratio* | *Kabbalae Christianae*, chap. 3, & chap. 7, § 26.[46]

Was with God *ʾytwhy hwʾ lwt ʾlhʾ*

Kabbalist Catecumen Am I mistaken or is there here indicated that intimate and, as you say, personal union of the soul, or of the created nature of the Messiah, with the divine nature ‖ communicated to him? For the preposition *lwt* ["with"] in both Aramaic and Syriac denotes conjunction | and a deeper mutual society.

Christian Clearly the [Greek] preposition *pros* ["with"] denotes rather an external aspect [of their] relationship, which is hardly adequate in the case of Christ. But suggest something about the noun *ʾlhʾ* [God].

Kabbalistic Catechumen The [Syriac] word *ʾlhʾ* [God] to which [the Hebrew] *ʾlhym* [*ʾelohim* (plural): God] is equivalent, (1) is indeed generally taken for all the Light, immanent in *Atsilut* from infinity, and communicated downwards from there |; thus this name extends through the whole system,

p. 13

---

43 Deletion: Annotatio 3
44 A red pencil square bracket inserted into the text ([particula) refers to an annotation in the left margin: 15.A/13
45 Another attempt to avoid this doctrine is made below on folio 4ʳ.
46 It is important to note that "Adumbratio kabbalæ christianæ" here deals with the introduction of the Christ by his Father into the world, the Verb made flesh and the two natures of Christ. Very little is made of the Virgin Mary. The text, however, considers at length the relationship between the Son and the Father, but never mentions the part taken by his Mother in his conception. A preliminary summary of the Virgin Mary in *Messias Puer* is to be found in Robert J. Wilkinson, "The Kabbalistic Treatment of the Virgin Mary in Christian Knorr von Rosenroth's *Historiae Evangeliae Initium secundum quatuor Evangelistas*: A Provisional Description", *art. cit.*

ita ut & Malchuth, & Thiphereth (intuitu Geburæ[47] *& Hod) & Binah illud sibi vindicent; & ratione* מ"י *(quæ est pars illius;) nec non ratione 32. semitarum sapientiæ, quæ sunt 32. Nomina Elohim historiæ Creationis; Chochmah etiam & Kether eò reducantur: sed tamen (2.) etiam specialiter sumitur quatenus severitatem & | dijudicationem insinuat.* |||

Christianus. Ad istos autem gradus, creationis tempore Messias potissimum inclinabat. Imò specialis quædam ratio, quare hoc unicum inter Divina Nomina plurali potius quam singulari nomine efferatur, nonne hæc esse posse videtur, quod eodem specialiùs indigitetur duarum Messiæ naturarum unio[48], ita ut ubicunque reperitur | hoc Nomen, geminæ hic Gigas substantiæ subinnuatur. Cui latior placet hoc loco exspatiandi campus, videre poterit de hac unione Adumbr. Cabb. Christ. cap. 11[49]. Part. II. p. 147. sqq. & p. 162. sqq.

---

47   BSB: Gebhuræ
48   Added in the right margin: ejusdemque per Spiritum suum in crea- ||-turis operatio. The addition has been integrated into the BSB version. A red pencil square bracket inserted into the correction in the right margin (crea[turis) refers to an annotation: 16.A/14.
49   Correction in the right margin: "cap." is replaced by "cap. 3.§. 9. De Nomine autem אלהים Excerpta quædam è Sohar Cabb. Denud. Tom.". Hence the reference reads as follows: "Adumbr. Cabb. Christ. cap. 3.§. 9. De Nomine autem אלהים Excerpta quædam è Sohar Cabbal. Denud. Tom. II, Part. II, p. 147. sqq. & p. 162. sqq." On the relationship between Christ and Light, "Adumbratio kabbalæ christianæ" says: "Hæc enim Messiæ Anima statim ab initio productionis suæ unita fuit cum Luce divinitatis sibi communicata: & quidem unione tam intellectus, quæ consistit in contemplatione; quam unione voluntatis, quæ consistit in amore. Et hæc omnia in gradu excellentissimo sub universalitate tam partium quam actuum." (p. 8) "Excerpta quædam è Sohar Cabbal. Denud. Tom. II, Part. II, p. 147. sqq. & p. 162. sqq." refers propably to *Kabbala denudata, II,* "Partis secundæ tractatus quintus qui continet Tres tractatus initiales Libri Sohar": "§. 4. Sic etiam Nomen אלהים istius loci se habet: (g) hoc enim postquàm primò illius facta est mentio (*Gen. 1. v. 1.*) producit tredecim voces, (h) quæ circundent Congregationem Israël, & custodiant illam, (i) & postea commemoratur vice alterâ" (p. 147) and "§. 3. Creavit ista: & quis est ille מי? ille qui vocatur Extremitas cœlorum Deut. 4. v. 32. superior, à cujus permissione omnia existunt, & quia ibi locum habet interrogatio, & ipse est in semita occulta, & non manifestatur, hinc appellatur מי: quis?" (Ibid., pp. 162–163).
50   On *my*, the Upper Edge of Heaven, see Zohar I, 1b–2a.
51   The Thirty-Two Paths of Wisdom occur at the very beginning of the *Sefer Yetsirah*: "With thirty-two mystical paths of Wisdom, Yh created his universe" and were subsequently of central concern. The number is that of the occurrences of the name Elohim in the first chapter of Genesis. It is obtained by adding the number of the twenty-two

SECTION II 143

p. 14 so that *Malkhut* and *Tiferet* (by contemplating *Gevurah* and *Hod*) and *Binah* [too] lay claim to it for themselves. Further, by reason of *my*[50] (which is part of it) and also by reason of the 32 Paths of Wisdom, which are the 32 [occurrences of the name] *'elohim* in the account of Creation[51], *Chokhmah* too and *Keter* are brought back to it: but none the less (2) it is also used specially to
45 suggest severity and | judgment[52]. ‖| fol. 4ʳ

Christian At the time of Creation, Messiah was most strongly inclined to these grades. The special reason why this unique plural [*'elohim*] amongst the divine names is used, rather than a singular name [e.g. Hebrew *'eloah*] can surely been seen to be because by this name [*'elohim*] the union of the two natures of Messiah ‖—and the operation of the same by his spirit in p. 14
5 creatures is indicated[53]—so that wherever this name occurs, | a Giant of Twin Substances is implied[54]. Whoever wants to learn more about this, can read about this union in *Adumbratio*, chap. 3, § 9 (*Cabb. Denud.*, Vol. 2, Part. 2, p. 147 et *seq.* & p. 162 et *seq.*).

---

letters of the alphabet to the number of the ten sefirot. The paths attracted the interest of earlier Christian Kabbalists. Francesco Georgio Veneto wrote his *Harmonia Mundi Totius* in 1525. It was translated into French by Guy le Fèvre de La Boderie in 1578 as *L'Harmonie du Monde*. Guy's brother Nicolas wrote a 19 page *in-folio* introduction to the translation which offers a theoretisation of the discovery of divinity by the Thirty-Two Paths of Wisdom (that is, thirty-two ways of reading developed from the four senses, but offering an enormous polysemic complexity). On this see: Marie-Madeleine Fragonard, "Les Trente-deux Sentiers de Sapience de Nicolas le Fèvre de La Boderie: une théorie de l'interprétation polysémique au XVIᵉ siècle" in *Mélanges sur la littérature de la Renaissance à la mémoire de V.-L. Saulnier* (Geneva: Droz, 1984), pp. 217–224.

52 Cf. Exodus Rabbah 3.6: "The Holy One, Blessed be He, said to them: You want to know my name? I am called according to my actions. When I judge creatures I am Elohim and when I have mercy upon my world I am named Yhwh".

53 This is perhaps best understood from a hierarchic perspective: in the same way as the Infinite (Ein Sof) / God projected light into Adam Kadmon / Messiah, that same light is in turn projected towards other creatures by the medium of Adam Kadmon / Messiah.

54 This "giant" comes from Ps 18.6 "*tanquam sponsus procedere de thalamo suo, exultavit ut gigas ad currendam viam*". The verse was popularised as an anti-Arian slogan by Ambrose's hymn "*Intende, qui regis Israel*", the fifth strophe of which has: "*Procedat de thalamo suo / pudoris aula regis / geminae gigas substantiae / alacris ut currat viam*". See *Ambroise de Milan: Hymnes*, edited by Jacques Fontaine et al. (Paris: Cerf, 1992), pp. 273–275. The phrase is common in Augustine: *En Ps* 18.6 1&2; *En Ps* 44.3; *En Ps* 77.10; *Cons Ev* 1.46.30; *Tr Joh* 2.3 et al. See Goulven Madec, *La Patrie et la Vie: le Christ dans la vie et la pensée de saint Augustin* (Paris: Desclée, 1989), pp. 191–192. For a study of this exegetical topos, R.E. Kaske, "Gigas the Giant in Piers Plowman", *Journal of English and Germanic Philology* 56 (1957): pp. 177–185.

[55]*Et Deus erat ipsum verbum*
ואלהא איתוהי הוא הו מלתא

Cabb. Cat. *Ex illa hypothesi*[56], *Nomen* אלהים *cui Moses adscribit creationem, non tantum habere sensum Divinæ Naturæ, sed & productæ, adeoque totius Messiæ.*

Christianus. *Nihil absurdi*[57]. *Imò augustius quid & adhuc longè excellentius de gloriosissimo hoc Domino statuendum, quod nempe non saltem nomen Elohim, sed omnia | cætera nomina Divina, ne Tetragrammato quidem excluso, insimul denotent Messiam, quippe qui totam habet naturarum*[58] *productarum Œconomiam atque directionem, sive ratione productionis, sive ratione informationis, (quô pertinent illa Nomina, quibus Divinitatem gradatim creaturis manifestavit:) sive tandem restitutionis ratione: conf. Joh. 17, 6.*

V. II. Hoc erat in principio apud Deum[59]:
הנא איתוהי הוא ברישית לות אלהא

Cabb. Cat. *Quem hîc putas esse sensum? Hocne vult Apostolus, quod Messiæ fiat*[60] *in principio Legis; &*[61] *quod in verbis* ‖ בראשית ברא אלהים *Messias seu verbum*[62] *sit ipsum illud Breschith*[63] *quod habetur penes nomen Elohim:*[64] *ita*[65] *idem dicatur principium causale, quo mediante creatio | instituta est; & quidem cum connotatione Unionis cum Divinitate? An verò vox* ברישית *hoc versiculo 2. aliam habet significationem, ne idem bis dici videatur: ut sensus sit,* ברישית. *Ab initio statim Messiam unitum fuisse cum Divinitate; & unionem illam non incepisse cum statu humiliationis?*

Christianus. *Uterque sensus*[66] *admitti posset, quamvis posterior mihi videatur facilior, | & majorem involvere connexionem cum subsequentibus.*

---

55   Deletion: Annotatio 4
56   Added in the right margin: *sequeretur*
57   Added above the line: in hoc invenirent Vestrates.
58   BSB: naturam (Printer's error)
59   BSB: DEum
60   Added above the line: mentio
61   Correction in the right margin: & remplaced by et
62   A red pencil square bracket inserted into the text (ver[bum) refers to an annotation in the right margin: Pr.B./17.
63   Added in the right margin: (materialiter sumendo hanc vocem;)
64   Deletion of a line and a half, now unreadable.
65   Correction: a crossed out word, now unreadable, replaced by ut.
66   Added in the right margin: à Vestratibus. BSB: â Vestratibus

SECTION II

And God was that Word w'lh' 'ytwhy 'wh hw mlt'

Kabbalist Catechumen From that hypothesis it follows that the name *'lhym* [*'elohim*] to which Moses ascribes the Creation has not so much the sense of divine nature but rather of produced [nature] and to that extent of the whole Messiah.[67]

Christian Your teachers would find nothing absurd in this. But there is something far more august and more excellent concerning this most glorious Lord to be considered, because truely not just the name Elohim, but all | the other divine names—not even to the exclusion of the Tetragrammaton—together designate Messiah in as much as he has the management and direction of the produced [i.e. created] natures, whether by reason of production or by reason of informing them (to which pertain those names by which he manifests Divinity progressively to creatures); or finally by reason of the Restitution (Jn 17.6).

Verse 2

This [First] Principle of Creation was with God hn' 'ytwhy hw' bryšyt lwt 'lh'

Kabbalist Catechumen What do you think is the meaning here? Does the Apostle want [to find] a mention of Messiah at the beginning of the Law so that in the [Hebrew] words ‖ *br'šyt br' 'lhym* Messiah or the Word becomes [materially] that same *Breschith* [by assuming this word]; and that it was in possession of the name Elohim in such a way that it is said to be the causal principle [*principium*] by means of which | creation was established; and that moreover with a connotation of union with Divinity? Or does the word *bryšyt* here in Verse 2 really have another meaning, so that the same thing does not appear to be said twice, and the sense is [Syriac] *bryšyt*: that right from the beginning the Messiah had been united with Divinity; and that that Union did not begin with his state of lowliness[68]?

Christian Either meaning could be admitted by your [teachers], although the second seems easier | to me and to involve a closer connection with what follows.

p. 15

---

67 This is evidently incompatible with Nicean orthodoxy.
68 That is, at the time of his birth from Mary. Once again, concern is shown not to concede that Messiah's existence began in Mary's womb.

V. III. ⁶⁹*Omnia per ipsum &c.* כל באידה

Christianus. Idem repetit Paulus Eph. 3, 9; Col. 1, 16.17; Hebr. 1, 2. Conf. Rom. 11, 36⁷⁰; 1 Cor. 8, 6.⁷¹

    Cabb. Cat. *Huc referri posset locus egregius Libri Sohar, quem retulisti | inter Commentationes in vocem* בראשית *inter Excerpta Centur. I. Loc. 3.*

⁷²*Quod factum est* מדם דהוא

p. 16   **Cabb. Cat.** *Quare tam seriò hæc inculcat Apostolus?* ||

    Christianus. Ut sub ista generalitate⁷³ non materialia saltem sed & immaterialia quævis comprehendantur. Vide de his Adumbrat. Cabb. Christianæ c. 4⁷⁴ & 6⁷⁵. Paterque | infinitus excluderetur solus.

V. IV. ⁷⁶*In ipso erat vita. &c.* בה חיא הוא

Cabb. Cat. *Num physicè hîc intelligenda est vox Vitæ; an moraliter?*

    Christianus. Uterque sensus quadrat. Physicè enim Messias est principium omnis vitæ, | id est omnis actus luminosi, in specie autem humani.

fol. 4ᵛ   Moraliter autem per⁷⁷ ||| vitam intelligitur Summum bonum, quod in alio non consistit, quam in influxu Messiæ; eodemque sensu vitæ vox accipitur Matth. 7, 14; c. 18, 8.9; c. 19, 17; Mar. 9, 43.45; Luc. 12, 15; Joh. 3, 36; c. 5, 24.40; c. 6, 33⁷⁸.51.63; c. 8, 12; c. 10, 10; c. 14, 6; c. 20, 31; 1 Joh. 5, 12. confer. loc. comm. Cabbal. in חיי⁷⁹. Sequentia autem naturam | hujus vitæ describunt, quod scilicet in illuminatione consistat.

---

69 Deletion: Annotatio 1

70 BSB: Rom. I, 136 (Printer's error)

71 For a similar, but more developed passage, cf. "Adumbratio kabbalæ christianæ", op. cit., p. 9.

72 Deletion: Annotatio 2

73 BSB: generalite (Printer's error)

74 Chapter IV is entitled: "De naturis productis & fine productionis earum".

75 Chapter VI is entitled: "De statu modernæ Constitutionis".

76 Deletion: Annotatio 1

77 In the right bottom corner appears a Hebrew letter ב presumably an indication of binding or pagination.

78 BSB: 32 (Printer's error)

79 "חי *Vivus*. Est Jesod. Sic in Raja Meh. R. Moscheh scribit: חי per pathach est cognomen Binah; per Zere, est Jesod. Vid. prolixè Schaare Zedek. In Sohar autem non distinguun-

Verse 3
Everything ... by his hand etc. kl bʾydh

Christian Paul repeats this Eph 3.9; Col 1.16, 17; Heb 1.2; Cf. Rm 11.36; 1 Cor 8.6.

Kabbalist Catechumen Here one can refer to that outstanding passage in the Book of the Zohar which you cited | amongst remarks on the word *brʾšyt* in Excerpta Cent. I Loc. 3.

Which was made mdm dhwʾ

Kabbalistic Catechumen Why does the Apostle introduce this in this context?

Christian ‖ So that under this general [specification] not only material things, but also anything immaterial may be embraced. See on this *Adumbratio*, chap. 4, § 6. Only the Infinite Father | should be excluded.

Verse 4
In Him was life etc. bh hyʾ hwʾ

Kabbalist Catechumen Should the word "Life" be understood physically here, or morally?

Christian Either meaning is satisfactory. For in physical terms Messiah is the [First] Principle of all Life, | that is, of every luminous act, but specifically of human [acts]. Morally, by ‖| "Life" is understood the *summum bonum* which consists in nothing else other than the influx of the Messiah. The word "Life" has this same sense in Mt 7.14; 18.8, 9; 19.17; Mk 9.43, 45; Lk 12.15; Jn 3.36; 5.24, 40; 6.33, 51, 63; 8.12; 10.10; 14.6; 20.31; 1Jn 5.12. Cf. Loc. Com. Cab. on *ḥyy*. What follows [in John] | describes the nature of this Life, namely that it consists of illumination.

---

tur. Omnes autem consentiunt, quod tunc vocetur חי, quando vita à Binah derivatur in Malchuth. In Sohar Cantici Canticorum. R. Schimeon ben Jochai hæc tradit; Cum tantum recipit influxum à supernis, vocatur חי, vivus: Cum verò vitam & influentiam demittit deorsum, tunc vocatur חי העולמים vivens pro æonibus, quia demittit vitam in æones seu mundos infra se locatos. Qua ex causa, juxta R. Moscheh, hoc nomen etiam tribuitur gradui Malchuth. [...]" ("Loci communes kabbalistici", op. cit., pp. 340–341).

Cabb. Cat. *Sanè tota Doctrina Cabbalistica nihil quasi est aliud, quam Doctrina de Luce, ejusque opposito. Sensus ergò istius versiculi hic esset; quod per Messiam omnes fideles V.F.*[80] *summam suam quæsiverint felicitatem; quæ in nulla re alia substiterit, quam in variis illuminationum generibus; quæ* | *vide*
p. 17   *Excerpt. Cent. I. Loc. 12.* ‖

[81]*Et ipsa Lux &c.* והו נוהרא

Christianus. [82]A cujus influxu hominibus lux oritur & vita æterna, nempe Messias, in statum hunc tenebrarum descendit per incarnationem suam; luxitque lumine doctrinæ, vitæque, & adhuc lucet lumine spiritus sui: & tenebræ non assecutæ sunt eum; id | est, in tenebras prolapsa Ecclesia vestra Judaica, luce propriâ nimium excœcatâ, non agnovit eum.

Cabb. Cat. *Annon generalior posset esse sensus, de toto tenebrarum, i. e. corticum genere, ut multò minus Gentiles excludantur?*

Christianus. Rectè, si per lucem spiritus, per tenebras caro intelligatur.

---

80   *Veteris Foederis* is abbreviated as V. F.
81   Deletion: Annotatio 2. A red pencil square bracket inserted into the text ([Et ipsa Lux) refers to an annotation in the left margin: Pr.B./17.
82   Added above the line: Ille

Kabbalist Catechumen Clearly the whole of kabbalistic teaching is nothing else than this teaching about Light and its opposite. The meaning therefore of this part of the verse here is: that through Messiah, all the faithful of the Old Covenant sought their greatest felicity, which subsisted in nothing else than in various types of illuminations. | On which see Excerpt. Cent. 1 Loc. 12.

And the Light ... whw nwhrʾ

Christian ‖ He from whose influx Light and Eternal Life are given to men—that is Messiah—came down into this state of darkness by his Incarnation. He illuminated it with the light of [his] doctrine and life and still illuminates it by the light of his Spirit. *"And the darkness did not follow him"*; that is, | your Jewish Church fell away into darkness, too much blinded by its own light, and did not recognise him[83].

p. 17

Kabbalist Catechumen Could the meaning not more generally include all darkness *i. e.* the descendants of the Shells[84]—so that the Gentiles are far less excluded?

Christian Yes: if the Spirit is understood by [the word] Light, [then] by Darkness we understand the Flesh.

---

[83] "*& tenebræ non assecutæ sunt eum*". This is not how the verb *drk* is usually understood here. It is usually taken to mean to "understand" or "overcome" with the Greek and Latin text. The aphel of *drk* can mean "to approach" in Syriac; perhaps von Rosenroth has found the sense "follow" from this. Notice that the "your Jewish Church" does not evidently refer here to Jews converted to Christianity, but Jews resisting the Gospel, though the Kabbalist Catechumen wants also to include the Gentiles.

[84] Within the Lurianic system the *kelipot* are the husks or shells which imprison the sparks of light that were exiled from God on account of "the breaking of the vessels". See Introduction.

[1]Luc. I.

[2]V. 5. Fuit in diebus Herodis Regis Jehudah Sacerdos quidam, cui nomen erat Zacharjah, ex ministerio familiæ Abiah: & uxor ejus ex filiabus Aharon[3], cujus | nomen erat Elischebahg[4].[5]

6. Ambo autem justi erant coram Deo, & incedentes in omnibus mandatis ejus & in rectitudine Domini, sine reprehensione.[6]

7. Soboles autem non erat eis, propterea, quod Elischebahg[7] sterilis esset, & ambo provecti in diebus suis essent.[8]

8. Factum est autem, cum ipse sacerdotio fungeretur in ordine ministerii sui coram | Deo;[9]

9. Secundum consuetudinem sacerdotii evenit ei, ut poneret aromata. Et ingressus est in templum Domini.[10] ||

10. [11]Omnis autem congregatio populi | orans erat foris tempore suffitus.[12]

11. Et conspectus est Zachariæ Angelus Domini, stans â dextra altaris suffimenti.[13]

12. Et conturbatus est Zacharjah cum videret eum, & timor incidit super eum.[14] |||

13[15]. Et dixit ei Angelus: Ne timeas, Zacharjah, quia exaudita est oratio tua, & uxor tua Elischeba pariet tibi filium, & vocabis nomen ejus Jochanan.[16,17]

---

1 Added in the left margin: Sectio III
2 On the left-hand half of the page, a fragment cut from Knorr's edition of the Peshittta New Testament of 1684 containing the Syriac version of the quoted Gospel of Luke is pasted in and crossed out. Text added in the left margin: Matth. 2, 1; 1 Par 24, 10.19; Neh. 12, 4.17. Deleted.
3 Aharon is not in the expected genitive case. Possibly Knorr was unconsciously remembering the Vulgate which also does not inflect here.
4 The last two letters crossed out (Elischebahg replaced by Elischeba).
5 Vulgate: Fuit in diebus Herodis, regis Iudææ, sacerdos quidam nomine Zacharias, de vice Abia, et uxor illius de filiabus Aaron, et nomen eius Elisabeth.
6 Vulgate: Erant autem iusti ambo ante Deum, incedentes in omnibus mandatis et iustificationibus Domini sine querela.
7 The last two letters crossed out (Elischebahg replaced by Elischeba).
8 Vulgate: Et non erat illis filius, eo quod esset Elisabeth sterilis, et ambo processissent in diebus suis.
9 Vulgate: Factum est autem, cum sacerdotio fungeretur in ordine vicis suæ ante Deum.
10 Vulgate: Secundum consuetudinem sacerdotii, sorte exiit ut incensum poneret, ingressus in templum Domini.
11 A red pencil square bracket inserted into the text ([10. Omnis) refers to an annotation in the left margin: 2.B./18.
12 Vulgate: Et omnis multitudo populi erat orans foris hora incensi.

Section III
Luke Chapter 1

5 There was in the days of Herod king of Jehudah [Judah] a priest, whose name was Zachariah, of the ministry of the family of Abiah and his wife, of the daughters of Aaron, whose name | was Elischeba.

6 Both were righteous before God and walked in all his commandments and in the uprightness[18] of the Lord without blame.

7 However they had no offspring because Elischeba was barren and both were well advanced in their days.

8 And it happened that when [Zachariah] was exercising his priesthood[19] in the order of his ministry before | God,

9 according to the custom of the priesthood, he was to offer the incense[20]. And he entered the Temple of the Lord,

10 ‖ and the whole congregation of the people | were praying outside at the time[21] of the incensing

p. 18

11 an Angel of the Lord appeared to Zachariah, standing to the right of the altar of incense,

12 and Zachariah was troubled when he saw him and fear fell upon him. ‖

fol. 5ʳ

13 And the Angel said to him, "Do not be afraid Zachariah, for you prayer has been heard and your wife Elischeba will bear you a son and you shall call his name Jochanan.

---

13 Vulgate: Apparuit autem illi angelus Domini, stans a dextris altaris incensi.

14 Vulgate: Et Zacharias turbatus est videns, et timor irruit super eum.

15 BSB: 14 (Printer's error)

16 Text in the right margin: 13. Inf. v. 60. Deleted.

17 Vulgate: Ait autem ad illum angelus: Ne timeas, Zacharia, quoniam exaudita est deprecatio tua; et uxor tua Elisabeth pariet tibi filium, et vocabis nomen eius Ioannem.

18 Text: *"in rectitudine"*. Vulgate: *"in justificationibus"*. The Syriac is k'nwt' meaning "uprightness", "justice", or "righteousness", which lacks important aspects of the "justification" in the Vulgate. Lightfoot, *Miscellanies and the Harmony of the Gospels*, op. cit., p. 149 on this verse disapproves of this word noting "the Romanists [i.e. Catholics] translate 'justifications:' and of the word would make no small advantage". It is possible that Knorr had this work to hand as he wrote, for similarities occur with what follows.

19 Here the Vulgate has *"sorte exiit"*. There is, however, no "lot" in the Syriac Peshitta, though it does appear in the comments below.

20 Vulgate: "He was chosen by lot to offer the incense".

21 The Vulgate, following the Greek, has *hora*. The Syriac is less specific, as the comment below makes clear.

14. *Eritque tibi gaudium & exultatio: & multi gaudebunt de ejus | nativitate.*[22,23]
15. *Erit enim magnus coram Domino, & vinum & temetum non bibet; et spiritu Sanctitatis implebitur adhuc existens in ventre matris suæ.*[24,25]
16. *Et multos ex filiis*[26] *Iisraël respicere faciet ad Dominum | Deum ipsorum.*[27,28]
17. *Et ipse præcedet eum in spiritu, & in virtute Elijah Prophetæ, ut reducat cor Patrum super filios, & eos qui sunt increduli ad cognitionem Justorum, & præparabit Domino populum perfectum.*[29,30]
18. *Et dixit Zacharjah ad Angelum, Quomodo noscam istud? Ego enim sum senex, & uxor mea provecta in diebus suis est.*[31,32]
19. *Et respondit Angelus, & dixit ei: Ego sum Gabriel, qui adsto coram Deo, & missus sum, ut loquar tecum, & nunciem tibi hæc.*[33,34]
20. *Deinceps silebis, neque poteris loqui, usque ad diem, quo hæc | fient, eò quod non credidisti*[35] *hisce sermonibus meis, qui implebuntur tempore suo.*[36]
21. *Populus autem stabat & expectabat Zacharjam, & mirabantur moram ejus, quâ in templo esset.*[37]
22. *Quum egressus autem esset Zacharjah, non poterat | loqui cum eis: & intellexerunt, quod visionem vidisset in templo, & ipse innuebat nutu eis, et*[38] *mansit mutus.*[39]
23. *Et cum impleti essent dies ministerii ejus, ivit in domum suam.*[40]
24. *Et factum est post dies eos in utero concepit Elischeba | uxor ejus: & occultabat seipsam mensibus quinque, ac dicebat:*[41]

---

22 Text in the right margin: 14. Inf. v. 58. Deleted.
23 Vulgate: Et erit gaudium tibi, et exultatio, et multi in nativitate eius gaudebunt.
24 Text in the right margin: 15. Num. 6, 3; Jud. 13, 4; Jer. 1, 5; Gal. 1, 15. Deleted.
25 Vulgate: Erit enim magnus coram Domino; et vinum et siceram non bibet, et Spiritu Sancto replebitur adhuc ex utero matris suæ.
26 BSB: filiiis (Printer's error)
27 Text in the right margin: v. 16. Mal. 4, 5; Matth. 11, 14. Deleted.
28 Vulgate: Et multos filiorum Israel convertet ad Dominum Deum ipsorum.
29 Text in the right margin: v. 17. Mal. 4, 6; Matt. 3, 1; Marc. 9, 12. Deleted.
30 Vulgate: Et ipse præcedet ante illum in spiritu et virtute Eliæ, ut convertat corda patrum in filios, et incredulos ad prudentiam iustorum, parare Domino plebem perfectam.
31 Text in the right margin: v. 18. Gen. 17, 17. Deleted.
32 Vulgate: Et dixit Zacharias ad angelum: Unde hoc sciam? ego enim sum senex, et uxor mea processit in diebus suis.
33 Text in the right margin: Dan. 9, 16. & 9, 21. Matth. 18, 10. Deleted.
34 Vulgate: Et respondens angelus, dixit ei: Ego sum Gabriel, qui asto ante Deum; et missus sum loqui ad te, et hæc tibi evangelizare.
35 BSB: credisti (Printer's error)

SECTION III   153

5   14 He shall be your joy and gladness and many will rejoice at his | birth.
    15 For he shall be great before the Lord and will not drink wine or intoxicating drink[42] and he shall be filled with the Spirit of Holiness while he is still in his mother's womb.
10 16 And he will make many of the sons of Israel turn again to the Lord | their God.
    17 And he shall go before him in the spirit and in the power of Elijah the Prophet to lead back the heart of fathers to their sons, and [to lead back] those who do not believe to the knowledge of the just[43], and he shall prepare a perfect people for the Lord".
15 18 And Zachariah said to the Angel "How shall I know that? For I am an old man, and my wife is well on in her days".
    19 And the Angel replied and said to him, "I am Gabriel who stands in the presence of God and I have been sent to speak with you and announce these things to you.
20 20 From now on you will be dumb and not able to speak until the day when | these things happen, because you did not believe these words of mine which will be fulfilled in their time".
    21 The people were standing waiting for Zachariah and wondered at his delay while he was in the temple.
25 22 But when Zachariah came out, he could not | speak to them and they realised that he had seen a vision in the Temple and he communicated with them by a gesture and remained speechless.
    23 And when the days of his ministry were over, he went home.
30 24 And it came to pass after those days that Elischeba | his wife conceived in her womb; and she hid herself for five months and used to say:

---

36   Vulgate: Et ecce eris tacens, et non poteris loqui usque in diem quo hæc fiant, pro eo quod non credidisti verbis meis, quæ implebuntur in tempore suo.
37   Vulgate: Et erat plebs expectans Zachariam; et mirabantur quod tarderet ipse in templo.
38   BSB: &
39   Vulgate: Egressus autem non poterat loqui ad illos, et cognoverunt quod visionem vidisset in templo. Et ipse erat innuens illis et permansit mutus.
40   Vulgate: Et factum est, ut impleti sunt dies officii eius, abiit in domum suam.
41   Vulgate: Post hos autem dies concepit Elisabeth uxor eius, et occultabat se mensibus quinque, dicens.
42   Here: "*temetum*." Vulgate: "*siceram*" which in fact derives from the Greek *skiera*, in turn derived from the Hebrew *shekar* which it translates in LXX.
43   Here: "ad cognitionem Justorum". Vulgate has: "ad prudentiam Justorum".

25. *Nempe hæc fecit mihi Dominus, in diebus quibus respexit me, ad auferendum opprobrium meum, quod (mihi erat) inter filios hominis.*[44,45] ‖

V. 5. [46]*Herodis* דהורדוס

Cabb. Cat. *Observasne occulta Exilii nostri Edomitici initia?*

Christianus. Sic est: Admiranda Dei directio hinc elucescit, quod populum suum nunc subjecerit Potentiæ Edomiticæ; Idumæus enim erat Herodes, Antipatris filius, qui â Romanis, sublato Chasmonæorum seu Maccabæorum ultimo Antigono, Judææ Rex declaratus fuerat, cum Galilææ â Patre Antipatre anno jam ætatis decimo ∣ quinto præfectus fuisset.

Cabb. Cat. *Quomodo hæc facta deducis è nostra de fluxu temporum hypothesi?*

Christianus. Ex hypothesi in Adumbratione Cabbalæ Christianæ proposita c. 10. §. 4.5.6[47] (cum quibus conferri possunt, quæ traduntur in Tractatu de Revolutionibus animarum[48] ∣ P. 1. c. 1. §. 10.11.12.14.15.16.17 & in specie

---

44 Text in the right margin: Gen. 30, 23; Es. 4, 1. Deleted.
45 Vulgate: Quia sic fecit mihi Dominus in diebus, quibus respexit auferre opprobrium meum inter homines.
46 Deletion: Annotatio 1. A red pencil square bracket inserted into the text ([Herodis) refers to an annotation in the right margin: 3.B./19.
47 "§. 4. Sicut autem Corporis humana mensura est ejusdem Caput, octies sumtum: ita & corporis hujus mystici mensura haud incongruè statui potest, illius caput Messias: & ita quidem, ut quoad durationem mundanam singulis capitum dimensionibus tribuantur mille anni: juxta illud Apoc. 1. v. 8 אלף אנא אנא [sic] Ego sum Aleph, &c. quasi subinnueretur millenarius. §. 5. Primum igitur Restitutionis gradum, Infirmationem scilicet Corticum Messias tribus instituit modis. 1. Animas per generationes producendo. 2. Productas accuratius secernendo. 3. Pertinaciores variis pœnis corrigendo. §. 6. Primò igitur Animas è corticibus per varias Generationes produxit: id quod vestrates fieri dicunt secundùm proportionem Corporis [Unde illud vestrum: *Non venturum Messiam, donec omnes Animæ prodierint è corpore.* Jcoamm. fol. 62. col. 1. Nidd. fol. 13. col. 2. Avoda sara fol. 5. col. 1.] Ita ut primò productæ fuerint animæ ad caput pertinentes: & sic porrò usque ad pedes. Et quia productio hæc vel concernit membra interna, vel externa, hinc juxta proportionem mensuræ supra dictæ, nimirum humani capitis, productio membrorum internorum & viscerum incepit cum Fidelibus, sive animabus nobilioribus, ab orbe condito, seu ab ipso capitis vertice; usque ad finem corporis propriè dicti; (demtis pedibus:) ad quod vos etiam aliàs stringitis Iisraëlem [sicut Abrahamum ad brachium dextrum, & Iizchacum ad sinistrum refertis.] Finitâ igitur corporis mensura, i.e. quatuor capitibus, quod est spatium quater mille annorum; censendum erit è corpore corticum jam productas fuisse omnes Animas nobiliores, Corporis Mes-

25 "*Surely, the Lord has done these things to me in the days when he looked again at me to take away my shame which I suffered among the sons of man*[49]".

Verse 5
Of Herod dhrwds

35 **Kabbalist Catechumen** ‖ Do you detect here the hidden beginnings of our Edomite [Roman] exile?[50]

p. 19

Christian That is so. The wonderful Providence of God shines out here, because he has now subjected his people to the Power of Edom—for Herod was an Idumean. He was the son of Antipater, who after the removal of Antigonus, the last of the Hasmoneans or Maccabees, had been made King of Judaea by the Romans when he had been put in charge of Galilee at the
40 age of fifteen | by his father Antipater.

Kabbalist Catechumen How do you deduce these facts from our hypothesis about the flow of the ages?

Christian From the hypothesis proposed in *Adumbratio* (chap. 10, §4, 5, 6)—with which may be compared the material in the *Tractate on the Revo-*
45 *lution of Souls*[51] | Part 1, chap. 1, §10, 11, 12, 14, 15, 16, 17 and specifically §18 and

---

siani antiqui: ad quas pertinet populus Fœderis antiqui: ita ut quicquid subsequentibus temporibus ex illis natum est, omne per revolutionis medium reversum sit: quod ego in hac hypothesi vestri causa admitto. §. 7. Finitâ autem Pedum mensurâ, qui sunt symbolum Graduum Nezach Hod, seu superationis & Gloriæ, quos vestrates appellant duas medietates corporis; productæ censendæ erunt omnes animæ exteriores & Gentilium." ("Adumbratio kabbalæ christianæ", op. cit., p. 60).

48 The text is published at the end of the *Kabbala denudata, II*, pp. 244–478, under the title of "Partis tertiæ tractatus secundus pneumaticus, de Revolutionibus Animarum, qui in hac materia à Judæis vocatur primus. È manuscripto haut ita pridem ex Oriente ad nos perlato ex Operibus R. Jitzchak Lorjensis Germani Cabbalistarum Aquilæ, latinitate donatus".

49 Vulgate: "amongst men".

50 Edom is frequently used as a cipher for Rome. R. Meir is said in Y. Taan 1.1; 64a to have read משא רמא for משא דמא in Isa 21.11 and ראמים in Isa 34.7 as Romans (Pesikta de Rav Kahana 7.11.). The names look very similar; Edom was thought to have burned the First Temple as Rome did the Second (1 Esd 4.45); and Herod as an Idumean was an Edomite. This commonplace identification of Edom with Rome will be further expounded in the forthcoming pages.

51 "De Revolutionibus animarum", one of the kabbalistic works translated by Knorr in *Kabbala Denudata II*.

18.20[52]) quod nempe[53] animæ populi Judaici è statu Corticum prodierint
fol. 5ᵛ secundum mensuram corporis Adamitici: ||| hactenus, quamdiu nondum
finita erat proportio corporis propriè dicti, (quo & referri solet in divinis
classibus Israël) dominium in populum hunc[54] adhuc habuerant Israëlitæ,
quamvis non è tribu Judah legitimi; sed sacerdotes illegitima possessione
ordinem Dei invertentes; (cum ad Benignitatis metrum pertinerent | non
p. 20 verò Regni.) Nunc finitâ Ani- || -marum Israëliticarum[55] (ad minimum nobi-
lissimarum) è corticibus productione, dominium in populum hunc[56] trade-
batur Corticibus, non ut antehac per intervalla; sed in perpetuam subjec-
tionem. Et quidem Cortici Edom, qui refertur ad judicia durissima: quod ut
melius innotescat[57] (Excerpta quædam è Sohar apponimus[58] de Esavo vid.
Excerpt.[59] Cent. 1. Loc. 13–20). Hic cortex dominium nunc | exercebat, non
tantum per Herodem, ita ut impleretur Isaaci vaticinium. Gen. 27.40. Sed &
per Romanos, qui juxta antiquissimam vestræ Gentis, ut nosti, traditionem
ab Idumæis descendunt.

Cabb. Cat. *Procul dubio notum tibi est ex Josepho Gorionide aliisque anti-*
quis libris, quod Tzepho filius Eliphæ, filii Esavi, cum Josepho et[60] *fratribus* |
ejus contenderit super sepultura Jacobi, quod ille se ex primogenitura natum
diceret; ubi tamen Tzepho cum suis bello victus inque Ægyptum deductus &
in carcere detentus fuerit omnibus diebus Josephi: mortuo autem Josepho ex
Ægypto fugerit, veneritque in Campaniam, ubi regnaverit super provinciam
Kitheorum ubi Roma: quodque hîc tandem regnaverit super Italiam, primus-

---

52 "§. 18. In omni itaque generationum sive ætatum periodo certæ quædam animæ bonæ
exeunt è malo illo supradicto, veniuntque in mundum hunc per præceptum illud
Gen. 1. v. 28. de prolificatione & multiplicatione, quod Sanctus ille Benedictus in hunc
finem nobis dedit: quod probè notandum. Prout igitur se habet generatio sive ætas illa,
sic eandem quoque proportionem observant animæ illæ, quæ prodeunt è corticibus:
quandoque nimirum animæ de membro capitis; quandoque alia, quæ ad pedes pertinent, exeunt. Eadem autem harum est ratio, quæ membrorum Gloriæ cohabitantis,
quæ nempe illo tempore intra cortices hærent: ejusdem enim generis sunt animæ illæ,
quæ seliguntur [...] atque illo tempore exinde prodeunt. Prout tandem deprehendi-
mus in postrema hac generatione, in qua nos vivimus, quod gloria cohabitans pedibus
nunc hic sistatur: unde omnes animæ, quæ nunc prodeunt de notione pedum Adami
protoplastæ sunt: quibus omnibus tandem ad finem usque secretis, deinde Meschiach
veniet. [...] §. 20. Ecce autem ultima illa generatione Regis Meschiach omnia erunt
selecta; nihilque erit residuum, quod secernatur de statura Adami protoplastæ, præter calcaneos ejus: quibus etiam selectis, Meschiach veniet, ut notum est. Vox א״ד״ם
etenim literis suis, involvit initiales nominum Adami, Davidis & Meschiach. Et huc
quoque pertinet, quod dicit scriptura Psal. 89. v. 52. Quod probris affecerunt calcaneos Messiæ tui. Ubi intelliguntur animæ generationis ultimæ. Hinc quoque sapientes
nostri dicunt: Cum perventum erit ad calcaneos Meschiach, protervia multiplicabi-
tur. Nam quia membra pedum admodum sunt materialia atque opaca; hinc animæ

SECTION III   157

20 [asserting that] that the souls of the Jewish people came forth from the
state of the Shells according to the measure of the Adamite Body ‖‖‖, as long as   fol. 5ᵛ
the proportion of that body properly so-called was not yet finished (by which
it is usually referred to in the divine classes of Israel), the Israelites still had
dominion over this people of yours, although not by legitimate rulers from
the tribe of Judah but by priests who were thus inverting the order of God
5 by their illegitimate possession. (For truly! Kingdoms | do not pertain to the
measure of *Kindness*!) Then after the production of the souls of the Israelites
(at least ‖ of the most noble) from the Shells, dominion over your people was   p. 20
handed over to the Shells, not periodically as previously, but in perpetual
subjection. And indeed, to the Shell Edom are assigned the harshest judg-
ments. (See, some Extracts from the Zohar about Esavus at Cent I Loc. 13–20).
10 This Shell was now exercising | dominion, not only through Herod, such that
the prophecy of Isaac (Gen 27.40) was fulfilled, but also through the Romans
who, as you know, according to the most ancient traditions of your people
descended from the Idumeans.

Kabbalist Catecumen Doubtless you know from Josippon and other ancient texts that Tzepho son of Elipha, son of Esavus contended with Joseph
15 and his brothers | over the tomb of Jacob, because he claimed to have the
right of primogeniture. Tzepho, however, was defeated in battle with all his
troops and taken to Egypt and was held in prison there all the days of Joseph.
When Joseph died, Tzepho fled from Egypt and went to Campania where he
ruled over the province of the Citthaei where Rome is located[61]. Here in time

---

abinde dependentes magis quoque sunt materiæ addictæ: unde augebitur protervia.
Hinc quoque dixerunt Magistri nostri: Non veniet filius David, donec plene exiverint
omnes animæ, quæ fuerunt in corpore [*nimirum protoplastæ*] quod probe notandum."
("De Revolutionibus animarum", op. cit., pp. 250–251). The text in square brackets is
Knorr's addition.

53 Word absent from the BSB. Probably due to printer's oversight.
54 Added above the line: vestrum
55 BSB: Israëlitarum
56 Correction above the line: hunc replaced by vestrum
57 Deletion: quod ut melius innotescat
58 Deleted word.
59 Deleted word.
60 BSB: &
61 The Scriptural text is Gen 36.11. Most of the material in the paragraph is taken from *Sefer Yosipon* Bk 1, ch. 2. Josephus Gorionides (or Josippon) is a tenth-century South Italian Hebrew text purporting to be by Josephus, subsequently expanded from Judah Leon ben Moses Musconi. *Sefer Yosipon* was first printed in Mantua in 1476 and has a printing by Sebastian Münster in Basel in 1541 and a Modern Hebrew edition by David Flusser (Jerusalem: Mossad Bialik, 1981). See also: Hayim Hominer, *Sepher Josippon of*

que fuerit, qui regnaverit | super Romam, templumque ibi primum construxe- 20
p. 21 *rit & maximum quod Romæ est. Et hæc quidem potissima est* ‖ [62]*ratio, quare Romani adhuc â Nostratibus*[63] *vocentur Edomitæ. Velim tamen ut etiam ex antiquitatibus Gentilium aliquid hîc haberemus adminiculi.*

Christianus. Non video quare in hac traditione plus lateat absurditatis, quam in pluribus hujuscemodi aliis, sive de Noacho, sive de Chamo, sive de Kittim ab | aliis proditis, qui pariter in Italiam venisse ibique regnasse dicun- 25
tur. Nec obstat, quod in Antiquitatibus Gentilium, nullum de hisce occurrere dicatur vestigium: notissimum enim est, quod antiquiora hæc secula fabulis plerumque fuerint occultata. Imò quamvis etiam narratio illa de Tzephone non admittatur, nihil tamen absurdi esset, si Idumæi colonias in Italiam usque duxisse dicerentur: | quamvis illius vix occurrant vestigia in Anti- 30
quitate Gentilium, non tamen propterea est rejicienda;[64] quia è Palæstina omnium quasi Maris Mediterranei accolarum origo est petenda; & Idumæi, quibus tam Mediterraneum patebat (in cujus vicinia urbs ipsorum Raphia) quam Erythreum (ab illis denominatum) artis nauticæ non censendi sunt fuisse imperiti; videatur 1. Reg. 9, 26. Unde facilè fieri | potuit, ut non minus 35
ab illis, quàm â Phœnicibus variæ ortum traxerint coloniæ. Adde quod & in Italia Rutulorum nomen sit notissimum, quod haud alienum est â Nomine Edom; et[65] Danaë & Acrisius, quibus illorum adscribitur origo, â judicio denominentur, quod est antiquissimum Nominis Edom Synonymon. Sic Tur-
p. 22 nus ille Ruffus[66], cui Vestrates adscribunt vastationem Templi, ejus- ‖ -dem[67] nominis est cum Turno Rutulorum | Rege, de quo Virgilius Æneid. 7. sqq.[68] 40

Yoseph Bar Gorion Hacohen, 4th ed. (Jerusalem 1967) and Saskia Dönitz, *Überleiferung und Rezeption des Sefer Yosippon* (Tübingen: Mohr Siebeck, 2013). There is also an Italian edition by Ariel Toaff, *Cronaca Ebraica del Sefer Yosephon*, (Rome: Barulli, 1969).

62 A red pencil square bracket inserted into the text ([ratio,) refers to an annotation in the left margin: 4.B./20.
63 BSB: nostratitibus (Printer's error)
64 Deletion: quamvis illius vix occurrant vestigia in Antiquitate Gentilium, non tamen propterea est rejicienda
65 BSB: &
66 Added in the left margin: seu Edomita
67 A red pencil square bracket inserted into the text (ejus[dem,) refers to an annotation in the left margin: 6.B./21.
68 "Sola domum et tantas seruabat filia sedes / iam matura uiro, iam plenis nubilis annis. / Multi illam magno e / Latio totaque petebant / Ausonia. Petit ante alios pulcherrimus omnis / Turnus, auis atauisque potens, quem regia coniunx / adiungi generum miro properabat amore. / Sed uariis portenta deum terroribus obstant. / [...] Continuo uates: 'Externum cernimus,' inquit, / 'aduentare uirum et partis petere agmen easdem / partibus ex isdem et summa dominarier arce.'" (VIRGIL, *Æneid*, 7, 52–70).

SECTION III 159

20 he ruled over Italy and was the first to rule over | the Romans. He built the first temple there which is the biggest in Rome. ‖ This is the principal reason why the Romans are still called Edomites by our people. I would like none the less to have some support here from Gentile antiquities too.

p. 21

Christian I do not see why this tradition should be considered any less plausible than several of this type related by others, whether about Noah
25 or Ham or the Kittim | who equally are said to have travelled to Italy and ruled there.[69] Nor is it an objection that no trace of this is reported in the antiquities of the Gentiles; for it is notorious that [the events of] those more ancient ages have frequently been obscured by legends. Even if this account of Tzepho is rejected, it is in no way absurd that the Idumeans are reported
30 to have planted colonies as far away as in Italy. |[70] For the origin of [all] the inhabitants of the [areas around] the Mediterranean is to be sought in Palestine. Moreover, the Idumeans—to whom the Mediterranean (close to their city Raphia) was as open as the Erythrean Sea (which was named for them[71])—are reckoned to have been skilled sailors. (See 1 Kgs 9.26[72].) | So
35 several colonies could have just as easily have been founded by them as by the Phoenicians. [Two additional points are:] that in Italy the name of the Rutuli is very well reknowned and is related to the name Edom; and that: both Danae and Acrisius from whom [the Rutuli] traced their origin are named for judgement, which is a very ancient synonym of the name Edom. Thus Turnus, that *red-haired man* or Edomite whom your people blame for the destruction of the Temple[73], has the same name as ‖ Turnus, king of the
40 Rutuli, | in Virgil, Aeneid 7 *seq*. Furthermore, Isaiah says the final liberation

p. 22

---

69 Annius da Viterbo (Giovanni Nanni, 1432–1502) forged texts precisely to describe the arrival of an Aramaic speaking Noah (also known as Janus) in Italy. The work was highly influential and contributed to Egidio da Viterbo's notions of an occult Aramaean tradition. See Wilkinson, *Orientalism*, op. cit., pp. 32–36.
70 There is a deletion here in the manuscript: "Although one finds few traces of the Idumaeans amongst the antiquities of the Gentiles, the theory should not however be rejected for that reason".
71 The Hebrew 'dm (Edom) and Greek *eruthros* both mean "red".
72 This is an error for verse 27.
73 Ta'anit 29a discussing disaster remembered on the 9th of Ab says: "The Mishnah taught that on the Ninth of Av the city of Jerusalem was ploughed. It is taught in a *baraita*: when the wicked Turnus Rufus (*twrnwś rwpwś*) ploughed the Sanctuary, a decree was issued against Rabban Gamliel for execution". In Yerushalmi he is just called Rufus. The reference is evidently to the aftermath of the Bar Kokhba Revolt in 135 AD when Quintus Tineius Rufus (c. 90–131 AD. Cos. Suf. 127 AD) was consular legate of Judaea from 130–133. He was also held responsible for the death of Rabbi Akiva.

& Jesaias liberationem ultimam fore dicit devictis Edomitis c. 63, 1. & Angelus seu Genius Romanorum Apoc. 12, 3 vocatur rufus Draco[74], quasi Edomiticus: et[75] nomen Roma valde est affine australi Idumæorum Regioni Daroma; quæ toties etiam occurrit apud Jonathanem in Obadiam v.9.19.20. Conferatur Targum Jonathanis & Hierosolym. in Num. 24, 24 & inter | Excerpta Centuriæ 1. Locus 21 & 86. |||.

Cabb. Cat. *Porrò nosti, â Doctoribus nostris curiosam institui solere seculorum collationem, ex illa nempe de Revolutionibus hypothesi, quod nihil sub sole novum, & qui in certa quadam periodo fatali clari fuerunt, jam olim quoque in theatro hoc mundano apparuisse credantur. Unde quæro, ad quam nam inter Antiquos personam | referri queat, Herodes iste?*

Christianus. In tui, tuorumque gratiam, ut dici haud queat, aliquid â me prætermissum esse, quod ad palatum vestrum sit; suggererem ultimum illum ê Regibus Edom, Gen. 36, 39. cui nomen Hadar; istius si Herodes dicatur Revolutio fuisse[76], nihil[77] absurdi: habent enim easdem radicales, quamvis transpositas: ut Kain et[78] Keni; Laban & | Nabal etc. Excerpt. Cent. 1. Loc. 59. Sic Herodes beneficum sese exhi- ||-buit[79] per structuram templi; juxta nomen מהיטבאל[80]; tyrannus fuit, juxta[81] nomen מטרד quod â benefaciendo descendit[82]. & dives juxta nomen מי זהב id est, Aquæ Auri. â טרד molestavit, afflixit, ursit, pressit.[83] Ad Regni gradum se applicuit, sicut ille &c.

Cabb. Cat. *Notum tibi etiam est ad sensus mysticos nos pronos esse; | Unde ad Hepar, Esavum; ad Cor Jacobum referunt Doctores nostri in Sohar (Excerptorum Cent. 1. Loc. 14 & 19). Quomodo specimen præberes commentatiunculæ cujusdam similis?*

Christianus. Eodem modo Herodem mysticè referrem ad regnum Hepatis seu ventris infimi, sive ad pravam concupiscentiam, quæ est vita brutalis in

---

74 Correction: a sign is placed above the line which indicates that the terms should be inverted. BSB: Draco rufus
75 BSB: &
76 Correction: a sign is placed above the line which indicates that the terms should be inverted. BSB: fuisse Revolutio
77 Added in the right margin: vobis erit
78 BSB: &
79 A red pencil square bracket inserted into the text (exhi[buit,) refers to an annotation in the right margin: 7.B./23.
80 Added in the right margin: quod a benefaciendo descendit:
81 BSB: juxtu (Printer's error)
82 Correction in the right margin: quod ê benefaciendo descendit replaced by quod derivatur â radice טרד molestavit, afflixit, ursit, pressit.
83 Deletion: quod derivatur â radice טרד molestavit, afflixit, ursit, pressit.
84 Targum Jonathan is also known as the Jerusalem Targum.

will come when the Edomites are defeated (63.1); also the Angel or Genius of the Romans (Rev 12.3) is called the Red Dragon as if it was Edomite, and the name *Roma* is very close to [that of] the Southern Idumean region of Daroma [often translated "South"] which occurs so many times in Targum Jonathan to Obed 9, 19, 20.[84] Cf. Targum Jonathan and the Jerusalem Targum on Num 24.24 and | Excerpts Cent. I Loc. 21 & 86. ‖

fol. 6ʳ

Kabbalist Catechumen Now progressing further, you know our teachers used carefully to draw up parallel ages on the basis of the Hypothesis of Revolutions—because there is "nothing new under the sun" [Eccl 1.9] and because those who in a certain fated period were once famous are now believed to have appeared repeatedly in the theatre of this world. For that reason I ask: to which personage amongst the ancients | can this Herod be linked?

Christian To please you and your people and so that it may not be said that I have omitted anything which interested you, I would suggest: the last king of Edom (Gen 36.39[85]), who was called Hadar. It will appear quite plausible to you if I say Herod was his *Reincarnation*[86]. For [their names] have the same letters (though transposed), like Kain and Keni [or] Laban | and Nabal. Excerpts Cent. I Loc. 59. Thus Herod showed himself to be a boon by building the ‖ Temple according to the name *mhyṭbʾl* which comes from "providing a benefit"; he was a tyrant according to the name *mṭrd* which comes from the root *ṭrd* "to molest, afflict, burn or crush". And also rich, according to the name *my zhb* which is "waters of gold"[87]. He attached himself to the degree of *Kingdom* just as [Hadar] did.

p. 23

Kabbalist Catechumen You know that we incline | to mystic meanings. That is why our teachers refer to Hepar, Esavus and the Heart of Jacob in *Zohar* (Excerpts Cent. I Loc. 14, 19). What short comment like these do you have to offer?

Christian In the same way, I would relate Herod mystically to the Kingdom of Hepar, or of the lower stomach, or to evil desire, which is the animal

---

85 "[…] and his [Hadar's] wife's name was Mehetabel, the daughter of Matred, the daughter of Mezahab".

86 John Locke used the word "Revolution" for *reincarnation* in his discussions of this doctrine. He had a copy of *Two hundred queries moderately proposed concerning the doctrine of the revolution of humane souls* (London: Robert Kettelwell, 1684) in his library which though published anonymously sets out the views of Francis Mercury van Helmont. See Victor Nuovo, *Christianity, Antiquity and Enlightenment: Interpretations of Locke* (Dortrecht: Springer, 2011), pp. 26–27.

87 The three names from the verse in Genesis 36.39 just cited are taken as suggestive of Hadar's character.

homine naturaliter | prædominans. Sicut autem sub Herode natus est Christus (anno nempe regni ejus 35: Ubi dehinc anno 37 venerunt Magi, post quorum adventum, perpetrato prius infanticidio, mortuus est Herodes:) ita sub regno Animæ infimæ, prædominante appetitu sensitivo, ejusque impetu concupiscibili nascitur vita in homine Divina, hujus persecutionibus & tentationibus obnoxia: Unde rectissimè, hîc in | anima quam primum moritur tyrannus. Imò sensu anagogico etiam dici posset per Herodem adumbrari hominem illum peccati 2. Thess. 2, 3.4. in suis initiis. Inclaruit enim re- ‖ -gnum[88] Herodianum per beneficia in templum: deinde per inspectionem in templum; tandemque absorptum est mero gentilismo. Paria autem sunt fata Ecclesiæ circa adventum Christi primum & secundum.

[89]Zacharias זכריא

Cabb. Cat. *Jam ad profundiora te accingas studii Cabbalistici specimina: ad quem nam gradum in Divinis Numerationibus referres Zachariam?*

Christianus. Si tu tam pronus eris ad amplectendam[90] veritatem Christianismi, | quam ego studiosus ero, ut satisfaciam pruritui aurium tuarum in illis (quas tu[91] putas esse[92],) ingenii vestri deliciis & acuminibus, uterque scopum attinget. Nomen ergo hoc derivatum â Recordatione, referrem ad gradum Jesod, juxta tradita Cabbalistarum vestrorum de quibus Apparat. in Libr. Sohar P. I, pp. 308, 309[93]. Nam quia sub isto statu Ecclesiæ vestræ

---

88   A red pencil square bracket inserted into the text (reg[num,) refers to an annotation in the right margin: 8.B./24.
89   Deletion: Annotatio 2
90   Correction above the line: amplectendam replaced by illustrandam
91   Added above the line: tales
92   Correction: a sign is placed above the line which indicates that the terms should be inverted. BSB: esse putas
93   "Apparatus in Librum Sohar" is the general title that appears at the beginning of the first volume of the *Kabbala denudata* (1677). The Christian here refers to the "Loci communes kabbalistici", op. cit.; "זכירה *Recordatio*. Omnes interpretes in eo consentiunt, quod recordatio sit in Jesod. Iste enim est Referendarius, qui in supernis omnia revocat in memoriam in loco Vitæ. Unde tempore Novi Anni precamur: *Memento nostri in vita.* [...] Nam זכירה habet etiam significationem קטורת suffiendi, vel potius connectendi, prout dicitur Levit. 6, 15. *Suffimentum vel connexionem Domino.* Et huc tendit David, dum inquit Ps. 38, 1. *Canticum David ad commemorandum,* id est, ad connexionem & colligationem τοῦ Malchuth cum reliquis Sephiris per Jesod. Forté tamen vox זכירה habet significationem masculinitatis, quia per naturam masculinam, quæ est Jesod, fit unio omnium Sephirarum; Porrò in Sohar Sect. Vajeze dicitur: sicut datur זכירה ex parte masculi in Sanctitate; ita est זכירה recordatio in malum ex parte Corticum in sinistra, sicut scriptum est Psal. 78, 39. *Et recordatus est, quod caro sunt.* Et similia plura.

SECTION III   163

20 life naturally | predominating in man. For just as Christ was born under Herod (in the 35th year of his reign; the Magi came later in his 37th year; and, after their arrival, having first massacred the infants, Herod died[94]), so the divine life was born in [a] man, liable to [Hepar's] persecutions and temptations, under the reign of the lower soul with its predominantly sensual appetite and the impulses of its desire. So it is most appropriate [in the nar-
25 rative] that the tyrant [Herod] died as soon as possible |. But in the analogical sense it could even be said that through Herod was foreshadowed || the Man   p. 24
of Sin (2 Thess 2.3, 4) in his beginnings[95]. For the rule of Herod was famous for his gifts for the Temple, then for his observance with respect to the Temple[96]. Finally it was absorbed by pure paganism. The same [fate] befalls the Church around the First—and Second—Coming of Christ.

30   *Zacharias*[97] *zkry'*

Kabbalist Catechumen Now stir yourself for some more profound examples of kabbalistic scholarship! To which of the divine numerations do you attach Zachariah?
35 **Christian** If you are going to be as eager to see Christian truth | illuminated as I am interested in satisfying your itching ears with the delights and subtleties (as you consider them) of your teachers, we shall both be satisfied. This name [Zachariah], which is derived from "Memory", I would relate to the degree *Yesod* [*Foundation*], according to the traditions of your Kabbalists (about which, see *Apparatus* in Lib. Zohar, Part 1, pp. 308, 309). For

---

Pardes Rimm. Tr. 23, c. 7. Vid. Sohar Sect. Jethro 41. & 42. Item Vajakhel 88, c. 350." ("Loci communes kabbalistici", op. cit., pp. 308–309).

94 Chronological data for this period is set out in more detail in *Harmonia Evangeliorum*. This two year gap is specified on pp. 10–11 citing Epiphanius.

95 By appealing to the analogical sense of Scripture Knorr evokes here the standard Medieval distinction of four senses, based itself upon patristic practice after Origen: the literal and the spiritual sense, the latter comprising the allegorical, the moral and the analogical, though the precise terms often vary. Augustine of Dacia O.P. (†1282) famously explained the four senses as *Littera gesta docet, quid credas allegorica: Moralis quid agas, quo tendes analogia*. The fundamental study is Henri de Lubac, *Exégèse médievale: Les quatre sens de l'Écriture*, 3 vols (Paris: Aubier, 1959). Jewish scholars similarly distinguished four senses: *Peshat, Remez, Drash* and *Sod* (or *PaRDeS*).

96 The phrase *per inspectionem in templum* is difficult to give a relevant meaning to here. We take it to be a Latin calque upon the Greek *epopteia*: the verb *epopteuō* being used of "observing laws".

97 The Latin spelling is used. The Syriac transcription used above appears to have been forgotten.

nulla fiebat illuminatio â gradu hoc | fundamenti, multò minus â Gradibus 40
Luminum superiorum: hinc etiam Gradus Regni, qui per se nullum habere
dicitur lumen proprium ut Luna, parum Lucis communicare poterat. Unde
si quid mystici in hoc textu observare vis, Zacharias (qui ad Fundamentum) & Elischeba (quæ ad Regnum referenda erit juxta p. 116 sq. Apparat.

p. 25 sup. cit.[98]) prole caruisse dicuntur. Cum autem (jam aures | arrige!) ad- ‖ 45
fol. 6ᵛ -veniente[99] in carnem Messia illuminatio Fundamenti nunc aperienda ‖‖
esset, mediante Zacharia, istud fiebat. Ubi simul mysticè nobis insinuatur
per nomen, statum, & opera Zachariæ, genuinum illud medium, quo Deus
permoveri queat, ut nostri recordetur: si nempe & in nobis frequens sit ipsius
memoria; si illius simus sacerdotes, & suffitu precum debitè illum colamus.
Hebr. 11, 39.40, | pateat, veteres sine nobis consummatos non fuisse.[100] 5

Cabb. Cat. *Si autem inter impios revolutionem antehac invenisti, quid si &*
inter pios periculum nunc faceres? Quoniam ex ipsa quoque Epistola vestra ad
Hebr. 11, 39.40 pateat[101], *veteres sine vobis*[102] *consummatos non fuisse.*

Christianus. Tu fortè facilè hîc admitteres, si assererem hunc Zachariam 10
fuisse revolutionem ipsius Aharonis; (fortè post[103] revolutiones in utroque
Zacharia, 2. Par. 24, 20[104]; Zach. 1, 1[105] vid. Apparat. Tom. II, P. III. Tract.
II. p. 405.406[106]) & uxorem Zachariæ revolutionem fuisse Uxoris Aharonis,
quæ etiam appellata fuit אלישבע Ex. 6,23. & juxta LXX. Ἐλισαβὲθ corruptè; ut
nostra | in Græco, rectè in Syriaco textu:[107] Porrò Nomen Abia ad Chochmah 15
pertinet; vid. Lexicon Cabbal. p. 7 & 377[108]. Status Sacerdotis ad Chesed, ibid.

---

98   "אלישבע In Sohar Sect. שמיני hoc nomen refertur ad *Malchuth* quia hæc influxum assu-
      git è septem gradibus superioribus" ("Loci communes kabbalistici", op. cit., p. 116).
99   A red pencil square bracket inserted into the text (reg[num,) refers to an annotation
      in the right margin: 9.B./25.
100   Deletion: Hebr. 11, 39.40, pateat veteres sine nobis consummatos non fuisse. The sen-
      tence was moved and attributed to the Cabbalist.
101   Correction: pateat replaced by patet
102   Correction: vobis replaced by nobis
103   Deletion: post (repetition)
104   Zacharia, the son of the priest Jehoiada.
105   Zacharia, the son of Berechiah.
106   "Postea autem revolutus est in Aharon adjecto Aleph nomini priori: atque necdum
      restitutus est: quoniam potius mortem sustinere debuisset, quam obedire plebi, fabri-
      cam vituli pro Idololatria exposcenti: quod tamen intermittebat, quoniam videbit
      quod Chur jugulatus coram ipso jaceret" ("De Revolutionibus animarum", op. cit.,
      pp. 405–406).

SECTION III

40 in that state | there was no illumination of your Church from this degree of *Foundation*, much less from the degrees of the higher lights. Even the degree *Kingdom* (which is said to have no light of its own, like the moon) was only able to illuminate [your Church] a little. If you wish to discover a secret [meaning] in this text, [notice] that Zachariah (who [is related] to *Foundation*) and Elischeba (who has to be related to *Kingdom* according to [*Loci communes kabbalistici*] p. 116 *seq. Apparat sup. cit.*) are said to lack off-

45 spring. But when (now prick up | your ears!) ‖ Messiah came in the flesh, the illumination of *Foundation* had to be manifested ⦀, and that happened by the mediation of Zachariah. There is thus mystically hinted to us (by the name, status and work of Zachariah together) the genuine medium by which God is able to be moved, when he remembers our [prayers], if we remember him truly and frequently and if we are his priests and entreat him duly with the incense of prayer.

p. 25
fol. 6ᵛ

Kabbalist Catechumen Up to now you have found Reincarnations only amongst the wicked. What if you now hazard [looking] also amongst the

5 pious! For it is clear from your Epistle to the Hebrews (11.39, 40) | that the ancients have not been made perfect without us.[109]

10 **Christian** I'm sure you will happily agree if I assert here that Zachariah was the reincarnation of Aaron himself (perhaps the reincarnations into the other two Zachariahs—2 Chron 24.20; Zech 1.1; see *Apparatus*, Tom. II, Part. 3, Tract. 2, p. 405, p. 406) and that the wife of Zachariah was the reincarnation of Aaron's wife. She was also called *'lyšb'* in [the Hebrew of] Ex 6.23

15 but, corruptly, '*Elisabeth*' in the Septuagint there, as in our | Greek [New Testament] where the Syriac text [*Elischeba*] is correct. [Aaron's wife] was of the tribe of Judah like this [New Testament Elischeba] (Lk 1.36). Moreover the name "Abiah" [the name of Zachariah's priestly course] has to do with *Wisdom* (*Lex. Cabb.*, pp. 7, 377). The status of priest [pertains] to *Chesed* (ibid.

---

107 Added in the left margin: & è tribu Jehudah erat, ut hæc; Luc. 1, 36.
108 Cf. "Loci communes kabbalistici", op. cit.: Knorr splits the name Abia into two: אב (to which is devoted page 7 of the *Loci*) and יה to which are devoted pages 377 sq.
109 The doctrine of the Revolution of Souls is boldly used to give new meaning to these verses.

p. 471.[110] genus Aharonis ad Hod; vid. Apparat. in Libr. Sohar P.II, p. 10[111]; P.IV, p. 248[112]. quibus denotari dicerem, Lumi- || -na[113] nunc â summis initiis per hos gradus in fundamentum & Regnum descensura. Nonne putas hæc omnia ex certa quadam ratione | nunc concurrere; statuique & characteri temporum, in quem nos adventum Messiæ referimus, egregiè convenire?

V. 6. *Justi* &c. צדיקין

Cabb. Cat. *Hæc est prima descriptio hominum justorum in vestris scriptis, quæ â nostra descriptione non variat: quare ergò vos aliam | urgetis justitiam quàm hanc realem?*

Christianus. Descriptio vestra & nostra non aliter variant, quam ratione exercitii moralis. Sicut enim, si juxta extremos perfectionis apices proponatur doctrina vestra Ethica, Justitia vobis nihil est aliud, quam continuata repetitio actuum legaliter bonorum, exercitorum prævia meditatione debita, | pro acquirendo influxu divino, ad singulos actus necessariò: ita nos pro nuda meditatione Fidem præreqvirimus; id est, ex verâ fide factam invocationem ad Patrem cœlestem, ut propter Jesum[114], quem Messiam credimus, auxilium Spiritus S. ad hunc actum nobis largiatur. Et talium actuum continuatio, Justitiæ similiter nomen habet, quamvis[115] actum fidei necessariò hîc præreqvisitum, | justitia hæc deinde vocetur Justitia fidei; Rom. 1, 17; c. 3, 22. Natura enim sibi relicta, citra impetratum || per[116] fidem auxiliorum gratiæ concursum ad istam bonitatis moralis excellentiam ascendere neqvit;

---

110 "כהן גדול: *Sacerdos magnus*. Pertinet ad Chesed, quia hæc maxima est ex omnibus diebus principii, istorumque Caput. Sacerdotes enim referuntur ad Chesed, juxta Deut. 33, 8. Et in R. Meh. dicit R. Schimeon ben Jochai, quod Michaël sit Sacerdos vulgaris: cum autem ministrat ut caput omnium circumstantium, vocetur Sacerdos magnus. Pardes Tract. 23, c. 11." ("Loci communes kabbalistici", op. cit., p. 471).

111 "Sphirah octava. Gloria seu Decus: quæ est femur sinistrum & pes sinister Brevi facie præditi: Eique tribuitur nomen Ehjeh valori 151. Cognomina & subordinata ejus sunt. 1. Elohim Zebaoth. 2. Aaron & ramus Aaron. 3. Disciplina domini. 4. Columna sinistra, Booz. 5. Serpens antiquus. 6. Molæ molentes. 7. Filii Regis. 8. Cherub. 9. Conclave Gazith. 10. Seraphin. &c. Ambæ dicuntur Prophetæ veri." (*Kabbala denudata, I*, Pars II, "Tabula secunda Clavis sublimioris Kabbalæ, de ordine divinorum Nominum pro resolutione difficiliorum Ænigmatum Libri Sohar", pp. 7–13, p. 10).

112 The reference is to "Apparatus in Librum Sohar Pars Quarta, quæ continet explicationem arborum seu tabularum quinque cabbalisticarum generalium. Cum Repræsentatione omnium & summorum totius Cabbalæ Capitum brevissima & perspicua, juxta diversas hypotheses", *Kabbala denudata, I*, Pars IV, pp. 195–255. Page 248 offers a table

SECTION III

p. 471) and the family of Aaron to *Hod* (*Apparatus in Lib. Zohar*, Part. 2, p. 10; Part. 4, p. 248). By this I would say is denoted the ‖ illumination now about to descend from the highest origins, through these degrees, into *Foundation* and *Kingdom*. Do you not think that all these things so certainly and logically | now converge and come together remarkably in the state and characteristics of the times in which we place the coming of Messiah?

p. 26

Verse 6
Righteous ... çdyqyn

Kabbalist Catechumen This is the first mention of righteous people in your Scriptures and it is not different from our notion. So why do you promote a righteousness | other than this, the real one?

Christian The only difference between your notion and ours lies in the question of moral practice. Your ethical teaching aims at the highest peaks of perfection. Righteousness[117] for you is nothing else than continual repetition of good works according to the Law with the antecedent meditation upon practice required | for acquiring the divine influx necessary for every single act. But we require Faith first before bare meditation—that is, an invocation of the Heavenly Father made from true faith, for on account of Jesus (whom we believe [to be] Messiah) the help of the Holy Spirit is vouchsafed to us in our action. Continuation in such actions is similarly called "righteousness", even though on account of the preceding act of faith necessary | here, this righteousness is then called the Righteousness of Faith (Rm 1.17; 3.22). For Nature left to itself, without ‖ the help of Grace through Faith, is not able to ascend to the excellence of moral goodness. That is why Abra-

p. 27

---

of the equivalences that exist between the sefirot, the divine names, and some biblical figures. Line 9 reads as follows: "9. Hod. הוה י" Aharon".

113   A red pencil square bracket inserted into the text (Lumi[na,) refers to an annotation in the left margin: 10.B./26.
114   BSB: JESUM
115   Added above the line: ob
116   A red pencil square bracket inserted into the text ([per fidem) refers to an annotation in the left margin: 11.B./27.
117   There are problems of translation here caused by the practice of the English Renaissance tradition of bible translation, which speaks of "righteousness", "good works" and of "justification". There terms have entered common theological discourse, but they conceal many of the associations of the Latin *justitia* and the Hebrew *zdkh*. One hopes the above makes sense in the English idiom. The nature of "righteousness" and the question of how it was obtained were, of course, contentious Reformation issues.

Unde est[118] Abraham & Sarah; Iizchak & Rebecca, item Elkanah & Hannah, qui mysticè denotant Animam & corpus; eodemque modo etiam Zacharias & | Elisabeth steriles fuerunt, ad denotandam Exercitiorum moralium tam quod[119] animam, quàm quoad corpus, si sibi relicta sit natura, sterilitatem. Conf. Excerpt. Centur. 1. Locus 94.95.

V. 7. Sterilis. עקרתא

Cabb. Cat. *Verum & aliud hîc mihi latere videtur mysterium, | quod magis est Cabbalisticum.* |||

fol. 7ʳ

Christianus. Recte quidem, nam sterilitas hæc etiam denotat Luminum divinorum ê Regno, sive Ecclesia absentiam. (videantur tamen etiam de sterilitate Excerpta quædam è Libro Sohar Cent. 1. Loc. 20 & 21).

V.8. *Cum ipse Sacerdotio fungeretur.*
כד מכהן הוא

Cabb. Cat. *Ab aliis jam demonstratum est (1.) quod Zacharias non fuerit Sacerdos magnus, sed è viginti quatuor ordinibus, de quibus 1. Par. 24, 18 & quidem ordine octavo, ib.*[120]*, v. 10.* || [121](*2.) Quod non omnes quidem sacerdotum familiæ è captivitate Babylonica redierint, cum Esr. 2, 36.37. tantum quatuor enumerentur: Sed ê redeuntibus tamen 24. ordines iterum constituti sint, retentis priorum | nominibus: Unde Zacharias de ordine quidem Abija*[122]*, sed non de familia, quippe quæ reversa non erat. (3.) Quod ordines isti hebdomatatim servitia præstiterint, accedentes in Sabbathum, in quo duo serviebant ordines, & post Sabbathum abeuntes. 2 Reg. 11, 7; 2. Par. 23, 4. In tribus autem solennitatibus maximis servierint omnes. (4.) Quod nunc cum Zacharias serviret, nullum fuisse dicatur festum majus. | (5.) Quod tempus ministerii ejus, & conceptio Johannis accuratè nequeat definiri. Attamen adhuc superest mysterium aliquod.*

p. 28

---

118   Correction above the line: est replaced by &
119   BSB: quoad
120   BSB: 16 (Printer's error)
121   A red pencil square bracket inserted into the text ([(2.) Quod) refers to an annotation in the right margin: 12.B./28.
122   Added above the line: est
123   The author reverts to this spelling which he has just criticised.
124   Lightfoot, *Miscellanies and the Harmony of the Gospels*, op. cit., p. 151 on Lk 1.9 is likely

ham and Sarah, Isaac and Rebecca, and Elkana and Hannah, who [as pairs] mystically denote Soul and Body in the same way as Zacharias and | Elizabeth[123], were also childless. This was to indicate the sterility of good works with respect of both Soul and Body, if Nature is left to itself. Conf. Excerpt. Cent. I Loc. 94, 95.

Verse 7

Barren ... 'qrt'

Kabbalist Catechumen In fact, I think there is another hidden mystery | here which is even more kabbalistic. ⫼   fol. 7ʳ

Christian Indeed for this sterility also denotes the absence of the holy illumination from *Kingdom* or the Church. (Some passages on sterility from the Book Zohar can be found in Cent. I Loc. 20, 21.)

Verse 8

While he was exercising his priesthood kd mkhn hw'

Kabbalist Catechumen It has previously been shown by others[124] that:

(1) Zachariah was not the High Priest, but [an ordinary priest] from the twenty four orders (concerning which 1 Chron 24.18) and in fact from the eighth order (*Ib.*, verse 10).

(2) ‖ Not all the priestly families had returned from exile in Babylon, since in Ezr (2.36, 37) only four are enumerated, but from these returnees none the less the 24 orders were reconstituted, keeping | their previous names. So Zachariah is of the order of Abiah, but not of [Abiah's] family—which in reality had not come back [from exile].   p. 28

(3) These [priestly] orders provided weekly periods of service, each arriving for the Sabbath (on which two orders served) and leaving after the [next] Sabbath (2 Kgs 11.7; 2 Chron 23.4.) On the three most holy feasts all priests served.

(4) At the time when Zachariah was serving, no major feast had been announced. |

(5) The time of the ministry and the conception of John cannot be precisely fixed.

However in spite of this [clarification], an [instructive] secret teaching does remain.

---

the source here. Knorr evidently consulted this work continuously in writing the following pages, though did not always agree with Lightfoot's comments.

Christianus. Nimirum, (6) notabile admodum est, quod abeunte ordine Abia, sub quo Zacharias erat, successerit ordo יֵשׁוּעַ Jesu[125], 1. Par. 24, 11. Unde sine mysterio factum non est, quod Præcursor Jesu ex octavo esset ordine; numeri | scilicet decrescentis sub omni multiplicatione: ipse autem Dominus erigeret sacerdotium Jesu, noni ordinis, numeri scilicet sub omni multiplicatione perennantis. ||.

[126] **Cabb. Cat.** *Rectè quidem. Sed & hoc observa: quod loco allegato 1. Par. 24.11. in verbis*

לישוע התשיעי לשכניהו העשרי (Jesu[127] nona; Schechanjahu decima:)[128] | Nomen a[129] ordinis decimi (id est perfectissimi) sit שכניהו; quod per metathesin est שכי״נה & ו״.

Christianus. Hic procul dubio tu colligeres, quod ו״ & שכינה veram copulam demum habituri sint ordine decimo: mihi tamen sufficit, quod & in illo reperiatur expressio Nominis ישוע, quod tu probè velim notes, nec[130] alium expectes Messiam, quàm | hunc nostrum.

V. 9. *Tangebat eum:* מטיהי

Cabb. Cat. *Antiquitas hæc optimè â me explicabitur; quod nempe hîc intelligatur sortitio in templo fieri solita: quia sine sorte in tanto sacerdotum numero confusio non potuisset evitari. Ut autem sortitio hæc eò rectius intelligatur, audiamus | verba Mischnæ ê tract. Joma cap. 2. In principio quisquis altare*

---

125 BSB: JESU
126 A red pencil square bracket inserted into the text ([Cabb.) refers to an annotation in the right margin: 13.B./29.
127 BSB: JESU
128 Two crossed out lines, now unreadable.
129 Deleted.
130 Added in the right margin: ut antehac. Absent from the BSB. Probably due to printer's oversight.
131 The KJV has "Jeshua".
132 So: 8, 16 (1+6=7), 24 (2+4=6), 32 (3+2=5), 40 (4+0=4) etc.
133 So: 9, 18 (1+8=9), 27 (2+7=9), 36 (3+6=9) etc.
134 Notice the apostrophes in the Hebrew lemma. This is consistent practice here, probably intended to prevent pronunciation of divine name. It may indicate that Jewish readers sensitive to this matter were expected to read the manuscript.
135 The KJV has "Shecaniah".
136 The Latin translation of the Syriac text of Lk 1.9 as given above omits any reference to being chosen by lot, which is not found in the Peshitta (or the Old Syriac), though the Vulgate has it clearly. The meaning of the Syriac word given there is "it happened to

Christian Undoubtedly.

(6) It is striking that as the order of Abiah (to which Zachariah belonged) departed, the order *yšwʿ* or "of Jesu" followed (1 Chron 24.11[131]). It is also of mystical significance that the precursor of [the order of] Jesu was of the eighth order |—for it is well-known that [8] is a number which when the digits of the product of its [successive multiplication] [are added together], the sum gets smaller every time.[132] But the Lord himself raised up the priesthood of Jesus, the ninth order. For it is well-known that [the sum of the digits of] progressive multiplications [of 9] always remains constant [at 9][133]. ‖

Kabbalist Catechumen Absolutely! And notice that in the passage we cited (1 Chron 24.11[134]) "Jesu the ninth; Schechanjahu the tenth", |[135] the name of the tenth order (that is of the most perfect [10, 20, 30, 40 etc.]) is *šknyhw* [Schechanjahu] which by metathesis is *šknh* and *w* [Shekhinah and *w*].

Christian Doubtless you see that *šknh* and *w* [*w*=and] are finally going to effect a true copula with the tenth order. However it is sufficient for me that here too is found an expression of the name *yšwʿ*. I would like you to note this carefully and to expect no other Messiah than this one | of ours.

p. 29

Verse 9
It happened to him *mṭyhy*[136]

Kabbalistic Catechumen I had better explain this ancient practice. This is the lot which used to be cast in the Temple, for without such a lottery confusion among so many priests could hardly be avoided. The better to understand this lottery, we should consult | Mishnah Treatise Yoma [The Day of Atonement] chapter 2:

---

him that …". The Latin gloss here "*Tangebat eum*" ("It was touching him") may mean the same as this, but though perhaps literally correct, is hardly clear. Here it may indeed be relevant to observe that the Italian *toccare a qualcuno* means "to take one's turn", which is possibly how we should take *tangebat eum* here. However although *tango* does not usually seem to be used of lots, the word is used below here for a number falling upon the priest who wins the lot. Also the Syriac verb properly translated here "it happened to him that …" does occur in some contexts where it is used (though not apparently absolutely) of lots (Robert Payne Smith, *A Compendious Syriac Dictionary* (Oxford: Clarendon, 1976) s.v., p. 266b. Also Michael Sokoloff, Carl Brockelmann (Eds.), *A Syriac lexicon* (Winona Lake, Indiana: Eisenbrauns; Piscataway, N.J.: Gorgias Press, 2009), p. 745 (4) gives "to be one's turn"). One is thus perhaps tempted to think that von Rosenroth considered both the Syriac and Latin he gives here to entail if not the idea of a lottery, at least a notion of "taking one's turn".

expurgare vellet, expurgabat. Quando plures erant, currebant & ascendebant per gradus: Qui autem socium suum quatuor cubitis, cum ad medium pervenisset, ‖ anteverterat[137]*, obtinebat. Si duo pares erant, dicebat illis præfectus; sortimini digitis. Quid istud? Unum aut duos digitos attollebant, pollicem autem non attollebant, in | sanctuario.*

2. Accidit aliquando, dum duo pares currerent & ascenderent per gradus, ut alter alterum deturbaret, ita ut caderet, & pes ejus frangeretur. Cum videret Synedrium magnum ipsos in periculo versari, statuerunt, ut sortitò deinceps altare expurgarent. Quatuor sortes erant ibi, & hæc fuit sors prima.

3. Sors secunda erat: Quis mactaret, quis spargeret, quis cinerem ab altari interiori abduceret, quis lucernas purgaret, quis portaret membra ad gradus, caput & ‖‖ pedem & duos armos, spinam dorsi & pedem, pectus & guttur, duas costas et interiora, similam & frixa & vinum; Tredecim sacerdotes hac sorte fungebantur &c.

4. Tertia Sors erat: Novi ad suffitum veniant & sortes projiciant. Quarta: Novi & etiam Veteres, quis portaret membra â gradibus ad altare. Hæc Mi- ‖ -schnah[138]*. Modus | ergò sortiendi inter duos hic erat, ut qui sortibus præfectus erat â reliquis sacerdotibus cinctus uni horum pileum detraheret, datoque numero quodam ab eo inciperet numerare, cujus pileum detraxisset. Postquam ergò hi unum aut duos erexissent digitos, hos digitos ordine numerabat, donec ad finem numeri pervenisset: Et quem ultima tetigisset unitas in illum sors dicebatur cecidisse. Si plures ad sortem | accederent, hi in corona consistere jubebantur, digitosque elevare, ubi detracto alicujus pileo, præfectus numeros proponebat, alium ad mactandum sacrificium, alium ad respargendum sanguinem &c. Ubi sumpto numerandi initio ab eo, cui detracta fuerat tiara, qui hoc vel illo tangebatur numero officium obtinebat. Numerabat autem digitos, quia homines numerare non licebat. Et sani quidem unum extollebant | digitum, infirmi duos, cum talibus facile simul assurgeret digitus alter. Sed unus tantùm digitus numerabatur. Ad suffiendum autem nemo admittebatur, qui antea hoc munere jam functus esset: Quia benedictionem huic negotio cense-*

---

137 A red pencil square bracket inserted into the text ([anteverterat) refers to an annotation in the right margin: 14.B./30.

138 A red pencil square bracket inserted into the text (Mi[schnah) refers to an annotation in the left margin: 15.B./31.

139 The translation of *The Mishnah* by Herbert Danby has been used here with minor adjustments. There are obscurities in both the Mishnah and our author's exposition.

140 That is a number chosen at random but naturally greater than the number of competing priests.

SECTION III

"[(1)] Beforetime whosoever was minded to clear the altar [of ashes] did so. If they were many, they ran and ascended the [altar] steps: and he who had preceded his colleague by four ‖ cubits, reaching the middle [of the steps] secured the task. If two were equal the officer said to them 'You are to be selected by your fingers'. What did that mean? They raised one or two fingers, but they did not raise their thumb in the sanctuary". |

p. 30

"(2) Once it happened that two [priests] were equal and ran and mounted the [altar] steps [together] and one of them pushed his fellow so that he fell and his foot was broken. When the Great Sanhedrin saw [the priests] incurred danger, they ordained that they should clear the altar [of ashes] one after another, after being chosen by lot. There were four lots and this was the first lot".

"(3) The second lot was [to determine] who should slaughter, who should sprinkle [the blood], who should take away the ash from the inner altar, who would clean the lamps, who should take the parts [of the whole-offering]— the head ‖‖ and the foot and the two fore-arms, the backbone and the foot, the breast and the neck and the two flanks and the inwards up to the altar steps; also [who should take up] the fine flour and the baked [cakes] and the wine. Thus by this lot thirteen priests secured a task".

fol. 7ᵛ

"(4) There was a third lot. New priests came for the incensing and cast their lots. [There was] a fourth [lot amongst] the new people and the previous ones [to select] who would take up the members [of the whole offering] from the [altar] steps up to the altar". Thus far the Mishnah[139].

This was how the lot was cast | between the two [contenders]: the officer responsible for the lottery was surrounded by the rest of the priests. He then pulled off the mitre of one of them and, allocating some number or other to him, began to count from the priest whose mitre he had pulled off. After the priests raised one or two fingers, he counted the fingers in order until he came to the last number[140]. The priest, upon whom the last number fell, won the lottery. If several [priests, rather than just two] came to the lottery, | these were ordered to stand in a circle and raise their fingers. When he had pulled off someone's mitre, the officer in charge allocated numbers, one for slaughtering the sacrifice, one for sprinkling the blood etc. Once numbering had started from the priest whose mitre had been pulled off, the priest who was selected by this or that number obtained the [corresponding] duty. [The officer] counted fingers because it was not permitted to number men. The fit held up one finger | and the weak two, since with such the second finger easily rises at the same time [as the first]. But only one finger was counted. However no one was admitted to the duty of incensing who had already performed this duty before, because a blessing was thought to attach to this

p. 31

p. 32   bant ad- ‖ -esse[141], ita ut dives inde fieret talis, ex Deut. 33, 10.11. Ut omnes igitur hac benedictione alternis vicibus fruerentur, novi semper sorte deligebantur.

Christianus. Ergò hæc est illa consuetudo sacerdotii, juxta quam Zacharias ad munus hoc suffitum faciendi, quod ante nondum habuerat, perveniebat; ubi benedictionem impetrabat omnibus abhinc speratis divitiis meliorem.

Aromata בסמא

Cabb. Cat. Quæ de suffitu tradant Cabbalistæ nostri, recte jam expressa | sunt Appar. in Lib. Soh. Tom. 1.P.1.p. 675.[142]

Christianus. Adiri tamen etiam potest inter Excerpta Locus 22. et[143] 23. Cent. 1.

V.10
וכלה כנשא דעמא מצלא הוא
Et omnis congregatio populi orans erat.

Cabb. Cat. Ut meliùs isti ritus antiqui intelligantur, evolvi potest | inter Excerpta Centur. 1. Loc 24. ubi invenientur quædam è capp. ultimis Tractatus
p. 33   Talmudi- ‖ -ci[144] Tamid seu de sacrificio jugi; qui[145] erat cultus quotidianus, de quo hic sermo est.[146]

Christianus. Jam tu tuas profer observationes.[147](1.) Observo, quod per *congregationem populi* intelligantur hoc loco Sacerdotes, Levitæ, stationarii Iisraëlitæ, & fortè | devoti quidam singulares. (2.) quod per orationem, quam in hoc textu orasse dicitur populus, non intelligi possint preces illæ statæ & ordinariæ matutinæ, de quibus mentio fit in Mischn. 1, c. 5. Tamid: quia istæ jam peractæ fuerant ante ministerium suffitus, juxta Misch. 3. c. 6 ej, sed pro-

---

141 A red pencil square bracket inserted into the text (ad[esse) refers to an annotation in the left margin: 16.B./32.

142 "קטורת *Suffitus.* Fumus est Tiphereth, qui ascendit, ut uniat mundos Chochmah & Binah. Dum ergò ascendit, vocatur *Fumus*; cum autem pervenit intra Chochmam; illa notio vocatur קטורת quasi à קשר quod nectendi sensum infert, quia tunc unio & nexus reperitur intra gradus Chochmah & Binah: ubi tunc in luce duarum harum facierum Chochmah & Binah, omnia vident lucem, & uniuntur unione perfectissima. Raja Meh. In Tikkunim autem Malchuth vocatur קטורת gradus Tiphereth, quia illa huic annectitur. Pard. vid. Soh. Vajikra 2, 5.6. Vajakhel 98." ("Loci communes kabbalistici", op. cit., p. 675).

SECTION III

work ‖, such that such a one might become rich (Deut 33.10,11). So that they might enjoy this blessing in turn, new priests were always chosen by the lot.

Christian That was the priestly custom according to which Zachariah won this duty of incensing. He obtained a duty he had not had previously and he received a blessing better than all the riches he had previously hoped for.

Incense bsmʿ

Kabbalist Catechumen The kabbalistic remarks of our sages about incense are already correctly related | in Appar in Book Zohar Vol. 1 Part. 1 p. 675.
Christian To which one can also add: Excerpta Cent. I Loc. 22 and 23.

Verse 10
And the whole congregation was praying wklh knšʾ dʿmʾ mçlʾ hwʾ

Kabbalist Catechumen The better to understand these ancient rites, you should consult | Excerpt Cent. I Loc. 24 where there are quotations from the last chapters of the Talmudic Tractate ‖ Tamid (or Concerning the Sacrifice of a Pair of Oxen) concerning the regular daily worship about which we are speaking. Now, please, make your observations.

Christian I notice that (1): by "congregation of the people" here is meant priests, levites and Jewish guards—and possibly | some devout individuals.

Also (2): that the prayer which the people are said to have prayed here, cannot be the fixed, regular morning prayers mentioned in Mishnah Tamid 1.5 because these had already been finished before the ministry of the incense. So Mishnah [Tamid] 3.6. Doubtless the reference is to prayers from the Eighteen [Benedictions][148].

---

143 BSB: &
144 A red pencil square bracket inserted into the text (Talmudi[ci]) refers to an annotation in the left margin: P.C./33.
145 BSB: quod
146 Added in the text: *Jam tu tuas profer observationes*. The sentence was initially attributed to the Christian.
147 Deletion: Jam tu tuas profer observationes.
148 The Eighteen Benedictions (called in Hebrew the *Shemoneh ʿEsreh* or "Eighteen") are the central prayer of the Jewish liturgy used three times every day, preferably while facing Jerusalem. It is also known simply as the Prayer (*Tefilah*) or the *ʿamidah* ("Standing [Prayer]"). It is traditionally ascribed to the Men of the Great Synagogue (bBer 33a) if not to those who preceded them way back to Moses (bMeg 17b. Cf. Mishnah Avot 1.1).

cul dubio reliquæ ex octodecim. (3.) quod vox ὥρα (quæ est in Græco) tempus saltem denotet, ut reddit Syrus: quia negotium suffiendi | haud longam requisivit moram. (4.) Quod tamen interea fuerit in templo silentium; quo etiam alludit visio Johannis Apoc. 8, 1.

V. 11. Angelus Domini &c.
מלאכא דמריא

Cabb. Cat. *Quid de Angelis sentiant nostrates, paucis vix expediri potest. Operæ tamen pretium erit pervolvere, quæ*[149] *| de his cumulata reperiuntur in Excerptis è Libro Sohar, Centur. 1*[150]. *â Loco XXVI. & ulterius usque ad locum 41.*

p. 34
fol. 8ʳ

Christianus. Hic autem specialiter observo, quod Denominatio hæc מלאכא דמריא ‖ ⦀ quæ[151] in textu Syriaco præter hunc locum etiam reperitur Matth. 2, 13.19; Act. 7, 30; c. 5, 19; c. 8, 26; c. 12, 7.23. quotiescunque in veteri Testamento Syriaco occurrit, ut Gen. 16, 7.9.10.11; Ex. 3, 2; Num. 22, 22.23.24.25.26.27.31.32.34.35; Jud. 2, 1.4; c. 5, 23; c. 6, 11.12.20.21.21.22.22; c. 13, 3.13.15.16.16.17.18.20.21.21; 1. Reg. 19, 7; | 2. Reg. 19, 35; 1. Par. 21, 15.30; Psal. 34, 8; Jes. 37, 36; Zach. 1, 11.12; c. 3, 1.6 & pluries, æquipollens sit phrasi Hebraicæ מלאך יה״וה. Unde certissimum est, quod & hic appellatio Nominis Tetragrammati subinnuatur. Cumque infra Luc. 1, 16.17 idem nomen *Domini*, Tetragrammato æquipollens, etiam tribuatur Messiæ; hinc colligo quod juxta sensum antiquum non tantum Nomen Tetragrammaton intellectum | fuerit de Messia; sed et Angelus Domini, idem sit, ac Angelus Messiæ; nimirum ad sellam illam curulem pertinens, quâ vectus est Messias Jes. 6, 1 coll. cum Joh. 12, 41; Jechesk. 1, 26.10 &c.

Cabb. Cat. *Adde & hoc, quod iste Angelus Domini Gabriel pertineat ad gradum Gebhurah S. Severitatis, sicut & Taurus in Mercabhâ*[152] *ad eundem |*

---

149   Deletion of a dozen words, now unreadable.
150   BSB: Cent. 21 (Printer's error)
151   A red pencil square bracket inserted into the text ([quæ) refers to an annotation in the right margin: 2.C./34.
152   BSB: *Nercabhâ* (Printer's error)
153   Knorr comments on Rev 8.1 in his *Apocalypse-Kommentar*, edited by Italo Michele Battafarano, op. cit., p. 89: "Denn der Engel / der itzo in dieser von Johanne geshenen himmlischen Hütten des Stiffs / den Priesterdienst verwaltete / wolte das Rauch-Opffer

SECTION III   177

That (3): the word *hōra* (which is in the Greek [New Testament text]) means only "time", as the Syriac [*b'dn'*] correctly renders it, [and not "an
40 hour"], because the business of incensing hardly | requires such a long period.

That (4): meanwhile there was silence in the Temple, to which John's vision also refers (Rev 8.1).[153]

Verse 11
An Angel of the Lord *ml'k' dmry'*

Kabbalist Catechumen What our sages have to say about angels can scarcely be presented in a few words! It will however be worth the effort to work
45 through the collected passages | which are found in Excerpts ex Lib. Zohar Cent. I from Locus 26 and onwards to Locus 41.

Christian What I particularly note is that this phrase *ml'k' dmry'* ||| which is found in the Syriac text || here and in Mt 2.13, 19; Acts 7.30; 5.19; 8.26; 12.7, 23, whenever it occurs in the Syriac Old Testament (as in Gen 16.7, 9, 10, 11; Ex 3.2; Num 22.22, 23, 24, 25, 26, 27, 31, 32, 34, 35; Judg 2.1, 4; 5. 23; 6.11, 12, 20,
5   21, [*bis*], 22, [*bis*]; 13. 3, 13, 15, 16, [*bis*], 17, 18, 20, 21, [*bis*]; 1 Kgs 19.7; | 2 Kgs 19.35; 1 Chron 21.15, 30; Ps 34.8; Isa 37.36; Zech 1.11, 12; 3.1,6 and many [other places]) is equivalent to the Hebrew phrase *ml'k yh-wh*[154]. Hence it is certain that by this word [*mry'*] the Name of the Tetragrammaton is signified. Below in Lk 1.16, 17 the same word "Lord" [*mry'*] (the equivalent of the Tetragrammaton) is also used of Messiah; from this I gather that according to the ancient
10 meaning not only was the name of the Tetragrammaton | understood of Messiah, but also that the Angel of the Lord was the same as the Angel of Messiah undoubtedly referring to the magisterial chair in which Messiah was carried Isa 6.1 compared with Jn 12.41 and Ezek 1.26, 10 etc.

fol. 8r
p. 34

Kabbalist Catechumen Add this also, that this Angel of the Lord, Gabriel, belongs to the degree *Gevurah* or *Severity*, just as also the Ox in the Mercabha

---

anzünden / darumb ward eine Stille / wie bey Jüdischen Ceremonien gebräuchlich war / Conf. Luc.1. 10."
154 The Tetragrammaton is broken by an apostrophe to prevent pronunciation. The text of the Syriac Old Testament was available in Walton's London Polyglot Bible, a copy of which is mentioned in the Sulzbach catalogue of 1734 now in the Bayerische Staatsbibliothek (BSB) in Munich (Cbm Cat 580.1 Repositorium A).

gradum pertinet. Et nota quæ tibi suggerit liber Sohar, Excerptorum Cent. 1. Loc. 90.

A dextra Altaris &c. מן ימינא דמרבחה

Cabb. Cat. *Hic iterum subministrabo Cab-* ‖ *-balistica*[155] *quædam. Dextrum latus Altaris incensi, & dextra sacerdotis*[156] *suffitum facientis respiciebat | latus templi septentrionale, & sinistram Schechinæ in Sancto sanctorum aliquo adhuc sui vestigio præsentis. Gabriel ergò hac ipsa statione sua situm observabat ab antiquitate Gentis nostræ Hebraicæ semper isti*[157] *tributum, nimirum gradus Gebhuræ, ad quem & septentrionis & sinistræ appellatio â nobis refertur (Vid. Lexicon Cabbalisticum p. 666*[158]. *voce* צפון *& p. 720*[159]. *| voce* שמאל*).*

Christianus. Denotari ergò videtur vehementissima Luminum divinorum manifestatio, cum subindicatione gravissimorum judiciorum adversus eos, qui futuri essent refractarii, imò hanc domum ipsam. Tempus enim aderat, quo Gradus Regni Messiani prævalere debebat, cujus Lumina pariter vehementissima | sunt, influxu Roboris illius sublimis lateris sinistri potissimum exsuscitata, juxta Matth. 11, 12. Unde & nomen ישוע, quod Messias assumsit habet numerum 386, id est. Nominis אלהים cujus numerus est 86 quatenus istud influit in tres mundos, ut decem singulorum Numerationes ascende-

---

155 A red pencil square bracket inserted into the text (Cab[balistica) refers to an annotation in the right margin: 3.C./35.
156 Added in the right margin: conversâ ad Sanctum Sanctorum facie
157 Correction in the right margin: isti replaced by ipsi
158 "צפון *Septentrio, reconditum.* Hoc interdum cognomen esse reperitur nominis Elohim: Nam cum à vivido Beneplaciti fonte metrum Chesed, quod semper apertum est, locupletissimè bonorum hauriat opes, ut inde flagitantibus elargiatur commoda; tunc varia illa emolumenta, in Septentrionis latere metrum sinistri attingentia, ibi sistunt, moramque ducunt, quatenus æquum de supplicante examen fiat, ut, si petitionis condignus extiterit, ejus adimpleantur vota, sin secus, nequaquam; sed tunc omnia illa bona in judicii oraculum suscepta, ibi in Aquilonis cellariis Thesaurisque reconduntur & asservantur, nec redeunt ad locum suum: unde hic judicii gradus צפון quasi *reconditorium* vocatur." ("Loci communes kabbalistici", op. cit., p. 666).
159 "שמאל *Sinistrum* ad Gebhurah pertinet; quamvis sæpè & ad Binah atque Hod extendatur. Prout & sinistri nomen Corticibus tribuitur. Pard. vid. Tezav. in f. Vaæra 12.46." (Ibid., p. 720).

belongs to the same | degree.[160] And note the suggestions the book Zohar makes in Excerpts Cent. I Loc. 90.

To the Right of the Altar mn ymyn' dmrbḥ'

Kabbalist Catechumen ‖ Here again I shall share some kabbalistic observations. The right side of the altar of incense and the right side of the face of the priest | doing the incensing, which was turned to the Holy of Holies, faced the northern side of the Temple and the left [side] of the Shekhinah, which was still at that time giving some evidence of its presence in the Holy of Holies.[161] So Gabriel in his proper station observed the site [of the Holy of Holies] from the early days of our Hebrew people, and certainly the degree *Gevurah* is always attributed to him to which we link both "north" and "left". (See *Lex. Cabb.*, p. 666 on *çpwn* and p. 720 | *sm'l*.)

Christian There seems therefore to be indicated here a very powerful manifestation of the Divine Lights with a warning of serious judgements against those who will be contentious—indeed against the Temple itself. For the time had come in which the degree of the *Kingdom of Messiah* should prevail, whose lights are equally most powerful | and aroused most strongly with the influx of the lofty left hand side of *Robur*, according to Mt 11.12[162]. Thus the name *yšw'* which Messiah assumed has the number 386, made up from the Name *'lhym* whose number is 86; and, in so far as that flows into the Three Worlds, as each of the ten numerations rises to the plenitude of its

p. 35

---

160 The Merkavah is the chariot throne in Ezek 1.26 etc which has just been alluded to. It has four faces, a man, a lion, an ox and an eagle.

161 Lightfoot, *Miscellanies and the Harmony of the Gospels*, op. cit., pp. 153–154 quotes "Massec. Jom 7" on the five items missing from the Second Temple. They are the Ark, Urim and Thummim, Fire from Heaven, The Divine Presence "or the Cloud of Glory" and the Holy Ghost "or Spirit of Prophecy and Power of Miracles." Evidently Knorr does not take this view above.

162 KJV: "And from the days of John the Baptist until now the kingdom of heaven suffereth violence, and the violent take it by force". This enigmatic verse is here newly interpreted of the influx of *Robur* (indicated by Gabriel and his position North and Left of the Holy of Holies). The following numerological calculation indicates that this will affect all three worlds.

rent ad plenitudinem Decadis suæ, unde 300[163]. Confer quæ in | hunc sen- 35
sum reperiuntur in Adumbratione Cabbalæ Christianæ cap. 11, §. 2.[164] ||

V. 12.[165] *Et conturbatus est &c. & timor cecidit &c.*
ואשתגש *&c.* ודחלתא נפלת

Cabb. Cat. *Egregia tibi hoc loco nascitur occasio, paululum | excurrendi circa* 40
materiam de Perturbationibus animi: nam primò perturbatio sive Affectus
Zachariæ in genere describitur; deinde affectus specialis nimirum Timoris ex-
primitur. Egregiè autem Syriaca hæc vox אשתגש *motus animæ nostræ denotat,*
sensui Chaldaico admodum conformis, qui non aliter se habent ac tumultus in
civitate Luc. 23, 5; Act. 19, 29; | *c. 14, 19; c. 21, 30; Act. 2, 6; Act. 19, 32.40*[166]*; Matth.* 45
26, 5; Marc. 14, 2; Act. 15, 2; Marc. 13, 8; Luc. 21, 9; 2 Cor. 6, 5 & in domo Matth. 9,
23 & in navi Matth[167]*.* ||| *14, 24, & mari Jac. 1, 6.*

Christianus. Recte mones, nam talis est tumultus in spiritu nostro ex
Affectu, confer. in Syriaco Jac. 1, 8; Joh. 12, 27; 1 Pet. 3, 14; 1 Cor. 13, 4; 1 Cor.
14, 33; Act. 20, 1; c. 23, 10; c. 24, 5.18; 2 Cor. 12, 20; & in V.T. Pr. 6, 14; c. 26,
22; Ex. 14, 24; | 1 Sam. 4, 3; 1. Reg. 1, 41; Prov. 26, 20.28; Ps. 35, 17; 1 Sam. 5, 11; 5
c. 14, 20 et in Chaldaico Ex. 14, 24; Jes. 44, 25; Esth. 9, 24; Ps. 144, 6; Deut. 7,
23; 1. Reg. 1, 41.45; Jer. 23, 19; c. 25, 27; Jes. 29, 9; (Nah, 2, 4; Jer. 25, 16) 1 Sam.
5, 11; Ps. 19, 4; Am. 3, 9; Deut. 28, 20; 1 Sam. 4, 14; Esth. 1, 10; c. 6, 1. Cumque primum non tantum Philosophi, sed & Christiani studium esse debeat

---

163   In addition to the three worlds of emanation, formation and creation, there is a forth
      one, the world of action. Each of the worlds contains the ten sefirot, and each of the
      sefiroth contains in itself the ten other sefirot, in such a way that they are nested in
      each other like Russian dolls.
164   "Atque hoc est Tempus Fœderis Novi, per sacrificum ipsius Messiæ sanciti ad impe-
      tranda pro animabus sanctificandis nova & ulteriora auxilia. Jamque Anima Messiæ
      in illo supponenda est Adami primi loco, in quo Regnum consistere concipitur, quo-
      niam ad Regnum à vestratibus refertur Messias: ita tamen, quatenus illud est in copula
      cum Microprosopo: unde etiam Agno tribuuntur omnia septem metra inferiora Apoc.
      5. vs. 12. (conf. Ap. 3. vs. 1.) Et omnia quidem Basiliæ & Messiæ attributa jam à rigoris
      & vehementiæ sive fortitudinis gradu (quæ Gebhurah vobis dicitur) influxum habue-
      runt, (juxta Matth. 11. vs. 12.) unde etiam Nomen ישוע, quod Messias assumsit, habet
      numerum 386. id est, Nominis אלהים cujus numerus est 86. quatenus istud influit in
      tres mundos, ut decem singulorum numerationes ascenderent ad plenitudinem Deca-
      dis suæ, unde 300. Hoc enim metro potissimùm opus fuit ad impugnandos cominùs
      Cortices. Quamvis alias nomen ישוע exhibeat totum systema emanativum: nimirum
      Jod cum Apice, coronam cum sapientia, prout in Tetragrammato. Schin intelligen-
      tiam (vid. Apparat. in lib. Soh. Part. I. p. 694. unde & tres literæ א"מש, de quibus
      Liber Iezirah, in Tikkunim, & in libro Pardes Rimmonim Tract. 27. c. 3. exponuntur de

decade, one gets another 300 [3×10×10]. Cf. what is said about this meaning | in *Adumbratio*, chap. 11, § 2. ‖

Verse 12
He was afraid etc. *and Fear fell* etc. *wʾštgš and wdḥltʾ nplt*

Kabbalist Catecumen You have an outstanding opportunity here, for launching forth somewhat | on the disturbances of the soul. First of all the perturbation of Zachariah is described generally [in this verse], then the specific emotion of excessive fear is expressed. Outstandingly, this Syriac word *ʾštgšʾ* (just like the [related] Aramaic [word]) denotes the movements of our soul, which are just like uprisings in a city (Lk 23.5; Acts 19. 29; | 14.19; 21.30; Acts 2.6; Acts 19. 32, 40; Mt 26.5; Mk 14.2; Acts 15.2; Mk 13.8; Lk 21.9; 2 Cor 6.5), in a home (Mt 9.23), on board [a ship] (Mt 14.24) ‖ or on the sea (Jam 1.6).

Christian You give good advice, for the tumult in our spirit [caused] by the passions is just like that. Cf. the Syriac of Jam 1.8; Jn 12.27; 1 Pet 3.14; 1 Cor 13.4; 14.33[168]; Acts 20.1; 23.10; 24.5, 18; 2 Cor 12.20 and in the Old Testament: Pro 6.14; 26.22; Ex 14.24; | 1 Sam 4.3; 1 Kgs 1.41; Pro 26.20, 28; Ps 35.17; 1 Sam 5.11; 14.20; and in the Aramaic [Targum] Ex 14.24; Isa 44.25; Esth 9.24; Ps 144.6; Deut 7.23; 1 Kgs 1.41, 45; Jer 23.19; 25.27; Isa 29.9 (Nah 2.4; Jer 25.16); 1 Sam 5.11; Ps 19.4; Amos 3.9; Deut 28.20; 1 Sam 4.14; Esth 1.10; 6.1. Not only a philosopher but also a Christian[169] needs to study to recognise the disturbances ‖ of his

---

tribus prioribus.) Vav autem denotat sex membra subsequentia. Et Ajin quidem denotat fundamentum, sed applicatum ad Regnum, ceu fons in mare influens. Ubi notandum, quia jam erat tempus, cum copula institueretur tam inferior quam superior; quod duæ Literæ Fœmininæ Tetragrammaticæ propterea mutatæ sint in tales, quæ connotant Masculinitatem: quoniam etiam Schin Matris, denotat tres Patres. (Unde & in nomine יהוןּ, qui erat alter à Messia, literæ Tetragrammaticæ tantùm masculinæ sunt). [...]" ("Adumbratio kabbalæ christianæ", op. cit., p. 62).

165　A red pencil square bracket inserted into the text ([V. 12.) refers to an annotation in the right margin: 4.C./36.

166　BSB reads Mt. 19, 32.40, which is impossible. The manuscript is hardly readable here, but the correct reading is probably Act. 19, 32.40, which has the appropriate vocabulary.

167　In the right bottom corner appears a Hebrew letter ג presumably an indication of binding or pagination.

168　The six following references refer to tumultuous public meetings of lively disputes and not to the life of the soul and thus illustrate the "uprisings in a city" mentioned immediately previously by the Kabbalist Catechumen.

169　Perhaps Knorr seeks here to make a contrast with "Adumbratio kabbalæ christianæ" and its more philosophic emphasis in which the Christian himself appeared as a philosopher.

p. 37 cognoscere perturbationes animæ suæ[170], non | inutilis ‖ erit[171] hæc digressio mea ad generalem quandam Affectuum nostrorum delineationem. Hi enim consistunt vel in parte Animæ

Concupiscibili, seu imâ, habentque pro Objecto Bonum aliquod, sivè verum sivè putativum; suntque

> 1. Amor, qui est eradiatio spiritus nostri ex ideâ pulchri, ceu centro, per | radios terebræ instar tortuosos, penetrantissimos ad unionem tendentes per implicationem cum striis redamantis.
> 2. Desiderium, quod est eradiatio spiritus nostri, ex ideâ commodi, ceu centro; per radios hamatos, lineis curvis ad centrum redeuntes, & ad fruitionem tendentes.
> 3. Spes, quæ est eradiatio spiritus nostri ex ideâ Prosperi, per radios rectos obfirmatos non redeundo in longissimum[172] tendentes; cujus species est Fides.
> 4. Lætitia, quæ est eradiatio spiritus nostri ex ideâ Jucundi, per radios veloces, in sui excitationem repercussos motu continuo.

Irascibili, seu mediâ: habentque pro objecto Malum aliquod, sive verum sive putativum, suntque vel

Prioribus oppositi, ut

> 1. Odium, quod est retractionis[173] spiritus nostri, ob ideam Tædiosi per radios tortuosus avertentes.
> 2. Fuga, quæ est retractio spiritus nostri ob ideam[174] Incommodi, per radios obliquos declinantes.[175]
> 3. Metus, qui est retractio spiritus nostri ob ideam Adversi per radios tremulos sibi invicem ‖ allisos[176]. Hujus species sunt Incredulitas, Pavor, Invidia, Desperatio.

p. 38

> 4. Tristitia, quæ est retractio spiritus nostri ob ideam ingrati, per radios centrum proprium supprimentes: cujus species est Misericordia &c.

---

170 Correction: animæ suæ replaced by animi sui
171 A red pencil square bracket inserted into the text ([erit) refers to an annotation in the left margin: 5.C./37.
172 Correction above the line: longissimum replaced by longinquum
173 Correction: retractionis replaced by retractio
174 Deleted word now unreadable.

SECTION III

own soul. So it will be useful | for me to digress into a general analysis of our Passions. These exist in the various parts of our Soul.[177]

[In the part of the Soul concerned with] Yearning (the lowest part), these affects have as their object some good (whether true or merely putative). They are:

1. Love—which is the eradiation of our spirit by the idea or centre of Beauty, with | very piercing rays (twisting like gimlets) which effect union by deep involvement with the grooves [of one who loves] in return.

2. Hope—which is the eradiation of our spirit by the idea of Prosperity with straight rays, strengthened by the fact that they generally do not have to return to a distant place (an example of which is Trust).

3. | Happiness—which is the eradiation of our spirit by the idea of Joy through swift rays repeatedly knocked into self-excitation by continual motion.

[In the] | Irascible (or middle) [part of the Soul], the following affects have some Evil, whether real or putative as an object and are, as it were, opposed to the preceding affects above. They are:

1. Hate—which is the contraction of our spirit on account of the idea of Disgust by twisting rays which turn away.

2. | Flight—which is the contraction of our spirit on account of the idea of the Inconvenient by downward slanting rays (an example of which is Shame).

3. Fear—which is the retraction of our spirit on account of the idea of Adversity by wobbly ‖ rays striking against each other. Examples of this are Incredulity, Fright, Envy and Desperation.

p. 38

4. | Sadness—which is the retraction of our spirit on account of the idea of Ingratitude by rays suppressing their own centre. Pity is an example of this.

---

175   Added into the text: *cujus species est Pudor*.
176   A red pencil square bracket inserted into the text ([erit) refers to an annotation in the left margin: 6.C./38.
177   The tri-partite division of the soul here is essentially that of Plato in the *Republic* and the Allegory of the Charioteer in the *Phaedrus*: the appetitive part *epithumētikon*; the "spirited" part *thumoeides* and the rational part *logistikon*.

Cum omnibus facilè commiscibilis, ut est Ira, quæ est crispatura
quædam et ebullitio spiritus nostri, ob ideam | mali præsentis, quod   40
repellere intendimus.

Rationali, seu summâ: ut Admiratio, quæ est aliqua spiritus nostri immobi-
litas, cujus species sunt superbia, abjectio, &c.

 Hinc facilè patebit, quis motus exortus fuerit in Anima Zachariæ, & quan-
ta exhinc subnata sit imbecillitas, unde dehinc vitium incredulitatis | prodiit.   45
Remedium autem hîc non datur validius, quam Firmitas animi crebris acti-

fol. 9ʳ bus in habitum deducta. ‖|

V. 13. Ne timeas &c. לא תדחל

Cabb. Cat. *Quid propriè indigitat hæc phrasis, quæ toties occurrit in historiis
apparitionum?*

 Christianus. Præparatio est ad fidem, cujus commotio contraria est mo-
tui | pavoris & metus, ut supra de spe diximus.   5

Quia exaudita est Oratio tua:
מטל דאשתמעת צלותך

p. 39 **Cabb. Cat.** *De exauditione precum juxta no-* ‖—*strates*[178] *quædam habentur in Idra Rabba §. 707–722*[179] *& in Idra min. §. 582*[180] *item in Comment.
p. 133*[181]*omnia in Cabbalæ Denud. Tom. II. Nec non Cabbal. denud. Tom. II,*

---

178 A red pencil square bracket inserted into the text (nostra[tes) refers to an annotation
  in the right margin: 7.C./39.
179 "§. 707. Didicimus. Scriptum est [2. Reg. 19. v. 16.] Inclina ô Deus aurem tuam & audi;
  hanc aurem scilicet quæ occultata est sub capillis; & capilli pendent super ea; & auris
  tamen est ad audiendum. §. 708. Et auris ab intra elaborata est cum signaturis con-
  cavis notantissimis, sicut sit scala cochlearis cum incurvatione, in utramque partem.
  §. 709. Quare autem cum curvaturis? Ut audiat bonum & malum. [...] §. 714. Ut col-
  ligatur vox interius nec prodeat foras; & sit custodita & occlusa ab omni latere: hinc
  est natura arcani. [...] §. 722. Cum ergo dicitur: Inclina Domine, aurem tuam: Aurem
  tuam i.e. Microprosopi." (*Kabbalah denudata*, II, "Partis secundæ, Tractatus Secundus
  qui est *Idra rabba seu Synodus areæ magna*, pp. 386–520", sectio XXXIII, §. 707–722, "De
  auribus Microposopi", pp. 470–472).
180 "§. 582. Duæ aures (*sunt ipsi*) ad audiendum bonum & malum; & ambæ reducuntur ad

Wrath is easily mixed with all these. It is a certain trembling and boiling of our spirit on account of | present evil which we intend to repel.

In the Rational (or highest) [part of the Soul] [we find] Admiration which is a certain motionlessness of our spirit. Examples of this are Pride, Abjection etc.

From this it is quite clear what movement was stirred up in the soul of Zachariah and how much weakness it gave rise to. From this | the fault of incredulity arose. No stronger remedy is given here than strength of mind become a habit by frequent actions. ‖

Verse 13
Don't be afraid l' tdḥl

Kabbalist Catechumen What does this phrase—which occurs so many times in accounts of visions—really mean?

Christian It is an encouragement to Faith, whose contrary motion | is Fear and Trembling (as we said above about Hope).

For He has heard your prayer mṭl d'štmʿt çlwtk

Kabbalist Catechumen You can find out something of what our sages ‖ say about God hearing prayer in *Idra Rabba*, § 707–722 and in *Idra Min.* § 582. Also in *Comment.* p. 133 and in *Cabb. Denud.*, II [*passim*]. Also [especially],

---

unam" (*Kabbalah denudata*, II, "Partis secundæ Tractatus Tertius qui est *Idra Suta*, seu Synodus minor", pp. 521–598, sectio XVI", p. 577).

181 "§. 225. Aures Microposopi sunt duæ dextra & sinistra. Datur enim auditus bonus in aure dextra, sicut dicitur: Quoniam audit egenos Dominus. Et in aure sinistra malus: juxta illud: Et audivit Dominus, & exarsit ira ejus. Et aures Microprosopi curvaturas habent, ut audire queant bonum & malum. [...] Unde necessum est, ut capilli ibidem dependeant ad contegendum foramen hoc cervicis, ne cortices aliquid exinde participent. Aures autem vacuæ esse debent à capillis, ne istæ impediantur ab exauditione precum nostrarum: unde de his dicitur: Inclina aurem tuam [...]" (*Kabbala denudata*, II, "Partis secundæ Tractatus quartus qui est in Siphra de Zeniutha seu Librum mysterii commentarius", pp. 1–144, p. 133).

Par. 1, p. 5, | *n. 44*[182]*; p. 37, n. 24–27.*[183] *Item in Excerpt. Loc. XXXV, c. 1, §. 5 sqq. Quæritur autem qualis hic intelligatur Zachariæ oratio: Utrum scilicet illa, quam nunc inter suffitum fuderit; an verò alia quædam præcedanea? Item an intelligenda sit oratio pro obtinendo filio; an verò*[184] *pro liberatione Iisraëlitarum & adventu* | *Messiæ? Ubi observes, velim, quoad primum; quod Sacerdos suffitum offerens preces tum simul Deo offerre non fuerit solitus, juxta ea, quæ supra tradita sunt ad v. 10 è Tamid c. 6 misch. 3, sed facta suffimenti exæquatione, exhibitaque prostrato corpore reverentiâ (id enim per adorationem intelligitur) exiverit: nisi forte suspiria quædam emisisset, quæ hic non possunt considerari.*

Christianus. Sicut Cornelius preces Deo plurimas obtulerat, antequam illi appareret Angelus Act. 10, 2.4 & Daniel jejunia quoque adjunxerat continuatis supplicationibus suis c. 9, 3.23, ita procul dubio Zacharias multum diuque ‖ supplicando[185] anteâc fatigaverat divinum Numen; præsertim cum non tam facile admittatur oratio solitaria, juxta Excerpt. Loc. XXXV, Cap. 1, §. 6. & è | textu Sohar Pekude §. 9.[186] Putarem igitur omninò intelligi orationes â Zachariâ aliquando fusas pro impetrando filio; de quarum exauditione ipse quidem jamjam desperavisset, ob subsecutam senectutem; coram Deo sanctissimo autem ob singulares quosdam precum illarum characteres earundem facta subinde fuisset commemoratio, donec emanaret decretum de descensu Animæ Eliæ in Johannem. | Quamvis enim dubium non sit, quin â Zachariâ (qui minimè censendus est plebejus fuisse Sacerdos, sed in Legis oralis doctrina peritissimus, cum ad Decretum tam singulare orando inflectere potuerit Dominum, & quidem penetrando ad sublimem illum Influen-

---

[182] "§. 44. Quicunque desiderat, ut accepta sit oratio ejus, is in Lege studeat. [Conf. Act. 10, 4. *Orationes tuæ & eleemosynæ tuæ ascenderunt in memoriam in conspectu DEI. 31. Corneli, exaudita est oratio tua, & eleemosynæ &c.*]" (Kabbala denudata, II, "Pars Prima ejusque Tractatus primus: quæ est Synopsis Celeberrimi illius Codicis Cabbalistici, qui vulgo dicitur Liber Sohar per novendecim titulos generales distributa, Autore R. Iisaschar F. Naphthali Sacerdote", pp. 1–150, p. 5). The text in square brackets is Knorr's addition to the translation.

[183] "§. 24. Dantur præfecti quidam, qui accipiunt illas preces, quæ emittuntur ab his, qui Dominum suum ritè sanctificare nôrunt. Et deinde alii quoque dantur præfecti, qui preces illorum accipiunt, qui sanctitatem nominis Divini non deprædicant, prout decet: & utræque preces simul uniuntur. col. 444. §. 25. Oratio requirit attentas cogitationes & propositum Spiritûs liberum, & pronunciationem verborum. col. 448. §. 26. In Oratorio sive Synagoga faciendæ sunt duodecim fenestræ. col. 450.—§. 27. Locus ille: Ezech. 1. v. 8. *Et manus hominis sub alis eorum &c.* sic explicatur, ut per manus has intelligatur officium accipiendi preces Iisraëlitarum, easdemque introducendi, per omnes portas supernas. col. 468." (Ibid., p. 37).

Cabb. Denud., II, Part. I, p. 5 | n. 44; p. 37 n. 24, 27. Similarly, in Excerpt Loc. 35, chap. 1, § 5 et *seq*. One wonders however what sort of prayer Zachariah offered here? Was it one he prayed there and then during the incensing, or was it rather some other preceding prayers? Similarly, should it be understood as a prayer for a son or one for the liberation of Israelites and the coming | of Messiah?[187] Notice initially, that the priest offering the incense did not usually at the same time offer prayers to God, (see the remarks on verse 10 above from Tamid 6. Mishn. 3), but rather having offered the incense and displayed his reverence by bodily prostration (for that is what is meant by adoration) he went out. Perhaps he breathed a sigh of relief, but we cannot consider that here.

Christian Just as Cornelius had offered many prayers to God before the angel appeared to him (Acts 10.2, 4) and Daniel had added fasting to his continual supplications (9.3, 23), so ‖ doubtless Zachariah had greatly wearied the Divine Power with his supplication, particularly as single prayers are not so easily granted (according to Excerpt Loc. 35. | chap. 1, § 6). I would consider therefore that the prayers Zachariah previously offered were requests for a son, but that he had long despaired of being heard on account of his old age. Remembrance of those prayers was suddenly made before the most holy God, on account of certain singular characteristics they had, and so there went out the decree concerning the decent of the soul of Elijah into John [the Baptist]. | There is no doubt that Zachariah was not an ordinary priest, but rather an expert in the teaching of the oral Law, since he had been able to incline the Lord to such a singular decree by praying and indeed by penetrating to that lofty degree of Gevurah [*Influentia*]. It is

p. 40

---

184 Absent from the BSB: an verò (probably due printer's oversight).
185 A red pencil square bracket inserted into the text ([supplicando) refers to an annotation in the right margin: 8.C./40.
186 Deletion: & è textu Sohar Pekude §. 9.
187 Lightfoot, *Miscellanies and the Harmony of the Gospels*, op. cit., p. 154: "Ver. 13: 'Thy prayer is heard,' &c.] Not that he was now praying for a child; for his age made him incredulous of having a child, when the angel told him of one; and then it is not like he would pray for one;—and in this place, and at this time, he was a person representative of the whole people; and, therefore, was not to make a private prayer for himself: but, either the prayers, which he had before made to that purpose, were now come into remembrance; or rather he was now praying for the delivery of Israel, the remission of their sins, and the coming of Christ, in which they without were joining with him; and this his prayer, the angel tells him, is so ready to be answered, that his wife should presently conceive a son, that should preach remission, convert the people, and go before the face of Christ."

tiæ gradum, â quo dependet liberorum concessio: sicut habet antiquum illud gentis vestræ: Liberorum, Vitæ, & alimentorum | causa non â Marito[188], sed ab Influentia dependet. Vid. Lex. Cabbalist. pp. 521, 522[189] & Sohar Pinchas P. III, Cremon, Col. 397) etiam oblatæ fuerint preces pro adventu Messiæ: non solent tamen largitiones beneficiorum universalium adscribi sollicitationibus singularium personarum.

Pariet tibi Filium &c. תאלדי לך ברא

Christianus. Hic filius communiter Eliæ dicitur similis. Quid tu hîc sentires?

p. 41   **Cabb. Cat.** *Juxta expressa verba Matth.* ‖ *11, 14*[190]. *Filius iste*[191] *fuit Elias, qui venturus esse credebatur & adhuc creditur ante adventum Messiæ ab omnibus nostratibus. Omnes autem Hebræi credebant & credunt, non similem quendam Eliæ, sed ipsum Eliam rediturum esse, juxta luculentissimum Eliæ*[192] |

fol. 9ᵛ   *vaticinium c. 4, 5. Ubi miror, Vos ab antiqua nostræ gentis Hypothesi re-* ‖‖- *cedere, aliumque sensum obtrudere velle Scriptoribus Hebræis: nonne enim hoc idem esset, ac ex Alcorano interpretari Platonem? Hic ergò præsupponitur Animarum non tantum Præexistentia, sed etiam metensomatosis sive revolutio, de qua quid fortuna*[193] *nostra tradat, videatur totus Tractatus Cabbalæ denudatæ* | *Tom. II, P. 3, tract. 2.*[194]

Christianus. Quânam autem specie revolutionis revolutus esset Elias, si hæc vestra hypothesis locum haberet?

Cabb. Cat. *Juxta nostrates alia est revolutio Psyches, quæ â nobis Nephesch dicitur; alia Spiritus seu Ruach; alia Mentis, seu Neschamah* | *&c. Apparet*

---

188   Correction above the line: Marito replaced by Merito
189   "מזל *Influentia*. Est Kether, quia influit in omnes Sephiras: sed hæc est è notionibus ejus manifestis. Pard. vid. Jethro 35, 138.64. Naso 70, 253. Pinchas 100, 397. In Schaare Orah sub Nominibus 3. & 4. de מזל extant sequentia post עצם השמים. Binah liberos producit à *Corona*, à loco scil. qui vocatur מזל *influentia*. Hæc est Influentia superna ob existentes ibidem 13. proprietates miserandi: & ab hac Influentia Liberi, Vita, & Alimenta proveniunt atque dependent, imò & ipse Liber Legis, qui in Templo. Ne enim cogites, à Planetarum & stellarum influxu dependere Librum Legis, quia totus mundus per Legem conditus; quomodo igitur Lex dependeret ab eo, quod ab ipsa est conditum. Sed à Corona dependent omnes Sephiroth & omnia creata. Dicitur autem מזל *Influentia*, quia ab ipsa profluunt vires in omnes Sephiras, & in omnes mundi filios: imò & Liber Legis ab hâc Influentiâ vires haurit atque recipit. [...] Unde dictum est: Circa liberos vitam & alimenta; non à merito, sed à Fortuna seu Influentia res dependet. [...]" ("Loci communes kabbalistici", op. cit., pp. 521–522).
190   A red pencil square bracket inserted into the text (Matth.[11, 14) refers to an annotation in the right margin: 9.C./41.

SECTION III

upon Gevurah that the gift of children depends. As that ancient saying of your people has it: "Children, Life and Food, | depend not upon deserts, but upon Gevurah". (*Lex. Cabb.*, pp. 521, 522; Zohar Phineas Part 3, Cremona [edition] col. 397). Prayers had [no doubt] also been offered [by Zachariah] for the coming of Messiah, however a gift of universal benefit is not usually attributed to the prayers of an individual person.

She shall bear you a son etc. *t'ldy lk br'*

Christian This son is commonly said to be like Elijah. What do you think about this?

Kabbalist Catechumen ‖ According to the express words of Mt 11.14, I must admit that this son was Elijah who was believed—and is still believed—by all our people to be going to come before the advent of Messiah. For all the Hebrews believed—and believe—Elijah himself (not someone *like* Elijah) will come according to the utterly clear prophecy of | Mal 4.5. Hence I am amazed that you wish to depart from the ancient understanding of our people ‖‖ and to introduce another meaning into the Hebrew writers. Surely this is the same as interpreting Plato from the Qur'an! For here is presupposed, not only the pre-Existence of Souls, but also their *metensōmatōsis*[195], (or reincarnation), the doctrine of which is found in our traditional teaching. (See the whole of Tract. of the *Cabb. Denud.*, | Vol. 2, Part. 3, Tract. 2.)

Christian What type of reimcarnation did Elijah experience, if this theory of yours is correct?

Kabbalist Catechumen According to our teachers, one type is the Reincarnation of the Psyche which we call [in Hebrew] *Nefesh*, another, the Reincarnation of the Spirit or [in Hebrew] *Ruach* and [a third], that of the Mind

p. 41

fol. 9ᵛ

---

191 Added in the right margin: fateor,
192 Correction in the right margin: Eliæ replaced by Malachiæ. Either reading is possible: the prophecy of Malachi concerns Elijah.
193 Correction above the line: fortuna replaced by Doctrina
194 Cf. "De Revolutionibus animarum".
195 The term is possibly taken from Origen's famous discussion of the soul in *The Commentary of Origen on S. John's Gospel. The Text Revised with a Critical Introduction and Indices*, edited by Allan England Brooke, 2 vols (Cambridge University Press, 1896), 6.85. In 6.86 Origen contrasts *metensōmatōsis* ("transmigration" or "re-embodiment in different bodies"), a doctrine of which he disapproved, with his own term *ensōmatōsis* ("incarnation" or "embodiment in only one body"). Plotinus used *metensōmatōsis* twice (Enn. 2.9.6; 4.3.9). See Geoffrey William Hugo Lampe, *A Patristic Greek Lexicon* (Oxford: Clarendon Press, 1961) p. 864a, *s.v.*

autem, admisso semel textu vestro, quod in Johanne fuerit revolutio non Psyches, sed ‖ *spiritus*[196] *Eliæ juxta verba Angeli Luc. 1, 17. De spiritu autem Eliæ Cabbalistæ nostri tradunt, quod ortum habeat â splendore superno Mundi Emanativi, quodque cum omni specie ad hunc splendorem pertinente, in Lapsu Animarum non immersus fuerit peccato & corticibus immundis,* | *sed tantum secesserit ab Adamo. Vide Tract. de Revolutionibus Animarum P. 1, c. 19, §. 16.*[197] *Deinde etiam Doctores nostri afferunt, quod Elias evaserit Angelus sicut Chanoch; unde ambo non sint mortui. Ibid. p. 382, §. 4*[198] *, & p. 408, §. 18, 20*[199]*; p. 450, c. 32*[200]*, vid. & Excerpta Cent. 1. Loc. XXVII. Et in specie, quod nomen ejus sit Sandalphon, vid. Pneumatica Cabbalist. Cabbal. Denud. Tom. II, P. 3, Tract. 1,* | *c. 3, §. 1, 2, p. 221. sqq. 227.*[201] *Conf. Excerpt. Cent. 1. Loc. XXXV, c. 1, §. 5, 15, 16. Item quod antehac fuerit Pinchas Ibid §. 10. & p. 406, c. 2, §. 3*[202] *sq. & p. 451, §. 5*[203] *sqq. Item* רל"ב"ג *ad. 1. Reg. 17, 1 quamvis hic traditur*[204] *Antiquorum minimè*

---

196 A red pencil square bracket inserted into the text (Matth.[11, 14) refers to an annotation in the left margin: 10.C./42.

197 "Porro tandem aliæ dantur animæ, quæ in protoplaste comprehensæ erant, quæ etiam dividuntur in plures species. Quoniam species splendoris superni de emanatione non immersæ fuerunt corticibus, sed tantum secesserunt ab Adamo. Atque hinc mens data est Chanocho; est Spiritus Eliæ; & psyche Caino & Hebeli. In altera specie trium nempe mundorum inferiorum etiam certæ sunt notiones, quæ pertinuerunt ad Chanochum & Eliam & Cainum atque Hebelem: Et cuilibet sua tradita est species." ("De Revolutionibus animarum", op. cit., p. 322).

198 "Elias autem b.m. accipiebat spiritum Emanativum; quare & ipse dignus fiebat, ut evaderet angelus sicut Chanoch: & ambo non moriebantur." (Ibid., p. 382).

199 "Alia tamen adhuc datur notio ipsius nempe portionis Adami, quam hæreditariò tradidit Kaino: in illa est assecutio omnium mundorum à Psyche Factiva usque ad Psychen Emanativam. Quicunque ergo à notione hac secunda descendit, magnæ admodum est excellentiæ, quoniam prima statim vice, qua in mundum venit, restitui potest usque ad Psychen Emanativam, & simul tota radix ejus ad hanc notionem pertinet secundam. Duæ enim sunt notiones, lux interna & ambiens. Et Elias erat de luce interna ejusdem, & tota radix ejus de luce hac interna erat. Et quia pertingere possunt, usque ad Emanationem, hinc vocantur Angeli. Quapropter & Elias p.m. vocatur Angelus. [...] Unde etiam de Pinchaso, qui erat unus exploratorum primorum, dicitur Jes. 2. v. 4. *Et occultabat eum*: quoniam erat Angelus, sicut dixerunt Magistri nostri bonæ memoriæ. [...] §. 20. Chanoch autem, quia accipiebat splendorem supernum i.e. mentem supernam, fiebat Angelus, & quidem excellentior quam Elias. Quicunque enim est de notione Emanativa, ascendere potest usque ad gradum Angelicum." (Ibid., pp. 408–409).

200 Ibid. Chapter 32 is entitled "Porta Angelorum" (pp. 450–453).

201 The reference is to *Kabbala denudata, II*, "Pars tertia Quæ est Pneumatica Kabbalistica. Seu Doctrina Hebræorum de Spiritibus, nempe Angelis Bonis & malis; itemque

or [in Hebrew] *Neshamah*. | It appears (to attend also to your own text at the same time) that in John [the Baptist] there was a Reincarnation not of the soul but ‖ of the spirit of Elijah (according to the words of the Angel in Lk 1.17). Concerning the Spirit of Elijah our Kabbalists teach that it had its origin in the heavenly splendour of the World of Emanation and that, together with every one belonging to this glory, did not sink in the fall of souls caused by sin and the worldly Shells, | but only seceded from Adam (Tract. *De Revol. Animarum*, Part. 1, chap. 19, § 16). For this reason our teachers also assert that Elijah became an angel like Enoch and thus neither of them died (ibid. p. 382, § 4 & p. 408, § 18, 20; p. 450, chap. 32. See also Excerpt Cent. I Loc. 27). And more particularly, that this angel's name was Sandalphon[205] (See *Pneumatica Cabbalistica, Cabb. Denud.*, II, Part. 3, Tract. 1 |, chap. 3, § 1, 2, pp. 221–227. Conf. Excerpt Cent. I Loc. 35, chap. 1, § 5, 15, 16). Similarly, that [Elijah] had already been Phineas ibid., § 10 & p. 406; chap. 2, § 3 *seq.* & p. 451, § 5 *seq.*. Also RL"BG[206] on 1 Kgs 17.1 (though this scarcely followed the ancient tradition).

p. 42

    de Anima. Partis tertiæ tractatus I. pneumaticus, Cui nomen בית אלהים, seu Domus Dei, conscriptus Lingua Lusitanicâ Auctore R. Abraham Cohen Irira Lusitano è dogmatibus R. Jizchak Lorjensis", pp. 188–242. Chapter III: "Angeli dividuntur inter eos, qui sub Sancto illo, qui benedictus sit! & inter eos, qui sub Schechinah; & inter eos, qui sub regimine duorum Capitaneorum, Metatronis & Sandalphonis; & quomodo alii ab aliis influxum accipiant."; Chapter IV: "Hic distinguuntur Animalia à Rotis: diciturque, quod Animalia locum habeant in mundo Angelorum; Rotæ autem quasi descendant in mundum Asiah: nec non de Sandalphone & Metatrone Capitaneis Angelorum"; Chapter V: "Ejusdem Argumenti"; Chapter VI: "De *decem Turmis Angelorum*" (pp. 221–227).

202 "In Eliah quoque erant animæ Nadab & Abihu. Hinc de pelle arietis Jizchak Elias sibi faciebat cingulum coriaceum circa lumbos suos. צחק" autem & פינחס numeris æquipollent. (Pinchas autem est Elias.)" ("De Revolutionibus animarum", op. cit., p. 406).

203 "§. 5. De Pinchaso autem dicitur: *Et Eleazar filius Aaron uxorem ducebat de filiabus Putiel, &c. ista sunt capita*, &c. ubi sensus hic est: quod Pinchas descenderit à duabus scintillis: nempe à radice Josephi, qui vicit (Hebr. פטפט) pravam suam concupiscentiam: & à radice Jethronis, qui saginaverat (Hebr. פטם) vitulos pro idololatria. Quod mirum tibi non videatur: quoniam Joseph denotat mysterium fundamenti, ubi omnes animæ, tam benignitatum quam severitatum commiscentur atque concurrunt: unde sæpè mixtura quædam datur animarum, ita ut & hic anima quædam aliena admisceri potuerit radici Josephi: Præsertim quod portio Jethronis, etiam esset de psyche emanativa. Unde Pinchas ex utroque hoc genere constabat." (Ibid., p. 451).

204 Correction: traditur replaced by tradita

205 This is the name of the archangel who Elijah became. He is often considered the twin of Metatron (who Enoch became) and presents the prayers of Israel to God.

206 The abbreviation refers to R. Levi ben Gershom. See Johannes Buxtorffius, *De Abbreviaturis Hebraicis*, 2nd ed. (Basel: Impensis Ludovici Regis, 1640), p. 183, s.v. A copy of the book is found in the Sulzbach library catalogue of 1734.

fuerit assecutus. Idem quod sæpius appareat sapientibus. Ibid. p. 453, §. 16[207],

p. 43   *vide Idra Rabba §. 1165*[208] *sqq.* ‖

Christianus[209]. *Johannes* יוחנן.[210] Hæc omnia si rectè perpenderetis[211], profectò negotium de incarnatione Messiæ vobis[212] tot non crearet difficultates. Si enim in carne nasci potuit Angelus; cur non Angelorum caput? Et si in gratiam Jesu Nazareni in carnem venit Elias; certè necesse est ut major sit illius Jesu autoritas, quàm â vobis hactenus statuitur. Ad minimum | insigniter hinc apparet eximia illa istius filii dignitas, de quo etiam Christus expressè dicit Matth. 11, 11 non surrexisse inter natos mulierum majorem Johanne.

Johannes יוחנן

Christianus. Velim ut in nomine hoc illa exquiras mysteria, quæ procul dubio | in ipso involuta latent; cum non frustra divinitus imponi soleant nomina. Et literaliter quidem sensus istius nominis est Deus gratiam exhibuit; ut indicetur character ille temporis Messiani, de quo Joh. 1, 17.

Cabb. Cat. *Supposito hoc, dicerem, quod in hunc finem, ut eò magis appareat istius gratiæ divinæ affluxus, literæ huic Nomini insertæ* | *sint Tetragrammaticæ masculinæ tantùm* (*vid. Adumbratio Cabbal. Christianæ c. 11, §. 2.*[213]) (2.) *Nomen hoc* יוחנן *numero minore exhibet numerum 7 qui eodem*

p. 44   *computi genere etiam in voce* אליהו[214] *apparet.* (3.) *Numerus ma-* ‖ *-jor*[215] *ejusdem Nominis 124, etiam reperitur in voce* עדן, *sive subintelligamus significationem temporis, quasi nunc inchoari dicatur nova Epocha* (*Matth. 11, 12.13.*[216])

---

207 "16. Elias ergo Thisbites, qui erat de tribu Gad, ascendit in cœlum, ibique relictus est, nec amplius descendit: residua igitur fuit portio Eliæ Benjaminitæ: qui revolutus est in illum, de quo scribitur 1. Paralipp. 8. v. 27. *Et Elias & Sichri Filii Jerocham*. Et deinde unitus est cum illo Elia Thisbite superno. Et hic est Elias ille de tribu Benjamin, qui ascendit & descendit, & loquitur cum sapientibus, & edit miracula. Unde intelligi potest illud, quod ipse dixit: se de posteris Rachelis descendere: quoniam illi nesciebant, quænam pars de supradictis ipse esset." ("De Revolutionibus animarum", op. cit., p. 453).

208 "§. 1165. Dixit R. Schimeon, Mirum est quod ille cinctus lumbis, indutus veste pilosa (*Elias*) non inventus sit in domo areæ nostræ, cum revelarentur res istæ sanctæ!" (*"Idra rabba* seu Synodus areæ magna", op. cit., p. 518).

209 A red pencil square bracket inserted into the text ([Christianus) refers to an annotation in the left margin: 11.C./43.

210 Deletion: *Johannes* יוחנן.

211 Correction above the line: perpenderetis replaced by perpenderent vestrates

212 Correction above the line: vobis replaced by illis

213 "Ubi notandum, quia jam erat tempus, cum copula institueretur tam inferior quam

Also that he rather frequently appeared to the sages ibid., p. 453, §16. See Idra Rabba, §1165 *seq.*.

Christian ‖ Your sages so rightly evaluated all these things, that, really, the business of the Incarnation of Messiah will not cause them many difficulties. For if an angel can be born in the flesh, why not the Chief of Angels? And if for the sake of Jesus of Nazareth, Elijah came in the flesh, it is surely necessary [to conclude] that the authority of this Jesus is greater than has thus far been admitted by you. At least, | from these passages is clearly apparent the distinguished dignity of that son, concerning which Christ also said expressly (in Mt 11.11) that there had "not arisen amongst the sons of women one greater than John".[217]

p. 43

Johannes ywḥnn

Christian I would like you to investigate the mysteries which doubtless | lie hidden, wrapped up in this name, since names are not usually divinely given in vain. Literally the meaning of this name is "God Showed Grace", to point to the character of the time of Messiah (about which Jn 1.17).

Kabbalist Catechumen Assuming this to be so, I would say that, the (masculine only) letters of the Tetragrammaton [*y, h*] are inserted | into this name, so that the afflux of that divine grace might be more apparent (See *Adumbratio*, chap. 11, §2).

(2) This name *ywḥnn* [John] indicates by its lower numerical value the number 7, which by the same type of reckoning appears in the word *'lyhw* [Elijah].

(3) ‖ The higher numerical value of the name [*ywḥnn*] is 124. It is also found in the word *'dn* [Eden] whether we detect here the meaning of time, as if a new epoch is said to be beginning now (Mt 11.12, 13; Mk 1,1); or

p. 44

---

superior; quod duæ Literæ Fœmininæ Tetragrammaticæ propterea mutatæ sint in tales, quæ connotant Masculinitatem: quoniam etiam Schin Matris, denotat tres Patres. (Unde & in Nomine יוחנן, qui erat alter à Messia, literæ Tetragrammaticæ tantum masculinæ sunt.)" ("Adumbratio kabbalæ christianæ", op. cit., p. 62).

214 BSB: אליחו (Printer's error)
215 A red pencil square bracket inserted into the text (ma[jor) refers to an annotation in the left margin: 12.C./44.
216 Added in the left margin: Mar. 1, 1.
217 This verse is not here treated as hyperbole but simple truth: the spirit of John had not rebelled and had become the angel Sandalphon. That he should come in the flesh to announce Jesus Messiah, enhances the status of the latter.

fol. 10ʳ

sive (4.) | Paradisi, cujus gaudia nunc in terram sese demittant (Luc. 1, 14) 45
(5.) *Eundem ||| numerum etiam efficiunt duæ plenitudines Tetragrammaticæ* ע״ב *72. &* ן״ב *52. (de quorum mysteriis plurima in Cabbala denudata Tom. 1, P. 1, p. 535*[218]*, 371*[219]*. item sub* ע״ב *&* ן״ב *& in Philosophia Cabbalistica p. 111 & sqq.*[220])[221].

V. 14. Gaudium: חדותא

Cabb. Cat. חדוה *Gaudium dicitur, quasi* ח״ד *unicum sunt,* ו״ה *duæ hæ literæ* 5
p. 45 *Tetragrammaticæ; masculus scilicet & fœ- || -mina*[222]*, Sponsus & Sponsa, Rex & Regina, in una nunc esse cupiunt copula.*

Christianus. *Addo, quod talem unionem nunc intenderit Messias etiam cum Ecclesia: nam ex unione graduum illorum potissimum quidem nunc resultabat Adventus | Messiæ, unde Gaudium oriebatur omni populo Luc. 2,* 10
10.

Cabb. Cat. *Sed ex eadem unione etiam in specie ortum habebat descensus Eliæ in Johannem, unde Gaudium speciale annunciatur Zachariæ. Et quia hic tanquam Sacerdos hactenus influxum saltem hauserat occultum ê gradu Benignitatis; nunc influxus etiam è gradu Vehementiæ opposito ipsi promittitur, | ad* 15
quem pertinet gaudium, ita ut Levitarum, (qui eodem pertinent;) simul sorte beetur, ubi mysticè impletum dici posset illud Ex. 4, 14. Nonne Aaron frater tuus Levita est?

---

218 "Nomen ע״ב refertur ad *Cerebra* & vocatur *Accentuum* nomine & correspondet *Systemati Aziluth*." ("Loci communes kabbalistici", op. cit., p. 535).
219 "טנ״תא 1. Est abbreviatura nominum טעמים seu *accentus*. נקודה seu *puncta*. תגין seu *apices*, & אותיות seu *literæ*, quibus denotantur conceptus sublimiores in *aziluthicis*, cognati quatuor *plenitudinibus* Tetragrammaticis h.m. ut Taamim pertineant ad ע״ב [...]." (Ibid., p. 371).
220 "Liber *Shaar ha-shamaïm* Seu Porta Coelorum", op. cit., pp. 111–120.
221 Added in the right margin: Christ. Adde quod Nomen Johannis plenius, quale describitur à Matthæo c. 3, 1 & Luca c. 3, 2 nimirum in Syriaco: יוחנן מעמדנא בר זכריא Johannes submersor Filius Zachariæ: & nomen Eliæ plenius, quod extat 1. Reg. 19, 1 nimirum אליהו התשבי Elias Tishbites: numeris æquipolleant, referantur singula numerum 769: qui numero minore exprimit 22. summam literarum Alphabethi; quæ Legis consummationem denotat Matth. 11, 13. (BSB: summa literarum Alphabethi).
222 A red pencil square bracket inserted into the text (fœ[mina) refers to an annotation in the right margin: 13.C./45.

45   (4) | [The meaning] of Paradise whose joys are now coming down to earth (Lk 1.14). ||| fol. 10ʳ

(5) Two full Tetragrammata make the same number: *'b* 72 and *bn* 52 [equals 124]. See more about these mysteries in Cabb Den Vol I. Part 1 p. 535, p. 371; also under *'b* [72] and *bn* [52] in *Philosophia Cabbalistica* p. 111 et seq..

Christian Add that the fuller name of John as given by Mt 3.1 and Lk 3.2 in Syriac *ywḥnn mʿndnʾ bn rkdy*[223], "John the Baptiser Son of Zachariah", and the fuller name of Elijah which stands [in Hebrew] in 1 Kgs 19.1 *ʾlyhw htšby*, "Elijah the Tishbite", have the same numerical value individually making the number 769[224], which by the lower numerical value is 22 the total number of the letters of the alphabet which denotes the end of the Law (Mt 11.13).[225]

Verse 14

Joy ḥdwtʾ

5   **Kabbalist Catechumen** [The Hebrew] *ḥdwh* is translated Joy as if *ḥd* [= one] is a unity and the || [other] two letters *w* and *h* are from the Tetragramma-   p. 45
ton. This denotes masculine and feminine, bridegroom and bride, King and Queen, now desiring to be joined in one uniting.

Christian I would add that Messiah now intends such a union with Eccle-
10 sia for, from the union of those Sefirot above all, there results the Advent | of Messiah, when Joy arose for all [the] people Lk 2.10.

Kabbalist Catechumen But from that same union also specifically came the descent of Elijah into John and so a particular Joy is [here] announced to Zachariah. This man who up to then merely in his capacity as a priest had imbibed a hidden influx from the degree Kindness, now was promised an
15 additional influx from the opposite degree of Strength, | to which pertains joy, so that from among the Levites (who [also] belong to the same [degree]) he was blessed at the same time by the lot: thus Ex 4.14 "Surely Aaron your brother is a levite?" can be said to be mystically fulfilled.

---

223   This is a conflation of John's name in the two passages cited, but with the Hebrew *bn* for the Aramaic *br* ("son of") and *rkdyʾ* as a printing error in the BSB fragment for *zkryʾ*.
224   The Hebrew letters for "John the Baptist, son of Zachariah" add up to 769 only if one gives terminal letters the value of their initial or medial forms.
225   The alphabet evoking the letter, rather than the spirit.

Et exultatio. ורוזאא

Cabb. Cat. רוזא *est summus Gaudii gradus in externos prorumpens | gestus.* 20
Christianus. Talis[226] affectus & Christo tribuitur Luc. 10, 21 & Act. 2, 26
p. 46 conf. Matth. 5, 12. ‖ Phil. 2, 17.18[227]; Pet. 1, 8; c. 4, 13; Act. 2, 46. Et Ps. 9, 3; c. 65, 14; c. 96, 11; Am. 6, 7 & Chaldaic. Prov. 13, 9; c. 11, 10; c. 23, 16.

Et multi gaudebunt &c. וסגיאא

Christianus. Obiter scire velim, annon in hac voce sublimior aliquis lateat 25
sensus?[228]
Cabb. Cat. *Mystico sensu* רבים *seu multi,* (1.) *sunt separati & dispersi; & qui extra unionem sunt. Et* (2.) *qui sub potestate Corticum immundorum sunt, vide Lexicon Cabbalisticum p.* 681[229] *&* 693[230]. *Conf. Joh. 11, 52; Matth. 26, 28; item Matth. 7, 13; c. 8, 11; c. 20, 16.28; Marc. 5, 9; Luc. 1, 16; c. 14, 16 &c.*

In vel super nativitate ejus במולדה 30

Christianus. Parum esset, si nihil hîc subintelligeretur, quam gaudium illud, de quo infra v. 58. Si verò latè sumatur nativitatis terminus pro toto tempore præsentiæ ejus; tunc huc pertineret illud Joh. 5, 35. Eodemque sensu accipitur vox מאתיתא παρουσία adventus Matth. 24, 37; 2 Cor. 10, 10; 2 Thess. 2, 9. | 35
Sed et strictè alicubi sumitur nativitatis terminus sicut Joh. 16, 21; Tit. 3, 5 & Græcum Matth. 1, 18[231].

---

226 BSB: Talius by error. This is a proper name.
227 A red pencil square bracket inserted into the text ([Phil. 2, 17.18) refers to an annotation in the right margin: 14.C./46.
228 BSB: sensus; (probably due to printer's oversight).
229 "רבים *Multi* in Raja Meh. dicuntur Patres, quia *multi* non dicuntur infra tres; ubi simul involvitur separatio, Unitati opposita: cum enim uniti sunt Patres, אגודה vocantur. Pard." ("Loci communes kabbalistici", op. cit., p. 681).
230 "רשות Denotat locum ubi licentia est aliquid agendi. Estque vel רשות הרבים Licentia plurium, aliàs Locus publicus: quo nomine appellantur lumina septem inferiora ex oculis Adam Kadmon prodeuntia separata aliud sub alio. Sed רבים κατ' ἐξοχὴν dicuntur Patres, nempe חגת sicut in Sohar & in Tikkunim traditur; vel est רשות היחיד Licentia unius aliàs locus privatus, cujus altitudo est 10. & latitudo 4. & hoc nomine appellatur ז"א postquam junctis Membris in unam coaluit personam, cujus latitudo est 4. quæ sunt 4. Literæ Tetragrammati & altitudo 10. quæ sunt 10. Literæ plenitudinis Alephatæ. Etz Chajim Part. Ozaroth Chajim Tract. Oroth, Nizuzoth & Kelim. Vid. מות 5.—רשות *Licentia*. Malchuth, quando copulata est cum marito, vocatur רשות היחיד

SECTION III

And Exultation *wrwz"*

Kabbalist Catechumen *rwz'* is the highest degree of Joy and reveals itself in external | gestures.

Christian This is also attributed to Christ: Lk 10.21; Acts 2.26; Cf. Mt 5.12; ‖ p. 46 Phil 2.17, 18; [1[232]]Pet 1.8; 4.13; Acts 2.46. Also: Ps 9.3 [KJV 2]; 65.14 [KJV 13]; 96.11; Amos 6.7[233]. Also: the Aramaic [Targum to] Pro 13.9; 11.10; 23.16.

And many shall rejoice *wsgy"*

Christian I would like to know whether something more sublime is hidden in this word.

Kabbalist Catechumen In a mystical sense, *rbym* (or "many") are [by definition] (1) separated and dispersed and take no part in any union.[234] And (2) are under the power of the Impure Shells. See *Lex. Cabb.*, p. 681 & p. 693. Cf. Jn 11.52; Mt 26.28. *Item* Mt 7.13; 8.11; 20.16, 28; Mk 5.9; Lk 1.16; 14.16 etc.

At his birth *bmwldh*

Christian It would hardly matter if nothing was implied here other than that joy [mentioned] below at verse 58. But if the term "his birth" is taken broadly [to mean] the whole time of his presence [here on earth], then Jn 5.35 is relevant here. The word *m'tyt'*, [or in Greek] *parousia* or advent has the same meaning in Mt 24.37; 2 Cor 10.10; 2 Thess 2.9. | But the term nativity is also taken elsewhere in its strict sense, as in Jn 16.21; Ti 3.5 and the Greek of Mt 1.18.

Licentia unius, quia in Eam licentiam habet unus ille 4. literis Nominis & decem plenitudinis constans. Sed רשות הרבים *Licentia plurium* est Serpens, mulier fornicatrix Samaëlis, sub quo multi, nempe 70. populi, qui omnes ab eo influxum habent. Pard." (Ibid., p. 693).

231 BSB: Matth. 1, 28 (Printer's error)
232 On occasion 1 Peter is cited merely as "Peter". This may be thought to indicate familiarity with the shorter and original Peshitta New Testament Canon, such as is printed in the Sulzbach 1684 Peshitta, which has only the First Letter of Peter (and which it therefore does not need to distinguish from a second letter). However reference is also found to "1 Peter".
233 The presence of the Hebrew *mrzḥ* is not always apparent in translations of the verse. Translate: "the shout of the banqueters shall cease" where *mrzḥ* is the revellers' cry.
234 That is the union mentioned immediately above in discussing the word "joy".

Cabb. Cat. *Ergò procul dubio gaudium hic subintelligitur aliquod occultum;* ‖ *Animarum*[235]*scilicet illarum, quæ post adventum Eliæ jamjam suam expectabant consummationem; vel liberationem è potestate corticum; scientes | descensum hunc è præconio illo, talibus in casibus publicari solito.*

V. 15. Magnus coram Domino. רב קדם מריא

Cabb. Cat. רב *est nomen officii sicut* רב טבחים *2. Reg. 25, 5.10.11.12.20* רב בית[236] *Esth*[237]. *1, 8. Conf. 2. Reg. 18, 17; Jes. 19, 20; Prov. 26, 10.*

Christianus. Sic procul dubio se habet et[238] Syriacum Matth. 20, 8; Luc. 8, 3; Rom. 16, 23; | Marc. 5, 35.36.38; Luc. 19, 2; 2 Cor. 11, 32; Heb. 4, 14.15; Luc. 12, 42; unde ‖ colligerem, quod Johannes vel Elias sit משנה secundus â Messiâ, cujus dignitas etiam describitur[239] Matth. 20, 23 & Apoc. 11, 4. Hinc sensus verborum Angelicorum non esset alius, quam Johannem fore Principem illum, primarium, qui minister sit proximus coram Messia. Conf. Matth. 11, 11.

Et vinum & temetum non bibet.
וחמרא ושכרא לא נשתא

Cabb. Cat. *Melius hic locus exponi non potest, quam ex Libro Sohar, cujus textus exprimitur inter Excerpta Cent.* ‖ *I. Loc. 43*[240]. *Unde apparet, quod sicera sit ex vino, confer. Targum in Jud. 13, 4, ubi Paraphrastæ*[241] שכר *est vinum vetus.*

Christianus. *Ergò procul dubio mysticè denotatur separatio à judicio: cum Gratiæ | dispensatio nunc præpolleret.* [**Cabb. Cat.**][242] *In specie autem, quod nullum ipsi commercium esse debeat cum illis gradibus, quibus ad peccandum impulsus est Adam.*[243]

---

235   A red pencil square bracket inserted into the text ([Phil. 2, 17.18) refers to an annotation in the right margin: 15.C./47.
236   BSB: וכ בית (Printer's error)
237   BSB: Est.
238   BSB: &
239   BSB: describur (Printer's error)
240   A red pencil square bracket inserted into the text (Cent.[I. Loc.) refers to an annotation in the left margin: 16.C./48.
241   BSB: Pharaphrastæ (Printer's error)
242   Added in the left margin: *Cabbal. Catech.* (which involves a change of speaker).
243   The sentence is underlined in order to give the speech to the Cabbalist.

SECTION III   199

Kabbalist Catechumen Doubtless joy here implies the hidden [joys] of those souls, who ‖ after the advent of Elijah, were then expecting their con- p. 47
summation and to be liberated from the power of the Shells. They would
40   know | of [Elijah's] descent from the proclamation usually made [in heaven]
in such cases.

Verse 15
Great before God rb qdm mry'

Kabbalist Catechumen *rb* is the name of an office like [the Hebrew] *rb ṭbḥym* ["Captain of the Guard"] 2 Kgs 25.5[244], 10, 11, 12, 20; *rb byt* ["Officer of the House"] Esth 1.8. Cf. 2 Kgs 18.17; Isa 19.20; Pro 26.10.

Christian Similarly, doubtless, also in the Syriac [text] of Mt 20.8; Lk 8.3;
45   Rm 16.23; | Mk 5.35, 36, 38; Lk 19.2; 2 Cor 11.32; Heb 4.14, 15; Lk 12.42 from
which ‖‖ I would gather that John or Elijah was [in Hebrew] *mšnh* or second   fol. 10ᵛ
to Messiah and that his glory is also described in Mt 20.23 and Rev 11.4. Thus
the meaning of the words of the angels was that John would be the chief, or
the foremost, who would be the closest minister before Messiah (Mt 11.11).

5   *And Wine and intoxicating liquor he will not drink wḥmr' wškr' l' nšt'*

Kabbalist Catechumen This verse cannot be better explained than from the Book Zohar ‖ whose text is printed among the Excerpt. Cent. I Loc. 43. From p. 48
there it appears that "strong liquor" is made from wine. Cf. The Targum to
Judg 13.4 where the *škr* [of the Hebrew text] is translated "old wine"[245].
Christian No doubt removal from Judgment is mystically indicated here,
10   since the dispensation | of Grace now has become more powerful.
Kabbalist Catechumen Precisely, in that there could be no commerce on his part with those degrees by which Adam was driven to sin.[246]

---

244   The phrase does not occur in this verse.
245   Hebrew Judges 13.4 "wine and strong liquor" is rendered in Aramaic as *ḥmr ḥdt w'tyq* "new wine and old".
246   About the intoxicating properties of a certain type of wine, which e.g. led Adam to commiting sin, see Joel Hecker, *Mystical Bodies, Mystical Meals: Eating and Embodiment in Medieval Kabbalah* (Wayne State University Press, 2005), pp. 214–215.

Et spiritu sancto implebitur &c. ורוחא דקורשא[247]

Cabb. Cat. *Exempla quædam similia habentur in Libro Sohar, quæ adducuntur Excerptorum Cent. 1. Loc. 44.45.46. Insigne autem hoc est argumentum | pro Animarum præexistentia: Operatio[248] enim spiritus sancti perficit intellectum Animæ potissimum & voluntatem; unde omninò legitimus istarum facultatum usus præsupponitur: qualem aliàs Embryones habere nequeunt, si vel per traducem vel immediatam creationem tum demum esse cœperunt.[249] Conferatur Exemplum Jeremiæ[250] c. 1, v. 5.* ‖

Christianus[251]. Argumentum hinc etiam sumi solet pro fide infantum, & effectu Baptismi in illis.

Cabb. Cat. *An autem à particularibus hisce ad universale concludi queat,[252] vos videritis.*

Christianus. Quid si et[253] vobis idem objiceretur?

Cabb. Cat. *Sufficit nos particulariter saltem concludere pro præexistentia ex exemplis his: quia & quarundam Animarum præexistentia hactenus non fuit admissa.*

V. 16. *Et multos ex filiis Israel respicere faciet etc.*
וסגיאא מן בני ישראל נפנא

Christianus. Vide quæ[254] de appellatione Multorum[255] dicta sunt ad v. 14. Converti autem | plurimos vel respicere fecit ad Messiam, dum digito in illum intentendo diceret, Ecce Agnus Dei &c. Joh. 1, 29.36.15.26.27.34; c. 5, 33. Quod enim per Dominum Deum suum intelligatur hôc loco Messias, expressè docet versiculus subsequens, dum dicitur: Et ipse præcedet eum, nempe

---

247   BSB: דקודשא. Here the writing in the manuscript is erroneous.
248   BSB: Opperatio (Printer's error)
249   The question received much attention in the "Adumbratio kabbalæ christianæ", in the discussion devoted to the hypothesis of the preexistence of the soul (chapter VII) and particularly to the question of how the soul enters the body: "Minor probatur: quia non nisi duæ sunt potissimum opiniones contrariæ. Una eorum, qui animam per traducem propagari dicunt, altera eorum qui, animam statuunt creari, data quacunque occasione. In priori occasione autem manifesta occurrit contradictio: Anima enim cum spiritus sit, essentiæ est indivisibilis id est indiscerpibilis. Altera sententia pronunciat quædam, quæ indigna sunt Majestate divina [...]". ("Adumbratio kabbalæ christianæ", op. cit., p. 33).
250   BSB: *Jer.*
251   A red pencil square bracket inserted into the text (Cent.[1. Loc.) refers to an annotation in the left margin: Pp.D./49.

SECTION III

And he will be filled with the Holy Spirit wrwḥʾ dqwdšʾ

Kabbalist Catechumen Some similar examples will be found in the Book *Zohar* and are adduced in Excerpt Cent. 1 Loc. 44, 45, 46. This is an outstanding argument | for the pre-existence of souls. For the operation of the Holy Spirit perfects particularly the intellect of the soul and the will, so that the entirely legitimate use of those faculties is presupposed, otherwise they would not be able to have embryos if they started to form either by transmission or immediate creation[256]. Cf. the example of Jer 1.5.

Christian ‖ One usually takes an argument from here concerning the faith of infants and the effect of baptism upon them.[257]   p. 49

Kabbalist Catechumen Do you think it is possible to draw a universal conclusion from these particulars?

Christian What if the same objection was put to you?

Kabbalist Catechumen It is good enough for us just to draw particular conclusions for the pre-existence [of souls] from these [words], since the pre-existence of any soul has not so far been admitted [by you].[258]

Verse 16

And he will make many of the sons of Israel turn to wsgyʾʾ mn bny yšrʾl npnʾ

Christian We have spoken about the term "many" in our discussion of verse 14. [John] | made many convert or turn to Messiah when he pointed him out and said "Behold the Lamb of God etc." (Jn 1.29, 36, 15, 26, 27, 34; 5.33). For in this verse the "Lord [their] God" is to be understood of Messiah. This is explicitly stated in the next verse when it says "and he shall go before him"

---

252 BSB: queat?
253 BSB: &
254 Deletion: Vide quæ
255 Added above the line: quædam
256 For "transmission" here (rather than "reincarnation"), see Vileno, *À l'ombre de la kabbale*, op. cit., pp. 172 *seq*.
257 Knorr remarks that the text just cited (Jer 1.5), where God declares that he knew Jeremiah before he framed him and sanctified him before he left the womb, was commonly used in discussions of infant baptism. So, for an example taken almost at random: Johannes Oecolampadius, *In Jeremiam Prophetam Commentariorum* (Geneva: Typographia Crispiniana, 1558), p. 3 on Jer 1.5.
258 Notice the discrete hesitation with respect to this doctrine on the part of the Christian, to which the Kabbalist Catechumen deliberately draws attention here.

p. 50 Dominum Deum Iisraël²⁵⁹. Non autem præcessit nisi Messiam: quod insignè est argumentum pro Deitate Messiæ. ‖

Cabb. Cat.²⁶⁰ *Contra vestrâtes certe, non verò contra illos ex nobis, qui Cabbalæ sunt ignari. Ego tamen omninò*²⁶¹ *annoto, quod etiam Nomen istud Divinum linguæ Syriacæ* מריא אלההון *omninò æquipollens sit*²⁶² *ille Hebraico* יהו״ה אלהיהם *Ex. 10, 7; c. 23, 33 & quod Nomen Elohim* אלהים י״י *denotet unionem graduum sexti & decimi, seu sponsi & sponsæ, quæ Messiæ temporibus*²⁶³ *in ∣ Ecclesia quàm maximè requiritur. (vid. Lexicon Cabbalist. p. 383*²⁶⁴ *sq.)*

V. 17. *Et ipse præcedet eum.* והו נאזל קדמוהי

Christianus. Ubicunque magnam instituit Redemptionem Messias, ibi suos habet Præcursores: In Ægyptiaca enim habebat Mosen; in Babylonicâ Josuam; in Universali Eliam. Eodemque modo & Pseudo-Messiæ suos sibi deligunt præcones: ∣ ut Barcochab R. Akibam.

Cabb. Cat. *Sic & Regnum Messiæ vicarium suum habebit Pseudoprophetam (Ap. 16, 13; c. 19, 20; c. 20, 10. Conf. Matth. 24, 24) & in ultima redemtione iterum præcedent eum Elias & Moses, Apoc. 11, 6.* ‖ ‖‖

p. 51
fol. 11ʳ

*In spiritu*²⁶⁵ &c. ברוחא

Cabb. Cat. *Excellentissimum illud, quod â summo splendore accepisse dicitur Elias, fuit Spiritus; idque tum demum cum peregisset*²⁶⁶ *Heroicum illud facinus in Sittim Num. 25, 7. Et hæc dicitur esse ratio, quare perpetuò cum de Elia sermo est, mentio tantum ∣ fiat spiritus, ut 1. Reg. 18, 12. Et spiritus Domini tollet te. Item 2. Reg. 2, 9. Sit mihi duplicatura spiritus tui. Et ibid, v. 15,*

---

259 BSB: Israel
260 A red pencil square bracket inserted into the text ([Cabb. Cat.) refers to an annotation in the left margin: 3.D./51.
261 Correction above the line: omninò replaced by simul
262 BSB: word lacking.
263 BSB: tomporibus (Printer's error)
264 "[…] Cum igitur combinatur יד״וד אד״ני quod est mysterium ידו״ד אלה״ים omnia sunt in perfectissima integritate […] Totum autem mysterium unionis consistit in ידוד אלהים: unde Deut. 6, 4. *Audi Iisraël*, יד״וד א״להינו, *est* י״דוד unus. […]" ("Loci communes kabbalistici", op. cit., pp. 383–384).
265 A red pencil square bracket inserted into the text ([In spiritu) refers to an annotation in the right margin: 3.D./51.

SECTION III

i.e. the Lord God of Israel. For [John] "went before" no one else other than Messiah—which is itself an outstanding argument for the deity of Messiah.

35 **Kabbalist Catechumen** ‖ For your own [Christian] people certainly, but not for those of us [Jews] who are ignorant of Kabbalah. I would want to add that at the same time the Divine Name in Syriac *mry' 'lhwn* is the full equivalent of the Hebrew *yhwh 'lhym* (Ex 10.7; 23.33) and that the name Elohim, *yy*[267] *'lhym*, denotes the union of the Sixth and Tenth Sefirot, or of groom
40 and bride, which is required in the times of Messiah |—most of all in Ecclesia (See *Lex. Cabb.*, pp. 383 *seq.*).

Verse 17
And he shall go before him whw n'zl qdmwhy

Christian Whenever Messiah institutes a great redemption, there he has his precursors. In Egypt he had Moses and in Babylon Joshua[268] and for the whole world, Elijah. In the same fashion pseudo-Messiahs also chose themselves heralds, | as Barcochba chose R. Akiba.
45 **Kabbalist Catechumen** The Kingdom of Messiah will have its own substitute false prophet (Rev 16.13; 19.20; 20.10. Cf. Mt 24.24) and in the final redemption Elijah and Moses will precede him again (Rev 11.6). ‖

In the Spirit *brwḥ'*

Kabbalist Catechumen That most wonderful thing which Elijah is said to have received from the Highest Splendour was the Spirit and that finally when he performed that heroic deed in Sittim [as Phineas] (Num 25.7). It
5 is said that whenever there is talk of Elijah [in the Hebrew Bible] | mention is also made of the Spirit as in 1 Kgs 18.12 "the Spirit of God will carry you". Also 2 Kgs 2.9 "Let a double portion of your spirit be upon me" and (v15) "the

---

266 BSB: per egisset
267 Abbreviated and distorted for pious reasons.
268 Joshua the High Priest mentioned in Zech 3.1–10 *et alibi*. Lightfoot, *Miscellanies and the Harmony of the Gospels*, op. cit., p. 163: "'Jesus': The same with 'Jehoshua' in Hebrew, and 'Joshua' in Chaldee. These were two renowned ones before: —the one whereof brought the people into Canaan, after the death of Moses; and the other brought them thither out of Babel; and so both were lively figures of our Jesus, that bringeth his people to the heavenly Canaan". Knorr would no doubt have dissented from the use of the word "heavenly" here.

Spiritus Eliæ quievit super Elischa. (vide Tract. de Revolutionibus Animarum, p. 382[269] *& 436*[270]*).*

Christianus. Et ille spiritus jam descendisse videtur in Johannem; tanquam receptaculum longè dignissimum, in quo commoraretur Spiritus Sanctus.

Et in virtute ובחילא

Christianus. Id est in eodem gradu Spiritus Sancti, qualem Elias habuit; quod enim vox ista cohabitationem Spiritus Sancti denotet, haud obscurè colligitur è locis sequentibus Luc. 24, 49; c. 4, 14; c. 1, 35; Act. 1, 8; c. 4, 33; Rom. 15, 19.

Cabb. Cat. *Scio quod communiter similitudo*[271] *saltem duorum istorum | Johannis ‖ & Eliæ*[272] *proponi soleat, nimirum (1.) quod uterque depravationem*[273] *religionem doluerit; (2.) & eandem restituerit; (3.) persecutione Regum similium pressus fuerit; (4.) loca deserta coluerit; (5.) austeritatem vitæ sustinuerit; (6.) eodem pallio & cingulo usus fuerit; (7.) apertum prope Jordanem cœlum habuerit. Ex hinc tamen Ego repetita potius unius personæ nunc revolutæ accidentia, quam duarum, colligerem, | prout similia & in aliis Revolutionibus observare solemus (juxta Tractatum de Revolutionibus passim).*

---

269 "Elias autem b.m. accipiebat spiritum Emanativum; quare & ipse dignus fiebat, ut evaderet angelus sicut Chanoch: & ambo non moriebantur. [...] Eodem modo Elias non merebatur partem illius spiritus accipere, donec (adhuc dum Pinchas) perfecisset factum illud in Sittim, Numer. 25. vers. 7. atque tunc istum spiritum accipiebat. Et hæc est ratio, quare perpetuo, cum de Elia sermo est, mentio tantum fiat spiritus. Exempli gratia: 1. Regum 18. v. 12. *Et spiritus Domini tollet te.* Item: 2. Regum 2. v. 9. *Sit mihi duplicatura Spiritus tui.* Item: 2. Regum 2. v. 15. *Spiritus Eliæ quievit super Elischah.* Quia autem Spiritus habitare non potest nisi in Psyche; hinc dignus non evadebat illo Spiritu, donec perfecisset opus illud cum Simri, Num. 25. v. 7. ubi accipiebat Psychen Nadab & Abihu: qui sunt Psyche Adami Protoplastæ, ut porro dicemus juvante Deo. [...]" ("De Revolutionibus animarum", op. cit., p. 382).

270 "§. 7. Elias autem suam portionem Spiritus accipere non merebatur, nisi per factum illud in Sittim Num. 25. v. 7: *Et tunc accipiebat eum.* Hinc de illo nunquam nisi istius Spiritus saltem fit mentio. Atque tunc dabatur ipsi *fœdus pacis* loc. cit. v. 13. Qui est Spiritus iste Emanativus: unde vocatur Pax, quia mysterium Spiritus ibidem in pulchritudine nempe & fundamento consistit; qui gradus ambo vocantur Pax. Confer Jesch. 57. v. 19: *Pacem, pacem longinquo & propinquo.*" (Ibid., p. 436).

271 BSB: *simililitudo* (Printer's error)

spirit of Elijah rested upon Elisha" (See the Tract. *De Revol. Animarum*, p. 382 and p. 436).

Christian And that Spirit is now seen to descend upon John, as upon a most worthy vessel in whom the Holy Spirit dwelt.

And in Righteousness wbḥyl'

Christian This is in the same degree of the Holy Spirit which Elijah had, for that the [Syriac] word [*ḥyl'*] ["Righteousness"] denotes the cohabitation of the Holy Spirit is clearly seen in the following verses: Lk 24.49; 4.14; 1.35; Acts 1.8; 4.33; Rm 15.19.

Kabbalist Catechumen ‖ I know that the similarity of John and Elijah | is   p. 52
usually asserted[274] because (1) each of them protested against a corrupted religion and (2) each restored it. Each (3) was heavily persecuted by a similar kingdom, and (4) lived in deserted places, and (5) taught a life of austerity. They both (6) wore the same cloak and belt and (7) both had the heavens opened by the Jordan. However, in all this I detect the accidents of one person who has been reincarnated, | rather than of two [different people]. Just as we usually see in the case of other transmigrations (according to Tract. *De Revol. Animarum, passim*).[275]

---

272 A red pencil square bracket inserted into the text ([& Eliæ) refers to an annotation in the right margin: 4.D./52.

273 Correction: depravationem replaced by depravatam

274 Lightfoot, *Miscellanies and the Harmony of the Gospels*, op. cit., pp. 154–155: "First, They both came, when religion was even perished and decaying: secondly, They both restored it, in an excellent measure; thirdly, They were both persecuted for it,—Elias by Ahab and Jezebel,—John, by Herod and Herodias; fourthly, They both conversed much in the wilderness; fifthly, They agreed in austerity of life; sixthly, In the wearing of a hairy garment, and a leathern girdle; seventhly, Both of them had heaven opened to them near Jordan."

275 The Kabbalist Catechumen's interpretation here departs from the usual typology which sees one person as a pre-figuration of another. Rather he draws on the doctrine of the "revolution" of souls, according to which parts of the same soul are found successively in both persons.

Ut reducat cor patrum super filios &c.
דנפנא לבא דאבהא על בניא

Cabb. Cat. *Sensum Philosophicum istorum verborum tradit R. Iizchak Lorja in Tractatu de Revolutionibus Animarum p. 373[276], 421[277] quod nempe per Eliam restituendæ | sint Animæ, per varios lapsus atque revolutiones mirum in modum â primo ordine suo disturbatæ ad radices suas singulæ, in qua opinione etiam fuit Syracides c. 48, 10. Præsupposito enim, (quod et in Adumbratione Cabbalæ Chri- ‖ -stianæ[278] supponitur cap. 10, §. 6.[279]) hoc ipso tempore è Corpore Animarum Messiano sive Adamitico prodiisse Animas Israëliticas omnes; nihil jam restabat, nisi earundem | adaptatio ad singula membrorum metra, cuilibet Animæ pro nativo gradu suo debita (Eph. 4, 15; Rom. 12, 5; 1 Cor. 12, 14–27).*

Christianus. Sensum autem Theologicum Ego puto esse talem: reducet motus cordis & inclinationes, id est, fidem seu pietatem Patriarcharum super Posteros eorum, ut non amplius pro justitiâ propriâ, traditionum inhæreant spinositatibus; sed | simplici fiducia ad bene agendum â Deo[280] sua expetant auxilia. Et hunc esse istorum verborum sensum etiam docet antithesis subsequens, quæ est paraphrasis verborum Malachiæ: quos enim Malachias dixerat filios & Patres[281], hos angelus appellat incredulos: & quos Propheta Patres vocaverat, hos Angelus Justos nuncupat. Phrasis enim דלא מתטפיסין potius denotat incredulos | & infideles, quam inobedientes & contumaces juxta Joh. 3, 36; Rom. 11, 30.31; Heb. 4, 11; Rom. 10, 22[282]; Act. 14, 2; c. 28, 24; Rom. 2, 8; c. 15, 31; Pet. 3, 1; c. 4, 17; Rom. 11, 30.32; Eph. 2, 2; c. 5, 6; Col. 3, 6. Et

---

276 "Et hæc sic permanebunt & continuabuntur usque ad adventum Messiæ: deinde autem quælibet anima redibit ad radicem suam, omnesque Psychæ abibunt ad Mentes & spiritus suæ radicis. Atque hoc efficietur per Eliam Prophetam bonæ memoriæ, sicut dicitur: Mal. 4. v. 6: *Et convertet cor Patrum ad filios &c.* quia jam etiam patres & filii non omnes sunt de radice una, ita ut quandoque pater sit Kainita, & filius Hebelita, & sic deinceps. Tunc autem omnes animæ redibunt ad radicem suam veram. Et quia etiam Elias talis erat, ut Psyche ejus de radice una, & spiritus de alia radice esset; hinc per illum restituentur omnia." ("De Revolutionibus animarum", op. cit., p. 373).

277 "Hæc autem durabunt usque ad adventum Messiæ, atque Eliæ bonæ memoriæ, tunc quilibet restituetur radici suæ, ita ut Spiritus Adamicus redeat ad Psychen Adamicam: & sic quoque Psyche Kainitica ad Spiritum Kainiticum. Quod Scriptura innuit verbis illis Mal. 4. v. ult. *Et convertet cor Patrum ad filios* &c. Id omne enim efficiet Elias p.m. Quoniam & ipse in hoc erat statu, ita ut Spiritus ejus esset ab Adamo Protoplaste; Psyche ejus autem à Nadabo & Abihu, qui erant radicis Kainiticæ. Tunc igitur ipse singulos restituet loco suo." (Ibid., p. 421).

SECTION III   207

That he may turn the hearts of the fathers back to their sons dnpn' lb' d'bh' 'l bny'

Kabbalist Catechumen R. Isaac Luria (in Tract. *De Revol. Animarum*, p. 373, p. 421) taught the philosophic meaning of these words, namely that through Elijah souls, | shaken awefully from their initial order by various falls and reincarnations, are to be restored to their individual roots. This was the opinion of Ben Sira (48.10).[283] For the presumption ‖ is (as in *Adumbratio*, chap. 10, § 6) that at one moment all the Israelite souls came forth from the Messianic or Adamite Body of Souls.[284] Nothing then remained other than their | adaptation to the individual measures of the members which was due to any soul on account of its rank at birth (Eph 4.15; Rm 12. 5; 1 Cor 12. 14–27). p. 53

Christian The theological meaning I take to be this: [Elijah] will lead back the movements of the heart and its inclinations (i.e. the faith or the piety of the Patriarchs) to their offspring, so that no more will they cling to the subtleties of tradition in their own righteousness, | but with simple trust will await help from God for well-doing. That this is the meaning of these words is shown by the following antithesis which is a paraphrase of the words of Malachi. For those whom Malachi had called sons, the angel called unbelieving; and those whom the prophet called fathers, these the angel called righteous. For the phrase *dl' mttpysyn* denotes unbelievers | and infidels rather than those who are disobedient and contumacious (according to Jn 3.36; Rm 11.30, 31; Heb 4.11; Rm 10.22; Acts 14.2; 28.24; Rm 2.8; 15.31; Pet 3.1; 4.17; Rm 11.30,

---

278   A red pencil square bracket inserted into the text (Chri[stianæ) refers to an annotation in the right margin: 5.D./53.
279   Cf. *supra*, pp. 154–155 ("Adumbratio kabbalæ christianæ", op. cit., p. 60).
280   BSB: â DEO
281   Deletion: & Patres.
282   The chapter only has 21 verses. The text probably refers to the last verse: "Ad Israel autem dicit: Tota die expandi manus meas ad populum non credentem, et contradicentem".
283   This verse from the Hymn to the Ancestors is concerned with Elijah and is a paraphrase of Mal 3.23–24: "[…] qui scriptus es in judiciis temporum, lenire iracundiam Domini, conciliare cor patris ad filium et restituere tribus Jacob?"
284   For a summary introduction to this doctrine, see Jean-Pierre Brach, "À propos de l'âme du Messie dans la kabbale chrétienne", *Annuaire de l'EPHE, Sciences religieuses* 115 (2006–2007): pp. 313–319, here pp. 313–316 and "Das Theorem der messianischen Seele in der christlischen Kabbala bis zur Kabbala Denudata", *art. cit.*

sicut membro istorum verborum[285] intelligi putarem doctiores Israëlitarum; ita membro altero plebejos, publicanosque & scorta intelligerem: juxta Matth. 21, 32; Luc. 3, 10 ‖.12.14.[286] quibus aliàs nulla erat cognitio vel eruditio; Joh. 7, 49 | cum nunc per Johannem ad eandem[287] adducerentur cognitionem Messiæ & virtutis, qua & Justi salvabantur. Joh. 17, 3. ‖|

Et præparabit Domino populum perfectum
ונטיב למריא עמא גמירא

Christianus. Per Dominum intelligitur Messias: per populum Israëlitæ. His enim sicuti[288] missus fuerat Messias Matth. 15, 24; c. 10, 5.6; Act. 1, 8 ita & Johannes | Act. 13, 24. Pauci enim illi milites Luc. 13, 14 si gentiles fuerunt, procul dubio fuerunt proselyti: sicut Centurio Luc. 7, 5 & Cornelius Act. 10, 2. [**Cabb. Cat.**][289] *Quodsi verò ad Gentilium conversionem aliquid cooperatus est Elias iste noster*[290]*, id præstitisse & adhuc præstare, & præstiturum esse, eundem putarem in disponendis & promovendis ad generationem intra Ecclesiam Christianam*[291] *Animabus in Ethnicismum prolapsis | præsertim illis, quæ antea ad populum Iisraëliticum pertinuerant: ut & hac ratione ad suam radicem reduceretur dispersum hoc genus; quod fortè simul subintelligi potest Joh. 11, 52; Jac. 1, 1; 1 Pet. 1, 1.*[292]

Cabb. Cat. Sanè[293] *nisi secretior quædam Johannis sive Eliæ accessit cooperatio, quam ministerium Prædi-* ‖ *-cationis*[294] *& Baptismi ejus, quomodo præparasse | dici potest populum perfectum? (ad tautologiam enim vix recurretis, dicendo* ἑτοιμάσαι λαὸν κατεσκευασμένον *esse: præparare populum præparatum.) Imò licet vox* גמירא *dicatur denotare perfectè idoneum, in quem scilicet introduceretur consummata Messiæ perfectio; tamen per publicum Johannis ministerium nec id præstitum fuit, quia pauci nimis tunc Jesum*[295] *| receperunt:*

---

285   Added above the line: primò
286   A red pencil square bracket inserted into the text (Luc. 3, 10.[12.14) refers to an annotation in the right margin: 6.D./54.
287   BSB: eundem by error.
288   BSB: sicut
289   Added above the line: *Cabb. Cat.* The speach, initially attributed to the Christian, is given to the Cabbalist.
290   Deletion: noster (To be understood in the light of the change of speaker).
291   Deletion: Christianam (To be understood in the light of the change of speaker).
292   Added at the end of the line: Imò, to make the link with the following text. The speech remains with the Cabbalist.

32; Eph 2.2; 5.6; Col 3.6). Just as by the first member of this contrast [fathers] I think the more learned of the Israelites are meant, so by the other word [sons], I understand the common people, the tax collectors ‖ and prostitutes (so Mt 21.32; Lk 3.10; 12,14) who otherwise had no understanding or learning
45 (Jn 7.49), | since now through John they were brought the same knowledge of Messiah and virtue by which even the righteous will be saved (Jn 17.3).[296] ⫼

And he will prepare a people ready for the Lord wntyb lmry' 'm' gmyr'

Christian By "Lord" here is meant Messiah; by "people" the Israelites. For just as Messiah had been sent to them (Mt 15.24; 10. 5, 6; Acts 1.8) so also had John
5 [the Baptist] | (Acts 13.24). For those few soldiers (in Lk 13.14), even if they were gentiles, were without doubt proselytes, like the centurion (in Lk 7.5) and Cornelius (in Acts 10.2).

Kabbalist Catechumen But what if Elijah did cooperate in some way towards the conversion of the gentiles—having proposed it, promoting it and then going on to do the same in the future—and [acted] similarly in disposing and prompting souls within Ecclesia to [spiritual] birth, especially
10 those who had lapsed | into paganism but were previously part of Israel? In this way this dispersed people might be brought back to its roots, which perhaps can be learned also from: Jn 11.52; Jam 1, 1; 1 Pet 1.1. Unless there was a more hidden cooperation of John or Elijah than the ministry of preaching
15 and baptising, how can he be said ‖ to have prepared a people | who were ready? (Please do not have recourse to the tautology [of the Greek New Testament at Lk 1.17] by saying "*etoimasai ... laon kataskeuasmenon*" "to prepare a people prepared"![297]) Although the [Syriac] word *gmyr'* is said to denote something perfectly suitable into which was introduced the complete perfection of Messiah, however that did not happen through the public ministry

---

293 Deletion: Cabb. Cat. Sanè
294 A red pencil square bracket inserted into the text (Prædi[catio]) refers to an annotation in the left margin: 6.D./55. The numeration is erroneous. It should be 7.D./55. But the problem is resolved in the next but one annotation.
295 BSB: JESUM
296 Here Knorr's interpretation quite diverges from that of Lightfoot ad loc. who considers the fathers Jews and the sons Gentiles and looks for the supercession of the former.
297 The superiority of the Peshitta is asserted here. For the use of Greek terms in translations of kabbalistic texts see Saverio Campanini, *The Book of Bahir Flavius Mithridates' Latin Translation* (Torino: Nino Aragno Editore, 2005), pp. 77 *seq*. Greek phrases are more to be expected in New Testament commentaries.

unde non immeritò concludi posset, ad totam Ecclesiæ colligendæ œconomiam secreto quodam ministerio concurrere Eliam hunc: (ut dictum supra).

V. 18. *Quomodo noscam istud &c.*
איכנא אדע הדא

Cabb. Cat. *Si Zacharias fuit revolutio Aharonis, mirum | non est, quod antiquum illud incredulitatis vitium Animæ ipsius adhuc inhæserit; Sicut Usia qui Usæ traditur fuisse revolutio, iterum ad illicita admovebat manum. 2 Chr. 26, 16; 2 Sam. 6, 6; vid. Tractat. de Revolut. Anim. p. 391*[298]. *Sicut enim non crediderat ipsi Domino, promittenti ê Petrâ ‖ aquas*[299] *Num. 20, 6.8.12 ita multò minus credebat Angelo, promittenti ê senio filium.*

Christianus. *Quare autem punitur (cum in simili dubio non punirentur Abram Gen. 15, 8; c. 17, 17 & Sarah Gen. 18, 12?)*

Cabb. Cat. *Quod scil. post tot revolutiones nondum correxisset nævum istum.*

V. 19. *Gabriel qui adsto coram Deo &c.*
גבריאל דקאם אנא קדם אלהא

Christianus. *In Loco 32. Centuriæ 1, Excerptorum ê Libro Sohar afferitur, quod Gabrielis nomen omnibus illis Angelis tribuatur, qui veniunt de latere sinistro: Unde & Angelo, qui Lailah aliàs dicitur, idem nomen competat, quique præfectus sit Animabus in corpora deducendis. Cumque*[300] *ergò dubitare potuisset Zacharias, an apparitio hæc tanti etiam sit momenti: Et annon ordinarius ille Animarum | deductor secum nunc loqueretur, hinc specialem suum characterem eidem manifestat Angelus; quod nempe non sit de communioribus, sed secretioribus illis ministris, qui coram Deo stant. Vide de istis in Excerptis Centur. I Loco 47.*

---

298 "1. Factum illud Usiæ Regis, qui leprosus fiebat, quod suffitum offerre vellet; 2. Paral. 26. v. 16. ita se habet: quod Usia esset revolutio illius Usæ, de quo scriptum est in libro Samuelis Prophetæ: 2. Sam. 6. v. 3.8. *Et Usa & Achio ducebant currum*: Unde literæ nominis utriusque plane sunt similes.—2. Venerat autem in mundum, ut expiaret peccatum istud primum, quod applicuisset manum suam ad arcam Dei, & propterea esset mortuus: & tamen non restituebatur, sed redibat ad vitium prius, ut manum suam admoveret ad rem quandam illicitam. Anima tamen ejus sciebat, quod antea fuisset sacerdos: hinc sacerdotium iterum appetebat: In hoc tamen errans, eò quod jam sacerdos non esset." ("De Revolutionibus animarum", op. cit., p. 391).

of John, for too few then accepted Jesus. | So, one may reasonably conclude that this Elijah [John] was working in a secret ministry towards the whole plan of the necessary gathering of Ecclesia (as was said above).[301]

Verse 18
How shall I know this etc. *'ykn' 'd' hd'*

Kabbalist Catechumen If Zachariah was the Reincarnation of Aaron, it is no | wonder that that ancient fault of incredulity should still adhere to his soul—just as Usia [Uzziah], who is said to have been the Revolution of Usa [Uzzah], again touched forbidden things (2 Chron 26.16; 2 Sam 6.6. See Tract. *De Revol. Animarum*, p. 391). For just as [Aaron] did not believe the Lord himself when he promised water ‖ from the rock (Num 20.6, 8, 12), so much less did he [in his reincarnation] believe the angel promising him a son in old age.

p. 56

Christian But why was he punished, when Abram (Gen 15.8; 17.17) and Sarah (Gen 18.12) who doubted just like him were not punished?

Kabbalist Catechumen Because after so many revolutions [reincarnations] he had still not yet corrected that flaw [of incredulity].

Verse 19
Gabriel who stands before God etc. *gbry'yl dq'm 'n' qdm 'lh'*

Christian In Locus 32 Centuriae 1 Excerpts from the Book *Zohar* it is said that the name Gabriel is given to all those angels who come from the Left Side, so [the name is also given] to the Angel who is elsewhere called Lailah and who is in charge of the souls descending into bodies. Therefore Zachariah could [reasonably] doubt whether this apparition was of such great importance and whether it was not the ordinary guide of souls | who was now talking to him. Thus the angel showed his special character to him because obviously those angels who stand before God do not carry out such common ministries, but more secret ones. See on this Excerpts Cent. 1 Loc. 47.

---

299 A red pencil square bracket inserted into the text ([aquas) refers to an annotation in the left margin: 7.D./56. The numeration is erroneous. It should be 8.D./56. But the problem is resolved in the next annotation.
300 Correction: Cumque replaced by Cum
301 This is a remarkable account of the work of the spirit of Elijah throughout time.

fol. 12ʳ   ***Cabb. Cat.*** *Quod autem tales Angeli, qui stant coram Domino, septem ‖‖ sal-*
p. 57   *tem sint, ‖ prout*[302] *habetur in latina versione Tob. 12, 15 communiter â nobis haud traditur: imò Jonathan F. Uziel in Paraphrasi suâ Chaldaica ad Gen. 11, 7. sic habet: Dixit Dominus* לשבעין מלאכיא דקיימין קימוי *ad septuaginta angelos, qui stant coram eo: Venite nunc & descendamus &c. Et manestatum*[303] *est Verbum Domini contra illam civitatem,* | *& cum eo septuaginta Angeli, ex adverso septuaginta populorum &c. conf. Jes. 6, 2; Dan. 7, 10.16; 1. Reg. 22, 19.*

     Christianus. Imò & Græcus Tobiæ textus aliter habet, & quidem ita: Ego sum Raphaël unus de septem Angelis sanctis, qui offerunt orationes sanctorum, καὶ εἰσπορεύονται ἐνώπιον τῆς δόξης τοῦ ἁγίου: & egrediuntur coram Gloria Sancti. De Gabriele autem | habentur plura inter Excerpta Loc. 27, 29, 31 sqq. & in Lexico Cabbalistico p. 229[304].

   Cabb. Cat. *Nomen quidem hoc Angelicum literaliter Virum Dei denotat; apud nostros autem Doctores Rigorosum Executorem mandatorum Dei.*

     Christianus. Hoc ergò procul dubio Zachariæ his verbis intimare vol-
p. 58   uit Angelus, ut vel ‖ ex[305] hoc quasi prooemio[306] prænosset incredulitatem suam pœnâ non carituram; | quam & verbis subsequentibus ulterius exprobare pergit; dum dicit: *missus sum*, non venio ut Dan. 9, 23; c. 10, 12.14.20 & legationem meam inanem esse putas? *Ut loquar tecum*; non ut in somnio appaream tibi, ut Matth. 1, 20; c. 2, 12.13.19; Gen. 31, 11. *Et lætum hoc nuncium tibi afferam*, non triste ut Matth. 2, 13 &c. Et tamen incredulus es?

     V. 20. *Eris silens &c.* תהוא שתיק

   Cabb. Cat. *Quæritur an Angelus propriâ vi & autoritate ita puniverit Zachariam; an ex mandato antecedaneo conditionali? an vero instantaneo?*

     Christianus. Probabilius est medium. Quamvis enim propriâ vi confortasse Danielem videatur Angelus Dan. 10, 10, puniendi tamen vis pro arbitrio non videtur concessa | illis. Requisito autem mandato, eodem instanti, quo peccabat Zacharias illud quidem dedisset Dominus, si in Templo tum

---

302   A red pencil square bracket inserted into the text ([prout) refers to an annotation in the right margin: 9.D./57.
303   BSB: manifestatum (Recte)
304   "גבריאל *Gabriel Angelus*. Vid. Talmud Tract. Schabbath c. 5. in f. fol. 50.c. 2. ubi invenies, quando hic Angelus baculum mari inseruerit, pro formandâ ex colluvie ejus Terra, in quâ deinde condita est Roma. & c. 1. f. 12. in Additamentis, ubi dicitur, Angelos cognoscere cogitationes hominum, & callere omnes linguas, Aramæa vel Syriacâ excepta: Gabrielem autem eandem scire, quia Josephum docuerit 70. linguas. [...]" ("Loci communes kabbalistici", op. cit., pp. 229–230).

Kabbbalist Catechumen These angels who stand before God are at least seven [in number] ‖‖ ‖ according to the Latin Tobit 12.15, but not commonly according to our tradition. Rather Jonathan ben Uziel in his Aramaic Targum on Gen 11.7 has: "The Lord said" *lśb'yn ml'ky' dqyymyn qymwy* "to the seventy angels who stand before him, Come now and let us go down [...]". And the Word of God appeared against that city [of Sodom] | and with him the 70 angels against the 70 peoples. Cf. Isa 6.2; Dan 7.10, 16; 1 Kgs 22.19.

fol. 12ʳ
p. 57

Christian But the Greek text of Tobit has it otherwise, thus: "I am Raphael, one of the seven holy angels who offer the prayers of the saints *kai ekporeuontai enōpion tēs doxēs tou hagiou* and go out from before the Glory of the Holy One". There is a lot | about Gabriel in Excerpts Loc. 27, 29, 31 *seq.* and in *Lex. Cabb.*, p. 229.

Kabbalist Catechecumen [Gabriel's] name means literally "Man of God". According to our scholars, he is a most rigorous executor of God's instructions.

Christian Doubtless Gabriel wished to convey this to Zachariah by his words, so that from ‖ the Angel's opening remarks he would know in advance that his incredulity would not go unpunished. | The angel went on to reproach him more thoroughly in the following words: "I have been sent" (not "I come" as in Dan 9.23; 10.12, 14, 20) and you consider my mission trivial; "to speak to you" (not "to appear to you in a dream", as in Mt 1.20; 2.12, 13, 19; Gen 31.11); "and bring you this joyful message" (not a sad one, as in Mt 2.13 etc.) and yet you still do not believe!

p. 58

Verse 20
You will be dumb etc. *thw' štyq*

Kabbalist Catechumen Did the angel punish Zachariah with his own strength and on his own authority? Or on the authority of a preceding command, and was that conditional or instantaneous?

Christian A command is the most probable. Although one angel does seem to have comforted Daniel from his own resources (Dan 10.10), the power of punishing according to their own judgment does not seem to have been given them. | God issued the command upon the [Angel's] request at the very moment Zachariah sinned—if, that is, God's Glory had at that time

---

305   A red pencil square bracket inserted into the text ([ex) refers to an annotation in the right margin: 10.D./58.
306   BSB: prœomio (Printer's error)

resedisset Gloria ejus, ut Jes. 6, 6.8; Ez. 10, 2.6. Sed in templo secundo illam habitasse ipsi negant vestrates: unde cum [suas] pœnas præcedere soleant judicia, in eodem simul consessu mandatum videtur datum Angelo, quo ablegabatur; ut si non crederet Zacharias privatione | loquelæ redargueretur.[307] Sed etiam quæritur: An simul[308] surditate percussus fuerit Zacharias? ||

    Cabb. Cat.[309] *Mihi neutiquam videtur asserendum: cum nullibi id asseratur, nec Angelus usus sit Hebraica phrasi* חרש *quæ etiam surditatem denotat: & si eâdem usus esset, neutiquam sanè evinceretur ista pœnæ exasperatio.*[310] [**Christianus.**] Nec solam illud | rem evincet, quod nutu Zachariam interrogasse dicuntur vicini. infra v. 62. ad eliciendam enim nominis declarationem non videtur sufficere potuisse nutus, nisi vox fuisset intermixta, quam ille auditu percepisset. Nec exaggeranda[311] sunt divina judicia, in quibus tanta adhuc gliscit gratiæ copia; ut & temporalis esset pœna, & beneficium promissum non excludens. Sic enim quandoque non obstante | incredulitate promissa implere solitus est Dominus, Jes. 7, 11 sqq.; Rom. 3, 3; Num. 20, 11; 2 Tim. 2, 13. [**Cabb. Cat.**][312] *Iterum quæritur, quare in pœnam hoc, & non aliud signum datum fuerit Zachariæ?*

    [**Christianus.**][313] Nimirum, quia de proprio corpore dubitaverat, in proprio corpore punitur; & quia obloquendo peccaverat lingua, obmutescendo | eadem corripitur.

    [**Cabb. Cat.**][314]. *Nisi & aliud subinnuitur mysterium: ut os Mosis Ex. 4, 16 nunc*[315] *|| obmu- ||| -tesceret*[316]*, cum mox locuturus esset Mosis Dominus. Heb. 1, 1; c. 3, 3. sqq.*

---

307 A correction was intended here (in the right margin: Cabb. Cat.) but Knorr changed his mind: the correction is itself deleted and no change of speaker occurs.
308 Added above the line: quoque
309 A red pencil square bracket inserted into the text ([Cabb. Cat.) refers to an annotation in the right margin: 11.D./59.
310 Added in the right margin: Christianus. Nec (Which gives the speach, initially attributed to the Cabbalist, to the Christian, until 2 Tim 2, 13 where a new change of speaker occurs).
311 BSB: ex aggeranda
312 Added above the line: Cabb. Cat. (which involves a change of speaker. The last sentence is underlined, in order to be attributed to the Cabbalist).
313 Correction: Cabb. Cat. replaced by Christ.
314 Correction: Christianus remplaced by Cabb. Cat.
315 In the right bottom corner appears a Hebrew letter ד presumably an indication of binding or pagination.
316 A red pencil square bracket inserted into the text ([obmutesceret) refers to an annotation in the right margin: 12.D./60.

returned to the Temple (so Isa 6.6, 8; Ezek 10. 2, 6.). But your sages deny that the Glory dwelt in the Second Temple. [In that case] although judgments usually precede the penalties [they bring with them], it seems that the instruction was given to the Angel in the same [heavenly] assembly from which he was sent, that if Zachariah did not believe, | he should be punished by loss of speech. But one might also ask: was Zachariah at the same time also struck with deafness?[317]

Kabbalist Catechumen ‖ I do not think we say that at all, since [Scripture] nowhere says so, and the Angel did not [apparently] use the [different] Hebrew word *ḥrš* which can also mean "deafness", and even if he did use it, it certainly did not indicate an increase in the penalty.   p. 59

Christian Nor does it prove | a single thing that the neighbours are said to have questioned Zachariah "with a gesture" (see verse 62 below). It hardly seems that a "gesture" could have been enough to elicit a declaration of the [child's] name from Zachariah unless it had been accompanied with speech which he was able to hear. Nor are divine judgments (which are often supplemented by great resources of Grace) to be overstated, for not only was the punishment temporary, but also it did not preclude the promised blessing [of a son]. For thus the Lord is accustomed at some point to fulfil his promises, | unbelief notwithstanding (Isa 7.11 *seq.*; Rm 3.3; Num 20.11; 2 Tim 2.13).

Kabbalist Catechumen Another question: why was Zachariah punished with dumbness and not with a different sign?

Christian Because he had entertained doubts about his own body, in his own body he was punished. And because his tongue had sinned by contradicting [the Angel], | his same [tongue] was punished by becoming mute.

Kabbalist Catechumen ‖ Unless another mystery is implied: it was when   p. 60
Moses' mouth (Ex 4.16) ‖‖ was growing dumb, that the Lord prepared shortly   fol. 12ᵛ
to speak to him (Heb 1.1; 3.3 *seq.*). [So, a similar situation might pertain here.]

---

317   Lightfoot, *Miscellanies and the Harmony of the Gospels*, op. cit., pp. 158–159: "Now, his punishment was twofold, 'deafness' and 'dumbness' both; for, because he had not hearkened to the angel's speech, he was struck deaf; and, because he had gainsaid it, he was made dumb. For, first, the Greek κωφός [*kōphos,*] ver. 22, and the word חרש [*ḥrš*] by which the Syrian rendereth it, do signify, both deaf and dumb. And, secondly, in ver. 62, it is said, 'They made signs to him'; which had not needed, if he could have heard". Knorr disagreed.

V. 21. *Super mora ejus &c.* על תוחרתה

Cabb. Cat. *Ordinarie, qui adolebat, nihil agebat, nisi quod suffimentum prunis in altari jam adæquatis injiceret illudque excæquaret, factâque | prostratione exiret. vid. sup. ad v. 10 è Tamid, c. 6, §. 2.3. quod*[318]

Christianus. Memini etiam me legisse, quod moram ibi nectere non licuerit, ne metus incuteretur populo. Vid. Excerpta Cent. 1. Loc. 49.

V. 22. *Non poterat loqui cum eis &c.*
לא משכח הוא דנמלל עמהון

Christianus. Nimirum cum interrogantibus, cur talem traxisset moram: sicut Simeon | Justus interrogatus fuisse legitur. An vero & benedictionem pronunciare[319] non potuit?

Cabb. Cat. *Ex Mischnah apparet, illum quidem simul substitisse in gradibus Vestibuli inter benedicendum: sed ita, ut manu teneret thuribulum cum operculo; unde manus elevare non potuit, quod reliquorum ministrantium erat, | dum be-* ‖ *-nedicerent.*[320] (*vide supra ad v. 10 è Tamid, c. 7, §. 2*)

Et ipse innuebat nutu eis &c.
והו מרמז רמז הוא להון

Cabb. Cat. *Quæritur an nutu totam visionem aperuerit; an verò sensus sit, quod coactus fuerit nutu saltem animi sensa in genere prodere?*

Christianus. Certe visionem ipsi obtigisse in genere jam cognoverant, partim ê | defectu sermonis, partim è signis consternati vultus: & nunc nutu ipsis aliquid significat; quid hoc esse potuit quam visionis argumentum?

---

318 Deletion: quod
319 Correction: benedictionem pronunciare replaced by benedictioni interesse
320 A red pencil square bracket inserted into the text (be[nedicerent) refers to an annotation in the left margin: 13.D./61.
321 Reference here is made to a famous baraita cited in the Palestinian Talmud (yYoma 5.142c) where it is introduced to illustrate the final line of Mishnah Yoma 5.1 which states that the high priest does not prolong his prayer in the sanctuary upon leaving the Holy of Holies on the Day of Atonement "lest he terrify Israel" by his delay in leaving the sanctuary: "A story of one [high priest] who prolonged [his prayer in the sanctuary when he left the Holy of Holies on the Day of Atonement] and they decided to enter after him—they said it was Simeon the Righteous. They said to him: 'Why did you prolong [your prayer]?' He said to them: 'I was praying for the sanctuary of your God that

SECTION III

Verse 21

Over his delay 'l twḥrth

Kabbalist Catechumen Normally the incensing priest did nothing other than toss the incense onto the altar when the coals were hot enough and level it out. He did | obeisance and then went out. See above on verse 10 from Tamid 6. 2, 3.

Christian I recall reading that it was forbidden to delay there, in case the people became frightened. See Excerpts Cent. I Loc. 49.

Verse 22

He could not speak with them etc. *l' mškḥ hw' dnmll 'mhwn*

Christian Evidently [he could not speak] with those asking why he had delayed so long. Just as we read Simon | the Righteous had been asked[321]. But surely he could not take part in giving the blessing [because he had become dumb]?[322]

Kabbalist Catechumen From the Mishnah it is clear he would have stopped on the steps of the Vestibule during the blessing, but in such a way that holding the thurible and its lid he ‖ could not lift his hand up [to bless], which was what the other ministers did | when they gave the blessing. (See above on verse 10 citing Tamid c7, § 2).

p. 61

And he communicated with them by a gesture whw mrmz rmz hw' lhwn

Kabbalist Catechumen I wonder whether he revealed the whole vision with a nod or whether it means that he was compelled by gesture to display the feelings of his soul in general terms only.

Christian Surely they now realised in general terms that he had had a vision—partly because | he could not speak and partly from the signs of consternation on his face—and now he was signalling something to them with a gesture. What could this be other than evidence of a vision? Because of the

---

it be not destroyed'. They said to him: 'Even so, you should not have prolonged [your prayer]'". For Simeon the Righteous in the Talmud, see Amram Tropper, *Simeon the Righteous in Rabbinic Literature. A Legend Reinvented* (Leiden: Brill, 2013). This translation here is from p. 155.

322   The answer seems to be that the incensing priest could not bless anyway because his hands were full.

Imò quod ob rei novitatem ipsum impulerint, ut scriptorem aperiret, quodque nec ipse abnuerit, crediderim. Non enim eadem die domum abibat (sed transacto demum Sabbatho, vide supra ad §. 8) & ipso poenæ suæ signo convictus, | non incredulus amplius erat; quidni igitur ad Acta rem omnem consignasse censendus erit?

Cabb. Cat. Non putarem tamen ad sortes ipsum, durantibus reliquis ministerii diebus, porrò admissum fuisse.

V. 24. Concepit &c. בטנת

Christianus. Signum est fidei & obedientiæ in Zacharia?[323] ‖

Cabb. Cat.[324] At quomodo Elisabeth nosse potuit se concepisse?

Christianus. Videtur sub momentum annunciationis marito factæ, domi eidem rediisse via mulierum (quæ ipsi esse desierat ut Saræ, Gen. 18, 12) quodsi redeunti significavit, & ipse scripto suum pariter fatum eidem apperuit[325]; expectatâ purificatione, gaudium | mandati observasse censendi erunt, de quo inter Excerpta Cent. 1. Loc. 50 signa ergò conceptionis esse potuerunt extumescentia uberum & cessatio, rejuvenescentiæ florum iterata.[326] (vid. & Excerpt. Cent. 1. Loc. 42[327]).

Et occultabat seipsam &c. ומטשיא הות נפשה

Cabb. Cat. Quæritur: An factum hoc sit occultando saltem uteri | ventrisque statum; an omninò subducendo sese ab hominum conspectu?

Christianus. Versio Arabica & Persica prius volunt. Sed posterius mihi probabilius est, eò quod & rationem aperit, procul dubio marito; â quo pariter interea separata mansisse videtur; nempe hanc: meritò cavere sese omnem pollutionis occasionem, dum totam nunc devotioni sese committat, quod non saltem sterilis esse | desinat; sed & tali modo, gestando nimirum foetum tam singularem, Nasiræatui devotum, quali in casu & olim mulieri custodiam sui injunxerit Angelus Jud. 13, 4. ‖‖ ‖

---

323 Correction: Zacharia? replaced by Zacharia.
324 A red pencil square bracket inserted into the text ([Cabb. Cat.) refers to an annotation in the left margin: 14.D./62.
325 Correction: apperuit replaced by aperuit
326 Correction: a sign is placed above the line which indicates that the order of the terms should be rearranged to be: iterata cessatio florum rejuvenescentiæ
327 BSB: Loc. 43. The reference cannot be checked as the book appears to be lost.
328 See footnote below on the Temple Archives. Knorr overlooks the fact that his reconstruction of events apparently requires Zachariah to write on the Sabbath.

strangeness of the event they compelled him to reveal what had happened in writing. I expect he complied. For he was not going home that same day (as the Sabbath had already started, see above at §8) and convinced by the very sign of his punishment, | he was no more unbelieving, so he may be expected to have recorded the whole business in the [Temple] Archives.[328]

Kabbalist Catechumen I would not think he would have been allowed to take part in the lots again for the remaining days of his ministry.

Verse 24
She conceived etc *bṭnt*

Christian This is a sign of faith and obedience in Zachariah.

Kabbalist Catechumen ‖ How could Elisabeth know she had conceived? p. 62

Christian It seems that as a result of the announcement made by her husband to her at home, the way of women (which had stopped for her as for Sara in Gen 18.12) returned, which was a clear indication. And [Zachariah] himself also told her of her destiny in writing. Awaiting purification, they thought to observe the joy | of the commandment (about which Excerpts Cent. I Loc. 50). The signs of conception could have been swelling breasts, repeated lethargy, rejuvenation of flowers etc. (see also Excerpts Cent. I Loc. 43).

And she hid herself etc. *wmṭsy' hwt npsh*

Kabbalist Catechumen A question. Was this done by merely concealing her growing size? | Or, by completely removing herself from the sight of men?

Christian The Arabic and Persian versions favour the first[329], but the second seems more likely to me, for it explains why she appears to have been separated from her husband too during this period. And also because she would be understandably fearful of every occasion of pollution as she was now committing herself totally to devotion because, not only had she ceased to be barren, | but in such a way as carry so singular a baby dedicated to Naziriteship.[330] In a similar case long ago, an angel had enjoined a baby's custody on a woman [by instructing her to avoid pollution] (Judg 13.4). ‖   fol. 13ʳ

---

329 Both versions are found in the London Polyglot Bible.
330 Lightfoot, *Miscellanies and the Harmony of the Gospels*, op. cit., p. 160: "[...] and for this it was, that she betook herself to this retiring and reclusiveness; partly, that she might ply her devotion so much the closer upon so great a benefit,—and chiefly, that she might sequester from all occasions of uncleanness, or defiling, since she carried one in her womb, that was to be so strict a Nazarite. As see the like, Judg. xiii. 14."

¹Luc I, v. 26–38

*V. 26. In mense autem sexto missus est Gabriel Angelus â Deo in Galilæam in civitatem, cujus nomen Nazareth.*²

*27. Ad virginem, quæ desponsata erat viro, cujus nomen erat Joseph de domo David: & nomen virgini erat Marjam.*³

*28. Et ingressus est ad eam Angelus, & dixit ei: Pax tibi, ô plena gratiâ: Dominus | noster tecum, benedicta inter mulieres.*⁴

*29. Illa verò cum vidisset, conturbata est per sermonem ejus, & cogitabat, cujusnam esset salutatio ista.*⁵

*30. Et dixit ei Angelus: Ne timeas Marjam; | invenisti enim gratiam apud Deum.*⁶

*31. Ecce enim concipies in utero, & paries filium, & vocabis nomen ejus Jeschua.*⁷

*32. Hic erit magnus, & filius Excelsi vocabitur; & dabit ei Dominus Deus solium David | patris ipsius.*⁸

*33. Et regnabit super domum Jaacob in æternum, & regno ejus finis non erit.*⁹

*34. Dixit Marjam ad Angelum: Quomodo fiet istud, quia vir non est cognitus mihi?*¹⁰

*35. Respondit Angelus & dixit ei: Spiritus Sanctitatis veniet & virtus Excelsi obteget*¹¹ *te. Propter hoc is qui nasciturus est ex te, sanctus est; & Filius Dei vocabitur.*¹²

*36. Et ecce Elischeba cognata tua etiam ipsa in utero concepit filium in senectute sua; & hic mensis sextus est ipsi, quæ vocatur | sterilis.*¹³

---

1 On the left-hand half of the page, a fragment cut from Knorr's edition of the Peshittta New Testament containing the Syriac version of the quoted passage in the Gospel of Luke is pasted in and crossed out. Added in the right margin: Sectio IV. A red pencil square bracket inserted into the correction in margin ([Sectio IV.) refers to an annotation in the right margin: 15.D./63.
2 Vulgate: In mense autem sexto, missus est angelus Gabriel a Deo in civitatem Galilææ cui nomen Nazareth.
3 Vulgate: Ad virginem desponsatam viro cui nomen erat Ioseph, de domo David, et nomen virginis Maria.
4 Vulgate: Et ingressus angelus ad eam, dixit: Ave gratia plena; Dominus tecum; benedicta tu in mulieribus.
5 Vulgate: Quæ cum audisset, turbata est in sermone eius, et cogitabat qualis esset ista salutatio. The Peshitta text supports *vidisset* against Vulgate *audisset*. Greek witnesses support both *vidisset* and *audisset*, but Nestle-Aland, *Novum Testamentum Graecum 27* chooses to omit the clause altogether.
6 Vulgate: Et ait Angelus ei: Ne timeas Maria, invenisti enim gratiam apud Deum.
7 Vulgate: Ecce concipies in utero, et paries filium, et vocabis nomen eius IESUM.
8 Vulgate: Hic erit magnus, et Filius Altissimi vocabitur, et dabit illi Dominus Deus sedem David patris eius; et regnabit in domo Iacob in æternum.

Section IV
Luke I v26–38

Verse 26 In the sixth month the angel Gabriel was sent by God to Galilee to a town whose name was Nazareth.

27 To a virgin who was betrothed to a man whose name was Joseph of the House of David and the virgin's name was Marjam.

28 And an Angel came in to her and said to her "Peace to you[14], O Thou full of grace. Our Lord | is with you, Thou blessed among women".

29 When she saw this, she was troubled by his words and wondered from whom came that greeting[15].

30 And the Angel said to her; "Do not be afraid, Marjam, | for you have found grace with God".

31 "For behold you will conceive in your womb and you will bear a son and you will call his name Jeschua[16]".

32 "He will be great and will be called Son of the Most High and the Lord God will give to him the throne of his father | David".

33 "And he shall rule over the house of Jacob forever and there will be no end to his kingdom".

34 Marjam said to the Angel "How will this be, for no man is known to me?"

35 The Angel replied and said to her; "The Spirit of Holiness will come[17] and the power of the Highest will cover you over. Because of this, he who will be born of you is holy and he will be called Son of God".

36 "And Look! Elischeba your relative has also herself conceived a son in her womb in her old age. And this is the sixth month [of pregnancy] for her who was called | barren".

---

9   Vulgate: Et regni eius non erit finis.
10 Vulgate: Dixit autem Maria ad angelum: Quomodo fiet istud, quoniam virum non cognosco?
11 Added above the line: super
12 Vulgate: Et respondens angelus dixit ei: Spiritus sanctus superveniet in te, et virtus Altissimi obumbrabit tibi. Ideoque et quod nascetur ex te Sanctum, vocabitur Filius Dei.
13 Vulgate: Et ecce Elisabeth cognata tua, et ipsa concepit filium in senectute sua: et hic mensis sextus est illi, quæ vocatur sterilis.
14 Vulgate: *Ave* or "Hail".
15 Vulgate: "What sort of greeting that was".
16 Vulgate: *Jesum.*
17 Vulgate adds: "into you".

37. *Quia non est difficile Deo quicquam.*[18]

38. *Dixit Marjam: Ecce ego sum ancilla Domini: fiat mihi juxta sermonem tuum; Et Angelus abiit ab ea.*[19]

V. 26. *In mense autem sexto* &.
בירחא דין דאשתא

Christianus. Iterum occasio tibi subnascitur mysteria quædam in numeris hisce observandi. ‖

Cabb. Cat.[20] *Elischeba quinque menses se occultans, literam* ה" *ultimam Tetragrammati insinuat; Et Messias mense sexto publicatæ Incarnationis suæ conceptus, literam* ו". *Illa Regnum denotat, hæc Regem: Illa Lunam,* | *hæc solem: Illa noctem, hæc diem.*

Christianus. Illa igitur occultatur, hæc manifestatur. Regnum nempe pristinum seu Ecclesia antiqui fœderis ad latibula tendit; Rex verus Messias Regnum novum inchoat; discedit Luna cum nocte sua; sol oriens ex alto[21] recentem aperit diem. Die sexto Adam primus prodit; mense sexto Adam adhuc prior, qui Kadmon dicitur. | Qualis autem & quotus anni mensis hic fuit?

Cabb. Cat. *Id frustra ex Ephemeriis sacerdotum disquiritur. Quia* ‖‖ (1.) *non saltem dubium est quotus ordo, post quascunque interruptiones sive pollutionum, sive desolationum, ministrandi rursus fecerit initium; utrum nimirum Jehojaribi primus, an verò ille, quem ex computo Sabbathorum*[22] *illius temporis ordo tangeret.* (2.) *quia intercalationes mensium Antiquis non tam juxta accuratum dierum horarumque* | *calculum, sed pro arbitrio instituebantur.* ‖

---

18   Vulgate: Quia non erit impossibile apud Deum omne verbum.
19   Vulgate: Dixit autem Maria: Ecce ancilla Domini, fiat mihi secundum verbum tuum. Et discessit ab illa angelus.
20   A red pencil square bracket inserted into the text ([Cabb. Cat.) refers to an annotation in the right margin: 16.D./64.
21   Deletion: ex alto
22   BSB: Sabbatorum
23   Vulgate has "impossible".
24   h =5.
25   w=6.
26   For the priestly archives alleged in Josephus and other sources, Catherine Hezser, *Jewish Literacy in Roman Palestine* (Tübingen: Mohr Siebeck, 2001), pp. 150–160.
27   According to 1 Chron 24.7, Jehoiarib's order served first of the 24 priestly orders established under King David. 1 Chron 9.10 mentions another Jehoiarib who returned from the exile with Zerubbabel and served under the High Priest Joshua. He was the ancestor

37 "For nothing is difficult²³ for God".
38 Marjam said: "See, I am the maid-servant of the Lord. Let it happen to me, according to your words". And the Angel left her.

Verse 26
In the sixth month etc *byrḥ' dyn d'št'*

Christian Once again you have an opportunity to remark upon the mysteries in these numbers.

Kabbalist Catechumen ‖ Elischeba hiding herself away for five months evokes the last letter h^{24} of the Tetragrammaton and Messiah conceived in the sixth month after the announcement of his incarnation [suggests] the letter w^{25}. The former denotes Kingdom, the later King; the former Moon, | the latter Sun; the former Night, the latter Day.

p. 64

Christian The first item [in these pairs] is hidden, [but] the last is revealed. The former Kingdom or Ecclesia of the Old Covenant slips away into hiding. The true King Messiah begins a new Kingdom. The moon departs with her night; the rising sun opens the new day. On the sixth day, the First Adam came forth, in the sixth month came forth the Adam who was even earlier, and who is called Adam Kadmon. | What sort of month of the year was this? Which one?

Kabbalist Catechumen One cannot find that in the records of the priests because ‖‖[26]:

fol. 13ᵛ

(1) It is uncertain which of the numbered orders [of the priests] began the newly restored ministry after so many interruptions caused by pollutions, and desolations. It may have been [begun again] by Jehoiarib or the [leader of the order of the priests] who was selected in order as a consequence of the computation of the Sabbaths at that time[27].

(2) The Ancients intercalated the months not so much according to an accurate reckoning of days and hours, | but by estimation.

---

of a priestly clan that was led by Mattenai when Joiakim was the High Priest in the days of Nehemiah. He was also called "Joiarib" (Nehem 11.10). For contemporary discussion: John Lightfoot, *Horae Hebraicae et Talmudicae impensae in Evangelium Sancti Lucae* on Lk 1.5 in *Omnia Opera*, edited by J. Leusden, 2nd ed. (Utrecht: Broedlet, 1699), p. 486 and Justus Heinrich Jungman, *Propheta Daniel modo novo* (Frankfurt am Main, 1681), pp. 489–490 who distinguishes three persons called Jehoiarib.

Christianus.[28] Addo & hoc, cum liturgia Zachariæ, sive ordinis Abiæ quotannis ad minimum bis recurreret, quod sciri interim nequeat utrum verbi gratia æstivo an hyemali recursu celebris hæc ipsi contigerit apparitio. Imò incertum etiam est, an immediatè post reditum Zachariæ è templo conceperit Elischeba, an post interpositum | quantulumcunque intervallum.

Missus est Gabriel &c. אשתלח גבריאל

Cabb. Cat. *Quæritur an idem ille, qui missus fuerat ad Zachariam, missus etiam sit ad Mariam? Dubium oritur ex eo, quod Gabrielis nomen pluribus sit commune, ut notatum est supra.*

Christianus. Quamvis Danieli idem Gabriel sæpius apparuerit Dan. 9, 21, ut nihil sit absurdi, si idem & â Lucâ sæpius apparuisse commemoretur: mihi tamen videtur ad immediata Messiæ ministeria immediatum illius adhibitum fuisse summumque legatum, qui certè Gabriel nullibi nomine proprio, sed Michael potius vocatur. Unde & princeps populi Dei dicitur Dan. 10, 21 & ê primis principibus primus ib. v. 13, | primoque impurorum spirituum opponitur. Judæ v. 9; Apoc. 12, 7 (vid. Pneumat. Cabbalistica Dissert. 2, c. 2, §. 1; 2[29], c. 5, §. 4[30]).

Cabb. Cat. *Sed summus omnium Angelorum nobis Cabbalistis dicitur Metatron,* || *qui*[31] *et Michaele superior esse ponitur (ibid. §. 3*[32]*).*

Christianus. Hic ipse tamen Metatron non tam ad legationes adhiberi reperitur, | quam ad usum familiarem. Michaël ergò, qui ad Gratiæ metrum ubique refertur, procul dubio ad gratiosum hoc nuncium adhibitus est;

---

28   A red pencil square bracket inserted into the text ([Christianus.) refers to an annotation in the left margin: Pr.E./65.

29   "§ 1. Sicut in nomine Tetragrammato continentur omnes decem Sephiroth, prout idem & plenè scriptum decem literas habet: Sic in quatuor Animalibus sanctis continentur omnes decem Chori Angelorum, prout declaratur Tikkun. 66. Ubi sermo est de 4. Spiritibus, quorum primus procedat à Corona summa, pergatque per Daath & Tiphereth & Jesod: alter procedat à Chochma, & pergat per Chesed ad Nezach: tertius veniat à Binah per Gebhura ad Hod: & quartus referatur ad Malchuth. Finitque quod sub istis sint Michaël, Gabriel, Nuriel & Raphaël, qui vestimenta sint quatuor Spirituum, & sese implicent in decem Choros Angelorum." ("Pneumatica Kabbalistica [...] Domus Dei", op. cit., pp. 219–220).

30   "§. 4. In intimo autem hujus Palatii sedes est Thronusque Gloriæ Divinæ, & sciendum, quod in Palatio sexto, quod est sub isto modo dicto, R. Schimeon Jochaides locet quatuor Principes Michaëlem, Gabrielem, Urielem, & Raphaëlem. Indicetque, quamvis isti sint Animalia sancta, quod tamen inferiores sint Sandalphone, qui est Rota: quodque Animalia & Rotæ unius sint gradus, & essentiâ sint unum & idem, quamvis differant conceptibus & operationibus." (Ibid., p. 226).

Christian ‖ I would add: it could not be known whether the order of Abijah (in which Zachariah ministered) would serve [once or] twice in the year. From this it follows it could not be calculated whether it would be a summer or winter turn in which the famous vision appeared to him. And it is also uncertain whether Elischeba conceived immediately after the return of Zachariah from the Temple or after some intervening | period of delay.

Gabriel was sent etc. *'štlḥ gbry'y'l*

Kabbalist Catechumen Is it the same angel who had been sent to Zachariah who was sent to Mary too? Doubt arises because Gabriel is a name common to several angels, as we noted above.

Christian Since the same Gabriel appeared quite often to Daniel (Dan 9.21), it would not be unreasonable if the same [Gabriel] was recorded by Luke too as appearing quite frequently. However I think this most lofty and unmediated delegation to direct ministration upon Messiah was given to the angel who is nowhere called Gabriel, but rather Michael. It is [Michael] who is called "Prince of the People of God" (Dan 10.21) and "First of the Foremost Princes" (Dan 10.13) | and who is opposed to the First of the Unclean Spirits. (Jude 9; Rev 12.7; see *Pneumatica Cabbalistica*, Dissert. 2, chap. 2, § 1, 2; chap. 5, § 4).

Kabbalist Catecumen But our Kabbalists say that the highest angel of all is called ‖ Metatron, who is considered superior even to Michael (ibid., § 3).

Christian But Metatron is not used on missions, | but rather [appointed to] domestic matters. Michael, therefore, who is everywhere linked to the measure of Grace, was no doubt appointed to this gracious announcement.

---

31   A red pencil square bracket inserted into the text ([qui) refers to an annotation in the left margin: 2.E./66.

32   "§. 3. Hoc autem velum sic interpretatur R. Moscheh Corduero, dum inquit: quod in Palatio septimo nempe summo, quod vocatur Sanctum Sanctorum, nulla sit forma, nec aliquid, quod comprehendi queat, sed omnia ibi sint occulta: quodque proximum sit mundo Aziluth. In medio autem hujus palatii aulæum quasi aliquod expandi, ut fiat distinctio inter Sanctum & inter Sanctum Sanctorum: in medio autem hujus aulæi locat duos Cherubim, qui sint Metatron & Sandalphon, ibique adducit locum istum è Sohar, addendo: quod Sandalphon consistat in Palatio Sancti Sanctorum, in aulæo dicto, quod aliis quoque textibus probat." ("Pneumatica Cabbalistica [...] Domus Dei", op. cit., p. 226).

Gabrielis autem nomine appellatur propter admirandam oppositorum illorum graduum in descendente nunc gradu medio unionem, quodque conceptio etiam virginis sine cooperatione metri sinistri minimè facta esse statuenda sit. Sed piæ hæ sunt meditationes, | nemini unquam obstruendæ. 30

A Deo &. מן לות אלהא

Cabb. Cat. *Sensus in Syriaco literalis conformis est Chaldaicæ phrasi, quæ occurrit apud Danielem c. 5, 24, ubi habetur:* באדין[33] & *קדמוהי חשלי* tunc[34] *â facie ejus missa est palma manus: adeoque & hic simul connotatur | locus* 35 *unde facta sit hæc ablegatio; nimirum è vicinia, sive è loco, qui apud Deum*[35] *est.*

Christianus. Simile quid observamus Joh. 16, 27. & Joh. 15, 26. bis & Luc. 2, 15. Non enim & de missione Johannis eadem adhibetur phrasis Joh. 1, 6.

Nazareth &c. נצרת

Christianus. Urbs Galilææ in tribu Za- ‖ -bulon[36], circa terminos tribus Isaschar | in monte sita, distante ab Urbe Hierosolymarum 16 ¼ milliaribus 40 versus septentrionem. Nomen autem habet â Radice נצר.

Cabb. Cat. *Hæc radix sensum habet observandi perpetuum*[37] *ut & Jes. 65, 4. observatoria magorum; & c. 1, 8. & c. 49, 6. in captivitatem abducti, qui bene observari solent: & Jesch. 60, 21; c. 11, 1; c. 14, 19; Dan. 11, 7. Surculus tenellus, qui ‖‖ ob speratos fructus obervarvi solet, intelligantur.*

Christianus. Ad quemnam locum communem Cabbalisticum urbem hanc referes[38]?

---

33 Deletion: באדין. This term (= tunc), the first word in the Aramaic text of Daniel, is deleted as it does not add to the explanation of the idiom used with "hand" under discussion here. Consequent upon this change, "*tunc*" was then removed from the Latin translation.

34 Suppresion: tunc. The term באדין no longer appears in the Aramaic version after its deletion here (see previous note). The Latin translation is adjusted to reflect this.

35 BSB: DEUM

36 A red pencil square bracket inserted into the text (Za[bulon) refers to an annotation in the left margin: 3.E./67.

37 Added above the line: , ita

38 Correction above the line: referes replaced by referres

39 The comment answers the question why the phrase is *mn lwt 'lh'* "from before God", rather than merely *mn 'lh'*, "from God".

40 Gabriel came "from before God" *mn lwt 'lh'* but John only *mn 'lh'*, "from God".

SECTION IV 227

He is called by the name of Gabriel on account of the wonderful union of those opposite grades in the descent at that time of the Middle Grade, because the conception of the Virgin had to be achieved without the cooperation of the Left [Hand Measure]. But these are merely pious meditations, | not ever to be forced upon on anyone.

From God etc. *mn lwt ʾlhʾ*

Kabbalist Catechumen The literal meaning of the Syriac is the same as the Aramaic phrase which occurs in Dan 5.24 where it has: *mn qdmwhy šlyḥ* "[the palm of the hand] was sent from his face" so that here there is denoted | the place from which the legation was sent—from near or out of the place which is with God[39].

Christian We observe something similar in Jn 16.27; 15.26 (*bis*) and Lk 2.15. However, the same preposition is not used of the mission of John (Jn 1.6)[40].

Nazareth etc. *nzrt*

Christian This was a town in Galilee in the tribal lands of Zebulon situated near the ‖ borders of the tribe of Issachar | in the hill country, 16¼ miles North of Jerusalem. Its name comes from the [Hebrew] root *nzr*.

Kabbalist Catechumen This root [*nzr*] means "perpetual observation". Thus Isa 65.4, "the observatories of the Magi"[41]; 1.8; and 49.6 "those taken into captivity" who are very closely watched [over][42]; and Isa[43] 60.21; 11.1; 14.19; Dan 11.7 where the word means a delicate shoot which is ⦀ carefully watched on account of the anticipated fruit[44].

Christian To which *locus communis* of the Kabbalists do you refer this town?

p. 67

fol. 14ʳ

---

41 The Hebrew text may mean "to lodge or spend the night amongst *the monuments*". This last word, a plural passive participle of *nṣr*, has evidently been understood to denote close observations made during the night, or, more precisely, the *observatories* of astrologers (Magi).

42 KJV has here "and to restore the preserved of Israel". The "preserved" (Kt *nṣyry*: Qr *nṣwry*) are taken to be the exiles and the etymology of the word is taken to be from *nṣr*, making them literally "the ones watched [over]".

43 The text has Ezekiel here by error. The words in the second group of citations from Isaiah are usually derived from a *nṣr* II and taken to mean a "shot" or "sprout". Our author considers these however an extended use of the first root.

44 In Dan 11.7, the word *mnṣr* "from a shoot" is similarly understood not from *nṣr* I but as an extended use of *nṣr* II whence the careful observation for anticipated fruit.

Cabb. Cat. Quia נצר *ferè æquipollet radici* שמר *quæ ad Regni gradum refertur; (Lex. Cabbalist. p. 720[45] sq.) hinc ad eundem gradum & hanc urbem referrem, | ut Symbolum esset Ecclesiæ, cui tam activa quam passiva Observationis significatio aptissimè congruit: adde & Animæ fidelis. Nec abludunt Symbola tribus, quæ â cohabitatione Nomen habet Gen. 30, 20.; 1. Reg. 8, 13.; Jes. 63, 15., et montis (vid. Lex Cabbalist. p. 277[46]. sq.) & vilitatis (Joh. 1 ‖, 47[47]; c. 7, 52.[48]) & regionis, quæ fuit Galilæa inferior â revolutione denominata, qualibus variè subjecta est Ecclesia | & Anima. Notandum autem, quod antiquissima fuerit Traditio, Messiam manifestatum iri in Galilæa: vid. in Excerptis Cent. 1, Loc. 70. & 74. sq. Ubi notandam*[49] *è Sohar P. I, col. 291. verba hæc: Post annum 66. cum dimidio manifestabitur Messias Rex in terra Galilæa. Et P. II, c. 11. Et manifestabitur in Galilæa, quia hic locus primus est, ubi devastatio terræ sanctæ incepit, unde in eo prius manifestabitur, quam | ullo loco alio. Quæ porrò quoque repetuntur ibidem col. 14. Item sect. Vajakel: ubi simul traditur in terra Galilæa primùm resurrecturos mortuos, quia ibi Rex Messias manifestandus sit. Hæc ibi.*

Christianus. Mysticè Galilæa denotat volubilem illam animæ partem, quæ aliàs τὸ ἐπιθυμητικὸν seu Concupiscibile dicitur, & infima est in homine, Amore, desiderio, | spe, gaudio, & hinc dependentibus affectibus occupata: ubi meritò primò hominem emendare debet vitæ Divinæ accessus.

Cabb. Cat. *Unum est, quod observatio-* ‖ *-nem[50] suam pariter meretur; quod cum Græci literam Hebraicam* צ *constanter per* σ *exprimant, ut patet in Saananim, Sabaoth, Sadoc, Salathi, Salmana, Salmona, Salphaad, Samarim, Senan, Saraa, | Sarath-asahar, Saredatha, Sarepta, Sarthan, Saruja, Sebeon, Sebia, Seboim, Sedada, Sedekias, Segon, Schesima, Seira, Sela, Seles, Seleph, Selethai, Selia, Selmon, Senna, Senneser, Seor, Sephath, Sephi, Sepho, Sephon, Sephor,*

---

45 "שמור *Custodi.* Magg. nostri cum dixerunt: τὸ זכור *memento*; & τὸ שמור *custodi* de unâ re dicuntur; intenderunt digitum ad duas Personas Tiphereth & Malchuth. Nam vocula זכור & quæ eundem habent sensum ad Præcepta affirmativa refertur ut Numer. 15, 40. Sed שמור & quicquid *cavendi* sensum infert, ad Negativa refertur, ut Gen. 2, 15. ubi verbis *colendi* & *custodiendi*, utrumque præceptorum genus denotatur. Affirmativa autem præcepta sunt רמ"ח 248, & ad Chesed pertinent, quo etiam inclinat masculus: sed 365. negativa ad Gebhuram referuntur; sicut & fœmina ad sinistram inclinat. Pard." ("Loci communes kabbalistici", op. cit., p. 720).

46 "הר *Mons.* Montes sunt multi. Sed Nomen hoc nudè positum quidam ad Jesod referunt, ut Liber Orah, & R. Moscheh in Libro Schem: qui etiam nomen הר ה" *Mons Domini*, ad Jesod refert. Sed in Sohar ad locum Jeschai. 2, 2. R. Chija sic commentatur: *Mons Domini est Bonum sine ullo malo; quia parti adversæ nullus ibi est locus, &c.* Discurrit autem de Malchuth, ut docet contextus." (Ibid., p. 277).

47 The reference is erroneous and should be Joh. 1,46.

48 A red pencil square bracket inserted into the text (Joh. 1,[47]) refers to an annotation in the right margin: 4.E./68.

SECTION IV

Kabbalist Catechumen Because the root *nzr* is almost equivalent to the root *šmr* which refers to the sefirah of *Kingdom* (*Lex. Cabb.*, pp. 720 *seq.*), I would refer this town also to that same Grade, | as a symbol of the Church (which fits most aptly both the active and passive meaning of "observation") and of the soul of the faithful. Similar are the symbols of the tribe [Zebulon] which gets its name from "cohabitation" (Gen 30.20; 1 Kgs 8.13; Isa 63.15) and [the symbol] of the hill-country (see *Lex. Cabb.*, pp. 277 *seq.*)[51]; || and that of its wretchedness (Jn 1.47[52]; 7.52); and [the symbol] of the region which was called *Lower* Galilee from a revolution [reincarnation]: all these are the sorts of things to which both Ecclesia | and the Soul are variously subjected. Note that there was a very ancient tradition that Messiah should appear in Galilee. Consider Excerpts Cent. 1 Loc. 70 and 74 *seq.* where these words of *Zohar* part 1 col 291 should be noted: "After 66½ years Messiah the King will be revealed in Galilee". And Part 2 chapter 11 "And he will be revealed in Galilee. This was the first place where the devastation of the Holy Land began, so he will be revealed there first before | anywhere else". This is found again ibid. column 14. Also in Section *Vajakel* where it is also handed down that the dead will be resurrected first in Galilee because there Messiah will appear. End of quotations.

p. 68

Christian Mystically Galilee denotes the spherical part of the soul which elsewhere is called [in Greek] *to epithumētikon* or [the seat of] desire and is the lowest [part] in mankind, occupied with love, | desire, hope, joy and the passions depending on these, where inevitably the arrival of the divine life has first to reform a man.[53]

Kabbalist Catechumen || Your interpretation is corroborated because the Greeks consistently transcribe the Hebrew letter /ç/ with an /s/ as one can see in the case of Saananim, Sabaoth, Sadoc, Salathi, Salmana, Salmona, Salphaad, Samarim, Senan, Saraa, | Sarath-asahar, Saredatha, Sarepta, Sarthan, Saruja, Sebeon, Sebia, Seboim, Sedada, Sedekias, Segon, Schesima, Seira, Sela, Seles, Seleph, Selethai, Selia, Selmon, Senna, Senneser, Seor, Sephath,

p. 69

---

49   Correction: notadam replaced by notanda
50   A red pencil square bracket inserted into the text (observatio[nem) refers to an annotation in the right margin: 5.E./69.
51   The tribe is Zebulon whose territory was to the West of the Sea of Galilee: the root *zbl* is used in the verses cited and this is taken to establish the symbolic significance explained here.
52   This should be: Jn 1.46.
53   Knorr has already introduced the tri-partite division of the soul above.

Sephora &c.&c. & per literam ζ, Hebræorum ז *denotent, ut innumeris pariter exemplis patet, quæ in onomasticis facilè observari possunt. In Nomine tamen* | *Nazareth loco* צ *quod in Syriaco constanter adhibetur retineant* ζ, *quasi in lingua originaria fuisse* ז; *& vox ista derivaretur â radice* נזר *quæ sensum habet separandi, abstrahendi, avertendi, abstinendi, sanctificandi.*

Christianus. Conjicio igitur Scriptores Sacros ob literarum unius organi facilem permutabilitatem utrumque sensum in eadem voce cumulare voluisse | (vid. plura ad Matth. 2, 23.)

V. 27. *Ad Virginem &c.* לות בתולתא

[**Christianus.**][54] Vide quæ de Messiæ Matre Vir- ‖ -gine[55] dicta sunt in Adumbratione Cabbalæ Christianæ, cap. 11, §. 5[56]. & in Excerptis Cent. I, Loc. 66.

Cabb. Cat. *Addo quod etiam voces* מרים[57] *Maria, &* בתולה | *virgo eundem habeant numerum minorem, quod apud Cabbalistas nostros non levis est momenti. Quare autem Messias â Virgine nasci debuit?*

Christianus. Ratio hæc esse videtur: Quia sanctissima illius Anima propterea in carnem descendebat, ut quatuor impugnaret & infirmaret Animarum hostes vel Cortices, 1. carnem ipsam, seu immediatum Animæ delapsæ vehiculum, | spiritum vitalem; 2. Carnis affectum sive peccatum; 3. Carnis Dominum seu Satanam; & 4. Carnis pœnam seu mortem. Cum igitur ordinariâ viâ in ge- ‖‖-nerationem veniunt Animæ, primò omnium â parentibus, eorumque vitali spiritu separatur sive traducitur particula illa lucida, quæ immediatum vehiculum est Animæ filii, seu spiritus ejus vitalis, quem ἀρχάιον seu progenitorem, sive primogenium dicunt: cujus natura semimaterialis

---

54 Added above the line (probably due to scribe's oversight).

55 A red pencil square bracket inserted into the text (observatio[nem) refers to an annotation in the right margin: 6.E./70.

56 "§. 5. Primus igitur congressus est, quem Messias instituit cum Materia, sive carne, ejusque amore: hanc enim (1.) Ipse assumsit. (2.) abnegavit. (3.) in aliis sanavit. (4.) passionibus subjecit. (5.) glorificavit. Assumsit autem pravâ libidinis concupiscentiâ (quam Jezer hara vocatis, & ad omnes generationes concurrere dicitis) non pollutam, sed à spiritu sancto in Matre Virgine ad polificationem fermentatam; quæ ultima dici posset primæ matris revolutio, ita ut, quæ virgo peccatum introduxerat, Virgo etiam salutem pareret. Et huc pertinet locus ille in Sohar sectione Beschallach col. 92. (Mart. fol. 52.b.) Fissio maris rubri à seniore dependet. [...]" ("Adumbratio kabbalæ christianæ", op. cit., p. 63). Mart. stands erroneously for "Mant." (the Mantuan edition of the Zohar). The exemplar held in the HAB offers a corrected text (by a red pencil, in the margins). Here, it reads: "Assumsit autem pravâ libidinis concupiscentiâ (quam Jezer hara vocatis, & ad

Sephi, Sepho, Sephon, Sephor, Sephora *etc.* etc. and with /z/ they transcribe the letter /z/ as may be shown from similar innumerable examples, which can easily be found in dictionaries[58].

In the name | Nazareth, in the place of /ç/ which appears consistently in the Syriac, they retain [the Greek zeta] /z/ as if in common speech it had been [Hebrew] /z/ [The word Nazareth] is thus derived from the root *nzr*, which [in contrast to the root mentioned above] means "to separate, to withdraw, to avoid, to abstain or to sanctify".

Christian I guess therefore that the holy writers, on account of the easy permutation of one of the letters, wished to embrace both meanings in the same word | (see further on Mt 2.23).

Verse 27
To a virgin etc. *lwt btwlt'*

Christian See what is said about the Virgin Mother of Messiah ‖ in *Adumbratio*, chap. 11, § 5 and Excerpts Cent. I Loc. 66.[59]   p. 70

Kabbalist Catechumen I would add that the words *mrym* "Maria" and *btwlh* "virgin" | have the same minor numerical value[60], which is important for our Kabbalists. But why did Messiah have to be born of a virgin?

Christian The reason seems to be that his most holy soul [had to] descend into the flesh to attack and weaken the four enemies of souls or "Shells", [namely]:

1 the Flesh itself or the immediate vehicle of the fallen soul, | the vital spirit;

2 the affect of the Flesh or sin;

3 the Lord of the Flesh or Satan;

4 the punishment of the Flesh or Death.

When souls are generated ‖‖ in the ordinary way, first of all from their parents, there is separated or transferred from the parents' vital spirit that bright particle, which is the immediate vehicle of the soul of the child or his vital spirit and which they call [in Greek] *archēgon* "progenitor" or "firstborn". The   fol. 14ᵛ

---

omnes generationes concurrere dicitis) non pollutam [carnem], sed à spiritu sancto in Matre Virgine ad p[r]olificationem fermentatam".

57   BSB: מתים (Printer's error)
58   Whence, evidently, this list was compiled.
59   The Virgin Birth in "Adumbratio kabbalæ christianæ" is discussed in the Introduction.
60   Calculation of the minor numerical value (קטנה גימטריה) requires one to skip the zeroes, or delete the tens, so that 40=4. Thus *mrym* = 4+2+1+4=11=1+1 =2 and *btwlh* = 2+4+6+3+5 =20 =2+0 =2. We are indebted here to Dr Judith Weiss of Ben-Gurion University of the Negev.

p. 71 est, eò quod â materiali cibo | & potu continuatur; unde etiam â parentum spiritu discerpi potest. Quoniam autem in eodem actu, quo particula hæc â parentum Archæo transfunditur, spiritus ille parentum in affectu libidinis est, qui est summus amoris motus excessivus, adeoque suâ naturâ propter excessum ‖ & exinde[61] natam offuscationem mentis, vitiosus; hinc istius affectus idea simul etiam | in parte traductâ permanet, & fomes est omnium in spiritu gliscentium idearum, & exhinc resultantium affectuum reliquorum, unde peccata. Cum ergò pro Anima Messiæ tale etiam præparandum esset vehiculum immediatum, seu Spiritus vitalis, is sanè omninò vacuus esse debebat ideis talibus; hinc non ex collisione spirituum progenerantium, quam semper concomitatur Jezer hara seu pruritus | ille libidinosus, separabatur Archæus ejus: nec â sola anima Matris, quamvis Virginis, quoniam & istius Spiritus vitalis ideis suis natisque exhinc motibus humanis non carebat, ut & ab officio docendi avocatura esset filium Matth. 12, 47. Spiritum igitur innatum hunc ipsi suppeditabat ipse Spiritus Sanctus[62]; eundemque cum spiritu Virgineo ita contemperabat, ut ab isto desumere | posset Spiritum ulteriorem influum, præpollente tamen semper luce Archæi illius Sanctioris, ut cum influo nullæ materiæ ideæ in ipsum derivari possent.

Cabb. Cat. [63]*Eodem omninò igitur*[64] *modo aliquando generabantur filii in Regno Messiano consummato Jes. 65, 20.23.*

Quæ desponsata erat. דמכירא

p. 72 [**Christianus.**][65] [66]Vid. ad Matth 1, 18[67]. ‖

Cabb. Cat.[68] *Quare â desponsatâ Virgine nasci voluit Messias?*

Christianus. Ratio hæc esse videtur, ut Satanas, cui ê præconio in cœlis publicato innotuerat ê Virgine jam nasciturum esse Messiam, hostem suum | infensissimum; veram ignoraret matrem, verumque partum; nec ante constitutum tentationum tempus hostiliter ipsum aggrederetur. Deinde etiam

---

61 A red pencil square bracket inserted into the text (observatio[nem) refers to an annotation in the left margin: 7.E./71.
62 Added in the left margin: quatenus est Spiritus Messiæ;
63 Added in the left margin: De spiritu hoc Messiæ innato profundiora quædam proferam infra ad Matth. 1, 1. verb. Filii David.
64 Correction above the line: omninò igitur replaced by autem
65 Added in the left margin: Christianus
66 Deletion: (
67 Deletion:)
68 A red pencil square bracket inserted into the text ([Cabb. Cat.) refers to an annotation in the left margin: 8.E./72.

nature of this is semi-material so that it is held together by material food | and drink and can be separated from the spirit of its parents. Since however in the same act [of coition] by which this [bright] particle is transferred from the parents into the Archegos ["progenitor" or "firstborn"], the spirit of the parents is in the affect of Desire which is the greatest movement of love, so by its own nature on account of its separation ‖ and the obfuscation of the mind born of this, it is flawed. Consequently the idea of this affect | remains even in the transferred part and is the tinder of all ideas flaring up in the spirit from which [come] the other consequent affects which produce sins.

When therefore such an unmediated vehicle or vital spirit had been prepared for the soul of Messiah, it clearly had to be absolutely void of any such notions. Consequently his Archegus was not separated by the coming together of the spirits of his parents which the *Yetser ha-ra* or "libidinous | desire" always accompanies, nor from the soul of his mother alone, although she was a virgin, because her vital spirit did not lack the notions and the human motivations which are born from this [manner of generation][69]. It was for this reason that she was called away from the responsibility of teaching her son (Mt 12.47). Therefore in her case the Holy Spirit itself supplemented the innate spirit (in as far as it is the spirit of Messiah) and so mixed it with the Virgin's spirit that she was able | to draw from it the highest spirit of the influxes, through the ever surpassingly powerful light of his more holy Archegus, so that no material ideas could arise in him with the influx.

Kabbalist Catechumen Concerning this inborn spirit of Messiah, I shall offer something more profound below on the words "Son of David" (Mt 1.1). In the same way children in the perfected kingdom of Messiah will at last be produced (Isa 65.20, 23[70]).

Who was betrothed dmkyr'

Christian See on Mt 1.18.

Kabbalist Catechumen ‖ Why did Messiah want to be born of a *betrothed virgin*?

Christian The reason seems to be so that Satan (who from the announcement published in heaven, had been made aware that Messiah, his most hostile | enemy, was now going to be born of a virgin) would not know the identity of the mother or indeed of the child. Consequently, he could not attack [Messiah] aggressively before the appointed time for [Messiah's]

---

69 This appears to be incompatible with the Immaculate Conception of the Virgin.
70 These verses are taken to refer to the spiritual birth envisaged in the comment.

ut defensor esset, testisque divinitùs edoctus virgini huic, Messiam in lucem edenti, contra qualescunque mundi calumnias.

Joseph de domo David. יוסף מן בית דויד

Christianus. Conjectare paululum, ad quamnam Revolutionem referri queat Josephus?

Cabb. Cat. *Nomenclaturam habet augentis vel Augusti juxta vulgarem hujus Nominis interpretationem: viderique posset Revolutio fuisse Josephi Patriarchæ, cum quo (1.) ratione castitatis egregiè convenit.* | *Adde (2.) quod Justus dicatur Matth. 1, 19. prout hoc ipso Epitheto à Cabbalistis nostris semper notatur Josephus (vid. Cabbal. denudatæ Tom. 1, P. ult. p. 248*[71]*; conf. Lex. Cabbalist. p. 430*[72] *& 440*[73]*, 659*[74]*, 369*[75]*; de Revolutionibus Animarum p. 382, §. 7.9*[76]*;*

---

[71] "10. Jesod. והיה. Joseph, qui vocatur justus". ("Explicatio Arborum seu Tabularum Quinque Cabbalisticarum Generalium", op. cit., p. 248).

[72] "יוסף *Joseph.* Est Jesod, qui gradus hoc nomine vocatur, quia Joseph est thronus ejus; unde in omnibus eidem similis, tam in eo, quod nutrivit totam domum Patris sui; sicut & Jesod nutrit universum mundum: quàm in aliis. Pard., Tr. 23. c. 10. Vid. Sohar Mikhez f. 112. c. 450. Vajechi 118. c. 467. Schlachlecha 77. c. 368." ("Loci communes kabbalistici", op. cit., p. 430).

[73] "יסוד *Fundamentum.* Omnes Interpretes Sephiram nonam propterea appellari hoc nomine dicunt, quod sit fundamentum τῆς Malchuth. Spiritualia enim corporalium contrarium obtinent; & cum corporalium fundamentum sit infra, in spiritualibus fundamentum est supra: Malchuth igitur quoad appetitum & desiderium suum ascendendi in isto gradu stabilitur, & per illum sustentatur. [...] Et in Sohar Sect. Noach indicium est, illum gradum propterea sic vocari, quia Malchuth nec influxum habet, nec vitam, nisi per illum; & si fortè subest ratio, ut hæc ejus notio cesset, status Malchuth insigniter diminuitur. Pardes Tr. 23. c. 10.–2. יסוד *Fundamentum.* In personis denotat membrum genitale utriusque sexus. [...]" (Ibid., pp. 439–440).

[74] "צדיק *Justus.* Penultimæ Sephirarum hoc sæpius ut cognomen inditur, quoniam hæc dimensio omnia sustinet inferiora: ex quo legitur Prov. 10, 25. *Et justus fundamentum mundi.* Justus autem dicitur, quod quæcunque inundationis bonique genera in nomen Adonai transfundit." (Ibid., pp. 659–660).

SECTION IV

temptations. And also so that [Satan] might be a witness that Messiah had been divinely brought forth into the light from the Virgin, and that thus [Messiah] has become a defender against all the calumnies of the world.

Joseph of the House of David ywsp mn byt dwyd

35 **Christian** Do you wish to speculate a little to which revolution [reincarnation] Joseph belonged?

Kabbalist Catechumen According to the popular interpretation, this name means "one increasing" or "distinguished". It can be seen as having been the revolution of the Patriarch Joseph with whom [our Joseph] shares
40 outstanding chastity[77]. | Add (2) that he is said to be Righteous (Mt 1.19) just as Joseph [the Patriarch] is always denoted by this epithet by our Kabbalists (See *Cabb. Denud.*, Vol. 1, Last part, p. 248; Cf. *Lex. Cabb.*, p. 430 and pp. 440,

---

75 "3. טוב *Bonus*. Habet ubique penultima Sephirarum boni Cognomen, ut illud: Jesch. 3, 16. Extollite justum, quoniam bonus: Tractus enim qui de supernis decurrunt Sephiris, imò & qui de fortitudinis timorisque mensura erumpunt, si per Justum incedunt, omnes in bonum perfectum & rei commodum inclinant, nullo intercedente malo." (Ibid., p. 369).

76 "7. Ista igitur portio mentis deinceps tribuebatur Josepho justo; quare etiam pulchritudo illa Adami, quam Chanochus accipiebat cum splendore superno in Josephum devolvebatur. Verum enim vero Josephus hanc Mentem accipere ultima demum merebatur nocte, qua finiebatur servitus ejus, quaque elevabatur ad regnum. Atque hinc intelligi potest mysticum illud, qua ratione septuaginta linguas didicerit illa nocte, quia nimirum dignus fiebat ista Mente, quæ Metatronis est, præfecti septuaginta populorum gnarique tot linguarum. [...] 9. Cùm autem mens istorum nondum gustasset mortem ab illo tempore, quo moriebatur Adam Protoplastes: sed ab illis auferebatur ante mortem suam: Josephus autem fratres suos somniis suis irritasset, ut ipsum venderent: hinc puniebatur, mentemque hanc revolvi oportebat in R. Jischmaël filio Elischah sacerdote magno; ut sufferret poenam mortis realiter. Hinc R. Jischmaël filius Elischah tanta excellebat pulchritudine, quanta Josephus justus. Quæ ratio est, quare eundem Metatron in libro suo, cui Palatiorum nomen est, semper vocet gloriam splendoris sui." ("De Revolutionibus animarum", op. cit., p. 382).

77 See Gen 39.

p. 73
fol. 15ʳ
p. 397, §. 2[78]*; p. 436, §. 5*[79]*; p. 463, §. 10*[80]*). Et (3.) notan-* ‖ *-dum*[81] *quod utrique revelationes factæ sint per somnia (Matth. 1, 20; c. 2, 13.19).* ‖‖ *Et (4.) quod sicut Joseph Patriarcha â Nostratibus dicitur Nutritor terræ seu Regni, ita Josephus iste nutritor fuerit Mariæ, quæ ad Regni metrum pariter referenda est.*

Christianus. In Theologia mystica per Josephum concipi potest Intellectus Animæ practicus; | Nam & hic augmenta semper quærit luminis, & de familia Amoris est: id est, de genere communicabilitatis. 5

Mariam מרים

[Vide ad Matth. 1, 17.22.][82]
Christianus. Quonam hanc refers?
Cabb. Cat. *Hæc statui posset Revolutio fuisse*[83] *Mirjam Sororis*[84] *Mosis.*[85] 10
notabile enim[86] *est (1.) utramque idem habere nomen. (2.) utramque habuisse dona spiritus sancti; (3.) utramque cecinisse canticum (4.) De Mirjam sorore Mosis traditio est, quod illâ mediante fons ille miraculosus castra Iisraelitica secutus sit; eò quod post mortem ejusdem, aqua hæc cessaverit. Num. 20, 1.2.* | 15
p. 74 *Rabboth, in Numer. in princ.* ‖ *Multò*[87] *magis de Maria hac dici potest, quod illa mediante in Ecclesiam influere cœperit fons ille salutis Joh. 7, 37; 1 Cor. 10, 4. Cum autem interposita fuerit Revolutio Prophetissæ Jeschajanæ Jes. 7, 14 hinc. (5.) omnibus tribus nomen* העלמה *tribuitur Ex. 2, 8; Jes. 7, 14; Matth. 1, 23.*

---

78 "2. Cum autem Jesepho (sic) justo accideret illud, ut guttæ seminis ipsi prodirent è digitis manuum pedumque ejus, juxta illud Genes. 49.v. 24. *Et dispersa sunt semina manuum ejus*; hinc quia Joseph repræsentat fundamentum superius; eodem tempore etiam in supernis scintillæ animarum prodierunt è fundamento masculino: quæ non deductæ sunt intra fœminam: sed in vanum prodierunt, ita ut iisdem adhæserint cortices." (Ibid., p. 397).

79 "Eadem autem pars Mentis deinceps derivata est in Josephum justum: unde pulchritudo Adami Protoplastæ, quam iste habuerat à Splendore hoc superno, spectanda postmodum erat in Josepho. Nimirum hic mentem illam assequebatur eadem nocte, qua finiebatur servitus ejus, & ipse extollendus erat in statum Regium. Unde dictum illud Gemaræ: Eum septuaginta linguas didicisse eadem nocte; quod nimirum acciperet Mentem Metatronis præfecti septuaginta populorum & linguarum, quas omnes callet. Et huc pertinet illud Psal. 81.v. 6. *Testimonium in Joseph posuit.* Quem locum conferas cum loco Job. 16.v. 19. *In cœlis testis meus.* Ubi per testem intelligitur Metatron, ita ut per testimonium illud in Josepho positum Metatron intelligatur, quoniam ע״די testis meus, & חנוך eundem referunt numerum; Et hæc portio tradita est Josepho. Cum autem sequitur Job. 16.v. 19. *Et testis meus in excelsis*; ibi intelligitur Elias, ut notum est. (Hic conferre aliquis posset locum Apoc. 11. v. 3.)" (Ibid., p. 436). The text in brackets is Knorr's addition to the translation.

80 "Circa prophetiam autem Jehoschuæ in dubio versor utrum à fundamento Microprosopi derivata fuerit; quia erat de tribu Joseph justi: an vero à parte posteriore duorum cerebrorum uxoris, ut dictum supra: Prout reperimus: faciem Jehoschuah fuisse ut

SECTION IV 237

659, 369; *De Revol. Animarum*, p. 382, §7.9; p. 397, §2; p. 436, §5; p. 463, §10). ‖ And (3), it is noteworthy that the revelations given to each of the two [Josephs] were made through dreams (Mt 1.20; 2.13, 19) ‖‖ and (4), just as the Patriarch Joseph is called by our Kabbalists "Nourisher of the Land" or "of the Kingdom"[88], so the other Joseph was the "Nourisher of Mary" who equally should be linked to the measure *of Kingdom*.

Christian In Mystical Theology[89] it is possible to understand by Joseph the practical intelligence of the soul, | for this is always seeking greater light and is of the family of Love, which is a type of sharing.

p. 73
fol. 15ʳ

Maria mrym

Christian Look at Mt 1.17, 22. To what do you refer this?

Kabbalist Catechumen It can be established that this [Miriam] was the latest reincarnation of the First Mother Eve after she had been incarnated into Miriam the sister of Moses. Concerning these [two Mariams], it is notable that: (1) they both have the same name; (2) both had the gifts of the Holy Spirit; (3) both sang a song and; (4) it is said of Miriam, Moses' sister, that by her mediation the miraculous spring followed the Israelite camp and that after her death this water dried up (Num 20.1.2, | Numbers Rabbah *initio*). ‖ Much more [than this] can be said of the other Miriam, because by her mediation the Fountain of Salvation began to flow into Ecclesia (Jn 7.37; 1 Cor 10.4). The Reincarnation of Isaiah's prophetess was interposed [between the two Mariams] (Isa 7.14) and this is why (5) the [Hebrew] word *h'lmh* [virgin] is applied to each of the three of them Ex 2.8; Isa 7.14; Mt 1.23.

p. 74

---

faciem Lunæ, eumque vaticinatum esse per speculum, cui non est lumen; per quod intelligitur Luna, quod est cognomentum uxoris." (Ibid., p. 463).

81 A red pencil square bracket inserted into the text (notan[dum) refers to an annotation in the left margin: 9.E./73.
82 Correction: the reference is moved to the beginning of the following sentence, so that the text reads as follows: Vide ad Matth. 1, 17.22. Quonam hanc refers?
83 Added in the right margin: ultima primæ Matris Evæ; postquam eadem revoluta fuisset in. The addition aims at extending the concatenation of the revolutions of the soul that are to be found in Mary.
84 Correction: sororis replaced by sorori
85 Correction: a few words, now unreadable, replaced by De hac autem
86 Deleted word: enim
87 A red pencil square bracket inserted into the text ([Multò) refers to an annotation in the right margin: 10.E./74.
88 Gen 41.52 ff. 45.11.
89 Knorr seems to use the term Mystical Theology to discuss the soul's turning in contemplation for illumination towards God.

Christianus. In Theologiâ mysticâ per Mariam intelligi potest voluntas Animæ, | ex quâ fœcundante Spiritu S. in lucem prodit vita divina. Perge autem, & de nomine hoc etiam quædam Cabbalistica suggere.

Cabb. Cat. *Prima nominis impositio videtur habuisse sensum amaritudinis, quod acerba tunc persecutio premeret Dei populum, ob filios in undas projectos cum Jochebed primogenitam hanc pareret filiam. Unde | Nomen hoc ad Regni gradum referri potest, ob amaritudinem corticum ibidem repertorum & connotationem Maris. Cabbalistis autem & aliæ allusiones concessæ sunt, prout Exempla habemus in* מור *myrrha (Lexic. Cabal. p. 517*[90]*) & Morijah (ibid. p. 279*[91]*) ubi admittitur sensus prædominii, & corona summa subinnuitur, item Gratiæ ‖ Gradus*[92]*: Unde sensum elicere possemus hunc*[93]*, quod nempe | prædominantes illi gradus Benevolentiæ summæ & Gratiæ, Mare hoc nostrum*[94] *nunc impleant.*

Et ingressus est &c. ועל

Christianus. Habesne, quod super ingressu & apparitione Angeli annotes?

Cabb. Cat. *Videtur Angelus ad ipsam intrasse in locum quendam â commercio plurium separatum, qui â nostratibus vocatur* רשות היחיד *| Licentia unius, (vid. Lexic. Cabb. p. 693*[95]*) non verò ut ad uxorem Manoach in agro; vel ut ad Sarah in præsentia mariti, ostioque tentorii Gen. 18, 10. Videtur etiam appa-*

---

[90] "מור *Myrrha*. In Raja M. ad Cant. 3, 6. מר dicitur Kether, quasi alluderetur ad significationem מר *Domini*. Corona enim prædominatur in Aziluth. Et ad Cant. 5, 1. ubi מור plenè, sic vocatur Chesed, quia sicut myrrha primarium est inter aromata, ita Chesed in structurâ. Et in Tikkunim myrrha vel ad Chesed, vel ad Nezach refertur. Pard." ("Loci communes kabbalistici", op. cit., p. 517).

[91] "10. Sed הר המוריה Mons Morijah sic vocatur ex parte Chesed, sic docet R. Schimeon ben Jochai ad locum illum Cant. 5, 1. collegi מורי myrrham meam: nam Myrrha ad Abraham pertinet, ut suo loco dicetur. Vocatur autem מוריה quatenus Chesed unita est tribus prioribus, comprehensis in י"ה, ut notum. Atque sic quoque Kether vocatur מור, ut tradit R. Schimeon ben Jochai ad locum illum Cant. 4, 6. *Ibo mihi ad montem Mor*, seu myrrhæ. Unde fortè ex istius parte Gedulah sic appellatur; & omnes quatuor simul, quando effundunt benedictionem & influentiam in montem istum, propter opus illud, quod ligaret Jizchak filium suum, nomine suo vocantur Mons Morijah." (Ibid., p. 279).

[92] A red pencil square bracket inserted into the text ([Gradus) refers to an annotation in the right margin: 11.E./75.

[93] Absent from the BSB: hunc (Probably due to printer's oversight).

[94] Deleted word: nostrum

[95] Cf. *supra*, pp. 196–197.

Christian In Mystical Theology by Mary can be understood the will of the soul | out of which by the fructifying of the Holy Spirit the divine life came forth into the light. Go on then, suggest something kabbalistic about this name too.

Kabbalist Catechumen The first giving of the name seems to have had the meaning of Bitterness [from the Hebrew root *mrr*] because at that time a harsh persecution pressed upon the people of God on account of the [Hebrew] baby boys who were being thrown into the waters [of the River Nile] at the time when Jochebed gave birth to her firstborn daughter [Miriam]. From | this the name can be related to the Grade of *Kingdom* on account of the bitterness of the Shells found there and the connotation of Sea.[96] Other allusions are allowed by the Kabbalists, in as much as we have examples in *mwr* myrrh (*Lex. Cabb.*, p. 517) and Morijah (ibid., p. 279) where the meaning of "Predominance" is admitted and the Highest Crown is implied. ‖ Also the Grade of *Grace* [is alluded to]; whence we can derive the meaning that those [powers] | predominating in the Grade of the greatest Kindness and Grace, now fill this Sea.

p. 75

And he went in etc. *w'l*

Christian Do you have something to say about the entrance and appearance of the angel?

Kabbalist Catechumen It seems that the angel came into her and into a place significantly out of the way of any traffic which our teachers call *rswt hyḥyd* | the "licence of one" (see *Lex. Cabb.*, p. 693): not as [an angel came] to the wife of Manoah in a field, but as [one appeared] to Sarah in the presence of her husband in the mouth of the tent (Gen 18.10). The Angel seems to have

---

[96] Miriam's name is here analysed as comprising the Hebrew root *mrr* ("bitterness") and *ym* ("sea"). But then in Mary's case, the first root is read as "predominance" and the sea evoked by the second name-bearer considered to be full of Kindness and Grace. Below on verses 36–38 (folio 18ʳ) in a summary of spiritual lessons (mystical meanings) to be learned from this passage, we are told that Mary's name indicates that "Will must have dominance over the Sea, that is Desire".

ruisse in forma hominis ordinariâ, quæ in se non esset terribilis, ut Dan. 10, 5–10[97] *cum Maria non tam fulgore, quam sermone ejus & salutatione terreatur.*

Pax tibi &c. שלם לכי 40

Christianus. Quâ linguâ facta est hæc salutatio; & quo effectu?

p. 76   **Cabb. Cat.** *Salutatio hæc aliâ linguâ facta non est, quàm Syriacâ, quæ illis locis erat vernacula: Unde omninò An-* ‖ *-gelus*[98] *dixit: Pax tibi; & non, Ave vel* χαίρε. *Cumque aliàs saltem confortandi ergò, hâc phrasi usi essent Angeli,* | 45 *ut Jud. 6, 23; Dan. 10, 19, jam salutem immediatè sic Virgini dicit Angelus, in signum familiaritatis & amicitiæ ut Luc. 24, 36; Joh. 20, 19.21.26. Sique effectum*

fol. 15ᵛ   *usquam habuisse* ‖ *dici potest, pacis hujuscemodi apprecatio, quemadmodum è salutationibus Apostolicis sperari poterat Matth. 10, 13; Luc. 10, 5.6. nunc sanè effectum quam maximè conspicuum habuit salutatio hæc Angelica.*

Gratiâ plena &c. מלית טיבותא

Christianus. Ad quemnam gradum divinarum numerationum hanc gratiam 5 refers?

Cabb. Cat. טיבותא *dicitur â* טוב *quod habet sensum Boni, & ad varios refertur gradus divinorum influxuum, nempe ad Benignitatem, Pulchritudinem, Fundamentum & Regnum (vid. Lex. Cabbalist. p. 368*[99] *seqq.) quibus omnibus* | 10 *repleta nunc Maria fuisse censeri potest: præcipuè vero Fundamenti; unde conceptio.*

p. 77   *Dominus noster tecum &c.* מרן עמבי ‖

Christianus.[100] Qualem Dominum hic intelligis, & qualem ejus præsentiam?

Cabb. Cat. *Hæc verba hunc habent sensum: Dominus Angelorum tecum* | 15 *est. Id est, Messias ipse præsens ad te descendit; sicut descenderat ad Gedeo-*

---

97   BSB: Dan. 10, 5–19 (Printer's error)
98   A red pencil square bracket inserted into the text (An[gelus) refers to an annotation in the right margin: 12.E./76.
99   "טוב *Bonus, Bonum.* Pertinet ad Chesed, habetque significationem *aptandæ Lucis*, juxta Exod. 30, 7. Deinde & Tiphereth ex parte Chesed vocatur *Bonus.* Item Jesod. Et Malchuth eôdem respectu dicitur Bona. [...] Secundum R. Moscheh tamen; etiam gradus Kether vocatur Bonus, quia benè adaptat omnes lucernas: quamvis huc non inclinent verba Sohar. [...]" ("Loci communes kabbalistici", op. cit., p. 368).
100   A red pencil square bracket inserted into the text ([Christianus.) refers to an annotation in the left margin: 13.E./77.

appeared in the form of an ordinary man which was not in itself terrible (as it was in Dan 10.5–10) since Mary was terrified not so much by his glory, as by his words and by his greeting.

40 *Peace be to you etc. slm lky*

Christian In what language was this greeting made and with what effect?

Kabbalist Catechumen This greeting was made in no other language than Syriac which was the vernacular in those regions[101]. ‖ Thus the angel said precisely "Peace to You" and not "Ave" or [in Greek] "Chaire". As elsewhere
45 angels used this phrase to give reassurance | (as in Judg 6.23; Dan 10.19), so now the Angel gave this greeting directly to the Virgin in such a way as to be a sign of familiarity and friendship (so Lk 24.36; Jn 20.19, 21, 26). To see that a prayer for peace of this kind can ever be said to have an effect, ⫼ consider the [expectations of a result] from the greeting of the Apostles in Mt 10.13, Lk 10.5.6. In this case, this Angel's salutation had the most obvious effect.

Full of Grace mlyt ṭybwt'

5 **Christian** To what grade of the Divine Numerations do you attribute this Grace?

Kabbalist Catechumen *ṭybwt'* is derived from *ṭwb* which means "good" and refers to various grades of divine influxes, particularly Kindness, Beauty,
10 Foundation and Kingdom (See *Lex. Cabb.*, pp. 368 *seq.*) with all of which | Mary can now be considered to have been filled, but especially with *Foundation* from which comes conception[102].

Our Lord is with you mrn 'mky

Christian ‖ What Lord is meant here and what is his presence like?

Kabbalist Catechumen These words mean here: The Lord of Angels is
15 with you. | That is: Messiah himself is present having descended to you, just

---

101 Syriac Christians have long held that Syriac was the vernacular of Jesus and his Mother. The conviction is reaffirmed on the title page of the *editio princeps* of the Peshitta New Testament, printed by Widmanstetter in Vienna in 1555.
102 "Foundation" corresponds to the sefirah *Yesod* which is associated with the *membrum virile*. This constitutes a subtle reflection upon the Virgin Birth. See Introduction.

nem Jud. 6, 12. Sed præsentiâ longè intimiore: ita ut tu nunc vocari queas civitas illa, cui nomen IHVH[103] ibidem. Jechesk. 48, 35.

Benedicta inter mulieres ברירת בנשא

Christianus. Quamnam esse putas emphasin istius benedictionis?

Cabb. Cat. Aptissimè huc quadrant, quæ de voce ברכה dicunt nostrates, quod illa stagnum denotet & Benedictionem (Lexic. Cabbalist. p. 215[104], 216[105]) ita ut ipsa receptaculum dicatur omnium benedictionum longè augustius, quàm de ulla unquam fœmina dici potuerit. Longè autem amplior est sensus modi indicativi, quàm si optativus esse intelligatur; nec intelligitur eventus acclamationum, ut Jud. 5, 24, | sed illuminationum copia. ||

V. 29.[106] & כד חזת אתרהבת במלתה
Cum vidisset conturbata est per sermonem ejus etc.

Christianus. Quis propriè est sensus radicis Syriacæ רהב?

Cabb. Cat. Convenit cum Arabico, sensumque terroris habet ac metus. | Maria ergò ob visum ignoti cujusdam secretius conclave suum subintrantis insolitamque ejus salutationem perterrita quidem est, prout vox eadem occurrit Luc. 24, 37 ut & vestes neglectius fortè assumtas colligeret, & utensilia ad usum variè dispersa curatius disponere conaretur, qualis est sensus Luc. 10, 41; Mar. 5, 39; conf. Joh. 21, 7. [**Christianus**][107] non[108] ita tamen expavit, ut non & visionem aliquam sibi fieri agnosceret, | & mentem servaret satis compositam atque attentam.

---

103 BSB: JHVH
104 "בְּרָכָה *Stagnum, Piscina.* Est Malchuth. Illa enim receptaculum illud est, quod colligit omnem influentiam ab omnibus locis supernis. Quandoque tamen & Binah vocatur stagni nomine. Scaturigo autem stagni inferioris est Tiphereth, per fontem, qui est Jesod. Et scaturigo stagni superioris est Kether per fontem, qui est Chochmah. […]" ("Loci communes kabbalistici", op. cit., p. 215).
105 "ברכה *Benedictio.* Itidem Malchuth est; sed tunc temporis, quando influxum affugit à dextra; quod ita traditur in Libro Raja Mehimna, locisque aliis. […]" (Ibid., p. 216).
106 A red pencil square bracket inserted into the text ([V. 29.) refers to an annotation in the left margin: 14.E./78.
107 Added in the left margin: Christian., (which involves a change of speaker, the rest of the passage being now attributed to the Christian).
108 Correction: non replaced by Non

SECTION IV   243

as he descended to Gideon (Judg 6.12) but with a far greater intimacy, so that now you can be called that city where the name JHVH is present (Ezek 48.35)[109].

Blessed among women brykt bnš'

Christian What do you consider to be the import of this blessing?

Kabbalist Catechumen This fits very neatly with what our teachers say about the word *brkh*—that it means "pool" and "blessing" (*Lex. Cabb.*, pp. 215, 216), so that she is said to be a far more august receptacle of all blessings than could ever have been said of any other woman. The sense is far greater if understood as an indicative rather than an optative. It does not mean the outcomes of the acclamations (as in Judg 5.24) | but the supply of illuminations ‖.   p. 78

Verse 29
When he saw she was troubled by his words etc. *kd ḥzt 'trhbt bmlth*

Christian What is the proper sense of the Syriac root *rhb*?

Kabbalist Catechumen. Like the Arabic, it means "terror" and "fear".[110] | Mary was thoroughly frightened by the sight of someone unknown penetrating her most private chamber and by his unusual greeting. The same word occurs in Lk 24.37. "To gather garments *removed rather carelessly by chance*, and utensils for various uses *scattered* and to try to arrange these more carefully"—such is the meaning[111] in Lk 10.41; Mk 5.39; Cf. Jn 21.7.

Christian But she was not so frightened that she did not recognise that she was having a vision | and she kept her mind sufficiently composed and attentive.

---

109   There is possibly a double reading here. The Hebrew Massoretic text at the end of the verse reads "The Lord is there". The LXX apparently read the same consonants as "will be its name". Knorr appears to conflate the two here.

110   This sort of Comparative Semitic Philology was easily facilated by Edmund Castell, *Lexicon Heptaglotton*, vol. 1 (London: Thomas Roycroft, 1669) column 3533, s.v. *rhb*. On this work H.T. Norris "Edmund Castell (1606–1686) and his *Lexicon Heptaglotton* (1669)" in *The 'Arabick' Interest of the Natural Philosophers in 17th Century England*, edited by G.A. Russell (Leiden: Brill, 1994), pp. 70–89.

111   Here, in the case of Martha.

Cujusnam hæc esset pacis apprecatio.
דמנו שלמא הנא

Christianus. Quare factum esse putas, ut miraretur salutationem hanc?

p. 79 **Cabb. Cat.** *Apud Priscos juxta Doctorum nostrorum tradita, nullo modo salutabatur* ‖ *fœmina*[112], *ne quidem mediante nuncio, imò nec mediante marito,* | *prout habet Gemara Kiddusch in fol. 70a.* [**Christianus**][113] Unde non immeritò mirabatur sponsa hæc, unde ista legatio; quia Domini sui mentionem fecerat Angelus: & quis ipsam per nuncium hunc salutari jusserit, casu tàm periculoso, ut in suspicionem adulterii incidere potuisset.

V. 30. *Ne timeas Marjam.* לא תדחלין מרים

Christianus. Nomine proprio ipsam compellat, ut timore seposito confidentiùs attendat, cum nihil periculi subsit: conf. Gen. 15, 1; c. 21, 17; c. 35, 10; c. 46, 3; Deut. 1, 21; Jos. 8, 1; Jud. 6, 23; Matth. 1, 20; c. 28, 5; Marc. 5, 36; Luc. 1, 13; Ap. fol. 16ʳ 1, 17. ‖‖

Cabb. Cat. *Si ad metrum Regni refertur Marjam; timore carere non poterat, quia hoc metrum Timoris nomine vocatur (Excerpt. Cent. 1. Loc. 10; Lexic. Cabbalist. in* יראה[114]). *Quia autem compositum est hoc metrum ex gratia & Vigore: illam nunc præponderare innuit.*

Invenisti enim gratiam &c. 5
אשכחתי גיר טיבותא

p. 80 **Christianus.** Illustra hoc exemplis. ‖

Cabb. Cat.[115] *Esther, prout nostrates tradunt, pulchra non fuit; Sed flavescens; invenit autem gratiam apud Regem. Esth. 2, 17 (conf. Lex. Cabbalist. p. 267).* **Christianus**][116] Idemque dicitur de Noah Gen. 6, 8 (Lexic. Cabbalist.

---

112 A red pencil square bracket inserted into the text ([fœmina,) refers to an annotation in the left margin: 15.E./79.

113 Added in the left margin: Christ. (which involves a change of speaker, the rest of the passage being now attributed to the Christian).

114 "יראה *Timor.* Hæc vox nudè posita est in Gebhurah; quia ab hac fundamentum timoris provenit: unde idem vocari solet *Timor Elohim.* Sed & Schechinah ex parte Gebhurah vocatur timor. [...]" ("Loci communes kabbalistici", op. cit., p. 451).

115 A red pencil square bracket inserted into the text ([Cabb. Cat.) refers to an annotation in the right margin: 16.E./80.

116 Added in the right margin: Christ. (which involves a change of speaker, the rest of the passage being now attributed to the Christian).

For which peace this was the prayer dmw šlm' hn'

Christian Why do you think it was that she wondered at this greeting?

Kabbalist Catechumen According to our sages, in olden times a ‖ woman was *never* greeted, not even by an intermediary messenger, nor even through the mediation of her husband | (so Talmud Kidushin 70a).

Christian This betrothed woman understandably wondered where this embassy came from, because the angel had made mention of her Lord[117], who had ordered her to be greeted by this message. It was a dangerous case because she could have fallen into suspicion of adultery.

Verse 30
Do not be afraid Mary l' tdḥlyn mrym

Christian He addresses her by her own name so that, putting fear aside, she may attend with more trust since she is not in any danger. (Cf. Gen 15.1; 21.17; 35.10; 46.3 Deut 1.21; Jos 8.1; Judg 6.23; Mt 1.20; 28.5 Mk 5.36; Lk 1.13; Rev 1.17.) ‖‖

Kabbalist Catechumen If Maria is related to the measure of *Kingdom* she could not lack fear because this degree is called by the name of Fear (Excerpts Cent. I Loc. 10; *Lex. Cabb.* on *yrʾh*). But because this Measure is composed of *Grace* and *Strength*, it is implied that [Grace] is now preponderant.

For you have found Grace etc. 'škḥ ty gyr ṭybwt'

Christian Illustrate this with examples, please.

Kabbalist Catechumen ‖ Esther, our teachers say, was not beautiful but *becoming fair* she found grace with the King (Esth 2.17; Cf. *Lex. Cabb.*, p. 267).

Christian The same [*finding* favour] is said of Noah in Gen 6.8 (*Lex.*

---

117 Or "his Lord". But "her Lord" follows pertinently after the immediately preceding remark that a woman was never greeted even through the agency of her husband. The angel, of course, had said "our Lord".

in voce | נוח)[118] & de David, Act. 7, 46. Sed & Esther & David ad Regnum refe- 10
runtur. (vid. Lex. Cabbal. in דוד[119]).

V. 31. *Conciples utero &c.* תקבלין בטנא

Christianus. Applicatio specialis esse videtur Prophetiæ Jes. 7, 14. ad personam Mariæ: Quid autem tu hic contribuis ê vestris dogmatibus?

Cabb. Cat. Si unquam alibi, quàm maximè hìc locum habet traditum illud 15
Doctorum nostrorum; quod, ut vitæ restitutio & alimentorum suppeditatio, ita
& liberorum progeneratio ab Influentiâ summâ occultâ dependeat. Egregiè[120]
etiam ex hac ipsâ phrasi fluit confirmatio opinionis nostræ antiquissimæ de
Animarum præexistentia: minimè enim hoc loco subintelligi | potest concep- 20
tio seminis masculini; & quia de motu dici non potest, quod concipiatur, sed
p. 81 *necessariò subauditur substantia quædam; nihil sanè super-* ‖ *-est*[121]*, quod*
concepisse utero suo potuit Virgo beata, quam Anima Messiæ, è sublimiore in
infimum hunc digressa mundum (vide ad Matth. 1, 18).

Et paries filium &c. ותאלדין ברא

Christianus. Hic quæritur, cujus respectu vocetur filius? Antiqui enim Chri- 25
stianorum adversarii, ex eo, quod Christus seipsum toties filium hominis
vocat, impugnabant Mariæ virginitatem. Sed certè nihil impedit, quin subintelligatur virgo ipsa; nam & istius filius vocatur Christus Matth. 1, 25; Mar. 6,
3; Luc. 2, 7.48; conf. Psal. 116, 16. Nihil tamen absurdi esset, si subintelligeretur David, cujus pariter filius idem dicitur | Matth. 20, 30.31; c. 21, 9; c. 22, 42; 30
&c. Unde & Justinus jam suo dixit ævo Tryphoni; quod progenitores filiarum,
istorum dicantur Patres, qui â filiabus progenerantur.

---

118 "נוח *Noach*; est Jesod, cujus vehiculum erat Noach; unde ingrediebatur in Arcam; eratque justus Gen. 6, 9. & ut Majores dicunt, circumcisus natus. Et per Jesod Malchuth invenit quietem; & (si Targumicè à נחת) per eum descendit influxus. Unde sic vocatur cum in unione est: atque tunc mundus est in tranquillitate & consolatione Gen. 5, 29. Pard. vid. Soh. Trumah 75, 297, Pinchas 102, 408. f. 121, 481." ("Loci communes kabbalistici", op. cit., pp. 568–569).
119 "דוד *David*. Ita vocatur Malchuth, quia David fuit vehiculum istius metri, Illudque (sic) condecoravit & donavit canticis suis: ad Ipsam enim spectant omnes laudes ejus. Illa tamen fuit metrum ejus, quatenus inclinat ad Hod; unde ד"וד cum voce æquipollet numero vocis ה"וד qui est 15. Et sic in Raja mehimna traditur, quod Metrum Davidis sit Hod. [...]" (Ibid., p. 247).
120 BSB: Egregiò (Printer's error)
121 A red pencil square bracket inserted into the text ([Cabb. Cat.) refers to an annotation in the right margin: Pr.F./81.

Cabb. | under *nwḥ*) and of David in Acts 7.46. Both Esther and David are also related to *Kingdom* (See *Lex. Cabb.* in *dwd*).

Verse 31
You will conceive in your womb etc. *tqblyn bṭn'*

Christian This seems to be a special application of the prophecy in Isa 7.14 to Mary personally.[122] But what do you have to say here from your teachings?

Kabbalistic Catechumen The teaching of our doctors that just as the restoration of life and the provision of food depend upon the highest hidden *Influentia*, so also does the generation of children is found nowhere more clearly than here. From this very phrase comes a striking confirmation of our oldest opinion about the pre-existence of souls, for a woman's conception with the assistance of a man can scarcely be | understood here. Because what is conceived cannot be said to be due to motion, some substance is here necessarily implied. So clearly nothing is left that the Blessed Virgin could have ‖ conceived in her womb [other] than the soul of Messiah come down from a more sublime world to this the lowest of worlds (See on Mt 1.18).

p. 81

And you will bear a child etc. *wt'ldyn br'*

Christian The question is: whose son will he be called? The ancient enemies of Christianity impugned the virginity of Mary because Christ so often called himself "Son of Man". But nothing prevents one from understanding here "[son of] the Virgin herself" for Christ is called her son: Mt 1.25; Mk 6.3; Lk 2.7, 48; Cf. Ps 116. 16. Nor is there anything absurd if [son of] David is implied as he is equally said to be his son: | Mt 20.30, 31; 21. 9; 22. 42 etc. As Justin said already in his time to Trypho: "the fathers of women are [likewise] called the fathers of those women who their daughters bear"[123].

---

[122] John Lightfoot, *Miscellanies and the Harmony of the Gospels*, op. cit., p. 163: "Ver. 31: 'Behold, thou shalt conceive,' &c.] From Isa. vii. 14; the angel giveth her to understand, that she is the virgin spoken of in that place: and of her apprehension of this, ariseth her question, ver, 4."

[123] Justin Martyr, *Dialogue with Trypho*, Chapter 100 Alexander Roberts and James Donaldson, eds., *The Ante-Nicene Fathers. I. The Apostolic Fathers—Justin Martyr—Irenæus* (New York: Charles Scribner, 1913), p. 249.

Cabb. Cat. *Imò, quid si & Adam connotaretur & Deus? Luc. 3, 38.*

Jeschua. ישוע

Christianus.[124] Procul dubio in aliquo conveniunt Nomina ישוע & עמנואל quia hoc | Messiæ tribuitur. Jesch. 7, 14. Quid tibi videtur? ‖

Cabb. Cat.[125] *Istud notavi, quod Nomen Jeschua* ישוע *cujus numerus est 386 & nomen* עמנואל *cujus numerus est 197 minori numero conveniant, qui est 17 & 8. Item quod utrumque nomen plenè scriptum referat eundem numerum 523: nempe* עי׳ן מם נו׳ן וי׳ו אל׳ף למ׳ד & יו׳ד שי׳ן ואיו עי׳ן *qui est numerus* חקת יה *Decretum | Domini. Conf. Psal 2, 7.*

V. 32. *Erit magnus &c.* נהוא רב

[**Cabb. Cat.**][126] *Quid de his verbis censes, nonne vaticinium quoddam in se includunt?*

[**Christianus**][127] Omninò hic deprehendo vaticinium, & quidem de triplici statu Messiæ (1.) exinanitionis: (2.) exaltationis inchoatæ (3.) & consummatæ. Ad statum[128] ‖‖ exinanitionis pertinent verba hæc: נהוא רב. Erit Raf: quæ vox significationem habet tam Doctoris, (Joh. 13, 13) quam Sacerdotis summi, (Matth. 26, 51; Hebr. 4, 14) ita ut utrumque status primi officium hic denotetur, propheticum nempe, & Sacerdotale; Ad statum exaltationis inchoatæ pertinent verba | hæc: Et filius altissimi vocabitur. Cum enim hoc ipsum propriè cogno- ‖ -men[129] sit Messiæ, (ut Matth. 4, 3.6; c. 8, 29; c. 14, 33; c. 16, 16; c. 26, 63; c. 27, 40.43.54; Marc. 1, 1; c. 3, 11; c. 5, 7; c. 15, 39; Luc. 8, 28; Joh. 1, 14.18.34; c. 3, 16.17.18; c. 6, 69; c. 11, 27; c. 20, 31; &c.&c.) Messias autem in hoc dignitatis gradu confirmatus non fuerit nisi post superatas tentationes atque passiones suas; hinc Nomen | hoc quoque filii Dei secundum excellentiam ipsi demum tributum fuit post resurrectionem (Act. 13, 32.33; Rom. 1, 4; Hebr. 2, 9; Act. 2, 36) idque ob hanc potissimum rationem, quod

---

124 Added in the right margin: (Vid. ad Matth. 1, 1 & 21).
125 A red pencil square bracket inserted into the text ([Cabb. Cat.) refers to an annotation in the right margin: 2.F./82.
126 Correction in the right margin: Christianus replaced by Cabb. Cat. Jam & tu quædam edissere (which involves the two speakers being changed over in the following exchange).

SECTION IV   249

Kabbalist Catechumen What if it means [son of] Adam and of God? (Lk 3.38)

Jeschua yšwʿ

35 **Christian** (See on Mt 1.1, 21) Doubtless there is some connection between the names *yšwʿ* and *ʿmnwʾl* [Emmanuel] since [Emmanuel] | is used of Messiah in Isa 7.14. What do you think?

Kabbalist Catechumen ‖ I have noticed that the numeral equivalent of   p. 82
[Jeshua] *yšwʿ* is 386 and that of [Emmanuel] *ʿmnwʾl* is 197 but they are related by the lesser numerical value which is 17 and 8. Also, either name written out fully [plene scriptum] comes to the same number 523. And also
40 ʿ/m/n/ʾ/l and y/š/ with no ʿayin which is the same numerical value of *ḥqt yʾh* "The Decree | of the Lord"[130] Cf. Ps 2.7.

Verse 32
And he shall be great etc. *nhwʾ rb*

Kabbalist Catchecumen. Now you say what you think about these words? Surely they contain some prophecy?

Christian I certainly see here a prophecy about the three states of Messiah: [that is,] of (1) his *kenosis* [self-emptying]; (2) his exaltation begun; and (3) his exaltation perfected. The words *nhwʾ rb* refer to the state ‖‖ of   fol. 16ᵛ
self-emptying and mean he will be a *"Rab"* a word that means the same as "scholar" (Jn 13.13) or High Priest (Mt 26.51; Heb 4.14) both of which here denote an office of the highest status—prophetic and priestly. To the state
5 of incipient exaltation refer the | words "And he shall be called Son of the Highest", for this is ‖ the proper family name of Messiah (So: Mt 4.3, 6; 8.29;   p. 83
14.33; 16.16; 26.63; 27.40, 43, 54; Mk 1.1; 3.11; 5.7; 15.39; Lk 8.28; Jn 1.14, 18, 34; 3.16, 17, 18; 6.69; 11.27; 20.31 *etc.* etc.). Messiah could not be confirmed in this grade of dignity until he had overcome temptations and his own passions. Hence
10 this name | Son of God in eminence was finally given him after the resurrection (Acts 13.32, 33; Rm 1.4; Heb 2.9; Acts 2.36) and this for the strongest

---

127   Correction above the line: Christianus replaced by Cabb. Cat. (as a consequence of the previous correction).
128   In the right bottom corner appears a Hebrew letter ה presumably an indication of binding or pagination.
129   A red pencil square bracket inserted into the text (cogno[men) refers to an annotation in the left margin: 3.F./83.
130   The divine name *yh* is piously broken by an apostrophe to prevent articulation.

sicut cum illo Divinitatis charactere, qui filius dicitur, (vide Adumbration. Cabbalæ Christianæ c. 3, §. 2[131] & c. 8, §. 6[132]) â primo statim productionis suæ initio unita fuerat Messiæ anima; ita in hâc | ipsa unione sub omnibus tentationibus gloriosè permanserit, nec defecerit sicut Adamus Protoplastes (Confer illud: *propterea* &c. Phil. 2, 9; Psal. 110, 7; Jes. 53, 12; Joh. 10, 17; c. 17, 4.5). Quod autem hanc ipsam cum Personâ Filii Divinitatis unionem, quatulacunque illa etiam fuerit, consequatur denominatio similis, exempla docent (1.) verorum Christianorum in mundo Asiah | seu materiali hoc, (ut Joh. 1, 12; Rom. 8, 15; Gal. 3, 26) (2.) Angelorum in mundo Jezirah seu Angelico (vid. Cabbal. Denudatæ Tom. 1. Part. 4. p. 246 sq.[133], Tom. II, Pneum. Cabbalist. p. 229[134]) (3.) Israëlis in mundo Briah, seu Animarum, (Ex. 4, 22; conf. Lex. Cabbal. p. 462 & p. 200[135]) quantò magis ergò (4.) Anima Messiæ hoc nomine Filii Dei gau- ‖ -debit[136], quæ ad mundum Aziluth | referenda est, imò ipse est Adam Kadmon; (vid. Adumbratio Cabbalæ Christianæ p. 8 sqq.[137] conf. Joh. 10, 36). [**Cabb. Cat.**][138]*Ad statum porrò*[139] *Exaltationis consummatæ*[140] *pertinebunt verba vaticinii hujus Angelici subsequentia: & dabit ipsi Dominus Deus thronum David Patris sui: & regnabit super domum Jaacob in secula & regni ejus non erit finis. Hæc omnia enim præsupponunt collectionem & con-*

---

131 "Phil. Christ. In statu hoc primo Deus ipse infinitus intelligi potest, per nomen Patris, quo scripta Novi Fœderis nostri tam sæpe utuntur. Lux autem ab Infinito in Adamum primum sive Messiam per canalem immissa, cumque ipso unita, applicari potest ad denominationem Filii. Et influxus ex hoc versus inferiora demissus referri potest ad characterem Spiritûs Sancti." ("Adumbratio kabbalæ christianæ", op. cit., p. 7).

132 "Philosoph. Christ. Cum Microprosopus à Vobis vocetur Filius, ita ut etiam generationis ejus, imò status ejus uterini, nec non lactationis & adolescendi, certi describantur modi (de quibus vid. Apparat. Par. 3. pag. 181.182. seqq.) dubium nullum est, quin ista applicari queant ad filium toties in Scriptis Evangelicis denominatum: quoniam in isto statu Anima Messiæ jam ulterius descendit in illum Adami prioris gradum, ad quem applicatur Microprosopus. Nec difficile foret, speciales illos Microprosopi status ad specialia Oeconomiæ Messianæ tempora applicare, ab orbe scilicet condito, usque ad tempora novissima." (Ibid., p. 55).

133 The reference is to the "Explicatio arborum seu tabularum quinque cabbalisticarum generalium", op. cit. Pages 243–255 deal with the commentary upon the last of the sixteen figures reported by Knorr at the end of the first volume of *Kabbala Denudata*. Pages 246 *seq.* are dedicated to the explanation of the relationship between the various angels and classes of angels and the sefirot.

134 The reference is to Chapter VI, entitled "De *decem Turmis Angelorum*": "Jamque de ordine decem Chororum Angelicorum dicendum nobis est: circa quem non parva inter Autores occurrit discrepantia. Nam R. Moscheh bar Maimon sic eos collocat, ut primò sint חיות, Animalia; secundò אופנים Rotæ: tertiò אראלים, Arelim: quartò חשמלים Chaschmalim: quintò שרפים Seraphim: sextò: מלאכים Angeli: septimò אלהים Dii: octavò:

reason: that straightaway from the first beginning of his creation the soul of Messiah had been united with that divine character which is called the Son (see *Adumbratio*, chap. 3, §2; chap. 8, §6). In this very union | he endured gloriously under all temptations, nor did he fail as [did] Adam Protoplast (q.v.) and see also Phil 2.9; Ps 110.7; Isa 53.12; Jn 10.17; 17.4, 5.[141] That a similar name [sons of God] is consequential upon this union with the character of the Son of the Divinity, however slight, is shown by the examples of: (1) true Christians in this world of *Asiah* | or the material [world] (as Jn 1.12; Rm 8.15; Gal 3.26); of (2) Angels in the world of *Yetsirah*, or the angelic [world] (*Cabb. Denud.*, Vol. 1 Part. 4, pp. 246 seq.; Vol. 2, *Pneumatica Cabbalistica*, p. 229); of (3) Israel in the world of *Briah*, or the [world] of the souls (Ex 4.22 Cf. *Lex. Cabb.*, p. 462 & p. 200). How much more therefore (4) the Soul of Messiah will rejoice ‖ in this name of Son of God, which must be referred to the world   p. 84
of *Atsilut* |—indeed he is Adam Kadmon (See *Adumbratio*, pp. 8 seq.. Cf. Jn 10.36).

Kabbalist Catechumen To the state of [Messiah's] perfect exaltation doubtless belong the following words of this prophecy of the Angel: "And the Lord God will give him the throne of his father David and he shall reign over the house of Jacob forever and of his kingdom there shall be no end". All

---

בני אלהים filii Dei: nonò כרובים Cherubim: decimò; אישים Viri. (...)" ("Pneumatica Kabbalistica. Domus Dei", op. cit., pp. 228–229).

135   "בכור *Primogenitus*. R. Moscheh scribit, per Primogenitum intelligi Coronam: quia huic tribuenda sit primogenitura præ totâ Aziluth; ut notum est. Alii hoc nomen de Chochmah exponunt. (...) Attamen & R. Moscheh *Primogeniti* nomen ad Chochmah refert & ad Malchuth. (...)" ("Loci communes kabbalistici", op. cit., p. 200). The references cited, both kabbalistic and from the New Testament, have to do with "sonship".

136   A red pencil square bracket inserted into the text (gau[debit) refers to an annotation in the left margin: 4.F./84.

137   The reference is to Chapter 3 of the "Adumbratio kabbalæ christianæ" dedicated to the comparison of the characteristics of Adam Kadmon and Christ. Pages 8 and following deal with the idea of Christ being the Son of God, the firstborn son of God.

138   Added in the left margin: Cabb. Cat., hence attributing the last lines to the Cabbalist.

139   Correction above the line: porrò replaced by autem (which is to be understood in the light of the change of speaker).

140   Added above the line: *procul dubio*

141   Messiah is called Son of God, because initially his soul was united with the divine character which is the Son, and also because he overcame temptation. Those others (men angel, Israelites) who are also called Sons of God are called so because of their enjoyment however slight of union with the character of the Son of God.

versionem Judaeorum[142] | quæ non continget nisi cum ingressu Millennii 30
illius sancti, de quo Apoc. 20, 4.5.6.7 (vid. Adumbrat. Cabbal. Christ. p. 70,
§. 2.3[143]).

Filius Summi &c. ברה דעליא

[**Cabb. Cat.**][144] *Quomodo tu hæc explicares secundum mentem Cabbalistarum*[145]*?*

[**Christianus**][146] Hoc loco nomine Summi sive Altissimi ut mihi videtur, | denotatur. Deus ipse Infinitus, quatenus vel extra mundum Aziluth sive 35
Emanationis consideratur, vel in illo sub notione Coronæ summæ denominationem habet (vide Lexicon Cabbalist. p. 223[147], 419[148], 683[149] & Cabbalæ
p. 85   Denud. Part. 2, p. 7[150]) ut non tam sit relatio inter Patrem & ‖ filium[151] è Personis Cabbalistarum; quam inter Æn-Soph seu Infinitum, & Adam Kadmon,
seu Messiam. VOCABITUR[152] | autem, idem est, ac declarabitur (ut Matth. 3, 40
17; 17, 5) & confirmabitur (Rom. 1, 4; Joh. 6, 27; Heb. 1, 3.4.5.)

---

142   Correction: Judaeorum replaced by Gentis nostræ (This is logical given the new speaker resulting from the correction). In the following sentence, the italic letters stop in the BSB and the text is not underlined in the manuscript. This is probably due to Knorr's oversight, after having made the correction.
143   "§. 2. Berviter (sic): circa finem Millennii sexti captivabitur satanas Apoc. 20. vf. 1.2.3.7. ita ut millennium septimum sit Regni Messiani Apoc. 3, 7–13; cap. 7, vs. 9–17; cap. 11, vs. 15.19; c. 20.vs. 6; c. 21, vs.1, 2–27; c. 22, 1–5; Matth. 13, vs. 8.23.30.43. ubi Messias ut filius David regnabit: & non humiliatus erit ut filius Joseph.—§. 3. Jam enim Regni metrum, prout vos dicitis, iterum ascendet in Coronam, i.e. Messias, qui sese demiserat ad ima Adami prioris, nunc iterum ascendet ad summitatem. Circa finem autem Millennii sexti, paulatim incipiet præparatio ad Regnum hoc divinissimum, & vita Christi variis in locis & gradibus evadet illustrior; ita ut manus Jacobi, i.e. initium Temporis venturi & calcaneus Esavi i.e. finis mundi corticosi Edomitici præsentis, in unam incidant periodum, juxta 4. Esdr. 6.vs.9 ad quam periodum spectare videtur Epistola Christi ad Sardenses Apoc. 3.vs.1." ("Adumbratio kabbalæ christianæ", op. cit., p. 70).
144   Correction in the left margin: Christianus replaced by Cabb. Cat. (which involves the two speakers being changed over in the following exchange).
145   Correction above the line: Cabbalistarum replaced by nostratium (to be understood in the light of the change of speakers).
146   Correction in the left margin: Cabb. Cat. replaced by Christianus (as a consequence of the previous correction).

these things presuppose the gathering and conversion of our people | which will not happen until the beginning of that holy millennium of which Rev 20.4, 5, 6, 7 speaks (Cf. *Adumbratio*, p. 70, § 2, 3).[153]

The Son of the Most High etc. brh d'ly'

Kabbalist Catechumen How do you explain this according to the doctrines of our teachers?

Christian Here the name of the Highest or Greatest seems to me | to indicate the Infinite God himself in so far as he is considered to be either outside the world of *Atsilut* or *Emanation* or is named within it by the notion of the Highest *Corona* (See *Lex. Cabb.*, pp. 223, 419, 683 and *Cabb. Denud.*, Part. 2, p. 7) so that there is not so much a ‖ relationship between Father and Son emerging between characters of the Kabbalists, as between *Ein Sof* or the Infinite and Adam Kadmon or Messiah. "He will be called" | is the same as "he will be declared" (as in Mt 3.17; 17.5) and "he will be confirmed" (Rm 1.4; Jn 6.27; Heb 1. 3, 4, 5.)

p. 85

---

147 "גבוה *Altus, elatus, excelsus*. Hoc nomen nudè positum, refertur ad Æn-Soph seu Infinitum, quippe qui Excelsus est super omnia in infinitum usque. Aliquando tamen accidentaliter etiam alii modi sic appellantur, sicut scribitur Eccl. 5, 7. *Quia Excelsus de super excelsum custodit, & excelsi super eos*. Pard. ib." ("Loci communes kabbalistici", op. cit., p. 223).

148 The reference is to a chart showing the symbolical equivalences of each of the three upper sefirot Keter, Chochmah and Binah: כתר Corona; רחמים Misericordia; יעקב Jaacobh; ודיי' Tetragrammaton; רוח Spiritus, aër, ventus; נורא Terribilis; [...] מרום Elatus; רם Altus [...]" (Ibid., p. 419).

149 "רום *Altitudo*, per Cholem refertur ad Kether: sed per Schurek ad Chochmah. Tikk. Pard." (Ibid., p. 683).

150 "Prima Sephirah Circulus Arich Anpin i.e. longa facie præditi (seu Longamini) & Coronæ summæ, quam denotat apex literæ Jod Nominis Tetragrammati: Hæc circa ima emanationis suæ, vocatur Longùs, & non Ens, circa summa verò Infinitum. In medio habet tria capita, propter quæ dicitur Antiquus dierum. Corona Coronæ summæ, Caput imperceptibile. Sapientia Coronæ summæ, Caput Infiniti. Intelligentia ejusdem, Caput Longa facie præditi. Reliquæ Sephiræ, Coronæ summæ, usque ad Regnum. (...)" ("Tabula secunda Clavis sublimioris Kabbalæ", op. cit., p. 7).

151 A red pencil square bracket inserted into the text ([filium) refers to an annotation in the left margin: 5.F./85.

152 BSB has italics here. The word is written in larger letters in the manuscript.

153 For this Jewish Messianic Millenial Kingdom, see Introduction.

Dominus Deus מריא אלהא

Christianus. Quodnam hoc est nomen inter Nomina divina linguæ Hebraicæ?[154]

Cabb. Cat. Est nomen יהו״ה אלה״ים ê Nominibus Divinis (de quo multa reperies in Lexic. Cabbalist. p. 383 sq.)[155] *Sensusque*[156] *est hic, quod illo tempore cum* ‖‖‖ *erigetur Regnum istud sacratissimum Messianum, influxus descensurus sit ex unione consummatissima graduum Tiphereth & Malchuth; qui dicuntur Sponsus & Sponsa*[157]; *ita ut restitutio similis fiat institutioni* Gen 2, 4.

Thronum Davidis Patris sui:
כורסיה דדויד אבוהי

Christianus. Quia vos adhuc Regnum aliquod Messianum in hoc mundo expectatis, & supra hæc verba de isto regno interpretatus es; quo quæso niteris fundamento?

Cabb. Cat. *Thronus successionem denotat: unde quale fuit Regnum Davidis, & qualis fuit successio aliorum ex* ‖ *posteris*[158] *ejus; tale etiam hîc intelligendum est Regnum Messiæ. Jam verò Regnum Davidis fuit in hoc mundo, & reliqui* | *posteri ejus ipsi successerunt in hoc mundo, adeoque politicè non figurativè. Ergò ita etiam sese habiturum est Regnum & successio Messiæ, qui est ê posteris Davidis. Cumque hoc ipsum Regum, & hæc ipsa successio politica nondum fuerit instituta, profectò vel adhuc speranda est: vel vaticinium hoc cariturum est impletione.*

V. 33. Super domum Jacob &c.
על ביתה דיעקוב

Christianus. Quare denominatur domus Jacob; annon[159] domus Iisraël, vel domus David?

Cabb. Cat. *Ne concipi queat distinctio illa Regnorum, quæ sub Rechabeamo exorta est; ita, ut si diceretur domus Israël, decem saltem subintelligerentur*

---

154 Correction in the left margin: Quodnam hoc est nomen inter Nomina divina linguæ Hebraicæ? replaced by *Supra* (ad Luc. 1, 16) dixisti quædam de hoc Nomine, quoad statum Ecclesiæ præsentem: cur idem & hoc loco repetitur?

155 Deletion of the entire sentence.

156 Correction: Sensusque replaced by Sensus (to be understood in the light of the correction).

SECTION IV 255

The Lord God *mry' 'lh'*

Christian You said earlier (above on Lk 1.16) something about this name with respect to the present state of the Church. Why is it repeated here?

45   **Kabbalist Catechumen** The meaning is this: that at that time ‖ when that   fol. 17ʳ
most holy Kingdom of Messiah will be established and an influx will descend from the most perfect union of the Grades *Tiferet* and *Malkhut*, there will be a restitution similar to the beginning in Gen 2.4.

The Throne of his father David *kwrsyh ddwyd 'bwhy*

5   **Christian** ‖ Why do you still expect the Messianic Kingdom in this world   p. 86
and understand these words to speak of it here? Upon what fundamental assumption are you relying here?

    Kabbalist Catechumen A throne indicates succession. So what sort of kingdom was David's and by what sort of succession did [later kings] inherit from their predecessors? That too is how the Kingdom of Messiah must be understood here. The Kingdom of David was in this world and his remain-
10   ing | posterity succeeded in this world politically (and not just figuratively). So too will be the Kingdom and succession of Messiah who is a descendant of David. Since this Kingdom and this political succession has not yet been instituted, it is entirely still to be hoped for, or this prophecy will lack any fulfilment.

15   Verse 33
And over the House of Jacob etc. *'l byth dy'qwb*

Christian Why is it called the House of Jacob and not the House of Israel or of David?

    Kabbalist Catechumen You must not think here of that division of the kingdoms which happened under Rehoboam, so that when the house of

---

157   Deletion: qui dicuntur Sponsus & Sponsa.
158   A red pencil square bracket inserted into the text ([posteris) refers to an annotation in the right margin: 6.F./86.
159   BSB: & non

Tribus: vel si diceretur domus David, Regnum saltem Judæ denotari videretur: | *hinc domus Jacob denominatur, ut omnes includerentur Tribus.*

Christianus. Quomodo autem hic subintelliguntur Gentiles? ||

Cabb. Cat.[160] *Sanè non aliter, quàm ut proselyti, prout & inter duodecim tribus proselyti è Gentilibus fuere plurimi, præsertim temporibus Davidis (Confer. Apoc. 21, 24.26; Jes. 60, 3).* Nulla tenus verò ut Judigenæ.[161]

Non erit finis &c. סוף לא נהוא

Christianus. Quomodo Regni ejus non erit finis; quia terminabitur millennio?

Cabb. Cat. *Quia finito millennio sancto succedet Regnum Paradisiacum citra interruptionem.* [**Christianus**][162] Et hoc regnum est[163] tempus illud Restitutionis omnium, (de quo loquitur Petrus Act. 3, 21).

V. 34. *Quomodo fiet istud? &c.*
איכנא תהוא הדא

Cabb. Cat. *Sed cur*[164] *Maria etiam non punitur,*[165] *sicut Zacharias?*

Christianus. Maria procul dubio sic intellexit verba Angeli, quasi conceptio hæc in eodem instanti futura esset: quia aliàs facile potuisset colligere se concepturam, postquam nupta esset Josepho sponso suo: sicut talis conceptio â viro | subindicata fuit Jud. 13, 3 & Jes. 7, 16. Si autem conceptio hæc eodem momento fieri deberet, prout forte commotiones || quasdam[166] intra sese jam tum persensit; non immeritò quærit: quomodo hoc sit eventurum, cum virum hactenus haud cognoverit ullum? Quæ verba non tam dubitationem involvunt & incredulitatem; quàm admirationem, tacitamque petitionem, ut plenius sibi adaperiatur hocce mysterium.

---

160 A red pencil square bracket inserted into the text ([Cabb. Cat.) refers to an annotation in the right margin: 7.F./87.
161 Deletion: Nulla tenus verò ut Judigenæ.
162 Added in the right margin: Christian. (which involves a change of speaker, the last sentence being now attributed to the Christian).
163 Correction: est replaced by erit

SECTION IV

Israel is mentioned, only the ten tribes are thereby meant; nor if the House of David is mentioned [should you consider] only the Kingdom Judah is in question. | Thus here the House of Joseph is mentioned in order to include all [his descendants] the tribes.

Christian How are the Gentiles to be imagined in all this?

Kabbalist Catechumen ‖ Clearly only as proselytes, in as much as among the Twelve Tribes there were many proselytes from the Gentiles especially at the time of David (Cf. Rev 21.24, 26; Isa 60.3).

p. 87

Shall have no end etc. *swp l' nhw'*

Christian How can his kingdom have no end? Since it will end in the Millennium.

Kabbalist Catechumen. Because when the Holy Millennium is over, it will be followed without interruption by the Kingdom of Paradise.

Christian And that Kingdom will be the "Time of the Restoration of All Things" of which Peter speaks in Acts 3.21.

Verse 34
How will this be? etc. *'ykn' thw' hd'*

Kabbalist Catechumen Why was Mary not punished [for disbelief] like Zachariah?

Christian Doubtless Mary so understood the words of the angel to mean the conception would take place in that very instant, for she would readily have assumed she was going to conceive at any another time after she had married Joseph her betrothed. Such a conception with the assistance of a man | is indicated in Judg 13.3 and Isa 7.16. If, however, this conception had to take place at that very moment, to the ‖ extent that perhaps she even then felt some commotion inside herself, she would then not have unreasonably asked: "How will this be?" as she had not yet known a man. These words do not contain doubt or incredulity, but rather wonder and a silent prayer that she might be more fully prepared for this mystery.

p. 88

---

164   Correction: Sed cur replaced by Cur
165   Correction: a sign is placed above the line which indicates that the terms should be inverted: Maria etiam non replaced by non etiam Maria
166   A red pencil square bracket inserted into the text ([quasdam) refers to an annotation in the right margin: 8.F./88.

V. 35. *Spiritus Sanctitatis veniet* &c.
רוחא דקודשא תאתא

Christianus. In Græco additur, super te; in Syriaco autem idem subintelligitur ê particula עליכי membri sequentis, ut indicetur non duos hic subinnui actus: sed unum saltem ad denotandam rem & modum, quo Spiritus Sanctus adveniens, vehementissimo & copiosissimo lumine ab Infinito ipso, cui nomen Altissimi competit, demisso, eandem ita cooperuerit, | ut quasi tentorium super ipsa formaret, eamque oculis spectantium quasi sub- |||-duceret. Nam (1.) hunc sensum infert vox חילא quæ sæpius denotat insignem luminis abundantiam, ut Act. 1, 8; c. 4, 33; c. 8, 10; Phil. 3, 21; Luc. 24, 49; Matth. 24, 30; c. 26, 64; Mar. 5, 30; c. 6, 5; c. 9, 1; Luc. 1, 17; Act 6, 8; c. 10, 38; Rom 1, 16; &c. (2.) Idem subindicat vox גנן super integet, â rad. גבן[167] quæ involvit connotationem Schechinæ, ut Joh. 1, 14 ubi | allegoria erecti tentorii sive tabernaculi subest: unde ab eâdem radice[168] denominatur גנונא coopertorium seu umbraculum illud nuptiale sub || quo[169] copulantur Sponsus & Sponsa Matth. 9, 15; Marc. 2, 19; Luc. 5, 34. Similique vi luminis spiritus S. obtexit credentes Act. 10, 44; c. 11, 15; c. 2, 3; conf. 2 Cor. 12, 9.

Cabb. Cat. *Sic quoque in Sohar Schechina dicitur apparuisse in tentoriis | Saræ & Rebeccæ.* (Evolvantur in Excerptis Cent. 1. Loc. 51.52.53).[170]

Christianus.[171] Unde & donum Prophetiæ accipiebat Maria; & totus Spiritus ejus fiebat lucidissimus Matth. 6, 22. purumque receptaculum incarnandæ jam animæ Messiæ. Jamque Spiritus Sanctus in illa statuebat pro Jesu Archæum seu Spiritum vitalem; Et hic spiritus vitalis insitus sibi corpusculum formabat beneficio | spiritus influi ê Maria.

---

167 BSB: גנן (Recte)
168 BSB: radic (Printer's error)
169 A red pencil square bracket inserted into the text ([quo) refers to an annotation in the left margin: 9.F./89.
170 Added in the left margin: Sed quomodo Spiritus S. venire dicitur cum tamen. Deus sit, sua natura omnipræsens?
171 Correction in the left margin, the entire speech of the Christian is replaced by: Spiritus Messiæ 1. consideratur juxta naturam ejus productam (1.) juxta divinam non productam. Ad illam facilè referre poteris omnes istos actus motusque quos locales. Quamvis & hi potius manifestationes aliquæ sint rei jam antea præsentis, sed non ita operantis quam lationes proprie dictæ.

40   Verse 35
        The Holy Spirit will come etc. *rwḥʾ dqwdšʾ tʾtʾ*

Christian The Greek text adds "upon you". In the Syriac the same meaning is understood from the preposition *ʿlyky* in the following part [of the verse] but in such a way as not to imply two separate actions here [as the Greek does], but just one denoting both the fact and the method of the Holy Spirit's Coming.[172] It descends with a great burst of very bright light, sent down from The
45 Infinite Himself (who is appropriately called The Highest). | So he covered her as if he had placed a tent over her and withdrawn her from prying eyes. ‖ fol. 17ᵛ
For (1) the word *ḥyl'* means this. It often denotes a great effulgence of light as in Acts 1.8; 4.33; 8.10; Phil 3.21; Lk 24.49; Mt 24.30; 26.64; Mk 5.30; 6.5; 9.1; Lk 1.17; Acts 6.8; 10.38; Rm 1.16 etc.. (2) The same is the meaning of the word *gnn* "to cover over" from the root *gnn* which carries a connotation of the Shekhi-
5 nah (as Jn 1.14[173]) where | the metaphor of a pitched tent or tabernacle is used. From the same root comes *gnwnʾ* a covering or the shady ‖ marriage p. 89
canopy under which groom and bride unite (Mt 9.15; Mk 2.19; Lk 5.34). With similarly bright light the Holy Spirit covered the believers in Acts 10.44; 11.15; 2.3. Cf. 2 Cor 12.9.

Kabbalist Catechumen That is how the Zohar says the Shekhinah ap-
10 peared in the tents | of Sarah and Rebecca (mentioned in Excerpts Cent. I Loc. 51, 52, 53). But how can the Holy Spirit be said "to come", when it is God, who is omnipresent by his very nature?

Christian The Spirit of Messiah is considered either according to its created nature or according to its uncreated divinity. To the first you can easily attribute all those, as it were, local, actions and motions, although these too are [better seen] rather as manifestations of something previously already
15 present, and not occurring quite as "coming", properly so called.[174] |

---

172 Lightfoot, *Miscellanies and the Harmony of the Gospels*, op. cit., p. 165: "In it, therefore, two actions are expressed to concur:—First, The 'Holy Ghost's coming' upon the Virgin. Secondly, The 'power of the Most High overshadowing' her: and two fruits, or consequents, of these two actions answerable to them:—First, 'The Holy Ghost shall come upon thee; therefore, that that is born of thee, shall be holy.' Secondly, The 'power of the Most High overshadowing' her: and two fruits, or consequents, of these two actions answerable to them: First, 'The Holy Ghost shall come upon thee; therefore, that that is born of thee, shall be holy.' Secondly, 'The power of the Most High shall overshadow thee; therefore, that that is born of thee, shall be called The Son of God.'" Again, Knorr specifically refutes this in the case of the Syriac.
173 The Greek verb here is *eskēnōsen*: "tabernacled".
174 The initial manuscript text, deleted by Knorr, was: "Hence Maria received the gift of

Cabb. Cat. [175]*Si ex me jam quæreret incredulus quidam è nostratibus, quia Anima Messiæ seu Adam Kadmon in se continere dicitur omnes mundos* (vid. Adumbratio Cabbal. Chr. p. 25, §. 54[176], col. 1, 17) *imò omnia portare* (Hebr. 1, 3)[177] & *movere* Act. 17, 28[178], *quisnam hoc tempore cum Anima Messiæ fuit in utero Virginis, ista omnia | præstiterit?* ‖

Christianus[179]. Quia hanc quæstionem etiam formant Cabbalistæ vestri de Metatrone, cum Chanochus esset, (vid. de Revol. Anim. p. 382, §. 6[180]; p. 436, §. 3[181]; conf. p. 414, §. 30[182] & p. 317, §. 5[183]). Responsio hîc illis dari posset similis, ê propriis Doctorum vestrorum principiis: nimirum Tres quidem gradus Messiariæ Animæ inferiores, | qui dicuntur Nephesch, Ruach Neschamah; seu Psyche, Spiritus et Mens, simul nunc ingressos esse, in statum hunc exinanitionis: duos verò superiores (qui tantum ambiunt hominem ab extra, per se autem in supernis[184] (vid. loc. cit. p. 414, §. 30[185] & Lex. Cabbal.

---

      prophecy; and all her spirit was made full of light (Mt 6.22) and [became] a pure receptacle to incarnate the soul of Messiah. And the Holy Spirit established in her the Archegus or the vital spirit for [welcoming] Jesus. And there the vital spirit, implanted in her, formed small corpuscula for the benefit of the spirit to be infused from Maria." It would appear that Knorr having sought to give an explanation of the Virgin Birth with the aid of small corpuscules formed in Mary, stepped back from such an audaciously bold attempt to specify the workings of the Holy Spirit in this regard.

175   Added in the left margin: *Quid;*
176   "Kabbal. Vigesimo tertiò: tandem Adam ille primus intra se dicitur continere quinque mundos; nempe mundum (1.) Infiniti, quem ipse constituit; (2.) Emanationis, cujus ipse est anima; & deinde tres mundos inferiores, qui ipsi sint loco corporis; ita ut (3.) mundus creationis quasi sit caput, (4.) mundus formationis corpus & brâchia; & (5.) mundus factionis duo crura & membrum fœderis ejus [ibid. pag. 130.131.] Quomodo applicabis ista ad Messiam vestrum?" ("Adumbratio kabbalæ christianæ", op. cit., p. 25).
177   BSB: Hebr. 13 (Printer's error)
178   BSB: Act. 17, 18 (Printer's error)
179   A red pencil square bracket inserted into the text ([Christianus) refers to an annotation in the left margin: 10.F./90.
180   "Mens igitur illa Emanativa etiam vocatur Dominus mundi: quoniam ab ipso mundo emanativo ortum habet; & dominium exercet in omnes mundos inferiores. Et quia cuilibet justo duo sunt spiritus, unus infra, & alter supra: Unde duplex illa appellatio, exempli gratia Gen. 22.v. 12. Abraham, Abraham: hinc non est quod objicias: cum Chanoch esset in terra; quisnam illo tempore fuerit Dominus mundi in supernis Metatronis loco?" ("De Revolutionibus animarum", op. cit., p. 382).
181   "Et quia in Sohar tract. Tosiphtah sect. Noach traditur: quod cuilibet justo duo sint Spiritus; unus inferius, & alter superius: unde duplex illa appellatio: Abraham, Abraham &c. Hinc nullum tibi exurget dubium: quis illo tempore, cum Chanoch esset in terris, fuerit Dominus mundi superius in mundo Metatronis." (Ibid., p. 436).

SECTION IV 261

Kabbalist Catechumen What if a certain unbeliever amongst our [Jewish] people now asked me why the Soul of Messiah or Adam Kadmon is said to contain in itself all the worlds (See *Adumbratio*, p. 25, §54; Col. 1.17), to "bear all things" (Heb 1.3), and "to move" them (Acts 17.28)? Who performed all these tasks when the soul of Messiah was in the womb of the Virgin? |

Christian ‖ Your Kabbalists posed this same question about Metatron when he was Enoch (See *De Revol. Animarum*, p. 382, §6; p. 436, §3. Cf. p. 414, §30 and p. 317, §5). A similar response can be given to them here from your sages' own principles: The three lower grades of the Messianic Soul | which are called Nefesh, Ruach and Neshamah (or Psyche, Spirit and Mind) entered together at the same time into the state of [kenosis or] "emptying". But the two superior [grades] (which surround a man externally but are in themselves in the higher region: see loc. cit., p. 414, §30 and *Lex. Cabb.*,

p. 90

---

182 "Quod ut rectius intelligatur, sciendum, nullum dari in mundo justum, qui non duas habeat animas: sicut dicitur in Sohar sectione Noach ad loca: Noach; Noach: Moscheh; Moscheh: Schmuel; Schmuel. Quorum sensus hic est: quod nempe animæ quædam dentur internæ, quæ cum homine nascuntur in mundum; & aliæ animæ tantum sunt ambientes alteram illam super caput hominis, quæ in supernis sunt, in mundo quodam superiore. Et hoc notorium est, quod homo superius habeat talem animam. Quod si igitur peccet homo iste, hoc ipso efficitur, ut anima ejus gradatim descendat intra cortices, donec tota eodem pervenerit, quæ omnia sic fiunt juxta naturam peccatorum: atque tunc anima ejus ambiens in interiora istius hominis descendit: unde patet, quod utraque harum animarum de gradu suo descendat: adeoque talis homo unam tantum habeat animam, eo quod prior illa descenderit in cortices. Cum è contrario justus utramque retineat, unam ambientem, & alteram internam. Unde intelligi poterit, quod in Sohar dicitur ad locum illum: Noach; Noach &c. In impio autem una tantum est anima; eò quod altera descendit in cortices. Quod innuit Scriptura dicendo Ex. 12, v. 15. *Anima autem illa exterminabitur.* Exscinditur enim intrando in cortices." (Ibid., p. 414).

183 "Jamque excellentiam Adami Protoplastæ, quam habuit ante lapsum, satis intelliges: quoniam major erat, quam nunc est Metatron: quia caput Protoplastæ in systemate creativo erat, ubi nunc Microprosopus emanativus extat: & gutturatque collum ejus in quatuor primis mundi formationis erant, qui locus dicitur hortus Eden: corpus autem consistebat in sex ultimis formativis, quæ vocantur terra Iisraëlis superior: ubi nunc sunt sex primæ creativæ. Et pedes ejus ad sex ultimas mundi factiones pertinebant, ubi nunc sunt sex primæ formationis." (Ibid., p. 317).

184 Added above the line: sunt;

185 Cf. *supra*, footnote 182.

p. 598 sq.[186])) mansisse in mundis sublimioribus: juxta Joh. 3, 13 ubi Christus dicit, se in cœlo esse, quamvis è cœlo descenderit.

Propter hoc id, quod nascitur ex te &c.
מטל הנא הו דמתילד מנכי

(vide ad Matth. 1, 20)[187]

Cabb. Cat. *Hic opus esset expressionibus quibusdam philosophicis de modo generationis.*

Christianus. Sensus esset hic: (1.) Illa ipsa Anima, quæ ex te vehiculum suscipit terrenum, non est ex illis, quæ cum Adamo lapsæ sunt: sed sancta est, sicut erat ab initio | creationis suæ. (2.) Ille etiam spiritus, qui nunc evadit Archæus corporis hujus, tam insitus, quam ex te influus, per illuminationem istam spiritus Sancti usque adeò purificatur ab omni qualiumcunque naturalium idearum labe, ut omninò Sanctus ‖ sit[188]: contra naturam omnium carnali generatione in lucem prodeuntium. Joh. 3, 6. Sequentia lucem habent ex iis, quæ ad v. 32 dicta sunt.[189]

V. 36.37.38. Elischeba &c. אלישבע

Cabb. Cat. [190]*Nostrates autem*[191] *hic*[192] *ad sensus | progrederentur mysticos, ut notum ex iis, quæ de Abrahamo, Isaaco &c. proferuntur in Sohar* (Excerpt. Cent. 1. Loc. 92 seqq.), *quid tu hîc suggereres?*

Christianus. Si jam mysticum quis hinc elicere velit sensum, de conceptione in Anima ⫴ vitæ divinæ; illi non deerunt notabilia quædam, ad disponendam Animam talem, requisita. Nam (1.) Angeli apparitio, denotat meditationes sublimiores; (2.) Gabrielis nomen; quod illæ robur suum obtinere debeant â Deo; (3.) Galilææ vox; quod meditationes hæ applicandæ sint ad volubilem Animæ concupiscentiam; (4.) | Nazareth; quod Anima talis debeat esse observationum studiosa; (5.) Virginis notio; quod puritatis;

---

186 "נר״נחי" Est abbreviatura vocum נפש רוח נשמה / חיה / יחידה de quibus in voce פרצופין de quibus in supernis ita philosophantur: Quælibet notio quadruplicem habet naturam, nempe vasa ab extra; Nephesch, Ruach, Neschamah, ab intra; נשמה לנשמה mens mentis ambiens; & א״א Arich Anpin ambientis ambiens. [...] Et in homine datur quidem vita interna, nempe Nephesch, Ruach, & Neschamah; ista autem lux non sufficit illuminando corpori materiali: unde opus habet Neschamâ Neschamæ, quæ dicitur Chaijah extrinsecus ambiens illud. [...]" ("Loci communes kabbalistici", op. cit., pp. 598–599).

187 Deletion: (vide ad Matth. 1, 20). The reference, after being corrected, is subsequently added at the end of the Christian's speech.

SECTION IV 263

pp. 598 *seq.*) remained in the higher worlds according to Jn 3.13 where Christ says that he is in heaven although he had [at that time] descended from heaven.[193]

30   *On account of this that which is born from you* etc. *mtl hn' hw dmtyld mnky*

Kabbalist Catechumen What we need here are some philosophical statements about how this generation took place.

Christian The meaning is this: (1) the Soul which according to you supports the earthly vehicle, is not one of those which fell with Adam, but is holy just as it was from its first | creation; (2) The Spirit which now goes out [as] Archegus of the body, (whether "implanted" or according to you "flowing in"), through the light of the Holy Spirit is purified from every stain of natural ideas whatsoever, so that it is ‖ entirely holy, contrary to the nature   p. 91
of everything brought forth into the light by carnal generation (Jn 3.6). The following here have light from these, which are spoken of in verse 32. (See on Mt 1.1, 20.)

40   Verses 36, 37, 38
                         Elischeba etc. *'lyšb'*

45   **Kabbalist Catechumen** Our teachers would here resort to mystic | meanings as you can see from what is said about Abraham, Isaac and Jacob etc. in *Zohar* (Excerpts Cent. 1 Loc. 92 *seq.*). What would you suggest here?

Christian If someone wished to extract some mystical meaning from here about the conception ‖‖ of the divine life in the Soul, they would have plenty   fol. 18ʳ
of noteworthy material suitable to the disposition of such a soul. For (1) the appearance of the angel indicates higher meditations; (2) the name of Gabriel [indicates] that they ought to obtain their strength from God; (3) the word Galilee [shows] these meditations are to be applied to the spherical seat of desire of the soul; (4) | Nazareth [indicates] that such a soul ought to be diligent in watching; (5) the idea of a virgin, that it should be a fol-

---

188   A red pencil square bracket inserted into the text ([sit) refers to an annotation in the left margin: 11.F./91.
189   Added into the text: (Vid. ad Matth 1, 1.20)
190   Deletion: three lines now unreadable.
191   Deleted word: autem
192   Deletion of several words now unreadable.
193   Knorr offers the same explanation for the heavenly location of the two superior parts of Elijah's soul whilst John the Baptist was on earth.

p. 92 sectatrix (6.) Desponsatio; quod voluntas talis debeat subesse dominio intellectus; (7.) Joseph, quod intellectus talis desiderare debeat augmenta luminis; (8.) Domus David; quod finem unicum propositum sibi habere debeat. Amorem & hinc progenerandam unionem Dei; (9.) Marjam; quod voluntas illa debeat | habere dominium Ma- ‖ -ris[194], id est concupiscentiæ; (10.) Jeschua; quod vita hæc divina unicum sit medium illud salutiferum pro summa Animæ beatitudine; (11.) Erit magnus &c. quod vitæ hujus divinæ magnoperè exoptanda sint incrementa; (12.) Sum ancilla &c. quod voluntas unicè subjicienda[195] Domino.

---

194 A red pencil square bracket inserted into the text (Ma[ris) refers to an annotation in the right margin: 12.F./92.
195 BSB: subjicenda (Printer's error)

lower of purity; (6) betrothal, that such a will ought to be under the control of the intellect; (7) Joseph [suggests] that such an intellect ought to desire greater light; (8) the House of David, that one ought to have one unique end set before oneself, the love of God and the union with God which is born of that; (9) Maria [indicates] that that || Will should | have dominion over the Sea—that is desire; (10) Jeschua, that this divine life was that sole salvation-bringing medium for the greatest blessing of the soul.; (11) "He will be great etc.", that increases of this divine light are greatly to be hoped for; (12) "I am the maid-servant etc.", that the Will particularly must be subject to the Lord.[196]

p. 92

---

196   Knorr seeks to extract mystical meanings (or spiritual lessons) about the divine life in the soul from the names of people and places in the passage just discussed. Part of his hermeneutic practice is to make use of the expositions he has established in this improving way. He does so below most noticeably after giving his exposition of Matthew's genealogy. He subsequently cut out that long passage (of 74 names) but this passage here gives an example of the motives which led him to draw up the Matthew list in the first place.

[^1]*Luc 1, v. 39.*[^2]

39. *Surrexit autem Marjam in diebus illis & profecta est sollicitè in Montana in Civitatem Judææ.*[^3]
40. *Et ingressa est in domum Zacharjah, & pacem apprecata est Elischebhæ.*[^4]
41. *Et factum est cum audiret Elischeba pacem Marjam, subsiliit infans in ventre ejus: & impleta est Spiritu Sanctitatis.*[^5]
42. *Et clamavit voce elatâ, dixitque Marjamæ: Benedicta tu inter mulieres: | & benedictus est fructus, qui in ventre tuo.*[^6]
43. *Unde mihi hoc, ut mater Domini veniat ad me?*[^7]
44. *Ecce enim cum incidit vox Pacis tuæ, in aures meas, cum gaudio magno subsultavit | infans in ventre meo:*[^8]
45. *Et beata illa, quæ credidit: quia impletio futura est illis, quæ dicta sunt illi è parte Domini.*[^9]
46. *Et dixit Marjam: Magnificat anima mea Dominum.*[^10]
47. *Et lætatur spiritus meus in Deo servatore meo.*[^11]
48. *Quia respexit humilitatem ancillæ suæ. Ecce enim deinceps beatitudinem tribuent mihi generationes omnes.*[^12]
49. *Quia fecit mihi magna, ille qui potens est; & sanctum nomen ejus.*[^13]

p. 93 50. *Et gratia ejus in progenies & generationes super eum, qui timent | ipsum.*[^14] ‖
51. *Fecit*[^15] *victoriam brachio suo, & dispersit superbos in cogitatione cordis ipsorum.*[^16]
52. *Detraxit potentes de thronis; & exaltavit humiles.*[^17]
53. *Esurientes saturavit bonis, & divites dimisit vacuè.*[^18]

---

1 On the left-hand half of the page, a fragment cut from Knorr's edition of the Peshittta New Testament containing the Syriac version of the quoted passage in the Gospel of Luke is pasted in and crossed out.
2 Added in the right margin: Sectio v.
3 Vulgate: Exurgens autem Maria in diebus illis abiit in montana cum festinatione in civitatem Iuda:
4 Vulgate: Et intravit in domum Zachariæ, et salutavit Elisabeth.
5 Vulgate: Et factum est, ut audivit salutationem Mariæ Elisabeth, exultavit infans in utero eius: et repleta est Spiritu sancto Elisabeth.
6 Vulgate: Et exclamavit voce magna, et dixit: Benedicta tu inter mulieres, et benedictus fructus ventris tui.
7 Vulgate: Et unde hoc mihi ut veniat mater Domini mei ad me?
8 Vulgate: Ecce enim ut facta est vox salutationis tuæ in auribus meis, exultavit in gaudio infans in utero meo.
9 Vulgate: Et beata, quæ credidisti, quoniam perficientur ea, quæ dicta sunt tibi a Domino.
10 Vulgate: Et ait Maria: Magnificat anima mea Dominum:
11 Vulgate: Et exultavit spiritus meus in Deo salutari meo.

Section v
Luke 1. 39–56

39 Now Mary arose in those days and went calmly[19] into the mountains to a city of Judaea.
40 And she entered the house of Zachariah, gave the blessing of peace to Elischebha
41 and it came to pass when Elischeba heard the peaceable greeting of Mary that the child leapt up in her womb and she was filled with the Spirit of Holiness
42 and she cried with a loud voice and said to Mary "Blessed are you among women | and blessed is the fruit which is in your womb.
43 And whence is this to me, that the Mother of the Lord[20] should come to me.
44 For See, when the sound of your peaceable greeting[21] fell upon my ears, the child in great joy | leapt in my womb.
45 And blessed is she who believed for there will be a fulfilment of those things which were said to her on the part of the Lord".
46 And Mary said, "My soul doth magnify the Lord
47 And my spirit rejoices in God my Saviour.
48 For he has regarded the low estate of his handmaiden. For Behold, from henceforth all generations will ascribe blessing to me.
49 For he that is mighty has done to be great things and holy is his name
50 and his grace [is shown] in offspring and [future] generations upon those who fear | him.
51 ‖ He made his arm victorious and scattered the proud in the thought of their hearts.   p. 93
52 He dragged the mighty from their thrones and exalted the humble.
53 He filled the starving with good things and sent the rich away empty.

---

12   Vulgate: Quia respexit humilitatem ancillæ suæ: ecce enim ex hoc beatam me dicent omnes generationes.
13   Vulgate: Quia fecit mihi magna qui potens est: et sanctum nomen eius.
14   Vulgate: Et misericordia eius a progenie in progenies timentibus eum.
15   A red pencil square bracket inserted into the text ([51. Fecit) refers to an annotation in the right margin: 13.F./93.
16   Vulgate: Fecit potentiam in brachio suo; dispersit superbos mente cordis sui.
17   Vulgate: Deposuit potentes de sede, et exaltavit humiles.
18   Vulgate: Esurientes implevit bonis: et divites dimisit inanes.
19   Vulgate: "with haste".
20   Vulgate: "my Lord".
21   Vulgate: "The voice (sound) of your greeting".

fol. 18ᵛ 54. *Adjuvit Israëlem servum suum; & recordatus est gratiæ suæ.*²² ‖‖‖   45
55. *Sicut locutus est cum patribus, cum Abraham, & cum semine ejus in æternum.*²³
56. *Mansit autem Marjam apud Elischebham quasi menses tres, & reversa est in domum suam.*²⁴

V. 39. *Ivitque sollicite &c.* ואזלת בטילאית   5

Cabb. Cat. *Habesne quod annotes de modo hujus itineris?*

Christianus. Ivit בטילאית, id est, omissis negotiis omnibus, â radice בטל cessavit: in domicilium Zachariæ: non sanè deducta â Josepho sponso; quia ille informatus de mysterio hoc â Prophetissis, non meditatus fuisset divortium Matth. 1, 19. Sed procul dubio in comitatu | plurium in festum quoddam   10
Hïerosolymas abeuntium: ita ut si circa festum tabernaculorum ascendisset, occasione festi Encæniorûm²⁵ exacto quasi trimestri occasionem habuisset domum redeundi.

In montem in civitatem Judææ.
לטורא למדינתא דיהוד

Cabb. Cat. *Jam de loco hoc quædam edissere.*

p. 94   **Christianus.** In Judæa nulla fuit in monte ‖ civitas²⁶ Sacerdotalis, ubi   15
Zacharias habitare potuisset, quam Chebron Jos. 21, 11, qui locus maximè notabilis est, ob mysteria, quæ ibidem manifestata fuêre plurima, & post Gen. 13, 18, variè commemorantur, nimirum primum exemplum fidei Gen. 15, 6, primum fœdus²⁷ Gen. 15, 18, prima nominis mutatio Gen. 17, 5.15, primum sacramentum ibid. v. 10, prima apparitio Messiæ & promissio | Isaaci, c. 18,   20
1.10, prima possessio terræ typicæ, c. 23, 2.17, primum sepulchrum patriarcharum ib. v. 19, nempe Abrahami & Saræ: Isaaci & Rebeccæ: Jacobi & Leæ c. 25, 9; c. 35, 27.29; c. 49, 31; c. 50, 13. Imò ut tradunt vestrates etiam Adami

---

22 Vulgate: Suscepit Israel puerum suum, recordatus misericordiæ suæ.
23 Vulgate: Sicut locutus est ad Patres nostros, Abraham et semini eius in sæcula.
24 Vulgate: Mansit autem Maria cum illa quasi mensibus tribus: et reversa est in domum suam.
25 Change in the handwriting: the word Encæniorum was written by Knorr, after a space was left empty for it, presumably because the secretary could not read it while copying.
26 A red pencil square bracket inserted into the text ([civitas]) refers to an annotation in the left margin: 14.F./94.

54 He helped Israel his servant and remembered his grace. ‖
55 as he spoke with the fathers, with Abraham and with his seed for ever".
56 Maria remained with Elischeba for about three months and then returned home.

Verse 39
And she went calmly w'zlt btyl'yt

Kabbalist Catechumen Do you have anything to say about the manner of this journey?

Christian She went *btyl'yt* "having laid aside all distractions" (from the root *btl* "to cease") and into the house of Zachariah. She had not been put away by her bethrothed Joseph for being informed of this mystery by the Prophetesses, he had not considered divorce (Mt 1.19). [She went] up almost certainly in the company | of many leaving for a feast in Jerusalem. If she went up about [the time of] the Feast of Tabernacles, she had an opportunity about three months later of going home after the Feast of Dedication.

Into the mountain into a city of Judaea ltwr' lmdynt' dyhwr

Kabbalist Catechumen Now please say something about this verse.

Christian In Judaea there was no priestly city in the hill country where Zachariah could have ‖ lived except Hebron (Josh 21.11), which is a very noteworthy place on account of the great number of mysteries which had been revealed there and following upon Gen 13.18 are variously mentioned [in the text][28]. These were as follows: the first example of faith (Gen 15.6); the first covenant (Gen 15.18); the first change of name (Gen 17.5, 15); the first oath (v. 10); the first appearance of Messiah and the promise | to Isaac (18.1, 10); the first possession of the land in type (23.2, 17); the first tomb of the Patriarchs (ibid. verse 19) namely of Abraham and Sarah, Isaac and Rebecca, Jacob and Leah (25.9; 35.27, 29; 49.31; 50.13). Your sages say, even of

---

27 Words not present in the BSB: Gen. 15, 6, primum fœdus (probably due to printer's oversight).
28 Lightfoot, *Miscellanies and the Harmony of the Gospels*, op. cit., p. 166: "This place had been excellently renowned in ancient time: Here was the promise given of Isaac; here was the institution of circumcision; here Abraham had his first land, and David his first crown; and here lay interred the three couples, Abraham and Sarah, Isaac and Rebekah, Jacob and Leah,—and, as antiquity hath held, Adam and Eve."

& Evæ. Hîc etiam David primam imposuit coronam, 2 Sam. 5, 3. Et hîc prima fuit Hebræorum Academia, nomen enim habet â חברים i.e. Studiosis. Ex his omnibus satis apparet, | quænam fuerint rationes, quare Maria visitaverit Elischebam: nimirum non tantùm (1.) ut inquireret, An vera esset Angeli narratio de conceptione cognatæ suæ sterilis; & (2.) ut eidem narraret miraculosam apparitionem & conceptionem suam. Sed & (3.) ut Messiæ incarnatio[29] primò manifestaretur in illo loco, ubi prima jacta erant fundamenta Ecclesiæ prisci | fœderis.

Cabb. Cat. Et quia fortassis urgerent nostrates illud Doctorum nostrorum traditum, quod Nephesch seu Psyche hominis maneat in sepulchro, ibidemque || nec[30] cognitione nec affectu careat (vid. Synopsin Libri Sohar Tit. 16 in Gen. n. 9[31], in Ex. n. 4.5[32]) *ut sepultis ibidem patribus innotesceret* | *Evangelium de concepto Messia, in spem statim secuturæ resurrectionis suæ* (vid. Matth. 27, 52).

Christianus. Quod autem Maria huc venerit, ut in loco tam celebri Messias conciperetur, propterea mihi non est probabile; quia sub primum statim ingressum Elischeba Spiritu S. plena, Mariam jam vocat Messiæ matrem. hoc loco v. 43.

V. 40. Et pacem apprecabatur Elischebæ.
ושאלת שלמה דאלישבע

Cabb. Cat. Quid tibi succurrit de modo hujus salutationis?
Christianus. Si fortè antiqua salutandi formula per modum interrogandi enunciata fuit; ut videtur innuere phrasis hæc interrogare de pace alterius, & exempla habemus Gen. 29, 5; 2. Reg. 9, 22.31; c. 10, 15, hoc loco tamen & aliis pluribus sensus apprecativus | potiùs locum habet, quod nempe petierit â Deo pacem omnemque prosperitatem Consangnineæ[33] suæ, idque pro-

---

29 Added in the left margin: sub initium novi fœderis (by scribe's hand, probably to correct an oversight).
30 A red pencil square bracket inserted into the text ([nec) refers to an annotation in the left margin: 15.F./95.
31 "De mortui noverunt præmium mundi venturi, & quæ fiant in hoc mundo. col. 230." (*Synopsis Celeberrimi illius Codicis Cabbalistici, qui vulgo dicitur Liber Sohar*, op. cit., p. 137).
32 "De mortui opera viventium nôrunt, & si cuidam casus aliquis tristis accidat, cognati ejus nullam in sepulchro quietem habent. Et nisi mortui orarent pro vivis, impossibile esset, ut mundus vel unicô momentô subsistere. col. 17." (Ibid., p. 138).

Adam and Eve. Here also David put on his first crown (2 Sam 5.3). Here was the Hebrews' first academy named from *ḥbrym* or students[34]. From all this it is sufficiently clear | there were several reasons why Mary visited Elischeba: not so much (1) so that she could ask whether the Angel's report about the conception by her barren relative was true; and not so much (2) to tell her about her own miraculous [visitation] and conception; but [particularly] (3) so that the Incarnation of Messiah at the beginning of the New Covenant might be first manifest in the place where the first foundations of the Church of the Old | Covenant were laid.

Kabbalist Catechumen And perhaps because our people value that tradition of our ‖ sages that the Nefesh or Psyche of a person remains in the grave, and in the grave enjoys both thought and emotion (See the synopsis of the Book *Zohar* Tit. 16 on Gen n. 9 in Ex n. 4, 5.), the Good News of the Conception of Messiah was made known to the fathers buried there in Hebron | to provide hope that their resurrection would immediately follow (Mt 27.52).

Christian That Mary came here so that Messiah might be conceived in such a celebrated place[35], does not seem probable to me, since immediately upon her first entrance, Elischeba, full of the Spirit of Holiness, [had] already called Mary the Mother of Messiah (verse 43 here).

p. 95

Verse 40
And she greeted Elischeba peaceably wšʾlt šlmh dʾlyšbʿ

Kabbalist Catechumen What occurs to you about this manner of greeting?

Christian If by chance the ancient formula of greeting was uttered as a question which seems implied here by the phrase "To ask about the peace of [someone or] other", we have other [similar] examples at Gen 29.5; 2 Kgs 9.22, 31; 10.15. In this place however and many others a prayerful meaning | rather takes over, in that she asked God for peace and all prosperity for her

---

33 BSB: Consaguinæ (Printer's error)
34 The Hebrew *hbr* is a "scholarly companion" or "fellow pupil". Here Hebron is derived from the same root and then the existence of a school is thought to be indicated.
35 Lightfoot, *Miscellanies and the Harmony of the Gospels*, op. cit., p. 167: "But I cannot but conceive this to be the very reason, indeed,—that "she might there conceive the Messias, where so many types, figures, and things, relating to him, had gone before,— namely, in Hebron." For, 1. This suited singularly with the harmony and consent which God used in his works, that the promise should begin to take place by the conception of Messias, even among those patriarchs, to whom the promise was first given."

fol. 19ʳ cul dubio ex intervallo spatii cujusdam cum ||| clamore, ut apparet ê v. 44
unde & Elischebha elatâ voce eidem acclamavit v. 42 prout solent familia-
p. 96 res. ||

V. 41[36]. Subsultavit infans &c. דץ עולא

Cabb. Cat. *Annon fortè naturalis fuit hæc commotio, ut quidam statuunt?*

Christianus. Mihi non videtur, quod infans hîc subsultaverit motu natu- 5
rali fortuito: quid enim miri nunciaret Mariæ; & quare impletio Spiritus
Sancti simul commemoraretur? imò quare Elischebha ipsamet v. 44 adde-
ret, quod בחדותא רבתא præ gaudio magno subsultasset Infans? (Conf. Luc.
6, 23). Sed in eo consistere puto miraculum, quod Johannes Spiritu S. reple-
tus dum adhuc in utero esset Luc. 1, 15. Messiam | agnosceret advenientem, 10
Dominumque & Regem suum salutaret. De infantibus enim in utero intellectu præditis jam supra dictum est ad Luc. 1, 15 (Confer. etiam, quæ leguntur
inter Excerpta Cent. 1, Loc. 15, n. 2).

Et impleta est Spiritu Sanctitatis.
ואתמלית רוחא דקודשא

Cabb. Cat. *Quid mirum? si Elischebha ad eum refertur gradum, ad quem & Spi-* 15
ritus Sanctus pertinet (vid. Lex. Cabbalist. p. 116[37], 682[38]) *quod Spiritu Sancto*
impleatur, & quidem donis ejusdem propheticis, ut occulta pernoscat, & ad
Messiæ arcana admittatur, qui nunc in Regni gradu primam sui edit manife-
stationem?[39]

---

36 A red pencil square bracket inserted into the text ([V. 41.) refers to an annotation in the
right margin: 16.F./96.
37 "אלישבע. In Sohar Sect. שמיני hoc nomen refertur ad *Malchuth*, quia hæc influxum
assugit è septem gradibus superioribus.—2. Estque magna differentia inter בתשבע
& inter אלישבע quia hoc posterius respectum habet ad *Chesed*, sicut Bathschebhah
gradum *Gebhurah* respicit. Nomen אלי enim ab אל descendit quod est nomen prædi-
camenti Chesed. Pardes ibid. h.t." ("Loci communes kabbalistici", op. cit., p. 116).
38 "רוח הקדש *Spiritus Sanctus* vel *Sanctitatis*, vocatur Malchuth, quando influxum habet à Hod, unde influentia promanat in eos, qui loquuntur per Spiritum Sanctum,
quippe qui inferiores sunt Prophetis, eo quod horum locus sit in Nezach. Soh. Sed
ib. Sect. Achare, dicitur, quod Malchuth tunc appelletur Spiritus Sanctus, quando influxum accipit à Chochmah, quæ vocatur קדש Sanctitas. Quæ procul dubio eodem

kinswoman and that doubtless over a period of time and with crying, as appears from verse 44, where Elischeba with a loud voice ||| also greets her (verse 42) as is usual amongst family members ||.

Verse 41
The child leapt etc. *dç 'wl'*

Kabbalist Catechecumen Perhaps this was a random natural movement, as some suggest?

Christian I do not think so, for if the infant leapt here because of a chance natural movement, why would that cause Mary to wonder and why was it recalled at the same time that she was full of the Holy Spirit? And why should Elischeba herself add that *bḥdwt' rbt'*, the child had leapt for great joy (Cf. Lk 6.23)? I think the miracle was that John, filled with the Holy Spirit while he was still in his mother's womb (Lk 1.15), recognised Messiah | as he arrived and greeted his Lord and King. That children in the womb enjoy intelligence was remarked above on Lk 1.15 (Cf. also the material in Excerpts Cent. I Loc. 15 n. 2).

And was filled with the Spirit of Holiness w'tmlyt rwḥ' dqwdš'

Kabbalist Catechumen It is no wonder, if Elischeba is related to the same sefirah as that to which the Holy Spirit belongs (See *Lex. Cabb.*, p. 116, p. 682), that she was filled with the Holy Spirit and also with its gifts of prophecy, so that she might know hidden things and be admitted to the secrets of Messiah who now first revealed himself in the sefirah of *Kingdom*.

---

recidunt; Chochmah enim influit in Hod, & Hod in Malchuth. [...]" (Ibid., pp. 682–683).

39 A handwritten note appears at the bottom of the last page of the BSB: "Plura non sunt impressa. Auctor operi est immortuus." None the less the bottom right corner of the page has a catchword: "Christ[ianus]" which anticipates the continuation of the book.

Christianus[40]. Res autem mysterio non caret, quod sicut post resurrectionem suam primò | fœminæ apparuit Dominus Joh. 20, 14 ita post incarnationem suam Fœminæ primò similiter sese manifestat. Gradus autem observat istos, quod Maria Magdalena sit me[r]etrix conversa: Elischebha uxor quidem sed sterilis: Mater ejus virgo. Solam ergò in anima requirit receptivitatem, cujus symbolum fœmininitas; et virilitatem seu activitatem propriam nullam: & illam quidem omni præconceptione va[c]uam.

V. 42. *Benedicta es tu etc.* מברכתא אנתי

Christianus. Motus est Indicativus, non optativus. Acclamat enim, quod docente Spiritu Sancto cognoscat, annunciationem istius benedictionis ab Angelo ipsi factam supra v. 28.

Cabb. Cat. *Unum autem & idem sunt benedictum esse, & unctum esse,* | *quia utraque phrasis affluxum luminis denotat.* (*vide Lex. Cabbal. p. 215*[41]. *216*[42].*721.722.*[43]) [**Christianus**][44] Dum igitur addit: *& benedictus fructus* etc. ad unctionem Messiæ digitum intendit, unde descenderat Mariæ benedictio. Et notanter dicit: *fructus qui in ventre tuo*; et non fructus ventris tui: ut non tam originem sese statueret Maria, conceptus tam admirandi, quam receptaculum & nutricem.

---

40 A red pencil square bracket inserted into the text ([Christianus.) refers to an annotation in the right margin: Pr.G./97.
41 Cf. *supra*, p. 242.
42 Cf. *supra*, ibid.
43 "שמן המשחה *Oleum unctionis*: hæc est influentia, quam cum Malchuth accipit è parte Chesed, illa vocatur Oleum unctionis Exod. 25, 6; 29, 7.21; 31, 11. &c. quod in Targum dicitur משחא רבות *Unguentum Magnificentiæ*, quod sensum Gedulah habet, quæ est Chesed. [...]" ("Loci communes kabbalistici", op. cit., pp. 721–722).
44 Added in the right margin: Christian (which involves a change of speaker).

No more was printed for the author of the work died ...
(Translation continued)

Christian There is another hidden teaching here for, just as the Lord after his Resurrection first | appeared to a woman (Jn 20.14), so, after his Incarnation he revealed himself similarly to a woman. He observed some distinctions, however, because Mary Magdalene was a repentant prostitute where as Elishebha was a wife—though barren. His mother was a virgin. He observed nothing other than receptivity of soul, the symbol of which is femininity, with no virility or activity of her own—and that she was indeed empty of every preconception.

Verse 42
Blessed are you etc. *mbrkt' 'nty*

Christian This is a statement of fact not a wish. She stated what she knew by the instruction of the Holy Spirit—an announcement of that Blessing given by the Angel himself (above v. 28).

Kabbalist Catechumen The blessing and anointing are one and the same | because both phrases denote the Influx of Light.[45] (See *Lex. Cabb.*, pp. 215, 216, 721 and 722).

Christian So when he added *"And blessed is the fruit etc."*, he referred to the anointing of Messiah from which had flowed down Mary's blessing. And deliberately he said [*the fruit*] *which is in your womb* and not the fruit *of your womb* so that Mary would not consider herself the origin of so marvellous a conception, but rather as a receptacle and wet-nurse.

---

[45] The Cosmic Light has unobtrusively become a constant theological theme in the preceding text, reaching back to the initial discussion of the word "Zohar".

V. 43.[46] Et beata ea quæ credidit[47] Mater Domini mei. אמה דמרי 35

Christianus. Quodnam hîc intelligis Nomen divinum?
Cabb. Cat. Sensus nominis אדני subest: quod quàm propriè tribuatur Messiæ in Regnum suum descendenti, nemini patet meliùs, quàm literaturæ nostrati addicto. (vide Lex. Cabbalist. pp. 32–41[48]. p. 386[49]. sq.)

V. 45. Et beata ea, quæ credidit. וטוביה לאידא דהימנת 40

Cabb. Cat. Egregius de fide locus!
Christianus. Nimirum sicut Chebrone prima manifestata fuit fides veteris pacti, nempe Abrahami; quæ ipsi imputata fuit in Justitiam Gen. 15, 6. sic eodem in loco nunc manifestatur prima fides Novi fœderis, nempe Mariæ: ut discamus veram fidem | sua requirere Studia, suam Academiam, in qua 45 vita divina, similitudo scilicet Christi manifestatur. Opponit autem Mariam marito suo, ob incredulitatem punito: ut do- |||-ceamur, nihil conferre ad Fidei gratiam obtinendam sive sexum, sive officium, sive ætatem, sive eruditionem, sive dignitatem; sed nudam & solam humilitatem.

fol. 19ᵛ

---

46 A red pencil square bracket inserted into the text ([V. 43.) refers to an annotation in the right margin: 2.G./98.
47 Deletion: Et beata ea quæ credidit
48 "אדני *Dominus*. [In Schaare Orah cum præfatione connectitur]. 1. Primum propiusque creatis omnibus nomen, quo ad Regem Tetragrammaton aditus patescit, est אדני: ad cujus notitiam animadverte; peculiare nomen Altissimi ידוד innuere summi opificis existentiam, à quo, quicquid continet universum, dependet. Sed portarum Claviumque prima quibus ad Tetragrammaton accedimus, est nomen Adonai: quod (cum sursum exordimur, vergimusque deorsum,) in toto Dei nominum ambitu, in extremo ordinem sortitur; & hucusque verum consummatumque unionis mysterium porrigitur. [...]" ("Loci communes kabbalistici", op. cit., p. 32).
49 "5. Sed cum Adonai præmittitur Tetragrammato utpote Gen. 15, 2. *Adonai Tetragrammaton* (prolatum Elohim) *quid dabis mihi, &c.* item Deut. 3, 24. c. 9, 26. &c. Tunc ab imis exorsi ea, quæ altiùs, ad *voluntatis* usque originem petimus. Nam per א״דני י״דוד Sephiræ ascendunt & uniuntur invicem, tanquam aspirantes ad locum lucis supernæ. Nomen Adonai enim ascendere desiderat & adhærere Sephiræ Binah, quæ vocatur ידוד cum punctis Elohim: qua voce præmissâ denotatur influentia Binæ, quæ descendit per canales, usque ad nomen Adonai, & tunc toti mundo benedicitur. Nec à memoria effluat per י״דוד Adonai semper justitiam altiorem, & Schechinam supernam simul & justitiam inferiorem & Schechinam inferiorem designari; quæ dum colligantur in

Verse 43
The Mother of my Lord etc. *'mh dmry*

Christian What do you understand of the divine name here?

Kabbalist Catechumen The [Hebrew] name *adonai* is intended here, which is the one most properly given to Messiah descending into his Kingdom—which does not appear more clearly to anyone than to [one who is] devoted to our literature. (*Lex. Cabb.*, pp. 32–41, pp. 386 *seq.*)

Verse 45
And blessed is she who believed wṭwbyh l'yd' dhymnt

Kabbalistic Catechumen An outstanding verse about faith![50]

Christian Indeed, just as the faith of the Old Covenant was first displayed at Hebron, namely that of Abraham, and it was "attributed to him for righteousness" (Gen 15.6), so in the same place [Hebron] is now revealed the first faith of the New Covenant, namely that of Mary, so that we may learn [in] her school[51], | in which the divine life (that is the likeness of Christ) is manifest, to seek true faith by her devotion. For Mary withstood her own husband who was punished on account of unbelief, so that we might learn ‖ fol. 19ᵛ that nothing contributes to obtaining the grace of faith, neither sex, function, age, learning nor dignity, but only naked humility[52].

---

unum, tunc universa machina opibus omnique bonorum largitate reficitur. In quod vergit illud Zach. 14, 9. *Erit Tetragrammaton unus, nomenque ejus unum.*" (Ibid., pp. 386–387).

50 Cumulatively, the insistence upon faith gathers momentum throughout *Messias Puer*.

51 Knorr picks up here the imagery of the "Academy" of scholars he has imagined above at Hebron.

52 This kind of Protestant declaration of faith and salvation *sola fide* appears in different parts of Knorr's work. See for example the remarks he inserted in his translation *"Tractatus de revolutionibus animarum"*, II, 7: *"Ex ungue hic Pharisaismum cognoscimus, quem Christus impugnat atque Apostoli, quod nempe non propriis viribus id fieri queat de per fidem atque preces, propter fœdus novum impetrato à Patre Spiritus auxiliô atque concursu"*. See also Ibid., IV, 5: "[...] *qua nimirum opera illa, quæ fidelis non propriis viribus, (quippe quas abnegavit,) sed per Spiritum Sanctum verà fide atque precibus à Patre per Filium Messiam impetratum, operatur* [...]; *eidem, in Justitiam imputantur, i.e. ac si ipse ea præstitisset, unde & pro iis merces promittitur.*"

Quia[53] *impletio futura est. etc.* דהוא שולמא

Cabb. Cat. *Nonne hæc connexio*[54] *cum præcedentibus quasi descriptionem | fidei, de qua Elisabeth loquitur?*

Christianus. Mihi hoc potius videtur vaticinium esse Elischebæ, confirmatorium dictori[s] Legati divini de statibus et officio, præsertim Regio Messiæ.

V. 46. *Et dixit Marjam &.* ואמרת מרים

Christianus. Nunc Spiritu Sancto se repletam similiter & altera declarat Prophetissa: | idque ordine admirando in duobus Cantici sui membris: quorum primo de se ipsa loquitur: altero de Ecclesia, ejusque statu futuro vaticinatur. [**Cabb. Cat.**][55] *Velim autem, ut tu in vestræ*[56] *gentis gratiam, Canticum hoc ad Cabbalæ trutinam paululum examines, quia, quæ â Nostratibus hîc traduntur, per se not[æ] sunt.*[57]

[**Christianus**][58] Membrum primum quatuor habet partes & ascendendo juxta literas Nominis Tetragrammati, seu quatuor mundorum systemata progreditur.

V. 46. respectum habet ad He ultimum, mundumque Asiah seu fabricæ & metrum Malchuth; quô etiam inter partes Animæ refertur Nephesch [vid. Lex. Cabbal. p. 589[59]. | Philosophia Cabbalisti. p. 72. § 5[60].] Unde de Nephesch sua, seu parte Animæ suæ infima primò loquitur, quod magnum prædicet Dominum: ubi ad nomen Tetragrammaton respicit, illiusque unionem cum gradu Regni seu Ecclesiæ extollit.

---

53 A red pencil square bracket inserted into the text ([Quia) refers to an annotation in the left margin: 3.G./99.
54 Correction: connexio replaced by connectis
55 Added in the left margin: Cabb. Cat. (which involves a change of speaker).
56 Correction into the text: vestræ replaced by nostræ
57 Deletion: quia, quæ â Nostratibus hîc traduntur, per se not[æ] sunt.
58 Correction in the left margin: Cabb. Cat. replaced by Christ.
59 "נפש *Psyche; Anima vegetativa; Pars animæ plastica;* seu *infima concupiscibilis*. In sublimiori conceptu hæc vox nudè posita est Malchuth Soh. Lechlecha. Quæ aliquando etiam vocatur נפש חיה *anima vivens*, in Tikk. quia ab illâ proveniunt נפשות Animæ vitales; & quia suctionem vitæ supernæ habet à Chochmah, à qua vita dependet. Dicitur autem Nephesch, quatenus supra se recipit Ruach, seu Spiritum & Neschamah, seu Mentem, quæ sunt Tiphereth & Binah; quo nexu mediante vitam habet à Chochmah: sed eodem cessante, dicenda esset mortua. Eademque quandoque vocatur

SECTION V

Because there will be a fulfilment etc. *dhw' šwlm'*

Kabbalist Catechumen Surely you connect these things with previous remarks as a description | of the faith about which Elisabeth spoke?

Christian To me this seems rather to be a prophecy of Elisabeth and a confirmation by the words of the Divine Ambassador of stations and role and especially about the Kingdom of Messiah.

Verse 46
And Mary said etc. *w'mrt mrym*

Christian Now [Mary] declares herself similarly full of the Holy Spirit and to be another[61] prophetess. | With an admirable order [she presents] the two parts of her Canticle. In the first of which she speaks of herself, [but] in the second she makes predictions about Ecclesia and its future status.

Kabbalist Catechumen I would like you out of kindness to our people to examine this Canticle a little in the scales of Kabbalistic teaching.[62]

Christian The first part [of the Canticle] has four parts and progresses by rising through the four letters of the name of the Tetragrammaton, or the four world-systems.[63]

Verse 46 has respect to the final [letter] *he* [*h*] [of the Tetragrammaton] and the [lower] world of Asiah (that of created things) and the degree Malkhut [or Kingdom]. Among the parts of the soul this is connected to Nefesh (See *Lex. Cabb.*, p. 589; | *Philosophia Cabbalistica*, p. 72, §. 5.) Thus she speaks first about her Nefesh, or the lower part of her soul, because she proclaims the Lord great: when she considers the name of the Tetragrammaton, she extols her union with the degree of Kingdom or Ecclesia.

Nephesch David, quia Istius gradus est. [...]" ("Loci communes kabbalistici", op. cit., p. 589).

60 "Cap. VIII. & IX. *Quomodo à Causa prima dependeant reliqua.* [...] §.5. Tandem autem Malchuth Jezirathica fabricarit mundum Asiah materialem." ("Liber porta cœlorum", op. cit., pp. 71–72).

61 In addition to Elisabeth.

62 Deletion: Because the things which are handed down here by our teachers are familiar [to them].

63 The four parts of the first part of the Canticle are correlated with the letters *yhwh*, the Worlds of Asiah, Yetsirah, Briah and Atsilut, the divisions of the soul, characteristic sefirot and their influxes into the soul of Mary, in a *tour de force* of exegesis.

V. 47. Respectum habet ad literam Vav Tetragrammati, & systema Iezirah, seu Formationis & metrum Tiphereth; quo inter partes Animæ referri solet Ruach | seu Spiritus [Lex. Cabbal. p. 682[64].] Unde Spiritus sui mentionem facit Maria quem lætari dicit in Deo vivificatore suo. Ubi respicit ad Nomen אל חי, quod ad Jesod, seu metrum influxus proximi pertinet, (vid. Lex. Cabb. p. 95[65]. sq. p. 340[66] vide & אלהים חיים Deus, unde vita, i.e. gradus Binah. ib. p. 112[67]. sq.) Nunc enim revera tempus erat, quo ad novam vitam influxum proximum accipiebat Ecclesia.

V. 48. Hunc habet sensum, quod Gradus iste Binah seu Matris Supernæ, cui competit nomen Dei vivificatoris, lumen suum immiserit in gradum Ecclesiæ infimæ cujus Maria typus erat: hujusque effectus sit Beatificatio. Respectus ergò sit ad He primum, mundumque Briah, & metrum Binah, quo etiam refertur Beatitudo. [vid. Lex. Cabbal. p. 166[68]. sq.]

V. 49. Respectum habet ad literam Iod Tetragrammati, mundumque Aziluth, et metrum Chochmah atque Kether; huc enim refertur Sanctitas [Lex. Cabbal. p. 670[69], 367[70].] Influx[um] autem se accepisse prædicat per partem

---

64 Cf. *supra*, footnote 36, p. 139.
65 "אל חי *Deus vivus*. [In Schaare Orah connectitur cum כנסת ישראל] Secundum (juxta gradus altitudinum ascendendo) ex dictionibus Sanctis est nomen *El Chai*: juxta illud Ps. 42, 3. *Sitivit anima mea, &c. ad Deum vivum*. Nam istud inter novem gradus, quos *novem specula* dicimus, extremùm obtinet locum, & à cunctis superioribus gratiam haurit & vitam, inque אדני diffundit, ac transfert. Quatenus igitur ipsam dimensionem Chesed suscipit, *El* appellatur; ex quo autem vitam sibi attrahit, *Vivus* dicitur; quæ duo cum invicem cohærent *Deus vivus* nuncupantur" ("Loci communes kabbalistici", op. cit., pp. 95–96).
66 Cf. *supra*, footnote 79, pp. 146–147.
67 "אלהים חיים *Deus vivus* seu *vitæ*. [In Schaare Orah connectitur cum אל חי]. 1. Ita nonnunquam *penultima Sephirarum* nempe *Jesod* vocari solet, ut dicitur Jirm. 10, 10. Ipse est *Elohim Chajim* i.e. *vitæ, vel vivens, & Rex Mundi*. [...] 2. Profertur autem Nomen *Elohim Chajim* de hac Sephira secunda; quamvis & metrum *Adonai* similiter cognominetur. Et illa quidem *Elohim* dicitur, quia judicii notionem involvit, sed ita, ut simul *vitam* impertiatur. [...]" ("Loci communes kabbalistici", op. cit., p. 112).
68 "אשר *Beatitudo*, item *qui*, &c. item *gressus*. 1. Hanc vocem R. Schimeon ben Jochai in Tikkunim duobus modis explicat. Primò enim ab illo, hoc nomine intelligitur *Binah*, juxta illud quod dicitur Genes. 30, 13. In *felicitate mea, quia beatificabunt me filiæ*; quæ sunt verba Leæ. Similia reperiuntur in Sohar Sectione Vajechi, his verbis: Veni, observa! *Ex Ascher*: (Gen. 49, 20.) iste est locus, quem omnes beatum prædicant; quis autem est locus ille? *Mundus qui venit*, quem superiores & inferiores beatum prædicant, & ad quem cum desiderio tendunt. Ubi quidem significatio gradiendi, tendendi, eundi locum haberet.—2. In Tikkunim autem expositio occurrit alia, priori tamen non adeo absimilis: quod nempe אשר pertineat ad *Kether*, seu Coronam, sed tamen quatenus

SECTION V 281

In Verse 47 has respect to the letter *wav* [*w*] of the Tetragrammaton, and the world-system of Yetsirah (or Formation) and the degree Tiferet which amongst the parts of the soul usually refers to Ruach | or Spirit (*Lex. Cabb.*, p. 682). So [Mary] makes mention of her spirit which she says rejoices in God who gives her life. When she refers to the [Hebrew] name *'l ḥy* [Living God] this is linked to Yesod or the degree with the closest influx. (See *Lex. Cabb.*, pp. 95 *seq.*, p. 340. See also [Hebrew] *'lhym ḥyym* (God who gives Life) i.e. the degree Binah, ibid., p. 112 *seq.*) for then truely was the time in which Ecclesia was receiving the closest influx for a new life.

Verse 48 means that the degree Binah (or of the Supernal Mother), to which is connected the name of the God who gives Life, sent its light into the degree of lower Ecclesia, of which Mary was a type. And its effect was Blessing. Therefore she makes reference to the first [letter] *he* [*h*] [of the Tetragrammaton], the world of Briah and the degree of Binah, to which also Blessing is linked (See *Lex. Cabb.* p. 166 *seq.*).

Verse 49 has respect to the [Hebrew] letter *yod* [*y*] in the Tetragrammaton and the world of Atsilut and the degrees, Chokhmah and Keter—for this is related to Holiness (*Lex. Cabb.*, pp. 670, 367). She declares she has

---

ista respicit *matrem*. Verba sunt hæc: אשר est אהיה, quod certum est: hæc autem est Corona summa ex parte fœmina: illi hoc nomen tribuitur, &c." (Ibid., p. 166).

69 "קדוש *Sanctus*: refertur ad Kether, ad Tiphereth, & ad Jesod; sed h.m. Cum enim hoc nomen nulli tribuatur gradui nisi ob mysterium Vav; hinc quando Tiphereth sub forma Vav ascendit ad Kether, sub mysterio Daath, tunc fit קדוש *Sanctus* per Vav. Tikkunim. Atque tunc Kether eodem vocatur nomine, cum nempe Daath illuc usque ascendit: Tiphereth autem, quando descendit à Kether & Sanctitatem secum defert: Item, Jesod, quando Sanctitas à capite Coronæ descendit intra Ipsum. Et quando Sanctus hic ingreditur in Malchuth, Ista vocatur קדושה *Sancta, Sanctitas*: quia tunc à Tiphereth in Ipsam influit Sanctitas; unde vox קדושה resolvitur in קדוש ה", quasi *Sanctum Domini*. [...]" (Ibid., p. 670).

70 "טהרה *Mundatio, mundities*. In Tikkunim Raja Mehim. & Sohar in genere refertur ad Chesed. Sed Sect. Kedoschim notio *Sancti* ad Sacerdotem, (Chesed) & *puri*, ad Levitam (Gebhurah) refertur. Et sic Sect. de Vacca rufa: Cum purum non dicatur, nisi respectu prioris impuritatis. Fundamentum ergò Sanctitatis est in Chesed, super qua Chochmah; cui nomen *Sancti* tribuitur; & hinc per dextram Sanctitas venit super omnia. Sed fundamentum puritatis est in Gebhurâ; quia Igne Gebhuræ omnia dealbantur. Unde Vacca perfectè rufa esse debuit ad denotandum rigorem judicii; ita ut ne duos quidem haberet pilos albos, ne vel tantillum miserationis intersit; nec nigros, ne Cortices adhærerent: & dein comburenda fuit violentia Ignis. Ut & fermentum expurgatum comburitur. Si ergò purificatio applicatur ad Chesed, id sit respectu exiguæ quantitatis Ignis, in dextra inclusi: Et si Sanctitas ad Levitam applicatur, id sit ob tantillum Aquarum, quæ in Gebhurâ. Pardes Tr. 23. c. 9. Vid. Sohar Æmor 47. c. 187." (Ibid., pp. 367–368).

dextram, unde mentionem facit Magnorum; respectu habito ad metrum[71] Nezach. [vid. ib. p. 589[72].] חיל enim, unde חילתן potens; sæpe exercitum denotat. De vaticinio tu edissere.[73]

[Christianus.][74] Versibus igitur[75] sequentibus Ecclesiæ depingit facta, & quomodo erga illam Messias se sit exhibiturus: idque phrasi ut plurimum temporis præteriti, cum significatione futuri, ut impletio tam certa subinnuatur, quasi jamjam facta esset. Unde in Græco Aoristi seu notæ temporis indefiniti adhibentur. Status autem Ecclesiæ describitur quintuplex; nimirum

V. 50. Denotatur status ille Christianismi primus, ab ipso Christo & Apostolis introductus, oppositus Judaismo & Pharisaismo illius temporis, qui nihil crepabat nisi merita: cum ||| Christus gratiam prædicaverit & prædicari jusserit Joh. 1,17; Luc. 4,18; Rom. 1, 5; c. 3, 24; c. 4, 16; c. 5, 2.15.17.20.21; c. 6, 14.15; c. 11, 5.6. &. Sensus ergò vaticinii est hic. Ante omnia in Ecclesia prædicabitur doctrina de Gratia per fidem cum timore [&] humiliatione sui obtinenda. Et hæc doctrina in Ecclesia continuabitur per omnes | generationes, quicquid contra moliantur illius hostes. Nam juxta

V. 51. Ante omnia[76] huic præconio Gratiæ[77], sese opponent Judæi superbi in cogitatione cordis ipsorum, descripti in parabola Luc. 18,11. conf. Matth. 23, 5. sqq. sed victoriosum sese erga illos exhibebit Messias; & non tantum politiam illorum [e]vertet, sed et totam gentem per varias mundi partes disperget. Porrò juxta

V. 52. Huic doctrinæ â Christo introductæ & ab Apostolis propagatæ sese opponent Dynastæ & Imperatores Romani in throno Monarchiæ sedentes, Ecclesiamque Christi omnibus modis persequentur. Sed Messias Ethnicum hoc Imperatorum genus â sede deturbabit: & ad Imperatoriam dignitatem elevabit illos, qui doctrinam de Gratia & humiliatione sui amplectentur, nempe Christianos, quod factum est | sub Constantino Magno & successoribus ejus.

---

71 Added in the left margin: Gedulah, item
72 "נצח *Superatio*. Sic vocatur Proprietas septima in descensu: quæ etiam quandoque dicitur נצח נצחים; Quælibet enim Proprietas tres habet notiones; ratione Receptionis, statûs sui, & influxûs; quarum media radicalis est, & hic vocatur Nezach; reliquæ duæ autem sunt Nezachim. Sic etiam se habet Hod: unde hæc *crura* dicuntur *columnæ senarii* Cant. 5, 15. quæ sunt sex istæ notiones ceu sex articuli. Eadem quandoque vocatur נצח ישראל *Superatio Iisraël*, cum adhæret corpori [...] י״י צבאות quod est mysterium Rotæ dextræ vocatur Nezach, *superatio* I. Chr. 29, 11. [...]" ("Loci communes kabbalistici", op. cit., p. 589).
73 Deletion: De vaticinio tu edissere.

received an influx through the right-hand side, so she makes mention of great [deeds], having in view the degree Netsach (see ibid., p. 589). For [the Hebrew word] *ḥyl*, whence *tyltn* [strong], often denotes an army. | In the subsequent verses, she depicts the deeds of Ecclesia and how Messiah will reveal himself towards her. As often [in Hebrew], the verb in the past tense has a future meaning, as if to indicate that its fulfilment is as certain as if it had already happened[78]. In Greek, aorists or indications of an indefinite time are used. The status of Ecclesia is described five times—remarkably.

Verse 50 describes the initial state of that Christianity which was ushered in by Christ and the Apostles and opposed to the Judaism and Pharisaism of that time which boasted nothing undeserved: for ||| Christ had both preached Grace and had ordered others to preach it (Jn 1.17; Lk 4.18; Rm 1.5; 3.24; 4.16; 5.2, 15, 17, 20, 21; 6.14, 15; 11.5, 6; etc.) The sense of the prophecy is that before all things there is preached in Ecclesia the doctrine of Grace through Faith to be obtained in fear and humility. And this teaching will continue in Ecclesia through all | generations, whatever her enemies undertake.

fol. 20ʳ

For according to Verse 51:[79]

The Jews, proud in the thoughts of their hearts, first opposed this herald of Grace. They are described in the parable in Lk 18.11 Cf. Mt 23.5 *seq.*. But Messiah will show himself victorious over them and will not only destroy their kingdom but will scatter the whole people throughout the various parts of the earth.

Now according to Verse 52, the Princes and Emperors of Rome, sitting on the throne of Monarchy, opposed this doctrine introduced by Christ and spread by the Apostles and persecuted the Ecclesia of Christ in every way. But Messiah shall cast down all these gentile emperors and raise to the imperial dignity those who embrace his doctrine of Grace and humility—namely, the Christians: which is what happened | with Constantine the Great and his successors.

---

74 Deletion: Christianus. The change of speaker initially intended is no longer needed, after the previous correction. The Christian remains the speaker.
75 Deleted word.
76 Deletion: Ante omnia
77 Added above the line: *primò*
78 For the so-called *perfectum propheticum*, see *Gesenius' Hebrew Grammar*, edited by Emil Kautzsch, translated by Arthur Ernest Cowley, 2nd ed. (Oxford: Clarendon, 1910), pp. 312–313, note 106; Paul Joüon, *Grammaire de l'hébreu biblique*, 2nd ed. (Rome: Institut Biblique Pontifical, 1947), pp. 298–299, 112 g–h.
79 Deleted: Before all things.

V. 53. Nec adhuc hostium erat finis: sed contra doctrinam hanc insurget certum quoddam Christianorum genus, multis præpollens divitiis magnoque superbiens dominatu, sub quo doctrina de meritis & justitia propria iterum præferetur. Sed & illos ad ultimum redactos egestatem, gratiâque suâ privatos exulare jubebit. Istos verò, qui hanc interea | doctrinam de Gratia propagabunt, esurientque & sitient veram illam, quæ ex Deo est, justitiam, Matth. 5,6. saturabit bonis gratiæ suæ atque spiritus. Conf. Luc. 6, 20.21.24.25.

V. 54–55. Tandem autem Iisraëlitas etiam auxilio suo beabit [eosque[80]] sicut olim Hebr. 8, 9; Jer. 31, 31. eosque ê dispersione sua collectos in corpus Ecclesiæ suæ inferet | [Rom.] 11, 24.25.26.27. & ad mysterium[81] suum applicabit in Regno suo Ap. 22, 3. c. 7, 15. ricordatus gratiæ huic populo toties promissæ atque exhibitæ â primis jam institutæ Ecclesiæ initiis. [**Cabb. Cat.**][82] *Eosque in terram illam Patribus quondam promissam reducet; quæ restitutio ultimata omninò subintelligenda est in promissionibus illis, quæ factæ Abrahæ Gen. 17, 7.8. & Isaaco Gen. 26, 3.4. & Iacobo Gen. 28, 13.14. Nisi enim subesset | vaticinium de ultimis hisce temporibus, pactum illud non esset pactum æternum Gen. 17, 7. nec possessio æterna ib. v. 8. Unde dubium nullum est, quin istæ promissiones sese extendant* לעלם *ut Maria dicit; in æternitatem usque, sub Regno nimirum illo Messiano beatissimo; prout & Angelus ipsi prædixerat Luc. 1, 33.*

V. 56. *Quasi menses tres &.* איך ירחא תלתא

Cabb. Cat. *An quasi dubitaret de imprægnatione sua; expectatetque trimestre illud apud Doctores nostros pro detegenda graviditate mulieris destinatum? Jebhamoth f. 33.2. & 34.2. & 35.1. Ketubboth c. 5.*

Christianus. Potiùs crederem id propterea factum esse, ut occasione festi | cujusdam commodius domum redire posset. Quia temporibus hisce, ubi non tantum Romani milites, sed & latrones (Luc. 10, 30. Matth. 27, 38; 2. Cor.

---

80   Deleted word.
81   Correction above the line: mysterium replaced by ministerium
82   Added in the right margin: Cabb. Cat. (which involves a change of speaker).
83   Knorr evidently believed that certain parts of the post-Constantinian Church had abandoned the crucial doctrine of Grace and taught a doctrine of merits and self-righteousness.
84   A correction takes the following messianic hope of a physical earthly Jewish kingdom away from the Christian.
85   The word is used in Gen 17.8 just cited.

SECTION V

Verse 53 This was not yet the end of the enemies, but rather against this doctrine [of Grace] there will arise a certain type of Christians, mighty in wealth and proud with great dominance, under whom the doctrine of merits and self-righteousness will once again be preferred.[83] But he will order them into exile to be reduced to ultimate poverty and to be deprived of his grace. But those meanwhile who will propagate | this doctrine of grace and hunger and thirst for that true righteousness which is from God (Mt 5.6.), he will fill with the good things of his own grace and spirit Cf. Lk 6. 20, 21, 24, 25.

Verses 54 & 55. But at length the Israelites also he will bless with his help, just as once [he did] (Heb 8.9, Jer 31.31) and will gather them from their dispersion and bring them into the body of his Ecclesia | Rm 11. 24, 25, 26, 27 and will turn them to his ministry in his Kingdom (Rev 22.3; 7.15) having remembered his Grace to this people so many times promised and shown right from the very beginnings of Ecclesia.

Kabbalist Catechumen[84] And he will lead them back into that land which he once promised to their fathers: the very last restitution is to be understood [here] which [is mentioned] in all his promises which [he made] to Abraham Gen 17.7, 8 and to Isaac Gen 26.3, 4 and to Jacob Gen 28.13, 14. For unless the prophecy is understood | about these last times, that covenant would not be "an everlasting covenant" (Gen 17.7), nor [the possession] "an eternal possession" (ibid., verse 8). So there is no doubt that [these] promises will last "for the age" (*l'lm*[85]) [or], as Mary says, "into eternity", that is obviously until [the coming of] that most blessed Messianic Kingdom—just as the Angel foretold to Mary (Lk 1.33).

Verse 56
For about three months etc. 'yk yrḥ' tlt'

Kabbalist Catechumen Is this because she was in doubt about her conception and waited for the three month period which, according to our teachers, is determined for the detection of a woman's pregnancy (Yevamot f.33.2 & 34.2 & 35.1; Ketuvot 5)?

Christian I would rather think she did it so that she might | be able to return home more conveniently at the time of one of the feasts. Because in those times when not only Roman soldiers but also bandits (Lk 10.30; Mt

fol. 20ᵛ 11, 26) metui poterant, Maria nullatenus sola tantum iter suscepisset; ut nihil superaddam de periculo famæ, & pudore virgineo, apud Hebræos[86] sanctè semper exculto.[87] |||

---

86 Correction: Hebræos replaced by gentem vestram
87 In the right bottom corner appears a Hebrew letter ו presumably an indication of binding or pagination.

27.38; 2 Cor 11.26) could cause fear, Mary would have in no way made such a long journey alone—to say no more about the danger to her reputation and maidenly modesty, always religiously cultivated with sanctity amongst your people. ‖

[1]Matthæi Cap. I. v. 1–25.
Evangelium Sanctum Prædicationis
Matthæi Apostoli.[2]

1. [3]*Descriptio generationis*[4] *Jeschua Meschicha, filii David, filii Abraham.*
2. *Abraham genuit Is-chak. Is-chak genuit Jaacob. Jaacob genuit Jehudah | & fratres ejus.*
3. *Jehudah genuit Phares & Zarah è Tamar. Phares genuit Chesron. Chesron genuit Aram.*
4. *Aram genuit Aminadab. Aminadab | genuit Nachschon. Nachschon genuit Salmon.*
5. *Salmon genuit Booz & Rachab. Booz genuit Obed è Ruth. Obed genuit Ischai.*
6. *Ischai genuit David Regem. David genuit Schlemon ex uxore Uriæ.*
7. *Schlemon genuit Rechebam. Rechebam genuit Abia. Abia genuit Assa.*
8. *Assa genuit Jehoschaphath. Jehoschaphath | genuit Joram. Joram genuit Uzia.*
9. *Uzia genuit Jotham. Jotham genuit Achaz. Achaz genuit Chezekja.*
10. *Chezekja genuit Menasche. Menasche genuit Amon. Amon genuit Joschia.*
11. *Joschia genuit Jochanja & fratres ejus in exilio Babel.*[5]
12. *Post exilium autem Babel Jochanjah genuit Schelatiel. Schelatiel genuit Zorbabel.*
13. *Zorbabel genuit Abiud. Abiud genuit Eliakim. Eliakim genuit Azur.*
14. *Azur genuit Zadok. Zadok genuit Achin. Achin genuit Eliud.*
15. *Eliud genuit Eleazar. Eleazar genuit Matthan. Matthan genuit Jaacob.*
16. *Jaacob genuit Joseph, virum Marjam, ex qua natus est Jeschua qui vocatur Meschicha.*
17. *Omnes igitur progenies*[6] *ab Abraham usque ad David, progenies quatuordecim: & à David usque ad Exilium*[7] *Babel progenies quatuordecim: & ab exilio Babel usque ad Meschicham progenies quatuordecim.*

---

1 Added in the left margin: Sectio VI.
2 The heading is a somewhat shortened version of the traditional heading at the beginning of the Peshitta Matthew which appears on the Syriac text stuck into the manuscript here.
3 On the left-hand half of the page, a fragment cut from Knorr's edition of the Peshittta New Testament containing the Syriac version of the quoted passage in the Gospel of Matthew is pasted in and crossed out.
4 Vulgate: liber generationis
5 Vulgate: in transmigratione Babylonis, consistently hereafter.

Section VI

Matthew 1.1–25

The Holy Gospel of the Preaching | of the Apostle Matthew

1. A record of the generation of Jeschua Meschicha, the son of David, the son of Abraham.

2. Abraham begat Issack[8]. Issack begat Jaacob. Jaacob begat Jehudah | and his brothers.

3. Jehudah begat Phares and Zerah by Tamar. Phares begat Chesron. Chesron begat Aram.

4. Aram begat Aminadab. Aminadab begat | Nachschon. Nachschon begat Salmon.

5. Salmon begat Booz & Rachab. Booz begat Obed by Ruth. Obed begat Ischai.

6. | Ischai begat King David. David begat Schlemon by Uria's wife.

7. Schlemon begat Rechebam. Rechebam begat Abiah. Abiah begat Assa.

8. Assa begat Jehoschaphath. Jehoschaphath | begat Joram. Joram begat Uziah.

9. Uziah begat Jotham. Jotham begat Achaz. Achaz begat Chezekja.

10. Chezekja begat Menasche. Menasche begat Amon. Amon begat Joschia.

11. | Joschia begat Jochanja and his brothers in exile in Babel [Babylon][9].

12. Then, after the exile in Babel [Babylon], Jochanjah begat Schelatiel. Schelatiel begat Zorababel.

13. Zorababel begat Abiud. Abiud begat Eliakim. Eliakim begat Azur.

14. | Azur begat Zadok. Zadok begat Achin. Achin begat Eliud.

15. Eliud begat Eleazar. Eleazar begat Matthan. Matthan begat Jaacob.

16. Jaacob begat Joseph, the husband of Maria, by whom was born Jeschua who is called Meschicha.

17. | So all the descendants from Abraham to David were fourteen generations; and from the Exile in Babel [Babylon] until Meschicha were fourteen generations.

---

6 Vulgate: generationes, consistently hereafter.

7 Vulgate: ad transmigrationem, consistently hereafter.

8 The names in the list have been given according to Knorr's Latin spellings which are taken from the Syriac. They are sometimes different from the spellings of the Vulgate. Subsequently in the translation, to avoid confusion, Old Testament names, if not obviously identifiable, are often silently corrected throughout to the forms in the KJV unless special attention is drawn in the text to another spelling for reasons of exposition, or the use of Syriac forms marks a significant distance from the Vulgate.

9 Vulgate: "in Babylon", consistently.

18. *Nativitas autem Meschichæ Jeschua*[10] *ita fuit: Cum desponsata | esset Mar-   45
jam, mater ejus Josepho, antequam consociarentur*[11] *inventa est in utero habere
ê Spiritu Sanctitatis.*

19. *Joseph autem maritus ejus justus erat, & non volebat diffamare eam medi-*
fol. 21ʳ *tabaturque, ut occultè dimitteret illam.*[12] |||

20. *Cum autem hæc meditaretur, apparuit ei Angelus Domini per somnium, &
dixit ei*[13]*: Joseph, fili David, ne metuas*[14] *assumere Marjam uxorem tuam*[15]*, is
enim, qui genitus est in eâ, ê spiritu Sanctitatis est*[16]*.*

21. *Pariet autem filium, & vocabis nomen ejus* JESCHVA: *ipse enim liberabit   5
populum suum â pœnis suis*[17]*.*

22. *Hoc autem totum, quod fuit, (factum est) ut impleretur, quod dictum fuerat
â Domino per Prophetam*[18]*:*

23. *Nempe*[19]*, ecce virgo in utero habebit & pariet filium, & vocabunt nomen | 10
ejus Emmanuel: quod exponitur; Nobiscum (est) Deus noster*[20]*.*

24. *Cum surrexisset autem Joseph ex somno suo, fecit sicut mandaverat ei
Angelus Domini & accepit uxorem suam*[21]*.*

25. *Et non cognovit*[22] *eam, donec peperisset filium suum primogenitum: &
(illa*[23]*) vocavit nomen ejus* JESCHUA.

Prædicationis Matthæi כרוזותא דמתי   15

Cabb. Cat. *Rem gratam faceres mihi meæque genti, si quæ de Evangelio Matthæi hîc controverti solent, & annon linguâ nostrate illud primitus conscriptum
fuerit expedires?*[24]

Christianus. Matthæum historiam hanc conscripsisse linguâ patriâ, quæ
tum | temporis in usu erat in Palæstina, eratque Chaldaico-Syriaca, ab aliis   20

---

10 Vulgate: Christi autem generatio sic erat.
11 Vulgate: convenirent.
12 Vulgate: Joseph autem vir eius, cum esset Justus, et nollet eam traducere, voluit occulte dimittere eam.
13 Vulgate: Haec autem eo cogitante ecce angelus Domini apparuit in somnis ei dicens.
14 Vulgate: noli timere.
15 Vulgate: accipere conjungem tuam
16 Vulgate: quod enim in ea natum est, de Spirito Sancto est.
17 Vulgate: ipse enim salvum fecit populum suum a peccatis eorum.
18 Vulgate: Hoc autem totum factum est, ut adimpleretur quod dictum est a Domino per prophetam dicentem.
19 Nempe is omitted in the Vulgate.
20 Vulgate: Nobiscum Deus.

SECTION VI

18. The birth of Meschicha Jeschua was like this: When Mary his Mother was betrothed | to Joseph before they came together she was found to have [a child] in her womb from the Holy Spirit.

19. But Joseph her husband was a righteous man and did not wish to damage her reputation and considered how he might send her away secretly. ‖

fol. 21ʳ

20. While he was considering these things, the Angel of the Lord appeared to him in a dream and said to him: "Joseph, Son of David, do not be afraid to take Mary for your wife, for [the child] which has been born in her is from the Holy Spirit.

21. | She will bear a son, and you will call his name JESCHUA: for he will free his people from their punishments.

22. All of this which happened (was done) so that what had been said by the Lord through the prophet might be fulfilled:

23. Namely: 'See! A virgin shall have [a child] in her womb and will bear a son and they shall call his name | Emmanuel which means Our God is with us.'"

24. When Joseph awoke from his dream, he did as he had been ordered by the Angel of the Lord and accepted his wife.

25. And he did not know her until she had born her first-born son and (she) called his name JESCHUA.

The Preaching of Matthew krwzwt' dmty

Kabbalist Catechumen[25] Was the Gospel of Matthew first written in our language?

Matthew seems to have written this history in his native language which was at that time | in use in Palestine which others correctly assert was Chaldean-Syriac. However I omit this controversy.

---

21   Vulgate: Exsurgens autem Joseph a somno fecit sicut praecepit ei angelus Domini et accepit conjungem suam.
22   Vulgate: cognoscebat
23   (illa) is not in the Vulgate, which consequently suggests that Joseph named the baby.
24   Correction: the entire sentence is replaced by: Evangelium Matthæi annon linguâ nostrate primitus conscriptum est?
25   Deleted: You would do a kindness to both me and my people if [you would tell us] what about the Gospel of Matthew is usually disputed here and whether it was originally written in our language.

rectè assertum videtur.²⁶Argumenta autem hujus sententiæ potiora sunt hæc (1.) Quia magno consensu antiquitas tradidit Apostolum hunc annos aliquam multos (octo minimum) in Palæstina mansisse: Unde probabile est, cum & Theophylactus tradat, Matthæum anno post Ascensionem Christi octavo jam scripsisse; scriptam ab eo Evangelicam | historiam eo sermone, qui ea in regione frequentabatur. (2.) Papias testis antiquissimus, qui de se ipso in proemio librorum suorum apud Eusebium testatur, quod ab illis acceperit ea, quæ fidei sunt, qui sectatores Apostolorum fuerunt; Idem testatur. (3.) Origenes ibidem affirmat, Evangelium hoc â Matthæo, Judaico sermone, sive Ebraicis literis fidelibus ex Judæis scriptum esse, apud Eusebium | lib. 6. c. 24. Ubi non intelligitur lingua Hebraica antiqua, quam fideles ex Judæis (qui rarius literati erant, ut pote non amplius usitatam, nisi in scholis disceretur;) non intellexissent. Sed lingua communis Hierosolymitana literis Hebraicis, sed vocibus iisdem scripta, qua hodierna Syriaca exstat, quamvis non iisdem vocalibus, quas Syri recentes adjecerunt: prout | eadem lingua vulgaris, Hebraica tamen â Græcis dicitur Joh. 19, 13; 17.20; Act. 21.40; c. 22, 2; c. 26, 14; Joh. 5.2. (4.) Idem asserit Irenæus l. 3, c.1. apud Euseb. l. 5. Hist. Eccles. c.8 (5.) Pantænus apud Eusebium l. 5. c. 9. asserit: Evangelium

25

30

35

---

26   Beginning of a long deletion. The following text is crossed out. A note in margin says: "Controversiam tamen ipsam hîc non tangam".

27   Most of the patristic evidence cited here and much more can be found assembled with commentaries and discussion of their significance for possible reconstruction of Jewish-Christian Gospel texts in: A.F.J. Klijn, *Jewish-Christian Gospel Tradition* (Leiden: Brill, 1992).

28   In the preface to his Commentary on Matthew, Theophylact of Orchrid (c. 1055—post 1107) remarks that: "Matthew, then, first wrote the Gospel, in the Hebrew language for the Jews who believed, eight years after Christ's Ascension". The Greek text of Theophylact was published in Rome in 1542, having been preceded in the 1520s by Latin versions by the Catholic Porsena and the Protestant Oecolampadius.

29   Papias, Bishop of Hierapolis belonged to the third Christian generation. He wrote an *Exposition of the Logia of the Lord* in five books which is now lost but which was cited by Eusebius in his *Ecclesiastical History*, 3.39. The date of the work is disputed but may lie between 110 and 130 AD. For an account of established scholarship, William R. Schoedel, "Papias" in *Anchor Bible Dictionary*, vol. 5, edited by David Noel Freedman (New York: Doubleday, 1992), pp. 140–142. For the fragments, Bart D. Ehrman, *The Apostolic Fathers, II: Epistle of Barnabas. Papias and Quadratus. Epistle to Diognetus. The Shepherd of Hermas* (Cambridge Mass.: Harvard University Press, 2003), pp. 92–118. The reference here is to fragment 3: "And this is what he says about Matthew: 'And so Matthew composed the sayings in the Hebrew tongue', and each one interpreted [*Or: translated*] them to the best of his ability". The phrase "In the Hebrew tongue" *hebraidi dialectōi* and the similar New Testament *hebraisti* are variously taken by New

[The preferable arguments however for this opinion are these[27]: (1) that with a great consensus, Antiquitity has handed down that this Apostle [Matthew] lived a good number of years (eight at least) in Palestine, which is probable, because Theophylact also hands down that Matthew, in the eighth year after Christ's Ascension, had already written a gospel | account in that language which was common in that region.[28] (2) The most ancient witness Papias, who gives evidence about himself at the beginning of his books quoted in Eusebius and says that he had received the details of the Faith from those who were eye-witnesses of the apostles, gives the same testimony[29]. (3) Origen in the same place affirms this Gospel was written by Matthew in the Jewish language, or with Hebrew letters by faithful Jews (so Eusebius | Ecclesiastical History 6.c24 [6.25.4])[30]. When the ancient Hebrew language was no longer understood, and the faithful among the Jews (who could even more rarely read it, since it was no longer used unless taught in the schools) did not understand it; [they used rather] the common Jerusalem language [of the time] written in Hebrew letters but with the same words which today's Syriac has, although not with those words which the modern Syriac speakers have subsequently added [to the language]. As far as | this common language goes, it is called "Hebrew" by the Greeks Jn 19.13; 17.20; Acts 21.40; 22.2; 26.14; Jn 5.2[31]. (4) Irenaeus says the same (Book 3.1) in Eusebius *Ecclesiastical History* book v chapter 8[32]. (5) Pantaenus at Eusebius Book 5 chapter 9[33] says that Matthew's Gospel in Hebrew letters had been

---

Testament and Patristic scholars to mean *either* Hebrew *or* Aramaic, which complicates the evaluation of these testimonia.

30   The reference should be 6.25.4 where Eusebius cites Origen *Commentary on the Gospel of Matthew* (Book I): "Concerning the four Gospels which alone are uncontroverted in the Church of God under heaven, I have learned by tradition that the Gospel according to Matthew, who was at one time a publican and afterwards an Apostle of Jesus Christ, was written first; and that he composed it in the Hebrew tongue and published it for the converts from Judaism". For some editions of the *Ecclesiastical History* available in Knorr's time, see: Andrew Pettegree and Malcolm Walsby, eds., *French Books III & IV. Books published in France before 1601 in Latin and Languages other than French*, 2 vols (Leiden: Brill, 2012), vol. 1 (A–G), pp. 782–783. C.G. Düring's 1734 *Novum Inventarum Bibliothecæ Sulzbaco-Palatino* (BSB Cbm 580 Repositorium A) records a copy in the library there: p. 22#16.

31   In the Greek of the New Testament: *Hebraisti*

32   *Ecclesiastical History* 5.8.2: "Matthew published a Gospel in writing also, among the Hebrews in their own language, while Peter and Paul were preaching the Gospel and founding the church in Rome".

33   This should be 5.10: "It is reported in the hands of some persons there [in India] who had come to know Christ, [Pantaenus] found the Gospel according to St. Matthew

Matthæi â Bartholomæo Apostolo in India literis Hebraicis relictum, ad suausque tempora ibi servatum fuisse. Ubi sane probabile | non est, Bartholomæum Indis Evangelium Hebraico sermone antiquo attulisse, cum Indi illum non intelligerent: ad illos autem Syriacam linguam ê Mesopotamia & vicinis regionibus[34] promanasse credibilius est, cum apud Christianorum reliquias, qui istis in locis ultimo seculo reperti sunt etiam Syriaca ||| lingua adhuc servata esse perhibeatur. Quin & Hieronymus in Catalogo scriptorum Eccles. c, 36 perhibet: Pantæum[35] istum Philosophum â Demetrio Episcopo Alexandrino in Judæam[36] missum reperisse Evangelium Matthæi Hebraicis literis scriptum, secundum quod Bartholomæus Apostolus fidem | Christi inter Indos plantaverat, hoc verò ipsum Alexandriam attulisse. (6.) Ipse Hieronymus in dicto Catalogo c. 3. sic scribit: Matthæus, qui & Levi, ex publicano Apostolus, primus in Judæa, propter eos, qui ex circumcisione crediderant, Evangelium Christi Hebraicis literis verbisque composuit. Quod quis postea in Græcum transtulerit, non satis certum est. Porrò ipsum Hebraicum | habetur usque hodiè in Cæsariensi Bibliotheca, quam Pamphilus martyr studiosissimè confecit. Mihi quoque â Nazaræis, qui in Berœa urbe Syriæ hoc volumine utuntur, describendi facultas fuit. In quo animadvertendum, quod ubicunque Evangelista sive ex persona sua, sive ex persone Domini Salvatoris veteris Scripturæ testimoniis utitur, non | sequatur septuaginta Translatorum autoritatem, sed Hebraicam, ê quibus illa duo sunt: Ex Ægypto vocavi filium meum. Et quoniam Nazaræus vocabitur. Hæc ille. Quod autem hoc ipsum Evangelium, cujus copiam habuit Hieronymus, non fuerit Hebraico antiquo, sed Syriaco sermone conscriptum, manifestum evadit, ex eo, quod idem refert Tomo IX in c. 6 | Matth. ad v. 34. in Evangelio Hebraico, quod

---

which had anticipated his arrival; for that Bartholomew, one of the apostles, had preached to them and left behind the writing of Matthew in the actual Hebrew characters, and that it was preserved up to the said time".

34 Added above the line: aliis
35 Correction above the line: Pantæum replaced by Pantænum
36 In error. It should be India.
37 For a very brief initial introduction to Syriac-speaking Christians in India, see Françoise Briquel-Chatonnet and Muriel Debié, *Le monde syriaque* (Paris: Les Belles Lettres, 2017), pp. 125–129. The earliest account of Thomas' evangelisation is that in the *Acts of Thomas* (A.F.J. Klijn, *The Acts of Thomas. Introduction, Text and Commentary*, (Leiden: Brill, 1962, 2003)). Europeans have been aware of these Christians ever since, but some were brought into full communion with Rome under the Latin episcopate of Goa during the Portuguese *Padroado* at the Synod of Diamper in 1599 (Robert Eric Frykenberg, *Christianity in India. From Beginnings to the Present* (Oxford University Press, 2008), pp. 122–134).

SECTION VI   295

left in India by the Apostle Bartholemew and had been preserved there to his
own day. It is not very probable | that Bartholemew had taken this Gospel in
the ancient Hebrew language to India, since the Indians do not understand
that [language]; but it is credible that the Syriac language from Mesopotamia
and [other] neighbouring regions had reached them, since among the rem-
nants of the Christians who were found last century in these places, Syriac ||| fol. 21ᵛ
appears to have been preserved upto now[37]. Does not Jerome in his *Catalogue of Ecclesiastical Writers* c. 36 say that Pantaenus the Philosopher sent
by Demetrius Bishop of Alexandria to India found a Gospel of Matthew
written in Hebrew letters, according to which the Apostle Bartholemew had
planted Faith | in Christ among the Indians—and that he took the [Gospel]
book itself to Alexandria[38]. (6) Jerome himself in the aforementioned Catalogue chapter 3 wrote thus: "Matthew who is also [called] Levi from being a
tax-collector [became] an apostle first in Judaea to those who had believed
from the circumcision, and composed a Gospel of Christ in Hebrew letters
and in the Hebrew language. Who later put this into Greek is not very clear.
But that Hebrew | exists up to today in the library in Caesarea which the
martyr Pamphilius so studiously assembled. I also had the opportunity of
examining the book given to me by the Nazaraeans, who use it in Beroea,
a town in Syria. In the [book] it was noteworthy that whenever the Evangelist used the testimony of the Old [Testament] Scriptures, either in his own
capacity (as narrator) or when quoting the words of the Lord Our Saviour,
he did not | follow the authority of the Septuagint translators but rather that
of the Hebrew text. Here are two [examples]: 'Out of Egypt have I called my
son' and 'For he shall be called a Nazarene'" (Thus far [Jerome][39]). But this
Gospel itself, a copy of which Jerome had, was not written in ancient Hebrew
but rather in the Syriac language, clearly escaped him, because he refers to it
again in Volume 9[40] on | Mt 6.34[41] [where he says] in a Hebrew Gospel which

---

38 Jerome, *Catalogus Scriptorum Ecclesiastorum* 36: "*Pantaenus Stoicae sectae Philosophus, juxta quamdam veterem in Alexandria consuetudinem, ubi a Marco Evangelista semper ecclesiastici fuere Doctores, tantae prudentiae & eruditionis tam in Scripturis divinis, quam in seculari litteratura fuit, ut in Indiam quoque rogatus ab illis gentis legatis, a Demetrio Alexandriae Episcopo, mitteretur. Ubi reperit, Bartholomaeum de duodecim Apostolis, adventum Domini nostri Iesu Christi juxta Matthaei Evangelium praedicasse, quod Hebraicis litteris scriptum, revertens Alexandriam, secum retulit.*"
39 The quotation of the whole chapter of Jerome here is complete and accurate.
40 This would appear to refer to the nine folio volumes of Erasmus's first edition of the complete works of Jerome produced at the Froben Press in Basel in 1516. A copy of this edition is recorded in C.G. Düring's 1734 *Novum Inventarium Bibliothecæ Sulzbaco-*

consuluit adhiberi vocem דמחר crastinum, pro Græco Ἐπιούσιος. Præfixum autem ד non Hebræorum est, sed Syrorum: quorum lingua Chaldaicæ admodum conformis est. Adde, quod idem Hieronymus alibi contra Pelagium tertio affirmet, hoc Evangelium scriptum fuisse Chaldæo & Syro sermone, sed Hebraicis | literis. (7.) Epiphanius etiam hæres. 29. ita refert: Nazaræi habent Matthæi Evangelium perfectissimum Hebraicè. Apud ipsos enim hoc clarè, quemadmodum ab initio scriptum est, Hebraicis literis adhuc servatur. (8.) Accedit Eusebius, qui l. 3. c. 24 sic ait: Matthæus cum primùm Ebræis prædicasset, & jam ad alios quoque transiturus erat, Evangelium | suum patrio sermone literis tradidit, & quod subtracta sua præsentia desiderare possent illi, â quibus discebat[42], per literas adimplevit. Nicephorus autem l. 2. c. 45. hoc ita expressit: Discedens absentiam suam scripto præsenti compensavit. Augustinus, quamvis non asserendo, ait tamen; perhibent illum cum Ebraico eloquio scripsisse. | l. 1. d. Cons. Evangel. c. 2. Et Nazianzenus, qui Ebræis Christi miracula scripsisse Matthæum ait. Et Chrysostomus, qui pariter ita scribit: homil. 1. in Matth. Matthæus scripsit accedentibus his qui ex Judæis

25

30

35

Palatino (BSB Cbm 580 Repositorium A), p. 16#35. On this edition, see Rice, *Saint Jerome in the Renaissance*, op. cit., pp. 116–136.

41 This should be verse 11. Jerome's *Commentary on the Gospel of Matthew* on 6.11 says "In the Gospel which is called 'According to the Hebrews' I have found instead of 'superstantial bread' *maar* which means 'tomorrow's'". Such a reading also occurs in some Coptic versions according to the apparatus ad loc. in Robert Weber and Roger Gryson, eds., *Biblia Sacra iuxta Vulgatam versionem* (Stuttgart: Deutsche Bibelgesellschaft, 2007).

42 Correction above the line: discebat replaced by discedebat

43 Jerome, *Dialogus adversus Pelagianos*, III, 2: "*In Evangelio juxta Hebraeos, quod Chaldaico quidem Syroque sermone sed Hebraicis litteris scriptum est, quo utuntur usque hodie Nazareni, secundum Apostolos, sive ut plerique autumnant, juxta Matthaeum, quod et in Caesariensi habetur bibliotheca, narrat historia: etc.*" ("In the Gospel according to the Hebrews which was written in the Chaldaic and Syriac language but with Hebrew letters, and is used up to the present day by the Nazaraeans, I mean that according to the Apostles, or, as many maintain, according to Matthew, which Gospel is also available in the Library of Caesarea, the story runs: etc.")

44 *The Panarion of Epiphanius of Salamis Book 1 (Sects 1–46)*, translated by Frank Williams, 2nd ed. (Leiden: Brill, 2009), p. 130.

45 Nicephorus Callistus Xanthopulus (c.1320) wrote an *Ecclesiastical History* from the birth of Christ to 610 A.D. from various sources. He writes: "Matthew first, who had been a publican, and had preached the saving word to Jews, when he was about to go abroad amongst the Gentiles, thought it best to write in his native language an account of his preaching, to supply the want of his presence; which he did about fifteen years after our Saviour's ascension". This passage is obviously dependant upon that of Eusebius just quoted. The text is found in *Patrologia Graeca*, vol. 145 (Paris: J.P. Migne,

he consulted there appeared the word *dmḥr* ("tomorrow's") for the Greek *epiousios*. The prefix /d/ is [characteristic] not of the Hebrews' [language] but rather of the Syrians' [language] which is pretty much the same as Chaldaean [or Aramaic]. Also consider as a third example what also Jerome says elsewhere against Pelagius[43]; that this Gospel had been written in the Chaldaean or Syriac language, but in Hebrew letters. | (7) Epiphanius also *Against Heresies* 29 says thus: The Nazaraeans have the Gospel according to Matthew in its entirety in Hebrew. For it is clear, that they still preserve this as it was originally written in the Hebrew alphabet[44]. (8) Add Eusebius, who in Book 3 chapter 24 [of his *Ecclesiastical History*] says as follows: 'Matthew when he had first preached to the Hebrews and then was about to go to others too, committed his | Gospel to writing in his native speech and its letters thus he made his writing compensate those from whom he was departing for the lack of his [bodily] presense'. Nicephorus however (Book 2 chapter 45) puts it like this: 'Upon his departure, he compensated for his absence by being present in his writing'[45]. Augustine, although not dogmatic, reports however that '*they say*' Matthew wrote in Hebrew | (*On the Agreement of the Evangelists* Book 1 ch. 2.[46]) And [Gregory] Nazianzenus says that Matthew wrote down Christ's miracles for the Hebrews[47]. Add Chrysostom who equally said [*Homily 1 on Matthew*[48]] that Matthew wrote for those believers from among

---

1865). The story of the printing of the sole manuscript of Nicephoros is found in Franco Mormando, "Pestilence, Apostasy and Heresy in Seventeenth Century Rome. Deciphering Michael Sweerts's 'Plague in an Ancient City'" in *Piety and Plague from Byzantium to the Baroque*, edited by Franco Mormando and Thomas Worcester (Kirksville: Truman State University Press, 2007), pp. 265–271. C.G. Düring's 1734 *Novum Inventarium Bibliothecæ Sulzbaco-Palatino* (BSB Cbm 580 Repositorium A) records a copy of Nicephorus, p. 22#19 in the Library at Sulzbach.

46 "Of these four, it is true, only Matthew is reckoned to have written in the Hebrew language; the others in Greek". Two copies of Froben's 1569 Basel edition of Augustine are recorded in C.G. Düring's 1734 *Novum Inventarium Bibliothecæ Sulzbaco-Palatino* (BSB Cbm 580 Repositorium A), pp. 13–14#5–12 in the Library at Sulzbach.

47 *Carmina dogmatica* 1.12.6–9. For Gregory's text see Margaret M. Mitchell, "Patristic Counter-Evidence to the claim that 'The Gospels were written for all Christians'", *New Testament Studies* 5, 1 (2005): pp. 36–79. Also *Opus Imperfectum in Mattheum 1* (53 homilies on first part of Matthew once attributed to Chrystostom) in *Patrologia Graeca*, vol. 56. (Paris: J.P. Migne, 1862). C.G. Düring's 1734 *Novum Inventarium Bibliothecæ Sulzbaco-Palatino* (BSB Cbm 580 Repositorium A), p. 16#31 records a Greek Nazianzenus and Lewenclavius' 1571 translation from Basel in the Library at Sulzbach.

48 "Of Matthew again it is said, that when those who from among the Jews had believed came to him, and besought him to leave to them in writing those same things, which he had spoken to them by word, he also composed his Gospel in the language of the

Christo crediderant & rogantibus, ut quæ verbis docuisset, hæc eis in literas servanda dimitteret. Ad hæc responderi quidem solet (1.) Papiam traditionibus magis | quam scripturis deditum, cum modici admodum juxta Eusebium fuerit judicii ab aliis persuasum fuisse, Matthæum Ebraica lingua scripsisse: cum & in aliis seductus sit ab hæreticis. Sed istud sane non sufficit asserere, nisi ||| opponi Papiæ queat autoritas alia æque antiqua, quod Græcè scripserit Matthæus. (2.) Dicunt Origenem & Irenæum ita persuasos fuisse, & secutos esse errantem Papiam. Sed & hoc frustra dicitur: cum antiquioribus illis patribus veritas hac de re melius innotescere potuerit quam nobis. Imò fidelibus ex Judæis in Palæstina frustrà | Græcè scripsisset Matthæus, quia lingua hæc vulgò ibidem haud erat familiaris. (3.) Reponunt: Exemplar illud, de quo Pantænus testatur, potuisse translatum esse ê Græco. Sed quare Bartholomæus Indis versionem potiùs commendasset, quam scriptum originarium; præsertim cum lingua Græca tam latè, imò latiùs innotuisset quàm Syriaca? imò quare non in Indicam | ipse linguam illud transtulisset potiùs, quam in Syriacam? (4.) Dicunt: Hieronymus nullum assertionis suæ testem laudat. At quis quæso illis testis est assertionis contrariæ: testis, inquam, ex antiquitate? (5.) Mirum fuerit, ajunt, quod Eusebius Cæsariensis Episcopus, Pamphilique amicissimus, cum sæpius meminerit Evangelii Matthæi Ebraici, de eo, quod liber iste in Cæsariensi Bibliotheca | asservaretur, ne verbum quidem mentionem fecerit. Proh fidem tuam Hieronyme; quæ ob istud Eusebii silentium tantopere in dubium vocatur! Verum enim vero, cum Eusebii tempore nemo dubitaret, utrum Evangelium Hebraicum extaret, an minus; hinc non opus habuit exemplum allegare rei per se in dubium haud vocatæ. Si autem quæstio fuisset, an Evangelii illius Hebraici Matthæus esset autor? nihil sanè ad | affirmandum hoc tum profuisset, provocare ad exemplar illud Bibliothecæ Pamphilianæ. (6.) Addunt: Chrysostomum Hieronymi Synchronum haud obscurè negasse, suo tempore extitisse Ebraicum Matthæi Evangelium. Sed quid Chrysostomo tribuendum est Græco homini, qui de linguis exoticis parum vel fuit vel esse potuit curiosus inter turbas ævi sui? Unde testi tanto asserenti opponi non poterit | ignorantia alteriùs multò inferioris

---

Hebrews. And Mark too, in Egypt, is said to have done this self-same thing at the entreaty of the disciples". C.G. Düring's 1734 *Novum Inventarium Bibliothecæ Sulzbaco-Palatino* (BSB Cbm 580 Repositorium A) records several copies of Chrystostom's works: p. 15#19; p. 17#40; p. 19#68–70 etc. in the Library at Sulzbach.

49 Eusebius considered Papias "a man of very little intelligence" (*Ecclesiastical History* 3.39.13) because he was a millenarian who expected an earthly kingdom at the Second Coming of Christ.

the Jews who had believed on Christ and were asking that what he had taught orally, might be passed down to them preserved in writing.

To these arguments the usual reply is: (1) that Papias was more given to traditions | than to Scripture and since, according to Eusebius, he was somewhat of modest judgment, he was persuded by others that Matthew wrote in the Hebrew language and was even more seduced by heretics[49]. But that clearly is insufficient grounds for the assertion unless it is possible ‖ to oppose to Papias another equally old authority [stating] that Matthew had written in Greek. (2) They say Origen and Irenaeus were persuaded of this and [so] followed the erring Papias. But this argument is equally ineffectual. The older Fathers were in a better position to know the truth about this matter than we are. Indeed to the faithful from among the Jews in Palestine, Matthew would have written in vain | in Greek, because that language was hardly familiar to the common people there. (3) [Opponents of this view] reply: That copy to which Pantaenus witnesses could have been translated from the Greek. But why would Bartholomew have commended this version to the Indians rather than the original writing; especially since the Greek language was so widely known, indeed more widely so than Syriac? Indeed why did he not put it into the Indian | language rather than into Syriac? (4) They [also] say: Jerome vouches no [historical] witness for his assertion. But who (I ask) is the witness of the contrary assertion—a witness (I insist) from antiquity? (5) It would have been amazing, they say, that Eusebius, Bishop of Caesarea and close friend of Pamphilius, when he quite frequently recalled the Hebrew Gospel of Matthew, should make not even a word of mention about the fact that the book itself was available for inspection in the Library of Caesarea! | Ah! Your trust in Jerome! Which, on account of the silence of Eusebius, is so much called into question! But really since Eusebius' time nobody questioned whether a Hebrew Gospel existed or not, so there was no reason to allege a copy for something not in itself called into question. But what if it had been a question of whether Matthew was the author of that Hebrew Gospel? Merely drawing attention to the copy in Pamphilius's Library | would have done nothing to confirm this! (6) They add: Chrystostom, a contemporary of Jerome, quite blatantly denied that at that time there existed a Hebrew Gospel of Matthew. But what weight should we place upon Chrystostom, a Greek [Father], who in the turmoil of his time, did not take and had little opportunity to take an interest [in exotic languages?] So against the testimony of such an assertive witness [Jerome], there cannot be opposed | the ignorance of another, [Chrysostom], much inferior in this type [of knowledge].

fol. 22r

in hoc genere. (7.) Ulterius superaddunt: Evangelium, quod Hieronymus descripsit, non fuisse Matthæi, sed Nazarenorum, quod isti venditarent, pro Matthæi Evangelio, unde Ebræo Evangelio aliis imposuerint: quod & Epiphanius crediderit. Sed rectè hic Grotius asserit, Nazaræos illos Berœenses genuinam fuisse progeniem eorum, qui primi in Palæstina Christi fidem | erant amplexi. Idque illis nomen primitùs fuisse inditum ê Christi nomine qui vulgò Nazaræenus vocabatur, juxta Act. 24, 5. Sicut qui lingua Græca Christum sunt amplexi vocabantur Christiani, Act. 11, 26. Additque, quod Epiphanius testetur, hos ipsos Nazaræos fuisse propaginem eorum, qui divinitùs admoniti Hierosolymis Pellam discesserant obsidii tempore. Et porrò subjungit: Nazaræi | non probantur in fidei negotio â cæteris Christianis discrepasse, quanquam ritus Judaicos traditâ â majoribus consuetudine observabant, Apostolis non prohibentibus. Bene enim notat Sulpitius in Palæstina Christianos penè omnes ad Adriani usque tempora Christum Deum sub Legis observatione credidisse. Et sane dubitat Epiphanius an aliquid hæreseos alerent: alii vero, qui de iis scribunt, | nihil plane illis tribuunt proprium, præter Hebræorum rituum observationem. Irenæus verò nullam eorum mentionem facit in recensu hæreseon: Unde in partem meliorem de iis judicandum est: eoque magis, quid Augustinus, qui vetustiores scriptores consuluit, dissertè affirmet, confiteri Nazaræos, Christum esse Dei filium. Ex quibus omnibus non immerito considerandum, annon injuria ||| fiat Nazaræis prædictâ assertione? (8.) Ad illud Hieronymi, quod Matthæus non tam autoritatem LXX. quàm Hebraicam sequatur: Reponunt: Esse quosdam qui eo argumento; quia plerumque dicta V.T. ex Græca versione asserat Mat-

fol. 22ᵛ

---

50   Hugo Grotius, *Annotationes in Libros Evangeliorum* (Amsterdam: J&C Blaev, 1641), p. 6, in commenting upon the superscription to Matthew's Gospel has: "*Adde quod et Epiphanius testatus, hos ipsos Nazaraeos fuisse propaginem eorum, qui Divinitus admoniti Hierosolymis Pellam discesserant obsidii tempore.*" Though the tradition has been contested historically, both Epiphanius and Eusebius assert that before the destruction of Jerusalem in AD 70, the Jerusalem Christians were divinely warned to flee to Pella across the Jordan in Decapolis. The flight is often associated with Lk 21.20–24. See, Craig Koester, "The Origin and Significance of the Flight to Pella Tradition", *Catholic Biblical Quarterly* 51, 1 (1989): pp. 90–106.

51   Not quite immediately.

52   Sulpicius Severus, *Chronica*, Book 2, 31, 3–5: "*sub Adriano deinde Iudaei rebellare voluerunt, Syriam ac Palaestinam diripere conati; misso exercitu subacti sunt. Qua tempestate Adrianus, existimans se Christianam fidem loci iniuria peremperturum, et in templo et loco Dominicae passionis daemonum simulacra constituit. Et quia Christiani ex Iudaeis potissimum putabantur—namque tum Hierosolymae non nisi ex circumcisione habebat ecclesia sacerdotem—militum cohortem custodias in perpetuum agitare iussit,*

(7) Finally they add: the Gospel which Jerome described was not Matthew's, but belonged to the Nazaraeans, which they hawked around as the real Matthew's Gospel. In this way they imposed the Hebrew Gospel on others: even Epiphanius believed in it. But Grotius rightly says[50] the Nazaraeans of Beroea were the genuine descendants of those in Palestine who had first embraced | Faith in Christ. They first got their name from the name of Christ who was commonly called "the Nazarene" according to Acts 24.5. Just as those who—in Greek—first embraced Christ were called "Christians" (Acts 11 26). He adds that Epiphanius testifies that these same Nazaraeans were the offspring of those who, divinely forewarned, had left Jerusalem for Pella at the time of the Siege [of Jerusalem]. And then he adds[51]: the Nazaraeans | are not proved to have differed in the matter of faith by other Christians although they observed Jewish rites by custom handed down from their forefathers, which the Apostles did not prohibit. For Sulpitius [Sulpicius Severus] notes well that in Palestine almost all Christians upto the time of [the Emperor] Hadrian believed Christ was God, while [at the same time] observing the Law[52]. And clearly Epiphanius doubts whether they supported heretics in any way[53]. Others who write about them | attribute to them nothing particularly special, other than their observation of Hebrew rites. Irenaeus however makes no mention of them in his list of heretics. So they should be given the benefit of the doubt; and the more so because Augustine, who consulted older writers, learnedly asserts that the Nazaraeans confess that Christ is the son of God[54]. From all of which, it should be rightly asked whether the Nazareans are unworthily defamed ||| by the aforementioned claim [that they were heretics].

fol. 22ᵛ

(8) To that point of Jerome, that Matthew follows not so much the authority of the LXX [Septuagint Greek Old Testament] as that of the Hebrew [text]: they reply that there are some who by pointing out that very often the words from the Old Testament Matthew cites are from the Greek version seek to

---

quae Iudaeos omnes Hierosolymae aditu arceret. Quod quidem Christianae fidei proficiebat, quia tum paene omnes Christum Deum sub legis observatione credebant. Nimirum id Domino ordinante dispositum, ut legis servitus a libertate fidei atque ecclesiae tolleretur."

53 Epiphanius' objections to them (see *Panarion*, translated by Williams, op. cit., pp. 123–130) amount mainly to their Jewish practices. He hesitates to accuse them of psilanthropy.

54 This would seem to be his view in Letters 75.13 & 82.15–16, translated in *The Works of St Augustine: A Translation for the Twenty-First Century. The Letters*, edited by John E. Rotelle (New York: New City Press, 2001). He however very much disapproved of their lingering Judaism.

thæus; utantur, ut ostendant non Ebraicè sed Græcè scripsisse illum in originali. Sed | (1.) Evangelium Matthæi Ebraicum non habemus: Syriacum autem hodiernum pro uno & eodem Codice cum antiquo etiam non omnino haberi potest, quamvis ad illum propius forte accedat, quam textus ullus alius. (2.) Conferat qui voluerit allegationes, & majorem cum Hebræo convenientiam, inveniet in locis Matth. 4, 15; c. 8, 17; c. 2, 18.15.6; c. 21, 5; c. 26, 31; c. 11, 18. quod quare fecerit qui Græcis | græcè scripsisset, non video. Loca autem Græco proximiora tam multa non sunt. Argumenta autem palmaria, quod Græcè scripserit Matthæus, sunt sequentia. (1.) Quod Ebraicum Evangelium Matthæi, Nazaræorum, Ebionitarum & Cerinthianorum fuerit, interque Apocrypha â Catholicis recensitum, qui Græcum amplectebantur unice. R[espondunt]. (1.) Nulla est sequela, Nazaræi, Ebionitæ & Cerinthiani habuerunt | Evangelium Ebraicum: E. vel Matthæus Ebraicum non scripsit; vel illud ipsum non fuit Matthæi. De Nazaræis enim ex Hieronymo patet, quod Evangelium suum â Matthæo profectum constantissime asseveraverint: quamvis fortè narrationes quædam auditu perceptæ paulatim assutæ fuerint. Sed & de Ebionæis & Cerinthianis Epiphanius dicit, usos eos Matthæi Evangelio: | prout Hieronymus idem commune facere videtur Nazaræis & Ebionitis: quamvis isti quædam expunxissent. (2.) Catholici dicebantur Christiani, cum Græcismus ubique prævaleret, & quicquid judaizare videtur, rejectum esset. Non sequitur autem; Græci græcum amplectebantur unicè; Ergò Hebraicè nihil primo scriptum erat: quia aliàs etiam negandum esset, libros V.T. Hebraice scriptos fuisse, quia inter | Christianos Græcos versio LXX unicè recipiebatur. Arg[umentum] (II.) est; quod traditio de originali Hebræo incerta sit, & non nisi autoritate Papiæ, non uno modo suspecta, inducta. R[espondunt]. Æque incertum esse, quod de originali Græco asseritur, cum ê veteribus nullum omnino habeat testem. Arg[umentum] (III.) quod ê veteribus nemo testetur se hebraicum textum authenticum | vidisse. R[espondunt]. Si authenticum idem est ac autographum, quid

---

55 Knorr has just presented eight numbered propositions and eight numbered responses (though has also sometimes introduced subsidiary number sequences within those numbered items). There follows now a numbered sequence which has no relation to the first two numbered sequences, but which simply presents a series of arguments on the original language of Matthew followed by immediate responses. To avoid any possible confusion of these remarks with the two previous numbered sequences we have substituted letters here for the manuscript's numbers.

56 These three Jewish-Christian groups are generally considered as heretics by Irenaeus, Epiphanius and others.

57 E.g. *In Matthaeum* 12.13. For further references see Klijn, *Jewish-Christian Gospels*, op. cit., p. 17.

show that he wrote the original not in Hebrew but in Greek. But | (1) we do not have a Hebrew Gospel of Matthew, and the contemporary Syriac one cannot be considered exactly one and the same book as the ancient [Hebrew Gospel] although it happens to approach more closely to that than any other text. (2) Anyone who wishes may compare these claims, but they will find a greater agreement with the Hebrew [Old Testament] in Mt 4.15; 8.17; 2.18, 15, 6; 21.5; 26.31; 11.18. I cannot see why someone who wrote in Greek | for Greeks should have done this. Citations [from the Old Testament] which are closer to the Greek are not so many.

But the decisive arguments that Matthew wrote in Greek are as follows:[55] (A) the Hebrew Gospel of Matthew belonged to the Nazaraeans, the Ebionites and the Cerinthians[56], but was reckoned amongst the Apocrypha by the Catholics who embraced Greek alone.

The reply is: (1) it does not follow that just because the Nazaraeans, Ebionites and Cerinthians [as heretics] | had a Hebrew Gospel, either that Matthew did not write a Hebrew [Gospel]; or that that very copy was not by Matthew. For concerning the Nazaraeans, it is clear from Jerome[57], they most constantly asserted that their gospel had been derived from Matthew although by chance certain narratives taught orally were little by little added. But also about the Ebionites and Cerinthians, Epiphanius says they use Matthew's Gospel[58]. | Jerome seems to consider it was shared in common by Nazaraeans and Ebionites although these removed certain passages. (2) The Catholics were called Christians when Greek [language and culture] was universally prevalent[59] and whatever seemed to be judaizing was rejected. But it does not follow that the Greeks embraced Greek alone: or that therefore nothing had been previously written in Hebrew. Otherwise it could even be denied that the books of the Old Testament had been written in Hebrew, just because amongst | Greek Christians the Septuagint version alone was received!

The Argument (B) is: that the tradition about the original Hebrew is uncertain and had it not been introduced with the authority of Papias nobody would have in any way suspected it. The reply is: what is being asserted about the original Greek is equally uncertain, since we have absolutely no testimony from the ancients.

Argument (C) is: that not one of the ancients said that they had seen | an authentic Hebrew text [of Matthew]. The response is: if "authentic" means

---

58 E.g. *Panarion*, Williams, 9.4.
59 Epiphanius (Ibid.) contends that by contrast all Christians originally and whenever thereafter they were Jews were called Nazaraeans.

judicandum erit de cæteris Scripturæ libris? Si vero intelligitur tale quid, quod autoritatem habet; Hieronymus sanè testatur, se vidisse & habuisse, & quidem ab iis inter quos hoc unicum habebat autoritatem. Arg[umentum] (IV.) Quod non consonent sententiæ etiam veterum. Nam Ebraicis literis scripsisse plerique dicunt; | at ex Hieronymo colligere est, quod Chaldaico vel Syriaco scriptum fuerit. R[espondunt]. Hebraicum omninò fuisse characterem, quali etiam usi sunt collectores Talmudis Hierosolymitani, & Libri Sohar, in quibus tamen multæ reliquæ veteris istius idiomatis Hierosolymitani. Ebraicum verò non fuisse sermonem, nisi sensus supra exposito; Unde contradictio nulla. Arg[umentum] (V.) Syriaco Antiocheno idiomate, | quo conscripta est N.T. paraphrasis Syriaca scripsisse Matthæum non est verisimile, quia isto tempore familiaris erat Judæis idiotismus Hierosolymitanus, maximè discrepans ab Antiocheno. Responsionis. loco hic adduco, quæ Waltonus de hac materia scribit Apparatus sui prolegomeno 13 n. 5. 35

40

fol. 23ʳ Controversia (de Lingua, quâ usus fuerit Christus) facilè dirimi potest ||| concedendo, dialecto Antiochena, quæ Syriacæ nomen κατ' ἐξοχὴν jam obtinuit, & in qua scripta est versio Syriaca, Christum usum non fuisse; sed Targumica, seu Chaldæo-Hierosolymitana, quæ tamen cum eadem esset lingua cum Syriaca, ut omnes uno ore affirmant, verissime dici possit Christo linguam Syriacam vernaculam fuisse, eamque sacro ore conferasse: | cum tam Antiochenum quam Hierosolymitanum idioma esset Chaldaicum sive Syriacum, ut qui Atticè vel Ionicè scripserunt, dici possint Græce scripsisse, eo quod utraque dialectus sit græca. Item paulò post. n. 7. Cur Antiocheni hanc scripturæ formam â Chaldaica & Judaica variantem introduxerint causam hanc reddidit Fabricius Boderianus Præf. ad Lexic. Syriacum, ut scil. Antiocheni Christiani Evangelium, quo | ipsi utebantur ab illo Nazaræorum & Ebionitarum, quod literis Hebraicis sive Chaldaicis exaratum erat, distinguerent, nihilque se commune cum istis hæreticis habere, testarentur. Arg[umentum] (VI.) Textum primigenium, originalem, authenticum & θεόπνευσον libri alicujus perpetuo Ecclesiæ Canoni consecrati divinitus, quale est Evange-

5

10

---

60 Brian Walton's London Polyglot Bible with its extensive range of languages and the quality of its ancillary matter marked a peak in oriental scholarship in the Sixteenth Century. A copy is mentioned in the Library in Sulzbach in C.G. Düring's 1734 *Novum Inventarium Bibliothecae Sulzbaco-Palatino* (BSB Cbm 580 Repositorium A), p. 1#1a.

61 Guy Lefèvre de la Boderie contributed a *Syriac Lexicon* to the Antwerp Polyglot

SECTION VI

the same as *an autograph*, what conclusion should we reach about the other books of Scripture? But if ["authentic"] is understood as something which has authority, then Jerome clearly says he had seen one and had one and that from those amongst whom it had unique authority.

Argument (D): that the opinions even of the ancients do not agree. For many say [Matthew] wrote in Hebrew letters, | but from Jerome one gathers that [the Gospel] was written in Aramaic or Syriac script. They reply: the script was entirely Hebrew like that used by the collectors of the Jerusalem Talmud and the Zohar, in which however are found many traces of the old Jerusalem dialect. But Hebrew but was not the vernacular (other than in the sense explained above). So there is no contradiction.

Argument (E): the Antiochene Syriac dialect | in which the [Peshitta] Syriac translation of the New Testament Matthew is written is not very likely to have been written at that time when the Jerusalem dialect, which is very different from Antiochene [Syriac], was the Jews' vernacular. In place of an answer, here I adduce what Walton wrote about this material in the *Apparatus to his Prolegomenon* 13 note 5[60]: "The controversy (about which language Christ used) may easily be separated ‖ from the subsequent Antiochene dialect which, considering that it has now obtained the name of Syriac *tout court* [Greek: *kat'exochēn*] and in which is written the Syriac translation [of the New Testament], Christ did not use; but [he used rather] Targumic Aramaic or Chaldaeo-Jerusalemite, which however, since it is the same language as Syriac, as everyone unanimously agrees, it can most truely be said that Syriac was Christ's vernacular and consecrated by his holy lips, | since both the Antiochene and the Jerusalemite dialect is Chaldean [Aramaic] or Syriac. Similarly those who wrote in Attic or Ionic may be said to have written in Greek, since each is a dialect of Greek". From the same author [Walton]— a little after note 7: Fabricius Boderianus explains why | the Antiochans introduced this form of script [i.e. the Syriac script] which is different from Chaldean [Aramaic] script or Jewish [script] in his *Preface to a Syriac Lexicon*: namely so that the Antiochene Christians might distinguish the Gospel which they used from that of the Nazaraeans & of the Ebionites which was written in Hebrew or Chaldaean letters, so that they might be seen to have nothing in common with those heretics[61].

fol. 23r

Argument (F): the first copy, original, authentic and *theopneuso[s]* [Greek: inspired] of any book divinely consecrated by the perpetual canon of the

---

Bible. For this and his assertion that the Syriac script was invented to distinguish its users from Ebionites, see: Wilkinson, *The Kabbalistic Scholars*, op. cit., pp. 81–85.

lium Matthæi, vel interire penitus, vel ita evanescere saltem, ut | ab Eccle- 15
sia legi consulique non possit, in ejusque informationem cedere, nunquam
permissura fuisset divina providentia. R[espondunt]. (1.) Si permittente divina providentia cessavit illa Christianorum species ceu normatum, in cujus
gratiam scilicet scripta fuit; cur non permitteret providentia eadem, ut et
norma cessaret, nulli in posterum inter Græcos futura usui; præsertim si
pro Græcis substituta | fuit norma alia, quæ θεόπνευσος similiter ab antiqui- 20
tate fuit habita; & pro orientalibus in usum venerit textus Syriacus quasi
idem, mutatis saltem literis & adjectis vocalibus Antiochenis: Unde non
dici potest evanuisse vel interiisse Matthæi Evangelium, si tam conforme
remansit apographon: sicut dici non potest interiisse libros Legis; quamvis
charactere antiquo Cuthæo | non amplius sint in usu. Imò si divinæ pla- 25
cuit providentiæ, ut magna part populi Judaici in Palæstina ad Christi fidem
converteretur, inque professione hac tria vel quatuor usque secula contin-
uaret, permittere ne potuit eadem Dei providentia, ut ista gens scriptura
careret theopneusta sui idiomatis, in quo sacra celebrabant? Arg[umen-
tum] (VII.) accedit, quod Ebraica & Syriaca cum | adducuntur in Matthæo 30
explicentur græco idiomate: cum non sit verisimile in textu græco quid
additum fuisse, quod in Archetypo non fuerit. R[espondunt]. Nihil esse
absurdi, quod vel Matthæus purè Hebraica Syriacè; vel interpres Hieroso-
lymitana græcè, vel Antiocheni eadem Syriacè expresserint: cum re ipsa
nihil mutetur. Arg[umentum] (VIII.) Non tantùm Ebræis scribendum &
proponendum fuerat | Evangelium Christi, sed etiam gentilibus; quorum 35
longè plures ad Ecclesiam Christi pertinent, quam Ebræi. Itaque in originali eam sine dubio linguam adhibere voluit Spiritus S. quæ etiam gentilibus familiaris & cognita fuerat; qualis erat potius græca quam Syriaca.
R[espondunt]. Admittitur igitur implicitè, quod Ebræis aliquid scriptum
fuerit: nihil autem istis scriptum fuisse antiquitas edocet, quam Matthæi | 40
Evangelium: sicut Græcis primariò scriptum fuit Evangelium Lucæ: cum
cæteris & Matthæi versione; quod istis sufficiebat. Arg[umentum]. (IX.)

---

62   The ancient Hebrew script used before the "square" or "Assyrian" characters repute-
     dly introduced by Ezra (which we today call paleo-Hebrew), was named for the *kwty*,
     Cuthaei or "Cuthites" by the scholars of the Talmud. By this they meant the Samari-
     tans (2 Kgs 17.24). See Talmud Sanh. 21b. (For the term "Assyrian", see J. Talmud Megil-
     lah 1.71b.) For patristic mentions of the script, see Samuel Rolles Driver, *Notes on the
     Hebrew Text and the Topography of the Books of Samuel*, 2nd ed. (Oxford: Clarendon
     Press, 1966), pp. i–iii. Paleo-Hebrew script was used commonly by Moabites, Hebrews,

Church, such as is the Gospel of Matthew, either perished entirely or so wore out little by little that | the Church could neither read nor consult it. But Divine Providence would never have allowed the information it contained to be lost. They reply (1): if the Divine Providence allowed that type of Christians to cease, or a canonised work for the sake of which the [information] had evidently been written, why should not that same Providence permit that a canon should cease which would be of no future use amongst the Greeks. Especially if for the Greeks were substituted | another canon, which similarly from antiquity had been considered *theopneusos* [Greek: inspired] and [further, if] for the Easterners there had come into use the Syriac text, much the same, just with the letters changed and the Antiochene vocabulary added? Thus one cannot say that Matthew's gospel "wore out" or "perished", if the copy remained so conformed [to the original]. Just as one cannot say the Books of the Law have perished, just because they no longer use | the ancient Samaritan script.[62] Rather, if Divine Providence had decided that a great part of the Jewish population of Palestine should convert to Faith in Christ and continue in that profession for three or four centuries, would the same Providence of God have permitted that that people would lack inspired Scripture in its own dialect in which they celebrated the liturgy?

Argument (G): Additionally: consider that Hebrew and Syriac [words and phrases] | when they are translated in [the extant canonical] Matthew, are explained in *Greek* phrases. It is not likely that material has been added to the Greek text which had not been in the archetype. They reply: it is not unreasonable that either Matthew correctly expressed the Hebrew in Syriac, or a Jerusalem translator [did so] in Greek, or the Antiochenes themselves expressed the same thing in Syriac, since the essential matter is not at all changed.

Argument (H): the Gospel of Christ was written and circulated | not only amongst Hebrews, but also amongst Gentiles, far more of whom belonged to the Church of Christ than of Hebrews. And so, in the original, the Holy Spirit doubtless wished to use that language which was also familiar and known to the Gentiles; and that was Greek rather than Syriac. To which the repost is: So! it is implicitly admitted that the Hebrews *did* have something written, but Antiquity teaches us of nothing written by them other than the Gospel of Matthew. | So similarly, the Gospel of Luke was initially written for the Greeks with the other [Gospels], and the translation of Matthew, which was sufficient for them.

Aramaeans and Phoenecians. It is attested in some scriptural scrolls found in the Judaean Desert and on coins of Bar-Kokhba.

fol. 23ᵛ

Cum cætera scripta omnia N.T. in Originali Græce sint proposita, non est, quod citra omnem rationem solum hocce Evangelium Matthæi Græce scriptum negemus. R[espondunt]. Non tantum esse petitionem ‖ principii, quia & de Epistola ad Hebræos aliter testantur veteres: Sed & iterum revolvi absurdum illud, quod fidelibus ê Judæis Palæstinæ nulla data fuerit scriptura. Arg[umentum] (x.) Peribit certe auctoritas Græci textus Matthæi, si admittatur hypothesis de archetypo hebraico. R[espondunt]. Textum græcum propterea non expungi | ê canone, quia ab antiquis etiam receptus fuit   5
tanquam Spiritu S. inspirante conscriptus; sive id factum fuit â Jacobo juxta Athanasium; sive â Johanne juxta Theophylactum sive â Lucâ & Paulo juxta Anastasium; sive â Barnab[e] sive â Marco, sive ab ipso Matthæo juxta alios. Incertitudo enim Autoris sicut nec aliis, ita nec huic N.T. scripto id detrahit, quod ipsi tribuit ipsius | sensus veritas atque sanctitas. Argumentum   10
adhuc superest aliud (xi.) Nec Matthæum, nec alios novi Fœderis amanuenses Syriaca lingua scripsisse: nisi linguâ ingrata gentis ingratæ eos scripsisse arbitremur, quod certe non arbitrandum. Cum enim jam rejiciendus esset populus Judaicus, incongruum certe admodum fuisset, linguam eorum, sive vernaculam Syram, sive affinem Chaldaicam | eô dignitatis [elevare]⁶³, ut   15
lingua originalis foret Novi Testamenti incongruum certè, Evangelium scribere eorum lingua, qui præ omnibus terrarum orbis incolis Evangelium maximè spernerent atque oppugnarent. R[respondunt] Evangelium Matthæi non scriptum esse in gratiam Judæorum convertendorum, sed jam in Palæstina conversorum, prout supra ex antiquitate Ecclesiastica | allegavi-   20
mus, quo ipso totus nervus istius argumenti incisus est. Annon autem iisdem Græca lingua fuit vernacula? Minimè. Nec id evincit locus Talmudis Hierosolym. Megil. fol. 71.b. ubi græca lingua vocatur לעז i.e. vernacula. Nam לעז idem potius est ac barbarum, non verò patrium. Nec aliquid confert ad istud paradoxum, locus alter Talmud. Hieros. Sotah f. 21, b. quod quidam

---

63   Word unreadable, but presumably "elevare".
64   Eusebius, *Ecclesiastical History* 6.14. 2–3 quotes Clement of Alexandria in his *Hypotyposeis*: "[Clement] says [The Epistle to the Hebrews] is Paul's, but that it was written for the Hebrews in the Hebrew tongue and that Luke carefully [*philotimōs*] translated it and published it for the Greeks".
65   For Athanasius' suggestion of James, see his *Synopsis Scripturae sacrae* (attributed to Athanasius), §76 in *Patrologia Graeca*, vol. 28 (Paris: J-P Migne, 1857), col. 433; for Theophylact's suggestion of John, see his *Preface to the Gospel of Matthew*. For contemporary considerations of the others: Isaac Casaubon (1559–1614), *De rebus sacris et ecclesiasticis exercitationes XVI, ad cardinal. Baronii Prolegomena in Annales et primam*

SECTION VI 309

Argument (I): just because all other New Testament Scriptures were circulated in Greek in the original, it [does not follow] that it is beyond all reason for us to assert that only this Gospel of Matthew was not written in Greek. They reply: this is not only to beg the question ||| (because the ancients tes-   fol. 23ᵛ
tify also that the Epistle to the Hebrews [was written in Hebrew][64]), but also to repeat again the absurdity that no Scripture had been given to the faithful from among the Jews of Palestine.

Argument (J): the authority of the Greek text of the Matthew will certainly be destroyed if the hypothesis of a Hebrew archetype is admitted. The
5 reply is: The Greek text cannot on that account be removed | from the canon, because it also had been received by the ancients as written by the inspiration of the Holy Spirit; whether it had been made either by James (according to Athanasius), or by John (according to Theophylact), or by Luke and Paul (according to Anastasius), or by Barnabus, or by Mark, or by Matthew himself according to others[65]. Uncertainty over the author, with this as with
10 other New Testament texts, does not detract from | the truth and holiness of its [message].

One other argument remains (K): neither Matthew nor any of the other writers of the New Testament wrote in Syriac, else we would consider them to have written in the graceless language of a graceless people. This is out of the question! For since the Jewish people were already going to be rejected, it would be clearly quite incongruous for their language, whether the Syr-
15 iac vernacular or the related Chaldean [Aramaic], | to rise to such a point of dignity that it should be the original language of the New Testament! Incongruous indeed to write a Gospel in the language of those who, ahead of all the inhabitants of the earth, most vehemently spurned the Gospel and fought against it! The reply is: The Gospel of Matthew was *not* written to convert Jews but for those in Palestine who were already converts, just as we showed
20 above from Church History, | which in itself quite destroys this argument. But was not Greek the vernacular of these people? No. Nor is this proved by that place in the Jerusalem Talmud (Megil fol. 71.b) where the Greek language is called *lʿz i. e.* the vernacular, as *lʿz* means rather "barbarian", and not "native". Nor is anything contributed to this unexpected fact by that other passage in
25 the Jerusalem Talmud (Sotah f. 21.b) [which says] that certain in Caesarea |

---

partem (Frankfurt: curantibus Ruland, typis Ioan Bring, 1615), p. 343; and for Richard Simon's remarks in 1689 upon the status of the Greek text of Matthew see Andrew W.R. Hunwick, *Richard Simon Critical History of the Text of the New Testament* (Leiden: Brill, 2013), p. 81ff.

Cæsareæ | lectionem Audi, recitarint Hellenisticè. Tales enim fuerunt Hel- 25
lenist[i] qui linguam Hebraicam ignorabant, quales in provinciis extraneis
erant plurimi. Non autem sequitur, quod lingua Græca etiam in Palæstina
fuerit vernacula. Sed hæc sufficiant de lingua istius Evangelii primigen[ii].
Utinam autem in gratiam convertendorum ê gente vestrâ textus ille adhuc, | 30
prout antiquitùs extitit extaret! In illius locum jam tamen non tum adhiberi
debet Hebraicum illud Munsterianum, vel Tilianum; sed Syriacum moder-
num, literis Hebraicis impressum, cum idiomate antiquo Hierosolymitano
multum concordans.[66]

Cabb. Cat. *Quid autem nos monet Matthæi nomen, quod Doni | etymon* 35
involvit?

Christianus. Donorum & Charismatum Divinorum hanc esse naturam,
ut â commercio mundano avulsos Christo totos mancipent, ita ut, qui illa
possident non tam historicè quam imitativè ad vivum exhibeant Dominum
suum.

V. 1. *Descriptio Genealogica &.* כתבא דילידותה

Cabb. Cat. Qualis hic est titulus? Et annon vertendum esset. Liber de nativi- 40
tate?[67]

Christianus. Titulus est non totius Evangelii Matthæi; sed descriptionis
fol. 24ʳ hujus singularis ||| Asservabantur enim tum temporis partim publicè, partim
privatim tales Tabulæ Genealogicæ ad conservandam familiarum purita-
tem ab Esdra introductam; prout passim docent scripta vestra Talmudica. E

---

66 End of deletion.
67 The text is not underlined in the manusucript, probably due to Knorr's oversight.
68 I.e. provinces outside Judaea.
69 The sixteenth-century Hebrew Matthew was the work of Ibn Shaprut, a thirteenth century Jewish polemicist, which Sebastian Münster popularised with his *Evangelium Secundum Matthaeum*, op. cit.. Another text was discovered in Italy by Jean du Til-let, Bishop of Brieu, in 1553 which Mercier published in 1555. For the question of a Hebrew Matthew thought to be associated with Postel, see Wilkinson, *Orientalism*, op. cit., pp. 105–106. On the question in general, see George Howard's article in the *Anchor Dictionary of the Bible*, vol. 5, pp. 642–643 and his subsequent *Hebrew Gospel of Matthew*, 2nd ed. (Macon: Mercer University Press, 1995).
70 Knorr had himself produced just such an edition of the Syriac Peshitta New Testament in Hebrew letters in 1689. See on this, Vileno and Wilkinson, "Die Peshitta von 1684", art. cit. The utility of the Peshitta is alluded to in the letter of 21 March 1684 which Pfalzgraf Christian Augustus sent to Herzog Rudolf August von Braunschweig-Lüneburg (1627–1704) to accompany the fine edition of the *Kabbala Denudata* he sent him for his library

SECTION VI   311

recited the reading of the Shema in Greek, as they were Greek speakers, who did not know Hebrew, like many in foreign[68] provinces. It does not follow that the Greek language was the vernacular even in Palestine. Now this is enough about the language of this first gospel. But, for the sake of those of
30   your people yet to be converted, I would [wish] that that [Hebrew] text | still existed today as it did in the past! In its place however should be provided, not so much the Hebrew version [of Matthew] of Münster or of Jean du Tillet[69], but the modern Syriac printed in Hebrew letters, which has so much in common with the ancient dialect of Jersualem[70].]

Kabbalist Catechumen Now what does Matthew's name teach us? What
35   gift | does the word conceal?[71]

Christian [It teaches that] it is the nature of divine gifts and charisms that they free those torn from the commerce of this world[72] entirely for Christ, so that those who possess them, may exhibit their Lord not so much by apeing the past but by imitating him in their lives.

Verse 1

A record of the genealogy etc. *ktbʾ dylydwth*

40   **Kabbalist Catechumen** What sort of a title is this? And should it not be translated, "The Book of the Nativity"?

Christian This is not the title of the whole Gospel of Matthew, but only of this specific record ‖. For at that time such records of genealogy were kept,   fol. 24ʳ both publically and privately, to preserve the purity of families which was established by Ezra,[73] just as your Talmudic writings teach throughout. This

---

in Wolfenbüttel (which is in fact named for his father (1579–1666)). The book is still in the library there. "... vnd dann anbey dieses Buch nunmehro auf eine solche Weise herausgegeben ist, dass dieienigen, so sich in etwas auf die Hebreische und Chaldeische Sprache verstehen (zumahlen, wenn sie sich das Syrische Neue Testament, so auch zur selbigen Zeit, und selbiger Land geschrieben ist, anbey bekand machen) darinnen gar leicht sollen fortkommen koennen: ...". Text in Finke, *Sulzbach im 17. Jahrhundert*, op. cit., pp. 206–207.

71   The Kabbalist Catechumen has here interpreted the name Matthew as meaning "a gift from the Lord".

72   A reference to Matthew's past as a tax-collector.

73   John Lightfoot, *Miscellanies and the Harmony of the Gospels*, op. cit., pp. 172–173: "Public registers of the tribe of Judah, and of the other tribes that adhered to it, were reserved even in the captivity and forward; as may be collected by the books of Ezra and Nehemiah: and from Luke's telling, that Anna was of the tribe of Aser,—and Paul's, that himself was of the tribe of Benjamin. From one of these doth Matthew fetch the latter end of his genealogy, and Luke from another the beginning of his, having then

quibus hæc una est, quam Matthæus historiæ suæ præmittit. Josephum quidem concernens: sed quæ illius ætatis homines convincere satis | poterat, Jesum quamvis in Galilæa habitaret, filium tamen Davidis esse posse: Unde ulterior enascebatur occasio inquirendi in veram historiam nativitatis ejusdem. Monentur autem fideles animæ in genuinas notas vitæ suæ (quæ divina esse debet, & Christum forma exprimere Gal. 4, 19.) quàm accuratissimè inquirere.

Cabb. Cat. Sed objicient nostrates; 1. Dubium non in eo versari, an | inquirere[74] *in Galilæa reperiri potuerit genus Davidicum; 2. nec sufficere, ut descriptio Genealogica occasionem præbeat ulterius inquirendi. 3. Sed tabularum istarum finem semper fuisse, ut clarè constaret de Nati prosapia: quod tamen ista non præstet. 4. Non sequi enim; Josephus fuit filius Davidis, ergo & Jesus Josephi nutritius; de illius sanguine haud natus. Nec 5. colligi consanguinitatem ex matrimonio: cum | & Elisabetha sanguine juncta dicatur Mariæ, Luc. 1, 36. & nupta tamen esset Sacerdoti. Adde, quod 6. etiam quatuordecim non sint generationes in classe tertiâ; quod tamen asseveret stemmatographus: Quæ mera sint vitia, in Genealogiis Hebræorum nunquiam tolerata.*

Christianus. Si cum aliquo ex infidelibus gentis tuæ mihi res sit, ipsius mihi liceat uti principiis; | quod nempe 1. Animæ humanæ existant antequam nascantur; 2. sæpius nasci possint. 3. quod sensus literalis in Scriptura non sit negligendus, licet ad mysteria transiri queat. Unde quid absurdi, si dixerim Josephum revera fuisse Mariæ patrem; sed ita, ut hæc ipsius filia paulò ante mortua quidem fuerit, sed mox renata ab Heli (Luc. 3, 23.) & sic

---

the civil records to avouch for them, if they should be questioned; which the Jews now wanting, do unjustly cavil."

74   Deleted word.
75   For an introduction to Early Modern debates on these genealogies, see Kirsten Macfarlane, "The Biblical Genealogies of the King James Version (1611): Their Purpose, Sources and Significance", *The Library* (7th series) 19, 2 (June 2018): pp. 131–158, especially pp. 131–141.
76   A point made long ago in the Christian tradition by Origen. Knorr's argument is highly structured here. He asks that the three initial points are conceded. He then cites the Zoharic treatment of reincarnation within the context of a levirate marriage. If a deceased man's wife marries his brother it is possible that the dead man's soul will be reincarnated in their offspring (thus preserving his name in Israel). In this case souls who were once spouses may become parent and child. So why could the situation not be reversed and souls which are spouses not have previously have been parent and child? He then hypothesises that Joseph the son of Eli had a daughter who died. Joseph subsequently married Mary into whom the dead child's soul had passed. Mary was the mother of Jesus. Joseph might legitimately—in as far as he was Jesus' grandfather (the

is one of those, which Matthew has placed at the beginning of his Gospel. It concerns Joseph, but was sufficiently capable of convincing the people of that time, | that although Jesus lived in Galilee, he could nonetheless be a Son of David. From this arose the subsequent opportunity of investigating the true story of his birth. For faithful souls sought to investigate as accurately as possible the genuine records of his life (which must be divine and express Christ by their form Gal 4.19).[75]

Kabbalist Catechumen But our teachers would object: (1) that one cannot escape the doubt whether | the family of David *could* be found in Galilee. (2) This is inadequate as a genealogical description to provide the basis of further enquiry. (3) The point of these [genealogical] tables was always that there could be clear agreement about the lineage of the neonate, which this account does not provide! (4) For it does not follow that because Joseph was a Son of David, therefore Jesus, whom Joseph merely brought up and was not born of his blood, was also one. Nor (5) can consanguinity be established from marriage: although | Elisabeth is said to be related by blood to Mary (Lk 1.36) she was nonetheless married to a priest. Additionally (6) there were *not* fourteen generations in the third group [of the genealogy], which however is what the writer of the genealogy asserts. These are pure errors which are never tolerated in the genealogies of the Hebrews!

Christian If I was dealing with one of the unbelievers amongst your people, I should be allowed to resort to first principles, | namely that: (1) human souls exist before they are born; and (2) they can be born several times. That (3) the literal sense in Scripture should not be neglected; one may be able to pass over [from it] to mysteries[76].

So what would be so absurd, if I had said that Joseph had truly been the father of Messiah; but specifically in the sense that his daughter, who had died a little before, was soon reborn from Heli (Lk 3.23)[77] and was thus

---

soul in Mary had previously been in his deceased daughter)—claim to be the father of Jesus. That is, because he was (in this way) his maternal grandfather. Note the audacity of this and also the systematic deployment of reincarnation to solve exegetical difficulties in the genealogy of Jesus in the New Testament.

[77] In Matthew Joseph is the son of Jacob, in Luke the son of Eli. If Joseph's dead daughter is reincarnated from Eli it is easy to see how, now as Joseph's father-in-law, he might reasonably be called his father—thus explaining the apparent contradiction between the genealogies. The recourse to the doctrine of the revolution of souls also solves the outstanding problem of why there are only thirteen generations in the last section of Matthew's genealogy. Once the revolution of the dead child's soul is allowed the extra generation is found as Joseph was her father.

desponsata Josepho. Si enim fieri potest, ut qui | fuerant conjuges, mox fiant filius & mater; quod in casu Leviratus factum fuisse expressè docet Liber Sohar, quidni fieri posset, ut qui fuerant filia & pater, mox evadant conjuges; præsertim suppositâ perpetuâ virginitate Mariæ? Atque sic primò propriè loquendo in tertiâ classe sunt quatuordecim generationes, cum & inter Josephum & Mariam intercesserit generatio. 2. proprie id efficit tabula | hæc, ut Jesum filium Davidis fuisse ostendat, ab Avo scilicet Josepho. 3. Ita discernenda sunt verba tabulæ â verbis Evangelistæ, ut cum generatione Josephi finem habeat tabula: quæ autem sequuntur, â Matthæo narrentur ceu Propheta (eodem sensu, qui extat Joh. 4, 19.) cui inspirante divino Spiritu hoc innotuerit paternitatis Josephi mysterium. (vid. Excerpta Libri Sohar de | Revolutionibus Animarum Cent.1. Loc. 54. usque ad 61.)

Jesu Messiæ &. דישוע משיחא

Christianus. Antiqua & genuina pronunciatio nominis יֵשׁוּעַ hodie in occidente nullibi in usu est: Unde mirum non est, neglecto Salvatoris nomine illius quoque vitam negligi. Literam autem primam recte exprimunt Latino-Germani | per suum Je. Secundam Galli per suum CE caudatum, per ç (quod sonum literæ S seu[78] ab initio Syllabæ duplicat: Sic enim literam Hebræorum שׁ cum puncto dextro semper expresserunt Græci per σ et non per χ.) Tertiam Græci per suum ου seu omicron Ypsilon; quod est OU Gallicum & U Germanicum. Quartum Arabes soli, expresso quàm lenissimè ex imo gutture, sono literæ G, ita ut Ain haud incongruè dici posset | Gimel gutturale; prout & LXX Interpretes idem alicubi per ע expresserunt in vocibus Gaza, Gazæi, Gomor, Gomorrha, Gothoniel &c. Igitur anomola quidem, sed accuratior[79] scri- |||-ptio illius esset Jesugh(a). (videantur plura de hoc nomine in Adumbratione Cabbalæ Christianæ, c. 11. §. 2.[80])

---

78   Deleted word.
79   In the right bottom corner appears a Hebrew letter ז presumably an indication of binding or pagination.
80   Cf. *supra*, footnote 164, pp. 180–181.
81   That is, as we have seen, the dead brother returns to life as the child of his former wife and his brother. The Zohar chapter (*Sava de Mishpatim*) on the Torah portion *Mishpatim* (Ex 21.1–24.18) is in great part devoted to levirate marriage understood in the context of "revolution" of souls. *The Zohar Pritzker Edition*, vol. 5, ed. by Daniel C. Matt (Standford University Press, 2009), 2.99b.

SECTION VI   315

25 betrothed to Joseph? For if it could happen that those | [souls], who had [once] been spouses, soon became son and mother—which is what the Zohar[81] expressly teaches happened in the case of Levirate marriage—why should it not happen that those [souls] who were father and daughter should shortly thereafter emerge as spouses?—especially on the assumption of the perpetual virginity of Mary.

And so, to speak first of all specifically about the third group [of the genealogy], there *are* fourteen generations, since [as has just been demonstrated] there was a generation between Joseph and Mary. (2) Specifically,
30 also, this table | achieves a demonstration that Jesus was a Son of David [by descent] from his grandfather i.e. Joseph. (3) The words of the table should be distinguished from the words of the Evangelist, in such a way that the table comes to an end with the generation of Joseph, but that the events which follow are told by Matthew or the Prophet (in the same sense as that found in Jn 4.19) who being inspired by the divine Holy Spirit recorded this mystery of the fatherhood of Joseph (See Excerpts from the Book of Zohar
35 about | the Revolution of Souls Cent. I Loc. 54 up to 61.)

Jesu Messiae etc. *dyšwʿ mšyḥʾ*

Christian The ancient and authentic pronunciation of the [Hebrew] name *Yeshuaʿ* is nowhere in use today in the West. So it is not surprising that where the Saviour's name has been neglected, his life is neglected also. The first let-
40 ter is correctly expressed by the Latin or German |/j/. The second, by the French /ç/ or /s/. (It is the same sound as /s/ at the beginning of a syllable. Thus the Hebrew letter *shin* with a dot on the right is always written by the Greeks as *sigma* and not as *xi*). The third letter is the Greek /ou/ or omicron [followed by] upsilon; which is /ou/ in French and /u/ in German. The fourth letter the Arabs alone express as gently as possible from the bottom of the throat with the sound of the letter /g/ so that ʿain [ʿ] can plausibly be described as a guttural *gimel*, to the extent that the LXX [Greek Septuagint] translators expressed this same letter [ʿayin] in some place by *gamma* in words [like] Gaza, Gazaei, Gomor Gomorrha Gothoniel[82] etc.. So [there is here something of an] anomaly, but a more accurate ||| transcription of this   fol. 24ᵛ
[name] would be *Jesugh(a)*. There is much more said about this name in *Abumbratio Cabbalae Christianae*, chap. 11, § 2.

---

82   Judith 6.15.

Cabb. Cat. *Sed & Messiæ potius nomen, qui convertendorum Judæorum studiosi esse volunt quam Christi, adhibere deberent: eò quod illud (1.) proprium quasi sit nostræ | Genti, cui hic promissus est: & (2.) proximius per illud pateat aditus ad vaticinia, Dan. 9, 25.26; Psal. 89, 52; Psal. 2, 2; Psal. 45, 5; Jes. 61, 1.2.*

Christianus. *Imò sic melius attingeretur scopus in quem collimant loca Act. 2, 36; 1 Joh. 2, 22; 1. Cor. 3, 11. porrò ad arcanas etiam Philo-Cabbalistæ meditationes, & fideles ad memoriam gratiosissimæ illius â capite suo in se derivatæ unctionis, (de qua 2. Cor. 1, 21; | 1. Joh. 2, 20.27; Psal. 133, 3.) peregrini hujus nominis sono eo citius recenti quadam impressione invitarentur.*

Filii David &c. ברה דדויד

Christianus. *Hoc apud vestrates est Nomen proprium Messiæ, conf. Matth. 9, 27; c. 12, 23; c. 15, 22; c. 20, 30.31; c. 21, 9.15; c. 22, 42.45; Marc. 10, 47.48; c. 12, 35; Luc. 18, 38.39; c. 20, 41.4[2]; | Luc. 1, 32; c. 3, 31; Joh. 7, 42; Rom. 1, 3; 2 Tim. 2, 8; Ap. 22, 16.* [**Cabb. Cat.**][83] *Sed â Doctoribus vestris*[84] *duo describuntur Messiæ, unus filius Joseph, & alter filius David: quid hîc consilii?*

---

83   Added in the left margin: Cabb. Cat. (which involves a change of speaker).
84   Correction above the line: vestris replaced by nostris (to be understood in the light of the change of speakers).
85   For the doctrine of the two messiahs, see Gustaf Dalman, *Der leidende und der sterbende Messias der Synagoge: Im ersten nachchristlichen Jahrtausend* (Berlin: H. Reuther, 1888) and the comprehensive David C. Mitchell, *Messiah ben Joseph* (Newton Means: Campbell, 2016). As well as passages in the Talmud and Midrashim, the Messiah ben Joseph is found in the *Book of Zerubbabel* (Martha Himmelfarb, *Jewish Messiahs in a Christian Empire A History of the Book of Zerubbabel* (Harvard University Press, 2017), pp. 99–119 on this Messiah's death here.) Abraham Abulafia used the notion of these two messiahs to contrast the Messiah ben Joseph who represents the body and Jesus (Joseph being Jesus' father), with the Messiah ben David, Abulafia himself. (Robert Sagerman, *The Serpent Kills Or the Serpent Gives Life. The Kabbalist Abraham Abulafia's Response to Christianity* (Leiden: Brill, 2011), p. 208; Moshe Idel, "Abraham Abulafia on the Jewish Messiah and Jesus" in Id., *Studies in Ecstatic Kabbalah* (Albany: Suny, 1988), pp. 45–61, at pp. 53–55 and 59–60. Both Luria himself and Haim Vital were considered by Safed kabbalists (or even considered themselves) to be the incarnation of Messiah ben Joseph in their time: Arthur Green, "Nahman of Bratslav's Messianic Strivings" in *Essential papers in Messianic Movements and Personalities in Jewish History*, edited by Marc Saperstein (New York University Press, 1992), pp. 389–432 at pp. 400–406 and Id., *Tormented Master: A Life of Rabbi Nathan of Bratslav* (University of Alabama Press, 1979), pp. 197–198. These pages note the association of the biblical and kabbalistic Joseph with Messiah ben Joseph in Lurianic sources (Cf. *Shaar ha Gilgulim*, chapter 13), Nathan of Gaza and other Sabbateans and also in the writings of Moses Hayyim Luzzato); D. Tamar, "Luria and Vital on the Messiah ben Joseph" (in Hebrew), *Sefunot* 7

SECTION VI   317

Kabbalist Catechumen But those who want to be active in converting Jews should use the name of Messiah rather than of Christ because (1) it is, as it were, proper to our | people, to whom he was promised; and (2) because its use facilitates a closer approach to the prophecies Dan 9.25, 26; Ps 89.52; Ps 2.2; 45.5; Isa 61. 1,2 [where the Hebrew word is used].

Christian Yes. In this way the goal towards which the passages Acts 2.36; 1Jn 2.22; 1Cor 3.11 aspire would be achieved much better and also [the goal to which] the philo-kabbalistic meditations upon the mysteries [which are] faithful to the memory of that most gracious anointing flowing down from his head over his body (concerning which 2Cor 1.21; | 1Jn 2.20, 27; Ps 133.3.) invite, [would be achieved] more quickly by the sound of this foreign name [Messiah] than by an more recent expression [Christ].

Son of David etc. brh ddwd

Christian This [Son of David] is the proper name of Messiah among your teachers Cf. Mt 9.27; 12.23; 15.22; 20.30, 31; 21.9, 15; 22.42, 45; Mk 10.47, 48; 12.35; Lk 18.38, 39; 20.41, 42; Lk 1.32; 3.31; Jn 7.42; Rm 1.3; 2Tim 2.8; Rev 22.16. |

Kabbalist Catechumen But our scholars describe *two* Messiahs, one the Son of Joseph and the other the Son of David; what [do you have to say] about this opinion?[85]

(1963): pp. 169–177. Arguing that Luria did see himself in this way, there is *Sefer Toledoth ha-Ari*, edited by Meir Benayahu (Jerusalem: Hebrew University Press, 1967), p. 199 and p. 258 (where Luria is said to die for the sins of others). Also, Hayyim Vital, *Shaar ha-Amidah* (Koretz, 1784), chapter 19, p. 526 which refers to Luria as Messiah Son of Joseph. Knorr indicates (folio 25ʳ) that he had collected Zoharic passages in *Excerpta* Cent. I Loc. 62 to 91 to illustrate the doctrine. Some probable passages may be found conveniently in Mitchell, *Messiah ben Joseph*, pp. 236–239. Amongst Christians, the doctrine was noted by Nicholas of Lyra (†1340) in his *Quaestiones contra hebraeos*, unpaginated *ad fin*: "Proper scripturas quae manifeste leguuntur de Christi humilitate et passion et propter illas quae loquuntur de eius eminate et postate, expectant duos messias, unum qui dicitur filius Joseph et ille passurus est et occidendus, alium filium David qui messiam filium Joseph resuscitabit et regnum Israel restaurabit." (*Biblia Cum Postillis Nicolai de Lyra ... Quaestiones disputatae contra Hebraeos* (Nuremburg: Anton Kolberger, 1485)). The Jewish convert to Christianity Anthonius Margaritha (1490–1542) rejected the doctrine, contrasting the simplicity of Christian doctrine with the later complications introduced by the rabbis. He considered the Jews lack of a homeland as evident proof that the one Messiah had come (Michael T. Walton, *Anthonius Margaritha and the Jewish Faith: Jewish Life and Conversion in Sixteenth Century Germany* (Detroit: Wayne State University, 2012), p. 43). Amongst the Christian kabbalists, Guillaume Postel took an interest in Messiah ben Joseph especially in his Hebrew Tractate *Ta'am HaTe'anim* which is now published with general bibliography on the topic, Guillaume Postel, *Tractate Ta'am HaTe'anim* (in Hebrew), edited by Judith Weiss (Jerusalem: Magnes,

[**Christianus.**][86] Ego quidem genuinum illius traditionis sensum hunc esse putarem, non duo fore individua; sed unius subjecti duplicem statum & adventum. Rectè ergò Jesus Nazarænus Messias quoque filius David[87] diceretur: (1.) Patris sui | putatitii ratione; quem supra Avum ipsius fuisse supposuisti[88]. (2.) ratione ipsius Josephi, filii Jaacob, quem ultimam suam revoltionem habuisse in hoc Josepho ad Luc. 1, 27. suspicati sumus. (3.) autem hic mysterium occurrit aliud: sicut enim Messias dicitur Rex super domum David Luc. 1, 32, 69. ita filius Joseph (l.) Ephraim idem etiam est ac Rex super domum Joseph: Regnum nempe illud secundarium | idololatricum Ephraimitarum, quo præfigurabantur Gentes idololatr[æ] externâ tantum specie ad Messiam conversi; prout illi Jehovam professi: Unde quicquid dicitur de Messia filio Joseph, etiam mors etc. applicari posset ad adventum Messiæ primum, cujus periodus adhuc durat, durabitque usque ad finem 1260. dierum apocalypticorum. Adventu autem potissimum secundario, | quem denotat nomen Schiloh Gen. 49, 10 (quasi â secundinis, post quas tranquillitas â doloribus Messianis.) Idem secundum excellentiam, dici poterit Filius

---

2018). Knorr would have found a note on the doctrine in Buxtorf's *Lexicon Chaldaicum*, s.v. משח col. 1267–1273, on col. 1273: *"Perro Messias duplex a Iudaeis fugitur: unus … Messias filium Joseph, alter … Messias filium Davidis. Priori tribunt quae humilia de Messia in Scriptura dicuntur; alteri, quae gloriosa. Prior bella geret & morietur; alter vivet in saeculum. Vide R. Sal Jesa 24v18. Messias ben Joseph vocatur etiam ben Ephrajim, qui fuit Josephi filius"*. A thesis defended before Christoph Cellarius by Johann Ferber was entitled *Specimen Anti-Judaicum de Gemino quem Judaei praestolantur Messia* (Weißenfels, 1668) and argued that there was only one Messiah. Knorr similarly takes the view that there is only one messiah, but integrates the two comings of the one Messiah into a chronological schema which allows for a Jewish messianic kingdom. The subject was also discussed by Gustav Peringer, *Dissertatio Philologia de Messia Judaico* (Stockholm: Nicolai Wankiif, 1676), pp. 56–71 (which is the whole of chapter 7 devoted to the subject).

86 Correction in the left margin: Cabb. Cat. replaced by Christianus.
87 Correction above the line: David replaced by Joseph
88 Correction above the line: supposuisti replaced by supposui
89 The quotation here is from 2 Kgs 11.28 where it is used of the first king of the Northern Kingdom (Jeroboam) who was an Ephraimite.
90 For this form of the divine name, see Robert J. Wilkinson, *Tetragrammaton. Western Christians and the Hebrew Name of God from the Beginnings to the Seventeenth Century* (Leiden: Brill, 2015), pp. 210–212. Knorr once again refers to Christian groups he evidently believed were converted "in external appearance only".
91 These are taken from Rev 12.6 where they are understood by Knorr as a period (600–1860 A.D.) between the two advents, corresponding to the Woman's' Sojourn in the

Christian I would consider the genuine sense of this tradition not to be that there will be two individuals, but a double status and a double advent of just one subject. Correctly therefore, Jesus of Nazareth, Messiah, is also said to be the Son of Joseph: (1) by reason of | his putative Father, whom above I supposed to be his Grandfather; (2) by reason of Joseph himself, son of Jacob, whom we suspected had his last incarnation in this Joseph (see on Lk 1.27 above). (3) However another hidden teaching arises: for just as Messiah is called 'king over the House of David' (Lk 1.32, 69), so the son of Joseph (Ephraim) is also similarly called the "king over the House of Joseph"[89]. That kingdom, of course, was the second-rate kingdom | of the idol-worshipping Ephraimites [i.e. the Kingdom of Israel rather than the Kingdom of Judah] by which the idolatrous Gentiles were prefigured, converted to Messiah in external appearance only, just as they [the Ephraimites] [deceitfully] confessed Jehovah[90]. From this we can conclude something about Messiah the Son of Joseph: even death etc. can be applied to the coming of the first Messiah whose period has lasted right up until now and will last until the end of the 1260 apocalyptic days[91]. [These will terminate] most importantly with his second advent | which is denoted by the name Shiloh in Gen 49.10 (as if "Shiloh" meant "after-birth" after which [there will be] tranquillity following the birth-pains of Messiah[92]). The same with respect to excellence

---

Wilderness described in Revelation. Knorr's prophetic interpretation of the Revelation may be immediately and conveniently grasped from the chart found in *Christian Knorr von Rosenroth Apokalypse-Kommentar*, op. cit., pp. 8–19.

92 The mention of "Shiloh" in Gen 49.10 is a notorious *crux interpretum*. For modern views, see John Adney Emerton, "Some Difficult Words in Genesis 49", in *Words and Meanings. Essays Presented to David Winton Thomas*, edited by Peter R. Ackroyd and Barnabas Lindars (Cambridge University Press, 1968), pp. 81–94. The use of Shiloh here as a name (as in the KJV), however, seems no older than Sebastian Münster in 1534. The versions (Septuagint, Vulgate, Peshitta) commonly take the half-line as meaning something like "[until he come] whose it is" and both the Targums and the Talmud tend to understand something similar of Messiah. An understanding of the name in terms of after-birth is thus initially surprising. An explanation is however found in William Robertson's, *Thesaurus Linguae Sanctae Compendiose scil. contractum* (London: Samuel Roycroft, 1680), p. 1196 a, b: "*R. Bechai scribit: Schilo i.e. filius eius, qui nascetur ex secundis mulieris, juxta viam omnium qui nascuntur: estque vox desumpta ex significatione vocis bšlyth Deut 28.57. Quod autem potius dicit šylwt quam bnw, eo innuit Jacob se de Messia perculiariter loqui etc. Vel h non est affectum pronomen et vocatur Messias kat'exochēn Schilo, quasi tranquillus et aeternae tranquilitatis author aut quod singulari modo ex secundis tantum, sine viri.*" ("R. Bechai wrote: Shilo i.e his son, who was born from the afterbirth of a woman, in the fashion of all who are born. The word is derived from the meaning of *bšlyth* Deut 28.57. However that [Jacob] says *šylwt* rather

David, i.e. Schlomoh (prout exponit nomen Schiloh Gen. 49, 10[93] textus Samaritanus:) adeò ut tunc implenda sint omnia, de feliciore statu Messiano vaticinia, tam pristini quàm Novi Fœderis. [**Cabb. Cat.**][94] *Porrò autem quæstio est | quid propriè hîc denotetur nomine Filii?* 35

Christianus. Vox illa idem denotat ac si diceretur ê posteris David, ut patet è Joh. 7, 42; Rom. 1, 3; 2 Tim. 2, 8; Ap. 22, 16; c. 5, 5. item successor Davidis ut colligitur ex Act. 15, 16; Apoc. 3, 7; Luc, 1, 32.69. item promissus Davidi, 2. Sam. 3, 12. item antitypus Davidis juxta Ezech. 34, 23.24; c. 37, 24; Hos. 3, 5; Jer. 30, 9. etc. (sub qua | significatione etiam Nomen Filii Joseph denotare posset, 40 Antitypum Joseph.)

Cabb. Cat. *Sed mysterium tamen subesse videtur aliud, quod ego tanquam conversus ê gente Hebræorum juxta nostra exponerem principia. Nimirum, quod in beatâ Virgine simul etiam revoluta & ultimo restituta fuerit Nephesch seu Psyche Davidis, ut et Nephesch seu Psyche Adam Protoplastæ, unde |* 45 *constitutus fuerit Spiritus vitalis Messiæ seu Archæus ille Messiani corporis, ita ut impletum nunc fuerit antiquum illud Doctorum nostrorum, quod literis nominis* א"ד"ם *denotetur* א"ד"ם *&* ד"ו"ד *&* מ"שיח, *quia in Messia futura esset tam Adami, quàm Davidis Revolutio. Quo etiam pertinet locus ille Libri Sohar*

fol. 25ʳ *in Gen. c. 232 ||| Cremon. Messias Rex, sive ê viventibus sive ê de mortuis oriatur, David vocabitur. Adde, quod & de Davide dicunt nostrates: Ipsum fuisse revolutionem Adami (vid. Yalkut Rubeni titul. David n. 3.5.10.) ille autem, â quo constituitur & traducitur Spiritus vitalis Filii, vocatur istius Pater. Et hæc vide-*

---

than *bnw* [his son] hints that he is specifically speaking of Messiah etc. Either both the /h/ is not a possessive suffix and Messiah is called *tout court* Shilo as if he were peaceful and the author of eternal peace, or because he was born from the afterbirth alone, without [the intervention] of a man.") The Spanish exegete Baḥya (Beḥai) ben Asher ibn Halawa (1255–1340) made use of Kabbalah in exposition in his Torah commentary. It was first printed in Naples in 1492 and repeatedly thereafter. The ten supercommentaries it attracted indicate its popularity with Jewish scholars and Robertson's *Thesaurus* indicates that it was known to Christian Hebraists.

93   Deletion: Gen. 49, 10 (in order to avoid repetition).
94   Added in the left margin: Cabb. Cat. (which involves a change of speaker).
95   The Samaritan transcript of the Hebrew text reads *sheloh*, "whose it is". This word however is often glossed as "peace" and this forms an etymological link with the name Solomon. A late but interesting example of this interpretation is found in John Wilson, "A Visit to the Samaritans", *The Visitor* (London: The Religious Tract Society, 1847), pp. 407–410, at p. 409 where Dr John Wilson engages in dialogue with a Samaritan: "W. What do you think of the passage, 'The sceptre shall not depart from Judah, nor

could have been said of the Son of David i. e. Solomon (as the Samaritan text explains the name *Shiloh*[95]) to the extent that then were fulfilled all the prophecies of the happier Messianic state both of the Old and the New Testaments.

Kabbalist Catechumen But the question is, | what does the name Son properly denote here?

Christian The word means the same as if were said "from the descendants of David" as is clear from Jn 7.42; Rm 1.3; 2 Tim 2.8; Rev 22.16; 5.5. It is used of the successor of David as is gleaned from Acts 15.16; Rev 3.7; Lk 1.32, 69. Also the one promised to David 2 Sam 3.12. And further, the antitype of David according to Ezek 34. 23, 24; 37.24; Hos 3.5; Jer 30.9 etc.. (Under which | meaning too, the name Son of Joseph could also denote the antitype of Joseph.)

Kabbalist Catechumen But another secret teaching seems to be hidden here, which I, although converted from the people of the Hebrews,[96] shall explain according to our principles. It is amazing that in the Blessed Virgin at one and the same time was the final reincarnation of the Nefesh or Psyche of David and also of the Nefesh or Psyche of Adam Kadmon. From this was formed the vital spirit of Messiah or the Archaeus of the Messianic body, in such a way that now has been fulfilled the ancient teaching of our Sages that the consonants of the name *'adam* denote *'adam* & *dwyd* & *msyḥ*, because in Messiah will be the reincarnated souls of both Adam and David. Also relevant here that passage of the Book Zohar on Genesis chap. 23 (Cremona edition) ‖: "Messiah the king, whether he rises from among the living or from the dead, will be called David". Add further that our teachers also say of David that he will be the reincarnation of Adam (see Yalkut Rubeni titul. David note 3, 5, 10). Now [generally] he from whom was composed and transmitted the vital spirit of the son is called his Father. And this seems to

fol. 25ʳ

---

a lawgiver from between his feet, until Shiloh come; and unto him shall the gathering of the people be?' To whom does this apply? Priest. 'Don't say Shiloh, but Shilah.' W. 'Take the word in either form you please.' Priest. 'Shalah is equivalent to Shalamah, (Solomon) [the peaceful one.]' W. 'How do you make the passage agree with the interpretation?' Priest. 'The sceptre did not depart from Judah till the days of Solomon, till the days of his son Rehoboam, as you may see even from those unworthy historical books that are in the hands of the Jews'".

96 Here it is clear that the *persona* of the Kabbalist Catechumen considers himself to have been already converted.

tur specialis illa esse ratio, quare non | tantum Filius David dicatur Jesus: sed & Filium Adam toties[97] *ipsum nominaverit idem: de quo suo loco Matth. 8, 20.*

Christianus. Nostrum interim est Jesus intueri ut Messiam Filium David, i.e. ut Regem nostrum; obediendo nempe præceptis ejus amorosis (quod innuit nomen David.) & militando cum ipso contra hostes spirituales, & sequendo ipsum in exilio, ut digni evadamus | cum ipso extolli in gloriæ regno. [Loca autem nonnulla ê Libro Sohar, ubi de utroque Messia agitur, evolvi possunt in Parallelismis atque Excerptis Soharisticis ad Nov. Testamentum.[98] Cent. 1. Loc. 62. usque ad 91.].

Filii Abraham ברה דאברהם

Christianus. Sensus quidem esse potest, quod Jesus dicatur filius Abraham, tanquam | originem ab eo ducens, eique promissus specialiter ceu tali, â quo Exordium habebat Fœdus antiquum.

Cabb. Cat. *Sed & subintelligi potest David, quod fuerit filius Abraham; prout in aliis Genealogiis relatio filiationis semper ad proximum spectat. Ubi sensus quidem planè idem prodit quoad literam: sed quoad mysterium id videtur subinnui, quod in | Davide aliquid Abrahami revolutum fuerit.* [**Christianus.**][99] Et quoad Theologiam secretiorem genus describi videtur virtutum illarum, unde prodit conformitas Christi: qui sunt Amor; (quod subindicat Davidis nomen) & quidem talis, qui natus sit ê Fide, (quod Abrahami mentio denotare videtur.) Quod autem sub Abrahamo allegoricè & antiqui gentis nostræ[100] Doctores intellexerint, Animam; specimina Excerptorum docent Cent. 1. loc. 92 | & sequentibus.

---

97   Added above the lline: se
98   Correction: Parallelismis atque Excerptis Soharisticis ad Nov. Testamentum replaced by Excerptis
99   Added in the right margin: Christian.
100 Correction above the line: nostræ replaced by vestræ
101 Jesus is called "son of Adam" in Lk 3.38. The New Testament phrase "Son of Man" probably derives from Dan 7.13, 14, though notoriously there appears to be no Jewish apocalyptic figure with a fixed identity and this name. Ragnar Leivestad, "Exit the Apocalyptic Son of Man", *New Testament Studies* 18 (1971): pp. 243–267; Geza Vermes, "The Use of *bar nasha / bar nash* in Jewish Aramaic" in *An Aramaic Approach to the Gospels and Acts*, edited by Matthew Black, 3rd ed. (Oxford University Press, 1967),

be the special reason why Jesus is not only called | Son of David but also Son of Adam [*i. e.* Son of Man] every time he names himself. And similarly [he called himself Son of Adam when he spoke] concerning his own [lack of] abode (Mt 8.20).[101]

Christian Meanwhile our people consider Jesus as Messiah the Son of David, *i. e.* as our king, by obeying the precepts of his love (which is what the name *David* means) [and] by fighting with him against spiritual enemies and by following him into exile so that we may be considered worthy to be | exalted with him in the Kingdom of his Glory. (Several places from the Zohar where both Messiahs are discussed can be found in Parallelismis atque Excerptis Zohariticis ad Nov. Testamentum[102] Cent. I Loc. 62 up to 91).

Son of Abraham brh d'brhm

Christian The sense could be that Jesus is called Son of Abraham as if taking | his origin from Abraham and as promised to him, either specifically or as the man from whom the Old Covenant took its origin.

Kabbalist Catecumen But David can be implied also because he was a Son of Abraham; just as in other genealogies, the reckoning of filiation always looks to the nearest [ancestor]. The meaning is clearly quite the same as far as the literal sense goes, but as far as hidden teaching is concerned, it seems to be hinted that in | David, Abraham was reincarnated.

Christian And as far as a more secret Theology goes, he seems to describe the type of virtues from which arises conformity to Christ:[103] which are Love (at which David's name hints) and such [other virtues] as are born from Faith (which the mention of Abraham seems to denote). And also that which the teachers of your ancient people understood as allegorically indicated by Abraham, namely the Soul. For instructive specimens Cf. Excerpt Cent. I Loc. 92 | et *seq.*.

---

pp. 310–330 showed that *bar nash* means "a human being", but his further contention that the emphatic form, *bar nasha*, was used to speak of oneself has yet to find decisive evidence. Knorr takes "Son of Man" to mean "a descendant of Adam".

102 Note what is, apparently, the full name of this book. Knorr subsequently deleted this title and substituted the single word Excerptis. See Introduction.

103 One notices again that Knorr moves from a literal sense, to a hidden meaning (an exemple of *revolutio*) to a "more secret Theology" which is an exhortation to Christian virtue.

V. 2. *Jehudah & fratres ejus* ליהודא ולאחוהי

Christianus. Mysterium istud hîc latere videtur, dum cæterorum fratrum in hac Genealogia mentio fit, ê quibus Messias tamen natus non est; quod istorum posteri, quamvis ê captivitate Babylonica nondum redierint, Messiæ tamen aliquando futuri | sint participes juxta Rom. 11, 26. Unde & Nomina illorum inscripta erant[104] portis Novæ[105] Hierosolymæ[106] Ap. 21, 12. Sive dicamus decem tribus alicubi superesse adhuc[107], ut in America seu[108] meridionali; in China & in planitie quadam Persiæ inter asperimos montes sita; sive Animas illarum per revolutionem regenitas esse inter Gentiles sub initium Novi Fœderis, qui deinde inter conversos ê Gentibus tam facilè admiserint | Evangelium; vel in hodiernâ Judæorum mixturâ; sive delitescere inter Gentiles; ut sunt Americani septentrionales. Quodsi ergò spes est talibus, quorum rejectio tam fuit diuturna; quidni spem habeant illi, qui adeò remoti â Messiæ cognitione non sunt?

Cabb. Cat. *Quod autem ê Jehuda pronasci debuerit Messias, ratio hæc traditur, in Sohar. In Gen. Crem. c. 503. Mant. f. 237. quod in nomine ejus contineatur Tetragrammaton,* | *& ipse pertinuerit ad He ultimum illius Nominis, quod est Regnum.* (Vid. inter Excerpta Centur. 1. Loco[109] 54. n. 40.41.)

30

35

40

---

104 Correction: erant replaced by erunt (in the context of the vision described in Revelation, chapter 21).
105 Added above the line: urbis
106 Correction above the line: Hierosolymæ replaced by urbis Hierosolymitanæ
107 Correction: a sign is placed above the line which indicates that the terms should be inverted: alicubi superesse adhuc replaced by adhuc superesse alicubi
108 Added in the right margin: septentrionali seu
109 Correction: Loco replaced by Locus
110 For the Ten Lost Tribes: Andrew Runni Anderson, *Alexander's Gate, Gog and Magog, and the Enclosed Nations* (Cambridge Mass.: Mediaeval Academy of America, 1932); Tudor Parfitt, *The Lost Tribes of Israel* (London: Weidenfeld and Nicolson, 2002), pp. 91–114 on North American Indians as the Lost Tribes. The earliest printed claim for this identification seems to be Joannes Fredericus Lumnius, *De Extremo Dei judicio et Indorum vocatione* (Antwerp, 1567). See Zvi Ben-Dor Benite, *The Ten Lost Tribes. A World History* (Oxford, 2009), pp. 135–141 for similar South American claims. Manasseh ben-Israel, *Hope of Israel* in 1650 spoke of Jews in China. On these, see Donald Daniel Leslie, *The Survival of the Chinese Jews* (Leiden: Brill, 1972). Knorr's correspondent Gottlieb Spizel (1639–1691) wrote an *Elevatio relationis Montezinianae de repertis in America tribus Israeliticis, et discussio argumentorum pro origine gentium Americanarum Israelitica a Menasseh ben Israel in Miqwe Jisrael seu Spe Israelis conquisitorum.* (Basel: Johannes König, 1661). By the middle of the Seventeenth Century these Jews

Verse 2
Judah and his brothers yhwd' wl'ḥwhy

Christian The following is the secret teaching which seems to be hidden here when mention is made in this genealogy of Judah's other brothers, from whom Messiah *was not* born: their descendants, although they have not yet returned from the Babylonian captivity, none the less will finally be | participators with Messiah according to Rm 11.26. That is why also their names will be written on the gates of the City of Jerusalem Rev 21.12. We may say that the Ten Tribes remain up to now [hidden] somewhere like America or the North or the South, in China[110]; even on a plain lying between rough mountains somewhere in Persia. [Alternatively we may say] their souls have been reborn by reincarnation amongst the Gentiles with the beginning of the New Covenant and that then amongst converts from the Gentiles they so easily accepted | the Gospel; or [they are to be found] in today's mixture of Jews; or are hiding themselves amongst the Gentiles as are the North American [Indians]. If therefore they have hope whose rejection was so long lasting; what [greater] hope do they have who are not so far from knowledge of the Messiah[111].

Kabbalist Catechumen The reason why Messiah had to descend from Judah is handed down in the Zohar on Genesis (Crem col. 503, Mant f. 237). It is because in Judah's name is contained in the Tetragrammaton [*yhwh*], | and he himself was related to the final [Hebrew letter] *he* of the [divine] name which is [the degree] Kingdom. (See in Excerpts Cent. I Loc. 54, n. 40.41).

---

were known from Nicolas Trigault's popular translation of Matteo Ricci's Journals, *De Christiana expeditione apud Sinas suscepta ab Societate Jesu* (Ausburg: Mang, 1615 and subsequently in several languages); Emmanuel Diaz, *Relazione della cose più notabili scritte ne gli anni 1619,1620, 1621 della Cina* (Rome: Zannetti, 1624) and Alvarez Semmedo, *Imperio del China* (Madrid: Printed for Iuan Sanchez at the expense of Pedro Coello, 1642). On these, Michael Pollak, *Mandarins, Jews and Missionaries. The Jewish Experience in the Chinese Empire* (New York: Weatherhill, 1998), pp. 20–30. For identification made of these with the Ten Tribes, Ibid. pp. 121–125. Sober historical probabilities are reflected in Ziva Shavitsky, *The Mystery of the Lost Tribes. A Critical Survey of Historical and Archaeological records relating to the People of Israel in Exile in Syria, Mesopotamia and Persia up to ca. 300 B.C.E.* (Newcastle upon Tyne: Cambridge Scholars Publishing, 2012).

111   Cf. Paul's argument in Rm 9–11.

V. 3. *Phares & Zarach â Tamar* לפרץ ולזרח מן תמר

Christianus. Mentio fit horum geminorum, quia fideles & pii erant: non verò cum Jacobo & Esavo[112] ob istius impietatem (conf. Psalm. 34, 17; Ps. 109, 5.)

Cabb. Cat. *Nostrates autem in Sohar ejusque historia de Sene Sect. Mischpatim, statuunt, hoc loco involvi mysterium de revolutione Animarum: ita ut Perez & Serach fuerint Er & Onan: & Tamar, quæ antea uxor eorum fue-* ‖‖‖ *rat, facta sit ipsorum mater. Quo posito, animas nempe aliunde accedere: quid mirum si anima Messiæ etiam aliunde ortum habeat, nascique voluerit ê virgine? (vide autem de his latius in Parallelismis & Excerptis Soharisticis Cent. 1. Loc. 54. n. 40.41.)*[113] *Ubi etiam observabitur, quod iidem redierint in Machlon & Chilion*[114]*: & quod in Boas fuerit | Jehudah dum generaretur Obed: quodque in hoc restitutum fuerit malum tâm Eris quàm Onanis: & per consequens in Obed fuerit tam Serach quam Perez; & hæc procul dubio est ratio, quare hîc commemoretur & Sarach, qui directè alias ad hanc Genealogiam non pertineret. Tamar autem â Nostratibus statuitur fuisse proselyta Justitiæ, ut Rahab & Ruth: & exinde nati dicuntur omnes Reges domus David, ipseque Messias, ut ê profundo | Corticum et impuritatum non illas tantum proselytas emersisse appareat; sicut etiam Abraham ex idololatrâ natus, multas animas fecerat, seu converterat in Charan Gen. 12, 5. Sed & per Messiam Animas multò copiosiores ê potestate corticum (i.e. Satanæ) eductas esse: inter quas & nos*[115] *ê Gentilibus conversi numerandi estis, qui ipsum vitâ vestrâ exprimitis.*

---

112   Correction above the line: Esavo replaced by Esavi
113   Correction: (vide autem de his latius in Parallelismis & Excerptis Soharisticis Cent. 1. Loc. 54. n. 40.41.) replaced by (Vide in Excerptis Cent. 1. Loc. 54. n. 40.41.)
114   Correction: Chilion replaced by Chiljon
115   Correction above the line: nos replaced by vos
116   Lightfoot, *Miscellanies and the Harmony of the Gospels*, op. cit., p. 173: "Ishmael and Esau,—the one, a brother to Isaac; the other, a twin to Jacob,—are not mentioned, because they were both wicked: but the brethren of Judah, and the twin to Phares, are named, because they are both good. At the birth of Jacob and Esau, it is said תומים twins, with the letter א wanting; because Esau, one of them, was evil: but, at the birth of Phares and Zara, it is said תאומים with that letter supplied: because both of them were good ("R. Sol. [i.e. Rashi] in Gen. xxv, and xxxviii.")".
117   Originally: *Zoharic Parallels and Excerpts*. This is the second of two references Knorr

Verse 3

Phares and Zarach by Thamah lprṣ wlzrḥ mn tmr

Christian Mention is made of these twins because they were faithful and pious, but not of Jacob and Esau on account of his [Esau's] impiety (Cf. Ps 34.17; 109.5).[116]

Kabbalist Catechumen Our teachers however in Zohar, and its account *About the Old Man* in Sect. Mishpatim, state that the mystery of the reincarnation of souls is hidden in this passage, in such a way that Perez and Serach [i.e. Zerach or Zara] were Er and Onan; and Tamar who previously had [successively] ‖ been their wife, became their mother. If this is granted, then souls clearly come from elsewhere. What wonder then, if the soul of Messiah also had its origin elsewhere and wished to be born from a virgin? But see more widely about this in Excerpta[117] Cent. I Loc. 54, n. 40, 41, where also it will be noticed that the same [souls] returned in Machlon and Chilion; and that Judah was in | Boaz when Obed was born; also in this was restitution made for the evil both of Er and of Onan and consequently in Obed was both Serach [Zerach or Zara] and Perez[118]. This without doubt is the reason why Sarach [Zerach or Zara] is mentioned here; who otherwise is does not directly belong in this genealogy. Tamar is considered by our teachers to have been a righteous proselyte like Rahab and Ruth and from her are said to be born all the kings of the House of David and Messiah himself.[119]

So that, in this way, out of the depths | of the Shards and from impurity, might be seen to have emerged not only those proselytes (just as also Abraham, born out of idolatry, had made many souls, or had converted them in Haran Gen 12.5), but also that by Messiah many more souls had been saved from the power of Shards (i.e. of Satan). Amongst whom also you converts from the Gentiles are to be numbered, who express him in your life.

---

makes to the name of this work. Like the first, this one was deleted. See Introduction.
118 The advantages of a theory of reincarnation for theodicy are apparent here.
119 Lightfoot, *Miscellanies and the Harmony of the Gospels*, op. cit., pp. 173–174: "'Of Thamar.'] Four women are named in this genealogy: women, once of notorious infamy. Thamar, incestuous; Rahab, a harlot; Ruth, a heathen; and Bath-sheba, an adulteress: to show, that Christ came to heal all sores, when he recured such sinners; and that he despised not our shame, when he shamed not to descend of such parents."

[**Christianus.**] Notetur[120] etiam, quod & Socer Jehudah procul dubio etiam[121] | fuerit proselytus; cumque nomen ejus שוע tres literas contineat ê nomine ישוע. Judas primam sui nominis, literam scilicet י, ipsi addidisse videtur, ut nomen hoc exsurgeret integrum, & salus oriretur ex hoc Nomine (Act. 4, 12.) etiam Cananæis, qui maledictionis quàm clarissimum erant exemplar ê Gen. 9, 25. omniumque quasi gentium typus. (vid. Tractat. de Revolutione Animarum cap. 2. in | fine, p. 255. §. 14[122].)

V. 5. *Ex Rahab &.* מן רחב

Cabb. Cat. *In Gemara Megillah fol. 14.b. quidem asseritur: quod Josua duxerit Rachab, & ex eâ tantum genuerit filias. Sed alia quoque ibidem opinio est, quod nempe ex ipsa prodierint octo sacerdotes & Prophetæ; quod ex alio matrimonio | fieri potuit. Jamque & tertium suggeritur Salmonis matrimonium, in tabula hac Genealogicâ, quæ procul dubio in asservatoriis publicis reperta fuit: & quàm tacitè confirmat locus jam citatus Libri Revolutionum.*

Christianus. In Targum autem Rachab dicitur cauponaria. Typusque est ad Jesum cum amplitudine (quem sensum habet nomen Rachab) convertendarum | gentium.

---

120 Correction in the left margin: Notetur replaced by Christianus. Videtur
121 Underlined in manuscript to have put in italics?
122 "Contingit autem quod anima illa robusta atque sancta insigniter excitetur operibusque bonis præcellat, ut penitus separetur à corticibus: neque id solum, sed etiam scintillas alias secum assumat, easque è profundis corticum educat. Id quod sic eveniebat in Abrahamo Patre nostro, super quo pax, qui erat filius Tarach idololatræ & magni Sacerdotis idolorum: & tamen è contrario de ipso dicitur Gen. 12. v. 5. & animas, quas [*proselytas*] fecerant in Charan. Quod similiter quoque accidit in omnibus proselytis justitiæ: quales erant Ruth & Thamar & Rachab; & omnes reges domus David, & ipse Meschiach: & R. Akiva & R. Meir & similes plures. Usque adeo, ut David, qui exinde prodierat, penitùs extirparet corticem illum, quo superindutus fuerat primitùs: nimirum corticem Moab, intra quem immersa fuerat Psyche Davidis, prout exponemus suo loco. Unde funiculis distribuerat terram Moab incolis occisis. Unde patet, quod Adam Belial dominium quidem habuerit in hominem sanctum; sed in malum sibi, perverso scilicet homini, ut dictum supra. Id quoque exhinc patet, quod anima quò sit excellentior, eò magis quoque immersa sit similibus corticibus; ita ut prava illius concupiscentia omnino magna sit atque insignis. Unde mirum non est, quod David tale quid perpetravit cum Bathschebah & Abigail: prout juvante Deo, gesta illa Davidis & Abrahami locis debitis explicabimus. Exhinc quoque perspicuum est, quare interdum justus quidam sit filius impii? cum tamen meritò omnes justi tantum generare deberent filios justos sibi similes." ("De Revolutionibus animarum", op. cit., p. 255).
123 Gen 38.2.

SECTION VI 329

15   **Christian** Evidently the father-in-law of Judah without doubt | was *also* a proselyte and [since] his name *šw'* [Shua[123]] contains three letters from the name yšw', Judah seems to have added the first letter of his own name—i.e. /y/ to it so that this name should arise whole and salvation in turn should arise from this name (Acts 4.12), even for the Canaanites who were the clearest example of a curse (Gen 9.25) and, as it were, a type of all the Gentiles
20   (see Tract. *De Revol. Animarum*, chap. 2 *in* | *fine*, p. 255, §14).

Verse 5
By Rahab etc. *mn rḥb*

Kabbbalist Catechumen In Gemarah Megilah folio 14b it is said that Joshua married Rahab and by her fathered very many daughters.[124] But there is another opinion on this too: that from her there came eight priests and
25   prophets, which could have come from another marriage.[125] | And also a third[126] suggestion is made of a marriage of [Rahab] to Salmon in this record of genealogy [here in Matthew] which without doubt had been found in the public archives[127] and which tacitly confirms the already cited passage in the Book of Revolutions.

Christian In the Targum, Rahab is called an inn-keeper[128] and the type refers to Jesus and the multitude (which is the meaning of [the name]
30   Rahab) of the Gentiles | who need saving.

---

124   Lightfoot, *Miscellanies and the Harmony of the Gospels*, op. cit., p. 174: "'Rahab'. It can little be doubted, but that he meaneth her, mentioned Josh. ii. Now the Jews [belike to deface the truth of Matthew, who, from ancient records, averreth her for the wife of Salmon] have broached this tenet,—that she was married unto Joshua."

125   Megillah 14b: "Rav Eina the Elder raised an objection from a *baraita* to Rav Naḥman's teaching. The *baraita* indicates that Huldah was in fact a descendant of Rahab, and seemingly not of Joshua: Eight prophets, who were also priests, descended from Rahab the prostitute, and they are: Neriah; his son Baruch; Seraiah; Mahseiah; Jeremiah; his father, Hilkiah; Jeremiah's cousin Hanamel; and Hanamel's father, Shallum. Rabbi Yehuda said: So too, Huldah the prophetess was a descendant of Rahab the prostitute, as it is written here with regard to Huldah: 'The son of Tikvah' and it is written elsewhere in reference to Rahab's escape from the destruction of Jericho: 'This cord of [*tikvat*] scarlet thread' (Joshua 2:18). See also Sifre Num 78."

126   Dinah marries into Judah (as here) also in *Yalkut Shimoni* on Joshua § 9.

127   See above for mentions of these records.

128   Targum Jonathan has *pwndqyt'* derived from the Greek *pandokeus*. The Hebrew *zonah* is usually taken as a harlot, but Josephus (*Ant*. V.1.2) considered her an inn-keeper (*katagōgion*) as did Rashi. Donald J. Wiseman, "Rahab of Jericho", *Tyndale Bulletin* 14 (1964): pp. 8–11 considered her establishment similar to the Old Babylonian *bît sābî(ti)* in the Laws of Hammurabi § 109 and later. He also made suggestions of different etymologies for *zonah*.

Ex Ruth מן רעות

Cabb. Cat. *Boas Doctoribus nostris habetur pro Ibsam, Jud. 12, 8. (vid. in Excerptis Cent. 1. Loc. 54. n. 41. & de Ruth ibid. Loc. 99.) Ruth autem Moabitis & Naëma Ammonitis, duæ neptes Lothi, in Gemara dicuntur duæ columbæ bonæ. (vid. Tract. de | Revolutionibus Anim. p. 424. §. 14*[129]*. & p. 465. c. 37. §. 1. p. 466. 467. 468*[130]*.) Liber Ser Sahab*[131]* in* ר״ *dicit, quod quicquid Cortex Moab abripuisset ê Sanctitate, illud Ruth reduxerit in Sanctitatem.*

Christianus. Quodsi ita se habet, facilè colligi posset eandem esse rationem in Thamar & Rachab, ratione Corticis Canaan; & in Bithia filia Pharaonis (1. Par. 4, 18.) ratione | Corticis Ægypti &c.

Obed genuit Ischai עוביד אולד לאישי

Christianus. Si ista generatio immediata fuit, ita ut Obed fuerit Pater & non Avus Iischai; res miraculo non caret: quia inter egressum ex Ægypto & fundatum templum sunt anni 480. 1. Reg. 6, 1. id est, inter Annum mundi verbi gratia 2453. & Annum mundi | 2933. Ponamus enim per Exodum ex Ægypto loco citato non intelligi annum transitus per mare rubrum, sed annum Transitus per Jordanem, ut Psal. 114, 1. Deut. 4, 45.46. qui sit Annus mundi 2492.

---

[129] "Hinc etiam reperimus, quod mysterium hujus pollicis repertum fuerit in Lot: quare ex illo prodiit Naëmah Ammonitis, quæ descendebat è Binah, cui etiam nomen Naëmah. In Lot autem continebantur duæ ejus neptes, quæ in Gemara dicuntur duæ columbæ bonæ; Naëmah scilicet & Ruth. Quæ ambæ commixtæ erant in Hebele. Quod patet ex verbis illis Genes. 11, vers. 31. Et Terach secum sumebat ה״רן ב ל״וט, Lot filium Haran, quorum literæ initiales sunt Hebel. Quamvis fundamentum radicis ejus esset è pollice dextro Adami. Et quia in ipso erat mysterium pollicis, quod denotat judicia rigorosa, sicut dictum est in Sohar Tract. Idra sect. Naso: hinc concupiscentia prava Hebelis in ipso dominium habebat: eumque accipiebat Abraham, ut ipsum emendaret." (Ibid., p. 424).

[130] "De Goliatho, quod longitudo ejus fuerit cubitorum sex & unius palmi 1. Schm. 17.v.4 notandum, quod mysterium sex illorum cubitorum pertineat ad cortices. Cortex enim Ruthæ erat Ophra (Mater Goliathi;) quæ etiam potuisset venire in sanctitatem, sed nolebat, Ruth. 1.v.14. Sicut contigerat Leæ & Racheli; ubi Leah etiam veniebat in sanctitatem. Quamvis enim Leah delapsa esset in partem Esavi; tamen per fletum suum redibat ad Jacobum. Sicut etiam acciderat Chavvæ primæ & Chavvæ secundæ; quarum hæc adhærebat Adamo. Sicut enim Chavva prima abibat ad externos; sic etiam fieri debuisset Leæ; Sec hæc tamen redibat ad sanctitatem, & inserta fuit Racheli. Eodem igitur modo facere potuisset Orpha; sed nolebat, & cervicem suam (עורף) obvertens abibat ad exteriores. Quicquid autem sanctitatis in ipsa erat, inserebatur in

SECTION VI

By Ruth mn rʿwt

Kabbalist Catechumen Boaz is taken by our Sages for Ibzan in Judg 12.8[132] (See in Excerpts Cent. I Loc. 54, n. 41; and for Ruth ibid. Loc. 99). Ruth however was a Moabitess and Naomi an Ammonitess, two nieces of Lot. In the Gemarah they are called two good doves[133] (See *Trac de | Revol. Animarum*, p. 424, §14; & p. 465, c. 37, §1; pp. 466, 467, 468). The Book Ser Sahab in Resh says that whatever the shard Moab[134] had snatched away from Sanctity, Ruth lead back into Sanctity.

Christian What if the same reason could easily be deduced in the case of Tamar and Rahab, with respect to the shard Canaan; and in [the case of] Bithiah the daughter of Pharoah (1 Chron 4.18) with respect to | the Shard of Egypt *etc..*

Obed begat Ischai [Jesse] ʿwbyd ʾwld lʾyšy

Christian If this begetting was immediate [without the insertion of another generation] so that Obed was the father and not the grand-father of Jesse, the matter was miraculous [on account of the age of the father] because between the Exodus from Egypt and the Foundation of the Temple were 480 years (1 Kgs 6.1)—that is between the Year of the World (AM [Annus Mundi]) 2453 (for example) and AM | 2933. For we contend that by "the Exodus out of Egypt" in the passage cited is not to be understood the year of the Crossing of the Red Sea, but the year of the Crossing of the Jordan as in Ps 114.1; Deut 4.45, 46 which was the Year of the World (AM) 2492. Let us

---

Ruth: Et quicquid mali erat in Ruth, inserebatur eidem. Sicut enim Rachel & Lea redigebantur in unam Synochen in Sanctitate: ita Sanctitas quæ erat in Orpha tota inserebatur in Ruth, unde dicitur, Ruth. 4,11. *Det Dominus mulierem venientem in domum tuam sicut Rachel & Lea, quæ ædificaverunt ambæ domum Iisraël.* Ubi sensus est, illas duas connexas esse in unum quasi subjectum; cujus intuitu adhibetur particula שתהם. Idem quoque denotatur per voculam את האשה quod nempe sanctitas Orphæ inserta fuerit Ruthæ, quod probe notandum. [...] Qui vero non usque adeo mali sunt, ut talem mentem (è corticibus) acceperint, illi per pœnitentiam possunt restitui. Qui vero Psychen, Spiritum & mentem (è corticibus) accepit, illius ossa putrescunt, & caro ejus absumitur. Et huc pertinet exemplum Ruth & Orpha: ubi Orpha redibat ad populum suum, & ad Deos suos." (Ibid., pp. 465–468).

131 A Dictionary published by Barukh ben David in Kraków in 1642, already referred to in the *Loci communes kabbalistici*.
132 Baba Bathra 91a.
133 *Baba Kammah* 38b (Cf. *Genesis Rabbah* on Gen 50.16).
134 Subsequently we shall find extensive reference to the shard of Edom.

fol. 26ʳ Demus quoque, quod Rachab tum vicennis post 26. demum ||| annos nupserit Salmoni & anno Mundi 2519. genuerit Boasum; huic sanè vix minus dari queunt quam Anni 120. ut anno mundi 2639. genuerit Obedum. Nec minus quàm totidem & huic tribui queunt, ut anno Mundi 2759. genuerit Ischai. Hunc ponamus anno ætatis suæ 100. & anno Mundi 2859. generasse Davidem, qui anno ætatis 70. & anno mundi | 2929. mortuus est, unde anno post quarto sequente & anno mundi 2933. Templum est fundatum. Cum ergò mirum omnino videri debeat Davidem septuaginta tantum; Mosen quoque centum & viginti, & Josuam centrum[135] & decem tantum annos vixisse, conf. Psal. 90, 10. Boasum autem & Obedum anno ætatis suæ centesimo adhuc generasse[136] & vigesimo, & Iischai anno ætatis suæ centesimo adhuc generasse; | delabemurne ad illud effugium, ut dicat non fuisse Obedum Patrem[137], sed Avum Iischai, ita ut integra generatio sit omissa, tam hoc Matthæi loco, quàm locis parallelis 1. Par. 2, 12; Ruth. 4, 22? (Quales omissiones nihilominus plures occurrent infra.)

Cabb. Cat. Si autem ad progenerandum Davidem effœta senectus per miraculum | toties fuit prolifera, id typus esset ante adventum filii Davidis fore, ut antiquitas potissimum concurrat ad veram vitæ ejus regenerationem. (vide autem de Obed inter Excerpta Cent. 1. Loc. 54. n. 39.40. & in Tractatu de Revolutionibus Animarum p. 286. §. 12[138]. De Iischai autem ibidem & p. 362. §. 12[139]. & p. 471. §. 6[140].)

---

135 Correction: centrum replaced by centum
136 Deletion: adhuc generasse (to prevent its unnecessary repetition in two successive clauses).
137 Correction: a sign is placed above the line which indicates that the terms should be inverted: non fuisse Obedum Patrem replaced by Obedum non fuisse Patrem
138 "Unde in Sohar pluries dicitur, quod David venerit de parte uxoris: quapropter etiam immersus est similiter in uxorem corticalem. Quod etiam innuitur in historia de sene, sectione Mischpatim fol. 23. ubi dicitur de Obed, Jischai & David, qui nempe dicitur arbor infima, quæ prodierit è ramis, &c. ubi vide latius, & intelliges quæ hic dicuntur. Quare etiam prodiit è Ruth Moabithide, quæ immersa fuerat in cortice Moab. Notum autem est, quod Ammon & Moab duo sint cortices oppositi numerationibus prudentiæ sive informatrici; & regni; de quibus suo loco: sicut etiam infra cap. 13. ubi de Davide agitur." ("De Revolutionibus animarum", op. cit., p. 286).
139 "Cum itaque quidam sint, qui ita non perficiuntur; illos redire oportet multis revolutionibus. Qui verò absoluti sunt penitus, ita ut in illis nihil remanserit, nisi labes Adamitica, illos purificari oportet per mortem. Atque huc pertinet illud, quod in Gemarah dicitur de quatuor illis, qui per totam vitam suam nullum perpetrarunt peccatum, inter quos est Jischai pater Davidis, &c. quos mori oportuit propter consilium serpentis.

SECTION VI   333

concede also that Rahab, then [say] a twenty year old |||, after 26 years finally   fol. 26ʳ
married Salmon [in AM 2418= 2492+26] and in AM 2519 gave birth to Boaz.
We can scarcely attribute less than 120 years to him, so that in AM 2639 [=
2519+120] he fathered Obed. We can scarcely reckon any fewer years to him,
so in AM 2759 [= 2639+120] he fathered Jesse. Let us imagine that he, aged
100 in AM 2859 [= 2759+100], fathered David, who died at 70 in AM | 2929
[= 2589+70]. Four years afterwards in AM 2933 [= 2929+4] the temple was
founded. So although it must seem completely amazing that David was only
70 [when he died]; that Moses too lived [only] 120 years and Joshua only 110
(Cf. Ps 90.10), Salmon fathered Boaz in his 120th year and Jesse when he was
just 100. | Shall we seek the escape from the problem whereby it is said that
Obed was not the father but the grandfather of Jesse, so that a whole generation is omitted, both in this place in Matthew and the parallel passages
1 Chron 2.12; Ruth 4.22? (Several such omissions do indeed occur below).

Kabbalist Catechumen If, however, in the generation of David the exhaustion of old age was so many times made miraculously | productive, this would be a type before the advent of the Son of David occurred, that antiquity collaborated most profoundly in the true regeneration of his life [For Obed, see Excerpts Cent. I Loc. 54, n. 39, 40 and in *Tract. De Revol. Animarum*, p. 286, § 12. For Jesse see ibid. also p. 362, § 12 and p. 471, § 6.]

Et quamvis id mirum videri queat; per supradicta tamen facile intelligi potest: quamvis enim ipsi nihil corruperint vel ulteriorem labem superaddiderint: nihilominus tamen vitium primum serpentis in Adamo Protoplaste obortum nondum fuit restitutum; unde moriendum ipsis fuit." (Ibid., p. 362).

140 "Omnes ergo Cortices, omnemque spurcitiem quam in se derivat homo per peccatum proprium, separare & emundare potest per conversionem pœnitentiæ: sed peccatum Adami protoplastæ multas ob causas magnum nimis est, quæ hic enarrari nequeunt. Hinc ne per pœnitentiam quidem multum separatur. Quamvis enim remissio detur peccatorum, & sine dubio Deus pœnitentiam Adami Protoplastæ susceperit: immundities tamen illa & cortex qui cuivis adhæsit, ab eodem tolli nequit nisi post mortem. Hinc quatuor illi Amram (Pater Mosis) Benjamin (filius Jacobi,) Et Calab (filius Davidis) Et Iischai (Pater Davidis [...]) quamvis fuerint justi perfecti; nihilominus tamen vis ista in tantum iisdem adhæsit, ut moriendum iis fuerit propter consilium serpentis: quoniam necesse fuit, ut restituerentur & purificarentur ab iisque separaretur cortex iste peccati Adami, cum quo cuivis adest cortex quidam de illa spurcitie serpentis." (Ibid., p. 471).

V. 6. *David Regem &.* לדויד מלכא

Christianus. Hic est perpetuus Titulus Davidis apud Scriptores vestros, quem hac exprimere solent abbreviaturâ: דהע״ה, i.e. דויד המלך עליו השלום David Rex Super quo pax[141] (De quo vide in Tractatu de Revolutionibus Animarum p. 248[142].251.286.287.293.335[143].349.368.374.417.418.419.426.434.445. 461.466.468.)

Cabb. Cat. *Connotatur autem hoc titulo, quod David pertineat ad | Regni gradum; sicut notum est. (vid. Lex. Cabb. tit.* דוד[144])

Ex uxore Uriæ מן אנתתה דאוריא

Christianus. Singularia illa ê scriptis vestris huc pertinentia, tu quæso enarres![145]

Cabb. Cat. *Bathscheba, quæ fuerat uxor Uriæ â nostratibus | statuitur fuisse compar Davidis propria: cujus peccatum in eo potissimum collocat, quod præponere illam duxerit cum homicidio per gladium Ammonitarum. Vid. Excerpta Cent. 1. Loc. 54. n. 46. & Loc. 98.* [**Christianus.**] Quibus[146] subjungi possunt ê Libro הפליאה sequentia: David Rex sciebat Animarum mutationes, noveratque quod ipse esset Adam primus, Urias autem Serpens; & Bathscheba Chavvah | &c: Quare autem punitus est David? Quia nimirum festinavit, nec expectavit donec Deus illum judicaret. Adde quod ad ipsam accesserit citra præparationem: quia primò ab ipsa tollenda fuisset immunditia serpentis, eò quod prius nupta fuerat plebejo &c. Unde filius ejus primus erat de spuritie[147] serpentis: Deinde autem filius ejus erat Rex super Iisraël, quia ipsa erat

---

141 Deletion: quem hac exprimere solent abbreviaturâ: דהע״ה, i.e. דויד המלך עליו השלום David Rex Super quo pax.

142 "Atque hinc intelligi potest id, quod dicitur in tractatu Talmudico de benedictionibus. Propterea Davidem Regem quinquies dixisse, laudet psyche mea Dominum Ps. 103. v.1.2.22; Ps. 104. v.1.35. quo scilicet indigitaret quinque nomina, quæ animæ tribuuntur: qualia sunt: nephesch seu psyche sive anima infima; Ruach seu spiritus sive anima media; Neschamah seu mens sive anima superior; Chajah seu vita nempe Divina, & Jechidah seu singularis, scilicet unio [...]" ("De Revolutionibus animarum", op. cit., p. 248). Pages 251, 286, 287, 293, 374 and 417 focuse on the soulf of David and on the various parts that compose it.

143 "Et sic etiam de Davide, qui pertinet ad Regnum, dicitur Psal. 89. v.28. *Ego ipsum primogenitum ponam*. Ubi in voce אתניהו *Ponam eum*, He præmittitur ante Vav, id est, uxor ante maritum. [...]". (Ibid., p. 335). Pages 349 and 368 deal with the numerous David's wifes.

144 "דוד *David*. Ita vocatur Malchuth, quia David fuit vehiculum istius metri, Illudque

Verse 6
David the King ldwyd mlkʾ

Christian This [King] is the consistent title of David in your Scriptures[148]. (About which see Tract. *De Revol. Animarum*, pp. 248, 251, 286, 287, 293, 335, 349, 368, 374, 417, 418, 419, 426, 434, 445, 461, 466, 468.)

Kabbalist Catechumen This title indicates that David is linked to the | degree Kingdom as we have seen (See *Lex. Cabb.* under *dwd*).

By the wife of Uriah mn'ntth d'wryʾ

[149]**Kabbalist Catechumen** Bathsheba, who had been the wife of Uriah, is considered by our scholars | to have been as David's very own wife. His sin with respect to her they locate primarily in that he married her too hastily [and had her husband killed] by the sword of the Ammonites.[150] See Excerpts Cent. I Loc. 54, n. 46 and Loc. 98.

Christian The following can be added from the *Sefer Haflaʾah*[151]:
"David the King knew about the migrations of souls and he knew that he was the first Adam, that Uriah was the Serpent and Bathsheba was Eve | etc. So why was David punished? Because he was too hasty and did not wait until God judged [Uriah]. Also because he went into her without preparation, for first the impurity of the Serpent [Uriah] should have been removed from her, because she had formerly been married to a commoner etc. That is why his first son was [born] of the filth of the Serpent[152]. Then his [next] son was King over Israel, because [Bathsheba] was his [intended] companion." End of quotation.

---

condecoravit & donavit canticis suis: ad Ipsam enim spectant omnes laudes ejus. Illa tamen fuit metrum ejus, quatenus inclinat ad Hod; unde דו״ד cum voce æquipollet numero vocis הו״ד qui est 15. [...]" ("Loci communes kabbalistici", op. cit., p. 247).

145 Deletion of the entire speech attributed to the Christian.
146 Correction: Quibus replaced by Christian. His etiam in the right margin.
147 Correction above the line: spuritie replaced by spurcitie
148 Deleted: which is usually expressed by the abbreviation *dhʿh* "David the King, Peace be upon him".
149 Deleted: Christian: Tell me the singularities from your scriptures which are relevant here.
150 Cf. Joseph Gikatilla, *Le secret du mariage de David et Bethsabée*, edited by Charles Mopsik (Paris: Éditions de l'Éclat, 2015) for a succinct but informed treatment of this theme.
151 The "Book of Utterances" from Maimonides' *Mishneh Torah*.
152 And died as a baby, 2 Sam 12.14–19.

compar ejus. Hæc ibi. Sic in Sohar in Gen. Crem. col. 216. | Mant. fol. 73.b. 40
Magnoperè caveant homines, ne peccent coram Domino. Cum enim peccat
homo, peccatum ejus designatur superius, nec deletur, nisi vi conversionis
maximâ: juxta illud Jerem. 2, 22. Veni vide! Cum homo primâ vice peccat
signum fit: cum secunda vice peccat; istud signum magis fit notabile: Si ter-
tiâ vice peccat; nota illa ab uno latere extenditur in alterum; & tunc scriptum
est: *Signata est iniquitas | tua coram me &c.*[153] David Rex igitur cum peccasset 45
in negotio Bathscheba putabat peccatum hoc sub perpetuo signo mansu-
rum: Hinc scriptum est: Abstulit Dominus peccatum tuum, non morieris;
i.e. sustulit notam illam coram se. Dixit illi R. Abba; Atqui traditum est,

fol. 26ᵛ quod Bathscheba Davidis fuerit ab initio mundi conditi: ||| quare ergò primi-
tus concessa est Uriæ Chitæo? Respondit ipsi: Hæc est via Sancti i.q.b.s.[154]!
quamvis uxor quædam destinata sit homini in matrimonium; sæpe tamen
alius antevertit eamque ducit: donec veniat tempus istius. Quodsi venerit,
expellitur ille qui eam duxit, ante alterum hunc sequentem, êque mundo
sustollitur. Durumque est | Deum[155] eundem ê mundo tollere, antequam 5
veniat tempus ejus. Mysterium autem Bathschebæ, quæ prius data fuit Uriæ,
si debitè inspexeris; rationem invenies, quare Terra Sancta prius data fuerit
Cananæis, antequam venirent Iisrælitæ: Omnia enim mysterium unum sunt,
& res una. &c. Confer. Sohar in Deut. col. 550. Mant. 284. a. Porrò ibidem in
Deut. Crem. col. 64. Mant. f. 37. nomen Bathscheba tribuitur | gradui Mal- 10
chuth, dum dicitur: Propterea Ecclesia Iisraëlis vocatur Bathscheba, i.e. filia
septimi ab illo septimo (gradu Jesod) qui in se continet sex alios, (â Binah,
unde initium unctionis â Chochmah defluentis:) Cum iste septimus comple-
tur sacerdotibus, tunc eos coronat, & ungit omnibus requisitis. Cum pervenit
ad Ecclesiam Israël, quæ est octava, mandaturque Aharoni, ut offerat | &c. 15
Et fol. seq. col. 68. ad Exod. 6, 23. Et accepit Aharon Elischeba filiam Aminadab &c. Omnia sicut oportuit: omnia sicut in supernis. Veni vide! Bathscheba

---

153   Underlined in the manuscript. The Vulgate has "*maculata es in iniquitate tua coram me*".
154   We resolve the abbreviation *i.q.b.s* here conjecturally as *is qui beatus sit*, and take it as a Latin form of the Hebrew abbreviation *hkbh* [*Hakadosh*] *Baruch-hu*, [The Holy One] Blessed be He!
155   Correction: Deum replaced by Deo
156   In this context at one point we remarked that he never cited his own edition of the Zohar. But then we subsequently reflected that perhaps he did—and that is how he had such a ready concordance of the different references in the two editions. Because we did not know anywhere else he could have looked that up easily.

SECTION VI

40   Thus [it says] in Zohar on Genesis Crem 216, | Mant folio 73b[156]:
"Let men be greatly afraid lest they sin before the Lord. For when a man sins, his sin is recorded in heaven and not deleted, other than by the mighty power of rependence, according to Jer 2.22. Come and See! When man sins the first time, a mark is made: when he sins a second time this mark becomes more noticeable. If he sins a third time that mark is extended from one side
45   to the other[157]. So thus it is written: *Marked is your | inquity before me etc.* King David, therefore, when he sinned in the matter of Bathsheba thought that this sin would remain [preserved] under a perpetual mark: For this reason it is written 'The Lord has removed your sin, you shall not die' [2 Sam 12.13] *i. e.* he has removed that record from before himself. R Abba said to him: None the less, it is handed down that Bathsheba was David's from the very foundation of the world ‖, so why was she first given to Uriah the Hittite?   fol. 26ᵛ He replied to him: this is the way of the Holy One, Blessed be He! Although a certain woman is destined for a man in marriage, often however another anticipates him and marries her until his time comes [to die]. And when it has come, he is expelled who married her before the other following him and
5   is taken from this world. But it is hard | for God to take him from the world before his time comes. If you examine properly the mystery of Bathsheba who was first given to Uriah, you will find the reason why the Holy Land was first given to the Canaanites before the Israelites arrived. For all things are but one mystery and one thing *etc*.." Cf. Zohar in Deut col. 550, Mant folio 284a.
     And likewise in Deut Crem col. 64 Mant folio 37—the name of Bathsheba
10   is attributed | to the degree of Kingdom, when it says:
"Because of this the Ecclesia of Israel is called Bathsheba i.e. 'the Daughter of the Seventh' from that seventh (degree of Yesod) which contains in itself the six others (from Binah [Understanding] whence begins the unction flowing down from Chokhmah [Wisdom]). When that Seventh One is filled with priests, then it crowns them and anoints them with all they need. When it comes to the Ecclesia of Israel which is the Eighth and it is commanded to
15   Aaron that he should offer | *etc*.".
     And on the following pages [of Zohar] col. 68 to Ex 6.23:
"And Aaron took Elischeba the daughter of Aminadab etc. All as it should be: everything as it is above. Come and see! Bathsheba was destined for

---

157   This phrase may refer to the stain of the record passing through the sheet of writing material from one side to the other.

destinata erat Davidi â die mundi conditi; Sic destinata erat Elischeba Aharoni â primordio mundi. Quænam inter has est differentia. Nimirum omnia unum, idemque sunt: (i.e. Elischeba & Bathscheba unum denotant | gradum Malchuth.) Verum ibi in judicii, hîc in misericordiæ signum. Cum jungeretur Davidi, in judicium; ut pugnaret in bellis & effunderet sanguinem: Hic autem in Aharone in pacem, in gaudium, in illuminationem faciei, in benedictionem. Et propterea (Malchuth) his nominibus appellatur ibi Bathscheba; hic Elischeba; quia conjuncta est cum gradu Benignitatis: Bathscheba | autem ob severitatem ad possidendum regnum, & ad corroborationem &c.

V.7. *Salomo genuit Rehabeam* שלימון אולד לרחבעם

Christianus. Ex Naëma Ammonitide 1. Reg. 14, 21. (de qua supra ad v. 5. ê Tract. de Revolutionibus p. 424. §. 14[158].) Et hæc est ê gentilibus quarta, quæ ad Genealogiam Messiæ pertinet, nimirum post Tamar, Rachab & Ruth.

Cabb. Cat. *Sic ê tribus Noæ filiis Messias quidem in Genealogiam suam admisit Semum & Chamum, filiumque hujus Canaan, unde Thamar & Rachab: quod validè mirum, ob istius maledictionem: Gen. 9, 25. Sed quare nihil admisit ê Japhato*[159]*? qui tamen medius fuisse dicitur in Sohar, Part.I. Edit. Crem. col. 215. Mant. fol. 73. pr.* [**Christianus.**][160] Propterea crederem posteros Japheth ex Javan, | qui sunt Græci & Romani, post adventum ejus, doctrinam Evangelii tàm prospera propagatione suscepisse.

V.8. *Joram genuit Uzia.* יורם אולד לעוזיא

Christianus. Non imediatè ceu pater: sed mediantibus Achasiâ, 2. Reg. 8, 24; 2. Reg. 11, 2. & Amaziâ 2. Reg. 12, 21; c. 14, 1.21. qui erat pater Asariæ, seu Uziæ, | c. 15, 1; 1. Par. 3, 12. Unde Joram illius tantum fuit Abavus. Tales autem omis-

---

158 Cf. *supra*, footnote 129, p. 330.
159 Correction: Japhato replaced by Japheto
160 Added in the left margin: Christian (which involves a change of speaker).
161 There is an allusion here to the words of the High Priest's blessing in Num 6.24–26.

SECTION VI

David from the day the world was founded. If Elischeba had been destined for Aaron from the beginning of the world, what difference is there between them? Indeed all things are one and the same (i.e. Elischeba and Bathsheba denote | the single degree Kingdom)—but in the one case for a mark of judgment, in the other for sign of mercy. [The degree] joined to David for judgment, so that he might fight in battles and shed blood. But [the degree] was in Aaron to produce peace, the brightness of the face and blessing[161]. For this reason (Kingdom) is called by these names—sometimes Bathsheba and some times Elischeba—the later because she is joined with the degree Kindness—but | Bathsheba, on account of the severity necessary for taking possession of the Kingdom and its strengthening etc."

Verse 7
Solomon begat Rehoboam šlymwn ʾwld lrḥbʿm

Christian [Solomon begat Rehoboam] by Naamah the Ammonitess (1 Kgs 14.21), (concerning whom, see above on verse 5 from Tract. *De Revol. Animarum*, p. 424, §14). And she is the fourth woman from the Gentiles who belongs to the genealogy of Messiah—after, that is, Tamar, Rahab and Ruth.

fKabbalist Catechumen Thus from the three sons of Noah, Messiah admitted into his genealogy Shem, Ham and Ham's son Canaan, from whom descended Tamar and Rahab. This is really remarkable in view of [Noah's] curse (Gen 9.25). But why did he admit no one from Japheth, who however is said to have been the middle son in Zohar Part. 1 Edit. Crem col. 215 Mant folio 73 pr.

Christian It is for this reason I would think the descendants of Japhet through Javan, | who are the Greeks and Romans, after Messiah's advent, took up the teaching of the Gospel with such a ready increase.[162]

Verse 8
Joram begat Uziah [Ozias] ywrm ʾwld lʿwzyʾ

Christian Not immediately—nor as a father, but by the intermission of Ahaziah (2 Kgs 8.24) and Joash (2 Kgs 11.2), who was also the father of Amaziah (2 Kgs 12.21; 14.1, 21), [and] who was the father of Azariah or Uziah | (2 Kgs 15.1; 1 Chron 3.12). So Joram was only his great-grandfather. Such omis

---

162 This is a distinctly Christian solution to the problem posed by the Kabbalist Catechumen.

siones in Genealogicis sæpius occurrunt, ut 1. Par. 6, 7. generationibus ab ipso aberat. Item Esr. 7, 3. collat cum[163] 1. Par. 6, 7. & Jos. 7, 1. coll. cum v. 24. cap. 22, 20. Et talis omissio etiam etiam[164] in Sohar invenitur, in Exordum Cremon. col. 151. Mant. fol. 85. Traditione didicimus ad 1. Par. 29, 23. & sedit Salomo super throno Domini, (i.e. Seir | Anpin) sicut scriptum est 2. Reg. 9, 18. sex gradus throno. R. Abba inquit; quia Luna tunc in plenilunio erat. Didicimus enim in diebus Salomonis Lunam fuisse in plenitudine. Quando autem plena sit? Die decima quinta prout didicimus: (quod ||| dies isti sint) 1. Abraham, 2. Isaac, 3. Jacob, 4. Jehudah, 5. Perez, 6. Chezron, 7. Ram, 8. Aminadab, 9. Nachson, 10. Salmon, 11. Boas, 12. Obed, 13. Iischai, 14. David, 15. Salomo. Cum ergò Salomo veniret, Luna erat in plenilunio; unde dicitur 1. Chron. 29, 23. eum sedisse super throno Tetragrammati. In diebus Zedekiæ defectum passam esse | Lunam, & obscuratam esse faciem Iisraëlis. Prodi enim & numera. 1. Rehabeam, 2. Abijah, 3. Assa, 4. Josaphath, 5. Joram, 6. Ahasia, 7. Amazia, (hic deficit Joas) 8. Usia, 9. Jotham, 10. Achas, 11. Hiskia, 12. Menasse, 13. Ammon[165], 14. Josias, 15. Zedekias. Cumque veniret Zedekias, Luna defectum patiebatur, inque defectu suo persistebat. Unde scriptum est Jerem. 52, 11. Et oculos Zedekiæ excæcabat &c. Causa autem primaria | omissionis trium videtur esse rotunditas numeri, ut mysterium tesseradecadis & hic resultaret. Sed quare hi tres omituntur & non alii? An quod tam abominabilis fuerit prosapia Achab, idololatrica, (1. Reg. 21, 21; 2. Reg. 9, 8.) quoniam Athalia Jorani uxor mater Achasiæ erat filia Achabi? Præsertim cum similes

---

163 Correction in the left margin: ut 1. Par. 6, 7. generationibus ab ipso aberat. Item Esr. 7, 3. collat cum replaced by ut 1. Par. 4, 1. collato cum c. 2, 50. ubi Schobal dicitur filius Judæ, qui tamen pluribus generationibus ab ipso aberat. Item Esr. 7, 3. collat. cum
164 Deleted word.
165 In error. It should be Amon, but was not corrected, probably due to oversight.
166 Examples deleted, see edition.
167 For a brief but authoritative introduction to Zeir Anpin (called Microprosopus in *Kabbala Denudata*), see Shaul Magid, *From Metaphysics to Midrash: Myth History and the Interpretation of Scripture in Lurianic Kabbalah* (Bloomington, Indiana University Press, 2008), pp. 16–34 "The Lurianic Myth", esp. pp. 24–29.
168 In error for 2 Chron 9.18. The references seem to be a little muddled here, 2 K 9.18 has nothing about the steps on the throne, but 1 K 10.19 and 2 Chron 9.18 have.
169 For moon and throne: Elliot. R. Wolfson, *Along the Path. Studies in Kabbalistic Myth, Symbolism and Hermeneutics* (State University of New York Press, 1995), p. 152.

sions in Genealogies often occur[166]. Thus, when 1 Chron 4.1 is compared with [1 Chron] 2.50, Schobal [= Shobal] who is said to be the son of Judah, is however separated from him by several generations. Similarly, when Ezra 7.3 is compared with 1 Chron 6.7; [and] Jos 7.1 with verse 24 and 22.20.

A similar omission is also found in Zohar on Exodus Crem col. 151, Mant folio 85:

"By tradition we have learned at 1 Chron 29.23 'And Solomon sat on the throne of the Lord' (i.e. Zeir | Anpin[167]). As it is written in 2 Kgs 9.18[168] [there were] six steps to the throne.[169] Rabbi Abba said: Because the moon was then full. For we say in the days of Solomon the moon was full. But when did it become full? On the fifteenth day, just as we have learned (because ||| these days are) 1 Abraham 2 Isaac 3 Jacob 4 Judah 5 Parez 6 Hezron 7 Ram 8 Aminadab 9 Nahshon 10 Salmon 11 Boaz 12 Obed 13 Jesse 14 David 15 Solomon[170]. So when therefore Solomon came along, the moon was full. Whence it says in 1 Chron 29.23, 'he sat on the throne of the Tetragrammaton'. In the days of Zedekiah the moon | had waned and the face of Israel was darkened. I set out the numbers: 1 Rehoboam 2 Abijah 3 Asa 4 Jehosaphath 5 Joram 6 Ahazia [Ozias] 7 Amazia (Joas is missing here) 8 Uzziah 9 Jotham 10 Ahaz 11 Hezekiah 12 Manasseh 13 Amon 14 Josiah 15 Zedekiah. And when Zediakiah came along the moon was obscured and it persisted in this state. Whence it is written: Jer 52.11 'And then he put out the eyes of Zedekiah'[171]etc."

fol. 27ʳ

The main cause | of the omission of the three seems to be the roundness of the number, to enable the Mystery of Fourteen to emerge here [in Matthew's genealogy]. But why were these three omitted and not others? Was it because the idolatrous descendants of Ahab were so abominable (1 Kgs 21.21; 2 Kgs 9.8), since Athalia, the wife of Joram and the mother of Achasia [Ahaziah 2 Chron 22.10] was the daughter of Ahab?[172] Especially

---

170   This sequence of numbered names and the similar list immediately below in the Zohar agrees with the order of Matthew's genealogy in chapter 1, but in the second list, after 6 Ahazia / Ozias until 9 Jotham, the names diverge. Matthew says Ozias begat Jotham and Jotham begat Ahaz. Amazia, Joas and Uzziah are thus missing from Matthew's list. The Christian below subsequently explains this as a measure to preserve the number fourteen in the list.

171   I.e. his eyes were darkened like the moon.

172   Some biblical verses suggest Athaliah was Ahab's daughter (2 Kgs 8.18; 2 Chron 21.6), others that she was his sister (2 Kgs 8.26; 2 Chron 22.2; 2 Kgs 8.27). See Winifred Thiel, "Athaliah" in *Anchor Bible Dictionary*, vol. 1, edited by David Noel Freedman (New York: Doubleday, 1992), pp. 511–512.

prætermissiones ob scelera similia suppeditent exempla, Simeonis, Deut. 33, & Danis, Apocal. 7. | & Joabi, 2. Sam. 23?

Cabb. Cat. *An vèro quod revera Jorami revolutio fuerit Amasia pater Uziæ? Sicut de Josiah dicunt nostrates, quod fuerit revolutio Achas: eò quod ad hunc dixerit Jesaias Propheta c. 7, 13. Audite nunc Domus David &c. De Josia autem dictum fuerit 1. Reg. 13, 2. Ecce filius nascetur pro Domo David, cui nomen | Josias &c.* (Emek Hammelech fol. 148. col. 4[173].)

Christianus. Nostrum interea est in id inniti, ne nomina nostra omittantur ê Catalogo viventium & vitam communicantium.[174]

V. 9. *Achaz genuit Chezekja.* אחז אולד לחזקיא

Christianus. Achaz erat annorum viginti, cum ad Regnum perveniret, 2. Par. 28, 1. & regnabat | annos sedecim, ita, ut anno ætatis 36. mortuus sit: quo tempore Hiskias filius ejus natus erat annos 25. 2. Par. 29, 1. quem propterea nasci oportuit anno Patris sui undecimo. Quid hîc statuemus? An cum Calvisio (ad Annum mundi 3196.) quod Hiskias vel privignus vel frater, vel adoptivus Achasi fuerit? An cum Lydiato ad A.M. 3262. quod Hiskias aliquot

---

173 The reference is to "Partis Secundæ Tractatus Quartus. Commentarius generalis methodicus in tres istos Libros: Librum Occultationis; & Synodos tam majorem, quam minorem. è Libro Emek Hammelech", *Kabbalah denudata II*, Pars II, pp. 47–144. The *Sefer Emek Ha-Melekh* written by Naphtali ben Jacob Barachah was published in Amsterdam. The reference given here does not refer to Knorr's Latin translation, rather to the Hebrew edition of the text.

174 Deletion of the entire speech of the Christian.

175 Simeon is conspicuously absent from the Blesssing of the Tribes by Moses in Deut 33. Possibly that tribe was absorbed into Judah (Samuel Rolles Driver, *The International Critical Commentary Deuteronomy* (Edinburgh: T&T Clark, 1951), pp. 395–396), but the omission is taken here as a sign of punishment, probably for Simeon's slaughter of the Shechemites after Hamor's violation of Dinah (Gen 34).

176 In this list of tribes Dan is absent. The mediaeval tradition has Antichrist born from this tribe. See Richard Kenneth Emmerson, *Antichrist in the Middle Ages. A Study of Medieval Apocalypticism, Art and Literature* (Manchester University Press, 1981), pp. 79–83; Wilhelm Bousset, *The Antichrist Legend* (London: Hutchinson, 1896), pp. 171–174.

177 Though Joab was King David's nephew and the commander of his army, he does not occur in the list of David's heroes in 2 Sam 23.8, 39; 1 Chron 11.11–41 (twelve of the names here also recur in 1 Chron 27.2–15 as those of the captains of the twelve divisions of David's army). He might be considered worthy of punishment for his ambush and murder of Abner (2 Sam 2.13–32; 3.27); his killing of Absalom (2 Sam 18.1–33); killing his replacement Amasa (2 Sam 20.8–13); or his final support of Adonijah (1 Kgs 1.1–27). David told Solomon to have him killed, which Solomon did by the hand of Bena-

SECTION VI   343

since examples of similar omissions on account evil doing are provided by
Simeon in Deut 33[175], by Dan in Rev 7[.5–8][176] | and by Joab in 2 Sam 23[177].

Kabballist Catechumen Or that, in fact, Joram was the reincarnation of
Amazia, the father of Uzziah? Just as our sages say Josiah was the reincarnation of Ahaz: Isaiah the Prophet 7.13 spoke about him: "Hear now, House of David"[178] etc. About Josiah it was said (1 Kgs 13.2) "Look, a son shall be born for the House of David whose name | shall be Josiah" etc..[179] (Emeq Hamelekh fol. 148 col. 4.)[180]

Verse 9
Ahaz begat Hezekiah 'ḥz 'wld lḥzqy'

Christian Ahaz was 20 years old when he came to the Kingdom (2 Chron 28.1) and he ruled | for 16 years, so he died at 36, at which time Hezekiah his son was 25 (2 Chron 29.1), who must have been born when his father was 11. What shall we decide here? Shall we say with Calvisius[181] (on AM[182] 3196) that Hezekiah was either a step-son or brother or adopted son of Ahaz? Or shall we say with Lydiat[183] (on AM 3262) that Hezekiah had some years pre-

---

iah (1 Kgs 2.29–34). Lightfoot, *Miscellanies and the Harmony of the Gospels*, op. cit., p. 174: "So Simeon is omitted in Moses's blessing, for his cruelty to Shechem, and to Joseph. So Dan, at the sealing of the Lord's people, because of idolatry, begun in his tribe: and so Joab, from among David's worthies, because of his bloodiness to Amasa and Abner."

178   The reference is to the Immanuel prophecy of which this is the beginning.
179   The wording of the announcement of Josiah's birth shows that he is the child promised in Isaiah 7.
180   Deleted: Christian But it is a characteristic of ours to struggle that no names of ours are lost from the list of the living and those sharing life.
181   Sethus Calvisius (1556–1615) was a German music theorist and composer and a significant mathematician and astronomer: in his *Opus chronologicum ex autoritate s. scripturae ad motum luminarium coelestium contextum* (Leipzig, 1605, with several editions elsewhere thereafter) he expounded a chronological system based on the records of nearly 300 eclipses: Arrey von Dommer, "Calvisius, Sethus" in *Allgemeine Deutsche Biographie*, vol. 3 (Leipzig: Duncker & Humblot, 1876), pp. 716–717. His entry for AM 3196 reads: "*Ezechias rex nascitur, cum Achas nondum esset decem annorum puer, idea privignus ipsius, vel frater, vel adoptivus filius potius, quam naturalis creditur 2. Reg 18.*"
182   *Anno Mundi*. The traditional Jewish chronological reckoning of the Mishnah and Talmud was formalised by R. Yose ben Ḥalaphta and is found in *Seder Olam*. To convert AM dates to Gregorian dates see, Heinrich W. Guggenheimer, *Seder Olam. The Rabbinic View of Biblical Chronology*, 2nd ed. (Lanham: Aronson, 2005), pp. 276–285.
183   Thomas Lydiat (1572–1646) published his *Emendatio Temporum ab initio Mundi ... contra Scaligerum et alios* in London in 1609 (London: F. Kyngston 1609). He remarks:

annis antea in Regni societatem cooptatus sit â patre, anno | ætatis suæ 20? 30
(videantur interim loca 2. Reg. 16, 1. coll. cum 2. Reg. 15 v. 27. & 33.) An vèro casum admittemus secundum literam?

[Cabb. Cat.][184] Sane incolæ illarum regionum multò citius pubuerunt quam qui in regionibus septentrionalibus vivunt. Ubi enim major est calor, copiosiores spiritus & vigor maturior ibi citior pubertas. Evincunt id exempla[185] Judæ; | Geris; Onanis; Selah; Perez; Benjamin; filiorum Ephraim; Salo- 35 monis; Amonis; Josiæ & aliorum. Nam inter annum Jacobi 130, Gen. 47, 9. (quo Joseph anno 14. servitutis Labaniticæ natus c. 30, 25. erat annorum 39. c. 45, 6; c. 41, 46. adeòque natus anno Patris 91.) & inter annum, quo Judah natus erat (id est servitutis undecimum Gen. 29, 20.32.33.34.35: & Jacobi 88.um) non | intercedunt nisi anni 42. intra quos tamen & Juda duxerat uxo- 40 rem, Gen. 38, v. 2. Et Ger; Onan; Selah pubuerant, atque post hujus pubertatem ê Judah natus Perez uxorem duxerat & duos Patri genuerat nepotes, Gen. 46, 12. Ubi intra 42 hosce annos ponatur Judam 14° ætatis anno duxisse uxorem: tunc 15° natus erit Ger: 16° Onan, 17° Selah. 26° Ger ducit uxorem Tamarem, anno | ætatis 12°. 27°. Onan eandem ducit. 28°. Selah est duodecennis & 45 Tamar ex Judâh concipit. 29°. Perez nascitur. 40°. Perez duodecennis ducit uxorem. 41°. Hebron ||| nascitur, 42°. Hamul nascitur & Jacob descendit in Ægiptum.

fol. 27^v

Ita & Benjamin anno ætatis 23°. jam genuerat filios decem Gen. 46, 21. Et Ephraim, cum filios vidisset octavæ generationis adhuc filium genuit, â quo usque ad Josuam filium Nun itidem numerantur octo generationis[186], 1. Par. 8, 20, ut | intra 215. annos factæ sint septendecim generationes. Et 5 Salomo cum gigneret Roboamum (sub initium imperii sui 1. Reg. 11, 42. collat. cum cap. 14, 22.) dicitur puer parvus 1. Reg. 3, 7. item puer & tenellus 1. Par. 23, 5; c. 30, 1. Amon autem annos natus 16. genuit Josiam. conf. 2. Reg. 21, 19. cum c. 22, 1. Et Josias annorum 14. maritus genuit Jehojakim conf. 2.

"A. 3262 m. [i.e. AM] mortuo Jothamo rege Judae postquam regnaverat 16 annos, successit eius filius Ahaz: aliquot tamen annis antea (ut apparet) in regni societatem cooptatus a patre, anno aetatis suae 20." Lydiat himself seems to have first dated the Creation to 4004 BC and to have influenced Ussher in this respect forty years later. See Jeremy Hughes, *Secrets of the Times Myth and History in Biblical Chronology* (Sheffield Academic Press, 1990), pp. 262–263.

184 Deletion: Cabb. Cat. so that the speech remains with the Christian.
185 Correction: a sign is placed above the line which indicates that the terms should be inverted: evincunt id exempla Judæ replaced by Id quod evincunt exempla Judæ
186 Correction: generationis replaced by generationes

viously, | when he was 20, been co-opted into a co-regency by his father? (In this context consider 2 Kgs 16.1 compared with 2 Kgs 15.27, 33.) Or should we take it all quite literally?

Clearly the inhabitants of those regions reached puberty much more quickly than those who live in Northern regions. For where the heat is greater, spirits are larger and vigour more mature and there puberty is earlier. Which is what is shown by the examples of Judah, | Gera, Onan, Selah, Perez, Benjamin, the sons of Ephraim, Solomon, Amon, Josiah and others. For between Jacob's 130th year (Gen 47, 9) [and the year] in which Joseph was born to him—[that is] in the 14th year of his [Jacob's] servitude to Laban (30.25)—were 39 years (45.6; 41.46) so that [Joseph] was born when his father [Jacob] was 91. And between the year in which Judah was born (that is the 11th of Jacob's servitude Gen 29.20, 32, 33, 34, 35 and Jacob's 88th year) [and Jacob's 130th year] there | were 42 years[187]. During [this time] Judah married (Gen 38.2). And Gera, Onan and Selah [Shelah[188]] reached puberty and after his puberty Perez [Pharez], born from Judah, took a wife and fathered two grandsons for his father (Gen 46.12). If within those 42 years[189] we say Judah took a wife in his fourteenth year, then in his fifteenth Gera will be born, in his sixteenth Onan, in his seventeenth Selah [Shelah] and in his twenty-sixth Gera marries Tamar when | he is twelve. In his twenty-seventh year Onan married the same Tamar and in his twenty-eighth year Selah [Shelah] is twelve and Tamar conceived by Judah. In his twenty-ninth year, Perez was born and in his fortieth year Perez, aged twelve, took a wife. In his forty-first year, Hebron ||| was born. In his forty-second year Hamul was born and Jacob went down into Egypt.

fol. 27ᵛ

So too Benjamin at 23 had already fathered ten sons (Gen 46.21). And Ephraim, when he had seen the sons of eight previous generations, fathered a son from whom up until Joshua, the son of Nun, are similarly reckoned eight generations (1 Chron 8.20), so that | in 215 years there were 17 generations. And Solomon, when Rehoboam was born at the beginning of his reign (1 Kgs 11.42 compared with 14.22) is called "a small boy" (1 Kgs 3.7) and "a boy" and "delicate" (1 Chron 23.5; 30.1). And Amon at sixteen fathered Josiah (Compare 2 Kgs 21.19 with 22.1.) And Josiah at 14 was married and fathered Jehoiakim (Compare 2 Kgs 22.1 with 23.36).

---

187 So: Judah was born in his father's 88th year (49 year's before his father's 130th year); Joseph was born three years later (in the 14 rather than the 11th year of Jacob's captivity) in his father's 91st year which was 39 years before his 130th year.
188 Names which may not be immediately recognisable are glossed with their KJV equivalent to aid identification.
189 That is, from the birth of Judah in his 88th year until Jacob's 130th year.

Reg, 22, 1. cum cap. 23, 36. [**Cabb. Cat.**]¹⁹⁰ *Sic Dinah cum | â Sichemo vitia-* 10
retur fuisse â nostratibus dicitur annorum septem, Chesed Abrahami Tract.
*4, cap. 49.*¹⁹¹ *verba sunt hæc : Dinah filia Jacobi nata fuit anno Jacobi nona-*
*gesimo*¹⁹²*: Joseph autem frater ejus anno nonagesimo primo. Cum ergo Dinah*
nata esset annos septem imprægnabatur â Sichemo, filio Hemor; & generabat
Asnath, cum nata esset octo annos. Cum autem habere[*t*] | *annos novem, ean-* 15
dem ducebat Simeon frater ejus, & generabat Saul, filium Cananitidis. Annos
habens quadraginta, cum Patre descendebat in Ægiptum anno ætatis Josephi
39. Cum autem Jacob moreretur Joseph erat annorum 56. & Dinah annorum 57.
Biennio post mortem Patris Dinah nubebat Jobo, annos nata 59. cum ipse esset
annorum 18. & nepos Uzi primogeniti | *Nachor fratris Abraham &c. Eratque* 20
Propheta & vir Sanctus ê Pii gentilibus: descenderatque in Ægiptum, & duxerat
Dinam agnatam suam (quarti gradus). Sed & Dinah Prophetissa erat, & scie-
bat, quod nuberet consanguineo suo, sciebatque, quod natus esset circumcisus,
unde etiam vocatur תם *integer &c. Et Dinah pariebat septem filios & tres filias*
&c. Et Rebecca | *cum nuberet Isaaco fuisse dicitur annorum trium in Sohar.* 25

[**Christianus.**]¹⁹³ Quin & hodiernum in India Orientali Benjanorum filii
& filiæ ante annum ætatis suæ decimum matrimonia contrahunt, quamvis
brevior quoque ipsis sit vita.

V. 11. *Joschia genuit Jeschonja.*¹⁹⁴ יושיא אולד ליוכניא

Christianus. Quid tibi videtur de hac difficultate?¹⁹⁵

Cabb. Cat. *Filii Josiæ juxta*¹⁹⁶ *1. Par. 3, 15.* fuerunt primogenitus Jochanan 30
(qui in Talmude Hierosol. Schækalim fol. 94, 4. explicatur fuisse Joachas,
de quo 2. Reg. 2. 23, 30.31. qui post patrem regnavit per trimestre spatium

---

190   Added in the left margin: *Cabb. Cat.* (which involves a change of speaker).
191   R. Abraham Ben Mordecai Azulai (1570–1643) *Chesed le-Abraham* was published in Amsterdam 1685 by Bloch with Knorr's assistance. The same year an inferior text, with lacunae and many errors, was printed in Amsterdam. C.G. Düring's 1734 *Novum Inventarum Bibliothecæ Sulzbaco-Palatino* (BSB Cbm 580 Repositorium A) records a copy in the library there: p. 29#19. According to the catalogue, that version was printed in Sulzbach in 1684.
192   Deletion of a word, now unreadable (probably primo).
193   Added in the left margin: Christian. (which involves a change of speaker).
194   Correction: Jeschonja replaced by Jechonja
195   Deletion of the entire speech of the Christian.
196   Deleted word.

SECTION VI 347

10 **Kabbalist Catechumen** Similarly our sages say | that Dinah when she was raped by Shechem was seven. *Chesed le-Abraham*, Tract. 4, chap. 49 runs as follows:

"Dinah the daughter of Jacob was born in Jacob's ninetieth year, but Joseph her brother in his ninety-first year. So when Dinah was seven years old, she was impregnated by Hemor the son of Shechem and gave birth
15 to Asnath when she was eight. However when she | was nine, Simeon her brother married her and fathered Saul [Shaul], the son of the Canaanitess[197]. When he was forty he went down into Egypt with his father in Joseph's thirty-ninth year. When Jacob died, Joseph was fifty-six and Dinah fifty-seven. Two years after the death of her father, Dinah married Job[198] when she was fifty-
20 nine and he was eighteen and the grandson of Uzi [Huz] the first born | of Nachor [Nahor][199], brother of Abraham etc. He was a prophet and a holy man from the godly Gentiles. He went down into Egypt and married Dinah his relative (of the fourth degree). But Dinah was also a prophetess and knew she was marrying a blood-relation and she knew because he was born circumcised which is why he is called *tm* 'whole'[200] etc. And Dinah had seven sons and three daughters etc.".

25 And Rebecca | when she married Jacob is said in Zohar to have been three years old.

Christian And today in Eastern India, the sons and daughters of the Benjani get married before they are ten, although their lives are also briefer[201].

Verse 11
Joschia [Josiah] begat Jechoniah ywšy' 'wld lywkny'

30 [202]**Kabbalist Catecumen** The sons of Josiah, according to 1 Chron 3.15 were the first born Johanan (who in the Jerusalem Talmud Shekalim fol. 94.4 is identified as Jehoahaz—concerning whom 2 Kgs 23.30, 31) who reigned after

---

197 Gen 46.10; Ex 6.15.
198 Midrashic texts (especially *Genesis Rabbah*) speak of Dinah's marriage to Job. See Mary Anna Bader, *Tracing the Evidence: Dinah in Post-Hebrew Bible Literature* (New York, Peter Lang, 2008). For *Genesis Rabbah*, see pp. 30–48.
199 Gen 22.20–21.
200 Job 1.1.
201 For the Benjanen, Johann Albrecht von Mandelslo, *Morgenländische Reyse Beschreibung* (Schleswig: Johan Holwein, 1658), ch. 36, p. 109 et seq.: "*Von der Benjanen Gestalt /Kleidung/ Natur ...*". On p. 110: "*Sie verheyrathen ihre Kinder gar jung / Knaben und Mädgen von 12, 9 und weniger Jahren.*"
202 Deleted: Christian What do you think about this difficulty?

deportatusque, in Ægiptum inibi mortuus est, ibid. v. 34.) Secundus Jehojakim (qui 2. Reg. 23, 34. Eliakim dicitur, & post regnum undecim annorum | deportatus in Babel in via mortuus est. 2. Par 36, 6; Jer. 22, 18.19; c. 36, 30.) Tertius Zidkijahu (qui ultimus fuit Regum Hierosolymitanorum, excæcatusque in Babel deportatus est. 2. Reg: 25, 7. liberis ejus occisis.) Quartus Schallum (quem Hierosolymitani loco allegato habent pro Zedekia: alii pro Joachaso ex Jerem. 22, 11, alii pro Jechonia, ut Kimchi.)[203] *Præter hos filios autem ê Jojakimo | Josiæ etiam nascebatur nepos Jehojachin seu Jechonjah octavo ante mortem anno, vide 2. Reg. 24, 6. conf. 2. Reg. 23. 34; 1 Par. 3, 16. quem avus adopt[as]se, & ad Regni consortium cum Patre declarasse videtur, quia anno jam ætatis octavo ad regnum pervenisse dicitur 2. Par. 36, 9. qui annus erat mortis Josiæ, & 25. patris quo & iste ad regnum perveniebat, ibid. v. 5. Hoc autem deinde | post undecim annos mortuo, Jechonia solus regnare incipiebat, completo anno ‖‖ ætatis decimo octavo 2. Reg. 24, 8. Atque hic est unitus ille, per quem Regium hoc semen durante captivitate propagatum est.* [**Christianus.**][204] Per vocem genuit igitur hoc loco non intelligitur generatio immediata, prout plerique statuunt, qui per Jechoniam intelligunt Jojakimum, absque ullâ tamen autoritate sive Historiæ; sive Traditionis; Sed mediata, nepotis scilicet, | iterumque omittitur Jehojakim ob maledictionem Jer. 22, v. 18.19. Reliqui autem filii Josiæ propterea dicuntur fratres ejus, quia ipse ab Avo adoptatus esse potuit in filium: illorumque propterea mentio fit, quia omnes miserè perierunt, hoc solo excepto Regii seminis propagatore, juxta 1. Par. 3, 17. Transportationis autem ideò fit mentio, quia Babylonem Jechonjah deductus est; ibique liberos genuit: postquam ê carcere | eductus esset & regiè haberetur in aula Babylonica, 2. Reg. 25, 27; Jer. 52, 31.

---

203   Correction: this first part of the Cabbalist's speech is deleted and replaced by simply: Filii Josiæ 1. Par. 3, 15. enumerantur
204   Added in the right margin: Christian. (which involves a change of speaker).
205   Lightfoot, *Miscellanies and the Harmony of the Gospels*, op. cit., pp. 174–175: "'Josias begat Jechonias.' So readeth the Syrian, Arabic, and the most and best Greek copies. And so the evangelist himself requireth that it be read, to make fourteen generations from David to the captivity into Babel. And so readeth D. Kimchi, on 1 Chron. iii. 15. Josias, indeed, begat Joachim; and Joachim begat Jechonias; but he, that was neither fit to be lamented, nor to be buried like one of the kings of Judah, was much more unfit to come into the line of the kings of Judah, that leadeth to Christ."
206   Knorr diverges markedly from Lightfoot, as might be expected, over the future of the Judaean kingly line. Lightfoot is eager that all temporal aspirations be extinguished with the arrival of Christ, whereas Knorr looks forward to an earthly Jewish messianic kingdom. Lightfoot, *Miscellanies and the Harmony of the Gospels*, op. cit., pp. 175–176: "The Jews, in their Talmud, give this rule for a fundamental point:— 'That there is no king to be for Israel, but of the house of David, and of the seed of Solomon only. And he that separateth against this family, denieth the name of the blessed God, and the words

his father for the space of three months and was deported to Egypt where he died (ibid. verse 34). The second was Jehoiakim who in 2 Kgs 23.34 is called Eliakim and after a reign of eleven years | was deported to Babyon and died on the way (2 Chron 36.6; Jer 22.18, 19; 36.30). The third was Zedekiah (who was the last king of the Jerusalemites and after being blinded was deported to Babylon (2 Kgs 25.7) after his sons were killed). The forth was Shallum whom the Jerusalemites had considered in the passage just cited to be Zedekiah, others, Jehoahaz (from Jer 22.11), and yet others like Kimchi to be Jechoniah.

In addition to these sons however, there was born of Jehoiakim | to Josiah his grandson Jehoiachin [Jehoiakin] (or Jeconiah) eight years before (See 2 Kgs 24.6 and Cf. 2 Kgs 23.34; 1 Chron 3.16) whom his grandfather adopted and seems to have been declared a consort in the Kingdom with his father, which was the year of the death of Josiah, for already in his eighth year he is said to have come to the throne (2 Chron 36.9). This was the year of the death of Josiah and the twenty-fifth of his father since he himself had also come to the throne (ibid. v5). When he died | eleven years later, Jechoniah began to reign alone, being ||| eighteen (2 Kgs 24.8) and it was through him alone whom the royal line was preserved during the Exile.

Christian By the word "fathered" here is not to be understood an immediate generation, as many think who by Jechoniah [Jeconiah] understand Jojakimum [Jehoiakim]—without any authority of History or of Tradition, but rather the mediation of a grandson.[205] | And, again, Jehoiakim is omitted on account of the curse in Jer 22.18, 19. The other sons of Josiah, moreover, are said to be his brothers because he was able to have been adopted by his grandfather as a son. For this reason mention is made of how wretchedly they all perished, with the sole exception of the preserver of the royal line according to 1 Chron 3.17. Mention of deportation is made because Jechonijah [Jeconiah] was taken to Babylon and there he fathered children; after he had been rescued from prison | he was treated royally and lived in the Babylonian palace (2 Kgs 25.27; Jer 52.31).[206]

fol. 28r

---

of his prophets, that are spoken in truth. (Sanhedr. cap. 10, and R. Samuel in Ner. Mitsvah, fol. 153). With this opinion, although Matthew seem to comply, at the first appearance, in that he deriveth our Saviour from Solomon; because of the Hebrews, for whom he wrote, which looked for him from thence:—yet the carnal sense of it, which aimeth only at the earthly kingdom of the Messias, and at the exact descent from Solomon, he closely confuteth, to the eyes of the intelligent reader, by these two things: 1. In that he bringeth the line along to Jechonias, in whom the seed of Solomon, and the regal dignity also with it, failed: 2. In that he deriveth the interest of Christ in that dignity, if it were any, only by Joseph: which, according to the flesh, had no relation at all to him, save the marriage of his mother."

V. 12. *Schelathielem.* לשלתאיל

[**Cabb. Cat.**][207] *Annon obstat locus Jer. 22, 30?*

[**Christianus.**][208] Neutiquam, id enim Gemara tribuit Conversioni ejus, vel etiam deportationi. Sanhedria[209] fol. 27. col. 2. quod decretum illud in melius conversum sit. | Idemque reperimus in Sohar Sect. Mischpatim Crem. col. 189. Mant. fol. 106.[210] Conferi[211] etiam 1. Par. 3, 17. ubi expressè Jechoniæ tribuuntur liberi.

Schelateel genuit Zorbabel. שלתאיל אולד [212]לזורבבל

[**Cabb. Cat.**][213] *Nonne obstat, quod 1. Par. 3, 19. Zerubabel dicatur filius Pedajah?*

[**Christianus.**][214] Neque hoc, jam enim respondit Kimchi ad h.l. versu 18. enarrari | filios Schealtiel, inter quos Pedajah: ita ut Zerubabel sit nepos Schealtielis, qui sæpissimè ponantur pro filiis. Conf. Esr. 3, 2; Neh. 12, 1; Hay. 1, 1. 12.14; c. 2, 3.24.

---

207 Correction above the line: Christianus replaced by Cabb. Cat. (which involves the two speakers being changed over in the following exchange).
208 Correction above the line: Cabb. Cat. replaced by Christianus (as a consequence of the previous correction).
209 Correction: Sanhedria replaced by Sanhedrin
210 Added in the right margin: Excerpt. Cent. 1. Loc. 54, n. 45.
211 Correction: Conferi replaced by Confer
212 Correction: לזורבבל replaced by לזרובבל
213 Correction above the line: Christianus replaced by Cabb. Cat. (which involves the two speakers being changed over in the following exchange).
214 Correction in the right margin: Cabb. Cat. replaced by Christian. (as a consequence of the previous correction).
215 Of Coniah [usually taken as Jeconiah] the son of Jehoiakim, Jeremiah says: "*Write this man childless ...*" Lightfoot, *Miscellanies and the Harmony of the Gospels*, op. cit., p. 175: "Jechonias was father to Salathiel, as Baasha was to Ahab, not by generation, but by predecession. For Jechonias, in very deed, was childless; and the natural father of Salathiel was Neri [Lk 3.27]: yet he is said to beget him, because he declared and owned him for his next heir and successor."

Verse 12
Schelathiel [Salathiel / Shealtiel] lšltʾyl

Kabbalist Catechumen Does not Jer 22.30 contradict this?[215]

Christian Not at all, for the Gemarah attributes it to his repentance or even his deportation (Sanhedrin fol. 27 col. 2)[216] because this judgment was turned into something better | and we find the same in the Zohar Sect Mishpatim Crem col. 189, Mant fol. 106; Excerpts Cent. I Loc. 54, n. 45. Compare also 1 Chron 3.17 where children are expressly allotted to Jechoniah [Jehoiachin].

Schaltiel [Salathiel] begot Zorbabel šltʾyl ʾwld lzrwbbl

Kabbalist Catechumen Surely an objection here is that in 1 Chron 3.19 Zerabbabel is said to be the son of Pedaiah?[217]

Christian Has Kimchi not already responded to the difficulty here? In verse 18 | the sons of Shealtiel are listed, amongst whom was Pedaiah; so that Zerubbabel was the grandson of Shealtiel (grandsons are very often referred to as sons Cf. Ezr 3.2; Neh 12.1; Hag 1.1, 12, 14; 2.3, 24).

---

216 Lightfoot, *Miscellanies and the Harmony of the Gospels*, op. cit., p. 176: "The Jews, to disgrace the Gospel of St. Luke, do hold, that Jechonias was the natural father of Salathiel; and that, upon his repentance in Babel, God gave him children, as Assir and Salathiel (D. Kimchi on 1 Chron 3). But God had sworn (Jer 22.23), and he will not repent (Ps 110.4), that he should die childless to the throne: and his repentance could no more repeal this oath of God, than the prayer of Moses did the decree of his not entering into the land."

217 Ibid., p. 176: "Salathiel begat Pedaiah, and Pedaiah begat Zorobabel (1 Chron 3.18–19). But because, when the masculine line of Solomon's house failed in Jechonias,—the dignity, turning over to the line of Nathan, first settled upon Salathiel, but first showed itself eminent in Zorobabel: therefore constantly, when mention is made of Zorobabel, he is not called the son of Pedaiah, a man of no action, but obscure,—but the son of Salathiel, in whom the honour of that family began. For 'Jechonias was a signet plucked off (Jer 22.24)', and Zorobabel was set on again in his stead (Hag 2.23)."

V. 13. *Zerubabel genuit Abiud.* לאביוד

[**Cabb. Cat.**][218] *Cur autem hujus Abiud inter filios Zerubabelis 1. Par. 3, 19. non fit | mentio; nec posterorum ejus?*

[**Christianus.**][219] Credo quod ibi illustriores enumerentur: apud Matthæum obscuriores.

V. 16. *Josephum maritum Marjam.* ליוסף [220] זברה דמרים

Christianus.[221] Josephi cum Maria contractum matrimonium[222] ostendit istum fuisse proximum | ejus agnatum ejusdem tribus, & familiæ ejusdem? sive Maria, prout ab antiquis præsertim Epiphanio asseritur, fuerit filia fratribus carens, soli tamen, fundive cujusdam hæres, ut legi Num. 36, 8.9. hîc locus esset: sive propter spem Messiæ promissionis[223] Davidi factas, tantum inter Davidigenas matrimonia proximorum agnatorum in usu essent: unde cognita Josephi stirpe & Mariæ atque Jesu genealogia | cognosci poterat[224]: quamvis ille pater hujus non esset? (vid. annot. ad Luc. 1, 27.)

Cabb. Cat. Sufficit autem[225], *quod aliunde constet (nempe ê Luc. 3, 23.*[226]*) Mariam ê stirpe Davidis oriundam: nam & ê Genealogia Hillelis in Juchasin f. 46. b. apparet, quod computetur inter Davidigenas ratione matris: | item f. 19. b. ibidem.*

---

218 Correction above the line: Christianus replaced by Cabb. Cat. (which involves the two speakers being changed over in the following exchange).
219 Correction above the line: Cab. Cat. replaced by Christianus (as a consequence of the previous correction).
220 Correction: זברה replaced by גברא
221 Added in the right margin: An ergò
222 Added above the line: non
223 Correction: promissionis replaced by promissiones
224 Correction: poterat replaced by potuerit
225 Deleted word.
226 Added in the right margin: ubi subinnuitur, Josephum fuisse generum Eli:
227 Knorr is inconsistent in his spelling of this name.
228 Epiphanius discusses the Antidicomarianites (Panarion 78) who deny the perpetual virginity of Mary and the Kollyridons (Panarion 79) who devote exaggerated veneration to Mary by offering her a kind of bread [*kollyra*] as to a god. The only comment apparently relevant to the question of her siblings is 79.5.1 and 7.1 where her birth to infertile parents is discussed (*The Panarion of Epiphanius of Salamis Books II & III De Fide*, trans. by Frank Williams, 2nd ed. (Leiden: Brill, 2013), pp. 641 and 643). Mary's own birth is first discussed in the *Proto-evangelium of James* (c. 145AD), a story of a bar-

SECTION VI 353

Verse 13
Zerubabel[227] *begat Abiud l'bywd*

Kabbalist Catechumen Why does 1Chron 3.19 make no | mention of this Abiud among the sons of Zerubbabel, nor of his descendents?

Christian I believe that there only the most illustrious are mentioned, but in Matthew the more obscure.

Verse 16
Joseph the husband of Mary lywsp gbr' dmrym

Christian Does the marriage Joseph contracted with Mary not show he was a close | relative of the same tribe and the same family? Or was Mary, as the ancient fathers—especially Epiphanius—assert, a daughter lacking brothers[228] but the heiress of some land or a farm (This would be an example of the law in Num 36.8,9 [about the daughters of Zelophehad]); or on account of the hope of Messiah and the promises made to David, did the descendants of David only make marriages with close relatives; so that, knowing the descent of Joseph and of Mary, Jesus' genealogy | could also be known, although Joseph was not his father (See the note on Lk 1. 27)?

Kabbalist Catechumen It is sufficient that elsewhere it is agreed (specifically from Lk 3. 23 where it is implied that Heli was the father-in-law of Joseph) that Mary was sprung from the descendants of David. Also from the genealogy of Hillel in Juchasin fol. 46b, it appears that he was considered amongst the descendant of David on account of his mother. | Also see fol. 19b of the same.

---

ren couple whose prayer for a child was answered and who devoted the child to the temple upon which Epiphanius relies. Their barrenness would apparently preclude siblings. However, some traditions consider Mary of Cleopas to be the sister of the Virgin: Agnes B.C. Dunbar, "St Mary of Clopas" in *A Dictionary of Saintly Women*, 2 vols, edited by Agnes B.C. Dunbar (London: George Bell & Sons, 1905), vol. 2, pp. 45–56. Others consider her the Virgin's sister-in-law (Fredrick G. Holweck, "Mary Cleophae" in *A Biographical Introduction of Saints with a General Introduction on Hagiology*, edited by Fredrick G. Holweck (London: B. Herder, 1924), p. 677). Mary Salome is also sometimes considered a daughter of St Anne by a third husband and thus a half-sister of the Virgin (*A Dictionary of Saintly Women*, op. cit., pp. 211–212). In this case St Anne is married successively to Joachim (Mary's father), to Cleopas by whom she had James the Less, Simon, Jude and Barsabas and finally to Salom, Joseph's brother (Holweck, "Mary Cleophae", *art. cit.*, p. 679). Further see Valerie Abrahamsen, "Human and Divine: The Marys in Early Christian Tradition" in *A Feminist Companion to Mariology*, edited by Amy-Jill Levine and Maria Mayo Robbins (London: T&T Clark, 2005), pp. 164–181 at p. 166.

Messias משיחא

Cabb. Cat. *Plerumque â nostratibus cum Epitheto appellatur* מלכא משיחא *Rex Messias; & ê nostra gente ceu restaurator omnis humanæ corruptionis semper expectatus est. Nomen hoc*[229] *per metaphoram ab unctione | denominari solet.*

Christianus. Merito autem tunc cum Matthæus hæc scriberet, Jesus dicebatur Messias, quia superatis tentationibus omnibus in hoc officio jam confirmatus erat. Act. 2, 36; Heb. 2, 9; Phil. 2, 9; Joh. 10, 17. (vide plura in Tractatu de Revolutionibus Animarum, p. 251.254.255.263.298.302.303.320.321.333 .361.363.364.373.[230] ||| 421.426.432.435.441.453. Et in Tractatu Vall. Reg. p. 174 .231.239.335.[231])

V. 17. Progenies שרבתא

Christianus. Membra intelliguntur Genealogica, sive personæ, partim generantes, partim generatæ, partim aliæ; quoniam inter membra ordinis tertii â Matthæo | connumeratur Maria, â qua genitus est Jesus: idque etiam propterea, ne Josephus videri posset aliquid ad ipsius nativitatem contribuisse. In novo enim hoc nascendi genere, novum etiam requirebatur Genealogiæ genus, ubi inter generantes numeraretur Mater contra gentis consuetudinem; & maritus ab uxore gradu discerneretur, quia carnis consuetudine nunquam facti erant caro una.

Cabb. Cat.[232] *Numerus autem iste quatuordecim juxta Cabbalistas nostros magna in se continet mysteria: Decadem nempe Sephriothicam, cum quaternario Tetragrammatico; vel mundorum; vel Patriarcharum; Et numerus totius Genealogiæ nempe 42. designat magnum Dei Nomen totidem literarum de quo prolixè agitur in Pardes Rimmonim Tract. 21, cap. 12, 13. fol. 123. d. sqq. Tres autem | classes denotare queunt tres mundos inferiores, vel tres infimos Animæ gradus.*

---

229 Added in the right margin: autem Babel à superfluo divinæ Naturæ, cum quæ unita est Anima hæc, influxu, qui

230 In the right bottom corner appears a Hebrew letter ח presumably an indication of binding or pagination.

231 Cf. *supra*, footnote 173, p. 342.

232 Added in the left margin: Ego autem iterum ad id respicis, quod dixeram ad Matth. 1, v.1.

233 The word "Messiah" and the word "Christ" mean "Anointed One".

234 Contrast Lightfoot, *Miscellanies and the Harmony of the Gospels*, op. cit., p. 177: "The whole sum of the three fourteens is the renowned number of two-and-forty: the number of the knops, and flowers, and branches, of the candlestick; of the journeys and sta-

Messiah *mšyḥ'*

Kabbalist Catechumen Frequently our sages use the epithet *mlk' mšyḥ'*, "Messiah the King", and we have always expected the Restorer of all Human Corruption from amongst our own people. This name, [Messiah], comes from the overflowing of divine nature with which the soul is united and is usually spoken of as a metaphor of | anointing.[233]

Christian Matthew is correct then when he writes these things. Jesus was called Messiah because, having overcome all temptations, he was then confirmed in this office (Act 2.36; Heb 2.9; Phil 2.9; Jn 10.17). (See more in Tract. *De Revol. Animarum*, pp. 251, 254, 255, 263, 298, 302, 303, 320, 321, 333, 361, 363, 364, 373, ||| 421, 426, 432, 435, 441, 453. And in *Tract Vall. Reg.*, pp. 174, 231, 239, 335.)   fol. 28v

Verse 17
Firstborn *šrbt'*

Christian Genealogical items are to be understood as characters—sometimes parents, sometimes children and sometime others—since amongst the members of [this] third group Matthew | reckons Mary from whom Jesus was born. And this is the case, so that Joseph should not appear to have contributed anything to [Jesus'] birth. For this new type of birth also required a new type of genealogy where the Mother was considered amongst those generating [new life], contrary to the practice of the people; and a husband was distinguished in status from his wife, because by the usage of the flesh they were never made one flesh.

Kabbalist Catechumen Meanwhile, I take up again that which I said on Mt 1.1. This number 14, according to our Kabbalists, contains in itself great mysteries: the ten grades and the four letters of the Tetragrammaton, or the four Worlds, or the Patriarchs.[234] The total number of [the items] in the genealogy, forty-two, designates the great name of God which has the same number of letters and which is dealt with—in great length!—in *Pardes Rimonim*, Tract. 21, chap. 12, 13, fol. 123d *seq*.[235]. The three | classes [of 14 in the genealogy] can denote the three inferior worlds or the three lowest parts of the soul.

---

tions of Israel, betwixt Egypt and Canaan (Num 33); and of the children of Bethel (savaged by Elisha's bear 2 Kgs 2.24)."

235 *Pardes Rimonim*, the first comprehensive and systematic exposition of Medieval Kabbalah, was written in Safed in 1548 by Moses ben Jacob Cordovero, a teacher of Isaac Luria.

Christianus.[236] Sensus autem mysticus talis esse videtur: frustra ad generandam in nobis vitam divinam eniti naturalia Animæ exercitia, sive ut corrigatur Psyche, quam Hebræi Nephesch vocant, Philosophi concupiscibile: sive ut spiritus emendetur, quem Hebræi Ruach | Philosophi irrascibile[237] dicunt: sive tandem, ut altius emergat Mens, quæ ab Hebræis Neschamah, â Philosophis Rationale dicitur: quia tandem divinitus in Mente hæc vita Christi enascatur.

Recte autem præmitti Ascetica hæc, per singula istius Genealogiæ membra denotata, ut quoad Classem primam, quæ proximum concernere videtur & Ecclesiam, (quamvis ad | alias quoque desuper instituendas meditationes via præclusa sit nemini.)

(1.) quis studeat esse *Membrum multitudinis* illius, quæ cum Deo in fœdere est. (Nam vox Abraham explicari potest, quasi dicatur אבר המון Membrum multitudinis, seposito, & ad alios casus reservato significatú, quod eadem vox & Patrem multitudinis denotet.)

(2.) *rideat* mundana & popularia: (Nam יצחק idem est ac ridebit.)

(3.) *supplantat*[238] *factitia* quævis. (Nam יעקוב idem est ac supplantabit; & עשה[239] â factura descendit.)

(4.) *Confiteatur* in publico *cum laudibus*, se eundem cum fideli hac multitudine DEUM invocare. (Nam יהודה Nomen confessionis & laudis est.)

(5.) *Perrumpat* obstacula quævis: (פרץ enim â perrumpendo dicitur.)

---

236 Beginning of a long deletion.
237 Correction: irrascibile replaced by irascibile
238 Correction: supplantat replaced by supplantet
239 Correction: עשה replaced by עשו
240 Knorr offered a similar extraction of "mystical meanings" or spiritual lessons based on names and places in Lk 1.5–38 (folio 18ʳ) above. One should not see the following attempt to turn his exposition into homiletic encouragement as anything other than an integral part of his exegetical programme.
241 This improving paragraph is compiled from sentences supposedly taken from the meanings of the Hebrew names. The glossing of Hebrew names in this way is exemplified by a fragmentary composition of the 3rd or 2nd century BC which appears to have provided a list of names in the LXX with glosses of their Hebrew meanings, *Oxyrhynchus Papyri* XXXVI, edited by Revel A. Coles et al. (London: Egypt Exploration Society, 1970), pp. 1–6. Jerome's *Liber interpretationis Hebraicorum nominum* or *Liber de nominibus Hebraicis* (389/391 AD), written in explicit rivalry with Philo and acknowledged dependency upon Origen just before the start of his major new translation project, aims "to make plain through consideration of the native language the etymologies of objects names and regions which do not resonate in our language" (*Questions on the Hebrew Genesis 1–2 in* Hieronymus: *Hebraicae quaestiones in libro Geneseos. Liber interpretationis hebraicorum nominum* .... CChr.SL72, edited by P. de Lagarde et

Christian The mystical sense seems to be this: the natural activities of the Soul struggle in vain to generate in us the divine life, so that either the psyche might be corrected (which the Hebrews call Nefesh and the Philosophers the desiring soul) or that the spirit (which the Hebrews call Ruach | and the Philosophers call the irascibile soul) should by emended, or, finally, that the mind (which the Hebrews call Neshamah and the Philosophers the rational soul), might be elevated because ultimately this life of Christ is born divinely in the mind.

The religious disciplines denoted through the individual parts of this genealogy are rightly to be promoted. The first group [of the three groups of 14] seems most closely relevant to Ecclesia although the way is open | to all to meditate further on these matters.[240]

1[241] *The one who desires to be a member of this multitude which is in covenant-relationship with God* (For the name of Abraham can be explained as if it meant 'br hmwn "a member of a multitude" by a separate meaning reserved for some cases, because the same word also means "Father of a Multitude")

2 *let him laugh at worldly and vulgar things* (for Issac means "he will laugh")

3 *let him replace whatever has been done* (for Jacob means "he will supplant" and Esau comes from "done")

4 *let him confess in public with praises that he calls upon the same God with this faithful multitude* (For Judah means "confession" and "praise")

5 *let him jump over every obstacle* (For Perez means "jump over")

---

al. (Brepols: Turnhout, 1959)); also *Liber de Nominibus Hebraicis*, in *Patrologia Latina*, vol. 23, edited by J.P. Migne (Paris: J.P. Migne 1846), col. 771–858 (1145–1206 for Greek fragments of the same). Jerome's *Liber exegetica ad Fabiolam De XLII mansiones Israelitarum in deserto* (which is attached to Letter 78, see *Patrologia Latina*, vol. 22, (Paris: J.P. Migne, 1845), col. 700ff.) derives spiritual exhortation for the Christian pilgrim from the meanings of the names of the Israelites' stopping-places in the wilderness. Alphabetic lists of Hebrew names are preserved in several Latin bibles and often grow beyond the number of names in the Hebrew Bible. A fine Latin incunabulum printed in Venice by Ottaviano Scotto in 1480 has at the end 73 pages marked: *Incipiunt interpretationes hebraiorum nominun in ordinem alphabeti*. On these Medieval *Interpretationes nominum Hebraeorum* see: Eyal Poleg, *Approaching the Bible in Medieval England* (Manchester University Press, 2013), pp. 118–124. One also finds the names in this genealogy glossed in the *Glossa Ordinaria* (on Mt 1) (*Biblia Latina cum Glossa ordinaria*, edited by A. Rusch (Strasburg, 1481), reproduced in Facsim. Brepols, V4 in Martin Movard *et alii*, eds., *Glossae Sacrae Scripturae electronicae* (Paris: CNRS-IRHT, 2016) accessed 10.4.2018. [http://gloss-e.irht.cnrs.fr]).

(6.) *Ad Atria* divinorum conventuum frequens advolet (Nam חצרון ab Atrio denominatur.)

(7.) *Celsus* sit animo, & ab infima terræ fœce abstractus. (Nam רם Excelsum denotat.)

(8.) *Spontaneis* officiis *populum* Dei fidelem prosequatur. (Sic enim vox אמינדב[242] | Populi & Spontaneitatis connotationem habet.)

(9.) *Experimentum* sæpe faciat sui. (נחשון enim â נחש expertus est, deducitur.)

(10.) *Pacificus* sit erga omnes. (שלמון enim â Pace descendit.)

(11.) *Fortis* sit erga hostes spirituales (בועז enim, idem est, ac In eo est fortitudo.)

(12.) *Libenter inserviat* proximo. (Nam עובד servum significat.)

(13.) Sit id, quod esse debet, absque fuco & simulatione. (ישי enim ab esse nomen habet.) ⦀

fol. 29ʳ

(14.) Et tandem *Amabilem* se omnibus præbeat, omnesque sincerè *diligat*. (דויד enim idem est ac dilectus.)

Porrò quoad classem secundam, antequam ad Christi specialia dogmata accedat, Patri trahendum se præbeat Joh. 6, 44.45. & generalia quædam præsupponat hypomnemata; Nimirum

(1.) Patrem cœlestem sibi esse propitium & *pacis* atque *felicitatis* suæ studiosum. (Nam שלמה Pacem infert significatu.)

(2.) Eundem *latitudinem* quandam & relaxationem concessurum *populo* suo, ne nimio hostium rigore obrutus occumbat, Gen. 26, 22. (רחבעם enim latitudinem populi in | se includit.)

(3.) Eundem *Dominum Patrem suum* fore (Nam אביה idem est ac Pater meus est Dominus: cujus nominis 1. Reg. 14, 31. quidem mutatur terminatio, sed non significatio.)

(4.) Eundem, *Medicum* animæ suæ futurum. (Nam אסה â medendo nomen habet.)

(5.) Eundem *Dominum benignum*, sibi fore *Judicem*. (Nam Nomen יהושפט Judicem quidem supponit Dominum, sed per literas Tetragrammati benigniores.)

(6.) Eundem *Dominum* unicam in se fore *Celsitudinem*. (Nam יהורם idem est, ac Dominus Celsus est.)

(7.) *Eundem* solum sibi fore fortitudinem atque robur. (Nam עזיהו idem est, ac Fortitudo | mea est Dominus.)

---

242   Correction: אמינדב replaced by עמינדב

SECTION VI

6 let him fly regularly to the halls of divine meetings (for Hezron comes from a word for "hall")

7 let him be lofty in mind and removed from the lowest filth of earth (For Ram means "high")

8 let him persue the faithful people of God with spontaneous kindnesses (For Aminadab | has the meaning of both "people" and "spontaneity")

9 let him often make trial of himself (For Nahshon comes from "tried")

10 let him be a peacemaker with all (For Solomon comes from "peace")

11 let him be strong against spiritual enemies (For Boaz means "strength is in him")

12 let him freely serve his neighbour (For Obed means "a servant")

13 let him be what he should be and separate from all concealment and deception (For Jesse means "to be separate") ‖

14 and finally let him show himself friendly to all and love all sincerely (For David means "beloved").

But as for the second group [:]

1 that the Heavenly Father was favourable to him and concerned about his peace and happiness (For Solomon means "peace")

2 that the same Heavenly Father allowed space and relaxation to his people, lest they perish, overcome by the strength of their enemies (Gen 26.22) (For Rehoboam embraces the meaning | "latitude of the people")

3 that the same Lord is his Father (For Abijah means "my father is Lord". The end of this name is changed in 1 Kgs 14.31 but not the meaning)

4 that He is the future Physician of his Soul (For Asa gets his name from "healing")

5 that the same Lord will be a kind judge to him (For Jehoshapat means "the Lord is judge" but the inclusion of the four letters of the Tetragrammaton in the name introduces the idea of a greater kindness)

6 that the same Lord will be in him a unique loftiness (For Joram means "the Lord is lofty")

7 that the same Lord will be his sole strength and might (For Uzziah means "the Lord is | my might")

fol. 29ʳ

(8.) Ab eodem *Domino* solo se expectare *perfectionem*. (Nam יותם idem est ac Perfectus est Dominus.)

(9.) Hunc solum nunc *prehendendum* & possidendum. (Nam אחז idem est, ac prehendit, possedit.)

(10.) Eundem *Dominum* solum *tenendum* nec dimittendum. (Nam חזקיה retentionem Domini involvit.)

(11.) Cætera omnia *oblivioni tradenda* & abneganda. (Nam מנשה oblivionem denotat.)

(12.) Quoniam ille solus *verax* sit atque fidelis (prout hæc significata habet nomen אמון.)

(13.) Atque nunc *desperare* se quoad cætera: *Domino* solo expectato. (Nam vox יאשיהו Desperationem involvit; & Tetragrammato suffulcitur.)

(14.) Ita ut hæc vera sit *præparatio* sui â *Domino* profecta. (Nam יכוניה idem est, ac Dominus præparabit.)

His factis præmissisque præparationibus ad tertiam accedat classem, in qua vita Christi | tandem emersura est. Ubi

(1.) Ita Christi similitudo ipsi apparebit, tanquam â *Deo* unicè *exoranda*. (Nam שאלתיאל idem est, ac Rogavi Deum.)

(2.) Videbit istam *alienam* esse[243] *omni confusione* Babelica, â qua propterea libentissimè exibit. (Nam זרבבל denotat alienum â confusione: seu talem, cui exaruit Babel.)

(3.) Illam unicè quærere *Patris* sui *gloriam*. (Nam אביהוד idem est, ac Pater meus gloriosus sit.)

(4.) *Deum* ipsum in anima sua *surrecturum* hâc Christi ideâ atque similitudine semel acquisitâ. (Nam אליקים idem est, ac Deus surget.)

(5.) Nunc *cingi* se ad sublimia peragenda. (Nam אזור cinctum dicit.)

(6.) Ex hoc se fore *justum* non aliter. (Nam צדוק Justi est appellatio.)

(7.) Nunc in ista rerum sublimium exstasi ê cœlis quasi acclamat Christus: *Parabo te*. (Nam est: Parabo.)

(8.) Respondet autem tam felix anima: *Deus meus sit gloriosus*. (Nam אליהוד hanc habet significationem.) |||

(9.) *Deus mihi sit adjutorium*, quia me totum abnegavi. (Nam אלעזר hanc involvit connotationem.)

(10.) Sic *dona* donis cumulantur. (Nam מתן Donum est.)

(11.) Sic repetitâ semper sui *supplantatione*; (Nam יעקוב hoc utitur etymo:)

(12.) Ad ultima tandem Luminis *augmenta* ascendit intellectus (יוסף enim ab augendo dicitur, & intellectum mysticè repræsentat.) Sed hîc virilia cessant, & omnis activitas propria deficit.

---

243 Added above the line: ab

SECTION VI

8 *that from the same Lord alone he awaits perfection* (For Jotham means "the Lord is perfect")

9 *that He alone must now be grasped and possessed* (For Ahaz means "grasp" or "possess")

10 *that He alone must be held on to and not dismissed* (For Hezekiah means "retaining the Lord")

11 *that all other things must be forgotten and denied* (For Manasseh means "forgetfulness")

12 *since He alone is truthful and faithful* (For that is the meaning of Amon)

13 *and that now he despairs of all other things and waits solely on the Lord* (For Josiah includes the idea of "despair" but also contains the four letters of the Tetragrammaton)

14 *so that these things are for him a true preparation, perfected by the Lord* (For Jeconiah means "the Lord will prepare").

By doing these things and these aforementioned preparations, one comes to the third class in which the life of Christ finally | emerges. When:

1 *the likeness of Christ himself will appear, as requested from God alone* (For Shealtiel means "I asked God")

2 *he will see that that likeness [of Christ] is alien to every Babel-like confusion, from which, for that reason, he will most willingly depart* (For Zerubbabel means "alien to confusion" or "one for whom [the attraction of] Babel has withered")

3 *to seek the unique glory of his Father* (For Abiud means "my Father is glorious")

4 *God himself will rise in his soul by this idea and likeness pattern of Christ once placed there* (For Eliakim means "God arises")

5 *when he girds himself for sublime tasks* (For Azor means "girt")

6 *because of which, he will be just and not otherwise* (For Zadok means "just")

7 *when now in the extasy of sublime things, Christ, as it were, cries fom heaven "I shall prepare you"* (For Akim means "I shall prepare")

8 *and the enraptured soul will reply "May my God be glorious"* (For this is what Eliud means) ‖

fol. 29ᵛ

9 *"May God be my helper, for I have totally denied myself"* (For that is what Eleazar means)

10 *Thus gifts will accumulate* (For Mattan means "gift")

11 Thus his replacing will always be repeated (which is what Jacob means)

12 *when finally his intellect ascends to the highest levels of increased light* (For Joseph comes from "increase" and mystically represents the intellect). But here human powers fail and all one's own activity ceases

(13.) Totamque se passivam & fœminam Deo subjicit Animæ voluntas, ita ut Dominus in eâ sit Deus. (Licet[244] enim nomen מרים sit interpretari, quasi diceretur | מריה Dominus est Jah, Deus: significatu Chaldaico illis temporibus prævalente; & liter[â] He finali sive aspirationis, sive respectus atque Religionis erga Nomen divinum habitæ causa in M mutata, prout exempla habemus in Abijam, pro Abijah: & Siloam pro Siloah: ita ut contrariam significationem habeat Martha, quasi ipsa sit Domina.)

(14.) Sic tandem morphosis illa Jesu, de qua Gal. 4, 19. sive habitus ejus, de quo Gal. 3, 27. sive facies ejus, de qua 2. Cor. 4, 6. &c. & uno verbo Analogia & similitudo ejus, quæ dicitur communicatio divinæ naturæ 2. Pet. 1, 4. â Spiritu Sancto concepta in lucem prodibit in voluntate, omnibusque actibus moralibus: ut appareat, sic *salvatam esse* â malis animam (quod nomen ישוע indigitat:) & unctionis influxuum divinorum factam esse | participem juxta 1. Joh. 2, 27. (quod nomen משיח infert.) Hic scopus sit omnium factorum dictorumque atque scriptorum & connotationum nostrarum, ut eò deducti nos primum ipsi, eôdem ex alios ducamus.[245]

V. 18. *Cum desponsata esset &c.* כד מכירא הות

Cabb. Cat. *Desponsatio est ritus antiquissimus (Gen. 19, 14; Deut. 20, 7; | c. 22, 23. Talmud toto Tractatu Kidduschim;) â domiductione & consortio maritali plerumque aliquantulum distans.*

Christianus. Quatenus autem hîc inter Josephum & Mariam præcessit mysticè id denotat; voluntatem hominis non vagari liberè, sed desponsatam Intellectui, ejusdem inspectioni & lumini subesse debere.

---

244 Correction above the line: licet replaced by liceat
245 End of the long deletion.
246 The name of Mary in Syriac, *mrym*, is derived as from *mr-yh*, understood here as "The Lord (*mr*) is Yah (*yh*)". The usual word for the Lord in Syriac is *mry'*. The Christian claims the final /h/ of Mary's name was changed to /m/ to avoid the resonance with "the Lord" and cites the names of Abijam and Siloam as a pious precedent. Alternatively he conjectures the substitution may have come about on account of the final /h/ being a light aspirate. The name of Martha, who elsewhere in the Gospels is con-

SECTION VI 363

13 and the will of the Soul subjects itself, passive and feminine, totally to God so that the Lord is God within it. (For Mary [*mrym*] may be understood as | [*mryh*] "the Lord is Jah, God". The Aramaic meaning was prevalent at that time and of the final [letter] he /*h*/, either because of the aspiration or from the customary religious respect towards the divine name, changed into a [letter] M. There is an example of this in Abijam for Abijah and Siloam for Siloah, so that Martha has the opposite meaning, as if she were "the Mistress"[246]).

14 Thus finally [we come to] that metamorphosis into Jesus about which Gal 4.19 speaks[247]; or to "putting him on as clothing" about which Gal 3.27 speaks[248]; or to "his face" (concerning which see 2 Cor 4.6 etc.)—in one word [to] his likeness and similitude, which is said in 2 Pet 1.4 to be a communication of the divine nature, conceived by the Holy Spirit which will illuminate the Will and all moral acts, so that the soul might appear thus saved from all ills (as the name Jesus indicates) and to be made a participant | according to 1Jn 2.27 of the unction of the divine influxes (as the name Messiah teaches[249]). It is this which was the goal of all the deeds, words, writing and exposition of of our people: that we ourselves might first be led to that place to which we shall lead yet others.

Verse 18

When she was betrothed etc. *kd mkyr' hwt*

Kabbalist Catechumen Betrothal is a very ancient ritual (Gen 19.14; Deut 20.7; | 22.23 and the whole of Talmud Tractate Kidushin) somewhat short of taking a woman into your home and full marital congress.

Christian To that extent this relationship between Joseph and Mary came first, it indicates mystically that the will of a man should not wander freely, but ought to be betrothed to the Intellect and to submit to its scrutiny and illumination.

---

trasted with another Mary, however, is derived from *mar* (Lord) with a femine ending, meaning "mistress".
247 The Greek in this verse has: *mechris hou morphōthēi Christos en humin.*
248 The Greek in this verse has: *Christon enedusasthe.*
249 Meaning "annointed".

Inventa est in utero habere &c. אשתכחת בטנא 30

[**Cabb. Cat.**][250] *Post spatium scilicet trimestre Gen. 38, 24. (vide ad Luc. 1, 56.) cum ab Elisabetha rediisset, Luc. 1, 56.*[251](*De hoc trimestri videatur Cabbalæ denudatæ Tomus 1, p. 619*[252].)

[**Christianus.**][253] Ista autem ingravidatio annon sequenti modo proces- 35
sit? Primo præsupponendum cum tota gentis nostræ[254] schola Animam Messiæ non ex Matre vel in Matre sumsisse initium, sed primum fuisse rerum conditarum (Apoc. 3, 14.) & cum omni spirituum genere simul ante mundi materialis primordia â Deo productam: unde in specie â Doctoribus nostris[255] inter ea, quæ ante mundum condita sunt, numeratur. | Imò 40
illam ipsam esse Principium hoc certum est, cum quo Moses historiam suam inchoat Gen. 1, 1. per quod condita sunt cætera, explicante Johanne, cap. 1, 1.3. ubi vide. Col. 1, 15.16; 1. Cor. 8, 6; Eph. 3, 9; Hebr. 1, 2. Et quoniam labentibus aliis ipsa in integritate, adeoque unita semper permanebat cum illo Divinitatis gradu, qui Filius dicitur, cumque quo ab initio | sese univerat, Heb. 13, 45
8. hinc tota antiqui Fœderis œconomia per illam ab initio Ecclesiæ administrabatur, 1 Cor. 10, 4.9. Donec tandem humana carne induta apparere & ministerium Novi Fœderis subire deberet.

Secundò assumo è Philosophia accuratiore, omnem generationem ex ovo esse, & in quadrupedibus quoque atque homine sua esse ovaria, quæ ad generationem instituendam non egeant, | nisi excitatore quodam spiritu, qui 50
fol. 30ʳ via ordinariâ â semine erumpit, corpore istius ||| omnino subducto. Videatur

---

250 Correction: Christianus replaced by Cabb. Cat. (which involves the two speakers being changed over in the following exchange).
251 Deletion of two lines, now unreadable.
252 "14. Sicut autem jam dictum, quod scintillæ perfectionem accipiant peractis 9. mensibus, ita si cuilibet mensi tribuas dies triginta, numerus dierum erit ר"ע 270. & infans nascetur die 271. qui numerus continetur in voce הריון conceptus. Quod ita intelligendum, quod triduo Coalitionis introeant 18. illæ scintillæ: reliqui autem dies 270. sint dies Conceptûs; quibus perficiantur 270. scintillæ, singulis diebus una; unde prodeunt ר"פח 288. Nizuzin sæpe memoratæ. Dies autem illi 270. computantur præter triduum coalitionis: unde in Gemara dicitur; Fœmina non parit nisi die 271. vel 272. vel 273. [...]—17. Deinde venit tempus trimestre, quo dignoscitur fœmina esse prægnans. Nunc enim superveniunt etiam 46. scintillæ Nominis ע"ב & totidem dies alii; ita ut numerus dierum formationis, cum hoc, jam exurgat in 86. quo tempore nunc ingressæ sunt omnes tres plenitudines Nominum ג"ס ב"ע ה"מ; ita ut nunc imprægnatio perfectè dignosci queat. Nec refert, quod menses hi tres non sunt completi; tempus hoc enim non adeo strictum est: adde quod menses etiam defectivi intelligi queant." ("Loci communes kabbalistici", op. cit., pp. 618–619).

SECTION VI 365

30 *She was found to be pregnant* etc. ʾštkḥt bṭnʾ

Kabbalist Catechumen After the period, that is, of three months (Gen 38.24[256]) (See on Lk 1.56) when she came back from Elisabeth (Lk 1.56). (For this three month period, see *Cabb. Denud.* Vol. I, p. 619).

35 **Christian** Is the following not the way this pregnancy progressed? First it should be presupposed with all the Academy of your people that the soul of Messiah was not from Mary, nor did it have its beginning in her womb, but was the First of Created Things (Rev 3.14) and together with whole race of spirits was created by God in a moment before the beginnings of the material world. That is why [the soul of Messiah] is specifically reckoned by your doctors amongst those things which were created before the foundation of
40 the world. | It is certain that [the Soul of Messiah] was the initial principle with which Moses began his account in Gen 1.1 and by which everything else was created, as John explains 1.1,3 (see also Col 1.15, 16; 1 Cor 8.6; Eph 3.9; Heb 1.2)[257]. And although others fell, the Soul of Messiah itself in its wholeness remained always united with the divine degree called The Son
45 and with which from the beginning | the Soul of Messiah had joined itself (Heb 13.8). Thus, from the beginning of the Ecclesia, the whole economy of the Old Covenant was administered through the Soul of Messiah (1 Cor 10.4, 9). Until at last, having put on human flesh, it was to appear and initiate the ministry of the New Convenant.

Secondly, let us assume from more accurate Science that all generation [comes] from an egg and that both in quadrupeds and in man it is their
50 ovaries which are necessary for effecting generation, [together with] | an excitement of the spirit which in the normal way comes from the seed and entirely overwhelms ‖ the mother's body. See Harvey *On the Generation of*   fol. 30ʳ
Animals.[258]

---

253   Correction in the left margin: Cabb. Cat. replaced by Christian. (as a consequence of the previous correction).
254   Correction: nostræ replaced by vestræ
255   Correction: nostris replaced by vestris
256   Where Tamar after three months is visibly pregnant and Judah decides to have her publically put to death.
257   See above on John 1.
258   *Exercitationes de Generatione Animalium* was published in London in March 1651 (London: Typis Du Gardianis at the expense of Octavian Pulleyn, St Paul's Cemetery, 1651). It

Harvæus de Generatione Animalium. Tertiò cum ovarium B. Virginis hoc modo excitaret Spiritus Sanctus, eidemque Archæum pro constituendo corpore Dominico, (quem alibi de Psyche Adami & Davidis desumtum fuisse notatui[259] ad Matth. 1, 1.) insereret, sciendum est in illam subintrasse prædictam Messiæ animam, atque | inibi proprium sibi construxisse templum atque tabernaculum, beneficio spiritus influi â Matre desumti; non concurrente ullatenus operâ virili, quod & Muhammedani credunt. Vid. Alcoran; Sur. 3, 35.41. & 4, 155. & 5, 19. 46.72. & 6, 87. & 19.

[Christianus][260] In generatione[261] Christi mystica in nobis, anima nostra locum Uxoris obtinet, quæ ima est Sephirah. Cæteræ novem novimestre spatium gestationis innuunt: | factoque initio â Jesod unde influxus generativus

---

was divided into seventy-two chapters on topics in development, and three additional chapters covering parturition, the structure of the uterus, and conception. Thirteen chapters describe the comparative anatomy of the reproductive organs of various animals. Thereafter Harvey discusses the day-by-day development of a chick in the egg and particularly the *cicatricula*, the area of the embryo that contains all the embryonic cells whence generation proceeds. Finally, he criticises previous theories including some of Aristotle and Galen. He denounced theories of spontaneous generation and insisted upon the doctrine of *ex ovo omnia*, rejecting equally Aristotle's formation of embryos from menstrual blood and semen and Galen's from both male and female semen.

259   Correction: notatui replaced by notasti
260   Deleted word. Because of the previous change of speaker, there is no need for a change of speaker here. The speech remains with the Christian.
261   Added above the line: autem
262   The Mother here is not Mary. *Abba* (Father) and *Ima* (Mother) and their descent into the body of *Zeir Anpin* are central features of Lurianic metaphysics. See Shaul Magid, *From Metaphysics to Midrash*, op. cit., p. 24.
263   On the Qur'an in Europe at this time, indispensible is Helmut Bobzin, *Der Koran im Zeitalter der Reformation* (Beirut: Franz Steiner Verlag, 1995). More briefly, for translations of the Qur'an available at this period, see Thomas E. Burman, "European Qur'an Translations. 1500–1700" in *Christian-Muslim Relations. A Bibliographical History*. vol. 6, Western Europe (1500–1600), edited by David Thomas et al. (Leiden: Brill, 2014), pp. 25–39. C.G. Düring's 1734 *Novum Inventarium Bibliothecae Sulzbaco-Palatino* (BAB Cbm 580 Repositorium A), p. 68#2 records the presence in the Sulzbach library of *L'Alcoran de Mahomet translaté d'Arabe en François par le Sieur du Ryer* (Paris: Antoine de Sommerville, 1649). On this vernacular translation see Alastair Hamilton and Francis Richard, *André du Ryer and Oriental Studies in Seventeenth-Century France* (Oxford University Press, 2004), pp. 110–119.

The following translations of (some of) the suras cited above are taken from Arthur

Thirdly, let us take it that when the Holy Spirit stimulated the ovaries of the Blessed Virgin in this way and, in order to form the Lord's body, it inserted into her the Archaeus (which elsewhere you noted on Mt 1.1 had been drawn from the Psyche [Soul] of Adam and David). It is necessary to know that the aforementioned Soul of Messiah | constructed for itself its own temple and tabernacle by the benefit of an influx of Spirit drawn from the Mother and without the concurrence or work of any human male, which even the Moslems believe.[262] See the Qur'an[263], suras: 3, 35, 41; and 4, 155; 5.19, 46, 72; and 6. 87, 19.

But in the mystical birth of Christ in us, our soul receives the place of the Wife which is the lowest degree. The other nine [degrees] hint at the nine month period of gestation | and the generative influx which begins

---

J. Arberry, *The Koran Interpreted* (Allen & Unwin, London 1955) and refer to Zachariah and John and the Virgin Birth.

Sura 3:35 'Lord,' said Zachariah, 'how shall I have a son, seeing I am an old man and my wife is barren?' 'Even so,' God said, 'God does what He will.' 'Lord,' said Zachariah, 'appoint to me a sign.' 'Thy sign,' God said, 'is that thou shalt not speak, save by tokens, to men for three days. And mention thy Lord oft, and give glory at evening and dawn.' 3:40 And when the angels said, 'Mary, God has chosen thee, and purified thee; He has chosen thee above all women. Mary; be obedient to thy Lord, prostrating and bowing before Him.' (That is of the tidings of the Unseen, that We reveal to thee; for thou wast not with them, when they were casting quills which of them should have charge of Mary; thou wast not with them, when they were disputing.) When the angels said, 'Mary, God gives thee good tidings of a Word from Him whose name is Messiah, Jesus, son of Mary; high honoured shall he be in this world and the next, near stationed to God. He shall speak to men in the cradle, and of age, and righteous he shall be.' 'Lord,' said Mary, 'how shall I have a son seeing no mortal has touched me?' 'Even so,' God said, God creates what He will. When He decrees a thing He does but say to it "Be," and it is.

Sura 4.155 ... and for their unbelief, and their uttering against Mary a mighty calumny, and for their saying, 'We slew the Messiah, Jesus son of Mary, the Messenger of God'—yet they did not slay him, neither crucified him, only a likeness of that was shown to them. Those who are at variance concerning him surely are in doubt regarding him; they have no knowledge of him, except the following of surmise; and they slew him not of a certainty—no indeed; God raised him up to Him; God is All-mighty, All-wise.

Sura 6:85 Zachariah and John, Jesus and Elias; each was of the righteous; Ishmael and Elisha, Jonah and Lot—each one We preferred above all beings; and of their fathers, and of their seed, and of their brethren; and We elected them, and We guided them to a straight path.

incipit, pergendo per Hod & Nezach id est, laudando & superando trimestre hoc innotescentis impraegnationis absolvitur.

E Spiritu Sanctitatis. מן רוחא דקודשא

Cabb. Cat. *Per Spiritum Sanctum nostrates illum repræsentatæ Divinitatis gradum intelligunt qui Malchuth seu Regnum dicitur: & gloriosam Dei cohabitationem cum Ecclesia concomitatur, quæ aliàs â nobis Schechinah dicitur & gloriosam Dei cohabitationem cum Ecclesia.*[264] *Semper autem generis Fœminini connotationem habet, unde & uxor Filii, & Sponsa ejusdem: & conceptu superiore Leah, inferiore Rachel vocatur.*

Christianus. Unde in ista Messiæ generatione nihil omninò masculini concurrisse apparet.[265]

V. 19. *Justus erat.* כאנא הוא

Cabb. Cat. *Id est æquitatis amans, exemplum præbens Benignitatis non secundum Legum rigorem omnia examinantis.*

Christianus. Quod nobis omnibus imitandum: ut nempe plerosque proximi actus in meliorem partem interpretemur, famæque ejus parcamus.

Ut occultè dimitteret eam. דמטשיאת נשריה

Cabb. Cat. *Quod præsentibus duobus testibus fieri poterat literis repudii vel in manum vel in sinum fœminæ datis. Talmud. Cod. Gittin.*

---

264 Deletion: & gloriosam Dei cohabitationem cum Ecclesia (to avoid the repetition due to oversight).

265 The manuscript has undergone several corrections here. It seems that Knorr intended, in the first place, to correct the text in order to attribute this remark about conception to the Kabbalist. But then, he changed his mind, and left the sentence with the Christian.

266 Associated with the *membrum virile*. This sefirah is above intimately connected with Knorr's sefirotic accounts of the Virgin Birth.

267 The meaning of the names of the two degrees just mentioned.

268 For an explanation of Rachel and Leah within the Lurianic system, see Magid, *From Metaphysics to Midrash*, op. cit., pp. 16–34, esp. p. 27: "… the female Rachel/ Leah/ Shekinah remains totally dependant on the male". The "Loci communes kabbalistici" in the entries devoted respectively to Leah and Rachel speak of their mutual relationship. Both are called wives, though Leah is the first wife ("*uxor superior*", p. 488) whilst Rachel is the true wife of Zeir Anpin ("*Rachel autem vocatur Uxor* ד"א *vera*"). Their hierarchic relationship is equally evident in physical terms within the cosmic body of Zeir Anpin,

SECTION VI 369

from Yesod[266] passes through Hod and Netsach, that is, by praising and endurance[267], and is fulfilled in the three month period of this increasingly conspicuous pregnancy.

From the Holy Spirit *mn ruḥʾ dqwdšʾ*

Kabbalist Catechumen By the Holy Spirit our teachers understood that degree | of the representation of God which is called Malkhut or Kingdom and the accompanying glorious cohabitation of God with Ecclesia which elsewhere we call Shekhinah. It always has the connotation of female gender, whence it is both the Wife of the Son and also his Betrothed—and by a more lofty conception is called Leah, but by a lower one is called Rachael.[268]
So in the conception of Messiah absolutely nothing male seems to have had any part.

Verse 19
was righteous kʾnʾ hwʾ

Kabbalist Catechumen Righteousness is loving equity, providing an example of kindness and not reckoning everything according to the rigor of the Laws.[269]
Christian This we all should imitate in such a way that we interpret most of our neighbour's acts in a favourable light and spare his reputation.

To send her away privily *dmṭšyʾt nšryh*

Kabbalist Catechumen That [dismissal] could happen in the presence of two witnesses, by a written repudiation placed in her hand or bosom (Talmud Cod. Gittin).

---

as Leah corresponds to the area between his head and his torso: *"Postquam per* א״ז *distributa esset vis Cerebrorum, lumina de istis non tantum ipsi inserviebant, pro usu proprio; sed & foras prodibant extra ipsum. Et quidem superius ubi verus est Cerebrorum Locus & magna est luminum copia, splendor aliquis prodibat ex parte ejus posteriore; unde fiebat persona Leæ à Tergo τῷ* א״ז *à Capite nempe usque ad pectus ejus"*, (Ibid., p. 488), whereas Rachel occupies the lower part of his body from his torso to his feet: *"Consistit autem à tergo* א״ז *ab initio productionis suæ: ejusque Tikkun seu formatio locum habet retro sub pectore* א״ז *usque ad finem pedum ejus, qua dimensione ipsius statura terminatur, cum tota decade suæ Sephirothica"*, (Ibid., p. 685).

269   That is Joseph did not act with the full rigour of the law, as he might have in a case of suspected adultery.

Christianus. Sic voluntas, cum â prava concupiscentia, quæ â nobis Jezer   30
hara appellatur, concepisse deprehenditur consensu Intellectus, in pravitate
non est confirmanda, sed repudio morali castiganda.

V. 20. *Angelus Domini.* מלאכא דמריא

Christianus. Quia Nomen Tetragrammaton Antiqui non pronunciabant nisi
per Nomen | Adonai, hinc & LXX Interpretes & scriptores Novi Fœderis illud   35
communiter efferunt per vocem Græcam κύριος DOMINUS; Syrus autem per
vocem מריא, (vide quæ ad Luc. 1, 11. annotata sunt.)

*Cabb. Cat. A Theologis nostris autem seu Cabbalistis nomen hoc divinum
primariò tribuitur illi Divinitatis revelatæ gradui, qui inter Numerationes, |*   40
Tiphereth; inter Personas autem Filii nomine & Seir Anpin nominatur: & mo-
derno in statu illud ipsum objectum est, cum quo Messiæ Anima unita fuit:
unde quotiescunque in antiquo Fœdere hoc Dei nomen occurrit semper Mes-
siæ connotatio involvitur.[270]

[Christianus.][271] *Non immeritò igitur*[272] *& hoc loco Angelus quidam ad Mes-*
siæ ministeria | destinatus intelligendus est; & idem fortè qui Mariæ, concep-   45
tionem Messiæ annunciavit.

In somnio בחלמא

fol. 30ᵛ *Cabb. Cat. Somniorum visio est infimus sublimiorum revelationum gradus, |||*
& â nostratibus ad Malchuth ejusque exhibitiones debiliores refertur; (vide
Lexic. Cabbalistic. p. 347[273]*.) unde conjicere licet Josephi animam altiorum tum*

---

270 Correction: Deletion of the entire speech of the Cabbalist, replaced by Quia supra jam dictum est quod semper Messiæ connotatio involvitur.
271 Deletion: Christianus (the speech remains thus with the Cabbalist).
272 Deleted word.
273 "חלום *Somnium.* In Raja Mehimna dicitur: quod Schechinah vocetur Visio, quæ vigilanti accidit, quando influxum accipit à quinque Sephiris supernis, Gedul. Geb. Tiph. Nez. Hod: quia Ipsa est filia seu pupilla oculi trium colorum, qui sunt 3. Patres; & duæ palpebræ Nezach & Hod; quæ si apertæ sint ad influxum dicitur Visio; מראה. Cum autem influxus Istorum Istorum ab Eâ tollitur, tunc vocatur *Visio per somnium.* Et hinc influxus provenit ad Prophetam; huc quoque Iste respicit, cum per somnium vaticinatur. Pard. l.c. vid. Soh. Behaaloth. 73. c.290. Et חלם est 78. ut: ה"יה והו"ה ו"יהיה." ("Loci communes kabbalistici", op. cit., p. 347).
274 The Evil Influence is taken from Gen 6.5 and 8.21. There is both a Good Influence and an Evil Impulse, but ultimately the individual is responsible for the decision of how to

SECTION VI 371

Christian Thus the Will when it is discovered to have, with the agreement of the Intellect, conceived by that wicked desire which you call the *Yetser hara* [Evil Impulse][274], is not to be encouraged in its sin but punished by moral repudiation.

Verse 20

The Angel of the Lord ml'k' dmry'

Christian Because the ancients did not pronounce the Name of the Tetragrammaton unless as the word | Adonai [Lord], the Septuagint translators and the writers of the New Testament both translated it by the Greek word *kurios* [Lord]. The Syriac however used *mry'* (see what was noted on Lk 1.11).

Kabbalist Catechumen[275] And we have already said above that allusion to Messiah is involved here. Not inappropriately an angel is to be understood here | as appointed to the ministry of Messiah and possibly it might chance to be the same one who announced the conception of Messiah to Mary.

in a dream bḥlm'

Kabbalist Catechumen A vision in a dream is the lowest grade of the more sublime revelations ||| and is attributed by our sages to [the grade] Kingdom and its weaker manifestations (See *Lex. Cabb.*, p. 347). So one may conjec-

fol. 30ᵛ

---

act. Mishnah Avot 3.18: "All things are forseen [by God], yet choice is given [to people] and the World is judged on its merits; Maimonides Mishnah Commentary (Berachot 9.5), All is given into the hand of Heaven [predetermined by God], except one's fear of Heaven [except one's choice of Good or Evil]."

275 Deletion: "This divine name is primarily attributed by our theologians or kabbalists to the degree of disclosed Divinity which amongst the degrees is called Tiferet, and among Persons is called by the name of The Son and Zeir Anpin: and in the modern dispensation it is the very object with which the soul of Messiah was united. This is why whenever this name of God occurs in the Old Covenant it always hints at Messiah." Probably this omission was made as it appeared on reflection too technical. Knorr very much spares his (Christian) readers many of the complexities of the Lurianic system. His only other references to Zeir Anpin in *Messias Puer* (other than in a cited Zoharic passage) are as glosses on the "Son", though the topic had been explored in *Kabbala Denudata*. It would appear that he felt here the extra complication would not be pursuasive, or perhaps was indiscrete.

non fuisse capacem: quia præter somnum etiam Angelus tantum cum ipso loquitur; non Deus ipse.

Christianus. Docemur igitur vitam divinam atque Christi in nobis non admittere inspectionem Intellectus superioris[276] subtilioris & excitatioris; ne id videatur ab humanis viribus oriri, quod â solo Deo est.

Fili David. &c. ברה דדויד

Cabb. Cat. *Mysterium regni Messiæ involvit insolita hæc compellatio.*

Christianus. Idemque mihi videtur, quasi diceret: Filius David seu Rex Messias cum nasciturus est[277] sit, ê filiis David aliquem requirit, qui sui curam habeat. Tu ergo divinarum promissionum Davidi factarum sis memor; & scito, Davidis dilecti sui nunc recordatum esse Altissimum, atque Tui simul.

Is enim, qui genitus est in eâ. הוגיר דאתילד בה[278]

Christianus. Genitum dicit, non conceptum: ut innuat, Animam Messiæ, gradusque ejus tres inferiores, qui â vestratibus vocantur Nephesch, Ruach, Neschamah, jam in fœturam illam sanctam ingressam esse (prout & in Johanne adhuc in utero existente iidem fuisse videntur, ut & spiritus Sancti capax esset Luc. 1, 15.) Cum in aliis unus saltem adveniat animæ gradus in corpus jam ex utero prodeuntis & auram mundanam haurientis, | juxta Pneumaticam vestram. Et quoniam duo adhuc alii Animæ sunt gradus superiores, Chajah nempe & Jechidah, seu vitalis & singularis quædam natura, qui â paucis obtinentur: illa in Messiâ Baptismi, hæc ultima transfigurationis tempore potissimum manifestata esse videtur: cum aliàs in mundis sublimioribus semper subsisterent. Vide ad Luc. 1, 35.

Cabb. Cat. *Verum enim vero, quia singulos hos Animæ gradus Cabbalistæ nostri in plures dividunt Nizzuzoth sive scintillas, quæ Animæ quædam subordinatæ sunt; circa Messiæ Animam si liceret, porrò præmitterem sequentia:*

---

276 Deleted word.
277 Deleted word.
278 Correction: הוגיר replaced by הו גיר. This is the correct Peshitta consonantal text. The correction seeks only properly to divide it into two words.
279 The name David means "beloved".

ture that, at that time, the soul of Joseph was not capable of higher things, since besides the dream, it was only an angel who spoke with him and not God Himself.

Christian By this we are also taught that the divine life of Christ in us does not admit scrutiny of the more subtle and stimulating Intellect, lest there seem to arise from human strength that which is from God alone.

Son of David etc. brh ddwyd

Kabbalist Catechumen The unusual mode of address conceals the mystery of the Kingdom of Messiah.

Christian It seems to me to mean that: the Son of David or Messiah the King, when he was about to be born, sought someone from the sons of David who might take care of him. So remember the divine promises made to David and know that the Most High now remembered David, his beloved[279] and yours also.

For the child which is born in her hw gyr d'tyld bh

Christian It says "born" not "conceived" in order to hint that the Soul of Messiah and its three inferior levels, which your scholars call Nefesh, Ruach and Neshamah had already entered into that holy foetus (just as when John was still in the womb, they seem to have entered him too, so that he was full of the Holy Spirit (Lk 1.15)) For according to your doctrine of Spirit in other cases too one level of the Soul enters the body when it is in the process of being born from the womb and inhales earthly air. | There are two other higher levels of the Soul, Chayah and Yechidah—or a certain vital and singular nature—which is obtained by few. The first seems to have occurred most forcefully in Messiah at his Baptism, the second at the time of the Transfiguration; although elsewhere in higher worlds they always subsisted. See on Lk 1.35.[280]

Kabbalist Catechumen Indeed, because our kabbalists divide these individual grades of Soul into many parts—Nitsutsot or sparks—which are subordinate souls. Concerning the Soul of Messiah, if I may be permitted, I shall

---

[280] The two outstanding incidents in the Gospels where Jesus receives supernatural recognition as the Son, the Baptism and the Transfiguration, are skilfully here interpreted in terms of the two higher portions of the Soul of Messiah.

(*1.*) *Adami Animam â Cabbalistis describi non ut singularem, sed ut totum omnium Animarum exercitum;* (vide Tract. de Revolutionibus Animarum p. 246.§.5[281].p. 248.§ 11[282]. | & simul confer pp. 249–252. 254–258. 260– 262. 276.277.280.300.301.304.sqq. 313.315.318.320.322.332.337.338.343.373.381. 386–390. 405.408.410.420.421.431.435.sqq. 440.442.450.453.465.sqq. 407.s. 478. Et in Tractatu Vallis Regia p. 159. n. 28.[283] p. 304. §.5[284].) *quarum Ipse esset Dux sive Capitaneus, quamvis non summus, quia in eo Messiæ phalanx Jechidæ locum obtinuit, seu locum summum.* (*2.*) *Cum Adam laberetur | & Exercitus iste ab Exercitu Corticum seu Adami Belialis subigeretur atque dispergeretur, Messiæ Animam cum cohorte sua Prætoria, ab eo, lapsisque omnibus discessisse: adeoque 3. lapsui illi non interfuisse, nec ejus fuisse participem.* (*4.*) *Eundem Messiam porrò de lumine suo quoque Jechidam communicasse Mosi, & postmodum Davidi sed sub utriusque lapsum istud lumen pariter*

---

281 "Cùm igitur sanctus ille εὐλογητὸς Rom. 9, 5. crearet Adamum Protoplastum; eo ipse seligebat partem illam Psycharum & spirituum quæ permixta erat cum malo septem istorum Regum: illamque accipiens, ex ea faciebat animam Adami Protoplastæ, constantem ex omnibus illis notionibus (animarum.) [*Sciendum enim, antiquo dogmate Hebræorum, per Adamum Protoplasten non intelligi personam unam individuam, sed totum animarum genus suis ordinibus atque gradibus variè distinctum, & sub formâ exercitûs cujusdam ab Adamo ceu Duce, sub Imperatore Messia, per signa membris humanis assimilata gubernatum, quod corpus intelligitur ab Apostolo, Eph. 4.v.13. & alibi, ubicunque Christus ab ipso caput nominatur, eo quod in statu restitutionis idem futurum sit regimen, quod erat in natura instituta, Eph. 4.v.16; Rom. 12.v.5; 1. Cor. 12.v.27; Eph. 5.v.23; Col. 1.v.24.&.*]" ("De Revolutionibus animarum", op. cit., p. 246). The text in square brackets is Knorr's addition to the translation.

282 "Res ipsa autem ita se habet, quod nempe omnes mentes & spiritus & psychæ nullâ exceptâ comprehensæ fuerint in Adamo protoplaste cum conderetur; ita ut quædam animæ pertinerent ad caput Adami; quædam ad oculos ejus; quædam ad ipsius nasum, & sic porrò ad omnia ejus membra, à quibus quasi dependebant. Atque hac ratione sub initium creationis Adami protoplastæ in illo existebant omnes animæ, quæcunque erant de parte boni; omnes, inquam, in illo continebantur & ab illo dependebant. Cum autem peccaret, bonoque malum immisceret; malum cum bono ita confundebatur, ut ex parte mali illius postmodum prodirent populi mundani. Unde apparet, quod fundamentum Adami protoplastæ saltem fuerit bonum: animæ nimirum Israëlitarum. Quare scriptura inquit loco citatô: Vos estis Adam. (Quasi diceret omnes Israëlitarum animas nihil aliud fuisse quàm Adamum nimirum protoplasten:) Et vos scintillæ illius atque membra ejus extitistis. Quapropter Israëlitæ 2. Samuel. 7.v.23. etiam vocantur gens unica in terra; prout verba sonant: Et quis sicut populus tuus; sicut Israël gens una in terra, &c. Populi mundani autem è contrario non vocatur Adam: id est, non prodierunt nisi ex parte mali, quod immixtum fuit Adamo protoplastæ." (Ibid., pp. 248–249).

283 "Omnes enim animæ dependebant ab Adamo primo, & postquam ipse eas peccato suo corrupit, ipse quoque easdem restituere tenetur. Et hoc est quod dicunt Magistri nostri bonæ memoriæ! in tract. Sanhedrim cap. חלק: Non venit filius David, donec consummentur omnes animæ, quæ in corpore Adami primi fuerunt: Ab ipso enim omnes

SECTION VI

emphasise the following:[285] 1. The Soul of Adam is described by the Kabbalists not as an individual but as the whole army of all souls (See Tract. *De Revol. Animarum*, p. 246, § 5; p. 248, § 11 | and also at the same time see pp. 249–252; 254–258; 260–262; 276; 277; 280; 300; 301; 304 *seq*.; 313, 315, 318, 320, 322, 332, 337, 338, 343, 373, 381, 386–390; 405, 408, 410, 420, 421; 431; 435 *seq*.; 440, 442, 450, 453, 465 *seq*.; 407, 478. And in *Tract. Vall. Reg.*, p. 159, n. 28, p. 304, § 5) of which he himself is the leader or Capitain, although not the greatest because in him the phalanx of Messiah has obtained the place of Yechidah, that is, the highest place. 2. When Adam fell | and that army was subdued and dispersed by the Army of the Shards or of Adam Belial[286], the Soul of Messiah with his praetorian guard departed from him [Adam] and from all the fallen. The result was that: 3. They neither attended the fallen nor participated in him. 4. The same Messiah from his own light also communicated [his] Yechidah to Moses and afterwards to David but upon the lapse of

dependent, ut restituantur. Et hoc est, quod dicitur *Jes.* 59, 20. *Et veniet ad Sion Redemptor & ad redeuntes ab iniquitate in Jacob, dixit Dominus.* In quibus verbis literæ initiales vocum פ"שע ו"לשבי ג"ואל constituunt vocabulum גוף, sicut diximus; ipsi enim incumbit restituere eas." ("Partis Primæ Tractatus Secundus, quæ est Introductio pro meliori intellectu Libri Sohar. E scripto R. Naphthali Hirtz, F.R. Jaacob Elchanan; quod vocat Vallem Regiam", *Kabbala denudata II*, Pars I, pp. 151–346, p. 159).

284 "Et scito, quod Seir sit Adam primus & Chanoch est ab umbilico ejus & deorsum, nempe Pulchritudo quæ in Seir. Nam Adam primus continebat omnes animas Israelitarum, juxta id quod dicunt Magistri nostri bonæ memoriæ super textum Job. 38, 4. *Ubi fuisti cum ego fundarem terram?* Unus pependit in capillo ejus, &c. Unde ipse est Lux spiritualis, quæ combinet omnem Lucem animarum Israëlis. Et sicut Seir est 7. Numerationes à Benignitate & deorsum, quarum fundamentum est Pulchritudo; ita Adam primus est Seir, & Chanoch est Pulchritudo: Et sicut Pulchritudo comprehendit Brachia & Pedes, sic Chanoch qui est Metatron, & ipse continet omnes 7. Et propterea vocatur Princeps faciei. Hoc tamen nomine etiam ob aliam vocatur rationem, nempe quia ipse est Princeps comprehendens omnes 7. videntes faciem Regis. Et ipse revera est forma Seir: Et sicut Seir continet 7. numerationes, ita Matatron (sic) continet 7. videntes faciem Regis; qui sunt intra velum, ubi facies Regis est sine omni cessatione & velo distinguente; & quilibet eorum suæ correspondet Numerationi. Et scito; quamvis Scriptura dicat Dan. 12, 1. *Michaël princeps magnus, qui stat pro filiis populis tui:* quod tamen Chanoch includat illum." (Ibid., pp. 304–305).

285 Knorr had previously treated of these topics, as the rather full citation here of passages from the *Tractate on the Revolutions of Souls* in *Kabbala Denudata II* indicates. None the less, the Kabbalist Catechumen here within the economy of eight numbered points summarises Luria's narrative of the origin of souls, the Soul of Messiah, the fall of souls and their salvation from the tyranny of the shards by reincarnations and their reincorporation in Messiah. One notices that the unfallen souls who would become Apostles and Martyrs entered the womb of Mary with him.

286 The name originates from Pro 6.12.

retraxisse (5.) Cæteras Animas | Adami partim ab illo delapsas immersas esse corticibus: partim corticibus inquinatas in ipso permansisse in liberos propagandas: partim inserviisse propriæ ipsius vitalitati. (6.) Omnes autem quotquot lapsæ sunt variis revolutionibus purificandas & ê corticibus seligendas esse. (7.) Officiumque Messiæ in eo potissimùm consistere, ut hanc selectionem instituat, atque perficiat, & in unum illud corpus atque rempublicam seu | Exercitum recolligat filios hos Dei dispersos. Joh. 11, 52; Eph. 4, 13; Rom. 12, 5; 1. Cor. 6, 15; c. 10, 16.17; c. 12, 12.13; sqq. 27. Eph. 1, 23; c. 2, 16; c. 4, 12.16; c. 5, 30; Col. 1, 18.24; c. 2, 19; c. 3, 15. (8.) Illas autem Animas non lapsas, sed Messiæ Cohortem Prætoriam constituentes ||| procul dubio partim cum ipso nunc intrasse Virginis uterum; ut deinde cum dicitur: virtus aliqua ab ipso prodiisse, tales intelligi queant scintillæ: Mar. 5, 30; Luc. 5, 17; c. 6, 19; c. 8, 46. partim verò eodem tempore incarnatas fuisse, ut tentationum examini subjicerentur sicut Ipse, & coronatæ martyrio ejusdem cum capite suo gloriæ fierent participes: & ex illis | fuisse Apostolos & Discipulos &c. (conf. Adumbratio Cabbal. Christian. p. 61. §. 8[287]*.)*

fol. 31ʳ

V. 21. *Pariet enim Filium &c.* תאלדי דין ברא

Christianus. Messias Filius Mariæ dicitur, ut alibi jam notatum est; ob assumtam in eâ cum Spiritu influo carnem: sed Filius Dei vocatur, ob primogenituram inter Naturas Spirituum & constantissimam unionem cum illo Divinitatis gradu, qui Filius vocatur. | (vide Adumbrat. Cabbal. Christ. cap. 3. §.2[288]; c.8. §.6[289].)

Cabb. Cat. *Nota autem, quod* ברא *filius cum voce, &* צדיק *Justus numeris æquipolleant.*

---

287 "Secundò Infirmationem Corticum Messias etiam instituit, animas ita productas accuratius secernendo: ita ut interiores ad peculiare Fœdus vocatas, methodo Legis ad vitam Divinam promoveret; easque vero & genuino DEI cultu à cæteris segregaret: atque ita præpararet ad perfectionem aliquando temporibus Messiæ obtinendam, (Hebr. 11.v.40; Dan. 12.v.13.) sive per revolutionem Matth. 11.v.14. sive per resurrectionem Matth. 27.v.52.53; Apoc. 20.v.6. Exteriores verò methodo Philosophiæ expoliit, vel ad proselytismum; vel ad revolutionem intra populum Fœderis obtinendam. Et hæc est Electio illa, quæ à vestratibus ברור: in Novo Fœdere ἐκλογή; & Syris צביות dicitur: Secretio scilicet ad Fœdus, & Ecclesiam tam priscam (Rom. 9.v.11.; cap. 11.vers.28; Actor. 13.vers.17) quam recentem (Act. 9.vs.15; Rom. 11.v.5.7; 1 Thess. 1.vs.4; 2. Pet. 1.vs.10; Act. 15.vs.7; 1. Cor. 1.vs.27.28; Ubi ἐκλογή & κλῆσις vs.26. pro synonymis habentur. Item. Jac. 2.vs.5; Matth. 24.vs.22.24.31; Marc. 13.vs.20.22.27; Luc. 18.vs.7; Rom. 8.vs.33; Col. 3.vs.12; 2. Tim. 2.vs.10; Tit. 1.vs.1; I. Pet. 1.vs.1; 1. Pet. 2.vs.1; Ap. 17.vs.14; sed Matt. 20.vs.16; & c. 22.v.14. Electi, idem sunt ac selectè Boni.) Prout similis selectio olim facta est post lapsum corticum, ubi animæ in unum corpus secretæ sunt sub capite Messia Eph. 1.vs.4. quæ deinde, postquam sub Adamo lapsæ essent vs.7. sub idem caput iterum reducebantur

SECTION VI

40   each similarly withdrew that light. 5. Of the other souls | of Adam, some fell from him and were overwhelmed by the shards, others, sullied by the shards, remained in him to have children, and yet others were enslaved by his own vitality. 6. But all who fell are purified and separated from the shards by reincarnations. 7. The office of Messiah most especially consists in this: that he should both institute and complete this selection and gather again these dispersed sons of God into that one body and republic | or army (Jn 11.52; Eph

45   4.13; Rm 12.5; 1 Cor 6.15; 10.16, 17; 12.12, 13 *seq.*, 27; Eph 1.23; 2.16; 4.12, 16; 5.30; Col 1.18, 24; 2.19; 3.15). 8. Of those souls which did not fall, but constituted Messiah's praetorian guard ‖, without doubt, some then entered the Virgin's   fol. 31ʳ
womb with him so that then, when it is said [in the Gospels] that a certain spirit went out from [Messiah], we can understand it as a reference to these "sparks" (Mk 5.30; Lk 5.17; 6.19; 8.46). Other [souls which did not fall] were at that same moment incarnated, so that they might undergo the trial of temptations like him and be crowned with his Martyrdom and might become

5   Partakers of His Glorious Head. Of such | were the Apostles and Disciples etc. (Cf. *Adumbratio*, p. 61, § 8).

Verse 21
For she will bare a son etc. *t'ldy dyn br'*

Christian Messiah is called the Son of Mary, as we have already noted elsewhere, on account of the fact that he took on flesh in her by the influx of the Holy Spirit.²⁹⁰ But he is called Son of God on account of being the firstborn amongst the natures of the spirits and on account of his constant union

10   with the divine degree which is called The Son | (See *Adumbratio*, chap. 3, § 2; chap. 8, § 6).

Kabbalist Catechumen But do note that [the Syriac word] *br'* [son] has the same numerical value as the [Hebrew] word *ṣadiq* [righteous]²⁹¹.

---

vs.10. & quidem certo ordine, ita ut quæ determinatæ & limitatæ quondam fuissent ad loca priora, adeoque ut caput pertinerent, priùs etiam purificarentur (tanquam eandem formam Capitis habentes. Rom. 8.vs.29.) per martyria scilicet. Hinc illud quod Syrus hic dicit קדם סס, priori loco posuit; קדם רשם sub priori signo collocavit &c. (confer. 2. Thess. 2.vs.13; 2. Tim. 1.vs.9; 1. Pet. 1.vs.2.)" ("Adumbratio kabbalæ christianæ", op. cit., p. 61).

288   Cf. *supra*, footnote 131, p. 250.
289   Cf. *supra*, footnote 132, ibid.
290   Knorr is careful not to say that Messiah took of Mary's flesh.
291   Syriac uses letters for numerals like Hebrew. However *br'* gives 2+200+1=203, but *ṣdyq* gives 90+4+10+100=204.

JESUM. ישוע

[Cabb. Cat.]²⁹² *Nomen illud est singulare characteristicum Novi Fœderis*²⁹³ *Act. 4, 12. & Animæ | Messiæ inditum â significatu radicis* ישע *vel* הושע²⁹⁴ *quod est eripere, liberare: id quod peculiariter tribuebatur sospitatoribus Judicibus Jud. 3, 9.15; 1. Sam. 10, 19; c. 11, 3; 2. Reg. 13, 3; Jes. 43, 11; c. 45, 15.17.21; Zach. 8, 7; Hos. 13, 4; Obed. 1, 21.*²⁹⁵ *Et*²⁹⁶ *hoc est Nomen illud, cujus variatâ scriptione ejiciebantur Dæmones &c. Matth. 7, 22; Mar. 9, 38.39; Luc. 9, 49; Mar. 16, 17; Luc. 10, 17.20.*

[Cabb. Cat.]²⁹⁷ *Vellim*²⁹⁸ *autem*²⁹⁹ *ut*³⁰⁰ *juxta Cabbalistarum methodum ad analogiam Tetragrammati principalis hoc tanquam Tetragrammaton secundarium considerares*³⁰¹ [Christianus.]³⁰² Et quidem³⁰³ (1.) quoad singulas literas: Ubi Jod cum Apice referetur ad Kether seu Coronam & Chochmah seu Sapientiam. Schin referri potuit ad Binah seu Intelligentiam (vid. Cabbal. denudat. p. 694³⁰⁴.) Atque sic literis istis יש Christianis³⁰⁵ exprimetur³⁰⁶ | Pater, (Cabbal. denudat. p. 457³⁰⁷.) vav denotabit sex Numerationes Filii,(Cabbala denudat. p. 285³⁰⁸.) Et Ajin Cabbalistis Christianis³⁰⁹ erit Mal-

---

292 Correction: Christianus replaced by Cabb. Cat. (which involves the two speakers being changed over in the following exchange).
293 Correction: *Nomen illud est singulare characteristicum Novi Fœderis* replaced by Communia sunt, quod nomen illud singulare & characteristicum sit Novi Fœderis
294 Correction: הושע replaced by הושע
295 Added in the right margin: sed quia
296 Deleted word.
297 Deletion: Cabb. Cat. The change of speaker initially intended is no longer needed, after the previous correction. The Christian remains the speaker.
298 Correction: Velim replaced by Vellem
299 Deleted word.
300 Deletion of several words now unreadable.
301 Correction: considerare[tur?] replaced by considerares
302 Added in the right margin: Christian. (which involves a change of speaker).
303 Correction in the right margin: Et quidem replaced by Illud igitur considerabo
304 "ש *Schin.* In Libro Temunah hæc litera refertur ad Binah, ita tamen ut tria Jodin denotent tres primas; tria Vavin autem tres Patres, & Caph infernum sit Malchuth cum Jesod, ut accipiat influxum ab illis Sephiris: fundamento ejus tamen constituto in Nezach, cujus beneficio hæc unio contingat. Dominium ejus autem ponitur sub hora Mercurii. Sed in Sohar hæc litera refertur ad tres Patres, cum allusione ad tria Vavin. Exod. 14, 19.20.21. inclusis tamen Nezach, Hod, Jesod, quæ sunt literarum illarum appendices. Pard. vid. Soh. Breschith 33, 132; 40, 159; Vajechi 119, 471; Mischpatim 53, 211. Pinchas 105, 106.119.120. Æthchannan 126." ("Loci communes kabbalistici", op. cit., p. 694).
305 Correction: Christianis replaced by nobis
306 Correction: exprimetur replaced by exprimeretur
307 "ש *Est; Sunt; Essentia.* Fundamentum hujus Nominis est Chochmah, cum hac tamen

SECTION VI 379

Jesus yšwʿ

[310]**Kabbalist Catechumen** This name is a specific characteristic of the New Testament (Acts 4.12)—and of the Soul of Messiah, | on account of the meaning of the root *yšw* or *hwš*ʿ which is "to remove" or "to liberate" (a role which is specifically attributed to other saviours [and] judges in Judg 3.9, 15; 1 Sam 10.19; 11.3; 2 Kgs 13.3[311]; Isa 43.11; 45.15, 17, 21; Zech 8.7; Hos 13.4; Obad 1.21) But [it is also well known] that this is that name by which, in its various spellings, daemons were expelled (Mt 7.22; Mk 9.38,39; Lk 9.49; Mk 16.17; Lk 10.27,20). | I would like after the method of the Kabbalists, for you, following the analogy of the principal Tetragrammaton, to consider this name [Jesus], as it were, a second Tetragrammaton.[312]

Christian I shall consider it so: (1) as far as the *individual letters* go, where [the letter] Yod with a tittle is linked to Keter (or the Crown) or Chokhmah (or Wisdom); [the letter] Shin can refer to Binah or Intellegence (See *Cabb. Denud.*, p. 694). And thus, for us, the Father | is denoted by these letters yš (*Cabb. Denud.*, p. 457). [The letter] Wav denotes the six degrees of the Son

---

sub eo comprehenditur Binah; literâ Jod enim denotatur Chochmah, & literâ Schin Binah, radix arboris. Atque sic vox איש hoc subindicat, quod illæ ambæ emanent à Kether, cui nomen א״ין, quasi diceretur י״ש provenit ab א״ין. Deinde etiam י״ש dicuntur, propter 310. mundos, qui in his duabus Sephiris continentur, & ab his promanant in Gedulah & Gebhurah, de quibus dictum est tit. אור. Atque hinc intelligitur locus Prov. 8, 21. Pardes Tract. 23.c.10." ("Loci communes kabbalistici", op. cit., p. 457).

308   "ו *Vav*. De Litera Vav sic scribitur in Libro Temunah, quod pertineat ad Tiphereth, quod certum est. Additur autem, quod propterea sit simpliciter oblonga, ut ostendatur, istum modum esse Columnam mundi. Quod clarius ex eo fit, quod primò mundus creatus fuit per Judicium; cum autem videret Deus, quod hoc modo substitere non posset, adjunxit illi misericordiam: unde, quia miserationes sunt causa, ut mundus subsistat, iisdem nomen columnæ tribuitur, cui innititur mundus. Porrò dicit, Istius literæ faciem aversam esse ab He; quia He denotat judicium, in quo nulla misericordia; Illa igitur ad Chesed conversa est, & à Judicio faciem avertit. [...] Tandem addit, dominium ipse esse in hora solis, juxta illud Ps. 84, 12. *Quia sol & Scutum Dominus*. Refertur autem ad Tiphereth, quia iste compositus est è sex membris, quæ sunt, Gedulah, Gebhurah, Tiphereth, Nezach, Hod, Jesod: ו enim est nota senarii. [...]" (Ibid., p. 285).

309   Deletion: Cabbalistis Christianis

310   Deletion: Christian. Also, it is general knowledge that.

311   This should be 2 Kgs 13.5.

312   Knorr shows familiarity here with Jewish kabbalistic manipulations of the Tetragrammaton and carries out similar operations upon the name of Jesus. It is informative to compare the sophistication of his treatment with the naive and jejune understanding of the name of Jesus as a Tetragrammaton with an inserted *shin*, popularised by Reuchlin. See Wilkinson, *Tetragrammaton*, op. cit., pp. 318–323.

chuth seu Regnum, in quo Spiritus Sanctus, qui est Fons ille, de quo Cabbal denud. p. 544³¹³. Zach. 13, 1; Joh. 3, 5; c. 4, 10 sqq.15; c. 7, 38; Apoc. 21, 6; c. 22, 17.

(2.) Idem Nomen considerari poterit quoad numerum suum. Si enim nomen hoc simplex | examinatur; numero refert 386. quem etiam habet nomen ש״כינה addita unitate vocis³¹⁴ (vide etiam Adumbrat. Cabbal. Christ. cap. 11.§.2³¹⁵.) Eundemque numerum quidem etiam habet Nomen ע״שיו prout plenè scribitur quibusdam in Libris Chronicorum: & עוש 1. Par. 1, 35. filius Esav: Unde nonnulli ê perversis inter nostrates³¹⁶ Sanctissimum Dominum nostrum ad Genus Esaviticum, illudque regnum Pravitatis relegant. Verum enim | vero eadem ratione etiam voces מ״שיח & נ״חש serpens numeris æquipollent, & 358 exhibent: non quasi ad unum Regnum atque consortium pertineant, sed quia Messias cortices eradicabit ê mundo Jes. 25, 8. Juxta ipsos Cabbalistas nostros³¹⁷. (Cabbalæ. Denud. Parte IV. p. 255³¹⁸.) Eodemque modo Jesus Messias destructurus est Regnum Esaviticum & Serpentis.

(3.) Hoc nomen etiam considerari potest quoad plenitudines suas & eorum numeros. Plenior autem | scriptio ejus triplex est: prima: ש״ין. ו״יו. ע״ין. י״וד cujus numerus est 532. Altera ש״ין. ו״או. ע״ין. י״וד cujus numerus est 523.

---

313   "מעין *Fons*. Binah vocatur *Fons hortorum*. Cant. 4, 15. Horti enim sunt Sephiræ insequentes; Scaturigo fontis autem est Chochmah. Sed Kether vocatur *Fons obsignatus* Cant. 4, 11. Vel si omnes tres supernæ dicuntur *fons*, primum punctum Scaturiens erit Kether; fistula aquam effundens, Chochmah; & fons ipse & aquarum effluxus ad exteriora est Binah; quæ hortos irrigat. Si autem Malchuth fontis nomine vocatur, id tunc fit, quando Tiphereth quam plurimum Influentiæ in Ipsam immittit, quo in casu Ipse est Scatebra; Jesod fistula seu canalis; & Malchuth fons. Pard. l.c.." ("Loci communes kabbalistici", op. cit., p. 544).

314   Added in the right margin: Notetur etiam, quod hîc numerus bis contineat numerum Nominis א״לוהים; nam 300 est numerus nominis hujus plenè scripti + Jud: & 86. est numerus Nominis simplicis.

315   Cf. *supra*, footnote 164, pp. 180–181.

316   Correction: nostrates replaced by vestrates

317   Without correction.

318   "Palatium septimum continet primò Jesod, cujus cortex vocatur גמליאל: item נחשיאל: item עבריאל. Et in Tikkunim huc locatur סמאל præputiatus. Huc ab aliis refertur draco cæcus. Secundò Malchuth, cujus cortex est לילית impia. Et in Sohar Sect. Acharemoth cortex decimus vocatur דורש אל המתים. Vide plura in Pardes Tr. 25.c.4. Sed nomen נחש serpens eundem habet numerum cum משיח, qui cortices eradicabit è mundo Jesch. 25, 8." ("Explicatio arborum seu tabularum quinque cabbalisticarum generalium", op. cit., p. 255).

319   Deletion: It should also be noted that this number is twice the numerical value of the name *'elohim*, for 300 is the value of this name [*'elohim*] written out fully with the [letter] Yod and 86 is the simple numerical value of the name. By *plene*, "fully", here is

SECTION VI
381

(*Cabb. Denud.*, p. 285) and [the letter] Ayin will be Malkhut or Kingdom in which [is found] the Holy Spirit, which is that Source concerning which *Cabb. Denud.*, p. 544, Zech 13.1; Jn 3.5; 4.10 *seq.*; 7.38; Rev 21.6; 22.17.

(2) The same name can be considered with respect to its *numerical values*. For if this name [*yšw'*] | is examined simply it adds up to 386 which is the same as the name Shekhinah [381] when the number of [Shekhinah's] letters [5] is also added [386].[319] (See also *Adumbratio*, chap. 11, § 2.) The same numberical value is also that of the name Esau when it is written *plene* [*'syw*] in certain places in the Book of Chronicles and of [*y'wš*] Jeush the son of Esau (1 Chron 1.35)[320]. On the basis of this, several of the perverse amongst [y]our[321] people relegate our most holy Lord to the Family of Esau and that Kingdom of Depravity [Edom].[322] But although | by the same reasoning, the words *mšyḥ* [Messiah] and *nḥš* [Nahash (the Serpent)] have the same numerical value and make 358, it is not that they belong to the same Kingdom and fellowship but rather that Messiah will eradicate the shards from the world (Isa 25.8) according these Kabbalists of [y]ours[323] (*Cabb. Denud.*, Part. 4, p. 255). And in the same way Jesus Messiah is going to destroy the Kingdom of Esau and the Serpent.

(3) This name can also be considered with respect *to its fuller values*, [that is, by spelling out the names of its individual letters in full and adding up their numerical values]. | There are three ways to spell out this writing of the fuller value[324]. The first is *y-o-d, š-y-n, w-y-w, '-y-n*—the sum of which is 532; the second is, *y-o-d, š-y-n, w-'-w, '-y-n* which makes 523; and the third

---

meant the calculation of the numerical values of all the letters of the names of the letters making up the word and summing them. So for "*elohim*": aleph=111, lamed =74, he=15; yod= 20 and mem=80, giving a total of 300.

320   The numerical value of Esau *plene* [*'syw*] is 386. His son's name, Jeush [*y'wš*] which occurs in 1 Chron 1.35 comprises the same letters (ignoring the difference between shin and sin) and also has a numerical value of 386.

321   This should have been corrected in the manuscript to "your".

322   One detects here a reference to the accusation found in the Talmud and the *Toledoth Yesu* that Jesus was the illegitimate son of Panthera, a Roman (and thus Edomite) soldier. In the Second Century, Origen *Contra Celsum* 1.32 reported a similar tale: "[...] and hear what the Jew says about the mother of Jesus: that she was driven out by her fiancé the carpenter, after being convicted of having committed adultery with a soldier Panthera" in J. Stevenson, *A New Eusebius Documents Illustrating the History of the Church to AD 337*, 2nd ed. (London: SPCK, 1987), p. 133.

323   This should have been corrected in the manuscript to "yours".

324   The difference between the three spellings is three different spellings of /w/: *wyw, w'w* and *ww*.

Tertia ע"ין. ו"ו. ש"ין. יו"ד. י'. cujus numerus est 522. Plenitudines autem Plenitudinum infinitæ ferè esse possunt: quas tamen Cabbalistæ Practici magni admodum æstimant: Videatur Liber Majan Chochmah[325].

(4.) Hîc etiam in considerationem veniunt quadraturæ & posteriorationes[326]: ut sunt: | ישוע. ישו. ש"ו. י'. cujus numerus est 1022. Si autem reflexio fiat ad pleniorem scriptio est hæc: יו"ד. י'. ש"ין. יו"ד. ש"ין. ו'. יו"ד. י'. ש"ין. יו"ד. ש"ין. ו'. יו"ד. ע"ין. cujus numerus est 1334. Et variari potest secundum triplicem plenitudinem. Ubi quæri possunt dictæ & voces eosdem numeros continentes. Pleniorum autem non esset numerus.

fol. 31ᵛ (5.) Occurrunt & variationes, quæ sunt 24. |||

1. ישוע	7. שיוע	13. וישע	19. עישו
2. ישעו	8. שיעו	14. ויעש	20. עיוש
3. יושע	9. שויע	15. וישעי	21. עשיו
4. יועש	10. שעיו	16. ועשי	22. עשוי
5. יעשו	11. שעיו	17. ועיש	23. עויש
6. יעוש	12. שעוי	18. ועשי	24. עושי

(6.) Observari possunt versiculi, ubi literæ hujus Nominis sunt initiales Vocum, vel finales, vel secundæ, vel tertiæ etc. vocum: assumtoque simul Nomine משיח materia erit meditandi abundantissima, & Arithmetica omni vulgari, imò vel ipsâ Algebrâ excellentior | atque divinior.

A peccatis suis.[327] מן חטהיהין

Christianus. Sicut nomen Hebraicum עון peccatum seu iniquitas, sæpe sumitur pro pœna: ut 1. Sam. 28, 10; Gen. 4, 13; c. 19, 15; Lev. 15, 1[328]; c. 16, 22. &.

---

325 The "Book of the Fount of Wisdom" is an introduction to Lurianic Kabbalah published in 1652 in Amsterdam by Abraham Kalmankes of Lubin.
326 "Et omnis quadratura vocatur posterioratio, & denominatur phrasi percutiendi: quoniam literæ collisæ & percussæ intra se invicem multiplicantur, & scintillas emittunt de grege sociorum suorum sub mysterio percussionis petræ, super qua puniebatur Moses Magister noster super quo pax. [...]". ("Introductio pro meliori intellectu libri Sohar Vallem regiam", op. cit., p. 336).
327 Added above the line: *s. pœnis*.
328 Correction: Lev. 15, 1 replaced by Lev. 5, 1 (recte).
329 This is, of course, an invitation to an exegetical and meditative *practice*. One may feel quite unable to predict what the outcome of such an exercise might be, but the very point is that it is also an invitation to kabbalistic exploration. On discovering numerical relations, one is driven to provide an account of them. Kabbalah here is not a repetition of tradition, but a lively exegetical and speculative *practice*.

SECTION VI 383

is *y-o-d, š-y-n, w-w, ʿ-y-n* which makes 522. Fuller values of fuller values [i. e. writing out in full the names of the letters which result from the previous operation] can be almost infinite; which the Practical Kabbalists consider of quite great significance. See Liber Mayyan Chokhmah. (4) Here also come into consideration *the four letters and their subsequent accumulation*. Thus |: *y – yš – yšw – yšwʿ* added up make 1022. But if one considers the writing of fuller value here (as we did above), the result is *y-o-d / y-o-d š-y-n / y-o-d š-y-n w-y-w / y-o-d š-y-n w-y-w ʿ-y /* which makes 1334. And this can be varied with *a triple fuller value*. Thus sayings and words can be sought which have the same numerical value [as each other]. But the number of fuller values is incalculable. (5) There are 24 variations [of the four letters]: ‖| fol. 31ᵛ

(*i*) *y-š-w-ʿ* (*ii*) *y-š-ʿ-w* (*iii*) *y-w-š-ʿ* (*iv*) *y-w-ʿ-š* (*v* |) *y-ʿ-š-w* (*vi*) *y-ʿ-w-š* (*vii*) *š-y-w-ʿ* (*viii*) *š-y-ʿ-w* (*ix*) *š-w-y-ʿ* (*x*) *š-w-ʿ-y* (*xi*) *š-ʿ-y-w* (*xii*) *š-ʿ-w-y* (*xiii*) *w-y-š-ʿ* (*xiv*) *w-y-ʿ-š* (*xv*) *w-š-y-ʿ* (*xvi*) *w-š-ʿ-y* (*xvii*) *w-ʿ-y-š* (*xviii*) *w-ʿ-š-y* (*xix*) *ʿ-y-š-w* (*xx*) *ʿ-y-w-š* (*xxi*) *ʿ-š-y-w* (*xxii*) *ʿ-š-w-y* (*xxiii*) *ʿ-w-y-š* (*xxiv*) *ʿ-w-š-y*.

(6) Verses can be observed where the letters of this name are the initial letters of words, or the final ones, or the second or third word.³²⁹ If one takes up consideration of the name *mšyḥ* [Messiah] at the same time, one will have the most abundant material to reflect upon and an Arithmetic more excellent and holy than all common reckonings and | even than Algebra itself.³³⁰

*From their punishments*³³¹ *mn ḥṭhyhyn*

Christian Just as the Hebrew word *ʿwn*, "sin" or "iniquity", is often used for punishment as in 1Sam 28.10; Gen 4.13; 19.15; Lev 15.1; 16.22 etc, so also is

---

330 People might at the time have conceded more to Algebra than one would commonly at present suppose. John Walker (1616–1703), algebraist and cofounder of the Royal Society, produced a *Treatise on Algebra* in 1685 (London: John Wallis, 1685). Rejecting the idea that one might restrict algebraic letters to being mere surrogates for numbers, he argued that Algebra was, in fact, a "Universal Art", "a discipline with more potency than Mathematicians or other conceded".

331 Correction to *suis poenis* from Vulgate *a peccatis eorum*. Thus "punishments" are substituted for "sins". In the "Adumbratio kabbalæ christianæ" also, Knorr makes a difference between *peccatum* and *pœna*. Jesus liberates souls from the punishments incurred by their primal fall. This is a very different view from that of the usual Augustinianism. It may be relevant (in a much wider perspective) to note that Knorr's friend Van Helmont translated Ottavio Pisani, *Lycurgus Italicus* (Sulzbach: Typis Abrahami Lichtenhaleri, 1666) before 1671, a book advocating the reform of the penal system (Allison P. Coudert, "Leibniz et Christian Knorr von Rosenroth: une amitié méconnue", *Revue de l'histoire des religions* 213, 4 (1996): pp. 467–484, p. 475).

ita quoque vox Græca ἁμαρτία ut Matth. 9, 2.5.6; Joh. 1, 29; c. 8, 21.24; c. 9, 41; c. 15, 22.24; c. 16, 8.9. Et Syriaca חטהא | his locis. Quia ergò hoc loco intelligitur totum officium Messiæ sospitatorium; hinc omne quoque malorum genus hîc subinnuitur, quo propter lapsum suum primævum punitæ sunt hominum Animæ: quod nempe immersæ sint immundis corticibus; careant primævo lumine atque influxu; subjectæ sint τῷ[332] Jezer hara seu pravæ concupiscentiæ; mortique & variis revolutionibus & involutionibus nascendi; torminibus quoque gehenna[libus] | &c. A quibus omnibus, & præcipuè â pronitate peccandi, Messias illas liberare vult & potest.

Cabb. Cat. Ut autem innotescat, quid Scriptores nostri intelligant per populum Messiæ, hoc loco uberius explicanda est illorum de Anima hypothesis. Nempe hominem Sanctitatis, id est Adamum Protoplastem[333] considerant ut integrum exercitum | Animarum: quasi nempe Animæ quædam tum pertinerent ad Caput ejus;[334] quædam ad oculos; quædam ad nasum &c. & sic ad singula ejus membra. Et huic alium opponunt Adam Belial, hominem perversitatis, qui ex ipse simile sit corpus, similisve Exercitus, sub Capite Samaële. Cumque alter hic & immundus jamque antehac lapsus exercitus, in tentatione illa Paradisiacâ prævaluisset, ita ut singula membra pravitate | singula sibi subjicerent analoga membra in Sanctitate: factumque[335] esse postmodum, dicunt ut eæ sub immunditiem delapsæ animæ, quæ in homine Sancto fuerant, dum in statum generationis descendunt, sint Populus Fœderis atque Iisraëliticus: illas autem, quæ antea jam lapsæ erant sub Samaële, Principe Spirituum immundorum; & tempore lapsus Adamitici corpori sancto immiscebantur, descendentes ad generationes evasisse volunt in Populos gentiles. | (vid. Tract. de Revolutionibus Animarum cap. 1. §. 11[336].14[337].) Quæ opinio correctius paulò proponitur in Adumbratione Cabbalæ Christianæ cap. 10. §.6.7[338]. Ubi notandum, quod juxta hanc hypothesin etiam Deteriorum pravitas & anomalia corticosa corrigi tamen etiam queat: ita ut temporibus Messianis ultimis privatio illa, & ad malum inclinatio, quam Scriptura <u>Mortem</u> appellat, (nempe Divinioris naturæ absentiam) penitus sit ê medio tollenda, ut | restitutio fiat plenaria. Jes. 25, 8;

---

332 Knorr frequently uses the Greek article to mark the case of transliterated Hebrew words when these are not susceptible to Latin case-endings and the meaning would otherwise be unclear.
333 Correction: Protoplastem replaced by Protoplaste
334 Added above the line: nimirum
335 Correction: factumque replaced by factum
336 Cf. infra, footnote 105, p. 419.
337 Cf. ibid.
338 Cf. *supra*, footnote 47, pp. 154–155.

the Greek word *harmartia* as in Mt 9.2,5,6; Jn 1.29; 8.21, 24; 9.41; 15.22, 24; 16.8, 9. Likewise, the Syriac [word] *ḥṭh'*, | in all these places. So here we should understand the whole saving work of Messiah. Thus all types of ills, by which on account of their primaeval fall the souls of men are punished, are implied here. They are overwhelmed by the filthy Shards; they lack the primal light and influx; and are subject to [*tōi* Greek] the *Yetser ha-ra* or the Evil Impulse; and to death, to being born with in various incarnations and envelopments; and to the torments of Gehennah | etc. from all of which, but mainly from their proneness to sin, Messiah both wishes and is able to free them.

Kabbalist Catechumen If what our writers mean by the People of Messiah is to become clear we need here to explain more fully their theory of the Soul. The Man of Holiness, that is Adam the Protoplast, they consider as a single army | of Souls; as if some Souls belonged to his head, evidently some to his eyes, some to his nose etc. and so on through his individual limbs. And to this [Adam] they oppose another—Adam Belial, the Man of Perversity,[339] who himself is also like a body and [constitutes] a similar army under the leadership of Samael. This alternate and impure army, which had already previously fallen, prevailed in the Temptation in Paradise with the consequence that that individual members [of this body], by specific | sins, subjected to themselves the corresponding members in [the body of] Holiness. Our writers say that it soon happened that those Souls which had been in the Holy Man which fell under pollution, then descended into the World of Generation to become the People of the Covenant and the Israelites. But those who before then had already fallen under Samael, the Prince of unclean spirits and by the time of the Fall were mixed into the holy body of Adam, as they descended to [the world] of Generation wanted to escape into the Gentile peoples | (Tract. *De Revol. Animarum*, 1§ 11, 14). This opinion is set forward a little more accurately in *Adumbratio*, chap. 10, § 6, 7, where it should be noted that according to this theory even the wickedness of the worse and the deviance of the shards can finally be corrected; so that in the Last Times of Messiah, that privation and inclination to evil which Scripture calls | *Death* (truely the absence of the diviner nature) will be utterly borne away, so that there will be a Complete Restitution (Isa 25.8; 1 Cor 15.26, 54, 55, 56).

---

[339] Also evoking the "Man of Sin" found in 2 Thess 3.10, though the Greek Codices Sinaiticus and Vaticanus prefer there the "Man of Lawlessness".

1. Cor. 15, 26.54.55.56. Primario ergò per populum Messiæ intelliguntur Animæ Fœderis antiqui, toties revolvendæ, donec Messiæ plenè subjiciantur: Secundariò autem omnes animæ reliquæ ad fœdus novum vel citius vel serius adducendæ: donec post revolutiones nativitatum & castigationes plurimas <u>Deus</u> *omnia sit in omnibus. 1. Cor. 15, 28.*

V. 22. *Ut impleretur* דנתמלא 45

Christianus. Sensus est hic: rem omnem ita gestam esse, ut dici potuerit, impletum nunc fuit vaticinium illud Jesaiæ. Innuitur autem potissimum concordantia facti, illius veteris & hujus novi: ubi difficultas quidem haud exigua, quomodo illud impletum sit in Maria & Jesu, ||| quod impleri debuit antequam perirent duo illi Reges Judæorum hostes, Jes. 7, 16. E Philosophia ergò vestra scire vellem, quid tu Calumniatoribus ê gente tua reponeres.

Cabb. Cat. *Res ita expediri posse videtur; ut saltem acquiescere cogantur nostrates: quod Eadem illa Virgo (Prophetæ dehinc uxor Jes. 8, 3. ex eâdem procul dubio Tribu | nempe Judah ê quâ Propheta natus erat, oriunda; & Prophetissa, quæ tempore Achasi prægnans futura & paritura erat filium, ante cujus annos discretionis Regna Syriæ & Israëlitarum suis Regibus essent privanda,) per Gilgul seu Revolutionem & reditum Animæ suæ in carnem futura esset illa ipsa virgo, quæ paritura esset Messiam. Nec obstat quod iidem Doctores nostri statuant, Mulieres non revolvi; sed certis pœnis gravioribus aliis | restitui. Id enim non simpliciter asserunt, & varios casus similium revolutionum muliebrium tradunt: inter quos citra absurditatem & hic referri posset, quamvis ab ipsa Mirjam sorore Mosis, & fortè ultra*[340]*, primordium hujus Matris repeteretur.*[341] [**Christianus.**][342] obiter id annoto, quod puer ille Immanuel, & postea Maher-Schalalchasbas nominatur[343] Jes. 8, 3. natus sit in magna annonæ caritate, ubi propter hostium | Judæam oppugantium copiam & pericula, Prophetissa coacta fuerit in altiora montium juga confugere, in quibus pecori sua erant pascua sicut hodiè in Alpibus: ubi, cum propter

fol. 32ʳ

5

10

15

---

340 Correction in the right margin: ultra replaced by ab ipsa Eva
341 Deletion of several words, now unreadable.
342 Addition in the right margin: Christian. Hîc (which involves a change of speaker).
343 Correction: nominatur replaced by nominatus
344 Lightfoot, *Miscellanies and the Harmony of the Gospels*, op. cit., p. 179: "The Jews seek to elude this prophecy of Isaiah, by expounding it, either of the prophet's wife, or of the king's wife; and, from Prov. xxx. 19, they plead, that *'lmh* doth not strictly signify 'a virgin', but 'a woman that hath known a man'." Lightfoot then offers his answers to all this.

First, therefore, by the People of Messiah we should understand the Souls of the Old Covenant reincarnated many times, until they are fully subject to Messiah. Second: all remaining Souls who sooner or later will be led to the New Covenant—until after reincarnated births and many punishments, God will be "all in all" (1 Cor 15.28).

Verse 22
To fulfil dntml'

Christian The sense is this: everything so happened that it could be said that then was fulfilled that prophesy of Isaiah. But there is forcefully implied a congruence of reality between the old and the new, from which arises no small difficulty: how was the prophecy fulfilled in Mary and Jesus ‖, when it had to be fulfilled before the deaths of those two kings who were enemies of the Judaeans in Isa 7.16? So I would like to know how you would reply from your philosophy to critics from your own people.[344]

fol. 32r

Kabbalist Catechumen It would appear that the matter can be addressed as follows: our teachers are compelled whatever to concede that that virgin is the same. (The wife of the prophet, we see from Isa 8.3, no doubt arose from the same tribe | of Judah from which the prophet himself had been born and this prophetess was to become pregnant and to give birth to a son in the time of Ahaz. Before the child reached the years of discretion, the kingdoms of Syria and of the Israelites would be deprived of their Kings). [The virgin is the same] by *Gilgul* or reincarnation and the return of her Soul into flesh would constitute that Virgin who was to give birth to Messiah. Nor is it an objection that our sages say that women are not reincarnated, but appointed to other heavier fixed punishments. | For they do not just simply assert that, but also [in contrast] hand down various different cases of the reincarnation of women; amongst whom we may reasonably include this case, although the origin of this mother might look back to Miriam, Moses' sister, and possibly to Eve herself.[345]

Christian I would also remark here that this boy, called Immanuel and afterwards Maher-Shalal-Hash-Baz in Isa 8.3, was born during a great corn famine when on account of the enemy forces attacking Judaea and the [consequential] dangers, the prophetess had been complelled to flee to the higher mountain ridges where the flocks grazed, just as today in the Alps,

---

345 That is, the Tradition is not consistent and counter-examples may be found.

hominum mulgentium defectum lac vaccis ex uberibus efflueret, quod in concavitatibus saxorum receptum, suum â sese separaret cremorem, huic puello talis spontè repertus cremor cum melle Sylvestri in scopulis hisce pariter reperto, in cibum concesserit. חמאה enim | non tam Butyrum est, quam cremor lactis; quia illis in terris, prout adhuc in regionibus calidioribus, butyri loco oleum abundabat, usuique erat. Conf. Gen. 18, 8; Jud. 5, 25. coll. cum c. 6, 38; Prov. 30, 33; 2. Sam. 17, 29; Job. 20, 17; c. 29, 6; Deut. 32, 14; Ps. 55, 22. Confer. R. Sal. ad Gen. 18, 8. ubi dicit, quod חמאה sit pinguedo lactis, quam colligunt â superficie ejus. Confer eandem annonæ caritatis descriptionem Jes. 7, 21–25.

V. 23. *Virgo &c.* בתולתא

Christianus. Vide quæ de Matre Messiæ Virgine adducta sunt in Adumbratione Cabbal. Christ. cap. 11, §.5. p. 63[346]. Et in Excerptis libri Sohar Cent. 1. Locum 16.n. 10. & loc. 66. ê Sect. Lechlecha Crem. c. 235. Quibus adde quæ ex Mornæo addicit Lightfoot in Luc. 1, 35.

Cabb. Cat. *Nota quod vox* מ"רים *contineat numerum vocis* עלמה *bis | sumtæ: quasi sensus sit, eam esse virginem ante partum; Virginem post partum.*

Et vocabunt &c. ונקרון

Cabb. Cat. *Eodem modo per tertiam pluralem, vocem* קראת *quæ hic apud Prophetam in Hebraico extat, exprimit Paraphrastes Chaldæus, in Jes. 60, 18. Et quamvis non dubitem filio illi Prophetico omninò impositum fuisse Nomen Immanuel; ad quem filium | signi loco etiam aliquoties provocat Jesaias c. 8,*

---

346 Cf. *supra*, footnote 56, pp. 230–231.
347 *Butyrum:* "butter", as in the Vulgate Isa 7.15.
348 *Rabbi Solomon ben Isaac* (Shlomo Yitzhaki), commonly known as Rashi.
349 On Lk 1.35 Lightfoot wrote: "Give me leave, for their sakes in whose hand the book is not, to transcribe some few things out of that noble author Morney, which he quotes concerning this grand mystery from the Jews themselves: 'Truth shall spring out of the earth.' 'R. Joden,' saith he, 'notes upon this place, that it is not said, Truth shall *be born*, but shall *spring out*; because the generation and nativity of the Messiah is not to be as other creatures in the world, but shall be begot without carnal copulation; and therefore no one hath mentioned his father, as who must be hid from the knowledge of men till himself shall come and reveal him.' And upon Genesis: 'Ye have said (saith the Lord), 'We are orphans, bereaved of our father'; such a one shall your Redeemer be, whom I shall give you.' So upon Zechariah, 'Behold my servant, whose name is

[and] where, in the absence of any sucklings, milk flowed from their teats, gathered in basins in the rocks and the curds separated out. The boy would have found these curds to eat of his own accord, together with wild honey from the same rocks. [The Hebrew word] *ḥm'h* is | not so much "butter"[347] as the "curd of the milk", since in those lands, just as still today in warmer climes, oil was a common substitute for butter Cf. Gen 18.8; Judg 5.25 compared with 6.38; Pro 30.33; 2 Sam 17.29; Job 20.17; 29.6; Deut 32.14; Ps 55.22. Cf. R. Solomon[348] on Gen 18.8 where he says that *ḥm'h* is the cream of the milk which they collect from its top. Cf. also, the description of the wheat famine in Isa 7.21–25.

Verse 23
A virgin etc. btwlt'

Christian Look up what is said about the Virgin Mother of Messiah in *Adumbratio*, chap. 11, § 5, p. 63. Also in Excerpts Cent. I Loc. 16, n. 10 & Loc. 66, from the section *Lech Lechah* Cremona, c. 235. To which add what Lightfoot on Lk 1.35 adduces from Mornaeus[349].

Kabbalist Catechumen Note that the [Hebrew] word *mrym* [Mary] has a numerical value of twice | that of [the Hebrew] *'lmh* [virgin], as if to say: she was a virgin before birth and afterwards too[350].

And they shall call etc. wnqrwn

Kabbalist Catechumen In the same way, the Aramaic Targum to Isa 60.18 renders the word *qr't* [you, (O Virgin), will call] here in the Hebrew text of Isaiah [7.14], by a third person plural [they will call][351]. And although I do not doubt that the name Immanuel was definitely given to that prophetic

---

Branch': and out of Psalm 110, 'Thou art a priest after the order of Melchizedek': he saith, R. Berachiah delivers the same things. And R. Simeon Ben Jochai upon Genesis more plainly; viz. 'That the Spirit, by the impulse of a mighty power, shall come forth of the womb, though shut up, that will become a mighty Prince, the King Messiah.' So he." *Hebrew and Talmudical Excercitations upon the Gospels of St. Luke & St. John* in vol. XII of Pitman's edition (London: J. Dove, 1823) pp. 25–26. Philippe Du Plessis-Mornay (1549–1623) was a Hugenot apologist and governor of Saumur at the time of the Hugenot rising in 1621. He learned his Hebrew in Padua in 1566.

350 *Mrym* gives 40+200+10+40=290. *'lmh* gives 70+30+40+5=145.
351 In Isa 60.18 *qr't* "you will call" in Hebrew is rendered by the Targum "they shall proclaim".

8.10. conf. ib. v. 18.[352] *Nihil tamen impedit, quin antitypus iste, licet non in nomine, tamen re ipsa cum typo suo conveniat.*

Christianus. Sanè haud rarò æquipollent vocari & esse, ut Jes. 1, 26; c. 9, 6; c. 14, 20; c. 56, 7; c. 60, 14; c. 62, 4; Jer. 3, 17; c. 23, 6; Ez. 48, 35; Zach. 8, 3; Luc. 19, 46; coll. cum Jes. 56, 7; Matth. 2, 23; | c. 5, 9.19; Matth. 21, 13; Mar. 11, 17; Luc. 1, 76; c. 2, 23; c. 15, 19.21; 1. Joh. 3, 1; Heb. 3, 13; Ap. 19, 11.

[Cabb. Cat.][353] Denotat autem hoc Nomen Immanuel unionem & copulam Mariti seu Sponsi in Divinis, (qui vocatur Filius in Divinitate & Seir Anpin) cum uxore sua, seu Ecclesia â Spiritu Sancto gubernatâ, (de qua videatur Cabbal. denud: P. 1. p. 305[354]. | & loca inibi, è Sohar allegata.) Unde â Cabbalistis Christianis[355] hoc nomen merito inter divina numeratur.

[Christianus.][356] Statum enim hunc, cum Deus per Messiam est cum Ecclesia, recte censemus pro felicisimo 2. Cor. 6, 16; Eph. 3, 17; Ap. 7, 15; c. 21, 3. (vide etiam, quæ notata sunt ad Luc. 1, 31.)[357] |||

fol. 32ᵛ

[Cabb. Cat.][358] Et hoc nomen Immanuel Matthæus, qui lingua Syriaco-Chaldæa sive vernacula sibi, scribebat, exponit & traducit in vernaculam; in quam omnis quoque lectio Textuum sacrorum â certis Interpretibus in Synagogis constitutis ê linguâ Hebraicâ vertebatur, de quibus Interpretibus vid. Gemarah, Megillah f. 25. &c.

V. 24. *Et accepit &c.* ודברה

Christianus. Exemplum spiritualis connubii Intellectus illuminati, cum voluntate Virgin[e], circa generandam in nobis cælitus vitam divinam.

Cabb. Cat. *Hoc consortium potius est, & adjutorium, nullum influxum & cooperationem involvens, quàm verum conjugium.*

---

352 Deletion: Et quamvis non dubitem (to avoid repetition).
353 Deletion: Cabb. Cat. The change of speaker initially intended is cancelled, the Christian keeps the speech.
354 "זיווג *Copula maritalis*. Item Tempus pubertatis, in quo congressus fieri potest. Ubi notandum in genere, quod זיוו seu status pubertatis dependeat à Cerebris, quæ sunt Chochmah cum sequentibus. Etz Chajim. Tract. Ozaroth Chajim. Sect. Olam Ha-Akü-dim. Vid. Titulos נפל n. 2. & מצח item נקודה. Vid. Sohar Lechlecha 82.c.245. sed. Vajeschebh 105.c.419. Vajiggasch 114.c.458. Vajechi 45.c.180. Mischpatim 46.c.182. Jethro 40.c.159. & Zav. 15.c.57." ("Loci communes kabbalistici", op. cit., p. 305).
355 Deletion: â Cabbalistis Christianis
356 Deletion: Christianus. The change of speaker initially intended is no longer needed, after the previous correction. The Christian remains the speaker.
357 In the right bottom corner appears a Hebrew letter ט presumably an indication of binding or pagination.

child to whom Isaiah | several times draws attention as a sign (Isa 8.8, 10 compared with 8.18), nothing however prevents this antetype agreeing with its type not merely in name but also in substance.

Christian Name and reality are often in agreement, as in Isa 1.26; 9.6; 14.20; 56.7; 60.14; 62.4; Jer 3.17; 23.6; Ezek 48.35; Zech 8.3; Lk 19.46 compared with Isa 56.7; Mt 2.23; | 5.9, 19; 21.13; Mk 11.17; Lk 1.76; 2.23; 15.19, 21; 1Jn 3.1; Heb 3.13; Rev 19.11. For this name Immanuel means the union and joining of the Father or Spouse in Divinity (which is called The Son in Divinity and Zeir Anpin) with his wife or the Ecclesia governed by the Holy Spirit.[359] (Concerning which see *Cabb. Denud.*, Part. 1, p. 305 | and the quotations collected from the Zohar there). So this name is rightly considered a divine name.[360]

For this state of affairs, when God through Messiah is with the Ecclesia, we certainly consider as the most felicitous. So, 2 Cor 6.16; Eph 3.17; Rev 7.15; 21.3. (See also what was remarked above on Lk 1.31). ||| fol. 32ᵛ

And Matthew who wrote in [the mixture of] Aramaic and Syriac which was his vernacular, expounded and translated this name Immanuel into that vernacular, into which also every Scriptural lection was translated from the Hebrew by translators installed in the synagogues[361]. Concerning these translators see Gemarah Megilah folio 25 etc.

Verse 24

And he took etc. *wdbrh*

Christian An example of the spiritual marriage of an illuminated Intellect with the Will of the Virgin for the heavenly generation of the divine life in us.

Kabbalist Catechumen This is rather [a matter of] company and assistance, involving no influx or cooperation, than real marriage.

---

358   Deletion: Cabb. Cat. The change of speaker initially intended is cancelled, the Christian keeps the speech.

359   The genderised pairings in Lurianic Kabbalah, together with the association of Zeir Anpin with "the Son" readily facilitate assimilation to the topos of Messiah and his bride Ecclesia.

360   Deletion: by the Christian Kabbalists. Here is a rather extraordinary deletion. Knorr's discression evidently led him to prefer not to suggest the existence of a category to which we would imagine he most obviously belonged!

361   The reference is to the Aramaic Targums provided as an (initially oral) gloss on the Hebrew lections. But notice the assumed continuum of Aramaic here.

V. 25. *Donec.* עדמא

Cabb. Cat. *Particula Hebraica* עד, & *Syriaca* עדמא & *Græca* Ἕως *Donec, tempora posteriora prioribus non semper opponunt: ut Gen. 8, 7; Gen. 28, 15; 1. Sam. 15, 35; 2. Sam. 6, 23; Job. 27, 5; Psal. 123, 2; Jes. 22, 14; Matth. 12, 20; c. 14, 22; Matth. 28, ult. imò si tractum aliquem temporis admitteret ista genitura primogeniti, | omninò dicerem ad tempus post partum pertinere hanc negationem, ut Rom. 5, 13. & ex præallegatis plura.*[362]

Christianus. Nec mysterio caret Josephi continentia: cesset enim perpetuò influxus humanus, ubi semel exorta est Naturæ divinioris excellentia. Sed &, si Antiquitatis testimomium hîc non concurreret, nec Maria perpetua Virgo mansisset, nihil tamen | exinde labefactaretur ipsius Jesu, adeoque Messiæ auctoritas.

Primogenitum. בוכרא

Cabb. Cat. *Nostratibus hæc vox eum tantum designat, qui uterum aperit: nec necessariò involvitur, dari sequentes. Sed Matth. 13, 55. ipsi tribuuntur fratres.*

Christianus. Nihil obstat: Nam Matth. 10, 3. Jacobus dicitur filius Alphæi: & Mar. 16, 1. Mariæ, quæ non potest fuisse Mater Domini. Ejusque etiam filius dicitur Joses Matth. 27, 56. conf. Mar. 15, 47. & Gen. 29, 12. Jacob dicitur frater Labanis, cum tamen Sororis tantum filius esset.

Et illa vocavit &c. וקרת

Christianus. In Græco ambiguum videtur, quis ipsi nomen hoc imposuerit; sed verbum Syriacum est fœminini generis, quamvis jussi essent ambo Matth. 1, 21; Luc. 1, 31.

Cabb. Cat. *Non ergò est humanæ impositionis Nomen istud, sed divinæ originis. Sicut nomen Immanuel, quamvis et illud â Matre esset imponendum Jesch. 7, 14.*

---

362 Deletion: imò si tractum aliquem temporis admitteret ista genitura, primogeniti, omninò dicerem ad tempus post partum pertinere hanc negationem, ut Rom. 5, 13. & ex præallegatis plura.

363 Deleted here: "But if this woman about to bear her first-born does admit of some passage of time, I would say that this negative related to the period after the birth, like Rm 5.13 and many other previously cited passages." The point of the remark about "until" in the text is to block an inference from the preposition that Joseph subsequently knew Mary.

Verse 25
Until 'dm'

Kabbalist Catechumen. The Hebrew conjunction '*d* [until] and the Syriac '*dm*' [until] and the Greek *heōs* [until] do not always oppose a later time to an earlier one, as [can be seen in] in Gen 8.7; Gen 28.15; 1 Sam 15.35; 2 Sam 6.23; Job 27.5; Ps 123.2; Isa 22.14 Mt 12.20; 14.22; Mt 28 *at the end*[363].

Christian Joseph's continence does not lack a mystery for the human influx would cease forever at once, when there arose the excellence of a diviner nature.[364] But even if the testimony of Antiquity does not agree here, or if Mary did not remain a perpetual virgin, this causes no | diminution in the authority of Jesus himself as Messiah.

First born bwkr'

Kabbalist Catechumen For our teachers this word only designates "one who opens the womb"[365] and does not necessarily involve the assumption of subsequent siblings. But in Mt 13.55 brothers are ascribed to Jesus.

Christian That is no objection. For in Mt 10.3 James is said to be the son of Alphaeus and in Mk 16.1 the son of Mary who cannot have been the Mother of the Lord. Her son is called Joses in Mt 27.56 Cf. Mk 15.47 and Gen 29.12 where Jacob is called the brother of Laban, when in fact he was the son of Laban's sister.

And she called etc. wqrt

Christian In the Greek it seems ambiguous who gave him his name, but in the Syriac the verb is femine, although both parents were righteous Mt 1.21, Lk 1.31[366].

Kabbalist Catechumen So this name was not given by any human imposition, but was of divine origin. Just like the name Immanuel, although that too was imposed by the mother (Isa 7.14).

---

364 The presence of a "diviner nature" in Mary's womb evidently terminally arrested Joseph's "human influx".
365 *peṭer reḥem*, "the womb-opener". This describes the child (in a polygamous society) from the perspective of its mother rather than its father. Cynthia R. Chapman, *The House of the Mother: The Social Roles of Maternal Kin in Hebrew Narrative and Poetry* (New Haven: Yale University Press, 2017), chapter 7, pp. 150–172.
366 In the Greek Mt 1.21 Joseph is told he will name the child, but in Lk 1.31 Mary is told she will.

Sectio VII.
De Nativitate & Circumsione[1] Johannis, & Restituto Zacharia, ê Luca 1, v. 57–80.

v. 57. Erat autem ipsi Elischevæ tempus ut pareret[2], & peperit filium.[3]

58. Et audiverunt vicini ejus & filii cognationis ejus[4], quod magnificasset Deus gratiam suam erga eam: & gaudebant cum eâ[5].

59. Et factum est in die octava, & venerunt ad circumcidendum puerum[6]: & vocabant eum nomine | Patris sui, Zacharja[7].

fol. 33ʳ *60. Et respondit mater illius, & dixit eis[8]: Non sic sed vocabitur Jochanan[9]. |||*

61. Et dixerunt ad eam[10]: Non est quisquam, qui vocetur in genere tuo nomine hoc[11].

62. Et innuerunt Patri ejus, quomodo vellet ut nominarent eum[12].

63. Et petiit tabellas, & scripsit ac dixit: Jochanan est nomen ejus. Et | miratus est quisque[13].

64. Et illicò apertum est os ejus, & lingua ejus: & locutus est, ac benedixit Deo[14].

65. Et extitit timor[15] super omnes vicinos eorum, & in universo monte Judææ ista dicebantur[16].

66. Et omnes, qui audiverunt, cogitabant in cordibus suis, & dicebant: Quidnam erit Puer iste? Et manus Domini erat cum eo[17].

67. Et impletus est Zacharja Pater ejus Spiritu Sanctitatis, prophetavitque ac dixit[18]:

68. Benedictus sit Dominus Deus Iisraël, qui visitavit populum suum, | & fecit ei salutem[19].

---

1 Sic. Probably in error. It should be "circumcisione".
2 Vulgate: Elizabeth autem impletum est tempus pariendi.
3 On the left-hand half of the page, a fragment cut from Knorr's edition of the Peshittta New Testament containing the Syriac version of the quoted passage in the Gospel of Luke is pasted in and crossed out.
4 Vulgate: vicini et cognatione eius.
5 Vulgate: quia magnificavit Dominus misericordiam suam cum illa, et congratulabantur ei.
6 Vulgate: venerunt circumcidere puerum.
7 Vulgate: Zachariam.
8 Vulgate: et respondens mater eius dixit.
9 Vulgate: Nequaquam sed vocabitur Ioannes.
10 Vulgate: illam.
11 Vulgate: Quia nemo est in cognatione tua qui vocetur hoc nomine.
12 Vulgate: Innuebant autem patri eius, quem vellet vocari eum.

Section VII
Concerning the Birth and Circumcision of John and the Restoration of Zachariah
From Luke Chapter 1 verses 57–80

57 It was the time for Elischeba [Elizabeth] to give birth and she gave birth to a son.

58 And her neighbours heard and the sons of her relatives heard that God had magnified his Grace towards her and they rejoiced with her.

59 And it came to pass of the eighth day that they came to circumcise the boy and they called him by the name | of his father Zachariah.

60 But his mother replied and said to them "Not so, but he will be called Jochanan [John]". ⦀. fol. 33ʳ

61 And they said to her "No one in your family is called by that name".

62 And they gestured to his father [asking] what he wanted them to call him.

63 And he found a writing tablet and wrote and said "His name is Jochanan" and | everyone was amazed.

64 And thereupon his mouth was opened and his tongue [freed] and he spoke and blessed God.

65 And fear fell upon all their neighbours and these things were spoken about in all the hill country of Judaea.

66 And all who heard pondered in their hearts and said "What will this boy be?" And the hand of the Lord was with him.[20]

67 And his father Zachariah was filled with the Spirit of Holiness and prophesied and said:

68 "Blessed be the Lord, the God of Israel who has visited his people | and wrought salvation for them.

---

13   Vulgate: Et postulans pugillarem scripsit, dicens: Joannes est nomen eius. Et mirati sunt universi.
14   Vulgate: Apertum est autem illico os eius et loquebatur benedicens Deum.
15   Vulgate: Et factus est timor.
16   Vulgate: et super omnia montana Judaeae divulgabantur omnia haec verba.
17   Vulgate: et posuerunt omnes qui audierant in corde suo, dicentes: Quis putas, puer iste erit? Etenim manus Domini erat cum illo.
18   Vulgate: Et Zacharias pater eius repletus est Spiritu Sancto et prophetavit dicens:
19   Vulgate: Benedictus Dominus Deus Israel, quia vistivit et fecit redemptionem plebis suae.
20   Lightfoot, *Miscellanies and the Harmony of the Gospels*, op. cit., p. 181: "Vulg. 'For the hand of the Lord was with him:' contrary to the original, Arabic, and Syriac."

69. *Et erexit nobis cornu salutis in domo David servi sui*[21].

70. *Sicut locutus est per os Prophetarum suorum sanctorum, qui (fuerunt) â seculo*[22].

71. *Quod redemturus esset nos ab inimicis nostris*[23], *& de manu | omnium osorum nostrorum*[24].

72. *Et exercuit gratiam cum Patribus nostris, & recordatus est pactorum suorum sanctorum*[25].

73. *Et juramenti, quod juravit Abrahæ Patri nostro, quod daturus esset nobis*[26]:

74. *Ut liberaremur de manu hostium nostrorum, & sine timore serviremus coram eo*[27].

75. *Omnibus diebus nostris in rectitudine (& justitia*[28].)

76. *Et tu Puer, Propheta Excelsi*[29] *vocaberis: ibis*[30] *enim ante faciem Domini, ut præpares vias ejus*[31].

77. *Ut det cognitionem vitæ populo suo, in remissionem peccatorum suorum*[32]:

78. *Per viscera gratiæ*[33] *Dei nostri, quibus*[34] *visitavit nos Oriens ab alto.*

79. *Ad lucendum iis*[35], *qui in tenebris, & in umbris*[36] *mortis | sedent: ut dirigeret*[37] *pedes nostros in viam pacis.*

80. *Puer autem crescebat et corroborabatur*[38] *Spiritu: & in deserto*[39] *erat, usque in diem ostensionis ejus apud Iisraël.*

V. 57. Tempus, ut pareret. זבנא דתאלדי

Christianus. Novimestre scilicet, quia Luc. 1, 26. numerantur sex ejus menses ante annunciationem | Mariæ, & v. 56. tres post eandem: quibus nondum absolutis Maria abiit.

Cabb. Cat. *Quare autem partus non fuit septimestris, vel duodecimestris majori cum miraculo? quod enim tales casus dentur ipsi ponunt Doctores*

---

21 Vulgate: Et erexit cornu salutatis nobis in domo David pueri sui.
22 Vulgate: os sanctorum qui a saeculo sunt, prophetarum eius.
23 Vulgate: salutem ex inimicis nostris.
24 Vulgate: qui oderant nos.
25 Vulgate: ad faciendam misericordiam cum patribus nostris et memorari testament sui sancti.
26 Vulgate: iusiurandum, quod iuravit ad Abraham patrem nostrum, daturus se nobis.
27 Vulgate: ut sine timore, de manu inimicorum nostrorum liberati, serviamus illi in sanctitate et iustitia coram ipso.
28 Vulgate omits *in rectitudine (& justitia.)* but cf Vulgate v74.
29 Vulgate: Altissimi.
30 Vulgate: praeibis.
31 Vulgate: parare vias eius.

SECTION VII

69 And has raised up a horn of salvation in the house of David his servant,
70 Just he said by the mouths of his holy prophets who (were) of old,
71 That he would redeem us from our enemies and from the hand | of all who hate us
72 And he showed Grace to our fathers and remembered his holy covenants.[40]
73 And the oath which he swore to our father Abraham, which will be given to us,
74 That we shall be freed from the hand of our enemies and minister before him without fear
75 All our days in uprightness (and righteousness).
76 And you, boy, will be called a prophet of the Most High, for you will go before the face of the Lord to prepare his ways,
77 So that he might give knowledge of life to his people by the remission of their sins
78 By the bowels of Grace of our God, with which he has visited us, rising from on high,
79 to lighten those who are in darkness and sit in the shadow of death, | so that he might guide our feet in the way of peace".
80 And the boy grew and became strong with the spirit and was in the desert until the day when he was shown to Israel.

Verse 57
The time that she should bear zbn' dt'ldy

Christian Nine months [later] obviously, since Lk 1.26 gives her six months before the Annunciation | to Mary and verse 56 three months after that. Before these later months were completely up, Mary left.

Kabbalist Catechumen Why [did not] the birth more miraculously [occur] in the seventh month or the twelfth month? For our teachers pro-

---

32 Vulgate: ad dandam scientiam salutis plebi eius, in remissionem peccatorum eorum.
33 Vulgate: misericordiae.
34 Vulgate: in quibus.
35 Vulgate: illuminare his.
36 Vulgate: in umbra.
37 Vulgate: ad dirigendos.
38 Vulgate: confortabatur.
39 Vulgate: in desertis.
40 Lightfoot, *Miscellanies and the Harmony of the Gospels*, op. cit., p. 181: "'syh ḥśd, as Josh. ii. 12; 2 Sam ix. 1, &c.. The Syriac reads conjunctively, 'And he hath showed mercy;' and so doth the Arabic the other clause, 'And he hath remembered.'"

fol. 33ᵛ *nostri (vid. Lexic. Cabbalist. p. 615. n. 2⁴¹.) Quodque etiam multi Justi & Pii nati sint mense septimo, ut Moscheh, Schmuel, Perez & Serah & similes, quamvis cum defectibus, ibidem asseritur | (p. 623.n. 28⁴².) |||* 45

Christianus. Procul dubio, ne viæ illius vel defectuosæ essent vel impeditæ, qui vias ut pararet Domino suo, missus erat.

Filium ברא

Cabb. Cat. *Si admittenda est Hypothesis Sapientum nostrorum, quod Elias |* 5
sit Sandalphon, princeps inter Angelos, (quod asseritur in Pneumatica Cabbalistica c. 3, §.2. p. 221⁴³.) notatu sane haud indignum est, quod tunc notionem habeat Naturæ fœmininæ, consistens in imagine atque forma gradus in Divinitate ultimi, nimirum Malchuth, seu Uxoris; & ita quidem, ut tanquam Domina, præfecta sit Mundo infimo: (prout ibidem traditur cap. 5. §. 7.8. p. 227⁴⁴.) Et illa tamen Natura fœminina, jam naturam | assumit Masculi? 10

Christianus. Nimirum quia Masculinum & Fœmininum nihil aliud sunt, quam Activum, seu communicativum, & Passivum seu receptivum. Elias,

---

41 "Tempus autem quo formantur tres istæ notiones non est æquale: Lumina enim non manent in statu Ibbur nisi septem menses. Et tunc formatio eorum consummata est. Scintillæ autem perficiuntur novem Mensibus: & vasa mensibus duodecim. Et sic triplex etiam est Tempus Uteri gestationis in mundo, nempe septimestre, novimestre & Mensium duodecim: sicut & in Gemara occurrit Exemplum mulieris, quæ uterum gestavit duodecim menses." ("Loci communes kabbalistici", op. cit., p. 615).

42 "Sequitur Ibbur 2. Cerebrorum, quoad Interna, qui est 7. mensium. Iste Ibbur enim occultus & sublimis est admodum, & consistit in eo, quod 7. inferiores τοῦ Attik Jomin investiantur intra 7. formationes Cranii τοῦ Arich; unde septimestris dicitur. Et in 7. his inferioribus attingi nequit medietas superna Chesedica; sed à medietate inferiore incipitur: unde dixerunt sapientes nostri b.m. omnem partum septimestrem esse defectivum etiam septem mensibus plenè exactis. Et sic multi Justi & Pii nati sunt cum defectibus mense septimo, ut Moscheh, Schmuel, Perez & Serah, & similes, qui omnes provenerunt à 7. istis formationibus Cranii τοῦ Arich. ibid. Vid. נוקבה 8. vid. Sohar Vajiggasch 115, 456." (Ibid., p. 623).

43 "Et duo isti Duces exercituum Metatron & Sandalphon sunt duo Cherubim, qui super arca fœderis DOMINI locati erant; alter mas & alter fœmina. Suntque quasi calceamenta Schechinæ: primus ad instar tibialium tenuium, quæ carni aptantur; & secundus tanquam sandalium crassius remotiorque & exterior. Et huc pertinet locus Cant. 7, 1. Suntque Chanoch & Elijahu, qui assumti sunt ad DEUM in mundum Jezirah." ("Pneumatica Kabbalistica [...] Domus Dei", op. cit., p. 221).

44 "§.7. Hinc ego colligerem, quod Metatron sit Psyche prima & universalis subsistens per se; Sandalphon autem Vita, quæ est in corpore primo, nempe cœlo illo, quod vocatur Araboth; alias etiam empyreum vel primum mobile, Orbis diurnus. Vel etiam ambo simul sumti vocari possent cor & cerebrum mundi, per quæ influxus sit in reliqua

pose that such cases do occur (See *Lex. Cabb.*, p. 615, n. 2). And also that many righteous and pious are born in the seventh month like Moses, Samuel, Perez, Zerah and similar, although it is said they had defects | (ibid., p. 623, n. 28).⁴⁵ ‖|

Christian No doubt his ways were neither defective nor hindered, because he had been sent to prepare the ways of the Lord.

Son br'

Kabbalist Catechumen If the theory of our wise men is allowed, Elijah | was Sandalphon, the leader of the angels (which is stated in *Pneumatica Cabbalistica*, chap. 3, §2, p. 221). It is worth noting that then he was imagined as female, consisting in the image and form of the last divine degree, *i. e.* Malkhut or Kingdom, and so, like a mistress, was set over the lower world (as it says ibid., chap. 5, §7, 8, p. 227). However, did that feminine nature, now | become masculine?⁴⁶

Christian No doubt yes, because masculine and feminine are respectively active or communicating and passive or receiving. Elijah, who under the

---

corpora, quæ reguntur virtute superiorum, & in specie virtute gradûs Tiphereth & sex Sephirarum structuræ: Sicut Sandalphon vitam & influxum præbet virtute Malchuth; estque fœmina in imagine atque forma istius, sicut Metatron masculus ad similitudinem Tiphereth. §.8. Unô verbô: Hic, nempe Metatron, est Princeps Mundi Jezirah, & hæc, nempe Sandalphon, est Domina præfecta mundo Asiah. Ille tanquam Intelligentia incorporea subsistit per se: hæc autem tanquam Phantasia & sensus, unitur cum corpore. Ille tanquam Intellectus & motor abstractus & separatus: hæc autem tanquam Psyche & motor compositus: Ille tanquam motionis finis; & hæc tanquam ejusdem executio. Et ex his intelligitur, quid sibi velint Talmudistæ, dum Metatronem vocant Principem facierum, & principem Mundi: nempe quod juxta nomen primum faciem convertat ad superiora, de quorum natura est; & ad inferiora, quorum quodammodo causa est, ita ut utraque duplici quasi facie simul intueatur. Et quod juxta nomen secundum involutus sit, & operetur in mundo corporeo, eumque formet & disponat ad modum intellectualium: estque causa motûs cœlorum, & conservator elementorum & specierum elementalium, generationisque & corruptionis, & alterationis individuorum, ex quibus constant. Unde dicendum est, quod Metatron & Sandalphon sint substantia & subjectum unum, cui competat nomen primum, quatenus consideratur in se; & secundum, quatenus involvitur in mundum Asiah, qui ab ipso formatur & regitur." (Ibid., p. 227).

45   For earlier remarks about seventh-month babies in Philo, see Philo of Alexandria, *On the Creation of the Cosmos*, introduced, translated and commented by David T. Runia (Leiden: Brill, 2001), pp. 292–293.

46   The problem and its specific and innovative solution arise only in this context where Sandalphon becomes John the Baptist.

qui sub Johannis nomine, jam communicare debebat Ecclesia mysteria plurima, in masculi forma nasci debuit. Quamvis Androgyneitatis naturâ interim non careret: unde & in cœlibatu mortuus est.[47]

V. 58. *Vicini ejus* &c. שבביה

Cabb. Cat. *E locis Jos. 21, 12. & 1. Chron. 7, 56. apparet, quod Ager circa Hebronem situs, datus fuerit Calebo; ipsa autem urbs tradita fuerit sacerdotibus.* [**Christianus.**][48] Hinc fortè colligi posset, quod per vicinos intelligantur posteri Calebi Laici: & per cognatos sacerdotes Hebronitæ. Hi digni fuerunt, quibus primum innotesceret recens hoc miraculum.

[**Christianus.**][49] Nota autem est Calebi fides & benedictio.

Quod magnificasset Deus gratiam suam. דאסגי אלהא חננה

Cabb. Cat. *In Gen. 19, 19: hanc phrasin ita reddit Syrus: Et maximum est beneficium tuum, quo usus est*[50] *es mecum.*

Christianus. Sanè aliquid fuisset, si solum sterilitatis opprobrium ab ipsa fuisset | sublatum: quod autem in senectute etiam partu miraculoso inclaresceret, quid quæso ab ipso[51] sperari potuisset majus? Conf. Ps. 18, 51; Ps. 126, 2.

V. 59. *In die octava* &c. ליומא דתמניא

Christianus. De circumcisione videri possunt varia in Excerptis Cent. 11 Loc. 1.2.3.4. Sed quia quædam Johannem in specie tangunt, hinc primò quæritur; quare non natus | sit circumcisus? prout Adam; Seth; Chanoch; Noach; Schem; Tarah; Jaacob; Joseph; Moscheh; Schmuel; David; Jeschajah; Jirmejah; qui ita recitantur in Midrasch Tehillim f. 10.b.

---

47 Deletion: Quamvis Androgyneitatis naturâ interim non careret: unde & in cœlibatu mortuus est.
48 Added in the left margin: Christian. (which involves a change of speaker).
49 Deletion: Christianus. The change of speaker initially intended is no longer needed, after the previous correction. The Christian remains the speaker.
50 Deleted word.
51 Correction: ipso replaced by ipsa
52 Lightfoot, *Miscellanies and the Harmony of the Gospels*, op. cit., p. 180: "Hebron was inhabited by Aaronites: but the fields and villages about, with children of Judah, Josh. xxi. 11. These two are Elisabeth's neighbours and cousins."

name of John now had to communicate very many mysteries to Ecclesia, had to be born in a masculine form. Although in between he was androgynous: this is why he died celebate.

Verse 58
Her neighbours etc. *šbbyh*

Kabbalist Catechumen From Jos 21.12 & 1 Chron 7.56 it appears that the land situated around Hebron had been given to Caleb. But the town itself had been given to the priests.

Christian From that it may perhaps be gathered that by "neighbours" are to be understood the lay descendants of Caleb and by "relatives", the priests of Hebron. These later were worthy to first hear of this new miracle. But also note the faith and blessing of Caleb.[52] |

Because God has magnified his favour d'šgy 'lh' ḥnnh

Kabbalist Catechumen In Gen 19.19 the Syriac gives this phrase as "And great is your benefit, which you have used with me".[53]

Christian Clearly, if only the shame of barrenness had been removed from her, | that would have been something [to be grateful for]. But also, she had been honoured in her old age by a miraculous birth. What more, I ask you, could she have hoped for? Cf. Ps 18.51; 126.1.

Verse 59
On the eighth day etc. *lywm' dtmny'*

Christian Various observations about circumcision can be found in Excert Cent. II Loc. 1, 2, 3, 4. Certain questions concern John specifically: first why was he not born | circumcised like Adam, Seth, Enoch, Noah, Shem, Terah, Jacob, Joseph, Moses, Samuel, David, Isaiah and Jeremiah who are listed in Midrash Tehilim folio 10.b.[54]

---

53   C.G. Düring's 1734 *Novum Inventarium Bibliothecae Sulzbaco-Palatino* (BAB Cbm 580 Repositorium A), p. 1 indicates the presence of Walton's Polyglot Bible in the library in Sulzbach in which the Old Testament could be consulted in Syriac.

54   On those born circumcised see Isaac Kalimi, "He was Born Circumcised: Some Midrashic Sources. Their Concept, Roots and Presumably Historical Context" in *Zeitschrift für Neutestamentiche Wissenschaft und die Kunde der Alten Kirche* 93, 1–2 (2002): pp. 1–12 which also appears in Id., *Early Jewish Exegesis and Theological Controversy Studies*

Cabb. Cat. *Responsio facilis erit, consideranti, quod Elias fuerit restaura-* 35
tor Circumcisionis, & propterea in omni circumcisione statuatur esse præsens |
tanquam Angelus fœderis: in quem finem etiam peculiaris ipsi locari solet sella:
unde mirum non est; quod multò minus subducere voluerit â circumcisione
seipsum.

Christianus. Iterum quæritur: Si Elias tanquam Angelus fœderis præsens
est omni circumcisionis actui; quis jam illius loco præsens fuerit in Circum-
cisione | corporis proprii? 40

Cabb. Cat. *Responsio iterum peti potest ex illis, quæ dicta sunt ad Luc. 1, 35*
fol. 34ʳ *quod nimirum Chajah & Jechidah Eliæ, quamvis reliquæ partes ||| Animæ ejus*
inferiores essent in Johanne, tamen manserint in mundo sublimiore; â quibus
hoc ipsius officium commodè potuerit suppleri.

Christianus. Notabile autem est, quod ista Circumcisio peracta fuerit
Hebreone[55], ubi circumcisionis fœdus primum fuerat institutum Gen. 17, 10.
coll. cum Gen. 13, 18.

Cabb. Cat. *An autem, ut prima circumcisio, prout statuunt nostrates, facta* 5
fuerit tempore Paschatis, certè affirmare cum quibusdam non ausim.[56]

Et vocarunt eum &c. וקרין הוו לה

Christianus. Sicut tempore primæ Circumcisionis Deus Abrahamo & Saræ
nova imposuit | Nomina Gen. 17, 5.15. ita tempore circumcisionis Nomina 10
etiam pueris imponebantur. Quod hîc factum videtur, non tam in honorem
Patris, quam boni ominis causa, præ gaudio, quod *Deus recordatus esset* precum, bonorumque operum Elisabethæ, ipsique dedisset filium hunc. Conf.
1. Sam. 1, 19; Act. 10, 31; Luc. 1, 72.

Cabb. Cat. *In Sohar impositio Nominum tribuitur Deo ê Psal. 46, 9. quæ |* 15
loca vide in Excerptis Cent. II Loc. 5.6.7. Exempla autem quod Nomina impo-
sita sunt ab Assistentibus, habemus Gen. 38, 29; c. 25, 25; Ruth. 4, 17.

---

in Scriptures in the Shadow of Internal and External Controversies (Assen: Royal van
Goricum, 2002), pp. 61–76.
55   Correction: Hebreone replaced by Hebrone
56   Deletion of an entire sentence (one line), now unreadable.
57   John is, of course, considered here as a reincarnation of Elijah.

SECTION VII 403

Kabbalist Catechumen The answer will be easy if one considers that Elijah[57] was the restorer of circumcision and therefore was considered to be present at every circumcision, | like the Angel of the Covenant.[58] For this reason a chair used to be set aside especially for him. So it is no surprise that he wished to be circumcised himself.

Christian Another question! If Elijah, like the Angel of the Covenant, was present at every act circumcision; who was now present in that capacity at his own | physical circumcision?

Kabbalist Catechumen The answer again can be sought from what said on Lk 1.35; that clearly the Chayah and Yechidah of Elijah, although the other parts ||| of his soul were below in John, nevertheless remained in the higher world.[59] They could easily perform this office.   fol. 34ʳ

Christian It is notable that this circumcision was performed at Hebron where the Covenant of Circumcision was first established. Gen 17.10 Cf. with Gen 13.18.

Kabbalist Catechumen Whether this took place at Passover, as our teachers assert was the case with the first circumcision, I would not presume to say with certainty.[60]

And call him etc. *wqr'n hww lh*

Christian Just as at the time of the first circumcision, God gave new names to Abraham and Sarah | Gen 17.5, 15, so at the time of a circumcision, names were also given to boys. This seems to have been done here not so much in honour of the father, than for the sake of a good omen and for joy that God had remembered the prayers and good works of Elisabeth and had given her this son. Cf. 1 Sam 1.19; Acts 10.31; Lk 1.72.

Kabbalist Catechumen In the Zohar the giving of names is attributed to God from Ps 46.9. See | more in Excerpt Cent. II Loc. 5, 6, 7. As examples of names given by by-standers, we have Gen 38.29; 25.25; Ruth 4.17.

---

58   Elijah restored the rite of circumcision when according to tradition based on 1 Kgs 19.9–10 it had been abrogated by the Ten Tribes after their separation from Judah. God thereafter decreed that he should attend every circumcision to testify that the covenant was now being kept (*Shir Hashirim Rabbah* 1.6; *Zohar* 1.93a). A chair is set aside for Elijah at a *brit milah*.
59   Similar to the case of the Chayah and Yechidah of Messiah discussed *supra*.
60   See, for example, *Pirke de Rabbi Eliezer* 29.

V. 60. *Non sic, sed vocabitur Jochanan.* יוחנן

Christianus. Hæc ita suggerit Mater, non tantum ad monitum Mariti, scripto procul dubio sibi traditum, sed & monente potissimum spiritu Sancto, quo ipso adhuc impleta | erat. Cum Johanne enim incipiebat Epocha Gratiæ, Matth. 11, 13. quam & ipse temporibus præterlapsis opponit Joh. 1, 17. ut & Petrus Act. 15, 10.11.

Cabb. Cat. *Adde quod ipsi etiam Talmudici Nomen Chaninah ê Jer. 16, 13, quod Gratiam denotat; tribuunt Messiæ Pesach. cap. 4. (vide plura de Nomine Jochanan in Adumbratione Cabbalæ Christianæ p. 62, §.2*[61]*. & ad Luc. 1, 13.)*

V. 61. *Non est quisquam &c.* דלית אנש

[**Cabb. Cat.**][62] *Quare hanc formant objectionem?*

[**Christianus.**][63] Videntur sic collegisse: Aut mysterium quærit; aut favorem cujusdam ê familia: prout exempla extant 1. Par. 3, 6.8; c. 23, 21.23. Mysterium autem jam subministravimus & familiæ exemplum non habemus.

V. 63. *Et scripsit & dixit.* וכתב ואמר

Cabb. Cat. *Miraculum insignius est, si Nomen hoc & scripto & verbo expressum statuatur; quæ etiam causa fuit, ut tanta omnnes*[64] *obrueret admiratio.*

Christianus. Et profectò tempus illud pœnæ ipsius ab Angelo præfinitum v. 20. h.c. nunc omninò elapsum erat: fidesque ejus non jam demum suum habuit initium, vid. ad. v. | 22. h. c. nisi & Mariæ narrata vel ignoravuit, vel non credidit; quod sanè probabile non est.

---

61 Cf. *supra*, footnote 164, pp. 180–181.
62 Correction above the line: Christianus replaced by Cabb. Cat. (which involves the two speakers being changed over in the following exchange).
63 Correction: Cabb. Cat. replaced by Christianus (as a consequence of the previous correction).
64 In error, it should be "omnes".
65 The connection here is to the chronographic / prophetic "Age of Grace" which John inaugurated.
66 Lightfoot, *Miscellanies and the Harmony of the Gospels*, op. cit., p. 184: "Rabbi Jochanan said, What is the name of the Messias? some said, Haninah, grace; as it is said, I will not

Verse 60
Not so, but he shall be called Jochanan ywḥnn

Christian His mother said this, not so much because of a warning admonition of her husband (doubtless conveyed to her in writing), but most probably by the Holy Spirit with which she herself had been now been filled. | For with John began the Age of Grace (Mt 11.13) which is contrasted with previous ages in Jn 1.17 as also by Peter in Acts 15.10, 11.

Kabbalist Catechumen Let me add that the Talmudists themselves attribute the name of Hananiah (which means "Grace"[65]) from Jer 16. 13 [36.12] to Messiah in Pesach 4[66] (See more about the name Jochanan [John] in *Adumbratio*, p. 62, §2 and on Lk 1.13).

Verse 61
There is nobody etc. dlyt 'nš

Kabbalist Catechumen Why do they raise this objection?

Christian They seem to have concluded that she was either seeking a mystery or the favour of someone's family as exemplified in 1 Chron 3.6, 8; 23.21, 23. We have now furnished the mystery, but we do not have an example of a family.

Verse 63
He wrote and said wktb w'mr

Kabbalist Catechumen It is a more striking wonder if he decided to express this name by both writing and speech, which was also the reason why so much amazement overcame everyone.

Christian And that period of his punishment which had been previously determined by the Angel in verse 20 of this chapter had now completely expired and his faith was not just beginning now at this late stage. See on verse | 22 of this chapter. Unless he either did not know, or did not believe Mary's account, which is clearly not very likely.

---

give you haninah, that is, the Messias, who shall be called gracious, Jer. xvi. 13. [In error for 36.12] (Talmud Bab. in Pesach. cap. 4.)"

V. 65. *Et in toto monte Judææ* ובכלה טורא דיהוד

Cabb. Cat. *In Talmude Hierosol. Tract. Schebiith. fol. 38. d. locus iste sic describitur: Quisnam est Mons qui in Judæa? Iste est Mons Regis: & Planities ejus est Planities quæ ad Austrum: & vallis ejus est ab Engedi usque ad Jericho. Et ibidem in | Tract. Taanith fol. 69. 1. in hoc monte extitisse dicitur Myrias urbium. Quod quamvis hyperbolicum sit; magnam tamen incolarum copiam denotat.*

 Christianus. Probabile itaque est, quod fama hujus rei quasi ad Hierosolymas usque pertigerit inter plebeios: inter sacerdotes autem in templo ministrantes nullo modo potuit esse incognita: quia Zacharias ad ministeria solita reversus est. |||

V. 66. *Et manus Domini &c.* ואידה דמריא

Christianus. Nihil absurdi reperiet aliquis ê vobis, si dicam, vim Prophetiæ in hoc puero statim eluxisse, Luc. 1, 76. ut in Jeremia c. 1, 5.6. quia ambo adhuc in utero existentes spiritum S. acceperant. Confer. Ez. 1, 3; c. 3, 22; c. 33, 22; c. 37, 1; c. 40, 1. & | forte Psal. 80, 17; 1. Chr. 28, 19.

 Cabb. Cat. *Sensum tamen simul adhibebimus*[67] *Cabbalisticum; ita ut Johannem, tanquam Amicum sponsi (sicut dicitur Joh. 3, 29.) collocemus in gradum Jesod, (quo & Josephus collocatur, & justi alii, qui sponsam deducunt ad maritum suum, videatur Sohar in Gen. Cremon. c. 431. circa f. & col. 30. circa f. quæ loca extant inter Excerpta Cent. | II. Loc. 8.9.) Jam ergò manus Domini, quæ cum ipso fuit, erunt quinque Sephiræ super ipsum extantes, influxuque suo ipsum illuminantes, nempe Gedulah, Geburah, Tiphereth, Nezach, & Hod. (vide Lexicon Cabbalisticum in voce* יד *manus. p. 375*[68].)

---

67 Correction above the line: adhibebimus replaced by indagabimus
68 "יד *Manus*. Quinque digiti in manu sunt quinque Sephiroth, Gedulah, Gebhurah, Tiphereth, Nez. Hod: suntque insertæ duabus manibus, quæ sunt duo Hehin, superum & inferum, alterum sinistrum, dextrum alterum denotans. Dextra autem ut plurimùm est Binah; & sinistra Malchuth; quia illa ad dextram inclinat & cum Malchuth collata Miserationes exhibet, unde vocatur חסידה, hæc ad sinistram. Tria autem sunt Manûs attributa, quæ quia utrique manui applicantur sunt sex: nempe quod sit גדולה *magna*; חזקה *fortis*; & רמה *excelsa*. Binah enim quando influit in Gedulah, ita ut hujus scatebræ aperiantur, dicitur manus *magna*: Influens autem in Gebhurah, *robusta*; & in Tiphereth *elata* dicitur. Idem de Malchuth dicendum, quatenus influxum ex his locis accipit. Et tria hæc Manus attributa continentur in Nomine 42. literarum. Et quinque *lumina* textus de luce, Gen. 1, 3. sunt quinque digiti manus *magnæ*: quinque *firmamenta* autem textus de firmamento Gen. 1, 6. sunt quinque digiti manus *elatæ*: & quod eodem in

Verse 65
And in all the hill country of Judaea wbklh ṭwrʾ dyhwd

Kabbalist Catechumen In the Jerusalem Talmud, Tractate Shevi'it folio 38d this place is described as follows: "What is the mountain which is in Judaea? It is the Mountain of the King and its plain is the plain which is to the West and its valley is from Ein-Gedi to Jericho". And there also in | Tractate Ta'anit, folio 69.1 there are said to have been thousands of cities in this mountain country. Although [this is] hyperbolic, it does however indicate a large number of inhabitants.

Christian And so it is probable that news of this matter reached almost as far as Jerusalem amongst the common people; and in no way could it have been unknown amongst the priests serving in the temple, because Zachariah had returned to his normal ministry. ‖ fol. 34ᵛ

Verse 66
And the hand of the Lord etc. *wʾydh dmryʾ*

Christian None of your people will think me foolish if I say that the power of prophecy was immediately apparent in his boy (Lk 1.76, as in Jer 1.5, 6), because both while still in the womb had received the Holy Spirit. Cf. Ezek 1.3; 3.22; 33.22; 37.1; 40.1 and | perhaps Ps 80.17; 1 Chron 28.19.

Kabbalist Catechumen We shall uncover a kabbalistic meaning at the same time. John as "the friend of the bridegroom" (as he is called in Jn 3.29) we place in the degree Yesod where Joseph is also located and the other righteous who led the bride to her husband. See the Zohar in Gen Crem. c. 431 (towards the end) & col. 30 (towards the end), which passages are found in Excerpt Cent. | II Loc. 8 & 9. So now the [five fingers of the] hand of the Lord which was with him will be the five degrees standing over him and illuminating him with their influx, namely: Gedulah, Gevurah, Tiferet, Netsach and Hod (See *Lex. Cabb.*, under *yd* [hand], p. 375).

---

textu quinquies mentio fit *aquarum* denotat 5. quinque digitos manus *robustæ*. Et qui in Gedulah & Gebhurah sunt rami particulares Istarum Sephirarum; sed qui in Manu *Elatâ* sunt Ipsæ quinque Sephiroth; quia hoc in loco nullum omninò accessum habent Klippoth, sicut in specialibus. Magna autem est differentia inter *brachium* & *manum*: quia ad manum pertingit vis Adversantium; unde lavandæ sunt manus: & hinc etiam ungues sunt in digitorum principiis, ubi scilicet Illis accessus patet. Brachium autem lotione non habet opus, quia denotat intimiorem Sephiræ naturam." ("Loci communes kabbalistici", op. cit., pp. 375–376).

V. 67. *Et vaticinatus est.* ואתנבי

[*Cabb. Cat.*]⁶⁹ *Explicationem Cantici hujus tibi relinquo.*

[**Christianus.**]⁷⁰ Vaticinium hoc Zachariæ duo potissimum continet membra: quorum primum agit de Adventu Messiæ; alterum de officio Præcursoris ejus. Membrum primum iterum bipartitum est, agitque (1.) de populi liberatione tam spirituali v. 68. quàm simul corporali v. 69. (2.) de promissionum impletione, iterumque tam spiritualium v. 70, 71. quàm simul corporalium v. 72.73.74.75. | Alterum membrum similiter respicit Regni Messiani vel initium v. 76.77. vel complementium v. 78.79. Ut igitur & specialius rem istam proponamus, præsertim nostratibus⁷¹, v. 68. Zacharias benedicit Domino, & quidem suo nomine יהוה אלהי ישראל, quod sæpius in scripturis occurrit, ut Jos. 7, 13; 1. Reg. 8, 23.25; 1. Par. 30, 10; 2. Par. 6, 14.16.17. &c. & â Sapientibus nostris⁷² ad gradum Tiphereth | refertur, (vid. Lexic. Cabbalist. p. 462⁷³. & p. 110⁷⁴.) Alias autem ad Nomina Messiæ pertinet, ad quem etiam omninò mentem dirigere videtur Zacharias: iste enim nunc adventu suo visitabat populum suum: (de qua phrasi visitandi specialem adduximus locum ê Sohar inter Excerpta Cent. II. loc. 10.) eidemque præstiturus erat liberationem. (Tempus enim omninò denotatur futurum, ut in vaticiniis sæpius observamus.) | ubi per vocem פורקנא intelligitur sospitatio illa, quam gens nostra⁷⁵ communiter â Messia expectabant⁷⁶, quaque⁷⁷ ordina-

---

69 Correction: Christianus replaced by Cabb. Cat. (which involves the two speakers being changed over in the following exchange).

70 Correction: Cabb. Cat. replaced by Christianus (as a consequence of the previous correction).

71 Correction: nostratibus replaced by vestratibus (to be understood in the light of the change of speaker).

72 Correction: nostris replaced by vestris (to be understood in the light of the change of speaker).

73 "ישראל *Iisraël*. Est Tiphereth, sed tunc, quando medium obtinet inter Chochmah & Binah, & lancem Binæ deflectit ad latus Chochmæ, prout solet cum ad Chesed inclinat. Atque sic resolvitur vox ישראל in א"ל, quod est Nomen ad latus Chochmah pertinens sub Chesed: & שיר *Canticum*, ad latus Binah pertinens sub mysterio cantûs Levitarum. Et sicut שמים dicitur quasi אש & מים ignis inclinans ad aquas: ita ישראל qs. שיר inclinans ad א"ל. Et hanc ob causam etiam vox שיר immutatur in ישר. Et quia hæc conciliatio non propriè est in Tiphereth, sed in Daath occulta; hinc dicitur: Iisraël ascendit in cogitationem: Ut denotetur, quod vocetur Iisraël, quatenus ascendit ad cogitationem, quæ est Chochmah. [...]" ("Loci communes kabbalistici", op. cit., p. 462).

74 "אלהי האלהים *Deus Deorum*. 1. R. Moscheh de *Tiphereth* explicat, quia iste gradus est princeps & præfectus septuaginta principium ambientium Thronum ejus, & ipse

Verse 67
And prophesied w'tnby

Kabbalist Catechumen I leave the explanation of this canticle to you.

Christian This prophecy of Zachariah has clearly two parts.[78] The first is about the coming of Messiah, the second about the role of his fore-runner. The first part is again divided into two and concerns (1) the liberation of the people both spiritual (v. 68) and physical (v. 69); and (2) the fulfilment of the prophecies, again both spiritual (v. 70, 71) and at the same time physical (v. 72, 73, 74, 75). | The second part likewise considers the Messianic kingdom, at its beginning (v. 76) and at its completion (v. 78, 79). Now therefore we can comment more particularly on the content, especially for your people. In verse 68 Zachariah blesses the Lord specifically by his [Hebrew] name [*yhwh 'lhy isr'l*] "The Lord God of Israel" which often occurs in the Scriptures (as in Jos 7.13; 1 Kgs 8.23, 25; 1 Chron 30.10; 2 Chron 6.14, 16, 17 etc.) and is associated by your sages with the degree Tiferet | (See *Lex. Cabb.*, p. 462 & p. 110). Elsewhere it is associated with the names of Messiah, towards whom Zachariah also appears to have entirely directed his mind [in this canticle]. For Messiah by his advent was now visiting his people (about this phrase "was visiting his people" we cite specifically a passage in the Zohar in Excerpt. Cent. II Loc. 10) and was going to bring them liberation. For a future time is altogether indicated, as we often observe in the prophecies | when by the [Aramaic] word *pwrqn'* is understood as that salvation which your people commonly

---

gubernat eos. 2. Quidam hoc Nomen putant continere totum systema aziluthicum, ita ut per vocem אלהי intelligantur Chochmah & Binah: per vocem האלהים septem dies structuræ. 3. Quidam de tribus primis exponunt: Ut Kether sub *Elohé*; Chochmah autem & Binah sub *ha-Elohim* intelligantur. 4. Præ cæteris tamen mihi videtur, quod hoc Nomen competat gradui *Binah*. Tres enim sunt significationes אלהים una in Binah: & duæ posteriores dependent à Binah: unde hæc vocatur *ha-Elohe ha-Elohim*. 5. Semper autem Nomen *Elohim* exponendum est secundum naturam loci sui; & sic per *Elohe Abraham* intelligitur Chesed, per *Elohe Jizchak* Gebhurah: per *Elohe Jaacob* Tiphereth. Ubi videtur nomen Elohe continere in se notionem Malchuth; quæ aliquando respectum habet ad Chesed, unde vocatur Elohe Abraham. Et sic quoque dicitur Gen. 35, 13: *Et ascendit Elohim, de loco in quo erat supra Abraham*. Ita se pariter habet in Jizchak & Gebhurah, quo pertinet illud: *Deus Jizchak*, & sic reliqua. [...]" (Ibid., p. 110).

75 Correction: nostra replaced by vestra (to be understood in the light of the change of speaker).
76 Correction: expectabant replaced by expectabat
77 Correction: quaque replaced by quæque
78 Compare the close analysis of Mary's *Magnificat* above.

rie גאולה dicitur (vide de hac Lexic. Cabbalisticum p. 222[79]. & inter Excerpta Cent. II. Locum 2.) In quibus autem consistat hæc Liberatio prolixius expositum est in Adumbratione Cabbalæ Christianæ c. 10. §. 3[80]. & c. 11. p.t. De spirituali ergò liberatione potissimum in hoc versiculo loquitur | Zacharias, quâ Messias Cortices, ê quibus liberandæ sunt Animæ partim infirmavit; partim oppugnavit. (de qua etiam intelligenda sunt loca Matth. 20, 28; Marc. 10, 45; Act. 4, 12; c. 28, 28; Rom. 3, 24; Eph. 1, 7.14; c. 6, 17; Col. 1, 14; 1. Tim. 2, 6; Heb. 9, 12.15.) Sequenti autem[81]

v. 69. intelligit liberationem simul corporalem, de qua etiam sumenda sunt loca Luc. | 2, 38; c. 21, 28; Rom. 8, 23; c. 4, 30. ad analogiam loci Act. 7, 25. ubi Messias Satanam captivabit, regnumque suum eriget singulare, de quo specialiter agitur. Apocal. 20, 1–6; c. 21. p.[82] 1. c. 22, 1–5. Vide & inter Excerpta de Messia Loca 68.69.70. & sqq. Cent. I. Sensus ergò hujus versiculi talis est: Non tantum spiritualem nunc instituet liberationem Messias, & inchoatam: sed futuro tandem tempore | ipsum Regnum sospitatorium eriget (sic enim pro Regno accipitur vox Cornu, 1. Sam. 2, 10; Jer. 48, 25. ubi sic etiam vertit Chaldæus Paraphrastes; conf. Zach. 1, 18.19; Dan. 7, 24; c. 8, 21; Ps. 89, 18; Ps. 92, 11; Ps. 132, 17; Ps. 148, 14.) idque in successione Davidis, quod etiam innuitur Ap. 3, 7. ubi etiam vaticinium est de hoc ipso Regno; ||| & Apoc. 22, 16.

fol. 35ʳ

v. 70. Jam pergit ad gratia[ru]m actionem pro impletione promissionum spiritualium, factarum per omnes ab ipso mundi initio Prophetas; ipso etiam Adamo & Chanocho non exceptis, quorum tunc Libri, vel saltem quoad

---

79 "גאולה *Redemptio, Liberatio*; est Binah, quippe quæ fundamentum est Liberationis juxta illud Lev. 25, 31. *Redemptio erit ei & in Jobel egredietur.* Judicia enim accusantia non ulteriùs adscendunt, quam usque ad Binah. Ab hoc autem modo Redemtionem haurit Jesod, qui vocatur Goël redemtor ex parte Binah, derivatque redemtionem in Malchuth; & huc pertinet illud: Ruth. 3, 13. *Si redemerit te, bonum*, sicut dicitur: *Elevate Justum, quia bonus.* Jesch. 3, 10. *Si noluerit redimere te, si vires desunt, & redimam te Ego, Binah*, ut dictum suo loco: ita tradit R. Schimeon ben Jochai in Tikkunim. In Sohar autem Sect. Æmor dicitur, quod Malchuth vocetur Goël Redemtor per Jesod, qui modus influxum immittit in eam per Nezach & Hod, qui sunt auxiliatores ad copulam, prout notum est, quod sint duo testiculi masculini. Diciturque quod respectu istorum quatuor, simul sumtorum, qui sunt Nezach, Hod, Jesod, Malchuth, vocentur quatuor Redemptiones. Pard. Tract. 23. c. 3. h.t.—2. Redemtio & precatio combinandæ sunt: Redemtio enim est modus Jesod, qui combinandus est cum precatione, quæ est Malchuth (Literæ enim initiales ס״גל denotant voces ס״מיכת ג״אולה ל״תפילה applicatio Redemtionis ad precationem) Tunc enim combinantur duo nomina י״דני א״דוד h.m. יאקד״ונקי. Quod si quis hanc intentionem prætermittat, idem est ac si Amhaarez atque idiota foret. Vide Sohar Chaje Sarah 79.c.314. & init. Vajiggasch. & Trumah 57.c.227. f.62.; c.245. f.70.; c.277. Achare. 34.c.135. Mischpatim 53.c.211. Vajakhel. 88.c.351. & f.97.c.388. & Tasria in sin. 23.c.92. & Naso 59. Pinchas 112.c.448. Ser Sahabh. h.l." ("Loci communes kabbalistici", op. cit., pp. 222–223).

expected from Messiah and which is usually called [in Hebrew] *gʾwlh* [See on this *Lex. Cabb.*, p. 222 and Excerpts Cent. 11 Loc. 2]. In what this liberation consiststs is more fully explained in *Adumbratio*, chap. 10, § 3 and chap. 11, *p.t.* In this verse Zachariah speaks rather about a *spiritual* liberation | by which Messiah partly weaked and partly attacked the shards from whom the souls are to be freed. Verses which are to be understood as concerning this are: Mt 20.28; Mk 10.45; Acts 4.12; 28.28; Rm 3.24; Eph 1.7, 14; 6.17; Col 1.14; 1 Tim 2.6; Heb 9.12, 15. In the following verse 69, he understands a liberation which is at the same time *physical*. Concerning this these references should be consulted: | Lk 2.38; 21.28; Rm 8.23 and 4.30, by analogy with the passage in Acts 7.25 where Messiah will capture Satan and establish his sole kingdom which is specifically treated of in Rev 20 1–6; 21.1; 22.1–5. See also about Messiah in Excerpts Cent. I Loc. 68, 69, 70 et *seq*. So the meaning of this verse is; Messiah not only institutes an incomplete and spiritual liberation now, but finally in the future | will establish this Kingdom of Saviours (thus the word "horn" [used by Zachariah in verse 69] is to be understood to mean "kingdom" in 1 Sam 2.10 and Jer 48.25 where this is how the Aramaic targum translates it, Cf. Zech 1.18, 19; Dan 7.24; 8.21; Ps 89.18; Ps 92.11; 132.17; 148.14). [This] kingdom in the line of David [is] in the succession which is also implied in Rev 3.7 where there is a prophecy about this very kingdom ‖ and in Rev 22.16. fol. 35ʳ

Verse 70

Now he moves on to his gracious action for the fulfilment of the spiritual promises made by all the prophets since the very beginning of the world, even by Adam himself and Enoch as their books (which are either not accepted today or remain only as fragments[83]) and certain texts | of the

---

80 "Itaque efficere voluit quatuor Gradibus: Nimirum (1.) Corpus corticum infirmando. (2.) Impugnando. (3.) Captivando. (4.) Destruendo. Ut tandem hoc modo iterum in unum corpus colligeret Filios Dei dispersos Joh. 11. vers. 52." ("Adumbratio kabbalæ christianæ", op. cit., p. 60).

81 Deletion of the numeration.

82 In error, it should be "v."

83 For knowledge of Enoch: Nathaniel Schmidt, "Traces of Early Acquaintance in Europe with the Book of Enoch", *Journal of the American Oriental Society* 42 (1922): pp. 44–52, where he discusses Pico, Reuchlin and Potken. For Guillaume Postel's considerable interest in Enoch, see Wilkinson, *Orientalism*, op. cit., p. 114, note 62. Now there is also, John C. Reeves and Annette Yoshiko Reed, eds., *Enoch from Antiquity to the Middle Ages*. vol. 1, Sources from Judaism, Christianity and Islam (Oxford University Press, 2018) which includes Zoharic material. For the Adamic literature, Michael E. Stone, *A History of the Literature of Adam and Eve* (Atlanta: Scholars Press, 1992) and for its

Fragmenta adhuc | extabant, textibus quibusdam Libri Sohar id testantibus. Quod autem per Prophetas locutus sit Messias, apparet ê Joh. 12, 41. conf. Joh. 8, 56; Ezech. 1, 26. &c.

v. 71. Argumentum autem generale omnium prisci ævi vaticiniorum est, Liberatio ab hostibus, & ab osoribus. Ubi sub hostium Nomine intelligi possunt Cortices leviores, Materia nempe & peccatum, (de quibus actum est in Adumbratione Cabbalæ Christianæ | c. 11. §. 4.5–1[9][84]) Sub osorum autem nomine, Satanas, cum omni exercitu Spirituum malignantium: (vid. ibid. §. 20[85].) unà cum Effectu istorum Morte, ibid. §. 21[86]. conf. 1. Cor. 15, 54–57; Heb. 2, 14.15. Sequitur

v. 72.73.74.75. Commemoratio promissionum simul corporalium; in Regno Messiæ supra commemorato specialiter ad implendarum: ubi sensus est hic; Quod Messias | hanc exhibiturus sit Gratiam Patribus, circa ultima tempora demum consummatè restituendis Hebr. 11, 39.40. ut recordetur fœderis prisci, cum Abrahamo, Isaaco, Jaacobo, & Iisraëlitis ad montem Sinai &c. pacti & Juramenti, quod juravit Abraham Gen. 22, 16.17. Effectus autem horum omnium consistere dicitur (1.) in liberatione ab hostibus, nimirum[87], nimirum etiam corporalibus, quod variè describitur Apoc. 14. 14. | & sequentibus versiculis & capitibus usque ad finem capitis 19. Confer, quæ de collectione exulum, reductione in terram sanctam, magnisque his victoriis &c. exhibuimus in Excerptis de Messiâ Cent. I. Loc. 74. (2.) in cessatione timoris; quia tunc ligatus[88] erit Satanas Ap. 20, 1.2.7. & impii â probis atque sanctis erunt separati, Ap. 21, 8; c. 22, 15; Matth. 13, 30.40.41.42.43.49.50. &c. (3.) in cultu beatissimo, Ap. 22, | 3.4.5; c. 7, 15. (4.) in justitia haud interruptâ. Jes. 60, 21; Matth. 13, 43; c. 25, 46; Luc. 14, 14; Act. 24, 15.

Medieval life, Brian Murdoch, *The Apocryphal Adam and Eve in Medieval Europe: Vernacular Translations and Adaptations of the Vita Adae et Evae* (Oxford University Press, 2009).

[84] "Et sicut quatuor potissimum sunt Corticum species: (de quibus videri potest Pneumaticæ Cabbalisticæ Tractatus prior:) qui in sacris Ezech. 1. v. 4. dicuntur: Negah s. splendor (quem indifferenter dicitis ad bonum & ad malum.); Ignis; Nubes magna; & Ventus turbinis veniens ab Aquilone. Item 1. Reg. 19. v. 11–12.; Vox silentii tenuis; Ignis; Terræ motus, & Spiritus grandis & fortis dissipans montes & confringens petras. Conf. Gen. 1. v. 2. Sic à scriptoribus Novi Fœderis iidem intelligi videntur per 1. Materiam seu carnem.; 2. Peccatum.; 3. Satanam, & 4. Mortem: (quorum Applicationem in aliud Tempus differimus:) Atque singulos hos Cortices aggressus est Messias; eosque aggredi suos edocuit; ut magno quasi exercitu impugnarentur." ("Adumbratio kabbalæ christianæ", op. cit., p. 63). Cf. *supra*, footnote 56, pp. 230–231 for § 5.

[85] "Tertia corticum species est Satanas, cum omni exercitu spirituum lapsorum: quos Christus impugnavit passim directè eosdem ex obsessis ejiciendo. (Luc. 11.v.22.) & ten-

SECTION VII 413

Zohar bear witness. That Messiah spoke by the prophets is apparent from Jn 12.41; Cf. Jn 8.56; Ezek 1.26 etc.

Verse 71: The general theme of all the prophecies of ancient times is liberation from their enemies and from those who hate them. In this context by the word "enemies" can be understood the shards of lighter substance and sin | (See the treatment of this in *Adumbratio*, chap. 11, § 4.5–19.) "Those who hate them" are Satan and all his army of evil spirits (see ibid. § 20) together with the effect of their afflictions (ibid. § 21. Cf. 1 Cor 15.54–57; Heb 2.14, 15).

There follow Verses 72, 73, 74, 75, a recollection of the promises—also *physical*—specifically to be fulfilled in the above mentioned Kingdom of Messiah. The meaning is this: that Messiah | will definitely show this favour to the fathers who are to be finally fully restored around the last times, Heb 11.39–40, in order to recall the Old Covenant with Abraham, Isaac, Jacob and the Israelites at Mount Sinai etc. and the covenant and the oath which he [Messiah[89]] swore to Abraham (Gen 22.16, 17). The effect of all these is said to consist:

(i) in liberation from enemies, even physical ones which is variously described in Rev 14.14, | the following verses [of that chapter] and in the chapters up to the end of chapter 19 [of Revelation]. Consult what we have quoted about the gathering of the exiles, their return to the Holy Land and these mighty victories in the Excerpt on Messiah Cent. I Loc. 74.

(ii) in the end of fear, because then Satan will be bound (Rev 20.1, 2, 7) and the impious will be separated from the good and holy (Rev 21.8; 22.15; Mt 13.30, 40, 41, 42, 43, 49, 50 etc.).

(iii) in the most blessed worship | (Rev 22.3, 4, 5; 7.15).

(iv) in uninterrupted righteousness (Isa 60.21; Mt 13.43; 25.46; Lk 14.14; Acts 24.15).

---

tationibus eorum, (præsertim Principis Edom, Matth. 4.vs. 8.9. Conf. Apoc. 12.v.3. Ubi idem vocatur Draco magnus Edomiticus) resistendo Hebr. 4.v.15. Unde in officio Messiano confirmatus est Act. 2.v.36. Heb. 2.v.9. Partim indirectè impugnato peccato & corticibus aliis. Col. 2. v.15. Joh. 12.vs.31. Eph. 4.v.8. Hebr. 2.v.14. Eumque sic ulterius impugnare etiam suos voluit. Eph. 6.v.11.12. Ap. 12.v.11. &c." (Ibid., p. 68).

86   "Quarta & ultima Corticum species est Mors, hostis ultimus. 1. Cor. 15. vers. 26. Nimirum vel corporalis, quam impugnavit non tantùm incorruptibilitate & resurrectione 1. Cor. 15 v.20.21.54. Sed & generosa vitæ suæ depositione. Joh. 10.vf.18. Qui gradus adhuc est sublimior, quam qui vobis dicitur, obitus per osculum: (ubi singulariter notari etiam velim tempus Minchah & Erebh Schabbath, de quibus alibi.) Ad quam & suos hortatur. Matth. 10.v.28. Joh. 5.v.24." (Ibid., p. 68).
87   Deletion (to avoid repetition).
88   Correction: ligatus replaced by legatus
89   It is God who swore this in Genesis.

v. 76. Sequitur alterum vaticinii hujus membrum de officio Johannis: Hoc quatenus respicit Regnum Messiæ inchoatum ista continet: (1.) quod futurus sit Propheta Altissimi: ubi Prophetæ vox sensum habet tam generalem, (denotans | hominem, qui impletus sit spiritu S. Luc. 1, 15. qui alloquia habeat divina Joh. 1, 33. qui â Deo missus sit, missione extraordinariâ, ibid. qui res præsentes ignotas sciat, & manifestet, sicut hic Messiam Joh. 1, 26. sqq. quique futura prædicat: ut Joh. 1, 29; Matth. 3, 10.11.12.) quam specialem, denotans Prophetam Eliam, qui promissus erat Malach. 4, 5. Per vocem Altissimi intelligitur Deus infinitus, | laudatus in secula, sicut Luc. 1, 32.35. ubi vide, & Lex. Cabbalisticum p. 92[90]. *Vocaberis* autem idem est, ac *eris*, vide ad Matth. 1, 23. (2.) quod præiturus sit ante faciem Messiæ, vid. supra ad v. 17. h.c. id est, quod futurus sit prænuncius ejus, & metator, quasi qui in supernis fuerat Sandalphon, nunc Metatron fiat coram Messia, (vide Lexicon Buxtorffii Talmudicum p. 1191[91]. sq. | in מטט. & Lexic. Cabbalist. p. 221. & sqq.[92]) Nomen

90 "אל ההודאות *Deus Laudum*. Interpp. hoc nomen referunt ad prædicamentum Hod: & ubicunque invenitur phrasis *Confessionis, Laudis, gratiarum actionis* illa ad eandem Classem referri solet.—אל עליון autem *Deus supremus*, est nomen quod juxta R. Moscheh refertur ad Coronam, quæ vocatur Deus supremus, quia summum locum habet in Aziluth. Attamen non aliam ob causam sic vocatur nisi quatenus operationes exercet in Chesed. 2. Unde etiam Chesed suprema dicitur, prout dictum est suo loco, & potissimum Tract. 20. libri Pardes. Ubi actum est de nominibus אל עליון *Deus supremus*, & אל מלך *Deus Rex*; & dictum, nomen אל semper pertinere ad prædicamentum Chesed. [...]" ("Loci communes kabbalistici", op. cit., p. 92).

91 The remarks there on Metatron are: "מטטרון Metatron. Nomen Angeli cuius passim mentio apud Rabbinos. In Targum Jonathanis; Et cultum exhibuit Enoch Domino in veritate & ecce non fuit amplius cum habitatoribus terrae, quia abreptus fuit & ascendit in caelum in verbo Domini, & vocatum fuit nomen eius מיטטרו Metatron ספרא רבא Scriba magnus Genes. 5.24. Idem citatur ex Medrafch Ruth in Zohar fol.181.in marginali nota. Vide Jevam.fol.16.2. & Cholin fol.60. Tosephos, ubi disputatur, An Metatron fit Enoch an vero fit שר העולם Princeps mundi (Angelus sic appellatus?) R. Levi scribit Prov.1.8.ad illud; Ne deseras legem matris tuae: Matris, id est השכל הפועל. Intellectus operantis, per cuius medium obtingit prophetia, &c. Ideoque vocarunt illum Rabbini p. m. Metatron, quod est in lingua Romana sive Latina אם Mater. R. Salomon in Illud, Nam nomen meus in medio eius est Ex. 23. V.21. scribit: Rabbini nostri inquiunt, Ille est Metatron, cuius nomen est sicut nomen Doctoris sui, nempe Dei שדי Omnipotentis. Nam שדי Gematrice 314 totidem מטטרון. Idem in libro Jalkut in hunc locum, & apud complures alios. Patres huius traditionis sunt Talmudici in Sanhaedrin cap. 4.fol.38.2. Hi ulterius respexisse videntur, ad Angelum nempe non creatum, (nulli enim hoc competit) sed increatum, Messiam nempe, sive Christum. In R. Bechai in locum Exodi legitur: Metatron nominator, quod in hoc nomine comprenduntur duo significata, nempe אדון Dominus, & שליח Nuncius, Legatus. Domini significatum, ex sermon Rabbinorum qui Heram sive Heroinam dominatricem vocant מטרונה Matronam. Legati ex sermone Graecorum, qui vocant Legatum מנטטור (si recte conjicio, respicit ad μηνυτής Nuncius, Nunciator, quod poetice dicitur μηνύτωρ.) Immo etiam tertia potest in

SECTION VII 415

From verse 76 there follows the next half of this prophecy, which concerns the role of John. Since this concerns the Kingdom of Messiah as yet unfinished, it contains the following:

(1) that John will be *a prophet of the Most High* where the word "prophet" has more a general sense (denoting | a man who is full of the Holy Spirit (Lk 1.15), who has divine communications (Jn 1.33), who has been sent by God with a very special mission (ibid.), who knows and reveals thing present yet otherwise unknown (as does Messiah in Jn 1.26 ff.) and who predicts the future (as in Jn 1.29; Mt 3.10, 11, 12)), rather than denoting specifically Elijah who had been promised in Mal 4.5. By the phrase "of the Highest" is understood the infinite God, | praised forever as in Lk 1.32,35 which see and also *Lex. Cabb.*, p. 92. "You will be called" is the same as "you will be": see on Mt 1.23.

---

eo esse significatio Custodiae sive custodis. Nam targum pro Hebraeo משמרת habet מטרת Custodia a נטר. Et quia custodit mundum, appellatur נוטר ישראל Custos Israelis. Ex his etymologiis patet, quod ipse est Dominus omnium quae sub eo sunt, & quod omnis exercitus superiorum & inferiorem in potestate eius sunt & sub eius manu. Est & nuncius omnium qui supra eum & sub eo sunt, quia fecit eum dominari super omnia, & posuit eum dominum domus suae & dominatorem omnium suorum. Est autem tibi observandum, quod ratione significati Dominii.ט in eo duplicatum est, & duo ט faciunt 18. id est, יח: iis sublatis remanet מרון, quod idem quod מרא, id est, אדון Dominus. Hactenus ille. Est ergo secundum Hebraeos triplex, aut quadruplex etymologia, quarum tamen nulla forfan est solida. Omnino enim videtur esse ex origine praecedentis vocis מיטטור Metator q.d. Metator, Legatus Dei. Hinc in Beres. Rabbah sect. 5. haec vox מיטטרון eodem sensu legitur, quo praecedens מיטטור, quae pure Latina. [...] Id est, Vox Domini facta est Metator Mosis eo tempore quo dixit ei, Ascende in montem Abarim, Deut 32.49. Vox Domini facta est Metator super aquis, sicut dicitur, Vox Domini super aquas, Psalm.29. Glossa לפני ומקים מנהיג. Ducens & praecedens eum; quod est officium metatorum. Porro Elias adducit in Tisbi, hunc Angelum vocari שר הפים Principem facierum, quod Deo simper praesens sit, in eius facie constitutus, & mandata eius suscipiens, Obrister Kammerer / Praesenswarter. Talmudici scribunt porro, [...] quod data site ei potestas, ut sedeat & conscribat merita Israelitarum: rursus quoque ei sit potestas [...] delere merita ipsorum, Chagiga fol. 15 col. 1. Hinc vocatur Cancellarius coelestis. Cabalistae scribunt [...] Praeceptor Mosis fuit Metatron, ut docet Reuchlinus lib 1 Cabalae. In libro Zezor hammor, cuius author R. Abraham Hispanus, litera ט 2.col 3 dicitur, Nomen Mosis abbreviate idem esse, quod מטטרון שר הגול Et adjicitur והוא שדי &c. In libro Zorobabelis: [...] Ego sum Metatron princeps facierum, & Michaelem est nomen meum."

92 Pages 221 et sq of the "Loci communes kabbalistici" deal with the letter ג. The entry dedicated to Metatron is at page 528 and reads as follows: "מטטרון *Metatron*. Si scribitur cum י, nempe מיטטרון Schechinam denotat: sed sine Jod est Angelus, Legatus Schechinæ, qui etiam vocatur נער *Puer*. (& Chanoch) de quo dicitur, quod nomen ejus se habeat sicut nomen Domini sui; quia æquipollet cum ש"די. Dicitur & habere 70. Nomina; sicut Deus; de quibus in Kabbalah practica. Et cum dicitur Exod. 23, 21. *Quia nomen meum in medio ejus*, intelligitur Schechinah, quæ in ipso occulta est. [...]" ("Loci communes kabbalistici", op. cit., p. 528).

מריא autem hoc loco procul dubio iterum denotat Tetragrammaton, ut sup. v. 17. sed pronunciatum per א״דני ut connotetur Schechinah sive Messiæ præsentia.

(3.) quod præparaturus sit vias ejus: vide infra ad Matth. 3, 3. Methodus ergò Messiæ intelligitur, quâ ipse Animarum intendat, primò quidem Iisraëlitarum[93], deinde tamen | & Proselyticarum restitutionem. Et hæc Methodus Messiana expressè describitur sequenti ||| v. 77. Quod nempe in eo consistat, ut Messias det cognitionem seu informet populum suum, tanquam supremus Academiæ Divinæ Rector (vide de Revolut. Animarum c. 1.§1.p. 244[94]. Adumbrat. Cabbal. Christ. c. 1.§.5.6[95]; c. 2.§.13[96]; c. 4.§.7[97].sqq.; c. 5.§.2[98], c. 6.§.2[99]; c. 8.§.2[100]. Et confer Joh. 3, 2; Matth. 8, 19; c.12, 38; c. 19, 16; c. 22,

fol. 35ᵛ

---

93 Correction: Iisraëlitarum replaced by Iisraëliticarum
94 "[...] Hinc ab Adamo supracœlesti seu Anima Messiæ, omnibus illis creatis, ceu discipulis, transcendentaliter atque Metaphysicè proponebantur sublimia illa veræ Theosophiæ Objecta, juxta Joh. 1.v.18. Hinc à Cabbalistis Spiritus illi creati, dicuntur Vasa. Realis autem illa Objectorum Divinissimorum repræsentatio & hinc factæ Ideæ, suo ordine digestæ, ab iisdem dicuntur Lumina. Jam suppone singulas Sephiras singulos esse spirituum illorum Choros, Academias, Synagogas, Hierarchias, Respublicas, Exercitus, Corpora, sive quocunque nomine vocentur alio, sub uno quodam singulæ Rege, Imperatore, Præside, Præfecto, Rectore, Doctore, &c. qui objecta illa à Messia proposita subordinatis sibi Catechumenis communicaret. [...]" ("De revolutionibus animarum", op. cit., p. 244).
95 "§.5. Kabbal. Ego qui ad symbolica magis feror, universum intueor ceu Academiam, ubi Doctor est causa causarum & Discipuli causata.—§.6. Phil. Chris. Id perinde sit: cum re ipsa concordemus. Istius igitur connexionis sive Academiæ cum non unus idemque semper fuerit status, hinc accuratius rem ipsam consideranti quatuor hic potissimum occurrunt diversitates: nimirum, primò status primævæ institutionis: secundò status secutæ destitutionis: tertiò status modernæ constitutionis: & quartò status postremæ restitutionis." ("Adumbratio kabbalæ christianæ", op. cit., pp. 3–4).
96 "Phil. Christ. Isthæc dijudicent alii, qui sive emanationem hic præferunt, sive productionem ex nihilo. Eidem autem Animæ Messiæ influendo se communicavit lucis Divinæ gradus summus, quæ nostratibus dicitur Natura Messiæ Divina. Adeoque quod vobis dicitur Adam Kadmon, nobis vocatur Christus: quod subjectum in hac unione consistens, erit supremus ille Academiæ tuæ Divinæ Director: hoc enim mediante deinceps intra eundem Adamum primum seu Messiam, productæ sunt creaturæ reliquæ, per certos ordines ditributæ, beatæque illi informationi submissæ. Illarum conditionem generalem conciperem fuisse talem: ut ceu centra existerent, quædam ampliora, quædam strictiora: seu potius globi tales modo majores modo minores ad puncti exiguitatem usque; quibus facultas esset à creatione sibi indita, sphæram emittendi luminosam, eandemque sive ampliandi sive restringendi, secundum varios sive primæ constitutionis, sive proprii moderaminis gradus: & ita quidem, ut istæ sphæræ sese invicem penetrare possent. Ipse vero Adam Kadmon seu Messias, ulteriores intra & infra se disposuit Divinitatis dispensationes, quæ in libro Zeniutha & Idra utrâque latius describuntur". (Ibid., p. 6).
97 "In secunda Classe locabatur totum corpus animarum humanarum, quarum Messias

(2) On "he will go before the face of" Messiah, see above on verse 17, loc. cit. It means that he would be his fore-runner and way-marker, as if he who in heaven had been Sandalphon now became Metatron before Messiah (See Buxtorff's *Lexicon Talmudicum* p. 1191 *seq* | on *mṭṭ* and *Lex. Cabb.*, pp. 221 et *seq.*). The [Syriac] name *mry'* [Lord] in this verse without doubt again denotes the Tetragrammaton as above in verse 17. But it is pronounced as "Adonai"[101], so that it indicates the Shekhinah or the presence of Messiah.

(3) On "he might prepare his ways": see below on Mt 3.3. So we grasp the method of Messiah by which he intends first the restitution of the souls of Israelites and then | the souls of proselytes too. And this Messianic method will be described in detail by the following ‖ verse 77. It requires that Messiah should give knowledge to or inform his people as the Supreme Rector of the Divine Assembly (see the *Revol. Animarum*, chap. 1, §1, p. 244; *Adumbratio*, chap. 1, §5, 6; chap. 2, §13; chap. 4, §7 *seq*; chap. 5, §2; chap. 6, §2;

fol. 35ᵛ

---

erat caput. Et hæ, sub forma unius corporis humani, quod vocatur Adam Protoplastes, informabantur in Collegio Sapientiæ, quæ etiam vocatur אדם id est homo; ob numerum מ"ה id est 45. (vide Apparatus Part.1. pag. 48)" (Ibid., p. 27).

98 "Phil. Christ. Cum in schola hac summâ, Lux illa objectorum divinissimorum afflueret copiosus, quam septem inferiores, etiam nimia affinitate in se arriperent; hinc factum esse dicitur, ut istæ faciem suam ab illa averterent, id est à contemplatione & amore illo cessarent; quod est mysterium lapsus & mortis. (Appar. Part.3. p. 160.) Vasa igitur illorum confracta dicuntur: ita ut ex hoc lapsu in mundo inferiore existerent spiritus maligni corticesque. (ibid. p. 161.) Et hoc ipsum est, quod in Epistola Judæ v.6. dicitur: *Angelos quosdam non servasse principium suum, sed deseruisse proprium suum domicilium*; classis scilicet illius, in qua commorantes studiis divinis invigilabant. Et hæc est ratio, quare Angeli illi dicantur, מלאכא דחטו *tales, qui peccaverunt*, 2. Pet. 2.v.4. atque huc etiam pertinet locus 1. Joh. 3.v.8. והו דסעד חטיתא מן סתנא הו מטול דמן רישיתא הו סתנא חטיא הו וגוי *Et is quis agit peccatum, ex Satana est; quia à principio ipse Satanas peccator est.* &c. Unde simul patet, in quo propriè consistat natura peccati. Atque hinc Christus etiam de Diabolo dicit Joh. 8.v.44. בשררא לא קאם מטול דשררא לית בה וגוי *In veritate non stetit, quia veritas non est in eo.*" (Ibid., pp. 27–28).

99 "Schola jam instituta est nova sub methodo alia, quæ vocatur Maris & Fœminæ; sive influxus & receptionis: ita ut objecta in minutiores distinguerentur Sectiones, nec obruerentur naturæ intelligentes." (Ibid., p. 30).

100 "His itaque spiritibus; tam Animabus scilicet, quam Angelis in certos ordines digestis, jam Dogmata Emanativa proponebantur, partim sub conceptibus Numerationum: partim & quidem potissimum per conceptus Personarum, sub forma maris & fœminæ propositarum: quarum sunt quinque apud vestrates: Macroprosopus scilicet: Pater & Mater: Microprosopus, & uxor ejus: ita ut prima referatur ad Coronam; secunda ad sapientiam: tertia ad intelligentiam: quarta ad sex subsequentes: & quinta ad ultimam. [...]" (Ibid., p. 54).

101 The Hebrew Tetragrammaton was commonly pronounced "*adonai*" and that is all Knorr means here. If he is taken to suggest the Syriac *mry'* was pronounced "*adonai*", the practice is apparently otherwise unattested and not very probable.

16.24.36; | c. 26, 18.&c.) Quod σωτηρία, sive יה‎ i.e. salutaris Animæ restitutio seu vita ejus (non consistat in actibus juxta normam Legis utriusque quàm studiosissimè exercitis, quia hi naturales tamen sint, prævitate primæva non omnino carentes, vid. Adumbrat. Cabbalæ Christianæ cap. 11, §.12[102] sed) requirat (1.) Remissionem peccatorum: quæ est[103] ut rectius intelligatur notandum est (a) Animam quamlibet, cum | in primâ creatione sua esset Globus lucidus, (in omnes formas adeoque & humanam transformabilis) tempore lapsus Adamitici captivatam fuisse â spiritu quodam impuritatis (vid. Revolut. Animarum p. 248. §.11.12.14[104].) tenebroso, cujus caligine offuscata fuit lux Animæ. (b.) Quod Anima in generationem deducta, magna[m] partem quidem ab illa caligine liberetur, deducta scil. in actum luminosum | quo antea carebat; multas tamen in se retineat maculas, sive Depravatoris sui reliquias atque partes (sunt enim suæ ut Animarum, ita & Corticum compositiones atque Nizzuzoth sive scintillæ variæ:) quæ sunt ideæ connatæ variorum affectuum i.e. motuum atque conformationum Animæ naturalium, principia. (c.) Quod ab extra quoque in Animam subintrent offuscationes variæ, quæ omnes | cum Spiritu quodam corticoso conjunctæ sint: sive â cibo & potu, unde nobis suppeditatur spiritus influus; sive â qualibet cujuscunque Affectus occasione, &c. unde Ideæ acquisitæ. (d.) Quod omnis Actus Animæ â quadam ideâ sit: & si peccaminosus est, ideam etiam pariat. Quotquot autem sunt in Anima Ideæ, tot in illa sunt spiritus; & qui-

---

102 "Methodus Christi ut evidentius appareat, sciendum est: triplicem esse in universum ad virtutum culturam methodum. Primæ est Philosophiæ & naturæ, qua quis ob finem Summi Boni per Actum virtutis moralis, Affectum moderari præsumit: per quam, ob nimiam Naturæ lapsæ imbecillitatem, & Corticum impedientium vigorem, omnisque auxili specialioris defectum, propriis viribus homo ad verum scopum eniti haud valet. Methodus secunda est Fœderis antiqui & Legis, qua quis ob speciales Dei promissiones & communicationes, expressiori Legis scriptæ viæ insistere; sacrificiorum beneficio vim Corticum infringere, & peculiaribus meditationibus, (quas vos Cawanoth appellatis) ad praxin virtutis sese dirigere contendit. In qua tamen ad perfectionem pariter haud patet via. (Conf. Matth. 5. vs. 20.) quia Natura hîc tamen, qua talis operatur; prava concupiscentia, quamvis commissa ejus per victimas expientur, ad similes actus sæpius recurrit, nec funditus infringitur, & auxilia saltem concurrunt inchoata non consummata. Tertia igitur est Christi methodus, qua quis (1.) Ob spem vitæ perfectissimæ in unione cum Deo consistentis (Matth. 5, 38; Joh. 17, 23.) (2.) Abnegata non saltem omni Equitate (Matth. 16, 24) sed & omnibus viribus propriis (Luc. 14, 28–33.) (3.) Circa omnem actum moralem ad primum affectus cujuscunque motum (Matth. 5, 22.28.29.30.) in cujus rei gratiam studium catecheticum de agnoscendis & observandis affectibus peculiare insigniter prodest:) (4.) Patrem cœlestem ardenti Fide. (5.) Ob fœdus novum per Messiam sacrificio proprii corporis sancitum, implorat. (6.) Ut Spiritus Sancti auxilio affectum præsentem subigat, (7.) Actumque hunc ad Christi præcepta, internum Mosaicæ Legis sensum ubique inculcantia (quæ à nobis specia-

SECTION VII 419

chap. 8, § 2. And compare Jn 3.2; Mt 8.19; 12.38; 19.16; 22.16, 24, 36; | 26.18 etc.).
Also that: [the Greek] *sōtēria* [salvation] or [the Aramaic] *ḥy'* [life] i.e. the
restoration of the *salvation* of the soul or its *life* (does not consist in deeds
as carefully as possible performed according to the norm of either Law since
these are natural and not entirely free from primaeval sin, see *Adumbratio*,
chap. 11, § 12 but) requires (1) the Remission of Sins which to be rightly understood requires us to note that:

(a) any given soul when | first created was a shining globe (which could take on any form, including the human), but at the time of Adam's fall was taken captive by a certain dark Spirit of Impurity (See *Revol. Animarum*, p. 248, § 11, 12, 14) whose blackness obscured the light of the soul.

(b) that the soul being drawn down into generation was liberated from a large part of that darkness—drawn down, that is, for bright action | which it previously lacked. However it retained many stains or remnants of its Perverter and parts (it has parts which are a mixture of both souls and shards and Nitsutsot or various sparks) which are ideas which come into existence with various affects i.e. the origins of the natural movements and organisation of the soul.

(c) that also various obfuscations enter the soul from outside. These are all | connected with a spirit of the Shards and may cause us an influx of spirit either from food or drink or the incidence of a certain feeling from which notions are formed.

(d) that every action of the soul arises from an idea and if it is sinful it only matches the idea. For all the ideas in a soul, there are an equal num-

---

liter excerpta & in jubentia, prohibentia & mystica distincta sunt, sicut vos præcepta vestra 613. excerpsistis: & exemplum conformet. [...]" (Ibid., pp. 65–66).

103 Deleted word.

104 "[...] sub initium creationis Adami protoplastæ in illo existebant omnes animæ, quæcunque erant de parte boni; omnes, inquam, in illo continebantur & ab illo dependebant. Cum autem peccaret, bonoque malum immisceret; malum cum bono ita confundebatur, ut ex parte mali illius post modum prodirent populi mundani. Unde apparet, quod fundamentum Adami protoplastæ saltem fuerit bonum: animæ nimirum Israëlitarum. [...] Cum enim ille comederet ex arbore cognitionis boni & mali; eo ipso immiscebat bono malum. Ita ut bonum illud, quod in Adamo protoplaste esset, confunderetur cum malo corticum masculinorum, nimirum Samaëlis, qui vocatur Adam Belial. Prov. 6. v. 12. Eademque ratione bonum illud, quod in Chavvah erat, immiscebatur malo uxoris ejus Lilith, quæ est spurcities serpentis; quoniam serpens rem habebat cum Chavvah. [...] Cum ergo peccaret Adam protoplastes, comederetque de arbore cognitionis boni & mali tunc prædictæ illæ animæ bonæ contentæ in membris Adami protoplastæ sic permiscebantur, & involvebantur atque implicabantur reliquis animabus in Adamo Beliale contentis [...]" ("De revolutionibus animarum", op. cit., pp. 248–250).

dem mali, si malæ sunt illæ; vide Tractat. de Anima Korduëri 6 | p. 146. sqq.[105]
& istæ sunt specificæ singulorum peccatorum pœnæ. (e.) Peccatorum ergò
remissio, non tantum in oblivione actuum illorum consistit; sed & in oblatione[106] pœnarum istarum, sive Spirituum horum corticosorum idealium. Et
hoc est illud Mich. 7, 19. quod peccata dicantur projici in profunda maris, i.e.
spiritus illi, peccatorum pœnæ, includi foramini Abyssi magnæ. Hæc igitur
ratione totum fundamentum | recentis hujus methodi Messianæ consistit in
Remissione peccatorum: i.e. in sublatione Pœnarum istarum; unde ex animâ
removentur ideæ illæ corruptrices, quæ aliàs non nisi generatrices erant plurium actuum similium. Et hoc est Vitæ sive restitutionis Animæ requisitum
primum. Sed &

(2.) requirit Salutaris ista restitutio, Gratiæ Dei miserantis influxum unicum: non | tantum ad prædictam pœnarum remissionem; sed & ad informationem omnium actuum Animæ moralium ulteriorum. Sensus ergò verborum Zachariæ breviter est hic: quod Messias informaturus sit Populum
suum; Vitam Animæ consistere in Remissione peccatorum, (quasi | dicat;
Lumen Animæ restitutum iri per ablationem obscuritatum corticalium:) &
in misericordia Gratiæ Dei: (quasi dicat, hoc lumen Animæ nec subsistere
posse, nec augeri, nisi per influxum illum nativum â Gradu Tiphereth, quo
pertinet vox רחמא, & â Gradu Chesed, quo pertinet vox חנגה; & â gradu
Binah; quo pertinet vox אלהן, (vide Lexic. Cabbalistic. p. 688.[107] & p. 349.[108]
& p. 109. n. 17.[109] p. 110.n. 2.3.4.[110] p. 111.n. 2.[111])).

v. 78.79. Jam tandem sequitur pars ultima hujus vaticinii, quæ respicit[112]
fol. 36ʳ Messiani ⫴ ultimum complementum. Ubi hic est sensus, Fore aliquando, ut

---

105 "Hinc patet, quæ sit animæ cognatio: Unde summa illa Neschamah, quatenus per gradus suos affinis facta est corpori, quamvis à corpori, quamvis à corpore semotior sit, omnes tamen corporis operationes persentiscit iisque necessariò corrumpitur. Sicut enim gradus sunt in Sanctitate, ita gradus sunt in impuritate; & sicut homo cum peccat, virtutem impuram in se derivat, ita similem derivat in Neschamah suam. Nam etiam in immunditie natura datur subtilior, quæ quasi Aziluth est impura: Unde qui seipsum inquinat, Neschamah suam inquinat, atque corticibus involvit tam tenuioribus quam crassioribus. [...]" ("Tractatus de Anima R. Moscheh Korduero", *Kabbala denudata 1*, Pars secunda, pp. 100–149, p. 146).

106 Correction: oblatione replaced by ablatione

107 "רחמים *Miserationes*. Vid. פנים. it. ישר. הכאה. נוקבה. Alias hoc nomen refertur ad Tiphereth, qui est linea dilectionum, seu lenitarum, seu miserationum. Kether autem quia istius lineæ radix est, vocatur רחמים גמורים Miserationes seu dilectiones meræ, ubi nihil intermixtum est rigoris. Pardes." ("Loci communes kabbalistici", op. cit., pp. 688–689).

108 "חסד *Benignitas, Gratia*. Sic Schaare Orah post Nomen El discurs. 7. Nomen El in Lege sæpissimè vocatur חסד Benignitas. Chesed autem est, cum quis aliquid facit, quod de

ber of spirits within it. And these are evil if the ideas are evil. (See *See Tract.*
de Anima by Rabbi Moses Cordovero, 6 | p. 146 *seq.*). These are the specific punishments for individual sins.

(e) that the remission of sins consists not so much in the forgetting of those acts, but also the removal of the punishments or the ideas of the shard spirits. This is what Mic 7.19 means when it says that sins "are thrown into the depths of the sea" *i. e.* those spirits which are the punishment of sins are shut into the depths of Great Abyss. So for these reasons the whole basis | of the new Messianic way of proceding is the remission of sins i.e. the removal of the punishments, which also removes those corrupting ideas which otherwise would produce many similar acts. This is the first requirement of life or the restoration of the soul.

But also required is (2) that saving restoration, the unique influx of the Grace of a merciful God, not merely | for the remission of sins which we have just been discussing, but also to inform all the subsequent moral acts of the soul. So briefly the meaning of Zachariah's words is this: that Messiah will inform his people; the life of the soul consists in the remission of sins (as if | he said "The Light of the Soul is restored by the removal of the darkness of the Shards") and in the mercy of the Grace of God (as if he said "This Light of the Soul cannot exist nor be increased unless born from the influx of the degree Tiferet [Glory]") to which is linked the [Aramaic] word *rḥmʾ* [mercy] and from the degree Chesed to which is linked the [Hebrew] word *ḥnnh* [Grace] and from the degree Binah to which is linked the word *ʾlhn* [God]. (See *Lex. Cabb.*, p. 688 & p. 349 & p. 109, n. 17; p. 110, n. 2, 3, 4; p. 111, n. 2.)[113]

Verses 78, 79: Now, finally, follows the last part of this prophecy which concerns the final completion of the Messianic ||| kingdom. The meaning is   fol. 36ʳ

---

rigore non esset necessarium, sed illud facit ex libera voluntate, & arbitrio, nemine cogente; & ex bonitate sua. Et huic opponitur id, quod sit necessariò. [...]" (Ibid., p. 349).

109 "[...] Quandoque etiam locus *Vitæ*, quæ vocatur *Vita æterna* (seu seculi venturi) exprimitur literis Tetragrammati, & legitur אלה״ים quia hæc est scaturigo illa, unde Gebhurah, quæ dicitur Tribunal supernum atque *Elohim*, influxus habet. Et, quia non est judicium perfectum, literis Tetragrammati scribitur. [...]" (Ibid., p. 109).

110 Cf. *supra*, footnote 75, pp. 408–409.

111 "אלהיך *Deus tuus*. Ad Malchuth referuntur hæc omnia. Quamvis etiam in *Binah* & *Gebhurah* locum habent pro re nata: quia nomen *Elohim* omnibus his tribus competit; prout diximus Tract. 20. Quidam de tota Aziluth explicant, quod minus placet. Pard. Tract. 23. c.1. h.t." (Ibid., p. 111).

112 Correction added above the line: regni

113 That is: the light of the soul is restored by the Grace and Mercy of God.

per hunc ipsum Misericordiæ Dei gratiosum influxum nos visitet idem Messiæ Lumen, non quidem, ut oriens, prout nunc; sed ex alto, & in meridie. Ut illuminet non illos tantum, quibus offuscata adhuc est caliginosis quibusdam maculis Anima; sed & illos, qui | omninò sedent in tenebris, (i.e. qui exortum hactenus Messiæ lumen nondum agnoverunt, sive sint ê Judæis dispersionis nostræ[114]; sive sint decem Tribuum posteri:) & in umbra mortis (i.e. qui adhuc convertendi sunt ê Gentilibus.) Nos autem, qui jam accepimus illuminationum initia, dirigat ad viam consummatæ prosperitatis. (vide Lexic. Cabbal. p. 717[115]. sq. & Apoc. 21, 23; | c. 22, 5; Jes. 60, 19.20.)

V. 80. *Et corroborabitur*[116] *Spiritu:* ומתחיל ברוחא

Christianus. Non video, quare non intelligi debeat spiritus Sanctus.

Cabb. Cat. Sic etiam in Sohar aliquid commemoratur, quod huic[117] planè est dissimile, quod vide in Excerptis Cent. *II.* loc. *13.*

In deserto &c. בחורבא

[*Cabb. Cat.*][118] Idemne fuit hoc Desertum cum eo, in quo Johannes prædicavit; Matth. *3, 1?*

[**Christianus.**][119] Non omnibus hoc videtur; sed quid obstat? Suprà enim ad v. 65. audivimus, quod vallis montis Jehudah fuerit ab Engedi usque ad Jericho. | In monte ergò cum natus esset Johannes, in vallim[120] saltem descendens jam in deserto fuit Engedi, de quo 1. Sam. 24, 1.2; Jos. 15, 61. conf. 2. Par. 20, 2. cujus deserti terminus orientalis fuit Mare mortuum; terminus occidentalis Mons Judææ; septrionalis[121] Jericho ad Jordanem; in medio autem planities fuit ingens, ubi & pascua & agri & villæ. Hîc igitur ob magnam graminis copiam, | locustarum etiam fuit abundantia, & simul palmarum; unde & Engedi cum sua planitie vocata fuit Sectio palmarum 2.

---

114 Correction above the line: nostræ replaced by modernæ
115 "שלהבת *Flamma.* In Tikk. per *prunam* intelligitur; & Chochmah; & per flammam ejus; Tiphereth, cum toto systemate sex membrorum; sed hæc omnia cum connotatione judicii. Sed שלהבת י"ה *Flamma Domini,* Cant. 8, 6. in Soh. Mezora dicitur esse Gebhurah prodiens à Binah per Chochmah. Fundamentum autem flammæ est excitare amorem, juxta Cant. 2, 6. Pard." ("Loci communes kabbalistici", op. cit., p. 717).
116 Correction: corroborabitur replaced by corroborabatur
117 Added above the line: non
118 Correction: Christianus replaced by Cabb. Cat. (which involves the two speakers being changed over in the following exchange).

SECTION VII 423

that in a little while, by the gracious influx of the mercy of God, we shall be visited by that same Light of Messiah, not merely in its rising as now, but from on high, as at mid-day, to illuminate not only those whose soul has up to now been obscured by the stains of darkness, but also those who | sit in complete darkness (i.e. who have not yet recognised the Light of Messiah that has arisen so far, or who are from the Jews of the modern dispersion; or are the descendants of the Ten Tribes) and in the shadow of death (i.e. who have up to now still to be converted from the Gentiles). But we who are already experiencing the beginnings of illumination he will lead to the way of complete prosperity. (See *Lex. Cabb.*, pp. 717 seq & Rev 21.23; | 22.5; Isa 60.19, 20.)

Verse 80
And was strong with the spirit wmtḥyl brwḥ'

Christian I do not see why the Holy Spirit should not be understood here.
Kabbalist Catechumen Something not at all dissimilar to this is indeed mentioned in the Zohar (See Excerpts Cent. II Loc. 13).

In the desert etc. *bḥwrb'*

Kabbalist Catechumen Was this the same desert as that in which John preached in Mt 3.1?
Christian Not everyone thinks so, but why not? For above on verse 65 we learned that the valley of the hill-country of Judaea ran from Ein-Gedi right up to Jericho. | Therefore although John had been born in the hill-country, he came down into the valley, and was then in the desert at Ein-gedi, concerning which 1 Sam 24.1, 2; Jos 15.61 Cf. 2 Chron 20.2. The eastern edge of the desert was the Dead Sea, the western edge the hill-country of Judaea and the northern boundary was Jericho on the Jordan. In the middle was a large plain with flocks and fields and farms. Here on account of the great supply of wheat, | was also an abundance also of locusts. And also palm-trees: which is why Ein-Gedi with its plain was called The Region of Palms in 2 Chron 20.2. From

---

119 Correction: Cabb. Cat. replaced by Christianus (as a consequence of the previous correction).
120 Correction: vallim replaced by vallem
121 In error, it should be "septentrionalis".

Par. 20.2. A palmis autem defluebat mel illud agreste, quo ad Locustas condiendas usus est Johannes, (sicut ê Maimonide allegat Lightfoot in Chorog. ad. Marc. c. 2. n. 5.) Non tamen ita in deserto fuit, ut non & festa solennia frequentaret. Hoc ipsum autem Desertum | fuit habitatio Essenorum, de quibus ita & Plinius l.5.c.17. Ab occidentali parte, (lacus Asphaltitis[122];) littora (istius lacus) Esseni fugitant, usque qua nocent; (i.e. tam procul in deserto versus montana habitant â littoribus remoti, quousque hæc sunt nociva.) Gens sola, & in toto orbe præter cæteras mira sine ulla fœmina, omni Venere abdicata, sine pecunia, socia Palmarum: in diem ex | æquo convenarum turba renascitur, largè frequentantibus, quos vitâ fessos ad mores eorum fortunæ fluctus agitat: ita per seculorum millia (incredibile dictu) gens æterna est, in qua nemo nascitur: tam fœcunda illis aliorum vitæ pœnitentia est. Infra hos Engadda oppidum fuit, secundum ab Hierosolymis fertilitate, palmetorumque nemoribus: nunc alterum bustum. Inde Masada castellum in rupe, & ipsum haud procul Asphaltite, | (conf. 1. Sam. 24, 1.) Et hactenus Judæa est. Hæc ibi: Istorum dogmata fusius prosequitur Josephus Antiquit. 18, 2. & Belli Judaic. lib. 2, 7. Nomen autem Essæus derivatur est â Syriaco, ipsis vernaculo חסי Sanctus Act. 2, 27; c.13, 35. Origo autem illorum haud obscurè colligi potest ê Libro Sohar Sect. Vajikra c. 13. (vid. Excerpta Cent. II. Loc. 20.) An ergò non inter illos vixerint Johannes[123], conside- ‖-ratione haud est indignum. Sane in monte Judææ Deserti appellatio locum non habet; cum Montanum illud incolis & urbibus fuerit frequentissimum, sicut supra dictum est ad v. 65.

---

122 The Dead Sea.
123 In the right bottom corner appears a Hebrew letter ׳ presumably an indication of binding or pagination.
124 "But that part that flowed, how did it flow with honey? Learn that from Rambam upon the place: 'When he saith, and honey, he understands *dbš šl tmrym*, 'the honey of palms'. For the palm-trees, which are in the plain and in the valleys, abound very much with honey." Translation in *J. Lightfoot, The Chorographic Works*, edited by John Rogers Pitman (London: J.F. Dove, 1823), p. 205.
125 This should be verse 73: "Ab occidente litora Esseni fugiunt usque qua nocent, gens sola et in toto orbe praeter ceteras mira, sine ulla femina, omni venere abdicata, sine pecunia, socia palmarum. in diem ex aequo convenarum turba renascitur, large frequentantibus quos vita fessos ad mores eorum fortuna fluctibus agit. Ita per saeculorum milia—incredibile dictu—gens aeterna est, in qua nemo nascitur. Tam fecunda illis aliorum vitae paenitentia est! Infra hos Engada oppidum fuit, secundum ab Hierosolymis fertilitate palmetorumque nemoribus, nunc alterum bustum. Inde Masada castellum in rupe, et ipsum haut procul Asphaltite. Et hactenus Iudaea est."

SECTION VII 425

those palms flowed that wild honey which John used to eat with the loqusts. (Just as Lightfoot, relying on Maimonides claims in his *Chorographia* on Mk 2, n. 5.[124]) The region was sufficiently a desert however, that it did not see the celebration of many religious festivals. But the desert itself | was the home of the Essenes [about whom also Pliny the Elder Book 5 Chap. 17[125]. From the western part of Lacus Asphaltis, the Essenes fled the shores (of the lake) for as far as they were noxious (i.e. they lived way into the desert towards the hill-country and remote from the shores, to the extent these were toxic). A solitary people and different from all others in the world, they lived without women, totally renouncing Venus, without money and as the companions of palm-trees. From one day to another, | a crowd of strangers would form there again with many people tired of life, whom the vicissitudes of fortune attracted to the Essene life-style. Thus (incredible to say) over millennia, this people—amongst whom nobody was born—remained eternal, so productive for them was other peoples' repentance of their lives. Below these was the town of Ein-Gedi, second only to Jerusalem in fertility and palm-groves, but now just another burned-out ruin. Near there is Masada, a fortress on a rock, not far away from the Ashphalt Lake itself | (Cf. 1 Sam 24.1). This far is all Judaea. Thus far Pliny: Josephus persues more fully (the [Essenes'] teachings *Ant.* 18.2 & *Bell Jud* Book 2.7][126]. Their name is derived from the Syriac, their vernacular, *ḥsy* [Holy]: Acts 2.27; 13.35[127]. Their origin can be obscurely gleaned from the Zohar Sect. Vayikra c. 13 (See Excerpta Cent. II Loc. 20)[128]. So to ask whether John lived among them ‖ is a reasonable question[129].   fol. 36ᵛ Clearly for the hill-country of Judaea the title of desert is inappropriate, since that same hill country was so very full of inhabitants and towns, as was said on verse 65.

---

126 Text conveniently in Alfred Adam, *Antike Berichte über Die Essener* (Berlin: De Gruyter, 1972).
127 To which may be added Ti 1.8. These are places where *ḥsy'* is used in the Peshitta to translate the Greek *hosios* [holy]. For a modern discussion of the etymology of "Essene" including this suggestion of a Syriac Source, see Joan E. Taylor, *The Essenes, the Scrolls and the Dead Sea* (Oxford University Press, 2012), pp. 26–27. It should be noted, however, that a Jewish Palestinian Aramaic form of the word is not attested, although sources are admittedly few. The corpus can be examined in Joseph A. Fitzmyer and Daniel J. Harrington, *A Manual of Palestinian Aramaic Texts* (Rome: Pontifical Biblical Institute, 2002), the glossary of which (pp. 307–355) gives no example of the word.
128 Unfortunately we have found this obscure hint inadequate in attempting to discover what Knorr had in mind here.
129 For a modern discussion of the question, Joan Taylor, *The Immerser. John the Baptist*

In diem ostensionis ejus &c. ליומא דתחויתה

[**Cabb. Cat.**][130] *Intelligiturne tempus illud, quo aptus esset ad ministeria templi, ibidemque examinatus in consortium sacerdotum admitteretur?*

[**Christianus.**][131] Non censeo: quia tum non tam ostendebatur Iisraëli, quam Sacerdotibus. Sed potius subintelligitur Tempus missionis ejus ad baptismus, conf. Joh. 1, 31. qui non erat annus ætatis ejus trigesimus, sed omninò largiori quodam | spatio prior, quoniam ex omnibus Evangeliis & præsertim Act. 13, 24.25. apparet, haud exiguo intervallo temporis Johannis Baptismum antecessisse Christi ministerium. Sique in mediâ septimanâ Danielis ultimâ passus est Christus Dan. 9, 27. procul dubio in medio ad minimum septimanæ penultimæ ministerium suum incepit Johannes.

---

    within Second Temple Judaism. A Historical Study (Cambridge: William B. Eerdmans, 1997), pp. 15–48.
130 Correction in the left margin: Christianus replaced by Cabb. Cat. (which involves the two speakers being changed over in the following exchange).
131 Correction: Cabb. Cat. replaced by Christianus (as a consequence of the previous correction).

SECTION VII 427

Until the day of his showing etc. *lywmʾ dthwyth*

Kabbalist Catechumen Should we take this to be when he was ready for his ministry in the Temple and was examined there by group of priests and was admitted [to the priesthood]?[132]

Christian I don't think so, because then he would not so much have been "shown to Israel" as "shown to the priests". But rather we should understand [a reference to] the time of his mission to baptise (Cf. Jn 1.31) which was not when he was thirty [the age of priestly ordination] but far | earlier, since from all the Gospels, and especially Acts 13.24, 25, it is clear that the baptism of John preceded the ministry of Christ by a considerable interval of time. And if in the middle of Daniel's last week, Christ suffered (Dan 9.27), there is no doubt that at the beginning of the penultimate week John began his ministry[133].

---

132   Lightfoot, *Miscellanies and the Harmony of the Gospels*, op. cit., p. 186: "'Till the day of his showing unto Israel': That is, when, at thirty years of age, he was to be brought to the sanctuary-service; to which he did not apply himself as the custom was, but betook himself to another course".

133   Dan 9.24–27 was commonly taken as a prophecy of Christ's Advent at the end of Daniel's Seventy Weeks. The standard exposition was that of Jerome in his *Commentary on Daniel* and he himself drew upon Julius Africanus on whom: Christophe Guignard, *La lettre de Julius Africanus à Aristide sur la généalogie du Christ. Analyse de la tradition textuelle, édition, traduction et étude critique* (Berlin: De Gruyter, 2011). Jerome's commentary is in *Patrologia Latina*, vol. 25 (Paris, J.P. Migne, 1845). An English version is Gleason L. Archer Jr, *Jerome's Commentary on Daniel* (Grand Rapids: Baker, 1997). See pp. 94–110 for Jerome's comment on this text.

Sectio VIII.
De Nativitate, Circumcisione & Oblatione Christi.
ê Luc. II, 1–39.

1. Factum[1] est autem in diebus illis, &[2] exiit edictum ab Augusto Cæsare[3], ut describeretur | universus populus[4] possessionis ejus[5].

2. (Hæc descriptio prima fuit in Præfectura Kyrini in Syria.[6])[7]

3. Et ibat quisque ut describeretur in | urbem suam[8].

4. Ascenderat autem Joseph quoque â Natzrath Galilææ, in Judæam in civitatem, quæ vocatur Bethlehem (quia erat ex domo & ex genere David[9])[10]

5. Cum Marjam sponsa | sua, quum in ventre haberet: ut ibi describeretur[11].

6. Et factum est, ut quum esset illic, complerentur dies ejus, ut pareret[12].

7. Et peperit filium suum primogenitum, ac | involvit eum linteolis, & posuit eum in stabulo campestri: quia non erat eis locus ubi habitabant.[13],[14]

8. Pastores autem erant in loco eo, qui degebant ibi, & custiebant[15] custodias noctis | pro gregibus suis[16].

9. Et ecce Angelus Dei venit ad eos, & gloria Domini resplenduit super eos[17], & timuerunt timore magno.

10. Et dixit eis[18] Angelus. Ne timeatis: ecce | enim annuncio vobis gaudium magnum quod erit universo mundo[19].

fol. 37ʳ *11. Natus enin est vobis hodiè Servator, ||| qui est Dominus Meschicha, in civitate David[20].*

---

1   On the left-hand half of the page, a fragment cut from Knorr's edition of the Peshittta New Testament containing the Syriac version of the quoted passage in the Gospel of Luke is pasted in and crossed out.
2   Vulgate omits &.
3   Vulgate: ab Caesare Augusto.
4   Vulgate: orbis.
5   Vulgate omits possessionis ejus.
6   Vulgate: facta est a praeside Syriae Cyrino.
7   Added in the left margin: 2.) Act. 5, 37. Crossed out.
8   Vulgate: Et ibant omnes ut profiterentur singuli in suam civitatem.
9   Vulgate: Ascendit autem et Joseph a Galilaea de civitate Nazareth in Judaeam in civitatem David quae vocatur Bethlehem, eo quod esset de domo et familia David.
10 Added in the left margin: 4.) Mich. 5, 1; Matth. 1.1.sqq. & 2, 6; Joh. 7, 42. Crossed out.
11 Vulgate: ut profiteretur cum Maria desponsa sibi uxore praegnante.
12 Vulgate: Factum est autem, cum essent ibi, impleti sunt dies ut pareret.
13 Added in the left margin: 7.) Matth. 1, 25. Crossed out.
14 Vulgate: et pannis eum involvit, et reclinavit eum in praesepio quia non erat eis locus in diversorio.

Section VIII
Concerning the Birth, Circumcision and Presentation of Christ
From Lk 2.1–39[21]

1 It came to pass in those days and there went out a decree from Caesar Augustus that the whole world | should be enroled.

2 This taxation first occurred during the prefectship of Kyrinus [Cyrinius] in Syria.

3 And each man went to his home town | to be taxed.

4 And Joseph went up also from Nazareth of Galilee to Judaea to the town which is called Bethlehem because he was of the house and lineage of David.

5 With Mary his espoused, | since she was pregnant, to be taxed there.

6 And it came to pass that while they were there, her days were fulfilled that she should give birth.

7 And she gave birth to her first-born son and | wrapped him in swaddling-bands and laid him in a field stall[22], because there was nowhere for them to stay.

8 And there were shepherds in that place who were staying there and were | guarding their flocks by night.

9 And behold! The Angel of the Lord came to them and the glory of the Lord shone upon them and they were afraid with great fear.

10 And the Angel said to them. Do not be afraid: | for here is an announcement of great joy which will be for the whole world.

11 For today is born for you a Saviour ||| who is the Lord Messiah in the town of David.   fol. 37ʳ

---

15   Correction: custiebant replaced by custodiebant
16   Vulgate: Et pastores erant in regione eadem vigilantes et custodientes vigilias noctis super gregem suam.
17   Vulgate: stetit juxta illos et claritas Dei circumfulsit illos.
18   Vulgate: illis.
19   Vulgate: Nolite timere: ecce enim evangelizo vobis gaudium magnum quod erit omni populo.
20   Vulgate: Quia natus est vobis hodie Salvator, qui est Christus Dominus, in civitate David.
21   A large number of citations from the Old Testament were adduced here and deleted from the manuscript.
22   Knorr seeks to displace the Vulgate "manger" (*praesepium*) with a "field-stall".

12. *Et hoc vobis signum: Invenies*[23] *puerum involutum linteolis, & positum in præsepi*[24,25].

13. *Et repente conspecti sunt cum Angelo exercitus | multi cœlorum laudantes Deum & dicentes:*[26,27]

14. *Gloria Deo in excelsis, & super terram pax, & opinio bona hominibus*[28].

15. *Et factum est, ut quum abivissent ab eis | Angeli in cœlum, loquerentur pastores unus cum alio, & dicerent, Descendamus usque in Bethlechem, & videmus*[29] *rem hanc quæ facta est, quemadmodum Dominus manifestavit nobis.*[30]

16. *Et venerunt festinanter, & invenerunt | Marjam & Joseph, & puerum qui positus erat in stabulo*[31].

17. *Et quum vidissent, manifestaverunt sermonem, qui dictus fuerat illis de puero illo*[32].

18. *Et omnes qui audierunt, mirati sunt de | his, quæ dicebantur sibi à pastoribus*[33].

19. *Marjam verò*[34] *conservabat omnia verba hæc, & conferebat*[35] *in corde suo.*

20. *Et reversi sunt pastores illi*[36] *glorificantes & laudantes Deum super orbus quæ | viderant & audierant, sicut dictum fuerat eis*[37].

21. *Et quum implerentur octo dies, ut circumcideretur puer, vocatum est nomen ejus Jeschua, quod vocatum fuerat ab Angelo, | priusquam conciperetur in ventre.*[38,39]

22. *Et quum impleti essent dies purificationis eorum, secundum legem Moscheh, adduxerunt eum in Urischelem, ut sisterent eum coram Domino.*[40,41]

23. *Sicut scriptum est in lege Domini, quod omnis masculus adaperiens*[42] *vulvam Sanctus Domini vocabitur.*[43,44]

---

23 Correction: invenies replaced by invenietis (closer to the Vulgate).
24 In error. It should be *præsepio*. Correction: *præsepi* replaced by stabulo campestri
25 Vulgate: Invenietis infantem pannis involutum et positum in praesepio.
26 Added in the right margin: 13.) Dan. 7, 10; Ap. 5, 11; Inf [i.e. Judges] 19, 30; Es. 57, 19; Eph. 1, 5. & 2, 17; Rom. 1, 5. Crossed out.
27 Vulgate: Et subito facta est cum angelo multitudo militiae caelestis, laudantium Deum et dicentium.
28 Vulgate: Gloria in altissimis Deo et in terra pax hominibus bonae voluntatis.
29 Correction: videmus replaced by videamus
30 Vulgate: Et factum est ut discesserunt ab eis angeli in caelum, pastores loquebantur ad invicem; Transeamus usque Bethlehem, et videamus hoc verbum quod factum est, quod Dominus ostendit nobis.
31 Vulgate: et infantem positem in praesepio
32 Vulgate: Videntes autem cognoverunt de verbo, quod dictum erat illis de puero hoc.
33 Vulgate: et de his quae dicta erant a pastoribus ad ipsos.
34 Vulgate: autem.
35 Vulgate: conferens.

SECTION VIII   431

12 And this will be a sign for you. You will find the boy wrapped in swaddling bands and placed in a field stall.
13 And suddenly they saw with the Angel | an army of many heavenly beings praising God and saying:
14 Glory to God in the Highest and on earth peace and good will to men.
15 And it came to pass that when the angels had gone from them | into heaven, the shepherds spoke one with another and said "Let us go down to Bethlehem and let us see this thing which has happened and which the Lord has shown to us".
16 And they came hurrying and found | Mary and Joseph and the boy who had been placed in a stable[45].
17 And when they had seen him, they disclosed what had been told them about the boy.
18 And all who heard were amazed | about the things which the shepherds told them.
19 But Mary kept all these words and pondered them in her heart.
20 And the shepherds returned glorifying and praising God for all the things which | they had seen and heard, just as had been told to them.
21 And when the eight days were completed, so that that the boy should be circumcised, his name was called Jeschua [Jesus] which he had been called by the Angel | before he was conceived in the womb.
22 And when the days of their purification according to the Law of Moses were fulfilled, they took him to Jerusalem to present him before the Lord.
23 As it is written in the Law of the Lord: every male who opens the womb will be called "a holy one of the Lord".

---

36   Vulgate omits illi.
37   Vulgate: in omnibus quae audierant et viderant, sicut dictum est ad illos.
38   Added in the right margin: 21.) Gen. 17, 12; Lev. 12, 3; sup. 1, 31; Matth. 1, 21. Crossed out.
39   Vulgate: Et postquam consummati sunt dies octo ut circumcideretur puer, vocatum est nomen eius Jesus, quod vocatum est ab angelo priusquam in utero conciperetur.
40   Added in the right margin: 22.) Lev. 12, 2.6. Crossed out.
41   Vulgate: Et postquam impleti sunt dies purgationis eius secundum legem Moysi, tulerunt illum in Jerusalem ut sisterent eum Domino.
42   Correction: adapariens replaced by adaperiens
43   Added in the right margin: 23.) Ex. 13, 2. & 22, 20. & 34, 19; Num. 3, 13. & 16, 17. Crossed out.
44   Vulgate: Quia omne masculinum adaperiens vulvam, sanctum Domino vocabitur.
45   In verse 12, "stable" is corrected to "field-stall", but its occurrence here has been overlooked.

24. *Et ut darent victimam*[46] *secundum id*[47], *quod dictum est in lege Domini, par turturum,* | *aut duos pullos columbæ.*[48,49]

25. *Vir autem quidam erat in Urischelem, cujus Nomen Schemeon, & vir iste erat rectus & justus, & expectabat consolationem Iisraël*[50]*, & Spiritus Sanctitatis* | *erat super eum.*[51]

fol. 37ᵛ

26. *Et dictum fuerat ei â Spiritu Sanctitatis, quod non visurus esset mortem, usque dum videret Messiam Domini.*[52] |||

27. *Hic ipse veniebat per spiritum*[53] *in templum: & quum adducerent parentes ipsum Jeschua puerum, ut facerent pro eo, sicut mandatum est in Lege*[54]*.*

28. *Accepit eum in ulnas suas, & benedixit Deo & dixit:*[55]

29. *Deinceps dimitte*[56] *servum tuum, Domine mei juxta sermonem tuum in pace.*[57,58]

30. *Quia ecce*[59] *viderunt oculi mei gratiosum tuum.*[60,61]

31. *Quem parasti ante faciem omnium gentium.*[62]

32. *Lumen ad revelationem populorum*[63] *& gloriam populo tuo*[64] *Iisraël.*[65]

33. *Joseph autem & mater ejus mirabantur super iis, quæ dicebantur de eo.*[66]

34. *Et benedixit eis Schemeon, & dixit Marjam matri ejus: Ecce hic positus est in casum & erectionem multorum in Israël, & in signum contradictionis.*[67,68]

35. *In animam autem tuam pertransibit* | *lancea, ut revelentur cogitationes cordium multorum.*[69,70]

36. *Channa autem Prophetissa, filia Penuil, ex tribu Aschir, ipsa quoque senior in diebus suis erat, & septem annis cum* | *viro suo vixerat â virginitate sua.*[71]

---

46   Vulgate: hostiam.
47   The Vulgate omits id.
48   Added in the right margin: 24.) Lev. 12, 6.8. Crossed out.
49   Vulgate: columbarum.
50   Added in the right margin: 25.) Jes. 49, 13; c. 52, 9; c. 66, 13; Jer. 31, 13; Zach. 1, 17; Thren. 1, 16. Crossed out.
51   Vulgate: Et ecce homo erat in Jerusalem, cui nomen Simeon, et homo iste Justus, et timoratus, expectans consolationem Israel, et Spritus Sanctus erat in eo.
52   Vulgate: Et responsum acceperat a Spiritu Sancto, non visurum se mortem nisi prius videret Christum Domini.
53   Added in the left margin: 27.) Matth. 4, 1; Luc. 4, 1; Act. 16, 7. Crossed out.
54   Vulgate: Et venit in spiritu in templum. Et cum inducerent puerum Jesum parentes eius, ut facerent secundum consuetudinem legis pro eo.
55   Vulgate: Et ipse accepit eum in ulnas suas et benedixit Deum et dixit.
56   Vulgate: Nunc dimittis.
57   Added in the left margin: 29.) Gen. 46, 30; Phil. 1, 23. Crossed out.
58   Vulgate: secundum verbum tuum in pace.
59   Vulgate omits ecce.

SECTION VIII

24 And to make a sacrifice according to that which is said in the Law of the Lord, a pair of pigeons | or two young doves.

25 But there was a certain man in Jerusalem, whose name was Simeon and this man was upright and righteous and was awaiting the consolation of Israel and the Spirit of Holiness | was upon him.

26 And it had been told him by the Spirit of Holiness that he would not see death until he saw the Lord's Messiah. |||

fol. 37ᵛ

27 He himself came by the Spirit into the Temple and when his parents brought the boy Jeschua [Jesus] that they might do for him according as the Law commands

28 Simeon took him in his arms and blessed God and said:

29 Lord, now dismiss your servant in peace,

30 For, behold, my eyes have seen your graciousness.

31 Which you prepared before the face of all peoples.

32 A light for revelation to the peoples and a glory for your people Israel.

33 Joseph and his mother were amazed at what was said about Jesus.

34 And Simeon blessed them and said to Mary his mother: behold this boy is placed for a falling and rising of many in Israel and for a sign to be spoken against.

35 A lance will pierce into your soul, | so that the thoughts of many hearts may be revealed.

36 Anna was a prophetess, a daughter of Penuil from the tribe of Asher and she was also advanced in her days and had lived seven years | with her husband from her virginity [i.e. after her marriage].

---

60 Added in the left margin: 30.) Ps. 98, 3; Es. 52, 10; inf. 3, 6. Crossed out.
61 Vulgate: salutare tuum.
62 Vulgate: quod parasti ante faciem omnium populorum.
63 Vulgate: gentium.
64 Vulgate: plebis tuae Israel.
65 Added in the left margin: 32.) Es. 42, 6; c. 49, 6; Act. 13, 47; c. 28, 28. sup. 1, 68. Crossed out.
66 Vulgate: et erat pater eius et mater mirantes super his quae dicebantur de illo.
67 Added in the left margin: 34.) Es. 8, 14; Rom. 9, 31.32; 1. Pet. 2, 6.7. Crossed out.
68 Vulgate: Et benedixit illis Simeon et dixit ad Mariam matrem eius: Ecce positus est hic in ruinam et in resurrectionem multorum in Israel, et in signum cui contradiceretur.
69 Added in the left margin: 35.) Act. 28, 22; Th. 3, 12; Job. 16, 12.13; Joh. 19, 25. Crossed out.
70 Vulgate: et tuam ipsam animam pertransibit gladius ut revelentur ex multis cordibus cogitationes.
71 Vulgate: Et erat Anna prophetissa, filia Phanuel de tribu Aser; haec processerat in diebus multis, et vixerat cum viro suo annos septem a virginitate sua.

37. Et erat vidua quasi annorum octoginta & quatuor. Et non abscedebat â templo: & in jejunio & in oratione serviebat die & nocte.[72,73]
38. Et ipsa quoque adstitit eadem hora, & confitebatur Dominum, & loquebatur de illo cum omni homine, qui expectabat[74] *Urischelem.*[75]
31[76]*. Et quum perfecissent omnia prout est in lege Domini, reversi sunt in Galilæam, | in Natzrath, civitatem suam.*[77]

In diebus illis &c. ביומתא הנון

[**Cabb. Cat.**][78] Quoto anno mundi?

[**Christianus.**][79] Dico, incertum omninò esse, nec ullo modo apodicticè Annum hunc designari posse. Quia

(1.) nondum convenêre Chronologi, utrum computus instituendus sit in annis Patriarcharum juxta Codices Græcos, an juxta Hebræum?

(2.) Utrum Annus Diluvii peculiariter sit computandus; an vero solis numeris Genealogiæ Patriarcharum nitatur calculus?

(3.) Utrum inter Patriarchas postdiluvianos cum Luca, c. 3, 36. inserendus sit | Cainam; an cum textu Hebræo Gen. 11, 12. omittendus?

(4.) Utrum Abraham dicendus sit natus esse Anno Patris 70; juxta Gen. 11, 26. ||| an verò Anno Patris 130, juxta Gen. 12, 40. collato cum Gen. 11, 32. item Act. 7, 4.

(5.) Utrum anni illi 430, de quibus Gal. 3, 17. computandi sint â Migratione Abrahæ ex Ur; an ê Charan; an â promissione Jacobo factâ descendenti in Ægyptum, Gen. 46, 2? juxta Ex. 12, 40?

(6.) Utrum Anni fundati Templi 1. Reg. 6, 1. computandi sint an initio Exitûs ex Ægypto: an â fine, ut Deut. 4, 45.46; Ps. 114, 1.3?[80]

---

72 Added in the left margin: 37.) 1. Sam. 1, 22. Crossed out.
73 Vulgate: Et haec vidua usque ad annos octoginta quatuor; quae non discedebat de templo, jejuniis et obsecrationibus serviens nocte ac die.
74 Added in the left margin: liberationem
75 Vulgate: Et haec ipsa hora superveniens, confitabatur Domino et loquebatur de illo omnibus qui expectabant redemptionem Israel.
76 In error, it should be 39.
77 Vulgate: Et ut perfecerunt omnia secundum legem Domini, reverse sunt in Galilaeam in civitatem suam Nazareth.
78 Correction in the left margin: Christianus replaced by Cabb. Cat. (which involves the two speakers being changed over in the following exchange).
79 Correction in the left margin: Cabb. Cat. replaced by Christian. (as a consequence of the previous correction).
80 Added in the right margin: (7.) Quomodo computandi sint Anni Regum Juda & Israël? Et quot annos steterit Templum primum?

37 And she was a widow of about eighty-four years old. And she did not leave the Temple but served in fasting and prayer, day and night.
38 And she too was present at the same hour and praised the Lord and spoke about him with every one who was expecting the liberation of Jerusalem.
39 And when they had completed all the requirements in the Law of the Lord, they returned to Galilee, | to Nazareth, their own town.

In those days bywmt' hnwn

Kabbalist Catechumen[81] What year of the world was this?

Christian That is quite uncertain, and there is no way this year can be definitively specified. Because:

1. | Chronologists have not yet agreed whether the dates of the Patriarchs should be reckoned according to the Greek copies [of the Old Testament] or according to the Hebrew ones[82].

2. Nor is it yet agreed whether the year of the Flood is independently calculable or whether the date can only be arrived at from the numbers in the genealogy of the Patriarchs.

3. There is also no agreement whether Cainan is to be included | among the Patriarchs after the Flood with Lk 3.36, or whether he is to be omitted with the Hebrew text of Gen 11.12.

4. Nor is it agreed whether Abraham should be considered to have been born in his father's seventieth year (according to Gen 11.26) ||| or rather in his father's one hundred and thirtieth year (according to Gen 12.40 when compared with Gen 11.32 and also Acts 7.4).

5. It is uncertain whether the 430 years about which Gal 3.17 speaks, should be counted from the migration of Abraham from Ur, or from Haran, or from the promise made to Jacob as he went down into Egypt (Gen 46.2 according to Ex 12.40).

6. | It is also uncertain whether the years of the founding of the Temple (1 Kgs 6.1) should be counted from the beginning of the departure from Egypt or from the end as in Deut 4.45, 46; Ps 114.1, 3.

fol. 38r

---

81 A correction in the manuscript reverses the order of the speakers.
82 The figures in the Septuagint are considerably greater than those in the Hebrew MT. Both antediluvian and post-deluvian ancestors in LXX Genesis 5 &11 have consistently higher ages of begetting. For a brief characterisation of the whole LXX chronology in comparison with both the MT and the Samaritan Pentateuch, Jeremy Hughes, *Secrets of the Times*, op. cit., pp. 238–241. Hughes' book provides a full account of the difficulties of the various chronologies and offers an explanation for the differences.

(8.) Quomodo computandi sint Anni Nebucadnezaris & captivitatis Babylonicæ; item Regum Persarum & septuaginta hebdomadum Danielis? Nec non anni Imperatorum Romanorum sub istius Monarchiæ initium?

(9.) Cum in Scriptura annorum aliqua summa describitur, (ut cum vixisse, vel regnasse quispiam tot annos dicitur) incertum est an numerus sit rotundus, an exactus? Et cum annus describitur aliquotus; v. g. tertius &c. dubium pariter est, an concipiendus sit currens, an verò, integer & absolutus?

Unde nihil restat, quàm ut dicatur, computum hunc omnem, non nisi ê verisimili quadam | conjectura colligi. Mihique omninò videtur Christum natum esse circa initium millennii quinti (juxta conjecturas illas propositas in Adumbratione Cabbalæ Christianæ cap. 10, §.4[83]. sqq.)

[Christianus.] Unde[84] etiam cum Calculo accuratiorum Chronologorum concordabit, si Lydiati secuti Emendationem usque ad fundatum Salomonis Templum cum | ipso numeremus annos 2988.

Abhinc autem usque ad Reditum ê captivitate, Cyri nempe primum fermè juxta Petavium Rationarii Temporum[85] P.II. l.2. c.11., annos 475.

Et â primo Cyri, usque ad natum Christum in Lydiato iterum ponamus annos, 537

Unde efficiuntur Anni. 4000
(vide infra v. 2 ad vocem Syria.)
[Cabb. Cat.] Minimè.[86]
[*Cabb. Cat.*][87] *Fortè major certitudo occurrit circa Nativitatis Christi diem.*
[Christianus.][88] Minime; Supponemus enim methodo omnium facillimâ;
1. Quod nostrates[89] habuerint annos Lunares, dierum 354. mensesque per vices plenos, i.e. 30. dierum: & defectivos, i.e. 29. dierum.

---

83 Cf. *supra*, footnote 47, p. 154.
84 Correction: Christianus. Unde. replaced by Quod. The change of speaker initially intended is no longer needed, since the speech was attributed to the Christian (cf. *supra*). Unde is replaced by Quod, in order to make the transition smoother.
85 The French Jesuit Dionysius Petavius (Denis Petau) (1583–1652) wrote his *Opus de docrina temporum* in Paris in 1627. It appeared in French and slightly abridged in 1633 (also in Paris) as *Rationarum Temporum* in two volumes.
86 Deletion: Cabb. Cat. Minimè.
87 Correction: Christianus replaced by Cabb. Cat. (which involves the two speakers being changed over in the following exchange).
88 Correction: Cabb. Cat. replaced by Christianus (as a consequence of the previous correction).
89 Correction: nostrates replaced by vestrates (to be understood in the light of the change of speaker).

SECTION VIII

7. We do not know how the years of the kingdoms of Judah and Israel should be counted, nor for how many years the first Temple stood.

8. Nor do we know how the years of Nebuchadnezzar and the Babylonian Captivity should be counted, nor [those of] the Kingdom of the Persians and Daniel's Seventy Weeks. Similarly the years of the Roman Emperors at the beginning of the Principate.

9. | When in Scripture a total of some years is described (as when someone is said to have lived so many years) it is uncertain whether this is a round number or a precise one. And when a year is given a specific [ordinal] number (e.g. third etc.) it is equally uncertain whether it should be considered merely a part of that year or [a] whole and complete [year].

From all this the only conclusion is to say that all of this calculation is based merely on | plausible conjecture. But it seems clear to me that Christ was born around the beginning of the fifth millenium (according to those conjectures proposed in *Adumbratio*, chap. 10, § 4 *seq.*). It will agree with the calculation of the more accurate chronologists, if we follow Lydiat's correction up to the foundation of Solomon's Temple, and with | him count 2,988 years[90].

From this to the Return from Captivity in the first year of Cyrus, according to Petavius' *Rationarii Temporum* P. ii l. 2.c. 11,

was 475 years.

And from the first year of Cyrus to the birth of Christ, again with Lydiat, let us say 537 years.

This makes 4,000 years.

[See below verse 2 on the word "Syria"]

Kabbalist Catechumen Perhaps there is greater certainty around the Day of Christ's Birth?

Christian Hardly! But let us set out the simplest solution of all. [Let us agree:]

1. | that your people had lunar years of 354 days and months by turn full with 30 days and defective with 29 days.

---

90   Lydiat has: "*Anno 2988m, utpote anno 480 ab Israelitarum Exodo ex Aegypto, mense secundo, secundo die mensis, incepit Salomon quarto anno regni sui aedificare templum Iehovae Hierosolymis. Rg 6c. quod 7 annis postea anno regni sui 11. sub festum tabernaculorum consumavit atque dedicavit.*"

II. Quod finito anno non etiam finita fuerit Septimana, & ministerium sacerdotale: quia si 354. dividantur per 7. prodeunt 50. Septimanæ & dies 4.

III. Quod propter inæqualitatem Anni Lunaris dierum 354. & solaris dierum | 365. ut æquationem tamen ne negligerent, soliti sint mensem intercalare, quem Ve-Adar dixerunt: Nimirum quando utriusque anni differentia quæ quotannis est undecim dierum adaucta fuit usque ad 30. dies, quod factum est anno quovis tertio. Quamvis enim ad[91] et alias prætendere soliti fuerint intercalandi causas; nempe, quod Paschate adveniente fruges non maturuissent; vel arbores | non florerent: vel pontes aquarum eluvionibus essent eversi; vel agni non satis adulti, &c. hæ omnes tamen exhinc ortum trahebant, quod neglectâ differentiâ illa undecim dierum, mensis Paschalis nimiùm anticiparet.

IV. Quod in anno hoc tertio Embolimali, cum fine Anni, finem quoque sortirentur hebdomadæ & ministeria sacerdotum: quia dies 354. ter sumti efficiunt dies | 1062; additis autem 30. diebus mensis embolimæi fiunt dies 1092. qui divisi per 7. efficiunt septimanas 156. die nullo residuo.

V. Quod ministeria sacerdotum numerari non possint in una serie, quia in ||| tribus festis majoribus ministrandum fuit Sacerdotibus omnibus, Ordine non observato. Unde absolutâ trieteride hâc non absoluti fuerunt sex cycli & 12. ministeria: sed sex cycli & 3. saltem ministeria: seu ministeria 147.

fol. 38ᵛ

VI. Supposito ergò ex Textu Talmudico Tract. Erachin. fol. 11. b. & Tract. Taanith, | fol. 29.a. quorum verba videantur inter Excerpta Cent. II. Loc. 14. Et ex Josepho, l. 7. de Bello c. 9. & c. 10. quod tempore destructi â Tito templi die 9. mensis Ab ministraverit Ordo Jehojarib seu primus sub exitum Sabbathi, jam quærendum est, quo mense ministraverit Ordo Abia seu Octavus, eô tempore, cum Zachariæ annunciaretur Johannes? Seu quis ordo ministraverit | die 9. mensis An, istius Anni?

VII. Instituto igitur calculo juxta accuratissimum inter modernos temporum Emendatorem Thomam Lydiatum Anglum; elapsi sunt â concepto Johanne usque ad destructum Templum anni 68. Si ergò uno triennio absoluta fuêre ministeria 147. sequitur, quod intra annos hosce 68. absoluta fuissent ministeria 3332. | Verum enim verò quia absolutâ cum intercalatione sua, trieteride unâ, dies tamen restant super numerarii tres, qui intra 30. annos iterum efficiunt mensem unum intercalandum: quæ intercalatio procul dubio etiam non fuit neglectui habita, quia aliàs odiosa illa mensis

---

91 Deleted word.

2. that the end of the year was neither the end of a week, nor of [that week's] priestly ministry, because if 354 is divided by 7, one gets 50 weeks and four days [left over].

3. that because of the inequality of the Lunar Year of 354 days and the Solar year | of 365 days they did not just ignore the difference, but used to intercalate [insert] a month which they called *Ve-Adar* when the difference between the lunar and solar year (which is eleven days a year) had increased to 30 days. This happened every third year. Although they used to give several reasons for intercalation, namely that the crops would not otherwise have matured when Passover came round, nor the trees | have flowered, or that the bridges [which the Jerusalem pilgrims used] would be washed away by flood water, or the lambs not sufficiently grown etc., all these reasons arise from the same fundamental issue, that if the difference of eleven days was ignored, Passover would come too early.

4. that in this third intercalated year with the end of the year, there ended also the week and the sacerdotal ministry because 354 days multiplied by 3 [years] makes 1,062 | days. The addition of the 30 days of the intercalated month makes 1,092 days, which when divided by 7 makes 156 weeks, with nothing left over.

5. that the priestly ministries cannot be numbered in a single series, because ||| on the three major [pilgrim] festivals all the priests had to serve, regardless of their order. So that, with the completion of this three year period, six cycles and 12 ministries had not been completed, but only six cycles and three ministries, which makes 147 ministries.

fol. 38ᵛ

6. So now let us suppose from the text of the Talmudic Tract. Arachin folio 11b & Tract. Ta'anit | folio 29a (which are cited in Except Cent. II Loc. 14) and from Josephus Book 7 of *de Bello* chap. 9 & chap. 10, that at the time of the destruction of the Temple by Titus on the Ninth Day of the Month Ab, the order of Jehojarib (or the first order) served at the end of the Sabbath. Now we must ask, in what month did the order of Abijah (or the eighth order) serve, which was the time when John was announced to Zachariah? Or what order served | on the Ninth of Ab of that year?

7. Let us follow in our calculation the most accurate of the modern chronographers, the Englishman Thomas Lydiat: there were 68 years from the conception of John to the Destruction of the Temple. So if in a three year period there were 147 ministries, it follows that in these 68 years there would have been 3,332 | ministries. But after the passage of one three-year period and its intercalation, there would remain three days over, which after the passage of 30 more years would mean a month had to be intercalated. This intercalation was doubtless never ignored, for otherwise within a short space

Paschalis anticipatio intra tam breve temporis spatium non potuisset evitari: hinc | suppono intra 68. hosce annos iterum intercalatos fuisse menses extraordinarios binos: qui efficiunt ministeria octo: ut[92] intra 68. hosce annos ministeria exercita fuissent 3340. Qui numerus divisus per Cyclum sacerdotalem 24; producit 139. cyclos integros & ministeria 4.

VIII. Retrogrediendo igitur â 9. die mensis Ab, (qui fuit Sabbathum,) anni â | concepto Johanne 68. usque ad annum propositum; initium faciendum est ab ordine Jehojaribi primo; & pergendum per 24. 23. 22. &c. usque ad secundum, cum quo finitus fuit Cyclus unus, seu ministeria 24. Unde in anno proposito, antequam veniret dies 9. mensis Ab, absolutus fuit cyclus, & ulterius ministrarunt Ordines quatuor, i.e. (1.) ordo primus Jehojarib. (2.) ordo vigesimus quartus, Mahaziah[93]. | (3.) Ordo vigesimus tertius Delajah: & (4.) ordo vigesimus secundus Gamul; qui ministerium habuit die nono mensis Ab anni concepti Johannis.

IX. Jam quæratur in specie[94] mensium & ordinum istius anni, quo mense ministraverit ordo octavus, adeoque Zacharias: & reperiemus; quod una vice series ipsum tetigerit circa 22. Tisri; septimanâ nempe illâ quæ festum Tabernaculorum | proximè secuta est. Et tunc conceptio Christi secuta sexto post mense, contigisset circa medium mensis Nisan, paulò ante, quam Maria abiisset ad Festum Paschatos; cujus occasione visitare potuisset Elisabetham: domumque redire post trimestre, occasione festi 10. Tamuz. Nativitas autem Christi nono postmodum mense secuta, incidisset circa medium Tebeth, quod â die modernæ | observationis, nimirum 25. Decembr. vel die Baptismi Dominici seu Epiphanias, Januar. 6. haud multum abesset. Altera autem vice series Zachariam tetigit circa 20. Nisan, septimanâ nempe illa, quæ festum Paschatos proximè secuta est. Et tunc conceptio Christi sexto post mense secuta incidisset in mensem Tisri, antequam Maria abiisset ad festum Tabernaculorum, | cujus occasione visitare potuisset Elisabetham; domumque redire occasione festi Encæniorum, quod erat 25. Kisleu. Nativitas autem Christi nono post mense festi secuta incidisset in mensem Tamuz, qui partim Junium, partim Julium nostrum tetigit. ‖

X. Si verò ille annus fuit mensium 13. adeoque embolimalis primum quidem Zachariæ ministerium nullam pateretur immutationem: alterum autem uno mense anticiparet. Verùm quis hîc non videt, quam incerta maneat conclusio, quamvis hæc omnia fundamento nitantur emendatiore? Interea

---

92   Added above the line: ita
93   Correction: Mahaziah replaced by Maaziah
94   Correction: specie replaced by serie

SECTION VIII

of time the unwelcome early arrival of Passover would be inevitable. Now | let us suppose that within these 68 years there were two more extra months intercalated, which would mean eight (extra) ministries, so the number of ministries served in those 68 years would be 3,340. This number divided by the priestly cycle of 24, gives 139 whole cycles and 4 ministries left over.

8. So let us work [forward] from the Ninth of Av (which was a Sabbath) in the year | John was conceived, 68 years to the year [of the Destruction of the Temple] we are talking about. We must begin with the (first) order of Jehojarib and work through 24, 23, 22 etc. to the second, with which finished one cycle or 24 ministries. Thus in the year we are talking about [AD 70] before the Ninth of Av there occurred one [full] cycle and four further orders ministered i.e. (1) the first order of Jehoiarib; (2) the twenty-fourth order of Maaziah; | (3) the twenty-third order of Delajah and (4) the twenty-second order of Gamul, who were exercising their ministry on the Ninth of Av in the year of the conception of John.

9. Now we must seek in the sequence of months and orders of that year, in what month the eighth order—and thus Zachariah—served. We shall find, on one reckoning, the series itself reached 22nd of Tishri, a week closely followed by the Feast of Tabernacles. | Then the conception of Christ, six months later, brings us to the middle of the month of Nisan, a little before Mary left for the Feast of Passover, which was the occasion when she may have visited Elizabeth and returned home after three months at the time of the Feast on 10th of Tamuz. So the Birth of Christ, nine months later, fell about the middle of [the month of] Tebet, which is not far from the date of the modern | observance, December 25th, or the Feast of the Baptism of the Lord[95], or Epiphany on 6th January. But, by another reckoning, the sequence reached Zachariah around the 20th of Nisan, the week closely followed by the feast of Passover. So the conception of Christ which followed six months later fell in the month of Tishri before Mary had gone to the Feast of Tabernacles | which may have been the occasion for her to visit Elizabeth and return home on the Feast of Lights [Chanukah] which was the 25th of Kislev. The Birth of Christ following nine months later would then have fallen in the month of Tamuz which falls between June and July. |||

fol. 39ʳ

10. But if that year was an intercalated year of thirteen months, the first ministry of Zachariah would have been unchanged, but the second a month later. But who cannot see how uncertain is the conclusion here, although based on a rigorously corrected foundation? None the less following this

---

95   January 8th.

juxta hanc methodum institui etiam | poterit supputatio ê calculo Chronologiæ communis, retrogrediendo â die Destructi Templi. Item â die Encæniorum Maccabaicorum progrediendo, si certum esset, quod tunc iterum factum esset exordium ministeriorum ab ordine Jehojarib.

[Christianus.][96] Certissimum sane[97] est, quod ex instituto divino Annus nativitatis Dominicæ | Christianis propositus non sit Epocham; sed potiùs Annus inchoati ministerii Johannitici, juxta Marc. 1, 4; Luc. 3, 1.2.3.4; Matth. 11, 12; Luc. 16, 16. Unde nec annus nec dies prædictæ Nativitatis admodum curæ fuit Antiquitati.

Edictum ab Augusto Cæsare &c. פוקדנא מן אגוסטוס קסר.

[Christianus.][98] Messias in generationem descendens dominio omnium Corticum sese subjecerat, ut omnes tandem vinceret: (vid. Adumbratio Cabbalæ Christianæ cap. 10. & 11. & 12.[99]) Inter illos Cortices haud minimus erat Primarius septuaginta Principum super populos mundanos constitutorum, Præfectus nimirum Imperii Romani, qui vocatur Satanas, & â nostratibus[100] aliàs Samaël. Cum ergò sicut præconio omnia publicantur | in subliminibus, ita & Descensus Messiæ publicè ibidem innotuisset, ut & Samaël eundem haud ignoraret, quamvis de persona ejus nihil certi pernôsset: consilium iniit de congreganda familia Davidicâ, unde Messiam proditurum vulgatissimum erat. Ad descriptionem igitur universalem concitavit clientem suum Imperatorem, ut de Persona Adversarii sui certior fieret, eundemque si | fieri posset, quantocujus è medio tolleret. Sub quadruplici igitur magistratu, quasi sub Corticibus totidem tunc degebat Messias; sub Herode, qui sub Kyrenio; qui sub Augusto; qui sub Genio Romanorum. Quod ergò hic ultimus inspirabat,

---

96 Deletion: Christianus. The change of speaker initially intended is no longer needed, after the previous correction. The Christian remains the speaker.
97 Correction: sane replaced by autem
98 Correction in the right margin: Cabb. Cat. replaced by Christianus. (which involves the two speakers being changed over in the following exchange).
99 The chapters 10, 11 and 12 of the "Adumbratio kabbalæ christianæ" deal with the salvation operated by Christ, in a very kabbalistic framework and vocabulary, as the titles of the chapters demonstrate: "Caput x. De statu postremæ Restitutionis, ejusque Gradu primo; Caput xi. De secundo Gradu Restitutionis Animarum; Caput 12. De duobus ultimis Restitutionis Meßianæ Gradibus".
100 Correction: nostratibus replaced by vestratibus (to be understood in the light of the change of speaker).
101 A change of speaker to the Christian is suppressed.

SECTION VIII 443

method one could make | a supposition from working back with commonly accepted dates from the day of the Destruction of the Temple. Similarly by working forwards from the Maccabbees' Feast of Chanukah, if it were certain that at that time also the ministery priests began with the order of Jehojarib.[101] But it is most certain that by divine providence the year of the Lord's nativity | was not made known to Christians at the time, but rather the year of the beginning of John's ministry [according to Mk 1.4; Lk 3.1, 2, 3, 4; Mt 11.12; Lk 16.16]. Thus neither the year nor the day of this birth was of much interest to Antiquity.

Ordered by Caesar Augustus etc. *pwqdn' mn 'gwsṭws qsr*

Christian Messiah descending [into the world of] generation submitted himself to the dominion of all the Shards, so that ultimately he might defeat them all [See *Adumbratio*, chap. 10, 11 and 12]. Not least amongst those shards was the leader of the seventy [angelic] princes set up over the peoples of the world,[102] namely the Head of the Roman Empire who is called Satan, or by your scholars elsewhere, Samael.[103] Now when, as if by a herald, everything was proclaimed | in heaven, so that the descent of Messiah was commonly known there and Samael was aware of the fact, although he knew nothing certain about the *persona* Messiah would assume, he devised a plan to gather together the family of David whence it was rumoured Messiah would be born.[104] Thus he incited his client, the [Roman] Emperor to a universal census, so he might be informed about the *persona* of his enemy and if | at all possible get rid of him. So Messiah lived under these four rulers, as if under four Shards; under Herod, who was under Cyrenius, who was under Augustus, who was under the Genius of the Romans. It was from this [Genius] that

---

102 The seventy nations of the world are found in Gen 10. Though MT of Deuteronomy 32.8 has the nations apportioned "according to the children of Israel", 4QDeutⁱ has "according to the number of the *bny 'l[hym]* sons of God" and LXX has "according to the number of *aggelōn theou* the angels of God". This is probably the correct reading and the root of the conviction that each nation had its own "prince" or angel. See: Dan 10.13.
103 Samael was appropriately the guardian angel of Esau (*Yalkut Shimoni* 1.110) and the patron of Edom: Howard Schwartz, *Tree of Souls: the Mythology of Judaism* (Oxford University Press, 2004), p. 361.
104 This is a most imaginative and innovative description of New Testament History as a strategy of Samael.

id Augustus mandabat, Kyrenius intimabat, Herodes publicabat. Secundum dogmata Doctorum nostrorum[105] autem, Benedictio superna non quiescit super re numeratâ; | unde Iisraëlitæ, cum numerabantur, lytron quoddam pendebant singuli, Exod. 30, 12. ut non capita, sed nummi numerarentur adjectis benedictionibus tam ante inchoatam, quàm post finitam numerationem. Cum autem describerentur â Davide sine lytro, 2. Sam. 24, 1. peste puniebantur. Nam quia sublatâ tum, ob numerationem erat benedictio, Pars adversa quiescebat super ipsis, illisque nocere | poterat, vide inter Excerpta Libri Sohar Cent. II. Loc. 15. Cum ergò in ista numeratione nec lytron penderetur, nec benedictiones accederent, procul dubio id intendit Satanas, quod intendebat, cum ad censum instigaret Davidem; in specie autem ut Davidis filium deprehenderet & submoveret.

[*Cabb. Cat.*][106] *Nec mirum est â Satana ad censum instigatum fuisse Augustum,* | *cum etiam â Satanæ directione, nimirum ab Augurio nomen acceperit: eò quod loca religiosa, & in quibus augurato quid consecratur, Augusta dicta sint.*

Populus possessionis ejus. עמא דאוחדנה

Cabb. Cat. *Meliùs exprimit rem ipsam quam Græcum* οἰκουμένη

Christianus. Vox ergò Universi in Græco hac ratione Orbem tantum sive Imperium | Romanum denotat.

fol. 39ᵛ

V. 2. *Prima erat* &c. קדמיתא הות ‖

Christianus. Sensus est ambiguus: vel enim ita dicitur prima, ut antea sub censum nondum acta fuerit Judæa. Vel ita, ut Kyrenius censum egerit etiam secundum; cum nempe Regnum Archelao ademptum est. Ter autem juxta Suetonium in Octav. c. 27. censum Populi egit Augustus, primum statim post

---

105 Correction: nostrorum replaced by vestrorum (to be understood in the light of the change of speaker).
106 Correction: Christianus replaced by Cabb. Cat.
107 That is, censuses are unacceptable.
108 Lightfoot, *Miscellanies and the Harmony of the Gospels*, op. cit., p. 19: "by the advice of Munatius Plancus, [Octavian] was named 'Augustus,' which importeth 'sacredness' and 'reverence'."
109 This is not however how Knorr translates the phrase above in the long citation of the text of Luke before these comments.

came the ultimate inspiration, then Augustus ordered it, Cyrenius passed it on, and Herod published it. According to the teaching of your sages the Heavenly Blessing does not come to settle upon the thing counted,[107] | which is why when the Israelites were being counted, individuals paid ransom money (Ex 30.12) so that coins rather than heads were counted with blessings added, blessings both at beginning and at the end of the count. When the Israelites were counted by David without the ransom money (2 Sam 24.1) they were punished. For because the Blessing was removed from them on account of the census, the Contrary Part [Satan] came to settle upon them and he was able to | harm them. (See in Excerpts Cent. II Loc. 15.) Since therefore in this census [under Augustus], they had neither paid ransom money nor received blessings, Satan no doubt had the same intention as previously when he incited David to take a census, but now specifically the capture and removal of the Son of David.

Kabbalist Catechumen It is no wonder that Augustus was led to hold the census by Satan, | or rather by the direction of Satan. His name comes from "Augury", so that religious sites where augury was practiced were called "*augusta*".[108]

People of his possession 'm' d'wḥdnh

Kabbalist Catechumen The Syriac [above] better expresses the reality than the Greek *oikoumenēi* [whole world].[109]

Christian The phrase "all the world" by this argument then means in Greek, either the globe or | the Roman Empire.

Verse 2
It was the first etc. *qdmyt' hwt* ‖‖‖   fol. 39ᵛ

Christian The meaning is ambiguous, for either by "first" it is intended to say that Judaea had never previously been subject to a census, or it means that Cyrenius conducted another, second, census, when indeed Archaelaus ruled the kingdom[110]. Three times, according to Suetonius in his *Octavius* ch. 27, Augustus subjected the people to a census: the first with his fellow

---

110 The subject of this census remains a matter of contention today and its resolution informs radically different views of Luke's historical reliability. As good an informed defense of Luke as any may be, I. Howard Marshall, *The Gospel of Luke. A Commentary on the Greek Text* (Exeter: Paternoster Press, 1978), pp. 99–104.

sublatum Antonium cum collega M. | Agrippa; secundum solus; qui est hic noster: tertium cum Tiberio.

Cabb. Cat. Si ergò sensus admittendus est primus, quæstio esset, quare sub censu Augusti primo Judæa non simul fuisset descripta?

Christianus. Fortè, quod census ille primus populi & civium tantum fuerit, non etiam subditorum.

In Præfectura &c. בהגמנותא

Christianus. Quirinius, (nempe Qu. & K veteribus æquipollebant) præfectus quidem Syriæ non fuit: Sed Legatus tamen Augusti in Syria; quod Tacitus innuit, dum l.3. Annal. scribit Quirinium ab Augusto datum esse Rectorem Cajo Cæsari Armeniam obtinenti. Videtur ergò terminus Præfecturæ latiùs sumi.

Cabb. Cat. Sed quare Josephus ejus non meminit ante relegatum Archelaum?

Christianus. Verùm Josephus nec Præfecturæ Caji Cæsaris in Syria, nec Lollii moderaturis ejus prioris meminit. Fortè autem neglexit hunc censum Josephus, quod tributa non simul indicerentur, tanquam rem haud satis memorabilem.

Cabb. Cat. At quare Tertullianus hunc censum tribuit Sentio Saturnino?

Christianus. Opinor hunc adjunctum fuisse Quirinio, tanquam illius temporis Syriæ Præsidem.

Kyrini in Syria. דקורינוס בסוריא

[*Cabb. Cat.*][111] *Vav hoc loco ut sæpius vocalem Kübbutz refert, & sonum requirit, quem habet u Gallicum & Ypsilon Græcorum habuit.*

[Cabb. Cat.] [112]*Quem locum autem habeat*[113] *Syria inter omnes mundi Terras?*[114] [**Christianus.**][115] apparet ex collatione Regionum Terræ cum corpore Adami, quæ videatur in Tractatu de Revolutione Animarum cap. 16.

---

111   Correction: Christianus replaced by Cabb. Cat. (which involves the two speakers being changed over in the following exchange).
112   Deletion: Cabb. Cat.
113   Correction: habeat replaced by habet
114   The phrase is underlined, in order to attribute it to the Cabbalist.
115   Added in the left margin: Christian. Id
116   The Greek of Lk 2.2 has *hēgemoneuontos*.
117   Tacitus Annals 3.48: "... datusque rector C. Caesari Armeniam obtinenti."
118   A similar census was carried out in Palestine on the banishment of Archelaus by Quirinius (Josephus, *Antiquities* 17.355; 18.1 ff.; 20.202; *Bellum Judaicum* 2.117 ff.; 7.253).

SECTION VIII

consul M. | Agrippa immediately after the removal of Anthony; the second on his own; and the third with Tiberius.

Kabbalist Catechumen If we accept the first sense, the question arises, why had Augustus not included Judaea in his first census?

Christian Perhaps, because that first census was only of the [Roman] people and citizens and not also of conquered peoples.

During the Prefectship etc. *bhgmnwt*'[116]

Christian Qurinius (notice that [the letters] /q/ & /k/ are equivalent amongst the ancients) was not in fact Prefect of Syria, but the Legate of Augustus in Syria; which is what Tacitus implies when in Annals Book 3 he writes that Qurinius had been given by Augustus as a mentor to Caius Caesar in capturing Armenia[117]. So it looks as if the term "Prefect" is being used rather imprecisely.

Kabbalist Catecumen But why did Josephus not mention it before Archelaus was relegated?[118]

Christian But Josephus mentions neither the prefecture of Caius Caesar in Syria, nor of Lollius, his first guide. Perhaps Josephus neglected this census because tribute was not leved at the same time, so that the thing was not sufficiently memorable.

Kabbalist Catecumen But why does Tertullian attribute this census to Sentius Saturninus?[119]

Christian I think he had been an assistant of Qurinius, and the Prefect of Syria of the time.

Kyrinius in Syria dqwrynws bswry'

Kabbalist Catechumen [The Letter] wav [/w/] here as quite often indicates the vowel *qibbuṣ* and has the same sound as /u/ in French and upsilon in Greek.

Where is Syria among all the lands of the earth?

Christian It appears from the correlation of the regions of the earth with the body of Adam, which is found in Tract. *De Revol. Animarum*, chap. 16,

---

[119] "Sed et census constat actos sub Augusto nunc in Iudaea per Sentium Saturninum, apud quos genus eius inquirere potuissent" (Tertullian, *Adversus Marcionem*, 2 vols, edited by Ernest Evans (Oxford University Press, 1972), 4.19. p. 362).

p. 309[120]. sqq. Nimirum | primum ibidem Terra Israëlitica locum habet; secundum Trans Jordanitica tertium Syria, quæ refertur ad finem corporis Adamici. Unde iterum confirmatur hypothesis mea[121] de tempore nati Salvatoris, quod nempe contigerit, circa finem mensurati corporis Adamitici, [juxta Adumbrationem Cabbalæ Christianæ cap. 10. §. 6[122].] Circa finem autem corporis hujus, Syria | Cortex finem etiam mox erat habiturus. Confer ea, pro confirmanda hac hypothesi de nato sub initium[123], cap. 14.§.23.[124] ubi expressè dicitur, quod bis mille anni posteriores relati antiquitus fuerint ad Messiam Filium David.

V. 3. *In urbem suam.* במדינתה

[**Cabb. Cat.**][125] *Quare hoc?*

[**Christianus.**][126] Hoc[127] quasi proscenium fuit restituendarum Animarum ad radices suas, (de qua restitutione temporibus Messiæ consummanda diximus ad Luc. 1, 17.)

V.4. *Bethlechem* &c. ביתלחם

[**Cabb. Cat.**][128] *Quid hic contribuunt scripta vestratium*[129]*?*

---

120 The text refers here to the "Schema Pro meliore intellectu Capitis 16" which shows, for each part of the earth (Terra Iisraëlitica; Transjordanitica; Syria; Extra terram) their origin in the body of Adam Kadmon. Syria is the last region reported for the chest.
121 Correction: mea replaced by nostra
122 Cf. *supra*, footnote 47, pp. 154–155.
123 Added in the left margin: Millennii quinti Messia, quæ in eodem Tractatum de Revolutionibus Animarum habentur.
124 "Postmodum sequuntur bis mille anni dierum Messiæ ratione mundi creationis. Notum enim est, quod mundus creationis correspondeat literæ Tetragrammaticæ He priori, qua denotatur Leah, ex qua provenit Meschiach filius David. Atque hinc respondere poteris ad objectionem illam, quare omnes bis mille anni dierum Messianorum tempus vocentur; cum jam plus quam mille anni effluxerint, & aliquot insuper secula è bis mille his annis, nec tamen filius David venit? unde mirum, quare omnes vocentur dies Messiæ? Respondetur autem ex illo, quod dixerunt Magistri nostri bonæ memoriæ: quod nempe tota redemptio procedat à matre superna, unde ortum trahat Meschiach filius David, qui est filius Leah: unde omnes illi bis mille anni destinantur ad restaurationem mundi creationis, qui in se continet bis mille gradus supradictos." ("De

SECTION VIII 449

30 p. 309 *seq.*, that | the land of the Israelites has first place, second Transjordan and Third Syria—which is placed at the extremity of the body of Adam. Here again is confirmed our hypothesis concerning the time of the Birth of the Saviour, which because it was located [geographically] at the extremity of the measure of the body of Adam (according to *Adumbratio*, chap. 10, § 6),
35 at the [geographical] extremity of this body also, the Shard of Syria | will soon have its end. For the confirmation of this hypothesis about the birth of Messiah at the beginning of the fifth millennium [i.e. in 4000 AM], look at the material in the same Tractate *De Revol. Animarum*, in chapters 14 §23 where is expressly said that the subsequent two thousand years had been long ago related to Messiah, Son of David.

Verse 3
To his own city bmdynth

40 **Kabbalist Catechumen** Why was that?
Christian This is, as it were, a theatrical stage setting for the restoration of souls to their roots. [We have remarked on this restoration to be accomplished in the days of Messiah on Lk 1.17.]

Verse 4
Bethlehem etc. bytlḥm

45 **Kabbalist Catechumen** What do the writings of our sages have to contribute here?

---

revolutionibus animarum", op. cit., pp. 303–304). The exemplar held at the HAB has an addition: "Respondetur autem ex illo, quod dixerunt Magistri nostri bonæ memoriæ: (*sed nullius judicii*) quod nempe tota redemptio procedat à matre superna".
125   Correction: Christianus replaced by Cabb. Cat. (which involves the two speakers being changed over in the following exchange).
126   Correction: Cabb. Cat. replaced by Christian. (as a consequence of the previous correction).
127   Added above the line: nimirum
128   Correction: Christianus replaced by Cabb. Cat. (which involves the two speakers being changed over in the following exchange).
129   Correction: vestratium replaced by nostratium (to be understood in the light of the change of speaker)

450 TEXT AND TRANSLATION

fol. 40ʳ
[**Christianus.**][130] Notabilis est locus in Midrasch איכה f. 48. c. Dicit Arabs quidam Judæo; Natus est Redemtor Judæorum. Et ille, quodnam ejus nomen? Menahem, inquit alter. Et quodnam nomen Patris ejus? Ezekia[s] ‖‖

Ubi nam verò illi habitant? In villa ovium in Bethlehem Jehudah; vel (ut in Talmude Hierosol. extat hæc narratio Berachoth, f. 5. a.) in Arce Regia, quæ in Bethlehem Jehudah. Locum autem ê Talmude Hierosolym. latius adducemus in Excerptis Centur. II. Loc. 16.

E domo, & ê familia David. מן ביתה ומן שרבתה דדויד   5

[**Christianus.**][131] Davidis Domus plures habebat familias; ê quarum unâ Josephus erat oriundus; nempe cujus caput fuerat Salomon; ex altera oriunda erat Maria, cujus caput fuerat Nathan Salomonis frater ex Bathscheba 1. Par. 3, 5. Ex alia ortus fuerat Hillel & Domus ejus; cujus caput fuerat | Schephatjak, filius Abitalæ. 1. Par. 3, 3. prout habetur in Juchasin f. 19, b.   10

[**Cabb. Cat.**][132] *Mirumque fuerit, nisi & quidam reliqui fuissent ex illis filiis David qui commemorantur Neh. 8, 2. item 1. Par. 3, 17–24. item Esr. 2, 21. coll. cum Neh. 7, 26.*

V. 7. *In stabulo campestri* &c. באוריא

[**Cabb. Cat.**][133] Quid vobis denotat אוריא?[134]   15

[**Christianus.**][135] Vox ista hoc loco non denotat Præsepe; sed stabulum, quod hoc loco in campo, inque spelunca quadam erat, pro pecoribus illius loci, quæ noctu & interdiu in pascuis degere solebant; unde pro illorum commoditate talia ibidem adornata erant in campestribus loca, ut contra inclementiam Æris ibidem | tutius morari possent. Et in hac significatione Vox ista   20

(1.) etiam adhibetur Esth. 6, 11. Ubi in secunda Paraphrasi Chaldaicâ hæc extant: Intrabatque לאוריא דמלכא in stabulum Regis: & accepit inde equum, qui stabat בריש אוריא. In primario loco stabuli. Et ibid v. 10. Et ingredere

---

130 Correction: Cabb. Cat. replaced by Christianus (as a consequence of the previous correction).
131 Correction: Cabb. Cat. replaced by Christian (which involves the two speakers being changed over in the following exchange).
132 Correction: Christianus replaced by Cabb. Cat. (as a consequence of the previous correction).
133 Correction: Christianus replaced by Cabb. Cat. (which involves the two speakers being changed over in the following exchange).
134 Correction: Quid vobis denotat אוריא? replaced by *Cur ita hac verbis?*

Christian Notable is the passage in Midrash *'ykh* [Lamentations] f48c: "An Arab says to a Jew 'The Saviour of the Jews is born'. But the Jew replies: 'What is his name?' 'Menahem', says the other. 'And what is his father's name?' 'Ezekias'. ‖ 'But where do they live?' 'In the town of sheep, in Bethlehem Judah', or (as in Jerusalem Talmud where this story also appears in Berachot folio 5a) *'in Arce Regia* [The Royal Citadel] which is in Bethlehem Judah'". The passage from the Jerusalem Talmud is more extensively quoted in Excerpts Cent. II Loc. 16.

fol. 40r

From the house and lineage of David mn byth wmn šrbth ddwyd

Christian The House of David had many familities. Joseph had sprung from one of them whose ancestor had been Solomon. From another whose ancestor had been Nathan the brother of Solomon by Bathsheba (1 Chron 3.5.) had sprung Mary. From another sprang Hillel and his house, whose ancestor had been | Shephatiah, the son of Abital (1 Chron 3.3), as it says in Juchasin folio 19.b.

Kabbalist Catechumen It would have been a wonder if they had not been a remnant of those Sons of David who are mentioned in Neh 8. 2, and also in 1 Chron 3.17–24 and Ezra 2, 21 (compared with Neh 7.26).

In a field stable etc. b'wry'

Kabbalist Catechumen Why do you translate it like that?

Christian The word here does *not* denote a manger, but rather a shelter, in this case in a field and also [perhaps] in a cave, for the flocks of the place which otherwise used to live [in the open] in the fields. These places were constructed there in the fields for the sake of the sheep, so that they might more safely shelter there | from the bad weather. In support of this meaning:

1. is the case of Esth 6.11, where the Second Aramaic Targum[136] says: "And he entered" *l'wry' dmlk'* "into the stable of the King and took a horse which was standing *bryš 'wry'* in the first stall in the stable". And ibid. verse 10

---

[135] Correction above the line: Cabb. Cat. replaced by Christianus (as a consequence of the previous correction).

[136] The *Targum Sheni* to Esther is an exuberant midrash of uncertain date but with similarities to Quranic material. An English translation may be found in Paulus Cassel, *An Explanatory Commentary on Esther* (Edinburgh: T. & T. Clarke, 1888), appendix I, pp. 263–344.

לאוריא in Equile Regis, & accipito inde Equum regium, qui stat דאוריתא | ברש. In principali loco stabuli.

(2.) Eodem sensu hæc vox etiam adhibetur in Hebraico 2. Par. 9, 25. ubi de Salomone dicitur: ויהי לשלמה ארבעת אלפים אריות סוסים Et fuerunt Salomoni quatuor millia stabula equorum. Qui procul dubio sustentati fuerunt in magnis Desertorum pascuis, ubi in usum eorundem destinata fuerunt stabula hæc, | pro denis singula; quod patebit conferenti locum 1. Reg. 4, 26.

(3.) Eodem[137] vocis acceptio etiam occurrit 2. Par. 32, 28. Ubi de Chiskiah dicitur, quod sibi fecerit ארות לכל בהמה ובהמה stabula pro quibusvis pecudibus ועדרים לאורות Et greges ad stabula. Ubi etiam in Græco reperitur vox φάτνη. Et hæc stabula, atque caulæ in desertis fuerunt, ubi pascuorum abundantia. | Conf. Joh. 6, 10; Matth. 14, 13. 15; Luc. 15, 4.

(4.) Sic & Jobi 39, 9. Nunquid volet רים (quæ est Caprea bicornis quæ utroque cornu ferit obvios, vid. Deut. 33, 17. ubi duo cornua denotant duas tribus. Consentiuntque & Arabes, quibus Rim est caprea inter Arabiæ arenas degens procera, summi candoris, capite & auribus plerumque sursum erectis, tam multa | sagina differta, ut caprearum ovis inde dicatur. Bochartus Hierozoici præf. l. 3. c. 27.) servire tibi? An pernoctabit (in Chaldaico) על אורותך ad stabula tua campestria? Jumentorum instar.

(5.) Eodem sensu hæc vox Urja etiam accipitur in Talmudico Tractatu Moed Katon fol. 10. b. ubi sermo est de erectione leviorum structurarum, quas in mediis | majorum festivitatum diebus peragere liceat: interque illas etiam referuntur hæc stabula, his verbis: & ad ædificandum אוריא stabula campestria; molas trusatiler &c.[138] |||

(6.) Sic in Tractatu Erubin fol. 55. b. inter similia campestria etiam referuntur אוריות stabula campestria & granaria, quæ sunt in Agris.

(7.) [Christianus.][139] Adde quod & Latina vox Præsepia eodem in sensu adhibita quondam fuerit, ut cum Virgilius dicit Æneid. 7.[140]

Stabant ter centum nitidi in præsepibus altis.

---

137 Correction: eodem replaced by eadem
138 In the right bottom corner appears a Hebrew letter כ presumably an indication of binding or pagination.
139 Deletion: Christianus. The change of speaker initially intended is no longer needed. The speech remains with the Christian.
140 Reference to the same appears *supra*, footnote 68, p. 158.
141 The Orientalist Samuel Bochart (1599–1667) was an illustrious scholarly representative of the French Reformed Church, and a pastor at Caen. A student of both Erpenius and Huet he wrote *Geographia Sacra seu Phaleg et Canaan* (Caen: Pierre de Cardonel, 1646) and his *Hierozoicon sive bipartium opus de animalibus Sacrae Scripturae*, 2 vols (London: Thomas Roycroft, 1663). Both were extensively used thereafter. The *Hierozoicon*

SECTION VIII 453

[that] he went into the stable of the King and had from there a royal horse, which stood *bryš* | *d'wryt'* "in the first stall of the stable".

2. the same meaning of this word also occurs in the Hebrew of 2 Chron 9.25 where it says of Solomon *wyhy lšlmh 'rb't 'lpym 'rywt* [vocalised *'uryôt*] *śuśym* "And Solomon had four thousand stalls for horses". The horses doubtless were kept in the large desert pastures and it was for their use these stables were intended, | one for every ten which can be seen by comparing 1 Kgs 4.26.

3. The same meaning of the word also occurs 2 Chron 32.28 where it is said of Hezekiah that "he made for himself *'rywt* [vocalised *uryôt*] *lkl bhmh wbhmh* stalls for various kinds of cattle *w'drym l'wrwh* and stalls for the flocks". Here the Greek has the word *phatnē* and these stalls and sheep-folds were in the desert where there were many flocks | Cf. Jn 6.10; Mt 14.13, 15; Lk 15.4.

4. thus also Job 39.9 "Will the *rym* consent [to serve you]" (This is the two-horned wild goat which strikes those it meets with either horn see Deut 33.17 where two horns denote two tribes. The Arabs concur, for whom a *rim* is a goat which lives in the sands of Arabia, lofty, very white, with its head and ears upright and erect and loaded with so much | meat that they call it "the sheep of the goats". *Bochartus Hierozoici*[141] praef. Book 3 c. 27). [Will it consent] to serve you? [means] "Will it stay by your field stall [Aramaic *'l 'wrwtk*] at night?" [as the stock does].

5. the same meaning of this word *urja* [Cf. *uryôt* above] is also found in Talmud Tract Mo'ed Qatan folio 10b where there is talk of erecting light structures in which it might be permitted to stay during | the greater feast days. Amongst these are also mentioned these stalls in these words: "and for building of *'wry'* country stalls, grindstones etc …" ‖

fol. 40ᵛ

6. Thus in Tract. Eruvin folio 55b, amongst similar field furniture, [one finds] *'wry'*, field stalls, and granaries which are in the fields mentioned.

7. Add the consideration that also the Latin word *praesepia* was once used in the same sence as when Virgil says in Book 7 [line 275] of the Aeneid | "*stabant ter centum nitidi in praesepibus altis*" "Three thousand resplendent animals were standing in the high stalls".

---

continues the tradition of Pliny the Elder, Conrad Gesner's *Historiae Animalium* and the inventive etymologies of Isidore of Seville. But Bochart was also an Arabist, having studied Queen Christina's Arabic manuscripts in Stockholm in 1652. He makes extensive and innovative use of the Arabic naturalists al-Damîrî and al-Qazwini as well as Hebrew and Syriac sources. The reference here is to *Partis primae Lib III De feris Quadrupeditis cap.* 27 which is devoted to the *rym* or *rim*.

(8.) Sic & apud Varronem de re Rustica lib. 9. ut citat Nonius: Contrà illic laudabatur Villa, si habeat culinam rusticam unam, præsepiam latam, cellam vinariam. Ubi Præsepia est stabulum, in quo equi, muli, & cætera id genus animalia continentur:

(9.) Ut & Apes, apud Virgilium Georgic. 4. Ignavum fucos pecus â | Præsepibus arcent.

(10.) Imò & homines vilioris conditionis, ut apud Horatium lib. 1. Ep[i], 16. Scurra vagus, non qui certum Præsepe teneret.

[Cabb. Cat.][142]Sensus ergò historiæ hujus breviter est hic: Josephus & Maria Bethlehemum venientes, in extremâ oppidi, muris haud quaquam cincti, (Joh. 7, 42.) domo, quippe quàm primum offenderant, secundum antiquum hospitalitatis | jus, diverterant, (quod Hebræis non fuisse inusitatum exempla docent Jos. 2, 15; Act. 9, 25; Act. 10, 6. conf. Heb. 13, 1; 1. Pet. 4, 9; 1. Tim. 5, 10; c. 3, 2; Tit. 1, 8; 3. Joh. v. 5; Matth. 25, 35.) Ubi cum plures divertissent hospites, nec locus esset puerperæ; in stabulum hoc campestre, in proximâ adornatum speluncâ discessit Maria: Unde & Pastoribus Angelus nunciat, Puellum repositum | esse in stabulo campestri; quem locum tanquam satis sibi cognitum illi in vallem descendentes, mox etiam reperiebant.[143] Animalia autem[144] tunc in eo fuisse, verisimile non est, quia & ovium greges sub dio agebant. Locus autem Chabac. 3, 2. unde juxta textum Græcum opinio illa fluxisse videtur, quod Dominus inter bovem, & asinum recubuerit, sensum tamen non suppeditat, qui in Græco | legitur: ἐν μέσῳ δύο ζῴων γνωσθήσῃ &c. in medio duorum animalium cognosceris. Sed verba illa

יהוה פעלך בקרב שנים חייהו בקרב שנים תודיע ברגז רחם תזכור ita vertenda sunt: Domine opus tuum in medio ruboris (excandescentiæ;) vivifica: in medio ruboris (iracundiæ) notum te fac: in ira misericordiæ recorderis.

---

142 Deletion: Cabb. Cat. The change of speaker initially intended is cancelled.
143 Added in the left margin but then crossed out: In spelunca autem natum esse Salvatorem ex Patrum etiam traditis notum est. Sed
144 Deleted word.
145 Wallace M. Lindsay, *Nonius Marcellus' Dictionary of Republican Latin* (Oxford, Parker, 1901).

SECTION VIII

8. Also in Varro *On Agriculture* Book 9, as cited in Nonius [Marcellus' Dictionary of Republican Latin¹⁴⁵], *"Contra illic laudabatur Villa si habeat culinam sufficum unam, praesepiam latam, cella vinariam"*. "On the other hand, a Farm is praised if it has one adequate kitchen, a wide stall and a wine-cellar". Here a *praesepia* is a stable in which horses, mules and other similar animals are housed.

9. The word is also used in this sense for bees in Virgil's Georgics 4, [168] *"ignavum fucos pecus a praesepibus arcent"*. "[The bees] | drive from their hives [*a praesepibus*] the drones, a lazy bunch".

10. It is also used for people of low estate as in Horace's Epistles, Book 1. [Letter] 15 [line 28]: *"scurra vagus, non qui certum praesepe teneret"*. "A wandering tramp, with no certain stall".

So the meaning of the narrative briefly is this: Joseph and Mary coming to Bethlehem, on the outskirts of the entirely unwalled town (Jn 7.42), had turned aside into a house, no doubt the first they came across, according to the ancient law of hospitality | (that this was not unusual among the Hebrews is shown by the examples of Jos 2.15; Acts 9.25; Acts 10.6. Cf. Heb 13.1; 1 Pet 4.9; 1 Tim 5.10; 3.2; Tit 1.8; 3 Jn 5; Mt 25.35). When many other guests had turned aside into the house and there was no room there to give birth, Mary left the house for this field stall, set up in a near-by cave. When the Angel made his announcement to the shepherds, the boy had been placed | in the field stall. The place was well enough known to them, and coming down into the valley they soon found it¹⁴⁶. It is not very likely that the animals were in the stall at the time, because flocks of sheep live outside. Hab. 3.2 in the Greek version seems to be the source of the belief that the Lord was laid between an ox and an ass, but this is not the meaning of what is written there [in Greek]: | *eni mesōi duo zōōn gnōthēsē etc.* "you will be recognised in the middle of two animals". But the Hebrew words *yhwh pʻlk bqrb šnym ḥyyhw bqrb šnym twdyʻ brgz rḥm tzkwr* should be translated as follows: "Lord, Revive your work in the midst of redness (irascibility), in the midst of redness (anger) make yourself known: in wrath remember mercy"¹⁴⁷.

---

146 Added and then deleted: "One notes that also according to Patristic tradition the Saviour was born in a cave. But ...". As the topic is taken up again below, the deletion merely avoids repetition.
147 The meaning of the Greek version of this difficult verse is quite different from the Hebrew. The Septuagint translation of Hab 3:2b contains an additional phrase not in the Hebrew: "You will be known between two living creatures". (For the Greek

[**Cabb. Cat.**][148] Sed in Græco Locus ille ubi diverterant vocatur καταλύμα, quasi â solutis jumentis; ergò ad minimùm asellus adfuit, quo vecta erat Maria.

[**Christianus.**][149] Non sequitur: Hac voce enim quilibet vocatur locus, ubi quis divertit[150] ut Marc. 14, 14; Luc. 22, 11. conf. Luc. 19, 7. Atque sic etiam vox Syriaca שרא, quæ alias solvendi habet significationem, divertendi | sensum habet Luc. 9, 12; Act. 28, 23; c. 10, 6.

V. 8. *Pastores autem* &c. רעותא דין

Cabb. Cat. *Hùc pertinet notabilis ille Locus Jonathanis F. Uziel in Targum ad Gen. 35, 21. ubi hac utitur paraphrasi: Et profectus Jacob extendit tabernaculum suum ultra Turrim Eder, (sive Gregis:) loco,* | *in quo manifestaturus est se Rex Messias in fine dierum.*

Christianus. In vicinia enim Bethlehemitici oppidi erat Turris Eder, ibid. v. 19. conf. Mich. 4, 8. cum c. 5, 1.

Habakkuk, see James A.E. Mulroney, *The Translation Style of the Old Greek Habakkuk* (Tübingen: Mohr Siebeck, 2016)). Methodius was evidently aware of the two versions of verse 2b and combined them: the "two living creatures" in the Greek referred to "cherubim" (Ex 25:22), and the reference to "years" [*šnym*] in the Hebrew suggested the Second Advent. (Methodius, "Oration Concerning Simeon and Anna on the Day That They Met in the Temple", in Alexander Roberts and James Donaldson (eds.) (rev. A. Cleveland Coxe), § 4; *The Ante-Nicene Fathers: Translations of the Writings of the Fathers Down to AD 325*, 10 vols (Eerdmans, Grand Rapids, 1956–1962 [1885–1896]) vol. 6, pp. 385–386).

The ox and the ass derive from Hab 3:2b and Isa 1:3. They are identified in Isa 1:3, but located on either side of baby Jesus in Hab 3:2 (LXX). The fifth-century Gospel of Pseudo-Matthew (a Latin adaptation of the Proto-Evangelium of Pseudo-James) chapter 14 sees the animals as the fulfillment of Habakkuk: *"And on the third day after the birth of our Lord Jesus Christ, the most blessed Mary went forth out of the cave, and entering a stable, placed the child in the stall, and the ox and the ass adored Him. Then was fulfilled that which was said by Isaiah the prophet, saying: The ox knoweth his owner and the ass his master's crib.* [2] *The very animals, therefore, the ox and the ass, having Him in their midst, incessantly adored Him. Then was fulfilled that which was said by Abacuc the prophet, saying:* [3] *Between two animals thou art made manifest. In the same place Joseph remained with Mary three days."* (*The Ante-Nicene Fathers*, vol. 8, pp. 368–384 at p. 375). However many of the Fathers do not take the Greek verse in this sense at

Kabbalist Catechumen But in the Greek the place into which they turned aside is called a *kataluma* as if meaning *"loosening* [the bridles of] the animals", so at least there was the ass there, on which Mary had travelled.

Christian It does not follow. For this word can indicate a place where someone turns aside and *loosens* their baggages as in Mk 14.14; Lk 22.11. Cf. Lk 19.7. And so also the Syriac word *šrʾ* (which elsewhere means loosing) has the meaning of | "turn aside" in Lk 9.12; Acts 28.23; 10.6.[151]

Verse 8

And Shepherds etc. *rʿwtʾ dyn*

Kabbalist Catechumen Relevant here is the notable passage of Jonathan Ben Uziel in his Targum on Gen 35.21 where this translation appears: "Jacob set out and pitched his tent beyond the Tower of Eder (or 'of the flock') | where at the end of days Messiah will appear".

Christian The Tower of Eder was in the neighbourhood of the town of Bethlehem (ibid., verse 19. Cf. Mic 4.8 with 5.1).[152]

---

all. In his translation of the Hebrew, Knorr renders the repeated word *šnym* as "red", a meaning the word has elsewhere. He then takes this metaphorically as "anger". It is more frequently taken here as meaning "years", so the Vulgate "*annos*".

148 Correction: Christianus replaced by Cabb. Cat., which involves the two speakers being changed over in the following exchange.

149 Correction: Cabb. Cat. replaced by Christian. (as a consequence of the previous correction).

150 Added in the right margin: & sarcinam solvit

151 The description of the semantic range of the Greek word is supported by finding a similar range in a Syriac word.

152 Lightfoot, *Miscellanies and the Harmony of the Gospels*, op. cit., p. 188: "It hath been held, that these shepherds were about the tower of Edar, Gen.xxxv.21: and that this was about a mile from Beth-lehem."

Qui ibi degebant &c. דשרין הוו תמן

Christianus. Nimirum sub dio juxta Textum Græcum.

 Cabb. Cat. *In Mischna ult. cap. ult. Tractatûs Jom tof, hæc traduntur:* Non potant ante mactationem pecudes eremi: sed potant ante mactationem domesticas[153]. Istæ autem sunt domesticæ, quæ pernoctant in urbe: pecudes eremi, quæ pernoctant in pascuo. *Ubi notetur vox* אפר *quæ pascuum significat: unde nomen traxisse videtur Ephrata, Bethlehemi cognomen;* | *quod ager illius loci pascuis abundaret. 1. Sam. 17, 13. Adhæc Gemara ibid. fol.* 4[o].*a.* Istæ sunt pecudes deserti, quæcunque exeunt Paschatis tempore, & pascuntur in pascuis; intrantque sub pluviam primam; (*tempore scilicet mensis Marchesuan, cujus pars una Octobrem, altera Novembrem tetigit.*) Et istæ sunt domesticæ, quæ ||| cunque exeunt, & pascuntur extra terminum (scil. Sabbathicum) & redeunt & pernoctant intra terminum. Rabbi inquit. Ambæ hæ sunt domesticæ; verum istæ sunt pecudes deserti, quæcunque exeunt & pascuntur in pascuo, nec reducuntur ad loca habitata, nec æstivo, nec pluviarum tempore. Hæc ibi.

fol. 41ʳ

 Ex quibus id saltem colligere licet, quod si verba illa de Ovium quoque gregibus, & non de bubulo saltem genere intelligenda sunt, sub dio pastores noctu non manserint, post Octobris finem.

V. 9. *Angelus Dei* &c. מלאכא דאלהא

[**Cabb. Cat.**][154] *Quem hoc loco intelligeres Angelum?*

[**Christianus.**][155] Si ad Zachariam, Gabriel; Luc. 1, 11.19. ad Mariam Michaël, ib. v. 26. ad Josephum pro medela suspicionis ejus Raphaël Matth. 1, 20. missus esse statueretur: (quippe qui etiam referri solet ad Regni gradum, quo & somnia pertinent, vid. Pneumatic. Cabbalist. c.3.§.5.[156] & c.5.§.4.[157]) &

---

153 In error. Should be domesticæ
154 Correction: Christianus replaced by Cabb. Cat., which involves the two speakers being changed over in the following exchange.
155 Correction: Cabb. Cat. replaced by Christian. (as a consequence of the previous correction).
156 "Quod etiam innuit R. Jizchak Lorjah, dum inquit: quod Malchuth quando vestitur tribus mundis inferioribus intra illos extendatur sub figura lit. ה Tetragrammati, quæ dividatur in duas literas ד & ו: quibus denotentur duo Cherubim, masculus & fœmina: Metatron nempe per ו, & Sandalphon per ד. Cumque conjungantur, contineant in sese tres mundos hôc modo: ut capita eorum relinquantur in mundo Briah, sintque illius anima; Corpora autem cum sex extremis existant in mundo Jezirah; & membra generationis extendantur in mundo Asiah, sintque illius Nephesch. Ubi porrò adducitur textus è cap. IV, capitulorum R. Elieser, ubi ad Orientem locat Hominem; ad Austrum

SECTION VIII 459

Who were abiding there etc. *dšryn hww tmn*

Christian In the open, according to the Greek text[158].

Kabbalist Catechumen In the Mishnah, in the last chapter of the Tractate Yom Tov, the following is handed down: The flocks of the desert do not drink before slaughter, but domesticated flocks do drink before they are slaughtered. Domesticated flocks are those which spend the night in a town, the flocks of the desert are those who spend the night in the pastures. Note the [Hebrew] word *'pr* here which means "pasture". Ephrata, the epithet of Bethlehem, | seems to derive from this word, because the countryside there abounds in pastures 1 Sam 17.13. On these things the Gemarah, ibid. folio 40a has: The flocks of the desert are those which go out at the time of Passover, graze in the pastures and come back with the first rain (that is the time of month Marcheshwan [or Cheshwan], which falls between October and November). Domesticated flocks are those which ‖ go out and feed outside the Sabbath boundary and return and spend the night inside the boundary. Rabbi [Judah] said: "Both of these are domesticated flocks, but the flocks of the desert are those which go out and eat in the pasture and are not brought back to inhabited areas, either in the summer or in the rainy season". Thus far the quotation. | From which it can be gathered, that if these words are also to be understood as concerning flocks of sheep and not just about cows, the shepherds did not stay under the open sky at night after the end of October.

fol. 41ʳ

Verse 9
The Angel of God etc. *ml'k' d'lh'*

Kabbalist Catecumen Who do you think the Angel is here?

Christian If Gabriel was sent to Zachariah (Lk 1.11, 19), Michael to Mary (ibid., verse 26), then Raphael can be thought to have been sent to Joseph

---

Leonem; ad Boream Bovem; ad Occasum Aquilam. In Sohar autem & ab omnibus Cabbalistis Michaël & facies Leonis ad Austrum & dextram, cum litera ʼ & aqua; Gabriel & facies Bovis ad Boream & sinistram, cum He primo & igne; Uriel & facies Aquilæ ad Orientem, & antrorsum cum ו & aëre; & Raphaël & facies hominis ad Occidentem, & retrorsum ponuntur cum He ultimo & terra: Quibus adjunguntur Metatron, tanquam summus Capitaneus; & Sandalphon, tanquam secundus ab eo, quingentis milliaribus, i.e. gradibus sociis suis altior." ("Pneumatica Kabbalistica [...] Domus Dei", op. cit., p. 222).

157 Cf. *supra*, footnote 30, p. 224.
158 Greek: *agraulountes*.

Angelus hic, qui pastoribus apparuit, Uriel fuisse diceretur, qui à luce nomen habet, jam | tota exhausta esset Mercava, sive Thronus Messiæ, cum ministris suis primariis: cumque hactenus ministrassent Bos, Leo & Aquila; jam cum Homo factus esset Messias Homo Angelicus ministrasse dici posset: & quidem cum magna illa luce, unde Nomen gerit; ubi si insimul consideretur statio ejus ad Orientem relata; orientem nunc illam lucem significasse videtur, quæ illuminat | omnem hominem venientem in mundum. Dicitur autem Syro Angelus Dei, ut Tetragrammati nomen perinde ab antiquis, sive per lectionem אדני sive per lectionem אלהים, Messiæ tributum fuisse appareat: quippe qui omninò etiam intelligitur, cum Gloria Domini resplenduisse super Pastores dicitur: & quidem in Aëre, elemento analogo Tetragrammato & Urieli. | Conf. Ezech. 1, 28; c. 3, 23; c. 8, 4; c. 10, 4.

V. 10. *Ne timeatis* &c. לא תדחלון

Cabb. Cat. *Quartum hoc est monitum Angelicum contra Timorem conf. Luc. 1, 13.30. & Matth. 1, 20.*

Christianus. Ut edoceamur Regnum filiationis non in timore consistere, | sed in fiducia hilari. Rom. 8, 15; 2. Tim. 1, 7.

Ego Evangelizo vobis &c. מסבר אנא לכון

Christianus. Quare vobis? De fœce plebis hominibus? Quod mirum foret, nisi mysterium subesset.

Cabb. Cat. *Ego hîc suspicarer Patriarcharum Davidisque Nizzuzoth | seu scintillas in his delituisse, qui Pastores omnes fuerant. Et quia cum illis Deus fœdus antiquum pepigerat, quid absurdum, si iisdem, fœdus novum prima*

---

159 Raphael's name means "God heals".
160 These are the four faces of the Cherubim on the chariot-throne in Ezekiel. On biblical Cherubim, see Alice Woods, *Of Wings and Wheels. A Synthetic Study of Biblical Cherubim* (Berlin, De Gruyter, 2008). This throne becomes an important focus for subsequent speculation. From an enormous bibliography: Gershom G. Scholem, *Jewish Gnosticism, Merkabah Mysticism and Talmudic Tradition* (New York: Jewish Theological Seminary Press, 2015); David J. Halperin, *The Merkabah in Rabbinic Literature* (New Haven: American Oriental Society, 1980); Timo Eskola, *Messiah and the Throne: Jewish Merkabah Mysticism and the Early Exaltation Discourse* (Tübingen: Mohr Siebeck, 2001).
161 This is a reference to Jn 1.9.

as a *cure*[159] for his doubt (Mt 1.20). He is also associated with [the degree] Kingdom to which dreams are linked (see *Pneumatica Cabbalistica*, 3, §5 etc. 5, §4). The Angel who appeared to the shepherds may be said to be Uriel who gets his name from [the Hebrew word for] "light". At this time | the Merkhabah, or Messiah's Throne, with his chief ministers was totally drained. Previously the Ox, the Lion and the Eagle[160] had ministered, but now the Man had been made Messiah, the Angelic Man could be said to have ministered and [to have done so] with that great light from which he derived his name. If also his station is considered to be related to the East, he would now seem to have signified that rising light which illuminates | every man who comes into the world[161]. He is called in the Syriac, the "Angel of the Lord", as the Tetragrammaton name (pronounced either as "*adonai*" or "*elohim*") appears from antiquity to have been applied to Messiah. This is to be fully understood, when it says the Glory of the Lord shone over the shepherds, and in the Air, an element related to both the Tetragrammaton and Uriel. | Cf. Ezek 1.28; 3.23; 8.4; 10.4.

Verse 10
Be not afraid etc. *l' tdḥlwn*

Kabbalist Catechumen This is the fourth angelic warning against fear (Cf. Lk 1.13, 30; Mt 1.20).
    Christian So that we should learn that the Kingdom of Sonship does not consist of fear, | but of joyful trust (Rm 8.15; 2 Tim 1.7).

I declare unto you etc. *mśbr 'n' lkwn*

Christian Why "to you", to men from the dregs of the people?[162] It would be a wonder if some secret teaching were not hidden here.
    Kabbalist Catechumen I would suspect here that *Nitsutsot* | or sparks of the Patriarchs and of David, who were all shepherds, were hidden in these men. And because God had made the Old Covenant with shepherds, how

---

162 Shepherds at times enjoyed a poor reputation: Philo, *On Husbandry* 61: "shepherds are considered mean and inglorious". F.H. Colston and G.H. Whitaker, *Philo in Ten Volumes. Loeb edition* (London: Heinemann, 1988), vol. 3. *On Husbandry* (*De Agricultura*) is found on pp. 108–207. The passage quoted is found in Greek and English pp. 139–141. Later in the Talmud they were considered disreputable, lax with repect to cleanness, likely to steal and inadmissible as witnesses in court. Knorr wishes to counter this prejudice in the case of these shepherds.

nunc habere fundamenta, cœlitus primò innotuisset? Quatuor autem fuisse videntur, pro quatuor noctis vigiliis, de quibus Thren[163]. *2, 19; Luc. 12, 38; Matth. 14, 25; Ex. 14, 24.*

Toti mundo. לכלה עלמא   40

Cabb. Cat. *Ita videtur originaliter dixisse Angelus: Scriptorem autem Græcum habuisse exemplar Fragmenti hujus, Syriacè primùm conscripti: (sic enim consignatæ primum fuisse videntur historiæ istæ, ut ê pluribus fragmentis, de hinc contexeretur volumen unicum.) Ubi pro* עלמא *legerit |* עמא *populo, non quidem cum sensu extensionis pro omni natione; sed potius cum restrictione ad populum Iisraëliticum, ut Joh. 11, 50; Act. 2, 47; c. 10, 41; Heb. 9, 19.*   45

Christianus. *Sicut autem verus est sensus Textus Græci; ita nihil est falsi in ||| Syriaco.*

fol. 41ᵛ

Cabb. Cat. *Imò Argumentum etiam hinc desumtum pro animarum revolutione, multò est amplius. Si enim Messiæ beneficia ad restitutionem non totius populi saltem, sed potius mundi tendunt; necesse est, ut & illorum | Animæ, qui demortui jam fuerant, in vitam redeant, quô ista beneficia ipsis innotescere queant.*   5

V. 11. *Natus est vobis* &c. אתיליד לכון

Christianus. *Vobis hîc dicitur in ampliatione; ut subintelligantur omnes, ad quos pertineat prædictum gaudium.*

Cabb. Cat. *Ita tamen, ut usus fit dispar: Patrum scilicet, ut perfectionem quàm proximè adipiscerentur Heb. 11, 40. Populi, atque mundi autem, ut suis gradibus paulatim nunc etiam restituantur.*   10

---

[163] Modern critical editions of the Vulgate call the book *Lamentationes*, but the traditional *Editio Clementina* has *Threni id est Lamentationes Jeremiae Prophetae*, thus preserving the name *threnoi* of the LXX.

[164] Lightfoot, *Miscellanies and the Harmony of the Gospels*, op. cit., p. 198: "The patriarchs, to whom Christ was more especially promised, were of this vocation, especially Abraham and David, to whom the promise was more clearly made; peculiarly David, who was feeding sheep near to Beth-lehem, when he was taken a father and type of Christ.

appropriate, if to similar shepherds was made the first heavenly announcement of the initial foundations of the New Covenant.[164] There seem to have been four shepherds, one for each watch of the night.[165] On these [watches], see Lam 2.19; Lk 12.38; Mt 14.25; Ex 14.24.

To the whole world lklh 'lm'

Kabbalist Catechumen This appears to have been what the Angel originally said [in Syriac]. The Greek [Gospel] writer had a copy of this fragment which had first been written in Syriac (For it seems that these accounts were first written down in this way and then a whole book was woven together from many fragments[166]) in which instead of *'lm'* "world" | he read *'m'* "people" and not with the sense of embracing all nations, but rather with a meaning restricted to the people of the Israelites (as in Jn 11.50; Acts 2.47; 10.41; Heb 9.19).

Christian So, just as the Greek text is true, there is nothing false in ||| the Syriac.   fol. 41ᵛ

Kabbalist Catechumen There is a much greater argument for the reincarnation of souls to be drawn from here. For if the benefits of Messiah extend to the restitution not of the whole people only, but rather of the [whole] world, then it is necessary that the souls of those | who had already died should return to life, so that these benefits can be made known to them.

Verse 11

There is born to you etc. *'tyld lkwn*

Christian "To you" is said in the widest sense, so that everyone may understand to whom belongs the promised joy.

Kabbalist Catechumen In such a way, however, that it will be appropriated differently: the perfection of the Fathers was obtained as soon as possible (Heb 11.40), but that of the people and of the [whole] world will be restored little by little in their stages.

  And it doth illustrate the exactness of the performance the more, and doth harmonize with the giving of it the better, when to shepherds it is first revealed, as to shepherds it was first promised."

165 To deduce four shepherds from four watches of the night is a bold move.
166 Such possibilities were envisaged as early as Papias' remarks.

Salvator &c. פרוקא

Cabb. Cat. *Hoc nomine in Sohar vocatur ille, qui Animam | defuncti fratris ê statu mortis liberat inque vitam reducit.* Vide Excerpta Cent. 1, Loc. 54. n. 21. sqq. *Eademque vox in Chaldaico hoc sensu occurrit* Ruth. 4, 6.4.3.1. conf. c. 3, 9. & c. 2, 20. &c. *Deinde simili appellatione in Chaldaico etiam vocatur, qui liberat fratrem ê servitute* Lev. 25, 26 *item qui liberat animam delinquentis ê reatu,* Num. 5, 5. *item qui liberat | animam occisi ab idea vindictæ, & â vinculo sanguinis.* Num. 35, 19.21.24.25.27. &c.

Christianus. Ita igitur hoc loco Messias etiam vocatur Reductor in vitam, in libertatem, in innocentiam, in quietem; uno verbo in restitutionem.

Dominus Messias &c. מריא משיחא

Cabb. Cat. *Pro eo, quod communiter dicebant* מלכא משיחא, *Rex Messias;* [*haud*[167] *sæpius occurrit in scriptis gentis nostræ &* Luc. 23, 2.] *Angelus ipsum vocat Divino Nomine, nimirum* Adonai, *sub quo intelligitur Tetragrammaton.*

Christianus. Annon huc etiam pertinet locus Act. 2, 36?

In civitate David. במדינתה דדויד

[**Christianus.**][168] Id est, intra terminum Sabbathi Bethlehemiticum.[169] [**Cabb. Cat.**][170] *Sic enim exponitur locus* Ex. 16, 29. *Ne exeat ullus ê loco suo septimo die: id est, juxta Targum Jonathanis. Non egrediatur quisquam ê loco | suo ad deambulandum nisi duo millia passuum.*

Christianus. Nimirum hæc efficiebant suburbium, Num. 35, 5. confer Luc. 9, 31; c. 13, 33; Jos. 5, 13; c. 10, 10; Luc. 5, 12; Matth. 2, 16.

---

167 Correction above the line: haud replaced by quod
168 Correction in the left margin: Cabb. Cat. replaced by Christianus.
169 The sentence had been underlined since it was initially attributed to the Cabbalist. But after the change of speaker, the underlining has been suppressed.
170 Added in the left margin: *Cabb. Cat.* (which involves a change of speaker).

A Saviour etc. *prwqʾ*

Kabbalist Catechumen This is the word the Zohar uses for a man who liberates the soul | of his dead brother from the state of death and restores him to life. See Excerpts Cent. I Loc. 54, n. 21 *seq*. The same word in Aramaic occurs in this sense in [the Targum to] Ruth 4.6, 4, 3, 1; Cf. 3.9; 2.20 etc. Someone who liberates his brother from servitude is designated by a similar word in Aramaic in [the Targum to] Lev 25.26. Similarly, one who frees the soul of a delinquent from accusation in [the Targum to] Num 5.5. Also, one who frees | the soul of the slain from the idea of revenge and from the bond of vendetta [in the Targum to] (Num 35.19, 21, 24, 25, 27 etc.).

Christian So in summary: in this verse Messiah is called the One who returns [souls] to life, to innocence and to quietness—in a word, [who brings them] Restoration.

The Lord Messiah etc. *mryʾ mšyḥʾ*

Kabbalist Catechumen [This phrase stands for] the One who is commonly called King Messiah *mlkʾ mšyḥʾ*, (which occurs quite often in the writings of our people and at Lk 23.2). The Angel names him with the Divine Name, that is *Adonai* [Lord], by which is to be understood the Tetragrammaton.

Christian Is not Acts 2.36 also relevant here?[171]

In the city of David *bmdynth ddwyd*

Christian That is, inside the Sabbath boundaries of Bethlehem.

Kabbalist Catecumen This verse is explained by Ex 16.29: "Let no one go out from his place on the Seventh Day": that is, according to Targum Jonathan: "Let no one go out from his | place to walk around for more than 2000 paces".

Christian These surely constituted the suburbs of the town (Num 35.5 Cf. Lk 9.31; 13.33; Jos 5.13; 10.10; Lk 5.12; Mt 2.16).

---

[171] "Therefore let all the House of Israel know assuredly that God hath made that same Jesus whom ye have crucified, both Lord and Christ". Knorr indicates that he understands the word "Lord" here also to be a translation of Adonai "by which is understood the Tetragrammaton".

V. 12. *Et hoc vobis signum*: והדא לכון אתא

[**Cabb. Cat.**][172] *Quidnam propriè characteris loco est, in his verbis?*
[**Christianus.**][173] Omne id, quo non tantum hunc infantem ab aliis dignoscerent: sed ex quo etiam partum hunc judicarent fuisse miraculosum. Invenietis enim, ait, Infantem involutum fasciis â matre sua, obstetrice & doloribus carente, nec puerperarum more decumbente, sed in spelæo in quo stabulum campestre est natum jam demum puellum suum curante.

V. 13. *Conspecti sunt.* &c. אתחזי

[**Christianus.**][174] Visio est haud minor illâ quam vidit Jecheskel Propheta, unde simul apparet in Prophetarum gradum admitti hos pastores, qui ||| exhinc non existimandi sunt plebeji fuisse & illiterati: unde primi etiam fuerunt Messiæ nati præcones infra v. 17. Viderunt autem[175] Schechinam cum Throno gloriæ omnibusque Angelis ministrantibus, confer Ezech. 1, 24; c. 3, 12. [**Cabb. Cat.**][176] *Licet enim Messias natus jam esset homo; Duo tamen Gradus Animæ ejus sublimiores, | qui dicuntur Chajah & Jechidah, sive vitalitas & singularitas in superis manebant, & jam in loco Messiæ nati cum ministerio suo Angelico dignissimis hisce Animabus, sese manifestabant.*

Christianus. Fortè hinc etiam pastores dicunt, quod Dominus hæc manifestaverit ipsis infra v. 15. Porrò etiam notabilis mihi videtur vox | חילותא quæ copias denotat & exercitus, sicut & Græcum δύναμις, Conf. Mar. 13, 25; 1. Pet. 3, 22. &. Unde & in Sohar frequentissimè de Angelorum Exercitibus sermo est. conf. 1. Reg. 22, 19; Job. 25, 3.

---

172   Correction in the left margin: Christianus replaced by Cabb. Cat. (which involves the two speakers being changed over in the following exchange).
173   Correction: Cabb. Cat. replaced by Christianus (as a consequence of the previous correction).
174   Correction in the left margin: Cabb. Cat. replaced by Christianus
175   Added in the right margin: (ut patet è v.9.)
176   Added in the right margin: Cabb. Cat. (which involves a change of speaker).
177   That Mary was delivered without pain is found in Gregory of Nyssa's *Homily on the Nativity* and in Jerome's *Homily* on the same topic. Also, in Aquinas *Summa theologica*, III q. 35 a 6. It is the traditional teaching of the Catechism of the Council of Trent. The Woman's travail and pain in Rev 12.2 is explained otherwise. An un-named midwife and compagnion of Salome is mentioned in the *Proto-evangelium of James* and they both appear in Orthodox icons of the Nativity, though have long disappeared from Western representations.

SECTION VIII

Verse 12

And this shall be to you a sign whd' lkwn 't'

Kabbalist Catechumen What do these words mean here specifically?

Christian Not only everything by which they would recognise this infant from all others, but also that by which they would judge this birth to have been miraculous. "For you will find the infant swaddled", it says, *by his mother*. She was without a mid-wife and had suffered no pain, nor was she lying down like women who have just given birth, but was already looking after her boy who had only just been born in the cave in which was the field stall[177].

Verse 13

And they saw etc. *'tḥzy*

Christian The sight is no less than that which Ezekiel the prophet saw[178], so it becomes immediately clear that these shepherds were admitted to the status of the prophets, so ||| consequently they should not be considered to have been common and illiterate men: for this reason they were also the first heralds of the new-born Messiah infra verse 17. For they saw (as verse 9 shows) the Shekhinah with the Throne of Glory and all the ministering angels. Cf. Ezek 1.24; 3.12.

fol. 42ʳ

Kabbalist Catechumen For although Messiah had now been born a man, the two higher parts of his soul | (called Chayah and Yechidah, or Vitality and Individuality) remained in heaven and now in the place where Messiah was born with his angelic ministers they revealed themselves to these most worthy souls.[179]

Christian Perhaps for this reason too the shepherds say that God had revealed these things to them below in verse 15. The [Syriac] word | *ḥylwt'* which means "forces" and "armies" (just like the Greek [word] *dunamis* Cf. Mk 13.25; 1 Pet 3.22 etc.) seems noteworthy to me. There is frequent mention in the Zohar of the armies of angels Cf. 1 Kgs 22.19; Job 25.3.

---

178   Ezek 1.4–28; 10.1–22.
179   The Glory is here apparently described as the Shekhinah on Messiah's Throne, the Merkavah, and the brightness of the two sublime degrees of the Soul of Messiah—Chayah and Yechidah. For a similar double explanation of the Magi's star, see on Mt 2.2 at folios 46ᵛ/47ʳ and on Mt 2.9 at folio 48ᵛ.

Laudantes Deum &c. כד משבחין לאלהא

[**Cabb. Cat.**][180] *Quis hic laudatur, & qua emphasi?*

[**Christianus.**][181] Messias intelligitur qui laudatus fuit ab Angelis, & hic vocatur Nomine Elohim; sicut eidem laudes canebantur â Seraphinis Jes. 6, 3; Joh. 12, 41. & â Cherubinis Ezech. 3, 12. coll. cum. c. 1, 26. conf. Heb. 1, 6. Sermo autem, quo usi sunt Angeli, procul dubio fuit Hebræus, quia juxta nostrates[182] Angeli non curant linguam Targumicam, Sohar Gen. Cremon. | c. 33. ad Jer. 10, 11. multò minus Syriacam juxta Tractatum Talmudicum Schabbath f. 12.b. &. Sota f. 33. a. Et tamen intellectus fuit â Pastoribus: unde iterum apparet eosdem non fuisse illiteratos. Si ergò examinem Canticum hoc Angelicum juxta linguam Hebraicam, sensum simul scrutatus Cabbalisticum, quia non nisi profundiora asscribi possunt | summis hisce spiritibus: vix errabo, si dixerim, quod nihil hæc verba præse ferunt, quam acclamationem encomiasticam ad Messiam; hujus sensus; Tu qui modo nasceris es, Gloria Deo in Excelsis; & super Terram pax; & opinio bona hominibus; i.e. Tu es horum causa: hic enim propriè dici possunt laudasse. Idemque sensus etiam occurrit | etiam[183] in Acclamatione illa Luc. 19, 38. Benedictus qui venit. Rex in nomine Domini: (qui est) Pax in cœlis, & gloria in excelsis. Conf. Eph. 2, 14; c. 1, 5. Hoc autem innuunt; Duplicem nunc pro emittendo Influxu abundantissimo institui copulam, (vide Lexicon Cabbalist. p. 305.[184] & locum ê Libro Sohar ibidem allegata.) nimirum inter Patrem & Matrem; | (nam כבוד seu Gloria est cognomen Matris supernæ, quando influxum habet â Sapientia seu Patre, vide Lexicon Cabbalisticum f. 464.[185]) & inter Mal-

---

180   Correction: Christianus replaced by Cabb. Cat. (which involves the two speakers being changed over in the following exchange).
181   Correction: Cabb. Cat. replaced by Christianus (as a consequence of the previous correction).
182   Correction above the line: nostrates replaced by vestrates (as a consequence of the change of speaker).
183   Deleted word (to avoid repetition).
184   Cf. *supra*, footnote 354, p. 390.
185   "כבוד *Gloria*. Secundum Interpretes quælibet Sephirah vocatur *Gloria*, respectu proximè inferioris; unde Chochmah dicitur Gloria prima, quia hæc est Principium Aziluth. Et sic Binah vocatur כבוד עליון Gloria summa, &c. Sed hæc omnia sine ratione. Sed juxta R. Schimeon ben Jochai, כבוד est Schechinah, quatenus unitur cum Amico suo & impletur decrementum ejus, ut fiat plenilunium. Ratio est, quia maritus ejus concedit ipsi vires 32. semitarum, qui est numerus כ"בוד; & fundamentum כבוד est in Chochmâh. Non enim in omni unione vocatur כ"בוד; sed quando ornatur, & dealbatur in palatio desiderabili, cui nomen כבוד juxta Ps. 29,9. atque tunc *plenitudo totius*

SECTION VIII

Praising God etc. *kd mšbḥyn l'lh'*

Kabbalist Catechumen Who is praised here and in what respect?

Christian It is understood to be Messiah who is praised by the Angels and here is called by the name *'elohim* [God], just as praises were sung to him by Seraphim in Isa 6.3; Jn 12.41 and also by Cherubim in Ezek 3.12 compared with 1.26 Cf. Heb 1.6. The language used by the angels was doubtless Hebrew, because according to your scholars the Angels do not use the Targumic dialect (Zohar Gen. Cremona | c. 33 on Jer 10.11) much less Syriac, according to Talmud Tractate Shabbat folio 12b & Sota folio 33a. None the less [the Hebrew] was understood by the Shepherds; whence it appears that they were not illiterate. So if we examine this angelic canticle on the assumption it was sung in Hebrew, the kabbalistic meaning will thereby be preserved: for only more profound meanings can be attributed | to these most lofty spirits. I shall hardly err, if I say that these words present nothing other than an acclamation of praise to Messiah. They mean to say: "You, who have just been born, *are* 'Glory to God in the highest and over the earth peace and good will to men'": *i. e.* "You are the cause of these things" and thus they can properly be said to have praised. The same meaning occurs | in the acclamation of Lk 19.38, "Blessed is the King who comes in the name of the Lord (*who is*) peace in the heavens and glory on high". Cf. Eph 2.14; 1.5 By this they imply that a double connection is established to send forth a most abundant influx (see *Lex. Cabb.*, p. 305 and the passage from the Zohar adduced there), namely, that between the Father and the Mother | (for *kbd* or Glory is the title of the supernal Mother when she receives an influx from Wisdom, or the Father,[186] see *Lex. Cabb.*, p. 464) and also between Malkhut, which is called Earth (see

---

terræ gloriâ ejus Jesch. 6,3. Quibus similia etiam occurrunt in Sohar Bresch. ad Ps. 19,2. Deinde & Binah vocatur כבוד, quia Chochmah in ipsâ exsuscitat semitas suas: unde etiam *Domus semitarum* dicitur Pr. 8,2. Et sic etiam כבודי *Gloria mea*, refertur ad Binah, ubi כבוד denotat 32. semitas; & י״י decem dicta: & quando illa his omnibus illustrata est, dicitur כבודי. Datur autem differentia inter כבוד Gloria; & ל״ב Cor; quamvis ambo denotent 32. semitas: Nam per כבוד intelliguntur 32. semitæ supernæ, quæ sunt in Chochmah per Binah: sed לב designat 32. semitas, quæ sunt in Malchuth: prout hoc docetur in Raja Mehimna. Et in Sohar Sect. Mikkez dicitur, quod semitæ deriventur in Malchuth per Jesod, quatenus vocatur שלום pax. Pardes Tract. 23. c. 11." ("Loci communes kabbalistici", op. cit., pp. 464–465).

186   Knorr has introduced the supernal Mother previously above.

chuth, quæ vocatur Terra (vid. Lex. Cabbal. p. 156.¹⁸⁷) & Jesod, quatenus vocatur שלום Pax (vide Lex Cabbalist. p. 465.¹⁸⁸ & p. 717.¹⁸⁹) Et exhinc resultare dicitur Bona patris voluntas, sive opinio Bona | pro hominibus: ubi in Hebræo procul dubio adhibita fuit vox רצון Benevolentia, quæ egregiam hic parit allusionem cum voce ארץ terra, (de qua vide Lexic. Cabbalist. p. 157.¹⁹⁰ & in specie p. 691. sq.¹⁹¹) summamque infert â primo Luminum principio illuminationem.

V. 15. *Descendamus usque ad* &c. נרדא עדמא

Cabb. Cat. *Hinc apparet, quod in valle qualicunque situm fuerit oppidum: quodque non in illo, sed prope illud depositus fuerit puellus.* [**Christianus.**]¹⁹² Locumque hunc passim Græci Latinique Patres appellant spelæum: sic enim ‖ habet Justinus vetus Auctor: (cui eò magis credendum est, quod non procul Judæa natus & educatus fuerit, quippe Samarites: & ejus temporibus satis recens esset rei memoria:) in spelæo quodam propè oppidum divertit.

fol. 42ᵛ

---

187 "ארץ *Terra*. Simpliciter sine addito, est Schechinah, seu Malchuth, quæ instar Terræ est respectu omnium Sephirarum. Atque sic quoque traditur in Tikkunim his verbis: Postquam expositum est per verba: את השמים intelligi Modos Tiphereth & Malchuth; item per ואת Jesod & Malchuth denotari; deinceps pergit Textus dicendo הארץ *Terra*. Hoc est vas omnium: id est, receptaculum eorum omnium, quæ superius sunt. Sicut se habet Terra, quæ in se recipit, quicquid effunditur à superis. Hæc ibi. Atque hæc jam exposuimus prolixius Tractatu libri Pardes 8. Porrò & in Raja Mehimna circa hanc materiam reperiuntur sequentia: O senior, senior! Schechinah vocatur Terra. Sicut dicitur Jeschai. 66, v. 1. *Terra est scabellum pedum meorum*. Respectu Chesed gaudet nomine, &c. Respectu Gebhuræ autem dicitur *Terra*, fundus omnium. Idque ratione partis Ejusdem infimæ, quæ est notio Ipius postrema; quoad naturam interiorem scilicet, juxta quam ab omnibus simul influxum recipit. Unde Vas quoque & receptaculum omnium dicitur. [...]" (Ibid., pp. 156–157).

188 Cf. *supra*, footnote 130, pp. 331.

189 "שלום *Pax*, refertur ad Kether, quia medium tenet inter extrema. It. ad Jesod, à quo Malchuth, irâ judiciali inflammata, per influxum 32. semitarum, pacatur. It. ad Tiphereth, qui idem efficit sub notione Daath, erga gradum Binah. Tikk. Pard. vid. Soh. Mikkez 111. Tezavveh 80. Vajikra 4. Korach in pr." ("Loci communes kabbalistici", op. cit., p. 717).

190 "2. Nomine ארץ autem insignitur, quatenus istud alludit ad etymon nominis רצון, quod est *Benevolentia, Gratia*: quia est κεχαριτωμένη gratiâ (è supernis) cumulata, propter optimam illam, quam suscepit influentiam. Et hanc explicationem debemus R. Schimeoni ben Jochai, qui in Sohar, Sectione Breschith, ad locum illum Gen. 1., v. 10. *Et vocavit Deus aridam Terram*, &c. sic inquit: Et quæ erat Arida, facta est ארץ *Terra*. ארעא autem *Terra* est רעוא *gratia seu benevolentia* perfecta, quanta Ipsi convenire potest. Hæc ibi. [...]" (Ibid., p. 157).

SECTION VIII 471

Lex. Cabb., p. 156) and Yesod in as much as it is called *šlwm* or Peace (See *Lex. Cabb.*, p. 465 & p. 717). This, it says, results in the goodwill or positive opinion | of the Father towards men. Here in the Hebrew no doubt the word *rzwn* (Benevolence) was used which gives rise here to a striking resonance with the [Hebrew] word *'rz* (Earth) (about which see *Lex. Cabb.*, p. 157 and especially pp. 691 *seq.*) and introduces great illumination from the First Principle of Light.[193]

Verse 15
Let us go down to etc. *nerde'* [vocalised] *'dm'*

Kabbalist Catechumen From this it appears that the town was situated in some valley or other, but not that the boy had been "laid" in the town, just near to it.

Christian This place the Greek and Latin Fathers generally call a cave. This is what the early writer Justin tells us ||| (he is particularly credible because he was born not far from Judaea, was brought up as a Samaritan and in his time memory of the matter was still sufficiently fresh): "he turned aside in a certain cave near the town"[194]. The place is described in the same way

fol. 42ᵛ

---

191 "רצון *Voluntas, Beneplacitum*. Cabbalistarum Sapientibus nonam Sephirarum ab imis adscendendo ita appellare placuit. Nam hic locus repræsentat ἐνέργειαν Beneplaciti Summi versus Sephiras, earumque manifestationem à Coronâ Summâ factam; ita tamen, ut nullo modo intelligi queat; eò quod nulla uspiam creatura scire queat, quomodo Beneplacitum illud sese exerat erga emanationem Sephirarum. [...] 2. Influentia descendens à Corona Summa contentas reddit & explet voluntatem & desiderium atque arbitrium omnium Sephirarum; & hinc vocatur רצון *Beneplacitum, acquiescentia* εὐδοκία: sicut enim homo in beneplacito est, cum comedit; sic Sephiræ saturantur beneplacito superno, cum influxum ab illo accipiunt. Fundamentum igitur τοῦ רצון quod acquiescentiam & beneplacitum producit, est in Kether: illud autem, quod contentum redditur, sunt Sephiroth; qualescunque hoc vel illo loco Scripturæ saturitatem experiri dicuntur, ut Ps. 85,2. i.e. influxu τοῦ רצון saturasti illam. Atque sic exponenda sunt & reliqua. Pard." (Ibid., pp. 691–692).
192 Added in the right margin: Christianus. (which involves a change of speaker).
193 An elegant return to the first theme of the Zohar and the initial comments of this commentary.
194 Justin Martyr (c. A.D.150) in *Dialogue with Trypho* (78): "But when the Child was born in Bethlehem, since Joseph could not find lodging in that village, he took up his quarters in a certain cave near the village; and while they were there Mary brought forth the Christ and placed Him in a manger, and here the Magi who came from Arabia found Him. I have repeated to you what Isaiah foretold about the sign which foreshadowed the cave; but for the sake of those who have come with us today, I shall again remind you of the passage". The testimonia of fathers on the point was com-

Ita hunc locum etiam appellant Origenes, Eusebius, Athanasius, Gregorius
Nyssenus, | Hieronymus, Epiphanius, Theodoretus &c. Observatque ê Strabone Casaubonus, totam regionem circa Hierosolyma ad sexagesimum
usque lapidem esse petrosam. Bethlehemum autem quatuor millia passuum, vel sex duntaxat ab urbe distabat. Sicque & Cyrillus putavit non in
urbe, sed ad urbem Bethlehem Mariam divertisse, atque ibi Christum peperisse.[195]

[Christianus.][196] Hoc[197] Casaubonus quidem impugnat: sed non video,
quâ soliditate.

Rem hanc: למלתא הדא

Christianus. Verbi appellatio in Græco sæpe rem denotat.
Cabb. Cat. Similiter apud Hebræos; atque sic & Syriacum. conf. Matth. 5, 32; Luc. 4, 36. &c.

V. 17. *Manifestarunt sermonem;* אודעו למלתא

[**Cabb. Cat.**][198] *Cui?*
[**Christianus.**][199] Nimirum præsentibus: non Mariæ tantùm & Josepho
sed & aliis, qui ê diversorio atque vicinia accurisse[200] videntur, ut colligitur
ê versu sequenti: *& omnes qui audierunt* (rem scilicet primitùs hîc in spelunca | narratam;) *mirati sint de his, quæ sibi dicebantur â Pastoribus.* Ubi per
voculam omnes, non possunt intelligi Maria & Joseph; de quibus etiam dici
non potest, quod mirati sint nuncium de Adventu Messiæ: quia idem jam
crediderant Luc. 1, 38; Matth. 1, 24. Quamvis deinde mirati sint vaticinium de
vocatione Gentium Luc. 1, 32.33. Nec intelligi possunt verba hæc de divulgatione | postmodum subsecuta: quia versu demum 20. reversi esse dicuntur
Pastores: ut hæc omnia in spelunca gesta esse credendum sit.

---

mon erudition at the time, see e.g. John Milner, *A Collection of the Church-History of Palestine* (London: Dring, 1688), p. 10 where much the same material is found (with references). C.G. Düring's 1734 *Novum Inventarium Bibliothecæ Sulzbaco-Palatino* (BSB Cbm 580 Repositorium A), p. 16#39, records a copy of Justin in the library in Sulzbach. The remarks of Casaubon are found in his *De Rebus Sacris et Ecclesiasticis Exercitationes* at Exercitatio II, Anni I, Num 2 (pp. 120–121 of that edition).

195 Added into the text: Et ... (in order to make the link with the following sentence: "Et hoc Casaubonus quidem ...").

196 Deleted word. The change of speaker is no longer needed as a consequence of the previous correction.

SECTION VIII   473

by Origen, Eusebius, Athanasius, Gregory of Nyssa, | Jerome, Epiphanius, Theodoret etc. and Casaubon noticed from Strabo that the whole region around Jerusalem as far as the 60th milestone was rocky. Bethlehem is only about four [Roman] miles and certainly no more than six from Jerusalem. Cyril also thought Mary had turned aside not in Bethlehem but only near to it and had there given birth to Christ. Causaubon disputes this, but I do not see on what grounds .

This thing *lmlt' hd'*

Christian The word "word" often denotes "thing" in Greek[201].

Kabbalist Catechumen Similarly in Hebrew and also in Syriac, Mt 5.32; Lk 4.36 etc.

Verse 17
And revealed the speech *'wd'w lmlt'*

Kabbalist Catechumen Revealed it to whom?

Christian To those there, naturally. Not just to Mary and Joseph but also to the others who seem to have run up from the inn and neighbourhood as one gathers from the following verse: "and all who heard" (the wonder first told here in the cave |) "were amazed at the things which were told them by the shepherds". In the word "all" here, we should not include Mary and Joseph of whom it cannot be said that they were amazed at the announcement of the coming of Messiah, because they had already believed in it (Lk 1.38; Mt 1.24) (although they subsequently wondered at the prophecy of the calling of the Gentiles in Lk 1.32, 33). Nor can these words be understood of the subsequent | spread of the news, because already by verse 20, the shepherds are said to have returned, so that we must believe all these things happened in the cave.

---

197   Correction: Hoc replaced by hoc (
198   Correction: Christianus replaced by Cabb. Cat. (which involves the two speakers being changed over in the following exchange).
199   Correction: Cabb. Cat. replaced by Christianus (as a consequence of the previous correction).
200   Correction: accurisse remplaced by accurrisse
201   Greek Lk 2.15: *to rēma touto*.

V. 19. *Et conferebat* &c. ומפחמא

Cabb. Cat. *Id est comparabat visionem Pastorum cum visione Zachariæ, & sua, atque Josephi.*
   Christianus. Cumque vaticiniis Veteris Testamenti &c. conf. 2. Cor. 10, 12; 1. Cor. 2, 13.

V. 20. *Sicut dictum fuerat eis.* איכנא דאתמלל עמהין

[**Cabb. Cat.** *A quibus?*][202]
   Christianus. Non tantum ab Angelo; sed & â Mariâ atque Josepho.
   [Cabb. Cat.][203] Et fortè ab aliis, qui Mariam viderant sine doloribus | parientem; sine obstetrice filiolum â secundinis dissolventem; & uberibus eundem sine doloribus admoventem. Ubi etiam addunt Saraceni, quod Puellus locutus sit sicut homo triginta quinque annorum, Alcoran Sur. 3. & Sur. 5. Non enim expressè dicit textus, quod Maria pepererit in stabulo, sed quod filium ibidem reposuerit. Unde nihil assereret absurdi, qui | diceret, illam peperisse filiolum in Diversorio; sed propter hominum accursum spatium non habuisse, ibi eundem reponeret; ut factum adulto, Matth. 8, 20.[34].[204]

V. 21. *Et cum implerentur* &c. [205]וכד מלו דנתגזר

Cabb. Cat. *Impleri dicitur cujus terminus initium habet; ut Mar. 1, 15; | Act. 2, 1; Luc. 9, 51; Gal. 4, 4; Eph. 1, 10; Joh. 7, 8.*

Ut circumcideretur &c. דנתגזר[206]

[**Christianus.**][207] Sed quare natus non fuit circumcisus? ut Justi alii, de quibus egimus ad Luc. 1, 59. ‖‖

fol. 43ʳ

---

202 Added in the left margin: *Cabb. Cat. A quibus?*
203 Deletion: Cabb. Cat. The change of speaker initially intended is cancelled. The speech remains with the Christian.
204 Deletion: Non enim expressè dicit textus, quod Maria peperit in stabulo, sed quod filium ibidem reposuerit. Unde nihil assereret absurdi, qui diceret, illam peperisse filiolum in Diversorio; sed propter hominum accursum spatium non habuisse, ibi eundem reponeret; ut factum adulto, Matth. 8, 20.34. (The last number of the reference [34] is not clear).
205 Deleted word: דנתגזר (to avoid repetition).
206 Deletion of the entire line.

SECTION VIII

Verse 19
And she pondered etc. *wmpḥm'*

Kabbalist Catechumen That is, she compared the vision of the shepherds with those of Zachariah, herself and Joseph.

Christian And [she also compared it] with the Old Testament promises etc. Cf. 2 Cor 10.12; 1 Cor 2.13.

Verse 20
As had been told them 'ykn' d'tmll 'mhyn

Kabbalist Catechumen By whom?

Christian Not only by the Angel, but also by Mary and Joseph. And perhaps by others, who had seen Mary giving birth without pain, | separating her little boy from the after-birth without a midwife and offering him her breasts without pain. The Moslems add that the boy spoke like a man of thirty-five years: Quran Sura 3 and 5.[208]

Verse 21
And when were fulfilled etc. *wkd mlw*

Kabbalist Catechumen Something is said to be fulfilled when it has both a beginning and an end: Mt 1.15; | Acts 2.1; Lk 9.51; Gal 4.4; Eph 1.10; Jn 7.8.[209]

But why was he not born circumcised as were the other righteous men about whom we spoke [in commenting upon] on Lk 1.59. ||| fol. 43ʳ

---

[207] Deletion: Christianus. The change of speaker initially intended is cancelled. The speech remains with the Cabbalist.

[208] Deletion in manuscript: "The text does not explicitly say that Mary gave birth in the stall, but that she placed her son there. So it is quite reasonable to say that she gave birth to her little boy in the inn, but because of the guests there was no room to put him. As happened when he was an adult (Mt 8.20)." There follows another illegible reference possibly to 8.34 where Jesus is expelled from the region of the Gadarenes. Presumably the passage was deleted as it raises for solution a problem, which perhaps would not otherwise occur to the reader.

[209] Here a whole lemma is deleted: *In order that he might be circumcised* etc. *dntgzr*.

[**Christianus.**][210] Quia omnibus sese subjecit corticibus; adeoque & carnis cortici, præputio; ut omnes frangeret. Et quamvis natus fuisset sine præputio; Denudatione tamen opus habuisset sanguinolentâ: hâc ipsa die octavâ: quâ caruere Job & Bileam, qui & ipsi nati dicuntur sine præputio. | Vide Excerpta Cent. II. Loc. 17.

Jeschua ישוע

[**Christianus.**][211] De variis Messiæ nominibus adducemus Locum quendam ê Talmude Hierosolym. Tractat. Berachoth f. 5.a. in Excerptis Cent. II. Loc. 18. ubi â quibusdam ipsi tribuitur Nomen David: ab aliis Zemach: ab aliis | Menachem. Nos verò id annotamus, quod si junxeris Nomina

24. ד״וד
138. צ״מח
138. מ״נחם
86. א״להים

Abhinc exsurgat numerus 386. i.e. ישוע

[**Christianus.**][212] Hinc iterum apparet, quam divina mysteria isthoc in nomine lateant. [**Cabb. Cat.**][213] *Quid si quis hoc Nomen revolvat per omnes Alphabethi rotationes, numerosque mutationum observet?*

V. 22. *Dies purificationis eorum.* יומתא דתדכיתהון

[**Christianus.**][214] De hac materia locum exscripsimus in Excerptis Cent.II. loc. 19. Per purificationem autem literaliter intelligitur Puritatis declaratio;

---

210   Correction: Cabb. Cat. replaced by Christianus.
211   Correction: Cabb. Cat. replaced by Christianus.
212   Deletion: Christianus. The change of speaker initially intended is no longer needed after the previous correction. The speech remains with the Christian.
213   Added in the right margin: Cabb. Cat. (which involves a change of speaker).
214   Correction: Cabb. Cat. replaced by Christian. (which involves the two speakers being changed over in the following exchange).
215   The "wicked" Balaam is considered (together with his father Beor, Job and Job's four friends) to be one of the seven Gentile prophets in *Bava Batra* 15b. Job's circumcised birth is mentioned in *Midrash Tanchuma* (Noach 5), but surprisingly *Avot de-Rabbi Nathan* (2.5) adds Balaam to the list. Perhaps this is an attempt to explain or justify why he was able to enjoy the gift of prophecy.

SECTION VIII

Christian Because he subjected himself to all the Shards, to the extent even of the Shard of the flesh, the foreskin, so that he might destroy them all. And even if he had been born without a foreskin, a bloody stripping away [of the flesh] would still have been necessary on that same eighth day which Job and Balaam, who are also themselves said to have been born without a foreskin, lacked.²¹⁵ | See Excerpt Cent. II Loc. 17.

Jeschua yšw'

Christian Concerning the various names of Messiah we adduce a passage from the Jerusalem Talmud Tractate Berachot folio 5a in Excerpt Cent. II Loc. 18, where some apply the name to David, others to Zemach, others | to Menachem. Add up the numerical value of these names together with that of *'elohim* [= God] and you get the numerical value of Jeschua. David =24; Zemach=138; Menachem 138; *'elohim* =86. The total is 386, the value of Jeschua. | From this it again emerges how divine mysteries are hidden is in this name.

Kabbalist Catechumen What if someone permuted this name through all the rotations of the alphabet and observed the numbers resulting from the changes?²¹⁶

Verse 22
The day of their purification ywmtʾ dtdkythwn

Christian We have written out a passage about this in Excerpt Cent. II Loc. 19. By purification literally is understood a *declaration* of purity; from this

---

216 Apparently the technique alluded to here, which is found as early as the *Sefer Yetsirah*, requires the combination of each letter of the Hebrew name Jeschua with each of the letters of the alphabet. Thus:

יא, יב, יג, יד ... ית

שא, שב, שג ... שת

וא, וב, וג ... ות

עא, אב ... עת

הא, הב ... הת

We are indebted to Dr Judith Weiss for advice here, but uncertain of what this might achieve. Perhaps once again this is an incitement to meditative practice and the creative discovery of further hidden depths.

unde non sequitur Messiam fuisse impurum, vel matrem ejus: sed sufficit hoc factum esse, non sui sed aliorum gratia, nimirum ne haberentur pro impuris.

[**Cabb. Cat.**]²¹⁷ *Et ut impleretur Præceptum Legis de Primogenitis.* [vide Excerpta Cent.II. Loc. 21.]

V. 25. *Simeon* &c. שמעון   25

Christianus. Nihil invenio absurdi in opinione Buxtorffii, in Abbreviaturis lit. ר״ quod Simeon iste fuerit filius Hillelis: cum non saltem eodem tempore vixerit; sed cum Præses esset Synedrii i.e. Vir juxta Legem utramque omnibus numeris absolutus, qualis & Pater ejus fuerat, mirum non est, quod spiritus | Sancti oraculo fuerit monitus. Adde quod ê tribu Judæ & familia   30
Davidis esset oriundus.

Cabb. Cat. *Et quia Doctores vestri*²¹⁸ *statuunt nullam dari Generationem in qua*²¹⁹ *reperiatur Moses:* [Vide Tract. de Revol. Anim. c. 11. §.8.²²⁰] *in hac sanè generatione nemo mihi videtur dignior, in quo Mosis Anima apparuerit,* | 35
quam Simeon iste.

---

217   Correction: Christianus replaced by Cabb. Cat. (as a consequence of the previous correction).
218   Correction: vestri replaced by nostri
219   Added above the line: non
220   "Et psyche illius justi quæ absolvit revolutiones suas, nec pluribus opus habet, saltem embryo sit in psyche tali ut dictum cap. 5. Atque tunc psyche illius justi sustinet vices Spiritus ratione psyches hujus imprægnatæ; quamvis restituta tantum sit sub notione psyches. Eo casu igitur quando homo restitutus est in psyche sua, fieri potest, ut eum imprægnet psyche quædam, è primis patribus: prout aliquando fieri potest, ut quidam sic imprægnetur psyche Abrahami patris nostri super quo pax: vel Mosis Magistri nostri super quo pax: Nempe omnia prout opus habet talibus, psyche illa. Unde dixerunt Magistri nostri p.m. nullam dari generationem in qua non sint justi quidam ut Abraham & Jizchak & Jaacob & Mosche & Schmuel & David. Atque sic explicuerunt dictum illud Gen. xv, 6. כה *sic erit semen tuum*, ut numerus voculæ כה est 25: quibus innui volunt in qualibet generatione dari 25. justos, qualis Abraham: quod clarum est intelligentibus." ("De revolutio animarum", op. cit., p. 293).
221   Further evidence, adduced by Knorr, that Jesus could not have been born as a result of congress between Joseph and Mary.
222   Ex 13.1–6.
223   It is, of course a common place that he was the son of Hillel, but this reference was used of this topic by Knorr in his Chronographical Introduction to his *Harmonia*,

SECTION VIII 479

it does not follow that Messiah was ever unclean nor his mother,[221] but it needed to be done not for his sake but for the sake of the others, so that they would not be considered unclean.

Kabbalist Catechumen And [also] that the precept of the Law of the Firstborn be kept (See Excerpt Cent. II Loc. 21).[222]

Verse 25
Simeon etc. *šmʿwn*

25

Christian I find nothing unreasonable in the opinion of Buxtorf in his book on Hebrew Abbreviations[223] that Simeon was himself the son of Hillel, since he not merely lived at the same time, but was [also] president of the Sanhedrin *i. e.* a man exact according to either Law just as his father had been.[224]
30 It would not be surprising if he had been warned | by a prophecy of the Holy Spirit. Add the point that he was descended from the tribe of Judah and the family of David.

Kabbalist Catechumen And because our teachers state that there is no generation in which Moses is *not* found (see Tract. *De Revol. Animarum*, 2, §8), nobody in that generation seems more worthy that the soul of Moses
35 should appear in them | than this Simeon.

---

p. 16. C.G. Düring's 1734 *Novum Inventarum Bibliothecæ Sulzbaco-Palatino* (BSB Cbm 580 Repositorium A), p. 53#q records a copy of the *Liber de abbreviaturis* of 1640 in the library there. Lightfoot, *Miscellanies and the Harmony of the Gospels*, op. cit., p. 200: "This Simeon seemeth to be he, whom the Jewish authors name for the son of Hillel: and who was the first that bare the title of 'Rabban,' the highest title that was given to their doctors, and which was given but to seven of them."

224 It is curious to note that in the letter Pfalzgraf Christian Augustus sent to Herzog Rudolf August von Braunschweig-Lüneburg on 21 March 1684 to accompany the copy of the *Kabbala Denudata* he was sending him, Christian Augustus suggests that Simeon here in the Gospel of Luke may indeed be Simeon ben Iochai, the "author" of the Zohar: "... indem der Auctor (von dessen Leben, Lehren vnd Thaten solches Buch am moisten handelt) rabbi Schimeon ben Iochai genanndt, zur Zeit vnsers Heilands selbst bis nach der Zerstoerung Ierusalem gelebet; vnd wohl gar davor gehalten werden will, dass dieses derjenige Simeon, welcher vnsern Herrn in seiner Kindheit im Tempel auf die Arme genommen; indem, ob derselbe damahls hohen oder mittlen Alters gewesen, der Evangelische Text nicht audsrucket [...]." (Text in Finke, *Sulzbach im 17. Jahrhundert*, op. cit., p. 206).

Consolationem Iisraël. [225] לבויאה דיסריל

Christianus. Lucas videtur Animo concepisse Syriacum נוחמא quod Resurrectionem significat Joh. 11, 24. illudque â radice Chaldaica expressisse per παράκλησις.

    Cabb. Cat. Eademque etiam mens videtur fuisse illorum apud Antiquos | juramentorum, אראה בנחמא, *prout videbo resurrectionem, ita vidi &c. Sanhedrin 37, 2. Chagigah 16, 2; Maccoth 5, 2; Ketubb. 67, 1. Schevuoth 34, 1.*   40

V. 26. *Quos non visurus esset mortem.* דלא נחזא מותא

Christianus. Propriènè hoc intelligendum an impropriè?
    Cabb. Cat. Sanè, quod moriturus videat Angelum mortis ante obitum | suum   45
fol. 43ᵛ   *tradunt Scriptores nostri. Vide Excerpta Cent. II. Loc. 22.* |||

Donec vidisset Messiam Domini. עדמא דנחזא למשיחא דמריא

Christianus. Non in apparitione ut Joh. 8, 11; c. 12, 41; Act. 9, 5. Nec ut justi morinbundi videre traduntur Schechinam, vid. Excerpta Cent. II. Loc. 23.24. Nec ut R. Iischmaël Ben Elischa, qui vidisse dicitur Schechinam cum suffimentum adoleret. Berachoth c.1. f. 7.a. | periitque in exitio urbis. Vide   5
Excerpta Cent. II. Loc. 25. sed talem, qualem consummata nunc plenitudine temporis in carne expectabat Luc. 17, 20; c. 19, 11. finitis enim nunc quatuor millenniis, tempora sequentia Messiana esse credebantur. Adde vaticinium Dan. 9, 26.27.

    Cabb. Cat. Sed & aliud hic latet mysterium in Nomine Messiæ. | Quamvis   10
enim Nomen hoc, Unctus Domini, olim & aliis tributum fuerit Regibus, ut 1. Sam. 24, 7; 2. Sam. 19, 21; Thr. 4, 20. certum tamen Simeoni impressisse videtur Spiritus S. characterem Cabbalisticum super persona Jesu: nam si computes vocem משיח *una cum voce, exurgit numerus 359. & si eâdem ratione compute-*

---

225   Israel is spelled *d'yśryl* here in Peshitta. Has Knorr missed out an aleph?
226   The Syriac word in Luke here *lbwy'* means "consolation" and is thus properly rendered by the Greek *paraklēsis*. Knorr suggests that the consolation anticipated is the resurrection and cites the use of the Syriac word for "resurrection", *nwḥm'* in Jn 11.24. Spector, *Francis Mercury van Helmont's Sketch of Christian Kabbalah*, op. cit., p. 164 suggests that van Helmont has "emended" the Syriac of Jn 11.24 from "consolation" to "resurrection", but that is not the case as the text of John already had resurrection. Rather Knorr appears to find in the etymology of the word for resurrection *nwḥm'* from the root *nḥm* "to consol" (Marcus Jastrow, *A Dictionary of the Targumim, the Talmud Babli and Yerushalmi and the Midrashic Literature* (New York: Judaica Press 1996) p. 895 has ניחם נחם meaning "to consol", "consolation") a confirmation of his interpretation that the Con-

SECTION VIII

The Consolation of Israel lbwy'h dyśryl

Christian Luke seems to have had in mind the Syriac *nwḥm'* which means Resurrection (Jn 11.24) and to have expressed it from the Aramaic root by *paraklēsis*.[226]

Kabbalist Catechumen The same thinking seems to be found in those oaths of the ancients | [which say] *'r'h bnḥm'* "As I will see Resurrection so I saw etc". Sanhedrin 37.2; Chagigah 16.2; Makot 5.2; Ketuvot 67.1; Shevu'ot 34.1.[227]

Verse 26
That he should not see death dl' nḥz' mwt'

Christian Should this be taken literally or not?
Kabbalist Catechumen Our writers hand down that, on the point of death, | he saw the Angel of Death before he died (see Excerpt Cent. II Loc. 22). ‖

fol. 43ᵛ

Until he saw the Lord's Messiah 'dm' dnḥz' lmšyḥ' dmry'

Christan Not in a vision as in Jn 8.11; 12.41; Acts 9.5, nor as the righteous before death are by tradition said to see the Shekhinah (Excerpt Cent. II Loc. 23, 24), nor as R. Ishmael ben Elicha who is said to have seen the Shekhinah when he was burning incense (Berachot, chap. 1, folio 7a) | and perished on leaving the City (see Excerpta Cent. II Loc. 25), but now with most of his days in the flesh behind him (Lk 17.20; 19.11), Simeon was waiting for just such a sight— for now the four thousand years were over, he believed the following period would be that of Messiah.[228]

Add the prophecy in Daniel 9.26, 27[229].

Kabbalist Catechumen Another mystery is here hidden in the name of Messiah. | For although this name, "Anointed of the Lord", had once been given also to other kings (as in 1 Sam 24.7; 2 Sam 19.21; Lam 4.20), the Holy Spirit certainly seems to have impressed upon Simeon the Kabbalistic character above the *persona* of Jesus. For if you add the numerical value of *mšyḥ*

---

solation of Israel is the Resurrection. Cf. Jerôme Rousse-Lacordaire, *Esquisse de la kabbale chrétienne* (Paris: Les Belles Lettres, 2018), p. 49, note 63, p. 156.

227 This idiom is illustrated in Buxtorf's *Lexicon Chaldaicum*, s.v. nhm in col. 1327 where the references to Chagigah 16.2 and Shevu'ot 34.1 (only) are given.
228 We are now familiar with this chronographic / prophetic schema.
229 This has been discussed above.

tur voc יהו״ה *unà cum voce, exurgit numerus 27. unde fit numerus 386.* | *Nominis* ישוע; *ad quod etiam ipse alludit Simeon infra v. 30.*

V. 29. *Dimitte* שרי

Christianus. Æquipollet Radici פטר, quæ tam in Chaldaico quam Syriaco significationem habet Dimissionis è vita, vide Phil. 1, 23.

    Cabb. Cat. *Unde argumentum suppeditatur pro opinione de Præexistentia* | *Animarum, quæ in corpore saltem tanquam in carcere subsistum, juxta antiquissimam gentis nostræ doctrinam.*

In Pace בשלמא

[**Cabb. Cat.**][230] *Quamnam emphasin habet hæc loquendi formula?*

[**Christianus.**][231] Noverant Antiqui ê Danielis 9, v. 26. quod post Adventum | Messiæ[232] vastandum esset Sanctuarium. Unde cum in Gemara Hierosolymitanâ Tract. Berachoth fol. 5. a. enarratur historia de Arabe quodam vastationem Sanctuarii & adventum Messiæ simul annunciante ibidem mox subjicit R. Bon: quod opus non sit ab Arabe isthæc discere: cum scriptura expressè dicat: Jes. c. 10, 34. Et Libanon (i.e. Sanctuarium) in forti | cadet. Mox autem sequatur (c. [11], v. 1.) Et egredietur virga de stirpe Jischai &c. Isthæc igitur & Simeon noverat; sed simul & hoc urget, ut nempe discessus sibi pateat pacificis adhuc temporibus, & antequam plenius irruant dolores Messiani.

V. 30. *Gratiosum suum.* חננך

Christianus. Simeon procul dubio locutus est lingua vernacula, i.e. Syriaca unde cum vox חננא tam abstracti, quàm concreti significationem habeat, talemque Gratiæ largitorem denotet, qui ipsa sit Gratia, Lucas in Græco

---

230   Correction in the left margin: Christianus replaced by Cabb. Cat. (which involves the two speakers being changed over in the following exchange).
231   Correction in the left margin: Cabb. Cat. replaced by Christianus (as a consequence of the previous correction).
232   Deletion of two words, now unreadable.
233   Peshitta: *šarā'*
234   This is a late reflex of the Platonic couple *sōma / sēma*.

[in Hebrew], and add one [for the number of words involved] the resulting number is [358+1=] 359. If in the same way you add the numerical value of *yhwh* together with one [for the number of words involved], the resulting number is [26+1=] 27. 359 and 27 make 386 | which is the numerical value of the name Jesus [10+300+6+70=386] to which also Simeon himself alludes below in verse 30.

Verse 29
Dismiss šāri [vocalized][233]

Christian This is equivalent to the root *ptr* which in both Aramaic and Syriac means "to depart from life". See Phil 1.23.

Kabbalist Catechumen From which an argument is gathered for our opinion about the preexistence | of souls which, according to the most ancient teaching of our people, live in the body as if in a prison.[234]

In Peace bšlm'

Kabbalist Catechumen What significance has this form of words?

Christian The Ancients knew from Dan 9.26 that after the advent | of Messiah, the sanctuary would be devastated. In the Jerusalem Talmud Tractate Berachot folio 5a there is told an account of a certain Arab who at the same moment announced both the Destruction of the Temple and the Advent of Messiah. R. Boni in the same place then adds that there was no need for the Arab to say this since Scripture states it expressly in Isa 10.34: "And Lebanon (i.e. the Sanctuary) shall fall | before the mighty one". But there soon follows (11.1): "And a rod shall arise from the stem of Jesse etc." So Simeon also knew this, but asked that he might be able to depart while the times were still peaceful and before the full onset of the Birthpains of Messiah.

Verse 30
Your Graciousness[235] *ḥnnk*

Christian Simeon doubtless spoke in the vernacular (i.e. Syriac) in which the word *ḥnn'* has both an abstract and a concrete meaning and denotes an abundance of largess which is Grace itself. Luke in Greek gives the neutral

---

235 Vulgate: "*salutare suum*"

adhibuit vocem neutram, σωτήριον. Quia autem salvatio Iisraëlitarum vel est gratiosa vel gloriosa: tacitè subinnuit Simeon gratiosum nunc se videre salvatorem, | gloriosum nondum.

Cabb. Cat. Ubi procul dubio simul allusit ad Nomen Messiæ חנינה, quod ê Jer. 16, 13. eruebant veteres. Item ad locum Joël 2, 13. ubi הוא ורחום וחנון, & Nomen ישוע numeris æquipollent. Adde quod חנון & ישועה ad idem Divinitatis metrum nempe Chesed, pertineant, [vide Lex. Cabbalist. p. 349.[236] & 460.[237]]

fol. 44ʳ   V. 31. *Quem parasti &c. lumen &c.* נוהרא &c הו דטיבת ||| 45

Cabb. Cat. Omnia alludunt ad istum gradum Chesed; ad quem etiam pertinet aptatio, seu bona constitutio lucis, juxta Exod. 30, 7. ubi similiter extat vox ejusdem radicis, in Hebraico & Syriaco [vide Lex. Cabbal. p. 368.[238]]

Christianus. Sed & allegoria de Sole subest. Sicut enim (1.) Sol oculis omnium populorum | expositus est: ita Messias; & hic Jesus, de quo Simeon ista 5 pronunciat universalis est Salvator Phil. 2, 11; Apoc. 5, 13. (2.) Sicut sol oriens ea revelat, quæ nocturno tempore occultata fuerant: ita sub initio temporum Messianorum Gentilibus, qui antea tenebræ fuerant Eph. 5, 8. obtigit revelatio veri Dei, veri cultus, veraque ad salutem methodi.

Cabb. Cat. Imò sicut Sol tempore meridiano lucem diffundit clarissimam: 10 ita Iisraëlitæ potissimum sub Messia sole suum habebunt meridiem, Regnumque gloriosissimum Matth. 13, 43; Ap. 21, 23.24; c. 22, 5. conf. Rom. 9, 4. Et iste procul dubio est sensus vaticinii hujus[239]. Ubi etiam aliena non est revelatio[240] illa Cabbalistarum, qua Seir Anpin dicitur Sol; & uxor ejus Luna: si subintel-

---

236 "חנון *Gratiosus, Clemens.* R. Moscheh refert hoc ad Chesed, ubi gratia & in indignos confertur. Sed videtur locus ille ubi dona gratis dantur in supernis esse, ubi judicium nullum. Pard. Tr. 23. c. 8." ("Loci communes kabbalistici", op. cit., p. 349).

237 "ישוע *Salus, Salvatio, auxilium.* Quicquid ad radicem ישע pertinet, ut הושיעה / ישועה / יושע &c. refertur ad Chesed, prout docetur in Sohar Section. Trumah his verbis: Quid est ישועות Psal. 18, 51? hæc est dextra, quæ salvat ab omnibus adversariis mundi, sicut scriptum est, Psal. 98, 1. &c. Pardes Tr. 23. c. 10." (Ibid., p. 460).

238 "טוב *Bonus, Bonum.* Pertinet ad Chesed, habetque significationem *aptandæ Lucis*, juxta Exod. 30, 7. Deinde & Tiphereth ex parte Chesed vocatur *Bonus.* Item Jesod. Et Malchuth eôdem respectu dicitur Bona. In Sohar Cantici Cant. Nomen boni applicatur ad Lucem primitivam; quæ notio est aliquantò superior quam Chesed. Unde in Soh. Sect. Trumah hæc habentur: Quando locum habet nomen Boni, & quando nomen Chesed? Nomen Boni, quando omnia in se continet, nec exserit se ut descendat: sed Chesed cum descendit, & benefacit omnibus creaturis. Et in historia de Puello Sect. Schemini ad Cant. 7, 10. dicitur, quod הטוב pertineat ad Chesed, *ad instar vini* cui admiscetur cum Aqua. [...]" (Ibid., p. 368).

word (between an abstract and concrete sence) *sōtērion*. Because the Salvation of the Israelites is both gracious and glorious, Simeon tacitly hints that then he saw the gracious Saviour, | but not yet the glorious one.

Kabbalistic Catechumen Doubtless at the same time he alludes to the [Hebrew] name of Messiah *ḥnynh* [Grace] which the ancients extracted from Jer 16.13. Likewise from Joel 2.13 where *ḥnwn wrḥwm hw'* [He is gracious and compassionate] and the name *yšw'* [Jeschua] have the same numerical value [of 386]. Additionally, both *ḥnwn* and *yšw'h* belong to the same divine degree Chesed (see *Lex. Cabb.*, pp. 349 &460).

Verse 31
Which you have prepared etc. *as a light* etc. *dṭybt* etc. *nwhr'* ‖‖ fol. 44ʳ

Kabbalist Catechumen Everything alludes to that same degree Chesed to which also belongs accommodation to or a good state of light according to Ex 30.7 where in both Hebrew and Syriac there is similarly used a word of the same root (see *Lex. Cabb.*, p. 368).

Christian But there is also an allegory of the Sun hidden here. For just as: (1) The Sun is exposed | to the eyes of all peoples, so Messiah and here Jesus about whom Simeon speaks these things is universal Saviour (Phil 2.11; Rev 5.13).

And just as (2) the rising Sun reveals those things which had been hidden during the night, so at the beginning of the Times of Messiah, the revelation of the true God, true worship and the true way of salvation came to the Gentiles who previously were in darkness (Eph 5.8).

Kabbalistic Catechumen But just as the sun at mid-day sheds the brightest light, so the Israelites most especially will have their mid-day and a most glorious kingdom under Messiah, their sun (Mt 13.43; Rev 21.23, 24; 22.5. Cf. Rm 9.4). And this is without question the meaning of this prophecy when it speaks of the Glory of Israel. Similar is the Kabbalists' account in which Zeir Anpin is called the Sun and his wife the Moon, if one understands that

---

239 Added in the right margin: cum de gloria populi Iisraël loquitur.
240 Correction: revelatio replaced by relatio. This is perhaps a most telling slip on Knorr's part. It seems clear that he was happy to consider the Lurianic tradition as indeed a revelation, but in correction modified the claim with discretion to speak of it as a mere "narrative".

ligantur | *Antiquorum more, Messias & Ecclesia.* [Vide Lexic. Cabbal. p. 576. n. 24.[241] & p. 723.[242]]

V. 33. *Mirabuntur* &c. תמיהין הוו

[**Cabb. Cat.**][243] *Quid jam demum mirabuntur, post tot apparitiones & revelationes?*

[**Christianus.**][244] Jam crediderant eum fore Jesum[245] Messiam: | sed mirabantur novam hanc officii Messiani ampliationem, quod nempe per illum peculiaris revelatio fieri debeat gentibus: cum hactenus creditum esset, Revelationem non superesse aliam, quam quæ facta fuisset Patribus Ps. 147, 20. nec salutem esse Gentilibus, nisi per proselytismum Jes. 60, 3.4. Unde etiam peculiaris hæc informatio Gentium facta ab Apostolis citra accessum ad Ecclesiam Iisraëlis ab Apostolo vocatur mysterium | hactenus absconditum Col. 1, 26; Rom. 16, 25.26; Eph. 1, 9; c. 3, 9. conf 2. Tim. 1, 9.10.11.

V. 14.[246] *Hic positus est* &c. הנא סים

[**Cabb. Cat.**][247] *Unde hæc Simeonis*[248] *phrasis?*

[**Christianus.**][249] Duplex hic est allusio ad Nomen ישוע: Sicut antiqui in benedictionibus | ad nomina alludere solebant conf. Gen. 27, 29; c. 49, 8.13.16.19.22. Primò igitur ita dividit hoc nomen Schimeon, ut respiciat ad literam י״ & ad voculam שוע. Sicut autem Litera Jod Cabbalistis denotare

---

241 "Sunt tamen & aliæ scintillæ *Uxoris Seiricæ*. Item omnes *Gebhuroth* & *Dinim* sunt duplices: unde dantur bis 320. in *Seir*; qua ex causa iste vocatur שמש Sol 640. & bis 320. in Uxore ejus ipsa vocatur תמר 640. *palma*. Omnesque hæ *Scintillæ* tam masculinæ quam fœmininæ in utero matris commixtæ ibique rursum formatæ sunt." ("Loci communes kabbalistici", op. cit., p. 576).

242 "שמש וירח *Sol & Luna*, sunt Tiphereth & Malchuth. Quanquam in Soh. Schemoth in pr. & Jesod vocatur Sol. Et in latere altero Sol & Luna sunt Samaël & Lilith, juxta Jesch. 24, 23. Pard. vid. Soh. Mikkez 112. Behaaloth. 71. Chuk. 87. Pinch. 100. Naso 61. שמש *Sol*. Vid. ניצוצות 24" (Ibid., p. 723). The ניצוצות are the *Scintillæ*, the "sparks".

243 Correction above the line: Christianus replaced by Cabb. Cat. (which involves the two speakers being changed over in the following exchange).

244 Correction in the right margin: Cabb. Cat. replaced by Christian (as a consequence of the previous correction).

245 Deleted word.

246 In error. It should be V. 34.

247 Correction: Christianus replaced by Cabb. Cat. (which involves the two speakers being changed over in the following exchange).

Messiah and Ecclesia are hidden here | in the fashion of the ancients (see *Lex. Cabb.*, p. 576, n. 24 & p. 723).[250]

Verse 33
They will wonder etc. *tmyhyn hww*

Kabbalist Catechumen What would [Mary and Joseph] now again wonder at after so many visions and revelations?

Christian They had already believed Jesus would be Messiah, | but they marvelled at this new expansion of the role of Messiah, that through him a peculiar revelation had to be given to the Gentiles. For up to then it had been believed that there was no further revelation to be made, other than that which had been made to the Fathers (Ps 147.20) and that there was no salvation for the Gentiles unless they became proselytes (Isa 60.3, 4). This specific revelation to the Gentiles, made by the Apostles after the entry of Israelites into the Ecclesia, is called by the Apostle "a mystery | previously hidden" (Col 1.26; Rm 16.25, 26; Eph 1.9; 3.9. Cf. 2 Tim 1.9, 10,11).

Verse 34
He is destined etc. *hn' śym*

Kabbalist Catechumen Why does Simeon say this?

Christian This is double allusion to the [Hebrew] name *yšw'* [Jesus].[251] Just as the ancients in benedictions | were accustomed to allude to names (Cf. Gen 27.29; 49.8, 13, 16, 19, 22), so Simeon first divides up this name and considers it [first] as the letter *yod* and the word *šw'*. The letter *yod* for the

---

248 Correction: Simeonis replaced by Simeoni
249 Correction in the right margin: Cabb. Cat. replaced by Christian. (as a consequence of the previous correction).
250 An identity facilitated not only by the gendered relationship between the sefirot, but also the association of Zeir Anpin with "the Son".
251 There follows another innovative kabbalistic interpretation of the name "Jesus" to explain Simeon's words.

solet Lapidem, & gradum Malchuth, [vide Lex. Cabbalist. p. 16.17.18.19.20.[252]]
ita & שועא Chaldæorum habet significationem Petræ & rupis Prov. 30, 19.
eodemque modo & Syriacum שועא Psal. 27, 5; Prov. 30, 19; | Matth. 7, 24.25; 35
c. 13, 5.20; Marc. 4, 5.16; c. 15, 46; Luc. 6, 48; c. 8, 6.13. Exhinc occasio suborta est
Simeoni pro allegoria de Parte Rupis in via prominula, ad quam alii pedem
offendentes laberentur: alii onerati lapsique erigerentur. Quasi diceret talem
nunc esse Messiæ statum, ut corticibus omninò esset immersus: unde istud
improvidis periculum.

Secundò litera Jod antiquis etiam denotavit signum vid. Lex. Cabbalist. 40
p. 65. f. 66. n. 1[253]; 67.n. 6.[254] Et שוע Hebræis est vociferatio. Unde Simeon
Jesum quidem professus est esse signum illud ad gradum Regni pertinens:
Nimirum illud את, quod initium sit finisque omnis illuminationis; sed cum
contentiosa & vociferante contradictione, qualis est sensus vocis חרינא Luc.
22, 24; Act. 15, 39; | Heb. 6, 16; c. 7, 7. Pergitque Propheta noster in hunc sen- 45
sum: Et istæ contra hunc filium tuum evibratæ calumniæ atque blasphemiæ,
quæ acutiores erunt omni gladio, lancea atque telo; (fortè & ad analogiam
soni Nominis respexit ad peregrinum illud teli genus, quod Gæsum dicebat,

---

252 "אבן *Lapis*. (Connectitur cum כל) 1. Sæpius Adonai Nomen Sephiræ ultimæ, & ipsa Malchuth, Regnum, ita dicitur; quoniam ipsa totius mundanæ fabricæ fundamentum extat; cui omnia, quæ in mundo, innituntur, & à quo sua expetunt commoda. [...] אבן *Lapis*. In hoc nomine perpetuò mysterium literæ י״י involvitur, & quidem ut plurimum in Malchuth, quatenus in ista existit litera Jod. Informis enim massa & figura τοῦ י״י figuram habet lapidis; & Malchuth est fundamentum & lapis cui totum ædificium superius superstruitur. De ea dicitur Zach. 3, 9. *Lapis unus septem oculorum*. Pardes Rimmonim Tract. 23, c.1.h.t. [...] אבן מאסו הבונים *Lapis quem reprobarunt ædificantes*. Ps. 118, 22. Exponitur autem ita: quod Patres Mundi (qui sunt filii quadrigæ,) omnes reprobaverint eam, receperintque pro portione sua Gedulah magnificentiam, Geburah fortitudinem seu Rigorem, & Tiphereth Pulchritudinem: cum tamen quandoque ipsa sit principalissima & caput omnium, quando scilicet ad Ænsoph usque adscendit. Et tunc vocatur Corona nempe Sacerdotii, quando est in Capite Chesed misericordiæ: Corona Levitica, quando est in Capite Gebhuræ; & Corona Legis, quando est in Capite Tiphereth. Et hoc est illud, quod in Textu allegato sequitur: *Factus est in Caput anguli*, seu Frontispicii. Quod commentatores ita exponunt: quod potissimum habeat aspectum atque intuitum, quodque omnia eam respiciant: superiora, ut influant in illam; inferiora verò, ut hauriant ex illa. Ibid. [...] אבן שלימה Deut. 25, 15; 1. Reg. 6, 7; Prov. 11, 1; Deut. 27, 6; Ios. 8, 31. *Lapis perfectus*; quatenus respectum habet ad Binah, & intelligitur per illud: Chochmah est Jod, & Malchuth est Jod. Huc etiam pertinet illud, quod R. Akibha dicebat ad discipulos suos, cum venirent ad lapides marmoris puri: cum videtis aquas, & aquas alias, ne dicite, duas esse aquarum species; quia omnia unum planè sunt, sicut dicitur Jes. 44, 6. *Ego primus & ego novissimus*. Unde etiam scriptum est Prov. 3, 19. *Dominus in Sapientia fundavit Terram*: quia Fundamentum Sephiræ Malchuth, quæ est Jod, provenit à Chochmah. Atque hujus intuitu vocatur lapis, simpliciter, propter figuram literæ Jod. Sed ratione Binæ vocatur lapis perfectus: quia tunc perfecta est

SECTION VIII 489

Kabbalists usually denotes a stone and the degree Malkhut [Kingdom] (See *Lex. Cabb.*, pp. 16, 17, 18, 19, 20). Also in Aramaic *šw'ʿ* means a stone or a rock (Pro 30.19) | and similarly the Syriac word *šw'ʿ* (Ps 27.5; Pro 30.19; Mt 7.24, 25; 13.5, 20; Mk 4.5, 16; 15.46; Lk 6.48; 8.6, 13). From this, the occasion arose for Simeon to create a metaphor of a rocky outcrop protruding in the road on which some people catch their foot and fall, but others along with their burdens not only fall but get up again. It is as if he was saying such is now the status of Messiah, that he is completely overwhelmed by the Shards and therefore a danger to those not looking where they are going. | Secondly: for the ancients the letter *yod* also denoted a sign (see *Lex. Cabb.*, pp. 65, 66.1; p. 67, n. 6). The Hebrew *šwʿ* means "to shout". So Simeon professed Jesus to be the sign belonging to the degree Kingdom, that *ʾoth* ["sign" in Hebrew] which is the beginning and end of every illumination, but meets with contentious and vociferous contradiction, such as is the meaning of the [Syriac] word *ḥryn'* in Lk 22.24; Acts 15.39; | Heb 6.16; 7.7. Our prophet [Simeon] goes on in this sense: "These calumnies and blasphemies excited against this your son, will be sharper than any sword, spear or weapon" (possibly because of the unaccustomed sound of the word he was thinking of that foreign weapon

---

in structura sua. Et de his dicitur Deut. 27, 6. *Lapidibus perfectis ædificabis altare Domini Dei tui*. Et cum ita perfecta est in Binah, tunc de ea dicitur ex Dan. 2, 34. *Videns eras, donec absissus est lapis* à Chochmah, secum ferens vim judicii ex parte Binah, & *percussit statuam* ut auferret idola è terra, & exscinderet Deos vanos, & tunc *factus est in montem magnum*, in loco suo, & *implevit totam terram*: quia hæc implet totam terram sub mysterio analogiæ quam cum Terra habet. Hæc omnia discuntur è verbis R. Schimeon ben Jochai in Tikkunim cum dicit: *Una hic altera ibi*, &. Ibid." ("Loci communes kabbalistici", op. cit., pp. 16–20).

253 "אות *Signum*. Hoc nomen Signi, sicut & אותו *Signum ejus*, ubique refertur ad Jesod: quia hic modus est signum fœderis. Et hoc modo multis in locis explicatur in Sohar & in Tikkunim. Verba ejus in Sectione וירא sunt hæc: ואותו & *signum ejus*, hoc est signum fœderis sancti, signum æternum. Sensus est: signi nomen referri ad Vav. Et sic אותות *Signa* sunt Vavin. Et sic datur signum in bonam, & aliud in malam partem. In bonam scilicet respectu benignitatis & miserationum: in malam autem respectu Gebhuræ. Ex parte Tiphereth autem vocatur signum longum, quia hic modus est medius & mundus longus. Sed in Raja Mehimna *Schechinah* vocatur *signum fœderis* respectu Jesod qui vocatur *Justus Mundi*. Eodemque in loco traditur quod per signum intelligatur Jod quod est super Vav. Et Schechinah vocatur אות ה"יא *Signum fœmininum*: Chochmah autem vocatur אות הוא *Signum masculinum* quia ambo vocantur Jodin prout expositum est in Pardes Tract. 14. c.3. & 4. Hinc dicitur quod signum sit Vav: & Schechinah respectu justi vocatur signum fœmininum: quia ipsa est Jod Corona super capite justi, qui est Vav. Pard. Tract. 23. c. 1. h.t." ("Loci communes kabbalistici", op. cit., pp. 65–66).

254 "Huc etiam pertinet quod Jod illud minutum, apex nempe inferior literæ Vav vocatur *signum parvum*, vel litera parva: diciturque signum fœderis sancti. Schaare Orah sub El Chai. [Connectitur cum ברית. Sequitur שבועה]". (Ibid., p. 67).

fol. 44ᵛ ut insolitam illam calumniandi[255] ‖‖ vehementiam eò penetrantius exprimeret. Sic enim acuta illa calumniantis linguæ mordacitas ab antiquis describi solebat Ps. 55, 22; Ps. 57, 5; Ps. 120, 4. Videatur & locus Sohar Cent. II. Loc. 26.) tuam ipsius animam penetrabunt. Unde id eneviet, ut multorum detegatur hypocrisis, qui cum Sancti videre[256] velint, sanctitatis | tamen hoc signum & exemplar perfectissimum omnibus viribus persequi non cessabunt.

V. 36. *Channa autem* &c. וחנא

Cabb. Cat. Ego hoc loco conjicerem, hanc fuisse revolutionem Channæ matris Samuelis, de qua tradunt Antiqui, quod fuerit ê revolutione Chavæ, | [vid. Tract. Vallis Regiæ p. 207. §. 12.[257]] Nam (1.) Nomine conveniunt. (2.) Hæc dicitur Prophetissa: qualis et mater Samuelis erat, quia de Messia vaticinabatur 1. Sam. 2, 10. (3.) Devota fuit utraque, cultusque divini studiosissima.

Christianus. Mysticè autem Channa hæc denotat Ecclesiam Israëliticam, quæ circa primum sui initium sub Mose â Gratiâ, juxta etymon Nominis, habuit | influxum; fuitque filia Pniel, i.e. facierum nominis אל, sive illuminationem habuit ab omnibus Sephiris sub Gradu El, i.e. Chesed contentis: ê tribu Asch[ir] i.e. felicitatis, contribuente sc. Lumen suum etiam Binah, seu Matre superna imò Corona ipsa: [vid. Lex. Cabbb. p. 166.[258]] dehinc intra annos virginitatis suæ mansit, donec David tabernaculum Domini Hierosolymas transferret, | ubi Hierosolyma inferior videtur nupsisse marito suo; abhinc si computentur anni usque ad excidium Templi, (sublatamque Schechinam, quod erat tempus inchoatæ viduitatis ejus,) 467, (nimirum 33. Davidis quatuor Salomonis ante templum & 43 usque ad destructionem templi juxta accuratissimum Lydiatum:) & abhinc tollant anni pravorum Regum

---

255 In the right bottom corner appears a Hebrew letter ל presumably an indication of binding or pagination.
256 Correction: videre replaced by videri
257 "Scito autem, quod Sarah, Channah, Sunamitis & Zarphitis omnes fuerint ex revolutione Chavæ, venerintque ut restituerent præcepta de menstruis, placenta & accensione candelæ. Et Sarah quidem restituit omnia, quoad ejus fieri poterat; istud enim est quod dixerunt Magistri nostri bonæ memoriæ, quod benedictionem invenerit in massa, id quod factum erat propter præceptum placentæ: Et lucernam accendit de una vespera Sabbathi in alteram: Et ratione menstruorum huc referendum, quod scriptum est Gen. 18, 11: *Cessaverat esse Saræ consuetudo mulierum.* Sed quia hoc saltem initium erat restitutionis, restitutio non fiebat pro requisitis; quare necessum erat, ut venirent 3. istæ mulieres cæteræ, quarum quælibet restitueret præceptum unum ex illis tribus. Channa restituit præceptum Nidda, quia scriptum est 1. Sam. 1, 18. *Et facies ejus ei non fuerunt ultra*: Sunamitis restituit candelam, sicut scriptum est 2. Reg. 4, 10. *Ponamusque*

called a *"gaesum"* [a Macedonian spear] to express more sharply the unaccustomed ||| vehemence of the calumnies). This is how the sharp mordacity of the tongue of the calumniator was usually described by the ancients (Ps 55.22; Ps 57.5; Ps 120.4). See also the passage in the Zohar (Cent. II Loc. 26).

fol. 44ᵛ

'will pierce your own soul also'.

So will be uncovered the hypocrisy of many, who, while they wish to seem holy, will not cease to persecute this | most perfect sign of holiness and example to all men.

Verse 36
Now Anna etc. *wḥn'*

Kabbalist Catechumen I imagine here that Anna was the reincarnation of Hannah the mother of Samuel, about whom the ancients taught that she was in turn the incarnation of Eve | (see Tract. *Vall. Reg.*, p. 207, § 12). For: (1) They have the same name; (2) Anna is called a prophetess, as was Hannah, the mother of Samuel, who prophesied about the Messiah in 1 Sam 2.10; (3) Each one of them was most attentively devoted to divine worship.

Christian Mystically here Anna denotes the Ecclesia of the Israelites, which around the time of its first beginning under Moses had an influx of Grace according to the meaning of the name, | [Anna]. Anna was the daughter of Phanuel (*i. e.* "of the faces of the name *'l* [El]") meaning she had illumination from all the degrees ranged under the degree of El (*i. e.* Chesed). She was of the tribe of Assher (*i. e.* Happiness) with Binah also, the supernal Mother, indeed Corona [Crown] herself, contributing her own light (see *Lex. Cabb.*, p. 166). "She then remained during the years of her virginity", until David transferred the Tabernacle of the Lord to Jerusalem | when the Lower Jerusalem seems to have married her husband. If we count the years from then until the [first] Destruction of the Temple (and the removal of the Shekhinah which was the time her widowhood began) we get 467. (That is: 33 for David, 4 for Solomon before the Temple and 430 up the Destruction of the Temple, according to the very accurate Lydiat). From this needs to

---

ipsi ibi lectum & mensam, & sellam, & candelabrum: Zarphitis autem restituit Challah, sicut scriptum est 1. Reg. 17, 14. *Cad farinæ non consumetur.*" ("Introductio pro meliori intellectu Libri Sohar. Vallem Regiam", op. cit., pp. 207–208).

258 Cf. *supra*, footnote 166, pp. 280–281.

Judæ, qui sunt quasi 125. remanent anni 342. Anni | autem 342.; efficiunt sep- 25
tem annos Jubilæos matrimonii; Dehinc â destructo templo usque ad natum
Christum, juxta Lydiati computum sunt anni 590. qui efficiunt annos quasi
duodecim Jubilæos, viduitatis seu absentiæ Schechinæ: sicuti Hanna vidua
fuisse dicitur duodecim annos Hebdomadicos sive 84. Nunc autem iterum
Prophetissa evadit, i.e. accessum habet Schechinæ, | Mal. 3, 1. 30

V. 37. *Et non abscedebat* &c. ולא פרקא

Christianus. Videturne inter illas pertinere, de quibus agitur Ex. 38, 8; 1. Sam.
2, 2[o] quippe quæ turmatim accedebant ad templum orandi vel sacrificiorum ob impuritatem offerendorum causa: iterumque recedebant?

Cabb. Cat. *Non mihi sed in templo*[259] *quodam* [*vaticinio*][260] *templi vicino* 35
Hierosolymis habitasse, ut omnibus sacris interesset: per totum diem jejunans,
studiisque legis incumbens, ut quædam filiæ Sapientum, & uxores ac viduæ
illorum, quamvis ad studia non essent obligata.

Et nocte ובלילה

Cabb. Cat. *Solebant enim Antiqui sub media nocte surgere, & studiis Legis* 40
incumbere: vide Excerpta Cent. II. Loc. 27. *Preces autem statæ non erant aliæ,*
quam matutinæ, vespertinæ & nocturnæ sub initium noctis fundi solitæ.

Christianus. Sed hæ erant arbitrariæ; & in specie fœminas minimè ob-
stringebant.

Cabb. Cat. *Ab accuratioribus & devotioribus tamen minimè negligebantur.* 45

fol. 45ʳ

V. 38. *Adstitit* &c. קמת |||

Christianus. Ubi?

Cabb. Cat. *Hæc omnia igitur gesta videntur in Atrio mulierum ubi Gazophy-*
lacium [vide Lightfoot. Centur. ante Matth. c. 29. item ad Matth. 8, 4. Item
Decad. ante Marc. c. 3, §.4.]

---

259 Correction above the line: templo replaced by loco
260 Deleted word (presumably vaticinio).
261 12×49=588.
262 The Peshitta has *wblly'*, but what Knorr has inadvertently written here *blylh* is Hebrew.
263 The reference here is to Lightfoot's *Chorographical Century* and to his *Chorographical Decad*. They are both found in *The Whole Works of Rev. John Lightfoot*, op. cit., vol. 10, pp. 3–183 and pp. 187–271 respectively.

SECTION VIII

be subtracted the 125 years of the wicked kings of Judah, leaving 342 years. Now 342 | years constitutes the seven jubilee years [49 years] of her marriage. From the Destruction of the Temple to the Birth of Christ according to Lydiat's reckoning is 590 years, which equals as it were[261], the 12 jubilee years of her widowhood, or the absence of the Shekhinah. So Anna is said to have been a widow for 12 Years of Weeks [*i. e.* 12 × 7] or 84 years, but now the prophetess "went out" again *i. e.* she had access to the Shekhinah | (Mal 3.1).

Verse 37
And she did not leave etc. wl' prq'

Christian Do Ex 38.8 and 1 Sam 2.20, where people go in crowds to the Temple to pray or offer sacrifices for uncleaness, *and then go out again*, not seem relevant here?

Kabbalist Catechumen Not to me. Rather [I imagine] she lived in a certain place near the Temple in Jerusalem, as she was involved in all the rites, fasting throughout the whole day and devoting herself to study of the Law, as did certain daughters of the sages and their wives and widows, although they had no legal obligation to study.

And night wblylh[262]

Kabbalist Catechumen The ancients used to get up in the middle of the night and devote themselves to study of the Law (see Excerpt Cent. II Loc. 27). The only fixed prayers offered were those in the morning, the evening and the beginning of the night.

Christian But these were optional and minimally affected women in particular.

Kabbalist Catechumen However they were not ignored by the most punctilious and devoted women.

Verse 38
She arose qmt ‖

fol. 45ʳ

Christian Where?

Kabbalist Catechumen All these things seem to have been done in the court of the Women [where the Treasury was] (See Lightfoot Centur. before Mt 29 and also on Mt 8.4. Also Decad. before Mk 3 § 4).[263]

Et confitebatur Dominum. ואודית למריא 5

[**Cabb. Cat.**]²⁶⁴ *Sensusne est, quod gratias egerit Deo?*

[**Christianus.**]²⁶⁵ Non putem: sed quod confessa sit Jesum hunc esse Messiam & Dominum deque illo locuta sit, nimirum quod nunc in carnem natus esset. Et hunc sensum istius vocis reperies Joh. 1, 20; Matth. 10, 32; Luc. 12, 8; Matth. 7, 23; | Rom. 14, 11; c. 10, 9.10; Act. 24, 14. 10

Liberationem Hierosolymarum. לפורקנה דאורשלם

[**Cabb. Cat.**]²⁶⁶ *Num intelligitur Liberatio urbis ab hostibus?*

[**Christianus.**]²⁶⁷ Neutiquam, sed liberatio totius populi Hierosolymis inchoanda, Luc. 24, 47; Rom. 11, 26; Jes. 59, 20. quod Antiquis erat notissimum, ex Prophetiis | passim. 15

V. 39. *Reversi sunt* &c. הפכו

[**Cabb. Cat.**]²⁶⁸ *Cur?*

[**Christianus.**]²⁶⁹ Non ut ibi habitarent, sed ut collectis reculis suis rem familiarem Bethlehemum transferrent, ubi credebant educandum esse Dominum, | quia in satis fuisset, ut ibi nasceretur. 20

---

264 Correction: Christianus replaced by Cabb. Cat. (which involves the two speakers being changed over in the following exchange).
265 Correction in the right margin: Cabb. Cat. replaced by Christianus (as a consequence of the previous correction).
266 Correction: Christianus replaced by Cabb. Cat. (which involves the two speakers being changed over in the following exchange).
267 Correction in the right margin: Cabb. Cat. replaced by Chr. (as a consequence of the previous correction).
268 Correction: Christianus replaced by Cabb. Cat. (which involves the two speakers being changed over in the following exchange).
269 Correction in the right margin: Cabb. Cat. replaced by Chr. (as a consequence of the previous correction).

SECTION VIII

        And gave thanks[270] *to God w'wdyt lmry'*

Kabbalist Catechumen Is the meaning that she thanked God?

Christian I don't think so, but rather that she confessed this Jesus was Messiah and Lord and had spoken of him as having been born in the flesh. This meaning of the word you will find in Jn 1.20; Mt 10.32; Lk 12.8; Mt 7.23; | Rm 14.11; 10.9, 10; Acts 24.14.

        The Liberation of Jerusalem lpwrqnh d'wršlm

Kabbalist Catechumen Surely not the liberation of the city from enemies?

Christian Not at all, but rather the beginning of the liberation of the whole people of Jerusalem (Lk 24.47; Rm 11.26; Isa 59.20), which the ancients had found salient throughout | the prophets.

        Verse 39
        They returned etc. *hpkw*

Kabbalist Catechumen Why?

Christian Not to live there, but to collect their [few] belongings and move their [new] family to Bethlehem, where, because it was appointed that the Lord should be born there, | they concluded he was also to be brought up.

---

270 Or: "confessed" since the Latin *confiteor* has both senses.

Sectio IX.
De Adventu Magorum & Fuga Christi: ex Matth. 2. p. t.

1.[1] Quum autem natus esset Jeschua in Bethlehem Jehuda[2], in diebus Herodis | Regis, venerunt Magi ab Oriente ad Jeruschalem.[3,4]

2. Et dixerunt, ubi est Rex Judæorum, qui natus est? Vidimus enim stellam ejus in Oriente, & venimus, ut summam reverentiam | exhibeamus ei.[5,6]

3. Audivit autem Hirodes[7] Rex, & conturbatus est & tota Jeruschalem cum eo.[8,9]

4. Et congregavit omnes Principes Sacerdotum & scribas populi, & percontabatur | eos, ubinam nasciturus esset Meschicha.[10]

5. Illi autem dixerunt, in Bethlehem Jehuda; ita enim scriptum est in Propheta:[11,12]

6. Etiam tu Bethlehem Jehuda non es | minima inter Reges Jehuda: ex te enim prodibit Rex, qui pascet populum meum Iisraël.[13,14]

7. Tunc Herodes clam vocavit. Magos, & didicit ab eis, quonam tempore apparuisset | eis stella.[15]

fol. 45ᵛ *8. Et misit eos in Bethlehem, dixitque ||| eis:[16] Ite, inquirite, de puero diligente & postquam inveneritis eum, venientes renunciate mihi, ut etiam ego profectus summam reverentiam exhibeam ei.[17]*

9. Illi autem cum audivissent â Rege, profecti sunt. Et ecce, stella illa, quam viderant in Oriente procedebat ante eos, usque dum progressa staret super illum locum, ubi erat puer.[18]

10. Quum autem vidissent stellam,[19] gavisi sunt gaudio magno valdè.

---

1   On the left-hand half of the page, a space was left, presumably for a fragment cut from Knorr's edition of the Peshittta New Testament containing the Syriac version of the quoted passage in the Gospel of Matthew.

2   Vulgate: cum ergo natus esset Jesus in Bethlehem Juda

3   Added in the right margin: Luc. 2, 4.6.7; Jud. 9, 1.2.18; Gen. 35, 5; Ruth. 1, 1; 1. Sam. 17, 12. Crossed out.

4   Vulgate: ecce Magi ab Oriente venerunt Jerosolymam.

5   Added in the right margin: Num. 24, 17; Matth. 21, 5; c. 25, 34.40; c. 27, 11.29.37.42. Crossed out.

6   Vulgate: dicentes: Ubi est qui natus est rex Judaeorum? Vidimus enim stellam eius in Oriente, et venimus adorare eum.

7   Correction: Hirodes replaced by Herodes

8   Added in the right margin: Matth. 8, 2; c. 9, 18; c. 14, 33; c. 15, 25; c. 18, 26; c. 20, 20; c. 28, 9.17. Crossed out.

9   Vulgate: Audiens autem Herodes rex turbatus est et omnis Jerosolyma cum illo.

10   Vulgate: Et congregans omnes principes sacerdotum et scribas populi, sciscitabatur ab eis ubi Christus nasceretur.

Section IX
The Arrival of the Magi and the Flight of Christ
From part of Mt 2

1 When Jeschua [Jesus] was born in Bethlehem Judah in the days of Herod | the King, Magi came from the East to Jerusalem.

2 And said "Where is he who is born the King of the Jews? For we have seen his star in the East and are come to show him | great reverence".

3 But King Herod heard and was disturbed and all of Jerusalem with him.

4 And he gathered all the chief priests and scribes of the people and asked | them where Messiah should be born.

5 And they said in Bethlehem Judah, for thus it is written in the Prophet:

6 "Thou Bethlehem Judah are not | least among the kings of Judah, for out of you will come a king who will feed my people Israel".

7 Then Herod secretly called the Magi and learned from them when the star had appeared | to them.

8 And he sent them to Behlehem, and said ||| to them "Go and inquire diligently about the boy and after you have found him come back and tell me, so that I also may show him deep reverence".   fol. 45ᵛ

9 And when they had listened to the King they set out and, behold, the star which they had seen in the East went before them until it moved and stood over the place where the boy was.

10 When they saw the star, they rejoiced with a very great joy.

---

11   Added in the right margin: Mich. 5, 1; Jon. 7, 42. Crossed out.
12   Vulgate: At illi dixerunt ei: in Bethlehem Judae: sic enim scriptum est per prophetam:
13   Added in the right margin: Heb. 2, 10. Crossed out.
14   Vulgate: Et tu, Bethlehem, terra Juda, nequaquam minima es in principibus Juda: ex te enim exiet dux, qui regat populum meum Israel.
15   Vulgate: Tunc Herodes clam vocatis Magis diligenter didicit ab eis tempus stellae, quae apparuit eis.
16   On the left-hand half of the page, a space was left, presumably for a fragment cut from Knorr's edition of the Peshittta New Testament containing the Syriac version of the quoted passage in the Gospel of Matthew.
17   Vulgate: Et mittens illos in Bethlehem, dixit: Ite, et interrogate diligenter de puero: et cum inveneritis, renunciate mihi ut et ego veniens adorem eum.
18   Vulgate: Qui cum audissent regem, abierunt: et ecce stella, quam viderant in Oriente, antecedebat eos, usque dum veniens staret supra ubi erat puer.
19   Vulgate: Videntes autem stellam.

11. Et ingressi sunt in domum, & viderunt puerum cum Mirjam matre ejus: & procedentes[20] *summam reverentiam exhibuerunt | ei: & aperuerunt conditoria sua obtuleruntque ei oblationes, aurum & myrrham & thus.*[21,22]

12. Et ostensum est eis per somnium, ne reverterentur ad Herodem;[23] *ac per viam aliam | profecti sunt*[24] *in regionem suam.*

13. Postquam autem abivissent, apparuit Angelus Domini per somnium Josepho, & dixit ei: Surge, accipe puerum & matrem ejus, & fuge in Ægyptum: & illis esto usque | dum dicam tibi. Futurum enim est, ut Herodes quærat puerum, ut perdat eum.

14. Joseph verò surgens[25] *accepit puerum & matrem ejus nocte & fugit*[26] *in Ægyptum.*

15. Mansitque illic, donec moreretur Herodes: | (ita) ut impleretur id, quod dictum est â Domino in Propheta, qui dixit:[27] *Ex Ægypto vocavi filium meum.*[28]

16. Tunc Herodes[29] *quum vidisset, quod illusus esset â Magis, excanduit valdè: | & mittens interficere fecit pueros omnes urbis Bethlechem, & omnium finium ejus â nato duos annos, & infra, juxta tempus, quod perquisiverat â Magis.*[30,31]

17. Tunc impletum est id,[32] *quod*[33] *| dictum erat per Jeremiam Prophetam, qui dixit:*[34,35]

18. Vox audita est in Rametha, fletus & ejulatus magnus. Rachel flens super filios suos, & noluit admittere consolationem, | propterea quod non extent.[36]

19. Postquam autem mortuus esset Herodes[37] *Rex, apparuit Angelus Domini per ⫾ somnium Josepho in Ægypto.*[38]

fol. 46ʳ

20. Et dixit ei: Surgens abducito puerum & matrem ejus, & proficiscere in terram Jisraël: mortui enim sunt illi[39]*, qui quæbant*[40] *| animam pueri.*

21. Et Joseph surgens abduxit puerum[41] *& matrem ejus, & venit in terram Iisraël.*

---

20 Correction: procedentes replaced by procidentes
21 Added in the left margin: Ps. 72, 10.11; Es. 60, 6. Crossed out.
22 Vulgate: Et intrantes domum, invenerunt puerum cum Maria matre eius, et procidentes adoraverunt eum: et apertis thesauris suis obtulerunt ei munera, aurum, thus, et myrrham.
23 Vulgate: Et responso accepto in somnis ne redirent ad Herodem.
24 Vulgate: reversi sunt.
25 Vulgate: Qui consurgens
26 Vulgate: secessit.
27 Vulgate: Et erat ibi usque ad obitum Herodis; ut adimpleretur quod dictum est a Domino per prophetam dicentem.
28 Added in the left margin: Os. 11, 1. Crossed out.
29 Correction: Herodes replaced by Herodis
30 Added in the left margin: Supr. 2, 7. Crossed out.

11 And they went into the house and saw the boy with Mary his mother and falling down they showed him great reverence: | and they opened their treasures and made offerings to him—gold, myrrh and frankincense.

12 And it was revealed to them in a dream not to return to Herod, so they set off home | by another route.

13 After they had gone away, the Angel of the Lord appeared in a dream to Joseph and said to him: "Arise, take the boy and his mother and flee to Egypt and stay there | until I tell you. For Herod will seek to kill the boy".

14 Joseph arose and took the boy and his mother by night and fled into Egypt.

15 And stayed there until Herod died, | (so) that it might be fulfilled what was written by the Lord in the Prophet, who said: "Out of Egypt have I called my son".

16 Then Herod when he saw that he had been tricked by the Magi was very angry | and he sent and had killed all the boys of the town of Bethlehem of two years of age and below, according to the time he had learned from the Magi.

17 Then was fulfilled that which | was spoken by the prophet Jeremiah who said:

18 "A voice was heard in Rametha, a weeping and great wailing, Rachel crying for her sons and she would accept no consolation | for they no longer were alive".

19 After the death of King Herod the Angel of the Lord appeared ||| in a dream to Joseph in Egypt.   fol. 46ʳ

20 And said to him: "Arise and take the boy and his mother away from here and go to the land of Israel, for those who sought | the boy's life are dead".

21 And Joseph rose up and took the boy and his mother and came to the land of Israel.

---

31   Vulgate: Tunc Herodes videns quoniam illusus est a magis, iratus erat valde, et mittens occidit omnes pueros qui erant in Bethlehem et in omnibus finibus eius, a bimatu et infra, secundum tempus quod exquisierat a Magis.

32   Vulgate: Tunc adimpletum est quod

33   Deleted word now unreadable.

34   Added in the left margin: Jer. 31, 15. Crossed out.

35   Vulgate: dicentem.

36   Vulgate: Vox in Rama audita est ploratus et ululates multus; Rachel plorans filios suos, et noluit consolari, quia non sunt.

37   Correction: Herodes replaced by Herodis.

38   Vulgate: Defuncto autem Herode, ecce angelus Domini apparuit in somnis Joseph in Aegypto.

39   Vulgate: dicens: surge et accipe puerum, et matrem eius, et vade in terram Israel; defuncti sunt enim.

40   Correction above the line: quæbant replaced by quærebant.

41   Vulgate: Qui consurgens, accepit puerum.

22. *Quum verò audivisset, quod Archelaus esset Rex in Judæa loco Herodis patris | sui, timuit proficisci illud; & ostensum est ei per somnium, ut proficisceretur in regionem GalilϾ.*⁴²

23. *Et veniens habitavit in civitate, quæ vocatur Natzrath*⁴³, *(ita) ut impleretur id, quod | dictum fuit in Propheta; quod Nazarenus vocaretur.*⁴⁴

V. 1. *Cum autem natus esset* &c. כד דין אתיליד

[*Cabb. Cat.*]⁴⁵ Quo tempore id factum esse statuis?

[**Christianus.**]⁴⁶ Non putandum est Magos statim advenisse post nativitatem | Domini, & adhuc infra 40. dies ante purificationem Mariæ, prout communis fert opinio. Nam (1.) Josephus testis est, eos qui supra Euphratem habitant, Hierosolyma demum venisse mensium quinque itinere: unde hi, sive Arabes, sive Chaldæi, sive Persæ fuerint, quinque Septimanarum spatio iter suum non potuerunt absolvere. (2.) Si post instructas jam ab Herode insidias occisosque pueros Bethlehemiticos | Christus in templum delatus est, mirum foret, Herodi nihil innotuisse de iis, quæ â Simeone & Channâ de ipso publico rumore propalabantur. De quo in hodiernum usque diem traditio peculiaris extat inter Christianos Orientis. (3.) Nec fuga in Ægyptum & reditus abinde includi possunt spatio illi 40. dierum. (4.) Matthæus expressè ait v. 16. Herodem occidisse infantes illius ætatis, qualem | Christus habere potuerit, juxta tempus accuratè â Magis perquisitum: quod spatium ille ad summum biennio determinabat ab exorta stella v. 7. & consequenter nato Christo.

---

42 Vulgate: Audiens autem quod Archelaus regnaret in Judaea pro Herode, patre suo, timuit illo ire; et admonitus in somnis, secessit in partes Galilaeae.

43 Vulgate: Nazareth.

44 Vulgate: ut adimpleretur quod dictum est per prophetas: Quoniam Nazaraeus vocabitur.

45 Correction: Christianus replaced by Cabb. Cat. (which involves the two speakers being changed over in the following exchange).

46 Correction in the right margin: Cabb. Cat. replaced by Chr. (as a consequence of the previous correction).

47 Lightfoot, *Miscellanies and the Harmony of the Gospels*, op. cit., p. 206: "It hath been generally held and believed, almost of every one, that the wise men came to Christ, when he was but thirteen days old; and it is written in red letters in the calendar, as if it were a golden truth, by the title of Epiphany, at the sixth of January." Lightfoot disagrees and argues otherwise at length pp. 206–212.

22 *But when he heard that Archelaus was King in Judaea in his father's place, | he was afraid to go there and was instructed in a dream to go to the region of Galilee*

23 *And he came and lived in a town called Natzrath, (so) that might be fulfilled that which | was said by the Prophet: "he shall be called a Nazarene".*

Verse 1
When Jesus was born etc. *kd dyn 'tyld*

Kabbalistic Catechumen When do you think this happened?

Christian It is not to be thought that the Magi came immediately after the Nativity | of the Lord and within the forty days before Mary's purification, as the common opinion has it.[47] For:

1. Josephus is a witness that some people who lived beyond the Euphrates finally arrived in Jerusalem after a journey of five months[48]. So these men whether they were Arabs, Chaldeans, or Persians could not have accomplished their journey in five weeks.

2. If after the ambush then laid by Herod and the slaughter of the boys of Bethlehem, | Christ was taken to the Temple it would be amazing if Herod had noticed nothing of those things [done] by Simeon and Anna and noised abroad by very public rumour. A special tradition about this exists amongst Eastern Christians right up until today[49].

3. Neither the flight to Egypt, nor the return from there can be fitted into that period of 40 days.

4. Matthew expressly states in verse 16 that Herod killed the children of the age that | Christ would have been, according to the time accurately inquired of by the Magi. That age had been determined as at most two years—from the rising of the star (verse 7) and consequently from the birth of Christ.

---

48   Apparently, this is a reference to *Antiquities* XI.5.2 recounting Ezra's journey from the Euphrates to Jerusalem "on the twelfth day of the first month of the seventh year of the reign of King Xerxes". They came to Jerusalem in the fifth month of the same year.

49   It is not obvious that there is a consistent Eastern tradition here. Epiphanius (*Adversus Haereses* 51.9) argued for the arrival of the Magi two years after the birth, in agreement with Knorr here, but Theophylact (*On Mt Gospel*, chap. 2) thought they arrived when Christ was still in the cave. Theophylact and Chrystostom (*Homily 6* on Mt 2.1–12) held the star appeared at the very moment of the Annunciation, the Descent of the Holy Spirit and the Incarnation of the Logos in the womb of Mary.

In Bethlechem Jehudah &c. בביתלחם דיהודא

Christianus. De hoc oppido, quod juxta Justinum Martyrem Apol. 2. stadiis triginta | quinque Hierosolymis distabat, id est, unico milliari Germanico majore; pauca inveniuntur apud vestrates.

Cabb. Cat. Nomen ipsum autem Cabbalistis nostris denotaret Receptaculum divinæ influentiæ; Regnumque seu Ecclesiam, quando cum illa unitur Tiphereth. [videatur Lex. Cabbalist. p. 500.⁵⁰] [**Christianus.**]⁵¹ ubi commodissimè intelligere possumus | Messiam venientem ad Ecclesiam, cum largissimo influxu supernarum saturitatum.

[Christianus.]⁵² Et sic quælibet Anima tunc est Domus Panis, seu Receptaculum divinæ Benedictionis quando vita Christi in illa generatur. Prov. 9, 5; Joh. 6, 32.33.35.48.50.51; Matth. 26, 26. Dicitur autem Bethlechem Jehudah, ad diffenretiam | Bethlechem tribus sebulon Jos. 19, 15. quasi per illam urbem Epulum Laudis & confessionis; per hanc domesticum saltem indigitaretur. 1. Cor. 11, 29.

Herodis &c. הרודס

Cabb. Cat. [Quis est sensus nominis?]⁵³ [**Christianus.**]⁵⁴ Hoc nomen si Chaldaicæ statuatur esse originis sensum habet diducendi & expandendi: si Syriacæ, solitudinem & vastitatem denotat; item ‖ tumultum: si Arabicæ autem⁵⁵, quod quàm maximè est probabile, lacerandi diffindendique & proscindendi significationem habet, sive vestis intelligatur, sive famæ.

---

50 "לחם *Panis*. Communiter refertur ad Malchuth è loco 1. Reg. 13, 19. Sed in Raja Meh. לחם dicitur esse Vav, scilicet in Tiphereth. Pro quorum conciliatione notetur è Tikkunim, quod Malchuth triplicem habeat notionem, nempe Cholem, Schurek, Chirek. Cholem autem dicitur, quando est supra Vav, tanquam corolla Tiphereth ratione Chochmah: & חלם per metathesin est לחם panis, & huc pertinet locus Psal. 78, 25. atque sic Malchuth & Tiphereth concipiuntur esse in unione. Quando igitur in Raja Meh. לחם dicitur Vav, ibi intelligitur Cholem. Sed Sect. Trumah, per Panem intelligitur Influentia, quæ demittitur in Malchuth. Dicendum ergo, quod Malchuth tunc dicatur Panis, quando repleta est influxu, quod sit per unionem ejus cum Tiphereth. Ubi si prævalet Tiphereth, Panis ille dicitur לחם פ״נג & Panis masculinus, & Vav: sed si prævalet Fœmina, erit לחם עוני Panis paupertatis, Deut. 16, 3. respectu Malchuth. [...]" ("Loci communes kabbalistici", op. cit., p. 500).

51 Added in the right margin: Chr. (which involves a change of speaker).

52 Deletion: Christianus. The change of speaker is no longer needed, as a consequence of the previous correction.

53 Question added in the right margin.

54 Added in the right margin: Christ. (in order to give the speech to the Christian).

In Bethlehem Judah etc. bbytlḥm dyhwdʾ

Christian The ancients have little to say about this town which according to Justin Martyr (Apol 2) is 35 | stades away from Jerusalem, which is one of Germanicus' greater milestones[56].

Kabbalist Catechumen For our Kabbalists, the name itself denotes a receptacle of divine influence and Kingdom, or Ecclesia when Tiferet is united with it [See *Lex. Cabb.*, p. 500].

Christian From which we can most conveniently learn | of Messiah coming to Ecclesia with a very great influx of supernal abundance.

And thus any Soul then becomes the House of Bread or Receptacle of Divine Blessing when the life of Christ is generated within it (Pro 9.5; Jn 6.32, 33, 35, 48, 50, 51; Mt 26.26). The text says "Bethlehem Judah" to distinguish it | from Bethehem of the tribe of Zebulon in Jos 19.15 as if by the first city was indicated a feast of praise and confession, but by the second, a mere domestic meal 1 Cor 11.29.[57]

Of Herod, etc. hrwdś

Kabbalist Catechumen What does this name mean?

Christian If this name is to be considered of Aramaic origin it has the meaning of stretching and expanding; if of Syriac origin, it denotes solitude and vast spaces, or ||| tumult. But if it is Arabic, which is the most likely it means to rip up, cut or tear and is used either of a garment or of a reputation[58].

fol. 46ᵛ

---

55   Deleted word.
56   A topic explored since 1970 by the Israel Milestone Committee, see briefly: Benjamin Isaac, "Milestones in Judaea: From Vespasian to Constantine" in *The Near East under Roman Rule—Selected Papers* (Leiden: Brill, 1988), pp. 48–75; I. Roll, "The Roman Road System in Judea", *Jerusalem Cathedra* 3 (1983): pp. 136–161. Lightfoot, *Miscellanies and the Harmony of the Gospels*, op. cit., p. 205: "Beth-lehem distant from Jerusalem thirty-five furlongs (Just. Mart. Apol. 2), four miles, and almost a half".
57   The meaning of Judah which first qualifies Bethlehem is "praise"; that of Zebulon, similarly modifying Bethlehem, is taken here to be a dwelling place. Hence, the feast of praise and confession, or an ordinary domestic meal.
58   Deletion: "All of which contributes very little to extracting the mystical sense here. [See more about Herod on Lk 1.5.]". The etymologies offered here for Herod's name are taken from Castell's *Lexicon Heptaglotton*, op. cit., col. 883–884. At the end of the entry Castell suggests the Arabic derivation of Herod's name.

[Christianus.] Quæ omnia haud parùm conducunt ad eruendum hoc loco sensum mysticum [vide plura de Herode ad Luc. 1, 5.][59]

Magi ab Oriente &c. מגושא מן מדנחא

Cabb. Cat. [*E qua regione?*][60] [**Christianus.**][61] Incertum quidem est, qua ê Regione isti venerint: quia per Kedem seu Orientem in sacris partim intelligitur Arabia, ut. Gen. 25, 6; Jud. 6, 3; c. 8, 10.11; Job. 1, 3; Jer. 49, 28. & fortè Jes. 11, 14; Ez. 25, 4.10. partim Mesopotamia Gen. 29, 1. & plures, 1. Reg. 4, 30. Et munera quidem illorum, fructus sunt Arabiæ: Mirum tamen | est, quod ipsi etiam Arabes suæ id Regioni non tribuant, quod patria horum Magorum fuerit; sed ab iis pro Persis habeantur, qui ignem adoraverint. Suntque de iis inter Orientales diversæ traditiones. Syri quidam hæc ipsi tribuunt Nomina: Aduphan; Horman; Tachsas. Alii hæc: Nudpurhon; Artachsasta; Lebuda; & Alpheza. Persis appellantur Amad; suo Amad; & Deusta Amad. In Dictionario | Syriaco Bar Bahluli hæc de his Magis extant. Erant 3. Magi filii Elam, Bar, Scham; quorum Genealogiæ per 3. secula sunt in Traditione, prout eas delinearunt Pictores quidam. Inde 3. eorum dona; numero autem duodecim. Ex principalioribus ac celeberrimis in universo Persiæ regno viris erant, ut sic perfectum atque sacrum, qui in scripturis occurrit numerum, complerent. Nomina | eorum hæc erant: Ahadojaad; Hadundat Bar Atbanan; Vastaph Bar Nudpar, Arsach, Bar Mahados; Zeronad; Vadvad Bar Veronad; Arihu Bar Cosro; Artachsasta Bar Cholith; Astanbuzan Bar Sisaron; Achsidas Bar Zibon; Zardanach Bar Baldaz; Merodach Bar Bel. Hæc ibi.

---

59   Deletion of the entire intervention of the Christian.
60   Question added in the left margin.
61   Added in the left margin: Christ. (in order to give the speech to the Christian).
62   Lightfoot, *Miscellanies and the Harmony of the Gospels*, op. cit., pp. 215–218 is of the same opinion concerning the provenance of the gifts. He takes the *magoi* as Arabian magicians.
63   Ugo Monneret de Villard, *Le leggende orientali sui magi evangelici* (Rome: Bibliotheca Apostolica Vaticana, 1973).
64   Witold Witakowski, "The Magi in Syriac Tradition" in *Malphono w-Rabo d-Malphone: Studies in Honour of Sebastian P. Brock*, edited by George Kiraz (Piscaway NJ: Gorgias, 2008), pp. 809–847. Also Kristian Heal, "The Magi in the Syriac Tradition: A Critical bibliography of Sources and Studies" made available at the Oxford Patristic Conference August 2011 and now available on edu.ac.

SECTION IX

5   *Magi from the East* etc. *mgwš' mn mdnḥ'*

Kabbalist Catechumen From what region?

Christian It is uncertain from which region they came. By *Kedem* or the *East* in Scripture is sometimes meant Arabia as Gen 25.6; Judg 6.3; 8.10, 11; Job 1.3; Jer 49.28 and perhaps Isa 11.14; Ezek 25.4, 10. Sometimes it means Mesopotamia, as in Gen 29.1 and many other places, 1 Kgs 4.30. The gifts
10 of the Magi are products of Arabia.[62] However, it is a wonder | that even the Arabs themselves do not consider that their own region was the home of the Magi. We take them to be Persians who worshipped fire. There are diverse traditions about the Magi amongst Easterners.[63] Syrians give them the names Adaphan, Horman and Tachsas.[64] Others [call them] Nudpurhon, Artachsasta, Lebuda and Alpheza. The Persians call them Amad Sudamad
15 and Deusta Amad. In the Syriac dictionary | of Bar Bahlul these words about these Magi are found[65]:

"There were three Magi [who were] sons of Elam, Bar and Scham (whose genealogies as some painters drew them up, went back through three centuries of tradition). Which is why they gave three types of gifts, although there were twelve men by number. They were from amongst the leading and famous men of the whole kingdom of Persia and thus they made up the most perfect and sacred number which occurs in Scripture, [twelve].
20 Their names | were Ahadojaad; Hadundat Bar Atbanan; Vastaph bar Nudpar, Arsach bar Mahados; Zeronad; Vadvad Bar Veronad; Arihu Bar Cosro; Artachsasta Bar Cholith; Astanbuzan Bar Sisaron; Achsidas Bar Zibon; Zardanach Bar Baldaz; Merodach Bar Bel." *End of Quotation.*[66]

---

65   Bar Bahlul's tenth-century Syriac Lexicon is one of the most common and distinguished of the native lexica. The quotation above is his entry under *mgwš'* [*magoi*]. Today the lexicon is read in the splendid edition of Rubens Duval, *Lexicon Syriacum auctore Hassano bar Bahlule*, 3 vols (Paris: E Reipublicae Typographaeo, 1901), vol. 2, col. 1002–1003. One is unaware of any printed edition of the Lexicon before Duval, so the question arises how Knorr knew this passage. Duval's third volume contains a description of the manuscripts he used. His manuscript M, Codex Marsh 198, now in the Bodleian, was sent to Jacobus Golius from his brother in the East in 1650 (page xxvii). Another manuscript (Duval's C) (page xxviii) was owned by Erpenius and at his death passed to the University Library in Cambridge. This was fully exploited there by Castell in his *Lexicon Heptaglotton*. Indeed the whole of our quotation is found in Castell s.v. *mgš* (col. 1991) which is clearly where Knorr got it from. Joannes D. Michaelis, *Edmundi Castelli Lexicon Syriacum ex eius Lexico Heptaglotto* (Göttingen: Sumptibus J. Christ. Dietrich, 1788) carried this citation well into the Nineteenth Century. It is found in his *Pars Prima*, pp. 482–483.

66   Deletion: Christian. It is unimportant to us, from which Eastern region they came.

[Christianus.] Nobis indifferens est, â quânam venerint Regione orientali.[67]

V.2. *Rex Judæorum* &c. מלכא דיהודיא

Christianus. Messiam intelligunt, in toto Oriente Traditionis fama & Mosis Prophetarumque, præsertim Danielis scriptis percelebrem: quique in scriptis veterum sæpius vocatur מלכא משיחא Rex Messias [vide in Excerptis Loca de Messia Cent. 1. Loc. 62. sqq.]

Cabb. Cat. *Notandum autem antiquissimam fuisse Traditionem nativitate in hunc mundum Messiam esse venturum, quo etiam pertinet Locus illæ Gemaræ Hierosolymitanæ, vid. Excerpta Cent. II. Loc. 16. Quamvis enim Messiæ animam jam ante mundi creationem productam esse inque Paradiso hactenus degere statuant Doctores nostri (videantur inter Excerpta Loca 62.74. etc. Cent. I.)* | *non tamen crediderunt illam Angelorum more descensuram assumto corpore aëreo; sed verum hominem futurum.*

Stellam ejus &c. כוכבה

[**Cabb. Cat.**][68] *Antiqua fuit Traditio, circa tempora Messiæ apparituram stellam quandam*[69] *cujus apparitionem quidem*[70] *ad Adventum Messiæ gloriosum referunt vestrates*[71]*; sed*[72] | *procul dubio sub velo Mosaico* [Videantur antiqua illa tradita inter[73] Excerpta Loc. 70.74. &c. Cent. I.]

[**Christianus.**][74] Hæc ipsa autem, quàm Magi in orientalibus suis regionibus viderunt stella, nec Cometa fuit, nec Angelus; sed Schechinah, seu[75] gloriosorum & sublimium Animæ Messianæ graduum, (de quibus diximus[76] ad Luc. 1. 35. & 59.) | singularis manifestatio. Sicut enim idem Messias apparebat Mosi in flamma ardentis rubi Ex. 3, 2. item Iisraëlitis in columna ignis, Ex. 14, 24. ita Pastoribus ||| similis fiebat manifestatio Luc. 2, 9. ubi vide

fol. 47ʳ

---

67 Deletion of the entire intervention of the Christian.
68 Correction in the left margin: Christianus replaced by Cabb. Cat. (which involves the two speakers being changed over in the following exchange).
69 Added in the left margin: sed
70 Deleted word.
71 Correction: vestrates replaced by nostrates (as a consequence of the change of speaker).
72 Deleted word.
73 Deletion: antiqua illa tradita inter

SECTION IX

Verse 2
King of the Jews etc. *mlkʾ dyhwdyʾ*

Christian In the whole of the East, by the report of Tradition and of Moses and of the Prophets, Messiah is understood [to be mentioned] here [in this passage] [and] specifically [as] that most celebrated personage in the writings of Daniel, who in the writings of the elders is more often called *mlkʾ mšyḥʾ* King and Messiah (see the passages on Messiah in Excerpts Cent. I Loc. 62 *seq.*).

Kabbalist Catechumen It is remarkable that there was a very ancient tradition that Messiah should come into this world by birth, to which is relevant a passage in the Jerusalem Talmud (see Excerpts Cent. II Loc. 16). For although the soul of Messiah had been created long before the Creation of the World and our sages state it lived previously in Paradise (see among the Excepts Cent. I Loc. 62, 74 etc.), | they did not however believe it would descend like an angel, assuming an arial body, but would be a real man.

His star etc. *kwkbh*[77]

Kabbalist Catechumen There was an ancient tradition that around the Time of Messiah a star would appear, whose appearance our sages connected to the Glorious Advent of Messiah, but | no doubt under the Mosaic veil[78]. (These ancient traditions can be found in Excerpts Cent. I Loc. 70, 74 etc.)

Christian The star which the Magi saw in their eastern regions was neither a comet nor an angel, but the Shekhinah, or a special manifestation of the glorious and sublime degrees of the Soul of Messiah (about which, [see] on Lk 1.35, 59).[79] | For just as Messiah appeared to Moses in the flame of the Burning Bush (Ex 3.2), or to the Israelites in the Pillar of Fire (Ex 14.24), so there was a similar appearance to the shepherds ||| (see the note   fol. 47ʳ

---

74   Correction in the left margin: Cabb. Cat. replaced by Christ.
75   Correction: seu replaced by sed
76   Deleted word.
77   For the extraordinary interest raised by the comets of 1680–1681 and a critique of Knorr's proposed authorship of a work *Cometa Scepticus*, see Finke, *Sulzbach im 17 Jahrhundert*, op. cit., pp. 225–230.
78   2 Cor 3.13.
79   For a similar explanation of the Glory that appeared to the shepherds in Lk 2.13–14, see folio 41ᵛ.

annotationem[80]: Eodemque modo Apparitio talis Schechinæ etiam facta est Magis. Non quod eodem tempore, cum Gloria Messiæ circumdaret Pastores, fulgorem eundem in stellæ forma & Magi viderint, quia ê remotis illis regionibus orientalibus humilior illa coruscatio conspici non | potuisset. Sed quod supra locum nati Messiæ splendor quidam continuò emicaret longe sublimior, & in extremitate Atmosphæræ constitutus, ê quo supra partum hunc semper ascenderent & descenderent Angeli, ministri Schechinæ proximi, Joh. 1, 52. Hic autem splendor propterea non fuit agnitus in Judæa, quia ibidem præter observationes Lunæ recentis nulla colebatur Astroscopia: & si fortè Pastores simile | quid ibidem observarunt; id sanè ab hisce pro recenti phænomeno non fuit habitum, sed inter reliquias conspecti sibi Exercitus Angelici relatum; cujus apparitionis famam & ipsi inter suos divulgabant. Hunc splendorem in ista altitudine haud aliter conspicere potuerunt, observatores Magi, quàm sub stellæ formâ, sed non caudatæ, quia aliàs & in Judæa fuisset agnita, pro cometa, sicut ille, | qui integro anno ante excidium urbis, supra Hierosolymis apparuit. Si autem in diversis Orientis Regionibus habitarunt, (quod admodum videtur probabile;) phænomenon hoc aliter observari non potuit, quam sub insigni parallaxi, unde dehinc factis pluribus inter se super ista apparitione communicationibus, exorta est prima inter illos conjectura de loco cui immineret, nempe Judæa; & postmodùm de ipsius | significatione, quod nempe natum denotaret Messiam. Sciendum autem in regionibus orientalibus tum temporis adhuc viguisse antiquissimam illam Religionem Gentilium, quæ dicta fuit Nabathæorum seu Chaldæorum seu Charanæorum &c. cui & Persæ addicti erant: quæque juxta Patricidem & Elmacinum scriptores Arabicos jam Serughi (qui proavus erat Abrahami,) temporibus exorta fuisse dicitur Autore quodam Zerodasto, | (qui Zoroaster est, cui & Epiphanius & alii Magiæ initium tribuunt:) unde & Abrahamum Sabæorum fuisse innutritum superstitionibus tradunt Euseb. Hist. Ecclesia-

---

80 Deleted word.
81 Josephus, *De Bello Judaico*, 6.5.3: "and at the ninth hour of the night so great a light shone round the altar and the holy house, that it appeared to be bright day-time; which light lasted for half an hour."

SECTION IX

on Lk 2.9). And in the same fashion a similar appearance of the Shekhinah was made to the Magi. It was not that, at the same time, when the Glory of Messiah surrounded the shepherds, the Magi too saw the same brightness but in the form of a star (since from those remote oriental regions a lower brightness could not | have been seen), but it was [rather] that above the place of the new-born Messiah, a far higher brightness shone out continually, and formed on the far edges of the Atmosphere from which, above this birth, angels, the closest ministers of the Shekhinah, ascended and descended (Jn 1.52). This Splendour was not noticed in Judaea, because there, other than sightings of the new moon, nobody was interested in observing the stars. And if by chance the shepherds | there observed something, it would not be taken by them for a new phenomenon, but considered a remnant of the angelic host they had seen, the report of which appearance they themselves were spreading amongst their people. This brightness at this height the Magi observers could not have perceived other than in the form of a star, but not with a tail which would have been recognised elsewhere, and in Judaea, for a comet, as was the one | which appeared over the city of Jerusalem, a whole year before its destruction[81]. But if the Magi lived in Eastern regions different [from each other] (which seems quite likely), this phenomenon could not have been observed other than as a striking parallax. So from many people communicating these facts about this appearance to each other, there arose among them an initial conjecture about the place it overhung, namely Judaea, and then [another conjecture] about its meaning, | namely that it indicated the birth of Messiah. One should know that in eastern regions at that time, the most ancient Gentile religion, which was said to be that of the Nabateans or Chaldeans or Haranites, to which the Persians adhered, was still flourishing. And which, according to the Arabic writers Patricides and Elmacinus[82] is said already in the days of Serug, the great-grandfather of Abraham, to have been promoted by a certain writer, Zerodestro, | (who is Zoroaster), to whom Epiphanius[83] and others attribute the origin of magic. So traditionally Abraham was brought up in the superstitions of the Sabaeans[84]: Eusebius, *Ecclesiastical History*

---

82 Elmacinus and Patricides are cited extensively in Johann H. Hottinger, *Smegma Orientale* (Heidelberg: A. Wyngaerden, 1658), Book I, chap. VIII. ("*De usu Linguarum Orientalium in Theologia Historica*"). This is likely the source of Knorr's knowledge. For Abraham as a Sabaean, and Zoroaster, pp. 279–280. However Knorr's report of the Sabaeans is based squarely on Maimonides.
83 *Panarion*, 1.1.6.
84 A learned introduction to the scholarship of early religion in the Seventeenth Cen-

sticæ l. 1 c.5. Arabes passim, Maimonidesque in More Nevoch. l. III. c. 29. Eidemque addicti fuerunt Nabathæi, Arabiæ Petreæ incolæ &c. item Chaldæi; item incolæ Charam in Mesopotamia; item Sabæi Arabiæ felicis incolæ &c. Nec abolita est in | hodiernum usque diem, cum adhuc in Persia vigeat inter Ignicolas, qui ibidem Gabri appellantur. Crediderunt[85] autem quod stellæ Dii sint, Sol autem Deorum maximus. Sacrificia obtulerunt Planetis, & Samaëli aliisque Dæmonibus & Geniis utriusque sexus: inter quæ etiam infantes mactabant. Preces statas ter quotidie fundebant. Lotiones adhibebant ob gonorrhæam, & abstinebant â menstruatis. | Ciborum observabant discrimina. Imagines fabricabant magicas quas Tilsemat Arabes vocant, vel Talismat.[86] Tradit[87] etiam[88] Maimonides, quod[89] varios habuerint libros de ratione stellarum, de magia, exorcismis, astris spiritualibus & Fateturque quod[90] multarum Legum Mosaicarum rationes & causæ sibi innotuerint ex cognitione fidei & cultus. Zabæorum, quippe cui | Religio Judaica expressè fuerit opposita. Porrò[91] de illis scribit, quod erexerint stellis imagines, & Soli quidem aureas, Lunæ verò argenteas; atque ita metalla & climata terræ inter stellas partiti sint. Item quod sacella ædificaverint, imaginesque in illis collo-

tury is Thomas Stanley, *The History of the Chaldaic Philosophy* (London: Thomas Dring, 1662).
85   Beginning of the deletion.
86   End of the deletion: Crediderunt autem quod stellæ Dii sint, Sol autem Deorum maximus. Sacrificia obtulerunt Planetis, & Samaëli aliisque Dæmonibus & Geniis utriusque sexus: inter quæ etiam infantes mactabant. Preces statas ter quotidie fundebant. Lotiones adhibebant ob gonorrhæam, & abstinebant â menstruatis. Ciborum observabant discrimina. Imagines fabricabant magicas quas Tilsemat Arabes vocant, vel Talismat.
87   Correction: Tradit replaced by Traditque
88   Deleted word.
89   Beginning of the deletion.
90   End of the deletion: quod varios habuerint libros de ratione stellarum, de magia, exorcismis, astris spiritualibus & Fateturque quod
91   Beginning of the deletion.
92   "It is well known that the Patriarch Abraham was brought up in the religion and the opinion of the Sabeans that there is no divine being except the stars. I will tell you in this chapter their works which are at present extant in Arabic translations, and also in their ancient chronicles; and I will show you their opinion and their practice according to these books. You will then see clearly that they consider the stars as deities, and the sun as the chief deity. They believe that all the seven stars are gods, but the two luminaries are greater than all the rest. They say distinctly that the sun governs the world, both that which is above and that which is below; these are exactly their expressions. In these books, and in their chronicles, the history of Abraham our father is given in the following manner [...]." (Translation taken from Michael Friedlander, *Moses Maimonides. The Guide for the Perplexed* (New York: Dover, 1905, 2000), ad loc.)

SECTION IX 511

Book I, chap. 5, Arab writers generally and Maimonides in his *Guide for the Perplexed* Book III, chap. 29.[92] To the same [Zoroaster] were devoted the Nabateans, the inhabitants of Arabia Petraea, the Chaldeans, the inhabitants of Haran in Mesopotamia, and the Sabaeans who live in Arabia Felix. Nor has the religion died out | even today when it still flourishes in Persia amongst inhabitants who are called there Gabri[93].

[Deletion: They believed that the stars are gods and the Sun the greatest of the gods. They offered sacrifices to the planets and to Samael and to other demons and genii of either sex, during which they slaughtered children. They offered fixed prayers three times a day. They had ritual washing for fluxes and kept away from menstruants. | They had food laws. They made magical images which the Arabs call Tilsemat or Talismat.] Maimonides says[94] [Deletion: they had various books about the movements of the stars, magic, exorcisms, astral spirits etc. It was said] that they knew many of the reasons and causes of the Mosaic laws they had noted for themselves from knowledge of the faith and worship of the Sabeans, although | the Jewish religion was explicitly opposed to this. [Deletion: It was written about them that erected images to the stars, golden ones to the Sun and silver ones to the Moon and in this way the metals and the zones of the earth were apportioned amongst the stars. Also that they built shrines and placed

---

93 This is a reference to the Zoroastrian Dari language.

94 "In accordance with the Sabean theories images were erected to the stars, golden images to the sun, images of silver to the moon, and they attributed the metals and the climates to the influence of the planets, saying that a certain planet is the god of a certain zone. They built temples, placed in them images, and assumed that the stars sent forth their influence upon these images, which are thereby enabled (to speak) to understand, to comprehend, to inspire human beings, and to tell them what is useful to them. They apply the same to trees which fall to the lot of these stars. When, namely, a certain tree, which is peculiar to a certain star, is dedicated to the name of this star, and certain things are done for the tree and to the tree, the spiritual force of that star which influences that tree, inspires men, and speaks to them when they are asleep. All this is written in their works, to which I will call your attention. It applies to the prophets of Baal, and the prophets of Asherah," mentioned in Scripture, in whose hearts the Sabean theories had taken root, who forsook God, and called, 'Baal, hear us' (1 Kings xviii. 26): because these theories were then general, ignorance had spread, and the madness with which people adhered to this kind of imaginations had increased in the world. When such opinions were adopted among the Israelites, they had observers of clouds, enchanters, witches, charmers, consulters with familiar spirits, wizards, and necromancers." (Translation taken from Friedlander, *Moses Maimonides. The Guide for the Perplexed*, Ibid.)

caverint, arbitrantes vires stellarum influere in illas imagines, easque intelligendi virtutem habere, hominibus Prophetiæ donum largiri, ac denique quæ ipsis | utilia & salutaria sunt, indicare. Cumque arbor quædam stellæ alicui dedicatur, nomini ejus plantatur, & hoc vel illo pacto colitur, quod virtutes spirituales stellæ in arbo- |||-rem illam infundantur, ita ut secundum modum Prophetiæ cum hominibus, ut prophetent, loquatur, & in somnio etiam illos alloquatur: Unde Prophetæ Baalis & lucorum, de quibus in libris sacris. Porrò quod inter illos fuerint מעוננים Præstigiatores מנחשים Augures; מכשפים Incantatores; חוברי חבר Magi, | & consulentes eos; ידעונים Arcoli &c. Item quod Solem adoraturi ad Orientem se converterint. Quod sanguinem commederint, quem Dæmonum crediderint cibum; ut familiares forent Dæmonibus: qui etiam, ut opinabantur, ad eos accedebant in somno, secreta iisdem indicabant, & multa commoda afferebant. Denique quod Ignicolæ fuerint, credentes, omnes illius liberos morituros, qui eos per ignem non | traducat. &c.[95] Huic religioni procul dubio, etiam addicti fuerunt Magi isti. [**Cabb. Cat.**][96] *Et cum eidem etiam addicti fuerint olim, Laban, Charanæus, habitans in terra filiorum Orientis Gen. 29, 1. nec non Bileam, qui dicit: de Aram adduxit me Balac, de montibus Orientis Num. 23, 7. item Balac, qui in Sohar fuisse dicitur Nepos Jethronis Arabis Proselyti, Soceri Mosis: hi omnes autem Magi fuerint | celeberrimi, quod ibidem in Sohar de ipsis asseritur; deque filiis Bileami Janne & Jombio; facilè hic conjicerem, hos Magos orientales fuisse revolutiones illorum.* [**Christianus.**][97] Nam[98] (1.) Animæ illorum admodum fuerunt insignes, & ad supremum quendam locum corporis pertinentes, licet profundius prolapsæ sint in impuritatem: unde Bileam oppositus dicitur Mosi

---

95 End of the deletion.
96 Added in the left margin: Cabb. Cat. (which involves a change of speaker).
97 Added in the left margin: Christian. (which involves a change of speaker).
98 Deleted word.
99 The classical Hebrew words for various kinds of magician are notoriously uncertain in their meaning. Here are given the traditional renderings of the KJV in Deut 18.10–11 (English has a similarly rich and equally vague vocabulary for these functions), followed by the Latin gloss Knorr provides. These are not the same as the Vulgate in Deut 18.

SECTION IX

the images in them, thinking that the forces of the stars flowed into the images and that they had power of understanding and gave the gift of
45 prophecy to men and finally revealed | useful and salutary things to them. And [they also believed that] when a tree was dedicated to a star, and planted for its name, and worshipped by some covenant or other, the spiritual forces of the star ||| were poured into the tree so that it spoke to men prophetically so that they might prophesy and also spoke to them in dreams. Hence the groves of the prophets of Baal about whom we read in Holy Scripture. Furthermore, amongst them were *m'wnnym* [observers of times / *praestigiatores*], *mnḥšym* [enchanters / *augurs*], *mkšpym* [witches / *incantors*] *ḥbry*
5 *ḥbr* [charmers / Magi | and those who consulted them], *yd'wnim* [necromancers / [*h*]*arioli* = soothsayers] etc.⁹⁹ Also when about to worship the Sun they turned to the East. They ate blood which they believed was the food of demons, to become familiar with demons who it was considered returned to them in dreams and revealed secrets to them and performed many useful tasks. Finally they were fire-worshippers and believed that all the children
10 of the man who did not pass them through the fire | would die. End of Deletion] This without doubt was the religion which these Magi [in Matthew] followed.

Kabbalist Catechumen Other adherents were once Laban living in Haran in the land of the Sons of East (Gen 29.1) and Balaam who says: "Balak brought me, from Aram, from the mountains of the East" (Num 23.7). The same Balak is said in the Zohar to have been the nephew of Jethro the Arab proselyte and Moses' father-in-law. All these were very famous | Magi, which
15 is also asserted of them in the Zohar. And with respect to Jannes and Jambres from among the sons of Balaam, it is an easy conjecture that these eastern Magi were their reincarnations¹⁰⁰.

Christian Clearly: (1) their souls were most distinguished and belonged to an exalted place in the body [of Adam], although they fell much further
20 into impurity. So Balaam is said to have opposed Moses (Tract. *De | Revol.*

fol. 47ᵛ

---

100 Jannes and Jambres are identified in 2 Tim 3.8 as the magicians who withstood Moses in Ex 7.10–12. Origen considered this a citation from an *Apocryphon of Jannes and Jambres* and fragments of such a work are now known in Greek and Ethiopic. They are also identified in the Targum to Num 22.22 as the two "young men" who accompanied Balaam when he was commissioned to curse the Israelites. They also appear in Zohar Balak 194, Cf. *Jerusalem Targum to Num* 31.8.

Tract. de | revolution. p. 389.[101] Vide & de Laban in Tr. Vallis Reg. p. 337.[102] (2.) Etiam in Bileamo superstites fuisse dicuntur aliquæ scintillæ animarum sanctarum. Tr. de Revol. p. 389.[103] ubi notetur illud, quod de filiis Bileam dicitur. (3.) Bileam jam antehac revolutus fuerat in Nabal adeoque in populo fœderis, Tract. de Revol. p. 418.[104] (4.) Ipse Bileam de sese vaticinatur: Videbo eum, & non nunc; | intuebor eum & non propè. Incessit stella ex Jaacob &c.[105] Num. 24, 16. ubi procul dubio Messiam intellexit. (5.) De similibus Revolutionibus in Sohar allegatur Locus Ps. 68, 23. Ex Basam redire faciam: redire faciam de profundis maris. Quæ intelligenda dicuntur de Tempore Messiano. Adde quod (6.) Deus ipse locutus est cum Labano & Bileamo &c. Semper autem Schechinah relinquere dicitur aliquid vestigii sui | Quæ loca ê Sohar de Bileam & similibus reperies inter Excerpta Cent. II. Loc. 28–33. [Cabb. Cat.][106] *Fortè autem nonnulli ex illis, (quia plures videntur fuisse) etiam fuerunt Revolutiones Regum Iisraël & Judæorum, qui â vero cultu prolapsi fuerunt ad superstitiones Sabæorum & artes magicas.*

V. 3. *Et conturbatus est* &c. ואתחזיע

Christianus. Rex regni amissionem: Populus novos metus metuit.

Cabb. Cat. *Et si Messiam advenire crediderunt, simul timuerunt calamitates illas, quæ ab ipsis Dolores Messiæ vocabantur:* [De quibus vide Excerpta Cent. I. Loc. 18.n. 4. & Loc. 69.74.85.]

---

101 "Sicut ergo Moses erat mysterium cognitionis supernæ, unde prodeunt guttæ seminales: idemque erat mysterium Hebelis filii Adami: ita colluvies hæc magna erant filii Bileam, sicut in Sohar traditur. Bileam autem oppositus erat Mosi in cognitione partis impuræ. Et hoc erat illud ipsum, quod separatum erat in purificatione istarum animarum: Ubi cortex relictus erat solus, quasi scoria, quæ erat anima Bileami: quamvis & in ipso superstites remanserint aliquæ scintillæ animarum sanctarum, prout inter nos vulgatum est. Unde Deus generationem hanc magnæ hujus colluviei vocabat populum Mosis: sicut dictum est: Deut. 9. v. 12. *Populus tuus rem perdidit.* Item: Exod. 34, v. 10. *Populus ille, in ejus medio tu es.* Ipse enim in medio illorum erat, sicut anima in corpore; eò quod ipsius radii & scintillæ essent. [...]" ("De revolutionibus animarum", op. cit., p. 389).

102 "Et si Sanctus ille qui benedictus sit, non creasset mundos & iterum destruxisset eos, non potuisset esse aliquid mali in mundo, sed omnia fuissent bona. Et notum est, quod à malo agnoscatur bonum, atque pariter non fuisset fructificatio & multiplicatio in mundo, sicut dicunt Sapientes nostri bonæ memoriæ in Tractatu Joma: Si concupiscentia prava captivaretur per triduum in foramine Abyssi magnæ, non inveniretur pro ægroto ovum unius diei. Quoniam appetitus nullam de se præberet influentiam, cum tamen dictum sit Jes. 45, 18. *Non inanem creavit illam, sed ut habitaretur, formavit illam.* Quia & tempore venturo vocabitur Laban, eò quod dealbabitur ab impuritate

Animarum, p. 389. See also on Laban in Tract. *Vall. Reg.*, p. 337). (2): even in Balaam some sparks of holy souls are said to have remained (Tract. *De Revol. Animarum*, p. 389, where that which is said about the sons of Balaam should be noted) (3): Balaam had already previously been reincarnated in Nabal and consequently in the people of the covenant (Tract. *De Revol. Animarum*, p. 418). (4): Balaam prophesied about himself: "I shall see him, but not now; | I shall look upon him, but not near. A star will rise from Jacob etc." in Num 24.16 where without doubt he understood Messiah. (5) The Zohar claims Ps 68.23 [22] is about similar reincarnations: "I shall make you return from Bashan, I shall make you return from the depths of the sea", which is said to have to be understood of the Time of Messiah. (6) Additionally; God himself spoke to Laban and to Balaam etc. and the Shekhinah is said always to leave [behind] some vestige of itself. | The passages in the Zohar about Balaam and those like him, you will find in Excerpts Cent. II Loc. 28–33.

Kabbalist Catechumen Perhaps some of them (for they seem to have been many) were also reincarnations of the Kings of Israel and Judah who had lapsed from the true worship into the superstitions of the Sabaeans and magic arts.

Verse 3
And was troubled etc. *w'ttzy'*

Christian The king was troubled about losing his kingdom, the people feared new horrors.

Kabbalist Catechumen And if they believed Messiah was coming, they would at the same time fear those calamities which are called "the birth-pangs" of Messiah (about which see Excerpts Cent. I Loc. 18, n. 4 & Loc. 69, 74, 85).

---

      sua & redibit ad dominium Israel, & orabunt Dominum, ut det ipsis appetitum concupiscentiæ pravæ ad generandum liberos, sicut invenimus in Midrasch Neelam Sectione Toledos in textum Gen. 25, 21. *Et rogavit Jizchak Dominum propter uxorem suam.*" ("Introductio pro meliori intellectu libri Sohar. Vallem regiam", op. cit., p. 337).

103 Cf. *supra*, footnote 110, p. 514.
104 "Qui autem maledicus est & calumniator, mutatur in lapidem silentem, unde de Nabale extimescente dictum est 1. Sam. 25, v. 37. *Et fiebat lapis.* Quoniam is revolutio erat Bileami, cujus veritas nonnisi in ore maledico consistebat: hinc in lapidem mutabatur." ("De revolutionibus animarum", op. cit., p. 418).
105 Vulgate: videbo eum, sed non modo; intuebor illum, sed non prope. Orietur stella ex Jacob ...
106 Added in the left margin: Cabb. Cat. (which involves a change of speaker).

V. 4. *Et congregavit* &c. ובנש

[**Cabb. Cat.**][107] *An Synedrium?*

[**Christianus.**][108] Sic videtur. Assessores enim Consilii hujus Synedrialis antea quidem plerosque occiderat, Joseph, Ant. 14, 17.[109] Gemara Tr. Bava bathra f. 37.b.[110] non tamen omnes: sed illos tantum, qui juri ipsius, quo Regnum obtinere volebat, opponebant Legem Deut. 17, 15. substitutis Proselytis. Philo de Temp. l. 2.

Principes Sacerdotum &c. רבי כהנא

Cabb. Cat. *Nomen hoc denotat (1.) Summum Sacerdotem Joh. 18, 24.* ||| *(2.) Ejusdem Vicarium Marc. 2, 26. (3.) Eos qui gesserant vel gesturi erant Pontificatum. Act. 4, 6. (4.) juxta quosdam, Capita viginta*[111] *quatuor Classium Sacerdotalium.*

Christianus. Hoc autem loco omnes intelligi possunt, quicunque hoc nomine membra | erant Synedrii.

Et scribas Populi &c. וספרא דעמא

Cabb. Cat. *Sopher nostratibus in genere denotabat Doctum quemvis & Legis peritum, ut Talm. Berachoth f. 45. b. Sotah f. 33. b. In specie Negotiis calami addictos ut scribendæ Legi Actis publicis, contractibus privatis & similibus.*

Christianus. Videtur autem scribæ populi hoc loco iidem esse, qui inter seniores Populi Matth. 26, 47; c. 27, 1; Luc. 22, 66. Primores populi Luc. 19, 47. Principes populi Act. 4, 8. erant eruditi; & inter Sanhedrin.

---

107 Correction in the left margin: Christianus replaced by Cabb. Cat. (which involves the two speakers being changed over in the following exchange).
108 Correction: Cabb. Cat. replaced by Chr. (as a consequence of the previous correction).
109 In error. The right reference is to 14, 16.
110 The reference is hardly readable and could be either 30.b. or 37.b.
111 Correction: viginta replaced by viginti
112 This is not a book by Philo. It appears in 1498 in Ioannes Annius (Giovanni Nanni), *Commentaria fratris Ioannis Annii Viterbensis ordinis praedicatorum Theologiae pro-*

Verse 4
And gathered together etc. *wknš*

40 **Kabbalist Catechumen** To the Sanhedrin?

Christian So it would seem. He had previously killed numerous members of this council of the Sanhedrin (Josephus, *Antiquities* 14.16; Gemarah Tract. Bava Batra folio 37b), not all of them but only those who opposed the law of Deut 17.15 to his right to obtain the kingdom. They were replaced by proselytes according to Philo, *De Temp*. Book 2[112].

Chief Priests etc. *rby khn'*

Kabbalist Catechumen This refers to: (1) the high priest in Jn 18.24; ||| (2) his substitute in Mk 2.26; (3) those who had been or would be high priest in Acts 4.6; (4) and, in addition to these, twenty four persons of the priestly classes.

fol. 48r

Christian Here they can all be meant. Whoever was called this, was a member | of the Sanhedrin.

And scribes of the people etc. *wśpr' d'm'*

Kabbalist Catechumen A *sopher* [scribe] for our people generally denotes a learned person and an expert in the law (as in Talmud Berachot folio 45b, Sota folio 33b). More especially it means a specialist in pen-work and writing laws, public acta, private contracts and such like.

Christian It seems the scribes of the people here are the same as those (found) amongst the elders of the people in Mt 26.47; 27.1; Lk 22.66. The chiefs of the people in Lk 19.47 and the rulers of the people in Acts 4.8 were both learned and members of the Sanhedrin.

---

fessoris super opera diversorum auctorum de Antiquitatibus loquentium (Rome: Eucharius Silber, 1498 and very frequently thereafter). The work is called *De temporibus or Brevarium de temporibus* and appears in sections G & H of his unpaginated book. It is Nanni's own work. He describes its contents as: *"promittimus commentaria super duos libellos Breviarii Philonis de temporibus: in quorum primo enumerat tempora ab Adam usque ad desolatum templum. & in secundo ab eadem desolationis usque ad suam etatem secula digerit."* For more on this see James R. Royse, *The Spurious Texts of Philo of Alexandria: A Study in Textual Transmission and Corruption* (Leiden: Brill, 1991), pp. 135–136.

Sic enim scriptum est per Prophetam &c. בכנא גיר כתיב בנביא

[**Cabb. Cat.** *Versiones & textus originarius hîc non concordant.*][113]

[Christianus.] Textus Hebræus ita habet: Et tu Bethehem Ephrathath, parvulane | es, ut sis in millibus Jehudah? Ex te mihi egredietur, ut sit Dominator in Israël; & egressiones ejus â primordio, â diebus Æternitatis. Paraphrasis Jonathanis ita traduxit. Et tu Bethlehem Ephrata quasi minima fuisti, adeò ut computareris inter millia domus Jehuda: ex te coram me prodibit Messias, ut sit dominium exercens in Israël: cujus nomen dictum est, ab æternitate, â diebus seculi. | Versio Græca ita habet: Et tu Bethlehem domus Ephrata minima es, ut sis in millibus Jehuda[114]. Ex te mihi egredriatur, ut sit in Principem Israël: & egressus ejus ab initio, ex diebus seculi: Hæc in Græco Matthæi ita sunt traductæ: Et tu Bethlehem terra Juda nequaquam minima es in Ducibus Juda: ex te enim exhibit Dux, qui pascat populum meum Israël. In Syriaco Matthæi Paraphrasin habemus | istam: Etiam tu Bethlehem Jehudæ non fuisti parvula inter Reges Jehudah: Ex te enim egredietur Rex, qui pascet populum meum Israël.[115]

[**Christianus.** Attamen][116] apparet (1.) Matthæum non esse secutum Versionem LXX. (2.) illum in Hebraico vocem אַלְפֵי intellexisse juxta sensum Jud 6, 15. de familia paterna, unde Duces belli prodierint. Nam & Reges apud antiquos bellandi causa potissimum constituebantur. | (3.) illum in Hebræo subintellixisse interrogationem; quam per negotionem expressit. (4.) notandum Prophetam describere Messiam ut Belli Ducem, qui non tunc primum sit egressurus cum nasciturus esset in Bethlehem; sed qui egressus sit (ad bella scilicet juxta sensum 1. Sam. 17, 55; 2. Par. 1, 10; c. 15, 5; Jer. 30, 21) jam pluries ab ipso mundi primordio: destinatusque ut ad plura genera | bellorum egrediatur. [videantur Excerpta de Messia.]

---

113 Beginning of the deletion. The entire intervention of the Christian hereafter is replaced, in the rifgt margin, by: *Cabb. Cat. Versiones & textus originarius hîc non concordant.*
114 Correction: Jehuda replaced by Juda
115 End of the deletion.
116 Correction in the right margin: Cabb. Cat. Unde replaced by Christian. Attamen
117 Lightfoot, *Miscellanies and the Harmony of the Gospels*, op. cit., pp. 225–226 discusses the textual issue at length. *En passant* he remarks about some who posit a Syriac original: "Whereas some talk of a Syriac edition, which the Jews used at that time more than the Hebrew, and which had this text of Micah as the evangelist hath cited it, and that he cited it according to that edition which was most in use;—here are two things presumed upon, which it is impossible ever to make good. For who ever read, in any Jew, of a Syrian edition of the prophets, besides the Chaldee paraphrast? who, we are sure,

SECTION IX

For thus it was written by the prophet etc. *bkn' gyr ktyb bnby'*

Kabbalist Catechumen The versions and the original text do not agree.[117]

[Deletion: **Christian** The Hebrew text [of Mic 2.6] has "But you Bethlehem Ephrathah, you are | small to be among the thousands of Judah? Out of you shall come forth for me one who will be Ruler in Israel and his goings out from the begining of the days of Eternity". Targum Jonathan puts it like this: "And you Bethlehem Ephratha although you were the smallest to be counted amongst the thousands of the tribe of Judah, from you shall come before me Messiah to exercise rule in Israel, whose name has been spoken from eternity, from days of old". | The Greek version has: "And you Bethlehem of the house of Ephratha, you are very small to be in the thousands of Judah. From you shall come forth to me one who will be a leader in Israel and his goings out are from the beginning from the days of old". This in the Greek Matthew is rendered: "And you Bethlehem, land of Judah, are by no means smallest among the tribes of Judah from out of you shall come a leader who will feed my people Israel". In the Syriac translation of Matthew, we have | this: "Even you Bethlehem of Judah were not smallest amongst the kings of Judah, for out of you will come a king who will feed my people Israel". [End of the deletion]

Christian However, it is clear: (1) Matthew was not following the [Greek] Septuagint; (2) he understood the Hebrew word "thousands" according to its meaning in Judg 6.15 [where it refers to] the paternal family from which the war leaders came. (For even kings amongst the ancients were mostly put in place to fight wars); | (3) he understood the Hebrew as a question expressed by a negative; (4) it is notable that the prophet describes Messiah as a war-leader who would not "come out" for the first time when he was born in Bethlehem[118], but who had come out (to fight, which is the meaning in 1 Sam 17.55; 2 Chron 1.10; 15.5; Jer 30.21) already many times from the very beginning of the world and was destined to go out for many different types | of battle (See Excerpts on Messiah).

---

readeth not thus:—or what Christian ever saw such an edition, that he could tell that it did so read? For this particular, therefore, in hand, it is to be answered, that the scribes, or the evangelists, or both, did thus differently quote the prophet, neither through forgetfulness, nor through the misleading of an erroneous edition, but purposely, and upon a rational intent."

118 This is the third occasion Knorr has chosen to emphasise that Messiah's life did not begin in Mary's womb.

V. 7. *Quo tempore* &c. באינא זבנא

[**Cabb. Cat.**][119] *Quare hoc?*

[**Christianus.**][120] Ut indagaret ætatem puelli, quem occisurus erat. De apparitionibus autem similium phænomenorum unde præsentia Schechinæ | colligeretur exempla adduximus inter Excerpta Loc. 52.53. Cent.I.   40

V. 8. *Et misit eos* &c. ושדר אנון

Cabb. Cat. *Non saltem dimisit: sed & autoritatem quandam sibi super illos tribuens, ablegatione*[121] *ablegatione sua illos honorare voluisse videtur,* [**Christianus.**][122] *ut occasio hinc sibi nasceretur illis nocendi quippe quos æque metuebat ac Messiam* | *ipsum, qui vel opes vel servitia ab iis sperare posse   45 credi poterat.*

Christianus.[123] Quod autem & se venturum dicit ut reverentiam ipsi exhibeat simulatio fuit politica, calliditatis serpentinæ progenies; mendaciorum mater, regni Satanici fulcrum unicum: & larva per lumen veritatis aliquando

fol. 48ᵛ   detrahenda.[124] |||

V. 9. *Procedebat ante eos* &c. אזל הוא קדמיהון

[**Cabb. Cat.**][125] *Opusne habebant stella ut invenirent Bethlehemum quod itinere paucarum saltem horarum ab urbe distabat, præsertim interdiu iter facientes?*

[**Christianus.**][126] Haud aliter nisi ut illius beneficio invenirent domum & puerum: | hunc in finem stella hæc, sive apparitio Gloriæ dominicæ ê summa   5 aëris regionis sese recepit in infimam, ut nunc ipsis appareret ut meteorum quoddam igneum.

---

119 Correction: Christianus replaced by Cabb. Cat. (which involves the two speakers being changed over in the following exchange).
120 Correction in the right margin: Cabb. Cat. replaced by Chr. (as a consequence of the previous correction).
121 Deleted word (to avoid repetition).
122 Added in the right margin: Chr. (which involves a change of speaker).
123 Beginning of the deletion: the entire intervention of the Christian is deleted.
124 End of the deletion. In the right bottom corner appears a Hebrew letter מ presumably an indication of binding or pagination.
125 Correction in the left margin: Christianus replaced by Cabb. Cat. (which involves the two speakers being changed over in the following exchange).

Verse 7
At what time etc. *b'yn' zbn'*

Kabbalist Catechumen Why this?

Christian So that he could try to find out the age of the boy he was going to kill. For the appearances of similar phenomena, from which the presence of the Shekhinah | was deduced, we have provided examples in Excerpts Cent. I Loc. 52, 53.

Verse 8
And sent them etc. *wšdr 'nwn*

Kabbalist Catechumen He did not just dismiss them but, assuming for himself a certain authority over them, he seemed to want to honour them by his mission.

Christian So that he would then have occasion to harm them, in as much as he feared them as much as Messiah | himself, who could be believed to be able to hope for resources or service from them.

[Deletion. **Christian** When he said that he also would come and do great reverence [to the child], this was a political deception, an offspring of the Serpent's cunning, the Mother of Lies, sole foundation of the Kingdom of Satan and the evil spirit shortly to be banished by the light of truth. End of the deletion] ‖ fol. 48ᵛ

Verse 9
Went before them etc. *'zl hw' qdmyhwn*

Kabbalist Catechumen Did they really need the star to find Bethlehem? Because it was only a journey of a few hours away from Jerusalem—and particularly if they were already going there!

Christian There was no other way they would have found the house and the boy | without the benefit of its light. To this end the star, or an appearance of Lordly Glory from the highest region of the *Aer*, descended to the lower regions and now appeared to them as a fiery meteor.

---

126 Correction in the left margin: Cabb. Cat. replaced by Chr. (as a consequence of the previous correction).

V. 11. *In domum* &c. לביתא

Cabb. Cat. *Hinc apparet, Parentes Domini non amplius fuisse in spelunca in qua Jesum depositum Patres antiquissimi edocent;*[127] *sed inquilinos fuisse*[128] *Bethlehemiticos, | translatâ ê Nazareth re sua familiari.*

Christianus. Utrum tamen absens fuerit, ob negotia forte domestica Josephus: an verò sensus sit, illos statim ê signis quibusdam fortassis fulgoris cujusdam ambientis agnovisse Dominum cum matre sua, ambiguum est. Id certè dubio omni caret, quod à Maria didicerint omnia circa miraculosam hanc nativitatem gesta tam antecedentia quàm consequentia: quodque relicta religione sua Magica facti | sint proselyti & membra Ecclesiæ Israëlis. Ubi autem circumcisi, (vel si ê circumcisis fortè fuerunt, detectionem glandis sanguinolentam passi) & baptizati, pro more proselytorum fuerint, ignoratur.

Et obtulerunt ipsi oblationes &c. וקרבו לה קורבנא

Christianus. An muneribus ipsum donando? An verò sacra ipsi facientes, ceu Numini | cuidam, & stellæ Domino, juxta sensum locorum Matth. 5, 23.24.24; c. 8, 4; c. 15, 5; c. 23, 18.19; Mar. 7, 11; Luc. 21, 1.4; Heb. 5, 1; c. 8, 3.4; c. 9, 9. Aurum sane ipsi in usum necessitatis offerebant, unguento myrrhæ ipsum ceu Regem inungebant (conf. Ps. 45, 9; Pr. 7, 16; Cant. 5, 6.13; Ex. 30, 23; Esth. 2, 14.) an & thure accenso ipsi sufficiebant[129]?

Cabb. Cat. *Crediderim. Nec mysterio res caret: nam juxta Cabbalistas Aurum referri solet ad Binah, seu intelligentiam: Thus ad Chochmah seu Sapientiam: & myrrha ad Kether seu Coronam,* [*vid. Lexic. Cabbalist. p. 298.*[130] *493*[131] *& 517.*[132]] *Quodsi quod*[133] *ex antiquis traditis noverunt Magi; (quamvis fortè ultra Numerationes Impuritatis non ascenderint:) septem numerationes*

---

127 Deletion: in qua Jesum depositum Patres antiquissimi edocent;
128 Deleted word.
129 Correction: sufficiebant replaced by suffiebant
130 "זהב *Aurum.* Est Symbolum Gebhurah sicut dicitur Ijobh 37, 22. *De Septentrione aurum venit.* Aliquando tamen etiam refertur ad Binah, de quo dictum est Tr. 10, c. 3. his verbis: Quidam colorem auri referunt ad Gebhurah, quia ad rubedinem inclinat; Et sic reperimus in aliquibus locis libri Sohar. Quidam eundem referunt ad Binah, quod etiam in quibusdam locis Libri Sohar invenimus. Conciliatio horum autem ita fieri potest: Si aurum dicitur exsuscitatio Gradûs Binah cum Gebhurah, & utriusque unio sub mysterio Judicii lætificantis. [...]" ("Loci communes kabbalistici", op. cit., p. 298).

SECTION IX   523

Verse 11
Into the house etc. *lbyt'*

Kabbalist Catechumen From this it appears that the parents of the Lord were no longer in the cave[134], but were living in Bethlehem, | having moved all their family affairs from Nazareth.

Christian Perhaps Joseph was absent for domestic affairs. [*i. e.* the text only speaks of the boy and his mother]. Whether the meaning is that the Magi immediately recognized the Lord and his mother, perhaps from the signs of a certain ambient glow, is uncertain. It is certain that they learned from Mary everything about this miraculous birth, what happened both before and afterwards, and that abandoning their own religion as Magi, | they became proselytes and members of the Ecclesia of Israel. Whether they were circumcised (or possibly they were already from a circumcised people and had already undergone the bloody uncovering of their glans) and were baptized in the fashion of proselytes is not known.

And they made offerings to him etc. *wqrbw lh qyrbn'*

Christian Either by giving him presents, or theselves performing holy rites to whatever power | was Lord of the Star, according to the meanings found in Mt 5.23,24 *bis*; 8.4; 15.5; 23.18, 19; Mk 7.11; Lk 21.1, 4; Heb 5.1; 8.3, 4; 9.9. Clearly they offered gold for use in necessity and they anointed him king with the liquid myrrh (Cf. Ps 45.9; Pro 7.16; Cant 5.6,13; Ex 30.23; Esth 2.14). Possibly they incensed him by burning the frankincense.

Kabbalist Catechumen. I think so. But the matter is not without some mystery, for according to the Kabbalists gold usually refers to Binah [or Intelligence], Frankincense to Chokhmah [or Wisdom] and myrrh to Keter [or Crown] (see *Lex. Cabb.*, pp. 298, 493 and 517). What if the Magi knew something of the ancient traditions (although perhaps they had not risen

---

131   "לבונה *Thus.* Cant. 4, 14. In Raj. Meh. ad Chochmah, in Tikkun. ad Hod refertur illud ob colorem, hoc ob saporem. Pard. Tr. 23. c. 12." (Ibid., p. 493).
132   Cf. *supra*, footnote 90, p. 238.
133   Correction: quod replaced by quid
134   Deletion: "in which the most ancient Fathers teach Jesus was laid." The observation is important in the argument over whether the Magi arrived shortly after the Circumcision or two years or so later.

inferiores | videntur in Messia deprehendisse; cum quibus unire voluissent tres supremas ad influxum longè faustissimum. 30

Christianus. Sensu alio mystico Aurum, Thus & myrrha referre videntur tres illas Philosophiæ antiquæ species; divinam scil. naturalem, & contentiosam seu Dialecticam: quas omnes vitæ huic divinæ subjici oportet.

V. 12. *Et visio ipsis facta est* &c. ואתחזי להון 35

Cabb. Cat. *Hinc notamus, quod vox χρηματίζω non inferat immediatum alloquium divinum (conf. Act. 10, 22.)*

Christianus. Adeoque procul dubio, his, qui circa diviniora minus erant exercitat[i] per gradus Angelicos facta est communicatio.

V. 13. *Et fuge in Ægyptum* &c. וערוק למצרין 40

Cabb. Cat. *Sicut primum exilium Populi Israëlitici, (cujus Præses semper fuit Anima Messiæ) in Ægypto fuit; ubi juxta Hebræorum dogmata*[135] *cum illis exulabat Schechinah: sic primum ipsius Messiæ exilium est in Ægypto: ut exitus ejus ex Ægypto præfiguraret, tempus nunc adesse, quo populus Messiæ ex angustiis (hæc enim | est significatio vocis* מצרים*) spiritualibus duci posset.* 45

fol. 49ʳ **Christianus.** Liberatio enim Messiæ sæpius talis fore dicitur, qualis fuerat ea, quâ li- ‖-berabantur ex Ægypto. Jesch. 10, 24.26; Jechesk. 20, 36; Mich. 7, 15; Chag. 2, 6.

V. 15. *Ex Ægypto* &c. מן מצרין

[**Cabb. Cat.**][136] Locus Prophetæ Hoseæ cap. 11. v. 1.2. ambiguus est, & prout solent textus Prophetici, plurium sensuum. Textus[137] Hebraicus ita habet: *Dum*[138] *puer (erat) | Iisraël, sanè dilexi eum, & ex Ægypto vocavi filium meum.* 5 *Vocaverunt eos (sc. Prophetæ;) sic abierunt à facie eorum: Baalim sacrifica-*

---

135 Suppression: juxta Hebræorum dogmata
136 Correction: Christianus replaced by Cabb. Cat. (which involves the two speakers being changed over in the following exchange). The handwriting is different from this point for approximatively half of a page. It is Knorr's handwriting (see Introduction).
137 Beginning of deletion.
138 The quotations are here underlined.
139 The intention here is to derive the Hebrew word *mṣrym* [Egypt] from a root *mzr* (2)

SECTION IX

above the degrees of impurity)? They seem to have grasped the seven lower degrees | in Messiah, with which they wanted to unite the three highest degrees for an influx by far most favourable.

Christian Another mystic meaning seems to relate gold, frankincense and myrrh to the three types of ancient philosophy: Divine Philosophy, of course; Natural Philosophy; and Argumentative Philosophy or Dialectic. All of which ought to be subordinated to this divine life.

Verse 12
And they had a vision etc. *w'tḥzy lhwn*

Kabbalist Catechumen From this we note that the [Greek] word *chrēmatizō* [used in the Greek text here] does not imply direct divine speech (Cf. Acts 10.22).

Christian To the extent, doubtless, that those who were less enthusiastic about divine matters were communicated with by the angelic grades.

Verse 13
And flee to Egypt etc. *w'rwq lmṣryn*

Kabbalist Catechumen Just like the first exile of the Israelites (whose Leader was always the soul of Messiah) to Egypt, where according to Hebrew teaching the Shekhinah was exiled with them. Thus the first exile of Messiah himself is in Egypt so that his departure from Egypt might pre-figure the time now present in which the people of Messiah can be lead out from spiritual straits (for this | is the meaning of the word *mṣrym* [Egypt][139]).

Christian The liberation of Messiah has quite often been said to be like the liberation ||| from Egypt (Isa 10.24, 26; Ezek 20.36; Mic 7.15; Hag 2.6). fol. 49ʳ

Verse 15
Out of Egypt etc. *mn mṣryn*

Kabbalist Catechumen This passage in the prophet Hosea [11.1, 2] is ambiguous and, as often with the prophetic texts, has several meanings.

[Deletion. The Hebrew text has: "When Israel was a boy, | I loved him and out of Egypt I called my son. They (*sc.* the prophets) called them thus they went out from the face of them, they sacrificed to Baal and offered incense to

---

"to shackle or imprison". See Francis Brown et al., eds., *A Hebrew and English Lexicon of the Old Testament* (Oxford University Press, 1972), p. 848b.

runt, & sculptilibus suffierunt. Targum Jonathan ita reddit: *Quando puer erat Iisraël, diligebam eum, & ex Ægypto vocavi eos filios. Misi prophetas meos ut erudirent eos; sed ipsi illorum conspectum refugerunt, idolis sacrificantes, & simulacris | adolentes aromata.* Græca versio sic traduxit: *Manè projecti sunt, projectus est rex Iisraël*[140]*; quia parvulus Israël: & ego dilexi eum, & ex Ægypto vocavi filios ejus. Sicut vocavi eos, ita abierunt â faciè mea: ipsi Baalim immolabant, & sculptilibus adolebant.* Syriaca ita legit: *In aurora admiratus est & obstupuit Rex Iisraëlis, quia dum puer esset Iisraël, dilexi | eum; & inde ab Ægypto vocavi eum filium meum. Prout vocaverunt eos, ita abierunt à conspectu meo, & Baali sacrificaverunt, & sculptilibus thura adhibuerunt.*[141]

[**Christianus.**][142] Notandum igitur, quod per vocem Iisraël, non tantum intelligantur Iisraëlitæ; sed & Dux atque Rector eorum Messias, sub | gradum Tiphereth: [vid. Lexic. Cabbalist. p. 460. f.[143]] Sensus[144] ergò mysticus verborum Propheticorum est hic: Circa illos gradus, ubi Israël dicitur puer (vide Kabba. Denudat. P. 2. p. 8.[145]) i.e. parte superiore circa initia Filii, qui Seir Anpin dicitur: ibi locus est amorum, seu Chesed. (vide Cabbal. Denudat. Par. 1. p. 43.[146]) et quamvis ibi locum habeant cortices anguste circumstantes, | (ut nomen Mizraim secum fert) evoco tamen filium meum, et per illum, influentiam præbeo inferioribus. Et sic quoque soleo in rebus Ecclesiæ et populi Fœderis mei procedere. Quando enim Populus fœderis mei, cui præsidet filius meus Messias, circa initia est, prout erat tempore exilii Ægyptiaci, et erit circa initia novi Fœderis, tum teneriore amore ejus curam habeo; et ex Ægypti corticibus | similibusque angustiis vocare soleo Messiam Filium meum, præfectum eorum, et illos cum atque sub ipso. Sed dum paulum senescit fœdus meum, in cortices velabuntur et ididololatriæ sese man-

---

140 Correction: Iisraël replaced by Israël
141 End of deletion.
142 Correction above the line: Cabb. Cat. replaced by Christian. (as a consequence of the previous correction).
143 "ישראל *Iisraël*. Est Tiphereth, sed tunc, quando medium obtinet inter Chochmah & Binah, & lancem Binæ deflectit ad latus Chochmæ, prout solet cum ad Chesed inclinat. [...]" ("Loci communes kabbalistici", op. cit., p. 462). The referece given by Knorr is probably erroneous since page 460 does not deal with the word "Israël".
144 Change of handwriting: a second secretarial hand appears for approximately one and a half folios.
145 "Pars superior vocatur Israël Puer eique tribuitur Tetragrammaton Valoris 45." ("Tabula secunda Clavis sublimioris Kabbalæ", op. cit., p. 8).
146 "האבה *Amor, dilectio*, 1. Est in *Chesed*. Unde Abraham vocatur אהבי *dilectus meus* Jeschai 41, 8. quia in sese derivaverat vim amoris. 2. Atque sic & Schechinah, quando sibi succum attrahit ex parte Chesed, vocatur Amor: & de hoc locus est in Tikkunim. Hoc nomen autem tunc ipsi tribuitur quando sugit è fibris Chesed, ut copulari queat

SECTION IX   527

carved images". Targum Jonathan renders it: "When Israel was a boy I loved him, and out of Egypt I called them sons. I sent my prophets to instruct them but they fled from the sight of them, sacrificing to idols and burning incense | to images". The Greek version has: "In the morning, they are thrown down and the king of Israel is thrown down because Israel was little and I loved | him and out of Egypt I called his sons. Just as I called them, so they went out from my face. They sacrificed to Baal and burned incense to carved images". The Syriac has[147]: "In the dawn the king of Israel wondered and was amazed, for when Israel was a boy I loved him and then from Egypt I called him my son. Just as they called them so they went out from my sight and sacrificed to Baal and offered incense to carved images." End of the deletion.]

Christian It is noteworthy that by the word "Israel" are understood not only the Israelites but also their General or Ruler, Messiah, | under the degree of Tiferet (see *Lex.Cabb.* p. 460).

The mystical sense of the prophet's words is this: Around those degrees where Israel is called "Boy" (See *Cabb. Denud.*, Part. 2, p. 8) (*i. e.* the higher part around the beginnings of the Son which is called Zeir Anpin, is the place of Love or Chesed (See *Cabb. Denud.*, Part. 1, p. 43)) and, although the surrounding Shards have there a narrow place | (as the name Egypt implies), nonetheless "I call out my Son and Boy" and through him provide an influx for lower creatures. And thus also I am accustomed to do in Ecclesia and among the people of my Covenant. For when the people of my Covenant, whose leader is my Son Messiah, was beginning around the time of the Exile in Egypt (and as it will be around the beginning of the New Covenant) then I care for them with a more tender love, and I call Messiah my Son, their leader, from the Shards of Egypt | and similar straits, and them with him and under him. But when my Covenant grows a little older, they will fall back into the Shards and enslave themselves to idolatry. This is what the Revo-

---

cum marito suo. [...] 3. Alio quodam in loco dicitur; illam tunc appellari hoc nomine, quando in se continet omnes Patres. Et dici quidem potest quod respectu Chesed dicatut (sic) amor atque dilectio; primò tamen influxum assugit à septentrione (i.e. Gebhurâ.) Hoc enim ordine amore nectitur cum marito suo; (vid. Pard. Tract. 8. c. 21.) & deinde influxum quoque accipit à meridie (i.e. Chesed,) atque tunc aperitur per Austrum & vocatur Ahabhah seu amor istius respectu; repleta tamen est & participationem habet ab omnibus." ("Loci communes kabbalistici", op. cit., pp. 43–44).

147 Knorr would have had ready access to a Syriac Peshitta text of the Old Testament in the copy of Walton's London Polyglot Bible which is mentioned in the 1734 catalogue of the library in Sulzbach.

cipiant[148]. Sic enim fert revolutio ævorum, ut quæ gessit Messias antiquitus atque passus est, eadem recurrant sæpius, donec restitutio sint plenaria (de qua Act. 3, 21.)

V. 16. *Excanduit valde*, אתחמה טב   35

Cabb. Cat. *Ut Edom persecutor erat Jacobi; sic Idumæus isto est Christi: et diaco Edom (Apoc 12, 3.)* **Christianorum. Christianus.**[149] Meminit autem hujus cædis Infantum et Macrobius scriptor Gentilis. l. 2. Saturnal. cap. 4. eorum-

fol. 49ᵛ   que 14,000 Misa Æthiopica numerat. ‖‖

V. 17. *Tunc impletum est* etc. הידין אתמלי

[**Cabb. Cat.**][150] *Quo sensu intelligenda est hæc impletio?* [**Christianus.**][151] Secundum dogmata Sapientum nostrorum[152], melius hæc impletio exponi nequit, quam per Revolutionem illorum qui occisi quondam à Babyloniis hoc loco, atque nunc | renati fuerant, iterumque occidebantur. Cumque   5
animæ essent mox plenius restituendæ, et propter Christum nunc è vivis sublatæ essent; citra absurditatem credi posset, quod regeniti fuerint quam primum, et statim post erectum Fœdus novum et deinceps effusum Spiritum Sanctum istius donis illuminati, per martyrium ultimatam adepti fue-

---

148   Correction: mancipiant replaced by mancipant
149   Change of speaker, but without new paragraph.
150   Correction in the left margin: Christianus replaced by Cabb. Cat. (which involves the two speakers being changed over in the following exchange).
151   Correction in the left margin: Cabb. Cat. replaced by Christ. (as a consequence of the previous correction). The change of speaker is not marked by a new paragraph.
152   Correction: nostrorum replaced by vestrorum
153   "*Cum audisset inter pueros quos in Syria Herodes rex Iudaeorum intra bimatum iussit interfici filium quoque eius occisum, ait: Melius est Herodis porcum esse quam filium.*"
154   Ernest A.W. Budge, *The Book of the Saints of the Ethiopian Church. A translation of the Ethiopic Synaxarium made from the manuscripts Oriental 660 and 661 in the British Museum*, 4 vols (Cambridge University Press, 1928) for Tir 3/ January 11 (p. 256). The

lution of the Ages brings; that what Messiah did and suffered of old, those same things recur quite often until the Final Full Restitution (about which Acts 3.21).

Verse 16
Was very angry 'tḥmh ṭb

Kabbalist Catechumen As Edom persecuted Jacob, so this Idumaean [Herod] will persecute Christ and the Dragon Edom (Rev 12.3) [Rome] [will persecute] the Christians.

Christian Macrobius, a Gentile writer, recalled this slaughter of the infants in his *Saturnalia* (Book II, chap. 4[153]) and the Ethiopic Mass gives their number as 14,000[154]. ‖‖

fol. 49ᵛ

Verse 17
Then was fulfilled etc. *hydyn 'tmly*

Kabbalist Catechumen How should we understand this "fulfillment"?

Christian According to the teachings of your sages, this fulfillment cannot be better explained than by the re-incarnation of those who were once killed by the Babylonians in this very place and then | had been reborn and were killed again. And since the souls are soon more fully to be restored and on account of Christ have now been taken from among the living, it is reasonable to believe that they were reborn as soon as possible and immediately after the establishment of the New Covenant and then after the pouring out of the Holy Spirit were illuminated by its gifts and through martyrdom

---

number is given as 18,000, but according to the Bodleian manuscript Budge cites it was 144,000. Knorr's own interest in Ethiopic is attested by a letter of Leibniz to Hiob Ludolph (1624–1704) seeking to establish a correspondence between Ludolph and Knorr: "He [Knorr] received with pleasure the continuation of your Ethiopian [history], which he had hoped for, as well as those things concerning the letters of the Samaritans, which I told you about, and your method for the comparing of different alphabets." (Cited and translated in Coudert, *Leibniz and the Kabbalah*, op. cit., p. 48). Ludolf produced a *Sciagraphia historiae aethiopicae* in Jena in 1676, and his *Historia aethopica* in Frankfurt in 1681. The volume Knorr was pleased to have read would seem to be the *Commentarius* of 1691, though if so Knorr must have read it in ms before his death in 1689. For an overview of Ethiopic studies in Germany: Ernst Hammerschmidt, "Die Äthiopistischen Studien in Deutschland (von ihren Anfängen bis zur Gegenwart)", *Annales d'Éthiopie* 6 (1965): pp. 255–277.

rint consummationem. De talibus autem | revolutionibus animarum[155] vide 10
Tractatum de Revolutionibus Animarum p. 423. §. 10.[156] p. 435. §.4.5.[157]

V. 18. *Vox in Ramah audita est* etc. קלא אשתמע ברמתה

Christianus.[158] Textus Hæbraicus Jer. 31, v. 15. ita se habet: Vox in Ramah audita est, querimonia, fletus amaritudinum, Rachel plorante super filios suos, renuit consolari | super filiis suis, quia non Ipse[159]. Targum Jonathan 15 hanc habet Paraphrasin: Vox in excelso mundi audita est, domus Israël flentis et gementis, post Jeremiam prophetam, quando misit cum Nebusaradam princeps occidentium ex Ramah. Lamentatio et plorantes; ob amaritudinem Jerusalem, plorat porpter filios suos, et renuit consolari super filiis suis, quia migraverunt. Versio Græca | hunc refert sensum: Vox in Ramah audita est, 20 lamentationis; et plorationis et fletus: Rachel deplorans, noluit conquiescere super filiis suis, quia non sunt.[160] **Cabb. Cat.**[161] *Antiqua autem traditione edocti sapientes nostri hunc locum circa adventum Messiæ*[162] *allegant: prout edocent loca Sohar inter Excerpta Cent. 1. Loc. 74. n. 17. et Cent. 2. l. 34.35.*[163]

---

155 Deleted word.
156 "Ratio autem, quare totô illo tempore filii Assai nemo fuerit tantæ excellentiæ, imò ne quidem Sacerdos magnus R. Jischmaël filius Elischa, qui erat scintilla Josephi justi, prout declaratum est; hæc est, quia in ipsa quoque radice decem illarum scintillarum guttarum Josephi seminalium, vitium erat, (eò quod Josephus passus sit Gonorrhæam:) hinc iste R. Jischmaël hoc idem præstare non poterat: imo potius ipse majori pœna dignus erat, quam reliqui omnes. Unde narratur, quod cutem ipsi abstraxerint per faciem ejus. Juxta illud Gen. 37, v. 23. *Et abstraxerunt Josepho tunicam.* Porrò quoque reperitur: quod sicut Joseph eleganti fuit forma; sic etiam R. Jischmaël: & sicut Joseph captivus fuit inter Ægyptos: ita R. Jischmaël inter Romanos. Unde cum eundem reperiret R. Jehoschua filius Chananjah, ipsique diceret Jesch. 42, v. 24. *Quis dedit Jacobum in conculcationem* &c. Ubi sensus est, quod conculcatio semper fiat sub pedibus: & quia omnes radices guttarum Josephi filii Jaacob descenderunt in profundum corticum, sub pedes: & intuitu illarum guttarum interrogabat R. Jehoschua filius Chananjah, dicens: Quis dedit Jacobum in conculcationem? Ubi respondebat R. Jischmaël (ex eodem loco:) *Quoniam peccavimus.*" ("De revolutionibus animarum", op. cit., p. 423).
157 "§.4. Et huc pertinet exemplum decem occisorum à Romanis; qui per necem suam meruerunt, ut colligere & in statum meliorem elevare potuerint omnes scintillas sibi subordinatas, è quo commodius possint restitui. §.5. Quamvis & alia subsit ratio insignis, de decem istis martyribus. Quoniam enim videbat Sanctus ille, qui benedictus

SECTION IX 531

10 obtained the final consummation. For such | reincarnations, see Tract. *De Revol. Animarum*, p. 423, §10.

Verse 18
A voice in Ramah etc. *qlʾ šʿ brmtʾ*

[Deletion **Christian** The Hebrew text of Jer 31.15 runs like this: "A voice was heard in Ramah wailing and bitterness of weeping, Rachel weeping for her
15 sons, she refuses to be consoled | for her sons because they are not". Targum Jonathan translates: "A voice was heard at the top of the world, of the house of Israel weeping and groaning after Jeremiah the prophet, when Nebusaradan, chief of the easterners, sent him from Ramah, lamentation and people for weeping bitterness, Jerusalem mourning for her sons and refusing to be consoled over her sons because they have left". The Greek version
20 [Septuagint] | has this sense: "A voice of lamentation and wailing was heard in Ramah, Rachel weeping did not wish to quiet grow over her sons because they are not". End of the deletion]

Kabbalist Catechumen By an ancient tradition our sages linked this verse with the advent of Messiah, just as is taught in the passages from the Zohar in Excerpt Cent. I Loc. 74, n. 17 and Cent. II Loc. 34, 35.

Christian No doubt, again under the Mosaic veil.[164]

---

sit! quod ab illorum tempore nullæ amplius futuræ sint Animæ, quæ inservire queant loco aquarum Fœmininarum: (quoniam ob peccata nostra in majorem semper ducimur egestatem, ut nulla nobis supersit facultas, restituendi animas nostras, easdemque elevandi sub mysterio aquarum fœmininarum.) Hinc illos occidi oportuit, ut istarum loco usui sint, ita ut per eos restitutio fiat scintillarum ipsis subordinatarum. Notum enim, quod illi fuerint universitas totius Jisraëlis. Illi quippe fuerunt decem tribus, & decem filii Joseph, sicut notum est nostratibus." (Ibid., p. 435).

158 Beginning of deletion.
159 In error, it should be "sunt"
160 End of deletion.
161 The change of speaker is not marked by a new paragraph.
162 Added above the line: ultimum
163 Added into the text: Christ. Nimirum sub velo Mosaico.
164 2 Cor 3.13.

V. 19. *Defuncto autem Herode* &c. כדמית דין הרודס 25

[*Cabb. Cat. Quando?*][165]
Christianus. Statim post Infanticidium juxta Eusebium. [Cabb. Cat.][166] Et secundum Josephum 17. Antiquit. ardore et cruciatu coli, atque prutredine intestinorum inexplebili comedendi desiderio; humore purulento circa pedes et abdomen; membri genitalis late et vermibus, sprirandi difficultate; spasmis et singul[ar]ibus crebris, | nervorum contractione etc. ad despera- 30
tionem et mortem usque ex agitatus: vindictæ divinæ exemplum incomparabile.

V. 20. *In Terram Israël* etc. לארעא דיסריל[167]

Cabb. Cat. Doctores nostri totum mundum dividunt in Erez Israël, seu Terram Israeliticam et chuzzah laarez, seu Extra Terram; [vide in Tract. de revolution. Animarum P. I. c. 16. | De Excellentia autem Terræ Israeliticæ præ 35
cæteris regionibus vid. Synopsin Libri Sohar Tit. 14.] **Christianus.**[168] Per illos autem, qui mortui hic [dicuntur] intelliguntur Herodes, et Antipater filius ejus crudelissimus, quinto ante illum die patris sententia ob læsam majestatem interfectus. Joseph. antiqu. 17, c. 8.9. Bell. Jud. I, c. 21. |||

fol. 50ʳ

V. 22.[169] *Archelaus* &c. ארכלאוס

Cabb. Cat. [*Cur istum metuebat?*][170] [**Christianus.**][171] Archelaus ab Augusto dimidiam partem regni Patris sui, & sub ea Judæam acceperat, cum titulo Ethnarchæ. Herodes Antipas autem, & Philippus duo fratres ejus, quartum singuli acceperant: nempe Herodes | Galilæam, & Philippus Iturææam & Tra- 5
chonitidem. In[172] Seder Olam et in Zemach David, Arkilos; Dioni Histor.

---

165 Added in the left margin: *Cabb. Cat. Quando?*
166 Deletion: Cabb. Cat. The speech remains with the Christian.
167 The Peshitta has an aleph in "Israel". Knorr has missed this out previously.
168 The change of speaker is not marked by a new paragraph.
169 Change of handwriting. Knorr's handwriting appears for a few lines.
170 Added in the right margin: Cur istum metuebat?
171 Added in the right margin: Christian. (which involves a change of speaker).
172 Change of handwriting: the second secretarial hand reappears for approximately two folios, before Knorr takes over at the top of folio 51ʳ until the end of the manuscript.

SECTION IX

Verse 19
when Herod was dead etc. *cdmyt dyn hrwdś*

Kabbalist Catechumen When was that?

Christian It was immediately after the killing of the children, according to Eusebius[173]. According to Josephus in *Antiquities* 17 [6.5], [he died] a burning, excruciating fate with the rotting of his insides and an insatiable desire to eat, with purulent puss around his feet and abdomen. His private parts were putrified and produced worms and he had difficulty breathing, and strong frequent convulsions | and the contraction of his nerves etc. driven to desperation and death as an incomparable example of divine punishment.

Verse 20
Into the land of Israel etc. *l'rṣ° dyśryl*

Kabbalist Catechumen Our scholars divide the whole world into *Erets Israel* or the Land of Israel and *chuzzah laaretz* or Outside the Land. (See in Tract. *De Revol. Animarum*, P. 1, c. 16.) | Concerning the excellence of the Land of Israel over all the other regions, see Synopsis Lib. Zohar Tit. 14.

Christian By those who here are said to have died are understood Herod and Antipater, his cruelest son, put to death five days before [Herod's own death] by his father's sentence of *lèse majesté*. So Josephus, *Antiquities* 17, c.8.9, and *De Bello Judaico*, 1, c. 21. ‖‖

fol. 50ʳ

Verse 22
Archelaus etc. *'rkl'wś*

Kabbalist Catechumen Why did he fear him?

Christian Archelaus had inherited half of his father's kingdom from Augustus including Judaea with the title of Ethnarch. Herod Antipas and Philip, his two brothers, had each received a quarter [of Herod's kingdom]. Antipas | had Galilee and Philip Ituraea and Trachontis[174].

---

173 See Eusebius, *Ecclesiastical History* 1.8.2–15 for a wonderful account of the end of Herod.
174 On Archelaus and the title of Ethnarch, see Geza Vermes et al., eds. *The History of the Jewish People in the Age of Jesus Christ* (175 BC to AD 135) *by Emil Schürer* (Edinburgh: T&T Clark, 1973), vol. 1, pp. 353–357. Mt 2.22 is inaccurate in suggesting he was king.

55. Herodes Palæstinus vocatur. Initio autem Archelaus calumniis Antipatris ita depressus fuit, ut pater eum, cum fratre Philippo testamenta præterierit: sed Delatore occiso, Pater eum omni modo hæredem, sed et post se Regem scripsit: Unde â Cohortibus Rex | salutatus est, et regiam dignitatem sibi vindicavit thronumque regium ad tempus occupavit. Augustus autem Judææ, Idumææ et Samariæ Ethnarcham saltem esse voluit, quia jam â Legatis ex Judæa crudelitatis accusatus erat, quod tria millia Judæorum. Hierosolymis occidisset. Joseph. Antiqu. 17. c. 11.12.13. [Christianus.][175] Hanc crudelitatem magis deinde magisque exerercitam[176] | (Antiqu. 17. c. 15. et 18. c. 1. 3.) merito Josephus metuebat: nomine quoque suspecto, quod Populi Principem innuit, qui Messiæ regnum emergere vix esset passurus.

In partes Galilææ etc. לאתרא דגלילא

Cabb. Cat. *In Antiquis nostris traditionibus Messiam in Galilæa* | *primo manifestatum iri docebatur, prout* apparet in Excerptis Libri Sohar Loc. 70. et 74. n. 11 Cent. I. **Christianus.**[177] Cum autem Galilæa vel superior esset, vel inferior; hæc campestris magis, illa magis montana, in hanc abiit Josephus. Nazaretha enim erat in Galilæa inferiore in confiniis tribuum Isaschar et Zebulon, quamvis potius in Zebulonitide sita fuisse putetur.

V. 23. *In Prophetis.* בנביא

Cabb. Cat. *Punctatio quidem Syriaca singularem numerum refert: sed scriptio prima videtur Græco conformis fuisse, ubi pluralis est.* [**Christianus.**][178] Præ-

---

175 Deletion: Christianus.
176 Correction: exerercitam replaced by exercitam
177 The change of speaker is not marked by a new paragraph.
178 Added in the right margin: Christ., (which involves a change of speaker).
179 David Gans (1541–1613) was author of *Tzemach David* (1592), a chronology divided into two parts. The first concerned Jewish history and the second innovatively addressed general history. The second part was first put into German in Prague in 1890 by Gutmann Klemperer as *David Gans Chronikartige Weltgeschichte unter dem Titel Zemach David* ... and printed by Gottlieb Schmelkes. The first part which is cited here was put into Latin by Wilhem Heinrich Vorst, *Chronologia Sacra-Profana a mundi conditu ad annum M 5352 vel Christi 1592 dicta Germen Davidis ... auctore R. David Gans* (Leiden: Joannis Mairie, 1644). Archelaus is mentioned on year 761 (of the third millennium AM) (see Vorst, pp. 86, 282). In neither place is Archelaus explicitly called a Palestinian. There seems to be no reference to Archelaus in *Seder Olam Rabbah* or *Seder Olam Zuta*.

SECTION IX 535

In Seder Olam and in Tsemach David[179] on *Arkilos* and Dio's History 55[180], Herod [= Archelaus[181]] is called a Palestinian. Initially Archelaus was so depressed by the calumnies of Antipater that his father passed him over with his brother Philip in his will. But when the informer [Antipater] was killed, his father made him [Archelaus] his heir in all respects and also specified he should be king after him. Then he was saluted king | by a cohort and claimed royal dignity for himself and in time sat on the royal throne. Augustus, in all events, wanted him to be Ethnarch of Judaea, Idumaea and Samaria, because he had already been accused of cruelty by an embassy from Judaea for killing three thousand Jews in Jerusalem [Josephus, *Antiquities* 17.2, 12, 13]. Joseph rightly feared this cruelty which grew worse and worse | (*Antiquities*, 17.15 and 18.1.9) and that suspect name which hinted at The Prince of the People [*Arche-laos*, read in Greek] who scarcely would suffer the Kingdom of Messiah to emerge.

In to the regions of Galilee etc. *l'tr' dglyl'*

Kabbalist Catechumen In our ancient traditions it was taught that Messiah would first appear in Galilee, | as appears in Excerpt Cent. I Loc. 70 & 74, n. 11.

Christian There is an Upper Galilee and a Lower Galilee. The former [is] fields, but the latter mountainous, which is where Joseph went, for Nazareth was in Lower Galilee, within the tribal borders of Assher and Zebulon, although it is thought more likely to have been in the territory of Zebulon.

Verse 23
In the prophets bnby'

Kabbalist Catecumen The Syriac vocalisation indicates one prophet. But the initial [consonantal] writing seems to be in conformity with the Greek which is plural[182].

---

180   Dio, *Histories* 55.27.6: "Herod of Palestine, who was accused by his brothers of some wrongdoing or other, was banished beyond the Alps and his portion of the domain was confiscated to the state."
181   Josephus never calls Archelaus Herod, but Dio does 55.27.6 (above). Also the coins bearing ΗΡΩΔΟΥ ΕΘΝΑΡΧΟΥ must be his, as no other Herod was Ethnarch.
182   Clearly Knorr is not looking at his own unvocalised edition of the Peshitta in Hebrew letters. It is possible he was using Aegidio Gutbirio, *Novum Domini Nostri Jesu Christi Testamentum Syriace* (Hamburg: Typis et Impensis Autoris, 1644). He may also have consulted Hutter's Polyglot New Testament which contained a Syriac version. C.G. Düring's 1734 *Novum Inventarum Bibliothecæ Sulzbaco-Palatino* (BSB Cbm 580 Reposito-

positio autem Græca dia[183] rectius hic qui IN exponitus ut Matth. 1, 22; c. 2, 5.16; c. 4; 14; c. 8, 17; c. 12, 17; c. 13, 35; c. 21, 4; c. 24, 12; c. 24, 15; c. 26, 61; c. 27, 9; 1. Tim. 2, 15. Et quia Prophetæ apud | nostrates[184] vel sunt priores, quo   30
referuntur omnia scripta Historica, vel posteriores, quo libri Prophetici referuntur: hinc puto utrumque genus hoc loco intelligi. Inter Prophetas enim priores refertur liber Judicum, in quem Evangelista videtur digitum intendere, typumque Samsonis allegare velle, ê Jud. 13, 5. Quasi Angelus ibidem dixisset: Ille Solis assecla (ut nomen Soham schon sonet.) non solus ea opera perpetrabit; sed in eo tanquam | Jechidah simul erit vis quædam Messiæ, veri   35
liberationis Populi sui, quo cum gradu Tiphereth, quem Solem apellant[185], originaliter unita est. Et sicut ille Heros; Naziræus erit, sic et Messias quon-

fol. 50ᵛ dam simili nomine vocabitur. [Christianus.][186] Quod et factum ||| Mar. 1, 24; c. 14, 67; c. 16, 6; Luc. 4, 34; Mar. 10, 47; Luc. 18, 37; c. 24, 19; Joh. 18, 5.7; c. 19, 19; Act. 2, 22; c. 3, 6; c. 4, 10; c. 6, 14; c. 22, 8; c. 26, 9. Non quasi vo[t]o legali Naziræus fuisset, quia vinum bibisse sæpius legitur: sed quod Deo, pro sanciendo fœdere novo sese devoverit, Joh. 17, 19.

[Cabbalista Catechumenus.[187]] Nec obstat, quod Syri Nomen urbis Naza-   5
reth; non scribant per ז ut scribitur נזיר: sed per צ. Notissimum enim est, quod litteræ[188] unius organi sæpius permutentur.[189] Deinde inter Prophetas posteriores, occurrit locus Jes. 11, v. 1. Ubi verba hæc: וְנֵצֶר et surculus etc. â Paraphraste Chaldæo sic redduntur: Et Messias de filis filiorum ejus ungetur.

---

rium A), p. 2#15, records a copy in the library in Sulzbach. For Hutter's eccentric edition, see Wilkinson, "Constructing Syriac in Latin", art. cit., pp. 169–283 at pp. 237–242. This version is vocalised and the word is vocalised as a singular. The consonantal text however is the same for singular and plural, so all Knorr can properly mean is that the consonantal text is capable of being vocalised as a plural, not that it must necessarily be so.

183 Correction in the right margin: dia replaced by διά
184 Correction: nostrates replaced by vestrates
185 In error. Should be appellant
186 Deleted word.
187 Beginning of the deletion. The speach remains with the Christian.
188 Correction: litteræ replaced by literæ
189 End of the deletion.

SECTION IX

Christian The Greek preposition *dia* ["through"] is more correctly rendered here by "in". See Mt 1.22; 2.5, 16; 4.14; 8.17; 12.17; 13.35; 21.4; 24.12; 24.15; 26.61; 27.9; 1 Tim 2.15. And since the prophets among | your people are either Former Prophets (that is all the Historical books) or Later Prophets, ([that is] the prophetic books [properly speaking]), I conclude that both categories can be understood here. For, amongst the Former Prophets is included the book of Judges, to which the evangelist seems to wish to point and to draw a type of Samson from Judg 13.5. As if the Angel there had said: This acolyte of the Sun (which the name "Soham Schon" sounds like[190]) will not only perform those feats, but in him, | as Yechidah, at the same time will be a power of Messiah, the true liberator of his people, which was originally united with the degree Tiferet (which they call the Sun). And just like that hero, he will be a Nazarite and thus Messiah will be called by a similar name. Which is what happened ‖: Mk 1.24; 14.67; 16.6; Lk 4.34; Mk 10.47; Lk 18.37; 24.19; Jn 18.5, 7; 19.19; Acts 2.22; 3.6; 4.10; 6.14; 22.8; 26.9. I do not wish to suggest [Jesus] was legally a Nazarite, for one often reads that he drank wine but [rather] that he devoted himself to God for the establishment of the New Covenant (Jn 17.19). | It is not an objection that the Syrians do not spell the name of the town of Nazareth with a /z/ as *nzyr* is written, but with a /ç/ [tsadhe]. It is very noticable that letters [representing the sounds] of one [vocal] organ are quite frequently exchanged. Then amongst the Later Prophets occurs (Isa 11.1) where this word appears in vocalized Hebrew *wᵉnēçer* "and a branch etc.". The Aramaic Targum gives this as: "And Messiah is anointed by his sons' sons".

fol. 50ᵛ

---

190   This is perhaps an attempt to pronounce "Samson" in Syriac: the Hebrew would be rather "Shimshon". But one would perhaps have expected "Shemson".

Sectio x.
De Sapientia Jesu Duodecennis in Templo Demonstrata
è Luc. 2, v. 40–52.

40. Puer autem crescebat, et corroborabatur Spiritu, ac implebatur sapientia, et gratia Dei erat super eum.[1,2,3]

41. Et homines illius quolibet anno ibant in Jeruschalem in festo Pascæ.[4,5]

42. Cumque esset filius annorum duodecim, ascenderunt sicut soliti erant ad festum.[6]

43. Et cum completi essent dies, reversi sunt. | Jeschua autem puer remansit in Jeruschalem et Josephus et mater ejus [recedebant].[7]

44. Existimabant enim quod cum comitibus eorum esset. Et cum ivissent itinere diei unius, quærebant eum apud homines suos, et apud quemcunque, | qui notus esset eis.[8]

45. Et non invenerunt eum: et reversi sunt iterum in Jeruschalem, et quærebant eum.[9]

46. Et post tres dies invenerunt eum in templo, sedentem in medio Doctorum, et audientem ab eis | et interrogantem eos.[10]

47. Et mirabantur omnes, qui audiebant eum super sapientia ejus et super responsis ipsius.[11,12]

48. Cumque vidissent eum, mirati sunt: et dixit ei mater ejus: Fili mi, quare fecisti nobis sic? Nam | ecce ego et pater tuus cum anxietate multa quærebamus te.[13]

49. Dixit eis, quid quærebatis me? Nesciebatis vos quod in domo patris mei oportet me esse.[14]

---

1 Added in the left margin: v. 40. *Supra* 1, 80; infr: v. 52. Deleted.
2 On the left-hand half of the page, a space was left, presumably for a fragment cut from Knorr's edition of the Peshittta New Testament containing the Syriac version of the quoted passage in the Gospel of Luke.
3 Vulgate: et confortabatur plenus sapientia; et gratia Dei erat in illo.
4 Added in the left margin: v. 41. Deut. 16, 1; Exod. 23, 15.17; c. 34, 23; Levit. 23, 5. Deleted.
5 Vulgate: Et ibant parentes eius per omnes annos in Jerusalem, in die solemni Paschae.
6 Vulgate: Et cum factus esset annorum duodecim, ascendentibus illis Jerosolymam secundum consuetudinem diei festi
7 Vulgate: consummatisque diebus, cum redirent, remansit puer Jesus in Jerusalem, et non cognoverunt parentes eius.
8 Vulgate: existimantes autem illum esse in comitatu, venerunt iter diei et requirebant eum inter cognatos et notos.

Section X

Concerning the Wisdom Jesus demonstrated in the Temple when he was 12 years old. Lk 2.40–52

40 The boy grew and was strong in the spirit and was filled with wisdom and the Grace of God was upon him.
41 And his people went to Jerusalem every year for the feast of Passover.
42 When the boy was twelve years old, they went up as they were accustomed to the feast.
43 And when the days were completed, | they came back. But the boy Jesus remained in Jerusalem [though] Joseph and his mother were going back.
44 For they thought that he was with their companions. And when they had gone a whole day's journey they looked for him amongst their folk and anyone | who was known to them.
45 And they did not find him, but returned again to Jerusalem and looked for him.
46 And after three days they found him in the temple sitting in the midst of the learned, listening to them | and asking questions.
47 And all were amazed who heard him at his wisdom and at his answers.
48 When they saw him they were amazed and his mother said to him, "My son why have you treated us like this. For | behold, I and your father have been most anxiously looking for you".
49 He replied to them, "Why were you looking for me? Did you not know I had to be in my father's house?"

---

9   Vulgate: Et non invenientes, regressi sunt in Jerusalem, requirentes eum.
10   Vulgate: et factum est, post triduum invenerunt eum in templo sedentem in medio doctorum, audientem illos, et interrrogantem eos.
11   Added in the left margin: v. 47. Matth. 7, 28; Marc. 1, 22; Luc. 4, 22.32; Joh. 7, 15.46. Deleted.
12   Vulgate: Stupebant autem omnes qui eum audiebant, super prudentia et responsis eius.
13   Vulgate: Et videntes admirati sunt. Et dixit mater eius ad illum: Fili, quid fecisti nobis sic? Ecce pater tuus et ego dolentes quaerebamus te.
14   Vulgate: Et ait ad illos: Quid est quod me quaerebatis? Nesciebatis quia in his quae Patris mei sunt oportet me esse?

50. Ipsi autem non intellexerunt sermonem, quem | dixerat eis.[15,16]   40
51. Et descendit cum eis, ac venit in[17] *Nazareth et erat subjectus eis*[18]. *Mater autem conservabat omnes sermones in corde suo*[19].
52. Jeschuah[20] *autem crescebat statura sua | et sapientia sua ac gratia apud*   45
fol. 51ʳ *Deum et filios hominis.*[21,22] |||

V. 40.[23] *Puer autem crescebat* &c. טליא דין רבא

[**Cabb. Cat.**][24] *Quamvis supremus hic omnium Spirituum Dominus nunc puer esset; omnes tamen quatuor adhuc implebat mundos.*

Christianus. Nempe in cœlis erat, etiam in mundo existens Joh. 3, 13.

[**Cabb. Cat.**][25]Idque non tantum quoad divinitatem, sed & quoad exten-   5
sionem graduum Animæ ejus. Et quid obstat, quò minus hoc in loco ad quatuor illos gradus alludi dicamus, ut hæc verba: *Puer autem crescebat*: referantur ad systema factivum. Sequentia: *Et corroborabatur spirutu*; ad formativum, seu angelicum: quasi Spiritu S.; (qui procul dubio hîc intelligitur, sicut in Johanne; | cum non minus, Sanctissimus Dominus noster eôdem imple-   10
tus fuerit adhuc in utero; quippe qui nunquam eo caruerit:) tali jam lumine in illo coruscasset, quale competit Systemati illi Angelico; sed Animabus in illis Paradisi Palatiis existentibus. Qua autem porrò sequuntur: *Ac implebatur sapientia*: referendum erit ad systema creativum: quasi sensus esset; specimina quædam | talis sapientiæ ab ipso eluxisse, qualis in Animabus   15
illis summis reperitur. Ubi haud inutile erit in Excerptis Exempla quædam inspicere Puerorum quorundam, multâ sapientiâ conspicuorum: Centur. II, loc. 36.37.38.39.40.41. Et forte sicut ratione systematis formativi ad ipsum descenderunt Angeli: ita è systemate Creativo è scholis illis omnium summis ad ipsum sæpius descenderunt Animæ quædam, prout | in Sohar sæpius   20
descendere ducuntur tales: vide Excerpta Centur. II. loc. 42.43. Et Cabbal.

---

15 Added in the left margin: v. 50. infr. 9, 45 et 18, 34. Deleted.
16 Vulgate: Et ipsi non intellexerunt verbum quod locutus est ad eos.
17 Vulgate omits in.
18 Vulgate: subditus illis.
19 Vulgate: Et mater eius conservabat omnia verba haec in corde suo.
20 Correction: Jeschuah replaced by Jeschua

SECTION X 541

40 *50 But they did not understand the words with which | he spoke to them.*
51 And he went down with them and came to Nazareth and was obedient to them. But his mother kept all his words in her heart.
45 *52 But Jeschua grew in his stature | and his wisdom and grace before God and the sons of men. |||*

fol. 51ʳ

Verse 40
The boy grew tly' dyn rb'

Kabbalist Catechumen Although the Supreme Lord of all Spirits was now [only] a boy, he still filled the Four Worlds.

5 **Christian** He was in heaven, though existing on earth (Jn 3.13). | And that not just with respect to his divinity, but also with respect to the extension of the grades of his soul. And what prevents us from saying that here there is an allusion to these four degrees? The words "The boy grew" refers to the Factive World. The following "and was strengthened by the spirit" refers to the Formative or Angelic World as if the Holy Spirit (which doubtless is under-
10 stood here, as in [the case of] John, | since our Most Holy Lord was no less filled [with it] while still in the womb, in as much as he never lacked it) now shone with a light in him which befitted that Angelic World, or the souls living in those Palaces of Paradise. What follows: "and was filled with Wisdom" will be a reference to the Creative World. It is as if the sense was: "exam-
15 ples | of such wisdom shone from him as are found only in the loftiest souls". Here it will be useful to examine some examples of boys conspicuous for their great wisdom (Cent. II Loc. 36, 37, 38, 39, 40, 41). And perhaps just as by the logic of the Formative World, the Angels descended upon him, so from the Creative World, from the greatest schools of all, there descended upon
20 him more often certain souls, as such | are quite often said to descend in the Zohar. See Excerpts Cent. II Loc. 42, 43 and *Cabb. Denud.*, Tom. 2, Part. 1,

---

21 Added in the left margin: v. 52. 1. Sam. 2, v. 26; *Supra* 1, 80. et 2, 40. Deleted.
22 Vulgate: Et Jesus proficiebat sapientia, et aetate, et gratia apud Deum et homines.
23 Change of handwriting. It is Knorr's hand again until the end of the manuscript.
24 Correction: Christianus replaced by Cabb. Cat.
25 Deletion: Cabb. Cat.

denudat. Tom. II P. I, p. 389. n. 14[26]; p. 428. n. 348[27]; p. 516. n. 1141. p. sq. n. 1148.[28]; p. 518. n. 1166.[29]; p. 524. n. 26.27.[30]; p. 525. n. 33.34.[31]

[**Cabb. Cat.**][32] *An verò Scholam frequentaverit quæri posset? Dubiumque oriri posset ex eo; quod Marc. 6, 3. ab ipsis Sympatriotis suis habitus fuerit pro idiota & plebejo, | qui procul dubio noverant educationem ejus. Conf. Matth. 13, 56. item quod Joh. 6, 45. haud obscurè innuat, se esse edoctum à Deo: unde etiam factum est, ut planè aliter doceret, ac communiter in Scholis discebatur.*

[**Christianus.**][33] Sed mirum foret, si parentes eius, qui tam ardua de ipso habebant promissa, planè ipsum reliquerint illiteratum: præsertim cum tribui Isasschar, in cuius | confinibus ipse educabatur, apud Antiquos semper tribuatur Amor studiorum: vide Excerpta Centur. II. loc. 44. Et Tract. de Revol. Anim. pag. 372. §.8.[34] Adde quod Luc. 4, v. 16.17. Legisse dicatur publicè: & preces quotidianæ jam tum temporis legerentur, ut paret Luc. 10, 26. item, quod ad Lectionem sæpius se referat Matth. 12, 2[35]; c. 19, 4; c. 21, 16.42; c. 22, 31. &c. Unde concludendum, eum omninò in tenera | hac ætate in Schola didicisse literas: quamvis deinceps non ita inhæreret studiis, ut

---

26 "Siluerunt & audiverunt vocem; & genua eorum invicem collisa sunt. Quæ (*fuit illa*) vox? vox congregationis superioris, quæ congregata erat. (*Animæ nempe Justorum è Paradiso accesserant, ut auscultarent; una cum Schechinah seu præsentia divina.*)" ("*Idra rabba* seu Synodus areæ magnæ", op. cit., p. 389).

27 "Didicimus. Antequam surgeret R. Chiskijah, vox prodiit & dixit: Unus angelus non exequitur duas legationes." (Ibid., p. 428).

28 "§. 1141. Audivit vocem: Beatus es tu R. Schimeon, & beata portio tua, & sociorum istorum, qui tecum sunt; revelatum enim vobis est, quod non revelatur toti exercitui superiori. §. 1142. Sed veni vide. Scriptum est [*Ios. 6.v.26*] Et in primogenito suo fundabit eam, & in minimo suo ponet portas ejus: multò magis hic, quia cum studio nimio & vehementi applicuerunt animas suas hoc tempore: & assumti sunt. §. 1143. Beata est portio eorum, certè enim in perfectione sublati sunt; & tales non fuerunt illi, qui fuerunt ante ipsos. §. 1144. Quare mortui sunt? Didicimus. Cum adhuc revelarentur verba, commota sunt superiora & inferiora illorum curruum, & vox personuit in 250 mundos, quod verba antiqua infra revelentur. §. 1145. Et antequam isti recolligerent animas suas, inter ista verba egressa est anima eorum cum osculo; & annexi sunt illi velo expanso, illosque deportarunt Angeli superni. §. 1146. Quare autem isti? quia ingressi erant, & nondum egressi altera vice ante hoc tempus. Omnes autem reliqui ingressi erant & egressi. §. 1147. Dixit R. Schimeon: quam beata est portio eorum trium, & beata portio nostra propterea. §. 1148. Exiit vox secunda vice & dixit: [*Deut. 4.v.4.*] Vos autem qui adhæretis in Domino Deo, vivitis omnes hodie." (Ibid., pp. 516–517).

29 "Interea veniebat Elias, & tres ictus lucebant in facie ejus." (Ibid., p. 518).

30 "§. 26. Dixit R. Schimeon, quàm diversum est tempus hoc à Synodo Areæ! Nam in Aream quidem adveniebat Deus ille Sanctissimus Benedictus! & quadriga ejus; §. 27. Nunc verò hic est Sanctus ille, qui benedictus sit! & accessit cum illis justis, qui in horto Eden sunt, quod non accidebat in Area." ("*Idra Suta*, seu Synodus Minor", op. cit., p. 524).

SECTION X   543

p. 389, n. 14; p. 428, n. 348; p. 516, n. 1141 et seq., n. 1148; p. 518, n. 1166; p. 524, n. 26, 27; p. 525, n. 33, 34.

Kabbalist Catecumen Can one ask whether he indeed attended a school? Doubt may possibly arise because in Mk 6.3 he was taken his very own countrymen, who no doubt knew his education, | for a lower-class ignoramus (Cf. Mt 13.56). Also because Jn 6.45 clearly shows he was taught by God, which suggests he was taught otherwise than commonly happens in schools.

Christian But it would be a wonder if his parents, who had such difficult things promised of him, simply left him illiterate. Especially since the tribe of Assher in whose | territory he was brought up always enjoyed a reputation among the ancients for a love of learning. See Excerpt Cent. 11 Loc. 44 and Tract. *De Revol. Animarum*, p. 372, § 8. Additionally one might point out that in Lk 4.16, 17 he is said to read in public. And daily prayers were already at this time read as Lk 10.26 shows [from the Shema]. Also he himself often mentions reading (Mt 12.[5]; 19.4; 21.16, 42; 22.31. etc.) from all of which we should conclude | that he was thoroughly, in youth and in age, taught his letters in a school. Although he was then not so absorbed in his studies as other who aspire to learning, but at the same time he cultivated a simple

---

31 "§.33. Dixit: Sanè Raf Hammenuna Senex hîc est, & circa eum 70 justi repræsentati in circuitu ejus, quorum quilibet radiat fulgore splendoris Senis Sanctissimi absconditi omnibus occultationibus. §. 33. Ille inquam venit, ut cum gaudio verba illa audiat, quæ ego eloquar. §. 34. Cumque sedisset, dixit: Certè R. Pinchaso F. Jair hic deputatus est locus." (Ibid., p. 525).

32 Correction: Christianus replaced by Cabb. Cat. (which involves the two speakers being changed over in the following exchange).

33 Correction in the right margin: Cabb. Cat. replaced by Christ. (as a consequence of the previous correction).

34 "Cum autem conduceret Leah Jacobum, verba hæc extant: Gen. 30.v.16. *Et cubuit cum illa eadem nocte*. Mysterium autem ita se habet: Quoniam Jacob est stipes arboris ligni vitæ: sed tribus & filii ejus, sunt rami sub mysterio duodecim signorum Zodiaci, & articulorum in manibus atque pedibus, sicut observatur in Sohar Sect. Vajechi. Jissaschar autem plus in lege studebat, quam omnes reliquæ tribus: & ipsa natura Jissascharis etiam erat de stipite arboris ipsa, cui est nomen legis scriptæ; sicuti Jacob pater noster: Et non pertinebat ad ramos, prout tribus reliquæ. Unde patet, quod Jissaschar quasi Jacob ipse fuerit, & corpus Jacobi. Unde dicitur: Et cubabat nocte ea cum illa. Id est, concubitus reliqui pro cæteris tribubus tantum erant sub conceptu ramorum: iste autem fiebat pro ipsa natura Jacobi: & contingebat sub mysterio istius calcanei, quem abstulerat Esavo, & propter quem dictus erat Jaacobh." ("De revolutionibus animarum", op. cit., p. 372).

35 In error. Matth. 12, 5 has the appropriate vocabulary.

alii, qui ad Doctoratum aspirabant; sed artem simul fabrilem excoleres. Jamque tandem restant verba ultima: *Et gratia Dei erat supra eum*: quæ omninò pertinere videntur ad systema Emanativum; ita ut per Gratiam intelligatur gradus Chesed; per nomen אלהא gradus Malchuth; quasi sensus sit: illum habuisse influxum | omnium septem inferiorum in ipsa puerilia sua: unde facilè concludi posset, quantus fuerit influxus eius ætate adultiore. ||| 40

fol. 51ᵛ

Et homines ejus: ואנשוה

[*Cabb. Cat.*][36] *Quid hoc sibi vult?*

[**Christianus.**][37] Lucas in Græco scripsit: οἱ γονεῖς, Parentes. Syrus, forte, ad evitandam suspicionem de concursu Josephi, sicut hoc cap. v.33. adhibuit vocem | generaliorem: quæ in specie non tantum[38] hoc loco, denotat 5 Josephum & Mariam; sed & cognatos alios, infra v. 44.

Quolibet anno ibant &c. בכל שנא אזלין הוו

[**Cabb. Cat.**][39] *Nihilne hîc mystici?*

[**Christianus.**][40] Quæ communia sunt de trina illa comparatione, hîc non attingemus. | Quæ autem mysticè de illa traduntur in Tikkunim, reperies 10 inter Excerpta Cent. II. l. 45.

In festum Paschatis; &c. לעדעדא דפצחא

[**Cabb. Cat.**][41] *Cur in festum Paschatis primum ascendit Jesus; &*[42] *non in festum Pentecostes; vel Tabernaculorum?*[43]

[**Christianus.**][44] Si dicam, primum hoc fuisse festum è majoribus post 15 absolutum annum ætatis duodecimum; concludi posset, illum in mensibus,

---

36 Correction: Christianus replaced by Cabb. Cat. (which involves the two speakers being changed over in the following exchange).
37 Correction: Cabb. Cat. replaced by Chr. (as a consequence of the following exchange).
38 Correction: a sign is placed above the line which indicates that the terms should be inverted: in specie non tantum replaced by non tantum in specie
39 Correction: Christianus replaced by Cabb. Cat., (which involves the two speakers being changed over in the following exchange).
40 Correction: Cabb. Cat. replaced by Christ. (as a consequence of the previous correction).
41 Correction: Christianus replaced by Cabb. Cat., (which involves the two speakers being changed over in the following exchange).

SECTION X

craft. Now finally there remain the last words: "And the Grace of God was upon him". These seem totally to have to do with the World of Emanations, so that by Grace is understood the degree of Chesed, by the name *'lh'* [God]
40　the degree Malkhut, as if the meaning was: he had an influx | of all seven of the lower degrees in his childhood. From which one may easily imagine how great the influx into him was when he was adult. ‖‖ fol. 51ᵛ

Verse 41
And his people w'nšwh

Kabbalist Catechumen What is this trying to say?
　Christian Luke writes in Greek *hoi goneis* "his parents". The Syriac perhaps attempts to remove any suspicion [here] that Joseph was his father, for
5　in a similar way in the same chapter at verse 33, it uses a more general | word which here not so much specifically denotes Joseph and Mary but also other relatives. See below on verse 44.

Every year they went etc. *bkl šn' 'zlyn hww*

Kabbalist Catechumen Is there anything mystical here?
　Christian What is generally said about those three feasts, we shall not
10　touch upon here. | What mystical traditions there are about them in Tikkunim you will find in Excerpt Cent. II Loc. 45.

In festum Paschatis etc. *b'd'd' dpṣḥ'*

Kabbalist Catechumen Why did Jesus first go up [to Jerusalem] at the feast of Passover and not at another feast[45]
15　**Christian** This was the first of the major feasts after Jesus became twelve years old. One may conclude that his birthday did not fall in the summer

---

42　Deletion: &
43　Correction: Pentacostes; vel Tabernaculorum replaced by aliud
44　Correction: Cabb. Cat. replaced by Chr. (as a consequence of the previous correction).
45　Deletion: Pentecost or Tabernacles

quæ inter Pascha & Scenopegiam interjacent æstivis, non fuisse natum. Si arbitrarium hoc ipse fuisse censebo; saltem id conjici posset, cum eo illum voluisse incipere, in quo habiturus esset finem.

V. 42. *Cumque esset filius annorum duodecim* &c.
וכד הוא בר שנין תרתעסרא

[Cabb. Cat.][46] *Quid indicatur hoc numero?*

[Christianus.] Inter Excerpta Centur. I. Locus 92. agit de Arbore Vitæ, quæ plantata dicitur sub duodecim limitibus. Hæc non incongruè applicari possunt ad Messiam, qui absoluto jam ætatis suæ anno duodecimo specimen edere voluit delitescentis | in se characteris huius duodenarii. Cumque communiter majus quid homini concedi dicatur post absolutum annum decimum tertium (vide Excerpt. Centur. II. loc. 46. Messias hic noster anno jam ætatis duodecimo longè se exhibet con[fir] matiorem). Et sicut juxta Antiquum illud,

—Pulchrum est digitu monstrari; & dicier HIC est:

ita hoc tempore Jesus puer revera ostendit, quod sit ille זה Hic: Jes. 25, 9. cujus numerus est 12; nempe Messias ille ad gradum Tiphereth pertinens. [Conferatur Lex. Cabbalist. pag. 297. h.l.[47]] Notetur etiam, quod duplex ז״ו, quæ alia est Dodecadis expressio, non tantum duplicem ipsius denotet naturam; sed scriptione sua defectiva etiam ipsius exinanitionem.

V. 43. *Remansit* &c. פש לה

[Cabb. Cat.][48] *Suntne & vobis exempla similia?*[49]

---

46 Correction: Christianus replaced by Cabb. Cat., (which involves the two speakers being changed over in the following exchange).

47 "זה *Hic, iste*. Est Tiphereth; vocaturque hoc Nomine, quia redundat in 12. Havajoth, qui sunt duodecim termini. Hoc זה autem unitur & copulatur cum זאת, tanquam masculus cum fœminâ. Atque sic traditur in Sohar Sect. Ba; his verbis: *Didicimus. Illa Corona, quæ vocatur* זאת, *vocatur mulier. Traditum enim est, quod* זאת *vocetur fœmina. Quare? quia scriptum est* Gen. 2, 23. *ex Viro sumta est* זאת. *Quis est Vir? Ille qui vocatur* זה, *Iste enim est Vir, nempe masculus, sicut dicitur* Exod. 32, 1.23. quia זה *Moscheh vir. Isch igitur est* זה, & זאת *desumta est ex.* זה. Hæc ibi. Ubi alluditur ad desumtionem Costæ, seu lateris, quæ est Sponsa Moscheh. Tiphereth ergo vocatur זה sub mysterio Gradûs Moscheh, qui in illo est, sub notione Daath, ut dictum Tr. 14." ("Loci communes kabbalistici", op. cit., p. 297).

months between Passover and Tabernacles. If I were to consider this a matter of his own choice, I would say that he wished to begin with the same feast as that on which he would end.

Verse 42
When their son was twelve years old etc. wkd hwʾ br šnyn trtʿ śrʾ

Kabbalist Catechumen What is the significance of this number?

Christian Excerpta Cent. I Loc. 92 concerns the Tree of Life, which is said to be planted at the junction of twelve paths[50]. These could be fittingly applied to Messiah who, now twelve years old, wished to provide an indication | of the descent into himself of this twelve-fold character. Since it is commonly said that something more is allowed a man after his thirteenth birthday (see Excerpt Cent. II Loc. 46), here our Messiah, now at twelve years old, shows himself more strengthed by far. And just as, according to the fashion of the ancients, it was desirable to be pointed out [and to have people say] "This is ...!", | so at this time the boy Jesus truly showed that he was the *zh* [this] of Isa 25.9 whose numerical value is twelve, Messiah clearly belonging to the degree Tiferet (Cf. *Lex. Cabb.*, p. 297 *h.l.*). Also note that *w w* [a double wav], which is another way of writing twelve [6+6], indicates not so much his double nature, but by its defective writing also his privation[51].

Verse 43
Stayed etc. pš lh

Kabbalist Catechumen Do you have any similar example from our teachers?

---

48   Correction: Christianus replaced by Cabb. Cat. (which involves the two speakers being changed over in the following exchange).
49   Correction: Suntne & vobis replaced by Habesne & è Nostratibus exempla similia?
50   The Lurianic Tree of Life diagram correlates the 22 paths of the tree with the 3 categories of letters in *Sefer Yetsirah*: the three horizontal paths with the three mother letters; the seven vertical paths with the 7 double letters; and the 12 horizontal paths with the 12 single letters.
51   See above in the explanation of the name of Jesus on Mt 1.21 where *wav* may be considered to be written plene as *w-ʾ-w* or *w-y-w*.

[**Christianus.**][52] Historiam de puero quodam erudito, qui neglecto Domino suo, cui serviebat, remansit cum Sapientibus, retulimus inter Excerpta Centur. II. Loc. 37.38. Historiam aliam, de singulari quodam Amore Sacrorum videsis ibidem Loc. 48. Cumque | & tam assidui fuerint Antiqui in 40
studiis, ut aliquando per biduum considerent, sine cibo & potû; [vide Historiam similem, inter Excerpta Centur. II. Loc. 47.] fortè suspicaretur quispiam, etiam Jesum puerum interea de cibo & potu non fuisse sollicitum. |||

fol. 52ʳ

V. 44. *Existimabant enim.* &c. סברין הוו

[**Cabb. Cat.** Subestne mysterium aliquid?][53]

Christianus. Neglectio Pueri Jesum per triduum, hoc mysterium aliquod[54] in se includere videtur Propheticum. Si enim, ut duodecim horæ diem naturalem, Job. 11, 9. ita duodecim anni diem unum vitæ Christi efficiunt; [conf. Luc. 13, 32.] consideranti | statim apparet, quod præsagium 5
hîc latuerit, fore scilicet, ut Christus ignotus maneret dodecade ætatis suæ primâ, & secundâ; nec innotesceret nisi sub finem tertiæ; tanquam Doctor Doctorum.

[**Cabb. Cat.**][55] Item; si ו' duplicatum denotavit dodecadem hanc mysticam, unius scilicet diei symbolum: triplicetur autem ו' idem; sed per characteres | Arithmeticæ gentilis, ut fiant 666; totidemque anni habeantur pro 10
die mystica alia Ecclesia & gentibus collectæ, Apoc. 13, 18. jam iterum patebit, quod die sui periodo primâ annorum scilicet 666 à Christo nato Messias ignoratus fuerit, nec inventus, (etiamsi quæreretur,) inter homines, sine cognatos suos, i.e. Judæos: nec inter illos, qui nosse se dicerent eum. Die autem secunda | & tertia; (id est, ab anno 666, usque ad 1332; & abhinc iterum 15
per secula subsequentia:) adhuc magis ignotus manserit. Spem tamen esse, ut sub finem diei tertia reperiatur in Nova Hierusalem; i.e. regno suo, Apoc. 21, 2.

---

52 Correction: Cabb. Cat. replaced by Christ. (as a consequence of the previous correction).
53 Added in the right margin: Cabb. Cat. Subestne mysterium aliquid?
54 Deletion: mysterium aliquod
55 Deletion: Cabb. Cat.

SECTION X   549

Christian We have related the story of a learned boy who, neglecting the master whom he served, remained with the wise men in Excerpta Cent. II Loc. 37, 38. You will see another story about a singular love of learning there
40 in Loc. 48. Since | the ancients were so assiduous in study that sometimes they sat together for two days without food or drink (see the story also in Excerpta at Cent. II Loc. 47), perhaps someone might suspect that Jesus too, though still a boy, was not worried about food and drink. ‖‖   fol. 52ʳ

Verse 44
For they thought etc. *śbryn hww*

Kabbalist Catechumen Is there any mystery here?

Christian The neglect of the boy Jesus for three days seems to involve a prophetic mystery. For if as twelve hours make a natural day (Job 11.9), so twelve years make one day of the life of Christ (Cf. Lk 13.32), it is imme-
5 diately obvious to one considering | the matter that a prophecy is hidden here, namely that Christ would remain unknown for the first and second twelve years of his life and would not become known until the end of the third twelve-year period and then as the Teacher of Teachers. Also if a double [Hebrew letter] wav denotes this mystical twelve years, a symbol of one
10 day, a triple [Hebrew letter] wav, written in | the numerals of the Gentiles, gives 666. The same number of years may be taken for another mystic day of the Ecclesia gathered from the Gentiles (Rev 13.18). Again it will already be clear that the period of his first day was the 666 years from the birth of Christ when Messiah was unknown and not found (even though looked for) amongst men, or his relatives, i.e. the Jews. Nor amongst those who claimed
15 to know him. The second | and third day (i.e. from 666 AD until 1332 AD and again through the following centuries) he remained still more unknown. But there is hope that at the end of the third day[56] he will be found in New Jerusalem *i. e.* in his Kingdom (Rev 21.2).

---

56   1998 AD. The periods of Jesus early life are matched here to larger chronographic / prophetic periods.

V. 46. *In medio Doctorum* &c. מצעת מלפנא

Cabb. Cat. *Quod Messias etiam in Paradiso visitet scholas Doctorum* | (*Excerpta nos docent Loc. 62. Cent. 1.*) [*Sed cur Jesus hoc fecit?*][57] [**Christianus.**][58] Cumque[59] severa esset Antiquorum Regula, Neminem debere esse αὐτοδιδάχτον, seu qui sine Magistro studia Legis tractaret, (vid. Synopsin Libri Sohar Titul. 1. in Gen. n. 4.[60] & in Levit. n. 6.[61]) An forte propterea Jesus audire voluit Doctores hos, ne[62] criminari postmodum exhinc possent? Sane Messiam sese esse profiteri non potuit, | cum nondum adesset tempus officii ejus. An professus sit se Messiam fu[it] dubitari similiter posset, ob metum nascituri sibi abinde periculi. Disputasse tamen ipsum, pro more tunc receptu, innuunt phrases, interrogandi & respondendi.||[63] Cœterum huc etiam referri potest Exemplum R. Elieseris f. Asarja, qui anno ætatis decimo tertio factus est Præses Synedrii; quique | anno jam ætatis decimo, quoad sapientiam similis fuit septuagenario. Vid. Tract. de Revolution. p. 376.[64] & Juchasin fol. 37.b.

Christianus.[65] Certe si ille tanti est æstimatus, multò sanè dignior fuit Jesus, qui esset Nasi; seu Synedrii Princeps, quales olim Reges erant: quippe qui & è tribû Judæ erat: cum ille sacerdos esset.[66]

57　Added in the right margin: Sed cur Jesus hoc fecit?
58　Added in the right margin: Chr. (which involves a change of speaker).
59　Correction: Cumque replaced by Cum
60　"Neminem debere noviter exponere verba Legis, nisi istud acceperit ad arbore quadam magna (i.e. Doctore quodam excellente.) col. 25." ("Synopsis Celeberrimi illius Codicis Cabbalistici, qui vulgo dicitur Liber Sohar", op. cit., p. 1).
61　"De præmio illius, qui pertigit ad gradum Magisterii, & informat secundum tradita. Et de pœna illius, qui gradum informandi non attigit, & tamen informat. col. 154." (Ibid., p. 20).
62　Added above the line: eum
63　Two vertical lines indicate that a paragraph is to be inserted.
64　"Illud quod in Gemara habetur, quod dixerit R. Elieser F. Asarjah: ecce ego quasi septuagenarius sum. Et quod Magistri nostri dixerunt, cum fuisse decimum ab Esra Scriba. Id sic intelligendum; quod ipse fuerit Esra ille. Si enim, exempli gratia, fata cujusdam

Verse 46
In the midst of the scholars etc. *mç't mlpn'*

Kabbalist Catechumen That even in Paradise, Messiah will visit the schools of the learned, | we discover from Excerpts Cent. I Loc. 62. But why did Jesus do it?

Christian It was a strict rule of the ancients that no one should be *autodidakton* [Greek "self-taught"] or undertake study of the Law without a master (see Synopsis Libri Sohar Tit. 1 in Gen n. 4 & in Lev n. 6). Perhaps for this reason Jesus wanted to hear those teachers, so that he could not later be charged on that account. Clearly he could not yet profess himself to be Messiah, | since the time of his office had not yet come. Whether he announced that he would be Messiah may similarly be doubted for fear of the danger to himself which would arise from that. However that he took part in the discussion is indicated, after the convention of the times, by the expressions "asking" and "answering". Otherwise this may be compared with the case of R. Eliezer ben Asarya[67], who at thirteen was made Leader of the Sanhedrin and when | he was only ten had the wisdom of a seventy year old. See Tract. *De Revol. Animarum*, p. 376 and Juchasin folio 37b. Certainly if he is greatly to be esteemed on account of that, Jesus was much more worthy because he was Nasi or Leader of the Sanhedrin as once the Kings were. Also he was from the tribe of Judah, whilst he [Eliezer] was a priest.

---

ferant, ut vivat septuaginta annos; & tamen aliquam ob causam dies ejus abbrevientur decennio; ille deinceps cum revolvitur, cum vixerit decem illos annos, perfectus est. Hinc dicebat R. Elieser F. Asarja: Ecce ego quasi septuagenarius sum (cum tamen decennis saltem esset:) Quia illo tempore completi erant anni ejus, qui ipsi defuerant in revolutione prima, ut tunc quasi septuagenarius esset." ("De revolutionibus animarum", op. cit., p. 376).

65 The entire intervention of the Christian is deleted.
66 End of deletion.
67 A famous first-century Tanna.

V. 48. *Ego & Pater tuus* &c. אנא ואבוך

[**Cabb. Cat.**][68] *Quare Mater præmittitur?*

[**Christianus.**][69] *Supra* v. 43. præmittitur Joseph: hoc loco verò Syrus præmittit Matrem. Simile quid observatur Exod. 20, v. 13. *Honora patrem tuum & matrem tuam*; ubi Pater præponitur. Et Lev. 19, v. 3. *Unusquisque matrem suam | & Patrem suum timeatis.* Ubi præfertur Mater. Rationem istius collocationis reperimus in Sohar: vide Excerpta Centur. II. loc. 49.[70] |||

fol. 52ᵛ

V. 49. *Quod in domo Patris mei* &c. דבית אבי

[**Christianus.**][71] Accuratissima est expresio textus Græci, qui generaliori phrasi utitur: observantibus præter recentiores & Origene, & Euthymio & Theophylacto. [***Cabb. Cat.*** *Quid autem obscurum hîc fuit parentibus?* **Christianus.** Jesus][72] Intelligit autem non saltem templum[73]; sed & gradum Regni | (Messiani;) qui in mysticis vocatur *Domus* (vid. Lex. Cabbal. pag.

---

68 Correction: Christianus replaced by Cabb. Cat. (which involves the two speakers being changed over in the following exchange).

69 Correction in the right margin: Cabb. Cat. replaced by Chr. (as a consequence of the previous correction).

70 In the right bottom corner appears a Hebrew letter נ presumably an indication of binding or pagination.

71 Correction in the left margin: Cabb. Cat. replaced by Christ.

72 Added in the left margin: Cabb. Cat. Quid autem obscurum hîc fuit parentibus? Christianus. Jesus

73 Correction: a sign is placed above the line which indicates that the terms should be inverted: Intelligit autem non saltem templum replaced by non saltem templum intelligit

74 *Homily on Luke*, chapter 20 on verse 49: "Therefore, in general terms, the Saviour taught in regard to everything that he should be nowhere else than among those who are his Father's."

Verse 48
I and your father etc. *'n' w'bwk*

Kabbalist Catechumen Why is his mother put first?

Christian Above in verse 43 Joseph is put first. Here the Syriac [unlike the Greek] puts his mother first. This is similar to what is observed in Ex 20.13 "Honour your father and mother" where the father is mentioned first and Lev 19.3 "Let each one of you fear his mother | and father", where the mother comes first. The reason for this order is found in the Zohar, see Excerpts Cent. II Loc. 49. ‖

fol. 52ᵛ

Verse 49
That ... in my father's house etc. *dbyt 'by*

Christian The expression of the Greek text is very accurate and uses a more general phrase [*en tois tou patros mou*. KJV: "about my father's business"], as is remarked by Origen[74], Euthymius[75] and Theophylact[76] in addition to more recent scholars.

Kabbalist Catechumen What did his parents not understand here?

Christian Jesus did not mean just the Temple, but also the degree of Kingdom | (of Messiah) which in mystical writings is called the House (See

---

75 The *Commentary on the Four Gosepels* by the tenth-century monk Euthymius Zigabenos is found in *Patrologia Græca*, vol. 129 (Paris: J.P. Migne, 1864). The comment on Lk 2.49 (col. 897) hardly supports the Christian here: "*elege de peri tou hierou*" ("He spoke about the temple"). The *Commentary* appeared in a Latin translation *Commentaria in sacrosancta quatuor Christi Euangelia ex Chrysostomi aliorum ueterum scriptis magna ex parte collecta* by Johannes Hintenius (Louvain, Ex officina R. Rescii, 1544). The Greek text was first printed in C.F. Mattäi's Leipzig edition of 1792. (*Euthymii Zigabeni, Commentarius in quatuor Evangelia graece et latine* (Leipzig: Impensis Weidmannianis 1792)).

76 "An explanation of the Holy Gospel according to St Luke", in *Patrologia Græca* (Paris: J.P. Migne, 1864), vol. 123, col. 734. Theophylact uses the Greek Gospel words: "*oti en tois tou patros mou dei einai me.*"

195.[77]) & *Domus El;* (ib. p. 196.[78]) & *Domus Elohim* (ibid.[79]) & Domus Sanctuarii (ib. p. 198.[80]) & Domus Regis: (p. 199.[81])

[Christianus.][82] & Hunc ergo[83] sensum obscurum mysticum non intellexerunt Parentes ejus: quamvis haud obscurum ipsis esset, quod filius Dei dicendus sit, ê Luc. 1, v. 35. | adeoque verba eius de Templo haud adeo essent obscura.

V. 51. *Et erat subjectus eis* &c. ומשתעבר הוא להון

Cabb. Cat. [*Quid hîc mysterii?* **Christianus.**][84] Quomodo occasione Præcepti de Timore Parentum sensus eruatur mysticus de Patre & Matre in divinis exhibemus inter Excerpta, Cent. II., Loc. 50.

V. 52. *Jeschua autem crescebat* &c. ישוע דין רבא

Cabb. Cat. *Qui profundius assuevit traditis Cabbalisticis, facilè hæc applicaret ad illa quæ traduntur de Seir Anpin, & Adolescentia eius, in Lex. Cabbalist. p. 314. sqq. n. 5.*[85] *sqq. Ita ut tres hosce gradus incrementi Christi quoad staturam, sapientiam & amicabilitatem, reduceret ad Nezach. Hod. Jesod; | Tebhuna, unde tria illa Cerebra.*

---

77 "בית *Domus*. Refertur ad *Malchuth* & ad *Binah*. Ratio est, quia ambæ habitacula sunt; nempe Binah modi Chochmah, qui Istius maritus est, sicut notum est; unde ambo dicuntur *Pater & Mater inferiorum*. Deinde sub alia quoque notione appellantur Domûs; quia Binah Domus est totius systematis Aziluthici infra se constituti: in Ipsâ enim fuerunt illæ Sephiræ, & ab Eâ exierunt, & in eam revertuntur. Malchuth autem illarum domus est, quatenus ad Illam eunt & redeunt. Notum enim est, quod omnes in Illam influxum demittant, omnesque in eam ingrediantur. Alia porrò & tertio ratio est in Malchuth: quia sicut Domus multas in se continet res, & vasa diversissima: ita Malchuth pariter multa in se continet, multasque notiones, atque Virtutes infinitas. [...]" ("Loci communes kabbalistici", op. cit., pp. 195–196).

78 "Aliquando huic voci adjunguntur Epithetha quædam alia; ex gr. בית אל *Domus El*. Quo nomine vocitatur Malchuth, quando influxum accipit à parte dextrâ, quæ vocatur אל." (Ibid., p. 196).

79 "Eâdem ratione Jizchak influxum demisit in sinistram, unde vocatur בית אלהים *Domus Elohim*. Quod cum videret Jaacobh, sic dicebat, Gen. 28, v. 17. *Non est hîc, nisi dodomus* (sic) *Elohim*: ex parte scilicet Jizchak, juxta mysticum illud Cant. 2, 6. *Sinistra ejus sub capite meo*. Talis explicatio quoque reperitur in Sohar, P. I, Sect. Vajeze. [...]" (Ibid., pp. 196–197).

80 "בתי המקדש *Domus Sanctuarii*; sic Eadem Malchuth vocitatur. Ratio hæc est, quod Ipsa sit ædes pro Illo Mikdasch seu Sanctuario, quod est Tiphereth. Domus enim ista Sanctuarii, quæ citò reædificetur in diebus nostris! erat similitudine Domûs Sanctuarii superioris, quæ est Malchuth, quæ etiam in hâc habitabat. [...]" ("Ibid., p. 198).

SECTION X

Lex. Cabb., p. 195), the House of El [God] (ibid. p. 196), the House of Elohim [God] (ibid.), the House of the Sanctuary (ibid., p. 198) and The House of the King (p. 199). It was this hidden mystical sense which his parents did not understand, although they knew he must be called Son of God from Lk 1.35 | and to that extent his words in the Temple were not that obscure.

Verse 51
And was obedient to them etc. *wmšt'bd hw' lhwn*

Kabbalist Catechumen What mystery is here?

Christian How by the opportunity of the commandment about fearing one's parents, Jesus taught mystically about the Father and Mother in the divine realm, we show in Excerpt Cent. II Loc. 50.

Verse 52
And Jesus grew etc. *yšw' dyn rb'*

Kabbalist Catechumen He who more deeply pursues the Kabbalistic traditions will easily apply these things to that which is said about Zeir Anpin and his youth in *Lex. Cabb.*, p. 314 *seq*, n. 5 *seq*, in such a way that he may relate these three aspects of the growing Christ (stature, wisdom and amiability) to Netsach, Hod and Yesod |—Tevunah, whence these three brains.[86]

---

81 "בית המלך *Domus Regis*. Ita ulteriùs vocatur Malchuth; cujus denominationis hanc exponit rationem R. Moscheh: quod nempe Illa sit Domus Regis superni, id est Gradûs Binah: sed citra necessitatem. Non enim alterius Regis Ipsa Domus est, quam Modi Tiphereth; cui etiam Regis nomen tribuitur. Et Ipsa (notoriè) est Domus ejus. Pardes Rimmon. ibid." (Ibid., p. 199).

82 Deletion: Christianus (the change of speaker is no longer needed.)

83 Deleted word.

84 Added in the left margin.

85 "Et iterum ulteriùs crescebant adscendebantque in Locum נ"הי Tebhunæ qui erat status Infantiæ quem קטנות vocant ibique sugebant è tribus Mediis ejusdem, qui est locus pectoris. Ista autem elevatio externa tantum erat, veluti cum Mater infantulo femoribus imposito lac propinat inter duo Brachia sua. Et hæc notio semper vocatur יניקה seu suctio atque lactatio; atque sic triplex est status τῶν זן nempe עיבור seu gestatio in utero, secundò יניקה seu lactatio, & tertiò, מוחין דגדלות seu pubertas & status perfecti cerebri in adolescentia. Atque hæc est vera illa Jenikah de qua toties in scriptis Cabbalisticis fit mentio: cui etiam plures aliæ involvuntur notiones." ("Loci communes kabbalistici", op. cit., pp. 314–315).

86 The relevant passage is cited in the Edition. The "three brains" generally refers to the three highest sefirot.

Christianus. Sanè & à cerebro dependent tria hæc in humanis. Nobis autem verum illud incrementum detur per quod perveniamus ad mensuram illam descriptam Eph. 4, 15 cuius ipse Christus[87] in nobis sit.[88]

FINIS.

---

87 Two deleted words, now hardly readable, but presumably cui nullus
88 Deletion of several words, now unreadable.

Christian Certainly in humans these three depend on the brain. But truly to us that growth is given by which we may attain the measure described in Eph 4.15—of Christ himself in us.

Finis

Bibliography

Manuscripts

Knorr von Rosenroth, Christian, *Collegium über Universal Historie* in HAB Cod. Guelf 149.13. Extrav.

Knorr von Rosenroth, Christian, *Commercium Epistolicum Knorrianum sive Litteræ Domini Knorrii à Rosenroth ad diversos scriptæ et à diversis acceptæ*, Herzog August Bibliothek, Wolfenbüttel, Cod. Guelf. 30.4 Extrav.

Knorr von Rosenroth, Christian, *Disputatio philologica de Theologia de Gentili*, Herzog August Bibliothek, Wolfenbüttel, Cod. Guelf. 87.20 Extrav.

Knorr von Rosenroth, Christian, *Peregrinatio academica*, Herzog August Bibliothek, Wolfenbüttel, Cod. Guelf. Extrav. 253.1.

Knorr von Rosenroth, Christian, *Historiæ Evangelicæ initium secundum quatuor Evangelistas*, Herzog August Bibliothek, Wolfenbüttel, Cod. Guelf. 126 Extrav.

Von Düring, Cilian Joseph, *Novum Inventarium Bibliothecæ Sulzbaco-Palatinæ*, Bayerische Staatsbibliothek, Cbm Cat. 580, 1734.

Before 1800

Anonymous, *A Short Enquiry concerning the Hermetic Art by a Lover of Philalethes. To which is annexed a Collection from Kabbala Denudata, and translation of the Chymical-cabbalistical treatise intituled Æsch Mezareph, or, Purifying Fire* (London: 1714).

Alsted, Johann Heinrich, *Diatribe de mille annis apocalypticis. Sumptibus Conradi Elfridi*, (Frankfurt am Main: Conrad Elfrid, 1627).

Amulo of Lyon, *Epistula seu Liber contra Judaeos ad Carolum Regem*, Patrologia Latina, vol. 116 (Paris: J.-P. Migne, 1852).

Annius, Ioannes, *Commentaria fratris Ioannis Annii Viterbensis ordinis praedicatorum Theologiae professoris super opera diversorum auctorum de Antiquitatibus loquentium* (Rome: Eucharius Silber, 1498).

Arnauld, Antoine, *Histoire et concorde des IV Evangelistes, contenant selon l'ordre des temps, la vie & les instructions de N.S. Jesus-Christ* (Paris: Veuve Charles Savreux, 1669).

Azulai, Abraham ben Mordecai, *Sefer Chesed le-Avraham* (Sulzbach: 1685).

Bayle, Pierre, *Nouvelles de la République des Lettres. Mois Janvier 1687* (Amsterdam: 1687).

Benzelius, Eric, *Notitiae Litterariae Sectionis Primae Pars II. exhibens Res Iudaeorum* (Upsala: Wernerianis, 1712–1716).

Bochart, Samuel, *Geographia Sacra seu Phaleg et Canaan* (Caen: Pierre de Cardonel, 1646).

Bochart, Samuel, *Hierozoicon sive bipartium opus de animalibus Sacrae Scripturae*, 2 vols (London: Thomas Roycroft, 1663).

Bodin, Jean, *Methodus ad facilem historiarum cognitionem* (Paris: Martinus Iuvenis, 1566).

Bodin, Jean, *Method for the Easy Comprehension of History*, transl. by B. Reynolds (New York: Norton, 1969).

Buxtorf, Johann, *De Abbreviaturis Hebraicis*, 2nd ed. (Basel: Impensis Ludovici Regis, 1640).

Buxtorf, Johann, *Lexicon Chaldaicum Talmudicum et Rabbinicum*, ed. by Bernard Fischer (London: Asher, 1875).

Calvisius, Sethus, *Opus chronologicum ex autoritate s. scripturae ad motum luminarium coelestium contextum* (Leipzig: Apelius, 1605).

Casaubon, Isaac, *De rebus sacris et ecclesiasticis exercitationes XVI, ad cardinal. Baronii Prolegomena in Annales et primam partem* (Frankfurt: curantibus Ruland, typis Ioan Bring, 1615).

Castell, Edmund, *Lexicon Heptaglotton*, vol. 1 (London: Thomas Roycroft, 1669).

De Baeza, Didaci, *Historia evangelica universa* (Cologne: Friess, 1684).

De la Carrera, Didaci, *Historia Evangelica metrice compacta ex ipsis Evangelistarum verbis* (Madrid, Ex typographia Didaci Diaz de la Carrera, 1651).

Diaz, Emmanuel, *Relazione della cose più notabili scritte ne gli anni 1619, 1620, 1621 della Cina* (Rome: Zannetti, 1624).

Draxe, Thomas, *The World's Restoration or Generall Calling of the Jews* (London: G. Eld for John Wright, 1608).

Erpenius, Thomas, *Novum D. N. J. Christi Testamentum Arabice ex bibliotheca Leidensi, edente Thoma Erpenio* (Leiden: Typographia Linguorum Orientalium, 1616).

Fabricius, Johann Albert *Historiae bibliothecae Fabricianae qua singuli eius libri eorumque contenta, VI* (Wolfenbüttel & Helmstadt: Sumptibus Ioan. Christ. Meiseneri, 1724).

Ferber, Johann, *Specimen Anti-Judaicum de Gemino quem Judaei praestolantur Messia* (Weißenfels: 1668).

Finch, Henry, *The Calling of the Jewes. A Present to Iudah and the Children of Israel* (London: Edward Griffin, 1621).

Foster, George, *The Pouring Forth of the Seventh and the Last Viall upon all Flesh and Fleshlines* ([London], 1650).

Georgio Veneto, Francesco, *Harmonia Mundi Totius* (Venise: In aedibus Bernardini de Vitalibus chalcographi, 1525).

Gikatilla, Joseph, *Le secret du mariage de David et Bethsabée*, ed. by Charles Mopsik (Paris: Éditions de l'Éclat, 2015).

Goodwin, Thomas, *An Exposition of the Revelation*, in *The Works of Thomas Goodwin* (Edinburgh: James Nichols, 1861), vol. 3.

Grotius, Hugo, *Annotationes in Libros Evangeliorum* (Amsterdam: J & C Blaev, 1641).

Gutbirio, Aegidio, *Novum Domini Nostri Jesu Christi Testamentum Syriace* (Hamburg: Typis et Impensis Autoris, 1644).

Harvey, William, *Exercitationes de Generatione Animalium* (London: Typis Du Gardianis at the expense of Octavian Pulleyn, St Paul's Cemetery, 1651).

Herrera, Abraham Cohen de, *Le portail des cieux*, trans. by Michel Attali (Paris: Éditions de l'Éclat, 2010).

Hintenius, Johannes, *Commentaria in sacrosancta quatuor Christi Euangelia ex Chrysostomi aliorum ueterum scriptis magna ex parte collecta* (Louvain: Ex officina R. Rescii, 1544).

Hottinger, Johann H., *Smegma Orientale* (Heidelberg: A. Wyngaerden, 1658).

Jungman, Justus Heinrich, *Propheta Daniel modo novo* (Frankfurt am Main: Typis Fredrici Herzogs, 1681).

Khunrath, Heinrich, *Amphitheatrum sapientiae* (Hamburg: 1595).

Khunrath, Heinrich, *Von Hylealischen, das ist Pri-materialischen Catholischen algemejnem naturljchen Chaos* (Magdeburg: 1567, Gehne, 1597).

Klaeden, Joachim, *De Lingua Domini nostri Jesu Christi vernacula dissertatio* (Jena: Bauhofen, 1672).

Knorr von Rosenroth, Christian, *Dissertatio De Antiquis Romanor. Numismatib. Consecrationem Illustrantibus* (Leipzig: Typis Hered. Colerianorum, 1660).

Knorr von Rosenroth, Christian, van Helmont, Francis Mercury, *Christlich-Vernunfftgemesser Trost und Unterricht, in Widerwertigkeit und Bestürtzung über dem vermeinten Wohl-oder Überlstand der Bösen und Frommen* (Sulzbach: Lichtenthaler, 1667).

Knorr von Rosenroth, Christian, *Harmonia Evangeliorum, Oder Zusamenfügung der vier H. Evangelisten* (Frankfurt: Zunner, 1672).

Knorr von Rosenroth, Christian *Kabbala Denudata I* (Sulzbach: A. Lichtenthaler, 1677).

Knorr von Rosenroth, Christian, *Aufgang der Artzney-Kunst. Mit Beiträgen von Walter Pagel und Friedhelm Kemp* (Reprint of 1683 edition; Munich: Kösel Verlag, 1971).

Knorr von Rosenroth, Christian, *Kabbala Denudata II* (Frankfurt: B.C. Wust for J.D. Zunner, 1684).

Knorr von Rosenroth, Christian, *Liber Sohar* (Sulzbach: Moysis Bloch and Johannes Holst, 1684).

Knorr von Rosenroth, Christian, *Novum domini nostri Jesu Christi Testamentum syriace. Ditika khadasha* (Sulzbach: J. Holst for W. Endter in Nürnberg, 1684).

[Knorr von Rosenroth, Christian], *A Genuine Explication of the Visions of the Book of Revelation: Full of New Christian Considerations wherein True and False Christendom is briefly and nakedly represented by A.B. Peganius* (London: W.G., n.d.).

Knorr von Rosenroth, Christian, *Apokalypse-Kommentar*, ed. by Italo Michele Battafarano (Bern: Peter Lang, 2004).
Laud, William, *The Works of the Most Reverend Father in God William Laud D. D.*, ed. by William Scott (Oxford: J.H. Parker, 1867).
Le Fèvre de La Boderie, Guy, *L'Harmonie du Monde* (Paris: Jean Macé, 1578).
Le Fèvre de La Boderie, Guy, *Novum Iesu Christi D. N. Testamentum* (Paris: Benenatus, 1584).
Le Sieur du Ryer, André, *L'Alcoran de Mahomet translaté d'Arabe en François* (Paris: Antoine de Sommerville, 1649).
Leibniz, Gottfried Wilhelm, *Sämtliche Schriften und Briefe*, edited by Deutsche Akademie der Wissenschaften (Darmstadt und Berlin: Akademie-Verlag, 1923).
Leibniz, Gottfried Wilhelm, *Reise-Journal 1687–1688* (Huldesheim: Facsimile G. Olms, 1966).
Leibniz, Gottfried Wilhelm, *Monatliche Unterredungen Einiger Guten Freunde Von Allerhand Büchern und andern annemlichen Geschichten* (Leipzig, 1690).
Lightfoot, John, *The harmony, chronicle and order of the New Testament, the text of the four evangelists methodized, story of the acts of the apostles analyzed, order of the epistles manifested, times of the revelation observed: all illustrated, with variety of observations upon the chiefest difficulties textuall & talmudicall, for clearing of their sense and language: with an additional discourse concerning the fall of Jerusalem and the condition of the Jews in that land afterward* (London: printed by A.M. for Simon Miller, 1655).
Lightfoot, John, *Horae hebraicae et talmudicae in quatuor evangelistas* (Leipzig: Friedrich Lanckisch, 1675).
Lightfoot, John, *Erubin; or Miscellanies and the Harmony of the Gospels. Parts I & II*, ed. by J.R. Pitman (London: J.F. Dove, 1822).
Ludolf, Hiob, *Sciagraphia historiae aethiopicae* (Jena: Samuel Krebs, 1676).
Ludolf, Hiob, *Historia aethopica* (Frankfurt: Johann David Zunner, 1681).
Lumnius, Joannes Fredericus, *De Extremo Dei judicio et Indorum vocatione* (Antwerp: Apud Antonium Tilenium Brechtanum, 1567).
Lydiat, Thomas, *Emendatio Temporum ab initio Mundi ... contra Scaligerum et alios* (London: F. Kyngston 1609).
Marckius, Johannes, *Scripturariae Exercitationes ad Quinque & Viginti Selecta Loca Veteris Testamenti* (Amsterdam: Borstius, 1709).
Meelführer, Rudolf Martin, *An Matthaeus Evangelium Graece scripserit?* (Altdorf: Literis Schönnerstaedtionis, 1696).
Michaelis, Joannes D., *Edmundi Castelli Lexicon Syriacum ex eius Lexico Heptaglotto* (Göttingen: Sumptibus J. Christ. Dietrich, 1788).
Milner, John, *A Collection of the Church-History of Palestine* (London: Dring, 1688).
Moréri, Louis, *Grand Dictionnaire Historique, vol. 5* (Basle: Pierre Roques 1740).

Münster, Sebastian, *Evangelium secundum Mattheum in Lingua Hebraica* (Basel: Henricus Petrus, 1537).

Nicholas of Lyra, *Biblia Cum Postillis Nicolai de Lyra ... Quaestiones disputatae contra Hebraeos* (Nuremburg: Anton Kolberger, 1485).

Oecolampadius, Johannes, *In Jeremiam Prophetam Commentariorum* (Geneva: Typographia Crispiniana, 1558).

Peringer, Gustav, *Dissertatio Philologia de Messia Judaico* (Stockholm: Nicolai Wankiif, 1676).

Petavius, Dionysius, *Opus de doctrina temporum* (Paris: S. Cramoisy, 1627).

Petavius, Dionysius, *Rationarum temporum* (Paris: S. Cramoisy, 1633).

Piscator, Johannes, *In Apocalypsin Johannis Commentarius* (Herborn: Christoph Rab, 1613).

Pisani, Ottavio, *Lycurgus Italicus*, trans. by Van Helmont (Sulzbach: Typis Abrahami Lichtenhaleri, 1666).

Postel, Guillaume, *Tractate Ta'am HaTe'anim* (in Hebrew), ed. by Judith Weiss (Jerusalem: Magnes, 2018).

Raimondi, Giovanni Battista, *Evangelium sanctus Domini Nostri Iesu Christi conscriptum a quatuor Evangelis sanctis id est Mattheo, Marco, Luca et Iohanne* (Rome: Medici Oriental Press, 1590).

Reiskius, Johannes Jacobus, *Dissertatio philologica de lingua vernacula Jesus Christi* (Jena: Bauhofer, 1670).

Reynolds, Beatrice (trans.), *Jean Bodin, Method for the Easy Comprehension of History*, translated by (New York: Norton, 1969).

Rhenferd, Jacob, *Dissertatio de Stylo Apocalypseos Cabbalistica* in Id., *Opera Philologica* (Utrecht: Guiliemus van der Water, 1722): pp. 1–33.

Ricci, Matteo, *De Christiana expeditione apud Sinas suscepta ab Societate Jesu* (Augsburg: Mang, 1615).

Robertson, William, *Thesaurus Linguae Sanctae Compendiose scil. contractum* (London: Samuel Roycroft, 1680).

Rusch, Adolphe (ed.) *Biblia Latina cum Glossa ordinaria*, (Strasburg, 1481), reproduced in Facsim. Brepols, V4 in Martin Movard ed., *Glossae Sacrae Scripturae electronicae* (Paris: CNRS-IRHT, 2016) accessed 10.4.2018. [http://gloss-e.irht.cnrs.fr].

Scaliger, Joseph, *Opus novum de emendatione temporum* (Paris: Robertus Stephanus, 1583).

Semmedo, Alvarez, *Imperio del China* (Madrid: Printed for Iuan Sanchez at the expense of Pedro Coello, 1642).

Simon, Richard, *Cérémonies et coustumes qui s'observent aujourd'huy parmi les Juifs. Seconde édition reveuë, corrigée & augmentée d'une seconde Partie qui a pour titre, Comparaison des Ceremonies des Juifs, & de la discipline de l'Eglise, avec un discours touchant les differentes Messes, ou Liturgies qui sont en usage dans tout le monde* (Paris: Louis Billaine, 1681).

Simon, Richard, *Histoire critique du Vieux Testament. Nouvelle édition qui est la première imprimée sur la copie de Paris, augmentée d'une apologie générale et de plusieurs remarques critiques* (Rotterdam: Reinier Leers, 1685).

Simon, Richard, *Histoire critique des versions du Nouveau Testament: où l'on fait connoître quel a été l'usage de la lecture des livres sacrés dans les principales églises du monde* (Rotterdam: Reinier Leers, 1690).

Spizel, Gottlieb, *Elevatio relationis Montezinianae de repertis in America tribus Israeliticis, et discussio argumentorum pro origine gentium Americanarum Israelitica a Menasseh ben Israel in Miqwe Jisrael seu Spe Israelis conquisitorum* (Basel: Johannes König, 1661).

Stanley, Thomas, *The History of the Chaldaic Philosophy* (London: Thomas Dring, 1662).

Tentzel, Wilhelm Ernst, *Monatliche Unterredungen Einiger Guten freunde Von Allerhand Büchern und aldermen annemlichen Geschichten [...] herausgeben von A.B. Aprilis 1689* (Leipzig: J.F. Gleditschen, 1689).

Trigault, Nicolas, *De Christiana expeditione apud Sinas suscepta ab Societate Jesu* (Ausburg: Mang, 1615).

Unger, Christian, "Vitae Knorrianae curriculum, ne pereat cum Historiae Litterariae Cultoribus communicat C.T.V [Christian Theophil Unger]", in *Nova Litteraria anni MDCCXVII in supplementum actorum eruditorum divulgata [...] auctore Io. Gottleib Kravsio* (Leipzig: Apud Io. Christ. Martini, 1718): pp. 191–200.

Van Helmont, Francis Mercury, *Two hundred queries moderately proposed concerning the doctrine of the revolution of humane souls* (London: Robert Kettelwell, 1684).

Vital, Hayyim, *Shaar ha-Amidah* (Koretz: 1784).

Vitringa, Campegius, *Sacrarum Observationum Libri Sex I* (Franeker: W. Bleck, 1712).

Von Mandelslo, Johann Albrecht, *Morgenländische Reyse Beschreibung* (Schleswig: Johan Holwein, 1658).

Vorst, Wilhem Heinrich, *Chronologia Sacra-Profana a mundi conditu ad annum M 5352 vel Christi 1592 dicta Germen Davidis ... auctore R. David Gans* (Leiden: Joannis Mairie, 1644).

Wagenseil, Johann Christoph, *Tela ignea Satanae* (Altdorf: J.H. Schönnerstaedt, 1681).

Wagenseil, Johann Christoph, *Exercitatio philologica de lingua authentica sive originali Novi Testamenti et praecipue Evangelii Matthaei* (Altdorf: Literis Schönnerstædtianis, 1691).

Wagenseil, Johann Christoph, *Hoffnung der Erlösung Israels* (Leipzig: Johann Heinichens Wittwe, 1705; Nürnberg and Altdorf: Jobst Wilhelm Kohles, 1707).

Walker, John, *Treatise on Algebra* (London: John Wallis, 1685).

Widmannstetter, Johann Albrecht, *Liber sacrosancti Evangelii de Iesu Christo Domino et Deo nostro* (Vienna: Michael Zimmerman, 1555).

Willet, Andrew, *De Universali et Novissima Iudaeorum vocatione* (Cambridge: John Legat, 1590).

Zacuto, Abraham ben Samuel, *Sefer Jucashin* (Tunisia: 1504; Cracow: 1581; London: 1857).

Zigabenus, Euthymius *Commentarius in quatuor Evangelia graece et latine*, ed. by Christian Friderick Mattäi (Leipzig: Impensis Weidmannianis 1792).

After 1800

Abrahamsen, Valerie, "Human and Divine: The Marys in Early Christian Tradition" in *A Feminist Companion to Mariology*, ed. by Amy-Jill Levine and Maria Mayo Robbins (London: T&T Clark, 2005): pp. 164–181.

Adam, Alfred, *Antike Berichte über Die Essener* (Berlin: De Gruyter, 1972).

Aiton, E.J., *Leibniz. A Biography* (Bristol: Adam Hilger, 1985).

Altmann, Alexander, "Eternality of Punishment: A Theological Controversy within the Amsterdam Rabbinate in the Thirties of the Seventeenth Century", *Proceedings of the American Academy for Jewish Research*, 40 (1972): pp. 1–88.

Altmann, Alexander, "Lurianic Kabbala in a Platonic Key: Abraham Cohen Herrera's *Puerta del Cielo*", *Hebrew Union College Annual Cincinnati* 53 (1982): pp. 317–355.

Ambrose of Milan, *Hymnes*, ed. by Jacques Fontaine (Paris: Cerf, 1992).

Anderson, Andrew Runni, *Alexander's Gate, Gog and Magog, and the Enclosed Nations* (Cambridge Mass.: Mediaeval Academy of America, 1932).

Archer, Gleason L., *Jerome's Commentary on Daniel* (Grand Rapids: Baker, 1997).

Arnold, Werner, "Jacob Burckhardt aus Sulzbach als Bibiothekar in Wolfenbüttel", *Morgen-Glantz* 19 (2009): pp. 53–70.

Asprem, Egil, "*Kabbalah Recreata*: Reception and Adaptation of Kabbalah in Modern Occultism", *The Pomegranate* 9/2 (2007): pp. 132–153.

Athanasius (attributed), *Synopsis Scripturae sacrae* (§ 76) in Patrologia Graeca, vol. 28 (Paris: J.-P. Migne, 1857).

Avivi, Joseph, "The Writings of Luria in Italy before 1620" (in Hebrew), *Alei Sefer* 11 (1984): pp. 91–134.

Backus, Irena, "The Beast: Interpretations of Daniel 7.2–9 and Apocalypse 13.1–4, 11–12 in Lutheran, Zwinglian and Calvinist Circles in the Late Sixteenth Century", *Reformation and Renaissance Review* 3 (2001): pp. 59–77.

Backus, Irena, *Reformation Readings of the Apocalypse* (Oxford: University Press, 2000).

Bader, Mary Anna, *Tracing the Evidence: Dinah in Post-Hebrew Bible Literature* (New York: Peter Lang, 2008).

Battafarano, Italo M. (ed.), *Christian Knorr von Rosenroth. Dichter und Gelehrter am Sulzbacher Musenhof. Festschrift zur 300 Wiederkehr des Todestages*, (Sulzbach-Rosenberg: Druckerei der Amberger Zeitung, 1989).

Battafarano, Italo M., "'Ob die Juden von Natur stincken'. Thomas Browne und Christian

Knorr von Rosenroth gegen die Gemeinplätze des Antisemitismus", *Morgen-Glantz* 2 (1992): pp. 51–63.

Battafarano, Italo M., "Gott als hermetischer Dichter. Christian Knorrs von Rosenroth ingeniös-barocker Kommentar der 'Johannesapokalypse' (1670)", *Morgen-Glantz* 7 (1997): pp. 15–65.

Battafarano, Italo M., "'Denn wenn Gott brüllet / wer wollte nicht weissagen' Christian Knorrs von Rosenroth Deutung der Weltgeschichte als Heilsgeschichte im *Apokalypse-Kommentar* (1670)", *Morgen Glantz* 15 (2005): pp. 13–26.

Baumgarten, Eliezer, "Comments on Rav Naftali Bachrach's Usage of Pre-Lurianic Sources", *Association for Jewish Studies Review*, 37/2 (2013): pp. 1–23.

Benayahu, Meir (ed.), *Sefer Toledoth ha-Ari*, (in Hebrew) (Jerusalem: Hebrew University Press, 1967).

Ben-Dor Benite, Zvi, *The Ten Lost Tribes. A World History* (Oxford: University Press, 2009).

Blastenbrei, Peter, *Johann Christoph Wagenseil und seine Stellung zum Judentum* (Erlangen: Harald Fischer, 2004).

Bobzin, Helmut, *Der Koran im Zeitalter der Reformation* (Beirut: Franz Steiner Verlag, 1995).

Bousset, Wilhelm, *The Antichrist Legend* (London: Hutchinson, 1896).

Brach, Jean-P., "À propos de l'âme du Messie dans la kabbale chrétienne", *Annuaire de l'EPHE, Sciences religieuses* 115 (2006–2007): pp. 313–319.

Brach, J.-Pierre, "Das Theorem der 'messianischen Seele' in der christlichen Kabbala bis zur *Kabbala Denudata*", *Morgen-Glantz* 16 (2006): pp. 244–258.

Brach, Jean-Pierre, "Paul Vuillaud (1875–1950) and Jewish Kabbalah", in *Kabbalah and Modernity*, ed. by Boas Huss, Marco Pasi and Kocku von Stuckrad (Leiden: Brill 2010): pp. 129–149.

Briquel-Chatonnet, Françoise and Debié, Muriel, *Le Monde syriaque* (Paris: Les Belles Lettres, 2017).

Brooke, A. England (ed.), *The Commentary of Origen on S. John's Gospel. The Text Revised with a Critical Introduction and Indices*, 2 vols (Cambridge: University Press, 1896).

Brown, Francis; Driver, Samuel Rolles; and Briggs, Charles A. (eds.), *A Hebrew and English Lexicon of the Old Testament* (Oxford: University Press, 1972).

Budge, Ernest Alfred Thompson Wallis, *The Book of the Saints of the Ethiopian Church. A translation of the Ethiopic Synaxarium made from the manuscripts Oriental 660 and 661 in the British Museum*, 4 vols (Cambridge: University Press, 1928).

Burman, Thomas E., "European Qur'an Translations. 1500–1700" in *Christian-Muslim Relations. A Bibliographical History*. vol. 6, Western Europe (1500–1600), ed. by David Thomas et al. (Leiden: Brill, 2014): pp. 25–39.

Burmistrov, Konstantin, "Die hebräischen Quellen der *Kabbala Denudata*", *Morgen-Glantz* 12 (2002): pp. 341–376.

Burnett, Stephen G., "Christian Hebrew Printing in the Sixteenth Century: Printers, Humanism and the Impact of the Reformation", *Helmantica: Revista de Filología Clásica y Hebrea*, 51/154 (2000): pp. 13–42.

Campanini, Saverio, *The Book of Bahir Flavius Mithridates' Latin Translation* (Torino: Nino Aragno Editore, 2005).

Campanini, Saverio, *"Francis Mercury van Helmont's Sketch of Christian Kabbalism*, edited by Sheila A. Spector", *Aries* 17/2 (2017): pp. 246–249.

Carmoly, Eliakim (ed.) "Jews in Sulzbach", *Revue orientale*, (Brussels) 3 (1843–1844): pp. 138–140.

Cassel, Paulus, *An Explanatory Commentary on Esther* (Edinburgh: T. & T. Clarke, 1888).

Chajes, Jeffrey H., "Durchlässige Grenzen: Die Visualisierung Gottes zwischen jüdischer und christlicher Kabbala bei Knorr von Rosenroth und van Helmont", *Morgen-Glantz* 27 (2017): pp. 99–147.

Chapman, Cynthia R., *The House of the Mother: The Social Roles of Maternal Kin in Hebrew Narrative and Poetry* (New Haven: Yale University Press, 2017).

Chrystostom, John [Pseudo-], *Opus Imperfectum in Mattheum 1*, Patrologia Graeca, vol. 56. (Paris: J.-P. Migne, 1862).

Cogley, Richard W., "The Fall of the Ottoman Empire and the Restoration of Israel in the 'Judeo-centric' Strand of Puritan Millenarianism", *Church History: Studies in Christianity and Culture* 72, 2 (2003): pp. 304–332.

Coles, Revel A. (ed.), *Oxyrhynchus Papyri* XXXVI (London: Egypt Exploration Society, 1970).

Coudert, Allison P. and Corse, Theodore *The Alphabet of Nature by F.M. van Helmont* (Leiden and Boston: Brill, 2007).

Coudert, Allison P., "Henry More, the Kabbalah, and the Quakers", in *Philosophy, Science, and Religion in England 1640–1700*, ed. by Perez Zagorin, Richard Ashcraft and Richard Kroll (Cambridge University Press, 1992): pp. 31–67.

Coudert, Allison P., "The *Kabbala denudata*: Converting Jews or Seducing Christians" in *Jewish Christians and Christian Jews. From the Renaissance to the Enlightenment*, ed. by Richard H. Popkin and G.M. Weiner (Dortrecht: Springer, 1994): pp. 73–96.

Coudert, Allison P., *Leibniz and the Kabbalah* (Dortrecht: Springer, 1995).

Coudert, Allison P., "Leibniz et Christian Knorr von Rosenroth: une amitié méconnue", *Revue de l'histoire des religions*, 213/4 (1996): pp. 467–484.

Coudert, Allison P., *The Impact of the Kabbalah in the Seventeenth Century: The Life and Thought of Francis Mercury van Helmont (1614–1698)* (Leiden: Brill, 1998).

Cowley, Arthur Ernest and Kautzsch, Emil (eds.), *Gesenius' Hebrew Grammar*, 2nd ed. (Oxford: Clarendon, 1910).

Crome, Andrew, *The Restoration of the Jews: Early Modern Hermeneutics, Eschatology and National Identity in the Works of Thomas Brightman* (Dordrecht: Springer, 2014).

Dahan, Gilbert, *La Polémique chrétienne contre le judaïsme* (Paris: Albin Michel, 1991).

Dalman, Gustaf, *Der leidende und der sterbende Messias der Synagoge: Im ersten nachchristlichen Jahrtausend* (Berlin: H. Reuther, 1888).

Danby, Herbert (trans.), *The Mishnah Translated from the Hebrew with Introduction and Brief Explanatory Notes* (London: Oxford University Press, 1933).

Darmon, Pierre, *Le mythe de la procréation à l'âge baroque* (Paris: Éditions du Seuil, 1981).

De Lubac, Henri, *Exégèse médievale: Les quatre sens de l'Écriture*, 3 vols (Paris: Aubier, 1959).

Dönitz, Saskia, *Überleiferung und Rezeption des Sefer Yosippon* (Tübingen: Mohr Siebeck, 2013).

Driver, Samuel Rolles, *The International Critical Commentary Deuteronomy* (Edinburgh: T&T Clark, 1951).

Driver, Samuel Rolles, *Notes on the Hebrew Text and the Topography of the Books of Samuel*, 2nd ed. (Oxford: Clarendon Press, 1966).

Dunbar, Agnes B.C., "St Mary of Clopas" in *A Dictionary of Saintly Women*, 2 vols, ed. by Agnes B.C. Dunbar (London: George Bell & Sons, 1905): vol. 2, pp. 45–56.

Duval, Rubens, *Lexicon Syriacum auctore Hassano bar Bahlule*, 3 vols (Paris: E Reipublicae Typographaeo, 1901).

Ehrman, Bart D., *The Apostolic Fathers, II: Epistle of Barnabas. Papias and Quadratus. Epistle to Diognetus. The Shepherd of Hermas* (Cambridge Mass.: Harvard University Press, 2003).

Elior, Rachel (ed.), *The Dream and its Interpretation: The Sabbatean Movement and Its Aftermath: Messianism Sabbatianism and Frankism* 2 vols. (in Hebrew) (Jerusalem, 2001).

Emerton, John Adney, "Some Difficult Words in Genesis 49", in *Words and Meanings. Essays Presented to David Winton Thomas*, edited by Peter R. Ackroyd and Barnabas Lindars (Cambridge: University Press, 1968): pp. 81–94.

Emmerson, Richard Kenneth, *Antichrist in the Middle Ages. A Study of Medieval Apocalypticism, Art and Literature* (Manchester: University Press, 1981).

Eskhult, Josef, *Andreas Norrelius' Latin translation of Johann Kemper's Hebrew Commentary on Matthew* (Uppsala: Acta Universitatis Upsaliensis, 2007).

Eskhult, Mats and Eskhult, Josef, "The Language of Jesus and Related Questions: a Historical Survey" in *KUSATU (Kleine Untersuchungen zur Sprache des Alten Testaments und seiner Umwelt)* 15 (2013): pp. 315–373.

Eskola, Timo, *Messiah and the Throne: Jewish Merkabah Mysticism and the Early Exaltation Discourse* (Tübingen: Mohr Siebeck, 2001).

Faivre, Antoine and Tristan, Frédéric (eds.) *Kabbalistes chrétiens* (Paris: Albin Michel, 1979).

Fine, Lawrence, *Physician of the Soul, Healer of the Cosmos. Isaac Luria and his Kabbalistic Fellowship* (Stanford University Press, 2003).

Finke, Manfred and Handschur, Erni, "Christian Knorrs von Rosenroth Lebenslauf aus dem Jahre 1718", *Morgen-Glantz* 1 (1991): pp. 33–48.

Finke, Manfred and Handschur, Erni, "Christian Knorrs von Rosenroth Lebenslauf aus dem Jahre 1718", *Morgen-Glantz* 1 (1991): pp. 33–48.

Finke, Manfred, *Sulzbach im 17. Jahrhundert. Zur Kulturgeschichte einer süddeutschen Residenz* (Regensberg: Friedrich Pustet, 1998).

Fitzmeyer, Joseph A. and Harrington, Daniel J., *A Manual of Palestinian Aramaic Texts* (Rome: Pontifical Biblical Institute, 2002).

Flusser, David, *Sefer Yosifon* (Jerusalem: Mosad Bialik, 1981).

Foucher de Careil, Louis-Alexandre, *Leibniz: La philosophie juive et la cabale* (Paris: Auguste, 1861).

Fragonard, Marie-Madeleine, "Les Trente-deux Sentiers de Sapience de Nicolas le Fèvre de La Boderie: une théorie de l'interprétation polysémique au xvie siècle" in *Mélanges sur la littérature de la Renaissance à la mémoire de V.-L. Saulnier* (Geneva: Droz, 1984): pp. 217–224.

Franck, Adolphe, *La kabbale ou la philosophie religieuse des Hébreux* (Geneva and Paris: Slatkine, 1981 [1843[1]]).

Fredriksen, Paula, *Augustine and the Jews. A Christian Defense of Jews and Judaism*, 2nd ed. (Yale: University Press, 2010).

Friedlander, Michael (ed.), *Moses Maimonides. The Guide for the Perplexed* (New York: Dover, 1905, 2000).

Friedman, Jerome, *The Most Ancient Testimony: Sixteenth-Century Christian-Hebraica in the Age of Renaissance Nostalgia* (Athens: Ohio University Press, 1983).

Frykenberg, Robert Eric, *Christianity in India. From Beginnings to the Present* (Oxford: University Press, 2008).

Fuchs, Arnold, "Christian Knorr von Rosenroth. Ein Beitrag zu seinem Leben und seinen Werken", *Zeitschrift für Kirchengeschichte*, 35 (1914): pp. 548–583.

Gesenius Wilhem, *Hebrew Grammar*, ed. by Emil Kautzsch, trans. by Arthur Ernest Cowley, 2nd ed. (Oxford: Clarendon, 1910).

Giller, Pinchas, *Reading the Zohar: The Sacred Text of the Kabbalah* (Oxford: University Press, 2000).

Goldish, Matt, *The Sabbatean Prophets* (Cambridge, Mass.: Harvard University Press, 2004).

Graetz, Heinrich, *Geschichte der Juden von den ältesten Zeiten bis auf die Gegenwart. Aus den Quellen neu Bearb*, vol. 10 (Leipzig: O. Leiner, 1897).

Grafton, Anthony, "Chronology and its Discontents in Renaissance Europe: The Vicissitudes of a Tradition" in *Time: Histories and Ethnologies*, ed. by Diane O. Hughes and Thomas R. Trautmann (Ann Arbor, 1995): pp. 139–167.

Grafton, Anthony, "From 'de Die Natali' to 'de Emendatione Temporum': The Origins and Setting of Scaliger's Chronology", *Journal of the Warburg and Courtauld Institutes* 48 (1985): pp. 100–143.

Grafton, Anthony, "Scaliger's Chronology: Philology, World History, Astronomy" in *Defenders of the Text in an Age of Science (1450–1800)*, ed. by Anthony Grafton (Cambridge Mass.: Harvard University Press, 1991): pp. 104–146.

Grafton, Anthony, *Joseph Scaliger: A Study in the History of Classical Scholarship. Vol. 2 Historical Chronology* (Oxford: Clarendon, 1993).

Grafton, Anthony, "Tradition and Technique in Historical Chronology" in *Ancient History and the Antiquarian: Essays in Memory of Arnaldo Momigliano*, ed. by Michael Crawford and Christopher R. Ligota (London: Warburg Institute, 1995): pp. 15–31.

Grafton, Anthony, "Some Uses of Eclipses in Early Modern Chronology", *Journal of the History of Ideas* 64, 2 (2003): pp. 213–229.

Green, Arthur, *Tormented Master: A Life of Rabbi Nathan of Bratslav* (University of Alabama Press, 1979).

Green, Arthur, "Nahman of Bratslav's Messianic Strivings" in *Essential papers in Messianic Movements and Personalities in Jewish History*, ed. by Marc Saperstein (New York: University Press, 1992): pp. 389–432.

Guggenheimer, Heinrich W. (ed.), *Seder Olam. The Rabbinic View of Biblical Chronology*, 2nd ed. (Lanham: Aronson, 2005).

Guignard, Christophe, *La Lettre de Julius Africanus à Aristide sur la généalogie du Christ. Analyse de la tradition textuelle, édition, traduction et étude critique* (Berlin: De Gruyter, 2011).

Elior, Rachel (ed.), *Ha-halom ve-shivro. Ha-tenu'ah ha-Shabbta'it u-sheluhoteha: meshihiyut, Shabbeta'ut u-Frankizm*, 2 vols. (in Hebrew) (Jerusalem: Magnes 2000)

Halperin, David J., *The Merkabah in Rabbinic Literature* (New Haven: American Oriental Society, 1980).

Hamilton, Alastair and Richard, Francis., *André du Ryer and Oriental Studies in Seventeenth-Century France* (Oxford: University Press, 2004).

Hammerschmidt, Ernst, "Die Äthiopistischen Studien in Deutschland (von ihren Anfängen bis zur Gegenwart)", *Annales d'Éthiopie* 6 (1965): pp. 255–277.

Hanegraaff, Wouter Jacobus, "The Beginnings of Occultist Kabbalah: Adolphe Frank and Élipas Lévi" in *Kabbalah and Modernity* ed. by Boas Huss, Marco Pasi and Kocku von Stuckrad (Leiden: Brill 2010): pp. 107–128.

Heal, Kristian, "The Magi in the Syriac Tradition: A Critical bibliography of Sources and Studies" made available at the Oxford Patristic Conference August 2011 and now available on edu.ac.

Hecker, Joel, *Mystical Bodies, Mystical Meals: Eating and Embodiment in Medieval Kabbalah* (Detroit: Wayne State University Press, 2005).

Hezser, Catherine, *Jewish Literacy in Roman Palestine* (Tübingen: Mohr Siebeck, 2001).

Himmelfarb, Martha, *Jewish Messiahs in a Christian Empire A History of the Book of Zerubbabel* (Cambridge Mass.: Harvard University Press, 2017).

Holweck, Fredrick G., "Mary Cleophae" in *A Biographical Introduction of Saints with a General Introduction on Hagiology*, ed. by Fredrick G. Holweck (London: B. Herder, 1924): p. 677.

Hominer, Hayim, *Sepher Josippon of Yoseph Bar Gorion Hacohen*, 4th ed. (Jerusalem: Hominer Publication, 1967).

Hotson, Howard, *Johann Heinrich Alsted (1588–1638): Between Renaissance, Reformation and Universal Reform* (Oxford: University Press, 2000).

Hotson, Howard, *Paradise Postponed: Johann Heinrich Alsted and the Birth of Calvinist Millenarianism* (Dordrecht: Springer, 2001).

Howard, George (ed.), *Hebrew Gospel of Matthew*, 2nd ed. (Macon: Mercer University Press, 1995).

Hughes, Jeremy, *Secrets of the Times Myth and History in Biblical Chronology* (Sheffield: Academic Press, 1990).

Hunwick, Andrew W.R., *Richard Simon Critical History of the Text of the New Testament* (Leiden: Brill, 2013).

Huss, Boaz, "Text und Context der Sulzbacher Zohar", *Morgen-Glantz* 16 (2002): pp. 135–159.

Huss, Boaz, "The Text and Context of the 1684 Sulzbach Edition of the Zohar", *Tradition, Heterodoxy and Religious Culture: Judaism and Christianity in the Early Modern Period*, ed. by Chanita R. Goodblatt and Howard Kreisel (Beer-Sheva: Ben-Gurion University of the Negev Press, 2006): pp. 117–138.

Huss, Boaz, "Translations of the Zohar: Historical Contexts and Ideological Frameworks", *Correspondances*, 4 (2016): pp. 81–128

Hutton, Sarah, *Anne Conway: A Woman Philosopher* (Cambridge: University Press, 2009).

Idel, Moshe, "Abraham Abulafia on the Jewish Messiah and Jesus" in Id., *Studies in Ecstatic Kabbalah* (Albany: Suny, 1988): pp. 45–61.

Idel, Moshe, "Concerning the Concept of *Tsimtsum* in Kabbalah and in Scholarship", *Mekhkarei Yerushalaym* 10 (1992): pp. 59–112.

Idel, Moshe, "'One from a Town, Two from a Clan'. The Diffusion of Lurianic Kabbala and Sabbateanism: A Re-Examination", *Jewish History* 7, 2 (1993): pp. 79–104.

Isaac, Benjamin H., "Milestones in Judaea: From Vespasian to Constantine" in *The Near East under Roman Rule—Selected Papers* (Leiden: Brill, 1988): pp. 48–75.

Jastrow, Marcus, *A Dictionary of the Targumim, the Talmud Babli and Yerushalmi and the Midrashic Literature* (New York: Judaica Press 1996).

Jerome, *Liber exegetica ad Fabiolam De XLII mansiones Israelitarum in deserto*, Patrologia Latina, vol. 22 (Paris: J.-P. Migne, 1845).

Jerome, *Liber de Nominibus Hebraicis*, Patrologia Latina, vol. 23 (Paris: J.-P. Migne 1846).

Jerome, *Commentary on Daniel*, Patrologia Latina, vol. 25 (Paris: J.-P. Migne, 1845).

Jerome, *Hebraicae quaestiones in libro Geneseos* ed. by Paul de Lagarde (Leipzig: Teubner, 1868)

Jerome, *Liber interpretationis hebraicorum nominum*, (CChr.SL72) ed. by Paul de Lagarde (Brepols: Turnhout, 1959).

Joüon, Paul, *Grammaire de l'Hébreu biblique*, 2nd ed. (Rome: Institut Biblique Pontifical, 1947).

Joyeux-Prunel, Béatrice, "'Les transferts culturels'. Un discours de la méthode", *Hypothèses* 1 (2002): pp. 149–162.

Kalimi, Isaac, "He was Born Circumcised: Some Midrashic Sources. Their Concept, Roots and Presumably Historical Context" in *Zeitschrift für Neutestamentiche Wissenschaft und die Kunde der Alten Kirche* 93, 1–2 (2002): pp. 1–12.

Kalimi, Isaac, *Early Jewish Exegesis and Theological Controversy Studies in Scriptures in the Shadow of Internal and External Controversies* (Assen: Royal van Goricum, 2002).

Kashouh, Hikmat, *The Arabic Versions of the Gospels. The Manuscripts and Their Families* (Berlin: De Gruyter, 2011).

Kaske, Robert E., "Gigas the Giant in Piers Plowman", *Journal of English and Germanic Philology* 56 (1957): pp. 177–185.

Kellner, S. and Spethmann, A. (eds.), *Historische Kataloge der Bayerischen Staatsbibliothek München. Münchner Hofbibliothek und andere Provenienzen* (Wiesbaden: Harrassowitz Verlag, 1996).

Kilcher, Andreas B., "Lexikographische Konstruktion der Kabbala. Die *Loci communes cabbalistici* der *Kabbala Denudata*", *Morgen-Glantz* 7 (1997): pp. 67–125.

Kilcher, Andreas B., "*Cabbala chymica*. Knorrs spekulative Verbindung von Kabbala und Alchemie", *Morgen-Glantz*, 13 (2003): pp. 97–119.

Kilcher, Andreas B., "Einleitung—Die *Kabbala Denudata* in Text und Kontext", *Morgen-Glantz*, 16 (2006): pp. 9–14.

Kilcher, Andreas B., "Verhüllung und Enthüllung des Geheimnisses. Die *Kabbala Denudata* im Okkultismus der Moderne", *Morgen-Glantz* 16 (2006): pp. 343–383.

Kilcher, Andreas B., "The Theological Dialectics of Christian Hebraism and Kabbalah in Early Modernity" in *The Jew as Legitimation. Jewish-Gentile Relations Beyond Antisemitism and Philosemitism*, ed. by David J. Wertheim (Amsterdam: Palgrave Macmillan, 2017): pp. 47–62.

Klemperer, Gutmann, *David Gans Chronikartige Weltgeschichte unter dem Titel Zemach David* (Prague: Gottlieb Schmelkes, 1890).

Klijn, Albertus Frederik Johannes, *Jewish-Christian Gospel Tradition* (Leiden: Brill, 1992).

Klijn, Albertus Frederik Johannes, *The Acts of Thomas. Introduction, Text and Commentary*, (Leiden: Brill, 1962, 2003).

Koester, C., "The Origin and Significance of the Flight to Pella Tradition", *Catholic Biblical Quarterly* 51, 1 (1989): pp. 90–106.

Kristeller, Paul Oskar, *Renaissance Thought: the Classic, Scholastic, and Humanist Strains* (New York: Harper and Row, 1961).

Kunert, Jeannine, *Der Juden Könige Zwei. Zum Deutschsprachigen Diskurs Über Sabbatai Zwi und Oliger Paulli. Nebst Systematischen Betrachtungen Zur Religionswissenschaftlichen Kategorie Endzeit und Soziodiskursiven Wechselwirkungen* (Unpublished Doctoral Thesis, Universität Erfurt, 2019).

Lampe, Geoffrey W.H., *A Patristic Greek Lexicon* (Oxford: Clarendon Press, 1961).

Leivestad, Ragnar, "Exit the Apocalyptic Son of Man", *New Testament Studies* 18 (1971): pp. 243–267.

Leslie, Donald D., *The Survival of the Chinese Jews* (Leiden: Brill, 1972).

Lévi, Éliphas, *Le livre des splendeurs: contenant le soleil judaïque, la gloire chrétienne et l'étoile flamboyante: études sur les origines de la Kabbale avec des recherches sur les mystères de la franc-maçonnerie suivies de la profession de foi et des éléments de la Kabbale* (Paris: Chamuel, 1894).

Lévi, Éliphas, *Das Buch der Weisen* (Wien: München-Planegg, 1928).

Lévi, Éliphas, *Dogme et rituel de la haute-magie* (Paris: Niclaus, 1967).

Liebes, Yehuda, "Toward a Study of the Author of *Emeq ha-Melech*: His Personality, Writings and Kabbalah" (in Hebrew), *Mekhkarei Yerushalaym* 11 (1993): pp. 101–137.

Liebes, Yehuda, "Myth *vs.* Symbol in the Zohar and in Lurianic Kabbalah", in *Essential Papers on Kabbalah*, ed. by Lawrence Fine (New York Press University, 2000): pp. 212–241.

Liebes, Yehuda, "Hebrew and Aramaic as Languages of the Zohar", *Aramaic Studies* 4/1 (2006): pp. 35–52.

Lindsay, Wallace Martin, *Nonius Marcellus' Dictionary of Republican Latin* (Oxford: Parker, 1901).

Livingstone, David N., *Adam's Ancestors Race: Religion and the Politics of Human Origins* (Baltimore: Johns Hopkins, 2008).

Macfarlane, Kirsten, *Hugh Broughton (1549–1612): Scholarship, Controversy and the English Bible* (Unpublished Doctoral Thesis, Oxford University, 2017).

Macfarlane, Kirsten, "The Biblical Genealogies of the King James Version (1611): Their Purpose, Sources and Significance", *The Library* (7th series) 19, 2 (June 2018): pp. 131–158.

Maciejko, Pawel, *Sabbatian Heresy: Writings on Mysticism, Messianism, and the Origins of Jewish Modernity* (Waltham, Massachusetts: University of New Hampshire Press, 2017).

Madec, Goulven, *La Patrie et la Vie: le Christ dans la vie et la pensée de saint Augustin* (Paris: Desclée, 1989).

Magid, S., "From Theosophy to Midrash: Lurianic Exegesis of the Garden of Eden", *AJS Review* 22, 1 (1997): pp. 37–75.

Magid, Shaul, *From Metaphysics to Midrash. Myth, History, and the Interpretation of Scripture in Lurianic Kabbalah* (Bloomington: Indiana University Press, 2008).

Mandelbrote, Scott, "'The Doors shall fly open': Chronology and Biblical Interpretation in England, 1630–1730", in *The Oxford Handbook of the Bible in Early Modern England, c.1530–1700*, ed. by Kevin Killeen, Helen Smith and Rachel Willie (Oxford: University Press, 2015): pp. 176–193.

Marigold, W. Gordon, "Die englische Übersetzung von Knorrs Kommentar zur Johannesapokalypse und die Rezeption deutscher Erbauungsschriften in England in 17. Jahrhundert", *Morgen-Glantz* 8 (1998): pp. 171–196.

Marshall, I. Howard, *The Gospel of Luke. A Commentary on the Greek Text* (Exeter: Paternoster Press, 1978).

Matar, Nabil I., "The Idea of the Restoration of the Jews in English Protestant Thought: From the Reformation until 1660", *Durham University Journal* 77 (1985): pp. 23–36.

Matar, Nabil I., "The Idea of the Restoration of the Jews in English Protestant Thought: From 1661–1701", *Harvard Theological Review* 78 (1985): pp. 115–148.

Matar, Nabil I., "The Controversy over the Restoration of the Jews in English Protestant Thought: 1701–1753", *Durham University Journal* 80 (1988): pp. 241–256.

Matar, Nabil I., "The Controversy over the Restoration of the Jews in English Protestant Thought: 1754–1809", *Durham University Journal* 87 (1990): pp. 29–44.

Matt, Daniel C., *The Zohar Pritzker Edition*, vol. 5, (Redwood City, California: Standford University Press, 2009).

Mc Namara, Martin, *Targum and Testament Revised* (Grand Rapids: Eerdmanns, 2010).

Mc Namara, Martin, "The Logos of the Fourth Gospel and the Memra of the Palestinian Targum (Ex 12.42)": in Id., *Targum and Testament Collected Essays* (Tübingen: Mohr Siebeck, 2011): pp. 439–443.

McIntosh, Christopher, *Eliphas Levi and the French Occult Revival* (London: Rider, 1972).

Meroz, Ronit, *The Teachings of Redemption in Lurianic Kabbalah* (in Hebrew) (Hebrew University of Jerusalem, 1988).

Meroz, Ronit, "Faithful Transmission Versus Innovation: Luria and His Disciples", in *Gershom Scholem's Major Trends in Jewish Mysticism 50 Years After*, ed. by Peter Schäfer and Joseph Dan (Tübingen: Mohr Siebeck, 1993): pp. 257–273.

Mingjun-Lu, *The Chinese Impact upon English Renaissance Literature: A Globalization and Liberal Cosmopolitan Approach to Donne and Milton* (London: Routledge, 2015).

Mitchell, David C., *Messiah ben Joseph* (Newton Means: Campbell, 2016).

Mitchell, Margaret M., "Patristic Counter-Evidence to the claim that 'The Gospels were written for all Christians'", *New Testament Studies* 5, 1 (2005): pp. 36–79.

Monneret de Villard, Ugo, *Le leggende orientali sui magi evangelici* (Rome: Bibliotheca Apostolica Vaticana, 1973).

Mopsik, Charles, "Late Judeo-Aramaic: The Language of Theosophic Kabbalah", *Aramaic Studies* 4/1 (2006): pp. 21–33.

Morlet, Sébastien (trans.), *Dialogue de Timothée et Aquila. Dispute entre un juif et un chrétien* (Paris: Les Belles Lettres, 2017).

Morlok, Elke, "*De Revolutionibus Animarum* in der *Kabbala Denudata* und dessen lurianische Vorlage *Sefer haGilgulim* von Chajjim Vital (1543–1620)", *Morgen-Glantz* 24 (2014): pp. 1–18.

Mormando, Franco, "Pestilence, Apostasy and Heresy in Seventeenth Century Rome. Deciphering Michael Sweerts's 'Plague in an Ancient City'" in *Piety and Plague from Byzantium to the Baroque*, ed. by Franco Mormando and Thomas Worcester (Kirksville: Truman State University Press, 2007): pp. 265–271.

Müller, Kurt and Krönert, Gisela, *Leben und Werke von Gottfried Wilhelm Leibnitz. Eine Chronick* (Frankfurt am Main: Vittorio Klostermann, 1969).

Mulroney, James A.E., *The Translation Style of the Old Greek Habakkuk* (Tübingen: Mohr Siebeck, 2016).

Murdoch, Brian, *The Apocryphal Adam and Eve in Medieval Europe: Vernacular Translations and Adaptations of the Vita Adae et Evae* (Oxford: University Press, 2009).

Nauert, Charles G., "Peter of Ravenna and the 'Obscure Men' of Cologne: A Case of Pre-Reformation Controversy", *Renaissance. Studies in Honor of Hans Baron* (DeKalb, IL: Northern Illinois University Press, 1971): pp. 609–640.

Nauert, Charles G., "The Clash of Humanists and Scholastics: An Approach to Pre-Reformation Controversies", *The Sixteenth Century Journal*, 4/1 (1973): pp. 1–18.

Necker, Gerold and Zeller, Rosemarie (eds.), *Morgen-Glantz. Die Präexistenz der Seelen. Eine interreligiöse Debatte im 17. Jahrhundert*, 24 (2014).

Necker, Gerold and Zeller, Rosmarie, "Einleitung", *Morgen-Glantz. Vater und Sohn Helmont*, 27 (2017): pp. 9–22.

Necker, Gerold, *Einfürung in die lurianische Kabbala* (Frankfurt am Main: Verl. Der Weltreligionen, 2008).

Necker, Gerold, *Humanistische Kabbala im Barock: Leben und Werk des Abraham Cohen de Herrera* (Berlin: De Gruyter, 2011).

Nicephorus, Callistus Xanthopulus, *Ecclesiastical History*, Patrologia Graeca, vol. 145 (Paris: J.-P. Migne, 1865).

Norris, Harry T., "Edmund Castell (1606–1686) and his *Lexicon Heptaglotton* (1669)" in *The 'Arabick' Interest of the Natural Philosophers in 17th Century England*, ed. by G.A. Russell (Leiden: Brill, 1994): pp. 70–89.

Nothaft, C. Phillip E., *Dating the Passion: The Life of Jesus and the Emergence of Scientific Chronology (200–1600)* (Leiden: Brill, 2012).

Nuovo, Victor, *Christianity, Antiquity and Enlightenment: Interpretations of Locke* (Dortrecht: Springer, 2011).

Oddos, Jean-Paul, *Isaac de Lapeyrère (1596–1676): Un intellectuel sur les routes du monde* (Paris: Honoré Champion, 2012).

Otte, Wolf-Dieter (ed.), *Kataloge der Herzog August Bibliothek Wolfenbüttel Die Neue Reihe; Die Neueren Handschriften, Der Gruppe Extravagantes II*, (Frankfurt: Vittorio Klostermann, 1987).

Overfield, James H., "A New Look at the Reuchlin Affair", *Studies in Medieval and Renaissance History*, 8 (1971): pp. 165–207.

Parfitt, Tudor, *The Lost Tribes of Israel* (London: Weidenfeld and Nicolson, 2002).

Patrides, Constantin Apostolos, "Renaissance Estimates of the Year of Creation", *Huntington Library Quarterly* 26, 4 (1963): pp. 315–322.

Payne Smith, Robert, *A Compendious Syriac Dictionary* (Oxford: Clarendon, 1976)

Pettegree, Andrew and Walsby, Malcolm (eds.), *French Books III & IV. Books published in France before 1601 in Latin and Languages other than French*, 2 vols (Leiden: Brill, 2012).

Phillips, David Nicholas, "Les canons des nouveaux testaments en syriaque" in *Le Nouveau Testament en syriaque*, ed. by Jean-Claude Haelewyck (Paris: Geuthner, 2017): pp. 7–26.

Philo of Alexandria. *Loeb edition*, ed. by F.H. Colston and G.H. Whitaker in ten volumes (Loeb Edition) (London: Heinemann, 1988).

Philo of Alexandria, *On the Creation of the Cosmos*, introduced, translated and commented by David T. Runia (Leiden: Brill, 2001).

Pietsch, Andreas Nikolaus, *Isaac La Peyrère: Bibelkritik, Philosemitismus Und Patronage in Der Gelehrtenrepublik Des 17. Jahrhunderts*. (Berlin De Gruyter, 2012).

Poleg, Eyal, *Approaching the Bible in Medieval England* (Manchester University Press, 2013).

Pollak, Michael, *Mandarins, Jews and Missionaries. The Jewish Experience in the Chinese Empire* (New York: Weatherhill, 1998).

Popkin, Richard H., *Isaac de La Peyrère (1596–1676). His Life, Works and Influence* (Leiden: Brill, 1987).

Postel, Guillaume, *Tractate Ta'am HaTe'anim* (in Hebrew), ed. by Judith Weiss (Jerusalem: Magnes, 2018).

Rapoport-Albert, Ada and Theodore Kwasman, "Late Aramaic: The Literary and Linguistic Context of the Zohar", *Aramaic Studies* 4/1 (2006): pp. 5–19.

Reeves, John C. and Yoshiko Reed, Annette (eds.), *Enoch from Antiquity to the Middle Ages*. vol. 1, Sources from Judaism, Christianity and Islam (Oxford: University Press, 2018).

Reid, William Stanford, "The Four Monarchies of Daniel in Reformation Historiography", *Historical Reflections* 8 (1981): pp. 115–123.

Reynolds, Beatrice (trans.), *Jean Bodin, Method for the Easy Comprehension of History* (New York: Norton, 1969).

Rice, Eugene F. Jr., *Saint Jerome in the Renaissance* (Baltimore: Johns Hopkins University Press, 1985).

Roberts, Alexander and Donaldson, James (eds.), *The Ante-Nicene Fathers. 1. The Apostolic Fathers—Justin Martyr—Irenæus* (New York: Charles Scribner, 1913).

Roling, Bernd, "Erlösung Im Angelischen Makrokosmos. Emanuel Swedenborg, Die *Kabbala Denudata* und Die Schwedische Orientalistik", *Morgen-Glantz*, 16 (2006): pp. 385–457.

Roll, Israel, "The Roman Road System in Judea", *Jerusalem Cathedra* 3 (1983): pp. 136–161.

Ronning, John, *The Jewish Targums and John's Logos Theology* (Peabody, Mass.: Hendrickson, 2010).

Rotelle, John E. (ed.), *The Works of St Augustine: A Translation for the Twenty-First Century. The Letters*, (New York: New City Press, 2001).

Rousse-Lacordaire, Jérôme, *Esquisse de la kabbale chrétienne* (Paris: Les Belles Lettres, 2018).

Royse, James Ronald, *The Spurious Texts of Philo of Alexandria: A Study in Textual Transmission and Corruption* (Leiden: Brill, 1991)

Sage, Athanase, "Le péché originel dans la pensée de saint Augustin, de 412 à 430", *Revue des Études Augustiniennes* 15, 1 (1969): pp. 75–112.

Sagerman, Robert J., *The Serpent Kills Or the Serpent Gives Life. The Kabbalist Abraham Abulafia's Response to Christianity* (Leiden: Brill, 2011).

Schmidt-Biggemann, Wilhelm, "Knorr von Rosenroths missionarische Intentionen", *Morgen-Glantz* 20 (2010): pp. 189–204.

Schmidt-Biggemann, Wilhelm, *Geschichte Der Christlichen Kabbala. Band I: 15. Und 16. Jahrhundert.* (Stuttgart-Bad Cannstatt: Frommann-Holzboog, 2012); *Band II: 1600–1660* (2013); *Band III: 1660–1850* (2013); *Band IV: Bibliographie* (2014).

Schmidt, Nathaniel, "Traces of Early Acquaintance in Europe with the Book of Enoch", *Journal of the American Oriental Society* 42 (1922): pp. 44–52.

Schoedel, William R., "Papias" in *Anchor Bible Dictionary*, vol. 5, ed. by David Noel Freedman (New York: Doubleday, 1992): pp. 140–142.

Scholem, Gershom, *Major Trends in Jewish Mysticism* (New York and Jerusalem: Schocken Books, 1954 [1941[1]]).

Scholem, Gershom, *Le Messianisme juif. Essais sur la spiritualité du judaïsme* (Paris: Calmann-Lévy, 1974).

Scholem, Gershom, *Avraham Cohen de Herrera's Shaar ha-shamayyim. His life, his work and his Influence* (in Hebrew) (Jerusalem: Mossad Bialik, 1978).

Scholem, Gershom, "Alchimie et kabbale" in *De la création du monde jusqu'à Varsovie* (Paris: Cerf, 1990 [1984[1]]): pp. 99–168.

Scholem, Gershom, *De la création du monde à Varsovie* (Paris: Cerf, 1990 [1984[1]]).

Scholem, Gershom, *Jewish Gnosticism, Merkabah Mysticism and Talmudic Tradition* (New York: Jewish Theological Seminary Press, 2015).

Scholem, Gershom, *Sabbatai Sevi. The Mystical Messiah 1626–1676* (Princeton: University Press, 2016 [1973¹])

Schwartz, Howard, *Tree of Souls: the Mythology of Judaism* (Oxford: University Press, 2004).

Secret, François, *Le Zohar chez les kabbalistes chrétiens de la Renaissance* (Paris: Durlacher, 1958; Paris: Mouton, 1964).

Secret, François, *Les kabbalistes chrétiens de la Renaissance*, (Paris: Dunod, 1964).

Secret, François, "Du 'De occulta philosophia' à l'occultisme du XIXe siècle", *Revue de l'histoire des religions* 186/1 (1974): pp. 55–81.

Secret, François, "Éliphas Lévi et la kabbale", *Charis. Archives de l'Unicorne* 1 (1988) pp. 81–89.

Seifert, Arno, *Der Rückzug der biblischen Prophetie von der neueren Geschichte: Studien zur Geschichte der Reichstheologie des frühneuzeitlichen deutschen Protestantismus* (Köln: Böhlau, 1990).

Shavitsky, Ziva, *The Mystery of the Lost Tribes. A Critical Survey of Historical and Archaeological records relating to the People of Israel in Exile in Syria, Mesopotamia and Persia up to ca. 300 B.C.E.* (Newcastle upon Tyne: Cambridge Scholars Publishing, 2012).

Slotkin, James S. (ed.), *Readings in Early Anthropology*, (London: Routledge, 2012).

Snobelen, Stephen, "'The Mystery of this Restoration of all Things': Isaac Newton on the Return of the Jews" in *Millenarianism and Messianism in Early Modern European Culture Vol III*, ed. by J.E. Force and Richard H. Popkin (Dordrecht: Springer, 2001): pp. 95–118.

Sokoloff, Michael and Brockelmann, Carl (eds.), *A Syriac Lexicon* (Winona Lake, Indiana: Eisenbrauns; Piscataway, N.J.: Gorgias Press, 2009).

Spector, Shiela A., *Francis Mercury van Helmont's Sketch of Christian Kabbalism* (Leiden: Brill, 2012).

Stevenson, James, *A New Eusebius Documents Illustrating the History of the Church to AD 337*, 2nd ed. (London: SPCK, 1987).

Stone, Michael E., *A History of the Literature of Adam and Eve* (Atlanta: Scholars Press, 1992).

Strauss, Leo, "On a Forgotten Kind of Writing", *Chicago Review* 8/1 (1954): pp. 64–75.

Strauss, Leo, *Persecution and the Art of Writing*, 2nd ed. (Chicago and London: University of Chicago Press, 1988).

Stroumsa, Guy Gedalyah, *A New Science: the Discovery of Religion in the Age of Reason* (Cambridge Mass.: Harvard University Press, 2010).

Strube, Julian, *Sozialismus, Katholizismus Und Okkultismus Im Frankreich Des 19. Jahrhunderts: Die Genealogie Der Schriften von Eliphas Lévi* (Berlin: de Gruyter, 2016).

Tamar, David, "Luria and Vital on the Messiah ben Joseph" (in Hebrew), *Sefunot* 7 (1963): pp. 169–177.

Taylor, Joan E., *The Immerser. John the Baptist within Second Temple Judaism. A Historical Study* (London: SPCK, 1997).

Taylor, Joan E., *The Essenes, the Scrolls and the Dead Sea* (Oxford University Press, 2012).

Tertullian, *Adversus Marcionem*, 2 vols, edited by Ernest Evans (Oxford: University Press, 1972).

Theisohn, Philipp, "Zur Rezeption von Naphtali Herz Bacharachs *Sefer Emeq ha-Melech* in der *Kabbala Denudata*", *Morgen-Glantz* 16 (2006): pp. 221–241.

Thiel, Winfried, "Athaliah" in *Anchor Bible Dictionary*, vol. 1, ed. by David Noel Freedman (New York: Doubleday, 1992), pp. 511–512.

Tischendorf, Constantin, *Novum Testamentum Graece*, vol. 3 (Leipzig: J.C. Hinrichs, 1894).

Tishby, Isaiah, *The Doctrine of Evil and of the Shard in the Kabbalah of Ari* (in Hebrew) (Jerusalem: Magnes, 1942).

Toaff, Arno, *Cronaca Ebraica del Sefer Yosephon*, (Rome: Barulli, 1969).

Toon, Peter (ed.), *Puritans, the Millenium and the Future of Israel: Puritan Eschatology 1600–1660*, 2nd ed. (Cambridge: James Clarke, 2002).

Tropper, Amram, *Simeon the Righteous in Rabbinic Literature. A Legend Reinvented* (Leiden: Brill, 2013).

Uzzel, Robert L., *Eliphas Lévi and the Kabbalah. The Masonic and French Connection of the American Mystery Tradition* (Cornerstone Book Publishers, 2006).

Van der Lugt, Maaike, *Le ver, le démon et la Vierge. Les théories médiévales de la génération extraordinaire* (Paris: L' Âne d' Or, 2004).

Van Gemert, Guillaume, "Frühe niederländische Stimmen zu Christian Knorr von Rosenroth und ihr Kontext. Knorr-Artikel in Lexiken aus der ersten Hälfte des 18. Jahrhunderts", *Morgen-Glantz* 1 (1991): pp. 79–90.

Van Gemert, Guillaume, "Zu Knorrs Evangelienharmonie von 1672 Vorlage, Verfasserfrage und Kontext", *Morgen-Glantz* 3 (1993): pp. 155–162.

Van Gemert, Guillaume, "Christian Knorr von Rosenroth und Petrus Serrarius Die Apokalypsekommentare in Deutungszusammenhang", *Morgen-Glantz* 11 (2001): pp. 205–227.

Van Gemert, Guillaume, "Christian Knorr von Rosenroth in Amsterdam. Die *Kabbala Denudata* und der niederländische Kontext", *Morgen-Glantz*, 16 (2006): pp. 111–133.

Van Gemert, Guillaume, "Knorrs Apokalypse-Kommentar und der niederländische Kontext. Breckling, Serrarius, Hiël und andere", *Morgen-Glantz* 21 (2011): pp. 211–225.

Vermès, Géza, "The Use of *bar nasha / bar nash* in Jewish Aramaic" in *An Aramaic Approach to the Gospels and Acts*, ed. by Matthew Black, 3rd ed. (Oxford University Press, 1967), pp. 310–330.

Vermès, Géza; Millar, Fergus; Black, Matthew and Goodman, Martin D. (eds.), *The History of the Jewish People in the Age of Jesus Christ (175 BC to AD 135) by Emil Schürer* (Edinburgh: T&T Clark, 1973).

Vileno, Anna M. and Wilkinson, Robert J., "Die Peshitta von 1684 im Kontext des Werkes von Christian Knorr von Rosenroth als Beitrag zu einem 'kabbalistischen Christentum'", *Morgen-Glantz*, 28 (2018): pp. 201–230.

Vileno, Anna M., *À l'ombre de la kabbale. Philologie et ésotérisme au XVIIe siècle dans l'œuvre de Knorr de Rosenroth* (Paris: Honoré Champion, 2016).

Vileno, Anna M., "Les noms divins dans l'œuvre de Knorr de Rosenroth: une présence voilée", *Accademia. Revue de la société Marsile Ficin* (forthcoming).

Vileno, Anna M., "Reincarnations of Messiah(s): Messianic Expectations in Christian Knorr von Rosenroth's Last Work", *Frankfurter Judaistische Beiträge* 43 (2019/2020): pp. 73–96.

Von Greyerz, Kaspar, "Das Nachdenken über die Apokalypse im England des späteren 17. Jahrhunderts", *Morgen-Glantz* 21 (2011): pp. 15–38.

Vulliaud, Paul, *Traduction intégrale du Siphra di-tzeniutha* (Paris: E. Nourry, 1930).

Waite, Arthur Edward, *Transcendental Magic. Its Doctrine and Ritual by Eliphas Levi. A Complete Translation of "Dogme et Rituel de la Haute Magie" with a Biographical Preface* (London: G. Redway, 1896).

Walker, David Pickering, *The Decline of Hell: Seventeenth-century Discussions of Eternal Torment* (Chicago: University of Chicago Press, 1964).

Walton, Michael T., *Anthonius Margaritha and the Jewish Faith: Jewish Life and Conversion in Sixteenth Century Germany* (Detroit: Wayne State University, 2012).

Wappmann, Volker, *Durchbruch zur Toleranz: die Religionspolitik des Pfalzgrafen Christian August von Sulzbach 1622–1708*, (Neustadt a.d. Aisch: Degener, 1998).

Wappmann, Volker, "Juden, Quäker, Pietisten. Die Irenik des Sulzbacher Kreises 1651–1708" in *Union-Konversion-Toleranz. Dimensionen der Annäherung zwischen den christlichen Konfessionen im 17 und 18. Jahrhundert* ed. by Heinz Duchhardt and Gerhard May (Mainz: P. von Zabern, 2000): pp. 119–138.

Weber, Camilla, "Jüdisches Leben in Sulzbach und Floß im 17. und 18. Jahrhundert", *Morgen-Glantz* 22 (2012): pp. 115–143.

Weber, Robert and Gryson, Roger (eds.), *Biblia Sacra iuxta Vulgatam versionem* (Stuttgart: Deutsche Bibelgesellschaft, 2007).

Weinberg, Magnus, "Die hebräischen Druckereien in Sulzbach", *Jahrbuch der Jüdisch-Literarischen Gesellschaft*, 1 (1903): pp. 25–32.

Weinberg, Magnus, "Die hebräischen Druckereien in Sulzbach" *Verbesserungen und Ergänzungen* (Frankfurt: Sänger & Friedberg, 1923).

Weinberg, Magnus, *Geschichte der Juden in der Oberpfalz* Volume 5 (Munich: Ewer-Buchhandl, 1927).

Weiss, Judith, "The Quality of Guillaume Postel's Zohar Latin Translation (1547–1553)", *Accademia: Revue de la Société Marsile Ficin* 15 (2013): pp. 63–82.

Weiss, Judith, *Guillaume Postel's First Latin Translation and Commentary of the Zohar*, 2 volumes (Hebrew PhD dissertation, Ben Gurion University of the Negev, 2013).

Weiss, Judith, *A Kabbalistic Christian Messiah in the Renaissance: Guillaume Postel and the Book of Zohar* (in Hebrew) (Tel Aviv: Hakibbutz Hameuchad, 2016).

Weiss, Judith, *On the Conciliation of Nature and Grace. A Latin Translation and Commentary on the Zohar by Guillaume Postel (1510–1581)* (in Hebrew) (Jerusalem: The Hebrew University, Magnes Press, 2017).

Welton, Daniel Morse, *John Lightfoot. The English Hebraist* (Leipzig: Ackermann and Glazer, 1878).

Werle, Fritz, "Éliphas Lévi. Versuch einer Biographie", in Éliphas Lévi, *Das Buch der Weisen* (Vienna: München-Planegg, 1928).

Wilcox, Donald J.J., *The Measure of Times Past. Pre-Newtonian Chronologies and the Rhetoric of Relative Time* (Chicago: University of Chicago Press, 1987).

Wilkinson, Robert J., *Orientalism, Aramaic and Kabbalah in the Catholic Reformation* (Leiden: Brill, 2007).

Wilkinson, Robert J., *The Kabbalistic Scholars of the Antwerp Polyglot Bible* (Leiden: Brill, 2007).

Wilkinson, Robert J., "Syriac Studies in Rome in the Second Half of the Sixteenth Century", *Journal for Late Antique Religion and Culture* 6 (2012): pp. 55–74.

Wilkinson, Robert J., *Tetragrammaton. Western Christians and the Hebrew Name of God from the Beginnings to the Seventeenth Century* (Leiden: Brill, 2015).

Wilkinson, Robert J., "Constructing Syriac in Latin: Establishing the Identity of Syriac in the West over a Century and a Half (c.1550-c.1700): An Account of Grammatical and Extra-Linguistic Determinants", *Babelao: Electronic Journal for Ancient and Oriental Studies* 5 (2016): pp. 169–283.

Wilkinson, Robert J., "Les Éditions imprimées de la Peshitta syriaque du Nouveau Testament" in *Le Nouveau Testament en syriaque*, ed. by Jean-Claude Haelewyck (Paris: Geuthner, 2017): pp. 269–289.

Wilkinson, Robert J., "The Kabbalistic Treatment of the Virgin Mary in Christian Knorr von Rosenroth's *Historiae Evangelicae initium secundum quatuor Evangelistas*. A Provisional Description", *Accademia. Revue de la société Marsile Ficin* (forthcoming).

William Whitaker, *A Disputation on Holy Scripture against the Papists*, edited by William Fitzgerald (Cambridge: University Press, 1849).

Williams, Frank (trans.), *The Panarion of Epiphanius of Salamis Book I (Sects 1–46)*, 2nd ed. (Leiden: Brill, 2009).

Williams, Frank (trans.), *The Panarion of Epiphanius of Salamis Books II & III De Fide*, 2nd ed. (Leiden: Brill, 2013).

Wilson, John, "A Visit to the Samaritans", *The Visitor* (London: The Religious Tract Society, 1847): pp. 407–410.

Wiseman, Donald J., "Rahab of Jericho", *Tyndale Bulletin* 14 (1964): pp. 8–11.

Witakowski, Witold, "The Magi in Syriac Tradition" in *Malphono w-Rabo d-Malphone:*

Studies in Honour of Sebastian P. Brock, ed. by George Kiraz (Piscaway NJ: Gorgias, 2008), pp. 809–847.

Wolfson, Elliot R., *Along the Path. Studies in Kabbalistic Myth, Symbolism and Hermeneutics* (State University of New York Press, 1995).

Woods, Alice, *Of Wings and Wheels. A Synthetic Study of Biblical Cherubim* (Berlin, De Gruyter, 2008).

Yosha, Nissim, *Myth and Metaphor. Avraham Cohen Herrera's Philosophic Interpretation of Lurianic Kabbalah* (in Hebrew) (Jerusalem: Magnes, 1994).

Zagorin, Perez, *Ways of Lying. Dissimulation, Persecution and Conformity in Early Modern Europe* (Cambridge, Mass.: Harvard University Press, 1990).

Zeller, Rosmarie., "Adamische Sprache, Natursprache und Kabbala. Überlegungen zur Sprachtheorie und Poesie in 17. Jahrhundert", *Morgen-Glantz* 6 (1996): pp. 133–154.

Zeller, Rosmarie, "Naturmagie, Kabbala, Millennium. Das Sulzbacher Projekt Um Christian Knorr von Rosenroth und der Cambridger Platoniker Henry More", *Morgen-Glantz* 11 (2001): pp. 13–76.

Zeller, Rosmarie, "Der Nachlaß Christian Knorr von Rosenroth in der Herzog August-Bibliothek in Wolfenbüttel", *Morgen-Glantz* 16 (2006): pp. 55–71.

Zeller, Rosmarie, "Die Kataloge der Sulzbacher Hofbibliothek", *Morgen-Glantz* 19 (2009): pp. 311–392.

Zeller, Rosmarie, "Knorr von Rosenroths Apokalypse Deutung und England", *Morgen-Glantz* 21 (2011): pp. 107–133.

Zeller, Rosmarie, "Knorrs Erklärung der Gesichter Johannis im Kontext der zeitgenössischen Apokalypse-Deutung", *Morgen-Glantz* 21 (2011): pp. 9–14.

Zeller, Rosmarie, "Die Lehre von der Präexistenz der Seelen bei Knorr und Helmont im Kontext der Diskussion in England", *Morgen-Glantz*, 24 (2014): pp. 133–154.

Zeller, Rosmarie, "Die Rolle von Franciscus Mercurius Van Helmont bei der Anseidlung der Juden in Sulzbach", *Morgen-Glantz* 25 (2015): pp. 383–401.

Zigabenos, Euthymios, *Commentary on the Four Gospels*, Patrologia Græca, vol. 129 (Paris: J.-P. Migne, 1864).

Index of Terms and Nouns

Aaron   151, 165, 195, 211, 337, 339
Abba   95, 337, 341, 366n262
Abiah   151, 165, 169, 171, 289
Abijah   225, 341, 359, 363, 439
Abital   451
Abiud   289, 353, 361
Abner   342n177
Abraham   11, 14, 77, 82n25, 84, 84n36, 98, 133, 133n84, 169, 211, 263, 269, 269n28, 277, 285, 289, 316n85, 323, 327, 341, 347, 357, 397, 403, 413, 435, 462n165, 509, 509n82, 510n92
Absalom   342n177
Abulafia, Abraham   316n85
Achaea   125
Adam   139, 143n53, 191, 199, 199n246, 223, 249, 251, 253, 261, 263, 269n28, 271, 321, 322n101, 335, 367, 375, 385, 401, 411, 411n84, 419, 424n125, 447, 513, 517n112
Adam Kadmon   47, 66, 74, 79, 81n23, 82, 87, 88, 93, 108, 109, 143n53, 223, 251
Adam Rishon   74, 87
Adonijah   342n177
Adumbratio   xiii, xiv, xvi, xx, xx n44, 8, 37, 44, 47, 50, 53, 56, 65, 66, 66n27, 66n29, 66n30, 66n31, 67n33, 68, 68n35, 68n38, 69, 71, 72n4, 85, 89, 90, 92, 93, 96, 99, 102, 108, 115, 120n21, 125n45, 136n28, 137n30, 141, 143, 147, 155, 181, 193, 207, 231, 251, 253, 261, 377, 381, 383n331, 385, 389, 405, 411, 413, 417, 437, 443, 449
Agrippa   447
Ahab   205n274, 341, 341n172, 350n215
Ahaz   341, 341n170, 343, 344n183, 361, 387
Ahaziah   339, 341
Akim   361
Al-Damîrî   453n142
Alexandria   119, 125, 295, 295n38, 308n64, 399n45, 517n112
Alkabetz, Salomon   x
al-Qazwini   453n142
Alsted, Johann Heinrich   99, 99n66
Altdorf   6n14, 46n11, 97n58
Amasa   342n177
Amazia   341, 341n170, 343
Ambrose   143n54

America   324n110, 325
Aminadab   289, 337, 341, 359
Ammonites   331, 335, 339
Amon   289, 341, 345, 361
Amsterdam   ix, ix n4, x, x n5, 1n2, 3, 3n6, 18, 39n18, 52n34, 84
Amulo of Lyon   121n28
Anastasius   309
Angel   151, 153, 161, 177, 191, 193, 211, 213, 215, 221, 223, 239, 241, 251, 271, 275, 285, 291, 371, 403, 405, 429, 431, 455, 459, 461, 463, 465, 469, 475, 481, 499, 537, 541
Anna   64, 99, 111, 112, 136n28, 311n73, 347n198, 433, 456n148, 491, 501
Annius, Ioannes (Giovanni Nanni)   159n69, 516n112
Anthony, Mark   447
Antidicomarianites   352n228
Antigonus   155
Antioch   125
Antipas   533
Antipater   155, 533, 535
Antwerp Polyglot Bible   45, 45n8
Apocalypse Commentary   56, 57, 68, 96
Apostle John   137
Aquinas   466n178
Arabia   453, 471n195, 505, 511
Arabic   xxi, 19, 30, 40, 47, 53, 124n42, 125, 219, 243, 348n205, 395n20, 397n40, 453n142, 503, 503n58, 509, 510n92
Archegus   101, 107, 231, 233, 260n174, 263
Archelaus   445, 446n119, 447, 501, 533, 533n174, 534n179, 535, 535n181
Aristotle   107, 366n258
Asa   341, 359
Asiah   251, 279, 279n63
Assher   491, 535, 543
Athanasius   308n65, 309, 473
Atsilut   141, 251, 253, 279n63, 281
Augustine   57n4, 96, 96n55, 143n54, 163n95, 297, 297n46, 301, 301n54
Augustus   429, 443, 444n109, 445, 447, 533, 535
Azariah   339
Azor   361

Babylon   169, 203, 289, 289n9, 349
Balaam   14, 15, 78, 477, 513
Baptism   2n4, 3n5, 5n11, 201, 373, 427, 441
Barcochba   203
Barnabus   309
Bartholemew   295
Bar Yochai, Simeon   xv, xv n25, 127
Bathsheba   335, 337, 451
Bayerische Staatsbibliothek   6n16, 24–26, 53n38, 82
Bayle, Pierre   7
Ben Asher ibn Halawa, Baḥya (Beḥai)   320n92
Ben Elicha, Ishmael   481
Ben Gershom, Levi   191n206
Ben Mordecai Azulai, Abraham   52n34
Ben Sira, Jesus   207
Ben Uri Schraga Bloch, Moses   26n19, 52n34
Benjamin   311n73, 345
Benjani   347
Beroea   295, 301
Bethlehem   429, 431, 449, 451, 455, 457, 459, 465, 471n195, 473, 495, 497, 499, 501, 503, 503n57, 519, 521, 523
Binah   139, 143, 281, 337, 379, 421, 491, 523
Bithiah   331
Blavatsky, Helena   xviii, xx
Boaz   120n22, 327, 331, 333, 341, 359
Bochart, Samuel   53, 452n142
Bodin, Jean   57, 58n5
Breton, André   xx
Briah   251, 279n63, 281
Bruno, Giordano   57n2
Burckhard, Jakob   16
Buxtorf, Johann   46, 51, 52, 121, 121n28, 318n85, 417, 479, 481n228

Caesarea   295, 296n43, 299, 309
Cainan   435
Caius Caesar   447
Caleb   401
Calvisius, Seth   59, 343, 343n181
Campania   157
Canaan   203n268, 331, 339, 355n234, 452n142
Casaubon, Isaac   308n65, 472n195, 473
Castell, Edmund   53, 243n110
Cellarius, Christoph   318n85
Cerinthians   303

Chaldean   291, 305, 309
Chaldeans   501, 509, 511
Chanukah   441, 443
Charter of Privileges   97
Chayah and *Yechidah*   95, 373, 403, 403n59, 467, 467n180
Chesed   165, 347, 421, 485, 491, 527, 545
Chilion   327
China   324n110, 325
Chokhmah   139, 143, 281, 337, 379, 383, 523
Christian Augustus, Pfalzgraf   21n6, 31, 31n1, 32n4, 50, 96, 310n70, 479n225
Chronography   57
Chrysostom, John   297, 299
Citthaei   157
Constantine the Great   283
Conway, Anne   68n36, 68n38, 98
Cordovero, Moshe   x
Cornelius   187, 209
Corona   109, 112, 253, 491
Crafft, Johan Daniel   1
Cuthites   306n62
Cyrene   123
Cyrenius   443, 445
Cyril   473
Cyrus   437

Dan   322n101, 342n176, 343n177, 427n134, 443n103
Daniel   187, 213, 223n27, 225, 314n81, 324n110, 425n126, 427, 427n134, 437, 507
Daroma   12, 13, 161
David   4, 14, 32n5, 51, 61, 61n15, 66n27, 77, 93, 103, 107, 112, 157n61, 221, 222n27, 233, 235, 247, 251, 255, 257, 265, 269n28, 271, 289, 291, 292n29, 313, 315, 316n85, 317, 319, 319n92, 321, 323, 327, 333, 335, 335n148, 335n150, 337, 339, 341, 341n172, 342n177, 343, 348n205, 348n206, 353, 359, 366n263, 367, 372n279, 373, 375, 397, 399n45, 401, 411, 429, 443, 449, 451, 460n161, 461, 462n165, 465, 477, 479, 491, 535
De Lapeyrère, Isaac   57
Descartes, René   xi
Dinah   329n126, 342n175, 347, 347n198
Draxe, Thomas   98
Du Plessis-Mornay, Philippe   389n349
Du Ryer, André   366n263

INDEX OF TERMS AND NOUNS 585

Du Tillet, Jean   310n69
Duke Anthony Ulrich of Brunswick   xii, 3, 62n19, 96

Ebionites   303, 305, 305n61
Ecclesia   73, 76n10, 94, 103, 104, 111, 137, 195, 203, 209, 223, 229, 237, 279, 281, 283, 285, 337, 357, 365, 369, 391, 391n359, 401, 487, 491, 503, 523, 527, 549
Edom   79, 155, 155n50, 157, 159, 159n71, 161, 331n134, 381, 443n104, 529
Egidio da Viterbo   45, 75n7, 159n69
Egypt   78, 79n18, 94, 157, 203, 295, 298n48, 331, 345, 347, 349, 356n241, 435, 499, 501, 524n139, 525, 527
Ein Sof   109, 139, 143n53, 253
Eleazar   289, 361
Eliakim   289, 349, 361
Elijah   12, 73, 76, 76n12, 95, 121, 121n24, 153, 187, 189, 191, 191n205, 193, 195, 199, 203, 205, 207, 207n283, 209, 211n301, 263n193, 399, 402n57, 403, 403n58, 415
Elisabeth / Elischeba   151, 153, 165, 219, 221, 223, 225, 263, 267, 269, 271, 273, 279, 279n61, 313, 337, 365, 395, 400n52, 403
Elisha   205, 355n234, 367n263
Elkana   169
Emmanuel   249, 291, 325n110
Ein-Gedi   407, 423, 425
Enoch   191, 191n205, 261, 401, 411, 411n84
Ephesus   125n43, 135
Ephraimites   319
Epiphanius   163n94, 296n44, 297, 300n50, 301, 301n53, 302n56, 303, 303n59, 352n228, 353, 473, 501n49, 509
Er   327
Erasmus   295n40
Ehrenbert, Karl Maria, Freiherr von Moll   6
Erpenius, Thomas   124n42, 452n142, 505n65
Esau (Esavus)   12, 326n116, 157, 161, 327, 357, 381, 381n320, 443n104
Esh Metsaref   xiii n18, xvii, xvii n30, xvii n32
Esotericism   xvi, xix, xx, 55, 55n43
Essenes   424n126, 425
Esther   245, 247, 451n137
Ethiopia   2
Ethiopian(s)   57, 528n154
Ethiopic   xxi, 53, 513n100, 529

Eusebius   57n4, 292n29, 293, 293n30, 296n45, 298n49, 299, 300n50, 308n64, 381n322, 473, 509, 533, 533n173
Euthymius   553, 553n75
Eve   76, 76n8, 237, 269n28, 271, 335, 387, 411n84, 491
Excerpta   xii n15, 2n2, 9, 9n26, 10, 10n27, 11, 16, 16n31, 24, 40n21, 51, 51n33, 53, 54, 56, 96, 43n30, 126n53, 133, 137, 147, 149, 161, 169, 175, 177, 187, 191, 199, 201, 211, 213, 219, 229, 231, 245, 259, 263, 273, 317n85, 323, 325, 327, 331, 333, 351, 389, 403, 407, 409, 413, 425, 465, 477, 479, 481, 493, 507, 515, 519, 521, 531, 535, 541, 543, 545, 547, 549, 551, 553, 555

Fabricius, Johan Christian   6, 24
Feast of Dedication   269
Feast of Lights   441
Feast of Tabernacles   269, 441, 547
Ferber, Johann   318n85
Finch, Henry   98
Findekeller, Christoph Daniel   1
Foundation   163, 167, 241, 241n102, 331
Franck, Adolphe   xvi

Gans, David   534n179
Georgio Veneto, Francesco   143n51
Gabri   511
Gabriel   120n23, 153, 177, 179, 179n162, 211, 213, 221, 225, 226n40, 227, 263, 459
Galen   107, 366n258
Galilee   155, 221, 227, 229, 229n51, 263, 313, 429, 435, 501, 533, 535
Gedulah   407
Geier, Martin   39n18
Gera   345
Gevurah   143, 177, 179, 187, 407
Giant of Twin Substances   143
Gideon   243
Głogów   ix
Goodwin, Thomas   98, 98n63
Graetz, Heinrich   xvi
Gregory of Nyssa   466n178, 473
Gutbirio, Aegidio   535n182

Hadrian   301
Ham   159, 339
Hamul   345

Hanamel 329n125
Hannah 169, 491
Hannover 1
Haran 327, 435, 509, 511, 513
Harmonia Evangeliorum 56, 57, 60, 63n23
Harvey, William 103, 107, 365, 366n258
Hasidism xiii
Hebron 269, 271, 271n34, 271n35, 277, 277n51, 345, 400n52, 401, 403, 39n19
Heli 313, 353
Hemor 347
Hepar 161
Herod 47, 53, 72n1, 79, 80, 151, 155, 155n50, 157, 161, 205n274, 443, 497, 499, 501, 503, 503n58, 529, 533, 533n173, 535, 535n180, 535n181
Herodias 205n274
Herzog August Bibliothek ix n1, ix n3, xxi n45, 6, 11, 18n2, 20, 26, 26n18
Hezekiah 341, 343, 361, 453
Hezron 341, 359
Hilkiah 329n125
Hillel 353, 451, 478n224, 479
Historiae Evangelicae initium 4n7, 5, 6, 8-10, 25, 35, 49n24, 99n67
Innocents (Holy) 53, 75, 78
Hominer, Hayim 157n61
Horace 455
Huldah 329n125
Huysmans, Joris-Karl xx
Huz 347

Ibn Shaprut, Hasdai 310n69
Ibzan 331
Idumean(s) 79, 157, 159, 161, 529
Imma 95
Immaculate Conception 101n73, 106, 233n69
Incense 151, 151n20, 165, 175, 179, 187, 217, 481, 525
India 293n33, 294n37, 295, 347
Irenaeus 247n123, 293, 299, 301, 302n56
Isaac 157, 169, 207, 263, 269, 269n28, 285, 308n65, 326n116, 341, 355n235, 388n348, 401n54, 413
Isaiah 131n76, 159, 227n43, 237, 343, 343n179, 386n344, 387, 389, 401, 456n148, 471n195
Issachar 227

Ituraea 533
Jacob 157, 161, 207n283, 221, 251, 255, 263, 269, 269n28, 285, 313n77, 319, 319n92, 326n116, 327, 341, 345, 345n187, 345n189, 347, 355n235, 357, 361, 393, 401, 413, 435, 457, 515, 529
Jannes and Jambres 78, 513, 513n100
Japheth 339
Javan 339
Jeconiah (Jechoniah, Jehoiachin) 347, 349, 350n215, 351, 361
Jehoahaz 347, 349
Johaiada 164
Jehoiakim 345, 349, 350n215
Jehoiarib 222n27, 223, 441
Jehosaphath 341, 359
Jeremiah 127, 201n257, 329n125, 350n215, 401, 499, 531
Jericho 329n125, 329n128, 407, 423
Jerome 125, 125n44, 295, 295n38, 295n39, 295n40, 296n41, 296n43, 299, 301, 303, 305, 356n241, 427n134, 466n178, 473
Jerusalem 122n35, 131, 157n61, 159n73, 160n84, 161, 175n148, 227, 269, 293, 300n50, 301, 305, 307, 309, 317n85, 325, 347, 407, 425, 431, 433, 435, 439, 451, 473, 477, 483, 491, 493, 495, 497, 501, 501n48, 503, 503n56, 507, 509, 513n100, 521, 531, 535, 539, 545, 549
Jesse 331, 333, 341, 359, 483
Jeush 381, 381n320
Jezebel 205n274
Joab 342n177, 343
Joash (Joas) 339, 341, 341n170
Job 347, 347n198, 347n200, 476n216, 477
Jochebed 239
Johanan 347
John 36, 64n25, 72, 76, 95, 111, 121n24, 122n35, 135, 135n18, 139, 140n39, 147, 169, 177, 179n162, 187, 189n195, 191, 193, 193n217, 195, 195n223, 195n224, 199, 201, 205, 205n274, 209, 223n27, 226n40, 227, 247n122, 263n193, 273, 301n54, 308n65, 309, 311n73, 319n92, 320n95, 365n257, 367n263, 373, 395, 399n46, 401, 402n57, 403, 404n65, 405, 407, 411n84, 415, 423, 425n130, 427, 439, 441, 443, 472n195, 480n227, 541

INDEX OF TERMS AND NOUNS

Joram   289, 339, 341, 343, 359
Joseph   32n4, 47, 53n38, 58, 58n7, 76, 77, 79,
   82n24, 100, 100n68, 104–106, 111, 157,
   221, 235, 237, 257, 265, 269, 289, 291,
   312n76, 313, 313n77, 315, 316n85, 317,
   319, 321, 335n150, 343n177, 345, 345n187,
   347, 349n206, 353, 353n228, 355,
   361, 363, 369n269, 373, 392n363, 393,
   393n364, 393n366, 401, 407, 425n126,
   429, 431, 433, 451, 455, 456n148, 459,
   471n195, 473, 475, 478n222, 487, 499,
   523, 535, 539, 545, 553
Josephus   157n61, 222n26, 329n128, 425, 439,
   446n119, 447, 501, 508n81, 517, 533, 535,
   535n181
Joshua   128n64, 203, 203n268, 222n27, 329,
   329n124, 329n125, 329n126, 333, 345
Josiah   341, 343, 343n179, 345, 347, 349, 361
Josippon (Yosipon)   79, 157, 157n61
Jotham   289, 341, 341n170, 361
Juchasin   123, 353, 451, 551
Judah   151, 157, 157n61, 165, 257, 311n73, 319,
   320n95, 325, 326n116, 327, 329, 329n126,
   341, 342n175, 345, 345n187, 345n189,
   348n205, 357, 365n256, 387, 400n52,
   403n58, 437, 451, 459, 479, 493, 497,
   503, 503n57, 515, 519, 551
Justin Martyr   247n123, 471n195, 503

Kabbala Denudata   ix, ix n4, x, xi, xii n15,
   xiii, xiii n16, xiv, xiv n19, xv, xv n24, xv
   n26, xvi, xvi n28, xvii, xvii n31, xvii n32,
   xix, xx, 6n12, 7, 8, 16n31, 35n12, 43, 53,
   56, 65, 66n27, 68n38, 70, 74, 77n13, 82,
   82n25, 82n27, 83–85, 85n40, 95, 97, 115,
   115n4
Kain   161
Keni   161
Kenosis   249, 261
Keter   139, 143, 281, 379, 523
Kiel   33
Kimchi, David   51, 348n205, 349, 351, 351n216
Kindness   157, 195, 239, 239n96, 241, 339
Kingdom   129, 139, 161, 165, 167, 169, 179,
   203, 223, 229, 237, 239, 241, 245, 247,
   253n153, 255, 257, 273, 277, 279, 285,
   318n89, 319, 323, 325, 335, 337, 339, 343,
   349, 369, 371, 373, 381, 399, 411, 413, 415,
   437, 461, 489, 503, 521, 535, 549, 553

Kircher, Athanasius   55
Kittim   159
Kollyridons   352n228
Khunrath, Heinrich   39n19

Laban   161, 345, 393, 513, 515
Laud, Archbishop   98, 98n62
Law   125, 127, 128n64, 128n65, 129, 131, 133,
   145, 167, 187, 195, 301, 307, 419, 431, 433,
   435, 479, 493, 551
Le Fèvre de La Boderie, Guy   45, 46n11, 49,
   49n28, 143n51, 305
Le Fèvre de La Boderie, Nicolas   143n51
Leibniz, Gottfried Wilhelm   xi, 1
Leipzig   123n35, 343n181, 553n75
Lévi, Éliphas   xviii, xviii n36, xix n40, xix
   n42
Levita, Elias   121n28, 123
Lichtenthaler, Abraham   26n19
Lightfoot, John   xxi, xxi n45, 36, 36n13, 51,
   52, 52n36, 54, 54n41, 60n14, 64, 64n26,
   71, 96, 122n35, 133n84, 151n18, 168n124,
   179n161, 187n187, 203n268, 205n274,
   209n296, 215n317, 219n330, 223n27,
   247n122, 259n172, 269n28, 271n35,
   311n73, 326n116, 327n119, 329n124,
   343n177, 348n205, 348n206, 350n215,
   351n216, 351n217, 354n234, 386n344,
   388n349, 389, 395n20, 397n40, 400n52,
   404n66, 425, 427n133, 444n109,
   457n153, 462n165, 479n224, 492n264,
   493, 500n47, 503n56, 504n62, 518n117
Loci communes (kabbalistici)   xiii, xiii n18,
   xvii n32, 35n12, 53, 56, 65, 70, 80, 81n23,
   82, 82n27, 83n29, 105, 115, 138n33,
   147n79, 163n93, 164n98, 165, 165n108,
   166n110, 174n142, 178n158, 188n189,
   194n218, 196n229, 202n264, 228n45,
   234n72, 238n90, 240n99, 242n104,
   244n114, 246n118, 251n135, 253n147,
   262n186, 272n37, 274n43, 276n48,
   279n59, 280n65, 282n72, 331n131,
   335n144, 364n252, 368n268, 370n273,
   378n304, 379n307, 380n313, 390n354,
   398n41, 407n69, 408n74, 410n80,
   414n91, 415n93, 420n108, 422n116,
   470n190, 484n237, 486n242, 489n253,
   502n50, 522n130, 526n143, 527n146,
   546n47, 554n77

Locke, John 161n86
Lollius 447
London Polyglot Bible 36, 44n5, 46n11, 48, 124n42, 177n154, 219n329, 304n60, 527n147
Lottery 171, 171n136, 173
Ludolph, Hiob 2, 529n154
Luïscius, A.G. 4
Luke 119, 119n11, 123, 124n43, 125, 125n44, 125n46, 151, 221, 225, 267, 307, 308n64, 309, 311n73, 313n77, 351n216, 395, 444n110, 445n111, 479n225, 480n227, 481, 483, 545, 552n74, 553n76
Lumnius, Joannes Fredericus 324n110
Luria, Isaac x, xiii, 71, 73, 80, 81, 83, 207, 316n85, 355n235, 375n285
Lurianic (Kabbalah, tradition, system) ix, x, xi, xiii, xiii n17, xviii, 38, 51, 64, 66, 67, 67n31, 73, 74, 75, 75n7, 80, 81, 81n24, 82, 83, 83n30, 83n32, 84, 84n36, 85, 86, 95, 316, 340, 382, 391
Lydiat, Thomas 112, 343, 343n183, 437, 437n90, 439, 491

Machlon 327
Mackenzie, Kenneth xx
Magdalene 275
Magi 36, 75, 78, 112, 163, 227, 227n41, 467n180, 471n195, 497, 499, 501, 501n49, 504n64, 505, 507, 513, 523, 523n134
Maimonides, Moses 41n24, 43, 335n151, 371n274, 425, 509n82, 510n92, 511, 511n94
Malkhut 139, 143, 255, 279, 369, 381, 399, 469, 489, 545
Manasseh 324n110, 341, 361
Manoah 239
Margaritha, Anthonius 317n85
Martha 49, 243n111, 316n85, 362n246, 363
Mary/ Maria /Marjam 3n5, 5n11, 25n15, 47, 48, 49n24, 66n29, 76, 76n8, 76n9, 77, 93, 94, 99, 99n67, 100, 100n68, 101, 101n72, 102, 103, 103n77, 104–107, 111, 141, 141n46, 145n68, 221, 225, 231, 237, 239, 239n96, 241, 243, 245, 247, 257, 259n174, 260n174, 265, 267, 269, 271, 273, 275, 277, 279, 279n63, 281, 285, 287, 289, 291, 312n76, 313, 315, 347n198, 352n228, 353, 353n228, 355, 362n246, 363, 365, 366n262, 367n263, 371, 375n285, 377, 377n290, 387, 389, 392n363, 393, 393n364, 393n366, 397, 405, 409n79, 429, 431, 433, 441, 451, 455, 456n148, 457, 459, 466n178, 471n195, 473, 475, 475n209, 478n222, 487, 499, 501, 501n49, 519n118, 523, 545
Mary of Cleopas 353n228
Mary Salome 353n228
Masada 425
Masius, Andreas 42
Mathers, Samuel Liddell MacGregor xvii
Mattan 361
Matthew 265n196, 289, 291, 291n25, 292n28, 292n29, 293, 293n30, 293n32, 293n33, 296n41, 296n43, 296n45, 297n46, 297n47, 297n48, 299, 300n50, 301, 302n55, 303, 305, 307, 308n65, 309, 310n69, 311, 311n71, 311n72, 313n77, 315, 322n101, 329, 329n124, 333, 341, 341n170, 349n206, 353, 355, 391, 456n148, 501, 513, 519
Meelführer, Rudolf Martin 46n11
Menachem 477
Merkhabah 177, 461
Messiah x, x n7, 5n11, 10, 12–15, 34, 35n10, 47, 48, 66n29, 66n30, 71, 72n4, 73, 74n5, 75, 77, 77n13, 78, 79, 80n20, 81n24, 88–96, 96n54, 99–110, 112, 121, 137, 137n28, 139, 141, 143, 143n53, 145, 145n68, 147, 149, 165, 167, 171, 177, 179, 187, 189, 193, 193n217, 195, 199, 201, 203, 209, 223, 225, 229, 231, 233, 241, 247, 249, 251, 251n141, 253, 255, 259, 260n174, 261, 269, 271, 273, 275, 277, 279, 283, 313, 316n85, 317, 319, 319n92, 321, 323, 325, 327, 339, 353, 354n233, 355, 363, 365, 367, 367n263, 369, 371, 371n275, 373, 373n280, 375n285, 377, 377n290, 379, 381, 383, 385, 387, 388n349, 389, 391, 391n359, 393, 403n59, 405, 409, 413, 415, 417, 421, 423, 429, 433, 443, 449, 457, 460n161, 461, 463, 465, 467, 467n180, 469, 473, 477, 479, 481, 483, 485, 487, 489, 491, 495, 497, 503, 507, 515, 519, 519n118, 521, 525, 527, 531, 535, 537, 547, 549, 551, 553

INDEX OF TERMS AND NOUNS

Messiah ben David   316n85
Messiah ben Joseph   316n85
Messias Puer   xi–xiii, xvi, xx, xxi, 1, 2, 2n2, 2n3, 2n4, 3, 3n5, 4, 4n7, 7, 7n19, 8, 8n20, 9n26, 10, 11, 16, 24, 30–34, 35n11, 37, 38, 38n18, 39, 40, 44, 50–55, 55n43, 56, 59, 63, 64, 64n25, 65, 66n29, 67, 68, 68n38, 69, 71–75, 76n9, 80, 81, 82n26, 82n28, 84, 85, 88, 90, 93–96, 99, 108, 113–115
Metatron   191n205, 225, 261, 417
Methodius   456n148
Michael   171n136, 225, 297n45, 317n85, 325n110, 411n84, 459, 510n92
Millennium   257
Miriam   76, 76n10, 237, 239, 239n96, 387
Moab   331
Molanus, Gehardt W.   2, 15
More, Henry   xi, xiv n19, 39, 65, 68n38, 90n47
Moréri, Louis   4
Morhof, Daniel Georg   33
Moses   52n34, 76, 76n10, 91, 103, 108, 111, 127, 128n64, 129, 141, 145, 157n61, 175n148, 203, 203n268, 215, 237, 316n85, 333, 342n175, 343n177, 351n216, 355n235, 365, 375, 387, 399, 401, 421, 431, 479, 491, 507, 510n92, 511n94, 513, 513n100
Münster, Sebastian   121n28, 157n61, 310n69, 319n92

Naamah   339
Nabal   161, 515
Nabateans   509, 511
Nahor   347
Nahshon   341, 359
Naomi   331
Nathan   316n85, 351n217, 451, 476n216
Nazaraeans   46, 295, 296n43, 297, 301, 303, 303n59, 305
Nazarene   501
Nazareth   123, 193, 221, 227, 231, 263, 319, 429, 435, 523, 535, 537, 541
Nazarite   219n330, 537
Nazianzenus, Gregory   297, 297n47
Nebuchadnezzar   437
Nebusaradan   531
Nefesh   76n12, 93, 189, 261, 271, 279, 321, 357, 373

Neshamah   76n12, 191, 261, 357, 373
Netsach   111, 283, 369, 407, 555
Nicephorus, Callistus Xanthopulus   57n4, 296n45, 297, 296n45
Nitsutsot   91, 373, 419, 461
Noah   159, 159n69, 245, 339, 401
Nonius, Marcellus   455
Nürnberg   6n14, 44n3, 97n58

Obed   161, 289, 327, 331, 333, 341, 359
Oecolampadius, Johannes   201n257
Onan   327, 345
Oral Law   11, 108, 127, 129
Origen   52n36, 88, 163n95, 189n195, 293, 293n30, 299, 312n76, 356n241, 381n322, 473, 513n100, 553

Pantaenus   293, 293n33, 295n38, 299
Panthera   381n322
Papias   292n29, 293, 298n49, 299, 303, 463n167
Paradise   195, 257, 385, 507, 541, 551
Parallelismi(s)   7, 8, 9, 322n98, 323, 326n113
Parez   341
Paris   124n42
Passover   403, 439, 441, 459, 539, 545, 547
Paths of Wisdom 32   109, 142n51
Paul   98, 121, 124n43, 125, 147, 283n78, 293n32, 308n64, 309, 311n73, 325n111, 365n258
Pedaiah   351, 351n217
Pella   300n50, 301
Perez   327, 345, 357, 399
Peringer, Gustav   318n85
Persia   325, 325n110, 505, 511
Persians   219, 437, 501, 505, 509
Peshitta   xiv, xiv n22, 8, 8n21, 9n26, 10, 21, 24, 35, 36n12, 44, 44n1, 44n2, 44n5, 45n7, 46, 47, 47n13, 48–50, 54, 99n67, 100, 108, 112, 114, 119n11, 135n18, 137n28, 151n19, 170n136, 197n232, 209n297, 241n101, 305, 310n70, 319n92, 424n126, 482n234, 492n263, 527n147, 535n182
Petavius, Dionysius   58, 58n6, 437
Phanuel   491
Phares   289, 326n116, 327
Pharisaism   283
Philip   533, 535
Philip Wilhelm, Duke of Pfalz-Neuburg   31

Philippi 125n43
Philo 356n241, 399n45, 461n163, 516n112, 517
Phoenicians 159
Pike, Albert xx
Pisani, Ottavio 383n331
Piscator, Johann 98
Plato 183n177, 189
Pliny the Elder 425, 453n142
Postel, Guillaume 45, 45n10, 49, 75n7, 120n22, 310n69, 317n85, 411n84
Principle of Creation 135, 145

Quintus Tineius Rufus 159n73
Qur'an 189, 366n263, 367, 475

Raban Maur 121n28
Rabbi Akiva 159n73, 203
Rahab 327, 327n119, 329, 329n124, 329n125, 329n128, 331, 333, 339
Ram 341, 359
Ramah 531
Raphael 213, 459, 460n160
Raphia 159
Rashi 326n116, 329n128, 388n348
Rebecca 169, 259, 269, 347
Rehoboam 255, 321n95, 339, 341, 345, 359
Reincarnation x n5, 64, 74, 76, 77n15, 78, 79, 88, 93, 121n24, 161n86, 165, 189, 201n256, 211, 229, 235, 237, 312n76, 321, 325, 327, 327n118, 343, 387, 402n57, 463, 491
Revolution of Ages 79, 80
Revolution(s) (of Souls) 74, 77, 78, 79, 155, 161, 165n109, 211, 315, 375
Rhenferd, Jacob 119n16
Ricci, Matteo 325n110
Robertson, William 319n92
Rome 124n42, 125n43, 155n50, 157, 158n61, 283, 283n78, 292n28, 293n32, 294n37, 297n45, 325n110, 425n126, 504n63, 517n112, 529
Ruach 76, 189, 261, 281, 357, 373
Rudolf August von Braunschweig-Lüneburg 310n70, 479n225
Ruth 289, 327, 327n119, 331, 339
Rutuli 159

Sabaeans 509, 509n82, 515
Safed x, 81, 316n85, 355n235
Salmon 289, 329, 329n124, 333, 341
Samael 385, 443, 443n104, 443n105, 511
Samaritan(s) 53, 60n12, 306n62, 307, 320n95, 321, 435n82, 471, 529n154
Samson 537, 537n190
Samuel 306n62, 319n92, 342n175, 349n206, 399, 401, 491
Sandalphon 73, 191, 193n217, 399, 399n46, 417
Sarah 12, 13, 169, 211, 239, 259, 269, 269n28, 403
Sarug 83, 83n32, 84, 86n41
Satan 231, 233, 327, 411, 413, 443, 445, 521
Scaliger, Joseph 58, 58n7
Schechanjahu 171
Scherzer, Johann Adam 39n18
Schuer, Jan Lodewijk 4
Scotto, Ottaviano 357n241
Sefirah, sefirot 47, 50, 71, 87, 103, 104, 108, 110, 111, 112, 113, 143n51, 167n112, 180n163, 195, 203, 229, 241n102, 250n133, 263n148, 273, 279n63, 368n266, 487n251, 555n86
Semmedo, Alvarez 325n110
Serpent 316n85, 335, 381, 521
Shallum 329n125, 349
Shards 78, 87–89, 91, 92, 327, 331, 375, 375n285, 377, 381, 385, 411, 413, 419, 421, 443, 449, 477, 489, 527
Shealtiel 351, 361
Shechem 343n177, 347
Shekhinah 112, 139, 141, 171, 179, 259, 369, 381, 417, 467, 481, 491, 493, 507, 509, 515, 521, 525
Shell(s) 67n33, 72, 73, 75, 79, 87, 149, 149n84, 157, 191, 197, 199, 231, 239
Shem 339, 401
Shema 311, 543
Shemoneh 'Esreh 175n148
Shephatiah 451
Shepherds 120n23, 429, 431, 455, 457n153, 459, 461, 461n163, 463n165, 463n166, 467, 473, 475, 507, 507n79
Shiloh 319, 319n92, 321n95
Shobal 341
Simeon 216n321, 342n175, 343, 343n177, 347, 389n349, 433, 456n148, 479, 479n224,

INDEX OF TERMS AND NOUNS   591

479n225, 481, 483, 485, 487, 487n252, 501
Simeon the Righteous   216n321
Simon, Richard   xi, xxi, 55, 309n65
Simultaneum   32
Solomon   133n84, 320n95, 321, 339, 341, 342n177, 345, 348n206, 351n217, 359, 388n348, 389, 437, 451, 453, 491
Soul of Messiah   71, 77n13, 78, 93, 94, 95, 101, 102, 103, 105, 106, 107, 233, 247, 251, 260, 261, 327, 365, 367, 371n275, 373, 375, 379, 467n180, 507, 525
Spizel, Gottlieb   324n110
Strabo   473
Strength   129, 195, 245
Suetonius   445
Sulzbach   ix n2, xi, xi n8, xii, xii n12, xii n13, xii n15, xiv, xiv n23, xv n24, 1, 1n1, 1n2, 3n5, 6n14, 6n16, 8n20, 8n21, 16, 16n34, 18, 21n6, 24, 26n19, 31, 31n1, 32, 32n3, 32n5, 38n18, 44, 44n3, 50n31, 51, 51n32, 52n34, 53, 54, 62n19, 68n38, 82, 82n26, 96, 97n56, 114, 120n22, 126n53, 177n154, 191n206, 197n232, 297n45, 297n46, 297n47, 298n48, 304n60, 311n70, 366n263, 383n331, 401n53, 472n195, 479n225, 507n77, 527n147, 536n182
Synod of Diamper   294n37
Syriac   xiv, xv, xx, 5, 7n19, 8, 8n20, 9, 9n26, 10, 21, 24, 25n15, 35, 40, 44, 44n1, 44n2, 45, 45n8, 46, 46n11, 47–50, 53, 53n37, 88, 100, 104, 108, 109, 112, 114, 119n16, 123, 124n42, 125, 127, 131, 135n19, 137, 137n28, 137n29, 141, 145, 149n83, 151n18, 151n19, 151n21, 163n97, 165, 170n136, 177, 177n154, 181, 195, 199, 203, 205, 209, 227, 231, 241, 241n101, 243, 259, 259n172, 289n8, 291, 293, 294n37, 296n43, 299, 303, 304n61, 305, 307, 309, 310n70, 362n246, 371, 377, 377n291, 385, 391, 393, 395n20, 397n40, 401, 401n53, 417, 417n102, 424n126, 425, 445, 453n142, 457, 457n152, 461, 463, 467, 469, 473, 480n227, 481, 483, 485, 489, 503, 504n64, 505, 505n65, 518n117, 519, 527, 527n147, 535, 535n182, 537n190, 545, 553

Syriac New Testament   xiv, xv, 8, 8n20, 35, 46

Tacitus   446n118, 447
Tamar   289, 316n85, 327, 331, 339, 345, 365n256
Targum   131, 139, 140n39, 160n84, 161, 181, 197, 199, 213, 329, 329n128, 389, 389n351, 451, 451n137, 457, 465, 513n100, 519, 527, 531, 537
Temple Archives   218n328
Ten Lost Tribes   78, 92, 324n110, 325, 325n110, 403n58, 423
Ten Words of Creation   139
Terah   401
Tetragrammaton   85, 95, 110, 111, 145, 177, 177n154, 193, 195, 223, 279, 281, 318n90, 325, 341, 355, 359, 361, 371, 379, 379n312, 417, 417n102, 461, 465, 465n172
Tevunah   555
Thamar   327n119, 328n122
The Father and the Mother   469
Theon, Max   xx
Theophilus   119, 133, 133n84
Theophylact   292n28, 293, 308n65, 309, 501n49, 553, 553n76
Thirty Years War   32, 32n5, 99
Thomas   243n110, 294n37, 297n45, 319n92, 343n183, 366n263, 439, 452n142, 510n84
Tiferet   92, 105, 108, 109, 110, 111, 139, 143, 255, 281, 371n275, 407, 409, 421, 503, 527, 537, 547
Titus   124n43, 439
Tobit   213
Trachontis   533
Tree of Life   547, 547n50
Tremellius, Immanuel   49
Trigault, Nicolas   325n110
Tsevi, Sabbatai   x
Turnus   159, 159n73
Tzepho, son of Elipha, son of Esavus   157

Uriah   335, 337
Uriel   461
Ussher, James   61, 61n16, 62n19
Uziah   289, 339
Uzzah   211
Uzziah   211, 341, 341n170, 343, 359

Van der Hardt, Hermann   62
Van Helmont, Jean-Baptiste   xii
Van Helmont, Francis Mercury   xii, xii
    n11, xiii, xiv, xiv n20, xxi n45, 1n2, 3,
    8n20, 18, 21n6, 26n19, 31, 31n2, 32, 32n3,
    39n18, 42, 47n15, 50n29, 51n32, 53n39,
    62n19, 67n31, 68, 68n35, 68n38, 69,
    69n39, 85n40, 90, 97n57, 98, 383n331
Van Hoogstraten, David   4
Varro   455
Ve-Adar   439
Virgil   158n68, 159, 453, 455
Vienna   1, 44, 49n27
Virgin   141n46, 221, 227, 231, 231n59, 233,
    233n69, 235, 237, 241, 241n102, 247,
    247n122, 259n172, 260n174, 261,
    263, 275, 291, 321, 327, 353n228, 367,
    367n263, 368n266, 377, 386n344, 387,
    389, 391, 393
Virgin Birth   66n29, 99, 106, 107
Vital, Hayyim   74, 81n24, 83, 83n30, 316n85
Vitringa, Campegius   5n12
Von Mandelslo, Johann Albrecht   347n201
Von Zesen, Philipp   39n18
Vulliaud, Paul   xvi, xvi n27, xix n39
Vulgate   119n13, 119n14, 119n15, 119n16, 135n19,
    135n20, 135n21, 135n22, 135n23, 137n29,
    151n18, 151n19, 151n20, 151n21, 153n42,
    153n43, 155n49, 170n136, 221n14, 221n15,
    221n16, 221n17, 222n23, 267n19, 267n20,
    267n21, 289n8, 289n9, 319n92, 383n331,
    388n347, 429n22, 457n148, 483n236,
    512n99

Wagenseil, Joseph Christoph   32n4, 46n11,
    97, 97n58, 121n28
Waite, Arthur Edward   xix, xx
Walker, John   383n330
Walton, Brian   36, 44n5, 46n11, 48, 53,
    177n154, 304n60, 305, 317n85, 401n53,
    527n147
Westcott, William Wynn   xvii
Widmanstetter, Johann Albrecht   44, 45n6,
    49, 49n27, 241n101

Willet, Andrew   98
Yesod   73, 103, 104, 105, 110, 111, 163, 241n102,
    281, 337, 369, 407, 471, 555
Yetser ha-ra   88, 101, 233, 371, 385
Yetsirah   142n51, 251, 279n63, 281, 477n217,
    477n217, 547n50

Zachariah   64, 72, 73, 90, 91, 99, 104, 105,
    106, 151, 153, 163, 165, 169, 171, 175, 181,
    185, 187, 189, 195, 195n224, 211, 213,
    215, 218n328, 219, 225, 257, 267, 269,
    367n263, 395, 407, 409, 411, 421, 439,
    441, 459, 475
Zacuto, Abraham   123n36
Zadok   289, 361
Zebulon   227, 229, 229n51, 503, 503n57, 535
Zedekiah   341, 349
Zeir Anpin   94, 95, 340n167, 366n262,
    368n268, 371n275, 391, 391n359, 485,
    487n251, 527, 555
Zemach   477, 534n179
Zerach   327
Zerubbabel   222n27, 316n85, 351, 353, 361
Zohar   x n6, xi n8, xiv, xiv n23, xv, xv n24, xv
    n25, xv n26, xvii–xix, xix n39, 2, 3n5,
    7, 7n19, 8, 8n20, 9, 9n22, 9n26, 11, 14,
    15, 15n30, 24, 26n19, 32n5, 33, 35n12,
    38n18, 39, 40, 45, 45n9, 45n10, 46, 50,
    50n31, 51, 51n33, 52, 54, 74, 74n6, 77,
    79, 82n24, 83, 83n30, 83n31, 83n33,
    84n35, 105, 110, 111, 114, 115n4, 120n22,
    121, 126n53, 127, 133, 135, 137, 139n38,
    142n50, 147, 157, 161, 163, 167, 169, 175,
    177, 179, 189, 199, 201, 211, 229, 259, 263,
    271, 275n45, 305, 314n81, 315, 321, 323,
    325, 327, 336n156, 337, 339, 341, 341n170,
    347, 351, 391, 403, 403n58, 407, 409,
    413, 423, 425, 465, 467, 469, 471n194,
    479n225, 491, 513, 513n100, 515, 531, 533,
    541, 553
Zoharic Aramaic   45n9, 50
Zoroaster   509

Index of Biblical References

Gen

1.1	365	27.40	157
2.4	255	28.13-14	285
4.13	383	28.15	393
6.8	245	28.20	139
8.7	393	28.21	139
9.25	329, 339	29.1	513
11.7	213	29.5	271
11.12	435	29.12	393
11.26	435	29.20	345
11.32	435	29.32-35	345
12.5	327	30.20	229
12.40	435	30.25	345
13.18	269, 403	31.11	213
15.1	245	35.10	245
15.6	269, 277	35.19	457
15.8	211	35.21	457
16.7	177	35.27	269
16.9	177	35.29	269
16.10	177	36.39	161
17.5	269, 403	38.2	345
17.7	285	38.24	365
17.7-8	285	38.25	403
17.8	285	38.29	403
17.10	269, 403	41.46	345
17.15	269, 403	45.6	345
17.17	211	46.2	435
17.51	403	46.3	245
18.1	269	46.12	345
18.8	389	46.21	345
18.10	239, 269	47.9	345
18.12	211, 219	49.8	487
19.14	363	49.10	319
19.15	383	49.13	487
19.19	401	49.16	487
21.17	245	49.19	487
22.16-17	413	49.22	487
23.2	269	49.31	269
23.17	269	50.13	269
23.19	269		
25.6	505	**Ex**	
25.9	269	2.8	237
25.25	403	3.2	177, 507
26.3-4	285	4.14	195
26.22	359	4.16	215
27.29	487	4.22	251
		6.23	165, 337

Ex (cont.)

10.7	203
12.40	435
14.24	181, 463, 507
16.29	465
19.17	139
20.13	553
23.33	203
30.12	445
30.23	523
38.8	493

Lev

15.1	383
16.22	383
19.3	553
25.26	465

Num

5.5	465
20.1-2	237
20.6	211
20.8	211
20.11	215
20.12	211
22.22-27	177
22.31-32	177
22.34-5	177
23.7	513
24.16	515
24.24	161
25.7	203
35.5	465
35.19	465
35.21	465
35.24	465
35.25	465
35.27	465
36.8-9	353

Deut

1.21	245
4.45-46	331, 435
17.15	517
20.7	363
22.23	363
28.20	181
32.14	389
33	343

33.10	175
33.11	175
33.17	453

Jos

2.15	455
5.13	465
7.1	341
7.13	409
7.24	341
8.1	245
10.10	465
15.61	423
19.15	503
21.11	269
21.12	401
22.20	341

Judg

2.1	177
2.4	177
3.9	379
3.15	379
5.23	177
5.24	243
5.25	389
6.3	505
6.11-12	177
6.12	243
6.15	519
6.20-22	177
6.23	241, 245
6.38	389
8.10-11	505
12.8	331
13.3	177, 257
13.4	199, 219
13.5	537
13.13	177
13.15-18	177
13.20-21	177

Ruth

2.20	465
3.9	465
4.1	465
4.3	465
4.4	465
4.6	465

INDEX OF BIBLICAL REFERENCES

4.17	403	19.7	177
4.22	333	21.21	341
		22.19	213, 467

1 Sam

1.19	403	**2 Kgs**	
2.3	379	2.9	203
2.10	411, 491	2.15	203
2.20	493	8.24	339
4.3	181	9.8	341
4.14	181	9.18	341
5.11	181	9.22	271
10.19	379	9.31	271
15.35	393	10.15	271
17.13	459	11.2	339
23.5	135	11.7	169
24.1	425	12.21	339
24.1-2	423	13.3	379
24.7	481	14.1	339
28.10	383	14.21	339
		15.1	339

2 Sam

		15.27	345
3.12	321	15.33	345
5.3	271	16.1	345
6.6	211	18.17	199
6.23	393	19.35	177
12.13	337	21.19	345
17.29	389	22.1	345
19.21	481	23.30-31	347
23	343	23.34	349
24.1	445	23.36	345
		24.6	349
		24.8	349

1 Kgs

1.41	181	25.5	199
3.7	345	25.7	349
4.26	453	25.10-12	199
4.30	505	25.20	199
6.1	331, 435	25.27	349
8.13	229		
8.23	409	**1 Chron**	
8.25	409	1.35	381
9.26	159	2.12	333
11.42	345	2.50	341
13.2	343	3.3	451
14.21	339	3.5	451
14.22	345	3.6	405
14.31	359	3.8	405
17.1	191	3.12	339
18.12	203	3.15	347
19.1	195	3.16	349

1 Chron (cont.)

3.17	349, 351
3.17-24	451
3.19	351, 353
4.1	341
4.18	331
6.7	341
7.56	401
8.20	345
21.15	177
21.30	177
23.5	345
23.21	405
23.23	405
24.10	169
24.11	171
24.18	169
28.19	407
29.23	341
30.1	345
30.10	409

2 Chron

1.10	519
6.14	409
6.16-17	409
9.25	453
15.5	519
20.2	423
22.10	341
23.4	169
24.20	165
26.16	211
28.1	343
29.1	343
32.28	453
36.6	349
36.9	349

Ezra

2.21	451
2.36	169
2.37	169
3.2	351
7.3	341

Neh

7.26	451
8.2	451
12.1	351

Esth

1.8	199
1.10	181
2.14	523
2.17	245
6.1	181
6.10	451
6.11	451

Job

1.3	505
11.9	549
20.17	389
25.3	467
27.5	393
29.6	389
39.9	453
41.2	135

Ps

2.2	317
2.7	249
9.2	197
12.3	393
18.51	401
19.4	181
27.5	489
34.8	177
34.17	327
40.10	121
45.5	317
45.9	523
46.9	403
55.22	389, 491
57.5	491
65.13	197
68.9	121
68.12	121
68.22	515
80.17	407
89.18	411
89.52	317
90.10	333
92.11	411

INDEX OF BIBLICAL REFERENCES 597

96.11	197	8.10	391
109.5	327	8.18	391
110.7	251	9.6	391
114.1	331, 435	10.24	525
114.3	435	10.26	525
116.16	247	10.34	483
120.4	491	11.1	227, 483, 537
126.1	401	11.14	505
132.17	411	14.19	227
133.3	317	14.20	391
147.20	487	19.20	199
148.14	411	22.14	393
		25.8	381, 385

Prov

		25.9	547
1.10	131	28.29	135
6.14	181	29.9	181
6.35	131	37.36	177
7.16	523	40.9	121
9.5	503	40.21	135
11.10	197	41.4	135
13.9	197	43.11	379
23.16	197	45.15	379
26.10	199	45.17	379
26.22	181	45.21	379
30.19	489	48.11	139
30.33	389	49.5	139
		49.6	227

Eccl

		49.15	139
1.9	161	51.5	139
		52.7	121

Cant

		53.12	251
5.6	523	56.7	391
5.13	523	59.20	495
		60.3	257

Isa

		60.3-4	487
1.8	227	60.14	391
1.14	139	60.19-20	423
1.16	139	60.21	227, 413
1.26	391	61.1-2	317
6.2	213	62.4	391
6.3	469	63.1	161
6.6	215	63.15	229
7.11	215	65.4	227
7.13	343	65.20	233
7.14	237, 247, 249, 389, 393	65.23	233
7.16	257, 387	66.9	135
7.21-25	389		
8.3	387		
8.8	391		

Jer

1.5	201
1.5-6	407
2.22	337
3.17	391
16.13	485
22.11	349
22.18-19	349
22.30	351
23.16	391
23.19	181
24.6	139
25.16	181
25.27	181
27.5	139
27.18	139
29.14	139
29.23	139
30.9	321
30.21	519
31.15	531
31.31	285
31.33	127
36.12	405
36.30	349
48.25	411
49.28	505
52.11	341
52.31	349

Lam

2.19	463
4.20	481

Ezek

1.3	407
1.10	177
1.24	467
1.26	413, 469
1.26 n	177
1.28	461
3.12	467, 469
3.22	407
3.23	461
8.4	461
10.2	215
10.4	461
10.6	215
20.36	525
25.4	505
25.10	505
33.22	407
34.23-24	321
37.1	407
37.24	321
40.1	407
48.35	243, 391

Dan

5.13	225
5.24	227
7.10	213
7.16	213
7.24	411
8.21	411
9.3	187
9.21	225
9.23	187, 213
9.25-26	317
9.26	483
9.26-27	481
9.27	427
10.5-10	241
10.10	213
10.12	213
10.19	241
10.21	225
11.7	227
14.20	213

Hos

1.7	139
1.9	139
3.5	321
11.1-2	525
13.4	379

Joel

2.13	485

Amos

3.9	181
6.7	197

Obad

1.9	161
1.21	379

INDEX OF BIBLICAL REFERENCES

Mic
2.6	519
4.8	457
5.1	457
7.15	525
7.19	421

Nah
2.4	181

Hab
3.2	455

Hag
1.1	351
1.12	351
1.14	351
2.3	351
2.6	525
2.24	351

Zech
1.1	165
1.11-12	177
1.18-19	411
2.5	139
3.1	177
3.6	177
8.3	391
8.7	379
13.1	381

Mal
3.1	493
4.5	189, 415

Ben Sira
48.10	207

Tobit
12.15	213

Mt
1.1	233, 263, 355, 367
1.15	475
1.17-22	237
1.18	197, 233, 247
1.19	235, 269
1.20	213, 237, 245, 263, 461
1.21	249, 393
1.22	537
1.23	237, 415
1.24	473
1.25	247
2.5	537
2.6	303
2.12-13	213
2.13	177, 213, 237
2.15	303
2.16	465, 537
2.18	303
2.19	177, 213, 237
2.23	231, 391
3.1	195, 423
3.3	417
3.10-12	415
3.17	253
4.3	249
4.6	249
4.14	537
4.15	303
4.23	121, 123
5.6	285
5.9	391
5.12	197
5.19	391
5.22	129
5.23-24	523
5.28	129
5.32	129, 473
5.34	129
5.39	129
5.44	129
6.34	295
7.14	147
7.22	379
7.23	495
7.24-25	489
8.4	493, 523
8.17	303, 537
8.19	419
8.20	323
8.29	249
9.2	385
9.5	385
9.6	385
9.15	259
9.22	247

Mt (*cont.*)

9.23	181	19.17	147
9.27	317	20.8	199
9.35	121, 123	20.20	247
9.42	247	20.23	199
10.3	393	20.28	411
10.5-6	209	20.30	247, 317
10.13	241	20.31	247, 317
10.32	495	21.4	537
11.11	193, 199	21.5	303
11.12	133, 179, 443	21.9	317
11.12-13	193	21.13	391
11.13	195, 405	21.15	317
11.14	189	21.16	543
11.18	303	21.32	209
12.5	543	21.42	543
12.17	537	22.16	419
12.20	393	22.24	419
12.23	317	22.31	543
12.38	419	22.36	419
12.47	233	22.42	317
13.5	489	22.45	317
13.11	129	23.5	283
13.20	489	23.18-19	523
13.30	413	24.12	537
13.35	129, 537	24.15	123
13.40-43	413	24.24	203
13.43	413, 485	24.30	259
13.49-50	413	24.37	197
13.52	127	25.15	537
13.55	393	25.35	455
13.56	543	25.46	413
14.13	453	26.5	181
14.15	453	26.13	123
14.22	393	26.18	419
14.24	181	26.26	503
14.25	463	26.31	303
14.33	249	26.47	517
15.5	523	26.51	249
15.9	131	26.61	537
15.22	317	26.63	249
15.24	209	26.64	259
16.16	249	27.1	517
17.5	253	27.9	537
18.8	147	27.38	285
18.9	147	27.40	249
19.4	137, 543	27.43	249
19.8	137	27.52	271
19.16	419	27.54	249
		27.56	393

INDEX OF BIBLICAL REFERENCES

27.57	127	**Lk**	
28.5	245	1.2	127
28.19	127	1.4	127
28.20	393	1.11	371, 459
29	493	1.13	245, 405, 461
		1.14	195
Mk		1.15	273, 373, 415
1.1	123, 193, 249	1.16	255
1.4	443	1.16-17	177
1.24	537	1.17	191, 209, 259, 449
2.19	259	1.19	121, 459
2.26	517	1.26	397, 459
3	493	1.27	353
3.11	249	1.30	461
4.5	489	1.31	391, 393
4.16	489	1.32	317, 319, 321, 415
5.7	249	1.32-33	473
5.30	259, 377	1.33	285
5.35-36	199	1.35	205, 373, 403, 415, 507, 555
5.36	245		
5.38	199	1.36	165, 313
5.39	243	1.38	473
6.3	247, 543	1.56	365, 397
6.5	259	1.59	475, 507
7.11	523	1.69	319, 321
9.1	259	1.72	403
9.38-39	379	1.76	391, 407
9.43	147	2.7	247
9.45	147	2.9	509
10.6	137	2.10	195
10.29	123	2.15	227
10.45	411	2.20	121
10.47	317, 537	2.23	391
10.48	317	2.38	411
11.17	391	2.48	247
12.35	317	3.1-4	443
13.8	181	3.2	195
13.25	467	3.10	209
14.2	181	3.18	121
14.14	457	3.23	313, 353
14.67	537	3.31	317
15.39	249	3.36	435
15.46	489	3.38	249
15.47	393	4.14	205
16.1	393	4.16	543
16.6	537	4.17	543
16.17	379	4.18	283
		4.34	537
		4.36	473

Lk (*cont.*)

5.12	465
5.17	377
5.34	259
6.19	377
6.20	283
6.20-21	285
6.23	273
6.24-25	285
6.48	489
7.5	209
8.3	199
8.6	489
8.13	489
8.28	249
8.46	377
9.12	457
9.31	129, 465
9.49	379
9.51	475
10.1	123
10.5-6	241
10.20	379
10.21	197
10.26	543
10.27	379
10.30	285
10.41	243
12.8	495
12.14	209
12.15	147
12.38	463
12.42	199
13.14	209
13.32	549
13.33	465
14.14	413
15.4	453
15.19	391
15.21	391
16.16	133, 443
17.20	481
18.11	283
18.37	537
18.38	317
18.39	317
19.2	199
19.7	457
19.11	481
19.38	469
19.46	391
19.47	517
20.41	317
20.42	317
21.1	523
21.4	523
21.9	181
21.28	411
22.11	457
22.24	489
22.66	517
23.2	465
23.5	181
24.4	495
24.19	537
24.27	129, 141
24.36	241
24.44	129
24.45	129
24.49	205, 259

Jn

1.1	365
1.3	365
1.6	227
1.12	251
1.14	249, 259
1.15	201
1.17	193, 283, 405
1.18	139, 249
1.19	201, 385
1.20	495
1.26	201, 415
1.27	201
1.29	415
1.31	427
1.34	201, 249
1.36	201
1.47	229
1.52	509
3.2	419
3.5	381
3.6	263
3.13	541
3.16-18	249
3.29	407
3.36	147, 207
4.10	381

INDEX OF BIBLICAL REFERENCES

4.19	315	17.3	209
5.2	293	17.4-5	251
5.24	147	17.6	145
5.33	201	17.19	537
5.35	197	17.20	293
5.39	129	18.5	537
5.40	147	18.7	537
5.46	141	18.24	517
6.10	453	19.13	293
6.27	253	19.19	537
6.32-33	503	20.14	275
6.33	147	20.19	241
6.35	503	20.21	241
6.45	543	20.26	241
6.48	503	20.31	147, 249
6.50-51	503	21.7	243
6.51	147		
6.63	147	**Acts**	
6.69	249	1.8	205, 259
7.8	475	1.18	209
7.37	237	2.1	475
7.38	381	2.3	259
7.42	317, 321, 455	2.6	181
7.49	209	2.22	537
7.52	229	2.26	197
8.11	481	2.27	425
8.12	147	2.36	249, 317, 355, 465
8.21	385	2.46	197
8.24	385	2.47	463
8.44	137	3.6	537
8.56	413	3.21	257
9.41	385	4.6	329, 517
10.10	147	4.8	517
10.17	251, 355	4.10	537
10.36	251	4.12	379, 411
11.24	481	4.33	205, 259
11.27	249	5.19	177
11.50	463	6.8	259
11.52	209, 377	6.14	537
12.27	181	7.4	435
12.41	177, 413, 469, 481	7.25	411
13.13	249	7.30	177
14.6	147	7.46	247
15.22	385	8.10	259
15.24	385	8.14	127
15.26	227	8.26	177
16.8-9	385	9.5	481
16.21	197	9.25	455
16.27	227	10.2	187, 209

INDEX OF BIBLICAL REFERENCES

Acts (*cont.*)

10.4	187
10.6	455, 457
10.22	525
10.31	403
10.38	259
10.41	463
10.44	259
11.15	259
11.19	127
11.26	301
11.30	133
12.7	177
12.23	177
13.1	123, 133
13.24	209
13.24-25	427
13.32-33	249
13.35	425
14.2	207
14.19	181
14.21	127
15.2	133, 181
15.4	133
15.6	133
15.10-11	405
15.16	321
15.22	133
15.23	133
15.39	489
16.4	133
17.28	261
18.2	181
18.25	127
19.29	181
19.32	181
19.40	181
20.1	181
21.30	181
21.40	293
22.2	293
22.8	537
23.10	181
24.5	181, 301
24.14	495
24.15	413
26.9	537
26.14	293
28.23	457
28.24	207
28.28	411

Rm

1.1	123
1.3	317, 321
1.4	249, 253
1.5	283
1.9	123
1.16	133, 259
1.17	167
2.8	207
2.18	127
3.3	215
3.22	167
3.24	283, 411
4.16	283
4.21	131
4.30	411
5.2	283
5.15	283
5.17	283
5.20-21	283
6.14-15	283
8.15	251, 461
8.23	411
9.4	485
10.9-10	495
10.16	123
10.22	207
11.2	495
11.5-6	283
11.24-27	285
11.26	325
11.30	207
11.30-31	207
11.32	209
11.36	147
12.5	207, 377
14.5	131
14.11	495
15.19	133, 205
15.31	207
16.21	123
16.23	199
16.25	129

INDEX OF BIBLICAL REFERENCES

1 Cor

1.18	133
1.24	133
2.4	133
2.5	133
2.13	475
3.11	317
4.20	133
6.15	377
8.6	147, 365
10.4	237, 365
10.9	365
10.16-17	377
11.29	503
12.10	133
12.12-13	377
12.14-27	207
12.27	377
12.28	133
12.29	133
13.4	181
14.19	127
14.33	181
15.26	385
15.28	387
15.54-56	385
15.54-57	413

2 Cor

1.21	317
3.3	129
3.6	129
3.7	129
3.7-11	121
3.18	121
4.6	121, 363
6.5	181
6.16	391
8.18	123
10.10	197
10.12	475
11.26	287
11.32	199
12.9	259
12.20	181
13 colophon	125

Gal

3.5	133
3.17	435
3.26	251
3.27	363
4.4	475
4.19	313, 363
4.24	129
6.6	127

Eph

1.5	469
1.7	411
1.9	487
1.10	475
1.14	411
1.23	377
2.2	209
2.14	469
2.16	377
3.9	129, 147, 365, 487
3.16	133
3.17	391
3.20	133
4.12	377
4.13	377
4.15	207, 557
4.16	377
5.6	209
5.8	485
5.30	377
6.17	411

Phil

1.23	483
2.9	251, 355
2.11	485
2.17-18	197
3.21	259

Col

1.11	133
1.14	411
1.15-16	365
1.16	147
1.17	147, 261
1.18	377
1.24	377
1.26	129, 487

Col (*cont.*)

1.29	133
2.2	131
2.19	377
3.6	209
3.15	377
4.14	123, 125

1 Thes

1.5	131

2 Thes

2.3	163
2.4	163
2.9	197

1 Tim

2.6	411
2.15	537
5.10	455

2 Tim

1.7	461
1.8	123
1.9-11	487
2.8	317, 321
2.13	215
4.11	123
4.17	131

Tit

1.8	455
3.5	197

Philem

24	123

Heb

1.1	215
1.2	147, 365
1.3	139, 261
1.3-5	253
1.6	469
1.10	137
2.9	249, 355
2.14-15	413
3.3	215
3.13	391
4.9	129
4.11	207
4.14	129, 249
4.14-15	199
5.1	523
6.16	489
7.1	129
7.7	489
8.3-4	523
8.5	129
8.9	285
9.1	129
9.8	129
9.9	523
9.12	411
9.15	411
9.19	463
10.7	141
11.39	165
11.39-40	413
11.40	165, 463
13.1	455
13.8	365

Jam

1.1	209
1.6	181
1.8	181
2.23	133

1 Pet

1.1	209
1.8	197
3.1	207
3.14	181
3.22	467
4.9	455
4.13	197
4.17	207

2 Pet

1.4	363

1 Jn

1.1	137
2.7	137
2.13	137
2.14	137
2.20	317
2.22	317

INDEX OF BIBLICAL REFERENCES

2.27	317, 363	13.18	549
3.1	391	14.14	413
5.12	147	16.13	203
		19.9	127
3Jn		19.11	391
5	455	19.20	203
		20.1-2	413
Jude		20.1-6	411
9	225	20.4-7	253
		20.7	413
Rev		20.10	203
1.17	245	21.1	411
1.19	127	21.2	549
2.1	127	21.3	391
2.8	127	21.6	381
2.12	127	21.8	413
2.18	127	21.12	325
3.1	127	21.23	423
3.7	127, 321, 411	21.23-24	485
3.14	127, 137, 365	21.24	257
5.5	321	21.26	257
5.13	485	22.1-5	411
7.5-8	343	22.3	285
7.15	285, 391, 413	22.3-5	413
8.1	177	22.5	423, 485
11.4	199	22.15	413
11.6	203	22.16	317, 321, 411
12.3	161, 529	22.17	381
12.7	225		